Literature for Composition

Page from Frost's notebooks, showing "The Silken Tent." (Printed with the permission of The Poetry/Rare Books Collection, University Libraries, State University of New York at Buffalo)

Literature for Composition

Essays, Fiction, Poetry, and Drama

FIFTH EDITION

Edited by

Sylvan Barnet
Tufts University

Morton Berman
Boston University

William Burto
University of Lowell

William E. Cain
Wellesley College

Marcia Stubbs
Wellesley College

LONGMAN

An imprint of Addison Wesley Longman, Inc.

New York • Reading, Massachusetts • Menlo Park, California • Harlow, England
Don Mills, Ontario • Sydney • Mexico City • Madrid • Amsterdam

Development Manager: Arlene Bessenoff
Development Editor: Katharine Glynn
Supplements Editor: Donna Campion
Marketing Manager: Melanie Goulet
Project Manager: Donna DeBenedictis
Design Manager: John Callahan
Text Designer: Alice Fernandes-Brown and Heather A. Peres
Cover Designer: Mary McDonnell
Cover Illustration: Pablo Picasso. *The Violin (Violin and Fruit)*. 1913. Paper, charcoal, gouache on paperboard. 25½″ × 19½″. Philadelphia Museum of Art. A. E. Gallatin Collection.
Art Studio (music): TTP International
Photo Researcher: Photosearch, Inc.
Technical Desktop Manager: Heather A. Peres
Print Buyer: Sheila Spinney
Electronic Page Makeup: Allentown Digital Systems, Inc.
Printer and Binder: RR Donnelley & Sons Company/Crawfordsville
Cover Printer: The Lehigh Press, Inc.

Library of Congress Cataloging-in-Publication Data

Literature for Composition : essays, fiction, poetry, and drama /
    edited by Sylvan Barnet . . . [et al.]. — 5th ed.
        p.   cm.
    Includes bibliographical references and indexes.
    ISBN 0-321-02153-3 (paper)
    1. College readers. 2. English Language—Rhetoric Problems,
exercises, etc. 3. Criticism—Authorship Problems, exercises, etc.
4. Academic writing Problems, exercises, etc.   I. Barnet, Sylvan
PE1417.L633 1999   99-16379
808'.0427—dc21   CIP

Please visit our website at http://www.awlonline.com

ISBN 0-321-02153-3

12345678910—DOC—02010099

Contents

CHAPTER 5 Reading Literature Closely: (2) Analysis 73

CHAPTER 6 Other Kinds of Writing About Literature 133

PART II Up Close: Thinking Critically About Literary Works and Literary Forms 147

CHAPTER 7 Critical Thinking: Asking Questions and Making Comparisons 149

CHAPTER 8 Reading (and Writing About) Essays 161

CHAPTER 9 Reading (and Writing About) Fiction 190

CHAPTER 10 Thinking Critically About a Short Story 239

CHAPTER 11 Reading (and Writing About) Drama 267

CHAPTER 12 Thinking Critically About Drama 344

CHAPTER 13 Reading (and Writing About) Poetry 397

PART IV A Thematic Anthology 519

CHAPTER 18 Love and Hate 521

✓ CHAPTER 19 Gender Roles: Making Men and Women 617

APPENDIX E *Glossary of Literary Terms 1369*

Alternate Contents

POETRY

DRAMA

List of Illustrations

Preface

This book is based on the assumption that students in composition or literature courses should encounter first-rate writing. By this we mean not simply competent prose but the powerful reports of experience that have been recorded by highly skilled writers past and present. We assume that the study of such writing offers pleasure and insight into life and that it also leads to increased skill in communicating.

In this preface we discuss the contents of the book at some length, but if we were asked to give, very briefly, the key features of *Literature for Composition,* here is what we would say:

KEY FEATURES

- **Extensive Instruction in Composition.** Students are given help in the entire process of writing, beginning with getting ideas (for instance by listing, or by annotating a text) and on through the final stages of documenting and editing. Many samples of student writing are included.
- **Mini-Genre Anthology.** After introductory chapters on getting ideas and thinking critically, students encounter chapters devoted to the essay, fiction, drama, and poetry.
- **Thematic Anthology.** Six themes are given including two new themes: "Gender Roles" and "Identity in Pluralistic America."
- **Casebooks.** Six casebooks—on the *Titanic,* Emily Dickinson, *Hamlet,* Ralph Ellison, Alice Munro, and American Indian Identity (included in the new theme on "Identity in Pluralistic America")—give a variety of perspectives and opportunities for writing and research.
- **New Material on Research and the Internet.** Because instructors are increasingly assigning research papers, the fifth edition has expanded the discussion of research. It now includes material on short, medium-length, and long research papers on literature and history, and it provides instruction on evaluating, using, and citing electronic sources.
- **Emphasis on Critical Thinking.** Critical thinking is at the heart of the first four chapters, and it is kept in view throughout the book, most visibly in the "Topics for Critical Thinking and Writing" that follow each literary selection.
- **Emphasis on Argument.** The apparatus in the fifth edition focuses on argument and evaluation, not only in the casebooks but in the topics that follow most of the readings.
- **Abundant Visual Material.** The book is conspicuously rich in photographs (not just head-shots), paintings, and facsimiles of manuscripts. *Examples:* The photos include the sinking *Titanic,* Huddie Ledbetter (Lead Belly), Buffalo Bill, and Sitting Bull. Among the facsimiles is the manuscript of a draft of E. E. Cummings's poem about Buffalo Bill (probably never before published in a textbook). These images support emphasis on visual learning and critical thinking.
- **Poems and Paintings.** The visual material includes a four-color insert, which has been amplified. Among the new items are Picasso's *Girl Before a Mirror,* and John Updike's highly accessible poem about the picture.

ORGANIZATION

Literature for Composition, Fifth Edition, is in large part an anthology of litera-ture, but it is more: It also offers instruction in writing.

Part One, "Getting Started," consists of six chapters with twenty-five short works of literature. The aim of all of the chapters in Part One is to help students to read and to respond—in writing—to literature. The first two chapters discuss such procedures as annotating, free writing, and listing; the third chapter ("What Is Lit-erature?") includes a casebook of prose, songs, and poems about the sinking of the *Titanic;* the fourth and fifth chapters discuss writing explications and analyses; the sixth chapter discusses other kinds of writing, including parody and stories based on stories and poems based on poems. These chapters include examples of stu-dent writing, several of which are accompanied by the preliminary journal entries and drafts that helped to produce them.

Part Two, "Up Close: Thinking About Literary Works and Literary Forms," begins (Chapter 7) with a discussion of critical thinking. This chapter in-vites students to analyze, especially by means of comparison, (1) a photograph of Buffalo Bill and Sitting Bull; (2) E. E. Cummings's poem, "Buffalo Bill 's"; (3) the manuscript draft of the poem; and (4) two encyclopedia articles on Sitting Bull. The next seven chapters introduce the students to four genres: the essay (Chapter 8), fiction (Chapters 9 and 10), drama (Chapters 11 and 12), and poetry (Chapters 13 and 14). The chapter on the essay includes six essays, ranging from the work of Jonathan Swift to Brent Staples and Sallie Bingham; the two chapters on fiction in-clude eight stories, with a casebook on Ralph Ellison's "Battle Royal"; the two chapters on drama include four plays (by playwrights from Sophocles to Harvey Fierstein); the two chapters on poetry include thirty-three poems, with a casebook on Emily Dickinson. Suggested topics for discussion and examples of student writ-ing (annotations, journal entries, drafts, final essays) help students to think criti-cally and to develop arguments about this material. Part Two, then, offers a small anthology of literature, organized by genre, and it also offers abundant guidance in thinking and writing about literature. The casebooks on works of literature include some critical commentaries, thereby allowing students to think about kinds of crit-icism and about evaluating interpretations. The casebook on Emily Dickinson in-cludes an essay by a student. We will talk a bit more about the casebooks later in this preface, when we summarize what is new in the fifth edition.

Part Three, "Standing Back: Arguing Interpretations and Evaluations, and Understanding Critical Approaches," consists of three chapters: Arguing an Interpretation (15), Arguing an Evaluation (16), and Writing About Literature: An Overview (17). Our idea is this: If instructors begin the course by assigning some or all of the chapters in Parts One and Two, by now the students have read enough literature to be in a good position to think further about the assumptions underlying the analytic interpretations and evaluations that they are writing.

About seventy-five literary texts appear in Parts One, Two, and Three; another two hundred appear in **Part Four, "A Thematic Anthology,"** where they are grouped into six themes: "Love and Hate"; "Gender Roles: Making Men and Women"; "Innocence and Experience"; "Identity in Pluralistic America"; "Literary Visions: Poems and Pictures"; and "Religion and Society." Here, as earlier, almost all of the essays, stories, plays, and poems are followed by questions that are meant to stimulate critical thinking and writing.

The book concludes with five **appendices:** "Remarks about Manuscript Form"; "Writing a Research Paper"; "New Approaches to the Research Paper: Literature, History, and the World Wide Web"; "Literary Research: Print and Electronic Sources"; and "Glossary of Literary Terms." The material on manuscript form may seem to be yet another discussion of writing, and some readers may wonder why it is put near the back of the book. But manuscript form is less a matter of drafting and revising than it is of editing. It is, so to speak, the final packaging of a product that develops during a complicated process, a process that begins with reading, responding, and finding a topic, a thesis (supported by evidence), and a voice, not with worrying about the width of margins or the form of citations. The last thing one does in writing an essay, and therefore almost the last thing in our book, is to set it forth in a physical form fit for human consumption.

WHAT IS NEW IN THE FIFTH EDITION?

Instructors familiar with earlier editions will notice major changes in this edition, some of which we have already mentioned. Here, for the convenience of instructors who have used an earlier edition, we will list the major changes:

Sample Essays and Checklists

We have amplified the material on writing, partly by giving additional advice of our own, especially on examining assumptions, evaluating evidence, and developing a thesis, but also by increasing the number of essays by students (usually prefaced with journal entries); the book now includes nineteen sample essays. We have also increased to nine the number of checklists concerned with writing.

Casebooks

We have changed somewhat the nature of the casebooks. We no longer give a single work accompanied by four or five interpretations; instead, we now sometimes accompany the work with contextual material. To take the first three examples:

- **The new casebook on the *Titanic*** contains an encyclopedia article, popular ballads by African Americans, four additional poems, and an essay on the recent film, all of which raise issues of fact versus literary creation, as well as issues of race and class.
- **The new casebook on Ralph Ellison's "Battle Royal"** follows the story with extracts from the writings of Booker T. Washington, W. E. B. Du Bois, Gunnar Myrdal, and Ellison himself.
- **The new casebook on *Hamlet*** contains the play and eight commentaries, but the commentaries do not essentially offer competing interpretations. Rather, they are varied, including a discussion by Claire Bloom on her performance in the BBC-TV production and a student's review of the Kenneth Branagh film.
- **The revised casebook devoted to poems about paintings** includes twelve works of art, shown in color, and the poems written about them.
- **A new casebook on representations of American Indians,** in poetry and in film, contains within it a smaller unit tracing the story of Pocahontas from John Smith's account through several poems to the Disney film.
- In addition to the casebooks on Emily Dickinson and Flannery O'Connor, there is **now a casebook on Alice Munro**, consisting of three of her stories, a lecture she delivered, and an interview.

Two New Thematic Units

We offer six themes; two are new. The new themes are "Gender Roles: Making Men and Women" and "Identity in Pluralistic America." We have also made many changes in the literary selections presented within those themes that we have retained.

Expanded Illustration Program

Photos. The number of color illustrations has increased from eight to twelve, and we have also included several important black-and-white illustrations (for instance a photograph of Buffalo Bill and Sitting Bull accompanies E. E. Cummings's poem, "Buffalo Bill 's," and three depictions of Pocahontas illustrate the casebook on representations of American Indians). These pictures themselves can be the subjects of analytic essays. We also reproduce the manuscript versions of several works, thereby allowing readers to think about changes the authors have introduced. Finally, nearly 100 photos of contemporary authors now accompany the author biographies to help students connect with the human qualities of the works they read.

Music. We've added the music for spirituals and folk songs as well as for popular ballads on the *Titanic.*

Research and Using the Internet

This edition now includes in two substantial appendices extensive coverage of how to locate, examine, evaluate, and cite Internet resources for literary research. Appendix C, "New Approaches to the Research Paper: Literature, History, and the World Wide Web," is keyed to a case study of the literature and history of the internment of Japanese Americans during World War II and describes in detail the process by which students can learn to integrate online and electronic resources with printed materials from the library. Appendix D is a substantial supplementary list and guide to resources in both print and electronic forms.

These extensive revisions have been made in the light of our own experience and the experience of many other instructors who have taught *Literature for Composition* and who have shared their thoughts with us.

SUPPLEMENTS

Instructor's Manual. An Instructor's Manual with detailed comments and suggestions for teaching each selection is available. This important resource also contains references to critical articles and books that we have found to be most useful.

Literature for Composition Website. The *Literature for Composition* website can be found at: *http://www.awlonline.com/barnetlfc.* This site includes in-depth information about the text as well as helpful links to literature and research sites.

Audio- and Videotapes. For qualified adoptors, an impressive selection of videotapes and Longman audiotapes is available to enrich students' experience of literature.

Penguin Program. In cooperation with Penguin Putnam Inc., one of our sibling companies, Longman is proud to offer a variety of Penguin paperbacks at a significant discount when packaged with any Longman title. Excellent additions to any literature course, Penguin titles give students the opportunity to explore contemporary and classic fiction and drama. The available titles include works by authors as diverse as Julia Alvarez and Mary Shelley, Shakespeare and Toni Morrison.

Daedalus Online. Daedalus Online is an Internet-based collaborative writing environment for students. The program offers prewriting strategies and prompts, computer-mediated conferencing, peer collaboration and review, and comprehensive writing support. For educators, Daedalus Online offers a comprehensive suite of online course management tools. For more information, visit *http://www.awlonline.com/daedalus,* or contact your Addison Wesley Longman sales representative.

English Pages (*http://www.longman.awl.com/englishpages*). This web site provides professors and students with continuously updated resources for reading, writing, and research practice in four areas: composition, literature, technical writing, and basic skills. Features include simulated searches, where students simulate the process of finding and evaluating information on the World Wide Web; first-person essays that show students how everyday men and women have applied what they learned in composition to a wide variety of situations; and annotated links that provide the best information on the widest variety of writing issues and research topics.

The Longman Guide to Columbia Online Style. This 32-page booklet includes an overview of Columbia Online Style (COS), guidelines for finding and evaluating electronic sources, and examples for citing electronic sources. COS is a documentation style developed specifically for citing electronic sources. *The Longman Guide to Columbia Online Style* is free when packaged with any Longman text.

Researching Online, 3rd edition. Students will find this companion indispensable to their navigation of the Internet. It includes detailed information on Internet resources such as e-mail, listservs, and Usenet newsgroups; advanced techniques for using search engines; tips on how to assess the validity of electronic sources; and a section on HTML that shows students how to create and post their own Web pages.

Analyzing Literature. This brief supplement provides critical reading strategies, writing advice, and sample student papers to help students interpret and discuss literary works in a variety of genres. Suggestions for collaborative activities and online research on literary topics are also featured, as well as numerous exercises and writing assignments.

The Essential Research Guide. A handy two-page laminated card, *The Essential Research Guide* features a table with guidelines for evaluating different kinds of print and on-line sources, a chart of editing and proofreading symbols, and a list of cross-curricular web site resources

ACKNOWLEDGMENTS

In preparing the first four editions of *Literature for Composition* we were indebted to Margaret Blayney, Bertha Norman Booker, John P. Boots, Pam Bourgeois, Robin W. Bryant, Kathleen Shine Cain, Diana Cardenas, Dennis Ciesielski, Arlene Clift-Pellow, Walter B. Connolly, Stanley Corkin, Linda Cravens, Donald A. Daiker, Beth DeMeo, Ren Draya, Bill Elliott, Leonard W. Engel, William Epperson, Elinor C.

Flewellen, Kay Fortson, Marie Foster, Donna Friedman, Larry Frost, Loris Galford, Chris Grieco, Sandra H. Harris, Syndey Harrison, Sally Harrold, Maureen Hoag, Clayton Hudnall, Joyce A. Ingram, Craig Johnson, Michael Johnson, Angela Jones, Bill Kelly, Cynthia Lowenthal, Timothy Martin, William McAndrew, Kathleen McWilliams, Zack Miller, JoAnna S. Mink, Dorothy Minor, Charles Moran, Patricia G. Morgan, Nancy Morris, Christina Murphy, Richard Nielsen, John O'Connor, James R. Payne, Don K. Pierstorff, Gerald Pike, Louis H. Pratt, Bruce A. Reid, Linda Robertson, Terry Santos, Jim Schwartz, Robert Schwegler, William Shelley, Janice Slaughter, Martha Smith, Tija Spitsberg, Judith Stanford, Darlene Strawser, Jim Streeter, Beverly Swan, Leesther Thomas, Raymond L. Thomas, Susan D. Tilka, Mary Trachsel, Dorothy Trusock, Billie Varnum, John Venne, Mickey Wadia, Nancy Walker, Linda Woodson, Kathy J. Wright, Dennis Young, and Gary Zacharias.

In preparing this latest edition we have been greatly aided by the suggestions of the following reviewers: Elizabeth Addison, Western Carolina University; James Allen, College of DuPage; Kathleen Andersen-Wyman, Idaho State University; Mary J. Balkun, Seton Hall University; Daniel Barwick, Alfred State College; David Beach, George Mason University; Phyllis Betz, La Salle University; Sara McKnight Boone, North Carolina State University; Carol Ann Britt, San Antonio College; William Carpenter, College of the Atlantic; Mike Chu, College of DuPage; John Desjarlais, Kishwaukee College; Emily Dial-Driver, Rogers State University; James Dubinsky, Virginia Polytechnic Institute; Gail Duffy, Dean College; Martin J. Fertig, Montgomery County Community College; Debbie Hanson, Augustana College; Dorothy Hardman, Fort Valley State University; Michael Hennessey, Southwest Texas State University; Mary Herbert, Long Island University; Natalie Herdman, Ohio State University; Mary Hickerson, Southwest State University; Rodney Keller, Ricks College; Beth Kemper, Campbellsville University; Alison Kuehner, Ohlone College; Regina Lebowitz, New York City Technical College; Margaret Lindgren, University of Cincinnati; Martin Meszaros, Ocean County College; Zack Miller, Brookhaven College; Nancy Moore, Edmonds Community College; David Norlin, Cloud County Community College; Marsha Nourse, Dean College; Chris Orchard, Indiana University of Pennsylvania; Suzanne Owens, Lorain County Community College; Stephanie Pelkowski, University of Kansas; Michael Punches, Oklahoma City Community College; Herbert Shapiro, Stanford University; David Sudol, Arizona State University; John H. Venne, Ball State University; Margaret Whitt, University of Denver; Rosemarie Winslow, Catholic University of America; Arthur Wohlgemuth, Miami-Dade Community College; Sallie Wolf, Arapahoe Community College; and Carlson Yost, Shawnee State University. All of these people have given us valuable advice.

Bill Cain would like to thank his wife Barbara and his daughters Julia and Isabel for their love and support.

At Longman, Katharine Glynn carefully watched over this project. We wish also to thank Virginia Creedan, who secured copyright permission—even for our last-minute and way-beyond-the-deadline inclusions—and Donna DeBenedictis, John Callahan, and Heather Peres, who converted a manuscript into a book.

Sylvan Barnet

Morton Berman

William Burto

William E. Cain

Marcia Stubbs

PART

1

Getting Started

The Writer as Reader: Reading and Responding

Interviewer: Did you know as a child you wanted to be a writer?

Toni Morrison: No. I wanted to be a reader.

Learning to write is in large measure learning to read. The text you must read most carefully is the one you write, an essay you will ask someone else to read. It may start as a jotting in the margin of a book you are reading or as a brief note in a journal, and it will go through several drafts before it becomes an essay. To produce something that another person will find worth reading, you must read each draft with care, trying to imagine the effect your words are likely to have on your reader. In writing about literature, you will apply some of the same critical skills to your reading; that is, you will examine your responses to what you are reading and will try to account for them.

Let's begin by looking at a very short story by Kate Chopin (1851–1904). (The name is pronounced in the French way, something like "show pan.") Kate O'Flaherty, born into a prosperous family in St. Louis, in 1870 married Oscar Chopin, a French-Creole businessman from Louisiana. They lived in New Orleans, where they had six children. Oscar died of malaria in 1882, and in 1884 Kate returned to St. Louis, where, living with her mother and children, she began to write fiction.

 **KATE CHOPIN**

Ripe Figs

Maman-Nainaine said that when the figs were ripe Babette might go to visit her cousins down on the Bayou-Lafourche where the sugar cane grows. Not that the ripening of figs had the least thing to do with it, but that is the way Maman-Nainaine was.

It seemed to Babette a very long time to wait; for the leaves upon the trees were tender yet, and the figs were like little hard, green marbles.

But warm rains came along and plenty of strong sunshine, and though Maman-Nainaine was as patient as the statue of la Madone, and Babette as restless as a humming-bird, the first thing they both knew it was hot summertime. Every day Babette danced out to where the fig-trees were in a long line against the fence. She walked slowly beneath them, carefully peering between the gnarled, spreading branches. But each time she came disconsolate away again. What she saw there finally was something that made her sing and dance the whole long day.

When Maman-Nainaine sat down in her stately way to breakfast, the following morning, her muslin cap standing like an aureole about her white, placid face, Babette approached. She bore a dainty porcelain platter, which she set down before her godmother. It contained a dozen purple figs, fringed around with their rich, green leaves.

"Ah," said Maman-Nainaine arching her eyebrows, "how early the figs have ripened this year!"

"Oh," said Babette. "I think they have ripened very late."

"Babette," continued Maman-Nainaine, as she peeled the very plumpest figs with her pointed silver fruit-knife, "you will carry my love to them all down on Bayou-Lafourche. And tell your Tante Frosine I shall look for her at Toussaint—when the chrysanthemums are in bloom."

[1893]

READING AS RE-CREATION

If we had been Chopin's contemporaries, we might have read this sketch in *Vogue* in 1893 or in an early collection of her works, *A Night in Acadie* (1897). But we are not Chopin's original readers, and, since we live more than a century later, we inevitably read "Ripe Figs" in a somewhat different way. And this gets us to an important truth about writing and reading. A writer writes, sets forth his or her meaning, and attempts to guide the reader's responses, as we all do when we write a letter home saying that we're thinking of dropping a course or asking for news or money. To this extent, the writer creates the written work and puts a meaning in it.

But the reader, whether reading that written work as a requirement or for recreation, *re-creates* it according to his or her experience and understanding. For instance, if the letter-writer's appeal for money is too indirect, the reader may miss it entirely or may sense it but feel that the need is not urgent. If, on the other hand, the appeal is direct or demanding, the reader may feel imposed upon, even assaulted. "Oh, but I didn't mean it that way," the writer later protests. Nevertheless, that's the way the reader took it. The letter is "out there," a physical reality standing between the writer and the reader, but its *meaning* is something the reader as well as the writer makes.

Since all readers bring themselves to a written work, they each bring something individual. Although many of Chopin's original readers knew that she wrote chiefly about the people of Louisiana, especially Creoles (descendants of the early French and Spanish settlers), Cajuns (descendants of the French whom the British had expelled from Canada in the eighteenth century), African-Americans, and mulattoes, those readers must have varied in their attitudes about such people. And many of today's readers do *not* (before they read a work by Chopin) know anything about her subject. Some readers may know where Bayou-Lafourche is, and they may have notions about what it looks like but most readers will not; indeed, many readers will not know that a bayou is a sluggish, marshy inlet or outlet of a river or lake. Moreover, even if a present-day reader in Chicago, Seattle, or Juneau knows what a bayou is, he or she may assume that "Ripe Figs" depicts a way of life still current, whereas a reader from Louisiana may see in the work a depiction of a lost way of life, a depiction of the good old days (or perhaps of the bad old days, depending on the reader's point of view). Much depends, we can say, on the reader's storehouse of experience.

To repeat: Reading is a *re*-creation; the author has tried to guide our responses, but inevitably our own experiences, including our ethnic background and education, contribute to our responses. You may find useful a distinction that E. D. Hirsch makes in *Validity in Interpretation* (1967). For Hirsch,

- the *meaning* in a text is the author's intended meaning;
- the *significance* is the particular relevance for each reader.

In this view, when you think about meaning you are thinking about what the author was trying to say and to do—for instance, to take an old theme and treat it in a new way. When you think about significance, you are thinking about what the work does for you—it enlarges your mind, deepens your understanding of love or grief, offends you by its depiction of women, or produces some other effect.

MAKING REASONABLE INFERENCES

Does this mean, then, that there is no use talking (or writing) about literature, since all of us perceive it in our relatively private ways, rather like the seven blind men in the fable? One man, you will recall, touched the elephant's tail (or was it his trunk?) and said that the elephant is like a snake; another touched the elephant's side and said the elephant is like a wall; a third touched the elephant's leg and said the elephant is like a tree, and so on. This familiar story is usually told in order to illustrate human limitations, but notice, too, that each of the blind men *did* perceive an aspect of the elephant—an elephant is massive, like a wall or a tree, and an elephant is (in its way) remarkably supple, as you know if you have given peanuts to one.

As readers we can and should make an effort to understand what an author seems to be getting at. For instance, we should make an effort to understand unfamiliar words. Perhaps we shouldn't look up every word that we don't know, at least on the first reading, but if certain unfamiliar words are repeated and thus seem especially important, we will want to look them up. It happens that in "Ripe Figs" a French word appears: "*Tante* Frosine" means "*Aunt* Frosine." Fortunately, the meaning of the word is not crucial, and the context probably makes it clear that Frosine is an adult, which is all that we really need to know about her. But a reader who does not know that chrysanthemums bloom in late summer or early autumn will miss part of Chopin's meaning. The point is this: The writer is pitching, and she expects the reader to catch.

On the other hand, although writers tell us a good deal, they cannot tell us everything. We know that Maman-Nainaine is Babette's godmother, but we don't know exactly how old Maman-Nainaine and Babette are. Further, Chopin tells us nothing of Babette's parents. It *sounds* as though Babette and her godmother live alone, but readers' opinions may differ. One reader may argue that Babette's parents must be dead or ill, whereas another may say that the status of her parents is irrelevant and that what counts is that Babette is supervised by only one person, a mature woman. In short, a text includes **indeterminacies** (passages that careful readers agree are open to various interpretations) and **gaps** (things left unsaid in the story, such as why a godmother rather than a mother takes care of Babette). As we work our way through a text, we keep reevaluating what we have read, pulling the details together to make sense of them, in a process called **consistency building.**

Whatever the gaps, careful readers are able to draw many reasonable inferences about Maman-Nainaine. What are some of these? We can list them:

> She is older than Babette.
> She has a "stately way," and she is "patient as the statue of la Madone."
> She has an odd way (is it exasperating, or engaging, or a little of each?) of connecting actions with the seasons.
> Given this last point, she seems to act slowly, to be very patient.
> She apparently is used to being obeyed.

You may at this point want to go back and reread "Ripe Figs," to see what else you can say about Maman-Nainaine.

And now what of Babette?

> She is young.
> She is active and impatient ("restless as a humming-bird").
> She is obedient.

And at this point, too, you may want to add to the list.

If you do add to the list, you might compare your additions with those of a classmate. The two of you may find that you disagree about what may reasonably be inferred from Chopin's words. Suppose, for instance, that your classmate said that although Babette is outwardly obedient, inwardly she probably hates Maman-Nainaine. Would you agree that this assertion is an acceptable inference? If you don't agree, how might you go about trying to convince your classmate that such a response is not justified? We are speaking here of an activity of mind called **critical thinking,** a topic discussed in the next chapter.

READING WITH PEN IN HAND

It's probably best to read a work of literature straight through, enjoying it and letting yourself be carried along to the end. But then, when you have an overall view, you'll want to read it again, noticing (for example) how certain innocent-seeming details given early in the work prove to be important later.

Perhaps the best way to read attentively is, after a first reading, to mark the text, underlining or highlighting passages that seem especially interesting, and to jot notes or queries in the margins. (*Caution:* Annotate and highlight, but don't get so carried away that you highlight whole pages.) Here is "Ripe Figs" once more, this time with the marks that a student added to it during and after a second reading.

KATE CHOPIN

Ripe Figs

Maman-Nainaine said that when the (figs) were ripe Babette might go to visit her cousins down on the <u>Bayou-</u> *?*
Lafourche where the sugar cane grows. Not that the ripening of figs had the least thing to do with it, but that is the *strange* way Maman-Nainaine was.

It seemed to Babette a very long time to wait; for the leaves upon the trees were tender yet, and the figs were like little hard, (green marbles.)

But warm rains came along and plenty of strong sunshine, and though Maman-Nainaine was as <u>patient as the statue</u> of la Madone, and Babette as <u>restless as a humming-bird,</u> the first thing they both knew it was hot summer-time. Every day Babette <u>danced out to where</u> the fig-trees were in a long line against the fence. She walked slowly beneath them, carefully peering between the gnarled, spreading branches. But each time she came disconsolate away again. What she saw there finally was something that made her sing and (dance) the whole long day.
contrast between M-N and B

When Maman-Nainaine (sat) down in her stately way to breakfast, the following morning, her muslin cap standing like an <u>aureole</u> about her white, placid face, Babette approached. <u>She bore a dainty porcelain platter,</u> which she set down before her godmother. It contained a dozen (purple) (figs) fringed around with their rich, green leaves.
Check? this
another contrast
ceremonious

nice echo. contrast like a song

("Ah,") said Maman-Nainaine arching her eyebrows, "how (early) the figs have ripened this year!"
time passes fast for M-N slowly for B

("Oh,") said Babette. "I think they have ripened very (late.")

is M-N herself like a plump fig?
"Babette," continued (Mama-Nainaine,) as she peeled the very plumpest figs with her pointed silver fruit-knife, "<u>you will carry my love</u> to them all down on Bayou-Lafourche. And tell your Tante Frosine I shall look for her at Toussaint—when the (chrysanthemums) are in <u>bloom.</u>"
B entrusted with a message of love

opens with figs; ends with chrys. (autumn)
fulfillment? Equivalent to figs ripening?

RECORDING YOUR FIRST RESPONSES

Another useful way of getting at the meaning of a work of literature is to jot down your initial responses to it, recording your impressions as they come to you in any order—almost as though you're talking to yourself. Since no one else is going to read your notes, you can be entirely free and at ease. You can write in sentences or not; it's up to you. You can jot down these responses either before or after you annotate the text. Some readers find that annotating the text helps to produce ideas for further jottings, but others prefer to jot down a few thoughts immediately after a first reading, and then, stimulated by these thoughts, they reread and annotate the text.

Write whatever comes into your mind, whatever the literary work triggers in your own imagination, whatever you think are the important ideas or values of your own experience.

Here is a student's first response to "Ripe Figs":

This is a very short story. I didn't know stories were this short, but I like it because you can get it all quickly and it's no trouble to reread it carefully. The shortness, though, leaves a lot of gaps for the reader to fill in. So much is not said. Your imagination is put to work.

But I can see Maman-N sitting at her table--pleasantly powerful--no one you would want to argue with. She's formal and distant--and definitely has quirks. She wants to postpone Babette's trip, but we don't know why. And you can sense B's frustration. But maybe she's teaching her that something really good is worth waiting for and that anticipation is as much fun as the trip. Maybe I can develop this idea.

Another thing. I can tell they are not poor--from two things. The pointed silver fruit knife and the porcelain platter, and the fact that Maman sits down to breakfast in a "stately" way. They are the leisure class. But I don't know enough about life on the bayous to go into this. Their life is different from mine; no one I know has that kind of peaceful rural life.

AUDIENCE AND PURPOSE

Now, suppose that you are beginning the process of writing about "Ripe Figs" for someone else, not for yourself. The first question to ask yourself is: "For whom am I writing?" That is, who is your *audience?* (Of course you probably are writing because an instructor has asked you to do so, but you must still imagine an audience. Your instructor may tell you, for instance, to write for your class-mates, or to write for the readers of the college newspaper.)

- If you are writing for people who already are familiar with some of Chopin's work, you won't have to say much about the author, but
- if you are writing for an audience who perhaps has never heard of Chopin, you may want to include a brief biographical note of the sort we gave.
- If you are writing for an audience who, you have reason to believe, has read several works by Chopin, you may want to make some compar-isons, explaining how "Ripe Figs" resembles or differs from Chopin's other work.

In a sense, the audience is your collaborator; it helps you to decide what you will say. You are also helped by your sense of *purpose.* If your aim is to introduce readers to Chopin, you will make certain points that reflect this purpose. If your aim is to tell people what you think "Ripe Figs" means to say about human rela-tionships, or about time, you will say some different things; if your aim is to have a little fun and to entertain an audience that is already familiar with "Ripe Figs," you may decide to write a parody (a humorous imitation) of the story.

A WRITING ASSIGNMENT ON "RIPE FIGS"

The Assignment

Let's assume that you want to describe "Ripe Figs" to someone who has not read it. You will briefly summarize the action, such as it is, and will mention where it takes place, who the characters are, including what their relationship is, and what, if anything, happens to them. Beyond that, you'll try to explain as honestly as you can what makes "Ripe Figs" appealing or interesting—or trifling, or boring, or whatever. That is, you will *argue* a thesis, even though you almost surely will not say anything as formal as "In this essay I will argue that . . ." or "This essay will attempt to prove that . . . ." Your essay nevertheless will essentially be an argument because (perhaps after a brief summary of the work) you will be pointing to the evidence that has caused you to respond as you did.

Here is an essay that a student, Marilyn Brown, wrote for this assignment.

A Sample Essay by a Student: "Ripening"

Ripening

Kate Chopin's "Ripe Figs" describes a growing season in a young girl's life. Maman-Nainaine agrees to allow young Babette to visit relatives away from home, but Babette must delay her trip until the figs ripen. Babette watches the signs of the natural world, impatiently observing, straining to have time pass at her own speed. At last, Babette finds that the figs have ripened, and she presents them to her godmother, Maman-Nainaine, who gives Babette her leave to go on the journey to Bayou-Lafourche.

Chopin sets the action within the context of the natural world. Babette, young and tender as the fig leaves, can't wait to "ripen." Her visit to Bayou-Lafourche is no mere pleasure trip but represents Babette's coming into her own season of maturity. Babette's desire to rush this process is tempered by a condition that Maman-Nainaine sets: Babette must wait until the figs ripen, since everything comes in its own season. Maman recognizes in the patterns of the natural world the rhythms of life. By asking Babette to await the ripening, the young girl is made to pay attention to these patterns as well.

In this work, Chopin asks her readers to see the relationship of human time to nature's seasons. Try as we may to push the process of maturity, growth or ripening happens in its own time. If we pay attention and wait with patience, the fruits of our own growth will be sweet, plump, and bountiful. Chopin uses natural imagery effectively, interweaving the young girl's growth with the rhythms of the seasons. In this way, the reader is connected with both processes in a very intimate and inviting way.

Marilyn wrote this paper for an assignment early in the semester, and it's worth noting that students were told to write "no more than a page." If "To whom am I writing" is the first question to ask, the second is, "What is the length of the assignment?" The answer to this second question will provide two sorts of guidance: It will give you some sense of how much time you should devote to preparing the paper—obviously an instructor expects you to spend more time on a ten-page paper than on a one-page paper—and, second, it will give you a sense of how much detail you can include. For a short paper—say, 1–2 pages— you will need to make your main point with a special kind of directness; you will not have space for lots of details, but just for those that support the main point. This is what Marilyn aims to achieve in her second and third paragraphs, where she highlights the term "ripens" and briefly, but effectively, develops its implications. For a longer paper, 3–5 pages, or one that is longer still, you can examine the characters, setting, and central themes in greater depth, and can focus on more details in the text to strengthen your analysis.

Other Possibilities for Writing

One might write a paper of a very different sort. Consider the following possibilities:

1. Write a sequel, moving from fall to spring.
2. Write a letter from Babette, at Bayou-Lafourche, to Maman-Nainaine.
3. Imagine that Babette is now an old woman, writing her memoirs. What does she say about Maman-Nainaine?
4. Write a narrative based on your own experience of learning a lesson in patience.

CHAPTER

2

The Reader as Writer: Developing a Thesis, Drafting and Writing an Argument

All there is to writing is having ideas. To learn to write is to learn to have ideas.

Robert Frost

PRE-WRITING: GETTING IDEAS

How does one "learn to have ideas"? Among the methods are these: reading with a pen or pencil in hand, so that (as we have already seen) you can annotate the text; keeping a journal, in which you jot down reflections about your reading; talking with others (including your instructor) about the reading. Let's take another look at the first of these, annotating.

Annotating a Text

In reading, if you own the book don't hesitate to mark it up, indicating (by highlighting or underlining or by making marginal notes) what puzzles you, what pleases or interests you, and what displeases or bores you. Later, you'll want to think further about these responses, asking yourself, on rereading, if you still feel that way, and if not, why not, but these first responses will get you started.

Annotations of the sort given on page 7, which chiefly call attention to contrasts, indicate that the student is thinking about writing an analysis of the story. That is, she is thinking of writing an essay in which she will examine the parts of a literary work either in an effort to see how they relate to each other or in an effort to see how one part relates to the whole.

More About Getting Ideas: A Second Story by Kate Chopin

Let's look at a story that is a little longer than "Ripe Figs," and then we'll discuss how in addition to annotating one might get ideas for writing about it.

11

The Story of an Hour

Knowing that Mrs. Mallard was afflicted with a heart trouble, great care was taken to break to her as gently as possible the news of her husband's death.

It was her sister Josephine who told her, in broken sentences, veiled hints that revealed in half concealing. Her husband's friend Richards was there, too, near her. It was he who had been in the newspaper office when intelligence of the railroad disaster was received, with Brently Mallard's name leading the list of "killed." He had only taken the time to assure himself of its truth by a second telegram, and had hastened to forestall any less careful, less tender friend in bearing the sad message.

She did not hear the story as many women have heard the same, with a paralyzed inability to accept its significance. She wept at once, with sudden, wild abandonment, in her sister's arms. When the storm of grief had spent itself she went away to her room alone. She would have no one follow her.

There stood, facing the open window, a comfortable, roomy armchair. Into this she sank, pressed down by a physical exhaustion that haunted her body and seemed to reach into her soul.

5   She could see in the open square before her house the tops of trees that were all aquiver with the new spring life. The delicious breath of rain was in the air. In the street below a peddler was crying his wares. The notes of a distant song which some one was singing reached her faintly, and countless sparrows were twittering in the eaves.

There were patches of blue sky showing here and there through the clouds that had met and piled above the other in the west facing her window. She sat with her head thrown back upon the cushion of the chair quite motionless, except when a sob came up into her throat and shook her, as a child who has cried itself to sleep continues to sob in its dreams.

She was young, with a fair, calm face, whose lines bespoke repression and even a certain strength. But now there was a dull stare in her eyes, whose gaze was fixed away off yonder on one of those patches of blue sky. It was not a glance of reflection, but rather indicated a suspension of intelligent thought.

There was something coming to her and she was waiting for it, fearfully. What was it? She did not know; it was too subtle and elusive to name. But she felt it, creeping out of the sky, reaching toward her through the sounds, the scents, the color that filled the air.

Now her bosom rose and fell tumultuously. She was beginning to recognize this thing that was approaching to possess her, and she was striving to beat it back with her will—as powerless as her two white slender hands would have been.

10   When she abandoned herself a little whispered word escaped her slightly parted lips. She said it over and over under her breath: "Free, free, free!" The vacant stare and the look of terror that had followed it went from her eyes. They stayed keen and bright. Her pulses beat fast, and the coursing blood warmed and relaxed every inch of her body.

She did not stop to ask if it were not a monstrous joy that held her. A clear and exalted perception enabled her to dismiss the suggestion as trivial.

She knew that she would weep again when she saw the kind, tender hands folded in death; the face that had never looked save with love upon her, fixed and gray and dead. But she saw beyond that bitter moment a long procession of years to come that would belong to her absolutely. And she opened and spread her arms out to them in welcome.

There would be no one to live for her during those coming years; she would live for herself. There would be no powerful will bending her in that blind persistence with which men and women believe they have a right to impose a private will upon a fellow creature. A kind intention or a cruel intention made the act seem no less a crime as she looked upon it in that brief moment of illumination.

And yet she had loved him—sometimes. Often she had not. What did it matter! What could love, the unsolved mystery, count for in face of this possession of self-assertion which she suddenly recognized as the strongest impulse of her being.

15 "Free! Body and soul free!" she kept whispering.

Josephine was kneeling before the closed door with her lips to the keyhole, imploring for admission. "Louise, open the door! I beg; open the door—you will make yourself ill. What are you doing, Louise? For heaven's sake open the door."

"Go away. I am not making myself ill." No; she was drinking in a very elixir of life through that open window.

Her fancy was running riot along those days ahead of her. Spring days, and summer days, and all sorts of days that would be her own. She breathed a quick prayer that life might be long. It was only yesterday she had thought with a shudder that life might be long.

She arose at length and opened the door to her sister's importunities. There was a feverish triumph in her eyes, and she carried herself unwittingly like a goddess of Victory. She clasped her sister's waist, and together they descended the stairs. Richards stood waiting for them at the bottom.

20 Some one was opening the front door with a latchkey. It was Brently Mallard who entered, a little travel-stained, composedly carrying his gripsack and umbrella. He had been far from the scene of accident, and did not even know there had been one. He stood amazed at Josephine's piercing cry; at Richards' quick motion to screen him from the view of his wife.

But Richards was too late.

When the doctors came they said she had died of heart disease—of joy that kills.

[1894]

Brainstorming for Ideas for Writing

Unlike annotating, which consists of making brief notes and small marks on the printed page, "brainstorming"—the free jotting down of ideas—asks that you jot down whatever comes to mind, without inhibition. Don't worry about spelling, about writing complete sentences, or about unifying your thoughts; just let one thought lead to another. Later you can review your jottings, deleting some, connecting with arrows others that are related, expanding still others, but for now you want to get going, and so there is no reason to look back. Thus you might jot down something about the title:

> Title speaks of an hour, and story covers an hour, but maybe takes five minutes to read.

And then, perhaps prompted "by an hour," you might happen to add something to this effect:

> Doubt that a woman who got news of the death of her husband could move from grief to joy within an hour.

Your next jotting might have little or nothing to do with this issue; it might simply say

Enjoyed "Hour" more than "Ripe Figs" partly because "Hour" is so shocking.

And then you might ask yourself

By shocking, do I mean "improbable," or what? Come to think of it, maybe it's not so improbable. A lot depends on what the marriage was like.

Focused Free Writing

Focused, or directed, free writing is a method related to brainstorming that some writers use to uncover ideas they may want to write about. Concentrating on one issue—for instance, a question that strikes them as worth puzzling over (What kind of person is Mrs. Mallard?)—they write at length, nonstop, for perhaps five or ten minutes.

Writers who find free writing helpful put down everything they can think of that bears on the one issue or question they are examining. They do not stop at this stage to evaluate the results, and they do not worry about niceties of sentence structure or of spelling. They just pour out their ideas in a steady stream of writing, drawing on whatever associations come to mind. If they pause in their writing, it is only to refer to the text, to search for more detail—perhaps a quotation—that will help them answer their question.

After the free-writing session, these writers usually go back and reread what they have written, highlighting or underlining what seems to be of value. Of course they find much that is of little or no use, but they also usually find that some strong ideas have surfaced and have received some development. At this point the writers are often able to make a rough outline and then begin a draft.

Here is an example of one student's focused free writing:

What do I know about Mrs. Mallard? Let me put everything down here I know about her or can figure out from what Kate Chopin tells me. When she finds herself alone after the death of her husband, she says, "Free. Body and soul free" and before that she said, "Free, free, free" Three times. So she has suddenly perceived that she has not been free; she has been under the influence of a "powerful will." In this case it has been her husband, but she says no one, man nor woman, should impose their will on anyone else. So it's not a feminist issue--it's a power issue. No one should push anyone else around is what I guess Chopin means, force someone to do what the other person wants. I used to have a friend that did that to me all the time; he had to run everything. They say that fathers--before the women's movement--used to run things, with the father in charge of all the decisions, so maybe this is an honest reaction to having been pushed around by a husband. I think Mrs. Mallard is a believable character, even if the plot is not all that believable--all those things happening in such quick succession.

Listing

In your preliminary thinking you may find it useful to make lists. In the previous chapter we saw that listing the traits of the two characters was helpful in thinking about Chopin's "Ripe Figs:"

Maman-Nainaine
  older than Babette
  "stately way"
  "patient as the statue of la Madone"
  connects actions with seasons
  expects to be obeyed
Babette
  young
  active
  obedient

For "The Story of an Hour" you might list Mrs. Mallard's traits; or you might list the stages in her development. (Such a list is not the same as a summary of the plot. The list helps the writer to see the sequence of psychological changes.)

weeps (when she gets the news)
goes to room, alone
"pressed down by a physical exhaustion"
"dull stare"
"something coming to her"
strives to beat back "this thing"
"Free, free, free!" The "vacant stare went . . . from her eyes"
"A clear and exalted perception"
rejects Josephine
"she was drinking in a very elixir of life"
gets up, opens door, "a feverish triumph in her eyes"
sees B, and dies

Unlike brainstorming and annotating, which let you go in all directions, listing requires that you first make a decision about what you will be listing—traits of character, images, puns, or whatever. Once you make the decision, you can then construct the list, and, with a list in front of you, you will probably see patterns that you were not earlier fully conscious of.

Asking Questions

If you feel stuck, ask yourself questions. (You'll recall that the assignment on "Ripe Figs" in effect asked the students to ask themselves questions about the work—for instance, questions about the relationship between the characters—and about their responses to it: "You'll probably try to explain as honestly as you can what makes 'Ripe Figs' appealing or interesting—or trifling, or boring."

If you are thinking about a work of fiction, ask yourself questions about the plot and the characters—are they believable, are they interesting, and what does it all add up to? What does the story mean *to you?* One student found it helpful to jot down the following questions:

Plot
    Ending false? Unconvincing? Or prepared for?
Character?
    Mrs. M. unfeeling? Immoral?
    Mrs. M. unbelievable character?
    What might her marriage have been like? Many gaps.
    (Can we tell what her husband was like?)

"And yet she loved him--sometimes" Fickle? Realistic?

What is "this thing that was approaching to possess her"?
Symbolism

Set on spring day = symbolic of new life?

You don't have to be as tidy as this student. You may begin by jotting down notes and queries about what you like or dislike and about what puzzles or amuses you. What follows are the jottings of another student, Janet Vong. They are, obviously, in no particular order—the student is "brainstorming," putting down whatever occurs to her—though it is equally obvious that one note sometimes led to the next:

Title nothing special. What might be a better title?
Could a woman who loved her husband be so heartless?
Is she heartless? Did she love him?
What are (were) Louise's feelings about her husband?
Did she want too much? What did she want?
Could this story happen today? Feminist interpretation?
Sister (Josephine)--a busybody?
Tricky ending--but maybe it could be true.
"And yet she had loved him--sometimes. Often she had not."
Why does one love someone "sometimes"?
Irony: plot has reversal. Are characters ironic too?

These jottings will help the reader-writer think about the story, find a special point of interest, and develop a thoughtful argument about it.

Keeping a Journal

A journal is not a diary, a record of what the writer did during the day ("today I read Chopin's 'Hour'"). Rather, a journal is a place to store some of the thoughts you may have inscribed on a scrap of paper or in the margin of the text, such as your initial response to the title of a work or to the ending. It is also a place to jot down further reflections, such as thoughts about what the work means to you, and what was said in the classroom about writing in general or specific works.

You will get something out of your journal if you write an entry at least once a week, but you will get much more if you write entries after reading each assignment and after each class meeting. You may, for instance, want to reflect on why your opinion is so different from that of another student, or you may want to apply a concept such as *character* or *irony* or *plausibility* to a story that later you may write about in an essay. Comparisons are especially helpful: How does this work (or this character, or this rhyme scheme) differ from last week's reading?

You might even make an entry in the form of a letter to the author or from one character to another. You might write a dialogue between characters in two works or between two authors, or you might record an experience of your own that is comparable to something in the work.

A student who wrote about "The Story of an Hour" began with the following entry in his journal. In reading this entry, notice that one idea stimulates another. The student was, quite rightly, concerned with getting and exploring ideas, not with writing a unified paragraph.

Apparently a "well-made" story, but seems clever rather than moving or real. Doesn't seem plausible. Mrs. M's change comes out of the blue--maybe <u>some</u> women might respond like this, but probably not most.

Does literature deal with unusual people, or with usual (typical?) people? Shouldn't it deal with typical? Maybe not. (Anyway, how can I know?) Is "typical" same as "plausible"? Come to think of it, prob. not.

Anyway, whether Mrs. M is typical or not, is her change plausible, believable? Think more about this.

Why did she change? Her husband dominated her life and controlled her actions; he did "impose a private will upon a fellow creature." She calls this a crime, even if well-intentioned. Is it a crime?

Critical Thinking: Arguing with Yourself

In our discussion of annotating, brainstorming, free writing, listing, asking questions, and writing entries in a journal, the emphasis has been on responding freely rather than in any highly systematic or disciplined way. Something strikes us (perhaps an idea, perhaps an uncertainty), and we jot it down. Maybe even before we finish jotting it down we go on to question it, but probably not; at this early stage it is enough to put onto paper some thoughts, rooted in our first responses, and to keep going.

The almost random play of mind that is evident in brainstorming and in the other activities already discussed is of course a kind of thinking, but the term **critical thinking** (which we addressed briefly in our first chapter) is reserved for something different. When we think critically, we skeptically scrutinize our own ideas—for example, by searching out our underlying assumptions, or by evaluating what we have quickly jotted down as evidence. We have already seen some examples of this sort of analysis of one's own thinking in the journal entries, where, for instance, a student wrote that literature should probably deal with "typical" people, then wondered if "typical" and "plausible" were the same, and then added "probably not."

Speaking broadly, critical thinking is rational, logical thinking. In thinking critically,

- one scrutinizes one's assumptions;
- one tests the evidence one has collected, even to the extent of looking for counterevidence;
- one revises one's thesis when necessary, in order to make the argument as complete and convincing as possible.

Let's start with assumptions. If I say that a story is weak because it is improbable, I ought to think about my assumption that improbability is a fault. I can begin by asking myself if all good stories—or all the stories that I value highly—are probable. I may recall that among my favorites is *Alice in Wonderland* (or *Gulliver's Travels* or *Animal Farm*)—so I probably have to withdraw my assumption that improbability in itself makes a story less than good. I may go on to refine the idea and decide that improbability is not a fault in satiric stories but is a fault in other kinds, but that is not the same as saying bluntly that improbability is a fault.

The second aspect of critical thinking that we have isolated—searching for counterevidence within the literary work—especially involves rereading the work to see if we have overlooked material or have taken a particular detail out of context. If, for instance, we say that in "The Story of an Hour" Josephine is a busybody, we should reexamine the work in order to make sure that she indeed is meddling needlessly and is not offering welcome or necessary assistance. Perhaps the original observation will stand up, but perhaps on rereading the story we may come to feel, as we examine each of Josephine's actions, that she cannot reasonably be characterized as a busybody.

Different readers may come to different conclusions; the important thing is that all readers should subject their initial responses to critical thinking, testing their responses against all of the evidence. Remember, your instructor probably expects you to hand in an essay that is essentially an **argument,** a paper that advances a thesis of your own, and therefore you will revise your drafts if you find counterevidence. The thesis might be that the story is improbable, or is typical of Chopin, or is anti-woman, or is a remarkable anticipation of contemporary feminist thinking. Whatever your thesis, it should be able to withstand scrutiny. You may not convince every reader that you are unquestionably right, but you should make every reader feel that your argument is thoughtful. If you read your notes and then your drafts critically, you probably will write a paper that meets this standard.

One last point, or maybe it's two. Just as your first jottings probably won't be the products of critical thinking, your first reading of the literary work probably *won't* be a critical reading. It is entirely appropriate to begin by reading simply for enjoyment. After all, the reason we read literature (or listen to music, or go to an art museum, or watch dancers) is to derive pleasure. It happens, however, that in this course you are trying (among other things) to deepen your understanding of literature, and therefore you are *studying* literature. On subsequent readings, therefore, you will read the work critically, taking careful note of the writer's view of human nature and the writer's ways of achieving certain effects.

This business of critical thinking is important, and we will discuss it yet again, on page 35, in talking about interpretations of literature.

Arriving at a Thesis, and Arguing It

If you think critically about your early jottings and about the literary work itself, you probably will find that some of your jottings lead to dead ends, but some will lead to further ideas that hold up under scrutiny. What the **thesis** of the essay will be— the idea that will be asserted and *argued* (supported with evidence)—is still in doubt, but there is no doubt about one thing: A good essay will have a thesis, a point, an argument. You ought to be able to state your point in a **thesis sentence.**

Consider these candidates as possible thesis sentences:

1. *Mrs. Mallard dies soon after hearing that her husband has died.*

True, but scarcely a point that can be argued or even developed. About the most the essayist can do with this sentence is amplify it by summarizing the plot of the story, a task not worth doing unless the plot is unusually obscure. An essay may include a sentence or two of summary to give readers their bearings, but a summary is not an essay.

2. *The story is a libel on women.*

In contrast to the first statement, this one can be developed into an argument. Probably the writer will try to demonstrate that Mrs. Mallard's behavior is despicable. Whether this point can be convincingly argued is another matter; the thesis may be untenable, but it is a thesis. A second problem, however, is this: Even if the writer demonstrates that Mrs. Mallard's behavior is despicable, he or she will have to go on to demonstrate that the presentation of one despicable woman constitutes a libel on women in general. That's a pretty big order.

3. *The story is clever but superficial because it is based on an unreal character.*

Here, too, is a thesis, a point of view that can be argued. Whether or not this thesis is true is another matter. The writer's job will be to support it by presenting evidence. Probably the writer will have no difficulty in finding evidence that the story is "clever"; the difficulty will be in establishing a case that the characterization of Mrs. Mallard is "unreal." The writer will have to set forth some ideas about what makes a character real and then will have to show that Mrs. Mallard is an "unreal" (unbelievable) figure.

4. *The irony of the ending is believable partly because it is consistent with earlier ironies in the story.*

It happens that the student who wrote the essay printed on page 24 began by drafting an essay based on the third of these thesis topics, but as she worked on a draft she found that she couldn't support her assertion that the character was unconvincing. In fact, she came to believe that although Mrs. Mallard's joy was the reverse of what a reader might expect, several early reversals in the story helped to make Mrs. Mallard's shift from grief to joy acceptable.

WRITING A DRAFT

After jotting down notes and then adding more notes stimulated by rereading and further thinking, you should be able to formulate a tentative thesis. At this point most writers find it useful to clear the air by glancing over their preliminary notes and by jotting down the thesis and a few especially promising notes— brief statements of what they think their key points may be. These notes may include some brief key quotations that the writer thinks will help to support the thesis.

Here are the selected notes (not the original brainstorming notes, but a later selection from them, with additions) and a draft (p. 20) that makes use of them.

title? Ironies in an Hour (?) An Hour of Irony (?) Kate Chopin's
    Irony (?)
thesis: irony at end is prepared for by earlier ironies
chief irony: Mrs. M. dies just as she is beginning to enjoy life
smaller ironies: 1. "sad message" brings her joy
                   2. Richards is "too late" at end;
                   3. Richards is too early at start

These notes are in effect a very brief **outline.** Some writers at this point like to develop a fuller outline, but most writers begin with only a brief outline, knowing that in the process of developing a draft from these few notes additional ideas will arise. For these writers, the time to jot down a detailed outline is *after* they have written a first or second draft. The outline of the written draft will, as we shall see, help them to make sure that their draft has an adequate organization, and that main points are developed.

A Sample Draft: "Ironies in an Hour"

Now for the student's draft—not the first version, but a revised draft with some of the irrelevancies of the first draft omitted and some evidence added.

The digits within the parentheses refer to the page numbers from which the quotations are drawn, though with so short a work as "The Story of an Hour," page references are hardly necessary. Check with your instructor to find out if you must always give citations. (Detailed information about how to document a paper is given on pp.1319–1329.)

Ironies in an Hour

After we know how the story turns out, if we reread it we find irony at the very start, as is true of many other stories. Mrs. Mallard's friends assume, mistakenly, that Mrs. Mallard was deeply in love with her husband, Brently Mallard. They take great care to tell her gently of his death. The friends mean well, and in fact they do well. They bring her an hour of life, an hour of freedom. They think their news is sad. Mrs. Mallard at first expresses grief when she hears the news, but soon she finds joy in it. So Richards's "sad message" (12), though sad in Richards's eyes, is in fact a happy message.

Among the ironic details is the statement that when Mallard entered the house, Richards tried to conceal him from Mrs. Mallard, but "Richards was too late" (13). This is ironic because earlier Richards "hastened" (12) to bring his sad message; if he had at the start been "too late" (13), Brently Mallard would have arrived at home first, and Mrs. Mallard's life would not have ended an hour later but would simply have gone on as it had before. Yet another irony at the end of the story is the diagnosis of the doctors. The doctors say she died of "heart disease--of joy that kills" (13). In one sense the doctors are right: Mrs. Mallard has experienced a great joy. But of course the doctors totally misunderstand the joy that kills her.

The central irony resides not in the well-intentioned but ironic actions of Richards, or in the unconsciously ironic words of the doctors, but in her own life. In a way she has been dead. She "sometimes" (13) loved her husband, but in a way she has been dead. Now, his apparent death brings her new life. This new life comes to her at the season of the year when "the tops of trees . . . were all aquiver with the new spring life" (12). But, ironically, her new life will last only an hour. She looks forward to "summer days" (13) but she will not see even the end of this spring day. Her years of marriage were ironic. They brought her a sort of living death instead of joy. Her new life is ironic too. It grows out of her moment of grief for her supposedly dead husband, and her vision of a new life is cut short.

[New page]

Work Cited

Chopin, Kate. "The Story of an Hour." Literature for Composition. Ed. Sylvan Barnet et al. 5th ed. New York: Longman, 2000, 12–13.

Revising a Draft

The draft, although thoughtful and clear, is not yet a finished essay. The student went on to improve it in many small but important ways.

First, the draft needs a good introductory paragraph, a paragraph that will let the **audience**—the readers—know where the writer will be taking them. (In Chapter 6 we discuss introductory paragraphs.) Doubtless you know from your own experience as a reader that readers can follow an argument more easily—and with more pleasure—if early in the discussion the writer alerts them to the gist of the argument. (The title, too, can strongly suggest the thesis.) Second, some of the paragraphs could be clearer.

In revising paragraphs—or, for that matter, in revising an entire draft—writers unify, organize, clarify, and polish.

1. **Unity** is achieved partly by eliminating irrelevancies. Notice that in the final version, printed on page 24 the writer has deleted "as is true of many other stories."
2. **Organization** is largely a matter of arranging material into a sequence that will assist the reader to grasp the point.
3. **Clarity** is achieved largely by providing concrete details and quotations to support generalizations and by providing helpful transitions ("for instance," "furthermore," "on the other hand," "however").
4. **Polish** is small-scale revision. For instance, one deletes unnecessary repetitions. In the second paragraph of the draft, the phrase "the doctors" appears four times, but it appears only three times in the final version of the paragraph. Similarly, in polishing, a writer combines choppy sentences into longer sentences and breaks overly long sentences into shorter sentences.

Later, after producing a draft that seems close to a finished essay, writers engage in yet another activity. They edit.

5. **Editing** includes checking the accuracy of quotations by comparing them with the original, checking a dictionary for the spelling of doubtful words, and checking a handbook for doubtful punctuation—for instance, whether a comma or a semicolon is needed in a particular sentence.

Outlining a Draft

Whether or not you draw up an outline as a preliminary guide to writing a draft, you will be able to improve your draft if you prepare an outline of what you have written. (If you write on a word processor it is probably especially important that you make an outline of your written draft. Writing on a word processor is—or seems—so easy, so effortless, that often we just tap away, filling screen after screen with loosely structured material.) For each paragraph in your draft, jot down the gist of the topic sentence or topic idea, and under each of these sentences, indented, jot down key words for the idea(s) developed in the paragraph. Thus, in an outline of the draft we have just looked at, for the first two paragraphs the writer might make these jottings:

> story ironic from start
>> friends think news is sad
>> Ms. M. finds joy
> some ironic details
>> Richards hastened, but "too late"
>> doctors right and also wrong

An outline of what you have written will help you to see if your draft is adequate in three important ways. The outline will show you:

1. the sequence of major topics
2. the degree of development of these topics
3. the argument, the thesis

By studying your outline you may see (for instance) that your first major point (probably after an introductory paragraph) would be more effective as your third point, and that your second point needs to be further developed.

An outline of this sort is essentially a brief version of your draft, perhaps even using some phrases from the draft. But consider making yet another sort of outline, an outline indicating not what each paragraph says but what each paragraph *does*. An attempt at such an outline of the three-paragraph draft of the essay on "The Story of an Hour" might look like something like this:

1. The action of the friends is ironic.
2. Gives some specific (minor) details about ironies.
3. Explains "central irony."

One ought to see a red flag here. The aim of this sort of outline is to indicate what each paragraph *does,* but the jotting for the first paragraph does not tell us what the paragraph does; rather, it more or less summarizes the content of the paragraph. Why? Because the paragraph doesn't *do* much of anything. It does not clearly introduce the thesis, or define a crucial term, or set the story in the context of Chopin's other work. An outline indicating the function of each paragraph will force you to see if your essay has an effective structure. We will see that the student later wrote a new opening paragraph for the essay on "The Story of an Hour."

Peer Review

Your instructor may encourage (or even require) you to discuss your draft with another student or with a small group of students. That is, you may be asked to get a review from your peers. Such a procedure is helpful in several ways. First, it gives the writer a real audience, readers who can point to what pleases or puzzles them, who make suggestions, who may often disagree (with the writer or with each other), and who frequently, though not intentionally, *misread.*

Though writers don't necessarily like everything they hear (they seldom hear "This is perfect. Don't change a word!"), reading and discussing their work with others almost always gives them a fresh perspective on their work, and a fresh perspective may stimulate thoughtful revision. (Having your intentions *misread* because your writing isn't clear enough can be particularly stimulating.)

The writer whose work is being reviewed is not the sole beneficiary. When students regularly serve as readers for each other, they become better readers of their own work and consequently better revisers. As we say in Chapter 1, learning to write is in large measure learning to read.

If peer review is a part of the writing process in your course, the instructor may distribute a sheet with some suggestions and questions. Here is an example of such a sheet.

QUESTIONS FOR PEER REVIEW   ENGLISH 125A

Read each draft once, quickly. Then read it again, with the following questions in mind.

1. What is the essay's topic? Is it one of the assigned topics, or a variation from it? Does the draft show promise of fulfilling the assignment?
2. Looking at the essay as a whole, what thesis (main idea) is stated or implied? If implied, state it in your own words.
3. Is the thesis plausible? How might the argument be strengthened?
4. Looking at each paragraph separately:
   a. What is the basic point? (If it isn't clear to you, ask for clarification.)
   b. How does the paragraph relate to the essay's main idea or to the previous paragraph?
   c. Should some paragraphs be deleted? Be divided into two or more paragraphs? Be combined? Be put elsewhere? (If you outline the essay by jotting down the gist of each paragraph, you will get help in answering these questions.)
   d. Is each sentence clearly related to the sentence that precedes and to the sentence that follows?
   e. Is each paragraph adequately developed?
   f. Are there sufficient details, perhaps brief, supporting quotations from the text?
5. What are the paper's chief strengths?
6. Make at least two specific suggestions that you think will assist the author to improve the paper.

THE FINAL VERSION (A SAMPLE ESSAY BY A STUDENT): "IRONIES OF LIFE IN KATE CHOPIN'S THE STORY OF AN HOUR'"

Here is the final version of the student's essay. The essay that was submitted to the instructor had been retyped, but here, so that you can easily see how the draft has been revised, we print the draft with the final changes written in by hand.

Ironies of Life in Kate Chopin's "The Story of an Hour"
~~Ironies in an Hour~~

Despite its title, Kate Chopin's "The Story of an Hour" ironically takes only a few minutes to read. In addition, the story turns out to have an ironic ending, but on rereading it one sees that the irony is not concentrated only in the outcome of the plot--Mrs. Mallard dies just when she is beginning to live--but is also present in many details.

After we know how the story turns out, if we reread it we
find irony at the very start. ~~as is true of many other stories.~~ *Because* Mrs.
and her sister   *she*
Mallard's friends assume, mistakenly, that ~~Mrs. Mallard~~ was

deeply in love with her husband, Brently Mallard. They take great
They
care to tell her gently of his death. ~~The friends~~ mean well, and in
ing   *joyous*
fact they do well. ~~They~~ bring her an hour of life, an hour of
but it is ironic that   *True,*
freedom. ~~They~~ think their news is sad. Mrs. Mallard at first
(unknown to her friends)
expresses grief when she hears the news, but soon she finds joy in

it. So Richards's "sad message" (12), though sad in Richards's

eyes, is in fact a happy message.
small but significant   *near the end of the story*
Among the ironic details is the statement that when Mallard

entered the house, Richards tried to conceal him from Mrs.
almost at
Mallard, but "Richards was too late" (13). This is ironic because
the start of the story, in the second paragraph,
~~earlier~~ Richards "hastened" (12) to bring his sad message; if he

had at the start been "too late" (13), Brently Mallard would have

arrived at home first, and Mrs. Mallard's life would not have ended

an hour later but would simply have gone on as it had before. Yet

another irony at the end of the story is the diagnosis of the

doctors. The doctors say she died of "heart disease--of joy that
they   *for the last hour*
kills" (13). In one sense ~~the doctors~~ are right: Mrs. Mallard

experienced a great joy. But of course the doctors totally

misunderstand the joy that kills her. *It is not joy at seeing her husband*
alive, but her realization that the great joy she
experienced during the last hour is over.

All of these ironic details add richness to the story, but
  The central irony resides not in the well-intentioned but

ironic actions of Richards, or in the unconsciously ironic words of
Mrs. Mallard's
the doctors, but in ~~her~~ own life. ~~In a way she has been dead.~~ She

"sometimes" (13) loved her husband, but in a way she has been

a body subjected to her husband's will

dead/, Now, his apparent death brings her new life. ^*Appropriately* ^This new

life comes to her at the season of the year when "the tops of

trees . . . were all aquiver with the new spring life" (12). But,

She is "free, free, free"--but only until her husband walks through the

ironically, her new life will last only an hour. ^She looks   *doorway.*

forward to "summer days" (13) but she will not see even the

end of this spring day. ^*If* Her years of marriage were ironic/,

bringing

~~They brought~~ her a sort of living death instead of joy/, ^Her

not only because

new life is ironic too/, ^It grows out of her moment of grief for

but also because her vision of "a long progression of years"

her supposedly dead husband, ~~and her vision of a new life~~ is ^"

cut short/ *within an hour on a spring day.*

[New page]

Work Cited

Chopin, Kate. "The Story of an Hour." Literature for Composition. Ed.

Sylvan Barnet et al. 5th ed. New York: Longman, 2000, 12–13.

A Brief Overview of the Final Version

Finally, as a quick review, let's look at several principles illustrated by this essay.

- The **title of the essay** is not merely the title of the work discussed; rather, it should give the reader a clue, a small idea of the essayist's topic. Because your title will create a crucial first impression, make sure that it is interesting.
- The **opening or introductory paragraph** does not begin by saying "In this story . . ." Rather, by naming the author and the title, it lets the reader know exactly what story is being discussed. It also develops the writer's thesis so readers know where they will be going.
- The **organization** is effective. The smaller ironies are discussed in the second and third paragraphs, the central (chief) irony in the last paragraph. That is, the essay does not dwindle or become anticlimatic; rather, it builds up from the least important to the most important point. Again, if you outline your draft you will see if it has an effective organization.
- Some **brief quotations** are used, both to provide evidence and to let the reader hear—even if only fleetingly—Kate Chopin's writing.
- The essay is chiefly devoted to **analysis** (how the parts relate to each other), not to summary (a brief restatement of the happenings). The writer, properly assuming that the reader has read the work, does not tell the plot in great detail. But, aware that the reader has not memorized the story, the writer gives helpful reminders.

- The **present tense** is used in narrating the action: "Mrs. Mallard dies"; "Mrs. Mallard's friends and relatives all assume."
- Although a **concluding paragraph** is often useful—if it does more than merely summarize what has already been clearly said—it is not essential in a short analysis. In this essay, the last sentence explains the chief irony and therefore makes an acceptable ending.
- Documentation is given according to the form set forth in Appendix B.
- There are no typographical errors. The author has proofread the paper carefully.

WRITING WITH A WORD PROCESSOR

In the preceding chapter we talked about "reading with pen in hand," and we really meant a pen—or a pencil—with which, in your early stage of interacting with the text, you will underline or circle or connect with arrows words and phrases. But when it comes to jotting down ideas, or sketching an outline, or drafting an essay, many students use a computer or a word processor. Further, you can receive valuable help from reference books and handbooks on style and usage, from computer programs (which check the spelling and grammar of documents), and from resources on the Internet. Users of this book, for example, can make good use of the many resources available at Longman's "English Pages" site:

> http://longman.awl.com/englishpages/

Here you will find a citation guide, advice on (and exercises for) developing your style, links to many additional sites and resources, and much more. Although no computer program or Internet site can write and revise a paper for you, it can help you to detect mistakes and weak spots in your work that you can then proceed to remedy.

✔ A Checklist for Writing with a Word Processor

Pre-writing

✔ Take notes. Try listing, then linking and clustering your ideas. Use an outline if you find it helpful.
✔ Check that your transcriptions are accurate if you quote.
✔ Keep your notes together in one file.
✔ Organize your sources in a bibliography.
✔ *Always back up your material.*
✔ Print out your notes.

Preparing a First Draft

✔ Use your notes—move them around in blocks. Expand on your ideas.
✔ Incorporate notes to yourself in your first draft.
✔ Read your draft on the screen to check for errors.
✔ Print out a copy of your first draft.

Working with Your Draft
✔ Revise your printed draft with pen or pencil. Incorporate these changes into your computer file.
✔ Read your corrected draft on the screen; then print out a fresh copy.
✔ Repeat these steps as many times as necessary.

Responding to Peer Review
✔ Give a copy to a peer for comments and suggestions.
✔ Respond appropriately to your reviewer, making changes in your computer file.
✔ Print out your revised version and reread it.

Preparing a Final Copy
✔ If there are only a few changes, make them on your printed copy. Otherwise, incorporate your changes in your computer file and print out your final copy.

A THIRD STORY BY KATE CHOPIN

Here is another of Chopin's stories, followed by some suggestions for writing.

The Storm

I

The leaves were so still that even Bibi thought it was going to rain. Bobinôt, who was accustomed to converse on terms of perfect equality with his little son, called the child's attention to certain sombre clouds that were rolling with sinister intention from the west, accompanied by a sullen, threatening roar. They were at Friedheimer's store and decided to remain there till the storm had passed. They sat within the door on two empty kegs. Bibi was four years old and looked very wise.

"Mama'll be 'fraid, yes," he suggested with blinking eyes.

"She'll shut the house. Maybe she got Sylvie helpin' her this evenin'," Bobinôt responded reassuringly.

"No; she ent got Sylvie. Sylvie was helpin' her yistiday," piped Bibi.

5   Bobinôt arose and going across to the counter purchased a can of shrimps, of which Calixta was very fond. Then he returned to his perch on the keg and sat stolidly holding the can of shrimps while the storm burst. It shook the wooden store and seemed to be ripping great furrows in the distant field. Bibi laid his little hand on his father's knee and was not afraid.

II

Calixta, at home, felt no uneasiness for their safety. She sat at a side window sewing furiously on a sewing machine. She was greatly occupied and did not notice the approaching storm. But she felt very warm and often stopped to mop her face on which the perspiration gathered in beads. She unfastened her white sacque at the throat. It began to grow dark, and suddenly realizing the situation she got up hurriedly and went about closing windows and doors.

Out on the small front gallery[1] she had hung Bobinôt's Sunday clothes to air and she hastened out to gather them before the rain fell. As she stepped outside, Alcée Laballière rode in at the gate. She had not seen him very often since her marriage, and never alone. She stood there with Bobinôt's coat in her hands, and the big rain drops began to fall. Alcée rode his horse under the shelter of a side projection where the chickens had huddled and there were plows and a harrow piled up in the corner.

"May I come and wait on your gallery till the storm is over, Calixta?" he asked.

"Come 'long in, M'sieur Alcée."

His voice and her own startled her as if from a trance, and she seized Bobinôt's vest. Alcée, mounting to the porch, grabbed the trousers and snatched Bibi's braided jacket that was about to be carried away by a sudden gust of wind. He expressed an intention to remain outside, but it was soon apparent that he might as well have been out in the open: the water beat in upon the boards in driving sheets, and he went inside, closing the door after him. It was even necessary to put something beneath the door to keep the water out.

"My! what a rain! It's good two years since it rain' like that," exclaimed Calixta as she rolled up a piece of bagging and Alcée helped her to thrust it beneath the crack.

She was a little fuller of figure than five years before when she married; but she had lost nothing of her vivacity. Her blue eyes still retained their melting quality; and her yellow hair, dishevelled by the wind and rain, kinked more stubbornly than ever about her ears and temples.

The rain beat upon the low, shingled roof with a force and clatter that threatened to break an entrance and deluge them there. They were in the dining room—the sitting room—the general utility room. Adjoining was her bed room, with Bibi's couch along side her own. The door stood open, and the room with its white, monumental bed, its closed shutters, looked dim and mysterious.

Alcée flung himself into a rocker and Calixta nervously began to gather up from the floor the lengths of a cotton sheet which she had been sewing.

"If this keeps up, *Dieu sait*[2] if the levees goin' to stan' it!" she exclaimed.

"What have you got to do with the levees?"

"I got enough to do! An' there's Bobinôt with Bibi out in that storm—if he only didn' left Friedheimer's!"

"Let us hope, Calixta, that Bobinôt's got sense enough to come in out of a cyclone."

She went and stood at the window with a greatly disturbed look on her face. She wiped the frame that was clouded with moisture. It was stiflingly hot. Alcée got up and joined her at the window, looking over her shoulder. The rain was coming down in sheets obscuring the view of far-off cabins and enveloping the distant wood in a gray mist. The playing of the lightning was incessant. A bolt struck a tall chinaberry tree at the edge of the field. It filled all visible space with a blinding glare and the crash seemed to invade the very boards they stood upon.

Calixta put her hands to her eyes, and with a cry, staggered backward.

---

[1]**gallery** porch, or passageway along a wall, open to the air but protected by a roof supported by columns   [2]***Dieu sait*** God only knows

Alcée's arm encircled her, and for an instant he drew her close and spasmodically to him.

"*Bonté!*"³ she cried, releasing herself from his encircling arm and retreating from the window, "the house'll go next! If I only knew w'ere Bibi was!" She would not compose herself; she would not be seated. Alcée clasped her shoulders and looked into her face. The contact of her warm, palpitating body when he had unthinkingly drawn her into his arms, had aroused all the old-time infatuation and desire for her flesh.

"Calixta," he said, "don't be frightened. Nothing can happen. The house is too low to be struck, with so many tall trees standing about. There! aren't you going to be quiet? say, aren't you?" He pushed her hair back from her face that was warm and steaming. Her lips were as red and moist as pomegranate seed. Her white neck and a glimpse of her full, firm bosom disturbed him powerfully. As she glanced up at him the fear in her liquid blue eyes had given place to a drowsy gleam that unconsciously betrayed a sensuous desire. He looked down into her eyes and there was nothing for him to do but to gather her lips in a kiss. It reminded him of Assumption.⁴

"Do you remember—in Assumption, Calixta?" he asked in a low voice broken by passion. Oh! she remembered; for in Assumption he had kissed her and kissed and kissed her; until his senses would well nigh fail, and to save her he would resort to a desperate flight. If she was not an immaculate dove in those days, she was still inviolate; a passionate creature whose very defenselessness had made her defense, against which his honor forbade him to prevail. Now— well, now—her lips seemed in a manner free to be tasted, as well as her round, white throat and her whiter breasts.

They did not heed the crashing torrents, and the roar of the elements made her laugh as she lay in his arms. She was a revelation in that dim, mysterious chamber; as white as the couch she lay upon. Her firm, elastic flesh that was knowing for the first time its birthright, was like a creamy lily that the sun invites to contribute its breath and perfume to the undying life of the world.

25   The generous abundance of her passion, without guile or trickery, was like a white flame which penetrated and found response in depths of his own sensuous nature that had never yet been reached.

When he touched her breasts they gave themselves up in quivering ecstasy, inviting his lips. Her mouth was a fountain of delight. And when he possessed her, they seemed to swoon together at the very borderland of life's mystery.

He stayed cushioned upon her, breathless, dazed, enervated, with his heart beating like a hammer upon her. With one hand she clasped his head, her lips lightly touching his forehead. The other hand stroked with a soothing rhythm his muscular shoulders.

The growl of the thunder was distant and passing away. The rain beat softly upon the shingles, inviting them to drowsiness and sleep. But they dared not yield.

The rain was over; and the sun was turning the glistening green world into a place of gems. Calixta, on the gallery, watched Alcée ride away. He turned and smiled at her with a beaming face; and she lifted her pretty chin in the air and laughed aloud.

---

³*Bonté!* Heavens!   ⁴**Assumption** a parish (i.e., a county) in southeast Louisiana

III

30 Bobinôt and Bibi, trudging home, stopped without at the cistern to make themselves presentable.

"My! Bibi, w'at will yo' mama say! You ought to be ashame'. You oughtn' put on those good pants. Look at 'em! An' that mud on yo' collar! How you got that mud on yo' collar, Bibi? I never saw such a boy!" Bibi was the picture of pathetic resignation. Bobinôt was the embodiment of serious solicitude as he strove to remove from his own person and his son's the signs of their tramp over heavy roads and through wet fields. He scraped the mud off Bibi's bare legs and feet with a stick and carefully removed all traces from his heavy brogans. Then, prepared for the worst—the meeting with an over-scrupulous housewife, they entered cautiously at the back door.

Calixta was preparing supper. She had set the table and was dripping coffee at the hearth. She sprang up as they came in.

"Oh, Bobinôt! You back! My! but I was uneasy. W'ere you been during the rain? An' Bibi? he ain't wet? he ain't hurt?" She had clasped Bibi and was kissing him effusively. Bobinôt's explanations and apologies which he had been composing all along the way, died on his lips as Calixta felt him to see if he were dry, and seemed to express nothing but satisfaction at their safe return.

"I brought you some shrimps, Calixta," offered Bobinôt, hauling the can from his ample side pocket and laying it on the table.

35 "Shrimps! Oh, Bobinôt! you too good fo' anything!" and she gave him a smacking kiss on the cheek that resounded. "*J'vous reponds,*[5] we'll have a feas' to night! umph-umph!"

Bobinôt and Bibi began to relax and enjoy themselves, and when the three seated themselves at table they laughed much and so loud that anyone might have heard them as far away as Laballière's.

IV

Alcée Laballière wrote to his wife, Clarisse, that night. It was a loving letter, full of tender solicitude. He told her not to hurry back, but if she and the babies liked it at Biloxi, to stay a month longer. He was getting on nicely; and though he missed them, he was willing to bear the separation a while longer—realizing that their health and pleasure were the first things to be considered.

V

As for Clarisse, she was charmed upon receiving her husband's letter. She and the babies were doing well. The society was agreeable; many of her old friends and acquaintances were at the bay. And the first free breath since her marriage seemed to restore the pleasant liberty of her maiden days. Devoted as she was to her husband, their intimate conjugal life was something which she was more than willing to forego for a while.

So the storm passed and everyone was happy.

[1898]

---

[5]*J'vous reponds* Take my word; let me tell you

✎ Writing About "The Storm"

As we said earlier, what you write will depend partly on your audience and on your purpose, as well as on your responses (for instance, pleasure or irritation). Consider the *differences* among these assignments:

1. Assume that you are trying to describe "The Storm" to someone who has not read it. Briefly summarize the action, and then explain why you think "The Storm" is (or is not) worth reading.
2. Assume that your readers are familiar with "The Story of an Hour" and "The Storm." Compare the implied attitudes, as you see them, toward marriage.
3. Write an essay arguing that "The Storm" is (or is not) immoral, or (a different thing) amoral. (By the way, because one of her slightly earlier works, a short novel called *The Awakening,* was widely condemned as sordid, Chopin was unable to find a publisher for "The Storm.")
4. In Part IV we are told that Alcée wrote a letter to Clarisse. Write his letter (500 words). Or write Clarisse's response (500 words).
5. You are writing to a high school teacher, urging that one of the three stories by Chopin be taught in high school. Which one do you recommend, and why?
6. Do you think "The Storm" would make a good film? Why? (And while you are thinking about Chopin and film, think about what devices you might use to turn "Ripe Figs" or "The Story of an Hour" into an interesting film.)

A NOTE ABOUT LITERARY EVALUATIONS

One other point—and it is a big one. Until a decade or two ago, Chopin was regarded as a minor writer who worked in a minor field. She was called a "local colorist," that is, a writer who emphasizes the unique speech, mannerisms, and ways of thinking of the charming and somewhat eccentric characters associated with a particular locale. Other late-nineteenth-century writers who are widely regarded as local colorists are Bret Harte (California), Sarah Orne Jewett and Mary E. Wilkins Freeman (New England), and Joel Chandler Harris (the old South). Because of the writer's alleged emphasis on the uniqueness and charm of a region, the reader's response is likely to be "How quaint" rather than "This is life as I feel it, or at least as I can imagine it."

Probably part of the reason for the relatively low value attributed to Chopin's work was that she was a woman, and it was widely believed that "serious and important literature" was (with a very few exceptions) written by men. In short, judgments, including literary evaluations, depend partly on cultural traditions.

A question: On the basis of the three stories by Chopin, do you think Chopin's interest went beyond presenting quaint folk for our entertainment? You might set forth your response in an essay of 500 words—after you have done some brainstorming, some thinking in a journal, and some drafting, revising, and editing.

What Is Literature?

Perhaps the first thing to say is that it is impossible to define *literature* in a way that will satisfy everyone. And perhaps the second thing to say is that in the last twenty years or so, some serious thinkers have argued that it is impossible to set off certain verbal works from all others, and on some basis or other to designate them as *literature.* For one thing, it is argued, a work is just marks on paper or sounds in the air. The audience (reader or listener) turns these marks or sounds into something with meaning, and different audiences will construct different meanings out of what they read or hear. There are *texts* (birthday cards, sermons, political speeches, magazines, novels that sell by the millions and novels that don't sell at all, poems, popular songs, editorials, and so forth), but there is nothing that should be given the special title of *literature.*

Although there is something to be said for the idea that *literature* is just an honorific word and not a body of work embodying eternal truths and eternal beauty, let's make the opposite assumption, at least for a start. Let's assume that certain verbal works are of a distinct sort—whether because the author shapes them, or because a reader perceives them a certain way—and that we can call these works *literature.* But what are these works like?

LITERATURE AND FORM

We all know why we value a newspaper (for instance) or a textbook or an atlas, but why do we value a verbal work that doesn't give us the latest news or important information about business cycles or the names of the capitals of nations? About a thousand years ago a Japanese woman, Shikibu Murasaki or Lady Murasaki (978?-1026), offered an answer in *The Tale of Genji,* a book often called the world's first novel. During a discussion about reading fiction, one of the characters gives an opinion as to why a writer tells a story:

> Again and again something in one's own life, or in the life around one,
> will seem so important that one cannot bear to let it pass into oblivion.
> There must never come a time, the writer feels, when people do not
> know about this.

Literature is about human experiences, but the experiences embodied in literature are not simply the shapeless experiences—the chaotic passing scene—captured by a mindless, unselective video camera. Poets, dramatists, and storytellers find or impose a shape on scenes (for instance, the history of two lovers), giving readers things to value—written or spoken accounts that are memorable not only for their content but also for their *form*—the shape of the speeches, of the scenes, of the plots. (In a little while we will see that form and content are inseparable, but for the moment, for textbook purposes, we can talk about them separately.)

Ezra Pound said that literature is "news that *stays* news." Now, "John loves Mary," written on a wall, or on the front page of a newspaper, is news, but it is not news that stays news. It may be of momentary interest to the friends of John and Mary, but it's not much more than simple information and there is no particular reason to value it. Literature is something else. The Johns and Marys in poems, plays, and stories—even though they usually are fairly ordinary individuals, and in many ways they often are rather like us—somehow become significant as we perceive them through the writer's eye and ear. The writer selects what is essential and makes us care about the characters. Their doings stay in our mind.

One reason literary works endure (whether they show us what we are or what we long for) is that their *form* makes their content memorable. The artist knows how to shape material—whether historical or fictional—into enduring forms. Because this discussion of literature is brief, we will illustrate the point by looking at one of the briefest literary forms, the proverb. (Our definition of literature is not limited to the grand forms of the novel, tragedy, and so on. It is wide enough, and democratic enough, to include brief, popular, spoken texts.) Consider this statement:

A rolling stone gathers no moss.

Now let's compare it with a **paraphrase** (a restatement, a translation into other words):

If a stone is always moving around, vegetation won't have a chance to grow on it.

What makes the original version more powerful, more memorable? Surely much of the answer is that the original is more concrete and its form is more shapely. At the risk of being heavy-handed, we can analyze the shapeliness thus: *Stone* and *moss* (the two nouns in the sentence) each contain one syllable; *rolling* and *gathers* (the two words of motion) each contain two syllables, with the accent on the first syllable. Notice, too, the nice contrast between stone (hard) and moss (soft).

The reader probably *feels* this shapeliness unconsciously rather than perceives it consciously. That is, these connections become apparent when one starts to analyze, but the literary work can make its effect on a reader even before the reader analyzes. As T. S. Eliot said in his essay on Dante (1929), "Genuine poetry can communicate before it is understood." Indeed, our *first* reading of a work, when, so to speak, we are all eyes and ears (and the mind is highly receptive rather than sifting for evidence), is sometimes the most important reading. Experience proves that we can feel the effects of a work without yet understanding *how* the effects are achieved.

Probably most readers will agree that

- the words in the proverb are paired interestingly and meaningfully;
- the sentence is not simply some information but is also (to quote one of Robert Frost's definitions of literature) "a performance in words";

- what the sentence *is,* we might say, is no less significant than what the sentence *says;*
- the sentence as a whole forms a memorable picture, a small but complete world, hard and soft, inorganic and organic, inert and moving;
- the idea set forth is simple—partly because it is highly focused and therefore it leaves out a lot—but it is also complex;
- by virtue of the contrasts, and, again, even by the pairing of monosyllabic nouns and of disyllabic words of motion, it is unified into a pleasing whole.

For all of its specificity and its compactness—the proverb contains only six words—it expands our minds.

A Brief Exercise: Take a minute to think about some other proverb, for instance "Look before you leap," "Finders keepers," "Haste makes waste," or "Absence makes the heart grow fonder." Paraphrase it, and then ask yourself why the original is more interesting, more memorable, than your paraphrase.

LITERATURE AND MEANING

We have seen that the form of the proverb pleases the mind and the tongue, but what about **content** or **meaning?** We may enjoy the images and the sounds, but surely the words add up to something. After all, they are not just "tra la la." Probably most people would agree that the contents or the meaning of "A rolling stone gathers no moss" is something like this: "If you are always on the move— if, for instance, you don't stick to one thing but you keep switching schools, or jobs—you won't accomplish much."

Now, if this statement approximates the meaning of the proverb, we can say two things:

- the proverb contains a good deal of truth, and
- it certainly is not always true.

Indeed this proverb is more or less contradicted by another proverb, "Nothing ventured, nothing gained." Many proverbs, in fact, contradict other proverbs. "Too many cooks spoil the broth," yes, but "Many hands make light work"; "Absence makes the heart grow fonder," yes, but "Out of sight, out of mind"; "He who hesitates is lost," yes, but "Look before you leap." The claim that literature offers insights, or illuminates experience, is not a claim that it offers irrefutable and unvarying truths, covering the whole of our experience. Of course literature does not give us *the* truth; rather it wakes us up, makes us see, helps us feel intensely some aspect of our experience, and perhaps to evaluate it. The novelist Franz Kafka said something to this effect, very strongly, in a letter of 1904:

> If the book we are reading does not wake us, as with a fist hammering on our skull, why then do we read it? . . . What we must have are those books which come upon us like ill-fortune, and distress us deeply, like the death of one we love better than ourselves. . . . A book must be an ice-axe to break the sea frozen inside us.

ARGUING ABOUT MEANING

Later we will discuss at length the question of whether one interpretation—one statement or formulation of the meaning of a work—is better than another, but a word should be said about it now. Suppose that while discussing "A rolling stone gathers no moss," someone said this to you:

> I don't think it means that if you are always on the move you won't accomplish anything. I think the meaning is something like the saying "There are no flies on him." First of all, what's so great about moss developing? Why do you say that the moss more or less represents worthwhile accomplishments? And why do you say that the implication is that someone should settle down? The way I see it is just the opposite: The proverb says that active people don't let stuff accumulate on them, don't get covered over. That is, active people, people who accomplish things (people who get somewhere) are always unencumbered, are people who don't stagnate.

What reply can be offered? Probably no reply will convince the person who interprets the proverb this way. Perhaps, then, we must conclude that (as the critic Northrop Frye said) reading is a picnic to which the writer brings the words and the reader brings the meanings. The remark is witty and is probably true. Certainly readers over the years have brought very different meanings to such works as the Bible and *Hamlet*.

Even if readers can never absolutely prove the truth of their interpretations, all readers have the obligation to make as convincing a case as possible. When you write about literature, you probably will begin (in your marginal jottings and in other notes) by setting down random expressions of feeling and even unsupported opinions, but later, when you are preparing to share your material with a reader, you will have to go further. You will have to try to show your reader *why* you hold the opinion you do. In short, as we have already said,

- You have to be aware of your assumptions.
- You have to offer plausible supporting evidence.
- You have to do so in a coherent and rhetorically effective essay.

That is, you'll have to make the reader in effect say, "Yes, I see exactly what you mean, and what you say makes a good deal of sense." You may not thoroughly convince your readers, but they will at least understand *why* you hold the views you do.

FORM AND MEANING

Let's turn now to a work not much longer than a proverb—a very short poem by Robert Frost (1874-1963).

The Span of Life

The old dog barks backward without getting up.
I can remember when he was a pup.

Read the poem aloud once or twice, physically experiencing Frost's "performance in words." Notice that the first line is harder to say than the second line, which more or less tolls off the tongue. Why? Because in the first line we must pause between *old* and *dog,* between *backward* and *without,* and between *without* and *getting*—and in fact between *back* and *ward.* Further, when we read the poem aloud, or with the mind's ear, in the first line we hear four consecutive stresses in *old dog barks back,* a noticeable contrast to the rather jingling "when he was a pup" in the second line. No two readers will read the lines in exactly the same way, but it is probably safe to say that most readers will agree that in the first line they may stress fairly heavily as many as eight syllables, whereas in the second line they may stress only three or four:

The óld dóg bárks báckward withoút gétting úp.
Í can remémber when hé was a pup.

And so we can say that the form (a relatively effortful, hard-to-speak line followed by a bouncy line) shapes and indeed is part of the content (a description of a dog that no longer has the energy or the strength to leap up, followed by a memory of the dog as a puppy).

Thinking further about Frost's poem, we notice something else about the form. The first line is about a dog, but the second line is about a dog *and* a human being ("*I* can remember"). The speaker must be getting on, too. And although nothing is said about the dog as a *symbol* of human life, surely the reader, prompted by the title of the poem, makes a connection between the life span of a dog and that of a human being. Part of what makes the poem effective is that this point is *not* stated explicitly, not belabored. Readers have the pleasure of making the connection for themselves—under Frost's careful guidance.

Everyone knows that puppies are frisky and that old dogs are not—though perhaps not until we encountered this poem did we think twice about the fact that "the old dog barks backward without getting up." Or let's put it this way:

- Many people may have noticed this behavior, but
- perhaps only Frost thought (to use Lady Murasaki's words), "There must never come a time . . . when people do not know about this." And,
- fortunately for all of us, Frost had the ability to put his perception into memorable words.

Part of what makes this performance in words especially memorable is, of course, the *relationship* between the two lines. Neither line in itself is anything very special, but because of the counterpoint the whole is more than the sum of the parts. Skill in handling language, obviously, is indispensable if the writer is to produce literature. A person may know a great deal about dogs and may be a great lover of dogs, but knowledge and love are not enough equipment to write even a two-line poem about a dog (or the span of life, or both). Poems, like other kinds of literature, are produced by people who know how to delight us with verbal performances.

Presumably Frost reported his observation about the dog not simply as a piece of dog lore, but because it concerns all of us. It is news that stays news. Once you have read or heard the poem, you can never again look at a puppy or an old dog in quite the way you used to—and probably the poem will keep coming to mind as you feel in your bones the effects of aging. If it at first seems odd to say that literature influences us, think of the debate concerning pornography.

The chief reason for opposing pornography is that it exerts a bad influence on those who consume it. If indeed books and pictures can exert a bad influence, it seems reasonable to think that other books and pictures can exert a good influence. Fairness requires us to mention, however, that many thoughtful people disagree and argue that literature and art entertain us but do not really influence us in any significant way. In trying to solve this debate, perhaps one can rely only on one's own experience.

We can easily see that Robert Frost's "The Span of Life" is a work of literature—a work that uses language in a special way—if we contrast it with another short work in rhyme:

> Thirty days hath September,
> April, June, and November;
> All the rest have thirty-one
> Excepting February alone,
> Which has twenty-eight in fine,
> Till leap year gives it twenty-nine.

This information is important, but it is only information. The lines rhyme, giving the work some form, but there is nothing very interesting about it. (This is a matter of opinion; perhaps you will want to take issue.) It is true and therefore useful, but it is not of compelling interest. It is not news that stays news, probably because it only *tells* us facts rather than *shows* or *presents* human experience. We all remember the lines, but they do not hold our interest. "Thirty days" does not offer either the pleasure of an insight or the pleasure of an interesting tune. It has nothing of what the poet Thomas Gray said characterizes literature: "Thoughts that breathe, and words that burn."

THE LITERARY CANON

You may have heard people talk about the **canon** of literature, that is, talk about the recognized body of literature. *Canon* comes from a Greek word for a reed (it's the same as our word *cane*); a reed or cane was used as a measuring stick, and certain works were said to measure up to the idea of literature. Many plays by Shakespeare fit the measure and were accepted into the canon early (and they have stayed there), but many plays by his contemporaries never entered the canon—in their own day they were performed, maybe applauded, and some were published, but later generations have not valued them. In fact, some plays by Shakespeare, too, are almost never taught or performed, for instance, *Cymbeline* and *Timon of Athens*.

Further, the canon—the group of works esteemed by a community of readers—keeps changing, partly because in different periods somewhat different measuring rods are used. For instance, Shakespeare's *Troilus and Cressida*—a play about war, in which heroism and worthy ideals are in short supply—for several hundred years was performed only rarely, but during the Vietnam War it became popular, doubtless because the play was seen as an image of that widely unpopular war. More important, however, than the shifting fortunes of individual works is the recent inclusion of material representing newly valued kinds of experiences. In our day we have increasingly become aware of the voices of women and of members of minority cultures, for instance, Native Americans,

African-Americans, Latinos, lesbians, and gays. As a consequence, works by these people—giving voice to identities previously ignored by the larger society—are now taught in literature classes.

What is or is not literature, then, changes over the years; in the language of today's criticism, "literature" as a category of "verbal production and reception" is itself a "historical construction" rather than an unchanging reality. Insofar as a new generation finds certain verbal works pleasing, moving, powerful, memorable, compelling—beautiful and true, one might say—they become literature. Today a course in nineteenth-century American literature is likely to include works by Harriet Beecher Stowe and Frederick Douglass—but it probably also includes works by long-established favorites such as Emerson, Hawthorne, and Whitman.

Some works have measured up for so long that they probably will always be valued, that is, they will always be part of the literary canon. But of course one cannot predict the staying power of new works. Doubtless some stories, novels, poems, and plays—as well, perhaps, as television scripts and popular songs—will endure. Most of the literature of *any* generation, however, measures up only briefly; later generations find it dated, uninteresting, unexciting. Lincoln's address at Gettysburg has endured as literature, but Kennedy's inaugural address—much praised in its day—now strikes many readers as thin, hollow, strained, even corny. (These adjectives of course imply value judgments; anyone who offers such judgments needs to support them, to argue them, not merely assert them. Elsewhere in this book we talk about arguing a thesis.) Even if Kennedy's inaugural address fades as literature, it will retain its historical importance. In this view, it belongs in a course in politics, but not in a course in literature.

LITERATURE, TEXTS, DISCOURSES, AND CULTURAL STUDIES

These pages have routinely spoken of *literature* and of literary *works,* terms recently often supplanted by *text.* Some say that *literature* is a word with elitist connotations. They may say, too, that a *work* is a crafted, finished thing, whereas a *text,* in modern usage, is something that in large measure is created (i.e., given meaning) by a reader. Further, the word *text* helps to erase the line between, on the one hand, what traditionally has been called literature—for instance, canonized material—and, on the other hand, popular verbal forms such as science fiction, westerns, sermons, political addresses, interviews, advertisements, comic strips, and bumper stickers (and, for that matter, nonverbal products such as sports events, architecture, fashion design, automobiles, and the offerings in a shopping mall). Texts or *discourses* of this sort (said to be parts of what is called a *discursive practice* or a *signifying practice*) in recent years have increasingly interested many people who used to teach literature ("great books") but who now teach *cultural studies.* In courses in cultural studies, the emphasis is not on objects inherently valuable and taught apart from the conditions of their production. Rather, the documents—whether plays by Shakespeare or comic books—are studied in their social and political contexts, especially in the light of the conditions of their production, distribution, and consumption. Thus, *Hamlet* would be related to the economic and political system of England around 1600, and *also* to the context today—the educational system, the theater industry, and so on—that produces the work. To study a work otherwise—to study a literary work as an esthetic object, something to be enjoyed and admired apart from its context—is, it is claimed, to "sacralize" it, to treat it as a sacred thing, and in effect to mummify it. (One might ask if it is really a bad thing to treat with respect—at least at the start—a work by, say, Shakespeare or George Eliot.)

IN BRIEF: A CONTEMPORARY AUTHOR SPEAKS ABOUT LITERATURE

Finally, in an effort to establish an idea of what literature is, let's listen to the words of John Updike, an author of stories, novels, and poems. Updike, as a highly successful writer, could of course be examined in the context of cultural studies: How are his novels promoted? To what extent do reviews of his books affect sales? To what extent do Updike's reviews of other people's books affect sales? What sorts of people (race, class, gender) read Updike? But Updike's own abundant comments about writing are almost entirely concerned with esthetic matters, as in the following passage. He is talking about stories, but we can apply his words to all sorts of literature:

> I want stories to startle and engage me within the first few sentences, and in their middle to widen or deepen or sharpen my knowledge of human activity, and to end by giving me a sensation of completed statement.

SUGGESTIONS FOR FURTHER READING

Subsequent chapters will cite a fair number of recent titles relevant to this chapter, but for a start a reader might first turn to an old but readable, humane, and still useful introduction, David Daiches, *A Study of Literature* (1948). Another book of the same generation, and still a useful introduction, is a businesslike survey of theories of literature by René Wellek and Austin Warren, *Theory of Literature*, 2nd ed. (1956). For a fairly recent, readable study, see Gerald Graff, *Professing Literature: An Institutional History* (1987).

Some basic reference works should be mentioned. C. Hugh Holman and William Harmon have written an introductory dictionary of movements, critical terms, literary periods, and genres: *A Handbook to Literature,* 7th ed. (1996). For fuller discussions of critical terms, see Wendell V. Harris, *Dictionary of Concepts in Literary Criticism and Theory* (1992), which devotes several pages to each concept (for instance, "author," "context," "evaluation," "feminist literary criticism," "narrative") and gives a useful reading list for each entry.

Fairly similar to Harris's book are Irene Makaryk, ed., *Encyclopedia of Contemporary Literary Theory: Approaches, Scholars, Terms* (1993), and Michael Groden and Martin Kreiswirth, eds., *The Johns Hopkins Guide to Literary Theory and Criticism* (1994). *The Johns Hopkins Guide,* though it includes substantial entries on individual critics as well as on critical schools, is occasionally disappointing in the readability of some of its essays and especially in its coverage, since it does not include critical terms other than names of schools of criticism. Despite its title, it does not have entries for "theory" or for "criticism," nor does it have entries for such words as "canon" and "evaluation." In coverage (and also in the quality of many entries) it is inferior to an extremely valuable work with a misleadingly narrow title, *The New Princeton Encyclopedia of Poetry and Poetics,* eds. Alex Preminger and T. V. F. Brogan (1993). Although *The New Princeton Encyclopedia* of course does not include terms that are unique to, say, drama or fiction, it does include generous, lucid entries (with suggestions for further reading) on such terms as "allegory," "criticism," "canon," "irony," "sincerity," "theory," and "unity," and the long entries on "poetics," "poetry," and "poetry theories of" are in many respects entries on "literature."

For a collection of essays on the canon, see *Canons,* ed. Robert von Hallberg (1984); see also an essay by Robert Scholes, "Canonicity and Textuality," in *Introduction to Scholarship in Modern Languages and Literatures,* ed. Joseph Gibaldi, 2nd ed. (1992), 238–158. Gibaldi's collection includes essays on related topics, for instance literary theory (by Jonathan Culler) and cultural studies (by David Bathrick).

A Casebook on the *Titanic:* Songs, Poems, and an Essay on a Film

This casebook contains (in addition to several illustrations) the following material:

1. an account from the *Columbia Encyclopedia*
2. a poem by Thomas Hardy
3. material on folk songs about the sinking, including the version by Huddie Ledbetter
4. three modern poems on the subject
5. a discussion of film and literature, with an essay by Katha Pollitt on the film *Titanic* (1997)

Continuing our examination of "What Is Literature?" let's look at the short account of the wreck of the *Titanic* in the admirable one-volume *Columbia Encyclopedia,* 5th ed. (1993).

Titanic (tītǎn'ĭk), British liner that sank on the night of April 14–15, 1912, after crashing into an iceberg in the N Atlantic S of Newfoundland. More than 1,500 lives were lost. The *Titanic,* thought to be the fastest ship afloat and almost unsinkable, was on her maiden voyage and carried many notables among the more than 2,200 persons aboard. These circumstances made the loss seem the more appalling to the public in England and the United States. Official and other investigations revealed that messages of warning had been sent but had either not been received by the commanding officers or had been ignored by them. The ship had continued at full speed even after the warnings were sent. She did not carry sufficient lifeboats, and many of the lifeboats were launched with only a few of the seats occupied. Other vessels in the vicinity were unable to reach the *Titanic* before she sank; one, only 10 mi (16km) away did not respond because her wireless operator had retired for the evening. The disaster did have some good effects in bringing about measures to promote safety at sea, particularly the establishment of a patrol to make known the location of icebergs and stringent regulations about the proper number and proper equipment of lifeboats to be carried by vessels. The catastrophe inspired a large literature. See Walter Lord, *A Night to Remember* (1959); Lawrence Beesley, *The Loss of the S. S. Titanic* (1912, repr. 1973); Archibald Gracie, *The Truth about the Titanic* (1913, repr. 1973).

This account is moderately interesting, but surely no one would call it "literature"— except in the sense that it is made out of letters of the alphabet, which is the way the word is used when we speak of "campaign literature" or "literature on the care of cats."

Why do people continue to find the *Titanic* disaster "appalling," to use the word provided by the *Columbia Encyclopedia?* Any loss of a ship evokes concern, and shipwrecks have been the subjects of many poems (Longfellow's "The Wreck of the Hesperus" was memorized by countless school children as late as the 1930s). Later in this book (page 423) we print a memorable ballad about a shipwreck, "Sir Patrick Spence." Perhaps we can say that the loss of the *Titanic*

Advertisement for the Titanic, 1912. (Private Collection. Photograph courtesy R.M.S. Titanic Inc.)

was especially memorable, and especially appalling, because, as we know even from the brief account in the encyclopedia,

- the ship was, in its day, the largest, most luxurious, and fastest ship ever built
- the ship carried many immensely wealthy people
- warnings were disregarded (accidentally? casually? arrogantly?)
- the ship was destroyed on its maiden voyage

The story, then, is rich in contrasts, rich in irony. Thoughts such as "Man proposes, God disposes" and "There's many a slip/ Twixt the cup and the lip" come easily to mind. All of this is evident even in the *Encyclopedia* account.

The *Encyclopedia* also mentions that "the disaster did have some good effects in bringing about measures to promote safety at sea," but it does not say anything about material that provided yet another sort of irony. Survivors reported certain acts of bravery, stories of manly behavior (the millionaire Isidor Straus, among other men, said he would not step into a lifeboat until all of the women and children had been taken off the ship), stories of wifely sacrificial de-

Front page of the *New York Times*, April 16, 1912. Although the ship was reputed to be unsinkable, when its stress signals abruptly ceased, the *Times* (in contrast to most other newspapers) concluded the ship had sunk, announced the sinking, and scored a journalistic scoop. (© 1912 by *The New York Times*. Reprinted by permission.)

votion (Straus's wife, Ida, said "We have been living together for many years, and where you go, I go"), and stories of stoic behavior or of Judeo-Christian faith (two prominent men, Major Archibald Butt and Francis Millet, calmly played cards almost to the end, and several survivors reported that the ship's musicians played lively tunes such as "Alexander's Ragtime Band" and "Great Big Beautiful Doll," and, shortly before the ship sank, "Nearer My God to Thee"). We can see in this disaster, then, aspects of loyalty and courage, reassuring aspects of human greatness—not the greatness of the massive wealth of the first-class passengers or even of the ship's unbelievably luxurious furnishings, but the greatness of men and women quietly but heroically responding to tragic circumstances. Don Lynch, in *Titanic: An Illustrated History* (1992), says, "There is no doubt that the bandsmen were heroes. There is no record of any one of them attempting to enter a lifeboat, and their efforts did indeed calm a number of passengers. Not one of them was saved" (p. 115). For such reasons, and doubtless for reasons that we have not thought of, the disaster of the *Titanic* belongs with those stories that Lady Murasaki (see p. 32) spoke of: "There must never come a time, the writer feels, when people do not know about this." Or, to quote again from page 33, the disaster of the *Titanic* is, in Ezra Pound's words, "News that *stays* news"; it was not simply a strange accident that happened and that should be recorded in a newspaper where it would live for a day. Rather, the many details seem to cohere into something that lodges itself permanently in the mind.

One memorable account of this memorable event was provided by Thomas Hardy (1840–1928), an Englishman who had already established himself as a major novelist, but who had turned, by the end of the nineteenth century, from writing prose to writing poetry.

Commemorative card, illustrating the ship and giving the text of a hymn that several survivors reported was played while the ship was sinking. Their report was disputed by other passengers, and there is no doubt that other music was also played. The question of which was the last song remains unsolved. (Collection of Richard Faber)

The Convergence of the Twain

Lines on the Loss of the Titanic

I

In a solitude of the sea
Deep from human vanity,
And the Pride of Life that planned her, stilly couches she.

II

Steel chambers, late the pyres
Of her salamandrine fires,
Cold currents thrid,° and turn to rhythmic tidal lyres.   5

III

Over the mirrors meant
To glass the opulent
The sea-worm crawls—grotesque, slimed, dumb, indifferent.

IV

Jewels in joy designed   10
To ravish the sensuous mind
Lie lightless, all their sparkles bleared and black and blind.

V

Dim moon-eyed fishes near
Gaze at the gilded gear
And query: "What does this vaingloriousness down here?"   15

VI

Well: while was fashioning
This creature of cleaving wing,
The Immanent Will that stirs and urges everything

---

⁶ **thrid** thread

VII

Prepared a sinister mate
For her—so gaily great—   20
A Shape of Ice, for the time far and dissociate.

VIII

And as the smart ship grew
In stature, grace, and hue,
In shadowy silent distance grew the Iceberg too.

IX

Alien they seemed to be: 25
No mortal eye could see
The intimate welding of their later history,

X

Or sign that they were bent
By paths coincident
On being anon twin halves of one august event,   30

XI

Till the Spinner of the Years
Said "Now!" And each one hears,
And consummation comes, and jars two hemispheres.

[1912]

✏ Topics for Critical Thinking and Writing

1. Does Hardy assign a cause to the disaster? What do you make of "The Immanent Will" (line 18) and "the Spinner of Years" (line 31)?
2. In line 19 Hardy speaks of the "sinister mate." What other words in the poem suggest that the ship and the iceberg participate in a marriage?
3. After you have read and thought carefully about the poem, consider the title and subtitle. Why, in your view, did Hardy use the phrase "The Convergence of the Twain" as his title? Would the poem be more effective if the title and subtitle were reversed? Explain.
4. Examine the form and structure of the poem, looking closely at the ways in which Hardy has organized his lines and stanzas. Stanza I, for example, could be rewritten with the final words coming first: "She couches stilly in a solitude of the sea." What poetic effects does Hardy achieve through this

change (and others like it) in normal or typical syntax and word order? And why does he use a series of three-line stanzas, each headed by a roman numeral? Why not simply present the poem as a single long stanza?

THE *TITANIC* AND FOLK SONGS

As we said on page 37, the literary canon changes. American folk songs and ballads, for instance, in 1900 were not generally admitted to the house of literature—or, at best, they were stigmatized as "folk literature" or "popular literature" and grudgingly allowed only in the attic, basement, or kitchen, while the products of educated people occupied (one might say) the royal suite. Today every college anthology of American literature includes such material, along with the works of Poe, Thoreau, Dickinson, Whitman, Hemingway, and Toni Morrison.

African-Americans especially created literature out of the story of the *Titanic,* partly by adapting songs about earlier shipwrecks. Oral poets—not only singers of folk songs but the singers of traditional epic poems such as Homer in ancient Greece—take earlier material and reshape it. The Victorian poet Rudyard Kipling, who saw himself as a poet of the people, put it this way:

> When 'Omer smote 'is blooming lyre,
> He'd 'eard men sing by land an' sea,
> An' what he thought 'e might require,
> 'E went an' took—the same as me!

Consider the following lines, said to be a "Negro" song from Mississippi, which were published in the *Journal of American Folk-lore* in 1909, three years before the *Titanic* sank. (The verse form is often found in blues.)

> O where were you when the steamer went down, Captain?
> O where were you when the steamer went down, Captain?
> O where were you when the steamer went down, Captain?
> I was with my honey in the heart of town.

On the Mississippi, exploding boilers, not icebergs, did the steamers in. Presumably the captain should have been with his ship, staying on board until the last passenger had gotten to safety. The song doesn't say that the captain was cowardly, only that he wasn't where he should have been at the moment he was needed. In four lines—really in two lines—we get the juxtaposition of disaster and joy, death and life, separated but connected by the Captain.

What the ship was, and who the captain was, are unknown, but the ship could have been any of several steamers that sank on the Mississippi. In any case, after the wreck of the *Titanic* an anonymous black singer transformed this song into:

> Where wus you when the big *Titanic* went down?
> Where wus you when the big *Titanic* went down?
> Where wus you when the big *Titanic* went down?
> Standin' on the deck, singin' "Alabama Boun."

And yet another version (there are several more):

O, what were you singing when the *Titanic* went down?
O, what were you singing when the *Titanic* went down?
O, what were you singing when the *Titanic* went down?
Sitting on a mule's back, singing "Alabama Bound."

One doesn't want to make too big a fuss, but surely these two anonymous lyrics about the *Titanic* lodge themselves in the mind, the first with its suggestion of an ocean voyager standing on the deck and singing about going home to Alabama, the second with its evocative contrast of the great ship sinking and the (presumably humble) person safe at home, sitting on a mule and singing of a happy voyage homeward.

In 1927 Carl Sandburg published a much longer song. "De Titanic," in a collection called *The American Songbag*. He prefaced it with these remarks:

The central facts of an immense sea tragedy are here. The main narrative lines of each stanza cadence a proud ship sailing at high speed, ending with a slow drawn drag, the silence of the empty sea that follows the "sinkin' down." As a poem, in accuracy of statement, in stresses of details, and in implicative quality, some would rate this above Longfellow's "Wreck of the Hesperus." The arrangement here is based on the singing of Miss Bessie Zaban, formerly of Georgia and now of Chicago; a number of verses were sent to her by C. H. Currie of Atlanta, Georgia. . . . The dialect is imperfectly rendered. Negro troops sang the song crossing the submarine zone and in the trenches overseas. The verses move smoothly, in even pulsations, like the stride of a great ocean liner with its turbines in good working order. The chorus words "ocean" and "Titanic" sway like a swiftly moving thing abruptly slowed down, struck, staggering and bewildered, while the words "sinkin' down" have the grave, quiet suspension of a requiem.

De Titanic

De rich folks 'cid-ed to take a trip On de fines'

ship dat was ev-er built. De cap-'n pre-sua-ded dese

peo-ples to think   Dis Ti - tan-ic too safe to sink.

CHORUS

Out on dat o - o - cean,   De great wide o -

- cean,   De   Ti -   tan - ic,   out on de o - cean,

slow

- Sink-in'   down! .   .   .

De rich folks 'cided to take a trip
On de fines' ship dat was ever built.
De cap'n presuaded dese peoples to think
Dis Titanic too safe to sink.

4

Chorus:

      Out on dat ocean,
      De great wide ocean,
      De Titanic, out on de ocean,
      Sinkin' down!

De ship lef' de harbor at a rapid speed,
'Twuz carryin' everythin' dat de peeples need.
She sailed six-hundred miles away,
Met an icebug in her way.   12

De ship lef' de harbor, 'twuz runnin' fas'.
'Twuz her fus' trip an' her las'.
Way out on dat ocean wide
An icebug ripped her in de side.   16

Up come Bill from de bottom flo'
Said de water wuz runnin' in de boiler do'.
Go back, Bill, an' shut yo' mouth,
Got forty-eight pumps to keep de water out!   20

Jus' about den de cap'n looked aroun',
He seed de Titanic wuz a-sinkin' down.
He give orders to de mens aroun':
"Get yo' life-boats an' let 'em down!"   24

De mens standin' roun' like heroes brave,
Nothin' but de wimin an' de chillun to save;
De wimin an' de chillun a-wipin' dere eyes,
Kissin' dere husbands an' friends good-bye.   28

On de fifteenth day of May nineteen-twelve,
De ship wrecked by an icebug out in de ocean dwell.
De people wuz thinkin' o' Jesus o' Nazaree,
While de band played "Nearer My God to Thee!"   32

✏ Topics for Critical Thinking and Writing

1. If the pronunciation was "corrected" (e.g., line 9, "The ship left the harbor at a rapid speed"), would the poem gain or lose anything? Why? What does the misnomer "icebug" (lines 12, 16, 30) suggest that "iceberg" lacks?
2. Why is the character Bill introduced (line 17)? What, if anything, does his presence add to the poem's account of the disaster's meaning?
3. Read "Sir Patrick Spence" (page 423), an older ballad. What characteristics do the poems share?
4. In its final stanza the song refers to Jesus and to a Christian hymn. What do these references contribute to the point of view that the song expresses?

We think that all of these verses, those of the anonymous African-Americans as well as those of Thomas Hardy are literature. And we think that the thoroughly respectable account in the *Columbia Encyclopedia,* on the other hand, is not literature. It is lucid and unified and interesting—worthy qualities—but it does not take possession of our minds. Furthermore, the truth it offers is that of a newspaper or of a case history, not the truth (if we can use that word about works that often are known to be fictional) of literature, where, as readers, we experience invented worlds that compel us to say, "Yes, I understand; yes, life—or at least some of life—is like this."

Here is yet another African-American version, this one sung by Huddie Ledbetter (better known as Lead Belly or Leadbelly). Like the first black version that we quoted ("O where were you when the steamer went down, Captain?") it implicates the captain, in this case "Captain Smith" (Edward John Smith was indeed the captain of the *Titanic*), and it connects the loss with the captain's racism: Allegedly the great black prize fighter Jack Johnson sought passage on the ship, and Captain Smith rejected him, saying "I ain' haulin' no coal," but there is absolutely no foundation to this legend.

We quote Leadbelly's version as it appears in *Negro Folk Songs as Sung by Lead Belly*, transcribed, selected, and edited by John A. Lomax and Alan Lomax (1936). The song is undoubtedly Leadbelly's, and yet.... Even without much knowledge of folk songs, one can guess (rightly) that line 3, "Cryin', 'Fare thee, *Titanic*, fare thee well!'" is adapted from some earlier song, with merely a change in the name, here a ship in place of a woman. Other lines, too—most obviously "Captain Smith, when he got his load, /Might 'a' heared him holl'in', 'All aboa'd!" and "It was midnight on the sea"—doubtless come from other songs. Further, in performance Leadbelly varied the song, adding or omitting stanzas, and slightly changing the wording. A version available on CD, *Lead Belly's Last Sessions,* includes a line, "Titanic was comin' round the curve," that clearly comes from an earlier song about a train wreck.

HUDDIE LEDBETTER

Huddie Ledbetter (c. 1888–1949), better known as Leadbelly, was born on a plantation north of Shreveport, Louisiana, on the Louisiana-Texas line. By the age of 15 he was playing the accordion and the guitar at local dances; at 16 he was in Fannin Street, a red-light district where he heard jazz and blues. In 1908 he moved to Dallas, where he met Blind Lemon Jefferson, regarded as the greatest blues singer of the period, and the two performed together for several years.

Huddie Ledbetter (Lead Belly or Leadbelly, 1888-1949), widely considered America's greatest folk singer. (American Folklife Center, Smithsonian Institution, Washington, D.C.)

In 1915 Ledbetter was convicted of assault and was sent to a chain gang, but he escaped. In 1917 he was convicted of murder and he was imprisoned, but he was pardoned in 1925 as a result of a song he sang to the governor in which he asked to be pardoned. In 1930 he was again convicted of assault, and in 1934 he was again pardoned, this time routinely. After leaving prison he was employed by John A. Lomax, who had heard him sing in prison in 1933 and who had recorded his songs for the Library of Congress. Lomax helped publicize Ledbetter in New York City, with radio shows, interviews, and bookings on college campuses. Ultimately Ledbetter made a series of recordings for Folkways. His greatest popularity in the late 1930s and '40s was with white socialist groups, though today his best-known songs, including "Irene" and "Midnight Special," are not overtly political.

De Titanic

Captain Smith, when he got his load,
Might 'a' heared him holl'in', "All aboa'd!"
Cryin', "Fare thee, *Titanic*, fare thee well!"

Captain Smith, when he got his load,
Might 'a' heared him holl'in', "All aboa'd!"   5
Cryin', "Fare thee, *Titanic,* fare thee well!"

Jack Johnson wanted to get on boa'd;
Captain Smith hollered, "I ain' haulin' no coal."
Cryin', "Fare thee, *Titanic,* fare thee well!"

It was midnight on the sea,   10
Band playin', "Nearer My God to Thee."
Cryin', "Fare thee, *Titanic,* fare thee well!"

Titanic was sinking down,
Had them lifeboats aroun'.
Cryin', "Fare thee, *Titanic,* fare thee well!"   15

Had them lifeboats aroun',
Savin' the women, lettin' the men go down.
Cryin', "Fare thee, *Titanic,* fare thee well!"

When the women got out on the land,
Cryin', "Lawd, have mercy on my man."   20
Cryin', "Fare thee, *Titanic,* fare thee well!"

Jack Johnson heard the mighty shock,
Might 'a' seen the black rascal doin' th' Eagle Rock."°
Cryin', "Fare thee, *Titanic,* fare thee well!"

Black man oughta shout for joy,   25
Never lost a girl or either a boy.
Cryin', "Fare thee, *Titanic,* fare thee well!"

Topics for Critical Thinking and Writing

1. As we mentioned in our introduction to this song, there is no historical truth
   to the assertion that Jack Johnson was refused passage because of his color.
   On the other hand, there were no persons of color on the ship—every passenger and every member of the crew was white. Is it reasonable, then, to
   say that although in its reference to Johnson the song is wrong, in a way it is
   right?
2. Reread the anonymous version and Leadbelly's version. Which do you prefer? Why?

THREE POEMS FOR STUDY

Thus far we have tried to indicate that "literature" on the one hand does not include every kind of writing (the entry in the *Columbia Encyclopedia* doesn't
make the cut) and, on the other hand, it does include the utterances of people
who probably would have been surprised to learn that they were producing literature. Here, now, are three works that easily fit the usual definition of literature.

²³**Eagle Rock** a dance step

 **MICHAEL DONAGHY**

Michael Donaghy, born in 1954 in New York City, lives in London and teaches at the University of London. He has published in numerous magazines, including The New Yorker *and* The Paris Review, *and he is the author of several volumes of poetry.*

Reliquary

The robot camera enters the Titanic
And we see her fish-cold nurseries on the news;
The toys of Pompeii trampled in the panic;
The death camp barrel of babyshoes;   4

The snow that covered up the lost girl's tracks;
The scapular she wore about her neck;
The broken doll the photojournalist packs
to toss into the foreground of the wreck.   8

[1993]

Topics for Critical Thinking and Writing

1. Exactly what is a reliquary? (If you are uncertain, check a good dictionary.) What effects do you suppose Donaghy sought to create by using this single-word title?
2. Closely examine, and comment on, specific uses of language in the poem, such as the image of "fish-cold nurseries" and the alliteration in "barrel of babyshoes." Where can we see signs in the text that Donaghy is using language for literary purposes and effects?
3. Is line 3, with its reference to Pompeii, a surprise? What happened at Pompeii—and when? In this line, and in the lines that follow, how is Donaghy relating the sinking of the *Titanic* to other events? Why do you suppose he does this?

WILLIAM DICKEY

William Dickey (1928–94) published his first book of poetry in 1958, when W. H. Auden awarded him the prize in the Yale Series of Younger Poets. Dickey went on to write several other volumes of poetry, taught English and creative writing at San Francisco State University, and served as poetry editor for the Hudson Review.

The Arrival of the *Titanic*

Gashed, from her long immobility on the sea-bed
gravid with the dreams of invertebrates, only half
here in the sense of consciousness, she pulls,
grey on a grey morning into New York Harbor,

bearing all of the dead in their attitudes, the old dead   5
in dinner jackets, bare feet encrusted with barnacles,
their pearls eyes, their old assurance of conquest
over the negligent elements, and walking thin and
perplexed among them the new dead who
never realized on what crossing they had embarked.   10

We are the photograph's negative, made after
the color print, made after the abyssal waters
took color out of the Liberty scarves,° the bright
upper atmosphere of tea dances, after the drift
downward, the pressures of winter. If it has been   15
abandoned, it is ours, it comes sailing silently
back with us. There were never enough
lifeboats, and never
enough gaiety to see us safely through past moonrise
and our monochrome exploration into the range of ice.   20

[1995]

✎ Topics for Critical Thinking and Writing

1. Skillful poets, like all other skillful writers, recognize the value of a good beginning. Do you find the title and first word of this poem effective? Why, or
   why not?
2. The first ten lines of this poem constitute one sentence. Three more sentences follow. As an experiment, type out the sentences as a single paragraph. Using this paragraph as a way to help you think about the form and
   structure of the poem that Dickey wrote, consider some of the poetic effects he gains by starting and ending his lines of verse as he does.
3. Who is the "We" referred to in line 11? At this point Dickey is making a transition, moving from the scene he imagines of the ship's arrival to something
   else. What is the nature of this something else, and what is the purpose of the
   images (for example, the photograph's negative) that Dickey has devised?
4. Do you agree with the student who argued in a class discussion that the
   poem is not really about the *Titanic* at all? Point to evidence in the text that
   could support this interpretation, and also to evidence that qualifies or chal-
   lenges it. Which body of evidence do you find more convincing?

📖 DAVID R. SLAVITT

*David R. Slavitt, born in 1935 and educated at Yale and Columbia, has
taught at several universities, including Rutgers. Slavitt has published
novels, plays, and several books of poetry, as well as translations of
Greek and Roman poets.*

---

[13]**Liberty scarves** Liberty is the name of a manufacturer of fashionable fabrics

Titanic

Who does not love the *Titanic?*
If they sold passage tomorrow for that same crossing,
who would not buy?

To go down . . . We all go down, mostly
alone. But with crowds of people, friends, servants,   5
well fed, with music, with lights! Ah!

And the world, shocked, mourns, as it ought to do
and almost never does. There will be the books and movies
to remind our grandchildren who we were
and how we died, and give them a good cry.   10

Not so bad, after all. The cold
water is anesthetic and very quick.
The cries on all sides must be a comfort.

We all go: only a few, first-class.

[1983]

 Topics for Critical Thinking and Writing

1. What would you say Slavitt's poem is about? The causes of the historical dis-
    aster? The way the passengers died? The death we ourselves are likely to ex-
    perience? Or what?
2. Thomas Hardy wrote "The Convergence of the Twain" in 1912, fifty-five
    years before Slavitt published this poem. What do you suppose Hardy would
    have said if he had seen Slavitt's poem? And what do you suppose Slavitt
    might say of Hardy's poem? (Consider writing a dialogue, about 500 words,
    in which the two poets converse.)
3. Slavitt suggests in this poem that in truth all of us find the idea of dying on
    the *Titanic* rather appealing. Do you agree with him? Do you think he really
    means what he says?

FILM AND LITERATURE

Perhaps one's first thought is that because film is primarily visual, it may be connected with painting but not with literary art. Yet most of the films that we see
tell a story, and therefore they in some degree resemble plays and novels or short
stories. And despite what one might at first think, films probably are closer to
novels and stories than they are to plays.

How can this be? After all, we *watch* a film, just as we watch a play. But
when we watch a play, we ourselves determine where to focus our attention,
whereas when we watch a film we can see only what the filmmaker chooses to
show us. In this sense, the director—who, perhaps gives us a close-up of one
character's face, or shows us only a hand crushing a cigarette in an ashtray, is
rather like the novelist, who has total control over what we see and hear. That is,
the writer of fiction lets us know only what he or she wishes to know. And

just as novelists do not simply write down whatever crosses their line of vision, so too filmmakers do not simply open the lens and shoot. As the great director V. I. Pudovkin said, "A film is not *shot*, but built, built up from the separate strips of celluloid that are its raw material."

Notice, too, that in speaking of film—whether in casual conversation or in a review of a film—we often use the language of literary criticism: We talk about *plot, character, motivation, foreshadowing, symbolism,* and we probably also talk about *theme* (though we may call it "the point," or "the idea"). We assume that everything in the film adds up to some sort of coherent whole. We are likely to be dissatisfied if after seeing a film we believe that we have seen merely certain imaginary people in certain imaginary situations that do not have a point, that do not (so to speak) say anything about life. Consider the comments of François Truffaut on the themes of *The 400 Blows* and *Jules and Jim,* and on the disastrous lack of a theme in *Shoot the Piano Player:*

> In *400 Blows,* I was guided by the desire to portray a child as honestly as possible, and to invest his actions with a moral significance. Similarly with *Jules and Jim,* my desire to keep the film from seeming either pornographic, indelicate, or conventional guided me. The trouble with *Shoot the Piano Player* was that I was able to do anything—that the subject itself didn't impose its own form. . . . As it stands, there are some nice bits in the film, but it can't be said, "This is the best work on this particular theme." There isn't any theme.

Now to return to the *Titanic.* A newspaper account (like an encyclopedia's account) of the sinking, insofar as it is news and not an editorial, cannot have a theme. It can only say, "X happened, Y, happened, Z happened." A newspaper account of the sinking of the *Titanic,* like a newspaper account of a wedding or of a ball game, can only report a happening. It may turn out to be mistaken in its presentation of what are supposed to be the facts, and it may turn out to reveal a decided bias, but ordinarily the aim is to report the news, not to interpret it, not to comment on it. And when we read the newspaper account we do not expect it to imply anything beyond itself. It tells us that something happened, but it does not tell us what ought to happen or what usually happens; it does not imply anything about the ways of people in general. When, however, we read a novel or see on the screen a happening, we inevitably feel—if only because we are asked to give the event an hour or more of our attention—that it is offered to us as noteworthy. It is not an example of what merely *happened,* such as might be reported in a newspaper—"Quintuplets Born in Brooklyn." It didn't happen; it's fictional, even if it claims to be connected to history. Rather, it is an example of what happens, of what life is like. The characters in the fictional work are (like the characters in newspaper items) individuals, not mere abstractions, but (unlike those in newspaper items) they are *significant* individuals, in some measure revealing to us a class of people or a way of life. Filmmakers, like novelists and poets and playwrights, draw on the world around us, and, like these other creators, they make another world, giving us a coherent representation that we relate to our own world.

An Essay on James Cameron's Film, *Titanic*

Films commonly are reviewed, and reviews usually are intended to tell readers whether to go to see the film or not. (On reviews, see p. 142.) But films often en-

gender essays that are somewhat more reflective, more meditative. Here is an example.

KATHA POLLITT

Katha Pollitt (b. 1949) often writes essays on literary, political, and social topics for The Nation, *a liberal journal that published the review we reprint below. Pollitt is also widely known as a poet; her first collection of poems,* Antarctic Traveller *(1982), won the National Book Critics Circle award for poetry.*

Women and Children First

People keep insisting that feminism is over and retro is *de retour*. Virginity is back, white weddings are back, chivalry and cigars are back. The fundamentalist Darwinians think women, or at least their genes, want to be taken care of by older men with thick necks and big incomes. The fundamentalist Christians think women want to be ordered around by dishwashing good old boys. It's been decades now since Hollywood thought about women at all—who cares what they want, as long as they tag along to the movies with their boyfriends?

This background chatter of complacent moralizing and conservative clap-trap is what makes the phenomenally popular success of *Titanic* so satisfying. In her *New York Times* review Janet Maslin hesitated to tag James Cameron's epic—a technological marvel and at $200 million in production costs supposedly the most expensive movie ever made—with the dreaded label "women's picture." But it's women—especially teenage girls—whose repeated viewings, often in groups of friends, have made *Titanic* the highest-grossing movie in history.

It *is* a women's picture, although men may like it too (lots of fancy computer imaging, technology, smashed furniture, and violent death, plus luscious Kate Winslet). That is, like so many great movies of the thirties and forties, it's a three-hankie romance centered on the female character, with tons of glamour and gorgeous clothes. But unlike any women's picture of recent years I can think of, the heroine does not have to choose between work and love or solitude and compromise. She does not have a violent husband, a fatal illness, a shaved head, a kidnapped child. She is not punished for being sexual—no back-alley abortion, stalker, AIDS, rape. She is not a perky sidekick or a long-suffering, tired-looking wife. We are not asked to believe that she would find Woody Allen attractive or enjoy being a prostitute, even for a night.

As you probably already know, *Titanic* is the story of 17-year-old Rose (Winslet), who is being sold into marriage to the very odious, very rich Cal (Billy Zane) by her heartless, snobbish and secretly penniless mother. Returning to America on the fatal ship for her wedding, frantic with boredom and dread, she is rescued from a halfhearted suicide attempt by Jack (Leonardo DiCaprio), a working-class artist and rover. They spend the rest of the movie falling in love, dining in first class and dancing in steerage, evading Cal and his evil manservant (David Warner) and rescuing each other from drowning. We know from the start that Rose survives, because we see her in the present-day framing story as a 101-year-old, still-beautiful bohemian (Gloria Stuart). And, without being told, we know Jack doesn't. It wouldn't be a movie if he did.

5   *Titanic* has been criticized for its silly plot, underwritten characters and wooden dialogue ("This is where we first met!" Rose tells Jack dreamily as they cling to the ship's stern, while people all around them slide off screaming into the sea). Also for its many anachronisms (Rose makes penis jokes and gives the finger, wears bright red lipstick day and night; has tête-à-têtes in her negligee with the villainous Cal. My daughter was sure she glimpsed F.D.R.'s head on a dime in one crucial scene). The 1958 British *A Night to Remember* made much better use of the wealth of knowledge about the liner and its sinking: in particular, the heroic telegraph operators and their desperate attempts to raise any of the several ships nearby; it gave, too, a much sharper sense of the various sorts of hubris—class, empire, industry, technology—that led to the disaster. Although my daughter was keen on the water-safety angle ("Don't go on a big boat or you might lose your lover" was her sarcastic version of the movie's message), Cameron's movie is more of a poetic meditation on class and gender and even, in its all-whiteness, race: The sinking of *Titanic* represents the onrushing destruction of the old order, in which a rapacious, cruel, and secretly sordid upper class suppresses proletarian and immigrant vigor and sells its own daughters into genteel bondage. It's hokum, of course; Cameron barely individualizes the steerage passengers he champions, and, according to the Nation Institute's Peter Meyer, a major *Titanic* buff, underplays the disproportionate death toll of steerage passengers and crew members. This is a pro-democracy movie, perhaps, in the sense that Diana was the people's princess.

Still, for millions of women Diana was exactly that, and within the context of Hollywood films, *Titanic* is a feminist movie. DiCaprio and Winslet are far from gender stereotypes. He has a pale, almost androgynous boyish beauty (you can't believe he needs to shave) and a sexiness from which the usual element of dominance and danger is entirely missing; she exudes a florid vitality, like a pre-Raphaelite angel who's been fed a lot of roast beef. She's flamboyant, even in a way titanic: There's a great scene of her tromping through the rising flood in her wispy gray-and-pink dinner dress, hefting a fire ax to rescue her Jack. She looks like a Valkyrie or a gorgeous fury, wild hair streaming.

Old Rose tells us Jack saved her "in every way that a woman can be saved." Through him she discovers herself as a sexual being and free spirit, abandons fiancé, mother, class for (bedside photos tell us) a long and exciting life as an actress, aviatrix, traveler, potter, mother. Fifteen hundred people perish in torment, but this is a movie with a happy ending and an optimistic vision of history. The twentieth century, which for so many men is a saga of loss, decline, and displacement, has told a different story to women.

So call *Titanic* a women's fantasy—of costless liberation brought to you by a devoted, selfless, charming, funny, incredibly handsome lover. He teaches you to spit, awakens you body and soul, points you toward a long, richly eventful future, and dies, beautifully, poetically, tragically—but not before he tells you that freezing to death in a sea full of corpses was worth it because it brought him you. "He had to die," said one friend of mine, "because otherwise he would have disappointed her down the road." I had the same thought: How many happy artists' wives can you think of?

Romantic feminism. It's what women want. See you at the movies.

✎ Topics for Critical Thinking and Writing

1. In paragraph 3 Pollitt says that the film *Titanic* is "a women's picture," but she goes on to give some reasons why men will also like it. Do you think her points here are well taken, or is she wrongly thinking in stereotypical terms? Explain.

2. If you have seen the movie, do you agree with Pollitt's assertion (paragraph 7) that it is "a movie with a happy ending and an optimistic sense of history"? Explain.

3. Pollitt ends her essay with a very short paragraph. It is just three sentences, and the first is not even a complete sentence. Is her strategy here effective? Would the essay be more effective if this paragraph were omitted?

CHAPTER

4

Reading Literature Closely: (1) Explication

READING IN SLOW MOTION

In this chapter, and in the next, we focus on the skills that careful study of literary language requires. "Close reading" is perhaps the most familiar name for this technique of heightened responsiveness to the words on the page. But another, employed by the literary critics Reuben A. Brower and Richard Poirier, may be even better. They refer to "reading in slow motion." Brower, for example, speaks of "slowing down the process of reading to observe what is happening, in order to attend very closely to the words, their uses, and their meanings." This sort of reading, he explains, involves looking and listening with special alertness, slowly, without rushing or feeling impatient if a work puzzles us at first encounter.[1]

As Brower and Poirier point out, sometimes we are so intrigued or moved by a writer's operations with words that we are led to "slow down" in our reading, lingering over verbal details and vivid images—"a watersmooth-silver / stallion" in Cummings's poem about Buffalo Bill (p. 153); the "icebug" in "De Titanic" (p. 47); or "Babette danced out to where the fig-trees were," in Chopin's "Ripe Figs" (p. 4). Or else, we find that we want to return to a poem, or to a key section of a story or scene in a play, to articulate—"slow motion" style—why it has affected us as powerfully as it did.

"Close" or "slow motion" reading can help you to understand and enjoy a work that at first seems strange or obscure. When we examine a piece of literature with care and intensity, we are not taking it apart in a destructive way but, instead, are seeking to satisfy our curiosity about how the writer organized it. And almost always, our increased *understanding* of the work results in increased *enjoyment*. There are very few poems that have been made worse by close reading, and many that have been made better—made, that is, more accessible and interesting, deeper, and more rewarding.

This point becomes clearer when we recall what it's like to watch a scene from a movie in slow motion, or a TV replay in slow motion of a touchdown run

---

[1] The quotation is taken from Brower's Introduction to *In Defense of Reading: A Reader's Approach to Literary Criticism,* ed. Reuben A. Brower and Richard Poirier (1962). See also Brower, *The Fields of Light: An Experiment in Critical Reading* (1951); and Poirier, *Poetry and Pragmatism* (1992).

60

in a football game. In slow-motion film we perceive details we might otherwise miss—the subtle changes in expression on an actress's face, for example, or the interplay of gestures among several performers at a climactic moment in the action. Similarly, seeing a touchdown multiple times in slow motion, and perhaps from a half-dozen camera angles, reveals to us how the play developed, who made the crucial blocks, where the defense failed. The touchdown was exciting when it took place; and it remains exciting—and frequently it becomes more so—when we slow it down in order to study and talk about it.

This chapter deals with explication, and the next with analysis. Both are based on the principle that responding well to literature means:

- acquiring the ability to read it closely
- practicing this skill to become better and better at it
- explaining and demonstrating in critical essays what we have learned.

But the two terms, while related to one another, differ in emphasis. An **explication** moves from beginning to end of an entire work (if it is fairly short) or of a section of a work; it is sustained, meticulous, thorough, systematic. An **analysis** builds upon the habits of attention that we have gained from explicating texts and passages of texts.

When we engage in analysis of literature, we are doing so as part of presenting an argument, a thesis, about a work. What is the central theme in this short story by Welty or that one by Updike? What is the most compelling insight into the nature of love that Rich offers in this or that group of poems about men and women? Does Hamlet delay and if he does, why? To deal with questions like these, we have to read the text closely and study its language carefully, but we must be selective in the pieces of textual evidence that we offer. To be sure, we can explicate a single speech in Hamlet, or an exchange between characters. But it would be a daunting assignment in a short critical essay to explicate an entire scene, and impossible to explicate the entire play from start to finish.

Analysis goes hand in hand with the job of presenting and proving a thesis; it goes hand in hand with explication as well, taking that form of close reading, of reading in slow motion, as its foundation. But rather than say more about analysis here, let's turn to explication first and learn what we can discover about literature through it. As you'll see, one of the things we quickly realize is that close reading of literary works makes us not only better readers, but also better writers attuned more sharply and sensitively to the organization of the language in our own prose.

EXPLICATION

A line-by-line or episode-by-episode commentary on what is going on in a text is an explication (literally, unfolding or spreading out). An explication does not deal with the writer's life and times, and it is not a paraphrase, a rewording—though it may include paraphrase. Rather, it is a commentary that reveals your sense of the meaning of the work and its structure. When we explicate a text, we ask questions about the meanings of words, the implications of metaphors and images, the speaker's tone of voice as we initially hear it and it develops and perhaps changes. How is this literary work put together? How did the writer organize it to prompt from me the response I had (and am having) to it? How does it begin, and what happens next, and next after that? And so on, through to the end.

It takes some skill to work one's way along in an explication without saying, "In line one. . . . In the second line. . . . In the third line . . . ." This sounds mechanical and formulaic. Make good use of transitional words and phrases, so that your commentary will feel to your reader more natural, with a better pace and rhythm. For example: "The speaker begins by suggesting. . . . The poem then shifts in direction. . . . In the next paragraph, however, the narrator implies . . . ."

A Sample Explication: Langston Hughes's "Harlem"

The following short poem is by Langston Hughes (1902–67), an African-American writer who was born in Joplin, Missouri, lived part of his youth in Mexico, spent a year at Columbia University, served as a merchant seaman, and worked in a Paris nightclub, where he showed some of his poems to Alain Locke, an influential critic, educator, and strong advocate of African-American literature. When he returned to the United States, Hughes went on to publish fiction, plays, essays, and biographies; he also founded theaters, gave public readings, and was, in short, an important force.

Harlem

What happens to a dream deferred?

    Does it dry up
    like a raisin in the sun?
    Or fester like a sore—   4
    And then run?
    Does it stink like rotten meat?
    Or crust and sugar over—
    like a syrupy sweet?   8

    Maybe it just sags
    like a heavy load.

    Or does it explode?

[1951]

Different readers will respond at least somewhat differently to any work. On the other hand, since writers want to communicate, they try to control their readers' responses, and they count on their readers to understand the denotations of words as they understand them. Thus, Hughes assumed that his readers knew that Harlem was the site of a large African-American community in New York City. A reader who confuses the title of the poem with Haarlem in the Netherlands will wonder what this poem is saying about the tulip-growing center in northern Holland. Explication is based on the assumption that the poem contains a meaning and that by studying the work thoughtfully we can unfold the meaning or meanings.

Let's assume that the reader understands Hughes is talking about Harlem, New York, and that the "dream deferred" refers to the unfulfilled hopes of African-Americans who live in a society dominated by whites. But Hughes does not say "hopes," he says "dream," and he does not say "unfulfilled," he says "deferred." You might ask yourself exactly what differences there are between these words. Next, after you have read the poem several times, you might think about which expression is better in the context, "unfulfilled hopes" or "dream deferred," and why.

Working Toward an Explication of "Harlem"

In preparing to write an explication, first write on a computer, or type or hand-write, the complete text of the work that you will explicate—usually a poem but sometimes a short passage of prose. *Don't* photocopy it; the act of typing or writing it will help you to get into the piece, word by word, comma by comma. Type or write it *double-spaced,* so that you will have plenty of room for annotations as you study the piece. It's advisable to make a few photocopies (or to print a few copies, if you are using a word processor) before you start annotating, so that if one page gets too cluttered you can continue working on a clean copy. Or you may want to use one copy for a certain kind of annotations—let's say those concerning imagery—and other copies for other kinds of notes—let's say those concerning meter or wordplay. If you are writing on a word processor, you can highlight words, boldface them, put them in capitals (for instance, to indicate accented syllables), and so forth.

Let's turn to an explication of the poem, a detailed examination of the whole. Here are the preliminary jottings of a student, Bill Horner.

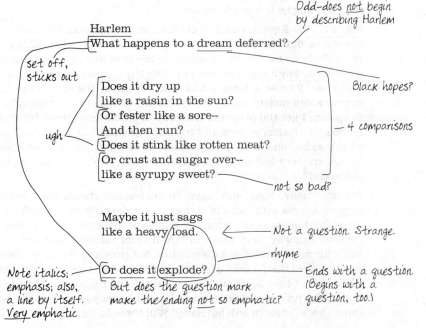

These annotations chiefly get at the structure of the poem, the relationship of the parts. Horner notices that the poem begins with a line set off by itself and ends with a line set off by itself, and he also notices that each of these lines is a question. Further, he indicates that each of these two lines is emphasized in other ways: The first begins farther to the left than any of the other lines—as though the other lines are subheadings or are in some way subordinate—and the last is italicized.

Some Journal Entries

Bill Horner later wrote an entry in his journal:

> Feb. 18. Since the title is "Harlem," it's obvious that the "dream" is by African-American people. Also, obvious that Hughes thinks that if the "dream" doesn't become real there may be riots ("explode"). I like "raisin in the sun" (maybe because I like the play), and I like the business about "a syrupy sweet"--much more pleasant than the festering sore and the rotten meat. But if the dream becomes "sweet," what's wrong with that? Why should something "sweet" explode?

> Feb. 21. Prof. McCabe said to think of structure or form of a poem as a sort of architecture, a building with a foundation, floors, etc., topped by a roof—but since we read a poem from top to bottom, it's like a building upside down. Title is foundation (even though it's at top); last line is roof, capping the whole. As you read, you add layers. Foundation of "Harlem" is a question (first line). Then, set back a bit from foundation, or built on it by white space, a tall room (7 lines high, with 4 questions); then, on top of this room, another room (lines, statement, not a question). Funny; I thought that in poems all stanzas are the same number of lines. Then--more white space, so another unit--the roof. Man, this roof is going to fall in--"explodes." Not just the roof, maybe the whole house.

> Feb. 21, p.m. I get it; one line at start, one line at end; both are questions, but the last sort of says (because it is in italics) that it is the most likely answer to the question of the first line. The last line is also a question, but it's still an answer. The big stanza (7 lines) has 4 questions: 2 lines, 2 lines, 1 line, 2 lines. Maybe the switch to 1 line is to give some variety, so as not to be dull? It's exactly in the middle of the poem. I get the progress from raisin in the sun (dried, but not so terrible), to festering sore and to stinking meat, but I still don't see what's so bad about "a syrupy sweet." Is Hughes saying that after things are very bad they will get better? But why, then, the explosion at the end?

> Feb. 23. "Heavy load" and "sags" in next-to-last stanza seem to me to suggest slaves with bales of cotton, or maybe poor cotton pickers dragging big sacks of cotton. Or maybe people doing heavy labor in Harlem. Anyway, very tired. Different from running sore and stinking meat earlier; not disgusting, but pressing down, deadening. Maybe worse than a sore or rotten meat--a hard, hopeless life. And then the last line. Just one line, no fancy (and disgusting) simile. Boom! Not just pressed down and tired, like maybe some racist whites think (hope?) blacks will be. Bang! Will there be survivors?

Drawing chiefly on these notes, Horner jotted down some key ideas to guide him through a draft of an analysis. (The organization of the draft posed no problem; the writer simply followed the organization of the poem.)

> 11 lines; short, but powerful; explosive
> Question (first line)
> answers (set off by space and also indented)

"raisin in the sun": shrinking ⎤
"sore"   ⎬ disgusting
"rotten meat"   ⎦
"syrupy sweet": relief from disgusting comparisons
final question (last line): explosion?
  explosive (powerful) because:
    short, condensed, packed
    in italics
    stands by self-like first line
    no fancy comparison; very direct

A SAMPLE ESSAY BY A STUDENT (THE FINAL DRAFT): "LANGSTON HUGHES'S 'HARLEM'"

Here is the final essay:

Langston Hughes's "Harlem"

"Harlem" is a poem that is only eleven lines long, but it is charged with power. It explodes. Hughes sets the stage, so to speak, by telling us in the title that he is talking about Harlem, and then he begins by asking, "What happens to a dream deferred?" The rest of the poem is set off by being indented, as though it is the answer to his question. This answer is in three parts (three stanzas, of different lengths).

In a way, it's wrong to speak of the answer, since the rest of the poem consists of questions, but I think Hughes means that each question (for instance, does a "deferred" hope "dry up / like a raisin in the sun?") really is an answer, something that really has happened and that will happen again. The first question, "Does it dry up / like a raisin in the sun?," is a famous line. To compare hope to a raisin dried in the sun is to suggest a terrible shrinking. The next two comparisons are to a "sore" and to "rotten meat." These comparisons are less clever, but they are very effective because they are disgusting. Then, maybe because of the disgusting comparisons, he gives a comparison that is not at all disgusting. In this comparison he says that maybe the "dream deferred" will "crust over-- / like a syrupy sweet."

The seven lines with four comparisons are followed by a stanza of two lines with just one comparison:

Maybe it just sags

like a heavy load.

So if we thought that this postponed dream might finally turn into something "sweet," we were kidding ourselves. Hughes comes down to earth, in a short stanza, with an image of a heavy load, which probably also calls to mind images of people bent under heavy loads, maybe of cotton, or maybe just any sort of heavy load carried by African-Americans in Harlem and elsewhere.

The opening question ("What happens to a dream deferred?") was followed by four questions in seven lines, but now, with "Maybe it just sags / like a heavy load," we get a statement, as though the poet at last has found an answer. But at the end we get one more question, set off by itself and in italics: "Or does it explode?" This line itself is explosive for three reasons: It is short, it is italicized, and it is a stanza in itself. It's also interesting that this line, unlike the earlier lines, does not use a simile. It's almost as though Hughes is saying, "O.K., we've had enough fancy ways of talking about this terrible situation; here it is, straight."

Topics for Critical Thinking

1. The student's explication suggests that the comparison with "a syrupy sweet" deliberately misleads the reader into thinking the ending will be happy, and it thus serves to make the real ending even more powerful. In class another student suggested that Hughes may be referring to African-Americans who play Uncle Tom, people who adopt a smiling manner in order to cope with an oppressive society. Which explanation do you prefer, and why? What do you think of combining the two?

   Does some method or principle help us decide which interpretation is correct? Can one, in fact, talk about a "correct" interpretation, or only about a plausible or implausible interpretation and an interesting or uninteresting interpretation?

2. In *The Collected Poems of Langston Hughes* (1994), the editors title this poem "Harlem." But in the *Selected Poems of Langston Hughes* (1959), published when the poet was still alive, the poem is titled "Dream Deferred." Which title do you think is more effective? Do you interpret the poem differently depending on how it is titled? How might a reader—who knew nothing about Hughes—respond to the poem if he or she came upon it with the title "Dream Deferred"?

Note: Another explication (of W. B. Yeats's "The Balloon of the Mind") appears in Chapter 13.

WHY WRITE? PURPOSE AND AUDIENCE

In Chapter 1 we briefly talked about audience and purpose, but a few further words may be useful. People write explications (as well as other essays on literature) not only to communicate with others but also to clarify and to account for their responses to material that interests or excites or frustrates them. In putting words on paper you will have to take a second and a third look at what is in front of you and at what is within you. And so the process of writing is a way of learning. The last word is never said about complex thoughts and feelings, but when we write we hope to make at least a little progress in the difficult but rewarding job of talking about our responses. We learn, and then we hope to interest our reader because we are communicating our responses to material that for one reason or another is worth talking about.

When you write, you transform your responses into words that will let your reader share your perceptions, your enthusiasms, and even your doubts. This sharing is, in effect, teaching. Students often think that they are writing for the teacher, but this is a misconception. When you write, *you* are the teacher. An essay on literature is an attempt to help someone to see something as you see it.

If you are not writing for the teacher, for whom are you writing? For yourself, of course, but also for others. Occasionally, in an effort to help you develop an awareness that what you write depends partly on your audience, your instructor may specify an audience, suggesting that you write for high school students or for the readers of *The Atlantic* or *Ms.* But if an audience is not specified, write for your classmates.

- If you keep your classmates in mind as your audience, you will *not* write, "William Shakespeare, England's most famous playwright," because such a remark seems to imply that your reader does not know Shakespeare's nationality or trade.
- On the other hand, you *will* write, "Sei Shōnagon, a lady of the court in medieval Japan," because you can reasonably assume that your classmates do not know who she is.

FIVE POEMS FOR EXPLICATION

The basis assignment is to explicate the poems, but your instructor may also ask you to respond to some or all of the questions that follow each poem.

WILLIAM SHAKESPEARE

William Shakespeare (1564–1616), born in Stratford-upon-Avon in England, is chiefly known as a dramatic poet, but he also wrote nondramatic poetry. In 1609 a volume of 154 of his sonnets was published, apparently without his permission. Probably he chose to keep his sonnets unpublished not because he thought that they were of little value, but because it was more prestigious to be an amateur poet (unpublished) than a professional (published) poet. Although the sonnets were published in 1609, they were probably written in the mid–1590s, when there was a vogue for sonneteering. A contemporary writer in 1598 said that Shakespeare's "sugred Sonnets [circulate] among his private friends."

Sonnet 73

That time of year thou mayst in me behold
When yellow leaves, or none, or few, do hang
Upon those boughs which shake against the cold,
Bare ruined choirs° where late the sweet birds sang.   4
In me thou see'st the twilight of such day
As after sunset fadeth in the west,
Which by-and-by black night doth take away,
Death's second self that seals up all in rest,   8
In me thou see'st the glowing of such fire
That on the ashes of his youth doth lie,
As the deathbed whereon it must expire,
Consumed with that which it was nourished by.   12
  This thou perceiv'st, which makes thy love more strong,
  To love that well which thou must leave ere long.

 **Topics for Critical Thinking and Writing**

1. In the first quatrain (the first four lines) to what "time of year" does Shake-speare compare himself? In the second quatrain (lines 5-8) to what does he compare himself? In the third? If the sequence of the three quatrains were reversed, what would be gained or lost?

2. In line 8, what is "Death's second self"? What implications do you perceive in "seals up all in rest," as opposed, for instance, to "brings most welcome rest"?

3. In line 13, exactly what is "This"?

4. In line 14, suppose in place of "To love that well which thou must leave ere long," Shakespeare had written "To love me well whom thou must leave ere long." What if anything would have been gained or lost?

WILLIAM BLAKE

William Blake (1757–1827) was born in London and at fourteen was apprenticed for seven years to an engraver. A Christian visionary poet, he made his living by giving drawing lessons and by illustrating books, including his own Songs of Innocence *(1789) and* Songs of Experience *(1794). These two books represent, he said, "two contrary states of the human soul." "London" comes from* Experience.*) In 1809 Blake exhibited his art, but the show was a failure. Not until he was in his sixties, when he stopped writing poetry, did he achieve any public recognition—and then it was as a painter.*

London

I wander through each chartered street,
Near where the chartered Thames does flow,

---

⁴ **choir** the part of the church where services were sung

And mark in every face I meet
Marks of weakness, marks of woe.   4

In every cry of every man,
In every Infant's cry of fear,
In every voice, in every ban,
The mind-forged manacles I hear.   8

How the Chimney-sweeper's cry
Every black'ning Church appalls;
And the hapless Soldier's sigh
Runs in blood down Palace walls.   12

But most through midnight streets I hear
How the youthful Harlot's curse
Blasts the new-born Infant's tear,
And blights with plagues the Marriage hearse.   16

[1794]

✎ Topics for Critical Thinking and Writing

1. What do you think Blake means by "mind-forged manacles" (line 8)? What might be some modern examples?
2. Paraphrase the second stanza.
3. Read the poem aloud, several times. How would you characterize the *tone*—sad, angry, or what? Of course the tone may vary from line to line, but what is the prevailing tone, if any?
4. An earlier version of the last stanza ran thus:

   But most the midnight harlots's curse
   From every dismal street I hear,
   Weaves around the marriage hearse
   And blasts the new-born infant's tear.

   Compare the two versions closely. Then consider which you think is more effective, and explain why.
5. Write a poem or a paragraph setting forth your response to a city or town that you know well.

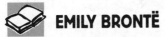 EMILY BRONTË

Emily Brontë (1818–48) spent most of her short life (she died of tuberculosis) in an English village on the Yorkshire moors. The sister of Charlotte Brontë (author of Jane Eyre*) and of Anne Brontë, Emily is best known for her novel* Wuthering Heights *(1847), but she was a considerable poet, and her first significant publication (1846) was in a volume of poems by the three sisters.*

Spellbound

The night is darkening round me,
The wild winds coldly blow;

But a tyrant spell has bound me
And I cannot, cannot go.   4

The giant trees are bending
Their bare boughs weighed with snow.
And the storm is fast descending,
And yet I cannot go.   8

Clouds beyond clouds above me,
Wastes beyond wastes below;
But nothing drear can move me;
I will not, cannot go.   12

[1837]

Topics for Critical Thinking and Writing

1. What exactly is a "spell," and what does it mean to be "spellbound"?
2. What difference, if any, would it make if the first line said "has darkened" instead of "is darkening"?
3. What difference would it make, if any, if lines 4 and 12 were switched?
4. What does "drear" (line 11) mean? Is this word too unusual? Should the poet have used a more familiar word?
5. Describe the speaker's state of mind. Have you ever experienced anything like this yourself? What was the situation and how did you move beyond it?

LI-YOUNG LEE

Li-Young Lee was born in 1957 in Jakarta, Indonesia, of Chinese parents. In 1964 his family brought him to the United States. He was educated at the University of Pittsburgh, the University of Arizona, and the State University of New York, Brockport. He now lives in Illinois, where he works as an artist.

I Ask My Mother to Sing

She begins, and my grandmother joins her.
Mother and daughter sing like young girls.
If my father were alive, he would play
his accordion and sway like a boat.   4

I've never been in Peking, or the Summer Palace,
nor stood on the great Stone Boat to watch
the rain begin on Kuen Ming Lake, the picnickers
running away in the grass.   8

But I love to hear it sung;
how the waterlilies fill with rain until
they overturn, spilling water into water,
then rock back, and fill with more.   12

Both women have begun to cry.
But neither stops her song.

[1986]

Topics for Critical Thinking and Writing

1. Why might the speaker ask the women to sing?
2. Why do the women cry? Why do they continue to sing?

GWENDOLYN BROOKS

Gwendolyn Brooks was born in Topeka, Kansas, in 1917, but was raised in Chicago's South Side, where she has spent most of her life. In 1950, when she won the Pulitzer Prize for Poetry, she became the first African-American writer to win a Pulitzer Prize.

Martin Luther King Jr.

A man went forth with gifts.

He was a prose poem.
He was a tragic grace.
He was a warm music.

He tried to heal the vivid volcanoes.   5
His ashes are
   reading the world.

His Dream still wishes to anoint
   the barricades of faith and of control.

His word still burns the center of the sun,   10
   above the thousands and the
   hundred thousands.

The word was Justice. It was spoken.

So it shall be spoken.
So it shall be done.   15

[1970]

Topics for Critical Thinking and Writing

1. You probably would not ordinarily say that someone "went forth." What does this somewhat unusual diction contribute to the poem?
2. Lines 2–4 offer three metaphors, asserting that King was "a prose poem," "a tragic grace," and "warm music." What do you take each of these metaphors to be saying about King?
3. Explain the meaning of line 5. What is the relationship of this line to lines 6–7?

4. In line 10 Brooks speaks of King's "word," but she does not tell us what that word was ("Justice") until line 13. What is the effect of delaying this information?
5. Is Brooks overstating her claim about King's power?
6. What is the effect of repeating "So it shall," in the last two lines of the poem? Let's think a bit further about this final stanza: It picks up a word, "spoken," from the preceding stanza. Suppose the final stanza omitted line 14 ("So it shall be spoken"), and the poem ended thus:

The word was Justice. It was spoken.
So it shall be done.

What might be gained, or lost?
7. Do you find this poem inspiring? Does it express for you the reason(s) you admire—assuming that you do—Martin Luther King, Jr.?

Reading Literature Closely: (2) Analysis.

ANALYSIS

Explication is a method used chiefly in the study of fairly short poems or brief extracts from essays, stories, novels, and plays. Of course, if one has world enough and time, one can set out to explicate all of *The Color Purple* or *Hamlet;* more likely, one will explicate only a paragraph or at most a page of the novel or a speech or two of the play. In writing about works longer than a page or two, a more common approach than explicating is **analyzing** (literally, separating into parts in order to better understand the whole). An analysis of, say, *The Color Purple* may consider the functions of the setting or the uses that certain minor characters serve; an analysis of *Hamlet* may consider the comic passages or the reasons for Hamlet's delay; an analysis of *Death of a Salesman* may consider the depiction of women or the causes of Willy Loman's failure.

Most of the writing that you will do in college—not only in your English courses but in courses in history, sociology, economics, fine arts, and philosophy—will be analytic. **Analysis** is a method we commonly use in thinking about complex matters and in attempting to account for our responses. Watching Steffi Graf play tennis, we may admire her serve, or her backhand, or the execution of several brilliant plays, and then think more generally about the concentration and flexibility that allow her to capitalize on her opponent's momentary weakness. And of course when we want to improve our own game, we try to analyze our performance. When writing is our game, we analyze our responses to a work, trying to name them and account for them. We analyze our notes, looking for ideas that connect, searching for significant patterns, and later we analyze our drafts, looking for strengths and weaknesses. Similarly, in peer review we analyze the draft of a fellow student, seeing how the parts (individual words, sentences, whole paragraphs, the tentative title, and so on) relate to one another and fit together as a whole.

To develop an analysis of a work, we tend, whether consciously or not, to formulate questions and then to answer them. We ask such questions as:

- What is the function of the setting in this story or play?
- Why has this character been introduced?
- What is the author trying to tell us?
- How exactly can I describe the tone?
- What is the difference in assumptions between this essay and that one?

This book contains an anthology of literary works for you to respond to and then write about, and after most of the works we pose some questions. We also pose general questions on essays, fiction, drama, and poetry. These questions may stimulate your thinking and thus help you write. Our concern as teachers of writing is not so much with the answers to these questions; we believe and we ask you to believe that there are in fact no "right answers," only more or less persuasive ones, to most questions about literature—as about life. Our aim is to help you to pose questions that will stimulate your thinking.

ANALYZING A STORY FROM THE HEBREW BIBLE

A brief analysis of a very short story about King Solomon, from the Hebrew Bible, may be useful here. Because the story is short, the analysis can consider all or almost all of the story's parts, and therefore the analysis can seem relatively complete. ("*Seem* relatively complete" because the analysis will in fact be far from complete, since the number of reasonable things that can be said about a work is almost as great as the number of readers. And a given reader might, at a later date, offer a different reading from what the reader offers today.)

The following story about King Solomon, customarily called "The Judgment of Solomon," appears in the Hebrew Bible, in the latter part of the third chapter of the book called 1 Kings or First Kings, probably written in the mid-sixth century BCE. The translation is from the King James version of the Bible (1611). Two expressions in the story need clarification: (1) The woman who "overlaid" her child in her sleep rolled over on the child and suffocated it; and (2) it is said of a woman that her "bowels yearned upon her son," that is, her heart longed for her son. (In Hebrew psychology, the bowels were thought to be the seat of emotion.)

The Judgment of Solomon

Then came there two women, that were harlots, unto the king, and stood before him. And the one woman said, "O my lord, I and this woman dwell in one house, and I was delivered of a child with her in the house. And it came to pass the third day after that I was delivered, that this woman was delivered also: and we were together; there was no stranger in the house, save we two in the house. And this woman's child died in the night; because she overlaid it. And she arose at midnight, and took my son from beside me, while thine handmaid slept, and laid it in her bosom, and laid her dead child in my bosom. And when I rose in the morning to give my child suck, behold, it was dead: but when I considered it in the morning, behold, it was not my son, which I did bear."

And the other woman said, "Nay; but the living is my son, and the dead is thy son." And this said, "No; but the dead is thy son, and the living is my son." Thus they spake before the king.

Then said the king, "The one saith, 'This is my son that liveth, and thy son is dead': and the other saith, 'Nay; but thy son is the dead, and my son is the living.'" And the king said, "Bring me a sword." And they brought a sword before the king. And the king said, "Divide the living child in two, and give half to the one, and half to the other."

Then spake the woman whose the living child was unto the king, for her bowels yearned upon her son, and she said, "O my lord, give her the living child, and in no wise slay it." But the other said, "Let it be neither mine nor thine, but divide it."

5   Then the king answered and said, "Give her the living child, and in no wise slay it: she is the mother thereof."

And all Israel heard of the judgment which the king had judged; and they feared the king, for they saw that the wisdom of God was in him to do judgment.

Analyzing the Story

Let's begin by analyzing the *form* or the shape of the story. One form or shape that we notice is this: The story moves from a problem to a solution. We can also say, still speaking of the overall form, that the story moves from quarreling and talk of death to unity and talk of life. In short, it has a happy ending, a form that (because it provides an optimistic view of life and also a sense of completeness) gives most people pleasure.

In thinking about a work of literature, it is always useful to take notice of the basic form of the whole, the overall structural pattern. Doubtless you are already familiar with many basic patterns, for example, tragedy (joy yielding to sorrow) and romantic comedy (angry conflict yielding to joyful union). If you think even briefly about verbal works, you'll notice the structures or patterns that govern songs, episodes in soap operas, political speeches (beginning with the candidate's expression of pleasure at being in Duluth, and ending with "God bless you all"), detective stories, westerns, and so on. And just as viewers of a western film experience one western in the context of others, so readers experience one story in the context of similar stories, and one poem in the context of others.

Second, we can say that "The Judgment of Solomon" is a sort of detective story: There is a death, followed by a conflict in the testimony of the witnesses, and then a solution by a shrewd outsider. Consider Solomon's predicament. Ordinarily in literature characters are sharply defined and individualized, yet the essence of a detective story is that the culprit should *not* be easily recognized as wicked, and here nothing seems to distinguish the two petitioners. Solomon is confronted by "two women, that were harlots." Until late in the story—that is, up to the time Solomon suggests dividing the child—they are described only as "the one woman," "the other woman," "the one," "the other."

Does the story suffer from weak characterization? If we think analytically about this issue, we realize that the point surely is to make the women as alike as possible, so that we cannot tell which of the two is speaking the truth. Like Solomon, we have nothing to go on; neither witness is known to be more honest than the other, and there are no other witnesses to support or refute either woman.

Analysis is concerned with

- seeing the relationships between the parts of a work, but it is also concerned with
- taking notice of what is *not* in the work.

A witness would destroy the story, or turn it into an utterly different story. Another thing missing from this story is an explicit editorial comment or interpretation, except for the brief remark at the end that the people "feared the king." If we had read the story in the so-called Geneva Bible (1557-60), which is the translation of the Bible that Shakespeare was familiar with, we would have found a marginal comment: "Her motherly affection herein appeareth that she had rather endure the rigour of the lawe, than see her child cruelly slaine." Would you agree that it is better, at least in this story, for the reader to draw conclusions than for the storyteller explicitly to point them out?

Solomon wisely contrives a situation in which these two claimants, who seem so similar, will reveal their true natures: The mother will reveal her love, and the liar will reveal her hard heart. The early symmetry (the identity of the two women) pleases the reader, and so does the device by which we can at last distinguish between the two women.

But even near the end there is a further symmetry. In order to save the child's life, the true mother gives up her claim, crying out, "Give her the living child, and in no wise slay it." The author (or, rather, the translator who produced this part of the King James Version) takes these very words, with no change whatsoever, and puts them into Solomon's mouth as the king's final judgment. Solomon too says, "Give her the living child, and in no wise slay it," but now the sentence takes on a new meaning. In the first sentence, "her" refers to the liar (the true mother says to give the child to "her"); in Solomon's sentence, "her" refers to the true mother: "Give her the living child . . . ." Surely we take pleasure in the fact that the very words by which the mother renounces her child are the words that (1) reveal to Solomon the truth, and that (2) Solomon uses to restore the child to its mother.

This analysis has chiefly talked about the relations of parts, and especially it has tried to explain why the two women in this story are *not* distinct until Solomon finds a way to reveal their distinctive natures: If the story is to demonstrate Solomon's wisdom, the women must seem identical until Solomon can show that they differ. But the analysis could have gone into some other topic. Let's consider several possibilities.

A student might begin by asking this question: "Although it is important for the women to be highly similar, why are they harlots?" (It is too simple to say that the women in the story are harlots because the author is faithfully reporting a historical episode in Solomon's career. The story is widely recognized as a folktale, found also in other ancient cultures.) One possible reason for making the women harlots is that the story demands that there be no witnesses; by using harlots, the author disposed of husbands, parents, and siblings who might otherwise be expected to live with the women. A second possible reason is that the author wanted to show that Solomon's justice extended to all, not only to respectable folk. Third, perhaps the author wished to reject or to complicate the stereotype of the harlot as a thoroughly disreputable person. The author rejected or complicated the harlot by introducing another (and truer?) stereotype, the mother as motivated by overwhelming maternal love.

Other Possible Topics for Analysis

1. Another possible kind of analytic essay might go beyond the structure of the individual work, to the relation of the work to some larger whole. For instance, one might approach "The Judgment of Solomon" from the point of view of gender criticism (discussed in Chapter 17): In this story, one might argue, wisdom is an attribute only of a male; women are either deceitful or emotional.

From this point one might set out to write a research essay on gender in a larger whole, certain books of the Hebrew Bible.

2. We might also analyze the story in the context of other examples of what scholars call Wisdom Literature (the Book of Proverbs, and Ecclesiastes, for instance). Notice that Solomon's judgment leads the people to *fear* him—because his wisdom is great, formidable, and God-inspired.

It happens that we do not know who wrote "The Judgment of Solomon," but the authors of most later works of literature are known, and therefore some critics seek to analyze a given work within the context of the author's life. For some other critics, the larger context would be the reading process, which includes the psychology of the reader. (Biographical criticism and reader-response criticism are discussed in Chapter 17.)

3. Still another analysis—again, remember that a work can be analyzed from many points of view—might examine two or more translations of the story. You do not need to know Hebrew in order to compare this early seventeenth-century translation with a twentieth-century version such as the New Jerusalem Bible or the Revised English Bible. You might seek to find which version is, on literary grounds, more effective. Such an essay might include an attempt, by means of a comparison, to analyze the effect of the archaic language of the King James Version. Does the somewhat unfamiliar language turn a reader off, or does it add mystery or dignity or authority to the tale, valuable qualities perhaps not found in the modern version? (By the way, in the Revised English Bible, Solomon does *not* exactly repeat the mother's plea. The mother says, "Let her have the baby," and Solomon then says, "Give the living baby to the first woman." In the New Jerusalem Bible, after the mother says, "Let them give her the live child," Solomon says, "Give the live child to the first woman." If you prefer one version to the other two, why not try to analyze your preference?)

Finally, it should be mentioned that an analysis of the structure of a work, in which the relationships of the parts to the whole are considered, allows the work to be regarded as independent of the external world. If we insist, say, that literature should in all respects reflect life, and we want to analyze the work against reality as we see it, we may find ourselves severely judging "The Judgment of Solomon." We might ask if it is likely that a great king would bother to hear the case of two prostitutes quarreling over a child, or if it is likely that the false claimant would really call for the killing of the child. Similarly, to take an absurd example, an analysis of this story in terms of its ability to evoke laughter would be laughable. The point: An analysis will be interesting and useful to a reader only insofar as the aim of the analysis seems reasonable.

ANALYZING A STORY FROM THE NEW TESTAMENT

Let's now look at another brief story from the Bible, this one from the Gospel according to St. Luke, in the New Testament. Luke, the author of the third of the four Gospels, was a second-generation Christian. He probably was a Roman, though some early accounts refer to him as a Syrian; in any case, he wrote in Greek, probably composing the Gospel about A.D. 80–85. In Chapter 15, verses

11–32, he reports a story that Jesus told. This story, which occurs only in Luke's Gospel, is of a type called a **parable,** an extremely brief narrative from which a moral may be drawn.

The Parable of the Prodigal Son

And he said, "A certain man had two sons: and the younger of them said to his father, 'Father, give me a portion of goods that falleth to me.' And he divided unto them his living. And not many days after, the younger son gathered all together, and took his journey into a far country, and there wasted his substance with riotous living.

"And when he had spent all, there arose a mighty famine in that land, and he began to be in want. And he went and joined himself to a citizen of that country, and he sent him into his fields to feed swine. And he would fain have filled his belly with the husks that the swine did eat: and no man gave unto him. And when he came to himself, he said, 'How many hired servants of my father's have bread enough and to spare, and I perish with hunger! I will arise and go to my father, and will say unto him, "Father, I have sinned against heaven, and before thee, and am no more worthy to be called thy son: make me as one of thy hired servants."'

"And he arose, and came to his father. But when he was yet a great way off, his father saw him, and had compassion, and ran, and fell on his neck, and kissed him. And the son said unto him, 'Father, I have sinned against heaven, and in thy sight, and am no more worthy to be called thy son.' But the father said to his servants, 'Bring forth the best robe, and put it on him, and put a ring on his hand, and shoes on his feet. And bring hither the fatted calf, and kill it, and let us eat, and be merry. For this my son was dead, and is alive again; he was lost, and is found.' And they began to be merry.

"Now his elder son was in the field, and as he came and drew nigh to the house, he heard music and dancing. And he called one of the servants, and asked what these things meant. And he said unto him 'Thy brother is come, and thy father hath killed the fatted calf, because he hath received him safe and sound.' And he was angry, and would not go in: therefore came his father out, and entreated him. And he answering said to his father 'Lo, these many years do I serve thee, neither transgressed I at any time thy commandment, and yet thou never gavest me a kid, that I might make merry with friends: but as soon as this thy son was come, which hath devoured thy living with harlots, thou hast killed for him the fatted calf.' And he said unto him, 'Son, thou art ever with me, and all that I have is thine. It was meet that we should make merry, and be glad: for this thy brother was dead, and is alive again: and was lost, and is found.'"

 Topics for Critical Thinking and Writing

1. In talking about the Judgment of Solomon we commented on certain repetitions (e.g., *two* women) and contrasts (e.g., troubled beginning, happy ending), which help to give shape to the story. What parallels or contrasts (or both) do you find in the Parable of the Prodigal Son? What *function* does the older brother serve? If he were omitted, what if anything would be lost? (Characterize him, partly by comparing him with the younger brother and with the father.)

2. Is the father foolish and sentimental? Do you approve or disapprove of his behavior at the end? Why?
3. Jesus told the story, so it must have had a meaning consistent with his other teachings. Christians customarily interpret the story as meaning that God (like the father in the parable) rejoices in the return of a sinner. What meaning, if any, can it have for readers who are not Christians? Explain.

COMPARISON: AN ANALYTIC TOOL

Analysis frequently involves comparing. A moment ago we asked you to compare the older brother with the younger brother and the father in the Parable of the Prodigal Son. When one compares, one examines things for their resemblances to and differences from other things. Strictly speaking, if one emphasizes the differences rather than the similarities, one is contrasting rather than comparing, but we need not preserve this distinction: we can call both processes *comparing*.

Although your instructor may ask you to write a comparison of two works of literature, the *subject* of the essay is the works; comparison is simply an effective analytic technique to show some of the qualities in the works. You might compare Chopin's use of nature in "The Story of an Hour" (page 12) with the use of nature in another story, in order to reveal the subtle differences between the stories, but a comparison of works utterly unlike can hardly tell the reader or the writer anything.

Something should be said about organizing a comparison, say between the settings in two stories, between two characters in a novel (or even between a character at the end of a novel and the same character at the beginning), or between the symbolism of two poems. Probably, a student's first thought after making some jottings is to discuss one half of the comparison and then go on to the second half. Instructors and textbooks (though not this one) usually condemn such an organization, arguing that the essay breaks into two parts and that the second part involves a good deal of repetition of categories set up in the first part. Usually, they recommend that the students organize their thoughts differently, somewhat along these lines:

1. First similarity
   a. First work (or character, or characteristic)
   b. Second work
2. Second similarity
   a. First work
   b. Second work
3. First difference
   a. First work
   b. Second work
4. Second difference
   a. First work
   b. Second work

and so on, for as many additional differences as seem relevant. If one wishes to compare *Huckleberry Finn* with *The Catcher in the Rye*, one may organize the material thus:

1. First similarity: the narrator and his quest
   a. Huck
   b. Holden
2. Second similarity: the corrupt world surrounding the narrator
   a. Society in *Huck*
   b. Society in *Catcher*
3. First difference: degree to which the narrator fulfills his quest and escapes from society
   a. Huck's plan to "light out" to the frontier
   b. Holden's breakdown

Another way of organizing a comparison and contrast:

1. First point: the narrator and his quest
   a. Similarities between Huck and Holden
   b. Differences between Huck and Holden
2. Second point: the corrupt world
   a. Similarities between the worlds in *Huck* and *Catcher*
   b. Differences between the worlds in *Huck* and *Catcher*
3. Third point: degree of success
   a. Similarities between Huck and Holden
   b. Differences between Huck and Holden

A comparison need not employ either of these structures. There is even the danger that an essay employing either of them may not come into focus until the essayist stands back from the seven-layer cake and announces in the concluding paragraph that the odd layers taste better. In one's preparatory thinking, one may want to make comparisons in pairs:

- good-natured humor: the clown in *Othello,* the clownish grave-digger in *Hamlet*
- social satire: the clown in *Othello,* the grave-digger in *Hamlet*
- relevance to main theme: —
- length of role: —

But before writing the final version one must come to some conclusions about what these add up to.

This final version should not duplicate the thought processes; rather, it should be organized so as to make the point—the thesis—clearly and effectively. After reflection, one may believe that

- although there are superficial similarities between the clown in *Othello* and the clownish grave-digger in *Hamlet,*
- there are essential differences.

In the finished essay, a writer will not wish to obscure the main point by jumping back and forth from play to play, working through a series of similarities and differences. It may be better to discuss the clown in *Othello* and then to point out that although the grave-digger in *Hamlet* resembles him in A, B, and C, the grave-digger also has other functions (D, E, and F) and is of greater consequence to *Hamlet* than the clown is to *Othello.* Some repetition in the second half of the essay ("The grave-digger's puns come even faster than the clown's . . .") will bind the two halves into a meaningful whole, making clear the degree of similarity or difference. The point of the essay is not to list pairs of similarities or differences but to illuminate a work or works by making thoughtful comparisons.

Although in a long essay one cannot postpone until page 30 a discussion of the second half of the comparison, in an essay of fewer than ten pages nothing is wrong with setting forth one half of the comparison and then, in light of it, the second half. The essay will break into two unrelated parts if the second half makes no use of the first or if it fails to modify the first half, but not if the second half looks back to the first half and calls attention to differences that the new material reveals. Students ought to learn how to write an essay with interwoven comparisons, but they ought also to know that a comparison may be written in another, simpler and clearer way.

Finally, a reminder: **The purpose of a comparison is to call attention to the unique features of something by holding it up against something similar but significantly different.** You can compare Macbeth with Banquo (two men who hear a prophecy but who respond differently), or Macbeth with Lady Macbeth (a husband and wife, both eager to be monarchs but differing in their sense of the consequences), or Hamlet and Holden Caulfield (two people who see themselves as surrounded by a corrupt world), but you can hardly compare Holden with Macbeth or with Lady Macbeth—there simply aren't enough points of resemblance to make it worth your effort to call attention to subtle differences.

If the differences are great and apparent, a comparison is a waste of effort. ("Blueberries are different from elephants. Blueberries do not have trunks. And elephants do not grow on bushes.") Indeed, a comparison between essentially and evidently unlike things can only obscure, for by making the comparison the writer implies that significant similarities do exist, and readers can only wonder why they do not see them. The essays that do break into two halves are essays that make uninstructive comparisons: the first half tells the reader about five qualities in Alice Walker, the second half tells the reader about five different qualities in Toni Morrison.

A SAMPLE ESSAY BY A STUDENT, MAKING A COMPARISON: "TWO NEW WOMEN"

A student in an introductory class was asked to compare any two of the three stories by Kate Chopin ("Ripe Figs," p. 3; "The Story of an Hour," p. 12; "The Storm," p. 27). She settled on "The Story of an Hour" and "The Storm." We print the final version of her essay, preceded by a page of notes (a synthesis of earlier notes) that she prepared shortly before she wrote her first draft.

Resemblances or differences greater?

Resemblances
Theme: release from marital bonds; liberated women
Setting: nature plays a role in both; springtime in "Hour," storm in "Storm"
Characterization: in both stories, no villains
    forces of nature compel;
    Clarisse presumably happier without husband
    both seem to emphasize roles of women

Differences

Ending: "Hour" sad (LM unfulfilled); "Storm" happy; all characters
    seem content

But endings different in that "Hour" ends suddenly, surprise; "Storm"
    not surprising at very end.

Overall view (theme?)

"Hour" very restricted view; only one person is of much interest (LM);
    Josephine interesting only in terms of LM (contrast).

In "Storm," Cal. and Alc. interesting; but also interesting are simple
    Bobinot and even the child, and also even Clarisse, who sort of
    has the last word

Possible titles

Two Women
New Women
Tragic Louise, Comic Calixta
Louise, Calixta, and Clarisse

Two New Women

It is not surprising that two stories by an author somewhat
resemble each other. What is especially interesting about Kate
Chopin's "The Story of an Hour" and "The Storm" is that although
they both deal with women who achieve a sense of new life or growth
outside of the bonds of marriage, the stories differ greatly in what we
call tone. "The Story of an Hour" is bittersweet, or perhaps even bitter
and tragic, whereas "The Storm" is romantic and in some ways comic.

The chief similarity is that Louise Mallard in "The Story of an
Hour" and Calixta in "The Storm" both experience valuable, affirming,
liberating sensations that a traditional moral view would condemn.
Mrs. Mallard, after some moments of deep grief, feels a great sense of
liberation when she learns of the death of her husband. She dies
almost immediately after this experience, but even though she is never
physically unfaithful to her husband, there is a sort of mental
disloyalty, at least from a traditional point of view. Calixta's disloyalty
is physical, not merely mental. Unlike Louise Mallard, Calixta does go
to bed with a man who is not her husband. But Calixta, as we will see,
is treated just about as sympathetically as is Mrs. Mallard.

Louise Mallard is sympathetic because she does grieve for her
husband, and because Chopin suggests that Mallard's sense of freedom

is natural, something associated with the spring, the "delicious breath of rain," and "the tops of trees that were all aquiver with the new spring life" (12). Furthermore, Chopin explicitly says that Mallard loved her husband. But Chopin also tells us that one aspect of the marriage was a "powerful will bending her" (13). For all of these reasons, then--Mrs. Mallard's genuine grief, the association of her new feeling with the power of nature, and the assertion that Mrs. Mallard loved her husband but was at least in some degree subject to his will-- the reader sympathizes with Mrs. Mallard.

In her presentation of Calixta, too, Chopin takes care to make the unfaithful woman a sympathetic figure. As in "The Story of an Hour," nature plays a role. Here, instead of nature or the outside world being a parallel to the woman's emotions, nature in the form of a storm exerts pressure on the woman. We are told that "the water beat in upon the boards in driving sheets" (28), and a bolt of lightning causes Calixta to stagger backward, into Alcée's arms. These forces of outside nature are parallel to a force of nature within Calixta. Chopin tells us that during the sexual union Calixta's "firm, elastic flesh . . . was knowing for the first time its birthright" (29). And in one additional way, too, Chopin guards against the reader condemning Calixta. We learn, at the end of the story, that Alcée's wife, Clarisse, is quite pleased to be free from her husband for a while:

> And the first free breath since her marriage seemed to restore
> the pleasant liberty of her maiden days. Devoted as she was to
> her husband, their intimate conjugal life was something which
> she was more than willing to forego for a while. (30)

Since Clarisse is portrayed as somewhat pleased to be relieved of her husband for a while, we probably do not see Alcée as a villainous betrayer of his wife. The story seems to end pleasantly, like a comedy, with everybody happy.

In Louise Mallard and in Calixta we see two women who achieve new lives, although in the case of Louise Mallard the reader is surprised to learn in the last sentence that the achievement lasts only a few moments. By "new lives" I mean emancipation from their husbands, but what is especially interesting is that in both cases Chopin guides the reader to feel that although in fact both women behave in ways that would be strongly condemned by the codes of Chopin's day, and even by many people today, neither woman (as Chopin presents her) is blameworthy. Mrs. Mallard is presented almost as a tragic victim, and Calixta is presented almost as a figure in a very pleasant comedy.

[New page]

Work Cited

Barnet, Sylvan, et al., eds. Literature for Composition. 5th ed. New

York: Longman, 2000.

EVALUATION IN EXPLICATION AND ANALYSIS

When we evaluate, we say how good, how successful, how worthwhile, something is. If you reread the student's essay on "Harlem," you'll notice that he implies that the poem is worth reading. He doesn't say "In this excellent poem," but a reader of the essay probably comes away with the impression that the student thinks the poem is excellent. The writer might, of course, have included a more explicit evaluation, along these lines:

In "Harlem," every word counts, and every word is effective. The image of the "heavy load" that "sags" is not as unusual as the image of the raisin in the sun, but it nevertheless is just right, adding a simple, powerful touch just before the explosive ending.

In any case, if an essay argues that the parts fit together effectively, it almost surely is implying a favorable evaluation. But only "*almost* surely." One might argue, for instance, that the parts fit, and so on, but that the work is immoral, or trivial, or unpleasant, or untrue to life. Even though one might grant that the work is carefully constructed, one's final evaluation of the work might be low. Evaluations are based on standards. If you offer an evaluation, make certain that your standards are clear to the reader.

Notice in the following three examples of evaluations of J. D. Salinger's *The Catcher in the Rye* that the writers let their readers know what their standards are. Each excerpt is from a review that was published when the book first appeared. In the first, Anne L. Goodman, writing in *The New Republic* (16 July 1951), began by praising Salinger's earlier short stories and then said of the novel:

But the book as a whole is disappointing, and not merely because it is a reworking of a theme that one begins to suspect must obsess the author. Holden Caulfield, the main character who tells his own story, is an extraordinary portrait, but there is too much of him. He describes himself early on and, with the sureness of a wire recording, he remains strictly in character throughout.

Goodman then quotes a longish passage from *The Catcher*, and says,

In the course of 277 pages the reader wearies of this kind of explicitness, repetition, and adolescence, exactly as one would weary of Holden himself.

Goodman lets us know that, in her opinion, (1) a book ought not simply to repeat a writer's earlier books, and also that, again in her opinion, (2) it's not enough to give a highly realistic portrait of a character; if the character is not a sufficiently interesting person, in the long run the book will be dull.

Another reviewer, Virgilia Peterson, writing in the *New York Herald Tribune Book Review* (15 July 1951), found the book realistic in some ways, but unrealistic and therefore defective because its abundant profanity becomes unconvincing:

> There is probably not one phrase in the whole book that Holden Caulfield would not have used upon occasion, but when they are piled upon each other in cumulative monotony, the ear refuses to believe.

Ms. Peterson concluded her review, however, by confessing that she did not think she was in a position to evaluate a book about an adolescent, or at least *this* adolescent.

> . . . it would be interesting and highly enlightening to know what Holden Caulfield's contemporaries, male and female, think of him. Their opinion would constitute the real test of Mr. Salinger's validity. The question of authenticity is one to which no parent can really guess the reply.

Here again the standard is clear—authenticity—but the writer confesses that she isn't sure about authenticity in this matter, and she defers to her juniors. Peterson's review is a rare example of an analysis offered by a writer who confesses an inability to evaluate.

Finally, here is a brief extract from a more favorable review, written by Paul Engle and published in the *Chicago Sunday Tribune Magazine of Books* (15 July 1951):

> The book ends with Holden in a mental institution, for which the earlier events have hardly prepared the reader. But the story is an engaging and believable one for the most part, full of right observations and sharp insight, and a wonderful sort of grasp of how a boy can create his own world of fantasy and live form.

The first sentence implies that a good book prepares the reader for the end, and that in this respect *The Catcher* is deficient. The rest of the paragraph sets forth other standards that *The Catcher* meets (it is "engaging and believable," "full of right observations and sharp insight"), though one of the standards in Engle's last sentence ("live form") strikes us as obscure.

CHOOSING A TOPIC AND DEVELOPING A THESIS IN AN ANALYTIC PAPER

Because Hughes's "Harlem" is very short, the analysis may discuss the entire poem. But a short essay, or even a long one, can hardly discuss all aspects of a play or a novel or even of a long story. If you are writing about a long work, you'll have to single out an appropriate topic.

What is an appropriate topic? First, it must be a topic that you can work up some interest in or your writing will be mechanical and dull. (We say "work up some interest" because interest is commonly the result of some effort.) Second, an appropriate topic is compassable—that is, it is something you can cover with reasonable attention to detail in the few pages (and few days) you have to devote to it. If a work is fairly long, almost surely you will write an analysis of some part.

Unless you have an enormous amount of time for reflection and revision, you cannot write a meaningful essay of 500 words or even 1000 words on "Shakespeare's *Hamlet*" or "The Fiction of Alice Walker." You cannot even write on "Character in *Hamlet*" or "Symbolism in Walker's *The Color Purple*." And probably you won't really want to write on such topics anyway. Probably *one* character or *one* symbol has caught your interest. Think of something in your annotations or "response" notes (described in Chapter 1) that has caught your attention. Trust your feelings; you are likely onto something interesting.

In Chapter 2 we talked about the value of asking yourself questions. To find an appropriate topic, ask yourself such questions as the following:

1. *What purpose does this serve?* For instance, why is this scene in the novel or play? Why is there a comic grave digger in *Hamlet?* Why are these lines unrhymed? Why did the author call the work by this title?
2. *Why do I have this response?* Why do I feel that this work is more profound (or amusing, or puzzling) than that work? How did the author make this character funny or dignified or pathetic? How did the author communicate the idea that this character is a bore without boring me?

The first of these questions, "What purpose does this serve?" requires that you identify yourself with the author, wondering, for example, whether this opening scene is the best possible for this story. The second question, "Why do I have this response?" requires that you trust your feelings. If you are amused or puzzled or annoyed, assume that these responses are appropriate and follow them up, at least until a rereading of the work provides other responses. If you jot down notes reporting your responses and later think about them, you will probably find that you can select a topic.

A third valuable way to find a thesis is to test a published comment against your response to a particular work. Perhaps somewhere you have seen—for instance, in a textbook—a statement about the nature of fiction, poetry, or drama. Maybe you have heard that a tragic hero has a "flaw." Don't simply accept the remark. Test it against your reading of the work. And interpret the word *published* broadly. Students and instructors publish their opinions—offer them to a public—when they utter them in class. Think about something said in class; students who pay close attention to their peers learn a great deal.

Given an appropriate topic, you will find your essay easier to write and the finished version of it clearer and more persuasive if, at some point in your preparation, in note taking or in writing a first draft, you have converted your topic into a *thesis* (a proposition, a point, an argument) and constructed a *thesis statement* (a sentence stating your overall point).

Let's dwell a moment on the distinction between a topic and a thesis. It may be useful to think of it this way: A topic is a subject (for example, "The Role of Providence in *Hamlet*"); to arrive at a thesis, you have to make an arguable assertion (for example, "The role of Providence in *Hamlet* is not obvious, but it is crucial").

Of course some theses are more promising than others. Consider this thesis:

The role of Providence in *Hamlet* is interesting.

This sentence indeed asserts a thesis, but it is vague and provides little direction, little help in generating ideas and in shaping your essay. Let's try again. It's almost always necessary to try again and again, for the process of writing is in large part a process of trial and error, of generating better and better ideas by evaluating—selecting or rejecting—ideas and options.

> The role of Providence is evident in the Ghost.

This is much better, and it could stimulate ideas for an interesting essay. Let's assume the writer rereads the play, looking for further evidence, and comes to believe that the Ghost is only one of several manifestations of Providence. The writer may stay with the Ghost or may (especially if the paper is long enough to allow for such a thesis to be developed) alter the thesis thus:

> The role of Providence is not confined to the Ghost but is found also in the killing of Polonius, in the surprising appearance of the pirate ship, and in the presence of the poisoned chalice.

Strictly speaking, the thesis here is given in the first part of the sentence ("The role of Providence is not confined to the Ghost"); the rest of the sentence provides an indication of how the argument will be supported.

Every literary work suggests its own topics for analysis to an active reader, and all essayists must set forth their own theses, but if you begin by seeking to examine one of your responses, you will soon be able to stake out a topic and to formulate a thesis.

A suggestion: With two or three other students, formulate a thesis about Kate Chopin's "The Storm" (in Chapter 2). By practicing with a group you will develop a skill that you will use when you have to formulate a thesis on your own.

AN ANALYSIS OF A STORY

If a story is short enough, you may be able to examine everything in it that you think is worth commenting on, but even if it is short you may nevertheless decide to focus on one element, such as the setting, or the construction of the plot, or the connection between two characters, or the degree of plausibility. Here is a story by James Thurber (1894–1961), the American humorist. It was first published in 1939.

JAMES THURBER
The Secret Life of Walter Mitty

"We're going through!" The Commander's voice was like thin ice breaking. He wore his full-dress uniform, with the heavily braided white cap pulled down rakishly over one cold gray eye. "We can't make it, sir. It's spoiling for a hurricane, if you ask me." "I'm not asking you, Lieutenant Berg," said the Commander. "Throw on the power lights! Rev her up to 8,500! We're going through!" The pounding of the cylinders increased: ta-pocketa-pocketa-pocketa-*pocketa-pocketa*. The Commander stared at the ice forming on the pilot window. He walked over and twisted a row of complicated dials. "Switch on No. 8 auxiliary!" he shouted. "Switch on No. 8 auxiliary!" repeated Lieutenant Berg. "Full strength in No. 3 turret!" shouted the Commander. "Full strength in No. 3 turret!" The crew, bending to their various tasks in the huge, hurtling eight-engined Navy hydroplane, looked at each other and grinned. "The Old Man'll get us through," they said to one another. "The Old Man ain't afraid of Hell!" . . .

"Not so fast! You're driving too fast!" said Mrs. Mitty. "What are you driving so fast for?"

"Hmm?" said Walter Mitty. He looked at his wife, in the seat beside him, with shocked astonishment. She seemed grossly unfamiliar, like a strange woman who had yelled at him in a crowd. "You were up to fifty-five," she said. "You know I don't like to go more than forty. You were up to fifty-five." Walter Mitty drove on toward Waterbury in silence, the roaring of the SN202 through the worst storm in twenty years of Navy flying fading in the remote, intimate airways of his mind. "You're tensed up again," said Mrs. Mitty. "It's one of your days. I wish you'd let Dr. Renshaw look you over."

Walter Mitty stopped the car in front of the building where his wife went to have her hair done. "Remember to get those overshoes while I'm having my hair done," she said. "I don't need overshoes," said Mitty. She put her mirror back into her bag. "We've been all through that," she said, getting out of the car. "You're not a young man any longer." He raced the engine a little. "Why don't you wear your gloves? Have you lost your gloves?" Walter Mitty reached in a pocket and brought out the gloves. He put them on, but after she had turned and gone into the building and he had driven on to a red light, he took them off again. "Pick it up, brother!" snapped a cop as the light changed, and Mitty hastily pulled on his gloves and lurched ahead. He drove around the streets aimlessly for a time, and then he drove past the hospital on his way to the parking lot.

5   . . . "It's the millionaire banker, Wellington McMillan," said the pretty nurse. "Yes?" said Walter Mitty, removing his gloves slowly. "Who has the case?" "Dr. Renshaw and Dr. Benbow, but there are two specialists here, Dr. Remington from New York and Dr. Pritchard-Mitford from London. He flew over." A door opened down a long, cool corridor and Dr. Renshaw came out. He looked distraught and haggard. "Hello, Mitty," he said. "We're having the devil's own time with McMillan, the millionaire banker and close personal friend of Roosevelt. Obstreosis of the ductal tract. Tertiary. Wish you'd take a look at him." "Glad to," said Mitty.

In the operating room there were whispered introductions: "Dr. Remington, Dr. Mitty, Mr. Pritchard-Mitford, Dr. Mitty." "I've read your book on streptothricosis," said Pritchard-Mitford, shaking hands. "A brilliant performance, sir." "Thank you," said Walter Mitty. "Didn't know you were in the States, Mitty," grumbled Remington. "Coals to Newcastle, bringing Mitford and me up here for a tertiary." "You are very kind," said Mitty. A huge, complicated machine, connected to the operating table, with many tubes and wires, began at this moment to go pocketa-pocketa-pocketa. "The new anesthetizer is giving way!" shouted an interne. "There is no one in the East who knows how to fix it!" "Quiet, man!" said Mitty, in a low, cool voice. He sprang to the machine, which was now going pocketa-pocketa-queep-pocketa-queep. He began fingering delicately a row of glistening dials. "Give me a fountain pen!" he snapped. Someone handed him a fountain pen. He pulled a faulty piston out of the machine and inserted the pen in its place. "That will hold for ten minutes," he said. "Get on with the operation." A nurse hurried over and whispered to Renshaw, and Mitty saw the man turn pale. "Coreopsis has set in," said Renshaw nervously. "If you would take over, Mitty?" Mitty looked at him and at the craven figure of Benbow, who drank, and at the grave, uncertain faces of the two great specialists. "If you wish," he said. They slipped a white gown on him: he adjusted a mask and drew on thin gloves; nurses handed him shining. . . .

"Back it up, Mac! Look out for that Buick!" Walter Mitty jammed on the brakes. "Wrong lane, Mac," said the parking-lot attendant, looking at Mitty closely. "Gee. Yeh," muttered Mitty. He began cautiously to back out of the lane marked "Exit Only." "Leave her sit there," said the attendant. "I'll put her away." Mitty got out of the car. "Hey, better leave the key." "Oh," said Mitty, handing the man the ignition key. The attendant vaulted into the car, backed it up with insolent skill, and put it where it belonged.

They're so damn cocky, thought Walter Mitty, walking along Main Street; they think they know everything. Once he had tried to take his chains off, outside New Milford, and he had got them wound around the axles. A man had had to come out in a wrecking car and unwind them, a young, grinning garageman. Since then Mrs. Mitty always made him drive to the garage to have the chains taken off. The next time, he thought, I'll wear my right arm in a sling; they won't grin at me then. I'll have my right arm in a sling and they'll see I couldn't possibly take the chains off myself. He kicked at the slush on the sidewalk. "Overshoes," he said to himself, and he began looking for a shoe store.

When he came out into the street again, with the overshoes in a box under his arm, Walter Mitty began to wonder what the other thing was his wife had told him to get. She had told him, twice, before they set out from their house for Waterbury. In a way he hated these weekly trips to town—he was always getting something wrong. Kleenex, he thought, Squibb's, razor blades? No. Toothpaste, toothbrush, bicarbonate, carborundum, initiative and referendum? He gave it up. But she would remember it. "Where's the what's-its-name?" she would ask. "Don't tell me you forgot the what's-its-name." A newsboy went by shouting something about the Waterbury trial.

10   . . . "Perhaps this will refresh your memory." The District Attorney suddenly thrust a heavy automatic at the quiet figure on the witness stand. "Have you ever seen this before?" Walter Mitty took the gun and examined it expertly. "This is my Webley-Vickers 50.80," he said calmly. An excited buzz ran around the courtroom. The Judge rapped for order. "You are a crack shot with any sort of firearms, I believe?" said the District Attorney, insinuatingly. "Objection!" shouted Mitty's attorney. "We have shown that the defendant could not have fired the shot. We have shown that he wore his right arm in a sling on the night of the fourteenth of July." Walter Mitty raised his hand briefly and the bickering attorneys were stilled. "With any known make of gun," he said evenly, "I could have killed Gregory Fitzhurst at three hundred feet *with my left hand.*" Pandemonium broke loose in the courtroom. A woman's scream rose above the bedlam and suddenly a lovely, dark-haired girl was in Walter Mitty's arms. The District Attorney struck at her savagely. Without rising from his chair, Mitty let the man have it on the point of the chin. "You miserable cur!" . . .

"Puppy biscuit," said Walter Mitty. He stopped walking and the buildings of Waterbury rose up out of the misty courtroom and surrounded him again. A woman who was passing laughed. "He said 'Puppy biscuit,'" she said to her companion. "That man said 'Puppy biscuit' to himself." Walter Mitty hurried on. He went into an A. & P., not the first one he came to but a smaller one farther up the street. "I want some biscuit for small, young dogs," he said to the clerk. "Any special brand, sir?" The greatest pistol shot in the world thought a moment. "It says 'Puppies Bark for It' on the box," said Walter Mitty.

His wife would be through at the hairdresser's in fifteen minutes, Mitty saw in looking at his watch, unless they had trouble drying it; sometimes they had trouble drying it. She didn't like to get to the hotel first; she would want him to be there waiting for her as usual. He found a big leather chair in the lobby, facing a window, and he put the overshoes and the puppy biscuit on the floor beside it. He picked up an old copy of *Liberty* and sank down into the chair. "Can Germany Conquer the World through the Air?" Walter Mitty looked at the pictures of bombing planes and of ruined streets.

. . . "The cannonading has got the wind up in young Raleigh, sir," said the sergeant. Captain Mitty looked up at him through tousled hair. "Get him to bed," he said wearily. "With the others. I'll fly alone." "But you can't, sir," said the sergeant anxiously. "It takes two men to handle that bomber and the Archies are pounding hell out of the air. Von Richtman's circus is between here and Saulier." "Somebody's got to get that ammunition dump," said Mitty. "I'm going over. Spot of brandy?" He poured a drink for the sergeant and one for himself. War thundered and whined around the dugout and battered at the door. There was a rending of wood and splinters flew through the room. "A bit of a near thing," said Captain Mitty carelessly. "The box barrage is closing in," said the sergeant. "We only live once, Sergeant," said Mitty, with his faint, fleeting smile. "Or do we?" He poured another brandy and tossed it off. "I never see a man could hold his brandy like you, sir," said the sergeant. "Begging your pardon, sir." Captain Mitty stood up and strapped on his huge Webley-Vickers automatic. "It's forty kilometers through hell, sir," said the sergeant. Mitty finished one last brandy. "After all," he said softly, "what isn't?" The pounding of the cannon increased; there was the rat-tat-tatting of machine guns, and from somewhere came the menacing pocket-pocketa-pocketa of the new flame-throwers. Walter Mitty walked to the door of the dugout humming "Auprès de Ma Blonde." He turned and waved to the sergeant. "Cheerio!" he said. . . .

Something struck his shoulder. "I've been looking all over this hotel for you," said Mrs. Mitty. "Why do you have to hide in this old chair? How did you expect me to find you?" "Things close in," said Walter Mitty vaguely. "What?" Mrs. Mitty said. "Did you get the what's-its-name? The puppy biscuit? What's in that box?" "Overshoes," said Mitty. "Couldn't you have put them on in the store?" "I was thinking," said Walter Mitty. "Does it ever occur to you that I am sometimes thinking?" She looked at him. "I'm going to take your temperature when I get you home," she said.

15   They went out through the revolving doors that made a faintly derisive whistling sound when you pushed them. It was two blocks to the parking lot. At the drugstore on the corner she said, "Wait here for me. I forgot something. I won't be a minute." She was more than a minute. Walter Mitty lighted a cigarette. It began to rain, rain with sleet in it. He stood up against the wall of the drugstore, smoking. . . . He put his shoulders back and his heels together. "To hell with the handkerchief," said Walter Mitty scornfully. He took one last drag on his cigarette and snapped it away. Then, with that faint, fleeting smile playing about his lips, he faced the firing squad; erect and motionless, proud and disdainful, Walter Mitty the Undefeated, inscrutable to the last.

[1939]

Some Journal Entries

Before reading the following entries about "The Secret Life of Walter Mitty," write some of your own. You may want to think about what (if anything) you found amusing in the story, or about whether the story is dated, or about some aspect of Mitty's character or of his wife's. But the choice is yours.

A student wrote the following entry in her journal after the story was discussed in class.

> March 21. Funny, I guess, especially the business about him as a doctor performing an operation. And that "pocketa-pocketa," but I don't think that it's as hysterical as everyone else seems to think it is. And how could anyone stand being married to a man like that? In fact, it's a good thing he has her to look after him. He ought to be locked up, driving into the "Exit Only" lane, talking to himself in the street, and having those crazy daydreams. No wonder the woman in the street laughs at him.
>
> March 24. He's certainly a case, and she's not nearly as bad as everyone was saying. So she tells him to put his overshoes on; well, he ought to put them on, since Thurber says there is slush in the street, and he's no kid anymore. About the worst I can say of her is that she seems a little unreasonable in always wanting him to wait for her, rather than sometimes the other way around, but probably she's really telling him not to wander off, because if he ever drifts away there'll be no finding him. The joke, I guess, is that he's supposed to have these daydreams because he's henpecked, and henpecked men are supposed to be funny. Would people find the story just as funny if she had the daydreams, and he bullied her?

List Notes

In preparation for writing a draft, the student reread the story and jotted down some tentative notes based on her journal and on material that she had high-lighted in the text. (At this point you may want to make your own list, based on your notes.)

> Mitty helpless: he needs her
> chains on tires
> enters Exit Only
> ~~Waterbury~~
> cop tells him to get going
> fantasies
> wife a nag?   causes his daydreams? Evidence?
> makes him get to hotel first
> overshoes
> backseat driver?
> "Does it ever occur to you that I am sometimes thinking?" Is he thinking, or just having dreams?
> M. confuses Richthoven with someone called Richtman.
> Funny--or anti-woman? Would it be funny if he nagged her, and she had daydreams?

Next, the student wrote a draft; then she revised the draft and submitted the revision (printed here) to some classmates for peer review. (The number enclosed within parentheses cites the source of a quotation.) Before reading the student's draft, you may want to write a draft based on your own notes and lists.

Sample Draft by a Student: "Walter Mitty Is No Joke"

Walter Mitty Is No Joke

James Thurber's "The Secret Life of Walter Mitty" seems to be highly regarded as a comic story about a man who is so dominated by his wife that he has to escape through fantasies. In my high school course in English, everyone found Mitty's dreams and his wife's bullying funny, and everyone seems to find them funny in college, too. Everyone except me.

If we look closely at the story, we see that Mitty is a pitiful man who <u>needs</u> to be told what to do. The slightest glimpse of reality sets him off on a daydream, as when he passes a hospital and immediately begins to imagine that he is a famous surgeon, or when he hears a newsboy shouting a headline about a crime and he imagines himself in a courtroom. The point seems to be that his wife nags him, so he escapes into daydreams. But the fact is that she <u>needs</u> to keep after him, because he <u>needs</u> someone to tell him what to do. It depends on what one considers nagging. She tells him he is driving too fast, and (given the date of the story, 1939) he probably is, since he is going 55 on a slushy or snowy road. She tells him to wear overshoes, and he probably ought to, since the weather is bad. He resents all of these orders, but he clearly is incompetent, since he delays when the traffic light turns from red to green, and he enters an "Exit Only" lane in a parking lot. We are also told that he can't put chains on tires.

In fact, he can't do anything right. All he can do is daydream, and the dreams, though they <u>are</u> funny, are proof of his inability to live in the real world. When his wife asks him why he didn't put the overshoes on in the store, instead of carrying them in a box, he says, "Does it ever occur to you that I am sometimes thinking?" (90). But he doesn't "think," he just daydreams. Furthermore, he can't even get things straight in his daydreams, since he gets everything mixed up, confusing Richthoven with Richtman, for example.

Is "The Secret Life of Walter Mitty" really a funny story about a man who daydreams because he is henpecked? Probably it is supposed to be so, but it's also a story about a man who is lucky to have a wife

who can put up with him and keep him from getting killed on the
road or lost in town.

Work Cited

Thurber, James. "The Secret Life of Walter Mitty." <u>Literature for</u>
<u>Composition</u>. Ed. Sylvan Barnet et al. 5th ed. New York:
Longman, 2000, 87-90.

INTRODUCTIONS, MIDDLES, ENDINGS

Introductory Paragraphs

As the poet Byron said, at the beginning of a long part of a long poem, "Nothing
so difficult as a beginning." Woody Allen thinks so, too. In an interview he said
that the toughest part of writing is "to go from nothing to the first draft."

We can give two pieces of advice:

1. *The opening paragraph is unimportant.* It's great if you can write a paragraph that will engage your readers and let them know where the essay will
be taking them, but if you can't come up with such a paragraph, just put
down anything in order to prime the pump.
2. *The opening paragraph is extremely important.* It must engage your readers, and probably by means of a thesis sentence it should let the readers
know where the essay will be taking them.

The contradiction is, however, only apparent, not real. The first point is relevant to the opening paragraph of a *draft;* the second point is relevant to the
opening paragraph of the *final version*. Almost all writers—professionals as
well as amateurs—find that the first paragraphs in their drafts are false starts.
Don't worry too much about the opening paragraphs of your draft; you'll want
to revise your opening later anyway. (Surprisingly often your first paragraph
may simply be deleted; your second, you may find, is where your essay truly begins.)

When writing a first draft you merely need something—almost anything
may do—to break the ice. But in your finished paper the opening cannot be
mere throat-clearing. The opening should be interesting.

Among the commonest **uninteresting openings** are these:

1. A dictionary definition ("Webster says . . .").
2. A restatement of your title. The title is (let's assume) "Romeo's Maturation,"
and the first sentence says, "This essay will study Romeo's maturation."
True, there is an attempt at a thesis statement here, but no information beyond what has already been given in the title. There is no information about
you, either, that is, no sense of your response to the topic, such as is present
in, say, "*Romeo and Juliet* covers less than one week, but within this short
period Romeo is impressively transformed from a somewhat comic infatuated boy to a thoughtful tragic hero."
3. A platitude, such as "Ever since the beginning of time men and women have
fallen in love." Again, such a sentence may be fine if it helps you to start
drafting, but because it sounds canned and because it is insufficiently interesting, it should not remain in your final version.

What is left? What *is* a good way for a final version to begin? Your introductory paragraph will be interesting if it gives information, and it will be pleasing if the information provides a focus—that is, if it goes beyond the title in letting the reader know exactly what your topic is and where you are headed.

Let's assume that you agree: An opening paragraph should be *interesting* and *focused*. Doubtless you will find your own ways of fulfilling these goals, but you might consider using one of the following time-tested methods.

1. *Establish a connection between life and literature* We have already suggested that a platitude (for instance, "Ever since the beginning of time men and women have fallen in love") usually makes a poor beginning because it is dull, but you may find some other way of relating the work to daily experience. For instance:

   > Doubtless the popularity of Romeo and Juliet (the play has been with us for almost four hundred years) is partly due to the fact that it deals with a universal experience. Still, no other play about love is so much a part of our culture that the mere mention of the names of the lovers immediately calls up an image. But when we say that So-and-so is "a regular Romeo," exactly what do we mean? And exactly what sort of lover is Romeo?

2. *Give an overview.* Here is an example:

   > Langston Hughes's "Harlem" is about the destruction of the hopes of African-Americans. More precisely, Hughes begins by asking "What happens to a dream deferred?" and then offers several possibilities, the last of which is that it may "explode."

3. *Include a quotation.* The previous example illustrates this approach, also. Here is another example:

   > One line from Langston Hughes's poem "Harlem" has become famous, "A raisin in the sun," but its fame is, in a sense, accidental; Lorraine Hansberry happened to use it for the title of a play. Doubtless she used it because it is impressive, but in fact the entire poem is worthy of its most famous line.

4. *Use a definition.* We have already suggested that a definition such as "Webster says . . ." is boring and therefore unusable, but consider the following:

   > When we say that a character is the hero of a story, we usually mean that he is the central figure, and we probably imply that he is manly. But in Kafka's "The Metamorphosis" the hero is most unmanly.

5. *Introduce a critical stance.* If your approach is feminist, or psychoanalytic, or Marxist, or whatever, you may want to say so at the start. Example:

> Feminists have called our attention to the unfunny sexism of mother-in-law jokes, comments about women hooking men into marriage, and so forth. We can now see that the stories of James Thurber, long thought to be wholesome fun, are unpleasantly sexist.

Caution: We are not saying that these are the only ways to begin, and we certainly are not suggesting that you pack all five into the opening paragraph. We are saying only that after you have done some brainstorming and written some drafts, you may want to think about using one of these methods for your opening paragraph

An Exercise: Write (either by yourself or in collaboration with one or two other students) an opening paragraph for an essay on one of Kate Chopin's stories and another for an essay on Hughes's "Harlem." (To write a useful opening paragraph you will, of course, first have to settle on the essay's thesis.)

Middle Paragraphs

The middle, or body, of your essay will develop your thesis by offering supporting evidence. Ideas for the body should emerge from the sketchy outline that you made after you reviewed your brainstorming notes or journal.

1. *Be sure that each paragraph makes a specific point* and that the point is sufficiently developed with evidence (a brief quotation is often the best evidence).
2. *Be sure that each paragraph is coherent.* Read each sentence, starting with the second sentence, to see how it relates to the preceding sentence. Does it clarify, extend, reinforce, add an example? If you can't find the relationship, the sentence probably does not belong where it is. Rewrite it, move it, or strike it out.
3. *Be sure that the connections between the paragraphs are clear.* Transitional words and phrases, such as "Furthermore," "On the other hand," and "In the next stanza," will often give readers all the help they need in seeing how your points are connected.
4. *Be sure that the paragraphs are in the best possible order.* A good way to test the organization is to jot down the topic sentence or topic idea of each paragraph, and then to see if your jottings are in a reasonable sequence.

Concluding Paragraphs

Concluding paragraphs, like opening paragraphs, are especially difficult, if only because they are so conspicuous. Readers often skim first paragraphs and last paragraphs to see if an essay is worth reading. With conclusions, as with openings, say something interesting. It is not interesting to say, "Thus we see that Mrs. Mitty . . ." (and here you go on to echo your title or your first sentence).

What to do? When you are revising a draft, you might keep in mind the following widely practiced principles. They are not inflexible rules, but they often work.

1. *Hint that the end is near.* Expressions such as "Finally," "One other point must be discussed," and "In short," alert the reader that the end is nigh and help to prevent the reader from feeling that the essay ends abruptly.
2. *Perhaps reassert the thesis, but put it in a slightly new light.* Not, "I have shown that Romeo and Hamlet are similar in some ways," but:

> These similarities suggest that in some respects Romeo is an early study for Hamlet. Both are young men in love, both seek by the force of their passion to shape the world according to their own desires, and both die in the attempt. But compared with Hamlet, who at the end of the play understands everything that has happened, Romeo dies in happy ignorance; Romeo is spared the pain of knowing that his own actions will destroy Juliet, whereas Hamlet dies with the painful knowledge that his kingdom has been conquered by Norwegian invaders.

3. *Perhaps offer an evaluation.* You may find it appropriate to conclude your analysis with an evaluation, such as this:

> Romeo is as convincing as he needs to be in a play about young lovers, but from first to last he is a relatively uncomplicated figure, the ardent lover. Hamlet is a lover, but he is also a good deal more, a figure whose complexity reveals a more sophisticated or a more mature author. Only five or six years separate Romeo and Juliet from Hamlet, but one feels that in those few years Shakespeare made a quantum leap in his grasp of human nature.

4. *Perhaps include a brief significant quotation from the work.* Example:

> Romeo has won the hearts of audiences for almost four centuries, but, for all his charm, he is in the last analysis concerned only with fulfilling his own passion. Hamlet, on the other hand, at last fulfills not only his own wish but that of the Ghost, his father. "Remember me," the Ghost says, when he first appears to Hamlet and asks for revenge. Throughout the play Hamlet does remember the Ghost, and finally, at the cost of his own life, Hamlet succeeds in avenging his dead father.

✔ ## A Checklist for Revising Paragraphs

✔ Does the paragraph *say* anything? Does it have substance?

✔ Does the paragraph have a topic sentence? If so, is it in the best place? If the paragraph doesn't have a topic sentence, might one improve the paragraph? Or does it have a clear topic idea?

✔ If the paragraph is an opening paragraph, is it interesting enough to attract and to hold a reader's attention? If it is a later paragraph, does it easily evolve out of the previous paragraph, and lead into the next paragraph?

✔ Does the paragraph contain some principle of development, for instance from general to particular?

✔ Does each sentence clearly follow from the preceding sentence? Have you provided transitional words or cues to guide your reader? Would it be useful to repeat certain key words, for clarity?

✔ What is the purpose of the paragraph? Do you want to summarize, or tell a story, or give an illustration, or concede a point, or what? Is your purpose clear to you, and does the paragraph fulfill your purpose?

✔ Is the closing paragraph effective, and not an unnecessary restatement of the obvious?

REVIEW: WRITING AN ANALYSIS

Each writing assignment will require its own kind of thinking, but here are a few principles that usually are relevant:

1. Assume that your reader has already read the work you are discussing but is not thoroughly familiar with it—and of course does not know what you think and how you feel about the work. Early in your essay name the author, the work, and your thesis.

2. Do not tell the plot (or, at most, summarize it very briefly); instead, tell your reader what the work is about (not what happens, but what the happenings add up to).

3. Whether you are writing about character or plot or meter or anything else, you will probably be telling your reader something about *how* the work works, that is, how it develops. The stages by which a work advances may sometimes be marked fairly clearly. For instance (to oversimplify), a poem of two stanzas may ask a question in the first and give an answer in the second, or it may express a hope in the first and reveal a doubt in the second. Novels, of course, are customarily divided into chapters, and even a short story may be printed with numbered parts. Virtually all works are built up out of parts, whether or not the parts are labeled.

4. In telling the reader how each part leads to the next, or how each part arises out of what has come before, you will probably be commenting on such things as (in a story) changes in a character's state of mind—marked perhaps by a change in the setting—or (in a poem) changes in the speaker's tone of voice—for instance from eager to resigned, or from

cautious to enthusiastic. Probably you will in fact not only be describing the development of character or of tone or of plot, but also (and more important) you will be advancing your own thesis.

A WORD ABOUT TECHNICAL TERMINOLOGY

Literature, like, say, the law, medicine, the dance, and, for that matter, cooking and baseball, has given rise to technical terminology. A cookbook will tell you to boil, or bake, or blend, and it will speak of a "slow" oven (300 degrees), a "moderate" oven (350 degrees), or a "hot" oven (450 degrees). These are technical terms in the world of cookery. In watching a baseball game we find ourselves saying, "I think the hit-and-run is on," or "He'll probably bunt." We use these terms because they convey a good deal in a few words; they are clear and precise. Further, although we don't use them in order to impress our hearer, in fact they do indicate that we have more than a superficial acquaintance with the game. That is, the better we know our subject, the more likely we are to use the technical language of the subject. Why? *Because such language enables us to talk precisely and in considerable depth about the subject.* Technical language, unlike jargon (pretentious diction that needlessly complicates or obscures), is illuminating—provided that the reader is familiar with the terms.

In writing about literature you will, for the most part, use the same language that you use in your other courses, and you will not needlessly introduce the technical vocabulary of literary study—but you *will* use this vocabulary when it enables you to be clear, concise, and accurate.

Example: A Lyric Poem and a Student's Essay

 APHRA BEHN

Aphra Behn (1640–89) is regarded as the first English woman to have made a living by writing. Not much is known of her life, but she seems to have married a London merchant of Dutch descent, and after his death to have served as a spy in the Dutch Wars (1665–67). After her return to England she took up playwrighting, and she gained fame with The Rover *(1677). Behn also wrote novels, the most important of which is* Oroonoko; or The Royal Slave *(1688), which is among the first works in English to express pity for enslaved Africans.*

Song: Love Armed

Love in fantastic triumph sate,
    Whilst bleeding hearts around him flowed,
For whom fresh pains he did create,
    And strange tyrannic power he showed:
From thy bright eyes he took his fire,   5
    Which round about in sport he hurled;
But 'twas from mine he took desire,
    Enough to undo the amorous world.

From me he took his sighs and tears:
  From thee, his pride and cruelty;   10
From me, his languishments and fears;
  And every killing dart from thee.
Thus thou and I the god have armed
  And set him up a deity;
But my poor heart alone is harmed,   15
  Whilst thine the victor is, and free.

[1676]

✏ Topics for Critical Thinking and Writing

1. The speaker talks of the suffering he is undergoing. Can we nevertheless feel that he enjoys his plight? *Why*, by the way, do we often enjoy songs of unhappy love?
2. The woman ("thee") is said to exhibit "pride and cruelty" (line 10). Is the poem sexist? Is it therefore offensive?
3. Do you suppose that men can enjoy the poem more than women? Explain.

Journal Entries

The subject is Aphra Behn's "song". We begin with two entries in a journal, kept by a first-year student, Geoffrey Sullivan, and we follow these entries with Sullivan's completed essay.

> October 10. The title "Love Armed" puzzled me at first; funny, I somehow was thinking of the expression "strong-armed" and at first I didn't understand that "Love" in this poem is a human--no, not a human, but the god Cupid, who has a human form--and that he is shown as armed, with darts and so forth.
> October 13. This god of "Love" is Cupid, and so he is something like what is on a valentine card--Cupid with his bow and arrow. But valentine cards just show cute little Cupids, and in this poem Cupid is a real menace. He causes lots of pain ("bleeding hearts," "tears," "killing dart," etc.). So what is Aphra Behn telling us about the god of love, or love? That love hurts? And she is singing about it! But we do sing songs about how hard life is. But do we sing them when we are really hurting, or only when we are pretty well off and just thinking about being hurt?
> When you love someone and they don't return your love, it hurts, but even when love isn't returned it still gives some intense pleasure. Strange, but I think true. I wouldn't say that love always has this two-sided nature, but I do see the idea that love can have two sides, pleasure and pain. And love takes two kinds of people, male and female. Well, for most people, anyway. Maybe there's also something to the idea that "opposites attract." Anyway, Aphra Behn seems to be talking about men vs. women, pain vs. pleasure, power vs. weakness, etc. Pairs, opposites. And in two stanzas (a pair of stanzas?).

A SAMPLE ESSAY BY A STUDENT: "THE DOUBLE NATURE OF LOVE"

The final essay makes use of some, but not of all, of the preliminary jottings, and it includes much that Sullivan did not think of until he reread his jottings, reread the poem, and began drafting the essay.

Geoffrey Sullivan

English 2G

15 October 1999

The Double Nature of Love

Aphra Behn's "Love Armed" is in two stanzas, and it is about two people, "me" and "thee," that is, you and I, the lover and the woman he loves. I think the speaker is a man, since according to the usual code men are supposed to be the active lovers and women are the (relatively) passive people who are loved. In this poem, the beloved--the woman, I think--has "bright eyes" (line 5) that provide the god of Love with fire, and she also provides the god with "pride and cruelty" (10). This of course is the way the man sees it if a woman doesn't respond to him; if she doesn't love him in return, she is (he thinks) arrogant and cruel. What does the man give to Love? He provides "desire" (7), "sighs and tears" (9), "languishments and fears" (11). None of this sounds very manly, but the joke is that the god of love--which means love--can turn a strong man into a crybaby when a woman does not respond to him.

Although both stanzas are clever <u>descriptions</u> of the god of love, the poem is not just a description. Of course there is not a plot in the way that a short story has a plot, but there is a sort of a switch at the end, giving the story something of a plot. The poem is, say, ninety percent expression of feeling and description of love, but during the course of expressing feelings and describing love something happens, so there is a tiny <u>story.</u> The first stanza sets the scene ("Love in fantastic triumph sate" [1]) and tells of some of the things that the speaker and the woman contributed to the god of Love. The woman's eyes provided Love with fire, and the man's feelings provided Love with "desire" (7). The second stanza goes on to mention other things that Love got from the speaker ("sighs and tears," etc. [9]), and other things that Love got from the beloved ("pride and cruelty," etc. [10]), and in line 13 the poet says, "Thus thou and I the god have armed," so the two humans share something. They have both given Love his weapons. But--and this is the story I spoke of--the poem ends by emphasizing their difference: Only the man is "harmed," and the woman is the "victor" because her heart is not captured, as the man's heart is. In the battle that Love presides over, the woman is the winner; the man's heart has fallen for the woman, but, according to the last line, the woman's heart remains "free."

We have all seen the god of Love on valentine cards, a cute little Cupid armed with a bow and arrow. But despite the bow and arrow that the Valentine Day Cupid carries, I think that until I read Aphra Behn's "Love Armed" I had never really thought about Cupid as powerful and as capable of causing real pain. On valentine cards, he is just cute, but when I think about it, I realize the truth of Aphra Behn's concept of love. Love is (or can be) two-sided, whereas the valentine cards show only the sweet side.

I think it is interesting to notice that although the poem is about the destructive power of love, it is fun to read. I am not bothered by the fact that the lover is miserable. Why? I think I enjoy the poem, rather than am bothered by it, because he is enjoying his misery. After all, he is singing about it, sort of singing in the rain, telling anyone who will listen about how miserable he is, and he is having a very good time doing it.

Work Cited

Behn, Aphra. "Love Armed." Literature and Composition. Ed. Sylvan Barnet et al. 5th ed. New York: Longman, 2000, 98.

 ## Topics for Critical Thinking and Writing

1. What do you think of the title? Is it sufficiently interesting and focused?
2. What are the writer's chief points? Are they clear, and are they adequately developed?
3. Do you think the writer is too concerned with himself, and that he loses sight of the poem? Or do you find it interesting that he connects the poem with life?

4. Focus on the writer's use of quotations. Does he effectively introduce and examine quoted lines and phrases?
5. What grade would you give the essay? Why?

 Editing Checklist: Questions to Ask Yourself

✔ Is the title of my essay at least moderately informative and interesting?

✔ Do I identify the subject of my essay (author and title) early?

✔ What is my thesis? Do I state it soon enough (perhaps even in the title) and keep it in view?

✔ Is the organization reasonable? Does each point lead into the next without irrelevancies and without anticlimaxes?

✔ Is each paragraph unified by a topic sentence or a topic idea? Are there adequate transitions from one paragraph to the next?

✔ Are generalizations supported by appropriate concrete details, especially by brief quotations from the text?

✔ Is the opening paragraph interesting and, by its end, focused on the topic? Is the final paragraph conclusive without being repetitive?

✔ Is the tone appropriate? No sarcasm, no apologies, no condescension?

✔ If there is a summary, is it as brief as possible, given its purpose?

✔ Are the quotations adequately introduced, and are they accurate? Do they provide evidence and let the reader hear the author's voice, or do they merely add words to the essay?

✔ Is the present tense used to describe the author's work and the action of the work ("Shakespeare *shows*," "Hamlet *dies*")?

✔ Have I kept in mind the needs of my audience, for instance, by defining unfamiliar terms or by briefly summarizing works or opinions that the reader may be unfamiliar with?

✔ Is documentation provided where necessary?

✔ Are the spelling and punctuation correct? Are other mechanical matters (such as margins, spacing, and citations) in correct form? Have I proofread carefully?

✔ Is the paper properly identified—author's name, instructor's name, course number, and date?

THREE SHORT STORIES FOR ANALYSIS

NATHANIEL HAWTHORNE

Nathaniel Hawthorne (1804–64) was born in Salem, Massachusetts, the son of a sea captain. Two of his ancestors were judges; one had persecuted Quakers, another had served at the Salem witch trials. After graduating from Bowdoin College in Maine he went back to Salem in order to write in relative seclusion. In 1832 he published "Roger Malvin's Burial"; in 1835 he published "Young Goodman Brown" (p.1207).

From 1839 to 1841 Hawthorne worked in the Boston Customs House and then spent a few months as a member of a communal society, Brook Farm. In 1842 he married. From 1846 to 1849 he was a surveyor at the Salem Customs House; from 1849 to 1850 he wrote The Scarlet Letter, *the book that made him famous. From 1853 to 1857 he served as American consul in Liverpool, England, a plum awarded him in exchange for writing a campaign biography of a former college classmate, President Franklin Pierce. In 1860, after living in England and Italy, he returned to the United States, settling in Concord, Massachusetts.*

In his stories and novels Hawthorne keeps returning to the Puritan past, studying guilt, sin, and isolation.

Roger Malvin's Burial

One of the few incidents of Indian warfare naturally susceptible of the moonlight of romance was that expedition undertaken for the defense of the frontiers in the year 1725, which resulted in the well-remembered "Lovell's Fight." Imagination, by casting certain circumstances judicially into the shade, may see much to admire in the heroism of a little band who gave battle to twice their number in the heart of the enemy's country. The open bravery displayed by both parties was in accordance with civilized ideas of valor; and chivalry itself might not blush to record the deeds of one or two individuals. The battle, though so fatal to those who fought, was not unfortunate in its consequences to the country; for it broke the strength of a tribe and conduced to the peace which subsisted during several ensuing years. History and tradition are unusually minute in their memorials of this affair; and the captain of a scouting party of frontier men has acquired as actual a military renown as many a victorious leader of thousands. Some of the incidents contained in the following pages will be recognized, notwithstanding the substitution of fictitious names, by such as have heard, from old men's lips, the fate of the few combatants who were in a condition to retreat after "Lovell's Fight."

The early sunbeams hovered cheerfully upon the tree-tops, beneath which two weary and wounded men had stretched their limbs the night before. Their bed of withered oak leaves was strewn upon the small level space, at the foot of a rock, situated near the summit of one of the gentle swells by which the face of the country is there diversified. The mass of granite, rearing its smooth, flat surface fifteen or twenty feet above their heads, was not unlike a gigantic gravestone, upon which the veins seemed to form an inscription in forgotten characters. On a tract of several acres around this rock, oaks and other hard-wood trees had supplied the place of the pines, which were the usual growth of the land; and a young and vigorous sapling stood close beside the travellers.

The severe wound of the elder man had probably deprived him of sleep; for, so soon as the first ray of sunshine rested on the top of the highest tree, he reared himself painfully from his recumbent posture and sat erect. The deep lines of his countenance and the scattered gray of his hair marked him as past the middle age; but his muscular frame would, but for the effect of his wound, have been as capable of sustaining fatigue as in the early vigor of life. Languor and exhaustion now sat upon his haggard features; and the despairing glance which he sent forward through the depths of the forest proved his own conviction that his pilgrimage was at an end. He next turned his eyes to the companion who reclined by his side. The youth — for he had scarcely attained the years of manhood — lay, with his head upon his arm, in the embrace of an unquiet sleep, which a thrill of pain from his wounds seemed each moment on the point of breaking. His right hand grasped a musket; and, to judge from the violent action of his features, his slumbers were bringing back a vision of the conflict of which he was one of the few survivors. A shout — deep and loud in his dreaming fancy — found its way in an imperfect murmur to his lips; and, starting even at the slight sound of his own voice, he suddenly awoke. The first act of reviving recollection was to make anxious inquiries respecting the condition of his wounded fellow-traveller. The latter shook his head.

"Reuben, my boy," said he, "this rock beneath which we sit will serve for an old hunter's gravestone. There is many and many a long mile of howling wilderness before us yet; nor would it avail me anything if the smoke of my own chimney were but on the other side of that swell of land. The Indian bullet was deadlier than I thought."

5   "You are weary with our three days' travel," replied the youth, "and a little longer rest will recruit you. Sit you here while I search the woods for the herbs and roots that must be our sustenance; and, having eaten, you shall lean on me, and we will turn our faces homeward. I doubt not that, with my help, you can attain to some one of the frontier garrisons."

"There is not two days' life in me. Reuben," said the other, calmly, "and I will no longer burden you with my useless body, when you can scarcely support your own. Your wounds are deep and your strength is failing fast; yet, if you hasten onward alone, you may be preserved. For me there is no hope, and I will await death here."

"If it must be so, I will remain and watch by you," said Reuben, resolutely.

"No, my son, no," rejoined his companion. "Let the wish of a dying man have weight with you; give me one grasp of your hand and get you hence. Think you that my last moments will be eased by the thought that I leave you to die a more lingering death? I have loved you like a father, Reuben; and at a time like this I should have something of a father's authority. I charge you to be gone that I may die in peace."

"And because you have been a father to me, should I therefore leave you to perish and to lie unburied in the wilderness?" exclaimed the youth. "No; if your end be in truth approaching, I will watch by you and receive your parting words. I will dig a grave here by the rock, in which, if my weakness overcome me, we will rest together; or, if Heaven gives me strength, I will seek my way home."

10   "In the cities and wherever men dwell," replied the other, "they bury their dead in the earth; they hide them from the sight of the living; but here, where no step may pass perhaps for a hundred years, wherefore should I not rest beneath the open sky, covered only by the oak leaves when the autumn winds shall strew them? And for a monument, here is this gray rock, on which my dying hand shall carve the name of Roger Malvin; and the traveller in days to come will know that here sleeps a hunter and a warrior. Tarry not, then, for a folly like this, but hasten away, if not for your own sake, for hers who will else be desolate."

Malvin spoke the last few words in a faltering voice, and their effect upon his companion was strongly visible. They reminded him that there were other and less questionable duties than that of sharing, the fate of a man whom his death could not benefit. Nor can it be affirmed that no selfish feeling strove to enter Reuben's heart, though the consciousness made him more earnestly resist his companion's entreaties.

"How terrible to wait the slow approach of death in this solitude!" exclaimed he. "A brave man does not shrink in the battle; and, when friends stand round the bed, even women may die composedly; but here" —

"I shall not shrink even here, Reuben Bourne," interrupted Malvin. "I am a man of no weak heart, and, if I were, there is a surer support than that of earthly friends. You are young, and life is dear to you. Your last moments will need comfort far more than mine; and when you have laid me in the earth, and are alone, and night is settling on the forest, you will feel all the bitterness of the death that may now be escaped. But I will urge no selfish motive to your generous nature. Leave me for my sake, that, having said a prayer for your safety, I may have space to settle my account undisturbed by worldly sorrows."

"And your daughter — how shall I dare to meet her eye?" exclaimed Reuben. "She will ask the fate of her father, whose life I vowed to defend with my own. Must I tell her that he travelled three days' march with me from the field of battle and that then I left him to perish in the wilderness? Were it not better to lie down and die by your side than to return safe and say this to Dorcas?"

15 "Tell my daughter," said Roger Malvin, "that, though yourself sore wounded, and weak, and weary, you led my tottering footsteps many a mile, and left me only at my earnest entreaty, because I would not have your blood upon my soul. Tell her that through pain and danger you were faithful, and that, if your life-blood could have saved me, it would have flowed to its last drop; and tell her that you will be something dearer than a father, and that my blessing is with you both, and that my dying eyes can see a long and pleasant path in which you will journey together."

As Malvin spoke he almost raised himself from the ground, and the energy of his concluding words seemed to fill the wild and lonely forest with a vision of happiness; but, when he sank exhausted upon his bed of oak leaves, the light which had kindled in Reuben's eye was quenched. He felt as if it were both sin and folly to think of happiness at such a moment. His companion watched his changing countenance, and sought with generous art to wile him to his own good.

"Perhaps I deceive myself in regard to the time I have to live," he resumed. "It may be that, with speedy assistance, I might recover of my wound. The foremost fugitives must, ere this, have carried tidings of our fatal battle to the frontiers, and parties will be out to succor those in like condition with ourselves. Should you meet one of these and guide them hither, who can tell but that I may sit by my own fireside again?"

A mournful smile strayed across the features of the dying man as he insinuated that unfounded hope, — which, however, was not without its effect on Reuben. No merely selfish motive, nor even the desolate condition of Dorcas, could have induced him to desert his companion at such a moment — but his wishes seized on the thought that Malvin's life might be preserved, and his sanguine nature heightened almost to certainty the remote possibility of procuring human aid.

"Surely there is reason, weighty reason, to hope that friends are not far distant," he said, half aloud. "There fled one coward, unwounded, in the beginning of the fight, and most probably he made good speed. Every true man on the frontier would shoulder his musket at the news; and, though no party may range so far into the woods as this, I shall perhaps encounter them in one day's march. Counsel me faithfully," he added, turning to Malvin, in distrust of his own motives. "Were your situation mine, would you desert me while life remained?"

20 "It is now twenty years," replied Roger Malvin, — sighing, however, as he secretly acknowledged the wide dissimilarity between the two cases, — "it is now twenty years since I escaped with one dear friend from Indian captivity

near Montreal. We journeyed many days through the woods, till at length over-come with hunger and weariness, my friend lay down and besought me to leave him; for he knew that, if I remained, we both must perish; and, with but little hope of obtaining succor, I heaped a pillow of dry leaves beneath his head and hastened on."

"And did you return in time to save him?" asked Reuben, hanging on Malvin's words as if they were to be prophetic of his own success.

"I did," answered the other. "I came upon the camp of a hunting party be-fore sunset of the same day. I guided them to the spot where my comrade was expecting death; and he is now a hale and hearty man upon his own farm, far within the frontiers, while I lie wounded here in the depths of the wilderness."

This example, powerful in affecting Reuben's decision, was aided, uncon-sciously to himself, by the hidden strength of many another motive. Roger Malvin perceived that the victory was nearly won.

"Now, go, my son, and Heaven prosper you!" he said. "Turn not back with your friends when you meet them, lest your wounds and weariness overcome you; but send hitherward two or three, that may be spared, to search for me; and believe me, Reuben, my heart will be lighter with every step you take to-wards home." Yet there was, perhaps, a change both in his countenance and voice as he spoke thus; for, after all, it was a ghastly fate to be left expiring in the wilderness.

25   Reuben Bourne, but half convinced that he was acting rightly, at length raised himself from the ground and prepared himself for his departure. And first, though contrary to Malvin's wishes, he collected a stock of roots and herbs, which had been their only food during the last two days. This useless supply he placed within reach of the dying man, for whom, also, he swept together a bed of dry oak leaves. Then climbing to the summit of the rock, which on one side was rough and broken, he bent the oak sapling downward, and bound his hand-kerchief to the topmost branch. This precaution was not unnecessary to direct any who might come in search of Malvin; for every part of the rock, except its broad, smooth front, was concealed at a little distance by the dense under-growth of the forest. The handkerchief had been the bandage of a wound upon Reuben's arm; and, as he bound it to the tree, he vowed by the blood that stained it that he would return, either to save his companion's life or to lay his body in the grave. He then descended, and stood, with downcast eyes, to receive Roger Malvin's parting words.

The experience of the latter suggested much and minute advice respecting the youth's journey through the trackless forest. Upon this subject he spoke with calm earnestness, as if he were sending Reuben to the battle or the chase while he himself remained secure at home, and not as if the human countenance that was about to leave him were the last he would ever behold. But his firmness was shaken before he concluded.

"Carry my blessing to Dorcas, and say that my last prayer shall be for her and you. Bid her to have no hard thoughts because you left me here," — Reuben's heart smote him, — "for that your life would not have weighed with you if its sacrifice could have done me good. She will marry you after she has mourned a little while for her father; and Heaven grant you long and happy days, and may your children's children stand round your death bed! And, Reuben," added he, as the weakness of mortality made its way at last, "return, when your wounds are healed and your weariness refreshed, — return to this wild rock, and lay my bones in the grave, and say a prayer over them."

An almost superstitious regard, arising perhaps from the customs of the Indians, whose war was with the dead as well as the living, was paid by the frontier inhabitants to the rites of sepulture; and there are many instances of the sacrifice of life in the attempt to bury those who had fallen by the "sword of the wilderness." Reuben, therefore, felt the full importance of the promise which he most solemnly made to return and perform Roger Malvin's obsequies. It was remarkable that the latter, speaking his whole heart in his parting words, no longer endeavored to persuade the youth that even the speediest succor might avail to the preservation of his life. Reuben was internally convinced that he should see Malvin's living face no more. His generous nature would fain have delayed him, at whatever risk, till the dying scene were past; but the desire of existence and the hope of happiness had strengthened in his heart, and he was unable to resist them.

"It is enough," said Roger Malvin, having listened to Reuben's promise. "Go, and God speed you!"

30   The youth pressed his hand in silence, turned, and was departing. His slow and faltering steps, however, had borne him but a little way before Malvin's voice recalled him.

"Reuben, Reuben," said he, faintly; and Reuben returned and knelt down by the dying man.

"Raise me, and let me lean against the rock," was his last request. "My face will be turned towards home, and I shall see you a moment longer as you pass among the trees."

Reuben, having made the desired alteration in his companion's posture, again began his solitary pilgrimage. He walked more hastily at first than was consistent with his strength; for a sort of guilty feeling, which sometimes torments men in their most justifiable acts, caused him to seek concealment from Malvin's eyes; but after he had trodden far upon the rustling forest leaves he crept back, impelled by a wild and painful curiosity, and, sheltered by the earthy roots of an uptorn tree, gazed earnestly at the desolate man. The morning sun was unclouded, and the trees and shrubs imbibed the sweet air of the month of May; yet there seemed a gloom on Nature's face, as if she sympathized with mortal pain and sorrow. Roger Malvin's hands were uplifted in a fervent prayer, some of the words of which stole through the stillness of the woods and entered Reuben's heart, torturing it with an unutterable pang. They were the broken accents of a petition for his own happiness and that of Dorcas; and, as the youth listened, conscience, or something in its similitude, pleaded strongly with him to return and lie down again by the rock. He felt how hard was the doom of the kind and generous being whom he had deserted in his extremity. Death would come like the slow approach of a corpse, stealing gradually towards him through the forest, and showing its ghastly and motionless features from behind a nearer and yet a nearer tree. But such must have been Reuben's own fate had he tarried another sunset; and who shall impute blame to him if he shrink from so useless a sacrifice? As he gave a parting look, a breeze waved the little banner upon the sapling oak and reminded Reuben of his vow.

Many circumstances combined to retard the wounded traveller in his way to the frontiers. On the second day the clouds, gathering densely over the sky, precluded the possibility of regulating his course by the position of the sun; and he knew not but that every effort of his almost exhausted strength was removing him farther from the home he sought. His scanty sustenance was supplied by the berries and other spontaneous products of the forest. Herds of deer, it is true, sometimes bounded past him, and partridges frequently whirred up before his footsteps; but his ammunition had been expended in the fight, and he had no means of slaying them. His wounds, irritated by the constant exertion in which lay the only hope of life, wore away his strength and at intervals confused his reason. But, even in the wanderings of intellect, Reuben's young heart clung strongly to existence; and it was only through absolute incapacity of motion that he at last sank down beneath a tree, compelled there to await death.

35   In this situation he was discovered by a party who, upon the first intelligence of the fight, had been despatched to the relief of the survivors. They conveyed him to the nearest settlement, which chanced to be that of his own residence.

Dorcas, in the simplicity of the olden time, watched by the bedside of her wounded lover, and administered all those comforts that are in the sole gift of woman's heart and hand. During several days Reuben's recollection strayed drowsily among the perils and hardships through which he had passed, and he was incapable of returning definite answers to the inquiries with which many were eager to harass him. No authentic particulars of the battle had yet been circulated; nor could mothers, wives, and children tell whether their loved ones were detained by captivity or by the stronger chain of death. Dorcas nourished her apprehensions in silence till one afternoon when Reuben awoke from an unquiet sleep, and seemed to recognize her more perfectly than at any previous time. She saw that his intellect had become composed, and she could no longer restrain her filial anxiety.

"My father, Reuben?" she began; but the change in her lover's countenance made her pause.

The youth shrank as if with a bitter pain, and the blood gushed vividly into his wan and hollow cheeks. His first impulse was to cover his face; but, apparently with a desperate effort, he half raised himself and spoke vehemently, defending himself against an imaginary accusation.

"Your father was sore wounded in the battle, Dorcas; and he bade me not burden myself with him, but only to lead him to the lakeside, that he might quench his thirst and die. But I would not desert the old man in his extremity, and, though bleeding myself, I supported him; I gave him half my strength, and led him away with me. For three days we journeyed on together, and your father was sustained beyond my hopes, but, awaking at sunrise on the fourth day, I found him faint and exhausted; he was unable to proceed; his life had ebbed away fast; and" —

40   "He died!" exclaimed Dorcas, faintly.

Reuben felt it impossible to acknowledge that his selfish love of life had hurried him away before her father's fate was decided. He spoke not; he only bowed his head; and between shame and exhaustion, sank back and hid his face in the pillow. Dorcas wept when her fears were thus confirmed; but the shock, as it had been long anticipated, was on that account the less violent.

"You dug a grave for my poor father in the wilderness, Reuben?" was the question by which her filial piety manifested itself.

"My hands were weak; but I did what I could," replied the youth in a smothered tone. "There stands a noble tombstone above his head; and I would to Heaven I slept as soundly as he!"

Dorcas, perceiving the wildness of his latter words, inquired no further at the time; but her heart found ease in the thought that Roger Malvin had not lacked such funeral rites as it was possible to bestow. The tale of Reuben's courage and fidelity lost nothing when she communicated it to her friends; and the poor youth, tottering from his sick chamber to breathe the sunny air, experienced from every tongue the miserable and humiliating torture of unmerited praise. All acknowledged that he might worthily demand the hand of the fair maiden to whose father he had been "faithful unto death;" and, as my tale is not of love, it shall suffice to say that in the space of a few months Reuben became the husband of Dorcas Malvin. During the marriage ceremony the bride was covered with blushes, but the bridegroom's face was pale.

45   There was now in the breast of Reuben Bourne an incommunicable thought — something which he was to conceal most heedfully from her whom he most loved and trusted. He regretted, deeply and bitterly, the moral cowardice that had restrained his words when he was about to disclose the truth to Dorcas; but pride, the fear of losing her affection, the dread of universal scorn, forbade him to rectify this falsehood. He felt that for leaving Roger Malvin he deserved no censure. His presence, the gratuitous sacrifice of his own life, would have added only another and a needless agony to the last moments of the dying man; but concealment had imparted to a justifiable act much of the secret effect of guilt; and Reuben, while reason told him that he had done right, experienced in no small degree the mental horrors which punish the perpetrator of undiscovered crime. By a certain association of ideas, he at times almost imagined himself a murderer. For years, also, a thought would occasionally recur, which, though he perceived all its folly and extravagance, he had not power to banish from his mind. It was a haunting and torturing fancy that his father-in-law was yet sitting at the foot of the rock, on the withered forest leaves, alive, and awaiting his pledged assistance. These mental deceptions, however, came and went, nor did he ever mistake them for realities, but in the calmest and clearest moods of his mind he was conscious that he had a deep vow unredeemed, and that an unburied corpse was calling to him out of the wilderness. Yet such was the consequence of his prevarication that he could not obey the call. It was now too late to require the assistance of Roger Malvin's friends in performing his long-deferred sepulture; and superstitious fears, of which none were more susceptible than the people of the outward settlements, forbade Reuben to go alone. Neither did he know where in the pathless and illimitable forest to seek that smooth and lettered rock at the base of which the body lay: his remembrance of every portion of his travel thence was indistinct, and the latter part had left no impression upon his mind. There was, however, a continual impulse, a voice audible only to himself, commanding him to go forth and redeem his vow; and he had a strange impression that, were he to make the trial, he would be led straight to Malvin's bones. But year after year that summons, unheard but felt, was disobeyed. His one secret thought became like a chain binding down his spirit and like a serpent gnawing into his heart; and he was transformed into a sad and downcast yet irritable man.

    In the course of a few years after their marriage changes began to be visible in the external prosperity of Reuben and Dorcas. The only riches of the former had been his stout heart and strong arm; but the latter, her father's sole heiress, had made her husband master of a farm, under older cultivation, larger, and better stocked than most of the frontier establishments. Reuben Bourne, however, was a neglectful husbandman; and, while the lands of the other settlers became annually more fruitful, his deteriorated in the same proportion. The discouragements to agriculture were greatly lessened by the cessation of Indian war, during which men held the plough in one hand and the musket in the other, and were fortunate if the products of their dangerous labor were not destroyed, either in the field or in the barn, by the savage enemy. But Reuben did not profit by the altered condition of the country; nor can it be denied that his intervals of industrious attention to his affairs were but scantily rewarded with success. The irritability by which he had recently become distinguished was another cause of his declining prosperity, as it occasioned frequent quarrels in his unavoidable intercourse with the neighboring settlers. The results of these were innumerable lawsuits; for the people of New England, in the earliest stages and wildest circumstances of the country, adopted, whenever attainable, the legal mode of deciding their differences. To be brief, the world did not go well with Reuben Bourne; and, though not till many years after his marriage, he was finally a ruined man, with but one remaining expedient against the evil fate that had pursued him. He was to throw sunlight into some deep recess of the forest, and seek subsistence from the virgin bosom of the wilderness.

The only child of Reuben and Dorcas was a son, now arrived at the age of fifteen years, beautiful in youth, and giving promise of a glorious manhood. He was peculiarly qualified for, and already began to excel in, the wild accomplishments of frontier life. His foot was fleet, his aim true, his apprehension quick, his heart glad and high; and all who anticipated the return of Indian war spoke of Cyrus Bourne as a future leader in the land. The boy was loved by his father with a deep and silent strength, as if whatever was good and happy in his own nature had been transferred to his child, carrying his affections with it. Even Dorcas, though loving and beloved, was far less dear to him; for Reuben's secret thoughts and insulated emotions had gradually made him a selfish man, and he could no longer love deeply except where he saw or imagined some reflection or likeness of his own mind. In Cyrus he recognized what he had himself been in other days; and at intervals he seemed to partake of the boy's spirit, and to be revived with a fresh and happy life. Reuben was accompanied by his son in the expedition, for the purpose of selecting a tract of land and felling and burning the timber, which necessarily preceded the removal of the household goods. Two months of autumn were thus occupied, after which Reuben Bourne and his young hunter returned to spend their last winter in the settlements.

It was early in the month of May that the little family snapped asunder whatever tendrils of affections had clung to inanimate objects, and bade farewell to the few who, in the blight of fortune, called themselves their friends. The sadness of the parting moment had, to each of the pilgrims, its peculiar alleviations. Reuben, a moody man, and misanthropic because unhappy, strode onward with his usual stern brown and downcast eye, feeling few regrets and disdaining to acknowledge any. Dorcas, while she wept abundantly over the broken ties by which her simple and affectionate nature had bound itself to everything, felt that the inhabitants of her inmost heart moved on with her, and that all else would be supplied wherever she might go. And the boy dashed one teardrop from his eye, and thought of the adventurous pleasures of the untrodden forest.

Oh, who, in the enthusiasm of a daydream, has not wished that he were a wanderer in a world of summer wilderness, with one fair and gentle being hanging lightly on his arm? In youth his free and exulting step would know no barrier but the rolling ocean or the snow-topped mountains; calmer manhood would choose a home where Nature had strewn a double wealth in the vale of some transparent stream; and when hoary age, after long, long years of that pure life, stole on and found him there, it would find him the father of a race, the patriarch of a people, the founder of a mighty nation yet to be. When death, like the sweet sleep which we welcome after a day of happiness, came over him, his far descendants would mourn over the venerated dust.

50   The tangled and gloomy forest through which the personages of my tale were wandering differed widely from the dreamer's land of fantasy; yet there was something in their way of life that Nature asserted as her own, and the gnawing cares which went with them from the world were all that now obstructed their happiness. One stout and shaggy steed, the bearer of all their wealth, did not shrink from the added weight of Dorcas; although her hardy breeding sustained her, during the latter part of each day's journey, by her husband's side. Reuben and his son, their muskets on their shoulders and their axes slung behind them, kept an unwearied pace, each watching with a hunter's eye for the game that supplied their food. When hunger bade, they halted and prepared their meal on the bank of some unpolluted forest brook, which, as they knelt down with thirsty lips to drink, murmured a sweet unwillingness, like a maiden at love's first kiss. They slept beneath a hut of branches, and awoke at peep of light refreshed for the toils of another day. Dorcas and the boy went on joyously, and even Reuben's spirit shone at intervals with an outward gladness; but inwardly there was a cold, cold sorrow, which he compared to the snowdrifts lying deep in the glens and hollows of the rivulets while the leaves were brightly green above.

Cyrus Bourne was sufficiently skilled in the travel of the woods to observe that his father did not adhere to the course they had pursued in their expedition of the preceding autumn. They were now keeping farther to the north, striking out more directly from the settlements, and into a region of which savage beasts and savage men were as yet the sole possessors. The boy sometimes hinted his opinions upon the subject, and Reuben listened attentively, and once or twice altered the direction of their march in accordance with his son's counsel; but, having so done, he seemed ill at ease. His quick and wandering glances were sent forward, apparently in search of enemies lurking behind the tree trunks; and, seeing nothing there, he would cast his eyes backwards as if in fear of some pursuer. Cyrus, perceiving that his father gradually resumed the old direction, forbore to interfere; nor, though something began to weigh upon his heart, did his adventurous nature permit him to regret the increased length and the mystery of their way.

On the afternoon of the fifth day they halted, and made their simple encampment nearly an hour before sunset. The face of the country, for the last few miles, had been diversified by swells of land resembling huge waves of a petrified sea; and in one of the corresponding hollows, a wild and romantic spot, had the family reared their hut and kindled their fire. There is something chilling, and yet heart-warming, in the thought of these three, united by strong bands of love and insulated from all that breathe beside. The dark and gloomy pines looked down upon them, and, as the wind swept through their tops, a pitying sound was heard in the forest; or did those old trees groan in fear that men were come to lay the axe to their roots at last? Reuben and his son, while Dorcas made ready their meal, proposed to wander out in search of game, of which that day's march had afforded no supply. The boy, promising not to quit the vicinity of the encampment, bounded off with a step as light and elastic as that of the deer he hoped to slay; while his father, feeling a transient happiness as he gazed after him, was about to pursue an opposite direction. Dorcas, in the meanwhile, had

seated herself near their fire of fallen branches, upon the moss-grown and mouldering trunk of a tree uprooted years before. Her employment, diversified by an
occasional glance at the pot, now beginning to simmer over the blaze, was the
perusal of the current year's Massachusetts Almanac, which, with the exception
of an old black-letter[1] Bible, comprised all the literary wealth of the family. None
pay a greater regard to arbitrary divisions of time than those who are excluded
from society; and Dorcas mentioned, as if the information were of importance,
that it was now the twelfth of May. Her husband started.

"The twelfth of May! I should remember it well," muttered he, while many
thoughts occasioned a momentary confusion in his mind. "Where am I? Whither
am I wandering? Where did I leave him?"

Dorcas, too well accustomed to her husband's wayward moods to note any
peculiarity of demeanor, now laid aside the almanac and addressed him in that
mournful tone which the tender hearted appropriate to griefs long cold and dead.

55
"It was near this time of the month, eighteen years ago, that my poor father
left this world for a better. He had a kind arm to hold his head and a kind voice
to cheer him, Reuben, in his last moments; and the thought of the faithful care
you took of him has comforted me many a time since. Oh, death would have
been awful to a solitary man in a wild place like this!"

"Pray Heaven, Dorcas," said Reuben, in a broken voice,—"pray Heaven that
neither of us three dies solitary and lies unburied in this howling wilderness!"
And he hastened away, leaving her to watch the fire beneath the gloomy pines.

Reuben Bourne's rapid pace gradually slackened as the pang, unintentionally inflicted by the words of Dorcas, became less acute. Many strange reflections, however, thronged upon him; and, straying onward rather like a sleep
walker than a hunter, it was attributable to no care of his own that his devious
course kept him in the vicinity of the encampment. His steps were imperceptibly led almost in a circle; nor did he observe that he was on the verge of a tract
of land heavily timbered, but not with pine-trees. The place of the latter was here
supplied by oaks and other of the harder woods; and around their roots clustered a dense and bushy under-growth, leaving, however, barren spaces between the trees, thick strewn with withered leaves. Whenever the rustling of the
branches or the creaking of the trunks made a sound, as if the forest were waking from slumber, Reuben instinctively raised the musket that rested on his arm,
and cast a quick, sharp glance on every side; but, convinced by a partial observation that no animal was near, he would again give himself up to his thoughts. He
was musing on the strange influence that had led him away from his premeditated course, and so far into the depths of the wilderness. Unable to penetrate to
the secret place of his soul where his motives lay hidden, he believed that a supernatural voice had called him onward, and that a supernatural power had obstructed his retreat. He trusted that it was Heaven's intent to afford him an opportunity of expiating his sin; he hoped that he might find the bones so long
unburied; and that, having laid the earth over them, peace would throw its sunlight into the sepulchre of his heart. From these thoughts he was aroused by a
rustling in the forest at some distance from the spot to which he had wandered.
Perceiving the motion of some object behind a thick veil of undergrowth, he
fired, with the instinct of a hunter and the aim of a practised marksman. A low

[1]**black-letter** a heavy typeface with thick ornamental serifs, also called "Gothic" and "Old
English" (editors' note)

moan, which told his success, and by which even animals can express their dying agony, was unheeded by Reuben Bourne. What were the recollections now breaking upon him?

The thicket into which Reuben had fired was near the summit of a swell of land, and was clustered around the base of a rock, which, in the shape and smoothness of one of its surfaces, was not unlike a gigantic gravestone. As if reflected in a mirror, its likeness was in Reuben's memory. He even recognized the veins which seemed to form an inscription in forgotten characters: everything remained the same, except that a thick covert of bushes shrouded the lower part of the rock, and would have hidden Roger Malvin had he still been sitting there. Yet in the next moment Reuben's eye was caught by another change that time had effected since he last stood where he was now standing again behind the earthy roots of the uptorn tree. The sapling to which he had bound the blood-stained symbol of his vow had increased and strengthened into an oak, far indeed from its maturity, but with no mean spread of shadowy branches. There was one singularity observable in this tree which made Reuben tremble. The middle and lower branches were in luxuriant life, and an excess of vegetation had fringed the trunk almost to the ground; but a blight had apparently stricken the upper part of the oak, and the very topmost bough was withered, sapless, and utterly dead. Reuben remembered how the little banner had fluttered on that topmost bough, when it was green and lovely, eighteen years before. Whose guilt had blasted it?

Dorcas, after the departure of the two hunters, continued her preparations for their evening repast. Her sylvan table was the moss-covered trunk of a large fallen tree, on the broadest part of which she had spread a snow-white cloth and arranged what were left of the bright pewter vessels that had been her pride in the settlements. It had a strange aspect, that one little spot of homely comfort in the desolate heart of Nature. The sunshine yet lingered upon the higher branches of the trees that grew on rising ground; but the shadows of evening had deepened into the hollow where the encampment was made, and the firelight began to redden as it gleamed up the tall trunks of the pines or hovered on the dense and obscure mass of foliage that circled round the spot. The heart of Dorcas was not sad; for she felt that it was better to journey in the wilderness with two whom she loved than to be a lonely woman in a crowd that cared not for her. As she busied herself in arranging seats of mouldering wood, covered with leaves, for Reuben and her son, her voice danced through the gloomy forest in the measure of a song that she had learned in youth. The rude melody, the production of a bard who won no name, was descriptive of a winter evening in a frontier cottage, when, secured from savage inroad by the high-piled snowdrifts, the family rejoiced by their own fireside. The whole song possessed the nameless charm peculiar to unborrowed thought, but four continually-recurring lines shone out from the rest like the blaze of the hearth whose joys they celebrated. Into them, working magic with a few simple words, the poet had instilled the very essence of domestic love and household happiness, and they were poetry and picture joined in one. As Dorcas sang, the walls of her forsaken home seemed to encircle her; she no longer saw the gloomy pines, nor heard the wind which still, as she began each verse, sent a heavy breath through the branches, and died away in a hollow moan from the burden of the song. She was aroused by the report of a gun in the vicinity of the encampment; and either the sudden sound, or her loneliness by the glowing fire, caused her to tremble violently. The next moment she laughed in the pride of a mother's heart.

60   "My beautiful young hunter! My boy has slain a deer!" she exclaimed, recollecting that in the direction whence the shot proceeded Cyrus had gone to the chase.

She waited a reasonable time to hear her son's light step bounding over the rustling leaves to tell of his success. But he did not immediately appear; and she sent her cheerful voice among the trees in search of him.

"Cyrus! Cyrus!"

His coming was still delayed; and she determined, as the report had apparently been very near, to seek for him in person. Her assistance, also, might be necessary in bringing home the venison which she flattered herself he had obtained. She therefore set forward, directing her steps by the long-past sound, and singing as she went, in order that the boy might be aware of her approach and run to meet her. From behind the trunk of every tree, and from every hiding-place in the thick foliage of the undergrowth, she hoped to discover the countenance of her son, laughing with the sportive mischief that is born of affection. The sun was now beneath the horizon, and the light that came down among the leaves was sufficiently dim to create many illusions in her expecting fancy. Several times she seemed indistinctly to see his face gazing out from among the leaves; and once she imagined that he stood beckoning to her at the base of a craggy rock. Keeping her eyes on this object, however, it proved to be no more than the trunk of an oak fringed to the very ground with little branches, one of which, thrust out farther than the rest, was shaken by the breeze. Making her way round the foot of the rock, she suddenly found herself close to her husband, who had approached in another direction. Leaning upon the butt of his gun, the muzzle of which rested upon the withered leaves, he was apparently absorbed in the contemplation of some object at his feet.

"How is this, Reuben? Have you slain the deer and fallen asleep over him?" exclaimed Dorcas, laughing cheerfully, on her first slight observation of his posture and appearance.

65   He stirred not, neither did he turn his eyes towards her; and a cold, shuddering fear, indefinite in its source and object, began to creep into her blood. She now perceived that her husband's face was ghastly pale, and his features were rigid, as if incapable of assuming any other expression than the strong despair which had hardened upon them. He gave not the slightest evidence that he was aware of her approach.

"For the love of Heaven, Reuben, speak to me!" cried Dorcas; and the strange sound of her own voice affrighted her even more than the dead silence.

Her husband started, stared into her face, drew her to the front of the rock, and pointed with his finger.

Oh, there lay the boy, asleep, but dreamless, upon the fallen forest leaves! His cheek rested upon his arm — his curled locks were thrown back from his brow — his limbs were slightly relaxed. Had a sudden weariness overcome the youthful hunter? Would his mother's voice arouse him? She knew that it was death.

"This broad rock is the gravestone of your near kindred, Dorcas," said her husband. "Your tears will fall at once over your father and your son."

70   She heard him not. With one wild shriek, that seemed to force its way from the sufferer's inmost soul, she sank insensibly by the side of her dead boy. At that moment the withered topmost bough of the oak loosened itself in the stilly air, and fell in soft, light fragments upon the rock, upon the leaves, upon Reuben, upon his wife and child, and upon Roger Malvin's bones. Then Reuben's heart

was stricken, and the tears gushed out like water from a rock. The vow that the wounded youth had made the blighted man had come to redeem. His sin was expiated, — the curse was gone from him; and in the hour when he had shed blood dearer to him than his own, a prayer, the first for years, went up to Heaven from the lips of Reuben Bourne.

[1832]

Topics for Critical Thinking and Writing

1. Near the beginning of the story, Reuben states, "resolutely," to Roger Malvin: "I will remain and watch by you." Trace the steps by which Reuben decides not to remain but, instead, to leave his companion behind. What leads Reuben to change his mind? Does he believe that he is making the right decision?
2. The Roman philosopher Seneca said a person is not guilty if he or she does not "will" the deed. What does this observation mean in the case of Reuben Bourne? Do you believe that Reuben should feel guilty for his action? Doesn't Roger Malvin himself bear much of the responsibility for what happens?
3. Why doesn't Reuben tell his wife what really took place? If he did nothing wrong, why does he allow her to believe that her father died and that Reuben did his best to bury him properly?
4. Write a journal entry of a page or two, in which you imagine Dorcas's feelings about the "moody" and "misanthropic" man her husband has become.
5. Isn't the conclusion of the story horrifying? Is it true that Reuben has sinned, and that only through the death of his own son can the sin be "expiated"? Is this Hawthorne's own position, or, rather, his account of Reuben's point of view?
6. Do you agree with Hawthorne's decision at the very end not to present Reuben's prayer? Should Hawthorne have told us what Reuben says at this climactic moment? What would such a prayer consist of and sound like? Try composing it yourself.

ALICE WALKER

Alice Walker was born in 1944 in Eatonton, Georgia, where her parents eked out a living as sharecroppers and dairy farmers; her mother also worked as a domestic. Walker attended Spelman College in Atlanta, and in 1965 she finished her undergraduate work at Sarah Lawrence College near New York City. She then became active in the welfare rights movement in New York and in the voter registration movement in Georgia. Later she taught writing and literature in Mississippi, at Jackson State College and Tougaloo College, and at Wellesley College, the University of Massachusetts, and Yale University.

Walker has written essays, poetry, and fiction. Her best known novel, The Color Purple *(1982), won a Pulitzer Prize and the National Book Award. She has said that her chief concern is "exploring the oppressions, the insanities, the loyalties, and the triumphs of black women."*

Everyday Use

For your grandmama

I will wait for her in the yard that Maggie and I made so clean and wavy yesterday afternoon. A yard like this is more comfortable than most people know. It is not just a yard. It is like an extended living room. When the hard clay is swept clean as a floor and the fine sand around the edges lined with tiny, irregular grooves, anyone can come and sit and look up into the elm tree and wait for the breezes that never come inside the house.

Maggie will be nervous until after her sister goes: she will stand hopelessly in corners homely and ashamed of the burn scars down her arms and legs, eyeing her sister with a mixture of envy and awe. She thinks her sister had held life always in the palm of one hand, that "no" is a word the world never learned to say to her.

You've no doubt seen those TV shows where the child who has "made it" is confronted, as a surprise, by her own mother and father, tottering in weakly from backstage. (A pleasant surprise, of course: What would they do if parent and child came on the show only to curse out and insult each other?) On TV mother and child embrace and smile into each other's faces. Sometimes the mother and father weep, the child wraps them in her arms and leans across the table to tell how she would not have made it without their help. I have seen these programs.

Sometimes I dream a dream in which Dee and I are suddenly brought together on a TV program of this sort. Out of a dark and soft-seated limousine I am ushered into a bright room filled with many people. There I meet a smiling, gray, sporty man like Johnny Carson who shakes my hand and tells me what a fine girl I have. Then we are on the stage and Dee is embracing me with tears in her eyes. She pins on my dress a large orchid, even though she has told me once that she thinks orchids are tacky flowers.

5   In real life I am a large, big-boned woman with rough, man-working hands. In the winter I wear flannel nightgowns to bed and overalls during the day. I can kill and clean a hog as mercilessly as a man. My fat keeps me hot in zero weather. I can work outside all day, breaking ice to get water for washing. I can eat pork liver cooked over the open fire minutes after it comes steaming from the hog. One winter I knocked a bull calf straight in the brain between the eyes with a sledge hammer and had the meat hung up to chill before nightfall. But of course all this does not show on television. I am the way my daughter would want me to be: a hundred pounds lighter, my skin like an uncooked barley pancake. My hair glistens in the hot bright lights. Johnny Carson has much to do to keep up with my quick and witty tongue.

But that is a mistake. I know even before I wake up. Who ever knew a Johnson with a quick tongue? Who can even imagine me looking a strange white man in the eye? It seems to me I have talked to them always with one foot raised in flight, with my head turned in whichever way is farthest from them. Dee, though. She would always look anyone in the eye. Hesitation was no part of her nature.

"How do I look, Mama?" Maggie says, showing just enough of her thin body enveloped in pink skirt and red blouse for me to know she's there, almost hidden by the door.

"Come out into the yard," I say.

Have you ever seen a lame animal, perhaps a dog run over by some careless person rich enough to own a car, sidle up to someone who is ignorant enough to be kind to him? That is the way my Maggie walks. She has been like this, chin on chest, eyes on ground, feet in shuffle, ever since the fire that burned the other house to the ground.

Dee is lighter than Maggie, with nicer hair and a fuller figure. She's a woman now, though sometimes I forget. How long ago was it that the other house burned? Ten, twelve years? Sometimes I can still hear the flames and feel Maggie's arms sticking to me, her hair smoking and her dress falling off her in little black papery flakes. Her eyes seemed stretched open, blazed open by the flames reflected in them. And Dee. I see her standing off under the sweet gum tree she used to dig gum out of; a look of concentration on her face as she watched the last dingy gray board of the house fall in toward the red-hot brick chimney. Why don't you do a dance around the ashes? I'd wanted to ask her. She had hated the house that much.

I used to think she hated Maggie, too. But that was before we raised the money, the church and me, to send her to Augusta to school. She used to read to us without pity; forcing words, lies, other folks' habits, whole lives upon us two, sitting trapped and ignorant underneath her voice. She washed us in a river of make-believe, burned us with a lot of knowledge we didn't necessarily need to know. Pressed us to her with the serious way she read, to shove us away at just the moment, like dimwits, we seemed about to understand.

Dee wanted nice things. A yellow organdy dress to wear to her graduation from high school; black pumps to match a green suit she'd made from an old suit somebody gave me. She was determined to stare down any disaster in her efforts. Her eyelids would not flicker for minutes at a time. Often I fought off the temptation to shake her. At sixteen she had a style of her own: and knew what style was.

I never had an education myself. After second grade the school was closed down. Don't ask me why: in 1927 colored asked fewer questions than they do now. Sometimes Maggie reads to me. She stumbles along goodnaturedly but can't see well. She knows she is not bright. Like good looks and money, quickness passed her by. She will marry John Thomas (who has mossy teeth in an earnest face) and then I'll be free to sit here and I guess just sing church songs to myself. Although I never was a good singer. Never could carry a tune. I was always better at a man's job. I used to love to milk till I was hoofed in the side in '49. Cows are soothing and slow and don't bother you, unless you try to milk them the wrong way.

I have deliberately turned my back on the house. It is three rooms, just like the one that burned, except the roof is tin; they don't make shingle roofs any more. There are no real windows, just some holes cut in the sides, like the portholes in a ship, but not round and not square, with rawhide holding the shutters up on the outside. This house is in a pasture, too, like the other one. No doubt when Dee sees it she will want to tear it down. She wrote me once that no matter where we "choose" to live, she will manage to come see us. But she will never bring her friends. Maggie and I thought about this and Maggie asked me, "Mama, when did Dee ever *have* any friends?"

She had a few. Furtive boys in pink shirts hanging about on washday after school. Nervous girls who never laughed. Impressed with her they worshiped the well-turned phrase, the cute shape, the scalding humor that erupted like bubbles in lye. She read to them.

When she was courting Jimmy T she didn't have much time to pay to us, but turned all her faultfinding power on him. He *flew* to marry a cheap gal from a family of ignorant flashy people. She hardly had time to recompose herself.

When she comes I will meet—but there they are!

Maggie attempts to make a dash for the house, in her shuffling way, but I stay her with my hand. "Come back here," I say. And she stops and tries to dig a well in the sand with her toe.

It is hard to see them clearly through the strong sun. But even the first glimpse of leg out of the car tells me it is Dee. Her feet were always neat-looking, as if God himself had shaped them with a certain style. From the other side of the car comes a short, stocky man. Hair is all over his head a foot long and hanging from his chin like a kinky mule tail. I hear Maggie suck in her breath. "Uhnnnh," is what it sounds like. Like when you see the wriggling end of a snake just in front of your foot on the road. "Uhnnnh."

20   Dee next. A dress down to the ground, in this hot weather. A dress so loud it hurts my eyes. There are yellows and oranges enough to throw back the light of the sun. I feel my whole face warming from the heat waves it throws out. Earrings, too, gold and hanging down to her shoulders. Bracelets dangling and making noises when she moves her arm up to shake the folds of the dress out of her armpits. The dress is loose and flows, and as she walks closer, I like it. I hear Maggie go "Uhnnnh" again. It is her sister's hair. It stands straight up like the wool on a sheep. It is black as night and around the edges are two long pigtails that rope about like small lizards disappearing behind her ears.

"Wa-su-zo-Tean-o!" she says, coming on in that gliding way the dress makes her move. The short stocky fellow with the hair to his navel is all grinning and he follows up with "Asalamalakim, my mother and sister!" He moves to hug Maggie but she falls back, right up against the back of my chair. I feel her trembling there and when I look up I see the perspiration falling off her chin.

"Don't get up," says Dee. Since I am stout it takes something of a push. You can see me trying to move a second or two before I make it. She turns, showing white heels through her sandals, and goes back to the car. Out she peeks next with a Polaroid. She stoops down quickly and lines up picture after picture of me sitting there in front of the house with Maggie cowering behind me. She never takes a shot without making sure the house is included. When a cow comes nibbling around the edge of the yard she snaps it and me and Maggie *and* the house. Then she puts the Polaroid in the back seat of the car, and comes up and kisses me on the forehead.

Meanwhile Asalamalakim is going through the motions with Maggie's hand. Maggie's hand is as limp as a fish, and probably as cold, despite the sweat, and she keeps trying to pull it back. It looks like Asalamalakim wants to shake hands but wants to do it fancy. Or maybe he don't know how people shake hands. Anyhow, he soon gives up on Maggie.

"Well," I say. "Dee."

25   "No, Mama," she says. "Not 'Dee,' Wangero Leewanika Kemanjo!"

"What happened to 'Dee'?" I wanted to know.

"She's dead," Wangero said. "I couldn't bear it any longer being named after the people who oppress me."

"You know as well as me you was named after your aunt Dicie," I said. Dicie is my sister. She named Dee. We called her "Big Dee" after Dee was born.

"But who was *she* named after?" asked Wangero.

30   "I guess after Grandma Dee," I said.

"And who was she named after?" asked Wangero.

"Her mother," I said, and saw Wangero was getting tired. "That's about as far back as I can trace it," I said. Though, in fact, I probably could have carried it back beyond the Civil War through the branches.

"Well," said Asalamalakim, "there you are."

"Uhnnnh," I heard Maggie say.

35   "There I was not," I said, "before 'Dicie' cropped up in our family, so why should I try to trace it that far back?"

He just stood there grinning, looking down on me like somebody inspecting a Model A car. Every once in a while he and Wangero sent eye signals over my head.

"How do you pronounce this name?" I asked.

"You don't have to call me by it if you don't want to," said Wangero.

"Why shouldn't I?" I asked. "If that's what you want us to call you, we'll call you."

40   "I know it might sound awkward at first," said Wangero.

"I'll get used to it," I said. "Ream it out again."

Well, soon we got the name out of the way. Asalamalakim had a name twice as long and three times as hard. After I tripped over it two or three times he told me to just call him Hakim-a-barber. I wanted to ask him was he a barber, but I didn't really think he was, so I didn't ask.

"You must belong to those beef-cattle peoples down the road," I said. They said "Asalamalakim" when they met you, too, but they didn't shake hands. Always too busy: feeding the cattle, fixing the fences, putting up saltlick shelters, throwing down hay. When the white folks poisoned some of the herd the men stayed up all night with rifles in their hands. I walked a mile and a half just to see the sight.

Hakim-a-barber said, "I accept some of their doctrines, but farming and raising cattle is not my style." (They didn't tell me, and I didn't ask, whether Wangero [Dee] had really gone and married him.)

45   We sat down to eat and right away he said he didn't eat collards and pork was unclean. Wangero, though, went on through the chitlins and corn bread, the greens and everything else. She talked a blue streak over the sweet potatoes. Everything delighted her. Even the fact that we still used the benches her daddy made for the table when we couldn't afford to buy chairs.

"Oh, Mama!" she cried. Then turned to Hakim-a-barber. "I never knew how lovely these benches are. You can feel the rump prints," she said, running her hands underneath her and along the bench. Then she gave a sigh and her hand closed over Grandma Dee's butter dish. "That's it!" she said. "I knew there was something I wanted to ask you if I could have." She jumped up from the table and went over in the corner where the churn stood, the milk in it clabber by now. She looked at the churn and looked at it.

"This churn top is what I need," she said. "Didn't Uncle Buddy whittle it out of a tree you all used to have?"

"Yes," I said.

"Uh huh," she said happily. "And I want the dasher, too."

50   "Uncle Buddy whittle that, too?" asked the barber.

Dee (Wangero) looked up at me.

"Aunt Dee's first husband whittled the dash," said Maggie so low you almost couldn't hear her. "His name was Henry, but they called him Stash."

"Maggie's brain is like an elephant's," Wangero said, laughing. "I can use the churn top as a centerpiece for the alcove table," she said, sliding a plate over the churn, "and I'll think of something artistic to do with the dasher."

When she finished wrapping the dasher the handle stuck out. I took it for a moment in my hands. You didn't even have to look close to see where hands pushing the dasher up and down to make butter had left a kind of sink in the wood. In fact, there were a lot of small sinks; you could see where thumbs and fingers had sunk into the wood. It was beautiful light yellow wood, from a tree that grew in the yard where Big Dee and Stash had lived.

55   After dinner Dee (Wangero) went to the trunk at the foot of my bed and started rifling through it. Maggie hung back in the kitchen over the dishpan. Out came Wangero with two quilts. They had been pieced by Grandma Dee and then Big Dee and me had hung them on the quilt frames on the front porch and quilted them. One was in the Lone Star pattern. The other was Walk Around the Mountain. In both of them were scraps of dresses Grandma Dee had worn fifty and more years ago. Bits and pieces of Grandpa Jarrell's paisley shirts. And one teeny faded blue piece, about the piece of a penny matchbox, that was from Great Grandpa Ezra's uniform that he wore in the Civil War.

"Mama," Wangero said sweet as a bird. "Can I have these old quilts?"

I heard something fall in the kitchen, and a minute later the kitchen door slammed.

"Why don't you take one or two of the others?" I asked. "These old things was just done by me and Big Dee from some tops your grandma pieced before she died."

"No," said Wangero. "I don't want those. They are stitched around the borders by machine."

60   "That's make them last better," I said.

"That's not the point," said Wangero. "These are all pieces of dresses Grandma used to wear. She did all this stitching by hand. Imagine!" She held the quilts securely in her arms, stroking them.

"Some of the pieces, like those lavender ones, come from old clothes her mother handed down to her," I said, moving up to touch the quilts. Dee (Wangero) moved back just enough so that I couldn't reach the quilts. They already belonged to her.

"Imagine!" she breathed again, clutching them closely to her bosom.

"The truth is," I said, "I promised to give them quilts to Maggie, for when she marries John Thomas."

65   She gasped like a bee had stung her.

"Maggie can't appreciate these quilts!" she said. "She'd probably be backward enough to put them to everyday use."

"I reckon she would," I said. "God knows I been saving 'em for long enough with nobody using 'em. I hope she will!" I didn't want to bring up how I had offered Dee (Wangero) a quilt when she went away to college. Then she had told me they were old-fashioned, out of style.

"But they're *priceless!*" she was saying now, furiously; for she has a temper. "Maggie would put them on the bed and in five years they'd be in rags. Less than that!"

"She can always make some more," I said. "Maggie knows how to quilt."

70   Dee (Wangero) looked at me with hatred. "You just will not understand. The point is these quilts, *these* quilts!"

"Well," I said, stumped. "What would *you* do with them?"

"Hang them," she said. As if that was the only thing you *could* do with quilts.

Maggie by now was standing in the door. I could almost hear the sound her feet made as they scraped over each other.

"She can have them, Mama," she said, like somebody used to never winning anything, or having anything reserved for her. "I can 'member Grandma Dee without the quilts."

75   I looked at her hard. She had filled her bottom lip with checkerberry snuff and it gave her face a kind of dopey, hangdog look. It was Grandma Dee and Big Dee who taught her how to quilt herself. She stood there with her scarred hands hidden in the folds of her skirt. She looked at her sister with something like fear but she wasn't mad at her. This was Maggie's portion. This was the way she knew God to work.

When I looked at her like that something hit me in the top of my head and ran down to the soles of my feet. Just like when I'm in church and the spirit of God touches me and I get happy and shout. I did something I never had done before: hugged Maggie to me, then dragged her on into the room, snatched the quilts out of Miss Wangero's hands and dumped them into Maggie's lap. Maggie just sat there on my bed with her mouth open.

"Take one or two of the others," I said to Dee.

But she turned without a word and went out to Hakim-a-barber.

"You just don't understand," she said, as Maggie and I came out to the car.

80   "What don't I understand?" I wanted to know.

"Your heritage," she said. And then she turned to Maggie, kissed her, and said, "You ought to try to make something of yourself, too, Maggie. It's really a new day for us. But from the way you and Mama still live you'd never know it."

She put on some sunglasses that hid everything above the tip of her nose and her chin.

Maggie smiled; maybe at the sunglasses. But a real smile, not scared. After we watched the car dust settle I asked Maggie to bring me a dip of snuff. And then the two of us sat there just enjoying, until it was time to go in the house and go to bed.

[1973]

✎ Topics for Critical Thinking and Writing

1. Alice Walker wrote the story, but the story is narrated by one of the characters, Mama. How would you characterize Mama?

2. At the end of the story, Dee tells Maggie, "It's really a new day for us. But from the way you and Mama still live you'd never know it." What does Dee mean? And how do Maggie and Mama respond?

3. In paragraph 76 the narrator says, speaking of Maggie, "When I looked at her like that something hit me in the top of my head and ran down to the soles of my feet." What "hit" Mama? That is, what does she understand at this moment that she had not understood before?

4. In "Everyday Use" why does the family conflict focus on who will possess the quilts? Why are the quilts important? What do they symbolize?

JOSÉ ARMAS

Born in 1944, José Armas has been a teacher (at the University of New Mexico and at the University of Albuquerque), publisher, critic, and community organizer. His interest in community affairs won him a fellowship, which in 1974–75 brought him into association with the Urban Planning Department at the Massachusetts Institute of Technology. In 1980 he was awarded a writing fellowship by the National Endowment for the Arts, and he now writes a column on Hispanic affairs for The Albuquerque Journal.

El Tonto del Barrio[1]

Romeo Estrado was called "El Cotorro"[2] because he was always whistling and singing. He made nice music even though his songs were spontaneous compositions made up of words with sounds that he liked but which seldom made any sense. But that didn't seem to bother either Romero or anyone else in the Golden Heights Centro where he lived. Not even the kids made fun of him. It just was not permitted.

Romero had a ritual that he followed almost every day. After breakfast he would get his broom and go up and down the main street of the Golden Heights Centro whistling and singing and sweeping the sidewalks for all the businesses. He would sweep in front of the Tortillería America,[3] the XXX Liquor Store, the Tres Milpas[4] Bar run by Tino Gabaldon, Barelas' Barber Shop, the used furniture store owned by Goldstein, El Centro Market of the Avila family, the Model Cities Office, and Lourdes Printing Store. Then, in the afternoons, he would come back and sit in Barelas' Barber Shop and spend the day looking at magazines and watching and waving to the passing people as he sang and composed his songs without a care in the world.

When business was slow, Barelas would let him sit in the barber's chair. Romero loved it. It was a routine that Romero kept every day except Sundays and Mondays when Barelas' Barber Shop was closed. After a period of years, people in the barrio got used to seeing Romero do his little task of sweeping the sidewalks and sitting in Barelas' Barber Shop. If he didn't show up one day someone assumed the responsibility to go to his house to see if he was ill. People would stop to say hello to Romero on the street and although he never initiated a conversation while he was sober, he always smiled and responded cheerfully to everyone. People passing the barber shop in the afternoons made it a point to wave even though they couldn't see him; they knew he was in there and was expecting some salutation.

When he was feeling real good, Romero would sweep in front of the houses

---

[1]**El Tonto del Barrio** the barrio dummy (in the United States, a barrio is a Spanish-speaking community) (all notes are by the editors)   [2]**El Cotorro** The Parrot   [3]**Tortillería America** America Tortilla Factory   [4]**Tres Milpas** Three Cornfields

on both sides of the block also. He took his job seriously and took great care to sweep cleanly, between the cracks and even between the sides of buildings. The dirt and small scraps went into the gutter. The bottles and bigger pieces of litter were put carefully in cardboard boxes, ready for the garbage man.

5   If he did it the way he wanted, the work took him the whole morning. And always cheerful—always with some song.

Only once did someone call attention to his work. Frank Avila told him in jest that Romero had forgotten to pick up an empty bottle of wine from his door. Romero was so offended and made such a commotion that it got around very quickly that no one should criticize his work. There was, in fact, no reason to.

Although it had been long acknowledged that Romero was a little "touched," he fit very well into the community. He was a respected citizen.

He could be found at the Tres Milpas Bar drinking his occasional beer in the evenings. Romero had a rivalry going with the Ranchera songs on the jukebox. He would try to outsing the songs using the same melody but inserting his own selection of random words. Sometimes, like all people, he would "bust out" and get drunk.

One could always tell when Romero was getting drunk because he would begin telling everyone that he loved them.

10   "I looov youuu," he would sing to someone and offer to compose them a song.

"Ta bueno, Romero. Ta bueno, ya bete,"[5] they would tell him.

Sometimes when he got too drunk he would crap in his pants and then Tino would make him go home.

Romero received some money from Social Security but it wasn't much. None of the merchants gave him any credit because he would always forget to pay his bills. He didn't do it on purpose, he just forgot and spent his money on something else. So instead, the businessmen preferred to do little things for him occasionally. Barelas would trim his hair when things were slow. The Tortillería America would give him menudo[6] and fresh-made tortillas at noon when he was finished with his sweeping. El Centro Market would give him the overripe fruit and broken boxes of food that no one else would buy. Although it was unspoken and unwritten, there was an agreement that existed between Romero and the Golden Heights Centro. Romero kept the sidewalks clean and the barrio looked after him. It was a contract that worked well for a long time.

Then, when Seferino, Barelas' oldest son, graduated from high school he went to work in the barber shop for the summer. Seferino was a conscientious and sensitive young man and it wasn't long before he took notice of Romero and came to feel sorry for him.

15   One day when Romero was in the shop Seferino decided to act.

"Mira, Romero. Yo te doy 50 centavos por cada día que me barres la banqueta. Fifty cents for every day you sweep the sidewalk for us. Qué te parece?"[7]

Romero thought about it carefully.

"Hecho! Done!" he exclaimed. He started for home right away to get his broom.

"Why did you do that for, m'ijo?"[8] asked Barelas.

---

[5]**Ta bueno, ya bete** OK, now go away   [6]**menudo** tripe soup   [7]**Qué te parece?** How does that strike you?   [8]**m'ijo** (mi hijo), my son

20   "It don't seem right, Dad. The man works and no one pays him for his work. Everyone should get paid for what they do."

"He don't need no pay. Romero has everything he needs."

"It's not the same, Dad. How would you like to do what he does and be treated the same way? It's degrading the way he has to go around getting scraps and handouts."

"I'm not Romero. Besides you don't know about these things, m'ijo. Romero would be unhappy if his schedule was upset. Right now everyone likes him and takes care of him. He sweeps the sidewalks because he wants something to do, not because he wants money."

"I'll pay him out of my money, don't worry about it then."

25   "The money is not the point. The point is that money will not help Romero. Don't you understand that?"

"Look, Dad. Just put yourself in his place. Would you do it? Would you cut hair for nothing?"

Barelas just knew his son was putting something over on him but he didn't know how to answer. It seemed to make sense the way Seferino explained it. But it still went against his "instinct." On the other hand, Seferino had gone and finished high school. He must know something. There were few kids who had finished high school in the barrio, and fewer who had gone to college. Barelas knew them all. He noted (with some pride) that Seferino was going to be enrolled at Harvard University this year. That must count for something, he thought. Barelas himself had never gone to school. So maybe his son had something there. On the other hand . . . it upset Barelas that he wasn't able to get Seferino to see the issue. How can we be so far apart on something so simple, he thought. But he decided not to say anything else about it.

Romero came back right away and swept the front of Barelas' shop again and put what little dirt he found into the curb. He swept up the gutter, put the trash in a shoe box and threw it in a garbage can.

Seferino watched with pride as Romero went about his job and when he was finished he went outside and shook Romero's hand. Seferino told him he had done a good job. Romero beamed.

30   Manolo was coming into the shop to get his hair cut as Seferino was giving Romero his wages. He noticed Romero with his broom.

"What's going on?" He asked. Barelas shrugged his shoulders. "Qué tiene Romero?9 Is he sick or something?"

"No, he's not sick," explained Seferino, who had now come inside. He told Manolo the story.

"We're going to make Romero a businessman," said Seferino. "Do you realize how much money Romero would make if everyone paid him just fifty cents a day? Like my dad says, 'Everyone should be able to keep his dignity, no matter how poor.' And he does a job, you know."

"Well, it makes sense," said Manolo.

35   "Hey, Maybe I'll ask people to do that," said Seferino. "That way the poor old man could make a decent wage. Do you want to help, Manolo? You can go with me to ask people to pay him."

"Well," said Manolo as he glanced at Barelas, "I'm not too good at asking people for money."

9**Qué tiene Romero?** What's with Romero?

This did not discourage Seferino. He went out and contacted all the businesses on his own, but no one else wanted to contribute. This didn't discourage Seferino either. He went on giving Romero fifty cents a day.

After a while, Seferino heard that Romero had asked for credit at the grocery store. "See, Dad. What did I tell you? Things are getting better for him already. He's becoming his own man. And look. It's only been a couple of weeks." Barelas did not reply.

But then the next week Romero did not show up to sweep any sidewalks. He was around but he didn't do any work for anybody the entire week. He walked around Golden Heights Centro in his best gray work pants and his slouch hat, looking important and making it a point to walk right past the barber shop every little while.

40   Of course, the people in the Golden Heights Centro noticed the change immediately, and since they saw Romero in the street, they knew he wasn't ill. But the change was clearly disturbing the community. They discussed him in the Tortillería America where people got together for coffee, and at the Tres Milpas Bar. Everywhere the topic of conversation was the great change that had come over Romero. Only Barelas did not talk about it.

The following week Romero came into the barber shop and asked to talk with Seferino in private. Barelas knew immediately something was wrong. Romero never initiated a conversation unless he was drunk.

They went into the back room where Barelas could not hear and then Romero informed Seferino, "I want a raise."

"What? What do you mean, a raise? You haven't been around for a week. You only worked a few weeks and now you want a raise?" Seferino was clearly angry but Romero was calm and insistent.

Romero correctly pointed out that he had been sweeping the sidewalks for a long time. Even before Seferino finished high school.

45   "I deserve a raise," he repeated after an eloquent presentation.

Seferino looked coldly at Romero. It was clearly a stand-off.

Then Seferino said, "Look, maybe we should forget the whole thing. I was just trying to help you out and look at what you do."

Romero held his ground. "I helped you out too. No one told me to do it and I did it anyway. I helped you many years."

"Well, let's forget about the whole thing then," said Seferino.

50   "I quit then," said Romero.

"Quit?" exclaimed Seferino as he laughed at Romero.

"Quit! I quit!" said Romero as he walked out the front of the shop past Barelas, who was cutting a customer's hair.

Seferino came out shaking his head and laughing.

"Can you imagine that old guy?"

55   Barelas did not seem too amused. He felt he could have predicted that something bad like this would happen.

Romero began sweeping the sidewalks again the next day with the exception that when he came to the barber shop he would go around it and continue sweeping the rest of the sidewalks. He did this for the rest of the week. And the following Tuesday he began sweeping the sidewalk all the way up to the shop and then pushing the trash to the sidewalk in front of the barber shop. Romero then stopped coming to the barber shop in the afternoon.

The barrio buzzed with fact and rumor about Romero. Tino commented that Romero was not singing anymore. Even if someone offered to buy him a beer he wouldn't sing. Frank Avila said the neighbors were complaining because he was leaving his TV on loud the whole day and night. He still greeted people but seldom smiled. He had run up a big bill at the liquor store and when the manager stopped his credit, he caught Romero stealing bottles of whiskey. He was also getting careless about his dress. He didn't shave and clean like he used to. Women complained that he walked around in soiled pants, that he smelled bad. Even one of the little kids complained that Romero had kicked his puppy, but that seemed hard to believe.

Barelas felt terrible. He felt responsible. But he couldn't convince Seferino that what he had done was wrong. Barelas himself stopped going to the Tres Milpas Bar after work to avoid hearing about Romero. Once he came across Romero on the street and Barelas said hello but with a sense of guilt. Romero responded, avoiding Barelas' eyes and moving past him awkwardly and quickly. Romero's behavior continued to get erratic and some people started talking about having Romero committed.

"You can't do that," said Barelas when he was presented with a petition.

60   "He's flipped," said Tino, who made up part of the delegation circulating the petition. "No one likes Romero more than I do, you know that Barelas."

"But he's really crazy," said Frank Avila.

"He was crazy before. No one noticed," pleaded Barelas.

"But it was a crazy we could depend on. Now he just wants to sit on the curb and pull up the women's skirts. It's terrible. The women are going crazy. He's also running into the street stopping the traffic. You see how he is. What choice do we have?"

"It's for his own good," put in one of the workers from the Model Cities Office. Barelas dismissed them as outsiders. Seferino was there and wanted to say something but a look from Barelas stopped him.

65   "We just can't do that," insisted Barelas. "Let's wait. Maybe he's just going through a cycle. Look. We've had a full moon recently, qué no?[10] That must be it. You know how the moon affects people in his condition."

"I don't know," said Tino. "What if he hurts . . . ."

"He's not going to hurt anyone," cut in Barelas.

"No, Barelas. I was going to say, what if he hurts himself. He has no one at home. I'd say, let him come home with me for a while but you know how stubborn he is. You can't even talk to him any more."

"He gives everyone the finger when they try to pull him out of the traffic," said Frank Avila. "The cops have missed him, but it won't be long before they see him doing some of his antics and arrest him. Then what? Then the poor guy is in real trouble."

70   "Well, look," said Barelas. "How many names you got on the list?"

Tino responded slowly, "Well, we sort of wanted you to start off the list."

"Let's wait a while longer," said Barelas. "I just know that Romero will come around. Let's wait just a while, okay?"

No one had the heart to fight the issue and so they postponed the petition.

There was no dramatic change in Romero even though the full moon had completed its cycle. Still, no one initiated the petition again and then in the middle of August Seferino left for Cambridge to look for housing and to register early for school. Suddenly everything began to change again. One day Romero began

---

[10]**qué no?** right?

sweeping the entire sidewalk again. His spirits began to pick up and his strange antics began to disappear.

75   At the Tortillería America the original committee met for coffee and the talk turned to Romero.

"He's going to be all right now," said a jubilant Barelas. "I guarantee it."

"Well, don't hold your breath yet," said Tino. "The full moon is coming up again."

"Yeah," said Frank Avila dejectedly.

When the next full moon was in force the group was together again drinking coffee and Tino asked, "Well, how's Romero doing?"

80   Barelas smiled and said, "Well. Singing songs like crazy."

[1982]

 Topics for Critical Thinking and Writing

1. What sort of man do you think Barelas is? In your response take account of the fact that the townspeople "sort of want" Barelas "to start off the list" of petitioners seeking to commit Romero.
2. The narrator, introducing the reader to Seferino, tells us that "Seferino was a conscientious and sensitive young man." Do you agree? Why, or why not?
3. What do you make of the last line of the story?
4. Do you think this story could take place in almost any community? If you did not grow up in a barrio, could it take place in your community?

THREE POEMS BY ELIZABETH BISHOP FOR ANALYSIS

 ELIZABETH BISHOP

Elizabeth Bishop (1911–79) was born in Worcester, Massachusetts. Because her father died when she was eight months old and her mother was confined to a sanitarium four years later, Bishop was raised by relatives in New England and Nova Scotia. After graduating from Vassar College in 1934, where she was co-editor of the student literary magazine, she lived (on a small private income) for a while in Key West, France, and Mexico, and then for much of her adult life in Brazil, before returning to the United States to teach at Harvard. Her financial independence enabled her to write without worrying about the sales of her books and without having to devote energy to distracting jobs.

Filling Station

Oh, but it is dirty!
—this little filling station,
oil-soaked, oil-permeated
to a disturbing, over-all
black translucency.
Be careful with that match!   5

Father wears a dirty,
oil-soaked monkey suit
that cuts him under the arms,
and several quick and saucy   10
and greasy sons assist him
(it's a family filling station),
all quite thoroughly dirty.

Do they live in the station?
It has a cement porch   15
behind the pumps, and on it
a set of crushed and grease-
impregnated wickerwork;
on the wicker sofa
a dirty dog, quite comfy.   20

Some comic books provide
the only note of color—
of certain color. They lie
upon a big dim doily
draping a taboret   25
(part of the set), beside
a big hirsute begonia.

Why the extraneous plant?
Why the taboret?
Why, oh why, the doily?   30
(Embroidered in daisy stitch
with marguerites, I think,
and heavy with gray crochet.)

Somebody embroidered the doily.
Somebody waters the plant,   35
or oils it, maybe. Somebody
arranges the rows of cans
so that they softly say:
ESSO°—so—so—so
to high-strung automobiles.   40
Somebody loves us all.

[1965]

Topics for Critical Thinking and Writing

1. Taking into account only the first 14 lines, how would you characterize the speaker?
2. Robert Lowell, a poet and a friend of Elizabeth Bishop, said of her poems that they have "a tone of . . . grave tenderness and sorrowing amusement." Do you agree? If so, illustrate his comment by calling attention to specific

---

39 **ESSO** a brand of gasoline, now Exxon (editors' note)

passages in "Filling Station." If you disagree, how would you describe the tone?

3. In lines 21–30, what evidence suggests that the speaker feels that her taste is superior to the taste of the family? Does she change her mind by the end of the poem, or not?

4. "High-strung" in the last stanza *is* a rather odd way to characterize automobiles. What else strikes you as odd in the last stanza?

5. In two or three paragraphs, characterize a store, or stand, or territory that you know. Focus on an aspect of it (as Bishop focuses on the dirt and oil) so that readers can see what you find odd, or interesting, or striking about it.

The Fish

I caught a tremendous fish
and held him beside the boat
half out of water, with my hook
fast in a corner of his mouth.
He didn't fight.   5
He hadn't fought at all.
He hung a grunting weight,
battered and venerable
and homely. Here and there
his brown skin hung in strips   10
like ancient wall-paper,
and its pattern of darker brown
was like wall-paper:
shapes like full-blown roses
stained and lost through age.   15
He was speckled with barnacles,
fine rosettes of lime,
and infested
with tiny white sea-lice,
and underneath two or three   20
rags of green weed hung down.
While his gills were breathing in
the terrible oxygen
—the frightening gills,
fresh and crisp with blood,   25
that can cut so badly—
I thought of the coarse white flesh
packed in like feathers,
the big bones and the little bones,
the dramatic reds and blacks   30
of his shiny entrails,
and the pink swim-bladder
like a big peony.
I looked into his eyes
which were far larger than mine   35
but shallower, and yellowed,
the irises backed and packed
with tarnished tinfoil

seen through the lenses
of old scratched isinglass.   40
They shifted a little, but not
to return my stare.
—It was more like the tipping
of an object toward the light.
I admired his sullen face,   45
the mechanism of his jaw,
and then I saw
that from his lower lip
—if you could call it a lip—
grim, wet, and weapon-like,   50
hung five old pieces of fish-line,
or four and a wire leader
with the swivel still attached,
with all their five big hooks
grown firmly in his mouth.   55
A green line, frayed at the end
where he broke it, two heavier lines,
and a fine black thread
still crimped from the strain and snap
when it broke and he got away.   60
Like medals with their ribbons
frayed and wavering,
a five-haired beard of wisdom
trailing from his aching jaw.
I stared and stared   65
and victory filled up
the little rented boat,
from the pool of bilge
where oil had spread a rainbow
around the rusted engine   70
to the bailer rusted orange,
the sun-cracked thwarts,
the oarlocks on their strings,
the gunnels—until everything
was rainbow, rainbow, rainbow!   75
And I let the fish go.

[1946]

Topics for Critical Thinking and Writing

1. In line 9 Bishop calls the fish "homely" and in succeeding lines compares him to a series of stained, scratched, and tarnished domestic objects. When (in line 45) she reports that she "admired his sullen face," did that take you by surprise, or had she prepared you for her admiration? Explain.

2. In lines 66–67 we're told that "victory filled up / the little rented boat." Whose victory was it? Or do you think the lines are deliberately ambiguous?

3. Why does the speaker pause in her story to describe the condition of the rented boat? Is a comparison between the boat and the fish implied?

4. What causes the "rainbow" in line 69? How do you understand "everything / was rainbow, rainbow, rainbow!" in lines 74–75?
5. Why does the speaker let the fish go? Is this ending a surprise, or has it been prepared for? Explain.

Brazil, January 1, 1502

. . . embroidered nature . . . tapestried landscape.

—*Landscape into Art,* by Sir Kenneth Clark

Januaries, Nature greets our eyes
exactly as she must have greeted theirs:
every square inch filling in with foliage—
big leaves, little leaves, and giant leaves,
blue, blue-green, and olive,   5
with occasional lighter veins and edges,
or a satin underleaf turned over;
monster ferns
in silver-gray relief,
and flowers, too, like giant water lilies   10
up in the air—up, rather, in the leaves—
purple, yellow, two yellows, pink,
rust red and greenish white;
solid but airy; fresh as if just finished
and taken off the frame.   15

A blue-white sky, a simple web,
backing for feathery detail:
brief arcs, a pale-green broken wheel,
a few palms, swarthy, squat, but delicate;
and perching there in profile, beaks agape,   20
the big symbolic birds keep quiet,
each showing only half his puffed and padded,
pure-colored or spotted breast.
Still in the foreground there is Sin:
five sooty dragons near some massy rocks.   25
The rocks are worked with lichens, gray moonbursts
splattered and overlapping,
threatened from underneath by moss
in lovely hell-green flames,
attacked above   30
by scaling-ladder vines, oblique and neat,
"one leaf yes and one leaf no" (in Portuguese).
The lizards scarcely breathe; all eyes
are on the smaller, female one, back-to,
her wicked tail straight up and over,   35
red as a red-hot wire.

Just so the Christians, hard as nails,
tiny as nails, and glinting,
in creaking armor, came and found it all,

not unfamiliar: 40
no lovers' walks, no bowers,
no cherries to be picked, no lute music,
but corresponding, nevertheless,
to an old dream of wealth and luxury
already out of style when they left home—   45
wealth, plus a brand-new pleasure.
Directly after Mass, humming perhaps
L'Homme armé or some such tune,
they ripped away into the hanging fabric,
each out to catch an Indian for himself—   50
those maddening little women who kept calling,
calling to each other (or had the birds waked up?)
and retreating, always retreating, behind it.

[1962]

✎ Topics for Critical Thinking and Writing

1. What is the function of the epigraph in the structure of the poem?
2. What is the effect of reading line 15 on your response to the description of the flowers in the previous lines? Why is Bishop doing this?
3. Line 21 suggests that the description in the second stanza is meant to be a symbolic one But symbolic of what? Focus on each element of the scene that the speaker describes, and explain as best you can the symbolic meaning of the scene as a whole.
4. In the final stanza, what is Bishop suggesting about the Christians? Is this poem primarily about the landscape and history of Brazil in the sixteenth century, or is it just as much or more a poem about the present?
5. Is the poem too obscure to be truly effective? Does Bishop succeed in communicating her feelings and insights to us?

Other Kinds of Writing about Literature

SUMMARY

The essay on "The Story of an Hour" in Chapter 2 does not include a *summary* because the writer knew that all of her readers were thoroughly familiar with Chopin's story. Sometimes, however, it is advisable to summarize the work you are writing about, thus reminding a reader who has not read the work recently, or even informing a reader who may never have read the work. A review of a new work of literature or of a new film, for instance, usually includes a summary, on the assumption that readers are unfamiliar with it.

A summary is a brief restatement or condensation of the plot. Consider this **summary** of Chopin's "The Story of an Hour."

> A newspaper office reports that Brently Mallard has been killed in a railroad accident. When the news is gently broken to Mrs. Mallard by her sister Josephine, Mrs. Mallard weeps wildly and then shuts herself up in her room, where she sinks into an armchair. Staring dully through the window, she sees the signs of spring, and then an unnameable sensation possesses her. She tries to reject it but finally abandons herself to it. Renewed, she exults in her freedom, in the thought that at last the days will be her own. She finally comes out of the room, embraces her sister, and descends the stairs. A moment later her husband--who in fact had not been in the accident-- enters. Mrs. Mallard dies--of the joy that kills, according to the doctors' diagnosis.

Here are a few principles that govern summaries:

1. A summary is **much briefer than the original.** It is not a paraphrase—a word-by-word translation of someone's words into your own. A paraphrase is usually at least as long as the original, whereas a summary is rarely longer than one-fourth of the original and is usually much shorter. A novel may be summarized in a few paragraphs, or even in one paragraph.
2. A summary **usually achieves its brevity by omitting almost all of the concrete details of the original** and by omitting minor characters and episodes. Notice that the summary of "The Story of an Hour" omits the

friend of the family, omits specifying the signs of spring, and omits the business of the sister imploring Mrs. Mallard to open the door.

3. A summary is **as accurate as possible,** given the limits of space. It has no value if it misrepresents the point of the original.

4. A summary is **normally written in the present tense.** Thus "A newspaper office reports . . . , Mrs. Mallard weeps . . . ."

5. If the summary is brief (say, fewer than 250 words), it **may be given as a single paragraph.** If you are summarizing a long work, you may feel that a longer summary is needed. In this case your reader will be grateful to you if you divide the summary into paragraphs. As you draft your summary, you may find **natural divisions.** For instance, the scene of the story may change midway, providing you with the opportunity to use two paragraphs. Or you may want to summarize a five-act play in five paragraphs.

6. The writer of a summary **need not make the points in the same order as that of the original.** If the writer of an essay has delayed revealing the main point until the end of the essay, the summary may rearrange the order, stating the main point first. Occasionally, for instance if the original author has presented an argument in a disorderly or confusing sequence, one writes a summary in order to disengage the author's argument from its confusing structure.

7. Because a summary is openly based on someone else's views, it is usually **not necessary to use quotation marks** around key words or phrases from the original. Nor is it necessary to repeat "he says" or "she goes on to prove." From the opening sentence of a summary it should be clear that what follows is what the original author says.

Summaries have their place in essays, but remember that a summary is not an analysis; it is only a summary.

PARAPHRASE

What Paraphrase Is

A **paraphrase** is a restatement—a sort of translation in the same language—of material that may in its original form be somewhat obscure to a reader. A native speaker of English will not need a paraphrase of "Thirty days hath September," though a non-native speaker might be puzzled by two things, the meaning of *hath* and the inverted word order. For such a reader, "September has thirty days" would be a helpful paraphrase.

Although a paraphrase seeks to make clear the gist of the original, if the original is even a little more complex than "Thirty days hath September" the paraphrase will—in the process of clarifying something—lose something, since the substitution of one word for another will change the meaning. For instance, "Shut up" and "Be quiet" do not say exactly the same thing; the former (in addition to asking for quiet) says that the speaker is rude, or perhaps it says that the speaker feels little respect for the auditor, but the paraphrase loses all of this.

The Value of Paraphrase

Still, a paraphrase can be a first step in helping a reader to understand a line that includes an obsolete word or phrase, or a word or phrase that is current only in one region. In a poem by Emily Dickinson (1830–86), the following line appears:

The sun engrossed the East. . . .

"Engrossed" here has (perhaps among other meanings) a special commercial meaning, "to acquire most or all of a commodity; to monopolize the market," so a paraphrase of the line might go thus:

The sun took over all of the east.

(It's worth mentioning, parenthetically, that you should have at your elbow a good desk dictionary, such as *The American Heritage Dictionary of the English Language,* third edition. Writers—especially poets—expect you to pay close attention to every word. If a word puzzles you, look it up.)

Idioms, as well as words, may puzzle a reader. The Anglo-Irish poet William Butler Yeats (1865-1939) begins one poem with

The friends that have it I do wrong. . . .

Because the idiom "to have it" (meaning "to believe that," "to think that") is unfamiliar to many American readers today, a discussion of the poem might include a paraphrase—a rewording, a translation into more familiar language, such as

The friends who think that I am doing the wrong thing. . . .

Perhaps the rest of the poem is immediately clear, but in any case here is the entire poem, followed by a paraphrase:

The friends that have it I do wrong
When ever I remake a song,
Should know what issue is at stake:
It is myself that I remake.

Now for the paraphrase:

The friends who think that I am doing the wrong thing when I revise one of my poems should be informed what the important issue is; I'm not just revising a poem—rather, I am revising myself (my thoughts, feelings).

Here, as with any paraphrase, the meaning is not translated exactly; there is some distortion. For instance, if "song" in the original is clarified by "poem" in the paraphrase, it is also altered; the paraphrase loses the sense of lyricism that is implicit in "song." Further, "Should know what issue is at stake" (in the original) is ambiguous. Does "should" mean "ought," as in "You should know better than to speak so rudely," or does it mean "deserve to be informed," as in "You ought to know that I am thinking about quitting"?

Granted that a paraphrase may miss a great deal, a paraphrase often helps you, or your reader, to understand at least the surface meaning, and the act of paraphrasing will usually help you to understand at least some of the implicit meaning. Furthermore, a paraphrase makes you see that the original writer's words (if the work is a good one) are exactly right, better than any words we might substitute. It becomes clear that the thing said in the original—not only the rough "idea" expressed but the precise tone with which it is expressed—is a sharply defined experience.

LITERARY RESPONSE

Anything that you write about a work of literature is a response, even if it seems to be as matter-of-fact as a summary. It's sometimes useful to compare your summary with that of a classmate. You may be surprised to find that the two summaries differ considerably—though when you think about it, it isn't really surprising. Two different people are saying what they think is the gist of the work, and their views are shaped, to some degree, by such things as their gender, their ethnicity, and their experience (including, of course, their *literary* experience).

But when we talk about writing a response, we usually mean something more avowedly personal, something like an entry in a journal, where the writer may set forth an emotional response, perhaps relating the work to one of his or her own experiences. (On journals, see pp. 16–17.)

Writing a Literary Response

You may want to rewrite a literary work, for instance by giving it a different ending or by writing an epilogue in which you show the characters 20 years later. (We have already talked about the possibility of writing a sequel to Chopin's "Ripe Figs," or writing a letter from Babette to Maman-Nainaine, or writing Babette's memoirs.) Or you might want to rewrite the work by presenting the characters from a different point of view. The student who in an essay on Thurber's "The Secret Life of Walter Mitty" argued that Mitty *needed* someone very much like Mrs. Mitty might well have rewritten Thurber's story along those lines. The fun for the reader would of course reside largely in hearing the story reinterpreted, in seeing the story turned inside out.

A Story, by a Student, Based on a Story: "The Ticket (A Different View of 'The Story of an Hour')"

Here is an example, written by Lola Lee Loveall for a course taught by Diana Muir at Solano Community College. Ms. Loveall's story is a response to Kate Chopin's "The Story of an Hour" (p. 12). Notice that Loveall's first sentence is close to her source—a good way to get started, but by no means the only way; notice, too, that elsewhere in her story she occasionally echoes Chopin—for instance, in the references to the treetops, the sparrows, and the latchkey. A reader enjoys detecting these echoes.

What is especially interesting, however, is that before she conceived her story Loveall presumably said to herself something like, "Well, Chopin's story is superb, but suppose we shift the focus a bit. Suppose we think about what it would be like, *from the husband's point of view,* to live with a woman who suffered from 'heart trouble,' a person whom one had to treat with 'great care'" (Chopin's words, in the first sentence of "The Story of an Hour"). "And what about Mrs. Mallard's sister, Josephine—so considerate of Mrs. Mallard? What, exactly, would *Mr.* Mallard think of her? Wouldn't he see her as a pain in the neck? And what might he be prompted to do? That is, how might this character in this situation respond?" And so Loveall's characters and her plot began to take shape. As part of the game, she committed herself to writing a plot that, in its broad outline, resembled Chopin's by being highly ironic. But read it yourself.

Lola Lee Loveall

English 6

The Ticket

(A Different View of "The Story of an Hour")

Knowing full well his wife was afflicted with heart trouble, Brently Mallard wondered how he was going to break the news about the jacket. As he strode along his boots broke through the shallow crust from the recent rain, and dust kicked up from the well-worn wagon road came up to flavor his breathing. At least, the gentle spring rain had settled the dusty powder even as it had sprinkled his stiffly starched shirt which was already dampened from the exertion of stamping along. The strenuous pace he set himself to cover the intervening miles home helped him regain his composure. Mr. Brently Mallard was always calm, cool, and confident.

However, he hadn't been this morning when he stepped aboard the train, took off his jacket and folded it neatly beside him, and settled in his seat on the westbound train. He had been wildly excited. Freedom was his. He was Free! He was off for California, devil take the consequences! He would be his old self again, let the chips fall where they may. And he would have been well on his way, too, if that accursed ticket agent hadn't come bawling out, "Mr. Mallard, you left your ticket on the counter!" just when Mallard himself had spied that nosy Jan Ardan bidding her sister goodbye several car lengths down the depot. How could he be so unfortunate as to run into them both twice this morning? Earlier, they had come into the bank just as the banker had extended the thick envelope.

"You understand, this is just an advance against the estate for a while?"

Only Mallard's persuasiveness could have extracted that amount from the cagey old moneybags. Mallard had carefully tucked it into his inside pocket.

This was the kind of spring day to fall in love--or lure an adventurer to the top of the next hill. Sparrows hovered about making happy sounds. Something about their movements reminded Mallard of his wife--quick, fluttering, then darting away.

He had loved her at first for her delicate ways. They had made a dashing pair--he so dark and worldly, she so fragile and fair--but her delicacy was a trap, for it disguised the heart trouble, bane of his life. Oh, he still took her a sip of brandy in bed in the morning as the doctor had suggested, although, of course, it wasn't his bed anymore. He had moved farther down the hall not long after her sister, Josephine, came to help, quick to come when Mrs. Mallard called, even in the middle of the night. After one such sudden appearance one night--"I thought I heard you call"--he had given up even sharing the same bed with his wife, although there had been little real sharing there for some time.

"No children!" the doctor had cautioned.

Mallard concentrated harder on the problem of the missing jacket. What to say? She would notice. Maybe not right away, but she would be aware. Oh, he knew Louise's reaction. She would apparently take the news calmly, then make a sudden stab toward her side with her delicate hands, then straighten and walk away--but not before he observed. A new jacket would cost money. Discussing money made the little drama happen more often, so now Mr. Mallard handled all the financial affairs, protecting her the best he could. After all, it was her inheritance, and he took great care with it, but there were the added costs: doctors, Josephine living with them, the medications, even his wife's brandy. Why, he checked it daily to be sure it was the proper strength. Of course, a man had to have a few pleasures, even if the cards did seem to fall against him more often than not. He manfully kept trying.

Everyone has a limit, though, and Mr. Mallard had reached his several days ago when the doctor had cautioned him again.

"She may go on like she is for years, or she may just keel over any time. However, the chances are she will gradually go downhill and need continual care. It is impossible to tell."

Mallard could not face "gradually go downhill." His manhood revolted against it. He was young, full of life. Let Josephine carry the chamber pot! After Louise's demise (whenever that occurred!) the simple estate which she had inherited reverted to Josephine. Let her earn it. Also, good old friend Richards was always about with a suggestion here or a word of comfort there for Louise. They'd really not care too much if Mallard were a long time absent.

As he drew nearer his home, Mallard continued to try to calm his composure, which was difficult for he kept hearing the sound of the train wheels as it pulled away, jacket, envelope, and all, right before his panic-stricken eyes: CALIFORNIA; California; california; california.

DUTY! It was his duty not to excite Louise. As he thought of duty he unconsciously squared his drooping shoulders, and the image of Sir Galahad flitted across his mind.

The treetops were aglow in the strange afterlight of the storm. A shaft of sunlight shot through the leaves and fell upon his face. He had come home.

He opened the front door with the latchkey. Fortunately, it had been in his pants pocket.

Later, the doctors did not think Mr. Mallard's reaction unusual, even when a slight smile appeared on the bereaved husband's face. Grief causes strange reactions.

"He took it like a man," they said.

Only later, when the full significance of his loss reached him, did he weep.

A Poem Based on a Poem

We begin with a poem by William Blake (1757–1827), an English Christian visionary poet.

The Tyger

Tyger! Tyger! burning bright
In the forests of the night,
What immortal hand or eye
Could frame thy fearful symmetry?   4

In what distant deeps or skies
Burnt the fire of thine eyes?
On what wings dare he aspire?
What the hand dare seize the fire?   8

And what shoulder, and what art,
Could twist the sinews of thy heart?

And, when thy heart began to beat,
What dread hand? and what dread feet?

12

What the hammer? what the chain?
In what furnace was thy brain?
What the anvil? What dread grasp
Dare its deadly terrors clasp?

16

When the stars threw down their spears,
And watered heaven with their tears,
Did he smile his work to see?
Did he who made the lamb make thee?

20

Tyger! Tyger! burning bright
In the forests of the night,
What immortal hand or eye,
Dare frame thy fearful symmetry?

24

[1794]

William Blake was the favorite poet of Allen Ginsberg (1926–97). Ginsberg, a New Yorker who established his fame in San Francisco, was noted for his declamatory poetry and his celebration of outsiders, especially protestors against the wars in Korea and Vietnam. He often chanted Blake's poems at his own poetry readings. In the following poem X. J. Kennedy pays homage to Ginsberg by adopting the form of one of Ginsberg's favorite poems. Kennedy alludes, in his poem, to Ginsberg's left-wing activities ("Taunter of the ultra right"), his view that his hearers should drop out of a corrupt and repressive society, his interest in Buddhist mantras (syllables laden with mystic power), his anti-war activity ("Mantra-minded flower child"), his homosexuality ("Queer," "Queen"), and his use of finger cymbals in some of his readings. *Om* (line 9) is a syllable that begins several mantras. Ginsberg often had his audience utter the sound.

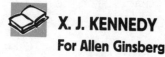

X. J. KENNEDY
For Allen Ginsberg

Ginsberg, Ginsberg, burning bright,
Taunter of the ultra right,
What blink of the Buddha's eye
Chose the day for you to die?

Queer pied piper, howling wild,
Mantra-minded flower child,
Queen of Maytime, misrule's lord
Bawling, *Drop out! All aboard!*

5

Finger-cymbaled, chanting *Om*,
Foe of fascist, bane of bomb,
Proper poets' thorn-in-side,
Turner of a whole time's tide,

10

Who can fill your sloppy shoes?
What a catch for Death. We lose
Glee and sweetness, freaky light,
Ginsberg, Ginsberg, burning bright.

15

PARODY

One special kind of response is the **parody,** a comic form that imitates the original in a humorous way. It is a caricature in words. A parody may imitate the style of the original—let's say, short, punchy sentences—but apply this style to a subject that the original author would not be concerned with. Thus, because Ernest Hemingway often wrote short, simple sentences about tough guys engaged in activities such as hunting, fishing, and boxing, parodists of Hemingway are likely to use the same style, but for their subject they may choose something like opening the mail or preparing a cup of tea.

We once heard on the radio a parody of an announcer doing a baseball game. It went something like this:

> Well, here's Bill Shakespeare now, approaching the desk. Like so many other writers, Bill likes to work at a desk. In fact, just about every writer we know writes at a desk, but every writer has a particular way of approaching the desk and sitting at it. Bill is sitting down now; now he's adjusting the chair, moving it forward a little. Oh, he's just pushed the chair back an inch or two. He likes his chair to be just right. Now he's picking up a pen. It's a gray quill. I think it's the pen he uses when he writes a tragedy, and he's due for a tragedy—of his last five plays, only one was a tragedy, and two were comedies and two were history plays. But you never can tell with Bill, or "The Bard" as his fans call him. Some people call him "The Swan of Avon," but I'm told that he really hates that. Well, he's at the desk, and, you know, in circumstances like these, he might even sneak in a sonnet or two. Oh, he's put down the gray quill, and now he's trying a white one. Oh boy, oh boy, he's written a *word. No,* he's going for *a whole sentence!"*

Parodies are, in a way, critical, but they are usually affectionate too. In the best parodies one feels that the writer admires the author being parodied. The distinguished sociologist Daniel Bell wrote a deliberate parody of sociological writing. It begins thus:

> The purpose of this scene is to present a taxonomic dichotomization which would allow for unilinear comparison. In this fashion we could hope to distinguish the relevant variables which determine the functional specificities of social movements.

The journalist H. L. Mencken (1880-1956), who had a love-hate relationship with what he called the Great American Booboisie, wrote a parody in which he set forth the Declaration of Independence as it might have been written (or spoken) by Joe Sixpack in the mid twentieth century. Here the target is not the original document but the twentieth-century American. The original document, you will remember, begins in this way:

> When in the Course of human events, it becomes necessary for one people to dissolve the political bands which have connected them with another, and to assume among the Powers of the earth, the separate and equal station to which the Laws of Nature and of Nature's God entitle them, a decent respect to the opinions of mankind requires that they should declare the causes which impel them to the separation.

Now for Mencken's version:

> When things get so balled up that the people of a country got to cut
> loose from some other country, and go it on their own hook, without
> asking no permission from nobody, excepting maybe God Almighty,
> then they ought to let everybody know why they done it, so that every-
> body can see they are not trying to put nothing over on nobody.

REVIEWING A DRAMATIC PRODUCTION

A review also is a response, since it normally includes an evaluation of the work,
but at least at first glance it may seem to be an analytic essay. We'll talk about a
review of a production of a play, but you can easily adapt what we say to a review of a book.

A review requires analytic skill, but it is not identical with an analysis. First
of all, a reviewer normally assumes that the reader is unfamiliar with the production being reviewed, and unfamiliar with the play if the play is not a classic.
Thus, the first paragraph usually provides a helpful introduction, along these
lines:

> Marsha Norman's recent play, *'night, Mother,* a tragedy with only two
> actors and one set, shows us a woman's preparation for suicide. Jesse
> has concluded that she no longer wishes to live, and so she tries to put
> her affairs into order, which chiefly means preparing her rather uncom-
> prehending mother to get along without her.

Inevitably some retelling of the plot is necessary if the play is new, and a summary of a sentence or two is acceptable even for a familiar play, but the review
will chiefly be concerned with

1. Describing,
2. Analyzing, and, especially,
3. Evaluating.

By the way, don't confuse description with analysis. Description tells what something—for instance, the set or the costumes—looks like; analysis tells us how it
works, what it adds up to, what it contributes to the total effect.) If the play is
new, much of the evaluation may center on the play itself, but if the play is a classic, the evaluation probably will be devoted chiefly to the acting, the set, and the
direction.

Other points:

1. **Save the playbill;** it will give you the names of the actors, and perhaps a
   brief biography of the author, a synopsis of the plot, and a photograph of
   the set, all of which may be helpful.
2. **Draft your review as soon as possible,** while the performance is still
   fresh in your mind. If you can't draft it immediately after seeing the play, at
   least jot down some notes about the setting and the staging, the acting, and
   the audience's responses.

3. If possible, **read the play**—ideally, before the performance and again after it.

4. **In your first draft, don't worry about limitations of space;** write as long a review as you can, putting down everything that comes to mind. Later you can cut it to the required length, retaining only the chief points and the necessary supporting details. But in your first draft try to produce a fairly full record of the performance and your response to it, so that a day or two later, when you revise, you won't have to trust a fading memory for details.

A Sample Review by a Student: "An Effective *Macbeth*"

If you read reviews of plays in *Time, Newsweek,* or a newspaper, you will soon develop a sense of what reviews do. The following example, an undergraduate's review of a college production of *Macbeth,* is typical except in one respect: Reviews of new plays, as we have already suggested, customarily include a few sentences summarizing the plot and classifying the play (a tragedy, a farce, a rock musical, or whatever), perhaps briefly putting it in the context of the author's other works. Because *Macbeth* is so widely known, however, the writer of this review chose not to risk offending her readers by telling them that *Macbeth* is a tragedy by Shakespeare.

Preliminary Jottings During the two intermissions and immediately after the end of the performance, the reviewer made a few jottings, which the next day she rewrote:

> Compare with last year's Midsummer Night's Dream
> occasionally exciting production, partly because the director,
>   pipe framework at rear. Duncan exits on it.
>   Useful?
>   witches: powerful, not funny
>   stage: battlefield? barren land?
>   costume: earth-colored rags
>   they seduce—even caress—Mac.
>   Macbeth
>   ~~witches caress him~~
>   strong; also gentle (with Lady M)
>   Lady Macb.
>   sexy in speech about unsexing her
>   too attractive? Prob. ok
>   Banquo's ghost: naturalistic; covered with blood
>   Duncan: terrible; worst actor except for Lady Macduff's boy
>   costumes: leather, metal; only Duncan in robes
>   pipe framework used for D, and murder of Lady Macduff
>   forest; branches unrealistic; stylized? or cheesy?

The Finished Version The published review appears below, accompanied by some marginal notes in which we comment on its strengths.

Title implies thesis

An Effective *Macbeth*

Opening paragraph is informative, letting the reader know the reviewer's overall attitude

Macbeth at the University Theater is a thoughtful and occasionally exciting production, partly because the director, Mark Urice, has trusted Shakespeare and has not imposed a gimmick on the play. The characters do not wear cowboy costumes as they did in last year's production of *A Midsummer Night's Dream.*

Reviewer promptly turns to a major issue

Probably the chief problem confronting a director of *Macbeth* is how to present the witches so that they are powerful supernatural forces and not silly things that look as though they came from a Halloween party. Urice gives us ugly but not absurdly grotesque witches, and he introduces them most effectively. The stage seems to be a bombed-out battlefield littered with rocks and great chunks of earth, but some of these begin to stir—the earth seems to come alive—and the clods move, unfold, and become the witches, dressed in brown and dark gray rags. The suggestion is that the witches are a part of nature, elemental forces that can hardly be escaped. This effect is increased by the moans and creaking noises that they make, all of which could be comic but which in this production are impressive.

First sentence of this paragraph provides an effective transition

The witches' power over Macbeth is further emphasized by their actions. When the witches first meet Macbeth, they encircle him, touch him, caress him, even embrace him, and he seems helpless, almost their plaything. Moreover, in the scene in which he imagines that he sees a dagger, the director has arranged for one of the witches to appear, stand near Macbeth, and guide his hand toward the invisible dagger. This is, of course, not in the text, but the interpretation is reasonable rather than intrusive. Finally, near the end of the play, just before Macduff kills Macbeth, a witch appears and laughs at Macbeth as Macduff explains that he was not "born of woman." There is no doubt that throughout the tragedy Macbeth has been a puppet of the witches.

Paragraph begins with a broad assertion and then offers supporting details

Stephen Beers (Macbeth) and Tina Peters (Lady Macbeth) are excellent. Beers is sufficiently brawny to be convincing as a battlefield hero, but he also speaks the lines sensitively, so the audience feels that in addition to being a hero, he is a man of gentleness. One can believe Lady Macbeth when she says that she fears he is "too full o' the milk of human kindness" to murder Duncan. Lady Macbeth is especially effective in the scene in which she asks the spirits to "unsex her." During this speech she is reclining on a bed and as she delivers the lines she be-

Reference to a particular scene

comes increasingly sexual in her bodily motions, deriving excitement from her own stimulating words. Her attachment to Macbeth is strongly sexual, and so is his attraction to her. The scene when she persuades him to kill Duncan ends with their passionately embracing. The strong attraction of each for the other, so evident in the early part of the play, disappears after the murder, when Macbeth keeps his distance from Lady Macbeth and does not allow her to touch him. The acting of the other performers is effective, except for John Berens (Duncan), who recites the lines mechanically and seems not to take much account of their meaning.

Description, but also analysis

The set consists of a barren plot, at the rear of which stands a spidery framework of piping of the sort used by construction companies, supporting a catwalk. This framework fits with the costumes (lots of armor, leather, heavy boots), suggesting a sort of elemental, primitive, and somewhat sadistic world. The catwalk, though effectively used when Macbeth goes off to murder Duncan (whose room is presumably upstairs and offstage), is not much used in later scenes. For the most part it is an interesting piece of scenery but not otherwise helpful. For instance, there is no reason why the scene with Macduff's wife and children is staged on it. The costumes are not in any way Scottish—no plaids—but in several scenes the sound of a bagpipe is heard, adding another weird or primitive tone to the production.

Concrete details to support evaluation

Summary

This *Macbeth* appeals to the eye, the ear, and the mind. The director has given us a unified production that makes sense and that is faithful to the spirit of Shakespeare's play.

Documentation

Work Cited

Macbeth. By William Shakespeare. Dir. Mark Urice. With Stephen Beers, Tina Peters, and John Berens. University Theater, Medford, MA. 3 Mar. 1998.

The Review Reviewed

The marginal notes call attention to certain qualities in the review, but three additional points should be made:

1. The reviewer's feelings and evaluations are clearly expressed, not in such expressions as "furthermore I feel," and "it is also my opinion," but in such expressions as "a thoughtful and occasionally exciting production," "excellent," and "appeals to the eye, the ear, and the mind."
2. The evaluations are supported by details. For instance, the evaluation that the witches are effectively presented is supported by a brief description of their appearance.

3. The reviewer is courteous, even when (as in the discussion of the catwalk, in the next-to-last paragraph) she is talking about aspects of the production she doesn't care for.

Note: Another review by a student (of a film version of *Hamlet*) appears in Chapter 20, which includes a casebook on *Hamlet*.

PART

II

Up Close:
Thinking Critically about
Literary Works and
Literary Forms

Critical Thinking: Asking Questions and Making Comparisons

WHAT IS CRITICAL THINKING?

The verb *to think* has several meanings, such as *to imagine* ("Think how he'll hit the ceiling when you tell him this"), *to expect or hope* ("I think I'll get the job"), and—the meaning we will chiefly be concerned with—*to consider closely, especially by exercising one's powers of reason* ("I've been thinking about why she did it, and I've come to some conclusions").

When we engage in this last sort of thinking, close consideration, we are keenly aware of what we are doing. We are, for instance, studying an effect and are searching for its causes. "This story bores me, but exactly *why* does it bore me?" Is the plot too familiar? Are the characters unrealistic? Is the language trite? Or so technical that I can't follow it? Does the author use too many words to say too little? Or: "I loved the book but hated the movie. Why?" And again we start to consider the problem closely, probably (again) by examining the parts that make up the whole. And here we are at the heart of *critical thinking*.

The words *critic, critical,* and *criticism* come from a Greek word *krinein,* meaning "to separate." Although in ordinary talk, *to criticize* is to find fault or to judge severely, in the sense with which we are concerned *to criticize* is to examine and to judge, not necessarily to find fault.

Having said that critical thinking does not necessarily involve fault-finding, we want to modify this statement. There is one writer whose work you should indeed judge severely. The writer is you. When you read a draft of your work, adopt a skeptical spirit. As you read the draft, ask yourself if assertions are supported with sufficient evidence, and ask if other interpretations of the evidence might reasonably be offered. If you engage in this process, you are engaged in critical thinking.

ASKING AND ANSWERING QUESTIONS

Critical thinking is a matter of separating the whole into parts, in order to see relationships. If you ask yourself questions about a work—whether the work is something reprinted in this book or is something that you have just drafted—you will almost surely set yourself thinking about how the parts relate to each other and to the whole, their context. Typical questions are:

- What expectations does the title arouse in a reader?
- Does the middle drag?
- Do certain characters or settings seem to be symbolic, suggesting more than themselves?
- Is the end satisfactory, and if so, why? Because it is surprising? Because, on the contrary, foreshadowing caused us to anticipate it, and it therefore fulfills our expectations?

When you ask yourself questions such as these, you will find that you are deepening your understanding of how a work (perhaps an essay, story, poem, or play in this book, perhaps an essay of your own) works. Because thinking about questions is an excellent way to deepen your understanding, we include questions along with most of the literature in this book. And we include numerous checklists—in effect, lists of questions for you to ask yourself when you are writing—in order to help you think about your own productions.

A process that in effect is synonymous with critical thinking is ***analysis,*** this word also comes from a Greek word, meaning *to separate into parts.* And because the point of analysis is to understand how things connect, how things work, and because the point of writing an analysis is to share your understanding with your readers, your essay normally will include a ***synthesis,*** "a putting together." One can almost say that essays based on critical thinking will propose a ***thesis,*** and will support the thesis by giving ***reasons,*** that is, by giving evidence: "X is so, *because. . . .*"

Writing of this sort, in which evidence is offered, commonly is the result of conscious reasoning, but it must be admitted that sometimes insights come unsought. Two examples are famous. Legend says that the Greek mathematician Archimedes (287–212 B.C.), asked by the ruler of Syracuse to determine if a gold crown really was pure gold or was alloyed with silver, was baffled. To relax, he visited a public bath, and idly observed the overflow of water. "*Eureka* ("I have found it"), he shouted, leaping out of the water and (in his excitement) running home naked. What he had found was not the soap but the solution to the problem: Since gold is denser than silver, a given weight of gold represents a smaller volume than an equal weight of silver. A one-pound crown of gold will therefore displace less water than a one-pound crown that is made of gold alloyed with silver. (The crown in question *was* alloyed.) A second (and better documented) example is the discovery by the great German chemist F. A. Kekulé, who, dozing in front of the fireplace, developed the ring theory of the molecular structure of benzene. Kekulé dreamed of a snake biting its own tail, and according to his report, he "awoke as though from a flash of lightning," and spent the rest of night in working out the consequences of the hypothesis.

Confronted with the difficult but exciting and rewarding job of writing a thoughtful paper, you cannot count on inspiration, no matter how many baths you take or how many fires you contemplate sleepily. You probably will find, like almost everyone else, that your best thoughts come to you when you start to put them into writing, whether with pencil and paper or with a keyboard and a computer. Although our chief concern in this book will be with writing about literature, and in a moment we will look at a short poem, let's start indirectly by thinking analytically, thinking critically, about a picture. (Our method will be in accord with Polonius's advice in *Hamlet*, "By indirections find directions out.")

This photograph of Sitting Bull and Buffalo Bill was taken by a Canadian photographer, William McFarlane Notman. Buffalo Bill—William F. Cody—got his name from his activities as a supplier of buffalo meat for workers on the Kansas Pacific Railway, but his fame came chiefly from his exploits as an army scout and a fighter against the Sioux Indians, and later from Buffalo Bill's Wild West. Buffalo Bill's Wild West was a show (though he never used this word because he insisted that the exhibition recreated recent Western history) consisting of mock battles with Indians, an attack on a stage coach, and feats of horsemanship and sharpshooting. Sitting Bull, a Sioux chief, had defeated Custer at the Battle of Little Bighorn ten years before this picture was taken, but he had fled to Canada soon after the battle. In 1879 he was granted amnesty and returned to the United States, and in 1885 he appeared in Buffalo Bill's Wild West. The photograph, entitled "Foes in '76, Friends in '85," was used to publicize the show.

William MacFarlane Notman, photograph of *Sitting Bull and Buffalo Bill.* The Sioux chief appeared for one season in William F. Cody's show, which was called *Buffalo Bill's Wild West.* Souvenir cards with this picture were sold. (Buffalo Bill Historical Center, Cody, WY)

COMPARING AND CONTRASTING

In Chapter 5 we talked about writing a comparison (pages 79–81), but we now want to add a few things. The writer Howard Nemerov once said, "If you really want to see something, look at something else." He was talking about the power of comparison to illuminate. We compare X and Y, not for the sake of making lists of similarities and differences, but for the sake of seeing X (or Y) more clearly. This book chiefly offers material for you to read with pleasure, and one source of pleasure is understanding. Your understanding of one work may be heightened by thinking about it in comparison with another work. We offer several *casebooks* that present a writer *in depth*. For example, we give three stories by Alice Munro, as well as a lecture by her and an interview; thinking about one story in comparison with another, or within this context, will enrich your understanding. Similarly, we offer several thematic chapters, for instance a chapter on "Love and Hate," where, again, works invite comparison.

Suppose we want to think about the picture of Sitting Bull and Buffalo Bill, in order to deepen our understanding of it and to share our understanding with others. To say that the photograph's dimensions are such-and-such or even to say that it shows two people is merely to *describe* it, not to do anything that can be called thinking. But if we look more closely, and compare the two figures, our mind is energized. (Strictly speaking, **to compare** is to take note of similarities, and **to contrast** is to take note of differences, but in ordinary usage *compare* covers both activities.) Comparing greatly stimulates the mind; by comparing X with Y, we notice things that we might otherwise pass over. Suppose we ask these questions:

- What resemblances and differences do we see in the clothes of the two figures?
- What about their facial expressions?
- How do their poses compare?
- Is the setting significant?

If we try to answer these and other questions that come to mind, we may find ourselves jotting down phrases and sentences along these lines:

> Buffalo Bill is in fancy clothing (shiny boots, a mammoth buckle, a decorated jacket)
>
> BB is striking a pose--very theatrical, his right hand on his heart, his head tilted slightly back, his eyes looking off as though he is gazing into the future. He seems to be working hard to present a grand image of himself.
>
> Sitting Bull simply stands there, apparently looking downward. One feels that he is going along with what is expected of him--after all, he had joined the show--but he refuses to make a fool of himself.
>
> Sitting Bull lets BB have upper hand (literally--on gun)
>
> BB in effect surrounds SB (Bills right shoulder is behind Sitting Bull and Bills left leg is in front of him).

ANALYZING AND EVALUATING EVIDENCE

If we continue to look closely, we probably notice that the landscape is fake, not the great outdoors but a set, a painted backdrop and probably a fake grass mat. If we see these things, we may formulate the thesis that Buffalo Bill here is all show biz, and that Sitting Bull retains his dignity. And if in our essay we support these assertions by pointing to **evidence,** we are demonstrating critical thinking.

Here, in fact, is the final paragraph from an essay that a student wrote on this picture:

> Buffalo Bill is obviously the dominant figure in this photograph, but he is not the outstanding one. His efforts to appear great only serve to make him appear small. His attempt to outshine Sitting Bull strikes us as faintly ridiculous. We do not need nor want to know any more about Buffalo Bill's personality; it is spread before us in the picture. Sitting Bull's inwardness and dignity make him more interesting than Buffalo Bill, and make us wish to prove our intuition and to ascertain that this proud Sioux was a great chief.

We think this analysis is excellent, but when we did some of our own research on Buffalo Bill we found that he was more complicated and more interesting than we at first thought. But this is to get ahead of the story.

THINKING CRITICALLY ABOUT A WORK OF LITERATURE, BY ASKING QUESTIONS AND BY COMPARING: E. E. CUMMINGS'S "BUFFALO BILL 'S"

Let's look now at a short poem by E. E. Cummings, probably written in 1917, the year Buffalo Bill died, but not published until 1920. Cummings did not give it a title, but included it in a group of poems called "Portraits." (In line 6, *pigeons* are clay targets used in skeet shooting or in exhibitions of marksmanship.)

```
Buffalo Bill 's
defunct
          who used to
          ride a watersmooth-silver
                              stallion                              5
and break onetwothreefourfive pigeonsjustlikethat
                                        Jesus
he was a handsome man
                    and what I want to know is
how do you like your blueeyed boy                         10
Mister Death
```

Manuscript of the draft of E. E. Cummings's poem (the final version is printed on page 153). (By permission of the Houghton Library, Harvard University. bMs Am 1823.7 (21), 80.)

Read the poem, preferably aloud, at least two or three times, and with as open a mind as possible. *Don't* assume that because the photograph shows us a man for whom we probably would not want to work, this poem necessarily conveys the same attitude.

Ultimately you will want to ask your own questions about the poem and about your responses, but for a start you may find it useful to put down tentative answers to some or all of these questions:

```
 1          buffalo Bill [i̶s̶]'s defunct
 2                        smooth silver  break one two three four five  one fell.
 3          who used to ride a ~white~ˌhorse and ~shoot~ˌpidgens ~before they fell.~
 4                                  streaming from
 5                                        ~xxx~
 6          with his long hair like reindeer moss,ˌi̶n̶ the old stone
 7                                       of his face

 8                              Buffalo Bill's        - - - -
 9                                  who used to
10      defunct who         defunct ~defunct~         - - - - -
11      used to ride a smooth    ~who~
12      silver stallion     ride a a smooth silver  ʳ - - - - -
13                          [h̶o̶r̶s̶e̶] stallion and

14                              break
15                          ~break one~
16      dead ‖Buffalo       ~two three~  one two three
17          'd
18    alo Bill who rode a      four ~xxxx~ five
19      smooth silver stallion    pidgens
20      he'd ~break~
21 how?      pidgens|    glissando down the (happy) shouting crowd as he passed
22      break ~break~
23              one     two|
24                      three four   five |        who'd ride smooth
25                                     |           silver ' stallion
26      pidgens ~pidgens being with his~ long      tossed by    glissandoing do
27      ax                              an indian
28      ~eighty two~
29      curls
30      hair like ‖ reindeer                        ~pidgens~
31              streaming
32      moss ~streaming~    from the        tossed by a Comanche brave
33                          face
34      *       old
35  ~xxx~ eighty year stone
36      stone ** 80 years ~xxx~ stone

37      his ~long~
38          how d'~you~
39      ~you [like]~ you like [i̶t̶] him  | blue ~boy~ eye[o̶]d boy
40                      death        |
41          the brave old           |
42          boy                     |
43              he had you always in his |ey[o̶s̶]e|
```

Modern transcription of the draft reproduced on page 154. (Used by permission of *Harvard Library Bulletin*. Originally published in Rushworth M. Kidder, "'Buffalo Bill's'—An Early E.E. Cummings Manuscript," *Harvard Library Bulletin* 24:4 (1976):373-380.)

1. What is the speaker's attitude toward Buffalo Bill? (How do you know? What *evidence* can you point to?)
2. In line 6, why do you suppose the poet ran the words together?
3. Why do you think Cummings spaced the poem as he does? One student suggested that the lines form an arrowhead pointing to the right. Do you find merit in this suggestion? If not, what better explanation(s) can you offer?

The Farewell Shot, 1910. A poster
from what was billed as a farewell
performance. (Buffalo Bill Historical
Center, Cody, WY)

4. What do you make out of the address to "Mister Death"? Why "Mister Death" rather than "Mr. Death" or "Death"? If Mister Death could speak, what answer do you think he might give to the speaker's question?

5. What do you make of the use of "defunct" (as opposed to "dead") in line 2?

6. What do you make of "Jesus" in line 7? What is the effect of placing the word on a line by itself? Is Cummings being blasphemous? Is he inviting us to compare Buffalo Bill with Jesus? Again, support your response with *evidence*.

7. Compare the published poem with the manuscript draft. In the manuscript (see page 154, and for a scholar's transcription of it, see page 155) you will notice that Cummings wrote, near the start, "with his long hair like reindeer moss streaming from the old stone of his face." These words do not appear in the final version. Do you think Cummings showed good judgment in deleting the line? Explain.

8. Some readers say that Cummings is satirizing Buffalo Bill, others that he is satirizing death. Do you agree with either of these views? Why? (In a sentence or two define satire—feel free to consult a dictionary—and perhaps give a clear example. By the way, one can satirize the common human fear of death, but can one satirize death? How might one do so? And what would be the point?)

You may want to discuss some or all of these questions, and others that you generate for yourself, with classmates and with your instructor. It will be interesting

Buffalo Bill on a favorite horse,
around 1910. (Buffalo Bill
Historical Center, Cody, WY)

to see whether at least some differences of opinion can be resolved by discussion, by pointing to evidence.

Finally, after you have thought about the preceding questions, and any questions that you may initiate, consider these two opinions, from published discussions of the poem:

1. Buffalo Bill, in the poem, functions as a destroyer, an agent of death.
2. The picture of Buffalo Bill on his "watersmooth-silver stallion," riding to the center of the tent to accept the adulation of the crowd before his demonstration of crack marksmanship is, I think, acidly ironic.

Do you agree with either, or with both? What evidence in the poem can you point to, in order to support or rebut these assertions?

Two Encyclopedia Accounts of Sitting Bull: An Exercise in Close Reading and Critical Thinking

As an exercise in close reading (normally the first stage in critical thinking about literature), study and compare these two anonymous accounts of Sitting Bull, one from the *Encyclopaedia Britannica* of 1911, the other from the *Britannica* of 1993. In an essay of about 250 words indicate what differences you notice, and offer a tentative explanation for the differences.

William McFarlane
Notman, photograph
of Sitting Bull.
Notman, a native of
Scotland who settled
in Canada, took this
picture during Sitting
Bull's Canadian stay.
(McCord Museum of
Canadian History,
Montreal)

Encyclopaedia Britannica 11th ed., 1911

SITTING BULL (c. 1837–1890), a chief and medicine man of the
Dakota Sioux, was born on Willow Creek in what is now North
Dakota about 1837, son of a chief named Jumping Bull. He gained
great influence among the reckless and unruly young Indians, and during the Civil War led attacks on white settlements in Iowa and Minnesota. Though he had pretended to make peace in 1866, from 1869
to 1876 he frequently attacked whites or Indians friendly to whites.
His refusal to return to the reservation in 1876, led to the campaign in
which General George A. Custer (q.v.) and his command were massa-
cred. Fearing punishment for his participation in the massacre, Sitting
Bull with a large band moved over into Canada. He returned to the
United States in 1881, and after 1883 made his home at the Standing
Rock Agency. Rumours of a coming Indian Messiah who should
sweep away the whites, and Indian dissatisfaction at the sale of their
lands, created such great unrest in Dakota in 1889–1890 that it was
determined to arrest Sitting Bull as a precaution. He was surprised and
captured by Indian police and soldiers on Grand river on the 15th of

December 1890, and was killed while his companions were attempting to rescue him.

Encyclopaedia Britannica, 1993

Sitting Bull, Indian name TATANKA IYOTAKE (b. *c.* 1831 near Grand River, Dakota Territory [now in South Dakota], U.S.—d. Dec. 15, 1890, on the Grand River in South Dakota), Teton Dakota Indian chief under whom the Sioux tribes united in their struggle for survival on the North American Great Plains. He is remembered for his lifelong distrust of white men and his stubborn determination to resist their domination.

Sitting Bull was born into the Hunkpapa division of the Teton Sioux. He joined his first war party at age 14 and soon gained a reputation for fearlessness in battle. He became a leader of the powerful Strong Heart warrior society and, later, was a participant in the Silent Eaters, a select group concerned with tribal welfare. As a tribal leader Sitting Bull helped extend the Sioux hunting grounds westward into what had been the territory of the Shoshone, Crow, Assiniboin, and other Indian tribes. His first skirmish with white soldiers occurred in June 1863 during the U.S. Army's retaliation against the Santee Sioux after the "Minnesota Massacre," in which the Teton Sioux had no part. For the next five years he was in frequent hostile contact with the army, which was invading the Sioux hunting grounds and bringing ruin to the Indian economy. In 1866 he became principal chief of the northern hunting Sioux, with Crazy Horse, leader of the Oglala Sioux, as his vice-chief. Respected for his courage and wisdom, Sitting Bull was made principal chief of the entire Sioux nation about 1867.

In 1868 the Sioux accepted peace with the U.S. government on the basis of the Second Treaty of Fort Laramie, which guaranteed the Sioux a reservation in what is now southwestern South Dakota. But when gold was discovered in the Black Hills in the mid-1870s, a rush of white prospectors invaded lands guaranteed to the Indians by the treaty. Late in 1875 those Sioux who had been resisting the whites' incursions were ordered to return to their reservations by Jan. 31, 1876, or be considered hostile to the United States. Even had Sitting Bull been willing to comply, he could not possibly have moved his village 240 miles (390 km) in the bitter cold by the specified time.

In March General George Crook took the field against the hostiles, and Sitting Bull responded by summoning the Sioux, Cheyenne, and certain Arapaho to his camp in Montana Territory. There on June 17 Crook's troops were forced to retreat in the Battle of the Rosebud. The Indian chiefs then moved their encampment into the valley of the Little Bighorn River. At this point Sitting Bull performed the Sun Dance, and when be emerged from a trance induced by self-torture, he reported that he had seen soldiers falling into his camp like grasshoppers from the sky. His prophecy was fulfilled on June 25, when Lieutenant Colonel George Armstrong Custer rode into the valley and he and all the men under his immediate command were annihilated in the Battle of the Little Bighorn.

Strong public reaction among whites to the Battle of the Little Bighorn resulted in stepped-up military action. The Sioux emerged the victors in their battles with U.S. troops, but though they might win battle after battle, they could never win the war. They depended on the buffalo for their livelihood, and the buffalo, under the steady encroachment of whites, were rapidly becoming extinct. Hunger led more and more Sioux to surrender, and in May 1877 Sitting Bull led his remaining followers across the border into Canada. But the Canadian government could not acknowledge responsibility for feeding a people whose reservation was south of the border, and after four years, during which his following dwindled steadily, famine forced Sitting Bull to surrender. After 1883 he lived at the Standing Rock Agency, where he vainly opposed the sale of tribal lands. In 1885, partly to get rid of him, the Indian agent allowed him to join Buffalo Bill's Wild West show, in which he gained international fame.

The year 1889 saw the spread of the Ghost Dance religious movement, which prophesied the advent of an Indian messiah who would sweep away the whites and restore the Indians' former traditions. The Ghost Dance movement augmented the unrest already stirred among the Sioux by hunger and disease. As a precaution, Indian police and soldiers were sent to arrest the chief. Seized on Grand River, Dec. 15, 1890, Sitting Bull was killed while his warriors were trying to rescue him. He was buried at Fort Yates, but his remains were moved in 1953 to Mobridge, S.D., where a granite shaft marks his resting place.

BIBLIOGRAPHY. Biographies include Stanley Vestal, *Sitting Bull, Champion of the Sioux* (1932, reissued 1989); and Alexander B. Adams, *Sitting Bull: An Epic of the Plains* (1973).

Reading (and Writing About) Essays

The word *essay* entered the English language in 1597, when Francis Bacon called a small book of ten short prose pieces *Essays*. Bacon borrowed the word from Michel de Montaigne, a French writer who in 1580 had published some short prose pieces under the title *Essais*—that is, "testings," or "attempts," from the French verb *essayer,* "to try." Montaigne's title indicated that his graceful and personal jottings—the fruit of pleasant study and meditation—were not fully thought-out treatises but rather sketches that could be amplified and amended.

If you keep a journal, you are working in Montaigne's tradition. You jot down your tentative thoughts, perhaps your responses to a work of literature, partly to find out what you think and how you feel. Montaigne said, in the preface to his book, "I am myself the subject of my book," and in all probability you are the real subject of your journal. Your entries—your responses to other writers and your reflections on those responses—require you to examine yourself.

SOME KINDS OF ESSAYS

If you have already taken a course in composition (or even if you haven't), you are probably familiar with the chief kinds of essays. Essays are usually classified—roughly, of course—along the following lines: meditation (or speculation or reflection), argument (or persuasion), exposition (or information), narration, and description.

Of these, the **meditative** (or **speculative** or **reflective**) **essay** is the closest to Montaigne. In a meditative essay, the writer seems chiefly concerned with exploring an idea or a feeling. The organization usually seems casual, not a careful and evident structure but a free flow of thought—what the Japanese (who wrote with brush and ink) called "following the brush." The essayist is thinking, but he or she is not especially concerned with arguing a case, or even with being logical. We think along with the essayist, chiefly because we find the writer's tentative thoughts engaging. Of course the writer may in the long run be pressing a point, advancing an argument, but the emphasis is on the free play of mind, not on an orderly and logical analysis.

In the **argumentative** (or **persuasive**) **essay,** the organization probably is apparent, and it is reasonable: for instance, the essay may announce a problem, define some terms, present and refute solutions that writer considers to be inadequate, and then, by way of a knockdown ending, offer what the writer considers to be the correct solution.

The **expository essay,** in which the writer is chiefly concerned with giving information (for instance on how to annotate a text, or how to read a poem, or how to use a word processor), ordinarily has an equally clear organization. A clear organization is necessary in such an essay because the reader is reading not in order to come into contact with an interesting mind that may keep doubling back on its thinking (as in a meditative essay), and not in order to come to a decision about some controversial issue (as in an argumentative essay), but in order to gain information.

Narrative and **descriptive essays** usually really are largely meditative essays. For instance, a narrative essay may recount some happening—often a bit of autobiography—partly to allow the writer and the reader to meditate on it. Similarly, a description, let's say of a spider spinning a web or of children playing in the street, usually turns out to be offered not so much as information—it thus is unlike the account of how to annotate a text—but rather as something for the writer and reader to enjoy in itself, and perhaps to think further about.

Of course most essays are not pure specimens. For instance, an informative essay, let's say on how to use a word processing program on a computer, may begin with a paragraph that seeks to persuade you to use this particular software. Or it might begin with a very brief narrative, an anecdote of a student who switched from program X to program Y, again in order to persuade the reader to use this software (Y, of course). Similarly, an argument—and probably most of the essays that you write in English courses will be arguments advancing a thesis concerning the meaning or structure of a literary work—may include some exposition, for instance a very brief summary in order to remind the reader of the gist of the work you will be arguing about.

THE ESSAYIST'S PERSONA

Many of the essays that give readers the most pleasure are, like entries in a journal, chiefly reflective. An essay of this kind sets forth the writer's attitudes or states of mind, and the reader's interest in the essay is almost entirely in the way the writer sees things. It's not so much *what* the writers see and say as *how* they say what they see. Even in essays that are narrative—that is, in essays that recount events, such as a bit of biography—our interest is more in the essayists' *responses* to the events than in the events themselves. When we read an essay, we almost say, "So that's how it feels to be you," and "Tell me more about the way you see things." The bit of history is less important than the memorable presence of the writer.

When you read an essay in this chapter or in a later chapter, try to imagine the kind of person who wrote it, the kind of person who seems to be speaking it. Then slowly reread the essay, noticing *how* the writer conveyed this personality or persona or "voice" (even while he or she was writing about a topic "out there"). The writer's persona may be revealed by common or uncommon words, for example, by short or long sentences, by literal or figurative language, or by familiar or erudite examples.

Let's take a simple, familiar example of words that establish a persona. Lincoln begins the Gettysburg Address with "Four score and seven years ago." He might have said "Eighty-seven years ago"—but the language would have lacked the biblical echo, and the persona would thus have been that of an ordinary person rather than that of a man who has about him something of the tone of an Old Testament prophet. This religious tone of "four score and seven years" is entirely fitting, since

- President Lincoln was speaking at the dedication of a cemetery for "these hallowed dead" and
- he was urging the members of his audience to give all of their energies to ensure that the dead men had not died in vain.

By such devices as the choice of words, the length of sentences, and the sorts of evidence offered, an author sounds to the reader solemn or agitated or witty or genial or severe. If you are familiar with Martin Luther King's "I Have a Dream," you may recall that he begins the piece (originally it was a speech, delivered at the Lincoln Memorial on the one-hundredth anniversary of Lincoln's Emancipation Proclamation) with these words: "Five score years ago. . . ." King is deliberately echoing Lincoln's words, partly in tribute to Lincoln, but also to help establish himself as the spiritual descendent of Lincoln and, further back, of the founders of the Judeo-Christian tradition.

Tone

Only by reading closely can we hear in the mind's ear the writer's tone—friendly, or bitter, or indignant, or ironic (characterized by wry understatement or overstatement). Perhaps you have heard the line from Owen Wister's novel *The Virginian:* "When you call me that, smile!" Words spoken with a smile mean something different from the same words forced through clenched teeth. But while speakers can communicate, or, we might say, can guide the responses of their audience, by body language and by gestures, by facial expressions and by changes in tone of voice, writers have only words in ink on paper. As a writer, you are learning control of tone as you learn to take pains in your choice of words, in the way you arrange sentences, and even in the punctuation marks you may find yourself changing in your final draft. These skills will pay off doubly if you apply them to your reading, by putting yourself in the place of the writer whose work you are reading. As a reader, you must make some effort to "hear" the writer's tone as part of the meaning the words communicate. Skimming is not adequate to that task. Thinking carefully about the works in this book means, first of all, reading them carefully, listening for the sound of the speaking voice, so that you can respond to the persona—the personality or character the author presents in the essay.

Consider the following paragraph from the middle of "Black Men and Public Space," a short essay by Brent Staples. Staples is talking about growing up in a tough neighborhood. Of course the paragraph is only a small example; the tone depends, finally, on the entire essay, which we will print in a moment.

> As a boy, I saw countless tough guys locked away; I have since buried several, too. They were babies, really—a teenage cousin, a brother of twenty-two, a childhood friend in his mid-twenties—all gone down in episodes of bravado played out in the streets. I came to doubt the virtues of intimidation early on. I chose, perhaps unconsciously, to remain a shadow—timid, but a survivor.

Judging only from these few lines, what sense of Staples do we get? Perhaps you will agree that we can probably say something along these lines:

- He is relatively quiet and gentle. We sense this not simply because he tells us that he was "timid" but because (at least in this passage) he does not raise his voice either in a denunciation of white society for creating a system that produces black violence or in a denunciation of those blacks of his youth who engaged in violence.
- He is perceptive; he sees that the "tough guys," despite the fact that some were in their twenties, were babies; their bravado was infantile and destructive.
- He speaks with authority; he is giving a firsthand report.
- He doesn't claim to be especially shrewd; he modestly says that he may have "unconsciously" adopted the behavior that enabled him to survive.
- In saying that he is a "survivor" he displays a bit of wry humor. The usual image of a "survivor" is a guy in a Banana Republic outfit, gripping a knife, someone who survived a dog-eat-dog world by being tougher than the others. But Staples almost comically says he is a "survivor" who is "timid."

If your responses to the paragraph are somewhat different, jot them down and in a few sentences try to explain them.

Pre-writing

Identifying the Topic and Thesis Although we have emphasized the importance of the essayist's personality, essayists also make a point. They have a thesis or argument, and an argument implies taking a specific viewpoint toward a topic. In reading an essay, then, try to identify the topic. The topic of "Do-It-Yourself Brain Surgery" can't really be brain surgery; it must be do-it-yourself books, and the attitude probably will be amused contempt for such books. Even an essay that is largely narrative, like Brent Staples's, recounting a personal experience or a bit of history, probably will include an attitude toward the event that is being narrated, and it is that attitude—the interpretation of the event rather than the event itself—that may be the real topic of the essay.

It's time to look at Staples's essay. (Following the essay you will find a student's outline of it and another student's version of its thesis.)

 **BRENT STAPLES**

Brent Staples, born in 1951, received a bachelor's degree from Widener University in Chester, Pennsylvania, and a Ph.D. from the University of Chicago. After working as a journalist in Chicago, he joined The New York Times in 1985, and he is now on the newspaper's editorial board, where he writes on politics and culture. His essay was first published in Ms. magazine in 1986 and reprinted in a slightly revised form—the form we give here—in Harper's in 1987.

Black Men and Public Space

My first victim was a woman—white, well dressed, probably in her late twenties. I came upon her late one evening on a deserted street in Hyde Park, a relatively affluent neighborhood in an otherwise mean, impoverished section of Chicago. As I swung onto the avenue behind her, there seemed to be a discreet, uninflammatory distance between us. Not so. She cast back a worried glance. To her, the youngish black man—a broad six feet two inches with a beard and billowing hair, both hands shoved into the pockets of a bulky military jacket—seemed menacingly close. After a few more quick glimpses, she picked up her pace and was soon running in earnest. Within seconds, she disappeared into a cross street.

That was more than a decade ago. I was twenty-two years old, a graduate student newly arrived at the University of Chicago. It was in the echo of that terrified woman's footfalls that I first began to know the unwieldy inheritance I'd come into—the ability to alter public space in ugly ways. It was clear that she thought herself the quarry of a mugger, a rapist, or worse. Suffering a bout of insomnia, however, I was stalking sleep, not defenseless wayfarers. As a softy who is scarcely able to take a knife to a raw chicken—let alone hold one to a person's throat—I was surprised, embarrassed, and dismayed all at once. Her flight made me feel like an accomplice in tyranny. It also made it clear that I was indistinguishable from the muggers who occasionally seeped into the area from the surrounding ghetto. That first encounter, and those that followed, signified that a vast, unnerving gulf lay between nighttime pedestrians—particularly women—and me. And I soon gathered that being perceived as dangerous is a hazard in itself. I only needed to turn a corner into a dicey situation, or crowd some frightened, armed person in a foyer somewhere, or make an errant move after being pulled over by a policeman. Where fear and weapons meet—and they often do in urban America—there is always the possibility of death.

In that first year, my first away from my hometown, I was to become thoroughly familiar with the language of fear. At dark, shadowy intersections, I could cross in front of a car stopped at a traffic light and elicit the *thunk*, thunk, thunk, thunk of the driver—black, white, male, or female—hammering down the door locks. On less traveled streets after dark, I grew accustomed to but never comfortable with people crossing to the other side of the street rather than pass me. Then there were the standard unpleasantries with policemen, doormen, bouncers, cabdrivers, and others whose business it is to screen out troublesome individuals *before* there is any nastiness.

I moved to New York nearly two years ago and I have remained an avid night walker. In central Manhattan, the near-constant crowd cover minimizes tense one-on-one street encounters. Elsewhere—in SoHo, for example, where sidewalks are narrow and tightly spaced buildings shut out the sky—things can get very taut indeed.

5   After dark, on the warrenlike streets of Brooklyn where I live, I often see women who fear the worst from me. They seem to have set their faces on neutral, and with their purse straps strung across their chests bandolier-style, they forge ahead as though bracing themselves against being tackled. I understand, of course, that the danger they perceive is not a hallucination. Women are particularly vulnerable to street violence, and young black males are drastically overrepresented among the perpetrators of that violence. Yet these truths are no solace against the kind of alienation that comes of being ever the suspect, a fearsome entity with whom pedestrians avoid making eye contact.

It is not altogether clear to me how I reached the ripe old age of twenty-two without being conscious of the lethality nighttime pedestrians attributed to me. Perhaps it was because in Chester, Pennsylvania, the small, angry industrial town where I came of age in the 1960s, I was scarcely noticeable against a backdrop of gang warfare, street knifings, and murders. I grew up one of the good boys, had perhaps a half-dozen fistfights. In retrospect, my shyness of combat has clear sources.

As a boy, I saw countless tough guys locked away; I have since buried several, too. They were babies, really—a teenage cousin, a brother of twenty-two, a childhood friend in his mid-twenties—all gone down in episodes of bravado played out in the streets. I came to doubt the virtues of intimidation early on. I chose, perhaps unconsciously, to remain a shadow—timid, but a survivor.

The fearsomeness mistakenly attributed to me in public places often has a perilous flavor. The most frightening of these confusions occurred in the late 1970s and early 1980s, when I worked as a journalist in Chicago. One day, rushing into the office of a magazine I was writing for with a deadline story in hand, I was mistaken for a burglar. The office manager called security and, with an ad hoc posse, pursued me through the labyrinthine halls, nearly to my editor's door. I had no way of proving who I was. I could only move briskly toward the company of someone who knew me.

Another time I was on assignment for a local paper and killing time before an interview. I entered a jewelry store on the city's affluent Near North Side. The proprietor excused herself and returned with an enormous red Doberman pinscher straining at the end of a leash. She stood, the dog extended toward me, silent to my questions, her eyes bulging nearly out of her head. I took a cursory look around, nodded, and bade her good night.

10   Relatively speaking, however, I never fared as badly as another black male journalist. He went to nearby Waukegan, Illinois, a couple of summers ago to work on a story about a murderer who was born there. Mistaking the reporter for the killer, police officers hauled him from his car at gunpoint and but for his press credentials would probably have tried to book him. Such episodes are not uncommon. Black men trade tales like this all the time.

Over the years, I learned to smother the rage I felt at so often being taken for a criminal. Not to do so would surely have led to madness. I now take precautions to make myself less threatening. I move about with care, particularly late in the evening. I give a wide berth to nervous people on subway platforms during the wee hours, particularly when I have exchanged business clothes for jeans. If I happen to be entering a building behind some people who appear skittish, I may walk by, letting them clear the lobby before I return, so as not to seem to be following them. I have been calm and extremely congenial on those rare occasions when I've been pulled over by the police.

And on late-evening constitutionals I employ what has proved to be an excellent tension-reducing measure: I whistle melodies from Beethoven and Vivaldi and the more popular classical composers. Even steely New Yorkers hunching toward nighttime destinations seem to relax, and occasionally they even join in the tune. Virtually everybody seems to sense that a mugger wouldn't be warbling bright, sunny selections from Vivaldi's *Four Seasons*. It is my equivalent of the cowbell that hikers wear when they know they are in bear country.

[1986]

Summarizing

Summary should be clearly distinguished from analysis. The word *summary* is related to *sum*, the total something adds up to. (We say "adds *up* to" because the Greeks and Romans counted upward and wrote the total at the top.)

A summary is a condensation or abridgement; it briefly gives the reader the gist of a longer work. It boils down the longer work, resembling the longer work as a bouillion cube resembles a bowl of soup. A summary of Staples's "Black Men and Public Space" will reduce the essay, perhaps to a paragraph or two or even to a sentence. It will not call attention to Staples's various strategies, and it will not evaluate his views or his skill as a writer; it will merely present the gist of what he says.

Summary and Analysis If, then, you are asked to write an analysis of something you have read, you should not hand in a summary. On the other hand, a very brief summary may appropriately appear within an analytic essay. Usually, in fact, the reader needs some information, and the writer of the essay will briefly summarize this information. For example, a student who wrote about Staples's essay is *summarizing* when she writes

> Staples says that he is aware that his presence frightens many whites, especially women.

She is summarizing because she is reporting, without personal comment, what Staples said.

On the other hand, she is *analyzing* when she writes

> By saying at the outset, "My first victim was a woman—white, well dressed, probably in her late twenties," Staples immediately catches the reader's attention and sets up expectations that will be undermined in the next paragraph.

In this sentence the writer is not reporting *what* Staples said but is explaining *how* he achieved an effect.

In Chapter 6 we discussed a few principles that govern summaries (see the list on pp. 133–134). Here is a summary of our comments on "summary":

> A summary is a condensation or abridgment. Its chief characteristics are that (1) it is rarely more than one-fourth as long as the original; (2) its brevity is usually achieved by leaving out most of the concrete details of the original; (3) it is accurate; (4) it may rearrange the organization of the original, especially if a rearrangement will make things clearer; (5) it normally is in the present tense; and (6) quoted words need not be enclosed in quotation marks.

Preparing a Summary If you are summarizing an essay, you may find that the essay includes its own summary, perhaps at the start or more likely near the end. If it does, you're in luck.

If it doesn't, we suggest that on rereading you jot down, after reading each paragraph, a sentence summarizing the gist of the paragraph. (A very long or poorly unified paragraph may require two sentences, but make every effort to boil the paragraph down to a dozen or so words.) Of course if a paragraph consists merely of a transitional sentence or two ("We will now turn to another example") you will lump it with the next paragraph. Similarly, if for some reason you encounter a series of very short paragraphs—for instance, three examples, each briefly stated, and all illustrating the same point—you probably will find that you can cover them with a single sentence. But if a paragraph runs to half a page or more of print, it's probably worth its own sentence of summary. In fact, your author may summarize the paragraph in the paragraph's opening sentence or in its final sentence.

Here is a student's paragraph-by-paragraph summary of Staples's "Black Men and Public Space." The numbers refer to Staples's paragraphs.

1. "First victim" was a white woman in Chicago, who hurried away.
2. Age 22, he realized--to his surprise and embarrassment-- that he (a "youngish black man") could be perceived by strangers as a mugger. And, since his presence created fear, he was in a dangerous situation.
3,4,5. At intersections he heard drivers of cars lock their doors, and elsewhere he sensed hostility of bouncers and others. In NY, lots of tension on narrow sidewalks. Women are esp. afraid of him; he knows why, but that's "no solace."
6. He's not sure why it took him 22 years to see that others fear him, but prob. because in his hometown of Chester, Pa., there was lots of adolescent violence, though he stayed clear of it.
7. As a boy, he saw young toughs killed, and he kept clear, "timid, but a survivor."
8,9,10. Though he is gentle, he looks fearsome. Once, working as a journalist, he was mistaken for a burglar. Another time, in a jewelry store, the clerk brought out a guard dog. Another black journalist was covering a crime, but the police thought the journalist was the killer. Many blacks have had such experiences.
11. He has learned to smother his rage--and he keeps away from nervous people.
12. Walking late at night, he whistles familiar classical music, trying to reassure others that he is not a mugger.

When you have written your sentence summarizing the last paragraph, you may have done enough if the summary was intended simply for your own private use, for example, to help you review material for an examination. But if you are going to use it as the basis of a summary within an essay you are writing, you probably won't want to include a summary longer than three or four sentences, so your job will be to reduce and combine the sentences you have jotted down. Indeed, you may even want to reduce the summary to a single sentence.

A Suggested Exercise: Assuming that you find the sentences summarizing "Black Men and Public Space" acceptable, reduce them to a summary no longer than four readable sentences. Then compare your version with the versions of two other students and, working as a group, produce a summary.

Stating the Thesis of an Essay Summarizing each stage of the essay forces a reader to be attentive and can assist the reader to formulate a **thesis sentence,** a sentence that (in the reader's opinion) sets forth the writer's central point. If an essay is essentially an argument—for example, a defense of (or an argument against) capital punishment—it will probably include one or more sentences that directly assert the thesis. "Black Men and Public Space," chiefly a narrative essay, is much less evidently an argument, but it does have a point, and some of its sentences come pretty close to summarizing the point. Here are three of those sentences:

> And I soon gathered that being perceived as dangerous is a hazard in itself. (2)
> The fearsomeness mistakenly attributed to me in public places often has a perilous flavor. (8)
> I now take precautions to make myself less threatening. (11)

We asked our students to formulate their own thesis sentence for Staples's essay. One student came up with the following sentence after first drafting a couple of tentative versions and then rereading the essay in order to modify them:

> In "Black Men and Public Space" Staples recognizes that because many whites fear a young black man and therefore may do violence to him, he may do well to try to cool the situation by making himself unthreatening.

Notice, again, that a thesis sentence states the *point* of the work. Don't confuse a thesis sentence with a summary of a narrative, such as "Staples at the age of twenty-two came to realize that his presence was threatening to whites, and he has since taken measures to make himself less threatening." This sentence, though true, doesn't clearly get at the point of the essay, the generalization that can be drawn from Staples's example.

Look again at the student's formulation of a thesis sentence (*not* the narrative summary sentence that we have just given). If you don't think that it fairly represents Staples's point, you may (if you are writing an essay about Staples's essay) want to come up with a sentence that seems more precise to you. Whether you use the sentence we have quoted or a sentence that you formulate for yourself, you can in any case of course disagree very strongly with what you take to be Staples's point. Your version of Staples's thesis should accurately reflect your understanding of Staples's point, but you need not agree with the point. You may think, for instance, that Staples is hypersensitive or (to mention only one other possibility) that he is playing the Uncle Tom.

A thesis sentence, then, whether the words are your own or the author's, is a very brief summary of the argument (not of the narrative) of the work. If you are writing an essay about an essay, you'll probably want to offer a sentence that reminds your reader of the point of the work you are discussing or gives the reader the gist of an unfamiliar work:

> Black males, however harmless, are in a perilous situation because whites, especially white women, perceive them as threatening.

Or:

> In "Black Men and Public Space" Staples recognizes that because many whites fear a young black man and therefore may do violence to him, a black man may do well to try to cool the situation by making himself nonthreatening.

Drafting a Summary   Sometimes, however, a fuller statement may be useful. For instance, if you are writing about a complex essay that makes six points, you may help your reader if you briefly restate all six. The length of your summary will depend on your purpose and the needs of your audience.

The following principles may help you to write your summary:

1. First, after having written sentences that summarize each paragraph or group of paragraphs, formulate the essay's thesis sentence. Formulating the sentence in writing will help you to stay with what you take to be the writer's main point.

2. Next, write a first draft by turning your summaries of the paragraphs into fewer and better sentences. For example, the student who wrote the paragraph-by-paragraph summary (page 168) of Staples's essay turned her first five sentences (on Staples's first paragraphs) into this:

> Staples's "first victim" was a white woman in Chicago. When she hurried away from him, he realized--to his surprise and embarrassment--that because he was large and black and young he seemed to her to be a mugger. And since his presence created fear, he was in a dangerous situation. Other experiences, such as hearing drivers lock their cars when they were waiting at an intersection, have made him aware of the hostility of others. Women are especially afraid of him, and although he knows why, this knowledge is "no solace."

The student turned the remaining sentences of the outline into the following summary:

> Oddly, it took him twenty-two years to see that others fear him. Perhaps it took this long because he grew up in a violent neighborhood, though he kept clear, "timid, but a survivor." Because he is black and large, whites regard him as fearsome and treat him accordingly (once a clerk in a jewelry store brought out a guard dog), but other blacks have been treated worse. He has learned to smother his rage, and in order to cool things he tries to reassure nervous people by keeping away from them and (when he is walking late at night) by whistling classical music.

3. Write a lead-in sentence, probably incorporating the gist of the thesis sentence. Here is an example:

> Brent Staples, in "Black Men and Public Space," tells how his awareness that many white people regarded him as dangerous caused him to realize that he was in danger. His implicitly recommended solution is to try to cool the anxiety by adopting nonthreatening behavior.

After writing a lead-in, revise the draft of your summary, eliminating needless repetition, providing transitions, and adding whatever you think may be needed to clarify the work for someone who is unfamiliar with it. You may rearrange the points if you think the rearrangement will clarify matters.

4. Edit your draft for errors in grammar, punctuation, and spelling. Read it aloud to test it once more for readability. Sometimes only by reading aloud do we detect needless repetition or confusing phrases.

Some Writing Assignments

1. In a paragraph or two set forth what you take to be Staples's *purpose*. Do you think he was writing chiefly to clarify some ideas for himself—for instance, to explore how he came to discover the "alienation that comes of being ever the suspect"? Or writing to assist blacks? Or to assist whites? Or what? (You may of course conclude that none of these suggestions, or all, are relevant.)

2. If you think the essay is effective, in a paragraph or two addressed to your classmates try to account for its effectiveness. Do certain examples strike you as particularly forceful? If so, why? Do certain sentences seem especially memorable? Again, why? For example, if the opening and concluding paragraphs strike you as effective, explain why. On the other hand, if you are unimpressed by part or all of the essay, explain why.

3. The success of a narrative as a piece of writing often depends on the reader's willingness to identify with the narrator. From an examination of "Black Men and Public Space," what explanations can you give for your willingness (or unwillingness) to identify yourself with Staples? (Probably you will want to say something about his persona as you sense it from the essay.) In the course of a 500-word essay explaining your position, very briefly summarize Staples's essay and state his thesis.

4. Have *you* ever unintentionally altered public space? For instance, you might recall an experience in which, as a child, your mere presence caused adults to alter their behavior—for instance, to stop quarreling.

    After a session of brainstorming, in which you produce some possible topics, you'll want to try to settle on one. After you have chosen a topic and produced a first draft, if you are not satisfied with your first paragraph—for instance, if you feel that it is not likely to get and hold the reader's attention—you may want to imitate the strategy that Staples adopted for his first paragraph.

5. If you have ever been in the position of one of Staples's "victims," that is, if you have ever shown fear or suspicion of someone who, it turned out, meant you no harm (or if you can imagine being in that position), write an essay from the "victim's" point of view. Explain what happened, what you did and thought. Did you think at the time about the feelings of the person you avoided or fled from? Has reading Staples's essay prompted further reflections on your experience? (Suggested length: 750 words.)

 ## A Checklist: Getting Ideas for Writing About Essays

Persona and Tone
  ✔ What sort of *persona* does the writer create?
  ✔ How does the writer create this persona? (For example, does the writer use colloquial language or formal language or technical language? Short sentences or long ones? Personal anecdotes? Quotations from authorities?)

✔ What is the *tone* of the essay? Is it, for example, solemn, or playful? Is the tone consistent? If not, how do the shifts affect your understanding of the writer's point or your identification of the writer's persona? Who is the *audience?*

Kind of Essay

✔ What kind of essay is it? Is it chiefly a presentation of facts (for example, an exposition, a report, a history)? Or is it chiefly an argument? Or a meditation? (Probably the essay draws on several kinds of writing, but which kind is it primarily? How are the other kinds related to the main kind?) What is the overall *purpose* of the essay?

✔ What does it seem to add up to? If the essay is chiefly meditative or speculative, how much emphasis is placed on the persona? That is, if the essay is a sort of thinking-out-loud, is your interest chiefly in the announced or ostensible topic, or in the writer's mood and personality? If the essay is chiefly a presentation of facts, does it also have a larger implication? For instance, if it narrates a happening (history), does the reader draw an inference—find a meaning—in the happening? If the essay is chiefly an argument, what is the thesis? How is the thesis supported? (Is it supported, for example, by induction, deduction, analogy, or emotional appeal?) Do you accept the assumptions (explicit and implicit)?

Structure

✔ Is the title appropriate? Propose a better title, if possible.

✔ Did the opening paragraph interest you? Why, or why not? Did the essay continue more or less as expected, or did it turn out to be rather different from what you anticipated?

✔ Prepare an outline of the essay. What effect does the writer seem to be aiming at by using this structure?

Value

✔ What is especially good (or bad) about the essay? Is it logically persuasive? Or entertaining? Or does it introduce an engaging persona? Or (if it is a narrative) does it tell a story effectively, using (where appropriate) description, dialogue, and commentary, and somehow make you feel that this story is worth reporting?

✔ Does the writer seem to hold values that you share? Or cannot share? Explain.

✔ Do you think that most readers will share your response, or do you think that for some reason—for example, your age, or your cultural background—your responses are unusual? Explain.

FIVE ESSAYS

 **JONATHAN SWIFT**

Jonathan Swift (1667–1745) was born in Ireland of an English family. He was ordained in the Church of Ireland in 1694, and in 1714 he became dean of St.

Patrick's Cathedral, Dublin. He wrote abundantly on political and religious topics, often motivated (in his own words) by "savage indignation." It is ironic that Gulliver's Travels, the masterpiece by this master of irony, is most widely thought of as a book for children.

From the middle of the sixteenth century the English regulated the Irish economy so that it would enrich England. Heavy taxes and other repressive legislation impoverished Ireland, and in 1728, the year before Swift wrote "A Modest Proposal," Ireland was further weakened by a severe famine. Swift, deeply moved by the injustice, the stupidity, and the suffering that he found in Ireland, adopts the disguise or persona of an economist and offers an ironic suggestion on how Irish families may improve their conditions.

A Modest Proposal

For Preventing the Children of Poor People in Ireland from Being a Burden to Their Parents or Country, and for Making Them Beneficial to the Public

It is a melancholy object to those who walk through this great town or travel in the country, when they see the streets, the roads, and cabin doors, crowded with beggars of the female sex, followed by three, four, or six children, all in rags and importuning every passenger for an alms. These mothers, instead of being able to work for their honest livelihood, are forced to employ all their time in strolling to beg sustenance for their helpless infants: who as they grow up either turn thieves for want of work, or leave their dear native country to fight for the pretender in Spain, or sell themselves to the Barbadoes.

I think it is agreed by all parties that this prodigious number of children in the arms, or on the backs, or at the heels of their mothers, and frequently of their fathers, is in the present deplorable state of the kingdom a very great additional grievance; and, therefore, whoever could find out a fair, cheap, and easy method of making these children sound, useful members of the commonwealth, would deserve so well of the public as to have his statue set up for a preserver of the nation.

But my intention is very far from being confined to provide only for the children of professed beggars; it is of a much greater extent, and shall take in the whole number of infants at a certain age who are born of parents in effect as little able to support them as those who demand our charity in the streets.

As to my own part, having turned my thoughts for many years upon this important subject, and maturely weighed the several schemes of our projectors,[1] I have always found them grossly mistaken in their computation. It is true, a child just dropped from its dam may be supported by her milk for a solar year, with little other nourishment; at most not above the value of 2s.,[2] which the mother may certainly get, or the value in scraps, by her lawful occupation of begging; and it is exactly at one year old that I propose to provide for them in such a manner as instead of being a charge upon their parents or the parish, or wanting food and raiment for the rest of their lives, they shall on the contrary contribute to the feeding, and partly to the clothing, of many thousands.

[1] **projectors** persons who devise plans [2] **2s.** two shillings. Later "£" is an abbreviation for pounds and "d" for pence.

5   There is likewise another great advantage in my scheme, that it will prevent those voluntary abortions, and that horrid practice of women murdering their bastard children, alas! too frequent among us! sacrificing the poor innocent babes I doubt more to avoid the expense than the shame, which would move tears and pity in the most savage and inhuman breast.

The number of souls in this kingdom being usually reckoned one million and a half, of these I calculate there may be about 200,000 couple whose wives are breeders; from which number I subtract 30,000 couple who are able to maintain their own children (although I apprehend there cannot be so many, under the present distress of the kingdom); but this being granted, there will remain 170,000 breeders. I again subtract 50,000 for those women who miscarry, or whose children die by accident or disease within the year. There only remain 120,000 children of poor parents annually born. The question therefore is, how this number shall be reared and provided for? which, as I have already said, under the present situation of affairs, is utterly impossible by all the methods hitherto proposed. For we can neither employ them in handicraft or agriculture; we neither build houses (I mean in the country) nor cultivate land; they can very seldom pick up a livelihood by stealing, till they arrive at six years old, except where they are of towardly parts; although I confess they learn the rudiments much earlier; during which time they can, however, be properly looked upon only as probationers; as I have been informed by a principal gentleman in the county of Cavan, who protested to me that he never knew above one or two instances under the age of six, even in a part of the kingdom so renowned for the quickest proficiency in that art.

I am assured by our merchants, that a boy or a girl before twelve years old is no salable commodity; and even when they come to this age they will not yield above 3£. or 3£. 2s. 6d. at most on the exchange; which cannot turn to account either to the parents or kingdom, the charge of nutriment and rags having been at least four times that value.

I shall now therefore humbly propose my own thoughts, which I hope will not be liable to the least objection.

I have been assured by a very knowing American of my acquaintance in London, that a young healthy child well nursed is at a year old a most delicious, nourishing, and wholesome food, whether stewed, roasted, baked, or broiled; and I make no doubt that it will equally serve in a fricassee or a ragout.

10   I do therefore humbly offer it to public consideration that of the 120,000 children already computed, 20,000 may be reserved for breed, whereof only one-fourth part to be males; which is more than we allow to sheep, black cattle, or swine; and my reason is, that these children are seldom the fruits of marriage, a circumstance not much regarded by our savages; therefore one male will be sufficient to serve four females. That the remaining 100,000 may, at a year old, be offered in sale to the persons of quality and fortune through the kingdom; always advising the mother to let them suck plentifully in the last month, so as to render them plump and fat for a good table. A child will make two dishes at an entertainment for friends; and when the family dines alone, the fore or hind quarter will make a reasonable dish, and seasoned with a little pepper or salt will be very good boiled on the fourth day, especially in winter.

I have reckoned upon a medium that a child just born will weigh 12 pounds, and in a solar year, if tolerably nursed, will increase to 28 pounds.

I grant this food will be somewhat dear, and therefore very proper for landlords, who, as they have already devoured most of the parents, seem to have the best title to the children.

Infant's flesh will be in season throughout the year, but more plentiful in March, and a little before and after: for we are told by a grave author, an eminent French physician, that fish being a prolific diet, there are more children born in Roman Catholic countries about nine months after Lent than at any other season; therefore, reckoning a year after Lent, the markets will be more glutted than usual, because the number of popish infants is at least three to one in this kingdom: and therefore it will have one other collateral advantage, by lessening the number of papists among us.

I have already computed the charge of nursing a beggar's child (in which list I reckon all cottagers, laborers, and four-fifths of the farmers) to be about 2s. per annum, rags included; and I believe no gentleman would repine to give 10s. for the carcass of a good fat child, which, as I have said, will make four dishes of excellent nutritive meat, when he has only some particular friend or his own family to dine with him. Thus the squire will learn to be a good landlord, and grow popular among the tenants; the mother will have 8s. net profit, and be fit for work till she produces another child.

15 Those who are more thrifty (as I must confess the times require) may flay the carcass; the skin of which artificially dressed will make admirable gloves for ladies, and summer boots for fine gentlemen.

As to our city of Dublin, shambles[3] may be appointed for this purpose in the most convenient parts of it, and butchers we may be assured will not be wanting: although I rather recommend buying the children alive, and dressing them hot from the knife as we do roasting pigs.

A very worthy person, a true lover of his country, and whose virtues I highly esteem, was lately pleased in discoursing on this matter to offer a refinement upon my scheme. He said that many gentlemen of this kingdom, having of late destroyed their deer, he conceived that the want of venison might be well supplied by the bodies of young lads and maidens, not exceeding fourteen years of age nor under twelve; so great a number of both sexes in every country being now ready to starve for want of work and service; and these to be disposed of by their parents, if alive, or otherwise by their nearest relations. But with due deference to so excellent a friend and so deserving a patriot, I cannot be altogether in his sentiments; for as to the males, my American acquaintance assured me from frequent experience that their flesh was generally tough and lean, like that of our schoolboys by continual exercise, and their taste disagreeable; and to fatten them would not answer the charge. Then as to the females, it would, I think, with humble submission be a loss to the public, because they soon would become breeders themselves: and besides, it is not improbable that some scrupulous people might be apt to censure such a practice (although indeed very unjustly), as a little bordering upon cruelty; which, I confess, has always been with me the strongest objection against any project, how well soever intended.

But in order to justify my friend, he confessed that this expedient was put into his head by the famous Psalmanazar,[4] a native of the island Formosa, who came from thence to London about twenty years ago: and in conversation told my friend, that in his country when any young person happened to be put to death, the executioner sold the carcass to persons of quality as a prime dainty;

---

[3]**shambles** slaughterhouses [4]**Psalmanazar** George Psalmanazer (c. 1679–1763), a Frenchman who claimed to be from Formosa (now Taiwan); wrote *An Historical and Geographical Description of Formosa* (1704). The hoax was exposed soon after publication.

and that in his time the body of a plump girl of fifteen, who was crucified for an attempt to poison the emperor, was sold to his imperial majesty's prime minister of state, and other great mandarins of the court, in joints from the gibbet, at 400 crowns. Neither indeed can I deny, that if the same use were made of several plump young girls in this town, who without one single groat to their fortunes cannot stir abroad without a chair, and appear at the playhouse and assemblies in foreign fineries which they never will pay for, the kingdom would not be the worse.

Some persons of a desponding spirit are in great concern about the vast number of poor people, who are aged, diseased, or maimed, and I have been desired to employ my thoughts what course may be taken to ease the nation of so grievous an encumbrance. But I am not in the least pain upon that matter, because it is very well known that they are every day dying and rotting by cold and famine, and filth and vermin, as fast as can be reasonably expected. And as to the young laborers, they are now in as hopeful a condition: they cannot get work, and consequently pine away for want of nourishment, to a degree that if at any time they are accidentally hired to common labor, they have not strength to perform it; and thus the country and themselves are happily delivered from the evils to come.

20　　I have too long digressed, and therefore shall return to my subject. I think the advantages by the proposal which I have made are obvious and many, as well as of the highest importance.

For first, as I have already observed, it would greatly lessen the number of papists, with whom we are yearly overrun, being the principal breeders of the nation as well as our most dangerous enemies; and who stay at home on purpose to deliver the kingdom to the Pretender, hoping to take their advantage by the absence of so many good Protestants, who have chosen rather to leave their country than stay at home and pay tithes against their conscience to an Episcopal curate.

Secondly, The poor tenants will have something valuable of their own, which by law may be made liable to distress and help to pay their landlord's rent, their corn and cattle being already seized, and money a thing unknown.

Thirdly, Whereas the maintenance of 100,000 children from two years old and upward, cannot be computed at less than 10s. a-piece per annum, the nation's stock will be thereby increased £50,000 per annum, beside the profit of a new dish introduced to the tables of all gentlemen of fortune in the kingdom who have any refinement in taste. And the money will circulate among ourselves, the goods being entirely of our own growth and manufacture.

Fourthly, The constant breeders beside the gain of 8s. sterling per annum by the sale of their children, will be rid of the charge of maintaining them after the first year.

25　　Fifthly, This food would likewise bring great custom to taverns, where the vintners will certainly be so prudent as to procure the best receipts for dressing it to perfection, and consequently have their houses frequented by all the fine gentlemen, who justly value themselves upon their knowledge in good eating; and a skilful cook who understands how to oblige his guests, will contrive to make it as expensive as they please.

Sixthly, This would be a great inducement to marriage, which all wise nations have either encouraged by rewards or enforced by laws and penalties. It would increase the care and tenderness of mothers toward their children, when they were sure of a settlement for life to the poor babes, provided in some sort by the public, to their annual profit instead of expense. We should see an honest emulation among the married women, which of them would bring the fattest child to the market. Men would become as fond of their wives during the time of their pregnancy as they are now of their mares in foal, their cows in calf, their sows when they are ready to farrow; nor offer to beat or kick them (as is too frequent a practice) for fear of a miscarriage.

Many other advantages might be enumerated. For instance, the addition of some thousand carcasses in our exportation of barreled beef, the propagation of swine's flesh, and improvement in the art of making good bacon, so much wanted among us by the great destruction of pigs, too frequent at our table, which are no way comparable in taste or magnificence to a well-grown, fat, yearling child, which roasted whole will make a considerable figure at a lord mayor's feast or any other public entertainment. But this and many others I omit, being studious of brevity.

Supposing that 1,000 families in this city would be constant customers for infants' flesh, besides others who might have it at merry-meetings, particularly at weddings and christenings, I compute that Dublin would take off annually about 20,000 carcasses; and the rest of the kingdom (where probably they will be sold somewhat cheaper) the remaining 80,000.

I can think of no one objection that will possibly be raised against this proposal, unless it should be urged that the number of people will be thereby much lessened in the kingdom. This I freely own, and it was indeed one principal design in offering it to the world. I desire the reader will observe, that I calculate my remedy for this one individual kingdom of Ireland and for no other that ever was, is, or I think ever can be upon earth. Therefore let no man talk to me of other expedients: of taxing our absentees at 5s. a pound: of using neither clothes nor household furniture except what is of our own growth and manufacture: of utterly rejecting the materials and instruments that promote foreign luxury: of curing the expensiveness of pride, vanity, idleness, and gaming in our own women: of introducing a vein of parsimony, prudence, and temperance: of learning to love our country, in the want of which we differ even from Laplanders and the inhabitants of Topinamboo: of quitting our animosities and factions, nor acting any longer like the Jews, who were murdering one another at the very moment their city was taken: of being a little cautious not to sell our country and conscience for nothing: of teaching landlords to have at least one degree of mercy toward their tenants: lastly, of putting a spirit of honesty, industry, and skill into our shopkeepers; who, if a resolution could now be taken to buy only our native goods, would immediately unite to cheat and exact upon us in the price, the measure, and the goodness, nor could ever yet be brought to make one fair proposal of just dealing, though often and earnestly invited to it.

30   Therefore I repeat, let no man talk to me of these and the like expedients, till he has at least some glimpse of hope that there will be ever some hearty and sincere attempt to put them in practice.

But as to myself, having been wearied out for many years with offering vain, idle, visionary thoughts, and at length utterly despairing of success, I fortunately fell upon this proposal; which, as it is wholly new, so it has something solid and real, of no expense and little trouble, full in our own power, and whereby we can incur no danger in disobliging England. For this kind of commodity will not bear exportation, the flesh being of too tender a consistence to admit a long continuance in salt, although perhaps I could name a country which would be glad to eat up our whole nation without it.

After all, I am not so violently bent upon my own opinion as to reject any offer proposed by wise men, which shall be found equally innocent, cheap, easy, and effectual. But before something of that kind shall be advanced in contradiction to my scheme, and offering a better, I desire the author or authors will be pleased maturely to consider two points. First, as things now stand, how they will be able to find food and raiment for 100,000 useless mouths and backs. And secondly, there being a round million of creatures in human figure throughout this kingdom, whose subsistence put into a common stock would leave them in debt 2,000,000£. sterling, adding those who are beggars by profession to the bulk of farmers, cottagers, and laborers, with the wives and children who are beggars in effect; I desire those politicians who dislike my overture, and may perhaps be so bold as to attempt an answer, that they will first ask the parents of these mortals, whether they would not at this day think it a great happiness to have been sold for food at a year old in the manner I prescribe, and thereby have avoided such a perpetual scene of misfortunes as they have since gone through by the oppression of landlords, the impossibility of paying rent without money or trade, the want of common sustenance, with neither house nor clothes to cover them from the inclemencies of the weather, and the most inevitable prospect of entailing the like or greater miseries upon their breed for ever.

I profess, in the sincerity of my heart, that I have not the least personal interest in endeavoring to promote this necessary work, having no other motive than the public good of my country, by advancing our trade, providing for infants, relieving the poor, and giving some pleasure to the rich. I have no children by which I can propose to get a single penny; the youngest being nine years old, and my wife past child-bearing.

Topics for Critical Thinking and Writing

1. In the fourth paragraph Swift speaks of proposals set forth by "projectors," that is, by advocates of other projects or proposals. Characterize the pamphleteer (not Swift but his persona, the invented "projector") who offers his "modest proposal." What sort of man does he think he is? What sort of man do we regard him as? Support your assertions with evidence.

2. In the first paragraph the speaker says that the sight of mothers begging is "melancholy." In this paragraph what assumption does the speaker make about women that in part gives rise to this melancholy? Now that you are familiar with the entire essay, explain Swift's strategy.

3. How might you argue that although this satire is primarily ferocious, it also contains some playful touches? What specific passages might support your argument?

4. Write your own "Modest Proposal," using some of Swift's strategies, exposing a topic of your own choice. Choose a serious topic (for instance, racism, anti-Semitism, environmental pollution, unemployment), and offer a solution that is outrageous but that is developed with relentless logic. Your essay should be about 750 words.

5. Swift's proposal is, in large measure, built on taking a metaphor literally: landlords devour the Irish poor. Take a metaphor (for example, "Certain people should be put in their place," or "It's a dog-eat-dog world") and set forth a modest proposal (250 words) in which you take the metaphor literally.

VIRGINIA WOOLF

Virginia Woolf (1882–1941) is known chiefly as a novelist, but she was also the author of short stories and essays, and in recent years the range of her power has been increasingly recognized.

Woolf was self-educated in the library of her father, Leslie Stephen, a distinguished man of letters. After her father's death she moved to Bloomsbury, an unfashionable part of London where she was part of a brilliant circle of friends—the Bloomsbury group—that included Clive Bell and Roger Fry (art critics), J. M. Keynes (an economist), Lytton Strachey (a biographer), and E. M. Forster (novelist and essayist). In 1907 she married Leonard Woolf, with whom ten years later she established the Hogarth Press, which published some of the most interesting literature of the period, including her own novels. Woolf experienced several mental breakdowns, and in 1941, fearing yet another, she drowned herself.

The Death of the Moth

Moths that fly by day are not properly to be called moths; they do not excite that pleasant sense of dark autumn nights and ivy-blossom which the commonest yellow-underwing asleep in the shadow of the curtain never fails to rouse in us. They are hybrid creatures, neither gay like butterflies nor somber like their own species. Nevertheless the present specimen, with his narrow hay-colored wings, fringed with a tassel of the same color, seemed to be content with life. It was a pleasant morning, mid-September, mild, benignant, yet with a keener breath than that of the summer months. The plow was already scoring the field opposite the window, and where the share had been, the earth was pressed flat and gleamed with moisture. Such vigor came rolling in from the fields and the down beyond that it was difficult to keep the eyes strictly turned upon the book. The rooks too were keeping one of their annual festivities; soaring round the tree tops until it looked as if a vast net with thousands of black knots in it had been cast up into the air; which, after a few moments, sank slowly down upon the trees until every twig seemed to have a knot at the end of it. Then, suddenly, the net would be thrown into the air again in a wider circle this time, with the utmost clamor and vociferation, as though to be thrown into the air and settle slowly down upon the tree tops were a tremendously exciting experience.

The same energy which inspired the rooks, the ploughmen, the horses, and even, it seemed, the lean bare-backed downs, sent the moth fluttering from side to side of his square of the windowpane. One could not help watching him. One was, indeed, conscious of a queer feeling of pity for him. The possibilities of pleasure seemed that morning so enormous and so various that to have only a moth's part in life, and a day moth's at that, appeared a hard fate, and his zest in enjoying his meager opportunities to the full, pathetic. He flew vigorously to one corner of his compartment, and, after waiting there a second, flew across to the other. What remained for him but to fly to a third corner and then to a fourth? That was all he could do, in spite of the size of the downs, the width of the sky, the far-off smoke of houses, and the romantic voice, now and then, of a steamer out at sea. What he could do he did. Watching him, it seemed as if a fiber, very thin but pure, of the enormous energy of the world had been thrust into his frail and diminutive body. As often as he crossed the pane, I could fancy that a thread of vital light became visible. He was little or nothing but life.

Yet, because he was so small, and so simple a form of the energy that was rolling in at the open window and driving its way through so many narrow and intricate corridors in my own brain and in those of other human beings, there was something marvelous as well as pathetic about him. It was as if someone had taken a tiny bead of pure life and decking it as lightly as possible with down and feathers, had set it dancing and zigzagging to show us the true nature of life. Thus displayed one could not get over the strangeness of it. One is apt to forget all about life, seeing it humped and bossed and garnished and cumbered so that it has to move with the greatest circumspection and dignity. Again, the thought of all that life might have been had he been born in any other shape caused one to view his simple activities with a kind of pity.

After a time, tired by his dancing apparently, he settled on the window ledge in the sun, and, the queer spectacle being at an end, I forgot about him. Then, looking up, my eye was caught by him. He was trying to resume his dancing, but seemed either so stiff or so awkward that he could only flutter to the bottom of the window-pane; and when he tried to fly across it he failed. Being intent on other matters I watched these futile attempts for a time without thinking, unconsciously waiting for him to resume his flight, as one waits for a machine, that has stopped momentarily, to start again without considering the reason of its failure. After perhaps a seventh attempt he slipped from the wooden ledge and fell, fluttering his wings, on to his back on the window sill. The helplessness of his attitude roused me. It flashed upon me that he was in difficulties; he could no longer raise himself; his legs struggled vainly. But, as I stretched out a pencil, meaning to help him to right himself, it came over me that the failure and awkwardness were the approach of death. I laid the pencil down again.

5　The legs agitated themselves once more. I looked as if for the enemy against which he struggled. I looked out of doors. What had happened there? Presumably it was midday, and work in the fields had stopped. Stillness and quiet had replaced the previous animation. The birds had taken themselves off to feed in the brooks. The horses stood still. Yet the power was there all the same, massed outside, indifferent, impersonal, not attending to anything in particular. Somehow it was opposed to the little hay-colored moth. It was useless to try to do anything. One could only watch the extraordinary efforts made by those tiny legs against an oncoming doom which could, had it chosen, have submerged an entire city, not merely a city, but masses of human beings; nothing, I knew, had any chance against death. Nevertheless after a pause of exhaustion the legs fluttered again. It was superb, this last protest, and so frantic that he succeeded at last in righting himself. One's sympathies, of course, were all on the side of life. Also, when there was nobody to care or to know, this gigantic effort on the part of an insignificant little moth, against a power of such magnitude, to retain what no one else valued or desired to keep, moved one strangely. Again, somehow, one saw life, a pure bead. I lifted the pencil again, useless though I knew it to be. But even as I did so, the unmistakable tokens of death showed themselves. The body relaxed, and instantly grew stiff. The struggle was over. The insignificant little creature now knew death. As I looked at the dead moth, this minute wayside triumph of so great a force over so mean an antagonist filled me with wonder. Just as life had been strange a few minutes before, so death was now as strange. The moth having righted himself now lay most decently and uncomplainingly composed. O yes, he seemed to say, death is stronger than I am.

[1941]

Topics for Critical Thinking and Writing

1. On the basis of the first paragraph, how would you describe Woolf's voice, or persona, in this essay? By what means does she try to engage our attention and interest?
2. Does the essay have a thesis sentence? If not, in a sentence or two of your own, try to state the essay's main point.
3. What is the season and the time span covered? How are these relevant to the thesis of the essay?
4. Reread the second paragraph, taking note as you do of the variety in sentence lengths. What sentences strike you as particularly effective? What makes them effective?
5. In paragraph 3 Woolf says, "One is apt to forget all about life, seeing it humped and bossed and garnished and cumbered so that it has to move with the greatest circumspection and dignity." What does she mean? Try to restate the idea in your own words.
6. Write an essay on an encounter with death or birth.

LANGSTON HUGHES

Langston Hughes (1902–67) was born in Joplin, Missouri. He lived part of his youth in Mexico, spent a year at Columbia University, served as a merchant seaman, and worked in a Paris nightclub, where he showed some of his poems to Dr. Alain Locke, a strong advocate of African-American literature. After returning to the United States, Hughes went on to publish poetry, fiction, plays, essays, and biographies.

Salvation

I was saved from sin when I was going on thirteen. But not really saved. It happened like this. There was a big revival at my Auntie Reed's church. Every night for weeks there had been much preaching, singing, praying, and shouting, and some very hardened sinners had been brought to Christ, and the membership of the church had grown by leaps and bounds. Then just before the revival ended, they held a special meeting for children, "to bring the young lambs to the fold." My aunt spoke of it for days ahead. That night I was escorted to the front row and placed on the mourners' bench with all the other young sinners, who had not yet been brought to Jesus.

My aunt told me that when you were saved you saw a light, and something happened to you inside! And Jesus came into your life! And God was with you from then on! She said you could see and hear and feel Jesus in your soul. I believed her. I had heard a great many old people say the same thing and it seemed to me they ought to know. So I sat there calmly in the hot, crowded church, waiting for Jesus to come to me.

The preacher preached a wonderful rhythmical sermon, all moans and shouts and lonely cries and dire pictures of hell, and then he sang a song about the ninety and nine safe in the fold, but one little lamb was left out in the cold. Then he said: "Won't you come? Won't you come to Jesus? Young lambs, won't you come?" And he held out his arms to all us young sinners there on the mourners' bench. And the little girls cried. And some of them jumped up and went to Jesus right away. But most of us just sat there.

A great many old people came and knelt around us and prayed, old women with jet-black faces and braided hair, old men with work-gnarled hands. And the church sang a song about the lower lights are burning, some poor sinners to be saved. And the whole building rocked with prayer and song.

5   Still I kept waiting to *see* Jesus.

Finally all the young people had gone to the altar and were saved, but one boy and me. He was a rounder's son named Westley. Westley and I were surrounded by sisters and deacons praying. It was very hot in the church, and getting late now. Finally Westley said to me in a whisper: "God damn! I'm tired o' sitting here. Let's get up and be saved." So he got up and was saved.

Then I was left all alone on the mourners' bench. My aunt came and knelt at my knees and cried, while prayers and songs swirled all around me in the little church. The whole congregation prayed for me alone, in a mighty wail of moans and voices. And I kept waiting serenely for Jesus, waiting, waiting—but he didn't come. I wanted to see him, but nothing happened to me. Nothing! I wanted something to happen to me, but nothing happened.

I heard the songs and the minister saying: "Why don't you come? My dear child, why don't you come to Jesus? Jesus is waiting for you. He wants you. Why don't you come? Sister Reed, what is this child's name?"

"Langston," my aunt sobbed.

10   "Langston, why don't you come? Why don't you come and be saved? Oh, Lamb of God! Why don't you come?"

Now it was really getting late. I began to be ashamed of myself, holding everything up so long. I began to wonder what God thought about Westley, who certainly hadn't seen Jesus either, but who was now sitting proudly on the platform, swinging his knickerbockered legs and grinning down at me, surrounded by deacons and old women on their knees praying. God had not struck Westley dead for taking his name in vain or for lying in the temple. So I decided that maybe to save further trouble, I'd better lie, too, and say that Jesus had come, and get up and be saved.

So I got up.

Suddenly the whole room broke into a sea of shouting, as they saw me rise. Waves of rejoicing swept the place. Women leaped in the air. My aunt threw her arms around me. The minister took me by the hand and led me to the platform.

When things quieted down, in a hushed silence, punctuated by a few ecstatic "Amens," all the new young lambs were blessed in the name of God. Then joyous singing filled the room.

15   That night, for the last time in my life but one—for I was a big boy twelve years old—I cried. I cried, in bed alone, and couldn't stop. I buried my head under the quilts, but my aunt heard me. She woke up and told my uncle I was crying because the Holy Ghost had come into my life, and because I had seen Jesus. But I was really crying because I couldn't bear to tell her that I had lied, that I had deceived everybody in the church, and I hadn't seen Jesus, and that

now I didn't believe there was a Jesus any more, since he didn't come to help me.

[1940]

✎ Topics for Critical Thinking and Writing

1. Do you find the piece amusing, or serious, or both? Explain.
2. How would you characterize the style or voice of the first three sentences? Childlike, or sophisticated, or what? How would you characterize the final sentence? How can you explain the change in style or tone?
3. Why does Hughes bother to tell us, in paragraph 11, that Westley was "swinging his knickerbockered legs and grinning"? Do you think that Westley too may have cried that night? Give your reasons.
4. Is the episode told from the point of view of someone "going on thirteen," or from the point of view of a mature man? Cite evidence to support your position.
5. One of the Golden Rules of narrative writing is "Show, don't tell." In about 500 words, report an experience—for instance, a death in the family, or a severe (perhaps unjust) punishment, or the first day in a new school—that produced strong feelings. Like Hughes, you may want to draw on an experience in which you were subjected to group pressure. Do not explicitly state what the feelings were; rather, let the reader understand the feelings chiefly through concretely detailed actions. But, like Hughes, you might state your thesis or basic position in your first paragraph and then indicate when and where the experience took place.

📖 SALLIE BINGHAM

Sallie Bingham, born in 1937, is known as an author (plays, fiction, a memoir) and as a strong supporter of feminist causes. She has, for instance, established the Kentucky Foundation for Women, which makes grants to women artists and which publishes a quarterly, The American Voice, *and she supports theater groups in Santa Fe and New York. By birth she is in a position to offer financial support; her grandfather, a man of immense wealth (derived largely from money he inherited from his second wife) founded the* Louisville Courier-Journal, *a major newspaper, and her father was the publisher of the paper. Sallie Bingham was active on the board of directors of the family's communications empire, but in the 1980s she was forced off the board, and she decided to sell her shares. Her memoir,* Passion and Prejudice *(1989), provides a view of life among the Binghams.*

Since 1991 Bingham has lived in Santa Fe, but "A Woman's Land" was published when she was living outside of Louisville.

A Woman's Land

Four years ago I bought a piece of wild land. Parts of it had been farmed in a haphazard sort of way, but most of it was woods, or fields on their way back to being woods. Since moving to this piece of land, which is often called a farm, I have begun to wonder about its appropriate uses and about my relation to it, as one of the very few women who own land.

So few women own land that the phrase, woman landowner, seems curious. At once we wonder how she came to own it, how she afforded it—and that recognition of the financial inequities women face obscures another question—can a woman *own* land?

We are in new territory here because we have no myths or legends, no sayings or parables to guide us. We few who own the half-acre our house stands on, or the several acres left from an old farm, or the piece of property that descended through the family, must weave our own theories; we have nothing to go on except the words of the land-patriarchs, and they have little to offer that does not offend.

Women do not usually exploit, even in situations where exploitation is possible or expected; we do not often sell our children, for example. Where poor women have been brought to barter their unborn babies for money, a concept vital to the community breaks down. The mother's heartbreak reflects the disease of her times.

5   Generally we are not farmers, but gardeners. We may raise a few flowers or some vegetables for the table. We take from the earth what we can use, or what we can enjoy without depleting the supply. Women are not usually hunters or real-estate developers. We do not always seek to convert gifts into power or cash.

The deer in the woods seems to me to have been placed there not for my purposes or for the purposes of the hunter, but to fulfill the law of her existence: to graze, sleep, procreate, or run away from danger, without reference even to my appreciation of her beauty.

The old fields in front of and behind my house seem to exist without reference to their potential productivity. Once they were treed; now, the trees and brush would return if the farmer who rents them for corn kept his machinery in the barn for one season. The land would be revitalized, no longer scoured and soured by chemical sprays and fertilizers. Perhaps in my lifetime those elements the soil has lost would be restored—if the machinery continued to stay in the barn. But soon the "field" would no longer be a field, but a wild place, accessible only to birds and small animals that can move through briars on their hidden paths.

Yet, this would not seem to me to be the land's intention either, but that cycle of change might, once again, bring beeches into maturity on this stretch. The land is given only to itself—it exists for me as the ground under my feet, but not as a possibility, a future, a hope of gain.

Does my attitude make the land into a luxury, affordable only by the very rich, who do not need to consider productivity? If so, women must find another way, for women are not rich, almost by definition, in a sexist society where we are always in charge of the spiritual and social work that holds the community together and pays poorly.

10   Perhaps I can form a theory based on the communal use of my land, which recognizes several purposes for this piece of common acreage: relief for my eyes and for my soul, a place for my husband's sheep to graze, a horizon for my sons to escape from and through, a place for the barn cat and her kitten to fatten off grain-fed mice, and for my friends to house and tend their special animals—the llama, the three-legged deer. These two curious animals bear, symbolically, the weight of the whole place: they exist outside of the money exchange. Does that make them the curiosities of the rich? Not quite. Their caretakers are not wealthy, and yet their wealth or lack of it does not enter into the exchange.

These animals live outside of the area of commerce, or are excluded from it. They are gifts.

The sheep are not gifts. They were bought with a certain end in view: to be converted into cash. However, the sheep's symbolic meaning has changed as they have begun to share the barn with the llama and the three-legged deer. They have names, or at least some of them do. Their purpose is no longer clear.

Is this sheer sentimentality? Again, a luxury of the rich, who do not toil, nor do they spin? Or is it a recognition of the ultimate independence of the sheep (an odd expression for such dumb and dumbly obedient beasts) from our aims or plans?

What defines the land is what escapes definition: the Canada geese who light on the pond and take off with a wild flurry of wings in the morning, always towards the south; the heron outside my studio window who stood for a short while on a stone in the river. These birds did not arrive here, and pause briefly, for our edification. They exist in their own worlds, which we can barely appreciate, which we cannot penetrate or convert into cash.

But what was the motive that brought a hunter to shoot one of our rare bald eagles, so well-marked with spray paint and electronic devices? Surely the hunter was a boy or a man. Surely he sought in the killing something he could take away with him, a talisman or a boast. The need to "make something out of" the experience perhaps defines the male. A woman might have wanted to make the sighting into a story or a painting. But she would not have figured, necessarily, in that story or painting, as the hunter must figure in the shooting of the eagle. The eagle would have lived to see another day, free of the woman—the artist—and her transitory usage; the eagle did not outlive the man's aim.

15   I am uncomfortable suggesting that a woman's use of the land might be better than a man's. Notions of women's superiority always have a sting in the tail. We carry enough weight in the world without taking on the weight of being morally superior. Yet, the fact remains that women do not destroy land, either as owners who sell off pastures for shopping centers or as employees who operate bulldozers that push down trees. Is it enough to say that we are powerless to commit this evil? I think not. A woman who is able to buy land probably learned something about its care from the way a woman without financial power tended her African violets.

But perhaps the difference in attitudes towards the land is not gender-related. Perhaps the artist, male or female, is able to see trees and open stretches as gifts, not as possibilities for conversion. Perhaps our addictive needs are satisfied by the manufacturing of words out of the landscape, rather than by the manufacturing of tract houses.

Artists who are men are often perceived as living on the fringes of their gender, stripling lads even in old age, Apollos without followers. Often they lack power and money. To the extent that their androgyny is corrupted by power and money, they become more male-like, more interested in conversion, in "making something out of." The rare successful artist who purchases land is perhaps more likely to sell off parts of it for subdivisions than the equally rare woman who can afford to buy and will preserve it.

If the gift survives the addiction, however, as it seems capable of doing, there will still be a need for a woman or an artist to appreciate it—although to all intents and purposes, that appreciation is inessential. Appreciation, if it is converted into action, can save land.

There will always be a few rich women who will endow a piece of land and will it to perpetuity, although for the land to survive, her heirs must accept that

it does not belong to them. In how many cases has a woman been able to sur-
mount her heirs' ideas of their rights and leave the land to continue "undevel-
oped"?

20   In the case of my land, the woman landowner's heirs despoiled it with their
motorcycles and logged out all the old trees and would have sold it to the highest bidder for any purpose whatsoever if the lack of city water and sewage had-
n't hampered their aims. It came to me almost by default.

Now, as I work on my will, I am trying to insure that the land remains open
forever. This means that it will not be inherited by my sons, but will remain, as it
is now, a gift. This is difficult, if not impossible, to do, first on a personal level. All
children long to inherit what is of value to the parent; it is a way of receiving
commitment and memories. In the case of my sons, their inevitable immersion in
the patriarchy means that they will want to "make something out of" the land,
should it pass to them. Leaving it to lie fallow, to grow up again with weeds,
would seem an eccentric choice for a male landowner.

On another level, the patriarchy itself is dead set against my decision. The
right of sons to inherit is fundamental to capitalism, and to the more secretive
continuation of a ruling class. How then can heirs be taught to see the land as a
gift? Only by stroking the three-legged deer and looking at the silent llama.

[1990]

Topics for Critical Thinking and Writing

1. What sort of persona does Bingham reveal? Point to specific passages that in
   your view especially clearly establish her persona.
2. Bingham says (paragraph 2) that "few" women own land. Think of the
   landowners whom you know. Do the men greatly outnumber the women?
   Do the women who own land seem different from those who don't? Explain.
3. In paragraph 10 Bingham very briefly introduces two "special animals—the
   llama, the three-legged deer." She goes on to say, in the same paragraph,
   "These two curious animals bear, symbolically, the weight of the whole
   place: they exist outside of the money exchange." What does she mean?
   (Notice that these animals return in the final—crucial—paragraph.)
4. In several passages Bingham wonders whether her views are possible only
   for the rich. Consider, for example, the first sentence in paragraph 9: "Does
   my attitude make the land into a luxury, affordable only by the very rich,
   who do not need to consider productivity?" Does she, in your view, have
   anything to say to persons who are not in a position to own land without
   putting it to use?
5. In the last sentence of paragraph 15 Bingham says, "A woman who is able to
   buy land probably learned something about its care from the way a woman
   without financial power tended her African violets." What does she mean?
   Do you think she is right? Explain.
6. In paragraph 4 Bingham says that "women do not usually exploit, even in situations where exploitation is possible or expected; we do not often sell our
   children, for example." Assuming the truth of Bingham's earlier assertion
   that women landowners are few, consider other areas for exploitation. As
   you think about this issue, consider whether you know women who exploit
   other women, or their spouses, or their children, or their parents, or their
   co-workers. And then consider the men whom you know, and the degree to

which they exploit land or people. Based on your firsthand knowledge, write an essay of about 250–500 words, evaluating Bingham's assertion that "women do not usually exploit."

 # LOUIS OWENS

Louis Owens, born in 1948, describes himself as "a mixed-blood American of Choctaw, Cherokee, and Irish-American heritage." He is a professor of English at the University of New Mexico, where he specializes in Native American writing, but before he became a teacher and a writer he worked as a fire fighter and wilderness ranger.

Owens's essay should be read in the context of the Wilderness Act of 1964, which defines a wilderness thus: "A wilderness, in contrast with those areas where man and his own works dominate the landscape, is hereby recognized as an area where the earth itself and its community of life are untrammeled by man, where man himself is a visitor who does not remain."

The American Indian Wilderness

In the center of the Glacier Peak Wilderness in northern Washington, a magnificent, fully glaciated white volcano rises over a stunningly beautiful region of the North Cascades. On maps, the mountain is called Glacier Peak. To the Salishan people who have always lived in this part of the Cascades, however, the mountain is *Dakobed,* or the Great Mother, the place of emergence. For more than eighty years, a small, three-sided log shelter stood in a place called White Pass just below one shoulder of the great mountain, tucked securely into a meadow between thick stands of mountain hemlock and alpine fir.

In the early fall of seventy-six, while working as a seasonal ranger for the U.S. Forest Service, I drew the task of burning the White Pass shelter. After all those years, the shelter roof had collapsed like a broken bird wing under the weight of winter snow, and the time was right for fire and replanting. It was part of a Forest Service plan to remove all human-made objects from wilderness areas, a plan of which I heartily approved. So I backpacked eleven miles to the pass and set up camp, and for five days, while a bitter early storm sent snow driving horizontally out of the north, I dismantled the shelter and burned the old logs, piling and burning and piling and burning until nothing remained. The antique, hand-forged spikes that had held the shelter together I put into gunny sacks and cached to be packed out later by mule. I spaded up the earth beaten hard for nearly a century by boot and hoof, and transplanted plugs of vegetation from hidden spots on the nearby ridge.

At the end of those five days, not a trace of the shelter remained, and I felt good, very smug in fact, about returning the White Pass meadow to its "original" state. As I packed up my camp, the snowstorm had subsided to a few flurries and a chill that felt bone-deep with the promise of winter. My season was almost over, and as I started the steep hike down to the trailhead my mind was on the winter I was going to spend in sunny Arizona.

A half-mile from the pass I saw the two old women. At first they were dark, hunched forms far down on the last long switchback up the snowy ridge. But as we drew closer to one another, I began to feel a growing amazement that, by the time we were face-to-face, had become awe. Almost swallowed up in their baggy wool pants, heavy sweaters and parkas, silver braids hanging below thick wool caps, they seemed ancient, each weighted with at least seventy years as well as a small backpack. They paused every few steps to lean on their staffs and look out over the North Fork drainage below, a deep, heavily forested river valley that rose on the far side to the glaciers and sawtoothed black granite of the Monte Cristo Range. And they smiled hugely upon seeing me, clearly surprised and delighted to find another person in the mountains at such a time.

5   We stood and chatted for a moment, and as I did with all backpackers, I reluctantly asked them where they were going. The snow quickened a little, obscuring the view, as they told me that they were going to White Pass.

"Our father built a little house up here," one of them said, "when he worked for the Forest Service like you. Way back before we was born, before this century."

"We been coming up here each year since we was little," the other added. "Except last year when Sarah was not well enough."

"A long time ago, this was all our land," the one called Sarah said. "All Indi'n land everywhere you can see. Our people had houses up in the mountains, for gathering berries every year."

As they took turns speaking, the smiles never leaving their faces, I wanted to excuse myself, to edge around these elders and flee to the trailhead and my car, drive back to the district station and keep going south. I wanted to say, "I'm Indian too. Choctaw from Mississippi; Cherokee from Oklahoma"—as if mixed blood could pardon me for what I had done. Instead, I said, "The shelter is gone." Cravenly I added, "It was crushed by snow, so I was sent up to burn it. It's gone now."

10   I expected outrage, anger, sadness, but instead the sisters continued to smile at me, their smiles changing only slightly. They had a plastic tarp and would stay dry, they said, because a person always had to be prepared in the mountains. They would put up their tarp inside the hemlock grove above the meadow, and the scaly hemlock branches would turn back the snow. They forgave me without saying it—my ignorance and my part in the long pattern of loss which they knew so well.

Hiking out those eleven miles, as the snow of the high country became a drumming rain in the forests below, I had long hours to ponder my encounter with the sisters. Gradually, almost painfully, I began to understand that what I called "wilderness" was an absurdity, nothing more than a figment of the European imagination. Before the European invasion, there was no wilderness in North America; there was only the fertile continent where people lived in a hard-learned balance with the natural world. In embracing a philosophy that saw the White Pass shelter—and all traces of humanity—as a shameful stain upon the "pure" wilderness, I had succumbed to a five-hundred-year-old pattern of deadly thinking that separates us from the natural world. This is not to say that what we call wilderness today does not need careful safeguarding. I believe that White Pass really is better off now that the shelter doesn't serve as a magnet to backpackers and horsepackers who compact the soil, disturb and kill the wildlife, cut down centuries-old trees for firewood, and leave their litter strewn about. And I believe the man who built the shelter would agree. But despite this unfortunate reality, the global environmental crisis that sends species into extinction daily and threatens to destroy all life surely has its roots in the Western pattern of thought that sees humanity and "wilderness" as mutually exclusive.

In old-growth forests in the North Cascades, deep inside the official Wilderness Area, I have come upon faint traces of log shelters built by Suiattle and Upper Skagit people for berry harvesting a century or more ago—just as the sisters said. Those human-made structures were as natural a part of the Cascade ecosystem as the burrows of marmots in the steep scree slopes. Our Native ancestors all over this continent lived within a complex web of relations with the natural world, and in doing so they assumed a responsibility for their world that contemporary Americans cannot even imagine. Unless Americans, and all human beings, can learn to imagine themselves as intimately and inextricably related to every aspect of the world they inhabit, with the extraordinary responsibilities such relationship entails—unless they can learn what the indigenous peoples of the Americas knew and often still know—the earth simply will not survive. A few square miles of something called wilderness will become the sign of failure everywhere.

 ## Topics for Critical Thinking and Writing

1. The Forest Service commissioned Owens to "dismantle" the shelter and then to burn the logs. Does it make sense to use human beings to create a "natural" space? Explain.
2. Suppose someone said to you that human beings are a part of nature, and that their creations—let's say the three-sided shelter at White Pass—are just as "natural" as a bird's nest. What response might you make?
3. In his second paragraph Owen tells us that the Forest Service had a plan "to remove all human-made objects from wilderness areas." What can be said in behalf of such a plan? What can be said against it? By the way, given the realities of life today, can we reasonably say that parts of the country can be unshaped by human activity? If, for instance, we restore wolves to a certain area that they have long been absent from, is this area of nature really natural?
4. In his final paragraph Owens says that unless people come to understand that they are "inextricably related to every aspect of the world, . . . a few square miles of something called wilderness will become the sign of failure everywhere." What does he mean?

Reading (and Writing About) Fiction

STORIES TRUE AND FALSE

The word *story* comes from *history;* the stories that historians, biographers, and journalists narrate are supposed to be true accounts of what happened. The stories of novelists and short-story writers, however, are admittedly untrue; they are "fiction," things made up, imagined, manufactured. As readers, we come to a supposedly true story with expectations different from those we bring to fiction.

Consider the difference between reading a narrative in a newspaper and one in a book of short stories. If, while reading a newspaper, we come across a story of, say, a subway accident, we assume that the account is true, and we read it for the information about a relatively unusual event. Anyone hurt? What sort of people? In our neighborhood? Whose fault? When we read a book of fiction, however, we do not expect to encounter literal truths; we read novels and short stories not for facts but for pleasure and for some insight or for a sense of what an aspect of life means to the writer. Consider the following short story by Grace Paley.

 ## GRACE PALEY

 Born in New York City, Grace Paley attended Hunter College and New York University but left without a degree. (She now is an affiliate faculty member at Sarah Lawrence College.) While raising two children she wrote poetry and then, in the 1950s, turned to writing fiction.

Paley's chief subject is the life of little people struggling in the Big City. Of life she has said, "How daily life is lived is a mystery to me. You write about what's mysterious to you. What is it like? Why do people do this?" Of the short story she has said, "It can be just telling a little tale, or writing a complicated philosophical story. It can be a song, almost."

Samuel

Some boys are very tough. They're afraid of nothing. They are the ones who climb a wall and take a bow at the top. Not only are they brave on the roof, but they make a lot of noise in the darkest part of the cellar where even the super hates to go. They also jiggle and hop on the platform between the locked doors of the subway cars.

Four boys are jiggling on the swaying platform. Their names are Alfred, Calvin, Samuel, and Tom. The men and the women in the cars on either side watch them. They don't like them to jiggle or jump but don't want to interfere. Of course some of the men in the cars were once brave boys like these. One of them had ridden the tail of a speeding truck from New York to Rockaway Beach without getting off, without his sore fingers losing hold. Nothing happened to him then or later. He had made a compact with other boys who preferred to watch: Starting at Eighth Avenue and Fifteenth Street, he would get to some specified place, maybe Twenty-third and the river, by hopping the tops of the moving trucks. This was hard to do when one truck turned a corner in the wrong direction and the nearest truck was a couple of feet too high. He made three or four starts before succeeding. He had gotten his idea from a film at school called *The Romance of Logging*. He had finished high school, married a good friend, was in a responsible job and going to night school.

These two men and others looked at the four boys jumping and jiggling on the platform and thought, It must be fun to ride that way, especially now the weather is nice and we're out of the tunnel and way high over the Bronx. Then they thought, These kids do seem to be acting sort of stupid. They *are* little. Then they thought of some of the brave things they had done when they were boys and jiggling didn't seem so risky.

The ladies in the car became very angry when they looked at the four boys. Most of them brought their brows together and hoped the boys could see their extreme disapproval. One of the ladies wanted to get up and say, Be careful you dumb kids, get off that platform or I'll call a cop. But three of the boys were Negroes and the fourth was something else she couldn't tell for sure. She was afraid they'd be fresh and laugh at her and embarrass her. She wasn't afraid they'd hit her, but she was afraid of embarrassment. Another lady thought, Their mothers never know where they are. It wasn't true in this particular case. Their mothers all knew that they had gone to see the missile exhibit on Fourteenth Street.

5   Out on the platform, whenever the train accelerated, the boys would raise their hands and point them up to the sky to act like rockets going off, then they rat-tat-tatted the shatterproof glass pane like machine guns, although no machine guns had been exhibited.

For some reason known only to the motorman, the train began a sudden slowdown. The lady who was afraid of embarrassment saw the boys jerk forward and backward and grab the swinging guard chains. She had her own boy at home. She stood up with determination and went to the door. She slid it open and said, "You boys will be hurt. You'll be killed. I'm going to call the conductor if you don't just go into the next car and sit down and be quiet."

Two of the boys said, "Yes'm," and acted as though they were about to go. Two of them blinked their eyes a couple of times and pressed their lips together. The train resumed its speed. The door slid shut, parting the lady and the boys. She leaned against the side door because she had to get off at the next stop.

The boys opened their eyes wide at each other and laughed. The lady blushed. The boys looked at her and laughed harder. They began to pound each other's back. Samuel laughed the hardest and pounded Alfred's back until Alfred coughed and the tears came. Alfred held tight to the chain hook. Samuel pounded him even harder when he saw the tears. He said, "Why you bawling? You a baby, huh?" and laughed. One of the men whose boyhood had been more watchful than brave became angry. He stood up straight and looked at the boys for a couple of seconds. Then he walked in a citizenly way to the end of the car, where he pulled the emergency cord. Almost at once, with a terrible hiss, the pressure of air abandoned the brakes and the wheels were caught and held.

People standing in the most secure places fell forward, then backward. Samuel had let go of his hold on the chain so he could pound Tom as well as Alfred. All the passengers in the cars whipped back and forth, but he pitched only forward and fell head first to be crushed and killed between the cars.

10   The train had stopped hard, halfway into the station, and the conductor called at once for the trainmen who knew about this kind of death and how to take the body from the wheels and brakes. There was silence except for passengers from other cars who asked, What happened! What happened! The ladies waited around wondering if he might be an only child. The men recalled other afternoons with very bad endings. The little boys stayed close to each other, leaning and touching shoulders and arms and legs.

When the policeman knocked at the door and told her about it, Samuel's mother began to scream. She screamed all day and moaned all night, though the doctors tried to quiet her with pills.

Oh, oh, she hopelessly cried. She did not know how she could ever find another boy like that one. However, she was a young woman and she became pregnant. Then for a few months she was hopeful. The child born to her was a boy. They brought him to be seen and nursed. She smiled. But immediately she saw that this baby wasn't Samuel. She and her husband together have had other children, but never again will a boy exactly like Samuel be known.

[1968]

You might think about the ways in which "Samuel" differs from a newspaper story of an accident in a subway. (You might even want to write a newspaper version of the happening.) In some ways, of course, Paley's story faintly resembles an account that might appear in a newspaper. Journalists are taught to give information about

- who,
- what,
- when,
- where, and
- why,

and Paley does provide this material. Thus, the *characters* (Samuel and others) are the journalist's Who; the *plot* (the boys were jiggling on the platform, and when a man pulled the emergency cord one of them was killed) is the What; the *setting* (the subway, presumably in modern times) is the When and the Where; the *motivation* (the irritation of the man who pulls the emergency cord) is the Why.

To write about fiction you would think about these elements of fiction, asking yourself questions about each, both separately and how they work together. Much of the rest of this chapter will be devoted to examining such words as *character* and *plot,* but before you read those pages notice the following questions we've posed about "Samuel" and try responding to them. Your responses will teach you a good deal about what fiction is, and some of the ways in which it works.

Topics for Critical Thinking and Writing

1. Paley wrote the story, but an unspecified person *tells* it. Describe the voice of this narrator in the first paragraph. Is the voice neutral and objective, or do you hear some sort of attitude, a point of view? If you do hear an attitude, what words or phrases in the story indicate it?

2. What do you know about the setting—the locale—of "Samuel"? What can you infer about the neighborhood?

3. In the fourth paragraph we are told that "three of the boys were Negroes and the fourth was something else." Is race important in this story? Is Samuel "Negro" or "something else"? Does it matter?

4. Exactly *why* did a man walk "in a citizenly way to the end of the car, where he pulled the emergency cord"? Do you think the author blames him? What evidence can you offer to support your view? Do *you* blame him? Or do you blame the boys? Or anyone? Explain.

5. The story is called "Samuel," and it is, surely, about him. But what happens after Samuel dies? (You might want to list the events.) What else is the story about? (You might want to comment on why you believe the items in your list are important.)

6. Can you generalize about what the men think of the jigglers and about what the women think? Is Paley saying something about the sexes? About the attitudes of onlookers in a big city?

Plot and Character

In some stories, such as adventure stories, the emphasis is on physical action—wanderings and strange encounters. In Paley's "Samuel," however, although there is a violent death in the subway, the emphasis is less on an unusual happening than on other things: for instance, the contrast between some of the adults, the contrast between uptight adults and energetic children, and the impact of the death on Samuel's mother.

The novelist E. M. Forster, in a short critical study entitled *Aspects of the Novel* (1927), introduced a distinction between **flat characters** and **round characters.** A *flat character* is relatively simple and usually has only one trait: loving wife (or jealous wife), tyrannical husband (or meek husband), braggart, pedant, hypocrite, or whatever. Thus, in "Samuel" we are told about a man "whose boyhood had been more watchful than brave." This man walks "in a citizenly way" to the end of the subway car, where he pulls the emergency cord. He is, so to speak, the conventional solid citizen. He is flat, or uncomplicated, but that is probably part of what the author is getting at. A *round character,* on the other hand, embodies several or even many traits that cohere to form a complex personality. Of course in a story as short as "Samuel" we can hardly expect to find fully rounded characters, but we can say that, at least by comparison with the "citizenly" man, the man who had once been a wild kid, had gone to night school, and now holds a "responsible job" is relatively round. Paley's story asserts rather than shows the development of the character, but much fiction does show such a development. Whereas a flat character is usually *static* (at the end of the story the character is pretty much what he or she was at the start), a round character is likely to be *dynamic,* changing considerably as the story progresses.

A frequent assignment in writing courses is to set forth a character sketch, describing some person in the story or novel. In preparing such a sketch, take these points into consideration:

- what the character says (but consider that what he or she says need not be taken at face value; the character may be hypocritical, or self-deceived, or biased—you will have to detect this from the context),
- what the character does,
- what other characters say about the character,
- What others *do.* (A character who serves as a contrast to another character is called a *foil.*)

A character sketch can be complex and demanding, but usually you will want to do more than write a character sketch. You will probably discuss the character's function, or trace the development of his or her personality, or contrast the character with another. (One of the most difficult topics, the narrator's personality, will be discussed later in this chapter under the heading "Narrative Point of View.") In writing on one of these topics you will probably still want to keep in mind the four suggestions for getting at a character, but you will also want to go further, relating your findings to additional matters that we discuss later.

Most discussions of fiction are concerned with happenings and with *why* they happen. Why does Samuel die? Because (to put it too simply) his youthful high spirits clash with the values of a "citizenly" adult. Paley never explicitly says anything like this, but a reader of the story tries to make sense out of the details, filling in the gaps.

Things happen, in most good fiction, at least partly because the people have certain personalities or character traits (moral, intellectual, and emotional qualities) and, given their natures, because they respond plausibly to other personalities. What their names are and what they look like may help you to understand them, but probably the best guide to characters is what they do and what they say. As we get to know more about their drives and goals—and especially about the choices they make—we enjoy seeing the writer complete the portraits, finally presenting us with a coherent and credible picture of people in action. In this view, plot and character are inseparable. Plot is not simply a series of happenings, but happenings that come out of character, that reveal character, and that influence character. Henry James puts it thus: "What is character but the determination of incident? What is incident but the illustration of character?" James goes on: "It is an incident for a woman to stand up with her hand resting on a table and look out at you in a certain way."

Foreshadowing

Although some stories depend heavily on a plot with a surprise ending, other stories prepare the reader for the outcome, at least to some degree. The **foreshadowing** that would eliminate surprise, or greatly reduce it, and thus destroy a story that has nothing else to offer, is a powerful tool in the hands of a writer of serious fiction. In "Samuel," the reader perhaps senses even in the first paragraph that these "tough" boys who "jiggle and hop on the platform" may be vulnerable, may come to an unfortunate end. When a woman says, "You'll be killed," the reader doesn't yet know if she is right, but a seed has been planted.

Even in such a story as Faulkner's "A Rose for Emily" (p. 557), where we are surprised to learn near the end that Miss Emily has slept beside the decaying corpse of her dead lover, from the outset we expect something strange; that is, we are not surprised by the surprise, only by its precise nature. The first sentence of the story tell us that after Miss Emily's funeral (the narrator begins at the end) the townspeople cross her threshold "out of curiosity to see the inside of her house, which no one save an old manservant . . . had seen in at least ten years." As the story progresses, we see Miss Emily prohibiting people from entering the house, we hear that after a certain point no one ever sees Homer Barron again, that "the front door remained closed," and (a few paragraphs before the end of the story) that the townspeople "knew that there was one room in that region above the stairs which no one had seen in forty years." The paragraph preceding the revelation that "the man himself lay in the bed" is devoted to a description of Homer's dust-covered clothing and toilet articles. In short, however much we are unprepared for the precise revelation, we are prepared for some strange thing in the house; and, given Miss Emily's purchase of poison and Homer's disappearance, we have some idea of what will be revealed.

The full meaning of a passage will not become apparent until you have read the entire story. In a sense, a story has at least three lives:

- when we read the story sentence by sentence, trying to turn the sequence of sentences into a consistent whole,
- when we have finished reading the story and we think back on it as a whole, even if we think no more than "That was a waste of time,"
- when we reread a story, knowing already even as we read the first line how it will turn out at the end.

Setting and Atmosphere

Foreshadowing normally makes use of **setting.** The setting or environment is not mere geography, not mere locale: it provides an **atmosphere,** an air that the characters breathe, a world in which they move. Narrowly speaking, the setting is the physical surroundings—the furniture, the architecture, the landscape, the climate—and these often are highly appropriate to the characters who are associated with them. Thus, in Emily Brontë's *Wuthering Heights* the passionate Earnshaw family is associated with Wuthering Heights, the storm-exposed moorland, whereas the mild Linton family is associated with Thrushcross Grange in the sheltered valley below.

Broadly speaking, setting includes not only the physical surroundings but also a point (or several points) in time. The background against which we see the characters and the happenings may be specified as morning or evening, spring or fall. In a good story, this temporal setting will probably be highly relevant; it will probably be part of the story's meaning, perhaps providing an ironic contrast to or exerting an influence on the characters.

Symbolism

When we read, we may feel that certain characters and certain things in the story stand for more than themselves, or hint at larger meanings. We feel, that is, that they are **symbolic.** But here we must be careful. How does one know that this or that figure or place is symbolic? In Hemingway's "Cat in the Rain" (p. 533), is the cat symbolic? Is the innkeeper? Is the rain? Reasonable people may differ in their answers. Again, in Chopin's "The Story of an Hour" (p. 12), is the railroad accident a symbol? Is Josephine a symbol? Is the season (springtime) a symbol? And again, reasonable people may differ in their responses.

Let's assume for the moment, however, that if writers use symbols, they want readers to perceive—at least faintly—that certain characters or places or seasons or happenings have rich implications, stand for something more than what they are on the surface. How do writers help us to perceive these things? By emphasizing them—for instance, by describing them at some length, or by introducing them at times when they might not seem strictly necessary, or by calling attention to them repeatedly.

Consider, for example, Chopin's treatment of the season in which "The Story of an Hour" takes place. The story has to take place at *some* time, but Chopin does not simply say, "On a spring day," or an autumn day, and let things go at that. Rather, she tells us about the sky, the trees, the rain, the twittering sparrows—and all of this in an extremely short story where we might think there is no time for talk about the setting. After all, none of this material is strictly necessary to a story about a woman who has heard that her husband was killed in an accident, who grieves, then recovers, and then dies when he suddenly reappears.

Why, then, does Chopin give such emphasis to the season? Because, we think, she is using the season symbolically. In this story, the spring is not just a bit of detail added for realism. It is rich with suggestions of renewal, of the new life that Louise achieves for a moment. But here, a caution. We think that the spring in this story is symbolic, but this is not to say that whenever spring appears in a story, it always stands for renewal, any more than whenever winter appears it always symbolizes death. Nor does it mean that since spring recurs, Louise will be reborn. In short, in *this* story Chopin uses the season to convey specific implications.

Is the railroad accident in "The Story of an Hour" also a symbol? Our answer is no—though we don't expect all readers to agree with us. We think that the railroad accident in "The Story of an Hour" is just a railroad accident. It's our sense that Chopin is *not* using this event to say something about (for instance) modern travel, or about industrialism. The steam-propelled railroad train could of course be used, symbolically, to say something about industrialism displacing an agrarian economy, but does Chopin give her train any such suggestion? We don't think so. Had she wished to do so, she would probably have talked about the enormous power of the train, the shriek of its whistle, the smoke pouring out of the smokestack, the intense fire burning in the engine, its indifference as it charged through the countryside, and so forth. Had she done so, the story would be a different story. Or she might have made the train a symbol of fate overriding human desires. But, again in our opinion, Chopin does not endow her train with such suggestions. She gives virtually no emphasis to the train, and so we believe it has virtually no significance for the reader.

What of Chopin's "Ripe Figs" (p. 3)? Maman-Nainaine tells Babette that when the figs are ripe Babette can visit her cousins. Of course Maman may merely be setting an arbitrary date, but as we read the story we probably feel—

because of the emphasis on the *ripening* of the figs, which occurs in the spring or early summer—that the ripening of the figs in some way suggests the maturing of Babette. If we do get such ideas, we will in effect be saying that the story is not simply an anecdote about an old woman whose behavior is odd. True, the narrator of the story, after telling us of Maman-Nainaine's promise, adds, "Not that the ripening of figs had the least thing to do with it, but that is the way Maman-Nainaine was." The narrator sees nothing special—merely Maman-Nainaine's eccentricity—in the connection between the ripening of the figs and Babette's visit to her cousins. Readers, however, may see more than the narrator sees or says. They may see in Babette a young girl maturing; they may see in Maman-Nainaine an older woman who, almost collaborating with nature, helps Babette to mature.

And here, of course, as we talk about symbolism we are getting into the theme of the story. An apparently inconsequential and even puzzling action, such as is set forth in "Ripe Figs," may cast a long shadow. As Robert Frost once said,

> There is no story written that has any value at all, however straightforward it looks and free from doubleness, double entendre, that you'd value at all if it didn't have intimations of something more than itself.

The stranger, the more mysterious the story, the more likely we are to suspect some sort of significance, but even realistic stories such as Chopin's "The Storm" and "The Story of an Hour" may be rich in suggestions. This is not to say, however, that the suggestions (rather than the details of the surface) are what count. A reader does not discard the richly detailed, highly specific narrative (Mrs. Mallard learned that her husband was dead and reacted in such-and-such a way) in favor of some supposedly universal message or theme that it implies. We do not throw away the specific narrative—the memorable characters or the interesting things that happen in the story—and move on to some "higher truth." Robert Frost went on to say, "The anecdote, the parable, the surface meaning has got to be good and got to be sufficient in itself."

Narrative Point Of View

An author must choose a **point of view** (or sometimes, several points of view) from which he or she will narrate the story. The choice will contribute to the total effect that the story will have.

Narrative points of view can be divided into two sorts: **participant** (or **first-person**) and **nonparticipant** (or **third-person**). That is, the narrator may or may not be a character who participates in the story. Each of these two divisions can be subdivided:

I. Participant (first-person narrative)
   A. Narrator as a major character
   B. Narrator as a minor character
II. Nonparticipant (third-person narrative)
    A. Omniscient
    B. Selective omniscient
    C. Objective

Participant Points of View Tony Bambara's "The Lesson" (p. 218) begins
thus:

> Back in the days when everyone was old and stupid or young and
> foolish and me and Sugar were the only ones just right, this lady
> moved on our block with nappy hair and proper speech and no
> makeup.

In this story, the narrator is a major character. Bambara is the author, but the narrator—the person who tells us the story—is a young girl who speaks of "me and
Sugar," and the story is chiefly about the narrator. One can say, then, that Bambara uses a first-person (or participant) point of view. She has invented a young
girl who tells us about the impact a woman in the neighborhood had on her:
"[Sugar] can run if she want to and even run faster. But ain't nobody gonna beat
me at nuthin." The narrator is a major character. She, and not Bambara, tells the
story.

But sometimes a first-person narrator tells a story that focuses on someone
other than the narrator; he or she is a minor character, a peripheral witness, for
example, to a story about Sally Jones, and we get the story of Sally filtered
through, say, the eyes of her friend or brother or cat.

Nonparticipant Points of View In a nonparticipant (third-person) point of
view, the teller of the tale does not introduce himself or herself as a character. If
the point of view is **omniscient,** the narrator relates what he or she wants to relate about the thoughts as well as the deeds of all the characters. The omniscient
teller can enter the mind of any character; whereas the first-person narrator can
only say, "I was angry" or "Jack seemed angry," the omniscient teller can say,
"Jack was inwardly angry but gave no sign; Jill continued chatting, but she
sensed his anger." Thus, in Paley's "Samuel," the narrator tells us that Samuel's
mother was "hopeful," but when the new baby was born "immediately she saw
that this baby wasn't Samuel."

Furthermore, a distinction can be made between **neutral omniscience**
(the narrator recounts deeds and thoughts but does not judge) and **editorial
omniscience** (the narrator not only recounts but also judges). An editorially omniscient narrator knows what goes on in the minds of all the characters and
might comment approvingly or disapprovingly: "He closed the book, having finished the story, but, poor fellow, he had missed the meaning."

Because a short story can scarcely hope to develop a picture of several
minds effectively, authors may prefer to limit their omniscience to the minds of
a few of their characters, or even to that of only one of the characters: that is,
they may use **selective omniscience** as the point of view. Selective omniscience provides a focus, especially if it is limited to a single character. When
thus limited, the author sees one character from outside and from inside, but
sees the other characters only from the outside and from the impact they have
on the mind of this selected receptor. When selective omniscience attempts to
record mental activity ranging from consciousness to the unconscious, from
clear perceptions to confused longings, it is sometimes labeled the **stream-of-
consciousness** point of view. The following example is from Katherine Anne
Porter's "The Jilting of Granny Weatherall" (p. 1218):

> Her eyelids wavered and let in streamers of blue-gray light like tissue
> paper over her eyes. She must get up and pull the shades down or she'd

never sleep. She was in bed again and the shades were not down. How could that happen? Better turn over, hide from the light, sleeping in the light gave you nightmares. "Mother, how do you feel now?" and a stinging wetness on her forehead. But I don't like having my face washed in cold water!

Finally, sometimes a third-person narrator does not enter even a single mind but records only what crosses an apparently dispassionate eye and ear. Such a point of view is **objective** (sometimes called the **camera** or **fly-on-the-wall** point of view). The absence of editorializing and of dissection of the mind often produces the effect of a play; we see and hear the characters in action. Much of Chekhov's "Misery" (p. 208) is objective, consisting of bits of dialogue that make the story look like a play:

> "My head aches," says one of the tall ones. "At the Dukmasovs' yesterday Vaska and I drank four bottles of brandy between us."
> "I can't make out why you talk such stuff," says the other tall one angrily. "You lie like a brute."
> "Strike me dead, it's the truth! . . ."
> "It's about as true as that a louse coughs."

Style and Point of View

Obviously a story told by a first-person narrator will have a distinctive style— let's say the voice of an adolescent boy, or an elderly widow, or a madman. The voice of a third-person narrator—especially the voice of a supposedly objective narrator—will be much less distinctive, but if, especially on rereading, you listen carefully, you will probably hear a distinctive tone. (Look, for instance, at the first paragraph of Grace Paley's "Samuel.") Put it this way: Even a supposedly objective point of view is not purely objective, since it represents the writer's choice of a style, a way of reporting material with an apparently dispassionate voice.

After reading a story, you may want to think at least briefly about what the story might be like if told from a different point of view. You may find it instructive, for instance, to rewrite "Samuel" from the "citizenly" man's point of view, or "Ripe Figs" from Babette's.

Determining and Discussing the Theme

First, we can distinguish between story (or plot) and theme in fiction. *Story* is concerned with "How does it turn out? What happens?" But **theme** is concerned with "What is it about? What does it add up to? What motif holds the happenings together? What does it make of life, and, perhaps, what wisdom does it offer?" In a good work of fiction, the details add up, or, to use Flannery O'Connor's words, they are "controlled by some overall purpose." In F. Scott Fitzgerald's *The Great Gatsby*, for example, there are many references to popular music, especially to jazz. These references contribute to our sense of the reality of Fitzgerald's depiction of America in the 1920s, but they do more: They help to comment on the shallowness of the white middle-class characters and they sometimes (very gently) remind us of an alternative culture. One might study Fitzgerald's references to music with an eye toward getting a deeper understanding of what the novel is about.

Suppose we think for a moment about the theme of Paley's "Samuel." Do we sense an "overall purpose" that holds the story together? Different readers inevitably will come up with different readings, that is, with different views of what the story is about. Here is one student's version:

Whites cannot understand the feelings of blacks.

This statement gets at an important element in the story—the conflict between the sober-minded adults and the jiggling boys—but it apparently assumes that all of the adults are white, an inference that cannot be supported by pointing to evidence in the story. Further, we cannot be certain that Samuel is black. And, finally, even if Samuel and his mother are black, surely white readers *do understand his youthful enthusiasm and his mother's inconsolable grief.*

Here is a second statement:

One should not interfere with the actions of others.

Does the story really offer such specific advice? This version of the theme seems to us to reduce the story to a too-simple code of action, a heartless rule of behavior, a rule that seems at odds with the writer's awareness of the mother's enduring grief.

A third version:

Middle-class adults, acting from what seem to them to be the best of motives, may cause irreparable harm and grief.

This last statement seems to us to be one that can be fully supported by checking it against the story, but other equally valid statements can probably be made. How would you put it?

✔️ A Checklist: Getting Ideas for Writing About Fiction

Here are some questions that may help to stimulate ideas about stories. Not every question is, of course, relevant to every story, but if after reading a story and thinking about it, you then run your eye over these questions, you will probably find some questions that will help you to think further about the story—in short, that will help you to get ideas.

As we have said in earlier chapters, it's best to do your thinking with a pen or pencil in hand. If some of the following questions seem to you to be especially relevant to the story you will be writing about, jot down—freely, without worrying about spelling—your initial responses, interrupting your writing only to glance again at the story when you feel the need to check the evidence.

Plot

✔ Does the plot grow out of the characters, or does it depend on chance or coincidence? Did something at first strike you as irrelevant that later you perceived as relevant? Do some parts continue to strike you as irrelevant?

✔ Does surprise play an important role, or does foreshadowing? If surprise is very important, can the story be read a second time with any interest? If so, what gives it this further interest?

✔ What conflicts does the story include? Conflicts of one character against another? Of one character against the setting, or against society? Conflicts within a single character?

✔ Are certain episodes narrated out of chronological order? If so, were you puzzled? Annoyed? On reflection, does the arrangement of episodes seem effective? Why, or why not? Are certain situations repeated? If so, what do you make out of the repetitions?

Character

✔ Which character chiefly engages your interest? Why?
✔ What purposes do minor characters serve? Do you find some who by their similarities and differences help to define each other or help to define the major character? How else is a particular character defined—by his or her words, actions (including thoughts and emotions), dress, setting, narrative point of view? Do certain characters act differently in the same, or in a similar, situation?
✔ How does the author reveal character? By explicit authorial (editorial) comment, for instance, or, on the other hand, by revelation through dialogue? Through depicted action? Through the actions of other characters? How are the author's methods especially suited to the whole of the story?
✔ Is the behavior plausible—that is, are the characters well motivated?
✔ If a character changes, why and how does he or she change? (You may want to jot down each event that influences a change.) Or did you change your attitude toward a character not because the character changes but because you came to know the character better?
✔ Are the characters round or flat? Are they complex, or, on the other hand, highly typical (for instance, one-dimensional representatives of a social class or age)? Are you chiefly interested in a character's psychology, or does the character strike you as standing for something, such as honesty or the arrogance of power?
✔ How has the author caused you to sympathize with certain characters? How does your response—your sympathy or lack of sympathy—contribute to your judgment of the conflict?

Point of View

✔ Who tells the story? How much does the narrator know? Does the narrator strike you as reliable? What effect is gained by using this narrator?
✔ How does the point of view help shape the theme? After all, the basic story of "Little Red Riding Hood"—what happens—remains unchanged whether told from the wolf's point of view or the girl's, but (to simplify grossly) if we hear the story from the wolf's point of view, we may feel that the story is about terrifying yet pathetic compulsive behavior; if from the girl's point of view, about terrified innocence.
✔ It is sometimes said that the best writers are subversive, forcing readers to see something they do not want to see—something that is true but that violates their comfortable conventional ideas. Does this story oppose comfortable conventional views?
✔ Does the narrator's language help you to construct a picture of the narrator's character, class, attitude, strengths, and limitations? (Jot down some evidence, such as colloquial or—on the other hand—formal expressions,

ironic comments, figures of speech.) How far can you trust the narrator? Why?

Setting

✔ Do you have a strong sense of the time and place? Is the story very much about, say, New England Puritanism, or race relations in the South in the late nineteenth century, or midwestern urban versus small-town life? If time and place are important, how and at what points in the story has the author conveyed this sense? If you do not strongly feel the setting, do you think the author should have made it more evident?

✔ What is the relation of the setting to the plot and the characters? (For instance, do houses or rooms or their furnishings say something about their residents?) Would anything be lost if the descriptions of the setting were deleted from the story or the setting were changed?

Symbolism

✔ Do certain characters seem to you to stand for something in addition to themselves? Does the setting—whether a house, a farm, a landscape, a town, a period—have an extra dimension?)

✔ If you do believe that the story has symbolic elements, do you think they are adequately integrated within the story, or do they strike you as being too obviously stuck in?

Style

✔ How has the point of view shaped or determined the style?

✔ How would you characterize the style? Simple? Understated? Figurative? Or what, and why?

✔ Do you think that the style is consistent? If it isn't—for instance, if there are shifts from simple sentences to highly complex ones—what do you make of the shifts?

Theme

✔ Is the title informative? What does it mean or suggest? Did the meaning seem to change after you read the story? Does the title help you to formulate a theme? If you had written the story, what title would you use?

✔ Do certain passages—dialogue or description—seem to you to point especially toward the theme? Do you find certain repetitions of words or pairs of incidents highly suggestive and helpful in directing your thoughts toward stating a theme? Flannery O'Connor, in *Mystery and Manners*, says, "In good fiction, certain of the details will tend to accumulate meaning from the action of the story itself, and when that happens, they become symbolic in the way they work." Does this story work that way?

✔ Is the meaning of the story embodied in the whole story, or does it seem stuck in, for example in certain passages of editorializing?

✔ Suppose someone asked you to state the point—the theme—of the story. Could you? And if you could, would you say that the theme of a particular story reinforces values you hold, or does it to some degree challenge them? Or is the concept of a theme irrelevant to this story?

SIX SHORT STORIES

📖 EDGAR ALLAN POE

Edgar Allan Poe (1809–49) was the son of traveling actors. His father abandoned the family almost immediately, and his mother died when Poe was two. The child was adopted—though never legally—by a prosperous merchant and his wife in Richmond, Virginia. The tensions were great, aggravated by Poe's drinking and heavy gambling, and in 1827 Poe left Richmond for Boston. He wrote, served briefly in the army, attended West Point but left within a year, and became an editor for the remaining eighteen years of his life. It was during these years, too, that he wrote the poems, essays, and fiction—especially detective stories and horror stories—that have made him famous.

The Cask of Amontillado

The thousand injuries of Fortunato I had borne as I best could, but when he ventured upon insult, I vowed revenge. You, who so well know the nature of my soul, will not suppose, however, that I gave utterance to a threat. At *length* I would be avenged; this was a point definitely settled—but the very definitiveness with which it was resolved precluded the idea of risk. I must not only punish, but punish with impunity. A wrong is unredressed when retribution overtakes its redresser. It is equally unredressed when the avenger fails to make himself felt as such to him who has done the wrong.

It must be understood that neither by word nor deed had I given Fortunato cause to doubt my good will. I continued, as was my wont, to smile in his face, and he did not perceive that my smile *now* was at the thought of his immolation.

He had a weak point—this Fortunato—although in other regards he was a man to be respected and even feared. He prided himself on his connoisseurship in wine. Few Italians have the true virtuoso spirit. For the most part their enthusiasm is adopted to suit the time and opportunity to practice imposture upon the British and Austrian *millionaires.* In painting and gemmary Fortunato, like his countrymen, was a quack, but in the matter of old wines he was sincere. In this respect I did not differ from him materially;—I was skillful in the Italian vintages myself, and bought largely whenever I could.

It was about dusk, one evening during the supreme madness of the carnival season, that I encountered my friend. He accosted me with excessive warmth, for he had been drinking much. The man wore motley. He had on a tight-fitting parti-striped dress, and his head was surmounted by the conical cap and bells. I was so pleased to see him, that I thought I should never have done wringing his hand.

5   I said to him—"My dear Fortunato, you are luckily met. How remarkably well you are looking to-day! But I have received a pipe[1] of what passes for Amontillado, and I have my doubts."

"How?" said he, "Amontillado? A pipe? Impossible! And in the middle of the carnival?"

"I have my doubts," I replied; "and I was silly enough to pay the full Amontillado price without consulting you in the matter. You were not to be found, and I was fearful of losing a bargain."

[1]**pipe** wine cask

"Amontillado!"

"I have my doubts."

10   "Amontillado!"

"And I must satisfy them."

"Amontillado!"

"As you are engaged, I am on my way to Luchesi. If any one has a critical turn, it is he. He will tell me—"

"Luchesi cannot tell Amontillado from Sherry."

15   "And yet some fools will have it that his taste is a match for your own."

"Come, let us go."

"Whither?"

"To your vaults."

"My friend, no; I will not impose upon your good nature. I perceive you have an engagement. Luchesi—"

20   "I have no engagement; come."

"My friend, no. It is not the engagement, but the severe cold with which I perceive you are afflicted. The vaults are insufferably damp. They are encrusted with nitre."

"Let us go, nevertheless. The cold is merely nothing. Amontillado! You have been imposed upon; and as for Luchesi, he cannot distinguish Sherry from Amontillado."

Thus speaking, Fortunato possessed himself of my arm. Putting on a mask of black silk, and drawing a *roquelaure*[2] closely about my person, I suffered him to hurry me to my palazzo.

There were no attendants at home; they had absconded to make merry in honor of the time. I had told them that I should not return until the morning, and had given them explicit orders not to stir from the house. These orders were sufficient, I well knew, to insure their immediate disappearance, one and all, as soon as my back was turned.

25   I took from their sconces two flambeaux, and giving one to Fortunato, bowed him through several suites of rooms to the archway that led into the vaults. I passed down a long and winding staircase, requesting him to be cautious as he followed. We came at length to the foot of the descent, and stood together on the damp ground of the catacombs of the Montresors.

The gait of my friend was unsteady, and the bells upon his cap jingled as he strode.

"The pipe," said he.

"It is farther on," said I; "but observe the white web-work which gleams from these cavern walls."

He turned towards me, and looked into my eyes with two filmy orbs that distilled the rheum of intoxication.

30   "Nitre?" he asked, at length.

"Nitre," I replied, "How long have you had that cough?"

"Ugh! ugh! ugh!—ugh! ugh! ugh!—ugh! ugh! ugh!—ugh! ugh! ugh!—ugh! ugh! ugh!"

My poor friend found it impossible to reply for many minutes.

"It is nothing," he said, at last.

---

[2] *roquelaure* short cloak

35   "Come," I said, with decision, "we will go back; your health is precious. You are rich, respected, admired, beloved; you are happy, as once I was. You are a man to be missed. For me it is no matter. We will go back; you will be ill, and I cannot be responsible. Besides, there is Luchesi—"

"Enough," he said; "the cough is a mere nothing: it will not kill me. I shall not die of a cough."

"True—true," I replied; "and, indeed, I had no intention of alarming you unnecessarily—but you should use all proper caution. A draught of this Medoc will defend us from the damps."

Here I knocked off the neck of a bottle which I drew from a long row of its fellows that lay upon the mould.

"Drink," I said, presenting him the wine.

40   He raised it to his lips with a leer. He paused and nodded to me familiarly, while his bells jingled.

"I drink," he said, "to the buried that repose around us."

"And I to your long life."

He again took my arm, and we proceeded.

"These vaults," he said, "are extensive."

45   "The Montresors," I replied, "were a great and numerous family."

"I forget your arms."

"A huge human foot d'or, in a field azure; the foot crushes a serpent rampant whose fangs are imbedded in the heel."

"And the motto?"

"Nemo me impune lacessit."[3]

50   "Good!" he said.

The wine sparkled in his eyes and the bells jingled. My own fancy grew warm with the Medoc. We had passed through walls of piled bones, with casks and puncheons intermingling, into the inmost recesses of the catacombs. I paused again, and this time I made bold to seize Fortunato by an arm above the elbow.

"The nitre!" I said; "see, it increases. It hangs like moss upon the vaults. We are below the river's bed. The drops of moisture tickle among the bones. Come, we will go back ere it is too late. Your cough—"

"It is nothing," he said; "let us go on. But first, another draught of the Medoc."

I broke and reached him a flagon of De Grâve. He emptied it at a breath. His eyes flashed with a fierce light. He laughed and threw the bottle upwards with a gesticulation I did not understand.

55   I looked at him in surprise. He repeated the movement—a grotesque one.

"You do not comprehend?" he said.

"Not I," I replied.

"Then you are not of the brotherhood."

"How?"

60   "You are not of the masons."[4]

"Yes, yes," I said, "yes, yes."

[3]*Nemo me impune lacessit* No one dare attack me with impunity (the motto of Scotland)   [4]**of the masons** i.e., a member of the Freemasons, an international secret fraternity

"You? Impossible! A mason?"

"A mason," I replied.

"A sign," he said.

65   "It is this," I answered, producing a trowel from beneath the folds of my *roquelaure*.

"You jest," he exclaimed, recoiling a few paces. "But let us proceed to the Amontillado."

"Be it so," I said, replacing the tool beneath the cloak, and again offering him my arm. He leaned upon it heavily. We continued our route in search of the Amontillado. We passed through a range of low arches, descended, passed on, and descending again, arrived at a deep crypt, in which the foulness of the air caused our flambeaux rather to glow than flame.

At the most remote end of the crypt there appeared another less spacious. Its walls had been lined with human remains piled to the vault overhead, in the fashion of the great catacombs of Paris. Three sides of this interior crypt were still ornamented in this manner. From the fourth the bones had been thrown down, and lay promiscuously upon the earth, forming at one point a mound of some size. Within the wall thus exposed by the displacing of the bones, we perceived a still interior recess, in depth about four feet, in width three, in height six or seven. It seemed to have been constructed for no especial use within itself, but formed merely the interval between two of the colossal supports of the roof of the catacombs, and was backed by one of their circumscribing walls of solid granite.

It was in vain that Fortunato, uplifting his dull torch, endeavored to pry into the depths of the recess. Its termination the feeble light did not enable us to see.

70   "Proceed," I said; "herein is the Amontillado. As for Luchesi—"

"He is an ignoramus," interrupted my friend, as he stepped unsteadily forward, while I followed immediately at his heels. In an instant he had reached the extremity of the niche, and finding his progress arrested by the rock, stood stupidly bewildered. A moment more and I had fettered him to the granite. In its surface were two iron staples, distant from each other about two feet, horizontally. From one of these depended a short chain, from the other a padlock. Throwing the links about his waist, it was but the work of a few seconds to secure it. He was too much astounded to resist. Withdrawing the key I stepped back from the recess.

"Pass your hand," I said, "over the wall; you cannot help feeling the nitre. Indeed it is *very* damp. Once more let me *implore* you to return. No? Then I must positively leave you. But I must first render you all the little attentions in my power."

"The Amontillado!" ejaculated my friend, not yet recovered from his astonishment.

"True," I replied; "the Amontillado."

75   As I said these words I busied myself among the pile of bones of which I have before spoken. Throwing them aside, I soon uncovered a quantity of building-stone and mortar. With these materials and with the aid of my trowel, I began vigorously to wall up the entrance of the niche.

I had scarcely laid the first tier of masonry when I discovered that the intoxication of Fortunato had in a great measure worn off. The earliest indication I had of this was a low moaning cry from the depth of the recess. It was *not* the cry of a drunken man. There was then a long and obstinate silence. I laid the second tier, and the third, and the fourth; and then I heard the furious vibrations of the chain. The noise lasted for several minutes, during which, that I might hearken to it with the more satisfaction, I ceased my labors and sat down upon the bones. When at last the clanking subsided, I resumed the trowel, and finished without interruption the fifth, the sixth, and the seventh tier. The wall was now nearly upon a level with my breast. I again paused, and holding the flambeaux over the masonwork, threw a few feeble rays upon the figure within.

A succession of loud and shrill screams, bursting suddenly from the throat of the chained form, seemed to thrust me violently back. For a brief moment I hesitated—I trembled. Unsheathing my rapier, I began to grope with it about the recess; but the thought of an instant reassured me. I placed my hand upon the solid fabric of the catacombs, and felt satisfied. I reapproached the wall. I replied to the yells of him who clamored. I re-echoed—I aided—I surpassed them in volume and in strength. I did this, and the clamorer grew still.

It was now midnight, and my task was drawing to a close. I had completed the eight, the ninth, and the tenth tier. I had finished a portion of the last and the eleventh; there remained but a single stone to be fitted and plastered in. I struggled with its weight; I placed it partially in its destined position. But now there came from out the niche a low laugh that erected the hairs upon my head. It was succeeded by a sad voice, which I had difficulty in recognizing as that of the noble Fortunato. The voice said—

"Ha! ha! ha!—he! he! he!—a very good joke indeed—an excellent jest. We will have many a rich laugh about it at the palazzo—he! he! he!—over our wine—he! he! he!"

80   "The Amontillado!" I said.

"He! he! he!—he! he! he!—yes, the Amontillado. But is it not getting late? Will not they be awaiting us at the palazzo, the Lady Fortunato and the rest? Let us be gone."

"Yes," I said, "let us be gone."

"For the love of God, Montresor!"

"Yes," I said, "for the love of God!"

85   But to these words I hearkened in vain for a reply. I grew impatient. I called aloud;

"Fortunato!"

No answer. I called again;

"Fortunato!"

No answer still, I thrust a torch through the remaining aperture and let it fall within. There came forth in return only a jingling of the bells. My heart grew sick—on account of the dampness of the catacombs. I hastened to make an end of my labor. I forced the last stone into its position; I plastered it up. Against the new masonry I reerected the old rampart of bones. For the half of a century no mortal has disturbed them. *In pace requiescat!*[5]

[1846]

✎ Topics for Critical Thinking and Writing

1. To whom does Montresor tell his story? The story he tells happened fifty years earlier. Do we have any clues as to why he tells it now?

---

[5]*In pace requiescat!* May he rest in peace!

2. At the end of the story we learn that the murder occurred fifty years ago. Would the story be equally effective if Poe had had Montresor reveal that fact at the outset? Why, or why not?

3. Poe sets Montresor's story at dusk, "during the supreme madness of the carnival season." What is the "carnival season"? (If you are uncertain as to the meaning of "carnival," consult a dictionary.) What details of the story derive from the setting?

4. In the justifiably famous first line Montresor declares. "The thousand injuries of Fortunato I had borne as I best could, but when he ventured upon insult, I vowed revenge." Do we ever learn what those injuries and that insult were? What do we learn about Montresor from this declaration?

5. How does Montresor characterize Fortunato? What details of his portrait unwittingly enlist our sympathy for Fortunato? Does Montresor betray any sympathy for his victim?

6. "The Cask of Amontillado" is sometimes referred to as a "horror tale." Do you think it has anything in common with horror movies? If so, what? (You might begin by making a list of the characteristics of horror movies.) Why do people take pleasure in horror movies? Does this story offer any of the same sorts of pleasure? In any case, why might a reader take pleasure in this story?

7. Construct a definition of madness (you may want to do a little research, but if you make use of your findings, be sure to give credit to your sources) and write an essay of 500–750 words arguing whether or not Montresor is mad. (*Note:* You may want to distinguish between Montresor at the time of the killing and Montresor at the present.)

 **ANTON CHEKHOV**

Anton Chekhov (1860–1904) was born in Russia, the son of a shopkeeper. While a medical student at Moscow University, Chekhov wrote stories, sketches, and reviews to help support his family and to finance his education. In 1884 he received his medical degree, began to practice medicine, published his first book of stories, and suffered the first of a series of hemorrhages from tuberculosis. In his remaining twenty years, in addition to writing several hundred stories, he wrote plays, half a dozen of which have established themselves as classics. He died from tuberculosis at the age of forty-four.

Misery

Translated by Constance Garnett

"To Whom Shall I Tell My Grief?"

The twilight of evening. Big flakes of wet snow are whirling lazily about the street lamps, which have just been lighted, and lying in a thin soft layer on roofs, horses' backs, shoulders, caps. Iona Potapov, the sledgedriver, is all white like a ghost. He sits on the box without stirring, bent as double as the living body can be bent. If a regular snowdrift fell on him it seems as though even then he would not think it necessary to shake it off. . . . His little mare is white and motionless too. Her stillness, the angularity of her lines, and the stick-like straightness of her legs make her look like a halfpenny gingerbread horse. She is probably lost in thought. Anyone who has been torn away from the plough, from the familiar gray landscapes, and cast into this slough, full of monstrous lights, of unceasing uproar and hurrying people, is bound to think.

It is a long time since Iona and his nag have budged. They came out of the yard before dinner-time and not a single fare yet. But now the shades of evening are falling on the town. The pale light of the street lamps changes to a vivid color, and the bustle of the street grows noisier.

"Sledge to Vyborgskaya!" Iona hears. "Sledge!"

Iona starts, and through his snow-plastered eyelashes sees an officer in a military overcoat with a hood over his head.

5   "To Vyborgskaya," repeats the officer. "Are you asleep? To Vyborgskaya!"

In token of assent Iona gives a tug at the reins which sends cakes of snow flying from the horse's back and shoulders. The officer gets into the sledge. The sledge-driver clicks to the horse, cranes his neck like a swan, rises in his seat, and more from habit than necessity brandishes his whip. The mare cranes her neck, too, crooks her stick-like legs, and hesitatingly sets off. . . .

"Where are you shoving, you devil?" Iona immediately hears shouts from the dark mass shifting to and fro before him. "Where the devil are you going? Keep to the r-right!"

"You don't know how to drive! Keep to the right," says the officer angrily.

A coachman driving a carriage swears at him; a pedestrian crossing the road and brushing the horse's nose with his shoulder looks at him angrily and shakes the snow off his sleeve. Iona fidgets on the box as though he were sitting on thorns, jerks his elbows, and turns his eyes about like one possessed, as though he did not know where he was or why he was there.

10   "What rascals they all are!" says the officer jocosely. "They are simply doing their best to run up against you or fall under the horse's feet. They must be doing it on purpose."

Iona looks at his fare and moves his lips. . . . Apparently he means to say something, but nothing comes out but a sniff.

"What?" inquires the officer.

Iona gives a wry smile, and straining his throat, brings out huskily: "My son . . . , er . . . my son died this week, sir."

"H'm! What did he die of?"

15   Iona turns his whole body round to his fare, and says:

"Who can tell! It must have been from fever. . . . He lay three days in the hospital and then he died. . . . God's will."

"Turn round, you devil!" comes out of the darkness. "Have you gone cracked, you old dog? Look where you are going!"

"Drive on! drive on! . . ." says the officer. "We shan't get there till tomorrow going on like this. Hurry up!"

The sledge-driver cranes his neck again, rises in his seat, and with heavy grace swings his whip. Several times he looks round at the officer, but the latter keeps his eyes shut and is apparently disinclined to listen. Putting his fare down at Vyborgskaya, Iona stops by a restaurant, and again.sits huddled up on the box. . . . Again the wet snow paints him and his horse white. One hour passes, and then another. . . .

20   Three young men, two tall and thin, one short and hunchbacked, come up, railing at each other and loudly stamping on the pavement with their galoshes.

"Cabby, to the Police Bridge!" the hunchback cries in a cracked voice. "The three of us, . . . twenty kopecks!"

Iona tugs at the reins and clicks to his horse. Twenty kopecks is not a fair price, but he has no thoughts for that. Whether it is a rouble or whether it is five kopecks does not matter to him now so long as he has a fare. . . . The three young men, shoving each other and using bad language, go up to the sledge, and all three try to sit down at once. The question remains to be settled: Which are to sit down and which one is to stand? After a long altercation, ill-temper, and abuse, they come to the conclusion that the hunchback must stand because he is the shortest.

"Well, drive on," says the hunchback in his cracked voice, settling himself and breathing down Iona's neck. "Cut along! What a cap you've got, my friend! You wouldn't find a worse one in all Petersburg . . . ."

"He-he! . . . he-he! . . ." laughs Iona. "It's nothing to boast of!"

25   "Well, then, nothing to boast of, drive on! Are you going to drive like this all the way? Eh? Shall I give you one in the neck?"

"My head aches," says one of the tall ones. "At the Dukmasovs' yesterday Vaska and I drank four bottles of brandy between us."

"I can't make out why you talk such stuff," says the other tall one angrily. "You lie like a brute."

"Strike me dead, it's the truth! . . ."

"It's about as true as that a louse coughs."

30   "He-he!" grins Iona. "Me-er-ry gentlemen!"

"Tfoo! the devil take you!" cries the hunchback indignantly. "Will you get on, you old plague, or won't you? Is that the way to drive? Give her one with the whip. Hang it all, give it her well."

Iona feels behind his back the jolting person and quivering voice of the hunchback. He hears abuse addressed to him, he sees people, and the feeling of loneliness begins little by little to be less heavy on his heart. The hunchback swears at him, till he chokes over some elaborately whimsical string of epithets and is overpowered by his cough. His tall companions begin talking of a certain Nadyezhda Petrovna. Iona looks round at them. Waiting till there is a brief pause, he looks round once more and says:

"This week . . . er . . . my . . . er . . . son died!"

"We shall all die, . . ." says the hunchback with a sigh, wiping his lips after coughing. "Come, drive on! drive on! My friends, I simply cannot stand crawling like this! When will he get us there?"

35   "Well, you give him a little encouragement . . . one in the neck!"

"Do you hear, you old plague? I'll make you smart. If one stands on ceremony with fellows like you one may as well walk. Do you hear, you old dragon? Or don't you care a hang what we say?"

And Iona hears rather than feels a slap on the back of his neck.

"He-he! . . ." he laughs. "Merry gentlemen . . . God give you health!"

"Cabman, are you married?" asks one of the tall ones.

40   "I? He-he! Me-er-ry gentlemen. The only wife for me now is the damp earth. . . . He-ho-ho! . . . The grave that is! . . . Here my son's dead and I am alive. . . . It's a strange thing, death has come in at the wrong door. . . . Instead of coming for me it went for my son . . . ."

And Iona turns round to tell them how his son died, but at that point the hunchback gives a faint sigh and announces that, thank God! they have arrived at last. After taking his twenty kopecks, Iona gazes for a long while after the revelers, who disappear into a dark entry. Again he is alone and again there is silence for him. . . . The misery which has been for a brief space eased comes back again and tears his heart more cruelly than ever. With a look of anxiety and suffering

Iona's eyes stray restlessly among the crowds moving to and fro on both sides of the street: can he not find among those thousands someone who will listen to him? But the crowds flit by heedless of him and his misery. . . . His misery is immense, beyond all bounds. If Iona's heart were to burst and his misery to flow out, it would flood the whole world, it seems, but yet it is not seen. It has found a hiding-place in such an insignificant shell that one would not have found it with a candle by daylight. . . .

Iona sees a house-porter with a parcel and makes up his mind to address him.

"What time will it be, friend?" he asks.

"Going on for ten. . . . Why have you stopped here? Drive on!"

45   Iona drives a few paces away, bends himself double, and gives himself up to his misery. He feels it is no good to appeal to people. But before five minutes have passed he draws himself up, shakes his head as though he feels a sharp pain, and tugs at the reins. . . . He can bear it no longer.

"Back to the yard!" he thinks. "To the yard!"

And his little mare, as though she knew his thoughts, falls to trotting. An hour and a half later Iona is sitting by a big dirty stove. On the stove, on the floor, and on the benches are people snoring. The air is full of smells and stuffiness. Iona looks at the sleeping figures, scratches himself, and regrets that he has come home so early. . . .

"I have not earned enough to pay for the oats, even," he thinks. "That's why I am so miserable. A man who knows how to do his work, . . . who has had enough to eat, and whose horse has had enough to eat, is always at ease . . . ."

In one of the corners a young cabman gets up, clears his throat sleepily, and makes for the waterbucket.

50   "Want a drink?" Iona asks him.

"Seems so."

"May it do you good. . . . But my son is dead, mate. . . . Do you hear? This week in the hospital. . . . It's queer business . . . ."

Iona looks to see the effect produced by his words, but he sees nothing. The young man has covered his head over and is already asleep. The old man sighs and scratches himself. . . . Just as the young man had been thirsty for water, he thirsts for speech. His son will soon have been dead a week, and he has not really talked to anybody yet. . . . He wants to talk of it properly, with deliberation. . . . He wants to tell how his son was taken ill, how he suffered, what he said before he died, how he died. . . . He wants to describe the funeral, and how he went to the hospital to get his son's clothes. He still has his daughter Anisya in the country. . . . And he wants to talk about her too. . . . Yes, he has plenty to talk about now. His listener ought to sigh and exclaim and lament. . . . It would be even better to talk to women. Though they are silly creatures, they blubber at the first word.

"Let's go out and have a look at the mare," Iona thinks. "There is always time for sleep. . . . You'll have sleep enough, no fear . . . ."

55   He puts on his coat and goes into the stables where his mare is standing. He thinks about oats, about hay, about the weather. . . . He cannot think about his son when he is alone. . . . To talk about him with someone is possible, but to think of him and picture him is insufferable anguish . . . .

"Are you munching?" Iona asks his mare, seeing her shining eyes. "There, munch away, munch away. . . . Since we have not earned enough for oats, we will eat hay. . . . Yes, . . . I have grown too old to drive. . . . My son ought to be driving, not I. . . . He was a real coachman. . . . He ought to have lived . . . ."

Iona is silent for a while, and then he goes on:

"That's how it is, old girl. . . . Kuzma Ionitch is gone. . . . He said goodby to me. . . . He went and died for no reason. . . . Now, suppose you had a little colt, and you were mother to that little colt. . . . And all at once that same little colt went and died. . . . You'd be sorry, wouldn't you? . . ."

60   The little mare munches, listens, and breathes on her master's hands. Iona is carried away and tells her all about it.

[1886]

Topics for Critical Thinking and Writing

1. What do you admire or not admire about Chekhov's story? Why?
2. Try to examine in detail your response to the ending. Do you think the ending is, in a way, a happy ending? Would you prefer a different ending? For instance, should the story end when the young cabman falls asleep? Or when Iona sets out for the stable? Or can you imagine a better ending? If so, what?

EUDORA WELTY

Eudora Welty was born in 1909 in Jackson, Mississippi. Although she earned a bachelor's degree at the University of Wisconsin, and she spent a year studying advertising in New York City at the Columbia University Graduate School of Business, she has lived almost all of her life in Jackson.

In the preface to her Collected Stories *she says:*

I have been told, both in approval and in accusation, that I seem to love all my characters. What I do in writing of any character is to try to enter into the mind, heart and skin of a human being who is not myself. Whether this happens to be a man or a woman, old or young, with skin black or white, the primary challenge lies in making the jump itself. It is the act of a writer's imagination that I set most high.

In addition to writing stories and novels, Welty has written a book about fiction, The Eye of the Story *(1977), and a memoir,* One Writer's Beginnings *(1984).*

A Worn Path

It was December—a bright frozen day in the early morning. Far out in the country there was an old Negro woman with her head tied in a red rag, coming along a path through the pinewoods. Her name was Phoenix Jackson. She was very old and small and she walked slowly in the dark pine shadows, moving a little from side to side in her steps, with the balanced heaviness and lightness of a pendulum in a grandfather clock. She carried a thin, small cane made from an umbrella, and with this she kept tapping the frozen earth in front of her. This made a grave and persistent noise in the still air, that seemed meditative like the chirping of a solitary little bird.

She wore a dark striped dress reaching down to her shoe tops, and an equally long apron of bleached sugar sacks, with a full pocket: all neat and tidy, but every time she took a step she might have fallen over her shoelaces, which dragged from her unlaced shoes. She looked straight ahead. Her eyes were blue with age. Her skin had a pattern all its own of numberless branching wrinkles and as though a whole little tree stood in the middle of her forehead, but a golden color ran underneath, and the two knobs of her cheeks were illuminated by a yellow burning under the dark. Under the red rag her hair came down on her neck in the frailest of ringlets, still black, and with an odor like copper.

Now and then there was a quivering in the thicket. Old Phoenix said, "Out of my way, all you foxes, owls, beetles, jack rabbits, coons, and wild animals! . . . Keep out from under these feet, little bob-whites. . . . Keep the big wild hogs out of my path. Don't let none of those come running my direction. I got a long way." Under her small black-freckled hand her cane, limber as a buggy whip, would switch at the brush as if to rouse up any hiding things.

On she went. The woods were deep and still. The sun made the pine needles almost too bright to look at, up where the wind rocked. The cones dropped as light as feathers. Down in the hollow was the mourning dove—it was not too late for him.

5   The path ran up a hill. "Seem like there is chains about my feet, time I get this far," she said, in the voice of argument old people keep to use with themselves. "Something always take a hold of me on this hill—pleads I should stay."

After she got to the top she turned and gave a full, severe look behind her where she had come. "Up through pines," she said at length. "Now down through oaks."

Her eyes opened their widest, and she started down gently. But before she got to the bottom of the hill a bush caught her dress.

Her fingers were busy and intent, but her skirts were full and long, so that before she could pull them free in one place they were caught in another. It was not possible to allow the dress to tear. "I in the thorny bush," she said. "Thorns, you doing your appointed work. Never want to let folks pass—no sir. Old eyes thought you was a pretty little *green* bush."

Finally, trembling all over, she stood free, and after a moment dared to stoop for her cane.

10   "Sun so high!" she cried, leaning back and looking, while the thick tears went over her eyes. "The time getting all gone here."

At the foot of this hill was a place where a log was laid across the creek.

"Now comes the trial," said Phoenix.

Putting her right foot out, she mounted the log and shut her eyes. Lifting her skirt, levelling her cane fiercely before her, like a festival figure in some parade, she began to march across. Then she opened her eyes and she was safe on the other side.

"I wasn't as old as I thought," she said.

15   But she sat down to rest. She spread her skirts on the bank around her and folded her hands over her knees. Up above her was a tree in a pearly cloud of mistletoe. She did not dare to close her eyes, and when a little boy brought her a little plate with a slice of marble-cake on it she spoke to him. "That would be acceptable," she said. But when she went to take it there was just her own hand in the air.

So she left that tree, and had to go through a barbed-wire fence. There she had to creep and crawl, spreading her knees and stretching her fingers like a baby trying to climb the steps. But she talked loudly to herself: she could not let her dress be torn now, so late in the day, and she could not pay for having her arm or leg sawed off if she got caught fast where she was.

At last she was safe through the fence and risen up out in the clearing. Big dead trees, like black men with one arm, were standing in the purple stalks of the withered cotton field. There sat a buzzard.

"Who you watching?"

In the furrow she made her way along.

20   "Glad this not the season for bulls," she said, looking sideways, "and the good Lord made his snakes to curl up and sleep in the winter. A pleasure I don't see no two-headed snake coming around that tree, where it come once. It took a while to get by him, back in the summer."

She passed through the old cotton and went into a field of dead corn. It whispered and shook and was taller than her head. "Through the maze now," she said, for there was no path.

Then there was something tall, black, and skinny there, moving before her.

At first she took it for a man. It could have been a man dancing in the field. But she stood still and listened, and it did not make a sound. It was as silent as a ghost.

"Ghost," she said sharply, "who be you the ghost of? For I have heard of nary death close by."

25   But there was no answer—only the ragged dancing in the wind.

She shut her eyes, reached out her hand, and touched a sleeve. She found a coat and inside that an emptiness, cold as ice.

"You scarecrow," she said. Her face lighted. "I ought to be shut up for good," she said with laughter. "My senses is gone. I too old. I the oldest people I ever know. Dance, old scarecrow," she said, "while I dancing with you."

She kicked her foot over the furrow, and with mouth drawn down, shook her head once or twice in a little strutting way. Some husks blew down and whirled in streamers about her skirts.

Then she went on, parting her way from side to side with the cane, through the whispering field. At last she came to the end, to a wagon track where the silver grass blew between the red ruts. The quail were walking around like pullets, seeming all dainty and unseen.

30   "Walk pretty," she said. "This the easy place. This the easy going."

She followed the track, swaying through the quiet bare fields, through the little strings of trees silver in their dead leaves, past cabins silver from weather, with the doors and windows boarded shut, all like old women under a spell sitting there. "I walking in their sleep," she said, nodding her head vigorously.

In a ravine she went where a spring was silently flowing through a hollow log. Old Phoenix bent and drank. "Sweet-gum makes the water sweet," she said, and drank more. "Nobody know who made this well, for it was here when I was born."

The track crossed a swampy part where the moss hung as white as lace from every limb. "Sleep on, alligators, and blow your bubbles." Then the track went into the road.

Deep, deep the road went down between the high green-colored banks. Overhead the live-oaks met, and it was as dark as a cave.

35   A black dog with a lolling tongue came up out of the weeds by the ditch. She was meditating, and not ready, and when he came at her she only hit him a little with her cane. Over she went in the ditch, like a little puff of milk-weed.

Down there, her senses drifted away. A dream visited her, and she reached her hand up, but nothing reached down and gave her a pull. So she lay there and presently went to talking. "Old woman," she said to herself, "that black dog come up out of the weeds to stall you off, and now there he sitting on his fine tail, smiling at you."

A white man finally came along and found her—a hunter, a young man, with his dog on a chain.

"Well, Granny!" he laughed. "what are you doing there?"

"Lying on my back like a June-bug waiting to be turned over, mister," she said, reaching up her hand.

40 He lifted her up, gave her a swing in the air, and set her down. "Anything broken, Granny?"

"No sir, them old dead weeds is springy enough," said Phoenix, when she had got her breath. "I thank you for your trouble."

"Where do you live, Granny?" he asked, while the two dogs were growling at each other.

"Away back yonder, sir, behind the ridge. You can't even see it from here."

"On your way home?"

45 "No, sir, I going to town."

"Why, that's too far! That's as far as I walk when I come out myself, and I get something for my trouble." He patted the stuffed bag he carried, and there hung down a little closed claw. It was one of the bob-whites, with its beak hooked bitterly to show it was dead. "Now you go on home, Granny!"

"I bound to go to town, mister," said Phoenix. "The time come around."

He gave another laugh, filling the whole landscape. "I know you old colored people! Wouldn't miss going to town to see Santa Claus!"

But something held Old Phoenix very still. The deep lines in her face went into a fierce and different radiation. Without warning, she had seen with her own eyes a flashing nickel fall out of the man's pocket onto the ground.

50 "How old are you, Granny?" he was saying.

"There is no telling, mister," she said, "no telling."

Then she gave a little cry and clapped her hands and said, "Git on away from here, dog! Look! Look at that dog!" She laughed as if in admiration. "He ain't scared of nobody. He a big black dog." She whispered, "Sic him!"

"Watch me get rid of that cur," said the man. "Sic him, Pete! Sic him!"

Phoenix heard the dogs fighting, and heard the man running and throwing sticks. She even heard a gunshot. But she was slowly bending forward by that time, further and further forward, the lids stretched down over her eyes, as if she were doing this in her sleep. Her chin was lowered almost to her knees. The yellow palm of her hand came out from the fold of her apron. Her fingers slid down and along the ground under the piece of money with the grace and care they would have in lifting an egg from under a sitting hen. Then she slowly straightened up, she stood erect, and the nickel was in her apron pocket. A bird flew by. Her lips moved. "God watching me the whole time. I come to stealing."

55 The man came back, and his own dog panted about them. "Well, I scared him off that time," he said, and then he laughed and lifted his gun and pointed it at Phoenix.

She stood straight and faced him.

"Doesn't the gun scare you?" he said, still pointing it.

"No, sir, I seen plenty go off closer by, in my day, and for less than what I done," she said, holding utterly still.

He smiled, and shouldered the gun. "Well, Granny," he said, "you must be a hundred years old, and scared of nothing. I'd give you a dime if I had any money with me. But you take my advice and stay home, and nothing will happen to you."

60   "I bound to go on my way, mister," said Phoenix. She inclined her head in the red rag. Then they went in different directions, but she could hear the gun shooting again and again over the hill.

     She walked on. The shadows hung from the oak trees to the road like curtains. Then she smelled wood-smoke, and smelled the river, and she saw a steeple and the cabins on their steep steps. Dozens of little black children whirled around her. There ahead was Natchez shining. Bells were ringing. She walked on.

     In the paved city it was Christmas time. There were red and green electric lights strung and crisscrossed everywhere, and all turned on in the daytime. Old Phoenix would have been lost if she had not distrusted her eyesight and depended on her feet to know where to take her.

     She paused quietly on the sidewalk where people were passing by. A lady came along in the crowd, carrying an armful of red-, green-, and silver-wrapped presents; she gave off perfume like the red roses in hot summer, and Phoenix stopped her.

     "Please, missy, will you lace up my shoe?" She held up her foot.

65   "What do you want, Grandma?"

     "See my shoe," said Phoenix. "Do all right for out in the country, but wouldn't look right to go in a big building."

     "Stand still then, Grandma," said the lady. She put her packages down on the sidewalk beside her and laced and tied both shoes tightly.

     "Can't lace 'em with a cane," said Phoenix. "Thank you, missy. I doesn't mind asking a nice lady to tie up my shoe, when I gets out on the street."

     Moving slowly and from side to side, she went into the big building and into a tower of steps, where she walked up and around and around until her feet knew to stop.

70   She entered a door, and there she saw nailed up on the wall the document that had been stamped with the gold seal and framed in the gold frame, which matched the dream that was hung up in her head.

     "Here I be," she said. There was a fixed and ceremonial stiffness over her body.

     "A charity case, I suppose," said an attendant who sat at the desk before her.

     But Phoenix only looked above her head. There was sweat on her face, the wrinkles in her skin shone like a bright net.

     "Speak up, Grandma," the woman said. "What's your name? We must have your history, you know. Have you been here before? What seems to be the trouble with you?"

75   Old Phoenix only gave a twitch to her face as if a fly were bothering her.

     "Are you deaf?" cried the attendant.

     But then the nurse came in.

     "Oh, that's just old Aunt Phoenix," she said. "She doesn't come for herself—she has a little grandson. She makes these trips just as regular as clockwork. She lives away back off the old Natchez Trace." She bent down. "Well, Aunt Phoenix, why don't you just take a seat? We won't keep you standing after your long trip." She pointed.

     The old woman sat down, bolt upright in the chair.

80   "Now, how is the boy?" asked the nurse.

     Old Phoenix did not speak.

     "I said, how is the boy?"

But Phoenix only waited and stared straight ahead, her face very solemn and withdrawn into rigidity.

"Is his throat any better?" asked the nurse. "Aunt Phoenix, don't you hear me? Is your grandson's throat any better since the last time you came for the medicine?"

85 With her hands on her knees, the old woman waited, silent, erect and motionless, just as if she were in armor.

"You mustn't take up our time this way, Aunt Phoenix," the nurse said. "Tell us quickly about your grandson, and get it over. He isn't dead, is he?"

At last there came a flicker and then a flame of comprehension across her face, and she spoke.

"My grandson. It was my memory had left me. There I sat and forgot why I made my long trip."

"Forgot?" The nurse frowned. "After you came so far?"

90 Then Phoenix was like an old woman begging a dignified forgiveness for waking up frightened in the night. "I never did go to school, I was too old at the Surrender," she said in a soft voice. "I'm an old woman without an education. It was my memory fail me. My little grandson, he is just the same, and I forgot it in the coming."

"Throat never heals, does it?" said the nurse, speaking in a loud, sure voice to Old Phoenix. By now she had a card with something written on it, a little list. "Yes. Swallowed lye. When was it—January—two-three years ago—"

Phoenix spoke unasked now. "No, missy, he not dead, he just the same. Every little while his throat begin to close up again, and he not able to swallow. He not get his breath. He not able to help himself. So the time come around, and I go on another trip for the soothing medicine."

"All right. The doctor said as long as you came to get it, you could have it," said the nurse. "But it's an obstinate case."

"My little grandson, he sit up there in the house all wrapped up, waiting by himself," Phoenix went on. "We is the only two left in the world. He suffer and it don't seem to put him back at all. He got a sweet look. He going to last. He wear a little patch quilt and peep out holding his mouth open like a little bird. I remembers so plain now. I not going to forget him again, no, the whole enduring time. I could tell him from all the others in creation."

95 "All right." The nurse was trying to hush her now. She brought her a bottle of medicine. "Charity," she said, making a check mark in a book.

Old Phoenix held the bottle close to her eyes and then carefully put it into her pocket.

"I thank you," she said.

"It's Christmas time, Grandma," said the attendant. "Could I give you a few pennies out of my purse?"

"Five pennies is a nickel," said Phoenix stiffly.

100 "Here's a nickel," said the attendant.

Phoenix rose carefully and held out her hand. She received the nickel and then fished the other nickel out of her pocket and laid it beside the new one. She stared at her palm closely, with her head on one side.

Then she gave a tap with her cane on the floor.

"This is what come to me to do," she said. "I going to the store and buy my child a little windmill they sells, made out of paper. He going to find it hard to believe there such a thing in the world. I'll march myself back where he waiting, holding it straight up in his hand."

She lifted her free hand, gave a little nod, turned round, and walked out of the doctor's office. Then her slow step began on the stairs, going down.

[1941]

Topics for Critical Thinking and Writing

1. If you do not know the legend of the phoenix, look it up in a dictionary or, better, in an encyclopedia. Then carefully reread the story, to learn whether the story in any way connects with the legend.
2. What do you think of the hunter?
3. What would be lost if the episode (with all of its dialogue) of Phoenix falling into the ditch and being helped out of it by the hunter were omitted?
4. Is Christmas a particularly appropriate time in which to set the story? Why or why not?
5. What do you make of the title?

TONI CADE BAMBARA

Toni Cade Bambara (1939–95), an African-American writer, was born in New York City and grew up in black districts of the city. After studying at the University of Florence in Italy and at City College in New York, where she received a master's degree, she worked for a while as a case investigator for the New York State Welfare Department. Later she directed a recreation program for hospital patients. After her literary reputation became established, she spent most of her time writing, though she also served as writer in residence at Spelman College in Atlanta.

The Lesson

Back in the days when everyone was old and stupid or young and foolish and me and Sugar were the only ones just right, this lady moved on our block with nappy hair and proper speech and no makeup. And quite naturally we laughed at her, laughed the way we did at the junk man who went about his business like he was some big-time president and his sorry-ass horse his secretary. And we kinda hated her too, hated the way we did the winos who cluttered up our parks and pissed on our handball walls and stank up our hallways and stairs so you couldn't halfway play hide-and-seek without a goddamn gas mask. Miss Moore was her name. The only woman on the block with no first name. And she was black as hell, cept for her feet, which were fish-white and spooky. And she was always planning these boring-ass things for us to do, us being my cousin, mostly, who lived on the block cause we all moved North the same time and to the same apartment then spread out gradual to breathe. And our parents would yank our heads into some kinda shape and crisp up our clothes so we'd be presentable for travel with Miss Moore, who always looked like she was going to church, though she never did. Which is just one of the things the grownups talked about when they talked behind her back like a dog. But when she came calling with some sachet she'd sewed up or some gingerbread she'd made or some book, why then they'd all be too embarrassed to turn her down and we'd get handed over all spruced up. She'd been to college and said it was only right that she should take responsibility for the young ones' education, and she not even related by marriage or blood. So they'd go for it. Specially Aunt Gretchen. She was the main gofer in the family. You got some ole dumb shit foolishness you want somebody to go for, you send for Aunt Gretchen. She been screwed into the go-along for so long, it's a blood-deep natural thing with her. Which is how she got saddled with me and Sugar and Junior in the first place while our mothers were in a la-de-da apartment up the block having a good ole time.

So this one day Miss Moore rounds us all up at the mailbox and it's puredee hot and she's knockin herself out about arithmetic. And school suppose to let up in summer I heard, but she don't never let up. And the starch in my pinafore scratching the shit outta me and I'm really hating this nappy-head bitch and her goddamn college degree. I'd much rather go to the pool or to the show where it's cool. So me and Sugar leaning on the mailbox being surly, which is a Miss Moore word. And Flyboy checking out what every-body brought for lunch. And Fat Butt already wasting his peanut-butter-and-jelly sandwich like the pig he is. And Junebug punchin on Q.T.'s arm for potato chips. And Rosie Giraffe shifting from one hip to the other waiting for somebody to step on her foot or ask her if she from Georgia so she can kick ass, preferably Mercedes'. And Miss Moore asking us do we know what money is, like we a bunch of retards. I mean real money, she say, like it's only poker chips or monopoly papers we lay on the grocer. So right away I'm tired of this and say so. And would much rather snatch Sugar and go to the Sunset and terrorize the West Indian kids and take their hair ribbons and their money too. And Miss Moore files that remark away for next week's lesson on brotherhood, I can tell. And finally I say we oughta get to the subway cause it's cooler and besides we might meet some cute boys. Sugar done swiped her mama's lipstick, so we ready.

So we heading down the street and she's boring us silly about what things cost and what our parents make and how much goes for rent and how money ain't divided up right in this country. And then she gets to the part about we all poor and live in the slums, which I don't feature. And I'm ready to speak on that, but she steps out in the street and hails two cabs just like that. Then she hustles half the crew in with her and hands me a five-dollar bill and tells me to calculate 10 percent tip for the driver. And we're off. Me and Sugar and Junebug and Flyboy hangin out the window and hollering to everybody, putting lipstick on each other cause Flyboy a faggot anyway, and making farts with our sweaty armpits. But I'm mostly trying to figure how to spend this money. But they all fascinated with the meter ticking and Junebug starts laying bets to how much it'll read when Flyboy can't hold his breath no more. Then Sugar lays bets as to how much it'll be when we get there. So I'm stuck. Don't nobody want to go for my plan, which is to jump out at the next light and run off to the first bar-b-que we can find. Then the driver tells us to get the hell out cause we there already. And the meter reads eighty-five cents. And I'm stalling to figure out the tip and Sugar say give him a dime. And I decide he don't need it as bad as I do, so later for him. But then he tries to take off with Junebug foot still in the door so we talk about his mama something ferocious. Then we check out that we on Fifth Avenue and everybody dressed up in stockings. One lady in a fur coat, hot as it is. White folks crazy.

"This is the place," Miss Moore say, presenting it to us in the voice she uses at the museum. "Let's look in the windows before we go in."

5   "Can we steal?" Sugar asks very serious like she's getting the ground rules squared away before she plays. "I beg your pardon," say Miss Moore, and we fall

out. So she leads us around the windows of the toy store and me and Sugar screamin, "This is mine, that's mine, I gotta have that, that was made for me, I was born for that," till Big Butt drowns us out.

"Hey, I'm goin to buy that there."

"That there? You don't even know what it is, stupid."

"I do so," he say punchin on Rosie Giraffe. "It's a microscope."

"Whatcha gonna do with a microscope, fool?"

10   "Look at things."

"Like what, Ronald?" ask Miss Moore. And Big Butt ain't got the first notion. So here go Miss Moore gabbing about the thousands of bacteria in a drop of water and the somethinorother in a speck of blood and the million and one living things in the air around us is invisible to the naked eye. And what she say that for? Junebug go to town on that "naked" and we rolling. Then Miss Moore ask what it cost. So we all jam into the window smudgin it up and the price tag say $300. So then she ask how long'd take for Big Butt and Junebug to save up their allowances. "Too long," I say. "Yeh," adds Sugar, "outgrown it by that time." And Miss Moore say no, you never outgrow learning instruments. "Why, even medical students and interns and," blah, blah, blah. And we ready to choke Big Butt for bringing it up in the first damn place.

"This here costs four hundred eighty dollars," say Rosie Giraffe. So we pile up all over her to see what she pointin out. My eyes tell me it's a chunk of glass cracked with something heavy, and different-color inks dripped into the splits, then the whole thing put into a oven or something. But for $480 it don't make sense.

"That's a paperweight made of semi-precious stones fused together under tremendous pressure," she explains slowly, and her hands doing the mining and all the factory work.

"So what's a paperweight?" asks Rosie Giraffe.

15   "To weigh paper with, dumbbell," say Flyboy, the wise man from the East.

"Not exactly," say Miss Moore, which is what she say when you warm or way off too. "It's to weigh paper down so it won't scatter and make your desk untidy." So right away me and Sugar curtsy to each other and then to Mercedes who is more the tidy type.

"We don't keep paper on top of the desk in my class," say Junebug, figuring Miss Moore crazy or lyin one.

"At home, then," she say. "Don't you have a calendar and a pencil case and a blotter and a letter-opener on your desk at home where you do your homework?" And she know damn well what our homes look like cause she nosys around in them every chance she gets.

"I don't even have a desk," say Junebug. "Do we?"

20   "No. And I don't get no homework neither," says Big Butt.

"And I don't even have a home," say Flyboy like he do at school to keep the white folks off his back and sorry for him. Send this poor kid to camp posters, is his specialty.

"I do," says Mercedes. "I have a box of stationery on my desk and a picture of my cat. My godmother bought the stationery and the desk. There's a big rose on each sheet and the envelopes smell like roses."

"Who wants to know about your smelly-ass stationery," say Rosie Giraffe fore I can get my two cents in.

"It's important to have a work area all your own so that . . . ."

25   "Will you look at this sailboat, please," say Flyboy, cuttin her off and pointin to the thing like it was his. So once again we tumble all over each other to gaze at this magnificent thing in the toy store which is just big enough to maybe sail two kittens across the pond if you strap them to the posts tight. We all start reciting the price tag like we in assembly. "Handcrafted sailboat of fiberglass at one thousand one hundred ninety-five dollars."

    "Unbelievable," I hear myself say and am really stunned. I read it again for myself just in case the group recitation put me in a trance. Same thing. For some reason this pisses me off. We look at Miss Moore and she lookin at us, waiting for I dunno what.

    "Who'd pay all that when you can buy a sailboat set for a quarter at Pop's, a tube of glue for a dime, and a ball of string for eight cents? It must have a motor and a whole lot else besides," I say. "My sailboat cost me about fifty cents."

    "But will it take water?" say Mercedes with her smart ass.

    "Took mine to Alley Pond Park once," say Flyboy. "String broke. Lost it. Pity."

30   "Sailed mine in Central Park and it keeled over and sank. Had to ask my father for another dollar."

    "And you got the strap," laugh Big Butt. "The jerk didn't even have a string on it. My old man wailed on his behind."

    Little Q.T. was staring hard at the sailboat and you could see he wanted it bad. But he too little and somebody'd just take it from him. So what the hell. "This boat for kids, Miss Moore?"

    "Parents silly to buy something like that just to get all broke up," say Rosie Giraffe.

    "That much money it should last forever," I figure.

35   "My father'd buy it for me if I wanted it."

    "Your father, my ass," say Rosie Giraffe getting a chance to finally push Mercedes.

    "Must be rich people shop here," say Q.T.

    "You are a very bright boy," say Flyboy. "What was your first clue?" And he rap him on the head with the back of his knuckles, since Q.T. the only one he could get away with. Though Q.T. liable to come up behind you years later and get his licks in when you half expect it.

    "What I want to know is," I says to Miss Moore though I never talk to her, I wouldn't give the bitch that satisfaction, "is how much a real boat costs? I figure a thousand'd get you a yacht any day."

40   "Why don't you check that out," she says, "and report back to the group?" Which really pains my ass. If you gonna mess up a perfectly good swim day least you could do is have some answers. "Let's go in," she say like she got something up her sleeve. Only she don't lead the way. So me and Sugar turn the corner to where the entrance is, but when we get there I kinda hang back. Not that I'm scared, what's there to be afraid of, just a toy store. But I feel funny, shame. But what I got to be shamed about? Got as much right to go in as anybody. But somehow I can't seem to get hold of the door, so I step away for Sugar to lead. But she hangs back too. And I look at her and she looks at me and this is ridiculous. I mean, damn, I have never ever been shy about doing nothing or going nowhere. But then Mercedes steps up and then Rosie Giraffe and Big Butt crowd in behind and shove, and next thing we all stuffed into the doorway with only Mercedes squeezing past us, smoothing out her jumper and walking right down the aisle. Then the rest of us tumble in like a glued-together jigsaw done all wrong. And people lookin at us. And it's like the time me and Sugar crashed into the Catholic

church on a dare. But once we got in there and everything so hushed and holy and the candles and the bowin and the handkerchiefs on all the drooping heads, I just couldn't go through with the plan. Which was for me to run up to the altar and do a tap dance while Sugar played the nose flute and messed around in the holy water. And Sugar kept givin me the elbow. Then later teased me so bad I tied her up in the shower and turned it on and locked her in. And she'd be there till this day if Aunt Gretchen hadn't finally figured I was lyin about the boarder takin a shower.

Same thing in the store. We all walkin on tiptoe and hardly touchin the games and puzzles and things. And I watched Miss Moore who is steady watchin us like she waitin for a sign. Like Mama Drewery watches the sky and sniffs the air and takes note of just how much slant is in the bird formation. Then me and Sugar bump smack into each other, so busy gazing at the toys, 'specially the sailboat. But we don't laugh and go into our fat-lady bumpstomach routine. We just stare at that price tag. Then Sugar run a finger over the whole boat. And I'm jealous and want to hit her. Maybe not her, but I sure want to punch somebody in the mouth.

"Whatcha bring us here for, Miss Moore?"

"You sound angry, Sylvia. Are you mad about something?" Givin me one of them grins like she tellin a grown-up joke that never turns out to be funny. And she's lookin very closely at me like maybe she plannin to do my portrait from memory. I'm mad, but I won't give her that satisfaction. So I slouch around the store bein very bored and say, "Let's go."

Me and Sugar at the back of the train watchin the tracks whizzin by large then small then gettin gobbled up in the dark. I'm thinkin about this tricky toy I saw in the store. A clown that somersaults on a bar then does chin-ups just cause you yank lightly at his leg. Cost $35. I could see me askin my mother for a $35 birthday clown. "You wanna who that costs what?" she'd say, cocking her head to the side to get a better view of the hole in my head. Thirty-five dollars could buy new bunk beds for Junior and Gretchen's boy. Thirty-five dollars and the whole household could go visit Granddaddy Nelson in the country. Thirty-five dollars would pay for the rent and the piano bill too. Who are these people that spend that much for performing clowns and $1000 for toy sailboats? What kinda work they do and how they live and how come we ain't in on it? Where we are is who we are, Miss Moore always pointin out. But it don't necessarily have to be that way, she always adds then waits for somebody to say that poor people have to wake up and demand their share of the pie and don't none of us know what kind of pie she talkin about in the first damn place. But she ain't so smart cause I still got her four dollars from the taxi and she sure ain't gettin it. Messin up my day with this shit. Sugar nudges me in my pocket and winks.

45   Miss Moore lines us up in front of the mailbox where we started from, seem like years ago, and I got a headache for thinkin so hard. And we lean all over each other so we can hold up under the draggy-ass lecture she always finishes us off with at the end before we thank her for borin us to tears. But she just looks at us like she readin tea leaves. Finally she say, "Well, what do you think of F. A. O. Schwarz?"

Rosie Giraffe mumbles, "White folks crazy."

"I'd like to go there again when I get my birthday money," says Mercedes, and we shove her out the pack so she has to lean on the mailbox by herself.

"I'd like a shower. Tiring day," say Flyboy.

Then Sugar surprises me by sayin, "You know, Miss Moore, I don't think all of us here put together eat in a year what that sailboat costs." And Miss Moore lights up like somebody goosed her. "And?" she say, urging Sugar on. Only I'm standin on her foot so she don't continue.

50   "Imagine for a minute what kind of society it is in which some people can spend on a toy what it would cost to feed a family of six or seven. What do you think?"

"I think," say Sugar pushing me off her feet like she never done before, cause I whip her ass in a minute, "that this is not much of a democracy if you ask me. Equal chance to pursue happiness means an equal crack at the dough, don't it?" Miss Moore is besides herself and I am disgusted with Sugar's treachery. So I stand on her foot one more time to see if she'll shove me. She shuts up, and Miss Moore looks at me, sorrowfully I'm thinkin. And somethin weird is goin on, I can feel it in my chest.

"Anybody else learn anything today?" lookin dead at me. I walk away and Sugar has to run to catch up and don't even seem to notice when I shrug her arm off my shoulder.

"Well, we got four dollars anyway," she says.

"Uh hunh."

55   "We could go to Hascombs and get half a chocolate layer and then go to the Sunset and still have plenty money for potato chips and ice cream sodas."

"Uh hunh."

"Race you to Hascombs," she say.

We start down the block and she gets ahead which is O.K. by me cause I'm going to the West End and then over to the Drive to think this day through. She can run if she want to and even run faster. But ain't nobody gonna beat me at nuthin.

[1972]

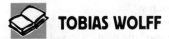

Topics for Critical Thinking and Writing

1. What is the point of Miss Moore's lesson? Why does Sylvia resist it?
2. Describe the relationship between Sugar and Sylvia. What is Sugar's function in the story?
3. What does the last line of the story suggest?
4. In a paragraph or two, characterize the narrator. Do not summarize the story—assume that your reader is familiar with it—but support your characterization by some references to episodes in the story and perhaps by a few brief quotations.

 **TOBIAS WOLFF**

Tobias Wolff was born in Alabama in 1945, but he grew up in the state of Washington. He left high school before graduating, served as an apprentice seaman and as a weight-guesser in a carnival, and then joined the army, where be served four years as a paratrooper. After his discharge from the army, he hired private tutors to enable him to pass the entrance examination to Oxford University. At Oxford he did spectacularly well, graduating with First Class Honors in English. Wolff has written stories, novels, and an autobiography (This Boy's Life); he now teaches writing at Syracuse University.

Powder

Just before Christmas my father took me skiing at Mount Baker. He'd had to fight for the privilege of my company, because my mother was still angry with him for sneaking me into a nightclub during his last visit, to see Thelonius Monk.

He wouldn't give up. He promised, hand on heart, to take good care of me and have me home for dinner on Christmas Eve, and she relented. But as we were checking out of the lodge that morning it began to snow, and in this snow he observed some quality that made it necessary for us to get in one last run. We got in several last runs. He was indifferent to my fretting. Snow whirled around us in bitter, blinding squalls, hissing like sand, and still we skied. As the lift bore us to the peak yet again, my father looked at his watch and said: "Criminey. This'll have to be a fast one."

By now I couldn't see the trail. There was no point in trying. I stuck to him like white on rice and did what he did and somehow made it to the bottom without sailing off a cliff. We returned our skis and my father put chains on the Austin-Healy while I swayed from foot to foot, clapping my mittens and wishing I were home. I could see everything. The green tablecloth, the plates with the holly pattern, the red candles waiting to be lit.

We passed a diner on our way out. "You want some soup?" my father asked. I shook my head. "Buck up," he said. "I'll get you there. Right, doctor?"

5   I was supposed to say, "Right, doctor," but I didn't say anything.

A state trooper waved us down outside the resort. A pair of sawhorses were blocking the road. The trooper came up to our car and bent down to my father's window. His face was bleached by the cold. Snowflakes clung to his eyebrows and to the fur trim of his jacket and cap.

"Don't tell me," my father said.

The trooper told him. The road was closed. It might get cleared, it might not. Storm took everyone by surprise. So much, so fast. Hard to get people moving. Christmas Eve. What can you do?

My father said: "Look. We're talking about four, five inches. I've taken this car through worse than that."

10   The trooper straightened up, boots creaking. His face was out of sight but I could hear him. "The road is closed."

My father sat with both hands on the wheel, rubbing the wood with his thumbs. He looked at the barricade for a long time. He seemed to be trying to master the idea of it. Then he thanked the trooper, and with a weird, old-maidy show of caution turned the car around. "Your mother will never forgive me for this," he said.

"We should have left before," I said. "Doctor."

He didn't speak to me again until we were both in a booth at the dinner, waiting for our burgers. "She won't forgive me," he said. "Do you understand? Never."

"I guess," I said, but no guesswork was required; she wouldn't forgive him.

15   "I can't let that happen." He bent toward me. "I'll tell you what I want. I want us to be all together again. Is that what you want?"

"Yes, sir."

He bumped my chin with his knuckles. "That's all I needed to hear."

When we finished eating he went to the pay phone in the back of the din-ner, then joined me in the booth again. I figured he'd called my mother, but he didn't give a report. He sipped at his coffee and stared out the window at the empty road. "Come on, come on," he said. A little while later he said, "Come on!" When the trooper's car went past, lights flashing, he got up and dropped some money on the check. "O.K. Vámanos."

The wind had died. The snow was falling straight down, less of it now; lighter. We drove away from the resort, right up to the barricade. "Move it," my father told me. When I looked at him he said, "What are you waiting for?" I got out and dragged one of the sawhorses aside, then put it back after he drove through. He pushed the door open for me. "Now you're an accomplice," he said. "We go down together." He put the car into gear and gave me a look. "Joke, doctor."

20   "Funny, doctor."

Down the first long stretch I watched the road behind us, to see if the trooper was on our tail. The barricade vanished. Then there was nothing but snow: snow on the road, snow kicking up from the chains, snow on the trees, snow in the sky; and our trail in the snow. I faced around and had a shock. The lie of the road behind us had been marked by our own tracks, but there were no tracks ahead of us. My father was breaking virgin snow between a line of tall trees. He was humming "Stars Fell on Alabama." I felt snow brush along the floorboards under my feet. To keep my hands from shaking, I clamped them between my knees.

My father grunted in a thoughtful way and said, "Don't ever try this yourself."

"I won't."

"That's what you say now, but someday you'll get your license and then you'll think you can do anything. Only you won't be able to do this. You need, I don't know—a certain instinct."

25   "Maybe I have it."

"You don't. You have your strong points, but not . . . this. I only mention it, because I don't want you to get the idea this is something just anybody can do. I'm a great driver. That's not a virtue, O.K.? It's just a fact, and one you should be aware of. Of course you have to give the old heap some credit, too—there aren't many cars I'd try this with. Listen!"

I listened. I heard the slap of the chains, the stiff, jerky rasps of the wipers, the purr of the engine. It really did purr. The car was almost new. My father couldn't afford it, and kept promising to sell it, but here it was.

I said, "Where do you think that policeman went to?"

"Are you warm enough?" He reached over and cranked up the blower. Then he turned off the wipers. We didn't need them. The clouds had brightened. A few sparse, feathery flakes drifted into our slipstream and were swept away. We left the trees and entered a broad field of snow that ran level for a while and then tilted sharply downward. Orange stakes had been planted at intervals in two parallel lines and my father steered a course between them, though they were far enough apart to leave considerable doubt in my mind as to where exactly the road lay. He was humming again, doing little scat riffs around the melody.

30   "O.K. then. What are my strong points?"

"Don't get me started," he said. "It'd take all day."

"Oh, right. Name one."

"Easy. You always think ahead."

True. I always thought ahead. I was a boy who kept his clothes on numbered hangers to insure proper rotation. I bothered my teachers for homework assignments far ahead of their due dates so I could make up schedules. I thought ahead, and that was why I knew that there would be other troopers waiting for us at the end of our ride, if we got there. What I did not know was that my father would wheedle and plead his way past them—he didn't sing "O Tannenbaum" but just about—and get me home for dinner, buying a little more time before my mother decided to make the split final. I knew we'd get caught; I was resigned to it. And maybe for this reason I stopped moping and began to enjoy myself.

35   Why not? This was one for the books. Like being in a speedboat, but better. You can't go downhill in a boat. And it was all ours. And it kept coming, the laden trees, the unbroken surface of snow, the sudden white vistas. Here and there I saw hints of the road, ditches, fences, stakes, but not so many that I could have found my way. But then I didn't have to. My father was driving. My father in his 48th year, rumpled, kind, bankrupt of honor, flushed with certainty. He was a great driver. All persuasion, no coercion. Such subtlety at the wheel, such tactful pedalwork. I actually trusted him. And the best was yet to come—the switchbacks and hairpins. Impossible to describe. Except maybe to say this: If you haven't driven fresh powder, you haven't driven.

[1992]

✐ Topics for Critical Thinking and Writing

1. How would you characterize the father?
2. How does the boy feel about his father?

📖 ALICE ELLIOTT DARK

Alice Elliott Dark received a B.A. in Oriental studies from the University of Pennsylvania, and an M.F.A. in creative writing from Antioch University. She has published a book of stories, Naked to the Waist *(1991), and she teaches at The Writer's Voice, in New York City.*

In the Gloaming

Her son wanted to talk again, suddenly. During the days, he still brooded, scowling at the swimming pool from the vantage point of his wheelchair, where he sat covered with blankets despite the summer heat. In the evenings, though, Laird became more like his old self—his *old* old self, really. He became sweeter, the way he'd been as a child, before he began to cloak himself with layers of irony and clever remarks. He spoke with an openness that astonished her. No one she knew talked that way—no man, at least. After he was asleep, Janet would run through the conversations in her mind, and realize what it was she wished she had said. She knew she was generally considered sincere, but that had more to do with her being a good listener than with how she expressed herself. She found it hard work to keep up with him, but it was the work she had pined for all her life.

A month earlier, after a particularly long and grueling visit with a friend who'd come up on the train from New York, Laird had declared a new policy: no visitors, no telephone calls. She didn't blame him. People who hadn't seen him for a while were often shocked to tears by his appearance, and, rather than having them cheer him up, he felt obliged to comfort them. She'd overheard bits of some of those conversations. The final one was no worse than the others, but he was fed up. He had said more than once that he wasn't cut out to be the brave one, the one who would inspire everybody to walk away from a visit with him feeling uplifted, shaking their heads in wonder. He had liked being the most handsome and missed it very much: he was not a good victim. When he had had enough he went into a self-imposed retreat, complete with a wall of silence and other ascetic practices that kept him busy for several weeks.

Then he softened. Not only did he want to talk again; he wanted to talk to *her*.

It began the night they ate outside on the terrace for the first time all summer. Afterward, Martin—Laird's father—got up to make a telephone call, but Janet stayed in her wicker chair, resting before clearing the table. It was one of those moments when she felt nostalgic for cigarettes. On nights like this, when the air was completely still, she used to blow her famous smoke rings for the children, dutifully obeying their commands to blow one through another or three in a row, or to make big, ropy circles that expanded as they floated up to the heavens. She did exactly what they wanted, for as long as they wanted, sometimes going through a quarter of a pack before they allowed her to stop. Incredibly, neither Anne nor Laird became smokers. Just the opposite; they nagged at her to quit, and were pleased when she finally did. She wished they had been just a little bit sorry; it was a part of their childhood coming to an end, after all.

5   Out of habit, she took note of the first lightning bug, the first star. The lawn darkened, and the flowers that had sulked in the heat all day suddenly released their perfumes. She laid her head back on the rim of the chair and closed her eyes. Soon she was following Laird's breathing, and found herself picking up the vital rhythms, breathing along. It was so peaceful, being near him like this. How many mothers spend so much time with their thirty-three-year-old sons? she thought. She had as much of him now as she had had when he was an infant; more, in a way, because she had the memory of the intervening years as well, to round out her thoughts about him. When they sat quietly together she felt as close to him as she ever had. It was still him in there, inside the failing shell. *She still enjoyed him.*

"The gloaming," he said, suddenly.

She nodded dreamily, automatically, then sat up. She turned to him. "What?" Although she had heard.

"I remember when I was little you took me over to the picture window and told me that in Scotland this time of day was called the 'gloaming.'"

Her skin tingled. She cleared her throat, quietly, taking care not to make too much of an event of his talking again. "You thought I said 'gloomy.'"

10   He gave a smile, then looked at her searchingly. "I always thought it hurt you somehow that the day was over, but you said it was a beautiful time because for a few moments the purple light made the whole world look like the Scottish Highlands on a summer night."

"Yes. As if all the earth were covered with heather."

"I'm sorry I never saw Scotland," he said.

"You're a Scottish lad nonetheless," she said. "At least on my side." She remembered offering to take him to Scotland once, but Laird hadn't been interested. By then, he was in college and already sure of his own destinations, which had diverged so thoroughly from hers. "I'm amazed you remember that conversation. You couldn't have been more than seven."

"I've been remembering a lot lately."

15   "Have you?"

"Mostly about when I was very small. I suppose it comes from having you take care of me again. Sometimes, when I wake up and see your face, I feel I can remember you looking in on me when I was in my crib. I remember your dresses."

"Oh, no!" She laughed lightly.

"You always had the loveliest expressions," he said.

She was astonished, caught off guard. Then, she had a memory, too—of her leaning over Laird's crib and suddenly having a picture of looking up at her own mother. "I know what you mean," she said.

20   "You do, don't you?"

He looked at her in a close, intimate way that made her self-conscious. She caught herself swinging her leg nervously, like a pendulum, and stopped.

"Mom," he said. "There are still a few things I need to do. I have to write a will, for one thing."

Her heart went flat. In his presence she had always maintained that he would get well. She wasn't sure she could discuss the other possibility.

"Thank you," he said.

25   "For what?"

"For not saying that there's plenty of time for that, or some similar sentiment."

"The only reason I didn't say it was to avoid the cliché, not because I don't believe it."

"You believe there is plenty of time?"

She hesitated; he noticed, and leaned forward slightly. "I believe there is time," she said.

30   "Even if I were healthy, it would be a good idea."

"I suppose."

"I don't want to leave it until it's too late. You wouldn't want me to suddenly leave everything to the nurses, would you?"

She laughed, pleased to hear him joking again. "All right, all right, I'll call the lawyer."

"That would be great." There was a pause. "Is this still your favorite time of day, Mom?"

35   "Yes, I suppose it is," she said, "although I don't think in terms of favorites anymore."

"Never mind favorites, then. What else do you like?"

"What do you mean?" she asked.

"I mean exactly that."

"I don't know. I care about all the ordinary things. You know what I like."

40   "Name one thing."

"I feel silly."

"Please?"

"All right. I like my patch of lilies of the valley under the trees over there. Now can we change the subject?"

"Name one more thing."

45   "Why?"

"I want to get to know you."

"Oh, Laird, there's nothing to know."

"I don't believe that for a minute."

"But it's true. I'm average. The only extraordinary thing about me is my children."

50   "All right," he said. "Then let's talk about how you feel about me."

"Do you flirt with your nurses like this when I'm not around?"

"I don't dare. They've got me where they want me." He looked at her. "You're changing the subject."

She smoothed her skirt. "I know how you feel about church, but if you need to talk I'm sure the minister would be glad to come over. Or if you would rather have a doctor . . ."

He laughed.

55   "What?"

"That you still call psychiatrists 'doctors.'"

She shrugged.

"I don't need a professional. Ma." He laced his hands and pulled at them as he struggled for words.

"What can I do?" she asked.

60   He met her gaze. "You're where I come from. I need to know about you."

That night she lay awake, trying to think of how she could help, of what, aside from her time, she had to offer. She couldn't imagine.

She was anxious the next day when he was sullen again, but the next night, and on each succeeding night, the dusk worked its spell. She set dinner on the table outside, and afterward, when Martin had vanished into the maw of his study, she and Laird began to speak. The air around them seemed to crackle with the energy they were creating in their effort to know and be known. Were other people so close, she wondered. She never had been, not to anybody. Certainly she and Martin had never really connected, not soul to soul, and with her friends, no matter how loyal and reliable, she always had a sense of what she could do that would alienate them. Of course, her friends had the option of cutting her off, and Martin could always ask for a divorce, whereas Laird was a captive audience. Parents and children were all captive audiences to each other; in view of this, it was amazing how little comprehension there was of one another's stories. Everyone stopped paying attention so early on, thinking they had figured it all out. She recognized that she was as guilty of this as anyone. She was still surprised whenever she went over to her daughter's house and saw how neat she was; in her mind, Anne was still a sloppy teenager who threw sweaters into the corner of her closet and candy wrappers under her bed. It still surprised her that Laird wasn't interested in girls. He had been, hadn't he? She remembered lying awake listening for him to come home, hoping that he was smart enough to apply what he knew about the facts of life, to take precautions.

Now she had the chance to let go of these old notions. It wasn't that she liked everything about Laird—there was much that remained foreign to her—but she wanted to know about all of it. As she came to her senses every morning in the moment or two after she awoke, she found herself aching with love and gratitude, as if he were a small, perfect creature again and she could look forward to a day of watching him grow. Quickly, she became greedy for their evenings. She replaced her half-facetious, half-hopeful reading of the horoscope in the daily newspaper with a new habit of tracking the time the sun would set, and drew satisfaction from seeing it come earlier as the summer waned; it meant she didn't have to wait as long. She took to sleeping late, shortening the day even more. It was ridiculous, she knew. She was behaving like a girl with a crush, behaving absurdly. It was a feeling she had thought she'd never have again, and now here it was. She immersed herself in it, living her life for the twilight moment when his eyes would begin to glow, the signal that he was stirring into consciousness. Then her real day would begin.

"Dad ran off quickly," he said one night. She had been wondering when he would mention it.

65   "He had a phone call to make," she said automatically.

Laird looked directly into her eyes, his expression one of gentle reproach. He was letting her know he had caught her in the central lie of her life, which was that she understood Martin's obsession with his work. She averted her gaze. The truth was that she had never understood. Why couldn't he sit with her for half an hour after dinner, or, if not with her, why not with his dying son?

She turned sharply to look at Laird. The word "dying" had sounded so loudly in her mind that she wondered if she had spoken it, but he showed no reaction. She wished she hadn't even thought it. She tried to stick to good thoughts in his presence. When she couldn't, and he had a bad night afterward, she blamed herself, as her efficient memory dredged up all the books and magazine articles she had read emphasizing the effect of psychological factors on the course of the disease. She didn't entirely believe it, but she felt compelled to give the benefit of the doubt to every theory that might help. It couldn't do any harm to think positively. And if it gave him a few more months . . .

"I don't think Dad can stand to be around me."

"That's not true." It was true.

70   "Poor Dad. He's always been a hypochondriac—we have that in common. He must hate this."

"He just wants you to get well."

"If that's what he wants, I'm afraid I'm going to disappoint him again. At least this will be the last time I let him down."

He said this merrily, with the old, familiar light darting from his eyes. She allowed herself to be amused. He had always been fond of teasing, and held no subject sacred. As the de facto authority figure in the house—Martin hadn't been home enough to be the real disciplinarian—she had often been forced to reprimand Laird, but, in truth, she shared his sense of humor. She responded to it now by leaning over to cuff him on the arm. It was an automatic response, prompted by a burst of high spirits that took no notice of the circumstances. It was a mistake. Even through the thickness of his terrycloth robe, her knuckles knocked on bone. There was nothing left of him.

"It's his loss," she said, the shock of Laird's thinness making her serious again. It was the furthest she would go in criticizing Martin. She had always felt it her duty to maintain a benign image of him for the children. He had become a character of her invention, with a whole range of postulated emotions whereby he missed them when he was away on a business trip and thought of them every few minutes when he had to work late. Some years earlier, when she was secretly seeing a doctor—a psychiatrist—she had finally admitted to herself that Martin was never going to be the lover she had dreamed of. He was an ambitious, competitive, self-absorbed man who probably should never have got married. It was such a relief to be able to face it that she wanted to share the news with her children, only to discover that they were dependent on the myth. They could hate his work, but they could not bring themselves to believe he had any choice in the matter. She had dropped the subject.

75   "Thank you, Ma. It's his loss in your case, too."

A throbbing began behind her eyes, angering her. The last thing she wanted to do was cry. There would be plenty of time for that. "It's not all his fault," she said when she had regained some measure of control. "I'm not very good at talking about myself. I was brought up not to."

"So was I," he said.

"Yes, I suppose you were."

"Luckily, I didn't pay any attention." He grinned.

80 "I hope not," she said, and meant it. "Can I get you anything?"

"A new immune system?"

She rolled her eyes, trying to disguise the way his joke had touched on her prayers. "Very funny. I was thinking more along the lines of an iced tea or an extra blanket."

"I'm fine. I'm getting tired, actually."

Her entire body went on the alert, and she searched his face anxiously for signs of deterioration. Her nerves darted and pricked whenever he wanted anything; her adrenaline rushed. The fight-or-flight response, she supposed. She had often wanted to flee, but had forced herself to stay, to fight with what few weapons she had. She responded to his needs, making sure there was a fresh, clean set of sheets ready when he was tired, food when he was hungry. It was what she could do.

85 "Shall I get a nurse?" She pushed her chair back from the table.

"O.K.," Laird said weakly. He stretched out his hand to her, and the incipient moonlight illuminated his skin so it shone like alabaster. His face had turned ashy. It was a sight that made her stomach drop. She ran for Maggie, and by the time they returned Laird's eyes were closed, his head lolling to one side. Automatically, Janet looked for a stirring in his chest. There it was: his shoulders expanded; he still breathed. Always, in the second before she saw movement, she became cold and clinical as she braced herself for the possibility of discovering that he was dead.

Maggie had her fingers on his wrist and was counting his pulse against the second hand on her watch, her lips moving. She laid his limp hand back on his lap. "Fast," she pronounced.

"I'm not surprised," Janet said, masking her fear with authority. "We had a long talk."

Maggie frowned. "Now I'll have to wake him up again for his meds."

90 "Yes, I suppose that's true. I forgot about that."

Janet wheeled him into his makeshift room downstairs and helped Maggie lift him into the rented hospital bed. Although he weighed almost nothing, it was really a job for two; his weight was dead weight. In front of Maggie, she was all brusque efficiency, except for the moment when her fingers strayed to touch Laird's pale cheek and she prayed she hadn't done any harm.

"Who's your favorite author?" he asked one night.

"Oh, there are so many," she said.

"Your real favorite."

95 She thought. "The truth is there are certain subjects I find attractive more than certain authors. I seem to read in cycles, to fulfill an emotional yearning."

"Such as?"

"Books about people who go off to live in Africa or Australia or the South Seas."

He laughed. "That's fairly self-explanatory. What else?"

"When I really hate life I enjoy books about real murders. 'True crime,' I think they're called now. They're very punishing."

100   "Is that what's so compelling about them? I could never figure it out. I just know that at certain times I loved the gore, even though I felt absolutely disgusted with myself for being interested in it."

"You need to think about when those times were. That will tell you a lot." She paused. "I don't like reading about sex."

"Big surprise!"

"No, no," she said. "It's not for the reason you think, or not only for that reason. You see me as a prude, I know, but remember, it's part of a mother's job to come across that way. Although perhaps I went a bit far . . ."

He shrugged amiably. "Water under the bridge. But go on about sex."

105   "I think it should be private. I always feel as though these writers are showing off when they describe a sex scene. They're not really trying to describe sex, but to demonstrate that they're not afraid to write about it. As if they're thumbing their noses at their mothers."

He made a moue.

Janet went on. "You don't think there's an element of that? I *do* question their motives, because I don't think sex can ever actually be portrayed—the sensations and the emotions are . . . beyond language. If you only describe the mechanics, the effect is either clinical or pornographic, and if you try to describe intimacy instead, you wind up with abstractions. The only sex you could describe fairly well is bad sex—and who wants to read about that, for God's sake, when everyone is having bad sex of their own?"

"Mother!" He was laughing helplessly, his arms hanging limply over the sides of his chair.

"I mean it. To me it's like reading about someone using the bathroom."

110   "Good grief!"

"Now who's the prude?"

"I never said I wasn't," he said. "Maybe we should change the subject."

She looked out across the land. The lights were on in other people's houses, giving the evening the look of early fall. The leaves were different, too, becoming droopy. The grass was dry, even with all the watering and tending from the gardener. The summer was nearly over.

"Maybe we shouldn't," she said. "I've been wondering. Was that side of life satisfying for you?"

115   "Ma, tell me you're not asking me about my sex life."

She took her napkin and folded it carefully, lining up the edges and running her fingers along the hems. She felt very calm, very pulled together and all of a piece, as if she'd finally got the knack of being a dignified woman. She threaded her fingers and laid her hands in her lap. "I'm asking about your love life," she said. "Did you love, and were you loved in return?"

"Yes."

"I'm glad."

"That was easy," he said.

120   "Oh, I've gotten very easy, in my old age."

"Does Dad know about this?" His eyes were twinkling wickedly.

"Don't be fresh," she said.

"You started it."

"Then I'm stopping it. Now."

125   He made a funny face, and then another, until she could no longer keep from smiling. His routine carried her back to memories of his childhood efforts to charm her: watercolors of her favorite vistas (unrecognizable without the captions), bouquets of violets self-consciously flung into her lap, chores performed without prompting. He had always gone too far, then backtracked to regain even footing. She had always allowed herself to be wooed.

Suddenly she realized: Laird had been the love of her life.

One night it rained hard. Janet decided to serve the meal in the kitchen, since Martin was out. They ate in silence; she was freed from the compulsion to keep up the steady stream of chatter that she used to affect when Laird hadn't talked at all; now she knew she could save her words for afterward. He ate nothing but comfort foods lately: mashed potatoes, vanilla ice cream, rice pudding. The days of his strict macrobiotic regime, and all the cooking classes she had taken in order to help him along with it, were past. His body was essentially a thing of the past, too; when he ate, he was feeding what was left of his mind. He seemed to want to recapture the cosseted feeling he'd had when he'd been sick as a child and she would serve him flat ginger ale, and toast soaked in cream, and play endless card games with him, using his blanket-covered legs as a table. In those days, too, there'd been a general sense of giving way to illness: then, he let himself go completely because he knew he would soon be better and active and have a million things expected of him again. Now he let himself go because he had fought long enough.

Finally, he pushed his bowl toward the middle of the table, signaling that he was finished. (His table manners had gone to pieces. Who cared?) She felt a light, jittery excitement, the same jazzy feeling she got when she was in a plane that was picking up speed on the runway. She arranged her fork and knife on the rim of her plate and pulled her chair in closer. "I had an odd dream last night," she said.

His eyes remained dull.

130   She waited uncertainly, thinking that perhaps she had started to talk too soon. "Would you like something else to eat?"

He shook his head. There was no will in his expression: his refusal was purely physical, a gesture coming from the satiation in his stomach. An animal walking away from its bowl, she thought.

To pass the time, she carried the dishes to the sink, gave them a good hot rinse, and put them in the dishwasher. She carried the ice cream to the counter, pulled a spoon from the drawer and scraped off a mouthful of the thick, creamy residue that stuck to the inside of the lid. She ate it without thinking, so the sudden sweetness caught her by surprise. All the while she kept track of Laird, but every time she thought she noticed signs of his readiness to talk and hurried back to the table, she found his face still blank.

She went to the window. The lawn had become a floodplain and was filled with broad pools; the branches of the evergreens sagged, and the sky was the same uniform grayish yellow it had been since morning. She saw him focus his gaze on the line where the treetops touched the heavens, and she understood. There was no lovely interlude on this rainy night, no heathered dusk. The gray landscape had taken the light out of him.

"I'm sorry," she said aloud, as if it were her fault.

135   He gave a tiny, helpless shrug.

She hovered for a few moments, hoping, but his face was slack, and she gave up. She felt utterly forsaken, too disappointed and agitated to sit with him and watch the rain. "It's all right," she said. "It's a good night to watch television."

She wheeled him to the den and left him with Maggie, then did not know what to do with herself. She had no contingency plan for this time. It was usually the one period of the day when she did not need the anesthesia of tennis games, bridge lessons, volunteer work, errands. She had not considered the present possibility. For some time, she hadn't given any thought to what Martin would call "the big picture." Her conversations with Laird had lulled her into inventing a parallel big picture of her own. She realized that a part of her had worked out a whole scenario: the summer evenings would blend into fall; then, gradually, the winter would arrive, heralding chats by the fire, Laird resting his feet on the pigskin ottoman in the den while she dutifully knitted her yearly Christmas sweaters for Anne's children.

She had allowed herself to imagine a future. That had been her mistake. This silent, endless evening was her punishment, a reminder of how things really were.

She did not know where to go in her own house, and ended up wandering through the rooms, propelled by a vague, hunted feeling. Several times, she turned around, expecting someone to be there, but, of course, no one ever was. She was quite alone. Eventually, she realized that she was imagining a person in order to give material properties to the source of her wounds. She was inventing a villain. There should be a villain, shouldn't there? There should be an enemy, a devil, an evil force that could be driven out. Her imagination had provided it with aspects of a corporeal presence so she could pretend, for a moment, that there was a real enemy hovering around her, someone she could have the police come and take away. But the enemy was part of Laird, and neither he nor she nor any of the doctors or experts or ministers could separate the two.

140 She went upstairs and took a shower. She barely paid attention to her own body anymore, and only noticed abstractly that the water was too hot, her skin turning pink. Afterward, she sat on the chaise longue in her bedroom and tried to read. She heard something; she leaned forward and cocked her head toward the sound. Was that Laird's voice? Suddenly she believed that he had begun to talk after all—she believed he was talking to Maggie. She dressed and went downstairs. He was alone in the den, alone with the television. He didn't hear or see her. She watched him take a drink from a cup, his hand shaking badly. It was a plastic cup with a straw poking through the lid, the kind used by small children while they are learning to drink. It was supposed to prevent accidents, but it couldn't stop his hands from trembling. He managed to spill the juice anyway.

Laird had always coveted the decadent pile of cashmere lap blankets she had collected over the years in the duty-free shops of the various British airports. Now he wore one around his shoulders, one over his knees. She remembered similar balmy nights when he would arrive home from soccer practice after dark, a towel slung around his neck.

"I suppose it has to be in the church," he said.

"I think it should," she said, "but it's up to you."

"I guess it's not the most timely moment to make a statement about my personal disbeliefs. But I'd like you to keep it from being too lugubrious. No lilies, for instance."

145 "God forbid."

"And have some decent music."

"Such as?"

"I had an idea, but now I can't remember."

He pressed his hands to his eyes. His fingers were so transparent that they looked as if he were holding them over a flashlight.

150 "Please buy a smashing dress, something mournful yet elegant."

"All right."

"And don't wait until the last minute."

She didn't reply.

Janet gave up on the idea of a rapprochement between Martin and Laird; she felt freer when she stopped hoping for it. Martin rarely came home for dinner anymore. Perhaps he was having an affair? It was a thought she'd never allowed herself to have before, but it didn't threaten her now. Good for him, she even decided, in her strongest, most magnanimous moments. Good for him if he's actually feeling bad and trying to do something to make himself feel better.

155 Anne was brave and chipper during her visits, yet when she walked back out to her car, she would wrap her arms around her ribs and shudder. "I don't know how you do it, Mom. Are you really all right?" she always asked, with genuine concern.

"Anne's become such a hopeless matron," Laird always said, with fond exasperation, when he and his mother were alone again later. Once, Janet began to tease him for finally coming to friendly terms with his sister, but she cut it short when she saw that he was blinking furiously.

They were exactly the children she had hoped to have: a companionable girl, a mischievous boy. It gave her great pleasure to see them together. She did not try to listen to their conversations but watched from a distance, usually from the kitchen as she prepared them a snack reminiscent of their childhood, like watermelon boats or lemonade. Then she would walk Anne to the car, their similar good shoes clacking across the gravel. They hugged, pressing each other's arms, and their brief embraces buoyed them up—forbearance and grace passing back and forth between them like a piece of shared clothing, designated for use by whoever needed it most. It was the kind of parting toward which she had aimed her whole life, a graceful, secure parting at the close of a peaceful afternoon. After Anne left, Janet always had a tranquil moment or two as she walked back to the house through the humid September air. Everything was so still. Occasionally there were the hums and clicks of a lawnmower or the shrieks of a band of children heading home from school. There were the insects and the birds. It was a straightforward, simple life she had chosen. She had tried never to ask for too much, and to be of use. Simplicity had been her hedge against bad luck. It had worked for so long. For a brief moment, as she stepped lightly up the single slate stair and through the door, her legs still harboring all their former vitality, she could pretend her luck was still holding.

Then she would glance out the window and there would be the heart-catching sight of Laird, who would never again drop by for a casual visit. Her chest would ache and flutter, a cave full of bats.

Perhaps she had asked for too much, after all.

160 "What did you want to be when you grew up?" Laird asked.

"I was expected to be a wife and mother. I accepted that. I wasn't a rebel."

"There must have been something else."

"No," she said. "Oh, I guess I had all the usual fantasies of the day, of being the next Amelia Earhart or Margaret Mead, but that was all they were—fantasies. I wasn't even close to being brave enough. Can you imagine me flying across the ocean on my own?" She laughed and looked over for his laughter, but he had fallen asleep.

A friend of Laird's had somehow got the mistaken information that Laird had died, so she and Martin received a condolence letter. There was a story about a time a few years back when the friend was with Laird on a bus in New York. They had been sitting behind two older women, waitresses who began to discuss their income taxes, trying to decide how much of their tip income to declare to sound realistic so they wouldn't attract an audit. Each woman offered up bits of folk wisdom on the subject, describing in detail her particular situation. During a lull in the conversation, Laird stood up.

165   "Excuse me, I couldn't help overhearing," he said, leaning over them. "May I have your names and addresses, please? I work for the IRS."

The entire bus fell silent as everyone watched to see what would happen next. Laird took a small notebook and pen from the inside pocket of his jacket. He faced his captive audience. "I'm part of a new IRS outreach program," he told the group. "For the next ten minutes I'll be taking confessions. Does anyone have anything he or she wants to tell me?"

Smiles. Soon the whole bus was talking, comparing notes—when they'd first realized he was kidding, and how scared they had been before they caught on. It was difficult to believe these were the same New Yorkers who were supposed to be so gruff and isolated.

"Laird was the most vital, funniest person I ever met," his friend wrote.

Now, in his wheelchair, he faced off against slow-moving flies, waving them away.

170   "The gloaming," Laird said.

Janet looked up from her knitting, startled. It was midafternoon, and the living room was filled with bright October sun. "Soon," she said.

He furrowed his brow. A little flash of confusion passed through his eyes, and she realized that for him it was already dark.

He tried to straighten his shawl, his hands shaking. She jumped up to help; then, when he pointed to the fireplace, she quickly laid the logs as she wondered what was wrong. Was he dehydrated. She thought she recalled that a dimming of vision was a sign of dehydration. She tried to remember what else she had read or heard, but even as she grasped for information, facts, her instincts kept interrupting with a deeper, more dreadful thought that vibrated through her, rattling her and making her gasp as she often did when remembering her mistakes, things she wished she hadn't said or done, wished she had the chance to do over. She knew what was wrong, and yet she kept turning away from the truth, her mind spinning in every other possible direction as she worked on the fire, only vaguely noticing how wildly she made the sparks fly as she pumped the old bellows.

Her work was mechanical—she had made hundreds of fires—and soon there was nothing left to do. She put the screen up and pushed him close, then leaned over to pull his flannel pajamas down to meet his socks, protecting his bare shins. The sun streamed in around him, making him appear trapped between bars of light. She resumed her knitting, with mechanical hands.

175   "The gloaming," he said again. It did sound somewhat like "gloomy," because his speech was slurred.

"When all the world is purple," she said, hearing herself sound falsely bright. She wasn't sure whether he wanted her to talk. It was some time since he had talked—not long, really, in other people's lives, perhaps two weeks—but she had gone on with their conversations, gradually expanding into the silence until she was telling him stories and he was listening. Sometimes, when his eyes closed, she trailed off and began to drift. There would be a pause that she didn't always realize she was making, but if it went on too long he would call out "Mom?" with an edge of panic in his voice, as if he were waking from a nightmare. Then she would resume, trying to create a seamless bridge between what she had been thinking and where she had left off.

"It was really your grandfather who gave me my love for the gloaming," she said. "Do you remember him talking about it?" She looked up politely, expectantly, as if Laird might offer her a conversational reply. He seemed to like hearing the sound of her voice, so she went on, her needles clicking. Afterward, she could never remember for sure at what point she had stopped talking and had floated off into a jumble of her own thoughts, afraid to move, afraid to look up, afraid to know at which exact moment she became alone. All she knew was that at a certain point the fire was in danger of dying out entirely, and when she got up to stir the embers she glanced at him in spite of herself and saw that his fingers were making knitting motions over his chest, the way people did as they were dying. She knew that if she went to get the nurse, Laird would be gone by the time she returned, so she went and stood behind him, leaning over to press her face against his, sliding her hands down his busy arms, helping him along with his fretful stitches until he finished this last piece of work.

Later, after the most pressing calls had been made and Laird's body had been taken away, Janet went up to his old room and lay down on one of the twin beds. She had changed the room into a guest room when he went off to college, replacing his things with guest room decor, thoughtful touches such as luggage racks at the foot of each bed, a writing desk stocked with paper and pens, heavy wooden hangers and shoe trees. She made an effort to remember the room as it had been when he was a little boy: she had chosen a train motif, then had to redecorate when Laird decided trains were silly. He had wanted it to look like a jungle, so she had hired an art student to paint a jungle mural on the walls. When he decided *that* was silly, he hadn't bothered her to do anything about it, but had simply marked time until he could move on.

Anne came over, offered to stay, but was relieved to be sent home to her children.

180   Presently, Martin came in. Janet was watching the trees turn to mere silhouettes against the darkening sky, fighting the urge to pick up a true-crime book, a debased urge. He lay down on the other bed.

"I'm sorry," he said.

"It's so wrong," she said angrily. She hadn't felt angry until that moment; she had saved it up for him. "A child shouldn't die before his parents. A young man shouldn't spend his early thirties wasting away talking to his mother. He should be out in the world. He shouldn't be thinking about me, or what I care about, or my opinions. He shouldn't have had to return my love to me—it was his to squander. Now I have it all back and I don't know what I'm supposed to do with it," she said.

She could hear Martin weeping in the darkness. He sobbed, and her anger veered away.

They were quiet for some time.

185 "Is there going to be a funeral?" Martin asked finally.

"Yes. We should start making the arrangements."

"I suppose he told you what he wanted."

"In general. He couldn't decide about the music."

She heard Martin roll onto his side, so that he was facing her across the narrow chasm between the beds. He was still in his office clothes. "I remember being very moved by the bagpipes at your father's funeral."

190 It was an awkward offering, to be sure, awkward and late, and seemed to come from someone on the periphery of her life who knew her only slightly. It didn't matter; it was perfectly right. Her heart rushed toward it.

"I think Laird would have liked that idea very much," she said.

It was the last moment of the gloaming, the last moment of the day her son died. In a breath, it would be night; the moon hovered behind the trees, already rising to claim the sky, and she told herself she might as well get on with it. She sat up and was running her toes across the bare floor, searching for her shoes, when Martin spoke again, in a tone she used to hear on those long-ago nights when he rarely got home until after the children were in bed and he relied on her to fill him in on what they'd done that day. It was the same curious, shy, deferential tone that had always made her feel as though all the frustrations and boredom and mistakes and rushes of feeling in her days as a mother did indeed add up to something of importance, and she decided that the next round of telephone calls could wait while she answered the question he asked her: "Please tell me—what else did my boy like?"

[1993]

✏ Topics for Critical Thinking and Writing

1. Good writers give careful attention to their choice of titles. Describe your response to the title of this story when you first encountered it. And then describe your response to the title after you had read the story and taken note of how the phrase "in the gloaming" is used.

2. Janet feels a special connection to her son. What is the nature of this connection, and how is their relationship different from that between Janet and Martin, and Martin and Laird?

3. How much does Dark tell us about Laird's illness and how he acquired it? Should she have given us more information and background than she does? Explain why you think she chose not to.

4. Why does Dark conclude with a scene between Janet and Martin? Is this ending an effective one, or would a different ending—perhaps one that focuses on the final moments between Janet and Laird—have been more effective?

Thinking Critically About a Short Story

A Casebook on Ralph Ellison's "Battle Royal"

In this section, we give a short story by the African-American writer and critic Ralph Ellison (1914–94), "Battle Royal," first published in 1947 and later included as Chapter One in the novel *Invisible Man* (1952), and we also give the following related material:

1. An influential, and controversial, speech delivered in 1895 by the African-American educator Booker T. Washington (1856–1915), founder in 1881 and first president of Tuskegee Normal and Industrial Institute. The speech was reprinted in Washington's book, *Up from Slavery* (1901), which was among the most widely read books of the period.
2. Excerpts from *The Souls of Black Folk* (1903), by the African-American historian, cultural critic, and man-of-letters W. E. B. Du Bois (1868–1963), which includes his critique of Washington's policies.
3. A photograph of the statue of Booker T. Washington at Tuskegee, to which Ellison's narrator refers.
4. A commentary on segregation in the South, from *An American Dilemma* (1944), a landmark study of race relations in the United States, written by the Swedish economist and sociologist Gunnar Myrdal (1898–1987).
5. An explanation by Ellison, from an interview published in 1955, of his use of folk material and myth in his fiction.
6. Ellison's reflections (1964) on his youth in Oklahoma and educational experiences at Tuskegee, where he was enrolled as a student in the 1930s.

RALPH ELLISON

Ralph Ellison (1914–94) was born in Oklahoma City. His father died when Ellison was three, and his mother supported herself and her child by working as a domestic. A trumpeter since boyhood, after graduating from high school Ellison went to study music at Tuskegee Institute, a black college in Alabama founded by Booker T. Washington. In 1936 he dropped out of Tuskegee and went to Harlem to study music com-

position and the visual arts; there he met Langston Hughes and Richard Wright, who encouraged him to turn to fiction. Ellison published stories and essays, and in 1942 became the managing editor of Negro Quarterly. During the Second World War he served in the Merchant Marine. After the war he returned to writing and later taught in universities.

"Battle Royal" was first published in 1947 and slightly revised (a transitional paragraph was added at the end of the story) for the opening chapter of Ellison's novel, The Invisible Man (1952), a book cited by Book-Week as "the most significant work of fiction written by an American" in the years between 1945 and 1965. In addition to publishing stories and one novel, Ellison published critical essays, which are brought together in The Collected Essays of Ralph Ellison (1995).

Battle Royal

It goes a long way back, some twenty years. All my life I had been looking for something, and everywhere I turned someone tried to tell me what it was. I accepted their answers too, though they were often in contradiction and even self-contradictory. I was naïve. I was looking for myself and asking everyone except myself questions which I, and only I, could answer. It took me a long time and much painful boomeranging of my expectations to achieve a realization everyone else appears to have been born with: That I am nobody but myself. But first I had to discover that I am an invisible man!

And yet I am no freak of nature, nor of history. I was in the cards, other things having been equal (or unequal) eighty-five years ago. I am not ashamed of my grandparents for having been slaves. I am only ashamed of myself for having at one time been ashamed. About eighty-five years ago they were told that they

Gordon Parks, *Ralph Ellison.*
Parks, an African-American photographer with an international reputation has published many books of photographs, including *Camera Portraits,* where this picture appears.

were free, united with others of our country in everything pertaining to the common good, and, in everything social, separate like the fingers of the hand. And they believed it. They exulted in it. They stayed in their place, worked hard, and brought up my father to do the same. But my grandfather is the one. He was an odd old guy, my grandfather, and I am told I take after him. It was he who caused the trouble. On his deathbed he called my father to him and said, "Son, after I'm gone I want you to keep up the good fight. I never told you, but our life is a war and I have been a traitor all my born days, a spy in the enemy's country ever since I give up my gun back in the Reconstruction. Live with your head in the lion's mouth. I want you to overcome 'em with yeses, undermine 'em with grins, agree 'em to death and destruction, let 'em swoller you till they vomit or bust wide open." They thought the old man had gone out of his mind. He had been the meekest of men. The younger children were rushed from the room, the shades drawn and the flame of the lamp turned so low that it sputtered on the wick like the old man's breathing. "Learn it to the younguns," he whispered fiercely; then he died.

But my folks were more alarmed over his last words than over his dying. It was as though he had not died at all, his words caused so much anxiety. I was warned emphatically to forget what he had said and, indeed, this is the first time it has been mentioned outside the family circle. It has a tremendous effect upon me, however. I could never be sure of what he meant. Grandfather had been a quiet old man who never made any trouble, yet on his deathbed he had called himself a traitor and a spy, and he had spoken of his meekness as a dangerous activity. It became a constant puzzle which lay unanswered in the back of my mind. And whenever things went well for me I remembered my grandfather and felt guilty and uncomfortable. It was as though I was carrying out his advice in spite of myself. And to make it worse, everyone loved me for it. I was praised by the most lily-white men of the town. I was considered an example of desirable conduct—just as my grandfather had been. And what puzzled me was that the old man had defined it as *treachery*. When I was praised for my conduct I felt a guilt that in some way I was doing something that was really against the wishes of the white folks, that if they had understood they would have desired me to act just the opposite, that I should have been sulky and mean, and that that really would have been what they wanted, even though they were fooled and thought they wanted me to act as I did. It made me afraid that some day they would look upon me as a traitor and I would be lost. Still I was more afraid to act any other way because they didn't like that at all. The old man's words were like a curse. On my graduation day I delivered an oration in which I showed that humility was the secret, indeed, the very essence of progress. (Not that I believed this—how could I, remembering my grandfather?—I only believed that it worked.) It was a great success. Everyone praised me and I was invited to give the speech at a gathering of the town's leading white citizens. It was a triumph for our whole community.

It was in the main ballroom of the leading hotel. When I got there I discovered that it was on the occasion of a smoker, and I was told that since I was to be there anyway I might as well take part in the battle royal to be fought by some of my schoolmates as part of the entertainment. The battle royal came first.

5　　All of the town's big shots were there in their tuxedoes, wolfing down the buffet foods, drinking beer and whiskey and smoking black cigars. It was a large room with a high ceiling. Chairs were arranged in neat rows around three sides of a portable boxing ring. The fourth side was clear, revealing a gleaming space of polished floor. I had some misgivings over the battle royal, by the way. Not from a distaste for fighting, but because I didn't care too much for the other fellows who were to take part. They were tough guys who seemed to have no grandfather's curse worrying their minds. No one could mistake their toughness. And besides, I suspected that fighting a battle royal might detract from the dignity of my speech. In those pre-invisible days I visualized myself as a potential Booker T. Washington. But the other fellows didn't care too much for me either, and there were nine of them. I felt superior to them in my way, and I didn't like the manner in which we were all crowded together into the servants' elevator. Nor did they like my being there. In fact, as the warmly lighted floors flashed past the elevator we had words over the fact that I, by taking part in the fight, had knocked one of their friends out of a night's work.

We were led out of the elevator through a rococo hall into an anteroom and told to get into our fighting togs. Each of us was issued a pair of boxing gloves and ushered out into the big mirrored hall, which we entered looking cautiously about us and whispering, lest we might accidentally be heard above the noise of the room. It was foggy with cigar smoke. And already the whiskey was taking effect. I was shocked to see some of the most important men of the town quite tipsy. They were all there—bankers, lawyers, judges, doctors, fire chiefs, teachers, merchants. Even one of the more fashionable pastors. Something we could not see was going on up front. A clarinet was vibrating sensuously and the men were standing up and moving eagerly forward. We were a small tight group, clustered together, our bare upper bodies touching and shining with anticipatory sweat; while up front the big shots were becoming increasingly excited over something we still could not see. Suddenly I heard the school superintendent, who had told me to come, yell. "Bring up the shines, gentlemen! Bring up the little shines!"

We were rushed up to the front of the ballroom, where it smelled even more strongly of tobacco and whiskey. Then we were pushed into place. I almost wet my pants. A sea of faces, some hostile, some amused, ringed around us, and in the center, facing us, stood a magnificent blonde—stark naked. There was dead silence. I felt a blast of cold air chill me. I tried to back away, but they were behind me and around me. Some of the boys stood with lowered heads, trembling. I felt a wave of irrational guilt and fear. My teeth chattered, my skin turned to goose flesh, my knees knocked. Yet I was strongly attracted and looked in spite of myself. Had the price of looking been blindness, I would have looked. The hair was yellow like that of a circus kewpie doll, the face heavily powdered and rouged, as though to form an abstract mask, the eyes hollow and smeared a cool blue, the color of a baboon's butt. I felt a desire to spit upon her as my eyes brushed slowly over her body. Her breasts were firm and round as the domes of East Indian temples, and I stood so close as to see the fine skin texture and beads of pearly perspiration glistening like dew around the pink and erected buds of her nipples. I wanted at one and the same time to run from the room, to sink through the floor, or go to her and cover her from my eyes and the eyes of the others with my body; to feel the soft thighs, to caress her and destroy her, to love her and murder her, to hide from her, and yet to stroke where below the small American flag tattooed upon her belly her thighs formed a capital V. I had a notion that of all in the room she saw only me with her impersonal eyes.

And then she began to dance, a slow sensuous movement; the smoke of a hundred cigars clinging to her like the thinnest of veils. She seemed like a fair bird-girl girdled in veils calling to me from the angry surface of some gray and threatening sea. I was transported. Then I became aware of the clarinet playing and the big shots yelling at us. Some threatened us if we looked and others if we did not. On my right I saw one boy faint. And now a man grabbed a silver pitcher from a table and stepped close as he dashed ice water upon him and stood him up and forced two of us to support him as his head hung and moans issued from his thick bluish lips. Another boy began to plead to go home. He was the largest of the group, wearing dark red fighting trunks much too small to conceal the erection which projected from him as though in answer to the insinuating low-registered moans of the clarinet. He tried to hide himself with his boxing gloves.

And all the while the blonde continued dancing, smiling faintly at the big shots who watched her with fascination, and faintly smiling at our fear. I noticed a certain merchant who followed her hungrily, his lips loose and drooling. He was a large man who wore diamond studs in a shirtfront which swelled with the ample paunch underneath, and each time the blonde swayed her undulating hips he ran his hand through the thin hair of his bald head and, with his arms upheld, his posture clumsy like that of an intoxicated panda, wound his belly in a slow and obscene grind. This creature was completely hypnotized. The music had quickened. As the dancer flung herself about with a detached expression on her face, the men began reaching out to touch her. I could see their beefy fingers sink into her soft flesh. Some of the others tried to stop them and she began to move around the floor in graceful circles, as they gave chase, slipping and sliding over the polished floor. It was mad. Chairs went crashing, drinks were spilt, as they ran laughing and howling after her. They caught her just as she reached a door, raised her from the floor, and tossed her as college boys are tossed at a hazing, and above her red, fixed-smiling lips I saw the terror and disgust in her eyes, almost like my own terror and that which I saw in some of the other boys. As I watched, they tossed her twice and her soft breasts seemed to flatten against the air and her legs flung wildly as she spun. Some of the more sober ones helped her to escape. And I started off the floor, heading for the anteroom with the rest of the boys.

10   Some were still crying and in hysteria. But as we tried to leave we were stopped and ordered to get into the ring. There was nothing to do but what we were told. All ten of us climbed under the ropes and allowed ourselves to be blindfolded with broad bands of white cloth. One of the men seemed to feel a bit sympathetic and tried to cheer us up as we stood with our backs against the ropes. Some of us tried to grin. "See that boy over there?" one of the men said. "I want you to run across at the bell and give it to him right in the belly. If you don't get him, I'm going to get you. I don't like his looks." Each of us was told the same. The blindfolds were put on. Yet even then I had been going over my speech. In my mind each word was as bright as flame. I felt the cloth pressed into place, and frowned so that it would be loosened when I relaxed.

But now I felt a sudden fit of blind terror. I was unused to darkness. It was as though I had suddenly found myself in a dark room filled with poisonous cottonmouths. I could hear the bleary voices yelling insistently for the battle royal to begin.

"Get going in there!"

"Let me at that big nigger!"

I strained to pick up the school superintendent's voice, as though to squeeze some security out of that slightly more familiar sound.

15   "Let me at those black sonsabitches!" someone yelled.

"No, Jackson, no!" another voice yelled. "Here, somebody, help me hold Jack."

"I want to get at that ginger-colored nigger. Tear him limb from limb," the first voice yelled.

I stood against the ropes trembling. For in those days I was what they called ginger-colored, and he sounded as though he might crunch me between his teeth like a crisp ginger cookie.

Quite a struggle was going on. Chairs were being kicked about and I could hear voices grunting as with a terrific effort. I wanted to see, to see more desperately than ever before. But the blindfold was as tight as a thick skin-puckering scab and when I raised my gloved hands to push the layers of white aside a voice yelled, "Oh, no you don't, black bastard! Leave that alone!"

20   "Ring the bell before Jackson kills him a coon!" someone boomed in the sudden silence. And I heard the bell clang and the sound of the feet scuffling forward.

A glove smacked against my head. I pivoted, striking out stiffly as someone went past, and felt the jar ripple along the length of my arm to my shoulder. Then it seemed as though all nine of the boys had turned upon me at once. Blows pounded me from all sides while I struck out as best I could. So many blows landed upon me that I wondered if I were not the only blindfolded fighter in the ring, or if the man called Jackson hadn't succeeded in getting me after all.

Blindfolded, I could no longer control my motions. I had no dignity. I stumbled about like a baby or a drunken man. The smoke had become thicker and with each new blow it seemed to sear and further restrict my lungs. My saliva became like hot bitter glue. A glove connected with my head, filling my mouth with warm blood. It was everywhere. I could not tell if the moisture I felt upon my body was sweat or blood. A blow landed hard against the nape of my neck. I felt myself going over, my head hitting the floor. Streaks of blue light filled the black world behind the blindfold. I lay prone, pretending that I was knocked out, but felt myself seized by hands and yanked to my feet. "Get going, black boy! Mix it up!" My arms were like lead, my head smarting from blows. I managed to feel my way to the ropes and held on, trying to catch my breath. A glove landed in my mid-section and I went over again, feeling as though the smoke had become a knife jabbed into my guts. Pushed this way and that by the legs milling around me, I finally pulled erect and discovered that I could see the black, sweat-washed forms weaving in the smoky-blue atmosphere like drunken dancers weaving to the rapid drum-like thuds of blows.

Everyone fought hysterically. It was complete anarchy. Everybody fought everybody else. No group fought together for long. Two, three, four, fought one, then turned to fight each other, were themselves attacked. Blows landed below the belt and in the kidney, with the gloves open as well as closed, and with my eye partly opened now there was not so much terror. I moved carefully, avoiding blows, although not too many to attract attention, fighting from group to group. The boys groped about like blind, cautious crabs crouching to protect their mid-sections, their heads pulled in short against their shoulders, their arms stretched nervously before them, with their fists testing the smoke-filled air like the knobbed feelers of hypersensitive snails. In one corner I glimpsed a boy violently punching the air and heard him scream in pain as he smashed his hand against a ring post. For a second I saw him bent over holding his hand, then going down as a blow caught his unprotected head. I played one group against the other, slipping and throwing a punch then stepping out of range while pushing the others into the melee to take the blows blindly aimed at me. The smoke was agonizing and there were no rounds, no bells at three minute intervals to relieve our exhaustion. The room spun round me, a swirl of lights, smoke, sweating bodies surrounded by tense white faces. I bled from both nose and mouth, the blood spattering upon my chest.

The men kept yelling, "Slug him, black boy! Knock his guts out!"

25   "Uppercut him! Kill him! Kill that big boy!"

Taking a fake fall, I saw a boy going down heavily beside me as though we were felled by a single blow, saw a sneaker-clad foot shoot into his groin as the two who had knocked him down stumbled upon him. I rolled out of range, feeling a twinge of nausea.

The harder we fought the more threatening the men became. And yet, I had begun to worry about my speech again. How would it go? Would they recognize my ability? What would they give me?

I was fighting automatically and suddenly I noticed that one after another of the boys was leaving the ring. I was surprised, filled with panic, as though I had been left alone with an unknown danger. Then I understood. The boys had arranged it among themselves. It was the custom for the two men left in the ring to slug it out for the winner's prize. I discovered this too late. When the bell sounded two men in tuxedoes leaped into the ring and removed the blindfold. I found myself facing Tatlock, the biggest of the gang. I felt sick at my stomach. Hardly had the bell stopped ringing in my ears than it clanged again and I saw him moving swiftly toward me. Thinking of nothing else to do I hit him smash on the nose. He kept coming, bringing the rank sharp violence of stale sweat. His face was a black bank of a face, only his eyes alive—with hate of me and aglow with a feverish terror from what had happened to us all. I became anxious. I wanted to deliver my speech and he came at me as though he meant to beat it out of me. I smashed him again and again, taking his blows as they came. Then on a sudden impulse I struck him lightly as we clinched, I whispered, "Fake like I knocked you out, you can have the prize."

"I'll break your behind," he whispered hoarsely.

30   "For *them?*"

"For *me,* sonofabitch!"

They were yelling for us to break it up and Tatlock spun me half around with a blow, and as a joggled camera sweeps in a reeling scene, I saw the howling red faces crouching tense beneath the cloud of blue-gray smoke. For a moment the world wavered, unraveled, flowed, then my head cleared and Tatlock bounced before me. That fluttering shadow before my eyes was his jabbing left hand. Then falling forward, my head against his damp shoulder, I whispered,

"I'll make it five dollars more."

"Go to hell!"

35   But his muscles relaxed a trifle beneath my pressure and I breathed, "Seven!"

"Give it to your ma," he said, ripping me beneath the heart.

And while I still held him I butted him and moved away. I felt myself bombarded with punches. I fought back with hopeless desperation. I wanted to deliver my speech more than anything else in the world, because I felt that only these men could judge truly my ability, and now this stupid clown was ruining my chances. I began fighting carefully now, moving in to punch him and out again with my greater speed. A lucky blow to his chin and I had him going too— until I heard a loud voice yell, "I got my money on the big boy."

Hearing this, I almost dropped my guard. I was confused: Should I try to win against the voice out there? Would not this go against my speech, and was not this a moment for humility, for nonresistance? A blow to my head as I danced about sent my right eye popping like a jack-in-the-box and settled my dilemma. The room went red as I fell. It was a dream fall, my body languid and fastidious as to where to land, until the floor became impatient and smashed up to meet me. A moment later I came to. An hypnotic voice said FIVE emphatically. And I lay there, hazily watching a dark red spot of my own blood shaping itself into a butterfly, glistening and soaking into the soiled gray world of the canvas.

When the voice drawled TEN I was lifted up and dragged to a chair. I sat dazed. My eye pained and swelled with each throb of my pounding heart and I wondered if now I would be allowed to speak. I was wringing wet, my mouth still bleeding. We were grouped along the wall now. The other boys ignored me as they congratulated Tatlock and speculated as to how much they would be paid. One boy whimpered over his smashed hand. Looking up front, I saw attendants in white jackets rolling the portable ring away and placing a small square rug in the vacant space surrounded by chairs. Perhaps, I thought, I will stand on the rug to deliver my speech.

40   Then the M.C. called to us, "Come on up here boys and get your money."

We ran forward to where the men laughed and talked in their chairs, waiting. Everyone seemed friendly now.

"There it is on the rug," the man said. I saw the rug covered with coins of all dimensions and a few crumpled bills. But what excited me, scattered here and there, were the gold pieces.

"Boys, it's all yours," the man said. "You get all you grab."

"That's right, Sambo," a blond man said, winking at me confidentially.

45   I trembled with excitement, forgetting my pain. I would get the gold and the bills, I thought. I would use both hands. I would throw my body against the boys nearest me to block them from the gold.

"Get down around the rug now," the man commanded, "and don't anyone touch it until I give the signal."

"This ought to be good," I heard.

As told, we got around the square rug on our knees. Slowly the man raised his freckled hand as we followed it upward with our eyes.

I heard, "These niggers look like they're about to pray!"

50   Then, "Ready," the man said. "Go!"

I lunged for a yellow coin lying on the blue design of the carpet, touching it and sending a surprised shriek to join those rising around me. I tried frantically to remove my hand but could not let go. A hot, violent force tore through my body, shaking me like a wet rat. The rug was electrified. The hair bristled up on my head as I shook myself free. My muscles jumped, my nerves jangled, writhed. But I saw that this was not stopping the other boys. Laughing in fear and embarrassment, some were holding back and scooping up the coins knocked off by the painful contortions of the others. The men roared above us as we struggled.

"Pick it up, goddamnit, pick it up!" someone called like a bass-voiced parrot. "Go on, get it!"

I crawled rapidly around the floor, picking up the coins, trying to avoid the coppers and to get greenbacks and the gold. Ignoring the shock by laughing, as I brushed the coins off quickly, I discovered that I could contain the electricity— a contradiction, but it works. Then the men began to push us onto the rug. Laughing embarrassedly, we struggled out of their hands and kept after the coins. We were all wet and slippery and hard to hold. Suddenly I saw a boy lifted into the air, glistening with sweat like a circus seal, and dropped, his wet back landing flush upon the charged rug, heard him yell and saw him literally dance upon his back, his elbows beating a frenzied tatoo upon the floor, his muscles twitching like the flesh of a horse stung by many flies. When he finally rolled off, his face was gray and no one stopped him when he ran from the floor amid booming laughter.

"Get the money," the M.C. called. "That's good hard American cash!"

55 And we snatched and grabbed, snatched and grabbed. I was careful not to come too close to the rug now, and when I felt the hot whiskey breath descend upon me like a cloud of foul air I reached out and grabbed the leg of a chair. It was occupied and I held on desperately.

"Leggo, nigger! Leggo!"

The huge face wavered down to mine as he tried to push me free. But my body was slippery and he was too drunk. It was Mr. Colcord, who owned a chain of movie houses and "entertainment palaces." Each time he grabbed me I slipped out of his hands. It became a real struggle. I feared the rug more than I did the drunk, so I held on, surprising myself for a moment by trying to topple *him* upon the rug. It was such an enormous idea that I found myself actually carrying it out. I tried not to be obvious, yet when I grabbed his leg, trying to tumble him out of the chair, he raised up roaring with laughter, and, looking at me with soberness dead in the eye, kicked me viciously in the chest. The chair leg flew out of my hand. I felt myself going and rolled. It was as though I had rolled through a bed of hot coals. It seemed a whole century would pass before I would roll free, a century in which I was seared through the deepest levels of my body to the fearful breath within me and the breath seared and heated to the point of explosion. It'll all be over in a flash, I thought as I rolled clear. It'll all be over in a flash.

But not yet, the men on the other side were waiting, red faces swollen as though from apoplexy as they bent forward in their chairs. Seeing their fingers coming toward me I rolled away as a fumbled football rolls off the receiver's fingertips, back into the coals. That time I luckily sent the rug sliding out of place and heard the coins ringing against the floor and the boys scuffling to pick them up and the M.C. calling, "All right, boys, that's all. Go get dressed and get your money."

I was limp as a dish rag. My back felt as though it had been beaten with wires.

60 When we had dressed the M.C. came in and gave us each five dollars, except Tatlock, who got ten for being the last in the ring. Then he told us to leave. I was not to get a chance to deliver my speech, I thought. I was going out into the dim alley in despair when I was stopped and told to go back. I returned to the ballroom, where the men were pushing back their chairs and gathering in groups to talk.

The M.C. knocked on a table for quiet. "Gentlemen," he said, "we almost forgot an important part of the program. A most serious part, gentlemen. This boy was brought here to deliver a speech which he made at his graduation yesterday . . . ."

"Bravo!"

"I'm told that he is the smartest boy we've got out there in Greenwood. I'm told that he knows more big words than a pocket-sized dictionary."

Much applause and laughter.

65 "So now, gentlemen, I want you to give him your attention."

There was still laughter as I faced them, my mouth dry, my eye throbbing. I began slowly, but evidently my throat was tense, because they began shouting, "Louder! Louder!"

"We of the younger generation extol the wisdom of that great leader and educator," I shouted. "who first spoke these flaming words of wisdom: 'A ship lost at sea for many days suddenly sighted a friendly vessel. From the mast of the unfortunate vessel was seen a signal: "Water, water; we die of thirst!" The answer from the friendly vessel came back: "Cast down your bucket where you are." The captain of the distressed vessel, at last heeding the injunction, cast down his bucket, and it came up full of fresh sparkling water from the mouth of the Amazon River.' And like him I say, and in his words. 'To those of my race who depend upon bettering their condition in a foreign land, or who underestimate the importance of cultivating friendly relations with the Southern white man, who is his next-door neighbor. I would say: "Cast down your bucket where you are"—cast it down in making friends in every manly way of the people of all races by whom we are surrounded . . . .'"

I spoke automatically and with such fervor that I did not realize that the men were still talking and laughing until my dry mouth, filling up with blood from the cut, almost strangled me. I coughed, wanting to stop and go to one of the tall brass, sand-filled spittoons to relieve myself, but a few of the men, especially the superintendent, were listening and I was afraid. So I gulped it down, blood, saliva and all, and continued. (What powers of endurance I had during those days! What enthusiasm! What a belief in the rightness of things!) I spoke even louder in spite of the pain. But still they talked and still they laughed, as though deaf with cotton in dirty ears. So I spoke with greater emotional emphasis. I closed my ears and swallowed blood until I was nauseated. The speech seemed a hundred times as long as before, but I could not leave out a single word. All had to be said, each memorized nuance considered, rendered. Nor was that all. Whenever I uttered a word of three or more syllables a group of voices would yell for me to repeat it. I used the phrase "social responsibility" and they yelled:

"What's the word you say, boy?"
70   "Social responsibility," I said.
"What?"
"Social . . ."
"Louder."
". . . responsibility."
75   "More!"
"Respon—"
"Repeat!"
"—sibility."
The room filled with the uproar of laughter until, no doubt, distracted by having to gulp down my blood, I made a mistake and yelled a phrase I had often seen denounced in newspaper editorials, heard debated in private.
80   "Social . . ."
"What?" they yelled.
". . . equality—"
The laughter hung smokelike in the sudden stillness. I opened my eyes, puzzled. Sounds of displeasure filled the room. The M.C. rushed forward. They shouted hostile phrases at me. But I did not understand.
A small dry mustached man in the front row blared out, "Say that slowly, son!"
85   "What sir?"
"What you just said!"
"Social responsibility, sir." I said.
"You weren't being smart, were you, boy?" he said, not unkindly.

"No, sir!"

90   "You sure that about 'equality' was a mistake?"

"Oh, yes, sir," I said. "I was swallowing blood."

"Well, you had better speak more slowly so we can understand. We mean to do right by you, but you've got to know your place at all times. All right, now, go on with your speech."

I was afraid. I wanted to leave but I wanted also to speak and I was afraid they'd snatch me down.

"Thank you, sir," I said, beginning where I had left off, and having them ignore me as before.

95   Yet when I finished there was a thunderous applause. I was surprised to see the superintendent come forth with a package wrapped in white tissue paper, and gesturing for quiet, address the men.

"Gentlemen, you see that I did not overpraise this boy. He makes a good speech and some day he'll lead his people in the proper paths. And I don't have to tell you that that is important in these days and times. This is a good, smart boy, and so to encourage him in the right direction, in the name of the Board of Education I wish to present him a prize in the form of this . . ."

He paused, removing the tissue paper and revealing a gleaming calfskin brief case.

". . . in the form of this first-class article from Shad Whitmore's shop."

"Boy," he said, addressing me, "take this prize and keep it well. Consider it a badge of office. Prize it. Keep developing as you are and some day it will be filled with important papers that will help shape the destiny of your people."

100   I was so moved that I could hardly express my thanks. A rope of bloody saliva forming a shape like an undiscovered continent drooled upon the leather and I wiped it quickly away. I felt an importance that I had never dreamed.

"Open it and see what's inside," I was told.

My fingers a-tremble, I complied, smelling the fresh leather and finding an official-looking document inside. It was a scholarship to the state college for Negroes. My eyes filled with tears and I ran awkwardly off the floor.

[1947]

 Topics for Critical Thinking and Writing

1. Now that you have read the entire story, the opening paragraph may be clearer than it was when you first read it. What does the narrator mean when he declares at the end of this paragraph, "I am an invisible man?" Explain how the events described in the story taught him this painful truth.

2. The narrator says of his grandfather's dying speech, "I could never be sure of what he meant." What do you think the grandfather meant by calling himself a traitor and a spy in the enemy's territory?

3. What is the significance of the scene involving the naked blonde woman? How is this scene related to the narrator's discovery that he is invisible?

4. This story is a powerful, indeed shocking study of racism, but in essays and interviews Ellison often noted that he intended his stories and his novel *Invisible Man* to illuminate "universal truths" about human experience as well. In your view, does "Battle Royal" achieve this goal? What insights does it offer about the nature of self-knowledge and human identity?

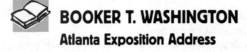

BOOKER T. WASHINGTON
Atlanta Exposition Address

MR. PRESIDENT AND GENTLEMEN OF THE BOARD OF DIRECTORS AND CITIZENS:

One-third of the population of the South is of the Negro race. No enterprise seeking the material, civil, or moral welfare of this section can disregard this element of our population and reach the highest success. I but convey to you, Mr. President and Directors, the sentiment of the masses of my race when I say that in no way have the value and manhood of the American Negro been more fittingly and generously recognized than by the managers of this magnificent Exposition at every stage of its progress. It is a recognition that will do more to cement the friendship of the two races than any occurrence since the dawn of our freedom.

Not only this, but the opportunity here afforded will awaken among us a new era of industrial progress. Ignorant and inexperienced, it is not strange that in the first years of our new life we began at the top instead of at the bottom; that a seat in Congress or the state legislature was more sought than real estate or industrial skill; that the political convention or stump speaking had more attractions than starting a dairy farm or truck garden.

A ship lost at sea for many days suddenly sighted a friendly vessel. From the mast of the unfortunate vessel was seen a signal, "Water, water; we die of thirst!" The answer from the friendly vessel at once came back, "Cast down your bucket where you are." A second time the signal, "Water, water; send us water!" ran up from the distressed vessel, and was answered, "Cast down your bucket where you are." And a third and fourth signal for water was answered, "Cast down your bucket where you are." The captain of the distressed vessel, at last heeding the injunction, cast down his bucket, and it came up full of fresh, sparkling water from the mouth of the Amazon River. To those of my race who depend on bettering their condition in a foreign land or who underestimate the importance of cultivating friendly relations with the Southern white man, who is their next-door neighbour, I would say: "Cast down your bucket where you are"—cast it down in making friends in every manly way of the people of all races by whom we are surrounded.

Cast it down in agriculture, mechanics, in commerce, in domestic service, and in the professions. And in this connection it is well to bear in mind that whatever other sins the South may be called to bear, when it comes to business, pure and simple, it is in the South that the Negro is given a man's chance in the commercial world, and in nothing is this Exposition more eloquent than in emphasizing this chance. Our greatest danger is that in the great leap from slavery to freedom we may overlook the fact that the masses of us are to live by the productions of our hands, and fail to keep in mind that we shall prosper in proportion as we learn to dignify and glorify common labour and put brains and skill into the common occupations of life; shall prosper in proportion as we learn to draw the line between the superficial and the substantial, the ornamental gewgaws of life and the useful. No race can prosper till it learns that there is as much dignity in tilling a field as in writing a poem. It is at the bottom of life we must begin, and not at the top. Nor should we permit our grievances to overshadow our opportunities.

5   To those of the white race who look to the incoming of those of foreign birth and strange tongue and habits for the prosperity of the South, were I permitted I would repeat what I say to my own race, "Cast down your bucket where you are." Cast it down among the eight millions of Negroes whose habits you know, whose fidelity and love you have tested in days when to have proved treacherous meant the ruin of your firesides. Cast down your bucket among these people who have, without strikes and labour wars, tilled your fields, cleared your forests, builded your railroads and cities, and brought forth treasures from the bowels of the earth, and helped make possible this magnificent representation of the progress of the South. Casting down your bucket among my people, helping and encouraging them as you are doing on these grounds, and to education of head, hand, and heart, you will find that they will buy your surplus land, make blossom the waste places in your fields, and run your factories. While doing this, you can be sure in the future, as in the past, that you and your families will be surrounded by the most patient, faithful, law-abiding, and unresentful people that the world has seen. As we have proved our loyalty to you in the past, in nursing your children, watching by the sick-bed of your mothers and fathers, and often following them with tear-dimmed eyes to their graves, so in the future, in our humble way, we shall stand by you with a devotion that no foreigner can approach, ready to lay down our lives, if need be, in defence of yours, interlacing our industrial, commercial, civil, and religious life with yours in a way that shall make the interests of both races one. In all things that are purely social we can be as separate as the fingers, yet one as the hand in all things essential to mutual progress.

There is no defence or security for any of us except in the highest intelligence and development of all. If anywhere there are efforts tending to curtail the fullest growth of the Negro, let these efforts be turned into stimulating, encouraging, and making him the most useful and intelligent citizen. Effort or means so invested will pay a thousand per cent interest. These efforts will be twice blessed—"blessing him that gives and him that takes."

There is no escape through law of man or God from the inevitable:—

> The laws of changeless justice bind
>   Oppressor with oppressed;
> And close as sin and suffering joined
>   We march to fate abreast.

Nearly sixteen millions of hands will aid you in pulling the load upward, or they will pull against you the load downward. We shall constitute one-third and more of the ignorance and crime of the South, or one-third its intelligence and progress; we shall contribute one-third to the business and industrial prosperity of the South, or we shall prove a veritable body of death, stagnating, depressing, retarding every effort to advance the body politic.

Gentlemen of the Exposition, as we present to you our humble effort at an exhibition of our progress, you must not expect overmuch. Starting thirty years ago with ownership here and there in a few quilts and pumpkins and chickens (gathered from miscellaneous sources), remember the path that has led from these to the inventions and production of agricultural implements, buggies, steam-engines, newspapers, books, statuary, carving, paintings, the management of drug-stores and banks, has not been trodden without contact with thorns and thistles. While we take pride in what we exhibit as a result of our independent efforts, we do not for a moment forget that our part in this exhibition would fall far short of your expectations but for the constant help that has come to our educational life, not only from the Southern states, but especially from Northern philanthropists, who have made their gifts a constant stream of blessing and encouragement.

10   The wisest among my race understand that the agitation of questions of social equality is the extremest folly, and that progress in the enjoyment of all the privileges that will come to us must be the result of severe and constant struggle rather than of artificial forcing. No race that has anything to contribute to the markets of the world is long in any degree ostracized. It is important and right that all privileges of the law be ours, but it is vastly more important that we be prepared for the exercises of these privileges. The opportunity to earn a dollar in a factory just now is worth infinitely more than the opportunity to spend a dollar in an opera-house.

In conclusion, may I repeat that nothing in thirty years has given us more hope and encouragement, and drawn us so near to you of the white race, as this opportunity offered by the Exposition; and here bending, as it were, over the altar that represents the results of the struggles of your race and mine, both starting practically empty-handed three decades ago, I pledge that in your effort to work out the great and intricate problem which God has laid at the doors of the South, you shall have at all times the patient, sympathetic help of my race; only let this be constantly in mind, that, while from representations in these buildings of the product of field, of forest, of mine, of factory, letters, and art, much good will come, yet far above and beyond material benefits will be that higher good, that, let us pray God, will come, in a blotting out of sectional differences and racial animosities and suspicions, in a determination to administer absolute justice, in a willing obedience among all classes to the mandates of law. This, this, coupled with our material prosperity, will bring into our beloved South a new heaven and a new earth.

[1895]

Charles Keck, *The Booker T. Washington Memorial* (1922). The statue shows Washington pulling away the veil of ignorance and revealing to the crouching black man the book of knowledge of life and the implements of industry that will enable African Americans to prosper. On the front of the pedestal are Washington's words, "We shall prosper in proportion as we learn to dignify and glorify labor and put brains and skill into the common occupations of life." (Courtesy of Tuskegee University. Photograph by Eric J. Sundquist)

W. E. B. DU BOIS
Of Our Spiritual Strivings

Between me and the other world there is ever an unasked question: unasked by some through feelings of delicacy; by others through the difficulty of rightly framing it. All, nevertheless, flutter round it. They approach me in a half-hesitant sort of way, eye me curiously or compassionately, and then, instead of saying directly, How does it feel to be a problem? they say, I know an excellent colored man in my town; or, I fought at Mechanicsville; or, Do not these Southern outrages make your blood boil? At these I smile, or am interested, or reduce the boiling to a simmer, as the occasion may require. To the real question, How does it feel to be a problem? I answer seldom a word.

And yet, being a problem is a strange experience,—peculiar even for one who has never been anything else, save perhaps in babyhood and in Europe. It is in the early days of rollicking boyhood that the revelation first bursts upon one, all in a day, as it were. I remember well when the shadow swept across me. I was a little thing, away up in the hills of New England, where the dark Housatonic winds between Hoosac and Taghkanic to the sea. In a wee wooden schoolhouse, something put it into the boys' and girls' heads to buy gorgeous visiting-cards—ten cents a package—and exchange. The exchange was merry, till one girl, a tall newcomer, refused my card,—refused it peremptorily, with a glance. Then it dawned upon me with a certain suddenness that I was different from the others; or like, mayhap, in heart and life and longing, but shut out from their world by a vast veil. I had thereafter no desire to tear down that veil, to creep through; I held all beyond it in common contempt, and lived above it in a region of blue sky and great wandering shadows. That sky was bluest when I could beat my mates at examination-time, or beat them at a foot-race, or even beat their stringy heads. Alas, with the years all this fine contempt began to fade; for the worlds I longed for, and all their dazzling opportunities, were theirs, not mine. But they should not keep these prizes, I said; some, all, I would wrest from them. Just how I would do it I could never decide: by reading law, by healing the sick, by telling the wonderful tales that swam in my head,—some way. With other black boys the strife was not so fiercely sunny: their youth shrunk into tasteless sycophancy, or into silent hatred of the pale world about them and mocking distrust of everything white; or wasted itself in a bitter cry, Why did God make me an outcast and a stranger in mine own house? The shades of the prison-house closed round about us all: walls strait and stubborn to the whitest, but relentlessly narrow, tall, and unscalable to sons of night who must plod darkly on in resignation, or beat unavailing palms against the stone, or steadily, half hopelessly, watch the streak of blue above.

After the Egyptian and Indian, the Greek and Roman, the Teuton and Mongolian, the Negro is a sort of seventh son, born with a veil, and gifted with second-sight in this American world,—a world which yields him no true self-consciousness, but only lets him see himself through the revelation of the other world. It is a peculiar sensation, this double-consciousness, this sense of always looking at one's self through the eyes of others, of measuring one's soul by the tape of a world that looks on in amused contempt and pity. One ever feels his two-ness,—an American, a Negro; two souls, two thoughts, two unreconciled strivings; two warring ideals in one dark body, whose dogged strength alone keeps it from being torn asunder.

The history of the American Negro is the history of this strife—this longing to attain self-conscious manhood, to merge his double self into a better and truer self. In this merging he wishes neither of the older selves to be lost. He would not Africanize America, for America has too much to teach the world and Africa. He would not bleach his Negro soul in a flood of white Americanism, for he knows that Negro blood has a message for the world. He simply wishes to make it possible for a man to be both a Negro and an American, without being cursed and spit upon by his fellows, without having the doors of Opportunity closed roughly in his face.

[1903]

W. E. B. DU BOIS
Of Mr. Booker T. Washington and Others

Mr. Washington represents in Negro thought the old attitude of adjustment and submission; but adjustment at such a peculiar time as to make his programme unique. This is an age of unusual economic development, and Mr. Washington's programme naturally takes an economic cast, becoming a gospel of Work and Money to such an extent as apparently almost completely to overshadow the higher aims of life. Moreover, this is an age when the more advanced races are coming in closer contact with the less developed races, and the race-feeling is therefore intensified; and Mr. Washington's programme practically accepts the alleged inferiority of the Negro races. Again, in our own land, the reaction from the sentiment of war time has given impetus to race-prejudice against Negroes, and Mr. Washington withdraws many of the high demands of Negroes as men and American citizens. In other periods of intensified prejudice all the Negro's tendency to self-assertion has been called forth; at this period a policy of submission is advocated. In the history of nearly all other races and peoples the doctrine preached at such crises has been that manly self-respect is worth more than lands and houses, and that a people who voluntarily surrender such respect, or cease striving for it, are not worth civilizing.

In answer to this, it has been claimed that the Negro can survive only through submission. Mr. Washington distinctly asks that black people give up, at least for the present, three things,—

First, political power,
Second, insistence on civil rights,
Third, higher education of Negro youth,—

and concentrate all their energies on industrial education, the accumulation of wealth, and the conciliation of the South. This policy has been courageously and insistently advocated for over fifteen years, and has been triumphant for perhaps ten years. As a result of this tender of the palm-branch, what has been the return? In these years there have occurred:

1. The disfranchisement of the Negro.
2. The legal creation of a distinct status of civil inferiority for the Negro.

3. The steady withdrawal of aid from institutions for the higher training of the Negro.

These movements are not, to be sure, direct results of Mr. Washington's teachings; but his propaganda has, without a shadow of doubt, helped their speedier accomplishment. The question then comes: Is it possible, and probable, that nine millions of men can make effective progress in economic lines if they are deprived of political rights, made a servile caste, and allowed only the most meagre chance for developing their exceptional men? If history and reason give any distinct answer to these questions, it is an emphatic *No*. And Mr. Washington thus faces the triple paradox of his career:

10

1. He is striving nobly to make Negro artisans business men and property-owners; but it is utterly impossible, under modern competitive methods, for workingmen and property-owners to defend their rights and exist without the right of suffrage.
2. He insists on thrift and self-respect, but at the same time counsels a silent submission to civic inferiority such as is bound to sap the manhood of any race in the long run.
3. He advocates common-school and industrial training, and depreciates institutions of higher learning; but neither the Negro common-schools, nor Tuskegee itself, could remain open a day were it not for teachers trained in Negro colleges, or trained by their graduates.

This triple paradox in Mr. Washington's position is the object of criticism by two classes of colored Americans. One class is spiritually descended from Toussaint the Savior, through Gabriel, Vesey, and Turner, and they represent the attitude of revolt and revenge; they hate the white South blindly and distrust the white race generally, and so far as they agree on definite action, think that the Negro's only hope lies in emigration beyond the borders of the United States. And yet, by the irony of fate, nothing has more effectually made this programme seem hopeless than the recent course of the United States toward weaker and darker peoples in the West Indies, Hawaii, and the Philippines,—for where in the world may we go and be safe from lying and brute force?

The other class of Negroes who cannot agree with Mr. Washington has hitherto said little aloud. They deprecate the sight of scattered counsels, of internal disagreement; and especially they dislike making their just criticism of a useful and earnest man an excuse for a general discharge of venom from small-minded opponents. Nevertheless, the questions involved are so fundamental and serious that it is difficult to see how men like the Grimkes, Kelly Miller, J. W. E. Bowen, and other representatives of this group, can much longer be silent. Such men feel in conscience bound to ask of this nation three things:

15

1. The right to vote.
2. Civic equality.
3. The education of youth according to ability.

They acknowledge Mr. Washington's invaluable service in counselling patience and courtesy in such demands; they do not ask that ignorant black men vote when ignorant whites are debarred, or that any reasonable restrictions in the suffrage should not be applied; they know that the low social level of the mass of the race is responsible for much discrimination against it, but they also know, and the nation knows, that relentless color-prejudice is more often a cause than a result of the Negro's degradation, they seek the abatement of this relic of barbarism, and not its systematic encouragement and pampering by all agencies of social power from the Associated Press to the Church of Christ. They advocate, with Mr. Washington, a broad system of Negro common schools supplemented by thorough industrial training; but they are surprised that a man of Mr. Washington's insight cannot see that no such educational system ever has rested or can rest on any other basis than that of the well-equipped college and university, and they insist that there is a demand for a few such institutions throughout the South to train the best of the Negro youth as teachers, professional men, and leaders.

This group of men honor Mr. Washington for his attitude of conciliation toward the white South; they accept the "Atlanta Compromise" in its broadest interpretation; they recognize, with him, many signs of promise, many men of high purpose and fair judgment, in this section; they know that no easy task has been laid upon a region already tottering under heavy burdens. But, nevertheless, they insist that the way to truth and right lies in straightforward honesty, not in indiscriminate flattery; in praising those of the South who do well and criticising uncompromisingly those who do ill; in taking advantage of the opportunities at hand and urging their fellows to do the same, but at the same time in remembering that only a firm adherence to their higher ideals and aspirations will ever keep those ideals within the realm of possibility. They do not expect that the free right to vote, to enjoy civic rights, and to be educated, will come in a moment; they do not expect to see the bias and prejudices of years disappear at the blast of a trumpet; but they are absolutely certain that the way for a people to gain their reasonable rights is not by voluntarily throwing them away and insisting that they do not want them; that the way for a people to gain respect is not by continually belittling and ridiculing themselves; that, on the contrary, Negroes must insist continually, in season and out of season, that voting is necessary to modern manhood, that color discrimination is barbarism, and that black boys need education as well as white boys.

In failing thus to state plainly and unequivocally the legitimate demands of their people, even at the cost of opposing an honored leader, the thinking classes of American Negroes would shirk a heavy responsibility,—a responsibility to themselves, a responsibility to the struggling masses, a responsibility to the darker races of men whose future depends so largely on this American experiment, but especially a responsibility to this nation,—this common Fatherland. It is wrong to encourage a man or a people in evil-doing; it is wrong to aid and abet a national crime simply because it is unpopular not to do so. The growing spirit of kindliness and reconciliation between the North and South after the frightful differences of a generation ago ought to be a source of deep congratulation to all, and especially to those whose mistreatment caused the war; but if that reconciliation is to be marked by the industrial slavery and civic death of those same black men, with permanent legislation into a position of inferiority, then those black men, if they are really men, are called upon by every consideration of patriotism and loyalty to oppose such a course by all civilized methods, even though such opposition involves disagreement with Mr. Booker T. Washington. We have no right to sit silently by while the inevitable seeds are sown for a harvest of disaster to our children, black and white.

[1903]

GUNNAR MYRDAL
On Social Equality*

I have heard few comments made so frequently and with so much emphasis and so many illustrations as the one that "Negroes are happiest among themselves" and that "Negroes really don't want white company but prefer to be among their own race." Even sociologists, educators, and interracial experts have informed me that, when the two groups keep apart, the wish for separation is as pronounced among Negroes as among whites. In the South, many liberals are eager to stress this assertion as part of the justification for their unwillingness to give up the Southern doctrine that the Negroes must not be allowed to aspire to "social equality." Southern conservatives will usually give a somewhat different twist to the argument and actually insist that Negroes are perfectly satisfied with their social status in the South. But the conservatives are more likely to contradict themselves bluntly in the next sentence by asserting that in the back of the Negro's mind there is a keen desire to be "like white people" and to "marry white girls."

For the moment, we shall leave it an open question whether the whites understand the Negroes correctly on this point. We shall start from the evident fact that—quite independent of whether or not, to what extent, and how the Negroes have accommodated themselves—*social segregation and discrimination is a system of deprivations forced upon the Negro group by the white group.* This is equally true in the North and in the South, though in this respect, as in all others, there is more segregation and discrimination in the South, and thus the phenomenon is easier to observe.

That segregation and discrimination are forced upon the Negroes by the whites becomes apparent in the *one-sidedness* of their application. Negroes are ordinarily never admitted to white churches in the South, but if a strange white man enters a Negro church the visit is received as a great honor. The guest will be ushered to a front seat or to the platform. The service will often be interrupted, an announcement will be made that there is a "white friend" present, and he will be asked to address the Negro audience, which will loudly testify its high appreciation. Likewise, a white stranger will be received with utmost respect and cordiality in any Negro school, and everything will be done to satisfy his every wish, whereas a Negro under similar circumstances would be pushed off the grounds of a white school. Whenever I have entered a Negro theater in the South, the girl in the ticket office has regularly turned a bewildered face and told me that "it is a colored movie." But she has apparently done this because she thought I was making a mistake and wanted to spare me embarrassment. When I answered that I did not care, the ticket office girls usually sold the ticket and received my visit as a courtesy. I have never been refused service in a Negro restaurant in the South.

When the white conductor in a train has told me occasionally that I was in the wrong car, the underlying assumption has also been the same, that the separation was made in order to save white people from having to tolerate Negro

*Editors' title

company. Contrary to the laws—which are all written on the fiction of equality—he has, with a shrug of his shoulders, always left me where I was after I told him I had gone there purposely to have a look at the Negroes. A Negro who would disclose a similar desire to observe whites would, of course, be dealt with in quite another way. In the streetcars and buses the separation seems to be enforced fairly well in both directions. When, however, the conductor tells me, a white man, that I have taken the wrong seat, it is done in a spirit of respect and in order to help me preserve my caste status. The assumption is that I have made a mistake with no intention of overstepping the rules. In the case of a Negro the assumption is usually the contrary, that he is trying to intrude. In public buildings or private establishments of the South, I have never encountered any objection to my entering the spaces set aside for the Negroes, nor to my riding in the elevator set apart for Negroes if, for any reason, the white car was not there or was filled.

5   The rules are understood to be for the protection of whites and directed against Negroes. This applies also to social rituals and etiquette. The white man may waive most of the customs, as long as he does not demonstrate such a friendliness that he becomes known as a "nigger lover"; the reaction then comes, however, from the white society. He can recognize the Negro on the street and stop for a chat, or he can ignore him. He can offer his hand to shake, or he can keep it back. Negroes often complain about the uncertainty they experience because of the fact that the initiative in defining the personal situation always belongs to the white man. It is the white man who chooses between the alternatives as to the character of the contact to be established. The Negro, who often does not know how the white man has chosen, receives surprises in one direction or the other, which constantly push him off his balance.

            . . . . .

      In his first encounter with the American Negro problem, perhaps nothing perplexes the outside observer more than the popular term and the popular theory of "no social equality." He will be made to feel from the start that it has concrete implications and a central importance for the Negro problem in America. But, nevertheless, the term is kept vague and elusive, and the theory loose and ambiguous. One moment it will be stretched to cover and justify every form of social segregation and discrimination, and, in addition, all the inequalities in justice, politics and breadwinning. The next moment it will be narrowed to express only the denial of close personal intimacies and intermarriage. The very lack of precision allows the notion of "no social equality" to rationalize the rather illogical and wavering system of color caste in America.

      The kernel of the popular theory of "no social equality" will, when pursued, be presented as a firm determination on the part of the whites to block amalgamation and preserve "the purity of the white race." The white man identifies himself with "the white race" and feels that he has a stake in resisting the dissipation of its racial identity. Important in this identification is the notion of "the absolute and unchangeable superiority of the white race." From this racial dogma will often be drawn the *direct* inference that the white man shall dominate in all spheres. But when the logic of this inference is inquired about, the inference will be made *indirect* and will be made to lead over to the danger of amalgamation, or, as it is popularly expressed, "intermarriage."

      It is further found that the ban on intermarriage is focused on white women.

For them it covers both formal marriage and illicit intercourse. In regard to white men it is taken more or less for granted that they would not stoop to marry Negro women, and that illicit intercourse does not fall under the same intense taboo. Their offspring, under the popular doctrine that maternity is more certain than paternity, become Negroes anyway, and the white race easily avoids pollution with Negro blood. To prevent "intermarriage" in this specific sense of sex relations between white women and Negro men, it is not enough to apply legal and social sanctions against . . . it—so the popular theory runs. In using the danger of intermarriage as a defense for the whole caste system, it is assumed both that Negro men have a strong desire for "intermarriage," and that white women would be open to proposals from Negro men, *if* they are not guarded from even meeting them on an equal plane. The latter assumption, of course, is never openly expressed, but is logically implicit in the popular theory. The conclusion follows that the whole system of segregation and discrimination is justified. Every single measure is defended as necessary to block "social equality" which in its turn is held necessary to prevent "intermarriage."

The basic role of the fear of amalgamation in white attitudes to the race problem is indicated by the popular magical concept of "blood." Educated white Southerners, who know everything about modern genetic and biological research, confess readily that they actually feel an irrational or "instinctive" repugnance in thinking of "intermarriage." These measures of segregation and discrimination are often of the type found in the true taboos and in the notion "not to be touched" of primitive religion. The specific taboos are characterized, further, by a different degree of excitement which attends their violation and a different degree of punishment to the violator: the closer the act to sexual association, the more furious is the public reaction. Sexual association itself is punished by death and is accompanied by tremendous public excitement; the other social relations meet decreasing degrees of public fury. Sex becomes in this popular theory the principle around which the whole structure of segregation of the Negroes—down to disfranchisement and denial of equal opportunities on the labor market—is organized. The reasoning is this: "For, say what we will, may not all the equalities be ultimately based on potential social equality, and that in turn on intermarriage? Here we reach the real *crux* of the question." In cruder language, but with the same logic, the Southern man on the street responds to any plea for social equality: "Would you like to have your daughter marry a Negro?"

10   This theory of color caste centering around the aversion to amalgamation determines, as we have just observed, the white man's rather definite rank order of the various measures of segregation and discrimination against Negroes. The relative significance attached to each of those measures is dependent upon their degree of expediency or necessity—in the view of white people—as means of upholding the ban on "intermarriage." In this rank order, (1) the ban on intermarriage and other sex relations involving white women and colored men takes precedence before everything else. It is the end for which the other restrictions are arranged as means. Thereafter follow: (2) all sorts of taboos and etiquettes in personal contacts; (3) segregation in schools and churches; (4) segregation in hotels, restaurants, and theaters, and other public places where people meet socially; (5) segregation in public conveyances; (6) discrimination in public services; and, finally, inequality in (7) politics, (8) justice and (9) breadwinning and relief.

The degree of liberalism on racial matters in the white South can be designated mainly by the point on this rank order where a man stops because he believes further segregation and discrimination are not necessary to prevent "intermarriage." We have seen that white liberals in the South of the present day, as a matter of principle, rather unanimously stand up against inequality in breadwinning, relief, justice and politics. These fields of discrimination form the chief battleground and considerable changes in them are, as we have seen, on the way. When we ascend to the higher ranks which concern social relations in the narrow sense, we find the Southern liberals less prepared to split off from the majority opinion of the region. Hardly anybody in the South is prepared to go the whole way and argue that even the ban on intermarriage should be lifted. Practically all agree, not only upon the high desirability of preventing "intermarriage," but also that a certain amount of separation between the two groups is expedient and necessary to prevent it. Even the one who has his philosophical doubts on the point must, if he is reasonable, abstain from ever voicing them. The social pressure is so strong that it would be foolish not to conform. Conformity is a political necessity for having any hope of influence; it is, in addition, a personal necessity for not meeting social ostracism.

. . .

The fixation on the purity of white womanhood, and also part of the intensity of emotion surrounding the whole sphere of segregation and discrimination, are to be understood as the backwashes of the sore conscience on the part of white men for their own or their compeers' relations with, or desires for, Negro women. These psychological effects are greatly magnified because of the puritan *milieu* of America and especially of the South. The upper class men in a less puritanical people could probably have indulged in sex relations with, and sexual day-dreams of, lower caste women in a more matter-of-course way and without generating so much pathos about white womanhood. The Negro people have to carry the burden not only of the white men's sins but also of their virtues. The virtues of the honest, democratic, puritan white Americans in the South are great, and the burden upon the Negroes becomes ponderous.

Our practical conclusion is that it would have cleansing effects on race relations in America, and particularly in the South, to have an open and sober discussion in rational terms of this ever present popular theory of "intermarriage" and "social equality," giving matters their factual ground, true proportions and logical relations. Because it is, to a great extent, an opportunistic rationalization, and because it refers directly and indirectly to the most touchy spots in American life and American morals, tremendous inhibitions have been built up against a detached and critical discussion of this theory. But such inhibitions are gradually overcome when, in the course of secularized education, people become rational about their life problems. It must never be forgotten that in our increasingly intellectualized civilization even the plain citizen feels an urge for truth and objectivity, and that this rationalistic urge is increasingly competing with the opportunistic demands for rationalization and escape.

There are reasons to believe that a slow but steady cleansing of the American mind is proceeding as the cultural level is raised. The basic racial inferiority doctrine is being undermined by research and education. For a white man to have illicit relations with Negro women is increasingly meeting disapproval. Negroes themselves are more and more frowning upon such relations. This all must tend to dampen the emotional fires around "social equality." Sex and race fears are, however, even today the main defense for segregation and, in fact, for the whole caste order. The question shot at the interviewer touching any point of this order is still: "Would you like to have your daughter (sister) marry a Negro?"

[1944]

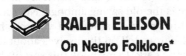

RALPH ELLISON
On Negro Folklore*

INTERVIEWERS: How representative of the American nation would you say Negro folklore is?

ELLISON: The history of the American Negro is a most intimate part of American history. Through the very process of slavery came the building of the United States. Negro folklore, evolving within a larger culture which regarded it as inferior, was an especially courageous expression. It announced the Negro's willingness to trust his own experience, his own sensibilities as to the definition of reality, rather than allow his masters to define these crucial matters for him. His experience is that of America and the West, and is as rich a body of experience as one would find anywhere. We can view it narrowly as something exotic, folksy or "low-down," or we may identify ourselves with it and recognize it as an important segment of the larger. American experience—not lying at the bottom of it, but intertwined, diffused in its very texture. I can't take this lightly or be impressed by those who cannot see its importance; it is important to *me*. One ironic witness to the beauty and the universality of this art is the fact that the descendants of the very men who enslaved us can now sing the spirituals and find in the singing an exaltation of their own humanity. Just take a look at some of the slave songs, blues, folk ballads; their possibilities for the writer are infinitely suggestive. Some of them have named human situations so well that a whole corps of writers could not exhaust their universality. For instance, here's an old slave verse:

Ole Aunt Dinah, she's just like me
She work so hard she want to be free
But old Aunt Dinah's gittin' kinda ole
She's afraid to go to Canada on account of the cold.

Ole Uncle Jack, now he's a mighty "good nigger,"
You tell him that you want to be free for a fac'
Next thing you know they done stripped the skin off your back.

Now old Uncle Ned, he want to be free
He found his way north by the moss on the tree
He cross that river floating in a tub
The patateroller† give him a mighty close rub.

It's crude, but in it you have three universal attitudes toward the problem of freedom. You can refine it and sketch in the psychological subtleties and historical and philosophical allusions, action and what not, but

---

*Editors' title   †Patroller.

I don't think its basic definition can be exhausted. Perhaps some genius could do as much with it as Mann has done with the Joseph story.

INTERVIEWERS: Can you give us an example of the use of folklore in your own novel?

5   ELLISON: Well, there are certain themes, symbols and images which are based on folk material. For example, there is the old saying amongst Negroes: If you're black, stay back; if you're brown, stick around; if you're white, you're right. And there is the joke Negroes tell on themselves about their being so black they can't be seen in the dark. In my book this sort of thing was merged with the meanings which blackness and light have long had in Western mythology: evil and goodness, ignorance and knowledge, and so on. In my novel the narrator's development is one through blackness to light; that is, from ignorance to enlightenment: invisibility to visibility. He leaves the South and goes North; this, as you will notice in reading Negro folktales, is always the road to freedom, the movement upward. You have the same thing again when he leaves his underground cave for the open.

It took me a long time to learn how to adapt such examples of myth into my work—also ritual. The use of ritual is equally a vital part of the creative process. I learned a few things from Eliot, Joyce and Hemingway, but not how to adapt them. When I started writing, I knew that in both *The Waste Land* and *Ulysses* ancient myth and ritual were used to give form and significance to the material, but it took me a few years to realize that the myths and rites which we find functioning in our everyday lives could be used in the same way. In my first attempt at a novel—which I was unable to complete—I began by trying to manipulate the simple structural unities of *beginning, middle* and *end,* but when I attempted to deal with the psychological strata—the images, symbols and emotional configurations—of the experience at hand, I discovered that the unities were simply cool points of stability on which one could suspend the narrative line, but beneath the surface of apparently rational human relationships there seethed a chaos before which I was helpless. People rationalize what they shun or are incapable of dealing with; these superstitions and their rationalizations become ritual as they govern behavior. The rituals become social forms, and it is one of the functions of the artist to recognize them and raise them to the level of art.

I don't know whether I'm getting this over or not. Let's put it this way: take the "Battle Royal" passage in my novel, where the boys are blindfolded and forced to fight each other for the amusement of the white observers. This is a vital part of behavior pattern in the South, which both Negroes and whites thoughtlessly accept. It is a ritual in preservation of caste lines, a keeping of taboo to appease the gods and ward off bad luck. It is also the initiation ritual to which all greenhorns are subjected. This passage which states what Negroes will see I did not have to invent; the patterns were already there in society, so that all I had to do was present them in a broader context of meaning. In any society there are many rituals of situation which, for the most part, go unquestioned. They can be simple or elaborate, but they are the connective tissue between the work of art and the audience.

INTERVIEWERS: Do you think a reader unacquainted with this folklore can properly understand your work?

ELLISON: Yes, I think so. It's like jazz; there's no inherent problem which pro-
hibits understanding but the assumptions brought to it. We don't all dig
Shakespeare uniformly, or even Little Red Riding Hood. The understanding
of art depends finally upon one's willingness to extend one's humanity and
one's knowledge of human life. I noticed, incidentally, that the Germans,
having no special caste assumptions concerning American Negroes, dealt
with my work simply as a novel. I think the Americans will come to view it
that way in twenty years—if it's around that long.

[1955]

RALPH ELLISON
Life in Oklahoma City*

. . .

In the loosely structured community of that time, knowledge, news of other
ways of living, ancient wisdom, the latest literary fads, hate literature—for years
I kept a card warning Negroes away from the polls, which had been dropped by
the thousands from a plane which circled over the Negro community—information of all kinds found its level, catch-as-catch-can, in the minds of those who
were receptive to it. Not that there was no conscious structuring—I read my first
Shaw and Maupassant, my first Harvard Classics in the home of a friend whose
parents were products of that stream of New England education which had been
brought to Negroes by the young and enthusiastic white teachers who staffed
the schools set up for the freedmen after the Civil War. These parents were both
teachers, and there were others like them in our town.

But the places where a rich oral literature was truly functional were the
churches, the schoolyards, the barbershops, the cotton-picking camps—places
where folklore and gossip thrived. The drug store where I worked was such a
place, where on days of bad weather the older men would sit with their pipes
and tell tall tales, hunting yarns and homely versions of the classics. It was here
that I heard stories of searching for buried treasure and of headless horsemen,
which I was told were my own father's versions told long before. There were
even recitals of popular verse, "The Shooting of Dan McGrew," and, along with
these, stories of Jesse James, of Negro outlaws and black United States marshals,
of slaves who became the chiefs of Indian tribes, and of the exploits of Negro
cowboys. There was both truth and fantasy in this, intermingled in the mysterious fashion of literature.

In their formative period, writers absorb into their consciousness much that
has no special value until much later, and often much which is of no special
value even then, perhaps, beyond the fact that it throbs with affect and mystery
and in it "time and pain and royalty in the blood" are suspended in imagery. So,
long before I thought of writing, I was claimed by weather, by speech rhythms,
by Negro voices and their different idioms, by husky male voices and by the high
shrill singing voices of certain Negro women, by music, by tight spaces and by
wide spaces in which the eyes could wander, by death, by newly born babies, by
manners of various kinds, company manners and street manners, the manners of

*Editors' title

white society and those of our own high society, and by interracial manners, by street fights, circuses and minstrel shows, by vaudeville and moving pictures, by prize fights and foot races, baseball games and football matches. By spring floods and blizzards, catalpa worms and jack rabbits, honeysuckle and snapdragons (which smelled like old cigar butts), by sunflowers and hollyhocks, raw sugar cane and baked yams, pigs' feet, chili and blue haw ice cream. By parades, public dances and jam sessions, Easter sunrise ceremonies and large funerals. By contests between fire-and-brimstone preachers and by presiding elders who got "laughing-happy" when moved by the spirit of God.

I was impressed by expert players of the "dozens" and certain notorious bootleggers of corn whiskey. By jazz musicians and fortunetellers and by men who did anything well, by strange sicknesses and by interesting brick or razor scars, by expert cursing vocabularies as well as by exalted praying and terrifying shouting, and by transcendent playing or singing of the blues. I was fascinated by old ladies, those who had seen slavery and those who were defiant of white folk and black alike, by the enticing walks of prostitutes and by the limping walks affected by Negro hustlers, especially those who wore Stetson hats, expensive shoes with well-starched overalls, usually with a diamond stickpin (when not in hock) in their tireless collars as their gambling uniforms.

5   And there were the blind men who preached on corners, and the blind men who sang the blues to the accompaniment of washboard and guitar, and the white junkmen who sang mountain music and the famous hucksters of fruit and vegetables.

And there was the Indian-Negro confusion. There were Negroes who were part Indian and who lived on reservations, and Indians who had children who lived in towns as Negroes, and Negroes who were Indians and traveled back and forth between the groups with no trouble. And Indians who were as wild as wild Negroes, and others who were as solid and as steady as bankers. There were the teachers, too: inspiring teachers and villainous teachers who chased after the girl students, and certain female teachers who one wished would chase after young male students. And a handsome old principal of military bearing who had been blemished by his classmates at West Point when they discovered on the eve of graduation that he was a Negro. There were certain Jews, Mexicans, Chinese cooks, a German orchestra conductor and an English grocer who owned a Franklin touring car. And certain Negro mechanics—"Cadillac Slim," "Sticks" Walker, Buddy Bunn and Oscar Pitman—who had so assimilated the automobile that they seemed to be behind a steering wheel even as they walked the streets or danced with girls. And there were the whites who despised us and the others who shared our hardships and our joys.

There is much more, but this is sufficient to indicate some of what was present even in a segregated community to form the background of my work and my sense of life.

And now comes the next step. I went to Tuskegee to study music, hoping to become a composer of symphonies, and there, during my second year, I read *The Waste Land* and that, although I was then unaware of it, was the real transition to writing.

Mrs. L. C. McFarland had taught us much of Negro history in grade school, and from her I'd learned of the New Negro Movement of the twenties, of Langston Hughes, Countee Cullen, Claude McKay, James Weldon Johnson and the others. They had inspired pride and had given me a closer identification with poetry (by now, oddly enough, I seldom thought of my hidden name), but with music so much on my mind it never occurred to me to try to imitate them. Still, I read their work and was excited by the glamour of the Harlem which emerged from their poems, and it was good to know that there were Negro writers. Then came *The Waste Land.*

10   I was much more under the spell of literature than I realized at the time. *Wuthering Heights* had caused me an agony of unexpressible emotion, and the same was true of *Jude the Obscure,* but *The Waste Land* seized my mind. I was intrigued by its power to move me while eluding my understanding. Somehow its rhythms were often closer to those of jazz than were those of the Negro poets, and even though I could not understand then, its range of allusion was as mixed and as varied as that of Louis Armstrong. Yet there were its discontinuities, its changes of pace and its hidden system of organization which escaped me.

There was nothing to do but look up the references in the footnotes to the poem, and thus began my conscious education in literature. For this, the library at Tuskegee was quite adequate and I used it. Soon I was reading a whole range of subjects drawn upon by the poet, and this led, in turn, to criticism and to Pound, Ford Madox Ford, Sherwood Anderson, Gertrude Stein, Hemingway and Fitzgerald and "round about 'til I was come" back to Melville and Twain—the writers who are taught and doubtless overtaught today. Perhaps it was my good luck that they were not taught at Tuskegee; I wouldn't know. But at the time I was playing, having an intellectually interesting good time.

Having given so much attention to the techniques of music, the process of learning something of the craft and intention of modern poetry and fiction seemed quite familiar. Besides, it was absolutely painless because it involved no deadlines or credits. Even then, however, a process which I described earlier had begun to operate. The more I learned of literature in this conscious way, the more the details of my background became transformed. I heard undertones in remembered conversations which had escaped me before, local customs took on a more universal meaning, values which I hadn't understood were revealed, some of the people whom I had known were diminished, while others were elevated in stature. More important, I began to see my own possibilities with more objective and in some ways more hopeful eyes.

The summer of 1936 I went to New York seeking work, which I did not find, and remained there, but the personal transformation continued. Reading had become a conscious process of growth and discovery, a method of reordering the world. And that world had widened considerably.

At Tuskegee I had handled manuscripts which Prokofiev had given to Hazel Harrison, a Negro concert pianist who taught there and who had known him in Europe, and through Miss Harrison I had become aware of Prokofiev's symphonies. I had also become aware of the radical movement in politics and art, and in New York had begun reading the work of André Malraux, not only the fiction but chapters published from his *Psychology of Art.* And in my search for an expression of modern sensibility in the works of Negro writers I discovered Richard Wright. Shortly thereafter I was to meet Wright, and it was at his suggestion that I wrote both my first book review and my first short story.

15   These were fateful suggestions. For although I had tried my hand at poetry while at Tuskegee, it hadn't occurred to me that I might write fiction, but once he suggested it, it seemed the most natural thing to try. Fortunately for me, Wright, then on the verge of his first success, was eager to talk with a beginner, and I was able to save valuable time in searching out those works in which writing was discussed as a craft. He guided me to Henry James's prefaces, to Conrad,

to Joseph Warren Beach and to the letters of Dostoevsky. There were other advisers and other books involved, of course, but what is important here is that I was consciously concerned with the art of fiction, and that almost from the beginning I was grappling quite consciously with the art through which I wished to realize myself. But this was not done in isolation; the Spanish Civil War was now in progress and the Depression was still on. The world was being shaken up, and through one of those odd instances which occur to young provincials in New York, I was to hear Malraux make an appeal for the Spanish Loyalists at the same party where I first heard the folk singer Leadbelly perform. Wright and I were there seeking money for the magazine which he had come to New York to edit.

Art and politics: a great French novelist and a Negro folk singer, a young writer who was soon to publish *Uncle Tom's Children,* and I who had barely begun to study his craft. It is such accidents, such fortuitous meetings, which count for so much in our lives. I had never dreamed that I would be in the presence of Malraux, of whose work I became aware on my second day in Harlem when Langston Hughes suggested that I read *Man's Fate* and *Days of Wrath* before returning them to a friend of his. And it is this fortuitous circumstance which led to my selecting Malraux as a literary "ancestor," whom, unlike a relative, the artist is permitted to choose. There was in progress at the time all the agitation over the Scottsboro boys and the Herndon Case, and I was aware of both. I had to be; I myself had been taken off a freight train at Decatur, Alabama, only three years before while on my way to Tuskegee. But while I joined in the agitation for their release, my main energies went into learning to write.

I began to publish enough, and not too slowly, to justify my hopes for success, and as I continued, I made a most perplexing discovery—namely, that for all his conscious concern with technique, a writer did not so much create the novel as he was created *by* the novel. That is, one did not make an arbitrary gesture when one sought to write. And when I say that the novelist is created by the novel, I mean to remind you that fictional techniques are not a mere set of objective tools, but something much more intimate: a way of feeling, of seeing and of expressing one's sense of life. And the process of *acquiring* technique is a process of modifying one's responses, of learning to see and feel, to hear and observe, to evoke and evaluate the images of memory and of summoning up and directing the imagination, of learning to conceive of human values in the ways which have been established by the great writers who have developed and extended the art. And perhaps the writer's greatest freedom, as artist, lies precisely in his possession of technique, for it is through technique that he comes to possess and express the meaning of his life.

[1964]

Reading (and Writing About) Drama

TYPES OF PLAYS

Most of the world's great plays written before the twentieth century may be regarded as one of two kinds: **tragedy** or **comedy.** Roughly speaking, tragedy dramatizes the conflict between the vitality of the individual life and the laws or limits of life. The tragic hero reaches a height, going beyond the experience of others but at the cost of his or her life. Comedy, on the other hand, dramatizes the vitality of the laws of social life. In comedy, the good life is seen to reside in the shedding of an individualism that isolates, in favor of a union with a genial and enlightened society. These points must be amplified a bit before we go on to the further point that, of course, any important play does much more than can be put into such crude formulas.

Tragedy

Tragic heroes usually go beyond the standards to which reasonable people adhere; they do some fearful deed which ultimately destroys them. This deed is often said to be an act of **hubris,** a Greek word meaning something like "overweening pride." It may involve, for instance, violating a taboo, such as that against taking life. But if the hubristic act ultimately destroys the man or woman who performs it, it also shows that person (paradoxically) to be in some way more fully a living being—a person who has experienced life more fully, whether by heroic action or by capacity for enduring suffering—than the other characters in the play. (If the tragic hero does not die, he or she is usually left in some deathlike state, as is the blind Oedipus in *Oedipus Rex.*) In tragedy we see humanity pushed to an extreme; the hero enters a world unknown to most and reveals magnificence. After the hero's departure from the stage, we are left in a world of littler people.

What has just been said may (or may not) be true of most tragedies, but it certainly is not true of all. If you are writing about a tragedy, you might consider whether the points just made are illustrated in your play. Is the hero guilty of hubris? Does the hero seem a greater person than the others in the play? An essay examining such questions probably requires not only a character sketch but also some comparison with other characters.

Tragedy commonly involves **irony** of two sorts: unconsciously ironic deeds and unconsciously ironic speeches. **Ironic deeds** have some consequence more or less the reverse of what the doer intends. Macbeth thinks that by killing Duncan he will gain happiness, but he finds that his deed brings him sleepless nights. Brutus thinks that by killing Caesar he will bring liberty to Rome, but he brings tyranny. In an **unconsciously ironic speech,** the words mean one thing to the speaker but something more significant to the audience, as when King Duncan, baffled by Cawdor's treason, says:

> There's no art
> To find the mind's construction in the face:
> He was a gentleman on whom I built
> An absolute trust.

At this moment Macbeth, whom we have already heard meditating the murder of Duncan, enters. Duncan's words are true, but he does not apply them to Macbeth, as the audience does. A few moments later Duncan praises Macbeth as "a peerless kinsman." Soon Macbeth will indeed become peerless, when he kills Duncan and ascends to the throne.[1] Sophocles' use of ironic deeds and speeches is so pervasive, especially in *Oedipus Rex,* that **Sophoclean irony** has become a critical term.

When the deed backfires or has a reverse effect, such as Macbeth's effort to gain happiness has, we have what Aristotle (the first—and still the greatest—drama critic) called a **peripeteia,** or a **reversal.** A character who comes to perceive what has happened (Macbeth's "I have lived long enough: my way of life / Is fall'n into the sere, the yellow leaf") experiences (in Aristotle's language) an **anagnorisis,** or **recognition.** Strictly speaking, for Aristotle the recognition was a matter of literal identification—for example, the recognition that Oedipus was the son of a man he killed. In *Macbeth,* the recognition in this sense is that Macduff, "from his mother's womb / Untimely ripped," is the man who fits the prophecy that Macbeth can be conquered only by someone not "of woman born."

In his analysis of drama, Aristotle says that the tragic hero comes to grief through his **hamartia,** a term sometimes translated as **tragic flaw** but perhaps better translated as **tragic error,** since *flaw* implies a moral fault. Thus it is a great error for Oedipus (however apparently justifiable his action) to kill a man old enough to be his father, and to marry a woman old enough to be his mother. If we hold to the translation *flaw,* we begin to hunt for a fault in the tragic hero's character; and we say, for instance, that Oedipus is rash, or some such thing. In doing this, we may diminish or even overlook the hero's grandeur.

Comedy

Although in tragedy the hero usually seems to embody certain values that are superior to those of the surrounding society, in comedy the fullest life is seen to re-

---

[1] **Dramatic irony** (ironic deeds, or happenings, and unconsciously ironic speeches) must be distinguished from **verbal irony,** which is produced when the speaker is *conscious* that his words mean something different from what they say. In *Macbeth* Lennox says, "The gracious Duncan / Was pitied of Macbeth. Marry, he was dead! / And the right valiant Banquo walked too late./.../ Men must not walk too late." He *says* nothing about Macbeth having killed Duncan and Banquo, but he *means* that Macbeth was killed them.

side *within* enlightened social norms: At the beginning of a comedy we find banished dukes, unhappy lovers, crabby parents, jealous husbands, and harsh laws; but at the end we usually have a unified and genial society, often symbolized by a marriage feast to which everyone, or almost everyone, is invited. Early in *A Midsummer Night's Dream,* for instance, we meet quarreling young lovers and a father who demands that his daughter either marry a man she does not love or enter a convent. Such is the Athenian law. At the end of the play the lovers are properly matched, to everyone's satisfaction.

Speaking broadly, most comedies fall into one of two classes: **satiric comedy** or **romantic comedy.** In satiric comedy, the emphasis is on the obstructionists—the irate fathers, hardheaded businessmen, and other members of the establishment who at the beginning of the play seem to hold all of the cards, preventing joy from reigning. They are held up to ridicule because they are repressive monomaniacs enslaved to themselves, acting mechanistically (always irate, always hardheaded) instead of responding genially to the ups and downs of life. The outwitting of these obstructionists, usually by the younger generation, often provides the resolution of the plot. Ben Jonson, Molière, and George Bernard Shaw are in this tradition; their comedy, according to an ancient Roman formula, "chastens morals with ridicule"—that is, it reforms folly or vice by laughing at it. On the other hand, in romantic comedy (one thinks of Shakespeare's *A Midsummer Night's Dream, As You Like It,* and *Twelfth Night*) the emphasis is on a pair or pairs of delightful people who engage our sympathies as they run their obstacle race to the altar. There are obstructionists here too, but the emphasis is on festivity.

In writing about comedy you may, of course, be concerned with the function of one scene or character, but whatever your topic, you may find it helpful to begin by trying to decide whether the play is primarily romantic or primarily satiric (or something else). One way of getting at this is to ask yourself to what degree you sympathize with the characters. Do you laugh *with* them, sympathetically, or on the other hand do you laugh *at* them, regarding them as at least somewhat contemptible?

ELEMENTS OF DRAMA

Theme

If we have read or seen a drama thoughtfully, we ought to be able to formulate its **theme,** its underlying idea, and perhaps we can even go so far as to say its moral attitudes, its view of life, its wisdom. Some critics, it is true, have argued that the concept of theme is meaningless. They hold that *Macbeth,* for example, gives us only an extremely detailed history of one imaginary man. In this view, *Macbeth* says nothing to you or me; it only says what happened to some imaginary man. Even *Julius Caesar* says nothing about the historical Julius Caesar or about the nature of Roman politics. Here we can agree; no one would offer Shakespeare's play as evidence of what the historical Caesar said or did. But surely the view that the concept of theme is meaningless, and that a work tells us only about imaginary creatures, is a desperate one. We *can* say that we see in *Julius Caesar* the fall of power, or (if we are thinking of Brutus) the vulnerability of idealism, or some such thing.

To the reply that these are mere truisms, we can counter: Yes, but the truisms are presented in such a way that they take on life and become a part of us rather than remain things of which we say, "I've heard it said, and I guess it's so." The play offers instruction, in a pleasant and persuasive way. And surely we are in no danger of equating the play with the theme that we sense underlies it. We recognize that the play presents the theme with such detail that our statement is only a wedge to help us enter into the play, so we can appropriate it more fully.

Some critics (influenced by Aristotle's statement that a drama is an imitation of an action) use **action** in a sense equivalent to theme. In this sense, the action is the underlying happening—the inner happening—for example, "the enlightenment of a character," or "the coming of unhappiness to a character," or "the finding of the self by self-surrender." One might say that the theme of *Macbeth,* for example, is embodied in some words that Macbeth himself utters: "Blood will have blood." Of course this is not to say that these words and no other words embody the theme or the action; it is only to say that these words seem to the writer (and, if the essay is effective, to the reader) to bring us close to the center of the play.

Plot

Plot is variously defined, sometimes as equivalent to *story* (in this sense a synopsis of *Julius Caesar* has the same plot as *Julius Caesar*), but more often, and more usefully, as the dramatist's particular *arrangement of the story.* Thus, because Shakespeare's *Julius Caesar* begins with a scene dramatizing an encounter between plebeians and tribunes, its plot is different from that of a play on Julius Caesar in which such a scene (not necessary to the story) is omitted.

Handbooks on drama often suggest that a plot (arrangement of happenings) should have a **rising action,** a **climax,** and a **falling action.** This sort of plot can be diagrammed as a pyramid: The tension rises through complications or **crises** to a climax, at which point the climax is the apex, and the tension allegedly slackens as we witness the **dénouement** (literally, *unknotting*). Shakespeare sometimes used a pyramidal structure, placing his climax neatly in the middle of what seems to us to be the third of five acts. In *Hamlet,* the protagonist proves to his own satisfaction Claudius's guilt in 3.2, with the play within the play; but almost immediately he begins to worsen his position, by failing to kill Claudius when he is an easy target (3.3) and by contaminating himself with the murder of Polonius (3.4). In *Romeo and Juliet,* the first half shows Romeo winning Juliet, but when in 3.1 he kills her cousin Tybalt, Romeo sets in motion the second half of the play, the losing of Juliet and of his own life.

Of course, no law demands such a structure, and a hunt for the pyramid usually causes the hunter to overlook all the crises but the middle one. William Butler Yeats once suggestively diagrammed a good plot not as a pyramid but as a line moving diagonally upward, punctuated by several crises. Perhaps it is sufficient to say that a good plot has its moments of tension, but the location of these will vary with the play. They are the product of **conflict,** but it should be noted that not all conflict produces tension; there is conflict but little tension in a ball game when the home team is ahead 10-0 and the visiting pitcher comes to bat in the ninth inning with two out and none on base.

Regardless of how a plot is diagrammed, the **exposition** is that part that tells the audience what it has to know about the past, the **antecedent action.** Two gossiping servants who tell each other that after a year away in Paris the young master is coming home tomorrow with a new wife are giving the audience the exposition. But the exposition may also extend far into the play, being given in small, explosive revelations.

Exposition has been discussed as though it consists simply of informing the audience about events, but exposition can do much more. It can give us an understanding of the characters who themselves are talking about other characters, it can evoke a mood, and it can generate tension. When we summarize the opening act, and treat it as "mere exposition," we are probably losing what is dramatic in it.

In fact, exposition usually includes **foreshadowing.** Details given in the exposition, which we may at first take as mere background, often turn out to be highly relevant to later developments. For instance, in the very short first scene of *Macbeth* the witches introduce the name of Macbeth, but in such words as "Fair is foul" and "when the battle's lost and won" they also give glimpses of what will happen: Macbeth will become foul, and though he will seem to win (he becomes king) he will lose the most important battle. Similarly, during the exposition in the second scene we learn that Macbeth has loyally defeated Cawdor, who betrayed King Duncan, and Macbeth has been given Cawdor's title. Later we will find that, like Cawdor, Macbeth betrays Duncan. That is, in giving us the background about Cawdor, the exposition is also telling us (though we don't know it, when we first see or read the play) something about what will happen to Macbeth.

In writing about an aspect of plot, you may want to consider one of the following topics:

- Is the plot improbable? If so, is the play therefore weak?
- Does a scene that might at first glance seem unimportant or even irrelevant serve an important function?
- If certain actions that could be shown onstage take place offstage, is there a reason? In *Macbeth,* for instance, why do you suppose the murder of Duncan takes place offstage, whereas Banquo and Macduff's family are murdered onstage? Why, then, might Shakespeare have preferred not to show us the murder of Duncan? What has he gained? (A good way to approach this sort of question is to think of what your own reaction would be if the action were shown on the stage.)
- If there are several conflicts—for example, between pairs of lovers or between parents and their children and also between the parents themselves—how are these conflicts related? Are they parallel? Or contrasting?
- Does the arrangement of scenes have a structure? For instance, do the scenes depict a rise and then a fall?
- Does the plot seem satisfactorily concluded? Are there loose threads? If so, is the apparent lack of a complete resolution a weakness in the play? Or does it serve a function?

Gestures

The language of a play, broadly conceived, includes the **gestures** that the characters make and the settings in which they make them. As Ezra Pound says, "The medium of drama is not words, but persons moving about on a stage using words." Because plays are meant to be seen, make every effort to visualize the action when you read a play. Ibsen is getting at something important when he tells us in a stage direction that Nora "walks cautiously over to the door to the study and listens." Her silent actions tell us as much about her as many of her speeches do.

Gesture can be interpreted even more broadly: The mere fact that a character enters, leaves, or does not enter may be highly significant. John Russell Brown comments on the actions and the absence of certain words that in *Hamlet* convey the growing separation between King Claudius and his wife, Gertrude:

> Their first appearance together with a public celebration of marriage is a large and simple visual effect, and Gertrude's close concern for her son suggests a simple, and perhaps unremarkable modification. . . . But Claudius enters without Gertrude for his "Prayer Scene" (3.2) and, for the first time, Gertrude enters without him for the Closet Scene (3.4) and is left alone, again for the first time, when Polonius hides behind the arras. Thereafter earlier accord is revalued by an increasing separation, often poignantly silent and unexpected. When Claudius calls Gertrude to leave with him after Hamlet has dragged off Polonius' body, she makes no reply; twice more he urges her and she is still silent. But he does not remonstrate or question; rather he speaks of his own immediate concerns and, far from supporting her with assurances, becomes more aware of his own fears:
>
> O, come away!
My soul is full of discord and dismay. (4.1.44–45)
>
> Emotion has been so heightened that it is remarkable that they leave together without further words. The audience has been aware of a new distance between Gertrude and Claudius, of her immobility and silence, and of his self-concern, haste, and insistence.[2]

Setting

Drama of the nineteenth and early twentieth centuries (for example, the plays of Henrik Ibsen, Anton Chekhov, and George Bernard Shaw) is often thought to be "realistic," but even a realistic playwright or stage designer selects from among many available materials. A **realistic setting** (indication of the **locale**), then, can say a great deal, and can even serve as a symbol. Over and over again in Ibsen we find the realistic setting of a nineteenth-century drawing room, with its heavy draperies and its bulky furniture, helping to convey his vision of a bourgeois world that oppresses the individual who struggles to affirm other values.

Twentieth-century dramatists are often explicit about the symbolic qualities of the setting. Here is an example from Eugene O'Neill's *Desire Under the Elms;* only a part of the initial stage direction is given:

> The house is in good condition but in need of paint. Its walls are a sickly grayish, the green of the shutters faded. Two enormous elms are on each side of the house. They bend their trailing branches down over the roof. They appear to protect and at the same time subdue. There is a sinister maternity in their aspect, a crushing, jealous absorption. . . .

---

[2] *Shakespeare's Plays in Performance* (New York: St. Martin's, 1967), p. 139.

They are like exhausted women resting their sagging breasts and hands and hair on its roof.

Not surprisingly, the action in the play includes deeds of "sinister maternity" (a mother kills her infant) and "jealous absorption."

In *The Glass Menagerie* Tennessee Williams tells us that

the apartment faces an alley and is entered by a fire-escape, a structure whose name is a touch of accidental poetic truth, for all of these huge buildings are always burning with the slow and implacable fires of human desperation.

Characterization and Motivation

Characterization, or personality, is defined, as in fiction (see p. 193-94), by what the characters do (a stage direction tells us that "Nora dances more and more wildly"), by what they say (she asks her husband to play the piano), by what others say about them, and by the setting in which they move. The characters are also defined in part by other characters whom they in some degree resemble or from whom they in some degree differ. Hamlet, Laertes, and Fortinbras have each lost their fathers, but Hamlet spares the praying King Claudius, whereas Laertes, seeking vengeance on Hamlet for murdering Laertes's father, says he would cut Hamlet's throat in church; Hamlet meditates about the nature of action, but Fortinbras leads the Norwegians in a military campaign and ultimately acquires Denmark.

Other plays, of course, also provide examples of such **foils,** or characters who set one another off. Macbeth and Banquo both hear prophecies, but they act and react differently; Brutus is one kind of assassin, Cassius another, and Casca still another. Any analysis of a character, then, will probably have to take into account, in some degree, the other characters who help to show what he or she is, and who thus help to set forth his or her **motivation** (grounds for action, inner drives, goals).

ORGANIZING AN ANALYSIS OF A CHARACTER

As you read and reread, you'll annotate the text and will jot down (in whatever order they come to you) your thoughts about the character you are studying. Reading, with a view toward writing, you'll want to

1. jot down traits as they come to mind ("kind," "forgetful," "enthusiastic");
2. look back at the text, searching for supporting evidence (characteristic actions, brief supporting quotations); and of course you will also look for counterevidence so that you may modify your earlier impressions.

Brainstorming leads to an evaluation of your ideas and to a shaping of them. Evaluating and shaping lead to a tentative outline, and a tentative outline leads to the search for supporting evidence—the material that will constitute the body of your essay.

When you set out to write a first draft, review your annotations and notes and see if you can summarize your view of the character in one or two sentences:

> X is . . . ,

or

> Although X is . . . , she is also . . . .

That is, try to formulate a thesis sentence or a thesis paragraph, a proposition that you will go on to support.

You want to let your reader know early, probably in your first sentence—and almost certainly by the end of your first paragraph—which character you are writing about and what your overall thesis is.

First Draft

Here is the first draft of an **opening paragraph** that identifies the character and sets forth a thesis:

> Romeo is a very interesting character, I think. In the beginning of the play Romeo is very adolescent. Romeo is smitten with puppy love for a woman named Rosaline. He desires to show all of his friends that he knows how a lover is supposed to act. When he sees Juliet he experiences true love. From the point when he sees Juliet he experiences true love, and from this point he steadily matures in Romeo and Juliet. He moves from a self-centered man to a man who lives not for himself but only for Juliet.

Revised Draft

Later the student edited the draft. We reprint the original, with the additional editing in handwriting:

> Romeo ~~is a very interesting character, I think. In the beginning~~ ^begins as an^ ~~of the play Romeo is very~~ adolescent, ~~Romeo is~~ smitten with puppy ^and a desire^ love for ~~a woman named~~ Rosaline/~~He desires~~ to show all of his friends ^however,^ that he knows how a lover is supposed to act. When he sees Juliet, he ^and^ ^this^ experiences true love, ~~From~~ the point ~~when he sees Juliet he~~ ~~experiences true love, and from this point~~ he steadily matures, in ^moving^ ^adolescent^ ~~Romeo and Juliet. He moves~~ from a self-centered ~~man~~ to a man who lives ~~not for himself but~~ only for Juliet.

Here is a revised version of another effective opening paragraph, effective partly because it identifies the character and offers a thesis:

In the last speech of Macbeth, Malcolm characterizes Lady Macbeth as "fiend-like," and indeed she invokes evil spirits and prompts her husband to commit murder. But despite her bold pose, her role in the murder, and her belief that she will be untroubled by guilt, she has a conscience that torments her and that finally drives her to suicide. She is not a mere heartless villain; she is a human being who is less strong—and more moral—than she thinks she is.

Notice that

- the paragraph quotes a word ("fiend-like") from the text. It happens that the writer goes on to argue that this word is *not* a totally accurate description, but the quotation nevertheless helps to bring the reader into close contact with the subject of the essay.
- in writing about literature we do not ordinarily introduce the thesis formally. We do not, that is, say "In this paper it is my intention to prove that . . . ." Such a sentence may be perfectly appropriate in a paper in political science, but in a paper on literature it sounds too stiff.

The body of your essay will be devoted, of course, to supporting your thesis. If you have asserted that although Lady Macbeth is cruel and domineering she nevertheless is endowed with a conscience, you will go on in your essay to support those assertions with references to passages that demonstrate them. This does *not* mean that you tell the plot of the whole work; an essay on a character is by no means the same as a summary of the plot. But since you must support your generalizations, you will have to make brief references to specific episodes that reveal her personality, and almost surely you will quote an occasional word or passage.

There are many possible **ways to organize** an essay on a character. Much will depend, of course, on your purpose and thesis. For instance

- you may want to show how the character develops—gains knowledge, or matures, or disintegrates. Or, again,
- you may want to show what the character contributes to the story or play as a whole. Or, to give yet another example,
- you may want to show that the character is unbelievable.

Still, although no single organization is always right, two methods are common and effective. One is to let the organization of your essay follow closely the sequence of the literary work; that is, you might devote a paragraph to Lady Macbeth as we perceive her in the first act, and then in subsequent paragraphs go on to show that her character is later seen to be more complex than it at first appears. Such an essay may trace your changing responses. This does not mean that you need to write five paragraphs, one on her character in each of the five acts. But it does mean that you might begin with Lady Macbeth as you perceive her in, say, the first act, and then go on to the additional revelations of the rest of the play.

A second effective way of organizing an essay on a character is to set forth, early in the essay, the character's chief traits—let's say the chief strengths and two or three weaknesses—and then go on to study each trait you have listed. Here the organization would (in order to maintain the reader's interest) probably begin with the most obvious points and then move on to the less obvious, subtler points. The body of your essay, in any case, is devoted to offering evidence that supports your generalizations about the character.

What about a **concluding paragraph?** The concluding paragraph ought *not* to begin with the obviousness of "Thus we see," or "In conclusion," or "I recommend this play because . . . ." In fact, after you have given what you consider a sound sketch of the character, it may be appropriate simply to quit. Especially if your essay has moved from the obvious traits to the more subtle and more important traits, and if your essay is fairly short (say, fewer than 500 words), a reader may not need a conclusion. Further, there probably is no reason to blunt what you have just said by adding an unnecessary and merely repetitive summary. But if you do feel that a conclusion is necessary, you may find it effective to write a summary of the character, somewhat as you did in your opening. For the conclusion, relate the character's character to the entire drama—that is, try to give the reader a sense of the role that the character plays.

✔ A Checklist: Getting Ideas for Writing About Drama

The following questions may help you to formulate ideas for an essay on a play.

Plot and Conflict

✔ Does the exposition introduce elements that will be ironically fulfilled? During the exposition do you perceive things differently from the way the characters perceive them?

✔ Are certain happenings or situations recurrent? If so, what significance do you attach to them?

✔ If there is more than one plot, do the plots seem to you to be related? Is one plot clearly the main plot and another plot a sort of subplot, a minor variation on the theme?

✔ Do any scenes strike you as irrelevant?

✔ Are certain scenes so strongly foreshadowed that you anticipated them? If so, did the happenings in these scenes merely fulfill your expectations, or did they also surprise you?

✔ What kinds of conflict are there? One character against another, one group against another, one part of a personality against another part in the same person?

✔ How is the conflict resolved? By an unambiguous triumph of one side or by a triumph that is also in some degree a loss for the triumphant side? Do you find the resolution satisfying, or unsettling, or what? Why?

Character

✔ A dramatic character is not likely to be thoroughly realistic, a copy of someone we might know. Still, we can ask if the character is consistent and coherent. We can also ask if the character is complex or is, on the other hand, a rather simple representative of some human type.

✔ How is the character defined? Consider what the character says and does and what others say about him or her and do to him or her. Also consider other characters who more or less resemble the character in question, because the similarities—and the differences—may be significant.

✔ How trustworthy are the characters when they characterize themselves? when they characterize others?

✔ Do characters change as the play goes on, or do we simply know them better at the end?

✔ What do you make of the minor characters? Are they merely necessary to the plot, or are they foils to other characters? Or do they serve some other functions?

✔ If a character is tragic, does the tragedy seem to you to proceed from a moral flaw, from an intellectual error, from the malice of others, from sheer chance, or from some combination of these?

✔ What are the character's goals? To what degree do you sympathize with them? If a character is comic, do you laugh *with* or *at* the character?

✔ Do you think the characters are adequately motivated?

✔ Is a given character so meditative that you feel he or she is engaged less in a dialogue with others than in a dialogue with the self? If so, do you feel that this character is in large degree a spokesperson for the author, commenting not only on the world of the play but also on the outside world?

Nonverbal Language

✔ If the playwright does not provide full stage directions, try to imagine for at least one scene what gestures and tones might accompany each speech. (The first scene is usually a good one to try your hand at.)

✔ What do you make of the setting? Does it help to reveal character? Do changes of scene strike you as symbolic? If so, symbolic of what?

The Play on Film

✔ If the play has been turned into a film, what has been added? What has been omitted? Why?

✔ Has the film medium been used to advantage—for example, in focusing attention through close-ups or reaction shots (shots showing not the speaker but a person reacting to the speaker)? Or do some of the inventions, such as outdoor scenes that were not possible in the play, seem mere busywork, distracting from the urgency or the conflict or the unity of the play?

FOUR PLAYS

A NOTE ON GREEK TRAGEDY

Little or nothing is known for certain of the origin of Greek tragedy. The most common hypothesis holds that it developed from improvised speeches during choral dances honoring Dionysos, a Greek nature god associated with spring, fertility, and wine. Thespis (who perhaps never existed) is said to have introduced an actor into these choral performances in the sixth century B.C. Aeschylus (525–456 B.C.), Greece's first great writer of tragedies, added the second actor, and Sophocles (496?–406 B.C.) added the third actor and fixed the size of the chorus at fifteen. (Because the chorus leader often functioned as an additional actor, and because the actors sometimes doubled in their parts, a Greek tragedy could have more characters than might at first be thought.)

All of the extant great Greek tragedy is of the fifth century B.C. It was performed at religious festivals in the winter and early spring, in large outdoor amphitheaters built on hillsides. Some of these theaters were enormous; the one at Epidaurus held about fifteen thousand people. The audience sat in tiers, looking down on the *orchestra* (a dancing place), with the acting area behind it and the *skene* (the scene building) yet farther back. The scene building served as dressing room, background (suggesting a palace or temple), and place for occasional entrances and exits. Furthermore, this building helped to provide good acoustics, for speech travels well if there is a solid barrier behind the speaker and a hard, smooth surface in front of him, and if the audience sits in tiers. The wall of the scene building provided the barrier; the orchestra provided the surface in front of the actors; and the seats on the hillside fulfilled the third requirement. Moreover, the acoustics were somewhat improved by slightly elevating the actors above the orchestra, but it is not known exactly when this platform was first constructed in front of the scene building.

Greek theater of Epidaurus. (Frederick Ayers/Photo Researchers)

A tragedy commonly begins with a *prologos* (prologue), during which the exposition is given. Next comes the *párodos,* the chorus's ode of entrance, sung while the chorus marches into the theater, through the side aisles, and onto the orchestra. The *epeisodion* (episode) is the ensuing scene; it is followed by a *stasimon* (choral song, ode). Usually there are four or five *epeisodia,* alternating with *stasima.* Each of these choral odes has a *strophe* (lines presumably sung while the chorus dances in one direction) and an *antistrophe* (lines presumably sung while the chorus retraces its steps). Sometimes a third part, an *epode,* concludes an ode. (In addition to odes that are *stasima,* there can be odes within episodes; the fourth episode of *Antigonê* (here called Scene IV) contains an ode complete with *epode.*) After the last part of the last ode comes the *exodos,* the epilogue or final scene.

The actors (all male) wore masks, and they seem to have chanted much of the play. Perhaps the total result of combining speech with music and dancing was a sort of music-drama roughly akin to opera with some spoken dialogue, like Mozart's *Magic Flute.*

SOPHOCLES

One of the three great writers of tragedies in ancient Greece, Sophocles (496?–406 B.C.) was born in Colonus, near Athens, into a well-to-do family. Well educated, he first won public acclaim as a tragic poet at the age of 27, in 468 B.C., when he defeated Aeschylus in a competition for writing a tragic play. He is said to have written some 120 plays, but only 7 tragedies are extant; among them are Oedipus Rex, Antigonê, *and* Oedipus at Colonus. *He died, much honored, in his ninetieth year, in Athens, where he had lived his entire life.*

Laurence Olivier in Oedipus Rex. (Photography by John Vickers)

Oedipus Rex

An English Version by Dudley Fitts and Robert Fitzgerald

LIST OF CHARACTERS

OEDIPUS
A PRIEST
CREON
TEIRESIAS
IOCASTÉ
MESSENGER
SHEPHERD OF LAÏOS
SECOND MESSENGER
CHORUS OF THEBAN ELDERS

SCENE: *Before the palace of* OEDIPUS, *King of Thebes. A central door and two lateral doors open onto a platform which runs the length of the facade. On the platform, right and left, are altars; and three steps lead down into the "orchestra," or chorus-ground. At the beginning of the action these steps are crowded by* SUPPLIANTS *who have brought branches and chaplets of olive leaves and who lie in various attitudes of despair.* OEDIPUS *enters.*

Prologue

OEDIPUS. My children, generations of the living
  In the line of Kadmos,° nursed at his ancient hearth;
  Why have you strewn yourselves before these altars
  In supplication, with your boughs and garlands?
  The breath of incense rises from the city   5
  With a sound of prayer and lamentation.
                              Children,
  I would not have you speak through messengers,
  And therefore I have come myself to hear you—
  I, Oedipus who bear the famous name.
  [*To a* PRIEST.] You, there, since you are eldest in the company,   10
  Speak for them all, tell me what preys upon you,
  Whether you come in dread, or crave some blessing:
  Tell me, and never doubt that I will help you
  In every way I can; I should be heartless
  Were I not moved to find you suppliant here.   15
PRIEST. Great Oedipus, O powerful King of Thebes!
  You see how all the ages of our people
  Cling to your altar steps: here are boys
  Who can barely stand alone, and here are priests
  By weight of age, as I am a priest of God,   20
  And young men chosen from those yet unmarried;
  As for the others, all that multitude,
  They wait with olive chaplets in the squares,

2 **Kadmos** mythical founder of Thebes

At the two shrines of Pallas,° and where Apollo°
Speaks in the glowing embers.

                         Your own eyes   25
Must tell you: Thebes is in her extremity
And cannot lift her head from the surge of death.
A rust consumes the buds and fruits of the earth;
The herds are sick; children die unborn,
And labor is vain. The god of plague and pyre   30
Raids like detestable lightning through the city,
And all the house of Kadmos is laid waste,
All emptied, and all darkened: Death alone
Battens upon the misery of Thebes.
You are not one of the immortal gods, we know;   35
Yet we have come to you to make our prayer
As to the man of all men best in adversity
And wisest in the ways of God. You saved us
From the Sphinx,° that flinty singer, and the tribute
We paid to her so long; yet you were never   40
Better informed than we, nor could we teach you:
It was some god breathed in you to set us free.

Therefore, O mighty King, we turn to you:
Find us our safety, find us a remedy,
Whether by counsel of the gods or the men.   45
A king of wisdom tested in the past
Can act in a time of troubles, and act well.
Noblest of men, restore
Life to your city! Think how all men call you
Liberator for your triumph long ago;   50
Ah, when your years of kingship are remembered,
Let them not say *We rose, but later fell—*
Keep the State from going down in the storm!
Once, years ago, with happy augury,
You brought us fortune; be the same again!   55
No man questions your power to rule the land:
But rule over men, not over a dead city!
Ships are only hulls, citadels are nothing,
When no life moves in the empty passageways.
OEDIPUS. Poor children! You may be sure I know   60
All that you longed for in your coming here.
I know that you are deathly sick; and yet,
Sick as you are, not one is as sick as I.
Each of you suffers in himself alone

---

24 Pallas Athena, goddess of wisdom, protectress of Athens   **Apollo** god of light and
healing   **39 Sphinx** a monster (body of a lion, wings of a bird, face of a woman) who
asked the riddle, "What goes on four legs in the morning, two at noon, and three in the
evening?" and who killed those who could not answer. When Oedipus responded correctly that man crawls on all fours in infancy, walks upright in maturity, and uses a staff in
old age, the Sphinx destroyed herself.

His anguish, not another's; but my spirit   65
Groans for the city, for myself, for you.

I was not sleeping, you are not waking me.
No, I have been in tears for a long while
And in my restless thought walked many ways.
In all my search, I found one helpful course,   70
And that I have taken: I have sent Creon,
Son of Menoikeus, brother of the Queen,
To Delphi, Apollo's place of revelation,
To learn there, if he can,
What act or pledge of mine may save the city.   75
I have counted the days, and now, this very day,
I am troubled, for he has overstayed his time.
What is he doing? He has been gone too long.
Yet whenever he comes back, I should do ill
To scant whatever hint the god may give.   80
PRIEST. It is a timely promise. At this instant
    They tell me Creon is here.
OEDIPUS.   O Lord Apollo!
    May his news be fair as his face is radiant!
PRIEST. It could not be otherwise: he is crowned with bay,
    The chaplet is thick with berries.
OEDIPUS.   We shall soon know;   85
    He is near enough to hear us now.

    Enter CREON.
                 O Prince:
Brother: son of Menoikeus:
    What answer do you bring us from the god?
CREON. It is favorable. I can tell you, great afflictions
    Will turn out well, if they are taken well.   90
OEDIPUS. What was the oracle? These vague words
    Leave me still hanging between hope and fear.
CREON. Is it your pleasure to hear me with all these
    Gathered around us? I am prepared to speak,
    But should we not go in?
OEDIPUS.   Let them all hear it.   95
    It is for them I suffer, more than myself.
CREON. Then I will tell you what I heard at Delphi.

    In plain words
The god commands us to expel from the land of Thebes
An old defilement that it seems we shelter.   100
It is a deathly thing, beyond expiation.
We must not let it feed upon us longer.
OEDIPUS. What defilement? How shall we rid ourselves of it?
CREON. By exile or death, blood for blood. It was
    Murder that brought the plague-wind on the city.   105
OEDIPUS. Murder of whom? Surely the god has named him?
CREON. My lord: long ago Laïos was our king,
    Before you came to govern us.

OEDIPUS.   I know;
  I learned of him from others; I never saw him.
CREON. He was murdered; and Apollo commands us now   110
  To take revenge upon whoever killed him.
OEDIPUS. Upon whom? Where are they? Where shall we find a clue
  To solve that crime, after so many years?
CREON. Here in this land, he said.
                                    If we make enquiry,
  We may touch things that otherwise escape us.   115
OEDIPUS. Tell me: Was Laïos murdered in his house,
  Or in the fields, or in some foreign country?
CREON. He said he planned to make a pilgrimage.
  He did not come home again.
OEDIPUS.   And was there no one,
  No witness, no companion, to tell what happened?   120
CREON. They were all killed but one, and he got away
  So frightened that he could remember one thing only.
OEDIPUS. What was that one thing? One may be the key
  To everything, if we resolve to use it.
CREON. He said that a band of highwaymen attacked them.   125
  Outnumbered them, and overwhelmed the King.
OEDIPUS. Strange, that a highwayman should be so daring—
  Unless some faction here bribed him to do it.
CREON. We thought of that. But after Laïos' death
  New troubles arose and we had no avenger.   130
OEDIPUS. What troubles could prevent your hunting down the killers?
CREON. The riddling Sphinx's song
  Made us deaf to all mysteries but her own.
OEDIPUS. Then once more I must bring what is dark to light.
  It is most fitting that Apollo shows,   135
  As you do, this compunction for the dead.
  You shall see how I stand by you, as I should,
  To avenge the city and the city's god,
  And not as though it were for some distant friend,
  But for my own sake, to be rid of evil.   140
  Whoever killed King Laïos might—who knows?—
  Decide at any moment to kill me as well.
  By avenging the murdered king I protect myself.
  Come, then, my children: leave the altar steps,
  Lift up your olive boughs!
                                    One of you go   145
  And summon the people of Kadmos to gather here.
  I will do all that I can; you may tell them that.

                                    [*Exit a* PAGE]

  So, with the help of God,
  We shall be saved—or else indeed we are lost.
PRIEST. Let us rise, children. It was for this we came,   150
  And now the King has promised it himself.
  Phoibos° has sent us an oracle; may he descend

152 Phoibos Phoebus Apollo, the sun god

Himself to save us and drive out the plague.
Exeunt OEDIPUS *and* CREON *into the palace by the central door. The* PRIEST
and the SUPPLIANTS *disperse right and left. After a short pause the*
CHORUS *enters the orchestra.*

Párodos

CHORUS. What is God singing in his profound   *Strophe 1*
  Delphi of gold and shadow?
What oracle for Thebes, the sunwhipped city?
Fear unjoints me, the roots of my heart tremble.
Now I remember, O Healer, your power, and wonder;   5
Will you send doom like a sudden cloud, or weave it
Like nightfall of the past?
Speak, speak to us, issue of holy sound:
Dearest to our expectancy: be tender!

Let me pray to Athenê, the immortal daughter of Zeus,   *Antistrophe 1* 10
And to Artemis her sister
Who keeps her famous throne in the market ring,
And to Apollo, bowman at the far butts of heaven—

O gods, descend! Like three streams leap against
The fires of our grief, the fires of darkness;   15
Be swift to bring us rest!

As in the old time from the brilliant house
Of air you stepped to save us, come again!
Now our afflictions have no end,   *Strophe 2*
Now all our stricken host lies down   20
And no man fights off death with his mind;

The noble plowland bears no grain,
And groaning mothers cannot bear—
See, how our lives like birds take wing,
Like sparks that fly when a fire soars,   25
To the shore of the god of evening.

The plague burns on, it is pitiless   *Antistrophe 2*
Though pallid children laden with death
Lie unwept in the stony ways,
And old gray women by every path   30
Flock to the strand about the altars

There to strike their breasts and cry
Worship of Phoibos in wailing prayers:
Be kind, God's golden child!

There are no swords in this attack by fire,   *Strophe 3* 35
No shields, but we are ringed with cries.
Send the besieger plunging from our homes
Into the vast sea-room of the Atlantic

Or into the waves that foam eastward of Thrace—
For the day ravages what the night spares—   40

Destroy our enemy, lord of the thunder!
Let him be riven by lightning from heaven!

Phoibos Apollo, stretch the sun's bowstring,   *Antistrophe 3*
That golden cord, until it sing for us,
Flashing arrows in heaven!
     Artemis, Huntress,   45
Race with flaring lights upon our mountains!
O scarlet god, O golden-banded brow,
O Theban Bacchos° in a storm of Maenads,°

 Enter Oedipus, *center.*
Whirl upon Death, that all the Undying hate!
Come with blinding cressets, come in joy!   50

Scene I

Oedipus. Is this your prayer? It may be answered. Come,
 Listen to me, act as the crisis demands,
 And you shall have relief from all these evils.

Until now I was a stranger to this tale,
As I had been a stranger to the crime.   5
Could I track down the murderer without a clue?
But now, friends,
As one who became a citizen after the murder,
I make this proclamation to all Thebans:
If any man knows by whose hand Laïos, son of Labdakos,   10
Met his death, I direct that man to tell me everything,
No matter what he fears for having so long withheld it.
Let it stand as promised that no further trouble
Will come to him, but he may leave the land in safety.

Moreover: If anyone knows the murderer to be foreign,   15
Let him not keep silent: he shall have his reward from me.
However, if he does conceal it, if any man
Fearing for his friend or for himself disobeys this edict,
Hear what I propose to do:

I solemnly forbid the people of this country,   20
Where power and throne are mine, ever to receive that man
Or speak to him, no matter who he is, or let him
Join in sacrifice, lustration, or in prayer.
I decree that he be driven from every house,

Being, as he is, corruption itself to us: the Delphic   25
Voice of Zeus has pronounced this revelation.

---

48 Bacchos Dionysos, god of wine, thus scarlet-faced   **48 Maenads** Dionysos's female
attendants

Thus I associate myself with the oracle
And take the side of the murdered king.

As for the criminal, I pray to God—
Whether it be a lurking thief, or one of a number— 30
I pray that that man's life be consumed in evil and wretchedness.
And as for me, this curse applies no less
If it should turn out that the culprit is my guest here,
Sharing my hearth.
                        You have heard the penalty.
I lay it on you now to attend to this 35
For my sake, for Apollo's, for the sick
Sterile city that heaven has abandoned.
Suppose the oracle had given you no command:
Should this defilement go uncleansed for ever?
You should have found the murderer: your king, 40
A noble king, had been destroyed!
                        Now I,
Having the power that he held before me,
Having his bed, begetting children there
Upon his wife, as he would have, had he lived—
Their son would have been my children's brother, 45
If Laïos had had luck in fatherhood!
(But surely ill luck rushed upon his reign)—
I say I take the son's part, just as though
I were his son, to press the fight for him
And see it won! I'll find the hand that brought 50
Death to Labdakos' and Polydoros' child,
Heir of Kadmos' and Agenor's line.
And as for those who fail me,
May the gods deny them the fruit of the earth,
Fruit of the womb, and may they rot utterly! 55
Let them be wretched as we are wretched, and worse!

For you, for loyal Thebans, and for all
Who find my actions right, I pray the favor
Of justice, and of all the immortal gods.
CHORAGOS.° Since I am under oath, my lord, I swear 60
    I did not do the murder, I cannot name
    The murderer. Might not the oracle
    That has ordained the search tell where to find him?
OEDIPUS. An honest question. But no man in the world
    Can make the gods do more than the gods will. 65
CHORAGOS. There is one last expedient—
OEDIPUS.   Tell me what it is.
    Though it seem slight, you must not hold it back.
CHORAGOS. A lord clairvoyant to the lord Apollo,
    As we all know, is the skilled Teiresias.

60 Choragos leader of the Chorus

One might learn much about this from him, Oedipus.   70
OEDIPUS. I am not wasting time:
   Creon spoke of this, and I have sent for him—
   Twice, in fact; it is strange that he is not here.
CHORAGOS. The other matter—that old report—seems useless.
OEDIPUS. Tell me. I am interested in all reports.   75
CHORAGOS. The King was said to have been killed by highwaymen.
OEDIPUS. I know. But we have no witnesses to that.
CHORAGOS. If the killer can feel a particle of dread,
   Your curse will bring him out of hiding!
OEDIPUS.   No.
   The man who dared that act will fear no curse   80

   Enter the blind seer TEIRESIAS *led by a* PAGE.
CHORAGOS. But there is one man who may detect the criminal.
   This is Teiresias, this is the holy prophet
   In whom, alone of all men, truth was born.
OEDIPUS. Teiresias: seer: student of mysteries,
   Of all that's taught and all that no man tells,   85
   Secrets of Heaven and secrets of the earth:
   Blind though you are, you know the city lies
   Sick with plague; and from this plague, my lord,
   We find that you alone can guard or save us.

   Possibly you did not hear the messengers?   90
   Apollo, when we sent to him,
   Sent us back word that this great pestilence
   Would lift, but only if we established clearly
   The identity of those who murdered Laïos.
   They must be killed or exiled.
                       Can you use   95
   Birdflight or any art of divination
   To purify yourself, and Thebes, and me
   From this contagion? We are in your hands.
   There is no fairer duty
   Than that of helping others in distress.   100
TEIRESIAS. How dreadful knowledge of the truth can be
   When there's no help in truth! I knew this well,
   But did not act on it: else I should not have come.
OEDIPUS. What is troubling you? Why are your eyes so cold?
TEIRESIAS. Let me go home. Bear your own fate, and I'll   105
   Bear mine. It is better so: trust what I say.
OEDIPUS. What you say is ungracious and unhelpful
   To your native country. Do not refuse to speak.
TEIRESIAS. When it comes to speech, your own is neither temperate
   Nor opportune. I wish to be more prudent.   110
OEDIPUS. In God's name, we all beg you—
TEIRESIAS.   You are all ignorant.
   No; I will never tell you what I know.
   Now it is my misery; then, it would be yours.
OEDIPUS. What! You do know something, and will not tell us?
   You would betray us all and wreck the State?   115

TEIRESIAS. I do not intend to torture myself, or you.
Why persist in asking? You will not persuade me.

OEDIPUS. What a wicked man you are! You'd try a stone's
Patience! Out with it! Have you no feeling at all?

TEIRESIAS. You call me unfeeling. If you could only see   120
The nature of your feelings . . .

OEDIPUS.   Why,
Who would not feel as I do? Who could endure
Your arrogance toward the city?

TEIRESIAS.   What does it matter!
Whether I speak or not, it is bound to come.

OEDIPUS. Then, if "it" is bound to come, you are bound to tell me.   125

TEIRESIAS. No, I will not go on. Rage as you please.

OEDIPUS. Rage? Why not!
                    And I'll tell you what I think:
You planned it, you had it done, you all but
Killed him with your own hands: if you had eyes,
I'd say the crime was yours, and yours alone.   130

TEIRESIAS. So? I charge you, then,
Abide by the proclamation you have made.
From this day forth
Never speak again to these men or to me;
You yourself are the pollution of this country.   135

OEDIPUS. You dare say that! Can you possibly think you have
Some way of going free, after such insolence?

TEIRESIAS. I have gone free. It is the truth sustains me.

OEDIPUS. Who taught you shamelessness? It was not your craft.

TEIRESIAS. You did. You made me speak. I did not want to.   140

OEDIPUS. Speak what? Let me hear it again more clearly.

TEIRESIAS. Was it not clear before? Are you tempting me?

OEDIPUS. I did not understand it. Say it again.

TEIRESIAS. I say that you are the murderer whom you seek.

OEDIPUS. Now twice you have spat out infamy. You'll pay for it!   145

TEIRESIAS. Would you care for more? Do you wish to be really angry?

OEDIPUS. Say what you will. Whatever you say is worthless.

TEIRESIAS. I say you live in hideous shame with those
Most dear to you. You cannot see the evil.

OEDIPUS. It seems you can go on mouthing like this for ever.   150

TEIRESIAS. I can, if there is power in truth.

OEDIPUS.   There is:
But not for you, not for you,
You sightless, witless, senseless, mad old man!

TEIRESIAS. You are the madman. There is no one here
Who will not curse you soon, as you curse me.   155

OEDIPUS. You child of endless night! You cannot hurt me
Or any other man who sees the sun.

TEIRESIAS. True: it is not from me your fate will come.
That lies within Apollo's competence,
As it is his concern.

OEDIPUS.   Tell me: 160
Are you speaking for Creon, or for yourself?

TEIRESIAS. Creon is no threat. You weave your own doom.
OEDIPUS. Wealth, power, craft of statesmanship!
    Kingly position, everywhere admired!
    What savage envy is stored up against these,   165
    If Creon, whom I trusted, Creon my friend,
    For this great office which the city once
    Put in my hands unsought—if for this power
    Creon desires in secret to destroy me!

    He has brought this decrepit fortune-teller, this   170
    Collector of dirty pennies, this prophet fraud—
    Why, he is no more clairvoyant than I am!
                      Tell us:
    Has your mystic mummery ever approached the truth?
    When that hellcat the Sphinx was performing here,
    What help were you to these people?   175
    Her magic was not for the first man who came along:
    It demanded a real exorcist. Your birds—
    What good were they? or the gods, for the matter of that?
    But I came by,
    Oedipus, the simple man, who knows nothing—   180
    I thought it out for myself, no birds helped me!
    And this is the man you think you can destroy,
    That you may be close to Creon when he's king!
    Well, you and your friend Creon, it seems to me,
    Will suffer most. If you were not an old man,   185
    You would have paid already for your plot.
CHORAGOS. We cannot see that his words or yours
    Have spoken except in anger, Oedipus,
    And of anger we have no need. How can God's will
    Be accomplished best? That is what most concerns us.   190
TEIRESIAS. You are a king. But where argument's concerned
    I am your man, as much a king as you.
    I am not your servant, but Apollo's.
    I have no need of Creon to speak for me.

    Listen to me. You mock my blindness, do you?   195
    But I say that you, with both your eyes, are blind:
    You cannot see the wretchedness of your life,
    Not in whose house you live, no, nor with whom.
    Who are your father and mother? Can you tell me?
    You do not even know the blind wrongs   200
    That you have done them, on earth and in the world below.
    But the double lash of your parents' curse will whip you
    Out of this land some day, with only night
    Upon your precious eyes.
    Your cries then—where will they not be heard?   205
    What fastness of Kithairon° will not echo them?

---

206 fastness of Kithairon stronghold in a mountain near Thebes

And that bridal-descant of yours—you'll know it then,
The song they sang when you came here to Thebes
And found your misguided berthing.
All this, and more, that you cannot guess at now, 210
Will bring you to yourself among your children.
Be angry, then. Curse Creon. Curse my words.
I tell you, no man that walks upon the earth
Shall be rooted out more horribly than you.

OEDIPUS. Am I to bear this from him?—Damnation 215
Take you! Out of this place! Out of my sight!

TEIRESIAS. I would not have come at all if you had not asked me.

OEDIPUS. Could I have told that you'd talk nonsense, that
You'd come here to make a fool of yourself, and of me?

TEIRESIAS. A fool? Your parents thought me sane enough. 220

OEDIPUS. My parents again!—Wait: who were my parents?

TEIRESIAS. This day will give you a father, and break your heart.

OEDIPUS. Your infantile riddles! Your damned abracadabra!

TEIRESIAS. You were a great man once at solving riddles.

OEDIPUS. Mock me with that if you like; you will find it true. 225

TEIRESIAS. It was true enough. It brought about your ruin.

OEDIPUS. But if it saved this town.

TEIRESIAS [*to the* PAGE]. Boy, give me your hand.

OEDIPUS. Yes, boy; lead him away.

—While you are here
We can do nothing. Go; leave us in peace.

TEIRESIAS. I will go when I have said what I have to say. 230
How can you hurt me? And I tell you again:
The man you have been looking for all this time,
The damned man, the murderer of Laïos,
That man is in Thebes. To your mind he is foreignborn,
But it will soon be shown that he is a Theban, 235
A revelation that will fail to please

A blind man
Who has his eyes now; a penniless man, who is rich now;
And he will go tapping the strange earth with his staff;
To the children with whom he lives now he will be
Brother and father—the very same; to her 240
Who bore him, son and husband—the very same
Who came to his father's bed, wet with his father's blood.

Enough. Go think that over.
If later you find error in what I have said,
You may say that I have no skill in prophecy. 245

Exit TEIRESIAS, *led by his* PAGE. OEDIPUS *goes into the palace.*

Ode 1

CHORUS. The Delphic stone of prophecies *Strophe 1*
Remembers ancient regicide
And a still bloody hand.
That killer's hour of flight has come.
He must be stronger than riderless 5

Coursers of untiring wind,
For the son of Zeus° armed with his father's thunder
Leaps in lightning after him;
And the Furies° follow him, the sad Furies.

Holy Parnossos' peak of snow   *Antistrophe 1*   10
Flashes and blinds that secret man,
That all shall hunt him down:
Though he may roam the forest shade
Like a bull gone wild from pasture
To rage through glooms of stone.   15
Doom comes down on him; flight will not avail him;
For the world's heart calls him desolate,
And the immortal Furies follow, for ever follow.

But now a wilder thing is heard   *Strophe 2*
From the old man skilled at hearing Fate in the wingbeat of a bird.   20
Bewildered as a blown bird, my soul hovers and cannot find
Foothold in this debate, or any reason or rest of mind.
But no man ever brought—none can bring
Proof of strife between Thebes' royal house,
Labdakos' line,° and the son of Polybos;°   25
And never until now has any man brought word
Of Laïos dark death staining Oedipus the King.

Divine Zeus and Apollo hold   *Antistrophe 2*
Perfect intelligence alone of all tales ever told;
And well though this diviner works, he works in his own night;   30
No man can judge that rough unknown or trust in second sight,
For wisdom changes hands among the wise.
Shall I believe my great lord criminal,
At a raging word that a blind old man let fall?
I saw him, when the carrion woman faced him of old,   35
Prove his heroic mind! These evil words are lies.

Scene II

CREON. Men of Thebes:
   I am told that heavy accusations
   Have been brought against me by King Oedipus.
   I am not the kind of man to bear this tamely.

   If in these present difficulties   5
   He holds me accountable for any harm to him
   Through anything I have said or done—why, then,
   I do not value life in this dishonor.
   It is not as though this rumor touched upon
   Some private indiscretion. The matter is grave.   10

Ode 1,7 son of Zeus Apollo   **9 Furies** avenging deities   **25 Labdakos' line** family of
Laïos   **son of Polybos** Oedipus (so the Chorus believes)

The fact is that I am being called disloyal
To the State, to my fellow citizens, to my friends.
CHORAGOS. He may have spoken in anger, not from his mind.
CREON. But did you hear him say I was the one
    Who seduced the old prophet into lying?   15
CHORAGOS. The thing was said; I do not know how seriously.
CREON. But you were watching him! Were his eyes steady?
    Did he look like a man in his right mind?
CHORAGOS.   I do not know.
    I cannot judge the behavior of great men.
    But here is the King himself.

    Enter OEDIPUS.

OEDIPUS.   So you dared come back.   20
    Why? How brazen of you to come to my house,
    You murderer!
              Do you think I do not know
    That you plotted to kill me, plotted to steal my throne?
    Tell me, in God's name: am I coward, a fool,
    That you should dream you could accomplish this?   25
    A fool who could not see your slippery game?
    A coward, not to fight back when I saw it?
    You are the fool, Creon, are you not? hoping
    Without support or friends to get a throne?
    Thrones may be won or bought: you could do neither.   30
CREON. Now listen to me. You have talked; let me talk; too.
    You cannot judge unless you know the facts.
OEDIPUS. You speak well: there is one fact; but I find it hard
    To learn from the deadliest enemy I have.
CREON. That above all I must dispute with you.   35
OEDIPUS. That above all I will not hear you deny.
CREON. If you think there is anything good in being stubborn
    Against all reason, then I say you are wrong.
OEDIPUS. If you think a man can sin against his own kind
    And not be punished for it, I say you are mad.   40
CREON. I agree. But tell me: what have I done to you?
OEDIPUS. You advised me to send for that wizard, did you not?
CREON. I did. I should do it again.
OEDIPUS.   Very well. Now tell me:
    How long has it been since Laïos—
CREON.   What of Laïos?
OEDIPUS. Since he vanished in that onset by the road?   45
CREON. It was long ago, a long time.
OEDIPUS.   And this prophet,
    Was he practicing here then?
CREON.   He was; and with honor, as now.
OEDIPUS. Did he speak of me at that time?
CREON.   He never did;
    At least, not when I was present.
OEDIPUS.   But . . . the enquiry?
    I suppose you held one?
CREON.   We did, but we learned nothing.   50

OEDIPUS. Why did the prophet not speak against me then?
CREON. I do not know; and I am the kind of man
 Who holds his tongue when he has no facts to go on.
OEDIPUS. There's one fact that you know, and you could tell it.
CREON. What fact is that? If I know it, you shall have it. 55
OEDIPUS. If he were not involved with you, he could not say
 That it was I who murdered Laïos.
CREON. If he says that, you are the one that knows it!—
 But now it is my turn to question you.
OEDIPUS. Put your questions. I am no murderer. 60
CREON. First, then: You married my sister?
OEDIPUS. I married your sister.
CREON. And you rule the kingdom equally with her?
OEDIPUS. Everything that she wants she has from me.
CREON. And I am the third, equal to both of you?
OEDIPUS. That is why I call you a bad friend. 65
CREON. No. Reason it out, as I have done.
 Think of this first. Would any sane man prefer
 Power, with all a king's anxieties,
 To that same power and the grace of sleep?
 Certainly not I. 70
 I have never longed for the king's power—only his rights.
 Would any wise man differ from me in this?
 As matters stand, I have my way in everything
 With your consent, and no responsibilities.
 If I were king, I should be a slave to policy. 75
 How could I desire a scepter more
 Than what is now mine—untroubled influence?
 No, I have not gone mad; I need no honors,
 Except those with the perquisites I have now.
 I am welcome everywhere; every man salutes me, 80
 And those who want your favor seek my ear,
 Since I know how to manage what they ask.
 Should I exchange this ease for that anxiety?
 Besides, no sober mind is treasonable.
 I hate anarchy 85
 And never would deal with any man who likes it.

 Test what I have said. Go to the priestess
 At Delphi, ask if I quoted her correctly.
 And as for this other thing: if I am found
 Guilty of treason with Teiresias, 90
 Then sentence me to death! You have my word
 It is a sentence I should cast my vote for—
 But not without evidence!
 You do wrong
 When you take good men for bad, bad men for good.
 A true friend thrown aside—why, life itself 95
 Is not more precious!
 In time you will know this well:
 For time, and time alone, will show the just man,
 Though scoundrels are discovered in a day.

CHORAGOS. This is well said, and a prudent man would ponder it.
    Judgments too quickly formed are dangerous.   100

OEDIPUS. But is he not quick in his duplicity?
    And shall I not be quick to parry him?
    Would you have me stand still, hold my peace, and let
    This man win everything, through my inaction?

CREON. And you want—what is it, then? To banish me?   105

OEDIPUS. No, not exile. It is your death I want,
    So that all the world may see what treason means.

CREON. You will persist, then? You will not believe me?

OEDIPUS. How can I believe you?

CREON.   Then you are a fool.

OEDIPUS. To save myself?

CREON.   In justice, think of me.   110

OEDIPUS. You are evil incarnate.

CREON.   But suppose that you are wrong?

OEDIPUS. Still I must rule.

CREON.   But not if you rule badly.

OEDIPUS. O city, city!

CREON.   It is my city, too!

CHORAGOS. Now, my lords, be still. I see the Queen,
    Iocastê, coming from her palace chambers;   115
    And it is time she came, for the sake of you both.
    This dreadful quarrel can be resolved through her.

    Enter IOCASTÊ.

IOCASTÊ. Poor foolish men, what wicked din is this?
    With Thebes sick to death, is it not shameful
    That you should rake some private quarrel up?   120
    [*To* OEDIPUS.] Come into the house.
                        —And you, Creon, go now:
    Let us have no more of this tumult over nothing.

CREON. Nothing? No, sister: what your husband plans for me
    Is one of two great evils: exile or death.

OEDIPUS.   He is right.
    Why, woman, I have caught him squarely   125
    Plotting against my life.

CREON.   No! Let me die
    Accurst if ever I have wished you harm!

IOCASTÊ. Ah, believe it, Oedipus!
    In the name of the gods, respect this oath of his
    For my sake, for the sake of these people here!   130

CHORAGOS. Open your mind to her, my lord. Be ruled   *Strophe 1*
    by her, I beg you!

OEDIPUS. What would you have me do?

CHORAGOS. Respect Creon's word. He has never spoken like a fool,
    And now he has sworn an oath.

OEDIPUS. You know what you ask?

CHORAGOS.   I do.

OEDIPUS.   Speak on, then.

CHORAGOS. A friend so sworn should not be baited so,   135
    In blind malice, and without final proof.

OEDIPUS. You are aware, I hope, that what you say
    Means death for me, or exile at the least.
CHORAGOS. No, I swear by Helios,° first in Heaven!   *Strophe 2*
    May I die friendless and accurst,   140
    The worst of deaths, if ever I meant that!
      It is the withering fields
        That hurt my sick heart:
      Must we bear all these ills,
        And now your bad blood as well?   145
OEDIPUS. Then let him go. And let me die, if I must,
    Or be driven by him in shame from the land of Thebes.
    It is your unhappiness, and not his talk,
    That touches me.
                As for him—
    Wherever he is, I will hate him as long as I live.   150
CREON. Ugly in yielding, as you were ugly in rage!
    Natures like yours chiefly torment themselves.
OEDIPUS. Can you not go? Can you not leave me?
CREON.   I can.
    You do not know me; but the city knows me,
    And in its eyes I am just, if not in yours.   155

                                       [*Exit* CREON.]
CHORAGOS. Lady Iocastê, did you not ask the King   *Antistrophe 1*
    to go to his chambers?
IOCASTÊ. First tell me what has happened.
CHORAGOS. There was suspicion without evidence; yet it rankled
    As even false charges will.
IOCASTÊ.   On both sides?
CHORAGOS.   On both.
IOCASTÊ.   But what was said?
CHORAGOS. Oh let it rest, let it be done with!   160
    Have we not suffered enough?
OEDIPUS. You see to what your decency has brought you:
    You have made difficulties where my heart saw none.
CHORAGOS. Oedipus, it is not once only I have told you—   *Antistrophe 2*
    You must know I should count myself unwise   165
    To the point of madness, should I now forsake you—
      You, under whose hand,
        In the storm of another time,
      Our dear land sailed out free,
        But now stand fast at the helm!   170
IOCASTÊ. In God's name, Oedipus, inform your wife as well:
    Why are you so set in this hard anger?
OEDIPUS. I will tell you, for none of these men deserves
    My confidence as you do. It is Creon's work,
    His treachery, his plotting against me.   175
IOCASTÊ. Go on, if you can make this clear to me.

139 Helios sun god

OEDIPUS. He charges me with the murder of Laïos.

IOCASTÊ. Has he some knowledge? Or does he speak from hearsay?

OEDIPUS. He would not commit himself to such a charge,
But he has brought in that damnable soothsayer   180
To tell his story.

IOCASTÊ.   Set your mind at rest.
If it is a question of soothsayers, I tell you
That you will find no man whose craft gives knowledge
Of the unknowable.

                Here is my proof.

An oracle was reported to Laïos once   185
(I will not say from Phoibos himself, but from
His appointed ministers, at any rate)
That his doom would be death at the hands of his own son—
His son, born of his flesh and of mine!

Now, you remember the story: Laïos was killed   190
By marauding strangers where three highways meet;
But his child had not been three days in this world
Before the King had pierced the baby's ankles
And left him to die on a lonely mountainside.

Thus, Apollo never caused that child   195
To kill his father, and it was not Laïos' fate
To die at the hands of his son, as he had feared.
This is what prophets and prophecies are worth!
Have no dread of them.

                It is God himself
Who can show us what he wills, in his own way.   200

OEDIPUS. How strange a shadowy memory crossed my mind,
Just now while you were speaking; it chilled my heart.

IOCASTÊ. What do you mean? What memory do you speak of?

OEDIPUS. If I understand you, Laïos was killed
At a place where three roads meet.

IOCASTÊ.   So it was said;   205
We have no later story.

OEDIPUS.   Where did it happen?

IOCASTÊ. Phokis, it is called: at a place where the Theban Way
Divides into the roads towards Delphi and Daulia.

OEDIPUS. When?

IOCASTÊ.   We had the news not long before you came
And proved the right to your succession here.   210

OEDIPUS. Ah, what net has God been weaving for me?

IOCASTÊ. Oedipus! Why does this trouble you?

OEDIPUS.   Do not ask me yet.
First, tell me how Laïos looked, and tell me
How old he was.

IOCASTÊ.   He was tall, his hair just touched
With white; his form was not unlike your own.   215

OEDIPUS. I think that I myself may be accurst
By my own ignorant edict.

IOCASTÊ.   You speak strangely.
   It makes me tremble to look at you, my King.
OEDIPUS. I am not sure that the blind man cannot see.
   But I should know better if you were to tell me—   220
IOCASTÊ. Anything—though I dread to hear you ask it.
OEDIPUS. Was the King lightly escorted, or did he ride
   With a large company, as a ruler should?
IOCASTÊ. There were five men with him in all: one was a herald;
   And a single chariot, which he was driving.   225
OEDIPUS. Alas, that makes it plain enough!
                                      But who—
   Who told you how it happened?
IOCASTÊ.   A household servant,
   The only one to escape.
OEDIPUS.   And is he still
   A servant of ours?
IOCASTÊ.   No; for when he came back at last
   And found you enthroned in the place of the dead king,   230
   He came to me, touched my hand with his, and begged
   That I would send him away to the frontier district
   Where only the shepherds go—
   As far away from the city as I could send him.
   I granted his prayer; for although the man was a slave,   235
   He had earned more than this favor at my hands.
OEDIPUS. Can he be called back quickly?
IOCASTÊ.   Easily.
   But why?
OEDIPUS. I have taken too much upon myself
   Without enquiry; therefore I wish to consult him.
IOCASTÊ. Then he shall come.
                             But am I not one also   240
   To whom you might confide these fears of yours!
OEDIPUS. That is your right; it will not be denied you,
   Now least of all; for I have reached a pitch
   Of wild foreboding. Is there anyone
   To whom I should sooner speak?   245
   Polybos of Corinth is my father.
   My mother is a Dorian: Meropê.
   I grew up chief among the men of Corinth
   Until a strange thing happened—
   Not worth my passion, it may be, but strange.   250

   At a feast, a drunken man maundering in his cups
   Cries out that I am not my father's son!

   I contained myself that night, though I felt anger
   And a sinking heart. The next day I visited
   My father and mother, and questioned them. They stormed,   255
   Calling it all the slanderous rant of a fool;
   And this relieved me. Yet the suspicion
   Remained always aching in my mind;
   I knew there was talk; I could not rest;

And finally, saying nothing to my parents,   260
I went to the shrine at Delphi.
The god dismissed my question without reply;
He spoke of other things.
                     Some were clear,
Full of wretchedness, dreadful, unbearable:
As, that I should lie with my own mother, breed   265
Children from whom all men would turn their eyes;
And that I should be my father's murderer.

I heard all this, and fled. And from that day
Corinth to me was only in the stars
Descending in that quarter of the sky,   270
As I wandered farther and farther on my way
To a land where I should never see the evil
Sung by the oracle. And I came to this country
Where, so you say, King Laïos was killed.
I will tell you all that happened there, my lady.   275

There were three highways
Coming together at a place I passed;
And there a herald came towards me, and a chariot
Drawn by horses, with a man such as you describe
Seated in it. The groom leading the horses   280
Forced me off the road at his lord's command;
But as this charioteer lurched over toward me
I struck him in my rage. The old man saw me
And brought his double goad down upon my head
As I came abreast.
                   He was paid back, and more!   285
Swinging my club in this right hand I knocked him
Out of his car, and he rolled on the ground.
                         I killed him.
I killed them all.
Now if that stranger and Laïos were—kin,
Where is a man more miserable than I?   290
More hated by the gods? Citizen and alien alike
Must never shelter me or speak to me—
I must be shunned by all.
                   And I myself
Pronounced this malediction upon myself!

Think of it: I have touched you with these hands,   295
These hands that killed your husband. What defilement!

Am I all evil, then? It must be so,
Since I must flee from Thebes, yet never again
See my own countrymen, my own country,
For fear of joining my mother in marriage   300
And killing Polybos, my father.
                 Ah,
If I was created so, born to this fate,
Who could deny the savagery of God?

O holy majesty of heavenly powers!
May I never see that day! Never!   305
Rather let me vanish from the race of men
Than know the abomination destined me!
CHORAGOS. We too, my lord, have felt dismay at this.
    But there is hope: you have yet to hear the shepherd.
OEDIPUS. Indeed, I fear no other hope is left me.   310
IOCASTÊ. What do you hope from him when he comes?
OEDIPUS.   This much:
    If his account of the murder tallies with yours,
    Then I am cleared.
IOCASTÊ.   What was it that I said
    Of such importance?
OEDIPUS.   Why, "marauders," you said,
    Killed the King, according to this man's story.   315
    If he maintains that still, if there were several,
    Clearly the guilt is not mine: I was alone.
    But if he says one man, singlehanded, did it,
    Then the evidence all points to me.
IOCASTÊ. You may be sure that he said there were several;   320
    And can he call back that story now? He cannot.
    The whole city heard it as plainly as I.
    But suppose he alters some detail of it:
    He cannot ever show that Laïos' death
    Fulfilled the oracle: for Apollo said   325
    My child was doomed to kill him; and my child—
    Poor baby!—it was my child that died first.

    No. From now on, where oracles are concerned,
    I would not waste a second thought on any.
OEDIPUS. You may be right.
                                    But come: let someone go   330
    For the shepherd at once. This matter must be settled.
IOCASTÊ. I will send for him.
    I would not wish to cross you in anything,
    And surely not in this.—Let us go in.   [*Exeunt into the palace.*]

Ode II

CHORUS. Let me be reverent in the ways of right,   *Strophe 1*
    Lowly the paths I journey on;
    Let all my words and actions keep
    The laws of the pure universe
    From highest Heaven handed down.   5
    For Heaven is their bright nurse,
    Those generations of the realms of light;
    Ah, never of mortal kind were they begot,
    Nor are they slaves of memory, lost in sleep:
    Their Father is greater than Time, and ages not.   10

    The tyrant is a child of Pride   *Antistrophe 1*
    Who drinks from his great sickening cup
    Recklessness and vanity,

Until from his high crest headlong
He plummets to the dust of hope.   15
That strong man is not strong.
But let no fair ambition be denied;
May God protect the wrestler for the State
In government, in comely policy,
Who will fear God, and on His ordinance wait.   20

Haughtiness and the high hand of disdain   *Strophe 2*
Tempt and outrage God's holy law;
And any mortal who dares hold
No immortal Power in awe
Will be caught up in a net of pain: 25
The price for which his levity is sold.
Let each man take due earnings, then,
And keep his hands from holy things,
And from blasphemy stand apart—
Else the crackling blast of heaven   30
Blows on his head, and on his desperate heart;
Though fools will honor impious men,
In their cities no tragic poet sings.

Shall we lose faith in Delphi's obscurities,   *Antistrophe 2*
We who have heard the world's core   35
Discredited, and the sacred wood
Of Zeus at Elis praised no more?
The deeds and the strange prophecies
Must make a pattern yet to be understood.
Zeus, if indeed you are lord of all,   40
Throned in light over night and day,
Mirror this in your endless mind:
Our masters call the oracle
Words on the wind, and the Delphic vision blind!
Their hearts no longer know Apollo,   45
And reverence for the gods has died away.

Scene III

Enter IOCASTÊ.

IOCASTÊ. Princes of Thebes, it has occurred to me
To visit the altars of the gods, bearing
These branches as a suppliant, and this incense.
Our King is not himself: his noble soul
Is overwrought with fantasies of dread,   5
Else he would consider
The new prophecies in the light of the old.
He will listen to any voice that speaks disaster,
And my advice goes for nothing.

She approaches the altar, right.

                          To you, then, Apollo,
Lycean lord, since you are nearest, I turn in prayer.   10
Receive these offerings, and grant us deliverance

From defilement. Our hearts are heavy with fear
When we see our leader distracted, as helpless sailors
Are terrified by the confusion of their helmsman.

   Enter MESSENGER.

MESSENGER. Friends, no doubt you can direct me: 15
   Where shall I find the house of Oedipus,
   Or, better still, where is the King himself?
CHORAGOS. It is this very place, stranger; he is inside.
   This is his wife and mother of his children.
MESSENGER. I wish her happiness in a happy house,   20
   Blest in all the fulfillment of her marriage.
IOCASTÊ. I wish as much for you: your courtesy
   Deserves a like good fortune. But now, tell me:
   Why have you come? What have you to say to us?
MESSENGER. Good news, my lady, for your house and your husband.   25
IOCASTÊ. What news? Who sent you here?
MESSENGER.   I am from Corinth.
   The news I bring ought to mean joy for you,
   Though it may be you will find some grief in it.
IOCASTÊ. What is it? How can it touch us in both ways?
MESSENGER. The people of Corinth, they say,   30
   Intend to call Oedipus to be their king.
IOCASTÊ. But old Polybos—is he not reigning still?
MESSENGER. No. Death holds him in his sepulchre.
IOCASTÊ. What are you saying? Polybos is dead?
MESSENGER. If I am not telling the truth, may I die myself.   35
IOCASTÊ [*to a* MAIDSERVANT]. Go in, go quickly; tell this to your master.

   O riddlers of God's will, where are you now!
   This was the man whom Oedipus, long ago,
   Feared so, fled so, in dread of destroying him—
   But it was another fate by which he died.   40

   Enter OEDIPUS, *center.*

OEDIPUS. Dearest Iocastê, why have you sent for me?
IOCASTÊ. Listen to what this man says, and then tell me
   What has become of the solemn prophecies.
OEDIPUS. Who is this man? What is his news for me?
IOCASTÊ. He has come from Corinth to announce your father's death! 45
OEDIPUS. Is it true, stranger? Tell me in your own words.
MESSENGER. I cannot say it more clearly: the King is dead.
OEDIPUS. Was it by treason? Or by an attack of illness?
MESSENGER A little thing brings old men to their rest.
OEDIPUS. It was sickness, then?
MESSENGER   Yes, and his many years.   50
OEDIPUS. Ah!
   Why should a man respect the Pythian hearth,° or

_____

52 Pythian hearth Delphi (also called Pytho because a great snake had lived there),
where Apollo spoke through a priestess

Give heed to the birds that jangle above his head?
They prophesied that I should kill Polybos,
Kill my own father; but he is dead and buried, 55
And I am here—I never touched him, never,
Unless he died in grief for my departure,
And thus, in a sense, through me. No Polybos
Has packed the oracles off with him underground.
They are empty words.

IOCASTÊ.   Had I not told you so? 60

OEDIPUS. You had; it was my faint heart that betrayed me.

IOCASTÊ. From now on never think of those things again.

OEDIPUS. And yet—must I not fear my mother's bed?

IOCASTÊ. Why should anyone in this world be afraid,
Since Fate rules us and nothing can be foreseen? 65
A man should live only for the present day.
Have no more fear of sleeping with your mother.
How many men, in dreams, have lain with their mothers!
No reasonable man is troubled by such things.

OEDIPUS. That is true; only— 70
If only my mother were not still alive!
But she is alive. I cannot help my dread.

IOCASTÊ. Yet this news of your father's death is wonderful.

OEDIPUS. Wonderful. But I fear the living woman.

MESSENGER Tell me, who is this woman that you fear? 75

OEDIPUS. It is Meropê, man; the wife of King Polybos.

MESSENGER Meropê? Why should you be afraid of her?

OEDIPUS. An oracle of the gods, a dreadful saying.

MESSENGER Can you tell me about it or are you sworn to silence?

OEDIPUS. I can tell you, and I will. 80
Apollo said through his prophet that I was the man
Who should marry his own mother, shed his father's blood
With his own hands. And so, for all these years
I have kept clear of Corinth, and no harm has come—
Though it would have been sweet to see my parents again. 85

MESSENGER And is this the fear that drove you out of Corinth?

OEDIPUS. Would you have me kill my father?

MESSENGER   As for that
You must be reassured by the news I gave you.

OEDIPUS. If you could reassure me, I would reward you.

MESSENGER I had that in mind, I will confess: I thought 90
I could count on you when you returned to Corinth.

OEDIPUS. No: I will never go near my parents again.

MESSENGER Ah, son, you still do not know what you are doing—

OEDIPUS. What do you mean? In the name of God tell me!

MESSENGER —If these are your reasons for not going home— 95

OEDIPUS. I tell you, I fear the oracle may come true.

MESSENGER And guilt may come upon you through your parents?

OEDIPUS. That is the dread that is always in my heart.

MESSENGER Can you not see that all your fears are groundless?

OEDIPUS. How can you say that? They are my parents, surely? 100

MESSENGER Polybos was not your father.

OEDIPUS.   Not my father?

MESSENGER No more your father than the man speaking to you.

OEDIPUS. But you are nothing to me!

MESSENGER   Neither was he.

OEDIPUS. Then why did he call me son?

MESSENGER   I will tell you:
    Long ago he had you from my hands, as a gift.   105

OEDIPUS. Then how could he love me so, if I was not his?

MESSENGER He had no children, and his heart turned to you.

OEDIPUS. What of you? Did you buy me? Did you find me by chance?

MESSENGER I came upon you in the crooked pass of Kithairon.

OEDIPUS. And what were you doing there?

MESSENGER   Tending my flocks.   110

OEDIPUS. A wandering shepherd?

MESSENGER   But your savior, son, that day.

OEDIPUS. From what did you save me?

MESSENGER   Your ankles should tell you that.

OEDIPUS. Ah, stranger, why do you speak of that childhood pain?

MESSENGER I cut the bonds that tied your ankles together.

OEDIPUS. I have had the mark as long as I can remember.   115

MESSENGER That was why you were given the name you bear.°

OEDIPUS. God! Was it my father or my mother who did it?
    Tell me!

MESSENGER I do not know. The man who gave you to me
    Can tell you better than I.   120

OEDIPUS. It was not you that found me, but another?

MESSENGER It was another shepherd gave you to me.

OEDIPUS. Who was he? Can you tell me who he was?

MESSENGER I think he was said to be one of Laïos' people.

OEDIPUS. You mean the Laïos who was king here years ago?   125

MESSENGER Yes; King Laïos; and the man was one of his herdsmen.

OEDIPUS. Is he still alive? Can I see him?

MESSENGER   These men here
    Know best about such things.

OEDIPUS.   Does anyone here
    Know this shepherd that he is talking about?
    Have you seen him in the fields, or in the town?   130
    If you have, tell me. It is time things were made plain.

CHORAGOS. I think the man he means is that same shepherd
    You have already asked to see. Iocastê perhaps
    Could tell you something.

OEDIPUS.   Do you know anything
    About him, Lady? Is he the man we have summoned?   135
    Is that the man this shepherd means?

IOCASTÊ.   Why think of him?
    Forget this herdsman. Forget it all.
    This talk is a waste of time.

OEDIPUS.   How can you say that,
    When the clues to my true birth are in my hands?

116 name you bear *Oedipus* means "swollen-foot"

IOCASTÊ. For God's love, let us have no more questioning!   140
   Is your life nothing to you?
   My own is pain enough for me to bear.

OEDIPUS. You need not worry. Suppose my mother a slave,
   And born of slaves: no baseness can touch you.

IOCASTÊ. Listen to me, I beg you: do not do this thing!   145

OEDIPUS. I will not listen; the truth must be made known.

IOCASTÊ. Everything that I say is for your own good!

OEDIPUS.   My own good
   Snaps my patience, then: I want none of it.

IOCASTÊ. You are fatally wrong! May you never learn who you are!

OEDIPUS. Go, one of you, and bring the shepherd here.   150
   Let us leave this woman to brag of her royal name.

IOCASTÊ. Ah, miserable!
   That is the only word I have for you now.
   That is the only word I can ever have.

                                        Exit into the palace.

CHORAGOS. Why has she left us, Oedipus? Why has she gone   155
   In such a passion of sorrow? I fear this silence:
   Something dreadful may come of it.

OEDIPUS.   Let it come!
   However base my birth, I must know about it.
   The Queen, like a woman, is perhaps ashamed
   To think of my low origin. But I   160
   Am a child of luck; I cannot be dishonored.
   Luck is my mother; the passing months, my brothers,
   Have seen me rich and poor. If this is so,
   How could I wish that I were someone else?
   How could I not be glad to know my birth?   165

Ode III

CHORUS. If ever the coming time were known   *Strophe*
   To my heart's pondering,
   Kithairon, now by Heaven I see the torches
   At the festival of the next full moon,
   And see the dance, and hear the choir sing   5
   A grace to your gentle shade:
   Mountain where Oedipus was found,
   O mountain guard of a noble race!
   May the god who heals us lend his aid,
   And let that glory come to pass   10
   For our king's cradling-ground.

   Of the nymphs that flower beyond the years.   *Antistrophe*
   Who bore you, royal child,
   To Pan of the hills or the timberline Apollo,
   Cold in delight where the upland clears   15
   Or Hermês for whom Kyllenês° heights are piled?

16 Hermês . . . Kyllenê's Hermês, messenger of the gods, was said to have been born on Mt. Kyllenê

Or flushed as evening cloud,
Great Dionysos, roamer of mountains,
He—was it he who found you there,
And caught you up in his own proud   20
Arms from the sweet god-ravisher°
Who laughed by the Muses' fountains?

Scene IV

OEDIPUS. Sirs: though I do not know the man,
   I think I see him coming, this shepherd we want:
   He is old, like our friend here, and the men
   Bringing him seem to be servants of my house.
   But you can tell, if you have ever seen him   5

   Enter SHEPHERD *escorted by servants.*
CHORAGOS. I know him, he was Laïos' man. You can trust him.
OEDIPUS. Tell me first, you from Corinth: is this the shepherd
   We were discussing?
MESSENGER   This is the very man.
OEDIPUS [*to* SHEPHERD]. Come here. No, look at me. You must answer
   Everything I ask.—You belonged to Laïos?   10
SHEPHERD. Yes: born his slave, brought up in his house.
OEDIPUS. Tell me: what kind of work did you do for him?
SHEPHERD. I was a shepherd of his, most of my life.
OEDIPUS. Where mainly did you go for pasturage?
SHEPHERD. Sometimes Kithairon, sometimes the hills near-by.   15
OEDIPUS. Do you remember ever seeing this man out there?
SHEPHERD. What would he be doing there? This man?
OEDIPUS. This man standing here. Have you ever seen him before?
SHEPHERD. No. At least, not to my recollection.
MESSENGER And that is not strange, my lord. But I'll refresh   20
   His memory: he must remember when we two
   Spent three whole seasons together, March to September,
   On Kithairon or thereabouts. He had two flocks;
   I had one. Each autumn I'd drive mine home
   And he would go back with his to Laïos' sheepfold.—   25
   Is this not true, just as I have described it?
SHEPHERD. True, yes; but it was all so long ago.
MESSENGER Well, then: do you remember, back in those days
   That you gave me a baby boy to bring up as my own?
SHEPHERD. What if I did? What are you trying to say?   30
MESSENGER King Oedipus was once that little child.
SHEPHERD. Damn you, hold your tongue!
OEDIPUS.   No more of that!
   It is your tongue needs watching, not this man's.
SHEPHERD. My King, my Master, what is it I have done wrong?
OEDIPUS. You have not answered his question about the boy,   35
SHEPHERD. He does not know . . . He is only making trouble . . .

21 the sweet god-ravisher the presumed mother, the nymph whom the god found irresistible

OEDIPUS. Come, speak plainly, or it will go hard with you.

SHEPHERD. In God's name, do not torture an old man!

OEDIPUS. Come here, one of you; bind his arms behind him.

SHEPHERD. Unhappy king! What more do you wish to learn?   40

OEDIPUS. Did you give this man the child he speaks of?

SHEPHERD.   I did.

  And I would to God I had died that very day.

OEDIPUS. You will die now unless you speak the truth.

SHEPHERD. Yet if I speak the truth, I am worse than dead.

OEDIPUS. Very well; since you insist upon delaying—   45

SHEPHERD. No! I have told you already that I gave him the boy.

OEDIPUS. Where did you get him? From your house?
   From somewhere else?

SHEPHERD. Not from mine, no. A man gave him to me.

OEDIPUS. Is that man here? Do you know whose slave he was?

SHEPHERD. For God's love, my King, do not ask me any more!   50

OEDIPUS. You are a dead man if I have to ask you again.

SHEPHERD. Then . . . Then the child was from the palace of Laïos.

OEDIPUS. A slave child? or a child of his own line?

SHEPHERD. Ah, I am on the brink of dreadful speech!

OEDIPUS. And I of dreadful hearing. Yet I must hear.   55

SHEPHERD. If you must be told, then . . .

                            They said it was Laïos' child,
   But it is your wife who can tell you about that.

OEDIPUS. My wife!—Did she give it to you?

SHEPHERD.   My lord, she did.

OEDIPUS. Do you know why?

SHEPHERD.   I was told to get rid of it.

OEDIPUS. An unspeakable mother!

SHEPHERD.   There had been prophecies . . .   60

OEDIPUS. Tell me.

SHEPHERD.   It was said that the boy would kill his own father.

OEDIPUS. Then why did you give him over to this old man?

SHEPHERD. I pitied the baby, my King,
   And I thought that this man would take him far away
   To his own country.

                        He saved him—but for what a fate!   65
   For if you are what this man says you are,
   No man living is more wretched than Oedipus.

OEDIPUS. Ah God!
            It was true!
            All the prophecies!
                        —Now,
   O Light, may I look on you for the last time!   70
   I, Oedipus,
   Oedipus, damned in his birth, in his marriage damned,
   Damned in the blood he shed with his own hand!

                                    He rushes into the palace.

                        Ode IV

CHORUS. Alas for the seed of men.   *Strophe 1*

What measure shall I give these generations
That breathe on the void and are void
And exist and do not exist?

Who bears more weight of joy   5
Than mass of sunlight shifting in images,
Or who shall make his thought stay on
That down time drifts away?

Your splendor is all fallen.

O naked brow of wrath and tears,   10
O change of Oedipus!
I who saw your days call no man blest—
Your great days like ghósts góne.

That mind was a strong bow.   *Antistrophe 1*
Deep, how deep you drew it then, hard archer,   15
At a dim fearful range,
And brought dear glory down!

You overcame the stranger—
The virgin with her hooking lion claws—
And though death sang, stood like a tower   20
To make pale Thebes take heart.

Fortress against our sorrow!

Divine king, giver of laws,
Majestic Oedipus!
No prince in Thebes had ever such renown,   25
No prince won such grace of power.

And now of all men ever known   *Strophe 2*
Most pitiful is this man's story:
His fortunes are most changed, his state
Fallen to a low slave's   30
Ground under bitter fate.

O Oedipus, most royal one!
The great door that expelled you to the light
Gave it night—ah, gave night to your glory:
As to the father, to the fathering son.   35

All understood too late.

How could that queen whom Laïos won,
The garden that he harrowed at his height,
Be silent when that act was done?

But all eyes fail before time's eye.   *Antistrophe 2* 40
All actions come to justice there.
Though never willed, though far down the deep past,
Your bed, your dread sirings,
Are brought to book at last.

Child by Laïos doomed to die,   45
Then doomed to lose that fortunate little death,
Would God you never took breath in this air
That with my wailing lips I take to cry:

For I weep the world's outcast.

I was blind, and now I can tell why: 50
Asleep, for you had given ease of breath
To Thebes, while the false years went by.

Exodos

Enter, from the palace, SECOND MESSENGER.
SECOND MESSENGER. Elders of Thebes, most honored in this land,
    What horrors are yours to see and hear, what weight
    Of sorrow to be endured, if, true to your birth,
    You venerate the line of Labdakos!
    I think neither Istros nor Phasis, those great rivers,   5
    Could purify this place of the corruption
    It shelters now, or soon must bring to light—
    Evil not done unconsciously, but willed.

The greatest griefs are those we cause ourselves.
CHORAGOS. Surely, friend, we have grief enough already;   10
    What new sorrow do you mean?
SECOND MESSENGER.   The Queen is dead.
CHORAGOS. Iocastê? Dead? But at whose hand?
SECOND MESSENGER.   Her own.
    The full horror of what happened you cannot know,
    For you did not see it; but I, who did, will tell you
    As clearly as I can how she met her death.   15

When she had left us,
    In passionate silence, passing through the court,
    She ran to her apartment in the house,
    Her hair clutched by the fingers of both hands.
    She closed the doors behind her; then, by that bed   20
    Where long ago the fatal son was conceived—
    That son who should bring about his father's death—
    We heard her call upon Laïos, dead so many years,
    And heard her wail for the double fruit of her marriage,
    A husband by her husband, children by her child.   25

Exactly how she died I do not know:
    For Oedipus burst in moaning and would not let us
    Keep vigil to the end: it was by him
    As he stormed about the room that our eyes were caught.
    From one to another of us he went, begging a sword,   30
    Cursing the wife who was not his wife, the mother
    Whose womb had carried his own children and himself.
    I do not know: it was none of us aided him,
    But surely one of the gods was in control!
    For with a dreadful cry   35

He hurled his weight, as though wrenched out of himself,
At the twin doors: the bolts gave, and he rushed in.
And there we saw her hanging, her body swaying
From the cruel cord she had noosed about her neck.
A great sob broke from him heartbreaking to hear,   40
As he loosed the rope and lowered her to the ground.

I would blot out from my mind what happened next!
For the King ripped from her gown the golden brooches
That were her ornament, and raised them, and plunged them down
Straight into his own eyeballs, crying, "No more,   45
No more shall you look on the misery about me,
The horrors of my own doing! Too long you have known
The faces of those whom I should never have seen,
Too long been blind to those for whom I was searching!
From this hour, go in darkness!" And as he spoke,   50
He struck at his eyes—not once, but many times;
And the blood spattered his beard,
Bursting from his ruined sockets like red hail.

So from the unhappiness of two this evil has sprung,
A curse on the man and woman alike. The old   55
Happiness of the house of Labdakos
Was happiness enough: where is it today?
It is all wailing and ruin, disgrace, death—all
The misery of mankind that has a name—
And it is wholly and for ever theirs.   60
CHORAGOS. Is he in agony still? Is there no rest for him?
SECOND MESSENGER. He is calling for someone to lead him to the gates
So that all the children of Kadmos may look upon
His father's murderer, his mother's—no,
I cannot say it!
                         And then he will leave Thebes,   65
Self-exiled, in order that the curse
Which he himself pronounced may depart from the house.
He is weak, and there is none to lead him,
So terrible is his suffering.
                         But you will see:
Look, the doors are opening; in a moment   70
You will see a thing that would crush a heart of stone.

The central door is opened; OEDIPUS, *blinded, is led in.*
CHORAGOS. Dreadful indeed for men to see.
Never have my own eyes
Looked on a sight so full of fear.

Oedipus!   75
What madness came upon you, what daemon°
Leaped on your life with heavier
Punishment than a mortal man can bear?

76 **daemon** a spirit, not necessarily evil

No: I cannot even
Look at you, poor ruined one.   80
And I would speak, question, ponder,
If I were able. No.
You make me shudder.

OEDIPUS. God. God.
Is there a sorrow greater?   85
Where shall I find harbor in this world?
My voice is hurled far on a dark wind.
What has God done to me?

CHORAGOS. Too terrible to think of, or to see.

OEDIPUS. O cloud of night,   *Strophe 1* 90
Never to be turned away: night coming on,
I cannot tell how: night like a shroud!
My fair winds brought me here.
                                   Oh God. Again
The pain of the spikes where I had sight,
The flooding pain   95
Of memory, never to be gouged out.

CHORAGOS. This is not strange.
You suffer it all twice over, remorse in pain,
Pain in remorse.

OEDIPUS. Ah dear friend   *Antistrophe 1* 100
Are you faithful even yet, you alone?
Are you still standing near me, will you stay here,
Patient, to care for the blind?
                                   The blind man!
Yet even blind I know who it is attends me,
By the voice's tone—   105
Though my new darkness hide the comforter.

CHORAGOS. Oh fearful act!
What god was it drove you to rake black
Night across your eyes?

OEDIPUS. Apollo. Apollo. Dear   *Strophe 2* 110
Children, the god was Apollo.
He brought my sick, sick fate upon me.
But the blinding hand was my own!
How could I bear to see
When all my sight was horror everywhere?   115

CHORAGOS. Everywhere; that is true.

OEDIPUS. And now what is left?
Images? Love? A greeting even,
Sweet to the senses? Is there anything?
Ah, no, friends: lead me away   120
Lead me away from Thebes.
                          Lead the great wreck
And hell of Oedipus, whom the gods hate.

CHORAGOS. Your fate is clear, you are not blind to that.
Would God you had never found it out!

OEDIPUS. Death take the man who unbound   *Antistrophe 2* 125
My feet on that hillside

And delivered me from death to life! What life?
If only I had died,
This weight of monstrous doom
Could not have dragged me and my darlings down.   130
CHORAGOS. I would have wished the same.
OEDIPUS. Oh never to have come here
    With my father's blood upon me! Never
    To have been the man they call his mother's husband!
    Oh accurst! O child of evil,   135
    To have entered that wretched bed—
                                    the selfsame one!
    More primal than sin itself, this fell to me.
CHORAGOS. I do not know how I can answer you.
    You were better dead than alive and blind.
OEDIPUS. Do not counsel me any more. This punishment   140
    That I have laid upon myself is just.
    If I had eyes,
    I do not know how I could bear the sight
    Of my father, when I came to the house of Death,
    Or my mother: for I have sinned against them both   145
    So vilely that I could not make my peace
    By strangling my own life.
                        Or do you think my children,
    Born as they were born, would be sweet to my eyes?
    Ah never, never! Nor this town with its high walls,
    Nor the holy images of the gods.
                        For I,   150
    Thrice miserable—Oedipus, noblest of all the line
    Of Kadmos, have condemned myself to enjoy
    These things no more, by my own malediction
    Expelling that man whom the gods declared
    To be a defilement in the house of Laïos.   155
    After exposing the rankness of my own guilt,
    How could I look men frankly in the eyes?
    No, I swear it,
    If I could have stifled my hearing at its source,
    I would have done it and made all this body   160
    A tight cell of misery, blank to light and sound:
    So I should have been safe in a dark agony
    Beyond all recollection.
                        Ah Kithairon!
    Why did you shelter me? When I was cast upon you,
    Why did I not die? Then I should never   165
    Have shown the world my execrable birth.

    Ah Polybos! Corinth, city that I believed
    The ancient seat of my ancestors: how fair
    I seemed, your child! And all the while this evil
    Was cancerous within me!
                        For I am sick   170
    In my daily life, sick in my origin.

O three roads, dark ravine, woodland and way
Where three roads met: you, drinking my father's blood,
My own blood, spilled by my own hand: can you remember
The unspeakable things I did there, and the things   175
I went on from there to do?

                      O marriage, marriage!
The act that engendered me, and again the act
Performed by the son in the same bed—

                           Ah, the net
Of incest, mingling fathers, brothers, sons,
With brides, wives, mothers: the last evil   180
That can be known by men: no tongue can say
How evil!

            No. For the love of God, conceal me
Somewhere far from Thebes; or kill me; or hurl me
Into the sea, away from men's eyes for ever.
Come, lead me. You need not fear to touch me.   185
Of all men, I alone can bear this guilt.

    Enter CREON.
CHORAGOS. We are not the ones to decide; but Creon here
    May fitly judge of what you ask. He only
    Is left to protect the city in your place.
OEDIPUS. Alas, how can I speak to him? What right have I   190
    To beg his courtesy whom I have deeply wronged?
CREON. I have not come to mock you, Oedipus,
    Or to reproach you, either.
    [*To* ATTENDANTS.]   —You, standing there:
    If you have lost all respect for man's dignity,
    At least respect the flame of Lord Helios: 195
    Do not allow this pollution to show itself
    Openly here, an affront to the earth
    And Heaven's rain and the light of day. No, take him
    Into the house as quickly as you can.
    For it is proper   200
    That only the close kindred see his grief.
OEDIPUS. I pray you in God's name, since your courtesy
    Ignores my dark expectation, visiting
    With mercy this man of all men most execrable:
    Give me what I ask—for your good, not for mine.   205
CREON. And what is it that you would have me do?
OEDIPUS. Drive me out of this country as quickly as may be
    To a place where no human voice can ever greet me.
CREON. I should have done that before now—only,
    God's will had not been wholly revealed to me.   210
OEDIPUS. But his command is plain: the parricide
    Must be destroyed. I am that evil man.
CREON. That is the sense of it, yes; but as things are,
    We had best discover clearly what is to be done.
OEDIPUS. You would learn more about a man like me?   215
CREON. You are ready now to listen to the god.

OEDIPUS. I will listen. But it is to you.
That I must turn for help. I beg you, hear me.

The woman in there—
Give her whatever funeral you think proper: 220
She is your sister.
                    —But let me go, Creon!
Let me purge my father's Thebes of the pollution
Of my living here, and go out to the wild hills,
To Kithairon, that has won such fame with me,
The tomb my mother and father appointed for me,   225
And let me die there, as they willed I should.
And yet I know
Death will not ever come to me through sickness
Or in any natural way: I have been preserved
For some unthinkable fate. But let that be.   230
As for my sons, you need not care for them.
They are men, they will find some way to live.
But my poor daughters, who have shared my table,
Who never before have been parted from their father—
Take care of them, Creon; do this for me   235
And will you let me touch them with my hands
A last time, and let us weep together?
Be kind, my lord,
Great prince, be kind!
                    Could I but touch them,
They would be mine again, as when I had my eyes.   240

Enter ANTIGONÉ *and* ISMENE, *attended.*
Ah, God!
Is it my dearest children I hear weeping?
Has Creon pitied me and sent my daughters?
CREON. Yes, Oedipus: I knew that they were dear to you
In the old days, and know you must love them still.   245
OEDIPUS. May God bless you for this—and be a friendlier
Guardian to you than he has been to me!

Children, where are you?
Come quickly to my hands: they are your brother's—
Hands that have brought your father's once clear eyes   250
To this way of seeing—
                    Ah dearest ones,
I had neither sight nor knowledge then, your father
By the woman who was the source of his life!
And I weep for you—having no strength to see you—,
I weep for you when I think of the bitterness   255
That men will visit upon you all your lives.
What homes, what festivals can you attend
Without being forced to depart again in tears?
And when you come to marriageable age,
Where is the man, my daughters, who would dare   260
Risk the bane that lies on all my children?

Is there any evil wanting? Your father killed
His father; sowed the womb of her who bore him;
Engendered you at the fount of his own existence!
That is what they will say of you.

                           Then, whom   265
Can you ever marry? There are no bridegrooms for you,
And your lives must wither away in sterile dreaming.
O Creon, son of Menoikeus!
You are the only father my daughters have,
Since we, their parents, are both of us gone forever.   270
They are your own blood: you will not let them
Fall into beggary and loneliness;
You will keep them from the miseries that are mine!
Take pity on them; see, they are only children,
Friendless except for you. Promise me this,   275
Great Prince, and give me your hand in token of it.

  CREON *clasps his right hand.*
Children:
I could say much, if you could understand me,
But as it is, I have only this prayer for you:
Live where you can, be as happy as you can—   280
Happier, please God, than God has made your father!
CREON. Enough. You have wept enough. Now go within.
OEDIPUS. I must; but it is hard.
CREON.   Time eases all things.
OEDIPUS. But you must promise—
CREON.   Say what you desire.
OEDIPUS. Send me from Thebes!
CREON.   God grant that I may!   285
OEDIPUS. But since God hates me . . .
CREON.   No, he will grant your wish.
OEDIPUS. You promise?
CREON.   I cannot speak beyond my knowledge.
OEDIPUS. Then lead me in.
CREON.   Come now, and leave your children.
OEDIPUS. No! Do not take them from me!
CREON.   Think no longer
That you are in command here, but rather think   290
How, when you were, you served your own destruction.

          Exeunt into the house all but the CHORUS;
          the CHORAGOS *chants directly to the audience.*
CHORAGOS. Men of Thebes: look upon Oedipus.
This is the king who solved the famous riddle
And towered up, most powerful of men.
No mortal eyes but looked on him with envy,   295

Yet in the end ruin swept over him.
Let every man in mankind's frailty
Consider his last day; and let none
Presume on his good fortune until he find
Life, at his death, a memory without pain.   300

                    [c. 430 B.C.*]*

Topics for Critical Thinking and Writing

1. On the basis of the Prologue, characterize Oedipus. What additional traits are revealed in Scene I and Ode I?

2. How fair is it to say that Oedipus is morally guilty? Does he argue that he is morally innocent because he did not intend to do immoral deeds? Can it be said that he is guilty of hubris but that hubris has nothing to do with his fall?

3. Oedipus says that he blinds himself in order not to look upon people he should not. What further reasons can be given? Why does he not (like his mother) commit suicide?

4. How fair is it to say that the play shows the contemptibleness of man's efforts to act intelligently?

5. How fair is it to say that in *Oedipus* the gods are evil?

6. Are the choral odes lyrical interludes that serve to separate the scenes, or do they advance the dramatic action?

7. Matthew Arnold said that Sophocles saw life steadily and saw it whole. But in this play is Sophocles facing the facts of life, or, on the contrary, is he avoiding life as it usually is and presenting a series of unnatural and outrageous coincidences?

8. Can you describe your emotions at the end of the play? Do they include pity for Oedipus? Pity for all human beings, including yourself? Fear that you might be punished for some unintended transgression? Awe, engendered by a perception of the interrelatedness of things? Relief that the story is only a story? Exhilaration?

SUSAN GLASPELL

Susan Glaspell (1882–1948) was born in Davenport, Iowa, and educated at Drake University in Des Moines. In 1903 she married George Cram Cook and, with Cook and other writers, actors, and artists, in 1915 founded the Provincetown Players, a group that remained vital until 1929. Glaspell wrote Trifles *(1916) for the Provincetown Players, but she also wrote stories, novels, and a biography of her husband. In 1931 she won a Pulitzer Prize for* Alison's House, *a play about the family of a deceased poet who in some ways resembles Emily Dickinson.*

Trifles

SCENE: *The kitchen in the now abandoned farmhouse of* JOHN WRIGHT, *a gloomy kitchen, and left without having been put in order—unwashed pans under the sink, a loaf of bread outside the breadbox, a dish towel on the table—other signs of incompleted work. At the rear the outer door opens, and the* SHERIFF *comes in, followed by the* COUNTY ATTORNEY *and* HALE. *The* SHERIFF *and* HALE *are men in middle life, the* COUNTY ATTORNEY *is a young man; all are much bundled up and go at once to the stove. They are followed by the two women—the* SHERIFF'S WIFE *first; she is a slight wiry woman, a thin nervous face.* MRS. HALE *is larger and would ordinarily be called more comfortable looking, but she is disturbed now and looks fearfully about as she enters. The women have come in slowly and stand close together near the door.*

Photo of the original production (1916) of *Trifles.* (New York Public Library)

COUNTY ATTORNEY [*rubbing his hands*]. This feels good. Come up to the fire, ladies.

MRS. PETERS [*after taking a step forward*]. I'm not—cold.

SHERIFF [*unbuttoning his overcoat and stepping away from the stove as if to the beginning of official business*]. Now, Mr. Hale, before we move things about, you explain to Mr. Henderson just what you saw when you came here yesterday morning.

COUNTY ATTORNEY. By the way, has anything been moved? Are things just as you left them yesterday?

SHERIFF [*looking about*]. It's just the same. When it dropped below zero last night, I thought I'd better send Frank out this morning to make a fire for us—no use getting pneumonia with a big case on; but I told him not to touch anything except the stove—and you know Frank.

COUNTY ATTORNEY. Somebody should have been left here yesterday.

SHERIFF. Oh—yesterday. When I had to send Frank to Morris Center for that man who went crazy—I want you to know I had my hands full yesterday. I knew you could get back from Omaha by today, and as long as I went over everything here myself—

COUNTY ATTORNEY. Well, Mr. Hale, tell just what happened when you came here yesterday morning.

HALE. Harry and I had started to town with a load of potatoes. We came along the road from my place; and as I got here, I said, "I'm going to see if I can't get John Wright to go in with me on a party telephone." I spoke to Wright about it once before, and he put me off, saying folks talked too much anyway, and all he asked was peace and quiet—I guess you know about how much he talked himself; but I thought maybe if I went to the house and talked about it before his wife, though I said to Harry that I didn't know as what his wife wanted made much difference to John—

COUNTY ATTORNEY. Let's talk about that later, Mr. Hale. I do want to talk about that, but tell now just what happened when you got to the house.

HALE. I didn't hear or see anything; I knocked at the door, and still it was all quiet inside. I knew they must be up, it was past eight o'clock. So I knocked again, and I thought I heard somebody say, "Come in." I wasn't sure, I'm not sure yet, but I opened the door—this door [*indicating the door by which the two women are still standing*], and there in that rocker—[*pointing to it*] sat Mrs. Wright. [*They all look at the rocker.*]

COUNTY ATTORNEY. What—was she doing?

HALE. She was rockin' back and forth. She had her apron in her hand and was kind of—pleating it.

COUNTY ATTORNEY. And how did she—look?

HALE. Well, she looked queer.

COUNTY ATTORNEY. How do you mean—queer?

HALE. Well, as if she didn't know what she was going to do next. And kind of done up.

COUNTY ATTORNEY. How did she seem to feel about your coming?

HALE. Why, I don't think she minded—one way or other. She didn't pay much attention. I said, "How do, Mrs. Wright, it's cold, ain't it?" And she said, "Is it?"—and went on kind of pleating at her apron. Well, I was surprised; she didn't ask me to come up to the stove, or to set down, but just sat there, not even looking at me, so I said, "I want to see John." And then she—laughed. I guess you would call it a laugh. I thought of Harry and the team outside, so I said a little sharp: "Can't I see John?" "No," she says, kind o' dull like. "Ain't he home?" says I. "Yes," says she, "he's home." "Then why can't I see him?" I asked her, out of patience. "'Cause he's dead," says she. "*Dead?*" says I. She just nodded her head, not getting a bit excited, but rockin' back and forth. "Why—where is he?" says I, not knowing what to say. She just pointed upstairs—like that [*himself pointing to the room above*]. I got up, with the idea of going up there. I walked from there to here—then I says, "Why, what did he die of?" "He died of a rope around his neck," says she, and just went on pleatin' at her apron. Well, I went out and called Harry. I thought I might—need help. We went upstairs, and there he was lyin'—

COUNTY ATTORNEY. I think I'd rather have you go into that upstairs, where you can point it all out. Just go on now with the rest of the story.

HALE. Well, my first thought was to get that rope off. I looked . . . [*Stops, his face twitches.*] . . . but Harry, he went up to him, and he said, "No, he's dead all right, and we'd better not touch anything." So we went back downstairs. She was still sitting that same way. "Has anybody been notified?" I asked. "No," says she, unconcerned. "Who did this, Mrs. Wright?" said Harry. He said it businesslike—and she stopped pleatin' of her apron. "I don't know," she says. "You don't *know?*" says Harry. "No," says she, "Weren't you sleepin' in the bed with him?" says Harry. "Yes," says she, "but I was on the inside." "Somebody slipped a rope round his neck and strangled him, and you didn't wake up?" says Harry. "I didn't wake up," she said after him. We must 'a looked as if we didn't see how that could be, for after a minute she said, "I sleep sound." Harry was going to ask her more questions, but I said maybe we ought to let her tell her story first to the coroner, or the sheriff, so Harry went fast as he could to Rivers' place, where there's a telephone.

COUNTY ATTORNEY. And what did Mrs. Wright do when she knew that you had gone for the coroner?

HALE. She moved from that chair to this over here . . . [*Pointing to a small chair in the corner.*] . . . and just sat there with her hands held together and looking down. I got a feeling that I ought to make some conversation, so I said I had come in to see if John wanted to put in a telephone, and at that she started to laugh, and then she stopped and looked at me—scared. [*The* COUNTY ATTORNEY, *who has had his notebook out, makes a note.*] I dunno, maybe it wasn't scared. I wouldn't like to say it was. Soon Harry got back, and then Dr. Lloyd came, and you, Mr. Peters, and so I guess that's all I know that you don't.

COUNTY ATTORNEY. [*looking around*]. I guess we'll go upstairs first—and then out to the barn and around there. [*To the* SHERIFF.] You're convinced that there was nothing important here—nothing that would point to any motive?

SHERIFF. Nothing here but kitchen things. [*The* COUNTY ATTORNEY, *after again looking around the kitchen, opens the door of a cupboard closet. He gets up on a chair and looks on a shelf. Pulls his hand away, sticky.*]

COUNTY ATTORNEY. Here's a nice mess. [*The women draw nearer.*]

MRS. PETERS [*to the other woman*]. Oh, her fruit; it did freeze. [*To the* LAWYER.] She worried about that when it turned so cold. She said the fir'd go out and her jars would break.

SHERIFF. Well, can you beat the women! Held for murder and worryin' about her preserves.

COUNTY ATTORNEY. I guess before we're through she may have something more serious than preserves to worry about.

HALE. Well, women are used to worrying over trifles.

[*The two women move a little closer together.*]

COUNTY ATTORNEY [*with the gallantry of a young politician*]. And yet, for all their worries, what would we do without the ladies? [*The women do not unbend. He goes to the sink, takes a dipperful of water from the pail and, pouring it into a basin, washes his hands. Starts to wipe them on the roller towel, turns it for a cleaner place.*] Dirty towels! [*Kicks his foot against the pans under the sink.*] Not much of a housekeeper, would you say, ladies?

MRS. HALE [*stiffly*] There's a great deal of work to be done on a farm.

COUNTY ATTORNEY. To be sure. And yet . . . [*With a little bow to her.*] . . . I know there are some Dickson county farmhouses which do not have such roller towels. [*He gives it a pull to expose its full length again.*]

MRS. HALE. Those towels get dirty awful quick. Men's hands aren't always as clean as they might be.

COUNTY ATTORNEY. Ah, loyal to your sex, I see. But you and Mrs. Wright were neighbors. I suppose you were friends, too.

MRS. HALE [*shaking her head*]. I've not seen much of her of late years. I've not been in this house—it's more than a year.

COUNTY ATTORNEY. And why was that? You didn't like her?

MRS. HALE. I liked her all well enough. Farmers' wives have their hands full, Mr. Henderson. And then—

COUNTY ATTORNEY. Yes—?

MRS. HALE [*looking about*]. It never seemed a very cheerful place.

COUNTY ATTORNEY. No—it's not cheerful. I shouldn't say she had the homemaking instinct.

MRS. HALE. Well, I don't know as Wright had, either.

COUNTY ATTORNEY. You mean that they didn't get on very well?

MRS. HALE. No, I don't mean anything. But I don't think a place'd be any cheerfuler for John Wright's being in it.

COUNTY ATTORNEY. I'd like to talk more of that a little later. I want to get the lay of things upstairs now. [*He goes to the left, where three steps lead to a stair door.*]

SHERIFF. I suppose anything Mrs. Peters does'll be all right. She was to take in some clothes for her, you know, and a few little things. We left in such a hurry yesterday.

COUNTY ATTORNEY. Yes, but I would like to see what you take, Mrs. Peters, and keep an eye out for anything that might be of use to us.

MRS. PETERS. Yes, Mr. Henderson.

[The women listen to the men's steps on the stairs, then look about the kitchen.]

MRS. HALE. I'd hate to have men coming into my kitchen, snooping around and criticizing. [*She arranges the pans under sink which the* LAWYER *had shoved out of place.*]

MRS. PETERS. Of course it's no more than their duty.

MRS. HALE. Duty's all right, but I guess that deputy sheriff that came out to make the fire might have got a little of this on. [*Gives the roller towel a pull.*] Wish I'd thought of that sooner. Seems mean to talk about her for not having things slicked up when she had to come away in such a hurry.

MRS. PETERS [*who has gone to a small table in the left rear corner of the room, and lifted one end of a towel that covers a pan*]. She had bread set. [*Stands still.*]

MRS. HALE [*eyes fixed on a loaf of bread beside the breadbox, which is on a low shelf at the other side of the room. Moves slowly toward it*]. She was going to put this in there. [*Picks up loaf, then abruptly drops it. In a manner of returning to familiar things.*] It's a shame about her fruit. I wonder if it's all gone. [*Gets up on the chair and looks.*] I think there's some here that's all right, Mrs. Peters. Yes—here; [*Holding it toward the window.*] this is cherries, too. [*Looking again.*] I declare I believe that's the only one. [*Gets down, bottle in her hand. Goes to the sink and wipes it off on the outside.*] She'll feel awful bad after all her hard work in the hot weather. I remember the afternoon I put up my cherries last summer. [*She puts the bottle on the big kitchen table, center of the room, front table. With a sigh, is about to sit down in the rocking chair. Before she is seated realizes what chair it is; with a slow look at it, steps back. The chair, which she has touched, rocks back and forth.*]

MRS. PETERS. Well, I must get those things from the front room closet. [*She goes to the door at the right, but after looking into the other room steps back.*] You coming with me, Mrs. Hale? You could help me carry them. [*They go into the other room; reappear,* MRS. PETERS *carrying a dress and skirt,* MRS. HALE *following with a pair of shoes.*]

MRS. PETERS. My, it's cold in there. [*She puts the cloth on the big table, and hurries to the stove.*]

MRS. HALE [*examining the skirt*]. Wright was close. I think maybe that's why she kept so much to herself. She didn't even belong to the Ladies' Aid. I suppose she felt she couldn't do her part, and then you don't enjoy things when you feel shabby. She used to wear pretty clothes and be lively, when she was Minnie Foster, one of the town girls singing in the choir. But that—oh, that was thirty years ago. This all you was to take in?

MRS. PETERS. She said she wanted an apron. Funny thing to want, for there isn't much to get you dirty in jail, goodness knows. But I suppose just to make her feel more natural. She said they was in the top drawer in this cupboard. Yes, here. And then her little shawl that always hung behind the door. [*Opens stair door and looks.*] Yes, here it is. [*Quickly shuts door leading upstairs.*]

MRS. HALE [*abruptly moving toward her*]. Mrs. Peters?

MRS. PETERS. Yes, Mrs. Hale?

MRS. HALE. Do you think she did it?

MRS. PETERS [*in a frightened voice*]. Oh, I don't know.

MRS. HALE. Well, I don't think she did. Asking for an apron and her little shawl. Worrying about her fruit.

MRS. PETERS [*starts to speak, glances up, where footsteps are heard in the room above. In a low voice*]. Mr. Peters says it looks bad for her. Mr. Henderson is awful sarcastic in speech, and he'll make fun of her sayin' she didn't wake up.

MRS. HALE. Well, I guess John Wright didn't wake when they was slipping that rope under his neck.

MRS. PETERS. No, it's strange. It must have been done awful crafty and still. They say it was such a—funny way to kill a man, rigging it all up like that.

MRS. HALE. That's just what Mr. Hale said. There was a gun in the house. He says that's what he can't understand.

MRS. PETERS. Mr. Henderson said coming out that what was needed for the case was a motive; something to show anger, or—sudden feeling.

MRS. HALE [*who is standing by the table*]. Well, I don't see any signs of anger around here. [*She puts her hand on the dish towel which lies on the table, stands looking down at the table, one half of which is clean, the other half messy.*] It's wiped here. [*Makes a move as if to finish work, then turns and looks at loaf of bread outside the breadbox. Drops towel. In that voice of coming back to familiar things.*] Wonder how they are finding things upstairs? I hope she had it a little more red-up there. You know, it seems kind of *sneaking.* Locking her up in town and then coming out here and trying to get her own house to turn against her!

MRS. PETERS. But, Mrs. Hale, the law is the law.

MRS. HALE. I s'pose 'tis. [*Unbuttoning her coat.*] Better loosen up your things, Mrs. Peters. You won't feel them when you go out.

[MRS. PETERS *takes off her fur tippet, goes to hang it on hook at the back of room, stands looking at the under part of the small corner table.*]

MRS. PETERS. She was piecing a quilt. [*She brings the large sewing basket, and they look at the bright pieces.*]

MRS. HALE. It's log cabin pattern. Pretty, isn't it? I wonder if she was goin' to quilt or just knot it?

[*Footsteps have been heard coming down the stairs. The* SHERIFF *enters, followed by* HALE *and the* COUNTY ATTORNEY.]

SHERIFF. They wonder if she was going to quilt it or just knot it. [*The men laugh, the women look abashed.*]

COUNTY ATTORNEY [*rubbing his hands over the stove*]. Frank's fire didn't do much up there, did it? Well, let's go out to the barn and get that cleared up.

[*The men go outside.*]

MRS. HALE [*resentfully*]. I don't know as there's anything so strange, our takin' up our time with little things while we're waiting for them to get the evidence. [*She sits down at the big table, smoothing out a block with decision.*] I don't see as it's anything to laugh about.

MRS. PETERS [*apologetically*]. Of course they've got awful important things on their minds. [*Pulls up a chair and joins* MRS. HALE *at the table.*]

MRS. HALE [*examining another block*]. Mrs. Peters, look at this one. Here, this is the one she was working on, and look at the sewing! All the rest of it has been so nice and even. And look at this! It's all over the place! Why, it looks as if she didn't know what she was about! [*After she has said this, they look at each other, then started to glance back at the door. After an instant* MRS. HALE *has pulled at a knot and ripped the sewing.*]

MRS. PETERS. Oh, what are you doing, Mrs. Hale?

MRS. HALE [*mildly*]. Just pulling out a stitch or two that's not sewed very good. [*Threading a needle.*] Bad sewing always made me fidgety.

MRS. PETERS [*nervously*]. I don't think we ought to touch things.

MRS. HALE. I'll just finish up this end. [*Suddenly stopping and leaning forward.*] Mrs. Peters?

MRS. PETERS. Yes, Mrs. Hale?

MRS. HALE. What do you suppose she was so nervous about?

MRS. PETERS. Oh—I don't know. I don't know as she was nervous. I sometimes sew awful queer when I'm just tired. [MRS. HALE *starts to say something, looks at* MRS. PETERS, *then goes on sewing.*] Well, I must get these things wrapped up. They may be through sooner than we think. [*Putting apron and other things together.*] I wonder where I can find a piece of paper, and string.

MRS. HALE. In that cupboard, maybe.

MRS. PETERS [*looking in cupboard*]. Why, here's a birdcage. [*Holds it up.*] Did she have a bird, Mrs. Hale?

MRS. HALE. Why, I don't know whether she did or not—I've not been here for so long. There was a man around last year selling canaries cheap, but I don't know as she took one; maybe she did. She used to sing real pretty herself.

MRS. PETERS [*glancing around*]. Seems funny to think of a bird here. But she must have had one, or why should she have a cage? I wonder what happened to it?

MRS. HALE. I s'pose maybe the cat got it.

MRS. PETERS. No, she didn't have a cat. She's got that feeling some people have about cats—being afraid of them. My cat got in her room, and she was real upset and asked me to take it out.

MRS. HALE. My sister Bessie was like that. Queer, ain't it?

MRS. PETERS [*examining the cage*]. Why, look at this door. It's broke. One hinge is pulled apart.

MRS. HALE [*looking, too*]. Looks as if someone must have been rough with it.

MRS. PETERS. Why, yes. [*She brings the cage forward and puts it on the table.*]

MRS. HALE. I wish if they're going to find any evidence they'd be about it. I don't like this place.

MRS. PETERS. But I'm awful glad you came with me, Mrs. Hale. It would be lonesome for me sitting here alone.

MRS. HALE. It would, wouldn't it? [*Dropping her sewing.*] But I tell you what I do wish, Mrs. Peters. I wish I had come over sometimes when *she* was here. I—[*Looking around the room.*]—wish I had.

MRS. PETERS. But of course you were awful busy, Mrs. Hale—your house and your children.

MRS. HALE. I could've come. I stayed away because it weren't cheerful—and that's why I ought to have come. I—I've never liked this place. Maybe because it's down in a hollow, and you don't see the road. I dunno what it is, but it's a lonesome place and always was. I wish I had come over to see Minnie Foster sometimes. I can see now—[*Shakes her head.*]

MRS. PETERS. Well, you mustn't reproach yourself, Mrs. Hale. Somehow we just don't see how it is with other folks until—something comes up.

MRS. HALE. Not having children makes less work—but it makes a quiet house, and Wright out to work all day, and no company when he did come in. Did you know John Wright, Mrs. Peters?

MRS. PETERS. Not to know him; I've seen him in town. They say he was a good man.

MRS. HALE. Yes—good; he didn't drink, and kept his word as well as most, I guess, and paid his debts. But he was a hard man, Mrs. Peters. Just to pass the time of day with him. [*Shivers.*] Like a raw wind that gets to the bone. [*Pauses, her eye falling on the cage.*] I should think she would 'a wanted a bird. But what do you suppose went with it?

MRS. PETERS. I don't know, unless it got sick and died. [*She reaches over and swings the broken door, swings it again; both women watch it.*]

MRS. HALE. You weren't raised round here, were you? [MRS. PETERS *shakes her head.*] You didn't know—her?

MRS. PETERS. Not till they brought her yesterday.

MRS. HALE. She—come to think of it, she was kind of like a bird herself—real sweet and pretty, but kind of timid and—fluttery. How—she—did—change. [*Silence; then as if struck by a happy thought and relieved to get back to everyday things.*] Tell you what, Mrs. Peters; why don't you take the quilt in with you? It might take up her mind.

MRS. PETERS. Why, I think that's a real nice idea, Mrs. Hale. There couldn't possibly be any objection to it, could there? Now, just what would I take? I wonder if her patches are in here—and her things. [*They look in the sewing basket.*]

MRS. HALE. Here's some red. I expect this has got sewing things in it [*Brings out a fancy box.*] What a pretty box. Looks like something somebody would give you. Maybe her scissors are in here. [*Opens box. Suddenly puts her hand to her nose.*] Why—[MRS. PETERS *bends nearer, then turns her face away.*] There's something wrapped up in this piece of silk.

MRS. PETERS. Why, this isn't her scissors.

MRS. HALE [*lifting the silk*]. Oh, Mrs. Peters—it's—[MRS. PETERS *bends closer.*]

MRS. PETERS. It's the bird.

MRS. HALE [*jumping up*]. But, Mrs. Peters—look at it. Its neck! Look at its neck! It's all—other side *to.*

MRS. PETERS. Somebody—wrung—its neck.

[*Their eyes meet. A look of growing comprehension of horror. Steps are heard outside.* MRS. HALE *slips box under quilt pieces, and sinks into her chair. Enter* SHERIFF *and* COUNTY ATTORNEY. MRS. PETERS *rises.*]

COUNTY ATTORNEY [*as one turning from serious things to little pleasantries*]. Well, ladies, have you decided whether she was going to quilt it or knot it?

MRS. PETERS. We think she was going to—knot it.

COUNTY ATTORNEY. Well, that's interesting, I'm sure. [*Seeing the birdcage.*] Has the bird flown?

MRS. HALE [*putting more quilt pieces over the box*]. We think the—cat got it.
COUNTY ATTORNEY [*preoccupied*]. Is there a cat?

[MRS. HALE *glances in a quick covert way at* MRS. PETERS.]

MRS. PETERS. Well, not now. They're superstitious, you know. They leave.
COUNTY ATTORNEY [*to* SHERIFF PETERS, *continuing an interrupted conversation*].
No sign at all of anyone having come from the outside. Their own rope.
Now let's go up again and go over it piece by piece. [*They start upstairs.*]
It would have to have been someone who knew just the—[MRS. PETERS *sits
down. The two women sit there not looking at one another, but as if
peering into something and at the same time holding back. When they
talk now, it is the manner of feeling their way over strange ground, as if
afraid of what they are saying, but as if they cannot help saying it.*]
MRS. HALE. She liked the bird. She was going to bury it in that pretty box.
MRS. PETERS [*in a whisper*]. When I was a girl—my kitten—there was a boy took
a hatchet, and before my eyes—and before I could get there—[*Covers her
face an instant.*] If they hadn't held me back, I would have—[*Catches herself, looks upstairs where steps are heard, falters weakly.*]—hurt him.
MRS. HALE [*with a slow look around her*]. I wonder how it would seem never to
have had any children around. [*Pause.*] No, Wright wouldn't like the
bird—a thing that sang. She used to sing. He killed that, too.
MRS. PETERS [*moving uneasily*]. We don't know who killed the bird.
MRS. HALE. I knew John Wright.
MRS. PETERS. It was an awful thing was done in this house that night, Mrs. Hale.
Killing a man while he slept, slipping a rope around his neck that choked
the life out of him.
MRS. HALE. His neck. Choked the life out of him.

[*Her hand goes out and rests on the birdcage.*]

MRS. PETERS [*with a rising voice*]. We don't know who killed him. We don't *know*.
MRS. HALE [*her own feeling not interrupted*]. If there'd been years and years of
nothing, then a bird to sing to you, it would be awful—still, after the bird
was still.
MRS. PETERS [*something within her speaking*]. I know what stillness is. When
we homesteaded in Dakota, and my first baby died—after he was two
years old, and me with no other then—
MRS. HALE [*moving*]. How soon do you suppose they'll be through, looking for
evidence?
MRS. PETERS. I know what stillness is. [*Pulling herself back.*] The law has got to
punish crime, Mrs. Hale.
MRS. HALE [*not as if answering that*]. I wish you'd seen Minnie Foster when she
wore a white dress with blue ribbons and stood up there in the choir and
sang. [*A look around the room*] Oh, I *wish* I'd come over here once in a
while! That was a crime! That was a crime! Who's going to punish that?
MRS. PETERS [*looking upstairs*]. We mustn't—take on.
MRS. HALE. I might have known she needed help! I know how things can be—for
women. I tell you, it's queer, Mrs. Peters. We live close together and we
live far apart. We all go through the same things—it's all just a different
kind of the same thing. [*Brushes her eyes, noticing the bottle of fruit,
reaches out for it.*] If I was you, I wouldn't tell her her fruit was gone. Tell

her it *ain't.* Tell her it's all right. Take this in to prove it to her. She—she
may never know whether it was broke or not.

MRS. PETERS [*takes the bottle, looks about for something to wrap it in; takes petticoat from the clothes brought from the other room, very nervously begins winding this around the bottle. In a false voice*]. My, it's a good
thing the men couldn't hear us. Wouldn't they just laugh! Getting all
stirred up over a little thing like a—dead canary. As if that could have anything to do with—with—wouldn't they *laugh!*

[The men are heard coming downstairs.]

MRS. HALE [*under her breath*] Maybe they would—maybe they wouldn't.

COUNTY ATTORNEY. No, Peters, it's all perfectly clear except a reason for doing it.
But you know juries when it comes to women. If there was some definite
thing. Something to show—something to make a story about—a thing that
would connect up with this strange way of doing it.

[The women's eyes meet for an instant. Enter HALE *from outer door.]*

HALE. Well, I've got the team around. Pretty cold out there.

COUNTY ATTORNEY. I'm going to stay here awhile by myself. [*To the* SHERIFF.] You
can send Frank out for me, can't you? I want to go over everything. I'm not
satisfied that we can't do better.

SHERIFF. Do you want to see what Mrs. Peters is going to take in?

[The LAWYER *goes to the table, picks up the apron, laughs.]*

COUNTY ATTORNEY. Oh I guess they're not very dangerous things the ladies have
picked up. [*Moves a few things about, disturbing the quilt pieces which
cover the box. Steps back.*] No, Mrs. Peters doesn't need supervising. For
that matter, a sheriff's wife is married to the law. Ever think of it that way,
Mrs. Peters?

MRS. PETERS. Not—just that way.

SHERIFF [*chuckling*]. Married to the law. [*Moves toward the other room.*] I just
want you to come in here a minute, George. We ought to take a look at
these windows.

COUNTY ATTORNEY [*scoffingly*]. Oh, windows!

SHERIFF. We'll be right out, Mr. Hale.

*[*HALE *goes outside. The* SHERIFF *follows the* COUNTY ATTORNEY *into the other
room. Then* MRS. HALE *rises, hands tight together, looking intensely at* MRS. PE-
TERS, *whose eyes take a slow turn, finally meeting,* MRS. HALE'S. *A moment* MRS.
HALE *holds her, then her own eyes point the way to where the box is concealed.
Suddenly* MRS. PETERS *throws back quilt pieces and tries to put the box in the bag
she is wearing. It is too big. She opens box, starts to take the bird out, cannot
touch it, goes to pieces, stands there helpless. Sound of a knob turning in the
other room.* MRS. HALE *snatches the box and puts it in the pocket of her big coat.
Enter* COUNTY ATTORNEY *and* SHERIFF.]*

COUNTY ATTORNEY [*facetiously*]. Well, Henry, at least we found out that she was
not going to quilt it. She was going to—what is it you call it, ladies?

MRS. HALE [*her hand against her pocket*]. We call it—knot it, Mr. Henderson.

Curtain

[1916]

Topics for Critical Thinking and Writing

1. Briefly describe the setting, indicating what it "says" and what atmosphere it evokes.
2. Even before the first word of dialogue is spoken, what do you think the play tells us (in the entrance of the characters) about the distinction between the men and the women?
3. How would you characterize Mr. Henderson, the county attorney?
4. In what way or ways are Mrs. Peters and Mrs. Hale different from each other?
5. Several times the men "laugh" or "chuckle." In their contexts, what do these expressions of amusement convey?
6. On page 324, *"the women's eyes meet for an instant."* What do you think this bit of action "says"? What do you understand by the exchange of glances?
7. On page 323, when Mrs. Peters tells of the boy who killed her cat, she says, "If they hadn't held me back, I would have—(*Catches herself, looks up- stairs where steps are heard, falters weakly.*)—hurt him." What do you think she was about to say before she faltered? Why do you suppose Glaspell included this speech about Mrs. Peters's girlhood?
8. On page 320, Mrs. Hale, looking at a quilt, wonders whether Mrs. Wright "was goin' to quilt it or just knot it." The men are amused by the women's concern with this topic, and the last line of the play returns to the issue. What do you make of this emphasis on the matter?
9. We never see Mrs. Wright on stage. Nevertheless, by the end of *Trifles* we know a great deal about her. In an essay of 500–750 words explain both what we know about her—physical characteristics, habits, interests, per- sonality, life before her marriage and after—and *how* we know these things.
10. The title of the play is ironic—the "trifles" are important. What other ironies do you find in the play? (On irony, see Glossary.)
11. Do you think the play is immoral? Explain.
12. Assume that the canary has been found, thereby revealing a possible motive, and that Minnie Wright is indicted for murder. You are the defense attorney. In 500 words set forth your defense. (Take any position you wish. For in- stance, you may want to argue that she committed justifiable homicide or that—on the basis of her behavior as reported by Mr. Hale—she is innocent by reason of insanity.)
13. Assume that the canary had been found and Minnie Wright convicted. Com- pose the speech you think she might have delivered before the sentence was given.

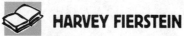 **HARVEY FIERSTEIN**

Harvey Fierstein was born in Brooklyn, New York, the son of parents who had emigrated from Eastern Europe. While studying painting at Pratt Institute he acted in plays and revues, and one of his plays was produced in 1973, but he did not achieve fame until his Torch Song Trilogy *(1976–1979) moved from Off Broadway to Broadway in 1982.* Torch Song Trilogy *won the Theatre World Award, the Tony Award, and the Drama Desk Award. In addition, Fierstein won the Best Actor*

Tony Award and the Best Actor Drama Desk Award. He later received a third Tony Award for the book for the musical version of La Cage aux Folles *(1983).*

On Tidy Endings

The curtain rises on a deserted, modern Upper West Side apartment. In the bright daylight that pours in through the windows we can see the living room of the apartment. Far Stage Right is the galley kitchen, next to it the multi-locked front door with intercom. Stage Left reveals a hallway that leads to the two bedrooms and baths.

Though the room is still fully furnished (couch, coffee table, etc.), there are boxes stacked against the wall and several photographs and paintings are on the floor leaving shadows on the wall where they once hung. Obviously someone is moving out. From the way the boxes are neatly labeled and stacked, we know that this is an organized person.

From the hallway just outside the door we hear the rattling of keys and two arguing voices:

JIM [*offstage.*] I've got to be home by four. I've got practice.
MARION [*offstage*] I'll get you to practice, don't worry.
JIM [*offstage.*] I don't want to go in there.
MARION [*offstage*] Jimmy, don't make Mommy crazy, alright? We'll go inside, I'll call Aunt Helen and see if you can go down and play with Robbie.

[The door opens. MARION *is a handsome woman of forty. Dressed in a business suit, her hair conservatively combed, she appears to be going to a business meeting.* JIM *is a boy of eleven. His playclothes are typical, but some-*

On Tidy Endings. (Photograph by Peter Cunningham)

one has obviously just combed his hair. MARION *recovers the key from the lock.]*

JIM. Why can't I just go down and ring the bell?
MARION. Because I said so.

[*As* MARION *steps into the room she is struck by some unexpected emotion. She freezes in her path and stares at the empty apartment.* JIM *lingers by the door.]*

JIM. I'm going downstairs.
MARION. Jimmy, please.
JIM. This place gives me the creeps.
MARION. This was your father's apartment. There's nothing creepy about it.
JIM. Says you.
MARION. You want to close the door, please?

[JIM *reluctantly obeys.]*

MARION. Now, why don't you go check your room and make sure you didn't leave anything.
JIM. It's empty.
MARION. Go look.
JIM. I looked last time.
MARION [*trying to be patient.*] Honey, we sold the apartment. You're never going to be here again. Go make sure you have everything you want.
JIM. But Uncle Arthur packed everything.
MARION [*less patiently.*] Go make sure.
JIM. There's nothing in there.
MARION [*exploding.*] I said make sure!

[JIM *jumps, then realizing that she's not kidding, obeys.]*

MARION. Everything's an argument with that one. [*She looks around the room and breathes deeply. There is sadness here. Under her breath:*] I can still smell you. [*Suddenly not wanting to be alone.*] Jimmy? Are you okay?
JIM [*returning.*] Nothing. Told you so.
MARION. Uncle Arthur must have worked very hard. Make sure you thank him.
JIM. What for? Robbie says, [*fey mannerisms*] "They love to clean up things!"
MARION. Sometimes you can be a real joy.
JIM. Did you call Aunt Helen?
MARION. Do I get a break here? [*Approaching the boy understandingly.*] Wouldn't you like to say good-bye?
JIM. To who?
MARION. To the apartment. You and your daddy spent a lot of time here together. Don't you want to take one last look around?
JIM. Ma, get a real life.
MARION. "Get a real life." [*Going for the phone.*] Nice. Very nice.
JIM. Could you call already?
MARION [*dialing.*] Jimmy, what does this look like I'm doing?

[JIM *kicks at the floor impatiently. Someone answers the phone at the other end.]*

MARION [*into the phone.*] Helen? Hi, we're upstairs. . . . No, we just walked in the door. Jimmy wants to know if he can come down. . . . Oh, thanks.

[Hearing that, JIM *breaks for the door.]*

MARION *[yelling after him.]* Don't run in the halls! And don't play with the elevator buttons!

[The door slams shut behind him]

MARION *[back to the phone.]* Hi. . . . No, I'm okay. It's a little weird being here. . . . No. Not since the funeral, and then there were so many people. Jimmy told me to get "a real life." I don't think I could handle anything realer. . . . No, please. Stay where you are. I'm fine. The doorman said Arthur would be right back and my lawyer should have been here already. . . . Well, we've got the papers to sign and a few other odds and ends to clean up. Shouldn't take long.

[The intercom buzzer rings.]

MARION. Hang on, that must be her. [MARION *goes to the intercom and speaks*] Yes? . . . Thank you. *[Back to the phone.]* Helen? Yeah, it's the lawyer. I'd better go. . . . Well, I could use a stiff drink, but I drove down. Listen, I'll stop by on my way out. Okay? Okay. 'Bye.

[She hangs up the phone, looks around the room. That uncomfortable feeling returns to her quickly. She gets up and goes to the front door, opens it and looks out. No one there yet. She closes the door, shakes her head knowing that she's being silly and starts back into the room. She looks around, can't make it and retreats to the door. She opens it, looks out, closes it, but stays right there, her hand on the doorknob. The bell rings. She throws open the door.]

MARION. That was quick.

*[*JUNE LOWELL *still has her finger on the bell. Her arms are loaded with contracts.* MARION*'s contemporary,* JUNE *is less formal in appearance and more hyper in her manner.]*

JUNE. *That* was quicker. What, were you waiting by the door?
MARION *[embarrassed.]* No. I was just passing it. Come on in.
JUNE. Have you got your notary seal?
MARION. I think so.
JUNE. Great. Then you can witness. I left mine at the office and thanks to gentrification I'm double-parked downstairs. *[Looking for a place to dump her load.]* Where?
MARION *[definitely pointing to the coffee table.]* Anywhere. You mean you're not staying?
JUNE. If you really think you need me I can go down and find a parking lot. I think there's one over on Columbus. So, I can go down, park the car in the lot and take a cab back if you really think you need me.
MARION. Well . . . ?
JUNE. But you shouldn't have any problems. The papers are about as straightforward as papers get. Arthur is giving you power of attorney to sell the apartment and you're giving him a check for half the purchase price. Everything else is just signing papers that state that you know that you signed the other papers. Anyway, he knows the deal, his lawyers have been over it all with him, it's just a matter of signatures.
MARION *[not fine.]* Oh, fine.

JUNE. Unless you just don't want to be alone with him . . . ?

MARION. With Arthur? Don't be silly.

JUNE [*laying out the papers.*] Then you'll handle it solo? Great. My car thanks you, the parking lot thanks you, and the cab driver that wouldn't have gotten a tip thanks you. Come have a quick look-see.

MARION [*joining her on the couch.*] There are a lot of papers here.

JUNE. Copies. Not to worry. Start here.

[MARION *starts to read.*]

JUNE. I ran into Jimmy playing Elevator Operator.

[MARION *jumps.*]

JUNE. I got him off at the sixth floor. Read on.

MARION. This is definitely not my day for dealing with him.

[JUNE *gets up and has a look around.*]

JUNE. I don't believe what's happening to this neighborhood. You made quite an investment when you bought this place.

MARION. Collin was always very good at figuring out those things.

JUNE. Well, he sure figured this place right. What, have you tripled your money in ten years?

MARION. More.

JUNE. It's a shame to let it go.

MARION. We're not ready to be a two-dwelling family.

JUNE. So, sublet it again.

MARION. Arthur needs the money from the sale.

JUNE. Arthur got plenty already. I'm not crying for Arthur.

MARION. I don't hear you starting in again, do I?

JUNE. Your interests and your wishes are my only concern.

MARION. Fine.

JUNE. I still say we should contest Collin's will.

MARION. June . . . !

JUNE. You've got a child to support.

MARION. And a great job, and a husband with a great job. Tell me what Arthur's got.

JUNE. To my thinking, half of everything that should have gone to you. And more. All of Collin's personal effects, his record collection . . .

MARION. And I suppose their three years together meant nothing.

JUNE. When you compare them to your sixteen-year marriage? Not nothing, but not half of everything.

MARION. [*trying to change the subject.*] June, who gets which copies?

JUNE. Two of each to Arthur. One you keep. The originals and anything else come back to me.[*Looking around.*] I still say you should've sublet the apartment for a year and then sold it. You would've gotten an even better price. Who wants to buy an apartment when they know someone died in it. No one. And certainly no one wants to buy an apartment when they know the person died of AIDS.

MARION [*snapping.*] June. Enough!

JUNE [*catching herself*] Sorry. That was out of line. Sometimes my mouth does that to me. Hey, that's why I'm a lawyer. If my brain worked as fast as my mouth I would have gotten a real job.

MARION [*holding out a stray paper.*] What's this?

JUNE. I forgot. Arthur's lawyer sent that over yesterday. He found it in Collin's safety-deposit box. It's an insurance policy that came along with some consulting job he did in Japan. He either forgot about it when he made out his will or else he wanted you to get the full payment. Either way, it's yours.

MARION. Are you sure we don't split this?

JUNE. Positive.

MARION. But everything else . . . ?

JUNE. Hey, Arthur found it, his lawyer sent it to me. Relax, it's all yours. Minus my commission, of course. Go out and buy yourself something. Anything else before I have to use my cut to pay the towing bill?

MARION. I guess not.

JUNE [*starting to leave.*] Great. Call me when you get home. [*Stopping at the door and looking back.*] Look. I know that I'm attacking this a little coldly. I am aware that someone you loved has just died. But there's a time and place for everything. This is about tidying up loose ends, not holding hands. I hope you'll remember that when Arthur gets here. Call me.

[*And she's gone.*]

[MARION *looks ill at ease to be alone again. She nervously straightens the papers into neat little piles, looks at them and then remembers:*]

MARION. Pens. We're going to need pens.

[*At last a chore to be done. She looks in her purse and finds only one. She goes to the kitchen and opens a drawer where* SHE *finds two more. She starts back to the table with them but suddenly remembers something else. She returns to the kitchen and begins going through the cabinets until she finds what she's looking for: a blue Art Deco teapot. Excited to find it, she takes it back to the couch. Guilt strikes. She stops, considers putting it back, wavers, then:*]

MARION [*to herself.*] Oh, he won't care. One less thing to pack.

[*She takes the teapot and places it on the couch next to her purse. She is happier. Now she searches the room with her eyes for any other treasures she may have overlooked. Nothing here. She wanders off into the bedroom. We hear keys outside the front door.* ARTHUR *lets himself into the apartment carrying a load of empty cartons and a large shopping bag.* ARTHUR *is in his mid-thirties, pleasant looking though sloppily dressed in work clothes and slightly overweight.* ARTHUR *enters the apartment just as* MARION *comes out of the bedroom carrying a framed watercolor painting. They jump at the sight of each other.*]

MARION. Oh, hi, Arthur. I didn't hear the door.

ARTHUR [*staring at the painting.*] Well hello, Marion.

MARION [*guiltily.*] I was going to ask you if you were thinking of taking this painting because if you're not going to then I'll take it. Unless, of course, you want it.

ARTHUR. No. You can have it.

MARION. I never really liked it, actually. I hate cats. I didn't even like the show. I needed something for my college dorm room. I was never the rock star poster type. I kept it in the back of a closet for years until Collin moved in here and took it. He said he liked it.

ARTHUR. I do too.

MARION. Well, then you keep it.

ARTHUR. No. Take it.

MARION. We've really got no room for it. You keep it.

ARTHUR. I don't want it.

MARION. Well, if you're sure.

ARTHUR [*seeing the teapot.*] You want the teapot?

MARION. If you don't mind.

ARTHUR. One less thing to pack.

MARION. Funny, but that's exactly what I thought. One less thing to pack. You know, my mother gave it to Collin and me when we moved in to our first apartment. Silly sentimental piece of junk, but you know.

ARTHUR. That's not the one.

MARION. Sure it is. Hall used to make them for Westinghouse back in the thirties. I see them all the time at antiques shows and I always wanted to buy another, but they ask such a fortune for them.

ARTHUR. We broke the one your mother gave you a couple of years ago. That's a reproduction. You can get them almost anywhere in the Village for eighteen bucks.

MARION. Really? I'll have to pick one up.

ARTHUR. Take this one. I'll get another.

MARION. No, it's yours. You bought it.

ARTHUR. One less thing to pack.

MARION. Don't be silly. I didn't come here to raid the place.

ARTHUR. Well, was there anything else of Collin's that you thought you might like to have?

MARION. Now I feel so stupid, but actually I made a list. Not for me. But I started thinking about different people; friends, relatives, you know, that might want to have something of Collin's to remember him by. I wasn't sure just what you were taking and what you were throwing out. Anyway, I brought the list. [*Gets it from her purse.*] Of course these are only suggestions. You probably thought of a few of these people yourself. But I figured it couldn't hurt to write it all down. Like I said, I don't know what you are planning on keeping.

ARTHUR [*taking the list.*] I was planning on keeping it all.

MARION. Oh, I know. But most of these things are silly. Like his high school yearbooks. What would you want with them?

ARTHUR. Sure. I'm only interested in his Gay period.

MARION. I didn't mean it that way. Anyway, you look it over. They're only suggestions. Whatever you decide to do is fine with me.

ARTHUR [*folding the list.*] It would have to be, wouldn't it. I mean, it's all mine now. He did leave this all to me.

[MARION *is becoming increasingly nervous, but tries to keep a light approach as she takes a small bundle of papers from her bag.*]

MARION. While we're on the subject of what's yours. I brought a batch of condolence cards that were sent to you care of me. Relatives mostly.

ARTHUR [*taking them.*] More cards? I'm going to have to have another printing of thank-you notes done.

MARION. I answered these last week, so you don't have to bother. Unless you want to.

ARTHUR. Forge my signature?

MARION. Of course not. They were addressed to both of us and they're mostly distant relatives or friends we haven't seen in years. No one important.

ARTHUR.   If they've got my name on them, then I'll answer them myself.

MARION.   I wasn't telling you not to, I was only saying that you don't have to.

ARTHUR.   I understand.

[MARION *picks up the teapot and brings it to the kitchen.*]

MARION.   Let me put this back.

ARTHUR.   I ran into Jimmy in the lobby.

MARION.   Tell me you're joking.

ARTHUR.   I got him to Helen's.

MARION.   He's really racking up the points today.

ARTHUR.   You know, he still can't look me in the face.

MARION.   He's reacting to all of this in strange ways. Give him time. He'll come around. He's really very fond of you.

ARTHUR.   I know. But he's at that awkward age: under thirty. I'm sure in twenty years we'll be the best of friends.

MARION.   It's not what you think.

ARTHUR.   What do you mean?

MARION.   Well, you know.

ARTHUR.   No I don't know. Tell me.

MARION.   I thought that you were intimating something about his blaming you for Collin's illness and I was just letting you know that it's not true. [*Foot in mouth, she braves on.*] We discussed it a lot and . . . uh . . . he understands that his father was sick before you two ever met.

ARTHUR.   I don't believe this.

MARION.   I'm just trying to say that he doesn't blame you.

ARTHUR.   First of all, who asked you? Second of all, that's between him and me. And third and most importantly, of course he blames me. Marion, he's eleven years old. You can discuss all you want, but the fact is that his father died of a "fag" disease and I'm the only fag around to finger.

MARION.   My son doesn't use that kind of language.

ARTHUR.   Forget the language. I'm talking about what he's been through. Can you imagine the kind of crap he's taken from his friends? That poor kid's been chased and chastised from one end of town to the other. He's got to have someone to blame just to survive. He can't blame you, you're all he's got. He can't blame his father; he's dead. So, Uncle Arthur gets the shaft. Fine, I can handle it.

MARION.   You are so wrong, Arthur. I know my son and that is not the way his mind works.

ARTHUR.   I don't know what you know. I only know what I know. And all I know is what I hear and see. The snide remarks, the little smirks. . . . And it's not just the illness. He's been looking for a scapegoat since the day you and Collin first split up. Finally he has one.

MARION [*getting very angry now.*]   Wait. Are you saying that if he's going to blame someone it should be me?

ARTHUR.   I think you should try to see things from his point of view.

MARION.   Where do you get off thinking you're privy to my son's point of view?

ARTHUR.   It's not that hard to imagine. Life's rolling right along, he's having a happy little childhood, when suddenly one day his father's moving out. No explanations, no reasons, none of the fights that usually accompany such things. Divorce is hard enough for a kid to understand when he's listened to years of battles, but yours?

MARION. So what should we have done? Faked a few months' worth of fights before Collin moved out?

ARTHUR. You could have told him the truth, plain and simple.

MARION. He was seven years old at the time. How the hell do you tell a seven-year-old that his father is leaving his mother to go sleep with other men?

ARTHUR. Well, not like that.

MARION. You know, Arthur, I'm going to say this as nicely as I can: Butt out. You're not his mother and you're not his father.

ARTHUR. Thank you. I wasn't acutely aware of that fact. I will certainly keep that in mind from now on.

MARION. There's only so much information a child that age can handle.

ARTHUR. So it's best that he reach his capacity on the street.

MARION. He knew about the two of you. We talked about it.

ARTHUR. Believe me, he knew before you talked about it. He's young, not stupid.

MARION. It's very easy for you to stand here and criticize, but there are aspects that you will just never be able to understand. You weren't there. You have no idea what it was like for me. You're talking to someone who thought that a girl went to college to meet a husband. I went to protest rallies because I liked the music. I bought a guitar because I thought it looked good on the bed! This lifestyle, this knowledge that you take for granted, was all a little out of left field for me.

ARTHUR. I can imagine.

MARION. No, I don't think you can. I met Collin in college, married him right after graduation and settled down for a nice quiet life of Kids and Careers. You think I had any idea about this? Talk about life's little surprises. You live with someone for sixteen years, you share your life, your bed, you have a child together, and then you wake up one day and he tells you that to him it's all been a lie. A lie. Try that on for size. Here you are the happiest couple you know, fulfilling your every life fantasy and he tells you he's living a lie.

ARTHUR. I'm sure he never said that.

MARION. Don't be so sure. There was a lot of new ground being broken back then and plenty of it was muddy.

ARTHUR. You know that he loved you.

MARION. What's that supposed to do, make things easier? It doesn't. I was brought up to believe, among other things, that if you had love that was enough. So what if I wasn't everything he wanted. Maybe he wasn't exactly everything I wanted either. So, you know what? You count your blessings and you settle.

ARTHUR. No one has to settle. Not him. Not you.

MARION. Of course not. You can say, "Up yours!" to everything and everyone who depends and needs you, and go off to make yourself happy.

ARTHUR. It's not that simple.

MARION. No. This is simpler. Death is simpler. [*Yelling out:*] Happy now?

[*They stare at each other.* MARION *calms the rage and catches her breath.* ARTHUR *holds his emotions in check.*]

ARTHUR. How about a nice hot cup of coffee? Tea with lemon? Hot cocoa with a marshmallow floating in it?

MARION. [*laughs.*] I was wrong. You *are* a mother.

[ARTHUR *goes into the kitchen and starts preparing things.* MARION *loafs by the doorway.*]

MARION. I lied before. He *was* everything I ever wanted.

[ARTHUR stops, looks at her, and then changes the subject as he goes on with his work.]

ARTHUR. When I came into the building and saw Jimmy in the lobby I absolutely freaked for a second. It's amazing how much they look alike. It was like seeing a little miniature Collin standing there.

MARION. I know. He's like Collin's clone. There's nothing of me in him.

ARTHUR. I always kinda hoped that when he grew up he'd take after me. Not much chance, I guess.

MARION. Don't do anything fancy in there.

ARTHUR. Please. Anything we can consume is one less thing to pack.

MARION. So you've said.

ARTHUR. So *we've* said.

MARION. I want to keep seeing you and I want you to see Jim. You're still part of this family. No one's looking to cut you out.

ARTHUR. Ah, who'd want a kid to grow up looking like me anyway. I had enough trouble looking like this. Why pass on the misery?

MARION. You're adorable.

ARTHUR. Is that like saying I have a good personality?

MARION. I think you are one of the most naturally handsome men I know.

ARTHUR. Natural is right, and the bloom is fading.

MARION. All you need is a few good nights' sleep to kill those rings under your eyes.

ARTHUR. Forget the rings under my eyes, *[grabbing his middle]* . . . how about the rings around my moon?

MARION. I like you like this.

ARTHUR. From the time that Collin started using the wheelchair until he died, about six months, I lost twenty-three pounds. No gym, no diet. In the last seven weeks I've gained close to fifty.

MARION. You're exaggerating.

ARTHUR. I'd prove it on the bathroom scale, but I sold it in working order.

MARION. You'd never know.

ARTHUR. Marion, *you'd* never know, but ask my belt. Ask my pants. Ask my underwear. Even my stretch socks have stretch marks. I called the ambulance at five A.M., he was gone at nine and by nine-thirty, I was on a firstname basis with Sara Lee. I can quote the business hours of every ice-cream parlor, pizzeria and bakery on the island of Manhattan. I know the location of every twenty-four-hour grocery in the greater New York area, and I have memorized the phone numbers of every Mandarin, Szechuan and Hunan restaurant with free delivery.

MARION. At least you haven't wasted your time on useless hobbies.

ARTHUR. Are you kidding? I'm opening my own Overeater's Hotline. We'll have to start small, but expansion is guaranteed.

MARION. You're the best, you know that? If I couldn't be everything that Collin wanted then I'm grateful that he found someone like you.

ARTHUR *[turning on her without missing a beat.]* Keep your goddamned gratitude to yourself. I didn't go through any of this for you. So your thanks are out of line. And he didn't find "someone like" me. It was me.

MARION *[frightened.]* I didn't mean . . .

ARTHUR. And I wish you'd remember one thing more: He died in my arms, not yours.

[MARION *is totally caught off guard. She stares disbelieving, openmouthed.* ARTHUR *walks past her as he leaves the kitchen with place mats. He puts them on the coffee table. As he arranges the papers and place mats he speaks, never looking at her.*]

ARTHUR. Look, I know you were trying to say something supportive. Don't waste your breath. There's nothing you can say that will make any of this easier for me. There's no way for you to help me get through this. And that's your fault. After three years you still have no idea or understanding of who I am. Or maybe you do know but refuse to accept it. I don't know and I don't care. But at least understand, from my point of view, who you are: You are my husband's *ex*-wife. If you like, the mother of *my* stepson. Don't flatter yourself into thinking you're any more than that. And whatever you are, you're certainly not my friend. [*He stops, looks up at her, then passes her again as he goes back to the kitchen.* MARION *is shaken, working hard to control herself. She moves toward the couch.*]

MARION. Why don't we just sign these papers and I'll be out of your way.

ARTHUR. Shouldn't you say *I'll* be out of *your* way? After all, I'm not just signing papers. I'm signing away my home.

MARION [*resolved not to fight, she gets her purse.*] I'll leave the papers here. Please have them notarized and returned to my lawyer.

ARTHUR. Don't forget my painting.

MARION. [*exploding.*] What do you want from me, Arthur?

ARTHUR. [*yelling back.*] I want you the hell out of my apartment! I want you out of my life! And I want you to leave Collin alone!

MARION. The man's dead. I don't know how much more alone I can leave him.

[ARTHUR *laughs at the irony, but behind the laughter is something much more desperate.*]

ARTHUR. Lots more, Marion. You've got to let him go.

MARION. For the life of me, I don't know what I did or what you think I did, for you to treat me like this. But you're not going to get away with it. You will not take your anger out on me. I will not stand here and be badgered and insulted by you. I know you've been hurt and I know you're hurting but you're not the only one who lost someone here

ARTHUR [*topping her.*] Yes I am! You didn't just lose him. I did! You lost him five years ago when he divorced you. This is not your moment of grief and loss, it's mine! [*Picking up the bundle of cards and throwing it toward her.*] These condolences do not belong to you, they're mine [*Tossing her list back to her.*] His things are not yours to give away, they're mine! This death does not belong to you, it's mine! Bought and paid for outright. I suffered for it, I bled for it.

I was the one who cooked his meals. I was the one who spoon-fed them. I pushed his wheelchair. I carried and bathed him. I wiped his backside and changed his diapers. I breathed life into and wrestled fear out of his heart. I kept him alive for two years longer than any doctor thought possible and when it was time I was the one who prepared him for death.

I paid in full for my place in his life and I will *not* share it with you. We are not the two widows of Collin Redding. Your life was not here. Your husband didn't just die. You've got a son and a life somewhere else.

Your husband's sitting, waiting for you at home, wondering, as I am what the hell you're doing here and why you can't let go.

*[*MARION *leans back against the couch. She's blown away.* ARTHUR *stands staring at her.]*

ARTHUR *[quietly.]* Let him go, Marion. He's mine. Dead or alive; mine.

[The teakettle whistles. ARTHUR *leaves the room, goes to the kitchen and pours the water as* MARION *pulls herself together.* ARTHUR *carries the loaded tray back into the living room and sets it down on the coffee table. He sits and pours a cup.]*

ARTHUR. One marshmallow or two?

*[*MARION *stares, unsure as to whether the attack is really over or not.]*

ARTHUR *[placing them in her cup.]* Take three, they're small.

*[*MARION *smiles and takes the offered cup.]*

ARTHUR *[campily.]* Now let me tell you how *I really* feel.

*[*MARION *jumps slightly, then they share a small laugh. Silence as they each gather themselves and sip their refreshments]*

MARION *[calmly.]* Do you think that I sold the apartment just to throw you out?
ARTHUR. I don't care about the apartment . . .
MARION. . . . Because I really didn't. Believe me.
ARTHUR. I know.
MARION. I knew the expenses here were too much for you, and I knew you couldn't afford to buy out my half . . . I figured if we sold it, that you'd at least have a nice chunk of money to start over with.
ARTHUR. You could've given me a little more time.
MARION. Maybe. But I thought the sooner you were out of here, the sooner you could go on with your life.
ARTHUR. Or the sooner you could go on with yours.
MARION. Maybe. *[Pauses to gather her thoughts.]* Anyway, I'm not going to tell you that I have no idea what you're talking about. I'd have to be worse than deaf and blind not to have seen the way you've been treated. Or mistreated. When I read Collin's obituary in the newspaper and saw my name and Jimmy's name and no mention of you. . . . *[Shakes her head, not knowing what to say.]* You know that his secretary was the one who wrote that up and sent it in. Not me. But I should have done something about it and I didn't. I know.
ARTHUR. Wouldn't have made a difference. I wrote my own obituary for him and sent it to the smaller papers. They edited me out.
MARION. I'm sorry. I remember, at the funeral, I was surrounded by all of Collin's family and business associates while you were left with your friends. I knew it was wrong. I knew I should have said something but it felt good to have them around me and you looked like you were holding up. . . . Wrong. But saying that it's all my fault for not letting go . . . ? There were other people involved.
ARTHUR. Who took their cue from you.

MARION. Arthur, you don't understand. Most people that we knew as a couple had no idea that Collin was Gay right up to his death. And even those that did know only found out when he got sick and the word leaked out that it was AIDS. I don't think I have to tell you how stupid and ill-informed most people are about homosexuality. And AIDS . . . ? The kinds of insane behavior that word inspires . . . ?

Those people at the funeral, how many times did they call to see how he was doing over these years? How many of them ever went to see him in the hospital? Did any of them even come here? So, why would you expect them to act any differently after his death?

So, maybe that helps to explain their behavior, but what about mine, right? Well, maybe there is no explanation. Only excuses. And excuse number one is that you're right, I have never really let go of him. And I am jealous of you. Hell, I was jealous of anyone that Collin ever talked to, let alone slept with . . . let alone loved.

The first year, after he moved out, we talked all the time about the different men he was seeing. And I always listened and advised. It was kind of fun. It kept us close. It kept me a part of his intimate life. And the bottom line was always that he wasn't happy with the men he was meeting. So, I was always allowed to hang on to the hope that one day he'd give it all up and come home. Then he got sick.

He called me, told me he was in the hospital and asked if I'd come see him. I ran. When I got to his door there was a sign, INSTRUCTIONS FOR VISITORS OF AN AIDS PATIENT. I nearly died.

ARTHUR. He hadn't told you?

MARION. No. And believe me, a sign is not the way to find these things out. I was so angry. . . . And he was so sick . . . I was sure that he'd die right then. If not from the illness then from the hospital staff's neglect. No one wanted to go near him and I didn't bother fighting with them because I understood that they were scared. I was scared. That whole month in the hospital I didn't let Jimmy visit him once.

You learn.

Well, as you know, he didn't die. And he asked if he could come stay with me until he was well. And I said yes. Of course, yes. Now, here's something I never thought I'd ever admit to anyone: had he asked to stay with me for a few weeks I would have said no. But he asked to stay with me until he was well and knowing there was no cure I said yes. In my craziness I said yes because to me that meant forever. That he was coming back to me forever. Not that I wanted him to die, but I assumed from everything I'd read. . . . And we'd be back together for whatever time he had left. Can you understand that?

[ARTHUR nods.]

MARION *[gathers her thoughts again.]* Two weeks later he left. He moved in here. Into this apartment that we had bought as an investment. Never to live in. Certainly never to live apart in. Next thing I knew, the name Arthur starts appearing in every phone call, every dinner conversation.

"Did you see the doctor?"

"Yes. Arthur made sure I kept the appointment."

"Are you going to your folks for Thanksgiving?"

"No. Arthur and I are having some friends over."

I don't know which one of us was more of a coward, he for not telling or me for not asking about you. But eventually you became a given. Then, of course, we met and became what I had always thought of as friends.

[ARTHUR *winces in guilt.*]

MARION. I don't care what you say, how could we not be friends with someone so great in common: love for one of the most special human beings there ever was. And don't try and tell me there weren't times when you enjoyed me being around as an ally. I can think of a dozen occasions when we ganged up on him, teasing him with our intimate knowledge of his personal habits.

[ARTHUR *has to laugh.*]

MARION. Blanket stealing? Snoring? Excess gas, no less? [*Takes a moment to enjoy this truce.*] I don't think that my loving him threatened your relationship. Maybe I'm not being truthful with myself. But I don't. I never tried to step between you. Not that I ever had the opportunity. Talk about being joined at the hip! And that's not to say I wasn't jealous. I was. Terribly. Hatefully. But always lovingly. I was happy for Collin because there was no way to deny that he was happy. With everything he was facing, he was happy. Love did that. You did that.

He lit up with you. He came to life. I envied that and all the time you spent together, but more, I watched you care for him (sometimes *overcare* for him), and I was in awe. I could never have done what you did. I never would have survived. I really don't know how you did.

ARTHUR. Who said I survived?

MARION. Don't tease. You did an absolutely incredible thing. It's not as if you met him before he got sick. You entered a relationship that you knew in all probability would end this way and you never wavered.

ARTHUR. Of course I did. Don't have me sainted, Marion. But sometimes you have no choice. Believe me, if I could've gotten away from him I would've. But I was a prisoner of love.

[*He makes a campy gesture and pose.*]

MARION. Stop.

ARTHUR. And there were lots of pluses. I got to quit a job I hated, stay home all day and watch game shows. I met a lot of doctors and learned a lot of big words. [ARTHUR *jumps up and goes to the pile of boxes where he extracts one and brings it back to the couch.*]

And then there was all the exciting traveling I got to do. This box has a souvenir from each one of our trips. Wanna see? [MARION *nods. He opens the box and pulls things out one by one. Holding up an old bottle.*]

This is from the house we rented in Reno when we went to clear out his lungs. [*Holding handmade potholders.*]

This is from the hospital in Reno. Collin made them. They had a great arts and crafts program. [*Copper bracelets.*]

These are from a faith healer in Philly. They don't do much for a fever, but they look great with a green sweater. [*Glass ashtrays.*]

These are from our first visit to the clinic in France. Such lovely people. [*A Bible.*]

This is from our second visit to the clinic in France. [*A bead necklace.*]

A Voodoo doctor in New Orleans. Next time we'll have to get there earlier in the year. I think he sold all the pretty ones at Mardi Gras. [*A tiny piñata.*]

Then there was Mexico. Black market drugs and empty wallets. [*Now pulling things out at random.*]

L.A., San Francisco, Houston, Boston. . . . We traveled everywhere they offered hope for sale and came home with souvenirs. [ARTHUR *quietly pulls a few more things out and then begins to put them all back into the box slowly. Softly as he works:*] Marion, I would have done anything, traveled anywhere to avoid . . . or delay. . . . Not just because I loved him so desperately, but when you've lived the way we did for three years . . . the battle becomes your life. [*He looks at her and then away.*] His last few hours were beyond any scenario I had imagined. He hadn't walked in nearly six months. He was totally incontinent. If he spoke two words in a week I was thankful. Days went by without his eyes ever focusing on me. He just stared out at I don't know what. Not the meals as I fed him. Not the TV I played constantly for company. Just out. Or maybe in.

It was the middle of the night when I heard his breathing become labored. His lungs were filling with fluid again. I knew the sound. I'd heard it a hundred times before. So, I called the ambulance and got him to the hospital.

They hooked him up to the machines, the oxygen, shot him with morphine and told me that they would do what they could to keep him alive.

But, Marion, it wasn't the machines that kept him breathing. He did it himself. It was that incredible will and strength inside him. Whether it came from his love of life or fear of death, who knows. But he'd been counted out a hundred times and a hundred times he fought his way back.

I got a magazine to read him, pulled a chair up to the side of his bed and holding his hand, I wondered whether I should call Helen to let the cleaning lady in or if he'd fall asleep and I could sneak home for an hour. I looked up from the page and he was looking at me. Really looking right into my eyes. I patted his cheek and said, "Don't worry, honey, you're going to be fine."

But there was something else in his eyes. He wasn't satisfied with that. And I don't know why, I have no idea where it came from, I just heard the words coming out of my mouth, "Collin, do you want to die?"

His eyes filled and closed, he nodded his head.

I can't tell you what I was thinking, I'm not sure I was. I slipped off my shoes, lifted his blanket and climbed into bed next to him. I helped him to put his arms around me, and mine around him, and whispered as gently as I could into his ear, "It's alright to let go now. It's time to go on." And he did.

Marion, you've got your life and your son. All I have is an intangible place in a man's history. Leave me that. Respect that.

MARION. I understand.

[ARTHUR *suddenly comes to life, running to get the shopping bag that he'd left at the front door.*]

ARTHUR. Jeez! With all the screamin' and sad storytelling I forgot something. [*He extracts a bouquet of flowers from the bag.*] I brung you flowers and everything.

MARION. You brought *me* flowers?

ARTHUR. Well, I knew you'd never think to bring me flowers and I felt that on an occasion such as this somebody oughta get flowers from somebody.

MARION. You know, Arthur, you're really making me feel like a worthless piece of garbage.

ARTHUR. So what else is new? [*He presents the flowers.*] Just promise me one thing: Don't press one in a book. Just stick them in a vase and when they fade just toss them out. No more memorabilia.

MARION. Arthur, I want to do something for you and I don't know what. Tell me what you want.

ARTHUR. I want little things. Not much. I want to be remembered. If you get a Christmas card from Collin's mother make sure she sent me one too. If his friends call to see how you are, ask if they've called me. Have me to dinner so I can see Jimmy. Let me take him out now and then. Invite me to his wedding. [*They both laugh.*]

MARION. You've got it.

ARTHUR [*clearing the table.*] Let me get all this cold cocoa out of the way. We still have the deed to do.

MARION [*checking her watch.*] And I've got to get Jimmy home in time for practice.

ARTHUR. Band practice?

MARION. Baseball [*Picking her list off the floor.*] About this list, you do what you want.

ARTHUR. Believe me, I will. But I promise to consider your suggestions. Just don't rush me. I'm not ready to give it all away. [ARTHUR *is off to the kitchen with his tray and the phone rings. He answers in the kitchen.*] "Hello? . . . Just a minute. [*Calling out.*] It's your eager Little Leaguer.

[MARION *picks up the living room extension and* ARTHUR *hangs his up]*

MARION [*into phone.*] Hello, honey. . . . I'll be down in five minutes. No. You know what? You come up here and get me. . . . No, I said you should come up here. . . . I said I want you to come up here. . . . Because I said so. . . . Thank you. [*She hangs the receiver.*]

ARTHUR [*rushing to the papers.*] Alright, where do we start on these?

MARION [*getting out her seal.*] I guess you should just start signing everything and I'll stamp along with you. Keep one of everything on the side for yourself.

ARTHUR. Now I feel so rushed. What am I signing?

MARION. You want to do this another time?

ARTHUR. No. Let's get it over with. I wouldn't survive another session like this.

[*He starts to sign and she starts her job.*]

MARION. I keep meaning to ask you; how are you?

ARTHUR [*at first puzzled and then:*] Oh, you mean my health? Fine. No. I'm fine. I've been tested, and nothing. We were very careful. We took many precautions. Collin used to make jokes about how we should invest in rubber futures.

MARION. I'll bet.

ARTHUR [*Stops what he's doing*] It never occurred to me until now. How about you?

MARION [*not stopping.*] Well, we never had sex after he got sick.

ARTHUR. But before?

MARION [*stopping but not looking up.*] I have the antibodies in my blood. No signs that it will ever develop into anything else. And it's been five years so my chances are pretty good that I'm just a carrier.

ARTHUR. I'm so sorry. Collin never told me.

MARION. He didn't know. In fact, other than my husband and the doctors, you're the only one I've told.

ARTHUR. You and your husband . . . ?

MARION. Have invested in rubber futures. There'd only be a problem if we wanted to have a child. Which we do. But we'll wait. Miracles happen every day.

ARTHUR. I don't know what to say.

MARION. Tell me you'll be there if I ever need you.

[Arthur gets up, goes to her and puts his arm around her. They hold each other. He gently pushes her away to make a joke.]

ARTHUR. Sure! Take something else that should have been mine.

MARION. Don't even joke about things like that.

[The doorbell rings. They pull themselves together.]

ARTHUR. You know we'll never get these done today.

MARION. So, tomorrow.

[Arthur goes to open the door as Marion gathers her things. He opens the doors and Jimmy is standing in the hall.]

JIM. C'mon, Ma. I'm gonna be late.

ARTHUR. Would you like to come inside?

JIM. We've gotta go.

MARION. Jimmy, come on.

JIM. Ma!

[She glares. He comes in. Arthur closes the door.]

MARION *[holding out the flowers.]* Take these for Mommy.

JIM *[taking them.]* Can we go?

MARION *[picking up the painting.]* Say good-bye to your Uncle Arthur.

JIM. 'Bye, Arthur. Come on.

MARION. Give him a kiss.

ARTHUR. Marion, don't.

MARION. Give your uncle a kiss good-bye.

JIM. He's not my uncle.

MARION. No. He's a hell of a lot more than your uncle.

ARTHUR *[offering his hand.]* A handshake will do.

MARION. Tell Uncle Arthur what your daddy told you.

JIM. About what?

MARION. Stop playing dumb. You know.

ARTHUR. Don't embarrass him.

MARION. Jimmy, please.

JIM *[He regards his MOTHER's softer tone and then speaks.]* He said that after me and Mommy he loved you the most.

MARION *[standing behind him.]* Go on.

JIM. And that I should love you too. And make sure that you're not lonely or very sad.

ARTHUR. Thank you.

[Arthur reaches down to the boy and they hug. Jim gives him a little peck on the cheek and then breaks away.]

MARION [_going to open the door._] Alright, kid, you done good. Now let's blow this joint before you muck it up.

[JIM _rushes out the door._ MARION _turns to_ ARTHUR.]

MARION. A child's kiss is magic. Why else would they be so stingy with them. I'll call you.

[ARTHUR _nods understanding._ MARION _pulls the door closed behind her._ ARTHUR _stands quietly as the lights fade to black._]

The End

NOTE: _If being performed on film, the final image should be of_ ARTHUR _leaning his back against the closed door on the inside of the apartment and_ MARION _leaning on the outside of the door. A moment of thought and then they both move on._

[1987]

Topics for Critical Thinking and Writing

1. We first hear about AIDS on page 329. Were you completely surprised, or did you think the play might introduce the subject? That is, did the author in any way prepare you for the subject? If so, how?
2. So far as the basic story goes, June (the lawyer) is not necessary. Marion could have brought the papers with her. Why do you suppose Fierstein introduces June? What function(s) does she serve? How would you characterize her?
3. On page 330 Marion says of the teapot, "One less thing to pack." Arthur says the same words a moment later, and then he repeats them yet again. A little later, while drinking cocoa, he repeats the words, and Marion says, "So you've said," to which Arthur replies, "So _we've_ said." Exactly what tone do you think should be used when Marion first says these words? When Arthur says them? And what significance, if any, do you attach to the fact that both characters speak these words?
4. A reviewer of the play said that Arthur is "bitchy" in many of his responses to Marion. What do you suppose the reviewer meant by this? Does the term imply that Fierstein presents a stereotype of the homosexual? If so, what is this stereotype? If you think that the term applies (even though you might not use such a word yourself), do you think that Fierstein's portrayal of Arthur is stereotypical? If it is stereotypical, is this a weakness in the play?
5. Arthur says that Jimmy blames him for Collin's death, but Marion denies it. Who do you think is right? Can a reader be sure? Why, or why not?
6. When Arthur tells Marion that she should have told Jimmy why Collin left her, Marion says, "How the hell do you tell a seven-year-old that his father is leaving his mother to go sleep with other men?" Arthur replies, "Well, not like that." What does Arthur mean? How _might_ Marion have told Jimmy? Do you think she should have told Jimmy?
7. Do you agree with a reader who found Marion an unconvincing character because she is "so passive and unquestioningly loving in her regard for her ex-husband"? If you disagree, how would you argue your case?

8. During the course of the play, what (if anything) does Marion learn? What (if anything) does Arthur learn? What (if anything) does Jimmy learn? What (if anything) does the reader or viewer learn from the play?

9. One reader characterized the play as "propaganda." Do you agree? Why, or why not? And if you think *On Tidy Endings* is propaganda, are you implying that it is therefore deficient as a work of art?

Thinking Critically About Drama

The college essays you write about plays will be similar in many respects to analytic essays about fiction. Unless you are writing a review of a performance, you probably won't try to write about all aspects of a play. Rather, you'll choose one significant aspect as your topic. For instance, if you are writing about Tennessee Williams's *The Glass Menagerie,* you might compare the aspirations of Jim O'Connor and Tom Wingfield, or you might compare Tom's illusions with those of his sister, Laura, and his mother, Amanda. Or you might examine the symbolism, perhaps limiting your essay topic to the glass animals but perhaps extending it to include other symbols, such as the fire escape, the lighting, and the Victrola. Similarly, if you are writing an analysis, you might decide to study the construction of one scene of a play or (if the play does not have a great many scenes) even the construction of the entire play.

The checklist on pages 276–77 in Chapter 11 may help you to find a topic for the particular play you choose to write about.

A SAMPLE ESSAY BY A STUDENT

The following essay discusses the structure of *The Glass Menagerie.* It mentions various characters, but since its concern is with the arrangement of scenes, it does not (for instance) examine any of the characters in detail. Of course an essay might well be devoted to examining (for example) Williams's assertion that "There is much to admire in Amanda, and as much to love and pity as there is to laugh at," but an essay on the structure of the play is probably not the place to talk about Williams's characterization of Amanda.

Preliminary Notes

After deciding to write on the structure of the play, with an eye toward seeing the overall pattern that the parts form, the student reread *The Glass Menagerie* (p. 350), jotted down some notes briefly summarizing each of the seven scenes, with an occasional comment, and then typed them. On rereading the typed notes, he added a few observations in handwriting.

nagging

1. begins with Tom talking to audience; ~~says he is a magician~~
   America, in 1930s
   "shouting and confusion"
   Father deserted
   Amanda nagging; ~~is she a bit cracked?~~
   Tom: bored, angry
   Laura: embarrassed, depressed
2. Laura: quit business school; sad, but Jim's name is mentioned, so, lighter tone introduced

out-and-out — 3. Tom and Amanda argue
battle   Tom almost destroys glass menagerie
                 Rage: Can things get any worse?

reconciliation, 4. T and A reconciled
and false   T to try to get a "gentleman caller"
hopes—then   5. T tells A that Jim will visit
final collapse   things are looking up
                 6. Jim arrives; L terrified still, A thinks things can work out
                 7. Lights go out (foreshadowing dark ending?) Jim a jerk, clumsy; breaks unicorn, but L doesn't seem to mind. Maybe he <u>is</u> the right guy to draw her into normal world. Jim reveals he is engaged:
                    "Desolation."
                 Tom escapes into merchant marine, but can't escape memories. Speaks to audience. L. blows out candles (does this mean he forgets her? No, because he is re-membering her right now. I don't get it, if the candles are supposed to be symbolic.)

These notes enabled the student to prepare a rough draft, which he then submitted to some classmates for peer review. (On peer review, see pages 22-23)

The Final Version: The Solid Structure of *The Glass Menagerie*

Notice that the final version of the essay, printed below, is *not* merely a summary (a brief retelling of the plot). Although it does indeed include summary, it chiefly is devoted to showing *how* the scenes are related.

Title is focused; it announces topic and thesis

Opening paragraph closes in on thesis

The Solid Structure of The Glass Menagerie

In the "Production Notes" Tennessee Williams calls The Glass Menagerie a "memory play," a term that the narrator in the play also uses. Memories often consist of fragments of episodes that are so loosely connected that they seem chaotic, and therefore we might think that The Glass Menagerie will consist of very loosely related episodes. However, the play covers only one episode, and though it gives the illusion of random talk, it really has a firm structure and moves steadily toward a foregone conclusion.

Reasonable organization; the paragraph touches on the beginning and the end

Tennessee Williams divides the play into seven scenes. The first scene begins with a sort of prologue, and the last scene concludes with a sort of epilogue that is related to the prologue. In the prologue Tom addresses the audience and comments on the 1930s as a time when America was "blind" and was a place of "shouting and confusion." Tom also

Brief but effective quotations

mentions that our lives consist of expectations, and though he does not say that our expectations are unfulfilled, near the end of the prologue he quotes a postcard that his father wrote to the family he deserted: "Hello--Goodbye!" In the epilogue Tom tells us that he followed his "father's footsteps," deserting the family. And just before the epilogue, near the end of Scene VII, we see what can be considered another desertion: Jim explains to Tom's sister Laura that he

Useful generalization based on earlier details

is engaged and therefore cannot visit Laura again. Thus the end is closely related to the beginning, and the play is the steady development of the initial implications.

Chronological organization is reasonable. Opening topic sentence lets readers know where they are going

The first three scenes show things going from bad to worse. Amanda is a nagging mother who finds her only relief in talking about the past to her crippled daughter Laura and her frustrated son Tom. When she was young she was beautiful and was eagerly courted by rich young men, but now the family is poor and this harping on the past can only bore or infuriate Tom and embarrass or depress Laura, who have no happy past to look back to, who see no happy future, and who can only be upset by

Brief plot summary supports thesis

Amanda's insistence that they should behave as she behaved long ago. The second scene deepens the despair: Amanda learns that the timorous Laura has not been attending a business school but has retreated in terror from this confrontation with the contemporary world. Laura's helplessness is made clear to the audience, and so is Amanda's lack of understanding. Near the end of the second scene, however, Jim's name is introduced; he is a boy Laura had a crush on in high school, and so the audience gets a glimpse of a happier Laura and a sense that possibly Laura's world is wider than the stifling tenement in which she and her mother and brother live. But in the third scene things get worse, when Tom and Amanda have so violent an argument that they are no longer on speaking terms. Tom is so angry with his mother that he almost by accident destroys his sister's treasured collection of glass animals, the fragile, lifeless world that is her refuge. The apartment is literally full of the "shouting and confusion" that Tom spoke of in his prologue.

Useful summary and transition

The first three scenes have revealed a progressive worsening of relations; the next three scenes reveal a progressive improvement in relations. In Scene IV Tom and his mother are reconciled, and Tom reluctantly--apparently in an effort to make up with his mother--agrees to try to get a friend to come to dinner so that Laura will have "a gentleman caller." In Scene V Tom tells his mother that Jim will come to dinner on the next night, and Amanda brightens, because she sees a possibility of security for Laura at last. In Scene VI Jim arrives, and despite Laura's initial terror, there seems, at least in Amanda's mind, to be the possibility that things will go well.

The seventh scene, by far the longest, at first
seems to be fulfilling Amanda's hopes. Despite the
ominous fact that the lights go out because Tom has
not paid the electric bill, Jim is at ease. He is an
insensitive oaf, but that doesn't seem to bother
Amanda, and almost miraculously he manages to
draw Laura somewhat out of her sheltered world.
Even when Jim in his clumsiness breaks the horn off
Laura's treasured glass unicorn, she is not upset. In
fact, she is almost relieved because the loss of the
horn makes the animal less "freakish" and he "will feel
more at home with the other horses." In a way, of
course, the unicorn symbolizes the crippled Laura,
who at least for the moment feels less freakish and
isolated now that she is somewhat reunited with
society through Jim. But this is a play about life in a
blind and confused world, and though in a previous
age the father escaped, there can be no escape now.
Jim reveals that he is engaged, Laura relapses into
"desolation," Amanda relapses into rage and
bitterness, and Tom relapses into dreams of escape. In
a limited sense Tom does escape. He leaves the family
and joins the merchant marine, but his last speech or
epilogue tells us that he cannot escape the memory of
his sister: "Oh, Laura, Laura, I tried to leave you
behind me, but I am more faithful than I intended to

*The essayist is
thinking and
commenting, not
merely summa-
rizing the plot*

be!" And so the end of the last scene brings us back
again to the beginning of the first scene: we are still
in a world of "the blind" and of "confusion." But now
at the end of the play the darkness is deeper, the
characters are lost forever in their unhappiness as
Laura "blows the candles out," the darkness being
literal but also symbolic of their extinguished hopes.

Numerous devices, such as repeated references
to the absent father, to Amanda's youth, to Laura's

Useful, thought-ful summary of thesis

Victrola, and of course to Laura's glass menagerie help to tie the scenes together into a unified play. But beneath these threads of imagery and recurring motifs is a fundamental pattern that involves the movement from nagging (Scenes I and II) to open hostilities (Scene III) to temporary reconciliation (Scene IV) to false hopes (Scenes V and VI) to an impossible heightening of false hopes and then, in a swift descent, to an inevitable collapse (Scene VII). Tennessee Williams has constructed his play carefully. G. B. Tennyson says that a "playwright must 'build' his speeches, as the theatrical expression

Effective quota-tion from an outside source

has it" (13). But a playwright must do more; the playwright must also build the play out of scenes. Like Ibsen, if Williams had been introduced to an architect he might have said, "Architecture is my business too."

Works Cited

Tennyson, G. B. An Introduction to Drama. New

Documentation

York: Holt, 1967.

Williams, Tennessee. The Glass Menagerie. Literature for Composition. Ed. Sylvan Barnet et al. 5th ed. New York: Longman, 2000, 350–94.

 ## TENNESSEE WILLIAMS

Tennessee Williams (1914–83) was born Thomas Lanier Williams in Columbus, Mississippi. During his childhood his family moved to St. Louis, where his father had accepted a job as manager of a shoe company. Williams has written that neither he nor his sister Rose could adjust to the change from the South to the Midwest, but the children had already been deeply troubled. Nevertheless, at the age of 16 he achieved some distinction as a writer when his prize-winning essay in a nationwide contest was published. After high school he attended the University of Missouri but flunked ROTC and was therefore withdrawn from school by his father. He worked in a shoe factory for a while, then attended Washington University, where he wrote several plays. He finally graduated from the University of Iowa with a major in playwrighting. After graduation he continued to write, supporting himself with odd jobs

The original cast of the New York production of *The Glass Menagerie* (1945). (New York Public Library)

such as waiting on tables and running elevators. His first commercial success was The Glass Menagerie *(produced in Chicago in 1944, and in New York in 1945); among his other plays are* A Streetcar Named Desire *(1947),* Cat on a Hot Tin Roof *(1955), and* Suddenly Last Summer *(1958).*

The Glass Menagerie

> *nobody, not even the rain, has such small hands.*
>
> —*e. e. cummings*

LIST OF CHARACTERS

AMANDA WINGFIELD, *the mother. A little woman of great but confused vitality clinging frantically to another time and place. Her characterization must be carefully created, not copied from type. She is not paranoiac, but her life is paranoia. There is much to admire in Amanda, and as much to love and pity as there is to laugh at. Certainly she has endurance and a kind of heroism, and though her foolishness makes her unwittingly cruel at times, there is tenderness in her slight person.*

LAURA WINGFIELD, *her daughter. Amanda, having failed to establish contact with reality, continues to live vitally in her illusions, but Laura's situation is even graver. A childhood illness has left her crippled, one leg slightly shorter than the other, and held in a brace. This defect need not be more than suggested on the stage. Stemming from this, Laura's separation increases till she is like a piece of her own glass collection, too exquisitely fragile to move from the shelf.*

TOM WINGFIELD, *her son. And the narrator of the play. A poet with a job in a warehouse. His nature is not remorseless, but to escape from a trap he has to act without pity.*

JIM O'CONNOR, *the gentleman caller. A nice, ordinary, young man.*

SCENE. *An alley in St. Louis.*

PART I. *Preparation for a Gentleman Caller.*

PART II. *The Gentleman Calls.*

TIME. *Now and the Past.*

Scene I

The Wingfield apartment is in the rear of the building, one of those vast hive-like conglomerations of cellular living-units that flower as warty growths in overcrowded urban centers of lower middle-class population and are sympto-matic of the impulse of this largest and fundamentally enslaved section of American society to avoid fluidity and differentiation and to exist and func-tion as one interfused mass of automatism.

The apartment faces an alley and is entered by a fire-escape, a structure whose name is a touch of accidental poetic truth, for all of these huge build-ings are always burning with the slow and implacable fires of human desper-ation. The fire-escape is included in the set—that is, the landing of it and steps descending from it.

The scene is memory and is therefore nonrealistic. Memory takes a lot of poetic license. It omits some details; others are exaggerated, according to the emotional value of the articles it touches, for memory is seated predominantly in the heart. The interior is therefore rather dim and poetic.

At the rise of the curtain, the audience is faced with the dark, grim rear wall of the Wingfield tenement. This building, which runs parallel to the foot-lights, is flanked on both sides by dark, narrow alleys which run into murky canyons of tangled clotheslines, garbage cans and the sinister latticework of neighboring fire-escapes. It is up and down these side alleys that exterior en-trances and exits are made, during the play. At the end of TOM's opening com-mentary, the dark tenement wall slowly reveals (by means of a transparency) the interior of the ground floor Wingfield apartment.

Downstage is the living room, which also serves as a sleeping room for LAURA, *the sofa unfolding to make her bed. Upstage, center, and divided by a wide arch or second proscenium with transparent faded portieres (or second curtain), is the dining room. In an old-fashioned what-not in the living room are seen scores of transparent glass animals. A blown-up photograph of the fa-ther hangs on the wall of the living room, facing the audience, to the left of the archway. It is the face of a very handsome young man in a doughboy's First World War cap. He is gallantly smiling, ineluctably smiling, as if to say, "I will be smiling forever."*

The audience hears and sees the opening scene in the dining room through both the transparent fourth wall of the building and the transparent gauze portieres of the dining-room arch. It is during this revealing scene that the fourth wall slowly ascends, out of sight.

This transparent exterior wall is not brought down again until the very end of the play, during TOM's final speech.

The narrator is an undisguised convention of the play. He takes whatever license with dramatic convention as is convenient to his purposes.

TOM *enters dressed as a merchant sailor from alley, stage left, and strolls across the front of the stage to the fire-escape. There he stops and lights a ciga-rette. He addresses the audience.*

TOM. Yes, I have tricks in my pocket, I have things up my sleeve. But I am the opposite of a stage magician. He gives you illusion that has the appearance of truth. I give you truth in the pleasant disguise of illusion. To begin with, I turn back time. I reverse it to that quaint period, the thirties, when the huge middle class of America was matriculating in a school for the blind. Their eyes had failed them, or they had failed their eyes, and so they were having their fingers pressed forcibly down on the fiery Braille alphabet of a dissolving economy. In Spain there was revolution. Here there was only shouting and confusion. In Spain there was Guernica. Here there were disturbances of labor, sometimes pretty violent, in otherwise peaceful cities such as Chicago, Cleveland, Saint Louis. . . . This is the social background of the play.

[Music.]

The play is memory. Being a memory play, it is dimly lighted, it is sentimental, it is not realistic. In memory everything seems to happen to music. That explains the fiddle in the wings. I am the narrator of the play, and also a character in it. The other characters are my mother, Amanda, my sister, Laura, and a gentleman caller who appears in the final scenes. He is the most realistic character in the play, being an emissary from a world of reality that we were somehow set apart from. But since I have a poet's weakness for symbols, I am using this character also as a symbol; he is the long delayed but always expected something that we live for. There is a fifth character in the play who doesn't appear except in this larger-than-life photograph over the mantel. This is our father who left us a long time ago. He was a telephone man who fell in love with long distances; he gave up his job with the telephone company and skipped the light fantastic out of town. . . . The last we heard of him was a picture post-card from Mazatlan, on the Pacific coast of Mexico, containing a message of two words— "Hello—Goodbye!" and no address. I think the rest of the play will explain itself . . . .

AMANDA*'s voice becomes audible through the portieres.*

[Legend on Screen: "Où Sont les Neiges?"]

He divides the portieres and enters the upstage area.

AMANDA *and* LAURA *are seated at a drop-leaf table. Eating is indicated by gestures without food or utensils.* AMANDA *faces the audience.* TOM *and* LAURA *are seated in profile.*

The interior has lit up softly and through the scrim we see AMANDA *and* LAURA *seated at the table in the upstage area.*

AMANDA *[calling]*. Tom?
TOM. Yes, Mother.
AMANDA. We can't say grace until you come to the table!
TOM. Coming, Mother. *[He bows slightly and withdraws reappearing a few moments later in his place at the table.]*
AMANDA *[to her son]*. Honey, don't *push* with your *fingers*. If you have to push with something, the thing to push with is a crust of bread. And chew— chew! Animals have sections in their stomachs which enable them to digest food without mastication, but human beings are supposed to chew

their food before they swallow it down. Eat food leisurely, son, and really enjoy it. A well-cooked meal has lots of delicate flavors that have to be held in the mouth for appreciation. So chew your food and give your salivary glands a chance to function!

TOM *deliberately lays his imaginary fork down and pushes his chair back from the table.*

TOM. I haven't enjoyed one bite of this dinner because of your constant directions on how to eat it. It's you that makes me rush through meals with your hawk-like attention to every bite I take. Sickening—spoils my appetite—all this discussion of animals' secretion—salivary glands—mastication!

AMANDA [*lightly*]. Temperament like a Metropolitan star! [*He rises and crosses downstage.*] You're not excused from the table.

TOM. I am getting a cigarette.

AMANDA. You smoke too much.

LAURA *rises.*

LAURA. I'll bring in the blanc mange.

He remains standing with his cigarette by the portieres during the following.

AMANDA [*rising*]. No, sister, no, sister—you be the lady this time and I'll be the darky.

LAURA. I'm already up.

AMANDA. Resume your seat, little sister—I want you to stay fresh and pretty—for gentlemen callers!

LAURA. I'm not expecting any gentlemen callers.

AMANDA [*crossing out to kitchenette. Airily*]. Sometimes they come when they are least expected! Why, I remember one Sunday afternoon in Blue Mountain—[*Enters kitchenette.*]

TOM. I know what's coming!

LAURA. Yes. But let her tell it.

TOM. Again?

LAURA. She loves to tell it.

AMANDA *returns with bowl of dessert.*

AMANDA. One Sunday afternoon in Blue Mountain—your mother received—*seventeen!*—gentlemen callers! Why, sometimes there weren't chairs enough to accommodate them all. We had to send the nigger over to bring in folding chairs from the parish house.

TOM [*remaining at portieres*]. How did you entertain those gentlemen callers?

AMANDA. I understood the art of conversation!

TOM. I bet you could talk.

AMANDA. Girls in those days *knew* how to talk, I can tell you.

TOM. Yes?

[*Image:* AMANDA *as a Girl on a Porch Greeting Callers.*]

AMANDA. They knew how to entertain their gentlemen callers. It wasn't enough for a girl to be possessed of a pretty face and a graceful figure—although I wasn't slighted in either respect. She also needed to have a nimble wit and a tongue to meet all occasions.

TOM. What did you talk about?

AMANDA. Things of importance going on in the world! Never anything coarse or common or vulgar. [*She addresses* TOM *as though he were seated in the vacant chair at the table though he remains by portieres. He plays this scene as though he held the book.*] My callers were gentlemen—all! Among my callers were some of the most prominent young planters of the Mississippi Delta—planters and sons of planters!

TOM *motions for music and a spot of light on* AMANDA.

Her eyes lift, her face glows, her voice becomes rich and elegiac. [Screen Legend: "Où Sont les Neiges?"]

There was young Champ Laughlin who later became vice-president of the Delta Planters Bank. Hadley Stevenson who was drowned in Moon Lake and left his widow one hundred and fifty thousand in Government bonds. There were the Cutrere brothers, Wesley and Bates. Bates was one of my bright particular beaux! He got in a quarrel with that wild Wainright boy. They shot it out on the floor of Moon Lake Casino. Bates was shot through the stomach. Died in the ambulance on his way to Memphis. His widow was also well-provided for, came into eight or ten thousand acres, that's all. She married him on the rebound—never loved her—carried my picture on him the night he died! And there was that boy that every girl in Delta had set her cap for! That beautiful, brilliant young Fitzhugh boy from Green County!

TOM. What did he leave his widow?

AMANDA. He never married! Gracious, you talk as though all of my old admirers had turned up their toes to the daisies!

TOM. Isn't this the first you mentioned that still survives?

AMANDA. That Fitzhugh boy went North and made a fortune—came to be known as the Wolf of Wall Street! He had the Midas touch, whatever he touched turned to gold! And I could have been Mrs. Duncan J. Fitzhugh, mind you! But—I picked your *father!*

LAURA [*rising*]. Mother, let me clear the table.

AMANDA. No dear, you go in front and study your typewriter chart. Or practice your shorthand a little. Stay fresh and pretty!—It's almost time for our gentlemen callers to start arriving. [*She flounces girlishly toward the kitchenette.*] How many do you suppose we're going to entertain this afternoon?

TOM *throws down the paper and jumps up with a groan.*

LAURA [*alone in the dining room*]. I don't believe we're going to receive any, Mother.

AMANDA [*reappearing, airily*]. What? No one—not one? You must be joking! [LAURA *nervously echoes her laugh. She slips in a fugitive manner through the half-open portieres and draws them gently behind her. A shaft of very clear light is thrown on her face against the faded tapestry of the curtains.*] [*Music: "The Glass Menagerie" Under Faintly.*] [*Lightly.*] Not one gentleman caller? It can't be true! There must be a flood, there must have been a tornado!

LAURA. It isn't a flood, it's not a tornado, Mother. I'm just not popular like you were in Blue Mountain. . . . [TOM *utters another groan.* LAURA *glances at him with a faint, apologetic smile. Her voice catching a little.*] Mother's afraid I'm going to be an old maid.

[The Scene Dims Out with "Glass Menagerie" Music.]

Scene II

"Laura, Haven't You Ever Liked Some Boy?"

On the dark stage the screen is lighted with the image of blue roses. Gradually LAURA's *figure becomes apparent and the screen goes out. The music subsides.*

LAURA *is seated in the delicate ivory chair at the small clawfoot table.*

She wears a dress of soft violet material for a kimono—her hair tied back from her forehead with a ribbon.

She is washing and polishing her collection of glass.

AMANDA *appears on the fire-escape steps. At the sound of her ascent,* LAURA *catches her breath, thrusts the bowl of ornaments away and seats herself stiffly before the diagram of the typewriter keyboard as though it held her spellbound. Something has happened to* AMANDA. *It is written in her face as she climbs to the landing: a look that is grim and hopeless and a little absurd.*

She has on one of those cheap or imitation velvety-looking cloth coats with imitation fur collar. Her hat is five or six years old, one of those dreadful cloche hats that were worn in the late twenties, and she is clasping an enormous black patent-leather pocketbook with nickel clasp and initials. This is her full-dress outfit, the one she usually wears to the D.A.R.

Before entering she looks through the door.

She purses her lips, opens her eyes wide, rolls them upward and shakes her head.

Then she slowly lets herself in the door. Seeing her mother's expression LAURA *touches her lips with a nervous gesture.*

LAURA. Hello, Mother, I was—[*She makes a nervous gesture toward the chart on the wall.* AMANDA *leans against the shut door and stares at* LAURA *with a martyred look.*]

AMANDA. Deception? Deception? [*She slowly removes her hat and gloves, continuing the swift suffering stare. She lets the hat and gloves fall on the floor—a bit of acting.*]

LAURA [*shakily*]. How was the D.A.R. meeting? [AMANDA *slowly opens her purse and removes a dainty white handkerchief which she shakes out delicately and delicately touches to her lips and nostrils.*] Didn't you go to the D.A.R. meeting, Mother?

AMANDA [*faintly, almost inaudibly*]. —No.—No. [*Then more forcibly.*] I did not have the strength—to go to the D.A.R. In fact, I did not have the courage! I wanted to find a hole in the ground and hide myself in it forever! [*She crosses slowly to the wall and removes the diagram of the typewriter keyboard. She holds it in front of her for a second, staring at it sweetly and sorrowfully—then bites her lips and tears it in two pieces.*]

LAURA [*faintly*]. Why did you do that, Mother? [AMANDA *repeats the same procedure with the chart of the Gregg Alphabet.*] Why are you—

AMANDA. Why? Why? How old are you, Laura?

LAURA. Mother, you know my age.

AMANDA. I thought that you were an adult; it seems that I was mistaken. [*She crosses slowly to the sofa and sinks down and stares at* LAURA.]

LAURA. Please don't stare at me, Mother.

AMANDA *closes her eyes and lowers her head. Count ten.*

AMANDA. What are we going to do, what is going to become of us, what is the future?

Count ten.

LAURA. Has something happened, Mother? [AMANDA *draws a long breath and takes out the handkerchief again. Dabbing process.*] Mother, has—something happened?

AMANDA. I'll be all right in a minute. I'm just bewildered—[*count five*]—by life. . . .

LAURA. Mother, I wish that you would tell me what's happened.

AMANDA. As you know, I was supposed to be inducted into my office at the D.A.R. this afternoon. [*Image: A Swarm of Typewriters.*] But I stopped off at Rubicam's Business College to speak to your teachers about your having a cold and ask them what progress they thought you were making down there.

LAURA. Oh. . . .

AMANDA. I went to the typing instructor and introduced myself as your mother. She didn't know who you were. Wingfield, she said. We don't have any such student enrolled at the school! I assured her she did, that you had been going to classes since early in January. "I wonder," she said, "if you could be talking about that terribly shy little girl who dropped out of school after only a few days' attendance?" "No," I said, "Laura, my daughter, has been going to school every day for the past six weeks!" "Excuse me," she said. She took the attendance book out and there was your name, unmistakably printed, and all the dates you were absent until they decided that you had dropped out of school. I still said, "No, there must have been some mistake! There must have been some mix-up in the records!" And she said, "No—I remember her perfectly now. Her hand shook so that she couldn't hit the right keys! The first time we gave a speed-test, she broke down completely—was sick at the stomach and almost had to be carried into the wash-room! After that morning she never showed up any more. We phoned the house but never got any answer"—while I was working at Famous and Barr, I suppose, demonstrating those—Oh! I felt so weak I could barely keep on my feet. I had to sit down while they got me a glass of water! Fifty dollars' tuition, all of our plans—my hopes and ambitions for you—just gone up the spout, just gone up the spout like that. [LAURA *draws a long breath and gets awkwardly to her feet. She crosses to the victrola and winds it up.*] What are you doing?

LAURA. Oh! [*She releases the handle and returns to her seat.*]

AMANDA. Laura, where have you been going when you've gone out pretending that you were going to business college?

LAURA. I've just been going out walking.

AMANDA. That's not true.

LAURA. It is. I just went walking.

AMANDA. Walking? Walking? In winter? Deliberately courting pneumonia in that light coat? Where did you walk to, Laura?

LAURA. It was the lesser of two evils, Mother. [*Image: Winter Scene in Park.*] I couldn't go back up. I—threw up—on the floor!

AMANDA. From half past seven till after five every day you mean to tell me you walked around in the park, because you wanted to make me think that you were still going to Rubicam's Business College?

LAURA. It wasn't as bad as it sounds. I went inside places to get warmed up.

AMANDA. Inside where?

LAURA. I went in the art museum and the bird-houses at the Zoo. I visited the penguins every day! Sometimes I did without lunch and went to the movies. Lately I've been spending most of my afternoons in the Jewel-box, that big glass house where they raise the tropical flowers.

AMANDA. You did all this to deceive me, just for the deception? [LAURA *looks down.*] Why?

LAURA. Mother, when you're disappointed, you get that awful suffering look on your face, like the picture of Jesus' mother in the museum!

AMANDA. Hush!

LAURA. I couldn't face it.

Pause. A whisper of strings.

[*Legend: "The Crust of Humility."*]

AMANDA [*hopelessly fingering the huge pocketbook*]. So what are we going to do the rest of our lives? Stay home and watch the parades go by? Amuse ourselves with the glass menagerie, darling? Eternally play those worn-out phonograph records your father left as a painful reminder of him? We won't have a business career—we've given that up because it gave us nervous indigestion! [*Laughs wearily.*] What is there left but dependency all our lives? I know so well what becomes of unmarried women who aren't prepared to occupy a position. I've seen such pitiful cases in the South— barely tolerated spinsters living upon the grudging patronage of sister's husband or brother's wife!—stuck away in some little mousetrap of a room— encouraged by one in-law to visit another—little birdlike women without any nest—eating the crust of humility all their life! Is that the future that we've mapped out for ourselves? I swear it's the only alternative I can think of! It isn't a very pleasant alternative, is it? Of course—some girls *do marry.* [LAURA *twists her hands nervously.*] Haven't you ever liked some boy?

LAURA. Yes. I liked one once. [*Rises.*] I came across his picture a while ago.

AMANDA [*with some interest*]. He gave you his picture?

LAURA. No, it's in the year-book.

AMANDA [*disappointed*]. Oh—a high-school boy.

[*Screen Image:* JIM *as a High-School Hero Bearing a Silver Cup.*]

LAURA. Yes. His name was Jim. [LAURA *lifts the heavy annual from the clawfoot table.*] Here he is in *The Pirates of Penzance.*

AMANDA [*absently*]. The what?

LAURA. The operetta the senior class put on. He had a wonderful voice and we sat across the aisle from each other Mondays, Wednesdays and Fridays in the Aud. Here he is with the silver cup for debating! See his grin?

AMANDA [*absently*]. He must have had a jolly disposition.

LAURA. He used to call me—Blue Roses.

[Image: Blue Roses.]

AMANDA. Why did he call you such a name as that?

LAURA. When I had that attack of pleurosis—he asked me what was the matter when I came back. I said pleurosis—he thought that I said Blue Roses! So that's what he always called me after that. Whenever he saw me, he'd holler, "Hello, Blue Roses!" I didn't care for the girl that he went out with. Emily Meisenbach. Emily was the best-dressed girl at Soldan. She never struck me, though, as being sincere. . . . It says in the Personal Section—they're engaged. That's—six years ago! They must be married by now.

AMANDA. Girls that aren't cut out for business careers usually wind up married to some nice man. *[Gets up with a spark of revival.]* Sister, that's what you'll do!

LAURA *utters a startled, doubtful laugh. She reaches quickly for a piece of glass.*

LAURA. But, Mother—

AMANDA. Yes? *[Crossing to photograph.]*

LAURA *[in a tone of frightened apology]*. I'm—crippled!

[Image: Screen.]

AMANDA. Nonsense! Laura, I've told you never, never to use that word. Why, you're not crippled, you just have a little defect—hardly noticeable, even! When people have some slight disadvantage like that, they cultivate other things to make up for it—develop charm—and vivacity—and—*charm!* That's all you have to do! *[She turns again to the photograph.]* One thing your father had *plenty of*—was *charm!*

TOM *motions to the fiddle in the wings.*

[The Scene Fades out with Music.]

Scene III

[Legend on the Screen: "After the Fiasco—"]

TOM *speaks from the fire-escape landing.*

TOM. After the fiasco at Rubicam's Business College, the idea of getting a gentleman caller for Laura began to play a more important part in Mother's calculations. It became an obsession. Like some archetype of the universal unconscious, the image of the gentleman caller haunted our small apartment. . . . *[Image: Young Man at Door with Flowers.]* An evening at home rarely passed without some allusion to this image, this specter, this hope. . . . Even when he wasn't mentioned, his presence hung in Mother's preoccupied look and in my sister's frightened, apologetic manner—hung like a sentence passed upon the Wingfields! Mother was a woman of action as well as words. She began to take logical steps in the planned direction. Late that winter and in the early spring—realizing that extra money would be needed to properly feather the nest and plume the bird—she conducted a vigorous campaign on the telephone, roping in subscribers to one of those magazines for matrons called *The Home-maker's Companion*, the type of journal that features the serialized sublimations of ladies of letters who think in terms of delicate cuplike breasts, slim, tapering waists, rich, creamy thighs, eyes like wood-smoke in autumn, fingers that soothe and caress like strains of music, bodies as powerful as Etruscan sculpture.

[Screen Image: Glamor Magazine Cover.]

AMANDA *enters with phone on long extension cord. She is spotted in the dim stage.*

AMANDA. Ida Scott? This is Amanda Wingfield! We *missed* you at the D.A.R. last Monday! I said to myself: She's probably suffering with that sinus condition! How is that sinus condition? Horrors! Heaven have mercy!—You're a Christian martyr, yes, that's what you are, a Christian martyr! Well, I just now happened to notice that your subscription to the *Companion's* about to expire! Yes, it expires with the next issue, honey!—just when that wonderful new serial by Bessie Mae Hopper is getting off to such an exciting start. Oh, honey, it's something that you can't miss! You remember how *Gone With the Wind* took everybody by storm? You simply couldn't go out if you hadn't read it. All everybody *talked* was Scarlett O'Hara. Well, this is a book that critics already compare to *Gone With the Wind*. It's the *Gone With the Wind* of the post-World War generation—What?—Burning?—Oh, honey, don't let them burn, go take a look in the oven and I'll hold the wire! Heavens—I think she's hung up!

[Dim Out.]

[Legend on Screen: "You Think I'm in Love with Continental Shoemakers?"]

Before the stage is lighted, the violent voices of TOM *and* AMANDA *are heard. They are quarreling behind the portieres. In front of them stands* LAURA *with clenched hands and panicky expression.*

A clear pool of light on her figure throughout this scene.

TOM. What in Christ's name am I—
AMANDA *[shrilly]*. Don't you use that—
TOM. Supposed to do!
AMANDA. Expression! Not in my—
TOM. Ohhh!
AMANDA. Presence! Have you gone out of your senses?
TOM. I have, that's true, *driven* out!
AMANDA. What is the matter with you, you—big—big—IDIOT!
TOM. Look—I've got *no thing*, no single thing—
AMANDA. Lower your voice!
TOM. In my life here that I can call my OWN! Everything is—
AMANDA. Stop that shouting!
TOM. Yesterday you confiscated my books! You had the nerve to—
AMANDA. I took that horrible novel back to the library—yes! That hideous book by that insane Mr. Lawrence. [TOM *laughs wildly.*] I cannot control the output of diseased minds or people who cater to them—[TOM *laughs still more wildly.*] BUT I WON'T ALLOW SUCH FILTH BROUGHT INTO MY HOUSE! No, no, no, no, no!
TOM. House, house! Who pays rent on it, who makes a slave of himself to—
AMANDA *[fairly screeching]*. Don't you DARE to—

TOM. No, no, *I* musn't say things! *I've* got to just—

AMANDA. Let me tell you—

TOM. I don't want to hear any more! [*He tears the portieres open. The upstage area is lit with a turgid smoky red glow.*]

AMANDA*'s hair is in metal curlers and she wears a very old bathrobe, much too large for her slight figure, a relic of the faithless Mr. Wingfield*

An upright typewriter and a wild disarray of manuscripts are on the dropleaf table. The quarrel was probably precipitated by AMANDA*'s interruption of his creative labor. A chair lying overthrown on the floor.*

Their gesticulating shadows are cast on the ceiling by the fiery glow.

AMANDA. You *will* hear more, you—

TOM. No, I won't hear more, I'm going out!

AMANDA. You come right back in—

TOM. Out, out, out! Because I'm—

AMANDA. Come back here, Tom Wingfield! I'm not through talking to you!

TOM. Oh, go—

LAURA [*desperately*]. Tom!

AMANDA. You're going to listen, and no more insolence from you! I'm at the end of my patience! [*He comes back toward her.*]

TOM. What do you think I'm at? Aren't I supposed to have any patience to reach the end of, Mother? I know, I know. It seems unimportant to you, what I'm *doing*—what I *want* to do—having a little *difference* between them! You don't think that—

AMANDA. I think you've been doing things that you're ashamed of. That's why you act like this. I don't believe that you go every night to the movies. Nobody goes to the movies night after night. Nobody in their right minds goes to the movies as often as you pretend to. People don't go to the movies at nearly midnight, and movies don't let out at two A.M. Come in stumbling. Muttering to yourself like a maniac! You get three hours' sleep and then go to work. Oh, I can picture the way you're doing down there. Moping, doping, because you're in no condition.

TOM [*wildly*]. No, I'm in no condition!

AMANDA. What right have you got to jeopardize your job? Jeopardize the security of us all? How do you think we'd manage if you were—

TOM. Listen! You think I'm crazy *about* the *warehouse*? [*He bends fiercely toward her slight figure.*] You think I'm in love with the Continental Shoemakers? You think I want to spend fifty-five *years* down there in that—*celotex interior!* with—*fluorescent—tubes!* Look! I'd rather somebody picked up a crowbar and battered out my brains—than go back mornings! *I go!* Every time you come in yelling that God damn "*Rise and Shine!*" "*Rise and Shine!*" I say to myself "How *lucky dead* people are!" But I get up. I *go!* For sixty-five dollars a month I give up all that I dream of doing and being *ever!* And you say self—*self's* all I ever think of. Why, listen, if self is what I thought of, Mother, I'd be where he is—GONE! [*Pointing to father's picture.*] As far as the system of transportation reaches! [*He starts past her. She grabs his arm.*] Don't grab at me, Mother!

AMANDA. Where are you going?

TOM. I'm going to the *movies!*

AMANDA. I don't believe that lie!

TOM [*crouching toward her, overtowering her tiny figure. She backs away, gasping*]. I'm going to opium dens! Yes, opium dens, dens of vice and criminals' hang-outs, Mother. I've joined the Hogan gang, I'm a hired assassin, I carry a tommy-gun in a violin case! I run a string of cat-houses in the Valley! They call me Killer, Killer Wingfield, I'm leading a double-life, a simple, honest warehouse worker by day, by night a dynamic *czar* of the *underworld, Mother.* I go to gambling casinos, I spin away fortunes on the roulette table! I wear a patch over one eye and a false mustache, sometimes I put on green whiskers. On those occasions they call me—*El Diablo!* Oh, I could tell you things to make you sleepless! My enemies plan to dynamite this place. They're going to blow us all sky-high some night! I'll be glad, very happy, and so will you! You'll go up, up on a broomstick, over Blue Mountain with seventeen gentlemen callers! You ugly—babbling old—*witch.* . . . [*He goes through a series of violent, clumsy movements, seizing his overcoat, lunging to the door, pulling it fiercely open. The women watch him, aghast. His arm catches in the sleeve of the coat as he struggles to pull it on. For a moment he is pinioned by the bulky garment. With an outraged groan he tears the coat off again, splitting the shoulders of it and hurls it across the room. It strikes against the shelf of* LAURA's *glass collection, there is a tinkle of shattering glass.* LAURA *cries out as if wounded.*]

[*Music Legend: "The Glass Menagerie."*]

LAURA [*shrilly*]. My glass!—menagerie. . . . [*She covers her face and turns away.*]

But AMANDA *is still stunned and stupefied by the "ugly witch" so that she barely notices this occurrence. Now she recovers her speech.*

AMANDA [*in an awful voice*]. I won't speak to you—until you apologize!

[*She crosses through portieres and draws them together behind her.* TOM *is left with* LAURA. LAURA *clings weakly to the mantel with her face averted.* TOM *stares at her stupidly for a moment. Then he crosses to shelf. Drops, awkwardly to his knees to collect the fallen glass, glancing at* LAURA *as if he would speak but couldn't.*)

"The Glass Menagerie" steals in as

[*The Scene Dims Out.*]

Scene IV

The interior is dark. Faint light in the alley.

A deep-voiced bell in a church is tolling the hour of five as the scene commences.

TOM *appears at the top of the alley. After each solemn boom of the bell in the tower, he shakes a little noise-maker or rattle as if to express the tiny spasm of man in contrast to the sustained power and dignity of the Almighty. This and the unsteadiness of his advance make it evident that he has been drinking.*

As he climbs the few steps to the fire-escape landing light steals up inside. LAURA *appears in night-dress, observing* TOM's *empty bed in the front room.*

Tom *fishes in his pockets for the door-key, removing a motley assortment of articles in the search, including a perfect shower of movie-ticket stubs and an empty bottle. At last he finds the key, but just as he is about to insert it, it slips from his fingers. He strikes a match and crouches below the door.*

TOM [*bitterly*].   One crack—and it falls through!

LAURA *opens the door.*

LAURA.   Tom! Tom, what are you doing?

TOM.   Looking for a door-key.

LAURA.   Where have you been all this time?

TOM.   I have been to the movies.

LAURA.   All this time at the movies?

TOM.   There was a very long program. There was a Garbo picture and a Mickey Mouse and a travelogue and a newsreel and a preview of coming attractions. And there was an organ solo and a collection for the milk-fund—simultaneously—which ended up in a terrible fight between a fat lady and an usher!

LAURA [*innocently*].   Did you have to stay through everything?

TOM.   Of course! And, oh, I forgot! There was a big stage show! The headliner on this stage show was Malvolio the Magician. He performed wonderful tricks, many of them, such as pouring water back and forth between pitchers. First it turned to wine and then it turned to beer and then it turned to whiskey. I know it was whiskey it finally turned into because he needed somebody to come up out of the audience to help him, and I came up— both shows! It was Kentucky Straight Bourbon. A very generous fellow, he gave souvenirs. [*He pulls from his back pocket a shimmering rainbow-colored scarf.*] He gave me this. This is his magic scarf. You can have it, Laura. You wave it over a canary cage and you get a bowl of gold-fish. You wave it over the gold-fish bowl and they fly away canaries. . . . But the wonderfullest trick of all was the coffin trick. We nailed him into a coffin and he got out of the coffin without removing one nail. [*He has come inside.*] There is a trick that would come in handy for me—get me out of this 2 by 4 situation! [*Flops onto bed and starts removing shoes.*]

LAURA.   Tom—Shhh!

TOM.   What you shushing me for?

LAURA.   You'll wake up Mother.

TOM.   Goody, goody! Pay 'er back for all those "Rise an' Shines." [*Lies down, groaning.*] You know it don't take much intelligence to get yourself into a nailed-up coffin, Laura. But who in hell ever got himself out of one without removing one nail?

As if in answer, the father's grinning photograph lights up.

[*Scene Dims Out*]

Immediately following: The church bell is heard striking six. At the sixth stroke the alarm clock goes off in AMANDA's *room, and after a few moments we hear her calling: "Rise and Shine! Rise and Shine!* LAURA, *go tell your brother to rise and shine!"*

TOM. [*sitting up slowly*].   I'll rise—but I won't shine.

The light increases.

AMANDA. Laura, tell your brother his coffee is ready.

LAURA *slips into front room.*

LAURA. Tom! it's nearly seven. Don't make Mother nervous. [*He stares at her stupidly. Beseechingly.*] Tom, speak to Mother this morning. Make up with her, apologize, speak to her!

TOM. She won't to me. It's her that started not speaking.

LAURA. If you just say you're sorry she'll start speaking.

TOM. Her not speaking—is that such a tragedy?

LAURA. Please—please!

AMANDA [*calling from kitchenette*]. Laura, are you going to do what I asked you to do, or do I have to get dressed and go out myself?

LAURA. Going, going—soon as I get on my coat! [*She pulls on a shapeless felt hat with nervous, jerky movement, pleadingly glancing at* TOM. *Rushes awkwardly for coat. The coat is one of* AMANDA's, *inaccurately made-over the sleeves too short for* LAURA.] Butter and what else?

AMANDA [*entering upstage*]. Just butter. Tell them to charge it.

LAURA. Mother, they make such faces when I do that.

AMANDA. Sticks and stones may break my bones, but the expression on Mr. Garfinkel's face won't harm us! Tell your brother his coffee is getting cold.

LAURA [*at door*]. Do what I asked you, will you, will you, Tom?

He looks sullenly away.

AMANDA. Laura, go now or just don't go at all!

LAURA [*rushing out*]. Going—going! [*A second later she cries out.* TOM *springs up and crosses to the door.* AMANDA *rushes anxiously in.* TOM *opens the door.*]

TOM. Laura?

LAURA. I'm all right. I slipped, but I'm all right.

AMANDA [*peering anxiously after her*]. If anyone breaks a leg on those fire-escape steps, the landlord ought to be sued for every cent he possesses!

[*She shuts door. Remembers she isn't speaking and returns to other room.*]

As TOM *enters listlessly for his coffee, she turns her back to him and stands rigidly facing the window on the gloomy gray vault of the areaway. Its light on her face with its aged but childish features is cruelly sharp, satirical as a Daumier print.*

[*Music Under: "Ave Maria."*]

TOM *glances sheepishly but sullenly at her averted figure and slumps at the table. The coffee is scalding hot; he sips it and gasps and spits it back in the cup. At his gasp.* AMANDA *catches her breath and half turns. Then catches herself and turns back to window.*

TOM *blows on his coffee, glancing sidewise at his mother. She clears her throat.* TOM *clears his. He starts to rise. Sinks back down again, scratches his head, clears his throat again.* AMANDA *coughs.* TOM *raises his cup in both hands to blow on it, his eyes staring over the rim of it at his mother for several moments. Then he slowly sets the cup down and awkwardly and hesitantly rises from the chair.*

TOM [*hoarsely*]. Mother. I—I apologize. Mother. [AMANDA *draws a quick, shuddering breath. Her face works grotesquely. She breaks into childlike tears.*] I'm sorry for what I said, for everything that I said, I didn't mean it.

AMANDA [*sobbingly*]. My devotion has made me a witch and so I make myself hateful to my children!

TOM. No you *don't.*

AMANDA. I worry so much, don't sleep, it makes me nervous!

TOM [*gently*]. I understand that.

AMANDA. I've had to put up a solitary battle all these years. But you're my right-hand bower! Don't fall down, don't fail!

TOM [*gently*]. I try, Mother.

AMANDA [*with great enthusiasm*]. Try and you will SUCCEED! [*The notion makes her breathless.*] Why, you—you're just *full* of natural endowments! Both of my children—they're *unusual* children! Don't you think I know it? I'm so—*proud!* Happy and—feel I've—so much to be thankful for but—Promise me one thing, son!

TOM. What, Mother?

AMANDA. Promise, son, you'll—never be a drunkard!

TOM [*turns to her grinning*]. I will never be a drunkard, Mother.

AMANDA. That's what frightened me so, that you'd be drinking! Eat a bowl of Purina!

TOM. Just coffee, Mother.

AMANDA. Shredded wheat biscuit?

TOM. No. No, Mother, just coffee.

AMANDA. You can't put in a day's work on an empty stomach. You've got ten minutes—don't gulp! Drinking too-hot liquids makes cancer of the stomach. . . . Put cream in.

TOM. No, thank you.

AMANDA. To cool it.

TOM. No! No, thank you, I want it black.

AMANDA. I know, but it's not good for you. We have to do all that we can to build ourselves up. In these trying times we live in, all that we have to cling to is—each other. . . . That's why it's so important to—Tom, I—I sent out your sister so I could discuss something with you. If you hadn't spoken I would have spoken to you. [*Sits down.*]

TOM [*gently*]. What is it, Mother, that you want to discuss?

AMANDA. Laura!

TOM *puts his cup down slowly.*

[Legend on Screen: "Laura."]

[Music: "The Glass Menagerie."]

TOM. —Oh.—Laura . . .

AMANDA [*touching his sleeve*]. You know how Laura is. So quiet but—still water runs deep! She notices things and I think she—broods about them. [TOM *looks up.*] A few days ago I came in and she was crying.

TOM. What about?

AMANDA. You.

TOM. Me?

AMANDA. She has an idea that you're not happy here.

TOM. What gave her that idea?

AMANDA. What gives her any idea? However, you do act strangely. I—I'm not criticizing, understand *that!* I know your ambitions do not lie in the warehouse, that like everybody in the whole wide world—you've had to—

make sacrifices, but—Tom—Tom—life's not easy, it calls for—Spartan endurance! There's so many things in my heart that I cannot describe to you! I've never told you but I—*loved* your father. . . .

TOM [*gently*]. I know that, Mother.

AMANDA. And you—when I see you taking after his ways! Staying out late—and—well, you *had* been drinking the night you were in that—terrifying condition! Laura says that you hate the apartment and that you go out nights to get away from it! Is that true, Tom?

TOM. No. You say there's so much in your heart that you can't describe to me. That's true of me, too. There's so much in my heart that I can't describe to *you!* So let's respect each other's—

AMANDA. But, why—*why,* Tom—are you always so *restless?* Where do you go to, nights?

TOM. I—go to the movies.

AMANDA. Why do you go to the movies so much, Tom?

TOM. I go to the movies because—I like adventure. Adventure is something I don't have much of at work, so I go to the movies.

AMANDA. But, Tom, you go to the movies *entirely too much!*

TOM. I like a lot of adventure.

AMANDA *looks baffled, then hurt. As the familiar inquisition resumes he becomes hard and impatient again.* AMANDA *slips back into her querulous attitude toward him.*

[*Image on Screen: Sailing Vessel with Jolly Roger.*]

AMANDA. Most young men find adventure in their careers.

TOM. Then most young men are not employed in a warehouse.

AMANDA. The world is full of young men employed in warehouses and offices and factories.

TOM. Do all of them find adventure in their careers?

AMANDA. They do or they do without it! Not everybody has a craze for adventure.

TOM. Man is by instinct a lover, a hunter, a fighter, and none of those instincts are given much play at the warehouse!

AMANDA. Man is by instinct! Don't quote instinct to me! Instinct is something that people have got away from! It belongs to animals! Christian adults don't want it!

TOM. What do Christian adults want, then, Mother?

AMANDA. Superior things! Things of the mind and the spirit! Only animals have to satisfy instincts! Surely your aims are somewhat higher than theirs! Than monkeys—pigs—

TOM. I reckon they're not.

AMANDA. You're joking. However, that isn't what I wanted to discuss.

TOM [*rising*]. I haven't much time.

AMANDA [*pushing his shoulders*]. Sit down.

TOM. You want me to punch in red at the warehouse, Mother?

AMANDA. You have five minutes. I want to talk about Laura.

[*Legend: "Plans and Provisions."*]

TOM. All right! What about Laura?

AMANDA. We have to be making plans and provisions for her. She's older than you, two years, and nothing has happened. She just drifts along doing nothing. It frightens me terribly how she just drifts along.

TOM. I guess she's the type that people call home girls.

AMANDA. There's no such type, and if there is, it's a pity! That is unless the home is hers, with a husband!

TOM. What?

AMANDA. Oh, I can see the handwriting on the wall as plain as I see the nose in the front of my face! It's terrifying! More and more you remind me of your father! He was out all hours without explanation—Then *left! Goodbye!* And me with the bag to hold. I saw that letter you got from the Merchant Marine. I know what you're dreaming of. I'm not standing here blindfolded. Very well, then. Then *do* it! But not till there's somebody to take your place.

TOM. What do you mean?

AMANDA. I mean that as soon as Laura has got somebody to take care of her, married, a home of her own, independent—why, then you'll be free to go wherever you please, on land, on sea, whichever way the wind blows! But until that time you've got to look out for your sister. I don't say me because I'm old and don't matter! I say for your sister because she's young and dependent. I put her in business college—a dismal failure! Frightened her so it made her sick to her stomach. I took her over to the Young People's League at the church. Another fiasco. She spoke to nobody, nobody spoke to her. Now all she does is fool with those pieces of glass and play those worn-out records. What kind of a life is that for a girl to lead!

TOM. What can I do about it?

AMANDA. Overcome selfishness! Self, self, self is all that you ever think of! [TOM *springs up and crosses to get his coat. It is ugly and bulky. He pulls on a cap with earmuffs.*] Where is your muffler? Put your wool muffler on! [*He snatches it angrily from the closet and tosses it around his neck and pulls both ends tight.*] Tom! I haven't said what I had in mind to ask you.

TOM. I'm too late to—

AMANDA [*catching his arms—very importunately. Then shyly*]. Down at the warehouse, aren't there some—nice young men?

TOM. No!

AMANDA. There *must* be—*some*.

TOM. Mother—

Gesture.

AMANDA. Find out one that's clean-living—doesn't drink and—ask him out for sister!

TOM. What?

AMANDA. For *sister!* To *meet!* Get *acquainted!*

TOM [*stamping to door*]. Oh, my *go-osh!*

AMANDA. Will you? [*He opens door. Imploringly.*] Will you? [*He starts down*] Will you? *Will* you dear?

TOM [*calling back*]. YES!

AMANDA *closes the door hesitantly and with a troubled but faintly hopeful expression.*

[Screen Image: Glamor Magazine Cover.]

Spot AMANDA *at phone.*

AMANDA. Ella Cartwright? This is Amanda Wingfield! How are you honey? How is that kidney condition? [*Count five.*] *Horrors!* [*Count five.*] You're a Christian martyr, yes, honey, that's what you are, a Christian martyr! Well, I just happened to notice in my little red book that your subscription to the *Companion* has just run out! I knew that you wouldn't want to miss out on the wonderful serial starting in this new issue. It's by Bessie Mae Hopper, the first thing she's written since *Honeymoon for Three*. Wasn't that a strange and interesting story? Well, this one is even lovelier, I believe. It has a sophisticated society background. It's all about the horsey set on Long Island!

[Fade Out.]

Scene V

[Legend on Screen: "Annunciation."] Fade with music.

It is early dusk of a spring evening. Supper has just been finished at the Wingfield apartment. AMANDA *and* LAURA *in light colored dresses are removing dishes from the table, in the upstage area, which is shadowy, their movements formalized almost as a dance or ritual, their moving forms as pale and silent as moths.*

TOM, *in white shirt and trousers, rises from the table and crosses toward the fire-escape.*

AMANDA [*as he passes her*]. Son, will you do me a favor?
TOM. What?
AMANDA. Comb your hair! You look so pretty when your hair is combed! [TOM *slouches on sofa with evening paper. Enormous caption "Franco Triumphs."*] There is only one respect in which I would like you to emulate your father.
TOM. What respect is that?
AMANDA. The care he always took of his appearance. He never allowed himself to look untidy. [*He throws down the paper and crosses to fire-escape.*] Where are you going?
TOM. I'm going out to smoke.
AMANDA. You smoke too much. A pack a day at fifteen cents a pack. How much would that amount to in a month? Thirty times fifteen is how much, Tom? Figure it out and you will be astounded at what you could save. Enough to give you a night-school course in accounting at Washington U! Just think what a wonderful thing that would be for you, son!

TOM *is unmoved by the thought.*

TOM. I'd rather smoke. [*He steps out on landing, letting the screen door slam.*]
AMANDA [*sharply*]. I know! That's the tragedy of it. . . . [*Alone, she turns to look at her husband's picture.*]

[Dance Music: "All the World Is Waiting for the Sunrise!"]

TOM [*to the audience*]. Across the alley from us was the Paradise Dance Hall. On evenings in spring the windows and doors were open and the music came outdoors. Sometimes the lights were turned out except for a large glass sphere that hung from the ceiling. It would turn slowly about and filter the dusk with delicate rainbow colors. Then the orchestra played a waltz or a tango, something that had a slow and sensuous rhythm. Couples would come outside, to the relative privacy of the alley. You could see them kissing behind ashpits and telephone poles. This was the compensation for lives that passed like mine, without any change or adventure. Adventure and change were imminent in this year. They were waiting around the corner for all these kids. Suspended in the mist over Berchtesgaden, caught in the folds of Chamberlain's umbrella—In Spain there was Guernica! But here there was only hot swing music and liquor, dance halls, bars, and movies, and sex that hung in the gloom like a chandelier and flooded the world with brief, deceptive rainbows. . . . All the world was waiting for bombardments!

AMANDA *turns from the picture and comes outside.*

AMANDA [*sighing*]. A fire-escape landing's a poor excuse for a porch. [*She spreads a newspaper on a step and sits down, gracefully and demurely as if she were settling into a swing on a Mississippi veranda.*] What are you looking at?

TOM. The moon.

AMANDA. Is there a moon this evening?

TOM. It's rising over Garfinkel's Delicatessen.

AMANDA. So it is! A little silver slipper of a moon. Have you made a wish on it yet?

TOM. Um-hum.

AMANDA. What did you wish for?

TOM. That's a secret.

AMANDA. A secret, huh? Well, I won't tell mine either. I will be just as mysterious as you.

TOM. I bet I can guess what yours is.

AMANDA. Is my head so transparent?

TOM. You're not a sphinx.

AMANDA. No, I don't have secrets. I'll tell you what I wished for on the moon. Success and happiness for my precious children! I wish for that whenever there's a moon, and when there isn't a moon, I wish for it, too.

TOM. I thought perhaps you wished for a gentleman caller.

AMANDA. Why do you say that?

TOM. Don't you remember asking me to fetch one?

AMANDA. I remember suggesting that it would be nice for your sister if you brought some nice young man from the warehouse. I think I've made that suggestion more than once.

TOM. Yes, you have made it repeatedly.

AMANDA. Well?

TOM. We are going to have one.

AMANDA. *What?*

TOM. A gentleman caller!

[The Annunciation Is Celebrated with Music.]

AMANDA *rises.*

[Image on Screen: Caller with Bouquet.]

AMANDA. You mean you have asked some nice young man to come over?

TOM. Yep. I've asked him to dinner.

AMANDA. You really did?

TOM. I did!

AMANDA. You did, and did he—*accept?*

TOM. He did!

AMANDA. Well, well—well, well! That's—lovely!

TOM. I thought that you would be pleased.

AMANDA. It's definite, then?

TOM. Very definite.

AMANDA. Soon?

TOM. Very soon.

AMANDA. For heaven's sake, stop putting on and tell me some things, will you?

TOM. What things do you want me to tell you?

AMANDA. Naturally I would like to know when he's *coming!*

TOM. He's coming tomorrow.

AMANDA. *Tomorrow?*

TOM. Yep. Tomorrow.

AMANDA. But, Tom!

TOM. Yes, Mother?

AMANDA. Tomorrow gives me no time!

TOM. Time for what?

AMANDA. Preparations! Why didn't you phone me at once, as soon as you asked him, the minute that he accepted? Then, don't you see, I could have been getting ready!

TOM. You don't have to make any fuss.

AMANDA. Oh, Tom, Tom, Tom, of course I have to make a fuss! I want things nice, not sloppy! Not thrown together. I'll certainly have to do some fast thinking, won't I?

TOM. I don't see why you have to think at all.

AMANDA. You just don't know. We can't have a gentleman caller in a pigsty! All my wedding silver has to be polished, the monogrammed table linen ought to be laundered! The windows have to be washed and fresh curtains put up. And how about clothes? We have to *wear* something, don't we?

TOM. Mother, this boy is no one to make a fuss over!

AMANDA. Do you realize he's the first young man we've introduced to your sister? It's terrible, dreadful, disgraceful that poor little sister has never received a single gentleman caller! Tom, come inside! [*She opens the screen door.*]

TOM. What for?

AMANDA. I want to ask you some things.

TOM. If you're going to make such a fuss, I'll call it off, I'll tell him not to come.

AMANDA. You certainly won't do anything of the kind. Nothing offends people worse than broken engagements. It simply means I'll have to work like a Turk! We won't be brilliant, but we'll pass inspection. Come on inside. [TOM *follows, groaning.*] Sit down.

TOM. Any particular place you would like me to sit?

AMANDA. Thank heavens I've got that new sofa! I'm also making payments on a floor lamp I'll have sent out! And put the chintz covers on, they'll brighten things up! Of course I'd hoped to have these walls repapered. . . . What is the young man's name?

TOM. His name is O'Connor.

AMANDA. That, of course, means fish—tomorrow is Friday! I'll have that salmon loaf—with Durkee's dressing! What does he do? He works at the warehouse?

TOM. Of course! How else would I—

AMANDA. Tom, he—doesn't drink?

TOM. Why do you ask me that?

AMANDA. Your father *did!*

TOM. Don't get started on that!

AMANDA. He *does* drink, then?

TOM. Not that I know of!

AMANDA. Make sure, be certain! The last thing I want for my daughter's a boy who drinks!

TOM. Aren't you being a little premature? Mr. O'Connor has not yet appeared on the scene!

AMANDA. But will tomorrow. To meet your sister, and what do I know about his character? Nothing! Old maids are better off than wives of drunkards!

TOM. Oh, my God!

AMANDA. Be still!

TOM [*leaning forward to whisper*]. Lots of fellows meet girls whom they don't marry!

AMANDA. Oh, talk sensibly, Tom—and don't be sarcastic! [*She has gotten a hair-brush.*]

TOM. What are you doing?

AMANDA. I'm brushing that cow-lick down! What is this young man's position at the warehouse?

TOM [*submitting grimly to the brush and the interrogation*]. This young man's position is that of a shipping clerk, Mother.

AMANDA. Sounds to me like a fairly responsible job, the sort of a job *you* would be in if you just had more *get-up.* What is his salary? Have you got any idea?

TOM. I would judge it to be approximately eighty-five dollars a month.

AMANDA. Well—not princely, but—

TOM. Twenty more than I make.

AMANDA. Yes, how well I know! But for a family man, eighty-five dollars a month is not much more than you can just get by on. . . .

TOM. Yes, but Mr. O'Connor is not a family man.

AMANDA. He might be, mightn't he? Some time in the future?

TOM. I see. Plans and provisions.

AMANDA. You are the only man that I know of who ignores the fact that the future becomes the present, the present the past, and the past turns into everlasting regret if you don't plan for it!

TOM. I will think that over and see what I can make of it.

AMANDA. Don't be supercilious with your mother! Tell me some more about this—what do you call him?

TOM. James D. O'Connor. The D. is for Delaney.

AMANDA. Irish on *both* sides! *Gracious!* And doesn't drink?

TOM. Shall I call him up and ask him right this minute?

AMANDA. The only way to find out about those things is to make discreet inquiries at the proper moment. When I was a girl in Blue Mountain and it was suspected that a young man drank, the girl whose attentions he had been receiving, if any girl *was,* would sometimes speak to the minister of his church, or rather her father would if her father was living, and sort of feel him out on the young man's character. That is the way such things are discreetly handled to keep a young woman from making a tragic mistake!

TOM. Then how did you happen to make a tragic mistake?

AMANDA. That innocent look of your father's had everyone fooled! He *smiled*—the world was *enchanted!* No girl can do worse than put herself at the mercy of a handsome appearance! I hope that Mr. O'Connor is not too good-looking.

TOM. No, he's not too good-looking. He's covered with freckles and hasn't too
    much of a nose.

AMANDA. He's not right-down homely, though?

TOM. Not right-down homely. Just medium homely, I'd say.

AMANDA. Character's what to look for in a man.

TOM. That's what I've always said, Mother.

AMANDA. You've never said anything of the kind and I suspect you would never
    give it a thought.

TOM. Don't be suspicious of me.

AMANDA. At least I hope he's the type that's up and coming.

TOM. I think he really goes in for self-improvement.

AMANDA. What reason have you to think so?

TOM. He goes to night school.

AMANDA [*beaming*]. Splendid! What does he do, I mean study?

TOM. Radio engineering and public speaking!

AMANDA. Then he has visions of being advanced in the world! Any young man who
    studies public speaking is aiming to have an executive job some day! And
    radio engineering? A thing for the future! Both of these facts are very illumi-
    nating. Those are the sort of things that a mother should know concerning
    any young man who comes to call on her daughter. Seriously or—not.

TOM. One little warning. He doesn't know about Laura. I didn't let on that we
    had dark ulterior motives. I just said, why don't you come have dinner
    with us? He said okay and that was the whole conversation.

AMANDA. I bet it was! You're eloquent as an oyster. However, he'll know about
    Laura when he gets here. When he sees how lovely and sweet and pretty
    she is, he'll thank his lucky stars he was asked to dinner.

TOM. Mother, you mustn't expect too much of Laura.

AMANDA. What do you mean?

TOM. Laura seems all those things to you and me because she's ours and we love
    her. We don't even notice she's crippled any more.

AMANDA. Don't say crippled! You know that I never allow that word to be used!

TOM. But face facts, Mother. She is and—that's not all—

AMANDA. What do you mean "not all"?

TOM. Laura is very different from other girls.

AMANDA. I think the difference is all to her advantage.

TOM. Not quite all—in the eyes of others—strangers—she's terribly shy and lives
    in a world of her own and those things make her seem a little peculiar to
    people outside the house.

AMANDA. Don't say peculiar.

TOM. Face the facts. She is.

[The Dance-Hall Music Changes to a Tango that Has a Minor and Some-
what Ominous Tone.]

AMANDA. In what way is she peculiar—may I ask?

TOM [*gently*]. She lives in a world of her own—a world of—little glass orna-
    ments, Mother. . . . [*Gets up.* AMANDA *remains holding brush, looking at*
    him, troubled.] She plays old phonograph records and—that's about all—
    [*He glances at himself in the mirror and crosses to door.*]

AMANDA [*sharply*]. Where are you going?

TOM. I'm going to the movies. [*Out screen door.*]

AMANDA. Not to the movies, every night to the movies! [*Follows quickly to screen door.*] I don't believe you always go to the movies! [*He is gone.* AMANDA *looks worriedly after him for a moment. Then vitality and optimism return and she turns from the door. Crossing to portieres.*] Laura! Laura! [LAURA *answers from kitchenette.*]

LAURA. Yes, Mother.

AMANDA. Let those dishes go and come in front! [*Laura appears with dish towel. Gaily.*] Laura, come here and make a wish on the moon!

LAURA [*entering*] Moon—moon?

AMANDA. A little silver slipper of a moon. Look over your left shoulder, Laura, and make a wish! [LAURA *looks faintly puzzled as if called out of sleep.* AMANDA *seizes her shoulders and turns her at angle by the door.*] Now! Now, darling, *wish!*

LAURA. What shall I wish for, Mother?

AMANDA. [*her voice trembling and her eyes suddenly filling with tears*]. Happiness! Good Fortune!

The violin rises and the stage dims out.

Scene VI

[Image: High School Hero.]

TOM. And so the following evening I brought Jim home to dinner. I had known Jim slightly in high school. In high school Jim was a hero. He had tremendous Irish good nature and vitality with the scrubbed and polished look of white chinaware. He seemed to move in a continual spotlight. He was a star in basketball, captain of the debating club, president of the senior class and the glee club and he sang the male lead in the annual light operas. He was always running or bounding, never just walking. He seemed always at the point of defeating the law of gravity. He was shooting with such velocity through his adolescence that you would logically expect him to arrive at nothing short of the White House by the time he was thirty. But Jim apparently ran into more interference after his graduation from Soldan. His speed had definitely slowed. Six years after he left high school he was holding a job that wasn't much better than mine.

[Image: Clerk.]

He was the only one at the warehouse with whom I was on friendly terms. I was valuable to him as someone who could remember his former glory, who had seen him win basketball games and the silver cup in debating. He knew of my secret practice of retiring to a cabinet of the washroom to work on poems when business was slack in the warehouse. He called me Shakespeare. And while the other boys in the warehouse regarded me with suspicious hostility, Jim took a humorous attitude toward me. Gradually his attitude affected the others, their hostility wore off and they also began to smile at me as people smile at an oddly fashioned dog who trots across their path at some distance.

I knew that Jim and Laura had known each other at Soldan, and I had heard Laura speak admiringly of his voice. I didn't know if Jim remembered her or not. In high school Laura had been as unobtrusive as Jim had been astonishing. If he did remember Laura, it was not as my sister, for when I asked him to dinner, he grinned and said, "You know, Shake-speare, I never thought of you as having folks!"

He was about to discover that I did . . . .

[Light up Stage]

[Legend on Screen: "The Accent of a Coming Foot."]

Friday evening. It is about five o'clock of a late spring evening which comes "scattering poems in the sky."

A delicate lemony light is in the Wingfield apartment.

AMANDA *has worked like a Turk in preparation for the gentleman caller. The results are astonishing. The new floor lamp with its rose-silk shade is in place, a colored paper lantern conceals the broken light fixture in the ceiling, new billowing white curtains are at the windows, chintz covers are on chairs and sofa, a pair of new sofa pillows make their initial appearance.*

Open boxes and tissue paper are scattered on the floor.

LAURA *stands in the middle with lifted arms while* AMANDA *crouches before her, adjusting the hem of the new dress, devout and ritualistic. The dress is colored and designed by memory. The arrangement of* LAURA's *hair is changed; it is softer and more becoming. A fragile, unearthly prettiness has come out in* LAURA: *she is like a piece of translucent glass touched by light, given a momentary radiance, not actual, not lasting.*

AMANDA [*impatiently*]. Why are you trembling?

LAURA. Mother, you've made me so nervous!

AMANDA. How have I made you nervous?

LAURA. By all this fuss! You make it seem so important!

AMANDA. I don't understand you, Laura. You couldn't be satisfied with just sitting home, and yet whenever I try to arrange something for you, you seem to resist it. [*She gets up.*] Now take a look at yourself. No, wait! Wait just a moment—I have an idea!

LAURA. What is it now?

AMANDA *produces two powder puffs which she wraps in handkerchiefs and stuffs in* LAURA's *bosom.*

LAURA. Mother, what are you doing?

AMANDA. They call them "Gay Deceivers"!

LAURA. I won't wear them!

AMANDA. You will!

LAURA. Why should I?

AMANDA. Because, to be painfully honest, your chest is flat.

LAURA. You make it seem like we were setting a trap.

AMANDA. All pretty girls are a trap, a pretty trap, and men expect them to be. [*Legend: "A Pretty Trap."*] Now look at yourself, young lady. This is the prettiest you will ever be! I've got to fix myself now! You're going to be surprised by your mother's appearance! [*She crosses through portieres, humming gaily.*]

LAURA *moves slowly to the long mirror and stares solemnly at herself.*

A wind blows the white curtains inward in a slow, graceful motion and with a faint sorrowful sighing.

AMANDA [*off stage*]. It isn't dark enough yet. [*She turns slowly before the mirror with a troubled look.*]

[*Legend on Screen: "This Is My Sister: Celebrate Her with Strings!" Music.*]

AMANDA [*laughing, off*]. I'm going to show you something. I'm going to make a spectacular appearance!

LAURA. What is it, Mother?

AMANDA. Possess your soul in patience—you will see! Something I've resurrected from that old trunk! Styles haven't changed so terribly much after all. . . . [*She parts the portieres.*] Now just look at your mother! [*She wears a girl-ish frock of yellowed voile with a blue silk sash. She carries a bunch of jonquils—the legend of her youth is nearly revived. Feverishly.*] This is the dress in which I led the cotillion. Won the cakewalk twice at Sunset Hill, wore one spring to the Governor's ball in Jackson! See how I sashayed around the ballroom, Laura? [*She raises her skirt and does a mincing step around the room.*] I wore it on Sundays for my gentlemen callers! I had it on the day I met your father—I had malaria fever all that spring. The change of climate from East Tennessee to the Delta—weakened resistance—I had a little temperature all the time—not enough to be serious— just enough to make me restless and giddy! Invitations poured in—parties all over the Delta!—"Stay in bed," said Mother, "you have fever!"—but I just wouldn't.—I took quinine but kept on going, going!—Evenings, dances!—Afternoons, long, long rides! Picnics—lovely!—So lovely, that country in May.—All lacy with dogwood, literally flooded with jonquils!— That was the spring I had the craze for jonquils. Jonquils became an ab-solute obsession. Mother said, "Honey, there's no more room for jonquils." And still I kept bringing in more jonquils. Whenever, wherever I saw them, I'd say, "Stop! Stop! I see jonquils!" I made the young men help me gather the jonquils! It was a joke, Amanda and her jonquils! Finally there were no more vases to hold them, every available space was filled with jonquils. No vases to hold them? All right, I'll hold them myself! And then I—[*She stops in front of the picture.*] [*Music.*] met your father! Malaria fever and jon-quils and then—this—boy. . . . [*She switches on the rose-colored lamp.*] I hope they get here before it starts to rain. [*She crosses upstage and places the jonquils in bowl on table.*] I gave your brother a little extra change so he and Mr. O'Connor could take the service car home.

LAURA [*with altered look*]. What did you say his name was?

AMANDA. O'Connor.

LAURA. What is his first name?

AMANDA. I don't remember. Oh, yes, I do. It was—Jim!

LAURA *sways slightly and catches hold of a chair.*

[*Legend on Screen: "Not Jim!"*]

LAURA [*faintly*]. Not—Jim!

AMANDA. Yes, that was it, it was Jim! I've never known a Jim that wasn't nice!

[*Music: Ominous.*]

LAURA. Are you sure his name is Jim O'Connor?

AMANDA. Yes. Why?

LAURA. Is he the one that Tom used to know in high school?

AMANDA. He didn't say so. I think he just got to know him at the warehouse.

LAURA. There was a Jim O'Connor we both knew in high school—[*Then, with effort.*] If that is the one that Tom is bringing to dinner—you'll have to excuse me, I won't come to the table.

AMANDA. What sort of nonsense is this?

LAURA. You asked me once if I'd ever liked a boy. Don't you remember I showed you this boy's picture?

AMANDA. You mean the boy you showed me in the year book?

LAURA. Yes, that boy.

AMANDA. Laura, Laura, were you in love with that boy?

LAURA. I don't know, Mother. All I know is I couldn't sit at the table if it was him!

AMANDA. It won't be him! It isn't the least bit likely. But whether it is or not, you will come to the table. You will not be excused.

LAURA. I'll have to be, Mother.

AMANDA. I don't intend to humor your silliness, Laura. I've had too much from you and your brother, both! So just sit down and compose yourself till they come. Tom has forgotten his key so you'll have to let them in, when they arrive.

LAURA [*panicky*]. Oh, Mother—*you* answer the door!

AMANDA [*lightly*]. I'll be in the kitchen—busy!

LAURA. Oh, Mother, please answer the door, don't make me do it!

AMANDA [*crossing into kitchenette*]. I've got to fix the dressing for the salmon. Fuss, fuss—silliness!—over a gentleman caller!

Door swings shut. LAURA is left alone.

[*Legend: "Terror!"*]

She utters a low moan and turns off the lamp—sits stiffly on the edge of the sofa, knotting her fingers together.

[*Legend on Screen: "The Opening of a Door!"*]

TOM *and* JIM *appear on the fire-escape steps and climb to landing. Hearing their approach,* LAURA *rises with a panicky gesture. She retreats to the portieres.*

The doorbell. LAURA *catches her breath and touches her throat. Low drums.*

AMANDA [*calling*]. Laura, sweetheart! The door!

LAURA *stares at it without moving.*

JIM. I think we just beat the rain.

TOM. Uh-huh. [*He rings again, nervously.*] JIM *whistles and fishes for a cigarette.*]

AMANDA [*very, very gaily*]. Laura, that is your brother and Mr. O'Connor! Will you let them in, darling?

LAURA *crosses toward kitchenette door.*

LAURA [*breathlessly*]. Mother—you go to the door!

AMANDA *steps out of kitchenette and stares furiously at* LAURA. *She points imperiously at the door.*

LAURA. Please, please!

AMANDA [*in a fierce whisper*]. What is the matter with you, you silly thing?

LAURA [*desperately*]. Please, you answer it, *please!*

AMANDA. I told you I wasn't going to humor you, Laura. Why have you chosen this moment to lose your mind?

LAURA. Please, please, please, you go!

AMANDA. You'll have to go to the door because I can't!

LAURA [*despairingly*]. I can't either!

AMANDA. Why?

LAURA. I'm *sick!*

AMANDA. I'm sick, too—of your nonsense! Why can't you and your brother be normal people? Fantastic whims and behavior! [TOM *gives a long ring.*] Preposterous goings on! Can you give me one reason-[*Calls out lyrically.*] COMING! JUST ONE SECOND!—why should you be afraid to open a door? Now you answer it, Laura!

LAURA. Oh, oh, oh . . . [*She returns through the portieres. Darts to the victrola and winds it frantically and turns it on.*]

AMANDA. Laura Wingfield, you march right to that door!

LAURA. Yes—yes, Mother!

A faraway, scratchy rendition of "Dardanella" softens the air and gives her strength to move through it. She slips to the door and draws it cautiously open.

TOM *enters with caller,* JIM O'CONNOR.

TOM. Laura, this is Jim. Jim, this is my sister, Laura.

JIM [*stepping inside*]. I didn't know that Shakespeare had a sister!

LAURA [*retreating stiff and trembling from the door*]. How—how do you do?

JIM [*heartily extending his hand*]. Okay!

LAURA *touches it hesitantly with hers.*

JIM. Your hand's *cold,* Laura!

LAURA. Yes, well—I've been playing the victrola. . . .

JIM. Must have been playing classical music on it! You ought to play a little hot swing music to warm you up!

LAURA. Excuse me—I haven't finished playing the victrola . . . .

She turns awkwardly and hurries into the front room. She pauses a second by the victrola. Then catches her breath and darts through the portieres like a frightened deer.

JIM [*grinning*]. What was the matter?

TOM. Oh—with Laura? Laura is—terribly shy.

JIM. Shy, huh? It's unusual to meet a shy girl nowadays. I don't believe you ever mentioned you had a sister.

TOM. Well, now you know. I have one. Here is the *Post Dispatch.* You want a piece of it?

JIM. Uh-huh.

TOM. What piece? The comics?

JIM. Sports! [*Glances at it*]. Ole Dizzy Dean is on his bad behavior.

TOM [*disinterest*]. Yeah? [*Lights cigarette and crosses back to fire-escape door.*]

JIM. Where are *you* going?

TOM. I'm going out on the terrace.

JIM [*goes after him*]. You know, Shakespeare—I'm going to sell you a bill of goods!

TOM. What goods?

JIM. A course I'm taking.

TOM. Huh?

JIM. In public speaking! You and me, we're not the warehouse type.

TOM. Thanks—that's good news. But what has public speaking got to do with it?

JIM. It fits you for—executive positions!

TOM. Awww.

JIM. I tell you it's done a helluva lot for me.

　　[Image: Executive at Desk.]

TOM. In what respect?

JIM. In every! Ask yourself what is the difference between you an' me and men in the office down front? Brains?—No!—Ability?—No! Then what? Just one little thing—

TOM. What is that one little thing?

JIM. Primarily it amounts to—social poise! Being able to square up to people and hold your own on any social level!

AMANDA [*off stage*]. Tom?

TOM. Yes, Mother?

AMANDA. Is that you and Mr. O'Connor?

TOM. Yes, Mother.

AMANDA. Well, you just make yourselves comfortable in there.

TOM. Yes, Mother.

AMANDA. Ask Mr. O'Connor if he would like to wash his hands.

JIM. Aw—no—no—thank you—I took care of that at the warehouse. Tom—

TOM. Yes?

JIM. Mr. Mendoza was speaking to me about you.

TOM. Favorably?

JIM. What do you think?

TOM. Well—

JIM. You're going to be out of a job if you don't wake up.

TOM. I am waking up—

JIM. You show no signs.

TOM. The signs are interior.

　　[Image on Screen: The Sailing Vessel with Jolly Roger Again.]

TOM. I'm planning to change. [*He leans over the rail speaking with quiet exhilaration. The incandescent marquees and signs of the first-run movie houses light his face from across the alley. He looks like a voyager.*] I'm right at the point of committing myself to a future that doesn't include the warehouse and Mr. Mendoza or even a night-school course in public speaking.

JIM. What are you gassing about?

TOM. I'm tired of the movies.

JIM. Movies!

TOM. Yes, movies! Look at them—[*a wave toward the marvels of Grand Avenue.*] All of those glamorous people—having adventures—hogging it all, gobbling the whole thing up! You know what happens? People go to the *movies* instead of *moving!* Hollywood characters are supposed to have all the adventures for everybody in America, while everybody in America sits in a dark room and watches them have them! Yes, until there's a war.

That's when adventure becomes available to the masses! *Everyone's* dish, not only Gable's! Then the people in the dark room come out of the dark room to have some adventures themselves—Goody, goody—It's our turn now, to go to the South Sea Island—to make a safari—to be exotic, far-off—But I'm not patient. I don't want to wait till then. I'm tired of the *movies* and I am *about* to *move!*

JIM [*incredulously*]. Move?

TOM. Yes.

JIM. When?

TOM. Soon!

JIM. Where? Where?

[Theme Three: Music Seems to Answer the Question, while TOM *Thinks it Over. He Searches among his Pockets.]*

TOM. I'm starting to boil inside. I know I seem dreamy, but inside—well, I'm boiling! Whenever I pick up a shoe. I shudder a little thinking how short life is and what I am doing!—Whatever that means. I know it doesn't mean shoes—except as something to wear on a traveler's feet [*Finds paper.*] Look—

JIM. What?

TOM. I'm a member.

JIM [*reading*]. The Union of Merchant Seamen.

TOM. I paid my dues this month, instead of the light bill.

JIM. You will regret it when they turn the lights off.

TOM. I won't be here.

JIM. How about your mother?

TOM. I'm like my father. The bastard son of a bastard! See how he grins? And he's been absent going on sixteen years!

JIM. You're just talking, you drip. How does your mother feel about it?

TOM. Shhh—Here comes Mother! Mother is not acquainted with my plans!

AMANDA [*enters portieres*]. Where are you all?

TOM. On the terrace, Mother.

They start inside. She advances to them. TOM *is distinctly shocked at her appearance. Even* JIM *blinks a little. He is making his first contact with girlish Southern vivacity and in spite of the nightschool course in public speaking is somewhat thrown off the beam by the unexpected outlay of social charm.*

Certain responses are attempted by JIM *but are swept aside by* AMANDA's *gay laughter and chatter.* TOM *is embarrassed but after the first shock* JIM *reacts very warmly. Grins and chuckles, is altogether won over.*

[Image: AMANDA *as a Girl.]*

AMANDA [*coyly smiling, shaking her girlish ringlets*]. Well, well, well, so this is Mr. O'Connor. Introductions entirely unnecessary. I've heard so much about you from my boy. I finally said to him, Tom—good gracious!—why don't you bring this paragon to supper? I'd like to meet this nice young man at the warehouse!—Instead of just hearing him sing your praises so much! I don't know why my son is so standoffish—that's not Southern behavior! Let's sit down and—I think we could stand a little more air in here! Tom, leave the door open. I felt a nice fresh breeze a moment ago. Where has it gone? Mmm, so warm already! And not quite summer, even. We're going to burn up when summer really gets started. However, we're having—we're having a very light supper. I think light things are better fo' this time of year. The same as light clothes are. Light clothes an' light food are what warm weather calls fo'. You know our blood gets so thick during th' winter—it takes a while fo' us to *adjust* ou'selves!—when the season changes. . . . It's come so quick this year, I wasn't prepared. All of a sudden—heavens! Already summer!—I ran to the trunk an' pulled out this light dress—Terribly old! Historical almost! But feels so good—so good an' co-ol, y'know. . . .

TOM. Mother—

AMANDA. Yes, honey?

TOM. How about—supper?

AMANDA. Honey, you go ask Sister if supper is ready! You know that Sister is in full charge of supper! Tell her you hungry boys are waiting for it. [*To Jim.*] Have you met Laura?

JIM. She—

AMANDA. Let you in? Oh, good, you've met already! It's rare for a girl as sweet an' pretty as Laura to be domestic! But Laura is, thank heavens, not only pretty but also very domestic. I'm not at all. I never was a bit. I never could make a thing but angel-food cake. Well, in the South we had so many servants. Gone, gone, gone. All vestiges of gracious living! Gone completely! I wasn't prepared for what the future brought me. All of my gentlemen callers were sons of planters and so of course I assumed that I would be married to one and raise my family on a large piece of land with plenty of servants. But man proposes—and woman accepts the proposal!—To vary that old, old saying a little bit—I married no planter! I married a man who worked for the telephone company!—that gallantly smiling gentleman over there! [*Points to the picture.*] A telephone man who—fell in love with long distance!—Now he travels and I don't even know where!—But what am I going on for about my—tribulations! Tell me yours—I hope you don't have any! Tom?

TOM [*returning*]. Yes, Mother?

AMANDA. Is supper nearly ready?

TOM. It looks to me like supper is on the table.

AMANDA. Let me look—[*She rises prettily and looks through portieres.*] Oh, lovely—But where is Sister?

TOM. Laura is not feeling well and she says that she thinks she'd better not come to the table.

AMANDA. What?—Nonsense!—Laura? Oh, Laura!

LAURA [*off stage, faintly*]. Yes, Mother.

AMANDA. You really must come to the table. We won't be seated until you come to the table! Come in, Mr. O'Connor. You sit over there and I'll—Laura? Laura Wingfield! You're keeping us waiting, honey! We can't say grace until you come to the table!

The back door is pushed weakly open and LAURA *comes in. She is obviously quite faint, her lips trembling, her eyes wide and staring. She moves unsteadily toward the table.*

[Legend: "Terror!"]

Outside a summer storm is coming abruptly. The white curtains billow inward at the windows and there is a sorrowful murmur and deep blue dusk.

LAURA *suddenly stumbles—She catches a chair with a faint moan.*

TOM. Laura!

AMANDA. Laura! [*There is a clap of thunder.*] [*Legend: "Ah!"*] [*Despairingly.*] Why, Laura, you *are* sick, darling! Tom, help you sister into the living room, dear! Sit in the living room, Laura—rest on the sofa. Well! [*To the gentleman caller.*] Standing over the hot stove made her ill!—I told her that it was just too warm this evening, but—TOM *comes back in.* LAURA *is on the sofa.*] Is Laura all right now?

TOM. Yes.

AMANDA. What is that? Rain? A nice cool rain has come up! [*She gives the gentleman caller a frightened look.*] I think we may—have grace—now . . . [TOM *looks at her stupidly.*] Tom, honey—you say grace!

TOM. Oh . . . "For these and all thy mercies—" [*They bow their heads.* AMANDA *stealing a nervous glance at* JIM. *In the living room* LAURA, *stretched on the sofa, clenches her hand to her lips, to hold back a shuddering sob.*] God's Holy Name be praised—

[*The Scene Dims Out.*]

Scene VII
A Souvenir

Half an hour later. Dinner is just being finished in the upstage area which is concealed by the drawn portieres.

As the curtain rises LAURA *is still huddled upon the sofa, her feet drawn under her, her head resting on a pale blue pillow, her eyes wide and mysteriously watchful. The new floor lamp with its shade of rose-colored silk gives a soft, becoming light to her face, bringing out the fragile, unearthly prettiness which usually escapes attention. There is a steady murmur of rain, but it is slackening and stops soon after the scene begins; the air outside becomes pale and luminous as the moon breaks out.*

A moment after the curtain rises, the lights in both rooms flicker and go out.

JIM. Hey, there, Mr. Light Bulb!

AMANDA *laughs nervously.*

[*Legend: "Suspension of a Public Service."*]

AMANDA. Where was Moses when the lights went out? Ha-ha. Do you know the answer to that one, Mr. O'Connor?

JIM. No, ma'am, what's the answer?

AMANDA. In the dark! [JIM *laughs appreciatively.*] Everybody sit still. I'll light the candles. Isn't it lucky we have them on the table? Where's a match? Which of you gentlemen can provide a match?

JIM. Here.

AMANDA. Thank you, sir.

JIM. Not at all, Ma'am!

AMANDA. I guess the fuse has burnt out. Mr. O'Connor, can you tell a burnt-out fuse? I know I can't and Tom is a total loss when it comes to mechanics. [*Sound: Getting Up: Voices Recede a Little to Kitchenette.*] Oh, be careful you don't bump into something. We don't want our gentleman caller to break his neck. Now wouldn't that be a fine howdy-do?

JIM. Ha-ha! Where is the fuse-box?

AMANDA. Right here next to the stove. Can you see anything?

JIM. Just a minute.

AMANDA. Isn't electricity a mysterious thing? Wasn't it Benjamin Franklin who tied a key to a kite? We live in such a mysterious universe, don't we? Some people say that science clears up all the mysteries for us. In my opinion it only creates more! Have you found it yet?

JIM. No, Ma'am. All these fuses look okay to me.

AMANDA. Tom!

TOM. Yes, Mother?

AMANDA. That light bill I gave you several days ago. The one I told you we got the notices about?

TOM. Oh.—Yeah.

[Legend: "Ha!"]

AMANDA. You didn't neglect to pay it by any chance?

TOM. Why, I—

AMANDA. Didn't! I might have known it!

JIM. Shakespeare probably wrote a poem on that light bill, Mrs. Wingfield.

AMANDA. I might have known better than to trust him with it! There's such a high price for negligence in this world!

JIM. Maybe the poem will win a ten-dollar prize.

AMANDA. We'll just have to spend the remainder of the evening in the nineteenth century, before Mr. Edison made the Mazda lamp!

JIM. Candlelight is my favorite kind of light.

AMANDA. That shows you're romantic! But that's no excuse for Tom. Well, we got through dinner. Very considerate of them to let us get through dinner before they plunged us into everlasting darkness, wasn't it, Mr. O'Connor?

JIM. Ha-ha!

AMANDA. Tom, as a penalty for your carelessness you can help me with the dishes.

JIM. Let me give you a hand.

AMANDA. Indeed you will not!

JIM. I ought to be good for something.

AMANDA. Good for something? [*Her tone is rhapsodic.*] *You?* Why, Mr. O'Connor, nobody, *nobody's* given me this much entertainment in years—as you have!

JIM. Aw, now, Mrs. Wingfield!

AMANDA. I'm not exaggerating, not one bit! But Sister is all by her lonesome. You go keep her company in the parlor! I'll give you this lovely old candelabrum that used to be on the altar at the church of the Heavenly Rest. It was melted a little out of shape when the church burnt down. Lightning struck it one spring. Gypsy Jones was holding a revival at the time and he intimated that the church was destroyed because the Episcopalians gave card parties.

JIM. Ha-ha.

AMANDA. And how about coaxing Sister to drink a little wine? I think it would be good for her! Can you carry both at once?

JIM. Sure. I'm Superman!

AMANDA. Now, Thomas, get into this apron!

The door of kitchenette swings closed on AMANDA's *gay laughter; the flick-ering light approaches the portieres.*

LAURA *sits up nervously as he enters. Her speech at first is low and breathless from the almost intolerable strain of being alone with a stranger.*

[Legend: "I Don't Suppose You Remember Me at All!"]

In her first speeches in this scene, before JIM's *warmth overcomes her paralyzing shyness,* LAURA's *voice is thin and breathless as though she has run up a steep flight of stairs.*

JIM's *attitude is gently humorous. In playing this scene it should be stressed that while the incident is apparently unimportant, it is to* LAURA *the climax of her secret life.*

JIM. Hello, there, Laura.

LAURA [*faintly*]. Hello. [*She clears her throat.*]

JIM. How are you feeling now? Better?

LAURA. Yes. Yes, thank you.

JIM. This is for you. A little dandelion wine. [*He extends it toward her with extravagant gallantry.*]

LAURA. Thank you.

JIM. Drink it—but don't get drunk! [*He laughs heartily.* LAURA *takes the glass uncertainly; laughs shyly.*] Where shall I set the candles?

LAURA. Oh—oh, anywhere . . .

JIM. How about here on the floor? Any objections?

LAURA. No.

JIM. I'll spread a newspaper under to catch the drippings. I like to sit on the floor. Mind if I do?

LAURA. Oh, no.

JIM. Give me a pillow?

LAURA. What?

JIM. A pillow!

LAURA. Oh . . . [*Hands him one quickly.*]

JIM. How about you? Don't you like to sit on the floor?

LAURA. Oh—yes.

JIM. Why don't you, then?

LAURA. I—will.

JIM. Take a pillow! [LAURA *does. Sits on the other side of the candelabrum.* JIM *crosses his legs and smiles engagingly at her.*] I can't hardly see you sitting way over there.

LAURA. I can—see you.

JIM. I know, but that's not fair, I'm in the limelight. [LAURA *moves her pillow closer.*] Good! Now I can see you! Comfortable?

LAURA. Yes.

JIM. So am I. Comfortable as a cow. Will you have some gum?

LAURA. No, thank you.

JIM. I think that I will indulge, with your permission [*Musingly unwraps it and holds it up.*] Think of the fortune made by the guy that invented the first piece of chewing gum. Amazing, huh? The Wrigley Building is one of the sights of Chicago.—I saw it summer before last when I went up to the Century of Progress. Did you take in the Century of Progress?

LAURA. No, I didn't.

JIM. Well, it was quite a wonderful exposition. What impressed me most was the Hall of Science. Gives you an idea of what the future will be in America,

even more wonderful than the present time is! [*Pause, Smiling at her.*]
     Your brother tells me you're shy. Is that right, Laura?
LAURA. I—don't know.
JIM. I judge you to be an old-fashioned type of girl. Well, I think that's a pretty
     good type to be. Hope you don't think I'm being too personal—do you?
LAURA [*hastily, out of embarrassment*]. I believe I *will* take a piece of gum, if
     you—don't mind. [*Clearing her throat.*] Mr. O'Connor, have you—kept
     up with your singing?
JIM. Singing? Me?
LAURA. Yes. I remember what a beautiful voice you had.
JIM. When did you hear me sing?

     [*Voice Offstage in the Pause*]

     Voice [*offstage*].

          O blow, ye winds, heigh-ho.
          A-roving I will go!
          I'm off to my love
          With a boxing glove—
          Ten thousand miles away!

JIM. You say you've heard me sing?
LAURA. Oh, yes! Yes, very often . . . I—don't suppose you remember me—at all?
JIM [*smiling doubtfully*]. You know I have an idea I've seen you before. I had
     that idea soon as you opened the door. It seemed almost like I was about to
     remember your name. But the name that I started to call you—wasn't a
     name! And so I stopped myself before I said it.
LAURA. Wasn't it—Blue Roses?
JIM [*springs up, grinning*]. Blue Roses! My gosh, yes—Blue Roses! That's what I
     had on my tongue when you opened the door! Isn't it funny what tricks
     your memory plays? I didn't connect you with the high school somehow
     or other. But that's where it was; it was high school. I didn't even know
     you were Shakespeare's sister! Gosh, I'm sorry.
LAURA. I didn't expect you to. You—barely knew me!
JIM. But we did have a speaking acquaintance, huh?
LAURA. Yes, we—spoke to each other.
JIM. When did you recognize me?
LAURA. Oh, right away!
JIM. Soon as I came in the door?   ou. I knew that Tom
LAURA. When I heard your name I thought it was pro᾿ou came in the door—
     used to know you a little in high school. So
          Well, then I was—sure.   ᾿as—too surprised!
JIM. Why didn't you *say* something, then? ᾿unny!
LAURA [*breathlessly*]. I didn't know wha᾿
JIM. For goodness' sakes! You know, ᾿ether?
LAURA. Yes! Yes, isn't it, though. .
JIM. Didn't we have a class in s᾿
LAURA. Yes, we did.
JIM. What class was that?
LAURA. It was—singin᾿
JIM. Aw!

LAURA. I sat across the aisle from you in the Aud.

JIM. Aw.

LAURA. Mondays, Wednesdays and Fridays.

JIM. Now I remember—you always came in late.

LAURA. Yes, it was so hard for me, getting upstairs. I had a brace on my leg—it clumped so loud!

JIM. I never heard any clumping.

LAURA [*wincing at the recollection*]. To me it sounded like—thunder!

JIM. Well, well, well. I never even noticed.

LAURA. And everybody was seated before I came in. I had to walk in front of all those people. My seat was in the back row. I had to go clumping all the way up the aisle with everyone watching!

JIM. You shouldn't have been self-conscious.

LAURA. I know, but I was. It was always such a relief when the singing started.

JIM. Aw, yes, I've placed you now! I used to call you Blue Roses. How was it that I got started calling you that?

LAURA. I was out of school a little while with pleurosis. When I came back you asked me what was the matter. I said I had pleurosis—you thought I said Blue Roses. That's what you always called me after that!

JIM. I hope you didn't mind.

LAURA. Oh, no—I liked it. You see, I wasn't acquainted with many—people. . . .

JIM. As I remember you sort of stuck by yourself.

LAURA. I—I—never had much luck at—making friends.

JIM. I don't see why you wouldn't.

LAURA. Well, I—started out badly.

JIM. You mean being—

LAURA. Yes, it sort of—stood between me—

JIM. You shouldn't have let it!

LAURA. I know, but it did, and—

JIM. You were shy with people!

LAURA. I tried not to be but never could—

JIM. Overcome it?

LAURA. No, I—I never could!

JIM. I guess being shy is something you have to work out of kind of gradually.

LAURA [*sorrowfully*]. Yes—I guess it—

JIM. Takes time!

LAURA. Yes—

JIM. People are not so dreadful when you know them. That's what you have to remember! And everybody has problems, not just you, but practically everybody has got some problems. You think of yourself as having the only problems, as being the only one who is disappointed. But just look around you and you'll see lots of people as disappointed as you are. For instance, I hoped when I was going to high school that I would be further along at this time, years after, than I am now—You remember that wonderful write-up I had in *The Torch*?

LAURA. Yes! [*She rises and crosses to table.*]

JIM. It said I was bound to succeed in anything I went into! [LAURA *returns with the annual.*] Holy Jeez! *The Torch!* [*He accepts it reverently. They smile across it with mutual wonder.* LAURA *crouches beside him and they begin to turn through it.* LAURA's *shyness is dissolving in his warmth.*]

LAURA. Here you are in *Pirates of Penzance!*

JIM [*wistfully*]. I sang the baritone lead in that operetta.

LAURA [*rapidly*]. So—*beautifully!*

JIM [*protesting*]. Aw—

LAURA. Yes, yes—beautifully—beautifully!

JIM. You heard me?

LAURA. All three times!

JIM. No!

LAURA. Yes!

JIM. All three performances?

LAURA [*looking down*]. Yes.

JIM. Why?

LAURA. I—wanted to ask you to—autograph my program.

JIM. Why didn't you ask me to?

LAURA. You were always surrounded by your own friends so much that I never had a chance to.

JIM. You should have just—

LAURA. Well, I—thought you might think I was—

JIM. Thought I might think you was—what?

LAURA. Oh—

JIM [*with reflective relish*]. I was beleaguered by females in those days.

LAURA. You were terribly popular!

JIM. Yeah—

LAURA. You had such a—friendly way—

JIM. I was spoiled in high school.

LAURA. Everybody—liked you!

JIM. Including you?

LAURA. I—yes, I—I did, too—[*She gently closes the book in her lap.*]

JIM. Well, well, well!—Give me that program, Laura. [*She hands it to him. He signs it with a flourish.*] There you are—better late than never!

LAURA. Oh, I—what a—surprise!

JIM. My signature isn't worth very much right now. But some day—maybe—it will increase in value! Being disappointed is one thing and being discouraged is something else. I am disappointed but I'm not discouraged. I'm twenty-three years old. How old are you?

LAURA. I'll be twenty-four in June.

JIM. That's not old age!

LAURA. No, but—

JIM. You finished high school?

LAURA [*with difficulty*]. I didn't go back.

JIM. You mean you dropped out?

LAURA. I made bad grades in my final examinations. [*She rises and replaces the book and the program. Her voice strained.*] How is—Emily Meisenbach getting along?

JIM. Oh, that kraut-head!

LAURA. Why do you call her that?

JIM. That's what she was.

LAURA. You're not still—going with her?

JIM. I never see her.

LAURA. It said in the Personal Section that you were—engaged!

JIM. I know, but I wasn't impressed by that—propaganda!

LAURA. It wasn't—the truth?

JIM. Only in Emily's optimistic opinion!

LAURA. Oh—

[Legend: "What Have You Done since High School?"]

JIM *lights a cigarette and leans indolently back on his elbows smiling at* LAURA *with a warmth and charm which light her inwardly with altar candles. She remains by the table and turns in her hands a piece of glass to cover her tumult.*

JIM *[after several reflective puffs on a cigarette]*. What have you done since high school? *[She seems not to hear him.]* Huh? *[*LAURA *looks up.]* I said what have you done since high school, Laura?

LAURA. Nothing much.

JIM. You must have been doing something these six long years.

LAURA. Yes.

JIM. Well, then, such as what?

LAURA. I took a business course at business college—

JIM. How did that work out?

LAURA. Well, not very—well—I had to drop out, it gave me—indigestion—

JIM *laughs gently.*

JIM. What are you doing now?

LAURA. I don't do anything—much. Oh, please don't think I sit around doing nothing! My glass collection takes up a good deal of my time. Glass is something you have to take good care of.

JIM. What did you say—about glass?

LAURA. Collection I said—I have one—*[She clears her throat and turns away again, acutely shy.]*

JIM *[abruptly]*. You know what I judge to be the trouble with you? Inferiority complex! Know what that is? That's what they call it when someone low-rates himself! I understand it because I had it, too. Although my case was not so aggravated as yours seems to be. I had it until I took up public speaking, developed my voice, and learned that I had an aptitude for science. Before that time I never thought of myself as being outstanding in any way whatsoever! Now I've never made a regular study of it, but I have a friend who says I can analyze people better than doctors that make a profession of it. I don't claim that to be necessarily true, but I can sure guess a person's psychology, Laura! *[Takes out his gum.]* Excuse me, Laura. I always take it out when the flavor is gone. I'll use this scrap of paper to wrap it in. I know how it is to get it stuck on a shoe. Yep—that's what I judge to be your principal trouble. A lack of confidence in yourself as a person. You don't have the proper amount of faith in yourself. I'm basing that fact on a number of your remarks and also on certain observations I've made. For instance that clumping you thought was so awful in high school. You say that you even dreaded to walk into class. You see what you did? You dropped out of school, you gave up an education because of a clump, which as far as I know was practically nonexistent! A little physical defect is what you have. Hardly noticeable even! Magnified thousands of times by imagination! You know what my strong advice to you is? Think of yourself as *superior* in some way!

LAURA. In what way would I think?

JIM. Why, man alive, Laura! Just look about you a little. What do you see? A world full of common people! All of 'em born and all of 'em going to die! Which of them has one-tenth of your good points! Or mine! Or anyone else's, as far as that goes—Gosh! Everybody excels in some one thing. Some in many! [*Unconsciously glances at himself in the mirror.*] All you've got to do is discover in *what!* Take me, for instance. [*He adjusts his tie at the mirror.*] My interest happens to he in electrodynamics. I'm taking a course in radio engineering at night school, Laura, on top of a fairly responsible job at the warehouse. I'm taking that course and studying public speaking.

LAURA. Ohhhh.

JIM. Because I believe in the future of television! [*Turning back to her.*] I wish to be ready to go up right along with it. Therefore I'm planning to get in on the ground floor. In fact, I've already made the right connections and all that remains is for the industry itself to get under way! Full steam—[*His eyes are starry.*] Knowledge—Zzzzzp! Money—Zzzzzzp!—Power! That's the cycle democracy is built on! [*His attitude is convincingly dynamic. Laura stares at him, even her shyness eclipsed in her absolute wonder. He suddenly grins.*] I guess you think I think a lot of myself!

LAURA. No—o-o-o, I—

JIM. Now how about you? Isn't there something you take more interest in than anything else?

LAURA. Well, I do—as I said—have my—glass collection—

A peal of girlish laughter from the kitchen.

JIM. I'm not right sure I know what you're talking about. What kind of glass is it?

LAURA. Little articles of it, they're ornaments mostly! Most of them are little animals made out of glass, the tiniest little animals in the world. Mother calls them a glass menagerie! Here's an example of one, if you'd like to see it! This one is one of the oldest. It's nearly thirteen. [*He stretches out his hand.*] [*Music: "The Glass Menagerie."*] Oh, be careful—if you breathe, it breaks!

JIM. I'd better not take it. I'm pretty clumsy with things.

LAURA. Go on, I trust you with him! [*Places it in his palm.*] There now—you're holding him gently! Hold him over the light, he loves the light! You see how the light shines through him?

JIM. It sure does shine!

LAURA. I shouldn't be partial, but he is my favorite one.

JIM. What kind of a thing is this one supposed to be?

LAURA. Haven't you noticed the single horn on his forehead?

JIM. A unicorn, huh?

LAURA. Mmm-hmmm!

JIM. Unicorns, aren't they extinct in the modern world?

LAURA. I know!

JIM. Poor little fellow, he must feel sort of lonesome.

LAURA [*smiling*]. Well, if he does he doesn't complain about it. He stays on a shelf with some horses that don't have horns and all of them seem to get along nicely together.

JIM. How do you know?

LAURA [*lightly*]. I haven't heard any arguments among them!

JIM [*grinning*]. No arguments, huh? Well, that's a pretty good sign! Where shall I set him?

LAURA. Put him on the table. They all like a change of scenery once in a while!

JIM [*stretching*]. Well, well, well, well—Look how big my shadow is when I stretch!

LAURA. Oh, oh, yes—it stretches across the ceiling!

JIM [*crossing to door*]. I think it's stopped raining. [*Opens fire-escape door.*] Where does the music come from?

LAURA. From the Paradise Dance Hall across the alley.

JIM. How about cutting the rug a little, Miss Wingfield?

LAURA. Oh, I—

JIM. Or is your program filled up? Let me have a look at it. [*Grasps imaginary card.*] Why, every dance is taken! I'll just have to scratch some out. [*Waltz Music: "La Golondrina."*] Ahhh, a waltz! [*He executes some sweeping turns by himself then holds his arms toward* LAURA.]

LAURA [*breathlessly*]. I—can't dance!

JIM. There you go, that inferiority stuff!

LAURA. I've never danced in my life!

JIM. Come on, try!

LAURA. Oh, but I'd step on you!

JIM. I'm not made out of glass.

LAURA. How—how—how do we start?

JIM. Just leave it to me. You hold your arms out a little.

LAURA. Like this?

JIM. A little bit higher. Right. Now don't tighten up, that's the main thing about it—relax.

LAURA [*laughing breathlessly*]. It's hard not to.

JIM. Okay.

LAURA. I'm afraid you can't budge me.

JIM. What do you bet I can't? [*He swings her into motion.*]

LAURA. Goodness, yes, you can!

JIM. Let yourself go, now, Laura, just let yourself go.

LAURA. I'm—

JIM. Come on!

LAURA. Trying!

JIM. Not so stiff—Easy does it!

LAURA. I know but I'm—

JIM. Loosen th' backbone! There now, that's a lot better.

LAURA. Am I?

JIM. Lots, lots better! [*He moves her about the room in a clumsy waltz.*]

LAURA. Oh, my!

JIM. Ha-ha!

LAURA. Goodness, yes you can!

JIM. Ha-ha-ha! [*They suddenly bump into the table.* JIM *stops.*] What did we hit on?

LAURA. Table.

JIM. Did something fall off it? I think—

LAURA. Yes.

JIM. I hope that it wasn't the little glass horse with the horn!

LAURA. Yes.

JIM. Aw, aw, aw. Is it broken?

LAURA. Now it is just like all the other horses.

JIM. It's lost its—

LAURA. Horn! It doesn't matter. Maybe it's a blessing in disguise.

JIM. You'll never forgive me. I bet that that was your favorite piece of glass.

LAURA. I don't have favorites much. It's no tragedy, Freckles. Glass breaks so easily. No matter how careful you are. The traffic jars the shelves and things fall off them.

JIM. Still I'm awfully sorry that I was the cause.

LAURA [*smiling*]. I'll just imagine he had an operation. The horn was removed to make him feel less—freakish! [*They both laugh.*] Now he will feel more at home with the other horses, the ones that don't have horns . . .

JIM. Ha-ha, that's very funny! [*Suddenly serious.*] I'm glad to see that you have a sense of humor. You know—you're—well—very different! Surprisingly different from anyone else I know! [*His voice becomes soft and hesitant with a genuine feeling.*] Do you mind me telling you that? [LAURA *is abashed beyond speech.*] You make me feel sort of—I don't know how to put it! I'm usually pretty good at expressing things, but—This is something that I don't know how to say! LAURA *touches her throat and clears it— turns the broken unicorn in her hands.*] [*Even softer*] Has anyone ever told you that you were pretty? [*Pause: Music.*] [LAURA *looks up slowly, with wonder, and shakes her head.*] Well, you are! In a very different way from anyone else. And all the nicer because of the difference, too. [*His voice becomes low and husky.* LAURA *turns away, nearly faint with the novelty of her emotions.*] I wish that you were my sister. I'd teach you to have some confidence in yourself. The different people are not like other people, but being different is nothing to be ashamed of. Because other people are not such wonderful people. They're one hundred times one thousand. You're one times one! They walk all over the earth. You just stay here. They're common as—weeds, but—you—well, you're *Blue Roses!*

[*Image on Screen: Blue Roses.*]

[*Music Changes.*]

LAURA. But blue is wrong for—roses . . .

JIM. It's right for you—You're—pretty!

LAURA. In what respect am I pretty?

JIM. In all respects—believe me! Your eyes—your hair—are pretty! Your hands are pretty! [*He catches hold of her hand.*] You think I'm making this up because I'm invited to dinner and have to be nice. Oh, I could do that! I could put on an act for you, Laura, and say lots of things without being very sincere. But this time I am. I'm talking to you sincerely. I happened to notice you had this inferiority complex that keeps you from feeling comfortable with people. Somebody needs to build your confidence up and make you proud instead of shy and turning away and—blushing— Somebody ought to—ought to—*kiss* you. Laura! [*His hand slips slowly up her arm to her shoulder.*] [*Music Swells Tumultuously.*] [*He suddenly turns her about and kisses her on the lips. When he releases her* LAURA *sinks on the sofa with a bright, dazed look.* JIM *backs away and fishes in his pocket for a cigarette.*] [*Legend on Screen: "Souvenir."*] Stumble-john! [*He lights the cigarette, avoiding her look. There is a peal of girlish laughter from* AMANDA *in the kitchen.* LAURA *slowly raises and opens her hand. It still contains the little broken glass animal. She looks at it with a tender, bewildered expression.*] Stumble-john! I shouldn't have done that—That was way off the beam. You don't smoke, do you? [*She looks up, smiling, not hearing the question. He sits beside her a lit-*

tle gingerly. She looks at him speechlessly—waiting. He coughs deco-
rously and moves a little farther aside as he considers the situation and
senses her feelings, dimly, with perturbation. Gently.] Would you—care
for a—mint? [*She doesn't seem to hear him but her look grows brighter*
even.] Peppermint—Life Saver? My pocket's a regular drug store—wherever I go . . . [*He pops a mint in his mouth. Then gulps and decides to*
make a clean breast of it. He speaks slowly and gingerly.] Laura, you
know, if I had a sister like you, I'd do the same thing as Tom. I'd bring out
fellows—introduce her to them. The right type of boys of a type to—appreciate her. Only—well—he made a mistake about me. Maybe I've got
no call to be saying this. That may not have been the idea in having me
over. But what if it was? There's nothing wrong about that. The only trouble is that in my case—I'm not in a situation to—do the right thing. I can't
take down your number and say I'll phone. I can't call up next week
and—ask for a date. I thought I had better explain the situation in case
you misunderstood it and—hurt your feelings. . . . [*Pause. Slowly, very*
slowly, LAURA'*s look changes, her eyes returning slowly from his to the*
ornament in her palm.]

AMANDA *utters another gay laugh in the kitchen.*

LAURA [*faintly*]. You—won't—call again?
JIM. No, Laura, I can't [*He rises from the sofa.*] As I was just explaining, I've—
got strings on me, Laura, I've—been going steady! I go out all the time with
a girl named Betty. She's a home-girl like you, and Catholic, and Irish, and
in a great many ways we—get along fine. I met her last summer on a moonlight boat trip up the river to Alton, on the *Majestic.* Well—right away
from the start it was—love! [*Legend: Love!*] [LAURA *sways slightly forward*
and grips the arm of the sofa. He fails to notice, now enrapt in his own
comfortable being.] Being in love has made a new man of me! [*Leaning*
stiffly forward, clutching the arm of the sofa, LAURA *struggles visibly with*
her storm. But JIM *is oblivious, she is a long way off.*] The power of love
is really pretty tremendous! Love is something that—changes the whole
world, Laura! [*The storm abates a little and* LAURA *leans back. He notices*
her again.] It happened that Betty's aunt took sick, she got a wire and had
to go to Centralia. So Tom—when he asked me to dinner—I naturally just
accepted the invitation, not knowing that you—that he—that I—[*He stops*
awkwardly.] Huh—I'm a stumble-john! [*He flops back on the sofa. The*
holy candles in the altar of LAURA'*s face have been snuffed out! There is*
a look of almost infinite desolation. JIM *glances at her uneasily.*] I wish
that you would—say something. [*She bites her lip which was trembling*
and then bravely smiles. She opens her hand again on the broken glass
ornament. Then she gently takes his hand and raises it level with her
own. She carefully places the unicorn in the palm of his hand, then
pushes his fingers closed upon it.] What are you—doing that for? You
want me to have him?—Laura? [*She nods.*] What for?
LAURA. A—souvenir . . .

She rises unsteadily and crouches beside the victrola to wind it up.

[*Legend on Screen: "Things Have a Way of Turning Out So Badly."*]

[*Or Image: "Gentleman Caller Waving Good-Bye!—Gaily."*]

At this moment AMANDA *rushes brightly back in the front room. She bears a pitcher of fruit punch in an old-fashioned cut-glass pitcher and a plate of macaroons. The plate has a gold border and poppies painted on it.*

AMANDA. Well, well, well! Isn't the air delightful after the shower? I've made you children a little liquid refreshment. [*Turns gaily to the gentleman caller.*] Jim, do you know that song about lemonade?

"Lemonade, lemonade
Made in the shade and stirred with a spade—
Good enough for any old maid!"

JIM [*uneasily*]. Ha-ha! No—I never heard it.

AMANDA. Why, Laura! You look so serious!

JIM. We were having a serious conversation.

AMANDA. Good! Now you're better acquainted!

JIM [*uncertainly*]. Ha-ha! Yes.

AMANDA. You modern young people are much more serious-minded than my generation. I was so gay as a girl!

JIM. You haven't changed, Mrs. Wingfield.

AMANDA. Tonight I'm rejuvenated! The gaiety of the occasion, Mr. O'Connor! [*She tosses her head with a peal of laughter. Spills lemonade.*] Oooo! I'm baptizing myself!

JIM. Here—let me—

AMANDA [*setting the pitcher down*]. There now. I discovered we had some maraschino cherries. I dumped them in, juice and all!

JIM. You shouldn't have gone to that trouble, Mrs. Wingfield.

AMANDA. Trouble, trouble? Why it was loads of fun! Didn't you hear me cutting up in the kitchen? I bet your ears were burning! I told Tom how outdone with him I was for keeping you to himself so long a time! He should have brought you over much, much sooner! Well, now that you've found your way, I want you to be a very frequent caller! Not just occasional but all the time. Oh, we're going to have a lot of gay times together! I see them coming! Mmm, just breathe that air! So fresh, and the moon's so pretty! I'll skip back out—I know where my place is when young folks are having a—serious conversation!

JIM. Oh, don't go out, Mrs. Wingfield. The fact of the matter is I've got to be going.

AMANDA. Going, now? You're joking! Why, it's only the shank of the evening, Mr. O'Connor!

JIM. Well, you know how it is.

AMANDA. You mean you're a young workingman and have to keep workingmen's hours. We'll let you off early tonight. But only on the condition that next time you stay later. What's the best night for you? Isn't Saturday night the best night for you workingmen?

JIM. I have a couple of time-clocks to punch, Mrs. Wingfield. One at morning, another one at night!

AMANDA. My, but you *are* ambitious! You work at night, too?

JIM. No, Ma'am, not work but—Betty! [*He crosses deliberately to pick up his hat. The band at the Paradise Dance Hall goes into a tender waltz.*]

AMANDA. Betty? Betty? Who's—Betty! [*There is an ominous cracking sound in the sky.*]

JIM. Oh, just a girl. The girl I go steady with! [*He smiles charmingly. The sky falls.*]

[Legend: "The Sky Falls."]

AMANDA *[a long-drawn exhalation]*. Ohhh . . . Is it a serious romance, Mr. O'Connor?

JIM. We're going to be married the second Sunday in June.

AMANDA. Ohhhh—how nice! Tom didn't mention that you were engaged to be married.

JIM. The cat's not out of the bag at the warehouse yet. You know how they are. They call you Romeo and stuff like that. *[He stops at the oval mirror to put on his hat. He carefully shapes the brim and the crown to give a discreetly dashing effect.]* It's been a wonderful evening, Mrs. Wingfield. I guess this is what they mean by Southern hospitality.

AMANDA. It really wasn't anything at all.

JIM. I hope it don't seem like I'm rushing off. But I promised Betty I'd pick her up at the Wabash depot, an' by the time I get my jalopy down there her train'll be in. Some women are pretty upset if you keep 'em waiting.

AMANDA. Yes, I know—The tyranny of women! *[Extends her hand.]* Good-bye, Mr. O'Connor. I wish you luck—and happiness—and success! All three of them, and so does Laura!—Don't you, Laura?

LAURA. Yes!

JIM *[taking her hand]*. Goodbye, Laura. I'm certainly going to treasure that souvenir. And don't you forget the good advice I gave you. *[Raises his voice to a cheery shout.]* So long, Shakespeare! Thanks again, ladies—good night!

He grins and ducks jauntily out.

Still bravely grimacing, AMANDA *closes the door on the gentleman caller. Then she turns back to the room with a puzzled expression. She and* LAURA *don't dare to face each other.* LAURA *crouches beside the victrola to wind it.*

AMANDA *[faintly]*. Things have a way of turning out so badly. I don't believe that I would play the victrola. Well, well—well—Our gentleman caller was engaged to be married! Tom!

TOM *[from back]*. Yes, Mother?

AMANDA. Come in here a minute. I want to tell you something awfully funny.

TOM *[enters with macaroon and a glass of the lemonade]*. Has the gentleman caller gotten away already?

AMANDA. The gentleman caller has made an early departure. What a wonderful joke you played on us!

TOM. How do you mean?

AMANDA. You didn't mention that he was engaged to be married.

TOM. Jim? Engaged?

AMANDA. That's what he just informed us.

TOM. I'll be jiggered! I didn't know about that.

AMANDA. That seems very peculiar.

TOM. What's peculiar about it?

AMANDA. Didn't you call him your best friend down at the warehouse?

TOM. He is, but how did I know?

AMANDA. It seems extremely peculiar that you wouldn't know your best friend was going to be married!

TOM. The warehouse is where I work, not where I know things about people!

AMANDA. You don't know things anywhere! You live in a dream; you manufacture illusions! [*He crosses to door.*] Where are you going?

TOM. I'm going to the movies.

AMANDA. That's right, now that you've had us make such fools of ourselves. The effort, the preparations, all the expense! The new floor lamp, the rug, the clothes for Laura! All for what? To entertain some other girl's fiancé! Go to the movies, go! Don't think about us, a mother deserted, an unmarried sister who's crippled and has no job! Don't let anything interfere with your selfish pleasure! Just go, go, go—to the movies!

TOM. All right, I will! The more you shout about my selfishness to me the quicker I'll go, and I won't go to the movies!

AMANDA. Go, then! Then go to the moon—you selfish dreamer!

TOM *smashes his glass on the floor. He plunges out on the fire-escape, slamming the door.* LAURA *screams—cut by door.*

Dance-hall music up. TOM *goes to the rail and grips it desperately, lifting his face in the chill white moonlight penetrating the narrow abyss of the alley.*

[Legend on Screen: "And So Good-Bye . . ."]

TOM*'s closing speech is timed with the interior pantomime. The interior scene is played as though viewed through sound-proof glass.* AMANDA *appears to be making a comforting speech to* LAURA *who is huddled upon the sofa. Now that we cannot hear the mother's speech, her silliness is gone and she has dignity and tragic beauty.* LAURA*'s dark hair hides her face until at the end of the speech she lifts it to smile at her mother.* AMANDA*'s gestures are slow and graceful, almost dancelike, as she comforts the daughter. At the end of her speech she glances a moment at the father's picture—then withdraws through the portieres. At close of* TOM*'s speech,* LAURA *blows out the candles, ending the play.*

TOM. I didn't go to the moon, I went much further—for time is the longest distance between two places—Not long after that I was fired for writing a poem on the lid of a shoe-box. I left Saint Louis. I descended the steps of this fire-escape for a last time and followed, from then on, in my father's footsteps, attempting to find in motion what was lost in space—I traveled around a great deal. The cities swept about me like dead leaves, leaves that were brightly colored but torn away from the branches. I would have stopped, but I was pursued by something. It always came upon me unawares, taking me altogether by surprise. Perhaps it was a familiar bit of music. Perhaps it was only a piece of transparent glass—Perhaps I am walking along a street at night, in some strange city, before I have found companions. I pass the lighted window of a shop where perfume is sold. The window is filled with pieces of colored glass, tiny transparent bottles in delicate colors, like bits of a shattered rainbow. Then all at once my sister touches my shoulder. I turn around and look into her eyes . . . Oh, Laura, Laura, I tried to leave you behind me, but I am more faithful than I intended to be! I reach for a cigarette, I cross the street, I run into the movies or a bar, I buy a drink, I speak to the nearest stranger—anything that can blow your candles out! [LAURA *bends over the candles.*]—for nowadays the world is lit by lightning! Blow out your candles, Laura—and so good-bye . . .

She blows the candles out.

[The Scene Dissolves.]

[1944]

Tennessee Williams's Production Notes

Being a "memory play," *The Glass Menagerie* can be presented with unusual freedom of convention. Because of its considerably delicate or tenuous material, atmospheric touches and subtleties of direction play a particularly important part. Expressionism and all other unconventional techniques in drama have only one valid aim, and that is a closer approach to truth. When a play employs unconventional techniques, it is not, or certainly shouldn't be, trying to escape its responsibility of dealing with reality, or interpreting experience, but is actually or should be attempting to find a closer approach, a more penetrating and vivid expression of things as they are. The straight realistic play with its genuine frigidaire and authentic ice cubes, its characters that speak exactly as its audience speaks, corresponds to the academic landscape and has the same virtue of a photographic likeness. Everyone should know nowadays the unimportance of the photographic in art: that truth, life, or reality is an organic thing which the poetic imagination can represent or suggest, in essence, only through transformation, through changing into other forms than those which were merely present in appearance.

These remarks are not meant as comments only on this particular play. They have to do with a conception of a new, plastic theater which must take the place of the exhausted theater of realistic conventions if the theater is to resume vitality as a part of our culture.

The Screen Device

There is *only one important difference between the original and acting version of the play* and that is the *omission* in the latter of the device which I tentatively included in my *original* script. This device was the use of a screen on which were projected magic-lantern slides bearing images or titles. I do not regret the omission of this device from the . . . Broadway production. The extraordinary power of Miss Taylor's performance made it suitable to have the utmost simplicity in the physical production. But I think it may be interesting to some readers to see how this device was conceived. So I am putting it into the published manuscript. These images and legends, projected from behind, were cast on a section of wall between the front-room and dining-room areas, which should be indistinguishable from the rest when not in use.

The purpose of this will probably be apparent. It is to give accent to certain values in each scene. Each scene contains a particular point (or several) which is structurally the most important. In an episodic play, such as this, the basic structure or narrative line may be obscured from the audience; the effect may seem fragmentary rather than architectural. This may not be the fault of the play so much as a lack of attention in the audience. The legend or image upon the screen will strengthen the effect of what is merely allusion in the writing and allow the primary point to be made more simply and lightly than if the entire responsibility were on the spoken lines. Aside from this structural value, I think the screen will have a definite emotional appeal, less definable but just as important. An imaginative producer or director may invent many other uses for this device than those indicated in the present script. In fact the possibilities of the device seem much larger to me than the instance of this play can possibly utilize.

The Music

Another extra-literary accent in this play is provided by the use of music. A single recurring tune, "The Glass Menagerie," is used to give emotional emphasis to suitable passages. This tune is like circus music, not when you are on the grounds or in the immediate vicinity of the parade, but when you are at some distance and very likely thinking of something else. It seems under those circumstances to continue almost interminably and it weaves in and out of your preoccupied consciousness; then it is the lightest, most delicate music in the world and perhaps the saddest. It expresses the surface vivacity of life with the underlying strain of immutable and inexpressible sorrow. When you look at a piece of delicately spun glass you think of two things: how beautiful it is and how easily it can be broken. Both of those ideas should be woven into the recurring tune, which dips in and out of the play as if it were carried on a wind that changes. It serves as a thread of connection and allusion between the narrator with his separate point in time and space and the subject of his story. Between each episode it returns as reference to the emotion, nostalgia, which is the first condition of the play. It is primarily Laura's music and therefore comes out most clearly when the play focuses upon her and the lovely fragility of glass which is her image.

The Lighting

The lighting in the play is not realistic. In keeping with the atmosphere of memory, the stage is dim. Shafts of light are focused on selected areas or actors, sometimes in contradistinction to what is the apparent center. For instance, in the quarrel scene between Tom and Amanda, in which Laura has no active part, the clearest pool of light is on her figure. This is also true of the supper scene. The light upon Laura should be distinct from the others, having a peculiar pristine clarity such as light used in early religious portraits of female saints or madonnas. A certain correspondence to light in religious paintings, such as El Greco's, where the figures are radiant in atmosphere that is relatively dusky, could be effectively used throughout the play. (It will also permit a more effective use of the screen.) A free, imaginative use of light can be of enormous value in giving a mobile, plastic quality to plays of a more or less static nature.

Topics for Critical Thinking and Writing

1. When produced in New York, the magic-lantern slides were omitted. Is the device an extraneous gimmick? Might it even interfere with the play, by oversimplifying and thus in a way belittling the actions?
2. What does the victrola offer to Laura? Why is the typewriter a better symbol (for the purposes of the play) than, say, a piano? After all, Laura could have been taking piano lessons. Explain the symbolism of the unicorn, and the loss of its horn. What is Laura saying to Jim in the gesture of giving him the unicorn?

3. Laura escapes to her glass menagerie. To what do Amanda and Tom escape? How complete is Tom's escape at the end of the play?

4. What is meant at the end when Laura blows out the candles? Is she blowing out illusions? Or life? Or both?

5. Did Williams make a slip in having Amanda say Laura is "crippled" on page 393?

6. There is an implication that had Jim not been going steady he might have rescued Laura, but Jim also seems to represent (for example, in his lines about money and power) the corrupt outside world that no longer values humanity. Is this a slip on Williams's part, or is it an interesting complexity?

7. On page 393 Williams says, in a stage direction, "Now that we cannot hear the mother's speech, her silliness is gone and she has dignity and tragic beauty." Is Williams simply dragging in the word "tragic" because of its prestige, or is it legitimate? "Tragedy" is often distinguished from "pathos": In the tragic, the suffering is experienced by persons who act and are in some measure responsible for their suffering; in the pathetic, the suffering is experienced by the passive and the innocent. For example, in discussing Aeschylus's *The Suppliants* (in *Greek Tragedy*), H. D. F. Kitto says, "The Suppliants are not only pathetic, as the victims of outrage, but also tragic, as the victims of their own misconceptions." Given this distinction, to what extent are Amanda and Laura tragic? pathetic?

Reading (and Writing About) Poetry

THE SPEAKER AND THE POET

The **speaker,** or **voice,** or **mask,** or **persona** (Latin for *mask*) that speaks a poem is not usually identical with the poet who writes it. The author assumes a role, or counterfeits the speech of a person in a particular situation. The nineteenth-century English poet Robert Browning, for instance, in "My Last Duchess" invented a Renaissance Italian duke who, in his palace, talks about his first wife and his art collection with an emissary from a count who is negotiating to offer his daughter in marriage to the duke.

In reading a poem, then, the first and most important question to ask yourself is this: Who is speaking? If an audience and a setting are suggested, keep them in mind too, although these are not always indicated in a poem. Consider, for example, the following poem.

EMILY DICKINSON (1830–1886)

I'm Nobody! Who are you?
Are you—Nobody—too?
Then there's a pair of us!
Don't tell! they'd banish us—you know!   4

How dreary—to be—Somebody!
How public—like a Frog—
To tell your name—the livelong June—
To an admiring Bog!   8

[1861?]

We can't quite say that the speaker is Emily Dickinson, though if we have read a fair number of her poems we can say that the voice in this poem is familiar, and perhaps here we *can* talk of Dickinson rather than of "the speaker of the poem," since this speaker (unlike Browning's Renaissance duke) clearly is not a figure utterly remote from the poet.

Let's consider the sort of person we hear in "I'm Nobody! Who are you?" (Read it aloud, to see if you agree with what we say. In fact, you should test each of our assertions by reading the poem aloud.)

- The voice in the first line is rather like that of a child playing a game with a friend.
- In the second and third lines the speaker sees the reader as a fellow spirit ("Are you—Nobody—too?") and invites the reader to join her ("Then there's a pair of us!"), to form a sort of conspiracy of silence against outsiders ("Don't tell!").

In "they'd banish us," however, we hear a word that a child would not be likely to use, and we probably feel that the speaker is a shy but (with the right companion) playful adult, who here is speaking to an intimate friend, the reader. By means of "banish," a word that brings to mind images of a king's court, the speaker almost comically inflates and thereby makes fun of the "they" who are opposed to "us."

In the second stanza, or we might better say in the space between the two stanzas, the speaker puts aside the childlike manner. In "How dreary," the first words of the second stanza, we hear a sophisticated voice, one might even say a world-weary voice or a voice perhaps with more than a touch of condescension. But since by now we are paired with the speaker in a conspiracy against outsiders, we enjoy the contrast that the speaker makes between the Nobodies and the Somebodies. Who are these Somebodies, these people who would imperiously "banish" the speaker and the friend? What are the Somebodies like?

> How dreary—to be—Somebody!
> How public—like a Frog—
> To tell your name—the livelong June—
> To an admiring Bog!

The last two lines do at least two things:

- They amusingly explain to the speaker's new friend (the reader) in what way a Somebody is public (it proclaims its presence all day), and
- they indicate the absurdity of the Somebody-Frog's behavior (the audience is "an admiring Bog").

By the end of the poem we are quite convinced that it is better to be a Nobody (like Dickinson and the reader?) than a Somebody (a loudmouth).

Dickinson did not always speak in this persona, however. In "Wild Nights," probably written in the same year as "I'm Nobody! Who are you?", Dickinson speaks as an impassioned lover, but we need not assume that the beloved is actually in the presence of the lover. In fact, since the second line says, "Were I with thee," the reader must assume that the person addressed is *not* present. The poem apparently represents a state of mind—a sort of talking to oneself—rather than an address to another person.

> Wild Nights—Wild Nights,
> Were I with Thee
> Wild Nights should be
> Our luxury

Futile—the Winds
To a Heart in port—
Done with the Compass—
Done with the Chart!   8

Rowing in Eden—
Ah, the Sea!
Might I but moor—Tonight—
In Thee.   12

[c. 1861]

Clearly the speaker is someone passionately in love. The following questions invite you to look more closely at how the speaker of "Wild Nights" is characterized.

✎ Topics for Critical Thinking and Writing

1. How does this poem communicate the speaker's state of mind? For example, in the first stanza (lines 1–4), what—beyond the meaning of the words—is communicated by the repetition of "Wild Nights"? In the last stanza (lines 9–12), what is the tone of "Ah, the Sea!"? ("Tone" means something like emotional coloring, as for instance when one speaks of a "businesslike tone," a "bitter tone," or an "eager tone.")
2. Paraphrase (that is, put into your own words) the second stanza. What does this stanza communicate about the speaker's love for the beloved? Compare your paraphrase and the original. What does the form of the original sentences (the *omission,* for instance, of the verbs of lines 5 and 6 and of the subject in lines 7 and 8) communicate?
3. Paraphrase the last stanza. How does "Ah, the Sea!" fit into your paraphrase? If you had trouble fitting it in, do you think the poem would be better off without it? If not, why not?

The voice speaking a poem may, of course, have the ring of the author's own voice, and to make a distinction between speaker and author may at times seem perverse. In fact, some poetry (especially contemporary American poetry) is highly autobiographical. Still, even in autobiographical poems it may be convenient to distinguish between author and speaker. The speaker of a given poem is, let's say, Sylvia Plath in her role as parent, or Sylvia Plath in her role as daughter, not simply Sylvia Plath the poet.

THE LANGUAGE OF POETRY: DICTION AND TONE

How is a voice or mask or persona created? From the whole of language, the author consciously or unconsciously selects certain words and grammatical constructions; this selection constitutes the persona's diction. It is, then, partly by the diction that we come to know the speaker of a poem. Just as in life there is a difference between people who speak of a "belly button," a "navel," or an "umbilicus," so in poetry there is a difference between speakers who use one word rather than another. Of course it is also possible that all three of these words are part of a given speaker's vocabulary, and the speaker's choice among the three would depend on the situation. That is, in addressing a child, the speaker would probably use the word "belly button"; in addressing an adult other than a family member or close friend, the speaker might be more likely to use "navel"; and if the speaker is a physician addressing an audience of physicians, he or she might be most likely to use "umbilicus." But this is only to say, again, that the dramatic situation in which one finds oneself helps to define oneself, helps to establish the particular role that one is playing.

Of course some words are used in virtually all poems: *I, see, and,* and the like. Still, the grammatical constructions in which they appear may help to define the speaker. In Dickinson's "Wild Nights," for instance, expressions such as "Were I with Thee" and "Might I" indicate a speaker of an earlier century than ours, and probably an educated speaker.

Speakers have attitudes toward

- themselves,
- their subjects, and
- their audiences,

and, consciously or unconsciously, they choose their words, pitch, and modulation accordingly; all these add up to their tone. In written literature, tone must be detected without the aid of the ear, although it's a good idea to read poetry aloud, trying to find the appropriate tone of voice. That is, the reader must understand by the selection and sequence of words the way the words are meant to sound—playful, angry, confidential, or ironic, for example. The reader must catch what Frost calls "the speaking tone of voice somehow entangled in the words and fastened to the page for the ear of the imagination."

Writing About the Speaker

Robert Frost once said that "everything written is as good as it is dramatic. . . . [A poem is] heard as sung or spoken by a person in a scene—in a character, in a setting. By whom, where and when is the question. By the dreamer of a better world out in a storm in autumn; by a lover under a window at night." Suppose, in reading a poem Frost published in 1916, we try to establish "by whom, where and when" it is spoken. We may not be able to answer all three questions in great detail, but let's see what the poem suggests. As you read it, you'll notice—alerted by the quotation marks—that there are *two* speakers; the poem is a tiny drama. Thus, the closing quotation marks at the end of line 9 signal to us that the first speech is finished.

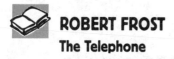 **ROBERT FROST**
The Telephone

"When I was just as far as I could walk
From here today
There was an hour
All still
When leaning with my head against a flower   5

I heard you talk.
Don't say I didn't, for I heard you say—
You spoke from that flower on the window sill—
Do you remember what it was you said?"

"First tell me what it was you thought you heard."   10
"Having found the flower and driven a bee away,
I leaned my head,
And holding by the stalk,
I listened and I thought I caught the word—
What was it? Did you call me by my name?   15
Or did you say—
Someone said 'Come'—I heard it as I bowed."

"I may have thought as much, but not aloud."

"Well, so I came."

[1916]

Suppose we ask: Who are these two speakers? What is their relationship? What's going on between them? Where are they? We don't think that these questions can be answered with absolute certainty, but we do think some answers are more probable than others. For instance, line 8 ("You spoke from that flower on the window sill") tells us that the speakers are in a room, probably of a home—rather than, say, in a railroad station—but we can't say whether the home is a farmhouse, or a house in a village, town, or city, or an apartment.

Let's put the questions (even if they may turn out to be unanswerable) into a more specific form.

✎ Topics for Critical Thinking and Writing

1. One speaker speaks lines 1–9, 11–17, and 19. The other speaks lines 10 and 18. Do you think you can tell the gender of each speaker? For sure, probably, or not at all? On what do you base your answer?
2. Try to visualize this miniature drama. In line 7 the first speaker says, "Don't say I didn't, . . ." What happens—what do you see in your mind's eye—after line 6 that causes the speaker to say this?
3. Why do you suppose the speaker of lines 10 and 18 says so little? How would you characterize the tone of these two lines? What sort of relationship do you think exists between the two speakers?
4. How would you characterize the tone of lines 11–17? Of the last line of the poem?

If you haven't jotted down your responses, we suggest that you do so before reading what follows.

Journal Entries

Given questions somewhat like the preceding ones, students were asked to try to identify the speakers by sex, to speculate on their relationship, and then to add whatever they wished to say. One student recorded the following thoughts:

These two people care about each other--maybe husband and wife, or lovers--and a man is doing most of the talking, though I can't prove it. He has walked as far as possible--that is, as far as possible and still get back on the same day--and he seemed to hear the other person call him. He claims that she spoke to him "from that flower on the window sill," and that's why I think the second person is a woman. She's at home, near the window. Somehow I even imagine she was at the window near the kitchen sink, maybe working while he was out on this long walk.

Then she speaks one line; she won't say if she did or didn't speak. She is very cautious, or suspicious: "First tell me what it was you thought you heard." Maybe she doesn't want to say something and then have her husband embarrass her by saying, "No, that's not what I thought." Or maybe she just doesn't feel like talking. Then he claims that he heard her speaking through a flower, as though the flower was a telephone, just as though it was hooked up to the flower on the window sill. But at first he won't say what he supposedly heard, or "thought" he heard. Instead, he says that maybe it was someone else: "Someone said 'Come'." Is he teasing her? Pretending that she may have a rival?

Then she speaks--again just one line, saying, "I may have thought as much, but not aloud." She won't admit that she did think this thought. And then the man says, "Well, so I came." Just like that; short and sweet. No more fancy talk about flowers as telephones. He somehow (through telepathy?) got the message, and so here he is. He seems like a sensitive guy, playful (the stuff about the flowers as telephones), but also he knows when to stop kidding around.

Another student also identified the couple as a man and woman and thought that this dialogue occurs after a quarrel:

As the poem goes on, we learn that the man wants to be with the woman, but it starts by telling us that he walked as far away from her as he could. He doesn't say why, but I think from the way the woman speaks later in the poem, they had a fight and he walked out. Then, when he stopped to rest, he thought he heard her voice. He really means that he was thinking of her and he was hoping she was thinking of him. So he returns, and he tells her he heard her calling him, but he pretends he heard her call him through a flower on their window sill. He can't admit that he was thinking about her. This seems very realistic to me; when someone feels a bit ashamed, it's sometimes hard to admit that you were wrong, and you want the other person to tell you that things are OK anyhow. And judging from line 7, when he says "Don't say I didn't," it seems that she is going to interrupt him by denying it. She is still angry, or maybe she doesn't want to make up too quickly. But he wants to pretend that she called him back. So when he says, "Do you remember what it was you said?" she won't admit that she was thinking of him, and she says, "First tell me what it was you thought you heard." She's testing him a little. So he goes on, with the business about flowers as telephones, and he says "someone" called him. He understands that she doesn't want to be pushed into forgiving him, so he backs off. Then she is willing to admit that she did think about him, but still she doesn't quite admit it. She is too proud to say openly that she wants him back but she does say, "I <u>may</u> have thought as much, . . ." And then, since they both have preserved their dignity, and also both have admitted that they care about the other, he can say, "Well, so I came."

Topics for Writing

1. In a paragraph or two or three, *evaluate* one of these two entries recorded by students. Do you think the comments are weak, plausible, or convincing, and *why* do you think so? Can you offer additional supporting evidence or, on the other hand, counterevidence? You may want to set forth your own scenario.
2. Two small questions: In a sentence or two, offer a suggestion as to why in line 11 Frost wrote, "and driven a bee away." After all, the bee plays no role in the poem. Second, in line 17 Frost has the speaker say, "I heard it as I bowed." Of course "bowed" rhymes with "aloud," but let's assume that the need for a rhyme did not dictate the choice of this word. Do you think "I heard it as I bowed" is better than, say, "I heard it as I waited," or "I heard it as I listened"? Why?
3. Write an essay of 500 words either about an uncanny experience of your own or about a quarrel or disagreement that was resolved in a way you had not expected.

FIGURATIVE LANGUAGE

Robert Frost has said, "Poetry provides the one permissible way of saying one thing and meaning another." This, of course, is an exaggeration, but it shrewdly suggests the importance of figurative language—saying one thing in terms of something else. Words have their literal meanings, but they can also be used so that something other than the literal meaning is implied. "My love is a rose" is, literally, nonsense, for a person is not a five-petaled, many-stamened plant with a spiny stem. But the suggestions of *rose* (at least for Robert Burns, who compared his beloved to a rose in the line "My love is like a red, red rose"), include "delicate beauty," "soft," and "perfumed," and thus the word *rose* can be meaningfully applied—figuratively rather than literally—to "my love." The girl is fragrant; her skin is perhaps like a rose in texture and (in some measure) color; she will not keep her beauty long. The poet, that is, has communicated his perception very precisely.

People who write about poetry have found it convenient to name the various kinds of figurative language. Just as the student of geology employs such special terms as *kames* and *eskers,* the student of literature employs special terms to name things as accurately as possible. The following paragraphs discuss the most common terms.

In a **simile**, items from different classes are explicitly compared by a connective such as *like, as,* or *than,* or by a verb such as *appears* or *seems.* (If the objects compared are from the same class, for example, "Tokyo is like Los Angeles," no simile is present.)

Float like a butterfly, sting like a bee.

—Muhammad Ali

It is a beauteous evening, calm and free.
The holy time is quiet as a Nun,
Breathless with adoration.

—William Wordsworth

All of our thoughts will be fairer than doves.

—Elizabeth Bishop

Seems he a dove? His feathers are but borrowed.

—Shakespeare

A **metaphor** asserts the identity, without a connective such as *like* or a verb such as *appears,* of terms that are literally incompatible.

Umbrellas clothe the beach in every hue.

—Elizabeth Bishop

                                                            The
whirlwind fife-and-drum of the storm bends the salt
marsh grass

—Marianne Moore

Two common types of metaphor have Greek names. In **synecdoche** the whole is replaced by the part, or the part by the whole. For example, *bread* in "Give us this day our daily bread" replaces all sorts of food. In **metonymy** something is named that replaces something closely related to it. For example, James Shirley names certain objects, using them to replace social classes (royalty and the peasantry) to which they are related:

Scepter and crown must tumble down
And in the dust be equal made
With the poor crooked scythe and spade.

The attribution of human feelings or characteristics or abstractions to inanimate objects is called **personification.**

            Memory,
that exquisite blunderer.

—Amy Clampitt

There's Wrath who has learnt every trick of guerilla warfare,
The shamming dead, the night-raid, the feinted retreat.

—W. H. Auden

Hope, thou bold taster of delight.

—*Richard Crashaw*

Crashaw's personification, "Hope, thou bold taster of delight," is also an example of the figure called **apostrophe,** an address to a person or thing not literally listening. Wordsworth begins a sonnet by apostrophizing Milton:

Milton, thou shouldst be living at this hour.

What conclusions can we draw about figurative language? First, figurative language, with its literally incompatible terms, forces the reader to attend to the **connotations** (suggestions, associations) rather than to the **denotations** (dictionary definitions) of one of the terms. Second, although figurative language is said to differ from ordinary speech, it is found in ordinary speech as well as in poetry and other literary forms. "It rained cats and dogs," "War is hell," "Don't be a pig," "Mr. Know-it-all," and other tired figures are part of our daily utterances. But through repeated use, these, and most of the figures we use, have lost whatever impact they once had and are only a shade removed from expressions which, though once figurative, have become literal: the *eye* of a needle, a *branch* office, the *face* of a clock. Third, good figurative language is usually concrete, condensed, and interesting.

We should mention, too, that figurative language is not limited to literary writers; it is used by scientists and social scientists—by almost everyone who is concerned with effective expression. Take, for instance, R. H. Tawney's *Religion and the Rise of Capitalism* (1926), a classic of economics. Among the titles of Tawney's chapters are "The Economic Revolution," "The Puritan Movement," and "The New Medicine for Poverty," all of which include metaphors. (To take only the last: Poverty is seen as a sick person or a disease.) Or take this sentence from Tawney (almost any sentence will serve equally well to reveal his bent for metaphor): "By the end of the sixteenth century the divorce between religious theory and economic realities had long been evident." Figures are not a fancy way of speaking. Quite the opposite: Writers use figures because they are forceful and exact. Literal language would not only be less interesting, it would also be less precise.

IMAGERY AND SYMBOLISM

When we read *rose* we may more or less call to mind a picture of a rose, or perhaps we are reminded of the odor or texture of a rose. Whatever in a poem appeals to any of our senses (including sensations of heat as well as of sight, smell, taste, touch, sound) is an image. In short, images are the sensory content of a work, whether literal or figurative. When a poet says "My rose" and is speaking about a rose, we have no figure of speech—though we still have an image. If, however, "My rose" is a shortened form of "My love is a rose," some would say that the poet is using a metaphor; but others would say that because the first term is omitted ("My love is"), the rose is a symbol. A poem about the transience of a rose might compel the reader to feel that the transience of female beauty is the larger theme even though it is never explicitly stated.

Some symbols are **conventional symbols**—people have agreed to accept them as standing for something other than their literal meanings: A poem about the cross would probably be about Christianity; similarly, the rose has long been a symbol for love. In Virginia Woolf's novel *Mrs. Dalloway,* the husband communicates his love by proffering this conventional symbol: "He was holding out flowers—roses, red and white roses. (But he could not bring himself to say he loved her; not in so many words.)" Objects that are not conventional symbols, however, may also give rise to rich, multiple, indefinable associations. The following poem uses the traditional symbol of the rose, but uses it in a nontraditional way:

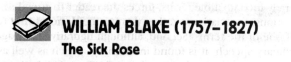 **WILLIAM BLAKE (1757–1827)**
The Sick Rose

O rose, thou art sick!
The invisible worm
That flies in the night,
In the howling storm,   4

Has found out thy bed
Of crimson joy,
And his dark secret love

Does thy life destroy.   8

[1794]

A reader might perhaps argue that the worm is invisible (line 2) merely because it is hidden within the rose, but an "invisible worm / That flies in the night" is more than a long, slender, soft-bodied, creeping animal; and a rose that has, or is, a "bed / Of crimson joy" is more than a gardener's rose. Blake's worm and rose suggest things beyond themselves—a stranger, more vibrant world than the world we are usually aware of. They are, in short, symbolic, though readers will doubtless differ in their interpretations. Perhaps we find ourselves half thinking, for example, that the worm is male, the rose female, and that the poem is about the violation of virginity. Or that the poem is about the destruction of beauty: Woman's beauty, rooted in joy, is destroyed by a power that feeds on her.

But these interpretations are not fully satisfying: The poem presents a worm and a rose, and yet it is not merely about a worm and a rose. These objects resonate, stimulating our thoughts toward something else, but the something else is elusive. This is not to say, however, that symbols mean whatever any reader says they mean. A reader could scarcely support, we imagine, an interpretation arguing that the poem is about the need to love all aspects of nature. All interpretations are not equally valid; it's the writer's job to offer a reasonably persuasive interpretation.

A symbol, then, is an image so loaded with significance that it is not simply literal, and it does not simply stand for something else; it is both itself *and* something else that it richly suggests, a kind of manifestation of something too complex or too elusive to be otherwise revealed. Blake's poem is about a blighted rose and at the same time about much more. In a symbol, as Thomas Carlyle wrote, "the Infinite is made to blend with the Finite, to stand visible, and as it were, attainable there."

VERBAL IRONY AND PARADOX

Among the most common devices in poems is **verbal irony**. The speaker's words mean more or less the opposite of what they seem to say. Sometimes verbal irony takes the form of **overstatement,** or **hyperbole,** as when Lady Macbeth says, while sleepwalking, "All the perfumes of Arabia will not sweeten this little hand." Sometimes it takes the form of **understatement,** as when Andrew Marvell's speaker in "To His Coy Mistress" (pp. 590–91) remarks with cautious wryness, "The grave's a fine and private place, / But none, I think, do there embrace," or when Sylvia Plath sees an intended suicide as "the big strip tease." Speaking broadly, intensely emotional contemporary poems like those of Plath often use irony to undercut—and thus make acceptable—the emotion presented.

Another common device in poems is **paradox:** the assertion of an apparent contradiction, as in Marvell's "am'rous birds of prey" in "To His Coy Mistress." Normally we think of amorous birds as gentle—doves, for example—and not as birds of prey, such as hawks. Another example of an apparent contradiction: In "Auld Lang Syne" there is the paradox that the remembrance of joy evokes a kind of sadness.

STRUCTURE

The arrangement of the parts, the organization of the entire poem, is its **structure.** Sometimes the poem is divided into blocks of, say, four lines each, but even if the poem is printed as a solid block it probably has some principle of organization. It may move, for example, from sorrow in the first two lines to joy in the next two or from a question in the first three lines to an answer in the last line.

Consider this short poem by an English poet of the seventeenth century.

ROBERT HERRICK (1591–1674)
Upon Julia's Clothes

Whenas in silk my Julia goes,
Then, then (methinks) how sweetly flows
That liquefaction of her clothes.

Next, when I cast mine eyes, and see
That brave° vibration, each way free   5
O, how that glittering taketh me.

[1648]

---

⁵**brave** splendid

A SAMPLE ESSAY BY A STUDENT:
"HERRICK'S JULIA, JULIA'S HERRICK"

One student, Stan Wylie, began thinking about this poem by copying it, double-spaced, and by making the following notes on his copy:

Upon Julia's Clothes

> Whenas in silk (my Julia) goes,   — *cool tone?*
>
> 3   Then, then (methinks) how sweetly flows
>
> That liquefaction of her clothes.

"Then, then" —
more
excited?
Almost at
a loss
for words?

> 3   Next, when I cast mine eyes, and see
>
> That brave vibration, each way free,
>
> O, how that glittering taketh me.
>   *emotional?*

free to do what?
free from what?

The student got some further ideas by thinking about several of the questions that, in the checklist on pages 420–22, we suggest you ask yourself while rereading a poem. Among the questions are these:

- Does the poem proceed in a straightforward way, or at some point or points does the speaker reverse course, altering his or her tone or perception?
- What is the effect on you of the form?

With such questions in mind, the student was stimulated to see if there is some sort of reversal or change in Herrick's poem, and if there is, how it is related to the structure. After rereading the poem several times, thinking about it in the light of these questions and perhaps others that came to mind, he produced the following notes:

Two stanzas, each of three lines, with the same structure
Basic structure of 1st stanza: When X (one line), then Y (two lines)
Basic structure of second stanza: Next (one line), then Z (two lines)

When he marked the text, after reading the poem a few times, he noticed that the last line—an exclamation of delight ("O, how that glittering taketh me")—is much more personal than the rest of the poem. A little further thought enabled him to refine this last perception:

Although the pattern of stanzas is repeated, the somewhat analytic, detached tone of the beginning ("Whenas," "Then," "Next") changes to an open, enthusiastic confession of delight in what the poet sees.

Further thinking led to this:

Although the title is "Upon Julia's Clothes," and the first five lines describe Julia's silken dress, the poem finally is not only about Julia's clothing but about the effect of Julia (moving in silk that liquefies or seems to become a liquid) on the poet.

This is a nice observation, but when the student looked again at the poem the next day, and started to write about it, he found that he was able to refine his observation.

Even at the beginning, the speaker is not entirely detached, for he speaks of "my Julia."

In writing about Herrick's "Upon Julia's Clothes," the student tell us, the thoughts did not come quickly or neatly. After two or three thoughts, he started to write. Only after drafting a paragraph, and rereading the poem, did he notice that the personal element appears not only in the last line ("taketh *me*") but even in the first line ("*my* Julia"). In short, for almost all of us, the only way to get to a good final essay is to read, to think, to jot down ideas, to write a draft, and to revise and revise again. Having gone through such processes, the student came up with the following excellent essay.

By the way, the student did not hit on the final version of his title ("Herrick's Julia, Julia's Herrick") until shortly before he typed his final version. His preliminary title was

Structure and Personality in
Herrick's "Upon Julia's Clothing"

That's a bit heavy-handed but at least it is focused, as opposed to such an uninformative title as "On a Poem." He soon revised his tentative title to

Julia, Julia's Clothing, and Julia's Poet

That's quite a good title: It is neat, and it is appropriate, since it moves (as the poem and the essay do) from Julia and her clothing to the poet. Of course it doesn't tell the reader exactly what the essay will be about, but it does stimulate the reader's interest. The essayist's final title, however, is even better:

Herrick's Julia, Julia's Herrick

Again, it is neat (the balanced structure, and structure is part of the student's topic), and it moves (as the poem itself moves) from Julia to the poet.

Herrick's Julia, Julia's Herrick

Robert Herrick's "Upon Julia's Clothes" begins as a description of Julia's clothing and ends as an expression of the poet's response not just to Julia's clothing but to Julia herself. Despite the apparently objective or detached tone of the first stanza and the first two lines of the second stanza, the poem finally conveys a strong sense of the speaker's excitement.

The first stanza seems to say, "Whenas" X (one line), "Then" Y (two lines). The second stanza repeats this basic structure of one line of assertion and two lines describing the consequence: "Next" (one line), "then" (two lines). But the logic or coolness of "Whenas," "Then," and "Next," and of such rather scientific language as "liquefaction" (a more technical-sounding word than "melting") and "vibration," is undercut by the breathlessness or excitement of "Then, then" (that is very different from a simple "Then"). It is also worth mentioning that although there is a personal rather than a fully detached note even in the first line, in "my Julia," this expression scarcely reveals much feeling. In fact, it reveals a touch of male chauvinism, a suggestion that the woman is a possession of the speaker's. Not until the last line does the speaker reveal that, far from Julia being his possession, he is possessed by Julia: "O, how that glittering taketh me." If he begins coolly, objectively, and somewhat complacently, and uses a structure that suggests a somewhat detached mind, in the exclamatory "O" he nevertheless at last confesses (to our delight) that he is enraptured by Julia.

Other things, of course, might be said about this poem. For instance, the writer says nothing about the changes in the basic iambic meter and their contributions to the poem. We have in mind not so much the trochees (a trochee is a metrical foot with a stressed syllable followed by an unstressed one) at the beginning of some lines, which is a fairly routine variation, but the spondees (two consecutive stresses) in "Then, then" and "O, how" and the almost-spondees in "Next, when," "each way free," and "that glittering." Also of interest are the two run-on lines (line 2 runs into 3, and 4 runs into 5) introducing related expressions, "That liquefaction" and "that brave vibration."

He also doesn't comment on the *s* and *z* sounds (*Whenas, silk, goes, thinks, sweetly flows*), which presumably imitate the sound of a silk gown in motion, a sound which can be said to resemble the sound of liquid, hence *liquefaction*—though the dress in motion also visually resembles flowing liquid. But the present essay seems excellent to us, and the neglected topics—sound effects in the poem—might be material for another essay.

CHRISTINA ROSSETTI (1830–1894)
In an Artist's Studio

One face looks out from all his canvases,
　One selfsame figure sits or walks or leans:
　We found her hidden just behind those screens,
That mirror gave back all her loveliness.　　　　　　4

A queen in opal or in ruby dress,
  A nameless girl in freshest summer-greens
  A saint, an angel—every canvas means
The same one meaning, neither more nor less.   8
He feeds upon her face by day and night,
  And she with true kind eyes looks back on him,
Fair as the moon and joyful as the light:
  Not wan with waiting, not with sorrow dim;   12
Not as she is, but was when hope shone bright;
  Not as she is, but as she fills his dream.

[1856]

This poem is a sonnet. We discuss the form later, on page 420, but if you study the rhymes here you will notice that the first eight lines are united by rhymes, and the next six by different rhymes. A reader might, for a start at least, think about whether what is said has any relation to these units. The first eight lines are about the model, but are the next six equally about her or about someone else?

Topics for Critical Thinking

1. What do we know about the model in the first eight lines? What do we know about her in the last two lines?
2. How are the contrasts (between then and now, between model and painter) communicated by the repetition of "Not as she is," in lines 13 and 14?

EXPLICATION

As we said in Chapter 4, a line-by-line commentary on what is going on in a text is an explication (literally, unfolding, or spreading out). Although your explication will for the most part move steadily from the beginning to the end of the selection, try to avoid writing along these lines (or, one might say, along this one line): "In the first line. . . . In the second line. . . . In the third line . . . ." That is, don't hesitate to write such things as

> The poem begins. . . . In the next line. . . . The speaker immediately adds. . . . He then introduces. . . . The next stanza begins by complicating the tone. . . .

And of course you can discuss the second line before the first if that seems the best way of handling the passage.

An explication is not a paraphrase (a rewording, a sort of translation)—though it may include paraphrase if a passage in the original seems unclear, perhaps because of an unusual word or an unfamiliar expression. On the whole, however, an explication goes beyond paraphrase, seeking to make explicit what the reader perceives as implicit in the work. It is chiefly concerned with

- the connotations of words—for instance, "look" versus "behold"
- the implications of syntax—for instance, whether it is notably complex (thereby implying one sort of speaker) or notably simple (implying a very different sort of speaker)

- the implications of rhyme—for instance, the implied connection in meaning between "throne" and "alone";
- patterns of imagery—for instance, commercial imagery in a love poem

As we said in Chapters 4 and 5, explication and analysis are not clearly distinct from each other; it is reasonable to think of explication as a kind of analysis operating on the level of verbal details.

An Example

Take this short poem (published in 1917) by the Irish poet William Butler Yeats (1865–1939). The "balloon" in the poem is a dirigible, a blimp.

 **WILLIAM BUTLER YEATS**
The Balloon of the Mind

Hands, do what you're bid:
Bring the balloon of the mind
That bellies and drags in the wind
Into its narrow shed.

[1917]

Annotations and Journal Entries

A student, Tina Washington, began thinking about the poem by copying it, double-spaced. Then she jotted down her first thoughts:

sounds abrupt

Hands, do what you're bid:

—balloon imagined by the mind? Or a mind like a balloon?

Bring the balloon of the mind

no real rhymes?

That bellies and drags in the wind

Into its narrow shed.

line seems to drag—it's so long!

Later she wrote some notes in a journal:

> I'm still puzzled about the meaning of the words "The balloon of the mind." Does "balloon of the mind" mean a balloon that belongs to the mind, sort of like "a disease of the heart"? If so, it means a balloon that the mind has, a balloon that the mind possesses, I guess by imagining it. Or does it mean that the mind is like a balloon, as when you say "he's a pig of a man," meaning he is like a pig, he is a pig? Can it mean both? What's a balloon that the mind imagines? Something like dreams of fame, wealth? Castles in Spain.
> Is Yeats saying that the "hands" have to work hard to make dreams a reality? Maybe. But maybe the idea really is that the mind is like a balloon—hard to keep under control, floating around. Very hard

to keep the mind on the job. If the mind is like a balloon, it's hard to get it into the hangar (shed).

"Bellies." Is there such a verb? In this poem it seems to mean something like "puffs out" or "flops around in the wind." Just checked The American Heritage Dictionary, and it says "belly" can be a verb, "to swell out," "to bulge." Well, you learn something every day.

A later entry:

OK; I think the poem is about a writer trying to keep his balloon-like mind from floating around, trying to keep the mind under control, trying to keep it working at the job of writing something, maybe writing something with the "clarity, unity, and coherence" I keep hearing about in this course.

A SAMPLE ESSAY BY A STUDENT: EXPLICATION OF W. B. YEATS'S "THE BALLOON OF THE MIND"

Here is the student's final version of the explication:

Yeats's "Balloon of the Mind" is about writing poetry, specifically about the difficulty of getting one's floating thoughts down in lines on the page. The first line, a short, stern, heavily stressed command to the speaker's hands, perhaps implies by its severe or impatient tone that these hands will be disobedient or inept or careless if not watched closely: the poor bumbling body so often fails to achieve the goals of the mind. The bluntness of the command in the first line is emphasized by the fact that all the subsequent lines have more syllables. Furthermore, the first line is a grammatically complete sentence, whereas the thought of line 2 spills over into the next lines, implying the difficulty of fitting ideas into confining spaces, that is, of getting one's thoughts into order, especially into a coherent poem.

Lines 2 and 3 amplify the metaphor already stated in the title (the product of the mind is an airy but unwieldy balloon), and they also contain a second command, "Bring." Alliteration ties this command, "Bring," to the earlier "bid"; it also ties both of these verbs to their object, "balloon," and to the verb that most effectively describes the balloon, "bellies." In comparison with the abrupt first line of the poem, lines 2 and 3 themselves seem almost swollen, bellying and dragging, an effect aided by using adjacent unstressed syllables ("of the," "[bell]ies and," "in the") and by using an eye rhyme ("mind" and "wind") rather than an exact rhyme. And then comes the short last line: almost before we could expect it, the cumbersome balloon--here, the idea that is to be packed into the stanza--is successfully lodged in its "narrow shed." Aside from the relatively colorless "into," the only words of more than one syllable in the poem are "balloon," "bellies," and "narrow," and all three emphasize the difficulty of the task. But after "narrow"--the word itself almost looks long and narrow, in this context like a hangar--we get the simplicity of the monosyllable "shed." The difficult job is done, the thought is safely packed away, the poem is completed--but again with an off-rhyme ("bid" and "shed"), for neatness can go only so far when hands and mind and a balloon are involved.

Note: The reader of an explication needs to see the text, and because the explicated text is usually short, it is advisable to quote it all. (Remember, your imagined audience probably consists of your classmates; even if they have already read the work you are explicating, they have not memorized it, and so you helpfully remind them of the work by quoting it.) You can quote the entire text at the outset, or you can quote the first unit (for example, a stanza), then explicate that unit, and then quote the next unit, and so on. And if the poem or passage of prose is longer than, say, six lines, it is advisable to number each line at the right for easy reference.

RHYTHM AND VERSIFICATION: A GLOSSARY FOR REFERENCE

Rhythm (most simply, in English poetry, stresses at regular intervals) has a power of its own. A highly pronounced rhythm is common in such forms of poetry as charms, college yells, and lullabies; all of them are aimed at inducing a special effect magically. It is not surprising that *carmen,* the Latin word for poem or song, is also the Latin word for *charm* and the word from which our word *charm* is derived.

In much poetry, rhythm is only half heard, but its presence is suggested by the way poetry is printed. Prose (from Latin *prorsus,* "forward," "straight on") keeps running across the paper until the right-hand margin is reached; then, merely because the paper has given out, the writer or printer starts again at the left, with a small letter. But verse (Latin *versus,* "a turning") often ends well short of the right-hand margin. The next line begins at the left—usually with a capital— not because paper has run out but because the rhythmic pattern begins again. Lines of poetry are continually reminding us that they have a pattern.

Note that a mechanical, unvarying rhythm may be good to put the baby to sleep, but it can be deadly to readers who want to stay awake. Poets vary their rhythm according to their purposes; they ought not to be so regular that they are (in W. H. Auden's words) "accentual pests." In competent hands, rhythm contributes to meaning; it says something. Ezra Pound has a relevant comment: "Rhythm *must* have meaning. It can't be merely a careless dash off, with no grip and no real hold to the words and sense, a tumty tum tumty tum tum ta."

Consider this description of Hell from John Milton's *Paradise Lost* (stressed syllables are marked by ´, unstressed syllables by ˘:

Rócks, cáves, lákes, féns, bógs, déns, aňd shádes ŏf déath.

The normal line in *Paradise Lost* is written in iambic feet—alternate unstressed and stressed syllables—but in this line Milton immediately follows one heavy stress with another, helping to communicate the "meaning"—the oppressive monotony of Hell. As a second example, consider the function of the rhythm in two lines by Alexander Pope:

Wȟen Ájax stríves soňe róck's vást wéight ťo thrów,
Tȟe líne tóo lábors, aňd tȟe wórds móve slów.

The stressed syllables do not merely alternate with the unstressed ones; rather the great weight of the rock is suggested by three consecutive stressed words, "rock's vast weight," and the great effort involved in moving it is suggested by another three consecutive stresses, "line too labors," and by yet another three, "words move slow." Note also the abundant pauses within the lines. In the first line, for example, unless one's speech is slovenly, one must pause at least slightly after "Ajax," "strives," "rock's," "vast," "weight," and "throw." The grating sounds in "Ajax" and "rock's" do their work, too, and so do the explosive *t*'s.

When Pope wishes to suggest lightness, he reverses his procedure, and he groups *un*stressed syllables:

Not so, when swift Camilla scours the plain,
Fliés o'ěr th'˘ unbéndiňg córn, aňd skíms ˘alŏng tȟe máin.

This last line has twelve syllables and is thus longer than the line about Ajax, but the addition of *along* helps to communicate lightness and swiftness because in this line (it can be argued) neither syllable of *along* is strongly stressed. If *along* is omitted, the line still makes grammatical sense and becomes more "regular," but it also becomes less imitative of lightness.

The very regularity of a line may be meaningful too. Shakespeare begins a sonnet thus:

Wȟen Í đo cóunt tȟe clóck tȟat ťells tȟe tíme.

This line about a mechanism runs with appropriate regularity. (It is worth noting, too, that "count the clock" and "tells the time" emphasize the regularity by the repetition of sounds and syntax.) But notice what Shakespeare does in the middle of the next line:

Aňd sée tȟe bráve dáy súnk ĭn hídeŏus níght.

The technical vocabulary of **prosody** (the study of the principles of verse structure, including meter, rhyme and other sould effects, and stanzaic patterns) is large. An understanding of these terms will not turn anyone into a poet, but it will enable you to write about some aspects of poetry more efficiently. The following are the chief terms of prosody.

Meter

Most poetry written in English has a pattern of stressed (accented) sounds, and this pattern is the **meter** (from the Greek word for "measure"). Strictly speaking, we really should not talk of "unstressed" or "unaccented" syllables, since to utter a syllable—however lightly—is to give it some stress. It is really a matter of *relative* stress, but the fact is that "unstressed" or "unaccented" are parts of the established terminology of versification.

In a line of poetry, the **foot** is the basic unit of measurement. It is on rare occasions a single stressed syllable; but generally a foot consists of two or three syllables, one of which is stressed. The repetition of feet, then, produces a pattern of stresses throughout the poem.

Two cautions:

* A poem will seldom contain only one kind of foot throughout; significant variations usually occur, but one kind of foot is dominant.
* In reading a poem, one chiefly pays attention to the sense, not to presupposed metrical pattern. By paying attention to the sense, one often finds (reading aloud is a great help) that the stress falls on a word that according to the metrical pattern would be unstressed. Or a word that according to the pattern would be stressed may be seen to be unstressed. Furthermore, by reading for sense one finds that not all stresses are equally heavy; some are almost as light as unstressed syllables, and sometimes there is a **hovering stress**—that is, the stress is equally distributed over two adjacent syllables. To repeat: One reads for sense, allowing the syntax to help indicate the stresses.

Metrical Feet.   The most common feet in English poetry are the six listed below. **Iamb** (adjective: **iambic**): one unstressed syllable followed by one stressed syllable. The iamb, said to be the most common pattern in English speech, is surely the most common in English poetry. The following example has four iambic feet:

My héart ĭs líke a síng-ĭng bírd.

—*Christina Rossetti*

Trochee (trochaic): one stressed syllable followed by one unstressed.

Wé wĕre vérỹ tĩred, wé wĕre vérỹ mérrỹ

—*Edna St. Vincent Millay*

Anapest (anapestic): two unstressed syllables followed by one stressed.

Thĕre ăre mán-y whŏ sáy thăt ă dóg hăs hĭs dáy.

—*Dylan Thomas*

Dactyl (dactylic): one stressed syllable followed by two unstressed. This trisyllabic foot, like the anapest, is common in light verse or verse suggesting joy, but its use is not limited to such material, as Longfellow's *Evangeline* shows. Thomas Hood's sentimental "The Bridge of Sighs" begins

Táke hĕr ŭp téndĕrly.

Spondee (spondaic): two stressed syllables; most often used as a substitute for an iamb or trochee.

Smárt lád, tŏ slíp bĕtimés ăwáy.

—A. E. Housman

Pyrrhic: two unstressed syllables; it is often not considered a legitimate foot in English.

Metrical Lines. A metrical line consists of one or more feet and is named for the number of feet in it. The following names are used:

monometer: one foot	**pentameter:** five feet
dimeter: two feet	**hexameter:** six feet
trimeter: three feet	**heptameter:** seven feet
tetrameter: four feet	

A line is scanned for the kind and number of feet in it, and the **scansion** tells you if it is, say, anapestic trimeter (three anapests):

Ăs Ĭ cáme tŏ thĕ édge ŏf thĕ wóods.

—Robert Frost

Or, in another example, iambic pentameter:

Thĕ súm -mĕr thún-dĕr, líke ă wóod-ĕn bĕll

—Louise Bogan

A line ending with a stress has a **masculine ending;** a line ending with an extra unstressed syllable has a **feminine ending.** The **caesura** (usually indicated by the symbol / /) is a slight pause within the line. It need not be indicated by punctuation (notice the fourth and fifth lines in the following quotation), and it does not affect the metrical count:

Awake, my St. John! / / leave all meaner things
To low ambition, / / and the pride of kings.
Let us / / (since Life can little more supply
Than just to look about us / / and to die)
Expatiate free / / o'er all this scene of Man;
A mighty maze! / / but not without a plan;
A wild, / / where weeds and flowers promiscuous shoot;
Or garden, / / tempting with forbidden fruit.

—Alexander Pope

The varying position of the caesura helps to give Pope's lines an informality that plays against the formality of the pairs of rhyming lines.

An **end-stopped line** concludes with a distinct syntactical pause, but a **run-on line** has its sense carried over into the next line without syntactical pause. (The running-on of a line is called **enjambment.**) In the following passage, only the first is a run-on line:

Yet if we look more closely we shall find
Most have the seeds of judgment in their mind:

Nature affords at least a glimmering light;
The lines, though touched but faintly, are drawn right.

—Alexander Pope

Meter produces **rhythm,** recurrences at equal intervals, but rhythm (from a Greek word meaning "flow") is usually applied to larger units than feet. Often it depends most obviously on pauses. Thus, a poem with run-on lines will have a different rhythm from a poem with end-stopped lines, even though both are in the same meter. And prose, though it is unmetrical, can have rhythm, too.

In addition to being affected by syntactical pause, rhythm is affected by pauses attributable to consonant clusters and to the length of words. Polysyllabic words establish a different rhythm from monosyllabic words, even in metrically identical lines. One can say, then, that rhythm is altered by shifts in meter, syntax, and the length and ease of pronunciation. But even with no such shift, even if a line is repeated verbatim, a reader may sense a change in rhythm. The rhythm of the final line of a poem, for example, may well differ from that of the line before, even though in all other respects the lines are identical, as in Frost's "Stopping by Woods on a Snowy Evening" (p. 462), which concludes by repeating "And miles to go before I sleep." One may simply sense that this final line ought to be spoken, say, more slowly and with more stress on "miles."

Patterns of Sound

Though rhythm is basic to poetry, **rhyme**—the repetition of identical or similar stressed sound or sounds—is not. Rhyme is, presumably, pleasant in itself; it suggests order; and it also may be related to meaning, for it brings two words sharply together, often implying a relationship, as in the now trite *dove* and *love,* or in the more imaginative *throne* and *alone.*

Perfect, or **exact, rhyme:** Differing consonant sounds are followed by identical stressed vowel sounds, and the following sounds, if any, are identical (*foe—toe; meet—fleet; buffer—rougher*). Notice that perfect rhyme involves identity of sound, not of spelling. *Fix* and *sticks,* like *buffer* and *rougher,* are perfect rhymes.

Half-rhyme (or **off-rhyme**): Only the final consonant sounds of the words are identical; the stressed vowel sounds as well as the initial consonant sounds, if any, differ (*soul—oil; mirth—forth; trolley—bully*).

Eye rhyme: The sounds do not in fact rhyme, but the words look as though they would rhyme (*cough—bough*).

Masculine rhyme: The final syllables are stressed and, after their differing initial consonant sounds, are identical in sound (*stark—mark; support—retort*).

Feminine rhyme (or **double rhyme**): Stressed rhyming syllables are followed by identical unstressed syllables (*revival—arrival; flatter—batter*). **Triple rhyme** is a kind of feminine rhyme in which identical stressed vowel sounds are followed by two identical unstressed syllables (*machinery—scenery; tenderly—slenderly*).

End rhyme (or **terminal rhyme**): The rhyming words occur at the ends of the lines.

Internal rhyme: At least one of the rhyming words occurs within the line (Oscar Wilde's "Each narrow *cell* in which we *dwell*").

Alliteration: sometimes defined as the repetition of initial sounds ("*A*ll the *a*wful *a*uguries," or "*B*ring me my *b*ow of *b*urning gold"), and sometimes as the prominent repetition of a consonant ("*a*fter li*f*e's *f*it*f*ul *f*ever").

Assonance: the repetition, in words of proximity, of identical vowel sounds preceded and followed by differing consonant sounds. Whereas *tide* and *hide* are rhymes, *tide* and *mine* are assonantal.

Consonance: the repetition of identical consonant sounds and differing vowel sounds in words in proximity (*fail—feel; rough—roof; pitter—patter*). Sometimes consonance is more loosely defined merely as the repetition of a consonant (*fail—peel*).

Onomatopoeia: the use of words that imitate sounds, such as *hiss* and *buzz*. There is a mistaken tendency to see onomatopoeia everywhere—for example, in *thunder* and *horror*. Many words sometimes thought to be onomatopoeic are not clearly imitative of the thing they refer to; they merely contain some sounds that, when we know what the word means, seem to have some resemblance to the thing they denote. Tennyson's lines from "Come down, O maid" are usually cited as an example of onomatopoeia:

> The moan of doves in immemorial elms
> And murmuring of innumerable bees.

Stanzaic Patterns

Lines of poetry are commonly arranged in a rhythmical unit called a stanza (from an Italian word meaning "room" or "stopping-place"). Usually all the stanzas in a poem have the same rhyme pattern. A stanza is sometimes called a **verse,** though *verse* may also mean a single line of poetry. (In discussing stanzas, rhymes are indicated by identical letters. Thus, *abab* indicates that the first and third lines rhyme with each other, while the second and fourth lines are linked by a different rhyme. An unrhymed line is denoted by *x*.) Common stanzaic forms in English poetry are the following:

Couplet: a stanza of two lines, usually, but not necessarily, with end-rhymes. *Couplet* is also used for a pair of rhyming lines. The **octosyllabic couplet** is iambic or trochaic tetrameter:

> Had we but world enough, and time,
> This coyness, lady, were no crime.

> *—Andrew Marvell*

Heroic couplet: a rhyming couplet of iambic pentameter, often "closed," that is, containing a complete thought, with a fairly heavy pause at the end of the first line and a still heavier one at the end of the second. Commonly, there is a parallel or an *antithesis* (contrast) within a line or between the two lines. It is called heroic because in England, especially in the eighteenth century, it was much used for heroic (epic) poems.

> Some foreign writers, some our own despise;
> The ancients only, or the moderns, prize.

> *—Alexander Pope*

Triplet (or **tercet**): a three-line stanza, usually with one rhyme:

Whenas in silks my Julia goes
Then, then (methinks) how sweetly flows
That liquefaction of her clothes.

—*Robert Herrick*

Quatrain: a four-line stanza, rhymed or unrhymed. The **heroic** (or **elegiac**) **quatrain** is iambic pentameter, rhyming *abab*. That is, the first and third lines rhyme (so they are designated *a*), and the second and fourth lines rhyme (so they are designated *b*).

Sonnet: a fourteen-line poem, predominantly in iambic pentameter. The rhyme is usually according to one of two schemes. The **Italian** (or **Petrarchan**[1]) **sonnet** has two divisions: The first eight lines (rhyming *abba abba* are the **octave,** and the last six (rhyming *cd cd cd,* or a variant) are the **sestet.** The second kind of sonnet, the **English** (or **Shakespearean) sonnet,** is usually arranged into three quatrains and a couplet, rhyming *abab cdcd efef gg.* (For examples see pages 586–87.) In many sonnets there is a marked correspondence between the rhyme scheme and the development of the thought. Thus an Italian sonnet may state a generalization in the octave and a specific example in the sestet. Or an English sonnet may give three examples—one in each quatrain—and draw a conclusion in the couplet.

Blank Verse and Free Verse

A good deal of English poetry is unrhymed, much of it in **blank verse,** that is, unrhymed iambic pentameter. Introduced into English poetry by Henry Howard, Earl of Surrey, in the middle of the sixteenth century, late in the century it became the standard medium (especially in the hands of Christopher Marlowe and Shakespeare) of English drama. In the seventeenth century, Milton used it for *Paradise Lost,* and it has continued to be used in both dramatic and nondramatic literature. For an example, see the first scene of *Hamlet* (p. 910), until the Ghost appears.

The second kind of unrhymed poetry fairly common in English, especially in the twentieth century, is **free verse** (or **vers libre**): rhythmical lines varying in length, adhering to no fixed metrical pattern and usually unrhymed. The pattern is often largely based on repetition and parallel grammatical structure. For an example, see T. S. Eliot's "The Love Song of J. Alfred Prufrock" (p. 602).

✔ A Checklist: Getting Ideas for Writing About Poetry

If you are going to write about a fairly short poem (say, under thirty lines), it's not a bad idea to copy out the poem, writing or typing it double-spaced. By writing it out you will be forced to notice details, down to the punctuation. After you have copied the poem, proofread it carefully against the original. Catching an error—even the addition or omission of a comma—may help you to notice a detail in the original that you might otherwise have overlooked. And of course, now that you have the poem with ample space between the lines, you have a worksheet with room for jottings.

---

[1]So called after Francesco Petrarch (1304-1374), the Italian poet who perfected and popularized the form.

A good essay is based on a genuine response to a poem; a response may be stimulated in part by first reading the poem aloud and then considering the following questions.

First Response

✔ What was your response to the poem on first reading? Did some parts especially please or displease you, or puzzle you? After some study—perhaps checking the meanings of some of the words in a dictionary and reading the poem several times—did you modify your initial response to the parts and to the whole?

Speaker and Tone

✔ Who is the speaker? (Consider age, sex, personality, frame of mind, and tone of voice.) Is the speaker defined fairly precisely (for instance, an older woman speaking to a child), or is the speaker simply a voice meditating? (Jot down your first impressions, then reread the poem and make further jottings, if necessary.)

✔ Do you think the speaker is fully aware of what he or she is saying, or does the speaker unconsciously reveal his or her personality and values? What is your attitude toward this speaker?

✔ Is the speaker narrating or reflecting on an earlier experience or attitude? If so, does he or she convey a sense of new awareness, such as of regret for innocence lost?

Audience

✔ To whom is the speaker speaking? What is the situation (including time and place)? (In some poems, a listener is strongly implied, but in others, especially those in which the speaker is meditating, there may be no audience other than the reader, who "overhears" the speaker.)

Structure and Form

✔ Does the poem proceed in a straightforward way, or at some point or points does the speaker reverse course, altering his or her tone or perception? If there is a shift, what do you make of it?

✔ Is the poem organized into sections? If so, what are these sections— stanzas, for instance—and how does each section (characterized, perhaps, by a certain tone of voice, or a group of rhymes) grow out of what precedes it?

✔ What is the effect on you of the form—say, quatrains (stanzas of four lines) or blank verse (unrhymed lines of ten syllables)? If the sense overflows the form, running without pause from (for example) one quatrain into the next, what effect is created?

Center of Interest and Theme

✔ What is the poem about? Is the interest chiefly in a distinctive character, or in meditation? That is, is the poem chiefly psychological or chiefly philosophical?

✔ Is the theme stated explicitly (directly) or implicitly? How might you state the theme in a sentence?

Diction

✔ Do certain words have rich and relevant associations that relate to other words and help to define the speaker or the theme or both?

✔ What is the role of figurative language, if any? Does it help to define the speaker or the theme?

✔ What do you think is to be taken figuratively or symbolically, and what literally?

Sound Effects

✔ What is the role of sound effects, including repetitions of sound (for instance, alliteration) and of entire words, and shifts in versification?

✔ If there are off-rhymes (for instance "dizzy" and "easy," or "home" and "come"), what effect do they have on you? Do they, for instance, add a note of tentativeness or uncertainty?

✔ If there are unexpected stresses or pauses, what do they communicate about the speaker's experience? How do they affect you?

FIFTEEN POEMS ABOUT PEOPLE, PLACES, AND THINGS

People

Folk ballads, or **popular ballads,** are anonymous stories told in song. They acquire their distinctive flavor by being passed down orally from generation to generation, each singer consciously or unconsciously modifying his or her inheritance. In Chapter 3 we print Huddie Ledbetter's version of a song about the sinking of the *Titanic,* but, as we point out, Ledbetter (better known as Leadbelly) was drawing in part on earlier songs about ships. Below we print a much older song about a shipwreck; it was written down in the eighteenth century, but before it was printed it doubtless had been circulating orally, passed down from singer to singer for at least two hundred years.

Among the usual characteristics of a work that circulates orally are these:

- It is impersonal; even if there is an "I" who sings the song, this "I" is usually characterless.

- Sometimes phrases are repeated, sometimes whole lines. In the poem we print here, notice "O wha is this has done this deid, / this ill deid don to me"; in Leadbelly's "The *Titanic*" (p. 50) notice the repetition of "Fare thee, *Titanic,* fare thee well." The repeated material doubtless eased the singer's burden of remembering the song, but it also serves to emphasize the important words or phrases; the singer is, so to speak, obsessed with the "deid" (deed) in "Sir Patrick Spence," or with bidding farewell to the vanished *Titanic.*

- The ballad often consists largely of sharply drawn scenes, with dialogue; presumably the weaker narrative passages were less memorable and therefore many of them disappeared over the years. You can see this characteristics in Leadbelly's "The Titanic" and equally in "Sir Patrick Spence."

Because until the mid-eighteenth century ballads were sung rather than printed, and even today they are chiefly transmitted orally rather than through print, and because singers consciously or unconsciously made alterations, no one version of a ballad is the "correct" one. As we point out in Chapter 3, Lead-belly varied his song each time he sang it, sometimes omitting one stanza or another, sometimes rearranging the stanzas, sometimes slightly changing the wording.

ANONYMOUS
Sir Patrick Spence

The king sits in Dumferling toune,
  Drinking the blude-reid wine:
"O whar will I get guid sailor,
  To sail this schip of mine?"   4

Up and spak an eldern knicht,
  Sat at the kings richt kne:
"Sir Patrick Spence is the best sailor,
  That sails upon the se."   8

The king has written a braid° letter,
  And signed it wi' his hand,
And sent it to Sir Patrick Spence,
  Was walking on the sand.   12

°braid broad, open

The first line that Sir Patgrick red,
    A loud lauch° lauched he;
The next line that Sir Patrick red,
    The teir blinded his ee.   16

"O wha is this has done this deid,
    This ill deid don to me,
To send me out this time o' the yeir,
    To sail upon the se?   20

"Mak hast, mak hast, my mirry men all,
    Our guid schip sails the morne":
"O say na sae, my master deir,
    For I feir a deadlie storme.   24

"Late late yestreen I saw the new moone,
    Wi' the auld moone to hir arme,
And I feir, I feir, my deir master,
    That we will cum to harme."   28

O our Scots nobles wer richt laith°
    To weet their cork-heild schoone;°
Bot lang owre° a' the play wer playd,
    Thair hats they swam aboone.°   32

O lang, lang may their ladies sit,
    Wi' thair fans into their hand,
Or eir° they se Sir Patrick Spence
    Cum sailing to the land.   36

O lang, lang may the ladies stand,
    Wi' thair gold kems in their hair,
Waiting for their ain deir lords,
    For they'll se thame na mair.   40

Have owre° have owre to Aberdour,
    It's fiftie fadom deip,
And thair lies guid Sir Patrick Spence,
    Wi' the Scots lords at his feit.   44

✎ Topics for Critical Thinking and Writing

1. The shipwreck occurs between lines 29 and 32, but it is not described. Does
the omission stimulate the reader to imagine the details of the wreck? Or
does it suggest that the poem is not so much about a shipwreck as about
kinds of behavior?

14 lauch laugh **29 laith** loath **30 cork-heild schoone** cork-heeled shoes
31 owre ere **32 aboone** above **35 eir** ere **41 Have owre** half over

2. Do you think that lines 17–18 warrant the inference that the "eldern knicht" (5) is Sir Patrick Spence's enemy?
3. What do you make of lines 13–16?
4. In place of lines 37–40, another version of this ballad has the following stanza:

> The ladies crack'd their fingers white,
> The maidens tore their hair,
> A' for the sake o' their true loves,
> For them they ne'er saw mair.

Which version do you prefer?
5. In the other version, the stanza that is here the final one (41–44) precedes the stanzas about the ladies (33–40). Which stanza do you think makes a better conclusion? Why?

 **BEN JONSON**

Ben Jonson (1572–1637), born in London, was Shakespeare's contemporary. Like Shakespeare, he wrote for the theater, and in fact Shakespeare acted in Jonson's first important play, Every Man in His Humor *(1598). But unlike Shakespeare, Jonson produced a fairly large body of non-dramatic poetry.*

Jonson's son, born in 1596, died on his birthday in 1603. Like the father, the boy was named Benjamin, which in Hebrew means "son of the right hand," a phrase Jonson draws on in the first line of the poem.

On My First Son

Farewell, thou child of my right hand and joy;
  My sin was too much hope of thee, loved boy.
Seven years thou wert lent to me, and I thee pay,
  Exacted by thy fate, on the just day.
O, could I lose all father now! For why   5
  Will man lament the state he should envy?
To have so soon 'scaped world's and flesh's rage,
  And, if no other misery, yet age?
Rest in soft peace, and asked, say here doth lie
  Ben. Jonson, his best piece of poetry: 10
For whose sake, henceforth, all his vows be such,
  As what he loves may never like too much.

[1616]

 Topics for Critical Thinking and Writing

1. In lines 6–9 Jonson sketches some of the pains of living, including the "misery" of old age. Why do we lament the loss of life, when we see the battering that most people ultimately undergo?
2. As a whole Jonson's language is plain and, it seems, eloquently straightforward. But his words and phrases in fact merit close study, and in certain

cases may even be somewhat obscure, at least at first. What, for example, does Jonson mean by the word "just" in line 4? In line 5, what is the meaning of his cry, "O, could I lose all father now"? In line 10, how do you interpret Jonson's statement that his son is "his best piece of poetry"? And in the final line, what is the distinction he makes between "loves" and "like"?

3. Later, in Chapter 16, we discuss several short poems about the deaths of children, and we suggest that sentimentality is usually regarded as a fault. You may want to glance at that discussion; in any event, would you call this poem sentimental, and, if so, do you think that the sentimentality is a fault?

 **ROBERT BROWNING**

Born in a suburb of London into a middle-class family, Browning (1812–89) was educated primarily at home, where he read widely. For a while he wrote for the stage, and in 1846 he married Elizabeth Barrett—herself a poet—and lived with her in Italy until her death in 1861. He then returned to England and settled in London with their son. Regarded as one of the most distinguished poets of the Victorian period, he is buried in Westminster Abbey.

My Last Duchess

Ferrara*

That's my last Duchess painted on the wall,
Looking as if she were alive. I call
That piece a wonder, now; Frà Pandolf's° hands
Worked busily a day, and there she stands.
Will't please you sit and look at her? I said   5
"Frà Pandolf" by design, for never read
Strangers like you that pictured countenance,
The depth and passion of its earnest glance,
But to myself they turned (since none puts by
The curtain I have drawn for you, but I)   10
And seemed as they would ask me, if they durst,
How such a glance came there; so, not the first
Are you to turn and ask thus. Sir, 'twas not
Her husband's presence only, called that spot
Of joy into the Duchess' cheek; perhaps   15
Frà Pandolf chanced to say "Her mantle laps
Over my lady's wrist too much," or, "Paint
Must never hope to reproduce the faint
Half-flush that dies along her throat." Such stuff
Was courtesy, she thought, and cause enough   20
For calling up that spot of joy. She had

*Ferrara** town in Italy   **3 Frà Pandolf** a fictitious painter

A heart—how shall I say?—too soon made glad,
Too easily impressed; she liked whate'er
She looked on, and her looks went everywhere.
Sir, 'twas all one! My favor at her breast,   25
The dropping of the daylight in the west,
The bough of cherries some officious fool
Broke in the orchard for her, the white mule
She rode with round the terrace—all and each
Would draw from her alike the approving speech,   30
Or blush, at least. She thanked men—good! but thanked
Somehow—I know not how—as if she ranked
My gift of a nine-hundred-years-old name
With anybody's gift. Who'd stoop to blame
This sort of trifling? Even had you skill   35
In speech—(which I have not)—to make your will
Quite clear to such an one, and say, "Just this
Or that in you disgusts me; here you miss,
Or there exceed the mark"—and if she let
Herself be lessoned so, nor plainly set   40
Her wits to yours, forsooth, and made excuse,
—E'en then would be some stooping; and I choose
Never to stoop. Oh, Sir, she smiled, no doubt,
Whene'er I passed her; but who passed without
Much the same smile? This grew; I gave commands;   45
Then all smiles stopped together. There she stands
As if alive. Will't please you rise? We'll meet
The company below, then. I repeat,
The Count your master's known munificence
Is ample warrant that no just pretense   50
Of mine for dowry will be disallowed;
Though his fair daughter's self, as I avowed
At starting, is my object. Nay, we'll go
Together down, Sir. Notice Neptune, though,
Taming a sea-horse, thought a rarity,   55
Which Claus of Innsbruck° cast in bronze for me!

[1842]

✎ Topics for Critical Thinking and Writing

1. Who is speaking to whom? On what occasion?
2. What words or lines especially convey the speaker's arrogance? What is our attitude toward the speaker? Loathing? Fascination? Respect? Explain.
3. The time and place are Renaissance Italy; how do they affect our attitude toward the duke? What would be the effect if the poem were set in the twentieth century?
4. Years after writing this poem, Browning explained that the duke's "commands" (line 45) were "that she should be put to death, or he might have

56 Claus of Innsbruck a fictitious sculptor

had her shut up in a convent." Should the poem have been more explicit? Does Browning's later uncertainty indicate that the poem is badly thought out? Suppose we did not have Browning's comment on line 45; could the line then mean only that he commanded her to stop smiling and that she obeyed? Explain.

5. Elizabeth Barrett (not yet Mrs. Browning) wrote to Robert Browning that it was not "by the dramatic medium that poets teach most impressively. . . . It is too difficult for the common reader to analyze, and to discern between the vivid and the earnest." She went on, urging him to teach "in the directest and most impressive way, the mask thrown off." What teaching, if any, is in this poem? If there is any teaching here, would it be more impressive if Browning had not used the mask of a Renaissance duke? Explain.

6. You are the envoy, writing to the Count, your master, a 500-word report of your interview with the duke. What do you write?

7. You are the envoy, writing to the count, advising—as diplomatically as possible—for or against this marriage. Notice that this exercise, unlike #6, which calls for a *report*, calls for an *argument*.

E. E. CUMMINGS

e. e. cummings was the pen name of Edwin Estlin Cummings (1894–1962), who grew up in Cambridge, Massachusetts, and was graduated from Harvard, where he became interested in modern literature and art, especially in the movements called cubism and futurism. His father, a conservative clergyman and a professor at Harvard, seems to have been baffled by the youth's interests, but Cummings's mother encouraged his artistic activities, including his use of unconventional punctuation and capitalization.

Politically liberal in his youth, Cummings became more conservative after a visit to Russia in 1931, but early and late his work emphasizes individuality and freedom of expression.

anyone lived in a pretty how town

anyone lived in a pretty how town
(with up so floating many bells down)
spring summer autumn winter
he sang his didn't he danced his did.   4

Women and men (both little and small)
cared for anyone not at all
they sowed their isn't they reaped their same
sun moon stars rain   8

children guessed (but only a few
and down they forgot as up they grew
autumn winter spring summer)
that noone loved him more by more   12

when by now and tree by leaf
she laughed his joy she cried his grief

bird by snow and stir by still
anyone's any was all to her   16

someones married their everyones
laughed their cryings and did their dance
(sleep wake hope and then) they
said their nevers they slept their dream   20

stars rain sun moon
(and only the snow can begin to explain
how children are apt to forget to remember
with up so floating many bells down)   24

one day anyone died i guess
(and noone stopped to kiss his face)
busy folk buried them side by side
little by little and was by was   28

all by all and deep by deep
and more by more they dream their sleep
noone and anyone earth by april
wish by spirit and if by yes.   32

Women and men (both dong and ding)
summer autumn winter spring
reaped their sowing and went their came
sun moon stars rain   36

[1940]

 ## Topics for Critical Thinking and Writing

1. Put into normal order (as far as possible) the words of the first two stanzas
   and then compare your version with cummings's. What does cummings
   gain—or lose?
2. Characterize the "anyone" who "sang his didn't" and "danced his did." In
   your opinion, how does he differ from the people who "sowed their isn't
   they reaped their same"?
3. Some readers interpret "anyone died" (line 25) to mean that the child matured and became as dead as the other adults. How might you support or refute this interpretation?

 # GWENDOLYN BROOKS

*Gwendolyn Brooks was born in Topeka, Kansas, in 1917 but was raised
in Chicago's South Side, where she has spent most of her life. Brooks
has taught in several colleges and universities and she has written a
novel (Maud Martha, 1953) and a memoir (Report from Part One,
1972), but she is best known as a poet. In 1950, when she won the
Pulitzer Prize for Poetry, she became the first African-American writer
to win a Pulitzer Prize. In 1985 Brooks became Consultant in Poetry to
the Library of Congress.*

The Mother

Abortions will not let you forget.
You remember the children you got that you did not get,
The damp small pulps with a little or with no hair,
The singers and workers that never handled the air.
You will never neglect or beat   5
Them, or silence or buy with a sweet.
You will never wind up the sucking-thumb
Or scuttle off ghosts that come.
You will never leave them, controlling your luscious sigh,
Return for a snack of them, with gobbling mother-eye.   10

I have heard in the voices of the wind the voices of my dim killed children.
I have contracted. I have eased
My dim dears at the breasts they could never suck.
I have said, Sweets, if I sinned, if I seized
Your luck   15
And your lives from your unfinished reach,
If I stole your births and your names,
Your straight baby tears and your games,
Your stilted or lovely loves, your tumults, your marriages, aches, and your deaths,
If I poisoned the beginnings of your breaths,   20
Believe that even in my deliberateness I was not deliberate,
Though why should I whine,
Whine that the crime was other than mine?—
Since anyhow you are dead
Or rather, or instead,   25
You were never made,
But that too, I am afraid,
Is faulty: oh, what shall I say, how is the truth to be said?
You were born, you had body, you died.
It is just that you never giggled or planned or cried.   30

Believe me, I loved you all.
Believe me, I knew you, though faintly, and I loved, I loved you
All.

[1945]

✎ Topics for Critical Thinking and Writing

1. The first ten lines sound like a chant. What gives them that quality? What makes them nonetheless serious?
2. In lines 20–23 the mother attempts to deny the "crime" but cannot. What is her reasoning here?
3. Do you find the last lines convincing? Explain.

SYLVIA PLATH

Sylvia Plath (1932–63) was born in Boston, the daughter of German immigrants. While still an undergraduate at Smith College, she published in Seventeen *and* Mademoiselle, *but her years at college, like her later years, were marked by manic-depressive periods. After graduating from college she went to England to study at Cambridge University, where she met the English poet Ted Hughes, whom she married in 1956. The marriage was unsuccessful, and they separated. One day she committed suicide by turning on the kitchen gas.*

Daddy

You do not do, you do not do
Any more, black shoe
In which I have lived like a foot
For thirty years, poor and white,
Barely daring to breathe or Achoo.   5

Daddy, I have had to kill you.
You died before I had time—
Marble-heavy, a bag full of God,
Ghastly statue with one gray toe
Big as a Frisco seal   10

And a head in the freakish Atlantic
Where it pours bean green over blue
In the waters off beautiful Nauset.
I used to pray to recover you.
Ach, du.°   15

In the German tongue, in the Polish town
Scraped flat by the roller
Of wars, wars, wars.
But the name of the town is common.
My Polack friend   20

Says there are a dozen or two.
So I never could tell where you
Put your foot, your root,
I never could talk to you.
The tongue stuck in my jaw.   25

It stuck in a barb wire snare.
Ich, ich, ich, ich,°
I could hardly speak.
I thought every German was you.
And the language obscene   30

---

15 Ach, du O, you (German)   **27 Ich, ich, ich, ich** I, I, I, I

An engine, an engine
Chuffing me off like a Jew.
A Jew to Dachau, Auschwitz, Belsen.°
I began to talk like a Jew.
I think I may well be a Jew.   35

The snows of the Tyrol, the clear beer of Vienna
Are not very pure or true.
With my gypsy ancestress and my weird luck
And my Taroc pack and my Taroc pack
I may be a bit of a Jew.   40

I have always been scared of *you,*
With your Luftwaffe,° your gobbledygoo.
And your neat moustache
And your Aryan eye, bright blue,
Panzer-man,° panzer-man, O You—   45

Not God but a swastika
So black no sky could squeak through.
Every woman adores a Fascist,
The boot in the face, the brute
Brute heart of a brute like you.   50

You stand at the blackboard, daddy,
In the picture I have of you,
A cleft in your chin instead of your foot
But no less a devil for that, no not
Any less the black man who   55

Bit my pretty red heart in two.
I was ten when they buried you.
At twenty I tried to die
And get back, back, back to you.
I thought even the bones would do   60

But they pulled me out of the sack,
And they stuck me together with glue,
And then I knew what to do.
I made a model of you,
A man in black with a Meinkampf° look   65

And a love of the rack and the screw.
And I said I do, I do.
So daddy, I'm finally through.
The black telephone's off at the root,
The voices just can't worm through.   70

If I've killed one man, I've killed two—
The vampire who said he was you
And drank my blood for a year,

---

33 Dachau, Auschwitz, Belsen concentration camps   **42 Luftwaffe** German airforce
45 Panzer-man member of a tank crew   **65 Mein Kampf** *My Struggle* (title of Hitler's
autobiography)

Seven years, if you want to know.
Daddy, you can lie back now.   75

There's a stake in your fat black heart
And the villagers never liked you.
They are dancing and stamping on you.
They always *knew* it was you.
Daddy, daddy, you bastard, I'm through.   80

[1965]

Topics for Critical Thinking and Writing

1. Many readers find in this poem something that reminds them of nursery
   rhymes. If you are among these readers, specify the resemblance(s).
2. Some critics have called parts of the poem "surrealistic." Check a college
   dictionary, and then argue in a paragraph or two why the word is or is not
   appropriate.
3. Is this a poem whose experience a reader can share? Explain.

LOUISE ERDRICH

*Louise Erdrich was born in Little Falls, Minnesota, in 1954 and raised
in North Dakota; her father (born in Germany) and her mother (French
Ojibwe) both worked for the Bureau of Indian Affairs. After graduating
from Dartmouth College in 1976, she returned to North Dakota to
teach in the Poetry in the Schools Program. In 1979 she received a
master's degree in creative writing from Johns Hopkins University. She
was married to late author and anthropologist Michael Dorris, a professor of Native American Studies at Dartmouth, and they successfully collaborated on
multicultural literature. She now lives in Minneapolis, Minnesota, with her youngest
three children. Although Erdrich is most widely known as a novelist, she has also won a
reputation as a poet.*

Indian Boarding School: The Runaways

Home's the place we head for in our sleep.
Boxcars stumbling north in dreams
don't wait for us. We catch them on the run.
The rails, old lacerations that we love,
shoot parallel across the face and break   5
just under Turtle Mountains.° Riding scars
you can't get lost. Home is the place they cross.
The lame guard strikes a match and makes the dark

6 Turtle Mountains mountains in North Dakota and Manitoba

less tolerant. We watch through cracks in boards
as the land starts rolling, rolling till it hurts
to be here, cold in regulation clothes. 10
We know the sheriff's waiting at midrun
to take us back. His car is dumb and warm.
The highway doesn't rock, it only hums
like a wing of long insults. The worn-down welts 15
of ancient punishment leagd back and forth.

All runaways wear dresses, long green ones,
the color you would think shame was. We scrub
the sidewalks down because it's shameful work.
Our brushes cut the stone in watered arcs 20
and in the soak frail outlines shiver clear
a moment, things us kids pressed on the dark
face before it hardened, pale, remembering
delicate old injuries, the spines of names and leaves.

[1984]

Topics for Critical Thinking and Writing

1. In line 4 the railroad tracks are called "old lacerations." What is the connection between the two?
2. What other imagery of injury do you find in the poem? In lines 20–24, what—literally—is "the dark / face" that "hardened, pale"?

Places

BASHO

If the name of any Japanese poet is known in the United States, it is probably Matsuo Basho (1644–94). He lived most of his life in Edo (now called Tokyo), but he enjoyed traveling on foot in Japan and writing about his experiences. His most famous work, The Narrow Road to the Deep North *(1694), is a poetic diary recording one of his extended journeys. (It is available in several English translations.)*

We give here, however, a short poem in the form known as **haiku.** *A haiku has 17 syllables, arranged in 3 lines of 5, 7, and 5 syllables. Japanese poetry is unrhymed, but English versions—which may or may not follow the Japanese syllabic pattern—sometimes rhyme the first and third lines, as in the following translation of one of Basho's haiku:*

> On the withered bough
> A crow alone is perching;
> Autumn evening now.

The American poet Langston Hughes (1902–1967) wrote a number of poems grouped under the title "Hokku" (a variant of haiku), one of which goes thus:

> Keep straight do wn this block
> Then turn right where you will find
> A peach tree blooming.

The subject matter of a haiku can be high or low—the Milky Way or the screech of automobile brakes—but usually it is connected with the seasons, and it is described objectively and sharply. Here is Basho's most famous haiku. (The translation does not preserve the syllabic count of the original.)

An Old Pond

An old pond;
A frog jumps in—
The sound of the water.

Topic for Writing

Write at least one haiku. You need not use the 5-7-5 system if you don't want to; on the other hand, you may use rhyme if you wish. Some tips:

1. For a start, take some ordinary experience—tying your shoelaces, or seeing a cat at the foot of the stairs, or glancing out a window and seeing unexpected snowflakes, or hearing the alarm clock—and present it interestingly.
2. One way to make the experience interesting is to construct the poem in two parts—the first line balanced against the next two lines, or the first two lines balanced against the last line. If you construct a poem on this principle, the two sections should be related to each other, but they should also in some degree make a contrast with each other. Here is an example: "This handsome rooster / Struts before the clucking hens; / Inside, the pot is boiling." A second example, this one offering a contrast between pleasant sociability (the first two lines) and loneliness: "Look, O look, there go / Fireflies," I would like to say— / But I am alone."

ALLEN GINSBERG

Allen Ginsberg (1926–97) was born in Newark, New Jersey and graduated from Columbia University in 1948. After eight months in Columbia Psychiatric Institute—Ginsberg had pleaded insanity to avoid prosecution when the police discovered that a friend stored stolen goods in Ginsberg's apartment—he worked at odd jobs and finally left the nine-to-five world for a freer life in San Francisco. In the 1950s he established a reputation as an uninhibited declamatory poet whose chief theme was a celebration of those who were alienated from a repressive America.

A Supermarket in California

What thoughts I have of you tonight, Walt Whitman, for I walked down the sidestreets under the trees with a headache self-conscious looking at the full moon.

In my hungry fatigue, and shopping for images, I went into the neon fruit supermarket, dreaming of your enumerations!

What peaches and what penumbras! Whole families shopping at night!
Aisles full of husbands! Wives in the avocados, babies in the tomatoes!—
and you, García Lorca,° what were you doing down by the watermelons?

I saw you, Walt Whitman, childless, lonely old grubber, poking among
the meats in the refrigerator and eyeing the grocery boys.
I heard you asking questions of each: Who killed the pork chops?
What price bananas? Are you my Angel?   5
I wandered in and out of the brilliant stacks of cans following you, and
followed in my imagination by the store detective.
We strode down the open corridors together in our solitary fancy tasting
artichokes, possessing every frozen delicacy, and never passing the cashier.

Where are we going, Walt Whitman? The doors close in an hour.
Which way does your beard point tonight?
(I touch your book and dream of our odyssey in the supermarket and
feel absurd.)
Will we walk all night through solitary streets? The trees add shade to
shade, lights out in the houses, we'll both be lonely.   10
Will we stroll dreaming of the lost America of love past blue automo-
biles in driveways, home to our silent cottage?

Ah, dear father, graybeard, lonely old courage-teacher, what America did
you have when Charon° quit poling his ferry and you got out on a smoking
bank and stood watching the boat disappear on the black water of Lethe?

[1956]

Topics for Critical Thinking and Writing

1. Ginsberg calls his poem "A Supermarket in California." Need the market be
   in California, or can it be anywhere?
2. In the second line, Ginsberg explains why he went into the supermarket. Is
   the explanation clear, or puzzling, or some of each? Explain.
3. In the third section ("What peaches and what penumbras!"), what *is* a
   penumbra? Are the aisles full of them?
4. In line 8 ("Where are we going, Walt Whitman? The doors close in an hour.
   Which way does your beard point tonight?"), is Ginsberg hopeful or not
   about where he and Walt Whitman will stroll?
5. Read two or three Whitman poems (reprinted elsewhere in this book, pages
   441, 597–98). In what ways does Ginsberg's poem resemble Whitman's
   poems? In what ways is "A Supermarket" pure Ginsberg?

[3]**García Lorca** Federico García Lorca (1899–1936), Spanish poet (and, like Whitman and
Ginsberg, a homosexual)   [12]**Charon** in classical mythology, Charon ferried the souls of
the dead across the river Styx, to Hades, where, after drinking from the river Lethe, they
forgot the life they had lived.

JAMES WRIGHT

*James Wright (1927–80) was born in Martins Ferry, Ohio, which pro-
vided him with the locale for many of his poems. He is often thought of
as a poet of the Midwest, but (as in the example that we give) his
poems move beyond the scenery. Wright was educated at Kenyon College in Ohio and at the University of Washington. He wrote several
books of poetry and published many translations of European and
Latin American poetry.*

Lying in a Hammock at William Duffy's Farm in Pine Island, Minnesota

Over my head, I see the bronze butterfly,
Asleep on the black trunk,
Blowing like a leaf in green shadow.
Down the ravine behind the empty house,
The cowbells follow one another   5
Into the distances of the afternoon.
To my right,
In a field of sunlight between two pines,
The droppings of last year's horses
Blaze up into golden stones.   10
I lean back, as the evening darkens and comes on.
A chicken hawk floats over, looking for home.
I have wasted my life.

[1963]

 ## Topics for Critical Thinking and Writing

1. How important is it that the poet is "lying in a hammock"? That he is at some
   place other than his own home?
2. Do you take the last line as a severe self-criticism, or as a joking remark, or as
   something in between, or what?
3. Imagine yourself lying in a hammock—perhaps you can recall an actual moment in a hammock—or lying in bed, your eye taking in the surroundings.
   Write a description ending with some sort of judgment or concluding comment, as Wright does. You may want to parody Wright's poem, but you
   need not. (Keep in mind the fact that the best parodies are written by people who regard the original with affection.)

X. J. KENNEDY

X. J. Kennedy was born in New Jersey in 1929. He has taught at Tufts University and is the author of several books of poems, books for children, and college textbooks.

Nothing in Heaven Functions as It Ought

Nothing in Heaven functions as it ought:
Peter's° bifocals, blindly sat on, crack;
His gates lurch wide with the cackle of a cock,
Not turn with a hush of gold as Milton° had thought;   4
Gangs of the slaughtered innocents keep huffing
The nimbus off the Venerable Bede°
Like that of an old dandelion gone to seed;
And the beatific choir keep breaking up, coughing.   8

But Hell, sleek Hell hath no freewheeling part:
None takes his own sweet time, none quickens pace.
Ask anyone, How come you here, poor heart?—
And he will slot a quarter through his face,   12
You'll hear an instant click, a tear will start
Imprinted with an abstract of his case.

[1965]

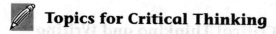

Topics for Critical Thinking

1. Roughly speaking, how does Kennedy characterize Heaven? Does his characterization strike you as disrespectful? Why, or why not?
2. In the octave (the first eight lines of the sonnet) Kennedy uses off-rhymes (*crack, cock; huffing, coughing*), but in the sestet (the last six lines) all the rhymes are exact. How do the rhymes help to convey the meaning?
3. "Nothing in Heaven" is a sonnet. How does the form of the poem help to convey the meaning?

2 Peter St. Peter, said to hold "the keys to the kingdom of Heaven" (Matt. 16.19)   **4 Milton** John Milton (1608–74), author of *Paradise Lost,* an epic poem that includes a description of heaven   **6 the Venerable Bede** English church historian (d. 735)

Things

WILLIAM WORDSWORTH

William Wordsworth (1770–1850), the son of an attorney, grew up in the Lake District of England. After graduating from Cambridge University in 1791, he spent a year in France, falling in love with a French girl, by whom he had a daughter. His enthusiasm for the French Revolution waned, and he returned alone to England where, with the help of a legacy, he devoted his life to poetry. With his friend, Samuel Taylor Coleridge, in 1798 he published anonymously a volume of poetry, Lyrical Ballads, *which changed the course of English poetry. In 1799 he and his sister Dorothy settled in Grasmere in the Lake District, where he married and was given the office of distributor of stamps. In 1843 he was appointed poet laureate.*

The World Is Too Much with Us

The world is too much with us; late and soon,
Getting and spending, we lay waste our powers;
Little we see in Nature that is ours;
We have given our hearts away, a sordid boon!°
This Sea that bares her bosom to the moon,   5
The winds that will be howling at all hours,
And are up-gathered now like sleeping flowers,
For this, for everything, we are out of tune;
It moves us not.—Great God! I'd rather be
A Pagan suckled in a creed outworn;   10
So might I, standing on this pleasant lea,
Have glimpses that would make me less forlorn;
Have sight of Proteus° rising from the sea;
Or hear old Triton° blow his wreathéd horn.

[1807]

Topics for Critical Thinking and Writing

1. How does the speaker clarify and explain the feeling expressed at the outset of the poem—that "the world is too much with us"? What does this phrase mean? Have you ever felt this way yourself? If so, what did you do about it?
2. Describe the tone of lines 1–9. Is the speaker angry? Depressed? Self-pitying?
3. Why does the speaker say he would rather be "a Pagan suckled in a creed outworn"? What's the point of referring to paganism?
4. Proteus and Triton: what is the purpose of these references to figures from classical mythology? How might such sights and sounds make the speaker feel better? But isn't the speaker also acknowledging that he knows that these figures do not really exist? What, then, is the meaning of the final

4 boon gift   **13, 14 Proteus, Triton** a sea god and a merman; Triton is often represented as blowing on a trumpet made out of a conch shell

lines? Does the speaker achieve a resolution of his problem (refer back to lines 1–9) or not?

EMILY DICKINSON

Emily Dickinson (1830–86) was born into a proper New England family in Amherst, Massachusetts. Although she spent her seventeenth year a few miles away, at Mount Holyoke Seminary (now Mount Holyoke College), in the next twenty years she left Amherst only five or six times, and in her last twenty years she may never have left her house. Her brother was probably right when he said that having seen something of the rest of the world—she had visited Washington with her father, when he was a member of Congress—"she could not resist the feeling that it was painfully hollow. It was to her so thin and unsatisfying in the face of the Great Realities of Life." Nevertheless, the following poem shows a keen interest in some things of the world.

I like to see it lap the Miles

I like to see it lap the Miles—
And lick the Valleys up—
And stop to feed itself at Tanks—
And then—prodigious step   4

Around a Pile of Mountains—
And supercilious peer
In Shanties—by the sides of Roads—
And then a Quarry pare   8

To fit its Ribs
And crawl between
Complaining all the while
In horrid—hooting stanza—
Then chase itself down Hill—   12

And neigh like Boanerges°—
Then—punctual as a Star
Stop—docile and omnipotent   16
At its own stable door—

[1862]

Topics for Critical Thinking and Writing

1. What is Dickinson describing?
2. Suppose someone argued that this poem is about literature, especially about poetry, which draws on the experiences of the mind ("stop to feed itself at Tanks"), threatens to go out of control ("prodigious step," "horrid—hooting

13 Boanerges a name said (in Mark 3.17) to mean "Sons of Thunder"

stanza," "chase itself down Hill"), but for the most part carefully orders its material ("pare," "crawl," "Stop—docile and omnipotent"). To what extent do you agree? Explain your position.

 WALT WHITMAN

Walt Whitman (1819–92) was born on Long Island, the son of a farmer. The young Whitman taught school and worked as a carpenter, a printer, a newspaper editor, and, during the Civil War, as a volunteer nurse on the Union side. After the war he supported himself by doing secretarial jobs. In Whitman's own day his poetry was highly contro-versial because of its unusual form (formlessness, many people said) and (though not in the following poem) its abundant erotic implications.

A Noiseless Patient Spider

A noiseless patient spider,
I mark'd where on a little promontory it stood isolated,
Mark'd how to explore the vacant vast surrounding,
It launch'd forth filament, filament, filament, out of itself,
Ever unreeling them, ever tirelessly speeding them.   5

And you O my soul where you stand,
Surrounded, detached, in measureless oceans of space,
Ceaselessly musing, venturing, throwing, seeking the spheres to connect them,
Till the bridge you will need be form'd, till the ductile anchor hold,
Till the gossamer thread you fling catch somewhere, O my soul.   10

[1862–63]

 **Topics for Critical Thinking and Writing**

1. How are the suggestions in "launch'd" (line 4) and "unreeling" (line 5) con-tinued in the second stanza?
2. How are the varying lengths of lines 1, 4, and 8 relevant to their ideas?
3. The second stanza is not a complete sentence. Why? The poem is un-rhymed. What effect does the near-rhyme (*hold: soul*) in the last two lines have on you?

 MARY OLIVER

Mary Oliver, born in Cleveland in 1935, attended Ohio State University and Vassar College. She is the author of six books of poetry—Ameri-can Primitive *received the Pulitzer Prize for Poetry in 1984, and* New and Selected Poems *received a National Book Award in 1992—and she has served as a visiting professor or a poet in residence at several colleges.*

Two of her prose comments may be of special interest. Of today's readers she has said, "The question asked today is: What does it mean? Nobody says, how does it feel?" And of her work she has said, "I am trying in my poems to vanish and have the reader be the experiencer. I do not want to be there. It is not even a walk we take together."

Hawk

This morning
   the hawk
      rose up
         out of the meadow's browse

and swung over the lake—   5
   it settled
      on the small black dome
         of a dead pine,

alert as an admiral,
   its profile   10
      distinguished with sideburns
         the color of smoke,

and I said: remember
   this is not something
      of the red fire, this is   15
         heaven's fistful

of death and destruction,
   and the hawk hooked
      one exquisite foot
         onto a last twig   20

to look deeper
   into the yellow reeds
      along the edges of the water
         and I said: remember

the tree, the cave,   25
   the white lily of resurrection,
      and that's when it simply lifted
         its golden feet and floated

into the wind, belly-first,
   and then it cruised along the lake—   30
      all the time its eyes fastened
         harder than love on some

unimportant rustling in the
   yellow reeds—and then it
      seemed to crouch high in the air, and then it   35
         turned into a white blade, which fell.

[1992]

Topics for Critical Thinking and Writing

1. As an experiment, rewrite the first eight lines, dividing them into two prose sentences. What is the difference between the two sentences in this form and the two stanzas of verse that Oliver has composed? How do the "same" words affect us differently?

2. The poem seems serious, even solemn (for example, lines 15–16), yet in places it seems witty, perhaps even on the edge of being comic, in its details (for example, lines 9–10, line 19). Do you find the speaker's tone and choices of language to be complicated and coherent, or simply confusing?

3. What is the nature of the speaker's relationship to the hawk? Does it mean something special to her, or is she really just concerned with giving a precise, accurate description of it?

4. How do you interpret lines 25–26? Are these lines to be understood in a secular or Christian context or both?

CHAPTER

14

Thinking Critically About Poetry

A Casebook on Emily Dickinson

In this casebook we give the texts of eleven poems and an essay by a student, on Dickinson's religious poetry.

Emily Dickinson (1830–86) was born into a proper New England family in Amherst, Massachusetts. Although she spent her seventeenth year a few miles away, at Mount Holyoke Seminary (now Mount Holyoke College), in the next twenty years she left Amherst only five or six times, and in her last twenty years she may never have left her house. Her brother was probably right when he said that having seen something of the rest of the world—she had visited Washington with her father, when he was a member of Congress—"she could not resist the feeling that it was painfully hollow. It was to her so thin and unsatisfying in the face of the Great Realities of Life." Dickinson lived with her parents (a somewhat reclusive mother and an austere, remote father) and a younger sister; a married brother lived in the house next door. She formed some passionate attachments, to women as well as men, but there is no evidence that they found physical expression.

By the age of twelve Dickinson was writing witty letters, but she apparently did not write more than an occasional poem before her late twenties. At her death—she died in the house where she was born—she left 1,775 poems, only seven of which had been published (anonymously) during her lifetime.

I heard a Fly buzz—when I died—

I heard a Fly buzz—when I died—
The Stillness in the Room
Was like the Stillness in the Air—
Between the Heaves of Storm—   4

The Eyes around—had wrung them dry—
And Breaths were gathering firm
For the last Onset—when the King
Be witnessed—in the Room—   8

I willed my Keepsakes—Signed away
What portion of me be
Assignable—and then it was
There interposed a Fly—   12

With Blue—uncertain stumbling Buzz—
Between the light—and me—
And then the Windows failed—and then
I could not see to see—   16

[c. 1862]

The Soul selects her own Society

The Soul selects her own Society—
Then—shuts the Door—
To her divine Majority—
Present no more—   4

Unmoved—she notes the Chariots—pausing—
At her low Gate—
Unmoved—an Emperor be kneeling
Upon her Mat—   8

I've known her—from an ample nation—
Choose One—
Then—close the Valves° of her attention—
Like Stone—

12

[1862]

11 Valves the two halves of a hinged door, such as is now found on old telephone booths. Possibly also an allusion to a bivalve, such as an oyster or a clam, having a shell consisting of two hinged parts

These are the days when Birds come back

These are the days when Birds come back—
A very few—a Bird or two—
To take a backward look.

These are days when skies resume
The old—old sophistries° of June—
A blue and gold mistake.

5

O fraud that cannot cheat the Bee—
Almost thy plausibility
Induces my belief.

Till ranks of seeds their witness bear—
And softly thro' the altered air
Hurries a timid leaf.

10

Oh Sacrament of summer days,
Oh Last Communion in the Haze—
Permit a child to join.

15

Thy sacred emblems to partake—
Thy consecrated bread to take
And thine immortal wine!

[1859]

5 sophistries deceptively subtle arguments

Papa above!

Papa above!
Regard a Mouse
O'erpowered by the Cat!
Reserve within thy kingdom
A "Mansion" for the Rat!

5

Snug in seraphic Cupboards
To nibble all the day,
While unsuspecting Cycles°
Wheel solemnly away!

[c. 1859]

8 Cycles long periods, eons

There's a certain Slant of light

There's a certain Slant of light,
Winter Afternoons—
That oppresses, like the Heft°
Of Cathedral Tunes—   4

Heavenly Hurt, it gives us—
We can find no scar,
But internal difference,
Where the Meanings, are—   8

None may teach it—Any—
'Tis the Seal Despair—
An imperial affliction
Sent us of the Air—   12

When it comes, the Landscape listens—
Shadows—hold their breath—
When it goes, 'tis like the Distance
On the look of Death—   16

[c. 1861]

3 Heft weight

This World is not Conclusion

This World is not Conclusion.
A Species stands beyond—
Invisible, as Music—
But positive, as Sound—
It beckons, and it baffles—   5
Philosophy—dont know—
And through a Riddle, at the last—
Sagacity, must go—
To guess it, puzzles scholars—
To gain it, Men have borne   10
Contempt of Generations
And Crucifixion, shown—
Faith slips—and laughs, and rallies—
Blushes, if any see—
Plucks at a twig of Evidence—   15
And asks a Vane, the way—
Much Gesture, from the Pulpit—
Strong Hallelujahs roll—
Narcotics cannot still the Tooth
That nibbles at the soul—   20

[c. 1862]

I got so I could hear his name—

I got so I could hear his name—
Without—Tremendous gain—
That Stop-sensation—on my Soul—
And Thunder—in the Room—   4

I got so I could walk across
That Angle in the floor,
Where he turned so, and I turned—how—
And all our Sinew tore—   8

I got so I could stir the Box—
In which his letters grew
Without that forcing, in my breath—
As Staples—driven through—   12

Could dimly recollect a Grace—
I think, they call it "God"—
Renowned to ease Extremity—
When Formula, had failed—   16

And shape my Hands—
Petition's way,
Tho' ignorant of a word
That Ordination°—utters—   20

My Business, with the Cloud,
If any Power behind it, be,
Not subject to Despair—

It care, in some remoter way,   24
For so minute affair
As Misery—
Itself, too great, for interrupting—more—

[1861]

20 Ordination the ministry

Because I could not stop for Death

Because I could not stop for Death—
He kindly stopped for me—
The Carriage held but just Ourselves—
And Immortality.   4

We slowly drove—He knew no haste
And I had put away
My labor and my leisure too,
For His Civility—   8

We passed the School, where Children strove
At Recess—in the Ring—

We passed the Fields of Gazing Grain—
We passed the Setting Sun—   12

Or rather—He passed Us—
The Dews drew quivering and chill—
For only Gossamer, my Gown—
My Tippet°—only Tulle°—   16

We paused before a House that seemed
A Swelling of the Ground—
The Roof was scarcely visible—
The Cornice—in the Ground—   20

Since then—'tis Centuries—and yet
Feels shorter than the Day
I first surmised the Horses' Heads
Were toward Eternity—   24

                                                                [c. 1863]

16 Tippet shawl **Tulle** net of silk

Those—dying, then

Those—dying, then
Knew where they went
They went to God's Right Hand—
The Hand is amputated now
And God cannot be found—   5

The abdication of Belief
Makes the Behavior small—
Better an ignis fatuus°
Than no illume at all—

                                                                  [1882]

8 ignis fatuus a phosphorescent light that hovers over swampy ground, hence something
deceptive

Apparently with no surprise

Apparently with no surprise
To any happy Flower
The Frost beheads it at its play—
In accidental power—
The blonde Assassin passes on—   5
The Sun proceeds unmoved
To measure off another Day
For an Approving God.

                                                                [c. 1884]

Tell all the Truth but tell it slant

Tell all the Truth but tell it slant—
Success in Circuit lies
Too bright for our infirm Delight
The Truth's superb surprise   4

As Lightning to the Children eased
With explanation kind
The Truth must dazzle gradually
Or every man be blind—   8

[c. 1868]

A SAMPLE ESSAY BY A STUDENT: RELIGION AND RELIGIOUS IMAGERY IN EMILY DICKINSON

Peter Gottsegen

English 150G

April 12, 1999

Religion and Religious Imagery in Emily Dickinson

Emily Dickinson was not a preacher but a poet, so if we read her poetry about God we should not be surprised if we do not find a simple, consistent view, or even a clear development from one view--for instance, belief--to another--for instance, loss of faith. Rather, judging from some examples of her poetry, she explored various views, and we should not try to convert this variety into unity.

We can begin by looking at extreme views, first two poems of faith, and then a poem of doubt. One of the poems of faith, "Papa above" (446), begins with a childlike or almost playful version of the Lord's Prayer. (In Matthew 6.9 Jesus begins a prayer by saying, "Our father who art in heaven.") I think this poem says that God will see to it that even a mouse or rat will get into heaven, and will remain there for eternity. But Dickinson's God is not always concerned for all of the creatures of the world. In another poem that expresses belief in the existence of God, "Apparently with no surprise" (449), Dickinson describes the frost as beheading a flower--that is, beauty perishes--and she goes on to make the point that this occurs under the eyes of "an Approving God." Here she seems to be saying that evil takes place, and God approves of it. It is important to realize that in this poem Dickinson still says that God exists, even if he is indifferent to suffering.

In another poem, "Those--dying, then" (449), Dickinson expresses doubt that God exists. In olden days, she says, people mistakenly thought that God would protect them, but now, she says, "God cannot be found." She uses a particularly terrifying image to convey the loss of God. In the past, Dickinson says, the faithful went to "God's Right Hand," but, she goes on to say, "The Hand is amputated now. . . ." The faith in God that earlier people had was an illusion, but it was something, and it was "better" than the nothingness we now experience. This nothingness, or something not much more than nothingness, is the subject of "I heard a Fly buzz--when I died" (444–45). In this poem, the speaker expects "the King" (God) to appear to her as she dies, but all she sees is a fly, and then she hears its buzz. God ("the King") never appears.

Even these few poems show that Dickinson held a variety of views about God and religion, and it is difficult or perhaps impossible for us to say exactly what her religious beliefs were. But what is certain is that religious ideas were so important to her, so much a part of her mind, that even when she was not explicitly writing about the existence of a benevolent God or the absence of God, she used religious imagery--for instance, to describe impressive things in the natural world around her. In "These are the days when Birds come back" (446), she talks about what we call Indian summer, fall days that are like summer days. But the poem is filled with religious words: "belief," "Sacrament," "Communion," "consecrated bread," "immortal wine." The fifth stanza goes like this:

> Oh Sacrament of summer days,
> Oh Last Communion in the Haze--
> Permit a child to join.

I don't think Dickinson is really talking about traditional religion here. Instead, she is using religious imagery to talk about a particular precious moment in the seasons. As a second example of her use of religious imagery in a poem that is about nature and not about God, we might look at "There's a certain Slant of light" (447). In this poem she says that on "Wintry Afternoons" this particular light has "the Heft / Of Cathedral Tunes." That is, the wintry light has the solidity, the feel, the "heft" of religious music. When we see this light, Dickinson says, we are moved, in a way that we are moved by music in church. She is not saying anything here about whether God is benevolent or not, or whether he exists or not. Rather, she is drawing on experiences in church--probably experiences shared by many people even today--to help us to see nature more effectively.

Speaking as someone who was brought up with traditional religious beliefs but who does not go to church now, I can say that Dickinson effectively represents the ideas of a believer and also of a non-believer. But what I think is especially impressive is that she sees that someone who no longer is a believer can't help but still think in religious terms when he or she sees something exceptionally beautiful, for instance on a winter day "a certain Slant of light."

Work Cited

Barnet, Sylvan, et al. Literature and Composition. 5th ed. New York: Longman, 2000.

✎ Topics for Critical Thinking and Writing

1. In this essay Gottsegen comments on the following poems: "Papa above," "Apparently with no surprise," "Those—dying, then," "I heard a Fly buzz—when I died," "These are the days when Birds come back," and "There's a certain Slant of light." Read or reread each of these poems to see if you agree with Gottsegen's interpretations.
2. Are there other poems in the casebook that you think Gottsegen could have used with better effect than some that he did use? Explain.
3. Reread the concluding paragraph. Do you think it is effective? Explain.

PART

III

Standing Back: Arguing Interpretations and Evaluations, and Understanding Critical Approaches

Arguing an Interpretation

In Chapter 2 we disucssed arguing with yourself as a way of developing ideas; in Chapter 3 we discussed arguing about meanings of interpretations; and in Chapter 7 we discussed supporting arguments with evidence. Nevertheless, we have more to say about writing an argument, and we will say some of it in this chapter and in the next two chapters where we will consider assumptions and evidence.

INTERPRETATION AND MEANING

We can define **interpretation** as

- a setting forth of the meaning, or, better,
- a setting forth of one or more of the meanings of a work of literature.

This question of *meaning* versus *meanings* deserves a brief explanation. Although some critics believe that a work of literature has a single meaning, the meaning it had for the author, most critics hold that a work has several meanings, for instance the meaning it had for the author, the meaning(s) it had for its first readers (or viewers, if the work is a drama), the meaning(s) it had for later readers, and the meaning(s) it has for us today. Take *Hamlet* (1600–01), for example. Perhaps this play about a man who has lost his father had a very special meaning for Shakespeare, who had recently lost his own father. Further, Shakespeare had earlier lost a son named Hamnet, a variant spelling of Hamlet. The play, then, may have had important psychological meanings for Shakespeare—but the audience could not have shared (or even known) these meanings.

What *did* the play mean to Shakespeare's audience? Perhaps the original audience of *Hamlet*—people living in a monarchy, presided over by Queen Elizabeth I—were especially concerned with the issue (specifically raised in *Hamlet*) of whether a monarch's subjects ever have the right to overthrow the monarch. But obviously for twentieth-century Americans the interest in the play lies elsewhere, and the play must mean something else. If we are familiar with Freud, we may see in the play a young man who subconsciously lusts after his mother and seeks to kill his father (in the form of Claudius, Hamlet's uncle). Or we may see the play as largely about an alienated young man in a bourgeois society. Or—but the interpretations are countless.

IS THE AUTHOR'S INTENTION A GUIDE TO MEANING?

Shouldn't we be concerned, one might ask, with the *intentions* of the author? The question is reasonable, but there are difficulties, as the members of the Supreme Court find when they try to base their decisions on the original intent of the writers of the Constitution. First, for older works we almost never know what the intention is. Authors did not leave comments about their intentions. We have *Hamlet,* but we do not have any statement of Shakespeare's intention concerning this or any other play. One might argue that we can deduce Shakespeare's intention from the play itself, but to argue that we should study the play in the light of Shakespeare's intention, and that we can know his intention by studying the play, is to argue in a circle. We can say that Shakespeare must have intended to write a tragedy (if he intended to write a comedy he failed), but we can't go much further in talking about his intention.

Even if an author has gone on record expressing an intention, we may think twice before accepting the statement as decisive. The author may be speaking facetiously, deceptively, mistakenly, or (to be brief) unconvincingly. For instance, Thomas Mann said, probably sincerely and accurately, that he wrote one of his novels merely in order to entertain his family—but we may nevertheless take the book seriously and find it profound.

IS THE WORK THE AUTHOR'S OR THE READER'S?

A good deal of recent critical theory argues that the writer's views are by no means definitive, especially since writers—however independent they may think they are—largely reflect the ideas of their age. In current terminology, to accept the artist's statements about a work is "to privilege intentionalism." The idea that the person who seems to have created the work cannot comment definitively on it is especially associated with Roland Barthes (1915–80), author of a much-reprinted essay entitled "The Death of the Author," and Michel Foucault (1926–84), author of an equally famous essay entitled "What Is an Author?" (Barthes's essay appears in his *Image-Music-Text* [1977], Foucault's in *Foucault Reader* [1984]). Foucault, for example, assumes that the concept of the author is a repressive invention designed to impede the free circulation of ideas. In Foucault's view, the work belongs—or ought to belong—to the *perceiver,* not to the alleged maker.

Much can be said on behalf of this idea—and much can be said against it. On its behalf, one can again say that we can never entirely recapture the writer's intentions and sensations. Suppose, for instance, we are reading a work by Langston Hughes (1902–67), the African-American poet, essayist, and dramatist. None of us can exactly recover Hughes's attitudes; we cannot exactly re-create in our minds what it was like to be Langston Hughes in the 1930s and 1940s—an age that preceded the civil rights movement. We can read his texts, but we necessarily read them through our own eyes and in our own times.

Similarly, we can read or see a performance of an ancient Greek tragedy (let's say Sophocles's *King Oedipus*), but surely we cannot experience the play as did the Greeks, for whom it was part of an annual ritual. Further, a Greek spectator probably had seen earlier dramatic versions of the story. The Oedipus legend was, so to speak, part of the air that the Greeks breathed. Moreover we know (or think we know) things that the Greeks did not know. If we are familiar with Freud's view of the Oedipus complex—the idea that males wish to displace their fathers by sleeping with their mothers—we probably cannot experience Sophocles's *King Oedipus* without in some degree seeing it through Freud's eyes.

However, *against* the idea that works have no inherent core of meaning that all careful readers can perceive, one can argue that a competent writer shapes the work so that his or her meaning is largely evident to a competent reader—that is, to a reader familiar with the language and with the conventions of literature. (Writers of course do not mindlessly follow conventions; they can abide by, challenge, or even violate conventions, putting them to fresh purposes. But to deeply enjoy and understand a given work—say, an elegy—one needs some familiarity with other works of a similar kind.) Many people who write about literature assume a community of informed readers, and indeed this assumption seems to be supported by common sense.

WHAT CHARACTERIZES A GOOD INTERPRETATION?

Even the most vigorous advocates of the idea that meaning is indeterminate do not believe that all interpretations are equally significant. Rather, they believe that an interpretive essay is offered against a background of ideas, shared by essayist and reader, as to what constitutes a *persuasive argument.* Thus, an essay (even if it is characterized as "interpretive free play" or "creative engagement") will have to be

- coherent,
- plausible, and
- rhetorically effective.

The *presentation*—the rhetoric—as well as the interpretation is significant. This means (to repeat a point made in Chapter 2) that the essayist cannot merely set down random expressions of feeling or unsupported opinions. The essayist must, on the contrary, convincingly *argue* a thesis—must point to evidence so that the reader will not only know what the essayist believes but will also understand why he or she believes it.

There are lots of ways of making sense (and even more ways of making nonsense), but one important way of helping readers to see things from your point of view is to do your best to face all of the complexities of the work. Put it this way: Some interpretations strike a reader as better than others because they are *more inclusive,* that is, because they *account for more of the details of the work.* The less satisfactory interpretations leave a reader pointing to some aspects of the work—to some parts of the whole—and saying, "Yes, but your explanation doesn't take account of . . . ." This does not mean, of course, that a reader must feel that a persuasive interpretation says the last word about the work. We always realize that the work—if we value it highly—is richer than the discussion, but, again, for us to value an interpretation we must find the interpretation plausible and inclusive.

Interpretation often depends not only on making connections among various elements of the work (for instance, among the characters in a story or among the images in a poem), and among the work and other works by the author, but also on making connections between the particular work and a **cultural context.** The cultural context usually includes other writers and specific works of literature, since a given literary work participates in a tradition. That is, if a work looks toward life, it also looks toward other works. A sonnet, for example, is about human experience, but it is also part of a tradition of sonnet writing. The more works of literature you are familiar with, the better equipped you are to interpret any particular work. Here is the way Robert Frost put it, in the preface to *Aforesaid:*

> A poem is best read in the light of all the other poems ever written. We read A the better to read B (we have to start somewhere; we may get very little out of A). We read B the better to read C, C the better to read D, D the better to go back and get something more out of A. Progress is not the aim, but circulation. The thing is to get among the poems where they hold each other apart in their places as the stars do.

Given the (debatable) views (1) that a work of literature may have several or even many meanings, (2) that some meanings may be unknowable to a modern spectator, and (3) that meaning is largely or even entirely determined by the viewer's particular circumstances, some students of literature prefer to say that they offer a "commentary" on the "significance" of a work rather than an "interpretation" of the "meaning."

AN EXAMPLE: INTERPRETING PAT MORA'S "IMMIGRANTS"

Let's think about interpreting a short poem by a contemporary poet, Pat Mora.

Immigrants

wrap their babies in the American flag,
feed them mashed hot dogs and apple pie,
name them Bill and Daisy,
buy them blonde dolls that blink   5
blue eyes or a football and tiny cleats
before the baby can even walk,
speak to them in thick English,
    hallo, babee, hallo.
whisper in Spanish or Polish   10
when the babies sleep, whisper
in a dark parent bed, that dark
parent fear, "Will they like
our boy, our girl, our fine american
boy, our fine american girl?"   15

[1986]

Perhaps most readers will agree that the poem expresses or dramatizes a desire, attributed to "immigrants," that their child grow up in an Anglo mode. (Mora is not saying that *all* immigrants have this desire; she has simply invented one speaker who says such-and-such. Of course *we* may say that Mora says all immigrants have this desire, but that is our interpretation.) For this reason the parents call their children Bill and Daisy (rather than, say, José and Juanita) and give them blonde dolls and a football (rather than dark-haired dolls and a soccer ball). Up to this point, the parents seem a bit silly in their mimicking of Anglo ways. But the second part of the poem gives the reader a more interior view of the parents, brings out the fear and hope and worried concern that lies behind the behavior: Some unspecified "they" may not "like / our boy, our girl." Who are "they"? Most readers probably will agree that "they" refers to native-born citizens, especially the blond, blue-eyed "all-American" Anglo types that until recently constituted the establishment in the United States.

One can raise further questions about the interpretation of the poem.

- Exactly what does the poet mean when she says that immigrants "wrap their babies in the American flag"? Are we to take this literally?
- If not, how are we to take it?
- And why in the last two lines is the word "american" not capitalized? Is Mora imitating the non-native speaker's uncertain grasp of English punctuation? (But if so, why does Mora capitalize "American" in the first line and "Spanish" and "Polish" later in the poem?) Or is she perhaps implying some mild reservation about becoming 100 percent American, some suggestion that in changing from Spanish or Polish to "american" there is some sort of loss?

A reader might seek Mora out and ask her why she didn't capitalize "american" in the last line, but Mora might not be willing to answer, or she might not give a straight answer, or she might say that she doesn't really know why—it just seemed right when she wrote the poem. Most authors do in fact take this last approach. When they are working as writers, they work by a kind of instinct, a kind of feel for the material. Later they can look critically at their writing, but that's another sort of experience.

To return to our basic question: What characterizes a good interpretation? The short answer is, *Evidence,* and especially evidence that seems to cover all relevant issues. In an essay it is not enough merely to assert an interpretation. Your readers don't expect you to make an airtight case, but because you are trying to help readers to understand a work—to see a work the way you do—you are obliged to

- offer reasonable supporting evidence.
- take account of what might be set forth as counterevidence to your thesis.

Of course your essay may originate in an intuition or an emotional response, a sense that the work is about such-and-such, but this intuition or emotion must then be examined, and it must stand a test of reasonableness. (It's usually a good idea to jot down in a journal your first responses to a work, and in later entries to reflect on them.) It is not enough in an essay merely to set forth your response. Your readers will expect you to *demonstrate* that the response is something that they can to a large degree share. They may not be convinced that the interpretation is right or true, but they must at least feel that the interpretation is plausible and in accord with the details of the work, rather than, say, highly eccentric and irreconcilable with some details.

This book includes seven casebooks, some of which include essays by critics advancing interpretations. When you read these interpretations, think about *why* you find some interpretations more convincing than others.

THINKING CRITICALLY ABOUT RESPONSES TO LITERATURE

Usually you will begin with a strong *response* to your reading—interest, boredom, bafflement, annoyance, shock, pleasure, or whatever. Fine. Then, if you are going to think critically about the work, you will go on to *examine* your response in order to understand it, or to deepen it, or to change it.

How can you change a response? Critical thinking involves seeing an issue from all sides, to as great a degree as possible. As you know, in ordinary language *to criticize* usually means to find fault, but in literary studies the term does not have a negative connotation. Rather, it means "to examine carefully." (The word *criticism* comes from a Greek verb meaning "to distinguish," "to decide," "to judge.") Nevertheless, in one sense the term *critical thinking* does approach the usual meaning, since critical thinking requires you to take a skeptical view of your response. You will, so to speak, argue with yourself, seeing if your response can stand up to doubts.

Let's say that you have found a story implausible. Question yourself:

- Exactly what is implausible in it?
- Is implausibility always a fault?
- If so, exactly why?

Your answers may deepen your response. Usually, in fact, you will find supporting evidence for your response, but in your effort to distinguish and to decide and to judge, try also (if only as an exercise) to find **counterevidence.** See what can be said against your position. (The best lawyers, it is said, prepare two cases—their own, and the other side's.) As you consider the counterevidence you will sometimes find that it requires you to adjust your thesis. Fine. You may even find yourself developing an entirely different response. That's also fine, though of course the paper that you ultimately hand in should clearly argue a thesis.

Critical thinking, in short, means examining or exploring one's own responses, by questioning and testing them. Critical thinking is not so much a skill (though it does involve the ability to understand a text) as it is a *habit of mind,* or, rather, several habits, including

- Open-mindedness
- Intellectual curiosity
- Willingness to work

It may involve, for instance, willingness to discuss the issues with others and to do research, a topic that will be treated separately in Appendix B, on writing a research paper.

TWO SAMPLE INTERPRETATIONS

Robert Frost, "Stopping by Woods on a Snowy Evening"

Read Frost's "Stopping by Woods on a Snowy Evening," and then read the first interpretation, written by a first-year student. This interpretation is followed by a discussion that is devoted chiefly to two questions:

- What is the essayist's thesis?
- Does the essayist offer convincing evidence to support the thesis?

A second essay by another first-year student, offering a different interpretation of the poem, provides further material for you to analyze critically.

ROBERT FROST (1874–1963)

Robert Frost (1874–1963) was born in California. After his father's death in 1885 Frost's mother brought the family to New England, where she taught in high schools in Massachusetts and New Hampshire. Frost studied for part of one term at Dartmouth College in New Hampshire, then did odd jobs (including teaching), and from 1897 to 1899 was enrolled as a special student at Harvard. He then farmed in New Hampshire, published a few poems in local newspapers, left the farm and taught again, and in 1912 left for England, where he hoped to achieve more

Manuscript version of Frost's "Stopping by Woods on a Snowy Evening." The first part is lost. (Courtesy of the Jones Library, Inc. Amherst, Mass.)

popular success as a writer. By 1915 he had won a considerable reputation, and he re-turned to the United States, settling on a farm in New Hampshire and cultivating the image of the country-wise farmer-poet. In fact he was well read in the classics, the Bible, and English and American literature.

Stopping by Woods on a Snowy Evening

Whose woods these are I think I know.
His house is in the village though;
He will not see me stopping here
To watch his woods fill up with snow.   4

My little horse must think it queer
To stop without a farmhouse near
Between the woods and frozen lake
The darkest evening of the year.   8

He gives his harness bells a shake
To ask if there is some mistake.
The only other sound's the sweep
Of easy wind and downy flake.   12

The woods are lovely, dark and deep.
But I have promises to keep,
And miles to go before I sleep,
And miles to go before I sleep.   16

[1923]

Sample Essay by a Student: Stopping by Woods—and Going On

Darrel MacDonald

Stopping by Woods—and Going On

Robert Frost's "Stopping by Woods on a Snowy Evening" is about what the title says it is. It is also about something more than the title says.

When I say it is about what the title says, I mean that the poem really does give us the thoughts of a person who pauses (that is, a person who is "stopping") by woods on a snowy evening. (This person probably is a man, since Robert Frost wrote the poem and nothing in the poem clearly indicates that the speaker is not a man. But, and this point will be important, the speaker perhaps feels that he is not a very masculine man. As we will see, the word "queer" appears in the poem, and, also, the speaker uses the word "lovely," which sounds more like the word a woman would use than a man.) In line 3 the speaker says he is "stopping here," and it is clear that "here" is by woods, since "woods" is mentioned not only in the title but also in the first line of the poem, and again in the second stanza, and still again in the last stanza. It is equally clear that, as the title says, there is snow, and that the time is evening. The speaker mentions "snow" and "downy flake," and he says this is "The darkest evening of the year."

But in what sense is the poem about more than the title? The title does not tell us anything about the man who is "stopping by woods," but the poem--the man's meditation--tells us a lot about him. In the first stanza he reveals that he is uneasy at the thought that the owner of the woods may see him stopping by the woods. Maybe he is uneasy because he is trespassing, but the poem does not actually say that he has illegally entered someone else's property. More likely, he feels uneasy, almost ashamed, of watching the "woods fill up with snow." That is, he would not want anyone to see that he actually is enjoying a beautiful aspect of nature and is not hurrying about whatever his real business is in thrifty Yankee style.

The second stanza gives more evidence that he feels guilty about enjoying beauty. He feels so guilty that he even thinks the horse thinks there is something odd about him. In fact, he says that the horse thinks he is "queer," which of course may just mean odd, but also (as is shown by The American Heritage Dictionary) it can mean "gay," "homosexual." A real man, he sort of suggests, wouldn't spend time looking at snow in the woods.

So far, then, the speaker in two ways has indicated that he feels insecure, though perhaps he does not realize that he has given himself away. First, he expresses uneasiness that someone might see him watching the woods fill up with snow. Second, he expresses uneasiness when he suggests that even the horse thinks he is strange, maybe even "queer" or unmanly, or at least unbusinesslike. And so in the last stanza, even though he finds the woods beautiful, he decides not to stop and to see the woods fill up with snow. And his description of the woods as "lovely"--a woman's word--sounds as though he may be something less than a he-man. He seems to feel ashamed of himself for enjoying the sight of the snowy woods and for seeing them as "lovely," and so he tells himself that he has spent enough time looking at the woods and that he must go on about his business. In fact, he tells himself <u>twice</u> that he has business to attend to. Why? Perhaps he is insisting too much. Just as we saw that he was excessively nervous in the first stanza, afraid that someone might see him trespassing and enjoying the beautiful spectacle, now at the end he is again afraid that someone might see him loitering, and so he very firmly, using repetition as a form of emphasis, tries to reassure himself that he is not too much attracted by beauty and is a man of business who keeps his promises.

Frost gives us, then, a man who indeed is seen "stopping by woods on a snowy evening," but a man who, afraid of what society will think of him, is also afraid to "stop" long enough to fully enjoy the sight that attracts him, because he is driven by a sense that he may be seen to be trespassing and also may be thought to be unmanly. So after only a brief stop in the woods he forces himself to go on, a victim (though he probably doesn't know it) of the work ethic and of an over-simple idea of manliness.

Let's examine this essay briefly.

The title is interesting. It gives the reader a good idea of which literary work will be discussed ("Stopping by Woods") *and* it arouses interest, in this case by a sort of wordplay ("Stopping . . . Going On"). A title of this sort is preferable to a title that merely announces the topic, such as "An Analysis of Frost's 'Stopping by Woods'" or "On a Poem by Robert Frost."

The opening paragraph helpfully names the exact topic (Robert Frost's poem) and arouses interest by asserting that the poem is about something more than its title. The writer's thesis presumably will be a fairly specific assertion concerning what else the poem is "about."

The body of the essay, beginning with the second paragraph, begins to develop the thesis. (The **thesis** perhaps can be summarized thus: "The speaker, insecure of his masculinity, feels ashamed that he responds with pleasure to the sight of the snowy woods.") The writer's evidence in the second paragraph is that the word "queer" (a word sometimes used of homosexuals) appears, and that the word "lovely" is "more like the word a woman would use than a man." Readers of MacDonald's essay may at this point be unconvinced by this evidence, but probably they suspend judgement. In any case, he has offered what he considers to be evidence in support of his thesis.

The next paragraph dwells on what is said to be the speaker's uneasiness, and the following paragraph returns to the word "queer," which, MacDonald correctly says, can mean "gay, homosexual." The question of course is whether *here,* in this poem, the word has this meaning. Do we agree with MacDonald's assertion, in the last sentence of this paragraph, that Frost is suggesting that "A real man . . . wouldn't spend time looking at snow in the woods"? Clearly this is the way MacDonald takes the poem—but is his response to these lines reasonable? After all, what Frost says is this: "My little horse must think it queer / To stop without a farmhouse near." Is it reasonable to see a reference to homosexuality (rather than merely to oddness) in *this* use of the word "queer"? Hasn't MacDonald offered a response that, so to speak, is private? It is *his* response—but are we likely to share it, to agree that we see it in Frost's poem?

The next paragraph, amplifying the point that the speaker is insecure, offers as evidence the argument that "lovely" is more often a woman's word than a man's. Probably most readers will agree on this point, though many or all might deny that only a gay man would use the word "lovely." And what do you think of MacDonald's assertions that the speaker of the poem "was excessively nervous in the first stanza" and is now "afraid that someone might see him loitering"? In your opinion, does the text lend much support to MacDonald's view?

The concluding paragraph effectively reasserts and clarifies MacDonald's thesis, saying that the speaker hesitates to stop and enjoy the woods because "he is driven by a sense that he may be seen to be trespassing and also may be thought to be unmanly."

The big question, then, is whether the thesis is argued *convincingly.* It certainly *is* argued, not merely asserted, but how convincing is the evidence? Does MacDonald offer enough to make you think that his response is one that you can share? Has he helped you to enjoy the poem by seeing things that you may not have noticed—or has he said things that, however interesting, seem to you not to be in close contact with the poem as you see it?

Here is another interpretation of the same poem.

Sample Essay by a Student: "Stopping by Woods on a Snowy Evening" as a Short Story

Sara Fong

"Stopping by Woods on a Snowy Evening" as a Short Story

Robert Frost's "Stopping by Woods on a Snowy Evening" can be read as a poem about a man who pauses to observe the beauty of nature, and it can also be read as a poem about a man with a death wish, a man who seems to long to give himself up completely to nature and thus escape his responsibilities as a citizen. Much depends, apparently, on what a reader wants to emphasize. For instance, a reader can emphasize especially appealing lines about the beauty of nature: "The only other sound's the sweep / Of easy wind and downy flake," and "The woods are lovely, dark and deep." On the other hand, a reader can emphasize lines that show the speaker is fully aware of the responsibilities that most of us agree we have. For instance, at the very start of the poem he recognizes that the woods are not his but are owned by someone else, and at the end of the poem he recognizes that he has "promises to keep" and that before he sleeps (dies?) he must accomplish many things (go for "miles").

Does a reader have to choose between these two interpretations? I don't think so; to the contrary, I think it makes sense to read the poem as a kind of very short story, with a character whose developing thoughts make up a plot with four stages. In the first stage, the central figure is an ordinary person with rather ordinary thoughts. His very first thought is of the owner of the woods. He knows who the owner is, and since the owner lives in the village, the poet feels safe in trespassing, or at least in watching the woods "fill up with snow." Then, very subtly, the poet begins to tell us that although this seems to be an ordinary person thinking ordinary thoughts, he is a somewhat special person in a special situation. First of all, the horse thinks something is strange. He shakes his bells, wondering why the driver doesn't keep moving, as presumably ordinary drivers would. Second, we are told that this is "The darkest evening of the year." Frost could simply have said that the evening is dark, but he goes out of his way to make the evening a special evening.

We are now through with the first ten lines, and only six lines remain, yet in these six lines the story goes through two additional phases. The first three of these lines ("The only other sound's the sweep / Of easy wind and downy flake" and "The woods are lovely, dark and deep") are probably the most beautiful lines, in the sense that they are the ones that make us say, "I wish I were there," or "I'd love to experience this." We feel that the poet has moved from the ordinary thoughts of the first stanza, about such businesslike things as who owns the woods and where the owner's house is, to less materialistic thoughts, thoughts about the beauty of the nonhuman world of nature. And now, with the three final lines, we get the fourth stage of the story, the return to the ordinary world of people, the world of "promises." But this world that we get at the end is not exactly the same as the world we got at the beginning. The world at the beginning of the poem is a world of property (who owns the woods, and where the house is), but the world at the end of the poem is a world of unspecified and rather mysterious responsibilities ("promises to keep," "miles to go before I sleep"). It is almost as though the poet's experience of the beauty of nature--a beauty that for a moment made him forget the world of property--has in fact served to sharpen his sense that human beings have responsibilities. He clearly sees that "The woods are lovely, dark and deep," and then he says (I add the italics) "<u>But</u> I have promises to keep." The "but" would be logical if after saying that the woods are lovely, dark and deep, he had said something like "But in the daylight they look different," or "But one can freeze to death in them." The logic of what Frost says, however, is not at all clear: "The woods are lovely, dark and deep, / But I have promises to keep." What is the logical connection? We have to supply one, something like "but, <u>because we are human beings we have</u> responsibilities; we can refresh ourselves by perceiving the beauties of nature, and we can even for a moment get so caught up that we seem to enter an enchanted forest ('the woods are lovely, dark and deep'), but we cannot forget our responsibilities."

My point is not that Frost ends with an important moral, and it is also not that we have to choose between saying it is a poem about nature or a poem about a man with a death wish. Rather, my point is that the poem takes us through several stages and that, although the poem begins and ends with the speaker in the woods, the speaker has undergone mental experiences--has, we might say, gone through a plot with a conflict (the appeal of the snowy woods versus the call to return to the human world). It's not a matter of good versus evil and of one side winning. Frost in no way suggests that it is wrong to feel the beauty of nature--even to the momentary exclusion of all other thoughts. But the poem is certainly not simply a praise of the beauty of nature. Frost shows us, in this mini-story or mini-drama, one character who sees the woods as property, then sees them as a place of almost overwhelming beauty, and then (maybe refreshed by this experience) rejoins the world of chores and responsibilities.

Topics for Critical Thinking and Writing

1. What is the thesis of the essay?
2. Does the essayist offer convincing evidence to support the thesis?
3. Do you consider the essay to be well written, poorly written, or something in between? On what evidence do you base your opinion?

ADDITIONAL POEMS FOR INTERPRETATION

ROBERT FROST
Mending Wall

Something there is that doesn't love a wall,
That sends the frozen-ground-swell under it,
And spills the upper boulders in the sun;
And makes gaps even two can pass abreast.
The work of hunters is another thing: 5
I have come after them and made repair
Where they have left not one stone on a stone,
But they would have the rabbit out of hiding,
To please the yelping dogs. The gaps I mean,
No one has seen them made or heard them made,   10
But at spring mending-time we find them there.
I let my neighbor know beyond the hill;
And on a day we meet to walk the line
And set the wall between us once again.
We keep the wall between us as we go.   15
To each the boulders that have fallen to each.
And some are loaves and some so nearly balls
We have to use a spell to make them balance:
"Stay where you are until our backs are turned!"
We wear our fingers rough with handling them.   20
Oh, just another kind of outdoor game,
One on a side. It comes to little more:
There where it is we do not need the wall:
He is all pine and I am apple orchard.
My apple trees will never get across   25
And eat the cones under his pines, I tell him.
He only says, "Good fences make good neighbors."
Spring is the mischief in me, and I wonder
If I could put a notion in his head:
"*Why* do they make good neighbors? Isn't it   30
Where there are cows? But here there are no cows.
Before I built a wall I'd ask to know
What I was walling in or walling out,
And to whom I was like to give offense.
Something there is that doesn't love a wall,   35

That wants it down." I could say "Elves" to him,
But it's not elves exactly, and I'd rather
He said it for himself. I see him there
Bringing a stone grasped firmly by the top
In each hand, like an old-stone savage armed.   40
He moves in darkness as it seems to me,
Not of woods only and the shade of trees.
He will not go behind his father's saying,
And he likes having thought of it so well
He says again, "Good fences make good neighbors."   45

[1914]

✏ Topics for Critical Thinking and Writing

1. The poem includes a scene, or action, in which the speaker and a neighbor are engaged. Briefly summarize the scene. What indicates that the scene has been enacted before and will be again?
2. Compare and contrast the speaker and the neighbor.
3. Notice that the speaker, not the neighbor, initiates the business of repairing the wall (line 12). Why do you think he does this?
4. Both the speaker and the neighbor repeat themselves; they each make one point twice in identical language. What do they say? And why does Frost allow the neighbor to have the last word?
5. "Something there is that doesn't love a wall" adds up to "Something doesn't love a wall." Or does it? Within the context of the poem, what is the difference between the two statements?
6. Write an essay of 500 words, telling of an experience in which you came to conclude that "good fences make good neighbors." Or tell of an experience that led you to conclude that fences (they can be figurative fences, of course) are "like to give offense" (see lines 32–34).

 **ROBERT FROST**
Nothing Gold Can Stay

Nature's first green is gold,
Her hardest hue to hold.
Her early leaf's a flower;
But only so an hour.
Then leaf subsides to leaf.
So Eden sank to grief,
So dawn goes down to day.
Nothing gold can stay.

[1923]

Topics for Critical Thinking and Writing

1. What does Frost mean in line 1 when he says, "nature's first green is gold"?
2. Can we confirm or disprove the first line? If so, how?
3. What meaning(s) does "gold" have in this poem? Support your assertion with argument(s).
4. If we say "This poem is by Robert Frost," the statement is either true or false, but if we say "Hello" to someone, or if we stub a toe and say "Ouch," the utterance is not true or false but simply is *expressive*. Do you think Frost's poem should be taken only as an expression of his emotions, or should it also be evaluated in terms of its degree of truth? Give *reasons* to support your answer.
5. Do you find the poem depressing? Why, or why not?
6. A poem begins not with its first line but with its title. What is the effect here of repeating the beginning—the title—in the final line? If you were reciting the poem aloud, might you speak the title and the final line differently? For instance, in speaking the title might you emphasize "gold" but in the final line emphasize "Nothing"? Why, or why not? Does a change in the way the line is said change the meaning?

WILLIAM WORDSWORTH

William Wordsworth (1770–1850) grew up in the Lake District in England. After graduating from Cambridge University in 1791, he spent a year in France, where he fell in love with a French girl and fathered her child. His enthusiasm for the French Revolution waned, and he returned alone to England, where be devoted his life to poetry. We print a poem, written in 1799, that is one of five poems customarily called "Lucy poems," even though this particular poem, unlike the other four, does not mention the woman's name. It is not known if the poems refer to a real person.

A Slumber Did My Spirit Seal

A slumber did my spirit seal;
  I had no human fears;
She seemed a thing that could not feel.
  The touch of earthly years.   4

No motion has she now, no force;
  She neither hears nor sees;
Rolled round in earth's diurnal course,
With rocks, and stones, and trees.   8

[1799]

Topics for Critical Thinking and Writing

Each of the following assertions represents a brief interpretation. Evaluate each, citing evidence to support or rebut it.

1. The first stanza expresses the speaker's comforting but naive view (his *spirit,* i.e., his intelligence, was in a *slumber*) that his beloved was exempt from the pressures of this world; the second stanza expresses his horrified realization that, now dead, she is mere inanimate matter mechanistically hurled into violent motion.

2. The poem, by a pantheist—someone who identifies the Deity with everything in the universe—is about the poet's realization that the woman whom he loved, and who seemed to be apart from everything else, is now (through her death) assimilated into the grandeur of all that is on the earth; her death is a return to the life of nature.

3. The poem is ambiguous—just as, say, the following sentence is ambiguous: "Martha's mother died when she was twenty." (Who was twenty, Martha or her mother?) There is no way to decide between the first and second views expressed.

4. The word *diurnal* ("daily") adds a solemnity that makes it impossible to see the poem as a statement about the brutality of Lucy's death. Further, *diurnal* contains the word *urn,* thereby affirming that the entire earth is her funeral urn.

5. Even if the second view correctly summarizes Wordsworth's pantheism, *for today's readers* the poem is about the brute fact of death.

6. The language is ambiguous, so the only intelligent way to decide between conflicting interpretations is to choose the interpretation that best fits in with what we know about the author.

7. Here, as in most poetry by males, the female is allowed no significant identity. She is a "thing" (line 3), she is the object of the poet's love, she seems to be above nature (thus she is the traditional woman on a pedestal), she is a nature spirit, she is the poet's inspiration—she is lots of things, but she is not a person.

If none of the preceding statements seems to you to be just what you would say if you were asked to summarize your interpretation, set forth your own view, in 50-75 words, and then support it by pointing to details in the poem.

CHAPTER

Arguing an Evaluation

CRITICISM AND EVALUATION

Although, as previously noted, in ordinary usage *criticism* implies finding fault, and therefore implies evaluation—"This story is weak"—in fact most literary criticism is *not* concerned with evaluation. Rather, it is chiefly concerned with *interpretation* (the setting forth of meaning) and with *analysis* (examination of relationships among the parts, or of causes and effects). For instance, an interpretation may argue that in *Death of a Salesman* Willy Loman is the victim of a cruel capitalistic economy, and an analysis may show how the symbolic setting of the play (a stage direction tells us that "towering, angular shapes" surround the salesman's house) contributes to the meaning. In our discussion of "What Is Literature?" we saw that an analysis of Robert Frost's "The Span of Life" (p. 35) called attention to the contrast between the meter of the first line (relatively uneven or irregular, with an exceptional number of heavy stresses) and the meter of the second (relatively even and jingling). The analysis also called attention to the contrast between the content of the first line (the old dog) and the second (the speaker's memory of a young dog):

> The old dog barks backward without getting up.
> I can remember when he was a pup.

In our discussion we did not worry about whether this poem deserves an A, B, or C, nor did we consider whether it was better or worse than some other poem by Frost, or by some other writer. And, to repeat, if one reads books and journals devoted to literary study, one finds chiefly discussions of meaning. For the most part, critics assume that the works they are writing about have value and are good enough to merit attention, so critics largely concern themselves with other matters.

Evaluative Language and the Canon

Still, some critical writing is indeed concerned with evaluation—with saying that works are good or bad, dated or classic, major or minor. (The language need not be as explicit as these words are: evaluation can also be conveyed through words like *moving, successful, effective, important,* or, on the other hand, *tedious, unsuccessful, weak,* and *trivial.*) In reviews of plays, books, movies, musical and dance performances, and films, professional critics usually devote much of their space to evaluating the work or the performance, or both. The reviewer seeks, finally, to tell readers whether to buy a book or a ticket—or to save their money and their time.

In short, although in our independent reading we read what we like, and we need not argue that one work is better than another, the issue of evaluation is evident all around us.

ARE THERE CRITICAL STANDARDS?

One approach to evaluating a work of literature, or, indeed, to evaluating anything at all, is to rely on personal taste. This approach is evident in a statement such as "I don't know anything about modern art, but I know what I like." The idea is old, at least as old as the Roman saying *De gustibus non est disputandum* ("There is no disputing tastes").

If we say "This is a good work" or "This book is greater than that book," are we saying anything beyond "I like this" and "I like this better than that"? Are all expressions of evaluation really nothing more than expressions of taste? Most people believe that if there are such things as works of art, or works of literature, there must be standards by which they can be evaluated, just as most other things are evaluated by standards. The standards for evaluating a scissors, for instance, are perfectly clear: it ought to cut cleanly, it ought not to need frequent sharpening, and it ought to feel comfortable in the hand. We may also want it to look nice (perhaps to be painted—or on the contrary to reveal its stainless steel), and to be inexpensive, rustproof, and so on, but in any case we can easily state our standards. Similarly, there are agreed-upon standards for evaluating figure skating, gymnastics, fluency in language, and so on.

But what are the standards for evaluating literature? In earlier pages we have implied one standard: In a good work of literature, all of the parts contribute to the whole, making a unified work. Some people would add that mere unity is not enough; a work of high quality needs not only to be unified but needs also to be complex. The writer offers a "performance in words" (Frost's words, again), and when we read, we can see if the writer has successfully kept all of the Indian clubs in the air. If, for instance, the stated content of the poem is mournful, yet the meter jingles, we can probably say that the performance is unsuccessful; at least one Indian club is clattering on the floor.

Here are some of the standards commonly set forth:

- Personal taste
- Truth, realism
- Moral content
- Esthetic qualities, for instance unity

Let's look at some of these in detail.

Morality and Truth as Standards

"It is always a writer's duty to make the world better." Thus wrote Samuel Johnson, in 1765, in his "Preface to Shakespeare." In this view, **morality** plays a large role: a story that sympathetically treats lesbian or gay love is, from a traditional

Judeo-Christian perspective, probably regarded as a bad story, or at least not as worthy as a story that celebrates heterosexual married love. On the other hand, a gay or lesbian critic, or anyone not committed to Judeo-Christian values, might regard the story highly because, in such a reader's view, it helps to educate readers and thereby does something "to make the world better."

But there are obvious problems. For one thing, a gay or lesbian story might strike even a reader with traditional values as a work that is effectively told, with believable and memorable characters, whereas a story of heterosexual married love might be unbelievable, awkwardly told, trite, sentimental. (More about sentimentality in a moment.) How much value does one give to the ostensible content of the story, the obvious moral or morality, and how much value does one give to the artistry exhibited in telling the story?

People differ greatly about moral (and religious) issues. Edward Fitzgerald's 1859 translation of *The Rubáiyát of Omar Khayyám* (a twelfth-century Persian poem) suggests that God doesn't exist, or—perhaps worse—if He does exist, He doesn't care about us. That God does not exist is a view held by many moral people: it is also a view opposed by many moral people. The issue then may become a matter of **truth.** Does the value of the poem depend on which view is right? In fact, does a reader have to subscribe to Fitzgerald's view to enjoy (and to evaluate highly) the following stanza from the poem, in which Fitzgerald suggests that the pleasures of this world are the only paradise that we can experience?

> A book of verses underneath the bough,
> A jug of wine, a loaf of bread—and thou
>   Beside me singing in the wilderness—
> Oh, wilderness were paradise enow!

Some critics can give high value to a literary work only if they share its beliefs, if they think that the work corresponds to reality. They measure the work against their vision of the truth.

Other readers can highly value a work of literature that expresses ideas they do not believe, arguing that literature does not require us to believe in its views. Rather, this theory claims, literature gives a reader a strong sense of *what it feels like* to hold certain views—even though the reader does not share those views. Take, for instance, a lyric poem in which Christina Rossetti (1830–94), a devout Anglican, expresses both spiritual numbness and spiritual hope. Here is one stanza from "A Better Resurrection":

> My life is like a broken bowl.
>   A broken bowl that cannot hold
> One drop of water for my soul
>   Or cordial in the searching cold:
> Cast in the fire the perished thing:
>   Melt and remould it, till it be
> A royal cup for Him, my King:
>   O Jesus, drink of me.

One need not be an Anglican suffering a crisis to find this poem of considerable interest. It offers insight into a state of mind, and the truth or falsity of religious belief is not at issue. Similarly, one can argue that although *The Divine Comedy* by Dante Alighieri (1265–1321) is deeply a Roman Catholic work, the non-Catholic reader can read it with interest and pleasure because of (for example) its rich portrayal of a wide range of characters, the most famous of whom perhaps are the pathetic lovers Paolo and Francesca. In Dante's view, they are eternally damned because they were unrepentant adulterers, but a reader need not share this belief.

Other Ways of Thinking About Truth and Realism

Other solutions to the problem of whether a reader must share a writer's beliefs have been offered. One extreme view says that beliefs are irrelevant, since literature has nothing to do with truth. In this view, a work of art does not correspond to anything "outside" itself, that is, to anything in the real world. If a work of art has any "truth," it is only in the sense of being internally consistent. Thus Shakespeare's *Macbeth,* like, say, "Rock-a-bye Baby," isn't making assertions about reality. *Macbeth* has nothing to do with the history of Scotland, just as (in this view) Shakespeare's *Julius Caesar* has nothing to do with the history of Rome, although Shakespeare borrowed some of his material from history books. These tragedies, like lullabies, are worlds in themselves—not to be judged against historical accounts of Scotland or Rome—and we are interested in the characters in the plays only as they exist *in the plays.* We may require, for instance, that the characters be consistent, believable, and engaging, but we cannot require that they correspond to historical figures. Literary works are neither true nor false; they are only (when successful) coherent and interesting. The poet William Butler Yeats (1865–1939) perhaps had in mind something along these lines when he said that you can refute a philosopher, but you cannot refute the song of sixpence. And indeed "Sing a song of sixpence, / Pocket full of rye" has endured for a couple of centuries, perhaps partly because it has nothing to do with truth or falsity; it has created its own engaging world.

The view that we should not judge literature by how much it corresponds to our view of the world around us is held by many literary critics, and there probably is something (maybe a great deal) to it. For instance, some argue that there is no fixed, unchanging, "real" world around us; there is only what we perceive, what we ourselves "construct," and each generation, indeed each individual, constructs things differently.

And yet one can object, offering a commonsense response: Surely when we see a play, or read an engaging work of literature, whether it is old or new, we feel that somehow the work says something about the life around us, the real world. True, some of what we read—let's say, detective fiction—is chiefly fanciful: we read it to test our wits, or to escape, or to kill time. But most literature seems to be connected to life. This commonsense view, that literature is related to life, has an ancient history, and in fact almost everyone in the Western world believed it from the time of the ancient Greeks until the nineteenth century, and of course many people—including authors and highly skilled readers—still believe it today.

For instance, a concern for accuracy characterizes much writing. Many novelists do a great deal of research, especially into the settings where they will place their characters. And they are equally concerned with style—with the exactness of each word that they use. Flaubert is said to have spent a day writing a sentence and another day correcting it. The German author Rainer Maria Rilke (1875–1926) has a delightful passage in *The Notebooks of Malte Laurids Brigge* (1910), in which he mentions someone who was dying in a hospital. The dying man heard a nurse mispronounce a word, and so (in Rilke's words) "he postponed dying." First he corrected the nurse's pronunciation. Rilke tells us, and "then he died. He was a poet and hated the approximate."

Certainly a good deal of literature, most notably the realistic short story and the novel, is devoted to giving a detailed picture that at least *looks like* the real world. One reason we read the fiction of Kate Chopin is to find out what "the real world" of Creole New Orleans in the late nineteenth century was like—as seen through Chopin's eyes, of course. (One need not be a Marxist to believe, with Karl Marx, that one learns more about industrial England from the novels of Dickens and Mrs. Gaskell than from economic treatises.) Writers of stories, novels, and plays are concerned to give plausible, indeed precise and insightful, images of the relationships between people. Writers of lyric poems presumably are specialists in presenting human feelings, the experience of love, for instance, or of the loss of faith. And presumably we are invited to compare the writer's created world to the world that we live in, perhaps to be reminded that our own lives can be richer than they are.

Even when a writer describes an earlier time, the implication is that the description is accurate, and especially that people *did* behave the way the writer says they did—and the way our own daily experience shows us that people do behave. Here is George Eliot at the beginning of her novel *Adam Bede* (1859):

> With a single drop of ink for a mirror, the Egyptian sorcerer undertook to reveal to any chance comer far-reaching visions of the past. This is what I undertake to do for you, reader. With this drop of ink at the end of my pen, I will show you the roomy workshop of Jonathan Burge, carpenter and builder in the village of Hayslope, as it appeared on the 18th of June, in the year of Our Lord, 1799.

Why do novelists like George Eliot give us detailed pictures, and cause us to become deeply involved in the lives of their characters? Another novelist, D. H. Lawrence, offers a relevant comment in the ninth chapter of *Lady Chatterley's Lover* (1928):

> It is the way our sympathy flows and recoils that really determines our lives. And here lies the vast importance of the novel, properly handled. It can inform and lead into new places the flow of our sympathetic consciousness, and it can lead our sympathy away in recoil from things gone dead. Therefore, the novel, properly handled, can reveal the most secret places of life.

In Lawrence's view, we can evaluate a novel in terms of its moral effect on the reader: the good novel, Lawrence claims, leads us into worlds—human relationships—that deserve our attention, and leads us away from "things gone dead," presumably relationships and values—whether political, moral, and religious—that no longer deserve to survive. To be blunt, Lawrence claims that good books improve us. His comment is similar to a more violent comment, quoted earlier, by Franz Kafka: "A book must be an ice-axe to break the frozen sea inside us."

Realism, of course, is not the writer's only tool. In *Gulliver's Travels* Swift gives us a world of Lilliputians, people about six inches tall. Is his book pure fancy, unrelated to life? Not at all. We perceive that the Lilliputians are (except for their size) pretty much like ourselves, and we realize that their tiny stature is an image of human pettiness, an *un*realistic device that helps us to see the real world more clearly.

The view that we have been talking about—that writers do connect us to the world—does not require realism, but it does assume that writers see, understand, and, through the medium of their writings, give us knowledge, deepen our understanding, and even perhaps improve our character. If, the argument goes, a work distorts reality—let's say because the author sees women superficially—the work is inferior. Some such assumption is found, for instance, in a comment by Elaine Savory Fido, who says that the work of Derek Walcott, a Caribbean poet and dramatist, is successful when Walcott deals with racism and with colonialism but is unsuccessful when he deals with women. "His treatment of women," Fido says in an essay in *Journal of Commonwealth Literature* (1986),

> is full of clichés, stereotypes and negativity. I shall seek to show how some of his worst writing is associated with these portraits of women, which sometimes lead him to the brink of losing verbal control, or give rise to a retreat into abstract, conventional terms which prevent any real treatment of the subject. (109)

We need not here be concerned with whether or not Fido's evaluations of Walcott's works about women and about colonialism are convincing: what concerns us is her assumption that works can be—should be—evaluated in terms of the keenness of the writer's perception of reality.

Although we *need* not be concerned with an evaluation, we may wish to be concerned with it, and, if so, we will probably find, perhaps to our surprise, that in the very process of arguing our evaluation (perhaps only to ourselves) we are also interpreting and reinterpreting. That is, we find ourselves observing passages closely, from a new point of view, and we may therefore find ourselves seeing them differently, finding new meanings in them.

IS SENTIMENTALITY A WEAKNESS—
AND IF SO, WHY?

The presence of **sentimentality** is often regarded as a sign that a writer has failed to perceive accurately. Sentimentality is usually defined as excessive emotion, especially an excess of pity or sorrow. But when one thinks about it, who is to say when an emotion is "excessive"? Surely (to take an example) parents can be grief-stricken by the death of a child; and just as surely they may continue to be grief-stricken for the rest of their lives. Well, how about a child's grief for a dead pet, or an adult's grief for the death of an elderly person, a person who has lived a full life, for whom death might serve as a relief? Again, can any of us say how someone else ought to feel?

What each reader can say, however, is that the *expression* of grief in a particular literary work is or is not successful, convincing, engaging, moving. Though readers may not be able to say that the emotion is proper or improper, they can say that the literary expression of that emotion is successful or not. Consider the following poem by Eugene Field (1850-95).

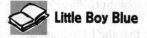 **Little Boy Blue**

The little toy dog is covered with dust,
    But sturdy and stanch he stands:
And the little toy soldier is red with rust.
    And his musket moulds in his hands.
Time was when the little toy dog was new.   5
    And the soldier was passing fair:
And that was the time when our Little Boy Blue
    Kissed them and put them there.

"Now, don't you go till I come," he said.
    "And don't you make any noise!"   10
So, toddling off to his trundle-bed,
    He dreamt of the pretty toys:
And, as he was dreaming, an angel song
    Awakened our Little Boy Blue—
Oh! the years are many, the years are long,   15
    But the little toy friends are true!

Ay, faithful to Little Boy Blue they stand,
    Each in the same old place—
Awaiting the touch of a little hand,
    The smile of a little face;   20
And they wonder, as waiting the long years through
    In the dust of that little chair,
What has become of our Little Boy Blue,
    Since he kissed them and put them there.

[1889]

Why do many readers find this poem sentimental, and of low quality? Surely not
because it deals with the death of a child. Many other poems deal with this subject sympathetically, movingly, interestingly. Perhaps one sign of weak writing
in "Little Boy Blue" is the insistence on the word *little*. The boy is little (five
times, counting the title), the dog is little (twice), the toy soldier is little (once),
the toys collectively are little (once), and Little Boy Blue has a little face, a little
hand, and a little chair. Repetition is not an inherently bad thing, but perhaps
here we feel that the poet is too insistently tugging at our sympathy, endlessly asserting the boy's charm yet not telling us anything interesting about the child
other than that he was little and that he loved his "pretty toys." Real writers don't
simply accept and repeat the Hallmark greeting card view of reality. Children are
more interesting than "Little Boy Blue" reveals, and adults react to a child's death
in a more complex way.

   Further, the boy's death is in no way described or explained. A poet of
course is not required to tell us that the child died of pneumonia or in an automobile accident, but since Field did choose to give us information about the
death we probably want something better than the assertion that when a child
dies it is "awakened" by an "angel song." One might ask oneself if this is an interesting, plausible, healthy way of thinking of the death of a child. In talking
about literature we want to be cautious about using the word *true*, for reasons al-

ready discussed, but can't we say that Field's picture of childhood and his explanation of death simply don't ring true? Don't we feel that he is talking nonsense?
And finally, can't we be excused for simply not believing that the speaker of the
poem, having left the arrangement of toys undisturbed for "many" years, thinks
that therefore "the little toy friends are true," and that they "wonder" while
"waiting the long years through." More nonsense. If we recall D. H. Lawrence's
comment, we may feel that in this poem the poet has *not* properly directed "the
flow of our sympathetic consciousness."

Let's look now at another poem on the death of a child, this one by X. J.
Kennedy (b. 1929):

 **Little Elegy**

for a child who skipped rope

Here lies resting, out of breath,
Out of turns, Elizabeth
Whose quicksilver toes not quite
Cleared the whirring edge of night.   4

Earth whose circles round us skim
Till they catch the lightest limb,
Shelter now Elizabeth
And for her sake trip up Death.   8

[1961]

This is a "little" elegy—literally, since it is only eight lines long—for another
child. We can't know for sure how the poet really felt, but will you agree that the
work itself (presumably the expression of feeling) is both tenderhearted and restrained? It is also—we can use the word—true: the passing days (alluded to here
in the reference to the ever-turning earth) really do finally catch everyone, even
someone with "the lightest limb." Further, the poem is also witty: In the first
stanza Elizabeth is said to be "Out of turns." a child's expression appropriately
describing a child at play, but here also meaning that Elizabeth is no longer turning about in this world, and also that she died too early, before her expected
time or turn. Notice, too, the fresh use of "out of breath," here meaning not only
"breathless from exertion" (as a girl skipping rope would sometimes be) but also
"unbreathing, dead."

In the second stanza the poet addresses the "Earth." Its revolutions (which
resemble the circular motion of the skipping rope) catch all of us, but the earth
will also "shelter" the dead girl, in a grave. The poem ends with a small, bitter
joke about tripping up Death, thus continuing the imagery of skipping rope. The
last line conveys (with great restraint) the unreconciled attitude most of us feel
when hearing of the death of a child. No such note of resentment occurs in
Field's poem: one almost believes that Field thinks the death of Little Boy Blue is
a very beautiful thing. His poem is all sweetness, uncomplicated by any perception of the pain that death causes.

Let's look at one more poem about death, although here the subject is not a
child but several young men.

GWENDOLYN BROOKS (b. 1917)
We Real Cool

The Pool Players.
Seven at the Golden Shovel

We real cool. We
Left school. We

Lurk late. We
Strike straight. We

Sing sin. We
Drink gin. We

Jazz June. We
Die soon.

[1960]

The subtitle pretty much tells us that the speakers are seven people who hang out at a pool hall called the Golden Shovel, and the last line tells us that they "Die soon," that is, while still young. The speaker uses Black English (one characteristic is the omission of the verb, as in "We real cool," instead of "We are real cool"), and he speaks for the group. The title and the first line of the poem each begin with the word "We," and the sense of group identity is emphasized by the fact that each line—except the last—ends with "We."

The death of these seven dropouts is communicated not only by what the poem explicitly says but also by what it does not say, or, rather, by what it shows. The "we" that occurs at the end of each of the first seven lines is missing from the eighth line; the group is no more. Beside the fact that they die—that we see them disappear—what can we say about them?

The young men have a strong sense of group identity but they have no connection with anyone else, except with June, a person who apparently exists only as a sexual object. There are no adults in the poem, and no whites. They live in an isolated world. We can say at least two other things about them: (1) They speak sentences of only three words, sentences of the utmost simplicity, and (2) the simplicity in fact is deceptive, because the language is vigorous, marked by strong rhythm and by interesting alliteration (repetition of initial sounds, as in "*L*urk *l*ate" and "*J*azz *J*une"). The speaker has something urgent to say, and he says it memorably. (Of course it is really Gwendolyn Brooks who is doing the talking, but Brooks has chosen to create this effective spokesperson, this character who holds our interest.) The poem, in short, communicates not only the group's severe limitations (behavior that will lead to early deaths) but also communicates the group's strengths (a sense of fellow feeling, a skill with language).

And can't we also say that the poem communicates the sadness of the waste of human lives, without tearfully tugging at our sleeve? Don't we feel that although the poet sympathizes with these seven young men (and all others who resemble them), she nevertheless does not try to sweeten the facts and take us into an unreal Little-Boy-Blue world where we can feel good about our response to death? She does not sentimentalize; she looks without flinching, and she tells it as it is. Perhaps we can even say that although the Golden Shovel and these seven young men may be inventions, the poem is a fiction that speaks the truth.

No one can tell you how you should feel about these three poems, but ask yourself

- if you agree with some or all of what has been said about them;
- on what standards you base your own evaluation of them;
- which of the first two poems ("Little Boy Blue" and "Little Elegy") you would prefer to read if you were so unfortunate as to have lost a child or a young sibling.
- Then explain *why* you answered as you did.

ADDITIONAL WORKS FOR EVALUATION

MATTHEW ARNOLD

Matthew Arnold (1822–88) was the son of a famous educator, Dr. Thomas Arnold, the headmaster of Rugby School. After graduating from Oxford, Matthew Arnold became an inspector of schools, a post he held until two years before his death. Besides writing poetry, Arnold wrote literary criticism and was appointed professor of poetry at Oxford from 1857 to 1867. He traveled widely on the Continent and lectured in the United States.

Dover Beach

The sea is calm to-night.
The tide is full, the moon lies fair
Upon the straits;—on the French coast the light
Gleams and is gone; the cliffs of England stand
Glimmering and vast, out in the tranquil bay.   5
Come to the window, sweet is the night-air!
Only, from the long line of spray
Where the sea meets the moon-blanch'd land,
Listen! you hear the grating roar
Of pebbles which the waves draw back, and fling,   10
At their return, up the high strand,
Begin, and cease, and then again begin,
With tremulous cadence slow, and bring
The eternal note of sadness in.

Sophocles long ago   15
Heard it on the Ægean, and it brought
Into his mind the turbid ebb and flow
Of human misery; we
Find also in the sound a thought,
Hearing it by this distant northern sea.   20

The Sea of Faith
Was once, too, at the full, and round earth's shore
Lay like the folds of a bright girdle furl'd.

But now I only hear
Its melancholy, long, withdrawing roar,   25
Retreating, to the breath
Of the night-wind, down the vast edges drear
And naked shingles° of the world.

Ah, love, let us be true
To one another! for the world, which seems   30
To lie before us like a land of dreams,
So various, so beautiful, so new,
Hath really neither joy, nor love, nor light,
Nor certitude, nor peace, nor help for pain;
And we are here as on a darkling plain   35
Swept with confused alarms of struggle and flight,
Where ignorant armies clash by night.

                                                                        [c. 1851]

²⁸**shingles** pebbled beaches

Topics for Critical Thinking and Writing

1. How would you characterize the speaker's tone of voice? Does the tone stay
   the same throughout?
2. What do we learn about the relationship between the speaker and the person whom he addresses? How is this relationship connected to the speaker's
   reflections on the general sorrow of life and the loss of faith?
3. What is your response to the simile that Arnold uses in line 23?
4. "Dover Beach" is included in many anthologies of literature and collections of
   verse. In your view, does this fact bear witness to the force of habit, or is there
   something about this poem that makes it especially important and memorable?

ANTHONY HECHT

*Anthony Hecht was born in New York City in 1923, and educated at
Bard College and Columbia University. He has taught at several institutions (since 1985 he has been at Georgetown University), and he has
served as poetry consultant to the Library of Congress.*

*Like "The Dover Bitch," which assumes a reader's familiarity with
Matthew Arnold's "Dover Beach," much of Hecht's work glances at
earlier literature.*

The Dover Bitch

A Criticism of Life
For Andrews Wanning

So there stood Matthew Arnold and this girl
With the cliffs of England crumbling away behind them,

And he said to her, "Try to be true to me,
And I'll do the same for you, for things are bad
All over, etc., etc."   5
Well now, I knew this girl. It's true she had read
Sophocles in a fairly good translation
And caught that bitter allusion to the sea.
But all the time he was talking she had in mind
The notion of what his whiskers would feel like   10
On the back of her neck. She told me later on
That after a while she got to looking out
At the lights across the channel, and really felt sad,
Thinking of all the wine and enormous beds
And blandishments in French and the perfumes.   15
And then she got really angry. To have been brought
All the way down from London, and then be addressed
As sort of a mournful cosmic last resort
Is really tough on a girl, and she was pretty.
Anyway, she watched him pace the room   20
And finger his watch-chain and seem to sweat a bit,
And then she said one or two unprintable things.
But you mustn't judge her by that. What I mean to say is,
She's really all right. I still see her once in a while
And she always treats me right.   25
We have a drink
And I give her a good time, and perhaps it's a year
Before I see her again, but there she is,
Running to fat, but dependable as they come,
And sometimes I bring her a bottle of *Nuit d'Amour*.   30

[1967]

 ## Topics for Critical Thinking and Writing

1. Do you think that the first six lines of Hecht's poem are too chatty and in-
   formal? What might be the poet's purpose in writing in this style?
2. Line 8 seems somewhat puzzling. Is "that bitter allusion to the sea" the kind
   of phrase that the speaker of the first few lines would use? Take note as well
   of the word "blandishments" in line 15, and the phrase "mournful cosmic
   last resort," line 18. Are the tone and diction of these lines consistent with
   that of the rest of the poem?
3. What, finally, is the point of Hecht's poem? Is he simply making fun of the
   stuffy, solemn author of "Dover Beach," or, beyond that, does he seek to
   present and explore a point of view of his own—for example, on the nature
   of male/female relationships?
4. Does "The Dover Bitch," to be effective, require that we know "Dover
   Beach"? If you came across Hecht's poem by itself, and had never read
   Arnold's poem, what do you imagine your response to "The Dover Bitch"
   would be?

 ## A. E. HOUSMAN

Alfred Edward Housman (1859–1936) was born near rural Shropshire, England, and educated in classics and philosophy at Oxford University. Although he was a brilliant student, his final examination was unexpectedly weak—in fact, he failed—and he did not receive the academic appointment that he had anticipated. He began working as a civil servant at the British Patent Office, but in his spare time he wrote scholarly articles on Latin literature, and these writings in 1892 won him an appointment as Professor of Latin at the University of London. In 1911 he was appointed to Cambridge. During his lifetime he published (in addition to his scholarly writings) only two thin books of poetry, A Shropshire Lad (1898) and Last Poems (1922), and a highly readable lecture called The Name and Nature of Poetry (1933). After his death a third book of poems, More Poems (1936), was published. The following poem is from this posthumous publication.

From the Wash the Laundress Sends

From the wash the laundress sends
My collars home with ravelled ends:
I must fit, now these are frayed,
My neck with new ones, London-made.
Homespun collars, homespun hearts,   5
Wear to rags in foreign parts.
Mine at least's as good as done,
And I must get a London one.

[1895]

Topics for Critical Thinking and Writing

1. Housman wrote this poem in 1895, but for some reason he did not publish it in his book of 1898 or in his second book, 1922. Do you think the poem is too trivial to merit publication? If you find it trivial, argue your case. If, on the other hand, you think it has serious implications, argue *that* case. Finally, evaluate the poem, perhaps on the basis of light verse (poetry that aims chiefly at entertaining), or perhaps on the basis that it is an effective or an ineffectual serious poem.

2. A small point, but one worth a moment's thought: When the poem was first published, in 1936, it was printed as two quatrains, that is with a space between lines 4 and 5, even though in Housman's manuscript nothing suggests a break. If you were printing the poem, would you print it as eight continuous lines (four couplets) or as two quatrains? Why?

IRA GERSHWIN

Ira (originally Israel) Gershwin (1896–1983) was born in the Lower East Side of New York City, of Russian-Jewish immigrant parents. He attended City College of New York for two years (1914–16), but dropped out so that he could concentrate on his work for musical comedies. A writer of lyrics, he collaborated with his younger brother George on some twenty Broadway musicals, as well as with others—notably Moss Hart, Kurt Weill, Jerome Kern, and Harold Arlen. In 1932 he and his collaborators (Morrie Ryskind and George S. Kaufman) received a Pulitzer Prize for the musical satire, Of Thee I Sing *(1931). Among his best-known songs (in addition to "The Man That Got Away") are "The Man I Love," "I Got Rhythm," "Embraceable You," and (from* Porgy and Bess *[1935]) "Summertime," "I Got Plenty o' Nuttin'," and "It Ain't Necessarily So." "The Man That Got Away" (music by Harold Arlen) was written for Judy Garland, in* A Star Is Born *(1954).*

Judy Garland (1922–69) is best known for her roles in such film musicals as The Wizard of Oz *(1939),* Meet Me in St. Louis *(1944), and* Easter Parade *(1948). In* A Star Is Born, *the tragic story of an aging actor who helps a young, aspiring actress to fame, Garland excelled in both her musical and dramatic work.*

The Man That Got Away

The night is bitter,
The stars have lost their glitter,
The winds grow colder
And suddenly you're older—
And all because of the man that got away.   5

No more his eager call,
The writing's on the wall;
The dreams you've dreamed have all
Gone astray.

The man that won you   10
Has run off and undone you.
That great beginning
Has seen the final inning.
Don't know what happened. It's all a crazy game.

No more that all-time thrill,   15
For you've been through the mill—
And never a new love will
Be the same.

Good riddance, good bye!
Ev'ry trick of his you're on to.   20
But, fools will be fools—
And where's he gone to?

The road gets rougher,
It's lonelier and tougher.
With hope you burn up—   25

Tomorrow he may turn up.
There's just no let-up the live-long night and day.

Ever since this world began
There is nothing sadder than
A one man woman looking for   30
The man that got away . . .
The man that got away.

[1954]

Topics for Critical Thinking and Writing

1. Are these lyrics trash as poetry but great as lyrics for a song? Explain. While you are thinking about this issue, you may want to ponder some words by Edgar Allan Poe: "There are few cases in which mere popularity should be considered a proper test of merit; but the case of song-writing is, I think, one of the few."

2. Is the speaker making too much of a fuss? After all, it's only a man that she has lost.

3. Gershwin, in *Lyrics on Several Occasions* (1973), comments on the song. He mentions that some reviewers mistakenly called it "The Man Who Got Away," but, Gershwin says, this title is unacceptable because (1) it sounds like a whodunit title, and (2) it loses the echo of the fisherman's "You should have seen the one that got away." How valuable do you find these comments?

4. Gershwin also mentions that the word "man" in the title of a song usually limits it to female vocalists. Even if one makes some minimal switches (in "The Man I Love," changing to "the girl I love," and so forth) one is still left with something like "the girl I love; / And she'll be big and strong," which, Gershwin says, gives her "some undesirable attributes." But because Frank Sinatra wanted to do a recording of "The *Gal* That Got Away," Gershwin changed the ending thus:

Ever since this world began
There is nothing sadder than
A lost, lost loser looking for
The gal that got away.

What do you think of this revision? Try your hand at producing a better one.

LOUISE BOGAN

Louise Bogan (1897–1970) was born in Maine, but the family moved to Boston, where she attended Girls' Latin School, a school noted for its academic excellence. Here she began her career as a poet, publishing not only in school journals but also in the Boston Evening Transcript. *Bogan married early and had a child, but the marriage was unhappy and the couple separated. Her husband died soon after, when Bogan was only twenty-three. She remarried, but this marriage ended in divorce. For most of her life she was an independent single woman, supporting herself by working in bookstores and libraries, and by writing reviews of poetry for magazines, including* The Atlantic Monthly *and* The New Yorker. *Most of her poems were written before 1940, and although she achieved considerable fame in her youth she was less visible as a poet in her later years. Since her death, however, she has been rediscovered.*

Women

Women have no wilderness in them,
They are provident instead,
Content in the tight hot cell of their hearts
To eat dusty bread.

They do not see cattle cropping red winter grass,   5
They do not hear
Snow water going down under culverts
Shallow and clear.

They wait, when they should turn to journeys,
They stiffen, when they should bend.   10
They use against themselves that benevolence
To which no man is friend.

They cannot think of so many crops to a field
Or of clean wood cleft by an axe.
Their love is an eager meaninglessness   15
Too tense, or too lax.

They hear in every whisper that speaks to them
A shout and a cry.
As like as not, when they take life over their door-sills
They should let it go by.   20

[1922]

 ## Topics for Critical Thinking and Writing

1. Bogan is much admired for her technical skills as a poet. What techniques do you observe in "Women," and how do they work?
2. Bogan writes of women as "they" rather than "we." Try substituting "we" in the poem. What is gained, or lost?

3. Write an imitation of "Women" called "Men." Observe as many of the structural features of the poem (line length, rhyme, metaphor) as you can. What
did you learn from this exercise about poetry? About your feelings about
men?

 **AMBROSE BIERCE**

*Ambrose Bierce (1842–1914?) was born in Horse Creek, Ohio, but soon his family
moved to Indiana, where at the age of nineteen he enlisted in the Union Army. In the
next four years he fought in several of the bloodiest battles of the Civil War, was
wounded twice, and rose to the rank of lieutenant. After the war he worked as a journalist in San Francisco, in England, and again in San Francisco. In 1912 he went to
Mexico to cover the Mexican Revolution, but he disappeared there and it is assumed
that he died in 1914.*

*Bierce's literary reputation rests chiefly on one story, reprinted here, but he wrote
other stories of interest—some about the supernatural—as well as a witty, cynical book
called* The Devil's Dictionary. *Sample definition: "Marriage. The state or condition
of a community consisting of a master, a mistress, and two slaves, making in all, two."*

An Occurrence at Owl Creek Bridge

1

A man stood upon a railroad bridge in northern Alabama, looking down into the
swift water twenty feet below. The man's hands were behind his back, the
wrists bound with a cord. A rope closely encircled his neck. It was attached to a
stout cross-timber above his head and the slack fell to the level of his knees.
Some loose boards laid upon the sleepers[1] supporting the metals of the railway
supplied a footing for him and his executioners—two private soldiers of the Federal army, directed by a sergeant who in civil life may have been a deputy sheriff.
At a short remove upon the same temporary platform was an officer in the uniform of his rank, armed. He was a captain. A sentinel at each end of the bridge
stood with his rifle in the position known as "support," that is to say, vertical in
front of the left shoulder, the hammer resting on the forearm thrown straight
across the chest—a formal and unnatural position, enforcing an erect carriage of
the body. It did not appear to be the duty of these two men to know what was
occurring at the center of the bridge; they merely blockaded the two ends of the
foot planking that traversed it.

Beyond one of the sentinels nobody was in sight; the railroad ran straight
away into a forest for a hundred yards, then, curving, was lost to view. Doubtless
there was an outpost farther along. The other bank of the stream was open
ground—a gentle acclivity topped with a stockade of vertical tree trunks, loop-
holed for rifles, with a single embrasure through which protruded the muzzle of
a brass cannon commanding the bridge. Midway of the slope between bridge
and fort were the spectators—a single company of infantry in line, at "parade
rest," the butts of the rifles on the ground, the barrels inclining slightly backward

[1]**sleepers** railroad crossties (All notes to this story are the editors'.)

against the right shoulder, the hands crossed upon the stock. A lieutenant stood at the right of the line, the point of his sword upon the ground, his left hand resting upon his right. Excepting the group of four at the center of the bridge, not a man moved. The company faced the bridge, staring stonily, motionless. The sentinels, facing the banks of the stream, might have been statues to adorn the bridge. The captain stood with folded arms, silent, observing the work of his subordinates, but making no sign. Death is a dignitary who when he comes announced is to be received with formal manifestations of respect, even by those most familiar with him. In the code of military etiquette silence and fixity are forms of deference.

The man who was engaged in being hanged was apparently about thirty-five years of age. He was a civilian, if one might judge from his habit, which was that of a planter. His features were good—a straight nose, firm mouth, broad forehead, from which his long, dark hair was combed straight back, falling behind his ears to the collar of his well-fitting frock-coat. He wore a mustache and pointed beard, but no whiskers; his eyes were large and dark gray, and had a kindly expression which one would hardly have expected in one whose neck was in the hemp. Evidently this was no vulgar assassin. The liberal military code makes provision for hanging many kinds of persons, and gentlemen are not excluded.

The preparations being complete, the two private soldiers stepped aside and each drew away the plank upon which he had been standing. The sergeant turned to the captain, saluted and placed himself immediately behind that officer, who in turn moved apart one pace. These movements left the condemned man and the sergeant standing on the two ends of the same plank, which spanned three of the crossties of the bridge. The end upon which the civilian stood almost, but not quite, reached a fourth. This plank had been held in place by the weight of the captain; it was now held by that of the sergeant. At a signal from the former the latter would step aside, the plank would tilt and the condemned man go down between two ties. The arrangement commended itself to his judgment as simple and effective. His face had not been covered nor his eyes bandaged. He looked a moment at his "unsteadfast footing," then let his gaze wander to the swirling water of the stream racing madly beneath his feet. A piece of dancing driftwood caught his attention and his eyes followed it down the current. How slowly it appeared to move! What a sluggish stream!

5   He closed his eyes in order to fix his last thoughts upon his wife and children. The water, touched to gold by the early sun, the brooding mists under the banks at some distance down the stream, the fort, the soldiers, the piece of drift—all had distracted him. And now he became conscious of a new disturbance. Striking through the thought of his dear ones was a sound which he would neither ignore nor understand, a sharp, distinct, metallic percussion like the stroke of a blacksmith's hammer upon the anvil; it had the same ringing quality. He wondered what it was, and whether immeasurably distant or near by—it seemed both. Its recurrence was regular, but as slow as the tolling of a death knell. He awaited each stroke with impatience and—he knew not why—apprehension. The intervals of silence grew progressively longer; the delays became maddening. With their greater infrequency the sounds increased in strength and sharpness. They hurt his ear like the thrust of a knife; he feared he would shriek. What he heard was the ticking of his watch.

He unclosed his eyes and saw again the water below him. "If I could free my hands," he thought, "I might throw off the noose and spring into the stream.

By diving I could evade the bullets and, swimming vigorously, reach the bank, take to the woods and get away home. My home, thank God, is as yet outside their lines; my wife and little ones are still beyond the invader's farthest advance."

As these thoughts, which have here to be set down in words, were flashed into the doomed man's brain rather than evolved from it the captain nodded to the sergeant. The sergeant stepped aside.

2

Peyton Farquhar was a well-to-do planter, of an old and highly respected Alabama family. Being a slave owner and like other slave owners a politician he was naturally an original secessionist and ardently devoted to the Southern cause. Circumstances of an impetious nature, which it is unnecessary to relate here, had prevented him from taking service with the gallant army that had fought the disastrous campaigns ending with the fall of Corinth, and he chafed under the inglorious restraint, longing for the release of his energies, the larger life of the soldier, the opportunity for distinction. That opportunity, he felt, would come, as it comes to all in war time. Meanwhile he did what he could. No service was too humble for him to perform in aid of the South, no adventure too perilous for him to undertake if consistent with the character of a civilian who was at heart a soldier, and who in good faith and without too much qualification assented to at least a part of the frankly villainous dictum that all is fair in love and war.

One evening while Farquhar and his wife were sitting on a rustic bench near the entrance to his grounds, a gray-clad soldier rode up to the gate and asked for a drink of water. Mrs. Farquhar was only too happy to serve him with her own white hands. While she was fetching the water her husband approached the dusty horseman and inquired eagerly for news from the front.

10 "The Yanks are repairing the railroads," said the man, "and are getting ready for another advance. They have reached the Owl Creek bridge, put it in order and built a stockade on the north bank. The commandant has issued an order, which is posted everywhere, declaring that any civilian caught interfering with the railroad, its bridges, tunnels or trains will be summarily hanged. I saw the order."

"How far is it to the Owl Creek bridge?" Farquhar asked.

"About thirty miles."

"Is there no force on this side the creek?"

"Only a picket post half a mile out, on the railroad, and a single sentinel at this end of the bridge."

15 "Suppose a man—a civilian and student of hanging—should elude the picket post and perhaps get the better of the sentinel," said Farqunar, smiling, "what could he accomplish?"

The soldier reflected. "I was there a month ago," he replied. "I observed that the flood of last winter had lodged a great quantity of driftwood against the wooden pier at this end of the bridge. It is now dry and would burn like tow."

The lady had now brought the water, which the soldier drank. he thanked her ceremoniously, bowed to her husband and rode away. An hour later, after nightfall, he repassed the plantation, going northward in the direction from which he had come. He was a Federal scout.

3

As Peyton Farquhar fell straight downward through the bridge he lost consciousness and was as one already dead. From this state he was awakened—ages later, it seemed to him—by the pain of a sharp pressure upon his throat, followed by a sense of suffocation. Keen, poignant agonies seemed to shoot from his neck downward through every fiber of his body and limbs. These pains appeared to flash along well-defined lines of ramification and to beat with an inconceivably rapid periodicity. They seemed like streams of pulsating fire heating him to an intolerable temperature. As to his head, he was conscious of nothing but a feeling of fulness—of congestion. These sensations were unaccompanied by thought. The intellectual part of his nature was already effaced; he had power only to feel, and feeling was torment. He was conscious of motion. Encompassed in a luminous cloud, of which he was now merely the fiery heart, without material substance, he swung through unthinkable arcs of oscillation, like a vast pendulum. Then all at once, with terrible suddenness, the light about him shot upward with the noise of a loud plash; a frightful roaring was in his ears, and all was cold and dark. The power of thought was restored; he knew that the rope had broken and he had fallen into the stream. There was no additional strangulation; the noose about his neck was already suffocating him and kept the water from his lungs. To die of hanging at the bottom of a river!—the idea seemed to him ludicrous. He opened his eyes in the darkness and saw above him a gleam of light, but how distant, how inaccessible! He was still sinking, for the light became fainter and fainter until it was a mere glimmer. Then it began to grow and brighten, and he knew that he was rising toward the surface—knew it with reluctance, for he was now very comfortable. "To be hanged and drowned," he thought, "that is not so bad; but I do not wish to be shot. No; I will not be shot; that is not fair."

He was not conscious of an effort, but a sharp pain in his wrist apprised him that he was trying to free his hands. He gave the struggle his attention, as an idler might observe the feat of a juggler, without interest in the outcome. What splendid effort!—what magnificent, what superhuman strength! Ah, that was a fine endeavor! Bravo! The cord fell away; his arms parted and floated upward, the hands dimly seen on each side in the growing light. He watched them with new interest as first one and then the other pounced upon the noose at his neck. They tore it away and thrust it fiercely aside, its undulations resembling those of a water-snake. "Put it back, put it back!" He thought he shouted these words to his hands, for the undoing of the noose had been succeeded by the direst pang that he had yet experienced. His neck ached horribly; his brain was on fire; his heart, which had been fluttering faintly, gave a great leap, trying to force itself out at this mouth. His whole body was racked and wrenched with an insupportable anguish! But his disobedient hands gave no heed to the command. They beat the water vigorously with quick, downward strokes, forcing him to the surface. He felt his head emerge; his eyes were blinded by the sunlight; his chest expanded convulsively, and with a supreme and crowning agony his lungs engulfed a great draught of air, which instantly he expelled in a shriek!

20 He was now in full possession of his physical senses. They were, indeed, preternaturally keen and alert. Something in the awful disturbance of his organic system had so exalted and refined them that they made record of things never before perceived. He felt the ripples upon his face and heard their separate sounds as they struck. He looked at the forest on the bank of the stream, saw the

individual trees, the leaves and the veining of each leaf—saw the very insects upon them: the locusts, the brilliant-bodied flies, the gray spiders stretching their webs from twig to twig. He noted the prismatic colors in all the dewdrops upon a million blades of grass. The humming of the gnats that danced above the eddies of the stream, the beating of the dragon-flies' wings, the strokes of water-spider's legs, like oats which had lifted their boat—all these made audible music. A fish slid along beneath his eyes and he heard the rush of its body parting the water.

He had come to the surface facing down the stream; in a moment the visible world seemed to wheel slowly round, himself the pivotal point, and he saw the bridge, the fort, the soldiers upon the bridge, the captain, the sergeant, the two privates, his executioners. They were in silhouette against the blue sky. They shouted and gesticulated, pointing at him. The captain had drawn his pistol, but did not fire; the others were unarmed. Their movements were grotesque and horrible, their forms gigantic.

Suddenly he heard a sharp report and something struck the water smartly within a few inches of his head, spattering his face with spray. He heard a second report, and saw one of the sentinels with his rifle at his shoulder, a light cloud of blue smoke rising from the muzzle. The man in the water saw the eye of the man on the bridge gazing into his own through the sights of the rifle. He observed that it was a gray eye and remembered having read that gray eyes were keenest, and that all famous markmen had them. Nevertheless, this one had missed.

A counter-swirl had caught Farquhar and turned him half round; he was again looking into the forest on the bank opposite the fort. The sound of a clear, high voice in a monotonous singsong now rang out behind him and came across the water with a distinctness that pierced and subdued all other sounds, even the beating of the ripples in his ears. Although no soldier, he had frequented camps enough to know the dread significance of that deliberate, drawling, aspirated chant; the lieutenant on shore was taking a part in the morning's work. How coldly and pitilessly—with what an even, calm intonation, presaging, and enforcing tranquility in the men—with what accurately measured intervals fell those cruel words:

25
"Attention, company! . . . Shoulder arms! . . . Ready! . . . Aim! . . . Fire!"

Farquhar dived—dived as deeply as he could. The water roared in his ears like the voice of Niagara, yet he heard the dulled thunder of the volley and, rising again toward the surface, met shining bits of metal, singularly flattened, oscillating slowly downward. Some of them touched him on the face and hands, then fell away, continuing their descent. One lodged between his collar and neck; it was uncomfortably warm and he snatched it out.

As he rose to the surface, gasping for breath, he saw that he had been a long time under water; he was perceptibly farther down stream—nearer to safety. The soldiers had almost finished reloading; the metal ramrods flashed all at once in the sunshine as they were drawn from the barrels, turned in the air, and thrust into their sockets. The two sentinels fired again, independently and ineffectually.

The hunted man saw all this over his shoulder; he was now swimming vigorously with the current. His brain was as energetic as his arms and legs; he thought with the rapidity of lightning.

"The officer," he reasoned, "will not make that martinet's error a second time. It is as easy to dodge a volley as a single shot. He had probably already given the command to fire at will. God help me, I cannot dodge them all!"

An appalling plash within two yards of him was followed by a loud, rushing sound, *diminuendo*, which seemed to travel back through the air to the fort and died in an explosion which stirred the very river to its deeps! A rising sheet of water curved over him, fell down upon him, blinded him, strangled him! The cannon had taken a hand in the game. As he shook his head free from the commotion of the smitten water he heard the deflected shot humming through the air ahead, and in an instant it was cracking and smashing the branches in the forest beyond.

30   "They will not do that again," he thought; "the next time they will use a charge of grape.[2] I must keep my eye upon the gun; the smoke will apprise me— the report arrives too late; it lags behind the missile. That is a good gun."

Suddenly he felt himself whirled round and round—spinning like a top. The water, the banks, the forests, the now distant bridge, fort and men—all were commingled and blurred. Objects were represented by their colors only; circular horizontal streaks of color—that was all he saw. He had been caught in a vortex and was being whirled on with a velocity of advance and gyration that made him giddy and sick. In a few moments he was flung upon the gravel at the foot of the left bank of the stream—the southern bank—and behind a projecting point which concealed him from his enemies. The sudden arrest of his motion, the abrasion of one of his hands on the gravel, restored him, and he wept with delight. He dug his fingers into the sand, threw it over himself in handfuls and audibly blessed it. It looked like diamonds, rubies, emeralds; he could think of nothing beautiful which it did not resemble. The trees upon the bank were giant garden plants; he noted a definite order in their arrangement, inhaled the fragrance of their blooms. A strange, roseate light shone through the spaces among their trunks and the wind made in their branches the music of aeolian harps. He had no wish to perfect his escape—was content to remain in that enchanting spot until retaken.

A whiz and rattle of grapeshot among the branches high above his head roused him from his dream. The baffled cannoneer had fired him a random farewell. He sprang to his feet, rushed up the sloping bank, and plunged into the forest.

All that day he traveled, laying his course by the rounding sun. The forest seemed interminable; nowhere did he discover a break in it, not even a woodman's road. He had not known that he lived in so wild a region. There was something uncanny in the revelation.

By nightfall he was fatigued, footsore, famishing. The thought of his wife and children urged him on. At last he found a road which led him in what he knew to be the right direction. It was as wide and straight as a city street, yet it seemed untraveled. No fields bordered it, no dwelling anywhere. Not so much as the barking of a dog suggested human habitation. The black bodies of the trees formed a straight wall on both sides, terminating on the horizon in a point, like a diagram in a lesson in perspective. Overhead, as he looked up through this rift in the wood, shone great golden stars looking unfamiliar and grouped in strange constellations. He was sure they were arranged in some order which had a secret and malign significance. The wood on either side was full of singular noises, among which— once, twice, and again—he distinctly heard whispers in an unknown tongue.

35   His neck was in pain and lifting his hand to it he found it horribly swollen. He knew that it had a circle of black where the rope had bruised it. His eyes felt congested; he could no longer close them. His tongue was swollen with thirst;

---

[2]**grapeshot** a cluster of small iron balls fired from a cannon

he relieved its fever by thrusting it forward from between his teeth into the cold air. How softly the turf had carpeted the untraveled avenue—he could no longer feel the roadway beneath his feet!

Doubtless, despite his suffering, he had fallen asleep while walking, for now he sees another scene—perhaps he has merely recovered from a delirium. He stands at the gate of his own home. All is as he left it, and all bright and beautiful in the morning sunshine. He must have traveled the entire night. As he pushes open the gate and passes up the wide white walk, he sees a flutter of female garments; his wife, looking fresh and cool and sweet, steps down from the veranda to meet him. At the bottom of the steps she stands waiting, with a smile of ineffable joy, an attitude of matchless grace and dignity. Ah, how beautiful she is! He springs forward with extended arms. As he is about to clasp her he feels a stunning blow upon the back of the neck; a blinding white light blazes all about him with a sound like the shock of a cannon—then all is darkness and silence!

Peyton Farquhar was dead; his body, with a broken neck, swung gently from side to side beneath the timbers of the Owl Creek bridge.

Topics for Critical Thinking and Writing

1. Is the story merely a clever trick, or is it a significant work of art, something with enduring power? You may find it useful to begin by thinking about a remark made by the poet and literary critic Samuel Taylor Coleridge, in which he asserts that *suspense* (or *expectation*) is superior to *surprise*. (In literature, suspense is usually achieved by foreshadowing—hints of what is to come.) Coleridge said that Shakespeare gives us not surprise but expectation, and then the satisfaction of perfect knowledge: "As the feeling with which we startle at a shooting star, compared with that of watching the sunrise at the pre-established moment, such and so low is surprise compared with expectation." Can you think of literary works (including films) that support or weaken his argument? Does Bierce's story support or weaken it?

2. Some readers of "An Occurrence at Owl Creek Bridge" have censured the story as sentimental, or as melodramatic, or as both. (You may want to check these terms in a good dictionary of literary terms, such as Meyer Abrams, *A Glossary of Literary Terms,* J. A. Cuddon, *A Dictionary of Literary Terms and Literary Theory,* C. Hugh Holman and William Harmon, *A Handbook to Literature,* or Ross Murfin and Supryia M. Ray, *The Bedford Glossary of Critical and Literary Terms.*) How much merit do you find in these accusations?

3. Presumably we can never know if in fact someone in the second before he or she dies can have a vision comparable to Farquhar's. Does our evaluation of Bierce's story depend on our view of whether or not it is psychologically sound? Explain. (You may want to argue, for example, that the experience may indeed be possible—just as it is possible for long-lost twins to be reunited on their one-hundredth birthday and to die at the same moment—but it is so freakish that it cannot speak to us in the way we expect art to speak to us.)

Writing About Literature: An Overview

THE NATURE OF CRITICAL WRITING

We have twice mentioned already that in everyday talk the commonest meaning of **criticism** is something like "finding fault." But a critic can see excellences as well as faults. Because we turn to criticism with the hope that the critic has seen something we have missed, the most valuable criticism is not that which shakes its finger at faults but that which calls our attention to interesting things going on in the work of art. Here is a statement by W. H. Auden (1907-73), suggesting that criticism is most useful when it calls our attention to things worth attending to:

> What is the function of a critic? So far as I am concerned, he can do me one or more of the following services:
>
> 1. Introduce me to authors or works of which I was hitherto unaware.
> 2. Convince me that I have undervalued an author or a work because I had not read them carefully enough.
> 3. Show me relations between works of different ages and cultures which I could never have seen for myself because I do not know enough and never shall.
> 4. Give a "reading" of a work which increases my understanding of it.
> 5. Throw light upon the process of artistic "Making."
> 6. Throw light upon the relation of art to life, science, economics, ethics, religion, etc.
>
> *The Dyer's Hand* (New York, 1963), pp. 8-9

Auden does not neglect the delight we get from literature, but he extends (especially in his sixth point) the range of criticism to include topics beyond the literary work itself. Notice too the emphasis on observing, showing, and illuminating, which suggests that the function of critical writing is not very different from the commonest view of the function of imaginative writing.

Auden begins by saying that a critic can "introduce" him to an author. How would a critic introduce a reader to an author? It's not enough just to name the author; almost surely the advocate would give *reasons* why we should read the book. "It will really grip you"; "It's the funniest thing I've read in months"; "I was moved to tears." Auden lets the cat out of the bag in his next two assertions: the critic may "convince" him of something, or may "show" him something. Criticism is largely a matter of convincing and showing—really, showing and thereby convincing. We can't just announce that we like or dislike something and expect people to agree; we have to point to evidence (that's the showing part) if we are going to convince.

In a moment we will return to the matter of evidence, but first let's hear another writer talk about criticism. The novelist D. H. Lawrence says,

> Literary criticism can be no more than a reasoned account of the feeling produced upon the critic by the book he is criticizing. Criticism can never be a science: it is, in the first place, much too personal, and in the second, it is concerned with values that science ignores.
>
> *Phoenix: The Posthumous Papers of D. H. Lawrence*
> (London, 1936), p. 539

We like Lawrence's assertion that criticism is *a reasoned account*—writing about literature is a rational activity, not a mere pouring out of emotion—but we equally like his assertion that it is rooted in *feeling*. As earlier chapters have suggested, when we read we respond (perhaps with an intense interest, perhaps with a yawn). Our responses are worth examining. *Why* do we find this character memorable, or that character unbelievable? As we examine our responses, and check the text to make sure that we have properly remembered it, we may of course find our responses changing, but finally we think we know what we think of the literary work, and we know *why* we think it. We are, in Lawrence's words, able to give "a reasoned account of the feeling produced . . . by the book."

CRITICISM AS ARGUMENT: ASSUMPTIONS AND EVIDENCE

In this process of showing and convincing (Auden's words) and of offering a reasoned account (Lawrence's words), even if we are talking about a so-so movie or television show, what we say depends in large measure on certain conscious or unconscious assumptions that we make:

- "I liked it because the characters were very believable" (here the assumption is that characters ought to be believable);
- "I didn't like it; there was too much violence" (here the assumption is that violence ought not to be shown, or it if is shown it should condemned);
- "I didn't like it; it was awfully slow" (here the assumption probably is that there ought to be a fair amount of physical action, perhaps even changes of scene, rather than character just talking in the kitchen);
- "I didn't like it; I don't think topics of this sort should be discussed publicly" (here the assumption is a moral one, that it is indecent to present certain topics);
- "I liked it partly because it was refreshing to hear such frankness" (here again the assumption is moral, and more or less the reverse of the previous one).

In short, whether we realize it or not, our responses are rooted in assumptions. These assumptions, we may believe, are so self-evident that they do not need to be stated. Our readers, however, may disagree.

If we are to hold our readers' interest, and perhaps convince them to see things the way we do, we must recognize our assumptions and must offer evidence—point to things in the work—that will convince the reader that our assumptions are reasonable. If we want to say that a short story ought to be realistic, we will call our reader's attention to unrealistic aspects in a particular story and will, with this evidence in front of the reader, argue that the story is not worth much. Or, conversely, we might say that in a satiric story realism of course is not a valid criterion; what readers want is (as in a political caricature in a newspaper) exaggeration and humor, and in our critical study we will call attention to the delight that this or that bit of exaggeration offers.

In brief, as we suggested in Chapters 15 and 16 ("Arguing an Interpretation," "Arguing an Evaluation"), argument consists of offering statements that are *reasons* for other statements ("The work means X *because* . . ."), and the words that follow "because" normally point to the evidence that we believe supports the earlier assertion.

SOME CRITICAL STANCES

Professional critics, like the ordinary moviegoer who recommends a movie to a friend, work from assumptions, but their assumptions are usually highly conscious, and the critics may define their assumptions at length. They regard themselves as, for instance, Freudians or Marxists or gay critics. They read all texts through the lens of a particular theory, and their focus enables them to see things that otherwise might go unnoticed. Most critics realize, however, that if a lens or critical perspective or interpretive strategy helps us to see certain things, it also limits our vision. They therefore regard their method not as an exclusive way of thinking but only as a useful tool.

What follows is a brief survey of the chief current approaches to literature. You may find, as you read these pages, that one or another approach sounds congenial, and you may want to make use of it in your reading and writing. On the other hand, it's important to remember that works of literature are highly varied, and we read them for various purposes—to kill time, to enjoy fanciful visions, to be amused, to learn about alien ways of feeling, and to learn about ourselves. It may be best, therefore, to try to respond to each text in the way that the text seems to require rather than to read all texts according to a single formula. You'll find, of course, that some works will lead you to want to think about them from several angles. A play by Shakespeare may stimulate you to read a book about the Elizabethan playhouse, and another that offers a Marxist interpretation of the English Renaissance, and still another that offers a feminist analysis of Shakespeare's plays. All of these approaches, and others, may help to deepen your understanding of the literary works that you read.

Formalist Criticism (New Criticism)

Formalist criticism emphasizes the work as an independent creation, a self-contained unity, something to be studied in itself, not as part of some larger context, such as the author's life or a historical period. This kind of study is called formalist criticism because the emphasis is on the *form* of the work, the relationships between the parts—the construction of the plot, the contrasts between characters, the functions of rhymes, the point of view, and so on.

Cleanth Brooks, perhaps America's most distinguished formalist critic, in an essay in the *Kenyon Review* (Winter 1951), reprinted in *The Modern Critical Spectrum,* eds. Gerald Jay Goldberg and Nancy Marmer Goldberg (1962), set forth what he called his "articles of faith":

> That literary criticism is a description and an evaluation of its object.
>
> That the primary concern of criticism is with the problem of unity—the kind of whole which the literary work forms or fails to form, and the relation of the various parts to each other in building up this whole.
>
> That the formal relations in a work of literature may include, but certainly exceed, those of logic.
>
> That in a successful work, form and content cannot be separated.
>
> That form is meaning.

If you have read the earlier pages of this book you are already familiar with most of these ideas, but in the next few pages we will look into some of them in detail.

Formalist criticism is, in essence, *intrinsic* criticism, rather than extrinsic, for it concentrates on the work itself, independent of its writer and the writer's background—that is, independent of biography, psychology, sociology, and history. The discussions of a proverb ("A rolling stone") and of a short poem by Frost ("The Span of Life") on pages 33–35 are brief examples. The gist is that a work of literature is complex, unified, and freestanding. In practice, of course, we usually bring outside knowledge to the work. For instance, a reader who is familiar with, say, *Hamlet* can hardly study some other tragedy by Shakespeare, let's say *Romeo and Juliet,* without bringing to the second play some conception of what Shakespearean tragedy is or can be. A reader of Alice Walker's *The Color Purple* inevitably brings unforgettable outside material (perhaps the experience of being an African-American, or some knowledge of the history of African-Americans) to the literary work. It is hard to talk only about *Hamlet* or *The Color Purple* and not at the same time talk, or at least have in mind, aspects of human experience.

Formalist criticism begins with a personal response to the literary work, but it goes on to try to account for the response by closely examining the work. It assumes that the author shaped the poem, play, or story so fully that the work guides the reader's responses. The assumption that "meaning" is fully and completely presented within the text is not much in favor today, when many literary critics argue that the active or subjective reader (or even what Judith Fetterley, a feminist critic, has called "the resisting reader"), and not the author of the text, makes the "meaning." Still, even if one grants that the reader is active, not passive or coolly objective, one can hold with the formalists that the author is active too, constructing a text that in some measure controls the reader's responses. Of course, during the process of writing about our responses we may find that our responses change. A formalist critic would say that we see with increasing clarity what the work is really like, and what it really means. (Similarly, when authors write and revise a text they may change their understanding of what they are doing. A story that began as a lighthearted joke may turn into something far more serious than the writer imagined at the start, but for the formalist critic the final work contains a stable meaning that all competent readers can perceive.)

Formalist criticism usually takes one of two forms, **explication** (the unfolding of meaning, line by line or even word by word) and **analysis** (the examination of the relations of parts). The essay on Yeats's "The Balloon of the Mind" (p. 413) is an explication, a setting forth of the implicit meanings of the words. The essays on Kate Chopin's "The Story of an Hour" (pp. 20 and 24) and on Tennessee Williams's *The Glass Menagerie* (p. 345) are analyses. The two essays on Frost's "Stopping by Woods on a Snowy Evening" (pp. 462-67) are chiefly analyses but with some passages of explication.

To repeat: Formalist criticism assumes that a work of art is stable. An artist constructs a coherent, comprehensible work, thus conveying to a reader an emotion or an idea. T. S. Eliot said that the writer can't just pour out emotions onto the page. Rather, Eliot said in an essay entitled "Hamlet and His Problems" (1919). "The only way of expressing emotion in the form of art is by finding an 'objective correlative': in other words, a set of objects, a situation, a chain of events which shall be the formula of the *particular* emotion." With this in mind, consider again Robert Frost's "The Span of Life," a poem already discussed on page 36:

> The old dog barks backward without getting up.
> I can remember when he was a pup.

The image of an old dog barking backward, and the speaker's memory—apparently triggered by the old dog's bark—of the dog as a pup, presumably are the "objective correlative" of Frost's emotion or idea: Frost is "expressing emotion" through this "formula." And all of us, as competent readers, can grasp pretty accurately what Frost expressed. Frost's emotion, idea, or meaning is "objectively" embodied in the text. Formalist critics explain how and why literary works—*these* words, in *this* order—constitute unique, complex structures that embody or set forth meanings.

Formalist criticism, also called the **New Criticism** (to distinguish it from the historical and biographical writing that in earlier decades had dominated literary study), began to achieve prominence in the late 1920s and was dominant from the late 1930s until about 1970, and even today it is widely considered the best way for a student to begin to study a work of literature. Formalist criticism empowers the student; that is, the student confronts the work immediately and is not told first to spend days or weeks or months in preparation—for instance reading Freud and his followers in order to write a psychoanalytic essay or reading Marx and Marxists in order to write a Marxist essay, or doing research on "necessary historical background" in order to write a historical essay.

Deconstruction

Deconstruction or deconstructive or poststructuralist criticism, can almost be characterized as the opposite of everything that formalist criticism stands for. Deconstruction begins with the assumptions that the world is unknowable and that language is unstable, elusive, unfaithful. (Language is all of these things because meaning is largely generated by opposition: *hot* means something in opposition to *cold*, but a hot day may be 90 degrees whereas a hot oven is at least 400 degrees, and a "hot item" may be of any temperature.) Deconstructionists seek to show that a literary work (usually called "a text" or "a discourse") inevitably is self-contradictory. Unlike formalist critics—who hold that a competent author constructs a coherent work with a stable meaning, and that competent readers can perceive this meaning—deconstructionists (e.g., Barbara Johnson in *The Critical Difference* [1980]) hold that a work has no coherent meaning at the center. Jonathan Culler, in *On Deconstruction* (1982), says that "to deconstruct a discourse is to show how it undermines the philosophy it asserts" (86). (Johnson and Culler provide accessible introductions, but the major document is Jacques Derrida's seminal, difficult work, *Of Grammatology* [1967, trans. 1976].) This view holds that the text is only marks on paper, and therefore so far as a reader goes the author of a text is not the writer but the reader; texts are "indeterminate," "open," and "unstable."

Despite the emphasis on indeterminacy, one sometimes detects in deconstructionist interpretations a view associated with Marxism. This is the idea that authors are "socially constructed" from the "discourses of power" or "signifying practices" that surround them. Thus, although authors may think they are individuals with independent minds, their works usually reveal—unknown to the authors—powerful social, cultural, or philosophic assumption. Deconstructionists "interrogate" a text, and they reveal what the authors were unaware of or had thought they had kept safely out of sight. That is, deconstructionists often find a rather specific meaning—though this meaning is one that might surprise the author.

Deconstruction is valuable insofar as—like the New Criticism—it encourages close, rigorous attention to the text. Furthermore, in its rejection of the claim that a work has a single stable meaning, Deconstruction has had a positive influence on the study of literature. The problem with Deconstruction, however, is that too often it is reductive, telling the same story about every text—that here, yet again, and again, we see how a text is incoherent and heterogeneous. There is, too, an irritating arrogance in some deconstructive criticism: "The author could not see how his/her text is fundamentally unstable and self-contradictory, but *I* can and now will interrogate the text and will issue my report." Readers should not prostrate themselves before texts, but there is something askew about an approach that often leads readers to conclude that they always know a good deal more than the benighted author.

Aware that their emphasis on the instability of language implies that their own texts are unstable or even incoherent, some deconstructionists seem to aim at entertaining rather than at edifying. They probably would claim that they do not deconstruct meaning in the sense of destroying it; rather, they might say, they exuberantly multiply meanings, and to this end they may use such devices as puns, irony, and allusions, somewhat as a poet might, and just as though (one often feels) they think they are as creative as the writers they are commenting on. Indeed, for many deconstructionists, the traditional conception of "literature" is merely an elitist "construct." All "texts" or "discourses" (novels, scientific papers, a Kewpie doll on the mantel, watching TV, suing in court, walking the dog, and all other signs that human beings make) are of a piece: all are unstable systems of signifying, all are fictions, all are "literature." If literature (in the usual sense) occupies a special place in deconstruction it is because literature delights in its playfulness, its fictiveness, whereas other discourses nominally reject playfulness and fictiveness.

Reader-Response Criticism

Probably all reading includes some sort of response—"This is terrific," "This is a bore," "I don't know what's going on here"—and almost all writing about literature begins with some such response, but specialists in literature disagree greatly about the role that response plays, or should play, in experiencing literature and in writing about it.

At one extreme are those who say that our response to a work of literature should be a purely aesthetic response—a response to a work of art—and not the response we would have to something comparable in real life. To take an obvious point: If in real life we heard someone plotting a murder, we would intervene, perhaps by calling the police or by attempting to warn the victim. But when we hear Macbeth and Lady Macbeth plot to kill King Duncan, we watch with deep *interest;* we hear their words with *pleasure,* and maybe with horror and fascination we even look forward to seeing the murder and to what the characters then will say and what will happen to the murderers.

When you think about it, the vast majority of works of literature do not have a close, obvious resemblance to the reader's life. Most readers of *Macbeth* are not Scots, and no readers are Scottish kings or queens. (It's not just a matter of older literature; no readers of Toni Morrison's *Beloved* are nineteenth-century African-Americans.) The connections that readers make between themselves and the lives in most of the books they read are not, on the whole, connections based on ethnic or professional identities, but, rather, connections with states of consciousness, for instance a young person's sense of isolation from the family, or a young person's sense of guilt for initial sexual experiences. Before we reject a work either because it seems too close to us ("I'm a man and I don't like the depiction of this man"), or on the other hand too far from our experience ("I'm not a woman, so how can I enjoy reading about these women?"), we probably should try to follow the advice of Virginia Woolf, who said, "Do not dictate to your author; try to become him." Nevertheless, some literary works of the past may today seem intolerable, at least in part. There are passages in Mark Twain's *Huckleberry Finn,* where African-Americans are stereotyped or called derogatory names, that deeply upset us today. We should, however, try to reconstruct the cultural assumptions of the age in which the work was written. If we do so, we may find that if in some ways it reflected its historical era, in other ways it challenged it.

Still, some of our experiences, some of *what we are,* may make it virtually impossible for us to read a work sympathetically or "objectively," experiencing it only as a work of art and not as a part of life. Take so humble a form of literature as the joke. A few decades ago jokes about nagging wives and mothers-in-law were widely thought to be funny. Our fairly recent heightened awareness of sexism today makes those jokes unfunny. Twenty years ago the "meaning" of a joke about a nagging wife or about a mother-in-law was, in effect, "Here's a funny episode that shows what women typically are." Today the "meaning"—at least as the hearer conceives it—is "The unfunny story you have just told shows that you have stupid, stereotypical views of women." In short, the joke may "mean" one thing to the teller and a very different thing to the hearer.

Reader-response criticism, then, says that the "meaning" of a work is not merely something put into the work by the writer; rather, the "meaning" is an interpretation created or constructed or produced by the reader as well as the writer. Stanley Fish, an exponent of reader-response theory, in *Is There a Text in This Class?* (1980), puts it this way: "Interpretation is not the art of construing but of constructing. Interpreters do not decode poems; they make them" (327).

Let's now try to relate these ideas more specifically to comments about literature. If "meaning" is the production or creation not simply of the writer but also of the perceiver, does it follow that there is no such thing as a "correct" interpretation of the meaning of a work of literature? Answers to this question differ. At one extreme, the reader is said to construct or reconstruct the text under the firm guidance of the author. That is, the author so powerfully shapes or constructs the text—encodes an idea—that the reader is virtually compelled to perceive or reconstruct or decode it the way the author wants it to be perceived. (We can call this view *the objective view,* since it essentially holds that readers look objectively at the work and see what the author put into it.) At the other extreme, the reader constructs the meaning according to his or her own personality—that is, according to the reader's psychological identity. (We can call this view *the subjective view,* since it essentially holds that readers inevitably project their feelings into what they perceive.) An extreme version of the subjective view holds that there is no such thing as literature: there are only texts, some of which some readers regard in a particularly elitist way.

Against the objective view one can argue thus: No author can fully control a reader's response to every detail of the text. No matter how carefully constructed the text is, it leaves something—indeed, a great deal—to the reader's imagination. For instance, when Macbeth says that life "is a tale / Told by an idiot, full of sound and fury / Signifying nothing," are we getting a profound thought from Shakespeare or, on the contrary, are we getting a shallow thought from Macbeth, a man who does not see that his criminal deeds have been played out against a heaven that justly punishes his crimes? In short, the objective view neglects to take account of the fact that the author is not continually at our shoulder making sure that we interpret the work in a particular way.

It is probably true, as Flannery O'Connor says in *Mystery and Manners* (1957), that good writers select "every word, every detail, for a reason, every incident for a reason" (75), but there are always *gaps* or *indeterminacies,* to use the words of Wolfgang Iser, a reader-response critic. Readers always go beyond the text, drawing inferences, and evaluating the text in terms of their own experience. In the Hebrew Bible, for instance, in Genesis, the author tells us (chap, 22) that God commanded Abraham to sacrifice his son Isaac, and then says that "Abraham rose up early in the morning" and prepared to fulfill the command. We are not explicitly told *why* Abraham "rose up early in the morning," or how he spent the intervening night, but some readers take "early in the morning" to signify (reasonably?) that Abraham has had a sleepless night. Others take it to signify (reasonably?) that Abraham is prompt in obeying God's command. And of course some readers fill the gap with both explanations, or with neither. Doubtless much depends on the reader, but there is no doubt that readers "naturalize"—make natural, according to their own ideas—what they read.

In an extreme form the subjective view denies that authors can make us perceive the meanings that they try to put into their works. This position suggests that every reader has a different idea of what a work means, an idea that reflects the reader's own ideas. Every reader, then, is Narcissus, who looked into a pool of water and thought he saw a beautiful youth but really saw only a reflection of himself. But does every reader see his or her individual image in each literary work? Of course not. Even *Hamlet,* a play that has generated an enormous range of interpretation, is universally seen as a tragedy, a play that deals with painful realities. If someone were to tell us that *Hamlet* is a comedy, and that the end, with a pile of corpses, is especially funny, we would not say, "Oh, well, we all see things in our own way." Rather, we would conclude that we have just heard a misinterpretation.

Many people who subscribe to one version or another of a reader-response theory would agree that they are concerned not with all readers but with what they call *informed readers* or *competent readers*. Informed or competent readers are familiar with the conventions of literature. They understand misinterpretation, that in a play such as *Hamlet* the characters usually speak in verse. Such readers, then, do not express amazement that Hamlet often speaks metrically, and that he sometimes uses rhyme. These readers understand that verse is the normal language for most of the characters in the play, and therefore such readers do not characterize Hamlet as a poet. Informed, competent readers, in short, know the rules of the game. There will still be plenty of room for differences of interpretation. Some people will find Hamlet not at all blameworthy, others will find him somewhat blameworthy, and still others may find him highly blameworthy. In short, we can say that a writer works against a background that is *shared* by readers. As readers, we are familiar with various kinds of literature, and we read or see *Hamlet* as a particular kind of literary work, a tragedy, a play that evokes (in Shakespeare's words) "woe or wonder," sadness and astonishment. Knowing (in a large degree) how we ought to respond, our responses are not merely private.

Consider taking, as a guide to reading, a remark made by Mencius (372–289 B.C.), the Chinese Confucian philosopher. Speaking of reading *The Book of Odes,* the oldest Chinese anthology, Mencius said that "a reader must let his thought go to meet the intention as he would a guest." Of course we often cannot be sure about the author's intention (we don't know what Shakespeare intended to say in *Hamlet;* we have only the play itself), and even those relatively few authors who have explicitly stated their intentions may be untrustworthy for one reason or another. Still, there is something attractive in Mencius's suggestion that when we read we should—at least for a start—treat our author not with suspicion or hostility but with goodwill and with the expectation of pleasure.

What are the implications of reader-response theory for writing an essay on a work of literature? Even if we agree that we are talking only about competent readers, does this mean, then, that *almost* anything goes in setting forth one's responses in an essay? Most all advocates of any form of reader-response criticism agree on one thing: There are agreed-upon rules of *writing* if not of reading. This one point of agreement can be amplified to contain two aspects: (1) we all agree (more or less) as to what constitutes evidence, and (2) we all agree that a written response should be coherent. If you say that you find Hamlet to be less noble than his adversary, Claudius, you will be expected to provide evidence by pointing to specific passages, to specific things that Hamlet and Claudius say and do. And you will be expected to order the material into an effective, coherent sequence, so that the reader can move easily through your essay and will understand what you are getting at.

Archetypal Criticism (Myth Criticism)

Carl G. Jung, the Swiss psychiatrist, in *Contributions to Analytical Psychology* (1928) postulates the existence of a "collective unconscious," an inheritance in our brains consisting of "countless typical experiences [such as birth, escape from danger, selection of a mate] of our ancestors." Few people today believe in an inherited "collective unconscious," but many people agree that certain repeated experiences, such as going to sleep and hours later awakening, or the perception of the setting and of the rising sun, or of the annual death and rebirth of vegetation, manifest themselves in dreams, myths, and literature—in these instances, as stories of apparent death and rebirth. This archetypal plot of death and rebirth is said to be evident in Coleridge's *The Rime of the Ancient Mariner* (1798), for example. The ship suffers a deathlike calm and then is miraculously restored to motion, and, in a sort of parallel rebirth, the mariner moves from spiritual death to renewed perception of the holiness of life. Another archetypal plot is the quest, which usually involves the testing and initiation of a hero, and thus essentially represents the movement from innocence to experience. In addition to archetypal plots there are archetypal characters, since an archetype is any recurring unit. Among archetypal characters are the scapegoat (as in Shirley Jackson's "The Lottery"), the hero (savior, deliverer), the terrible mother (witch, stepmother—even the wolf "grandmother" in the tale of Little Red Riding Hood), and the wise old man (father figure magician).

Because, the theory holds, both writer and reader share unconscious memories, the tale an author tells (derived from the collective unconscious) may strangely move the reader, speaking to his or her collective unconscious. As Maud Bodkin puts it, in *Archetypal Patterns in Poetry* (1934), something within us "leaps in response to the effective presentation in poetry of an ancient theme" (4). But this emphasis on ancient (or repeated) themes has made archetypal criticism vulnerable to the charge that it is reductive. The critic looks for certain characters or patterns of action and values the work if the motifs are there, meanwhile overlooking what is unique, subtle, distinctive, and truly interesting about the work. That is, a work is regarded as good if it closely resembles other works, with the usual motifs and characters. A second weakness in some archetypal criticism is that in its search for the deepest meaning of a work the critic may crudely impose a pattern, seeing (for instance) the quest in every walk down the street. But perhaps to say this is to beg the question; it is the critic's job to write so persuasively that the reader at least tentatively accepts the critic's view. In a wide-ranging study of one particular motif, *In Search of the Swan Maiden* (1994), Barbara Fass Leavy discusses the legend of a swan maiden who is forced to marry a mortal because he possesses something of hers, usually a garment or an animal skin. Leavy analyzes several versions of the story, which she takes to be a representation not only of female rage against male repression but also a representation of male fear of female betrayal. Leavy ends her book by examining this motif in Ibsen's *A Doll's House* (1879). Her claim is that when Nora finds a lost object, the dance costume, she can flee from the tyrannical domestic world and thus regain her freedom.

If archetypal criticism sometimes seems farfetched, it is nevertheless true that one of its strengths is that it invites us to use comparisons, and comparing is often an excellent way to see not only what a work shares with other works but what is distinctive in the work. The most successful practitioner of archetypal criticism was Northrop Frye (1912-91), whose numerous books help readers to see fascinating connections between works. For Frye's explicit comments about archetypal criticism, as well as for examples of such criticism in action, see especially his *Anatomy of Criticism* (1957) and *The Educated Imagination* (1964). On archetypes see also Chapter 16, "Archetypal Patterns," in Norman Friedman, *Form and Meaning in Fiction* (1975).

Historical Scholarship

Historical scholarship studies a work within its historical context. Thus, a student of *Julius Caesar, Hamlet,* or *Macbeth*—plays in which ghosts appear—may try to find out about Elizabethan attitudes toward ghosts. We may find that the Elizabethans took ghosts more seriously than we do, or, on the other hand, we may find that ghosts were explained in various ways, for instance sometimes as figments of the imagination and sometimes as shapes taken by the devil in order to mislead the virtuous. Similarly, a historical essay concerned with *Othello* may be devoted to Elizabethan attitudes toward Moors, or to Elizabethan ideas of love, or, for that matter, to Elizabethan ideas of a daughter's obligations toward her-father's wishes concerning her suitor. The historical critic assumes (and one can hardly dispute the assumption) that writers, however individualistic, are shaped by the particular social contexts in which they live. One can put it this way: The goal of **historical criticism** is to understand how people in the past thought and felt. It assumes that such understanding can enrich our understanding of a particular work. The assumption is, however, disputable, since one may argue that the artist may *not* have shared the age's view on this or that. All of the half-dozen or so Moors in Elizabethan plays other than *Othello* are villainous or foolish, but this evidence does not prove that *therefore* Othello is villainous or foolish.

Marxist Criticism

One form of historical criticism is **Marxist criticism,** named for Karl Marx (1818–83). Actually, to say "one form" is misleading, since Marxist criticism today is varied, but essentially it sees history primarily as a struggle between socioeconomic classes, and it sees literature (and everything else, too) as the product of the economic forces of the period.

For Marxists, economics is the "base" or "infrastructure"; on this base rests a "superstructure" of ideology (law, politics, philosophy, religion, and the arts, including literature), reflecting the interests of the dominant class. Thus, literature is a material product, produced—like bread or battleships—in order to be consumed in a given society. Marxist critics are concerned, for instance, with Shakespeare's plays as part of a market economy—show *business,* the economics of the theater, including payments to authors and actors. and revenue from audiences. See Steven Mullaney, *The Place of the Stage: License, Play and Power in Renaissance England* (1995), and Douglas Bruster, *Drama and Market in the Age of Shakespeare* (1993). Like every other product, literature is the product of work, and it *does* work. A bourgeois society, for example, will produce literature that in one way or another celebrates bourgeois values, individualism for example. These works serve to assure the society that produces them that its values are secure, natural, even universal. The enlightened Marxist writer or critic, on the other hand, exposes the fallacy of traditional values and replaces them with the truths found in Marxism. In the heyday of Marxism in the United States, during the depression of the 1930s, it was common for such Marxist critics as Granville Hicks, in *The Great Tradition* (1933), to assert that the novel must show the class struggle.

Few critics would disagree that works of art in some measure reflect the age that produced them, but most contemporary Marxist critics go further. First, they assert—in a repudiation of what has been called "vulgar Marxist theory"— that the deepest historical meaning of a literary work is to be found in what it does *not* say, what its ideology does not permit it to express. Second, Marxists take seriously Marx's famous comment that "the philosophers have only *interpreted* the world in various ways: the point is to *change* it." The critic's job is to change the world, by revealing the economic basis of the arts. Not surprisingly, most Marxists are skeptical of such concepts as "genius" and "masterpiece." These concepts, they say, are part of the bourgeois myth that idealizes the individual and detaches art from its economic context. For an introduction to Marxist criticism, see Terry Eagleton, *Marxism and Literary Criticism* (1976).

New Historicism

A recent school of scholarship, called **New Historicism,** insists that there is no "history" in the sense of a narrative of indisputable past events. Rather, New Historicism holds that there is only our version—our narrative, our representation—of the past. In this view, each age projects its own preconceptions on the past: historians may think they are revealing the past, but they are revealing only their own historical situation and their personal preferences. Thus, in the nineteenth century and in the twentieth almost up to 1992, Columbus was represented as the heroic benefactor of humankind who discovered the New World. But even while plans were being made to celebrate the five-hundredth anniversary of his first voyage across the Atlantic, voices were raised in protest: Columbus did not "discover" a New World; after all, the indigenous people knew where they were, and it was Columbus who was lost, since he thought he was in India. In short, people who wrote history in, say, 1900 projected onto the past their current views (colonialism was a good thing), and people who wrote history in 1992 projected onto that same period a very different set of views (colonialism was a bad thing). Similarly, ancient Greece, once celebrated by historians as the source of democracy and rational thinking, is now more often regarded as a society that was built on slavery and on the oppression of women. And the Renaissance, once glorified as an age of enlightened thought, is now often seen as an age that tyrannized women, enslaved colonial people, and enslaved itself with its belief in witchcraft and astrology. Thinking about these changing views, one feels the truth of the witticism that the only thing more uncertain than the future is the past.

New Historicism is especially associated with Stephen Greenblatt, who popularized the term in 1982 in the preface to a collection of essays published in a journal called *Genre.* Greenblatt himself has said of New Historicism that "it's no doctrine at all" (*Learning to Curse* [1990]) but the term is nevertheless much used, and, as preceding remarks have suggested, it is associated with power, most especially with revealing the tyrannical practices of a society that others have glorified. New Historicism was shaped by the 1960s: the students who in that decade protested against the war in Vietnam by holding demonstrations protested in the 1980s against Ronald Reagan by writing articles exposing Renaissance colonialism. (In its most doctrinaire form, New Historicism assumes that a centralized authority creates cultural meanings.) Works of literature were used as a basis for a criticism of society. Academic writing of this sort was not dry, impartial, unimpassioned scholarship: rather, it connected the past with the present, and it offered value judgments. In Greenblatt's words.

> Writing that was not engaged, that withheld judgments, that failed to connect the present with the past seemed worthless. Such connection could be made either by analogy or causality: that is, a particular set of historical circumstances could be represented in such a way as to bring out homologies with aspects of the present or, alternatively, those circumstances could be analyzed as the generative forces that led to the modern condition. (*Learning to Curse,* p. 167)

On the New Historicism, see H. Aram Veeser, ed., *The New Historicism* (1989), and Veeser, *The New Historicism Reader* (1994).

Biographical Criticism

One kind of historical research is the study of *biography*, which for our purposes includes not only biographies but also autobiographies, diaries, journals, letters, and so on. What experiences did (for example) Mark Twain undergo? Are some of the apparently sensational aspects of *Huckleberry Finn* in fact close to events that Twain experienced? If so, is he a "realist"? If not, is he writing in the tradition of the "tall tale"?

The really good biographies not only tell us about the life of the author—they enable us to return to the literary texts with a deeper understanding of how they came to be what they are. If, for example, you read Richard B. Sewall's biography of Emily Dickinson, you will find a wealth of material concerning her family and the world she moved in—for instance, the religious ideas that were part of her upbringing.

Biographical study may illuminate even the work of a living author. If you are writing about the poetry of Adrienne Rich, for example, you may want to consider what she has told us in many essays about her life, in *On Lies, Secrets, and Silence* (1979) and *Blood, Bread, and Poetry* (1986), especially about her relations with her father and her husband.

Psychological or Psychoanalytic Criticism

One form that biographical study may take is **psychological criticism** or *psychoanalytic criticism*, which usually examines the author and the author's writings in the framework of Freudian psychology. A central doctrine of Sigmund Freud (1856–1939) is the Oedipus complex, the view that all males (Freud seems not to have made his mind up about females) unconsciously wish to displace their fathers and to sleep with their mothers. According to Freud, hatred for the father and love of the mother, normally repressed, may appear disguised in dreams. Works of art, like dreams, are disguised versions or repressed wishes.

Consider, for instance, Edgar Allan Poe. An orphan before he was three years old, he was brought up in the family of John Allan, but he was never formally adopted. His relations with Allan were stormy, though he seems to have had better relations with Allan's wife and still better relations with an aunt, whose daughter he married. In the Freudian view, Poe's marriage to his cousin (the daughter of a mother figure) was a way of sleeping with his mother. Psychoanalytic critics allege that if we move from Poe's life to his work, we see this hatred for his father and love for his mother. Thus, the murderer in "The Cask of Amontillado" is said to voice Poe's hostility to his father, and the wine vault in which much of the story is set (an encompassing structure associated with fluids) is interpreted as symbolizing Poe's desire to return to his mother's womb. In Poe's other works, the longing for death is similarly taken to embody his desire to return to the womb.

Other psychoanalytic interpretations of Poe have been offered. Kenneth Silverman, author of a biography entitled *Edgar Allan Poe* (1991) and the editor of a collection entitled *New Essays on Poe's Major Tales* (1993), emphasizes the fact that Poe was orphaned before he was three and was separated from his brother and his infant sister. In *New Essays* Silverman relates this circumstance to the "many instances of engulfment" that he finds in Poe's work. Images of engulfment, he points out, "are part of a still larger network of images having to do with biting, devouring, and similar oral mutilation." Why are they common in Poe? Here is Silverman's answer:

> Current psychoanalytic thinking about childhood bereavement explains the fantasy of being swallowed up as representing a desire, mixed with dread, to merge with the dead; the wish to devour represents a primitive attempt at preserving loved ones, incorporating them so as not to lose them. (p. 20)

Notice that psychoanalytic interpretations take us away from what the author consciously intended; they purport to tell us what the work reveals, whether or not the author was aware of this meaning. The "meaning" of the work is found not in the surface content of the work but in the author's psyche.

One additional example—and it is the most famous—of a psychoanalytic study of a work of literature may be useful. In *Hamlet and Oedipus* (1949) Ernest Jones, amplifying some comments by Freud, argued that Hamlet delays killing Claudius because Claudius (who has killed Hamlet's father and married Hamlet's mother) has done exactly what Hamlet himself wanted to do. For Hamlet to kill Claudius, then, would be to kill himself.

If this approach interests you, take a look at Norman N. Holland's *Psychoanalysis and Shakespeare* (1966) or Frederick Crews's study of Hawthorne, *The Sins of the Fathers* (1966). Crews finds in Hawthorne's work evidence of unresolved Oedipal conflicts, and he accounts for the appeal of the fictions thus: The stories "rest on fantasy, but on the shared fantasy of mankind, and this makes for a more penetrating fiction than would any illusionistic slice of life" (263). For applications to other authors, consider Simon O. Lesser's *Fiction and the Unconscious* (1957), or an anthology of criticism, *Literature and Psychoanalysis,* edited by Edith Kurzweil and William Phillips (1983).

Psychological criticism can also turn from the author and the work to the reader, seeking to explain why we, as readers, respond in certain ways. Why, for example, is *Hamlet* so widely popular? A Freudian answer is that it is universal because it deals with a universal (Oedipal) impulse. One can, however, ask whether it appeals as strongly to women as to men (again, Freud was unsure about the Oedipus complex in women) and, if so, why it appeals to them. Or, more generally, one can ask if males and females read in the same way.

Gender Criticism (Feminist, and Lesbian and Gay Criticism)

This last question brings us to **gender criticism.** As we have seen, writing about literature usually seeks to answer questions. Historical scholarship, for instance, tries to answer such questions as "What did Shakespeare and his contemporaries believe about ghosts?" or "How did Victorian novelists and poets respond to Darwin's theory of evolution?" Gender criticism, too, asks questions. It is especially concerned with two issues, one about reading and one about writing: "Do men and women read in different ways?" and "Do they write in different ways?"

Feminist criticism can be traced back to the work of Virginia Woolf (1882–1941). but chiefly it grew out of the women's movement of the 1960s. The women's movement at first tended to hold that women are pretty much the same as men and therefore should be treated equally, but much recent feminist criticism has emphasized and explored the differences between women and men. Because the experiences of the sexes are different, the argument goes, their values and sensibilities are different, and their responses to literature are different. Further, literature written by women is different from literature written by men. Works written by women are seen by some feminist critics as embodying the experiences of a minority culture—a group marginalized by the dominant male culture. (If you have read Susan Glaspell's *Trifles* [page 315] you'll recall that this literary work itself is largely concerned about the differing ways that males and females perceive the world.) Of course, not all women are feminist critics, and not all feminist critics are women. Further, there are varieties of feminist criticism, but for a good introduction see *The New Feminist Criticism: Essays on Women, Literature, and Theory* (1985), edited by Elaine Showalter, and *Feminism: An Anthology of Literary Theory and Criticism,* ed. Robyn R. Warhol and Diane Price Herndl, 2nd ed. (1997). For the role of men in feminist criticism, see *Engendering Men,* edited by Joseph A. Boone and Michael Cadden (1990). At this point it should also be said that some theorists, who hold that identity is socially constructed, strongly dispute the value of establishing "essentialist" categories such as *gay* and *lesbian*—a point that we will consider in a moment.

Feminist critics rightly point out that men have established the conventions of literature and that men have established the canon—that is, the body of literature that is said to be worth reading. Speaking a bit broadly, in this patriarchal or male-dominated body of literature, men are valued for being strong and active, whereas women are expected to be weak and passive. Thus, in the world of fairy tales, the admirable male is the energetic hero (Jack, the Giant-Killer) but the admirable female is the passive Sleeping Beauty. Active women such as the wicked stepmother or—a disguised form of the same thing—the witch are generally villainous. (There are of course exceptions, such as Gretel in "Hansel and Gretel.") A woman hearing or reading the story of Sleeping Beauty or of Little Red Riding Hood (rescued by the powerful woodcutter). or any other work in which women seem to be trivialized, will respond differently than a man. For instance. a woman may be socially conditioned into admiring Sleeping Beauty, but only at great cost to her mental well-being. A more resistant female reader may recognize in herself no kinship with the beautiful, passive Sleeping Beauty and may respond to the story indignantly. Another way to put it is this: The male reader perceives a romantic story, but the resistant female reader perceives a story of oppression.

For discussions of the ways in which, it is argued, women *ought* to read, you may want to look at *Gender and Reading,* edited by Elizabeth A. Flynn and Patrocino Schweikart, and especially at Judith Fetterley's book *The Resisting Reader* (1978). Fetterley's point, briefly, is that women should resist the meanings (that is, the visions of how women ought to behave) that male authors—or female authors who have inherited patriarchal values—embed in their books. "To read the canon of what is currently considered classic American literature is perforce to identify as male," Fetterley says. "It insists on its universality in specifically male terms." Fetterley argues that a woman must read as a woman, "exorcising the male mind that has been implanted in women." In resisting the obvious meanings—for instance, the false claim that male values are universal values—women may discover more significant meanings. Fetterley argues that Faulkner's "A Rose for Emily"

is a story not of a conflict between the South and the North or between the old order and the new; it is a story of the patriarchy North and

South, new and old, and of the sexual conflict within it. As Faulkner himself has implied, it is a story of a woman victimized and betrayed by the system of sexual politics, who nevertheless has discovered, within the structures that victimize her, sources of power for herself. . . . "A Rose for Emily" is the story of how to murder your gentleman caller and get away with it. (34–35)

Fetterley contends that the society made Emily a "lady"—society dehumanized her by elevating her. Emily's father, seeking to shape her life, stood in the doorway of their house and drove away her suitors. So far as he was concerned, Emily was a nonperson, a creature whose own wishes were not to be regarded; he alone would shape her future. Because society (beginning with her father) made her a "lady"—a creature so elevated that she is not taken seriously as a passionate human being—she is able to kill Homer Barron and not be suspected. Here is Fetterley speaking of the passage in which the townspeople crowd into her house when her death becomes known:

When the would-be "suitors" finally get into her father's house, they discover the consequences of his oppression of her, for the violence contained in the rotted corpse of Homer Barron is the mirror image of the violence represented in the tableau, the back-flung front door flung back with a vengeance. (42)

"A Rose for Emily" is reprinted on pages 557–62.

Feminist criticism has been concerned not only with the depiction of women and men in a male-determined literary canon and with women's responses to these images but also with yet another topic: women's writing. Women have had fewer opportunities than men to become writers of fiction, poetry, and drama—for one thing, they have been less well educated in the things that the male patriarchy valued—but even when they *have* managed to write, men sometimes have neglected their work simply because it was written by a woman. Feminists have further argued that certain forms of writing have been especially the province of women—for instance journals, diaries, and letters; and predictably, these forms have not been given adequate space in the traditional, male-oriented canon.

In 1972, in an essay entitled "When We Dead Awaken: Writing as Re-Vision," the poet and essayist Adrienne Rich effectively summed up the matter:

A radical critique of literature, feminist in its impulse, would take the work first of all as a clue to how we live, how we have been living, how we have been led to imagine ourselves, how our language has trapped as well as liberated us: and how we can begin to see—and therefore live—afresh. . . . We need to know the writing of the past and know it differently than we have ever known it; not to pass on a tradition but to break its hold over us.

Much feminist criticism concerned with women writers has emphasized connections between the writer's biography and her work. Suzanne Juhasz, in her introduction to *Feminist Critics Read Emily Dickinson* (1983), puts it this way:

The central assumption of feminist criticism is that gender informs the nature of art, the nature of biography, and the relation between them.

Dickinson is a woman poet, and this fact is integral to her identity. Feminist criticism's sensitivity to the components of female experience in general and to Dickinson's identity as a woman generates essential insights about her. . . . Attention to the relationship between biography and art is a requisite of feminist criticism. To disregard it further strengthens those divisions continually created by traditional criticism, so that nothing about the woman writer can be seen whole. (1–5)

Feminist criticism has made many readers—men as well as women—increasingly aware of gender relationships within literary works.

Lesbian criticism and **gay criticism** have their roots in feminist criticism; that is, feminist criticism introduced many of the questions that these other, newer developments are now exploring.

In *On Lies, Secrets, and Silence,* Adrienne Rich reprinted a 1975 essay on Emily Dickinson, "Vesuvius at Home." In her new preface to the reprinted essay she said that a lesbian-feminist reading of Dickinson would not have to prove that Dickinson slept with another woman. Rather, lesbian-feminist criticism "will ask questions hitherto passed over; it will not search obsessively for heterosexual romance as the key to a woman artist's life and work" (157–58). Obviously such a statement is also relevant to a male artist's life and work. It should be mentioned, too, that Rich's comments on lesbian reading and lesbianism as an image of creativity have been much discussed. For a brief survey, see Marilyn R. Farwell, "Toward a Definition of the Lesbian Literary Imagination," *Signs* 14 (1988): 100–18.

Before turning to some of the questions that lesbian and gay critics address, it is necessary to say that lesbian criticism and gay criticism are not symmetrical, chiefly because lesbian and gay relationships themselves are not symmetrical. Straight society has traditionally been more tolerant of—or blinder to—lesbianism than male homosexuality. Further, lesbian literary theory has tended to see its affinities more with feminist theory than with gay theory: that is, the emphasis has been on gender (male/female) rather than on sexuality (homosexuality/bisexuality/heterosexuality). On the other hand, some gays and lesbians have been writing what is now being called queer theory.

Now for some of the questions that this criticism addresses: (1) Do lesbians and gays read in ways that differ from the ways straight people read? (2) Do they write in ways that differ from those of straight people? (For instance, Gregory Woods argues in *Lesbian and Gay Writing: An Anthology of Critical Essays* [1990], edited by Mark Lilly, that "modern gay poets . . . use . . . paradox, as weapon and shield, against a world in which heterosexuality is taken for granted as being exclusively natural and healthy" [176]. Another critic, Jeffrey Meyers, writing in *Journal of English and Germanic Philology* 88 [1989]: 126–29, in an unsympathetic review of a book on gay writers contrasts gay writers of the past with those of the present. According to Meyers, closeted homosexuals in the past, writing out of guilt and pain, produced a distinctive literature that is more interesting than the productions of today's uncloseted writers.) (3) How have straight writers portrayed lesbians and gays, and how have lesbian and gay writers portrayed straight women and men? (4) What strategies did lesbian and gay writers use to make their work acceptable to a general public in an age when lesbian and gay behavior was unmentionable?

Questions such as these have stimulated much critical writing especially about bisexual and lesbian and gay authors (for instance Virginia Woolf,

Gertrude Stein, Elizabeth Bishop, Walt Whitman, Oscar Wilde, E. M. Forster, Hart Crane, Tennessee Williams), but they have also led to interesting writing on such a topic as Nathaniel Hawthorne's attitudes toward women. "An account of Hawthorne's misogyny that takes no account of his own and his culture's gender anxieties," Robert K. Martin says in Boone and Cadden's *Engendering Men,* "is necessarily inadequate" (122).

Shakespeare's work—and not only the sonnets, which praise a beautiful male friend—has prompted a fair amount of gay criticism. Much of this criticism consists of "decoding" aspects of the plays. Seymour Kleinberg argues in *Essays on Gay Literature* (1985), ed. Stuart Kellogg, that Antonio in *The Merchant of Venice,* whose melancholy is not clearly accounted for by Shakespeare, is melancholy because (again, this is according to Kleinberg) Antonio's lover, Bassanio, is deserting him, and because Antonio is ashamed of his own sexuality:

> Antonio is a virulently anti-Semitic homosexual and is melancholic to the point of despair because his lover, Bassanio, wishes to marry an immensely rich aristocratic beauty, to leave the diversions of the Rialto to return to his own class and to sexual conventionality. Antonio is also in despair because he despises himself for his homosexuality, which is romantic, obsessive, and exclusive, and fills him with sexual shame. (113)

Several earlier critics had suggested that Antonio is a homosexual, hopelessly pining for Bassanio, but Kleinberg goes further and argues that Antonio and Bassanio are lovers, not just good friends, and that Antonio's hopeless and shameful (because socially unacceptable) passion for Bassanio becomes transformed into hatred for the Jew, Shylock. The play, according to Kleinberg, is partly about "a world where . . . sexual guilt is translated into ethnic hatred" (124).

Examination of gender by gay and lesbian critics obviously can help to illuminate literary works, but it should be added, too, that some—perhaps most—gay and lesbian critics write also as activists, reporting their findings not only to enable us to understand and to enjoy the works of (say) Whitman, but also to change society's view of sexuality. Thus, in *Disseminating Whitman* (1991), Michael Moon is impatient with earlier critical rhapsodies about Whitman's universalism. It used to be said that Whitman's celebration of the male body was a sexless celebration of brotherly love in a democracy, but the gist of Moon's view is that we must neither whitewash Whitman's poems with such high-minded talk nor reject them as indecent; rather, we must see exactly what Whitman is saying about a kind of experience that society had shut its eyes to, and we must take Whitman's view seriously. Somewhat similarly, Gregory Woods in *Articulate Flesh* (1987) points out that until a few years ago discussions of Hart Crane regularly condemned his homosexuality, as is evident, for instance, in L. S. Dembo's characterization of Crane (quoted by Woods) as "uneducated, alcoholic, homosexual, paranoic, suicidal" (140). Gay and lesbian writers don't adopt this sort of manner. But it should also be pointed out that today there are straight critics who study lesbian or gay authors and write about them insightfully and without hostility.

One assumption in much lesbian and gay critical writing is that although gender greatly influences the ways in which we read, reading is a skill that can be learned, and therefore straight people—aided by lesbian and gay critics—can learn to read, with pleasure and profit, lesbian and gay writers. This assumption also underlies much feminist criticism, which often assumes that men must stop ignoring books by women and must learn (with the help of feminist critics) how to read them, and, in fact, how to read—with newly opened eyes—the sexist writings of men of the past and present.

In addition to the titles mentioned earlier concerning gay and lesbian criticism, consult Eve Kosofsky Sedgwick, *Between Men: English Literature and Male Homosocial Desire* (1985), and an essay by Sedgwick, "Gender Criticism," in *Redrawing the Boundaries,* ed. Stephen Greenblatt and Giles Gunn (1992).

While many in the field of lesbian and gay criticism have turned their energies toward examining the effects that an author's—or a character's—sexual identity may have upon the text, others have begun to question, instead, the concept of sexual identity itself.[1] Drawing upon the work of the French social historian Michel Foucault, critics such as David Halperin (*One Hundred Years of Homosexuality and Other Essays on Greek Love* [1990]) and Judith Butler (*Gender Trouble* [1989]) explore how various categories of identity, such as "heterosexual" and "homosexual," represent ways of defining human beings that are distinct to particular cultures and historical periods. These critics, affiliated with what is known as the social constructionist school of thought, argue that the way a given society (modern American, for instance, or ancient Greek) interprets sexuality will determine the particular categories within which individuals come to understand and to name their own desires. For such critics the goal of a lesbian or gay criticism is not to define the specificity of a lesbian or gay literature or mode of interpretations, but to show how the ideology, the normative understanding, of a given culture makes it seem natural to think about sexuality in terms of such identities as lesbian, gay, bisexual, or straight. By challenging the authority of those terms, or "denaturalizing" them, and by calling attention to moments in which literary (and nonliterary) representations make assumptions that reinforce the supposed inevitability of those distinctions, such critics attempt to redefine our understandings of the relations between sexuality and literature. They hope, in short, to make clear that sexuality is always, in a certain sense, "literary"; it is a representation of a fiction that society has constructed in order to make sense out of experience.

Because such critics have challenged the authority of the opposition between heterosexuality and homosexuality, and have read it as a historical construct rather than as a biological or psychological absolute, they have sometimes resisted the very terms *lesbian* and *gay.* Many now embrace what is called Queer Theory as an attempt to mark their resistance to the categories of identity they see our culture as imposing upon us.

Works written within this mode of criticism are often influenced by deconstructionist or psychoanalytic thought. They examine works by straight authors as frequently as they do works by writers who might be defined as lesbian or gay. Eve Kosofsky Sedgwick's reading of *Billy Budd* in her book *Epistemology of the Closet* (1990) provides a good example of this type of criticism. Reading Claggart as "the homosexual" in the text of Melville's novella, Sedgwick is not interested in defining his difference from other characters. Instead, she shows how the novella sets up a large number of oppositions—such as public and private, sincerity and sentimentality, health and illness—all of which have a relationship to the way in which a distinct "gay" identity was being produced by

---

[1]This paragraph and the next two are by Lee Edelman of Tufts University.

American society at the end of the nineteenth century. Other critics whose work in this field may be useful for students of literature are D. A. Miller, *The Novel and the Police* (1988); Diana Fuss, *Essentially Speaking* (1989) and *Identification Papers* (1995); Judith Butler, *Bodies That Matter* (1993); and Lee Edelman, *Homographesis: Essays in Gay Literary and Cultural Theory* (1993).

In this book, works that concern gay or lesbian experience include those by A. E. Housman, Gloria Naylor, Adrienne Rich, Walt Whitman, and Oscar Wilde.

This chapter began by making the obvious point that all readers, whether or not they consciously adopt a particular approach to literature, necessarily read through particular lenses. More precisely, a reader begins with a frame of interpretation and from within the frame selects one of the several competing methodologies. Critics often make great—even grandiose—claims for their approaches. For example, Frederic Jameson, a Marxist, begins *The Political Unconscious: Narrative as a Socially Symbolic Act* (1981) thus:

> This book will argue the priority of the political interpretation of literary texts. It conceives of the political perspective not as some supplemental method, not as an optional auxiliary to other interpretive methods current today—the psychoanalytic or the myth-critical, the stylistic, the ethical, the structural—but rather as the absolute horizon of all reading and all interpretation. (7)

Readers who are chiefly interested in politics may be willing to assume "the priority of the political interpretation . . . as the absolute horizon of all reading and all interpretation," but other readers may respectfully decline to accept this assumption.

In talking about a critical approach, sometimes the point is made by saying that readers decode a text by applying a grid to it: the grid enables them to see certain things clearly. Good; but what is sometimes forgotten is that a lens or a grid—an angle of vision or interpretive frame and a methodology—also prevents a reader from seeing certain other things. This is to be expected. What is important, then, is to remember this fact, and thus not to deceive ourselves by thinking that our keen tools enable us to see the whole. A psychoanalytic reading of, say, *Hamlet* may be helpful, but it does not reveal all that is in *Hamlet,* and it does not refute the perceptions of another approach, let's say a historical study. Each approach may illuminate aspects neglected by others.

It is too much to expect a reader to apply all useful methods (or even several) at once—that would be rather like looking through a telescope with one eye and through a microscope with the other—but it is not too much to expect readers to be aware of the limitations of their methods. If one reads much criticism, one finds two kinds of critics. There are, on the one hand, critics who methodically and mechanically peer through a lens or grid, and they of course find what one can easily predict they will find. On the other hand, there are critics who (despite what may be inevitable class and gender biases) are at least relatively open-minded in their approach—critics who, one might say, do not at the outset of their reading believe that their method assures them that they have got the text's number and that by means of this method they will expose the text for what it is. The philosopher Richard Rorty engagingly makes a distinction somewhat along these lines, in an essay he contributed to Umberto Eco's *Interpretation and Overinterpretation* (1992). There is a great difference, Rorty suggests, between kno ing what you want to get out of a person or thing or text in advance and [on the other hand] hoping that the person or thing or text will help you want something different—that he or she or it will help you to change your purposes, and thus to change your life. This distinction, I think, helps us highlight the difference between methodical and inspired readings of texts. (106)

Rorty goes on to say he has seen an anthology of readings on Conrad's *Heart of Darkness,* containing a psychoanalytic reading, a reader-response reading, and so on. "None of the readers had, as far as I could see," Rorty says,

been enraptured or destabilized by *Heart of Darkness.* I got no sense that the book had made a big difference to them, that they cared much about Kurtz or Marlow or the woman "with helmeted head and tawny cheeks" whom Marlow sees on the bank of the river. These people, and that book, had no more changed these readers' purposes than the specimen under the microscope changes the purpose of the histologist. (107)

The kind of criticism that Rorty prefers he calls "unmethodical" criticism and "inspired" criticism. It is, for Rorty, the result of an "encounter" with some aspect of a work of art "which has made a difference to the critic's conception of who she is, what she is good for, what she wants to do with herself . . ." (107). This is not a matter of "respect" for the text, Rorty insists. Rather, he says "love" and "hate" are better words, "for a great love or a great loathing is the sort of thing that changes us by changing our purposes, changing the uses to which we shall put people and things and texts we encounter later" (107).

SUGGESTIONS FOR FURTHER READING

Because a massive list of titles may prove discouraging rather than helpful, it seems advisable here to give a short list of basic titles. (Titles already mentioned in this chapter—which are good places to begin—are *not* repeated in the following list.)

A good sampling of contemporary criticism (60 or so essays or chapters from books), representing all of the types discussed in this commentary except lesbian and gay criticism, can be found in *The Critical Tradition: Classic Texts and Contemporary Trends,* ed. David H. Richter, 2nd ed. (1998).

For a readable introduction to various approaches, written for students who are beginning the study of literary theory, see Steven Lynn, *Texts and Contexts,* 2nd ed. (1998). For a more advanced survey, that is, a work that assumes some familiarity with the material, see a short book by K. M. Newton, *Interpreting the Text: A Critical Introduction to the Theory and Practice of Literary Interpretation* (1990). A third survey, though considerably longer than the books by Lynn and Newton, is narrower because it confines itself to a study of critical writings about Shakespeare: Brian Vickers, *Appropriating Shakespeare: Contemporary Critical Quarrels* (1993), offers an astringent appraisal of deconstruction, New Historicism, psychoanalytic criticism, feminist criticism, and Marxist criticism. For collections of essays on Shakespeare written from some of the points of view that Vickers deplores, see Patricia Parker and Geoffrey Hartman, eds., *Shakespeare and the Question of Theory* (1985), and John Drakakis, ed., *Shakespearean Tragedy* (1992).

Sympathetic discussions (usually two or three pages long) of each approach, with fairly extensive bibliographic suggestions, are given in the appropriate articles in the four encyclopedic works by Harris, Makaryk, Groden and Kreiswirth, and Preminger and Brogan, listed on page 39, in Chapter 3, though only Groden and Kreiswirth (*Johns Hopkins Guide*) discuss lesbian and gay criticism (under "Gay Theory and Criticism"). For essays discussing feminist, gender, Marxist, psychoanalytic, deconstructive, New Historicist, and cultural criticism—as well as other topics not covered in this chapter—see Stephen Greenblatt and Giles Gunn. eds., *Redrawing the Boundaries: The Transformation of English and American Literary Studies* (1992).

Formalist Criticism (New Criticism)

Cleanth Brooks, *The Well Wrought Urn: Studies in the Structure of Poetry* (1947), especially Chapters 1 and 11 ("The Language of Paradox" and "The Heresy of Paraphrase"); W. K. Wimsatt, *The Verbal Icon* (1954), especially "The Intentional Fallacy" and "The Affective Fallacy"; Murray Krieger, *The New Apologists for Poetry* (1956); and, for an accurate overview of a kind of criticism often misrepresented today, Chapters 9–12 in Volume 6 of René Wellek, *A History of Modern Criticism: 1750-1950.*

Deconstruction

Christopher Norris, *Deconstruction: Theory and Practice,* rev. ed. (1991); Vincent B. Leitch, *Deconstructive Criticism: An Advanced Introduction and Survey* (1983); Christopher Norris, ed., *What Is Deconstruction?* (1988); Christopher Norris and Andrew Benjamin, *Deconstruction and the Interests of Theory* (1989).

Reader-Response Criticism

Wolfgang Iser, *The Act of Reading: A Theory of Aesthetic Response* (1978); Wolfgang Iser, *Prospecting: From Reader Response to Literary Anthropology* (1993); Susan Suleiman and Inge Crossman, eds., *The Reader in the Text* (1980); Jane P. Tompkins, ed., *Reader-Response Criticism* (1980); Norman N. Holland, *The Dynamics of Literary Response* (1973, 1989); Steven Mailloux, *Interpretive Conventions: The Reader in the Study of American Fiction* (1982).

Archetypal Criticism

G. Wilson Knight, *The Starlit Dome* (1941); Richard Chase, *Quest for Myth* (1949); Murray Krieger, ed., *Northrop Frye in Modern Criticism* (1966); Frank Lentricchia, *After the New Criticism* (1980). For a good survey of Frye's approach: Robert D. Denham, *Northrop Frye and Critical Method* (1978).

Historical Criticism

For a brief survey of some historical criticism of the first half of this century, see René Wellek, *A History of Modern Criticism: 1750-1950,* Volume 6, Chapter 4 ("Academic Criticism"). E. M. W. Tillyard, *The Elizabethan World Picture* (1943), and Tillyard's *Shakespeare's History Plays* (1944), both of which relate

Elizabethan literature to the beliefs of the age, are good examples of the historical approach.

Marxist Criticism

Raymond Williams, *Marxism and Literature* (1977); Tony Bennett, *Formalism
and Marxism* (1979); Lydia Sargent, ed., *Women and Revolution: A Discussion
of the Unhappy Marriage of Marxism and Feminism* (1981); and for a brief survey of American Marxist writers of the 1930s and 1940s, see Chapter 5 of Volume 6 of René Wellek, *A History of Modern Criticism* (1986). Also helpful:
Daniel Aaron, *Writers on the Left: Episodes in American Literary Communism*
(1961, new ed., 1992); and Barbara Foley, *Radical Representations: Politics and
Form in U. S. Proletarian Fiction, 1929–1941* (1993).

New Historicism

Stephen Greenblatt, *Renaissance Self-Fashioning from More to Shakespeare*
(1980), especially the first chapter; Brook Thomas, *The New Historicism and
Other Old-Fashioned Topics* (1991).

Biographical Criticism

Leon Edel, *Literary Biography* (1957); Estelle C. Jellinek, ed., *Women's Autobiography: Essays in Criticism* (1980); James Olney, *Metaphors of Self: The Meaning of Autobiography* (1981); and *Women, Autobiography, Theory: A Reader*,
ed. Sidonie Smith and Julia Watson. Among the most distinguished twentieth-
century literary biographers is Richard Ellmann, *James Joyce* (1959, rev. ed.
1982), and, more recently, Hermione Lee, *Virginia Woolf* (1997).

Psychological (or Psychoanalytical) Criticism

Edith Kurzweil and William Phillips, eds., *Literature and Psychoanalysis*
(1983); Maurice Charney and Joseph Reppen, eds., *Psychoanalytic Approaches
to Literature and Film* (1987); Madelon Sprengnether, *The Spectral Mother:
Freud, Feminism, and Psychoanalysis* (1990); Frederick Crews, *Out of My System* (1975).

Gender (Feminist, and Lesbian and Gay) Criticism

Gayle Greene and Coppèlia Kahn, eds., *Making a Difference: Feminist Literary
Criticism* (1985), including an essay by Bonnie Zimmerman on lesbian criticism;
Catherine Belsey and Jane Moore, eds., *The Feminist Reader: Essays in Gender
and the Politics of Literary Criticism* (1989); Toril Moi, ed., *French Feminist
Thought* (1987); Elizabeth A. Flynn and Patrocinio P. Schweikart, eds., *Gender
and Reading: Essays on Readers, Texts, and Contexts* (1986); Barbara Christian,
Black Feminist Criticism: Perspectives on Black Women Writers (1985);
Shoshana Felman, *What Does a Woman Want? Reading and Sexual Difference*
(1993); Robert Martin, *The Homosexual Tradition in American Poetry* (1979).
Henry Abelove et al., eds., *The Lesbian and Gay Studies Reader* (1993) has only
a few essays concerning literature, but it has an extensive bibliography on the
topic.

Valuable reference works include: *Encyclopedia of Feminist Literary Theory,* ed. Beth Kowaleski-Wallace (1997); and *The Gay and Lesbian Literary Heritage: A Reader's Companion to the Writers and Their Works, From Antiquity to the Present,* ed. Claude J. Summers (1995).

For discussion of queer theory: Annamarie Jagose, *Queer Theory: An Introduction* (1996); Alan Sinfield, *Cultural Politics—Queer Reading* (1994); and *Feminism Meets Queer Theory,* ed. Elizabeth Weed and Naomi Schor (1997).

A last word: If you want to read only a few pages about the nature and value of criticism, look at Helen Vendler's introduction and "The Function of Criticism" in a collection of her essays, *The Music of What Happens* (1988). Vendler is aware that most criticism today is ideological and it is therefore concerned with the interpretation of meaning—but she is less concerned with ideology and meaning than with the causes of "the aesthetic power of the art work":

> It is natural that people under new cultural imperatives should be impelled to fasten new interpretations (from the reasonable to the fantastic) onto aesthetic objects from the past. But criticism cannot stop there. The critic may well begin, "Look at it this way for a change," but the sentence must continue, "and now don't you see it as more intelligibly beautiful and moving?" That is, if the interpretation does not reveal some hitherto occluded aspect of the aesthetic power of the art work, it is useless as art criticism (though it may be useful as cultural history or sociology or psychology or religion). (2)

Vendler describes and exemplifies her approach in *Poems, Poets, Poetry: An Introduction and Anthology* (1997).

PART

IV

A
Thematic
Anthology

Love and Hate

ESSAYS

 **SEI SHŌNAGON**

Sei Shōnagon was a Japanese woman who, in the tenth century, served for some ten years as a lady-in-waiting to the empress in Kyoto. Her Pillow Book—*a marvelous collection of lists, eyewitness reports, and brief essays—established the Japanese tradition of* zuihitsu, *"spontaneous writing" (literally, "to follow the brush").*

Not much is known about Sei Shōnagon Her book tells us nothing of her early years, and the date and circumstances of her death are unknown. Scholars conjecture that she was born about 965 and that she became a lady-in-waiting during the early 990s. It is evident from her book that she was witty, snobbish, and well versed in the etiquette of love at court.

The passage that we here reprint appears in a list entitled "Hateful Things."

A Lover's Departure

A lover who is leaving at dawn announces that he has to find his fan and his paper. "I know I put them somewhere last night," he says. Since it is pitch dark, he gropes about the room, bumping into the furniture and muttering, "Strange! Where on earth can they be?" Finally he discovers the objects. He thrusts the paper into the breast of his robe with a great rustling sound; then he snaps open his fan and busily fans away with it. Only now is he ready to take his leave. What charmless behavior! "Hateful" is an understatement.

Equally disagreeable is the man who, when leaving in the middle of the night, takes care to fasten the cord of his headdress. This is quite unnecessary; he could perfectly well put it gently on his head without tying the cord. And why must he spend time adjusting his cloak or hunting costume? Does he really think someone may see him at this time of night and criticize him for not being impeccably dressed?

A good lover will behave as elegantly at dawn as at any other time. He drags himself out of bed with a look of dismay on his face. The lady urges him on: "Come, my friend, it's getting light. You don't want anyone to find you here." He gives a deep sigh, as if to say that the night has not been nearly long enough and that it is agony to leave. Once up, he does not instantly pull on his trousers. Instead he comes close to the lady and whispers whatever was left unsaid during the night. Even when he is dressed, he still lingers, vaguely pretending to be fastening his sash.

Presently he raises the lattice, and the two lovers stand together by the side door while he tells her how he dreads the coming day, which will keep them apart; then he slips away. The lady watches him go, and this moment of parting will remain among her most charming memories.

5   Indeed, one's attachment to a man depends largely on the elegance of his leave-taking. When he jumps out of bed, scurries about the room, tightly fastens his trouser-sash, rolls up the sleeves of his Court cloak, overrobe, or hunting costume, stuffs his belongings into the breast of his robe and then briskly secures the outer sash—one really begins to hate him.

✎ Topics for Critical Thinking and Writing

1. What are your first responses to this passage? Later—even if only thirty minutes later—reread the passage and think about whether your responses change.
2. On the basis of this short extract, how would you characterize Sei Shōnagon? Can you imagine that you and she might become close friends or lovers?
3. Write a journal entry or two on the topic "Hateful Things."

📖 JUDITH ORTIZ COFER

Born in Puerto Rico in 1952 of a Puerto Rican mother and a United States mainland father who served in the Navy, Judith Ortiz Cofer was educated both in Puerto Rico and on the mainland. After earning a bachelor's and a master's degree in English, she did further graduate work at Oxford and then taught English in Florida. She has published seven volumes of poetry.

The following selection comes from an autobiography, Silent Dancing *(1990).*

I Fell in Love, Or My Hormones Awakened

I fell in love, or my hormones awakened from their long slumber in my body, and suddenly the goal of my days was focused on one thing: to catch a glimpse of my secret love. And it had to remain secret, because I had, of course, in the great tradition of tragic romance, chosen to love a boy who was totally out of my reach. He was not Puerto Rican; he was Italian and rich. He was also an older man. He was a senior at the high school when I came in as a freshman. I first saw him in the hall, leaning casually on a wall that was the border line between girl-side and boyside for underclassmen. He looked extraordinarily like a young Marlon Brando—down to the ironic little smile. The total of what I knew about the boy who starred in every one of my awkward fantasies was this: that he was the nephew of the man who owned the supermarket on my block; that he often had parties at his parents' beautiful home in the suburbs which I would hear about;

that this family had money (which came to our school in many ways)—and this fact made my knees weak: and that he worked at the store near my apartment building on weekends and in the summer.

My mother could not understand why I became so eager to be the one sent out on her endless errands. I pounced on every opportunity from Friday to late Saturday afternoon to go after eggs, cigarettes, milk (I tried to drink as much of it as possible, although I hated the stuff)—the staple items that she would order from the "American" store.

Week after week I wandered up and down the aisles, taking furtive glances at the stock room in the back, breathlessly hoping to see my prince. Not that I had a plan. I felt like a pilgrim waiting for a glimpse of Mecca. I did not expect him to notice me. It was sweet agony.

One day I did see him. Dressed in a white outfit like a surgeon: white pants and shirt, white cap, and (gross sight, but not to my love-glazed eyes) blood-smeared butcher's apron. He was helping to drag a side of beef into the freezer storage area of the store. I must have stood there like an idiot, because I remember that he did see me, he even spoke to me! I could have died. I think he said, "Excuse me," and smiled vaguely in my direction.

5   After that, I *willed* occasions to go to the supermarket. I watched my mother's pack of cigarettes empty ever so slowly. I wanted her to smoke them fast. I drank milk and forced it on my brother (although a second glass for him had to be bought with my share of Fig Newton cookies which we both liked, but we were restricted to one row each). I gave my cookies up for love, and watched my mother smoke her L&M's with so little enthusiasm that I thought (God, no!) that she might be cutting down on her smoking or maybe even giving up the habit. At this crucial time!

I thought I had kept my lonely romance a secret. Often I cried hot tears on my pillow for the things that kept us apart. In my mind there was no doubt that he would never notice me (and that is why I felt free to stare at him—I was invisible). He could not see me because I was a skinny Puerto Rican girl, a freshman who did not belong to any group he associated with.

At the end of the year I found out that I had not been invisible. I learned one little lesson about human nature—adulation leaves a scent, one that we are all equipped to recognize, and no matter how insignificant the source, we seek it.

In June the nuns at our school would always arrange for some cultural extravaganza. In my freshman year it was a Roman banquet. We had been studying Greek drama (as a prelude to church history—it was at a fast clip that we galloped through Sophocles and Euripedes toward the early Christian martyrs), and our young, energetic Sister Agnes was in the mood for spectacle. She ordered the entire student body (it was a small group of under 300 students) to have our mothers make us togas out of sheets. She handed out a pattern on mimeo pages fresh out of the machine. I remember the intense smell of the alcohol on the sheets of paper, and how almost everyone in the auditorium brought theirs to their noses and inhaled deeply—mimeographed handouts were the school-day buzz that the new Xerox generation of kids is missing out on. Then, as the last couple of weeks of school dragged on, the city of Paterson becoming a concrete oven, and us wilting in our uncomfortable uniforms, we labored like frantic Roman slaves to build a splendid banquet hall in our small auditorium. Sister Agnes wanted a raised dais where the host and hostess would be regally enthroned.

She had already chosen our Senator and Lady from among our ranks. The Lady was to be a beautiful new student named Sophia, a recent Polish immigrant, whose English was still practically unintelligible, but whose features, classically perfect without a trace of makeup, enthralled us. Everyone talked about her gold hair cascading past her waist, and her voice which could carry a note right up to heaven in choir. The nuns wanted her for God. They kept saying that she had vocation. We just looked at her in awe, and the boys seemed afraid of her. She just smiled and did as she was told. I don't know what she thought of it all. The main privilege of beauty is that others will do almost everything for you, including thinking.

10   Her partner was to be our best basketball player, a tall, red-haired senior whose family sent its many offspring to our school. Together, Sophia and her senator looked like the best combination of immigrant genes our community could produce. It did not occur to me to ask then whether anything but their physical beauty qualified them for the starring roles in our production. I had the highest average in the church history class, but I was given the part of one of many "Roman Citizens." I was to sit in front of the plastic fruit and recite a greeting in Latin along with the rest of the school when our hosts came into the hall and took their places on their throne.

On the night of our banquet, my father escorted me in my toga to the door of our school. I felt foolish in my awkwardly draped sheet (blouse and skirt required underneath). My mother had no great skill as a seamstress. The best she could do was hem a skirt or a pair of pants. That night I would have traded her for a peasant woman with a golden needle. I saw other Roman ladies emerging from their parents' cars looking authentic in sheets of material that folded over their bodies like the garments on a statue by Michaelangelo. How did they do it? How was it that I always got it just slightly wrong, and worse, I believed that other people were just too polite to mention it. "The poor little Puerto Rican girl," I could hear them thinking. But in reality, I must have been my worst critic, self-conscious as I was.

Soon, we were all sitting at our circle of tables joined together around the dais. Sophia glittered like a golden statue. Her smile was beatific: a perfect, silent Roman lady. Her "senator" looked uncomfortable, glancing around at his buddies, perhaps waiting for the ridicule that he would surely get in the locker room later. The nuns in their black habits stood in the background watching us. What were they supposed to be, the Fates? Nubian slaves? The dancing girls did their modest little dance to tinny music from their finger cymbals, then the speeches were made. Then the grape juice "wine" was raised in a toast to the Roman Empire we all knew would fall within the week—before finals anyway.

All during the program I had been in a state of controlled hysteria. My secret love sat across the room from me looking supremely bored. I watched his every move, taking him in gluttonously. I relished the shadow of his eyelashes on his ruddy cheeks, his pouty lips smirking sarcastically at the ridiculous sight of our little play. Once he slumped down on his chair, and our sergeant-at-arms nun came over and tapped him sharply on his shoulder. He drew himself up slowly, with disdain. I loved his rebellious spirit. I believed myself still invisible to him in my "nothing" status as I looked upon my beloved. But toward the end of the evening, as we stood chanting our farewells in Latin, he looked straight across the room and into my eyes! How did I survive the killing power of those dark pupils? I trembled in a new way. I was not cold—I was burning! Yet I shook from the inside out, feeling light-headed, dizzy.

The room began to empty and I headed for the girls' lavatory. I wanted to relish the miracle in silence. I did not think for a minute that anything more would follow. I was satisfied with the enormous favor of a look from my beloved. I took my time, knowing that my father would be waiting outside for me, impatient, perhaps glowing in the dark in his phosphorescent white Navy uniform. The others would ride home. I would walk home with my father, both of us in costume. I wanted as few witnesses as possible. When I could no longer hear the crowds in the hallway, I emerged from the bathroom, still under the spell of those mesmerizing eyes.

15   The lights had been turned off in the hallway and all I could see was the lighted stairwell, at the bottom of which a nun would be stationed. My father would be waiting just outside. I nearly screamed when I felt someone grab me by the waist. But my mouth was quickly covered by someone else's mouth. I was being kissed. My first kiss and I could not even tell who it was. I pulled away to see that face not two inches away from mine. It was he. He smiled down at me. Did I have a silly expression on my face? My glasses felt crooked on my nose. I was unable to move or to speak. More gently, he lifted my chin and touched his lips to mine. This time I did not forget to enjoy it. Then, like the phantom lover that he was, he walked away into the darkened corridor and disappeared.

I don't know how long I stood there. My body was changing right there in the hallway of a Catholic school. My cells were tuning up like musicians in an orchestra, and my heart was a chorus. It was an opera I was composing, and I wanted to stand very still and just listen. But, of course, I heard my father's voice talking to the nun. I was in trouble if he had had to ask about me. I hurried down the stairs making up a story on the way about feeling sick. That would explain my flushed face and it would buy me a little privacy when I got home.

The next day Father announced at the breakfast table that he was leaving on a six month tour of Europe with the Navy in a few weeks and that at the end of the school year my mother, my brother, and I would be sent to Puerto Rico to stay for half a year at Mamá's (my mother's mother) house. I was devastated. This was the usual routine for us. We had always gone to Mamá's to stay when Father was away for long periods. But this year it was different for me. I was in love, and . . . my heart knocked against my bony chest at this thought . . . he loved me too? I broke into sobs and left the table.

In the next week I discovered the inexorable truth about parents. They can actually carry on with their plans right through tears, threats, and the awful spectacle of a teenager's broken heart. My father left me to my mother who impassively packed while I explained over and over that I was at a crucial time in my studies and that if I left my entire life would be ruined. All she would say was, "You are an intelligent girl, you'll catch up." Her head was filled with visions of *casa*[1] and family reunions, long gossip sessions with her mamá and sisters. What did she care that I was losing my one chance at true love?

In the meantime I tried desperately to see him. I thought he would look for me too. But the few times I saw him in the hallway, he was always rushing away. It would be long weeks of confusion and pain before I realized that the kiss was nothing but a little trophy for his ego. He had no interest in me other than as his adorer. He was flattered by my silent worship of him, and he had *bestowed* a kiss

[1]home

on me to please himself, and to fan the flames. I learned a lesson about the battle of the sexes then that I have never forgotten: the object is not always to win, but most times simply to keep your opponent (synonymous at times with "the loved one") guessing.

20   But this is too cynical a view to sustain in the face of that overwhelming rush of emotion that is first love. And in thinking back about my own experience with it, I can be objective only to the point where I recall how sweet the anguish was, how caught up in the moment I felt, and how every nerve in my body was involved in this salute to life. Later, much later, after what seemed like an eternity of dragging the weight of unrequited love around with me, I learned to make myself visible and to relish the little battles required to win the greatest prize of all. And much later, I read and understood Camus'[2] statement about the subject that concerns both adolescent and philosopher alike: if love were easy, life would be too simple.

[1990]

 ## Topics for Critical Thinking and Writing

1. If you agree with us that Cofer's essay is amusing, try to analyze the sources of its humor. *Why* are some passages funny?
2. In paragraph 9 Cofer says, "The main privilege of beauty is that others will do almost everything for you, including thinking." Do you agree that the beautiful are privileged? If so, draw on your experience (as one of the privileged or the unprivileged) to recount an example or two. By the way, Cofer seems to imply (paragraph 10) that the academically gifted should be privileged, or at least should be recognized as candidates for leading roles (e.g., that of "a perfect, silent Roman lady") in school productions. Is it any fairer to privilege brains than to privilege beauty? Explain.
3. In her final paragraph Cofer speaks of the experience as a "salute to life." What do you think she means by that?
4. Cofer is describing a state that is (or used to be) called "puppy love." If you have experienced anything like what Cofer experienced, write your own autobiographical essay. (You can of course amplify or censor as you wish.) If you have experienced a love that you think is more serious, more lasting, write about *that.*

 ## GARY SOTO

Gary Soto was born in Fresno, California, in 1952. While at Fresno State College he studied poetry with Philip Levine, and in his senior year he published his first poem, in the Iowa Review. *He has published several books of poetry since then, and he has won numerous prizes and grants. Since 1977 he has taught English and Chicano studies at the University of California, Berkeley.*

The following essay comes from Small Faces *(1986), a collection of autobiographical sketches.*

---

[2]Albert Camus (1913–1960), French novelist and philosopher

Like Mexicans

My grandmother gave me bad advice and good advice when I was in my early teens. For the bad advice, she said that I should become a barber because they made good money and listened to the radio all day. "Honey, they don't work como burros,"[1] she would say every time I visited her. She made the sound of donkeys braying. "Like that, honey!" For the good advice, she said that I should marry a Mexican girl. "No Okies, hijo"[2]—she would say—"Look, my son. He marry one and they fight every day about I don't know what and I don't know what." For her, everyone who wasn't Mexican, black, or Asian were Okies. The French were Okies, the Italians in suits were Okies. When I asked about Jews, whom I had read about, she asked for a picture. I rode home on my bicycle and returned with a calendar depicting the important races of the world. "Pues si, son Okies tambien!"[3] she said, nodding her head. She waved the calendar away and we went to the living room where she lectured me on the virtues of the Mexican girl: first, she could cook and, second, she acted like a woman, not a man, in her husband's home. She said she would tell me about a third when I got a little older.

I asked my mother about it—becoming a barber and marrying Mexican. She was in the kitchen. Steam curled from a pot of boiling beans, the radio was on, looking as squat as a loaf of bread. "Well, if you want to be a barber—they say they make good money." She slapped a round steak with a knife, her glasses slipping down with each strike. She stopped and looked up. "If you find a good Mexican girl, marry her of course." She returned to slapping the meat and I went to the backyard where my brother and David King were sitting on the lawn feeling the inside of their cheeks.

"This is what girls feel like," my brother said, rubbing the inside of his cheek. David put three fingers inside his mouth and scratched. I ignored them and climbed the back fence to see my best friend, Scott, a second-generation Okie. I called him and his mother pointed to the side of the house where his bedroom was, a small aluminum trailer, the kind you gawk at when they're flipped over on the freeway, wheels spinning in the air. I went around to find Scott pitching horseshoes.

I picked up a set of rusty ones and joined him. While we played, we talked about school and friends and record albums. The horseshoes scuffed up dirt, sometimes ringing the iron that threw out a meager shadow like a sundial. After three argued-over games, we pulled two oranges apiece from his tree and started down the alley still talking school and friends and record albums. We pulled more oranges from the alley and talked about who we would marry. "No offense, Scott," I said with an orange slice in my mouth, "but I would never marry an Okie." We walked in step, almost touching, with a sled of shadows dragging behind us. "No offense, Gary," Scott said, "but I would *never* marry a Mexican." I looked at him: a fang of orange slice showed from his munching mouth. I didn't think anything of it. He had his girl and I had mine. But our seventh-grade vision was the same: to marry, get jobs, buy cars and maybe a house if we had money left over.

5   We talked about our future lives until, to our surprise, we were on the downtown mall, two miles from home. We bought a bag of popcorn at Penneys

---

[1]**como burros** like burros   [2]**hijo** son   [3]**Pues si, son Okies tambien** Well, yes, they're Okies too

and sat on a bench near the fountain watching Mexican and Okie girls pass. "That one's mine," I pointed with my chin when a girl with eyebrows arched into black rainbows ambled by. "She's cute," Scott said about a girl with yellow hair and a mouthful of gum. We dreamed aloud, our chins busy pointing out girls. We agreed that we couldn't wait to become men and lift them onto our laps.

But the woman I married was not Mexican but Japanese. It was a surprise to me. For years, I went about wide-eyed in my search for the brown girl in a white dress at a dance. I searched the playground at the baseball diamond. When the girls raced for grounders, their hair bounced like something that couldn't be caught. When they sat together in the lunchroom, heads pressed together, I knew they were talking about us Mexican guys. I saw them and dreamed them. I threw my face into my pillow, making up sentences that were good as in the movies.

But when I was twenty, I fell in love with this other girl who worried my mother, who had my grandmother asking once again to see the calendar of the Important Races of the World. I told her I had thrown it away years before. I took a much-glanced-at snapshot from my wallet. We looked at it together, in silence. Then grandma reclined in her chair, lit a cigarette, and said, "Es pretty." She blew and asked with all her worry pushed up to her forehead: "Chinese?"

I was in love and there was no looking back. She was the one. I told my mother who was slapping hamburger into patties. "Well, sure if you want to marry her," she said. But the more I talked, the more concerned she became. Later I began to worry. Was it all a mistake? "Marry a Mexican girl," I heard my mother say in my mind. I heard it at breakfast. I heard it over math problems, between Western Civilization and cultural geography. But then one afternoon while I was hitchhiking home from school, it struck me like a baseball in the back: my mother wanted me to marry someone of my own social class—a poor girl. I considered my fiancee, Carolyn, and she didn't look poor, though I knew she came from a family of farm workers and pull-yourself-up-by-your-bootstraps ranchers. I asked my brother, who was marrying Mexican poor that fall, if I should marry a poor girl. He screamed "Yeah" above his terrible guitar playing in his bedroom. I considered my sister who had married Mexican. Cousins were dating Mexican. Uncles were remarrying poor women. I asked Scott, who was still my best friend, and he said, "She's too good for you, so you better not."

I worried about it until Carolyn took me home to meet her parents. We drove in her Plymouth until the houses gave way to farms and ranches and finally her house fifty feet from the highway. When we pulled into the drive. I panicked and begged Carolyn to make a U-turn and go back so we could talk about it over a soda. She pinched my cheek, calling me a "silly boy." I felt better, though, when I got out of the car and saw the house: the chipped paint, a cracked window, boards for a walk to the back door. There were rusting cars near the barn. A tractor with a net of spiderwebs under a mulberry. A field. A bale of barbed wire like children's scribbling leaning against an empty chicken coop. Carolyn took my hand and pulled me to my future mother-in-law who was coming out to greet us.

10   We had lunch: sandwiches, potato chips, and iced tea. Carolyn and her mother talked mostly about neighbors and the congregation at the Japanese Methodist Church in West Fresno. Her father, who was in khaki work clothes, excused himself with a wave that was almost a salute and went outside. I heard a truck start, a dog bark, and then the truck rattle away.

Carolyn's mother offered another sandwich, but I declined with a shake of my head and a smile. I looked around when I could, when I was not saying over and over that I was a college student, hinting that I could take care of her daughter. I shifted my chair. I saw newspapers piled in corners, dusty cereal boxes and vinegar bottles in corners. The wallpaper was bubbled from rain that had come in from a bad roof. Dust. Dust lay on lamp shades and window sills. These people are just like Mexicans, I thought. Poor people.

Carolyn's mother asked me through Carolyn if I would like a *sushi*. A plate of black and white things were held in front of me. I took one, wide-eyed, and turned it over like a foreign coin. I was biting into one when I saw a kitten crawl up the window screen over the sink. I chewed and the kitten opened its mouth of terror as she crawled higher, wanting in to paw the left-overs from our plates. I looked at Carolyn who said that the cat was just showing off. I looked up in time to see it fall. It crawled up, then fell again.

We talked for an hour and had apple pie and coffee, slowly. Finally, we got up with Carolyn taking my hand. Slightly embarrassed, I tried to pull away but her grip held me. I let her have her way as she led me down the hallway with her mother right behind me. When I opened the door, I was startled by a kitten clinging to the screen door, its mouth screaming "cat food, dog biscuits, *sushi*. . . ." I opened the door and the kitten, still holding on, whined in the language of hungry animals. When I got into Carolyn's car, I looked back: the cat was still clinging. I asked Carolyn if it were possibly hungry, but she said the cat was being silly. She started the car, waved to her mother, and bounced us over the rain-poked drive, patting my thigh for being her lover baby. Carolyn waved again. I looked back, waving, then gawking at a window screen where there were now three kittens clawing and screaming to get in. Like Mexicans, I thought. I remembered the Molinas and how the cats clung to their screens— cats they shot down with squirt guns. On the highway, I felt happy, pleased by it all. I patted Carolyn's thigh. Her people were like Mexicans, only different.

[1986]

 ## Topics for Critical Thinking and Writing

1. Do you agree that Soto implies that the differences between his Mexican-American family and Carolyn's Japanese-American family are slight? Judging only from what he says in the essay, do their differences seem slight to you? Explain.

2. If you are familiar with a couple who are from different ethnic backgrounds, write an essay discussing the degree to which ethnicity is evident in their lives. For instance, do the two people enjoy the same foods, and do they share the same religious beliefs? If not, do the differences make for richness or for difficulty?

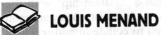 ## LOUIS MENAND

Louis Menand, educated at Pomona College and Columbia University, and a specialist in Victorian and modern literature, teaches at the Graduate Center, City University of New York. We reprint an essay that originally appeared in The New Yorker, *in 1997.*

Love Stories

All the world loves a lover? Not necessarily. In real life, few emotions are less sociable than romantic passion. A person who has valentines dancing in his eyes is
a person generally avoided by those not identically smitten, which is to say, in
most cases, by the rest of humanity. Passion of the unrequited sort can be an acceptable subject of conversation if your advice is being sought; but does anyone
ever listen? "He's a *complete jerk*," you say. "Forget about him." "Oh, you're so
right," she says. "Thank you for helping me face the truth." Later on, you learn
she's marrying the guy.

You can talk with other people about their romantic misery, but there is really no way to have a decent conversation about romantic bliss. Not that love affairs aren't interesting; on the contrary. It's usually both more enjoyable and
more efficient, though, to learn about them from a third party. The lover himself
has a tendency to ignore the ordinary limits of the human faculty for paying attention. And he somehow expects you to share all his feelings for the beloved, although, of course, if you actually did share them he'd want to murder you. Having a friend who is madly in love is one of the reasons people get call waiting.

What all the world really loves is not a lover. It's a love story. People can't
get enough of love stories. What people flee from in reality (where the stuff is
available for nothing) they flock to bookstores, theatres, and cinemas to seek out
and pay for. A love story is usually a story not about how happy two people are
but about how unhappy they are. It's about either the difficulty they are having
in getting together or the difficulty they are having in staying together. End of difficulty, generally speaking, end of story. The repertoire of dénouements is fairly
limited: marriage, splitsville, murder, and mutual annihilation. But audiences
keep coming back for more.

There are so many love stories—it's hard to think of a novel or a movie or a
play, or even an epic poem, that is *not* in some way a love story—that categoriz-
ing them might seem impossible. One way to do it, though, is to employ a simple
lovability index. It's a straightforward and logical tripartite scale. In the first category are love stories in which you find neither of the lovers particularly lovable;
in the second category are love stories in which you find one but not both of the
lovers lovable; and in the third category are the stories in which you find the
lovers nearly as irresistible as they find each other—stories that give you a feeling
for their feeling.

5   One surprising thing the lovability index reveals is that the more famous the
love story the less lovable the lovers. Who actually cares about Romeo? Only
Juliet. And vice versa. They're so busy being infatuated with each other that neither has a spare moment to waste on seducing us. Romeo and Juliet, Tristam and
Isolde, Lancelot and Guinevere are world-famous couples, but they don't evoke
the emotion of love; they symbolize it. Their stories invite us to thrill to the force
of a passion we cannot share.

The last question we would ever think of asking about the lovers in a story
of this type is: What is the basis of their relationship? These people don't have
"relationships," any more than a magnet has a "relationship" with the North
Pole. They are acting under the compulsion of a blind fate. They are mutually-at-
tracting force fields, missiles preprogrammed to collide in midair, effects without causes. In the Hollywood version, if he is fabulous-looking and she is fabulous-looking, they don't need a better reason for getting together. And, most of
the time, we don't need a better one for watching them get together.

The love stories that make us wonder about "the basis of the relationship" are stories of the second type—stories in which our feelings for the lovers are asymmetrical. It's easy to fall in love with Emma Woodhouse;[1] it's hard to feel anything more tender than respect for Mr. Knightley. Anna Karenina[2] is wonderful, but what in the world does she see in Vronsky? Second-category love stories are not force-of-nature stories. They are force-of-circumstance stories, Mr. Knightley just happens to be the best card in the hand society has dealt. In a movie Emma could probably have done better—and in "Clueless," actually, she did do better: Alicia Silverstone's Mr. Knightley turned out to be a sweet college kid named Josh.

Third-category love stories—stories that evoke something that resembles the sensation of romantic love most poignantly—are the rarest. These usually seem to involve odd couples—Leopold Bloom and Molly, Harold and Maude, the Owl and the Pussycat[3]—or just everyday, charismatically challenged people. There is something about the spectacle of two ordinary, slightly mismatched characters ending up together which triggers an involuntary gush of sentiment much more quickly and effectively than does the spectacle of two statuesque godlings who can't keep their hands off each other. "When Harry Met Sally," in which the lovers end by getting married, is more moving than "The English Patient," in which they both so glamorously die.

Is it the purpose of love stories to teach us how to be lovers? This is sometimes suggested, by people who take the view that the essential purpose of culture is to acculturate. That seems implausible. People don't require much tutelage to fall in love; it just happens. And when the attraction is mutual the learning curve is short. Amatory awkwardness is quickly forgiven. Lovers tend to find a way to love. Insofar as the lessons learned from love stories do enter into real life, the results are usually disastrous. Few romantic come-ons backfire more humiliatingly than come-ons picked up from books or movies, including come-ons picked up from books or movies (e.g., "Play It Again, Sam") in which characters successfully employ come-ons picked up from books or movies. Only Bogart could be Bogart, only Garbo Garbo, and only Gable Gable; and even they had better luck in the movies.

10   Maybe the purpose of culture is not to acculturate. Maybe it's not a stealth indoctrination program at all. Maybe art and literature are just what people take them to be: a means of providing a particular and complex kind of pleasure. Love stories are there to allow us to indulge our instinctive fascination with this most exquisite of human emotions, and to do it in a form that has a beginning, a middle, and, unlike certain phone calls, an end.

 ## Topics for Critical Thinking and Writing

1. In paragraph 5 Menand suggests that none of us cares about Romeo and Juliet or certain other famous lovers who, he says, "don't evoke the emotion

[1]**Emma Woodhouse ... Mr. Knightley** characters in Jane Austen's novel, *Emma* (1816) [2]**Anna Karenina ... Vronsky** characters in Leo Tolstoy's novel *Anna Karenina* (1873-76) [3]**Leopold ... Pussycat** Leopold and Molly Bloom are characters in James Joyce's novel *Ulysses* (1922); *Harold and Maude* (1971) is a film; "The Owl and the Pussycat" (1871) is a poem by Edward Lear

of love; they symbolize it." If you have read or seen *Romeo and Juliet*, or a film version of it, evaluate this view. If you are not familiar with the play, choose some other work with lovers, and explain to what degree the lovers evoke our love.

2. In paragraph 4 Menand divides stories about lovers into three groups. Drawing on your own experience of such stories—whether in books or films—come up with one story in each group, and, devoting a paragraph to each story, explain why it fits the group.

3. Menand says (paragraph 9) that some people believe "the essential purpose of culture is to acculturate." What does this mean? (See also paragraph 10, where the term is repeated, and where Menand suggests that "love stories are there to allow us to indulge our instinctive fascination with this most exquisite of human emotions, and to do it in a form that has a beginning, a middle, and, unlike certain phone calls, an end.")

4. In paragraph 9 Menand says, "People don't require much tutelage to fall in love; it just happens." Do you agree? In responding, consider an opposite view: "People would never fall in love if they hadn't heard about it."

5. Menand does not discuss the possibility that the responses of men differ from the responses of women. What are your thoughts on this subject?

6. Consider the following assertions:

I can understand companionship. I can understand bought sex in the afternoon. I cannot understand the love affair.

—Gore Vidal

In love, there is always one who kisses and one who offers the cheek.

—French proverb

For what is love itself, for the one we love best?—an enfolding of immeasurable cares which yet are better than any joys outside our love.

—George Eliot

It has ever been since time began,
And ever will be, till time lose breath
That love is a mood—no more—to man,
And love to a woman is life or death.

—Ella Wheeler Wilcox

Lovers should also have their days off.

—Natalie Clifford Barney

Take any one of these quotations and either show its relevance or irrelevance to any of the literary works in this chapter, or write a response to it, in the persona of a character in one of the works (including the speaker of a poem).

FICTION

 ## ERNEST HEMINGWAY

Ernest Hemingway (1899–1961) was born in Oak Park, Illinois. After graduating from high school in 1917 he worked on the Kansas City Star, *but left to serve as a volunteer ambulance driver in Italy, where he was wounded in action. He returned home, married, and then served as European correspondent for the* Toronto Star, *but he soon gave up journalism for fiction. In 1922 he settled in Paris, where he moved in a circle of American expatriates that included Ezra Pound, Gertrude Stein, and F. Scott Fitzgerald. It was in Paris that he wrote stories and novels about what Gertrude Stein called a "lost generation" of rootless Americans in Europe. (For Hemingway's reminiscences of the Paris years, see his posthumously published* A Moveable Feast.) *He served as a journalist during the Spanish Civil War and during the Second World War, but he was also something of a private soldier.*

After the Second World War his reputation sank, though he was still active as a writer (for instance, he wrote The Old Man and the Sea *in 1952). In 1954 Hemingway was awarded the Nobel Prize in Literature, but in 1961, depressed by a sense of failing power, he took his own life.*

Cat in the Rain

There were only two Americans stopping at the hotel. They did not know any of the people they passed on the stairs on their way to and from their room. Their room was on the second floor facing the sea. It also faced the public garden and the war monument. There were big palms and green benches in the public garden. In the good weather there was always an artist with his easel. Artists liked the way the palms grew and the bright colors of the hotels facing the gardens and the sea. Italians came from a long way off to look up at the war monument. It was made of bronze and glistened in the rain. It was raining. The rain dripped from the palm trees. Water stood in pools on the gravel paths. The sea broke in a long line in the rain and slipped back down the beach to come up and break again in a long line in the rain. The motor cars were gone from the square by the war monument. Across the square in the doorway of the café a waiter stood looking out at the empty square.

The American wife stood at the window looking out. Outside right under their window a cat was crouched under one of the dripping green tables. The cat was trying to make herself so compact that she would not be dripped on.

"I'm going down and get that kitty," the American wife said.

"I'll do it," her husband offered from the bed.

5   "No, I'll get it. The poor kitty out trying to keep dry under a table."

The husband went on reading, lying propped up with the two pillows at the foot of the bed.

"Don't get wet," he said.

The wife went downstairs and the hotel owner stood up and bowed to her as she passed the office. His desk was at the far end of the office. He was an old man and very tall.

"Il piove,"[1] the wife said. She liked the hotel-keeper.

10   "Si, si, Signora, brutto tempo. It is very bad weather."

He stood behind his desk in the far end of the dim room. The wife liked him. She liked the deadly serious way he received any complaints. She liked his dignity. She liked the way he wanted to serve her. She liked the way he felt about being a hotel-keeper. She liked his old, heavy face and big hands.

Liking him she opened the door and looked out. It was raining harder. A man in a rubber cape was crossing the empty square to the café. The cat would be around to the right. Perhaps she could go along under the eaves. As she stood in the doorway an umbrella opened behind her. It was the maid who looked after their room.

"You must not get wet," she smiled, speaking Italian. Of course, the hotel-keeper had sent her.

With the maid holding the umbrella over her, she walked along the gravel path until she was under their window. The table was there, washed bright green in the rain, but the cat was gone. She was suddenly disappointed. The maid looked up at her.

15   "Ha perduto qualque cosa, Signora?"[2]

"There was a cat," said the American girl.

"A cat?"

"Si, il gatto."

"A cat?" the maid laughed. "A cat in the rain?"

20   "Yes," she said, "under the table." Then. "Oh. I wanted it so much. I wanted a kitty."

When she talked English the maid's face tightened.

"Come, Signora," she said. "We must get back inside. You will be wet."

"I suppose so," said the American girl.

They went back along the gravel path and passed in the door. The maid stayed outside to close the umbrella. As the American girl passed the office, the padrone bowed from his desk. Something felt very small and tight inside the girl. The padrone made her feel very small and at the same time really important. She had a momentary feeling of being of supreme importance. She went on up the stairs. She opened the door of the room. George was on the bed, reading.

25   "Did you get the cat?" he asked, putting the book down.

"It was gone."

"Wonder where it went to," he said, resting his eyes from reading.

She sat down on the bed.

"I wanted it so much," she said. "I don't know why I wanted it so much. I wanted that poor kitty. It isn't any fun to be a poor kitty out in the rain."

30   George was reading again.

She went over and sat in front of the mirror of the dressing table looking at herself with the hand glass. She studied her profile, first one side and then the other. Then she studied the back of her head and her neck.

"Don't you think it would be a good idea if I let my hair grow out?" she asked, looking at her profile again.

George looked up and saw the back of her neck, clipped close like a boy's.

"I like it the way it is."

35   "I get so tired of it," she said. "I get so tired of looking like a boy."

[1]**Il piove** It's raining (Italian)   [2]**Ha . . . Signora** Have you lost something, Madam?

George shifted his position in the bed. He hadn't looked away from her since she started to speak.

"You look pretty darn nice," he said.

She laid the mirror down on the dresser and went over to the window and looked out. It was getting dark.

"I want to pull my hair back tight and smooth and make a big knot at the back that I can feel," she said. "I want to have a kitty to sit on my lap and purr when I stroke her."

40   "Yeah?" George said from the bed.

"And I want to eat at a table with my own silver and I want candles. And I want it to be spring and I want to brush my hair out in front of a mirror and I want a kitty and I want some new clothes."

"Oh, shut up and get something to read," George said. He was reading again.

His wife was looking out of the window. It was quite dark now and still raining in the palm trees.

"Anyway, I want a cat," she said, "I want a cat. I want a cat now. If I can't have long hair or any fun, I can have a cat."

45   George was not listening. He was reading his book. His wife looked out of the window where the light had come on in the square.

Someone knocked at the door.

"Avanti,"[3] George said. He looked up from his book.

In the doorway stood the maid. She held a big tortoise-shell cat pressed tight against her and swung down against her body.

"Excuse me," she said, "the padrone asked me to bring this for the Signora."

[1925]

[3]**Avanti** Come in

A STUDENT'S ANNOTATIONS AND JOURNAL ENTRIES ON "CAT IN THE RAIN"

When you read a story—or, perhaps more accurately, when you reread a story before discussing it or writing about it—you'll find it helpful to jot an occasional note (for instance, a brief response or a question) in the margins and to underline or highlight passages that strike you as especially interesting. Here is part of the story, with a student's annotations.

The cat was trying to make herself so compact that she would not be dripped on.

"I'm going down and get that kitty," the American wife said.

"I'll do it," her husband offered from the bed.

"No, I'll get it. The poor kitty out trying to keep dry under a table."

The husband went on reading, lying propped up with the two pillows at the foot of the bed.

"Don't get wet," he said.

[marginal annotations:] He doesn't make a move

still doesn't move

Is he making a joke? Or maybe he just isn't even thinking about what he is saying?

contrast — The wife went downstairs and the <u>hotel owner stood</u>
with the <u>up and bowed to her</u> as she passed the office. His desk was
husband at the far end of the office. He was an old man and very tall.

"Il piove," the wife said. She liked the hotel-keeper.

"Si, si, Signora, brutto tempo. It is very bad weather."

He stood behind his desk in the far end of the dim *She re-*
room. <u>The wife liked him.</u> She liked the deadly serious way *spects*
he received any complaints. <u>She liked his dignity.</u> She liked *him and*
the way he wanted to serve her. She liked the way he felt *she is*
about being a hotel-keeper. She liked his old, heavy face and *pleased*
big hands. *by the*

to em- Liking him she opened the door and looked out. It was *atten-*
phasize) raining harder. <u>A man in a rubber cape</u> was crossing the *tion he*
the bad / <u>empty square</u> to the café. The cat would be around to the *shows*
weather?? right.

ASKING QUESTIONS ABOUT A STORY

Everything in a story presumably is important, but having read the story once, probably something has especially interested (or puzzled) you, such as the relationship between two people, or the way the end of the story is connected to the beginning. On rereading, then, pen in hand, you'll find yourself noticing things that you missed or didn't find especially significant on your first reading. Now that you know the end of the story, you will read the beginning in a different way.

And of course if your instructor asks you to think about certain questions, you'll keep these in mind while you reread, and you will find ideas coming to you. In "Cat in the Rain," suppose you are asked (or you ask yourself) if the story might just as well be about a dog in the rain. Would anything be lost?

Here are a few questions that you can ask of almost any story. (On pages 200–202, in Chapter 9, we give a fuller list.) After scanning the questions, you will want to reread the story, pen in hand, and then jot down your responses on a sheet of paper. As you write, doubtless you will go back and reread the story or at least parts of it.

1. *What happens?* In two or three sentences—say 25–50 words—summarize the gist of what happens in the story.
2. *What sorts of people are the chief characters?* In "Cat in the Rain" the chief characters are George, George's wife, and the innkeeper (the padrone). Jot down the traits that each seems to possess, and next to each trait briefly give some supporting evidence.
3. *What especially pleased or displeased you in the story?* Devote at least a sentence or two to the end of the story. Do you find the end satisfying? Why or why not?
4. *Have you any thoughts about the title?* If so, what are they? If the story did not have a title, what would you call it?

After you have made your own jottings, compare them with these responses by a student. No two readers will respond in exactly the same way, but all readers can examine their responses and try to account for them, at least in part. If your responses are substantially different, how do you account for the differences?

1. A summary. A young wife, stopping with her husband at an Italian hotel, from her room sees a cat in the rain. She goes to get it, but it is gone, and so she returns empty-handed. A moment later the maid knocks at the door, holding a tortoise-shell cat.

2. The characters: The woman.
   kind-hearted (pities cat in rain)
   appreciates innkeeper's courtesy ("liked the way he wanted to serve her") and admires him ("She liked his dignity")
   unhappy (wants a cat, wants to change her hair, wants to eat at a table with her own silver)
   The husband, George.
   not willing to put himself out (says he'll go to garden to get cat but doesn't move)
   doesn't seem very interested in wife (hardly talks to her--he's reading; tells her to "shut up")
   but he does say he finds her attractive ("You look pretty darn nice")
   The innkeeper.
   serious, dignified ("She liked the deadly serious way he received any complaints. She liked his dignity")
   courteous, helpful (sends maid with umbrella; at end sends maid with cat)

3. Dislikes and likes. "Dislikes" is too strong, but I was disappointed that more didn't happen at the end. What is the husband's reaction to the cat? Or his final reaction to his wife? I mean, what did he think about his wife when the maid brings the cat? And, for that matter, what is the wife's reaction? Is she satisfied? Or does she realize that the cat can't really make her happy? Now for the likes. (1) I guess I did like the way it turned out; it's sort of a happy ending, I think, since she wants the cat and gets it. (2) I also especially like the innkeeper. Maybe I like him partly because the wife likes him, and if she likes him he must be nice. And he is nice--very helpful. And I also like the way Hemingway shows the husband. I don't mean that I like the man himself, but I like the way Hemingway shows he is such a bastard--not getting off the bed to get the cat, telling his wife to shut up and read.

Another thing about him is that the one time he says something nice about her, it's about her hair, and she isn't keen on the way her hair is. She says it makes her look "like a boy," and she is "tired" of looking like a boy. There's something wrong with this marriage. George hardly pays attention to his wife, but he wants her to look like a boy. Maybe the idea is that this macho guy wants to keep her looking like an inferior (immature) version of himself. Anyway, he certainly doesn't seem interested in letting her fulfill herself as a woman.

I think my feelings add up to this: I like the way Hemingway shows us the relation between the husband and wife (even though the relation is pretty bad), and I like the innkeeper. Even if the relation with the couple ends unhappily, the story has a sort of happy ending, so far as it goes, since the innkeeper does what he can to please his guest: he sends the maid, with the cat. There's really nothing more that he can do.

More about the ending. The more I think about it, the more I feel that the ending is as happy as it can be. George is awful. When his wife says "I want a cat and I want a cat now," Hemingway tells us "George was not listening." And then, a moment later, almost like a good fairy the maid appears and grants the wife's wish.

4. The title. I don't suppose that I would have called it "Cat in the Rain," but I don't know what I would have called it. Maybe "An American Couple in Italy." Or maybe "The Innkeeper." I really do think that the innkeeper is very important, even though he only has a few lines. He's very impressive--not only to the girl, but to me (and maybe to all readers), since at the end of the story we see how careful the innkeeper is.

But the more I think about Hemingway's title, the more I think that maybe it also refers to the girl. Like the "poor kitty" in the rain, the wife is in a pretty bad situation. "It isn't any fun to be a poor kitty out in the rain." Of course the woman is indoors, but her husband generates lots of unpleasant weather. She may as well be out in the rain. She says "I want to have a kitty to sit on my lap and purr when I stroke her." This shows that she wants to be affectionate and that she also wants to have someone respond to her affection. She is like a cat in the rain.

The responses of this student probably include statements that you want to take issue with. Or perhaps you feel that the student did not even mention some things that you think are important. You may want to jot down some notes and raise some questions in class.

A SAMPLE ESSAY BY A STUDENT: "HEMINGWAY'S AMERICAN WIFE"

The responses that we have quoted were written by Bill Yanagi, who later wrote an essay developing one of them. Here is the essay.

Bill Yanagi

English 10B

20 October 1996

Hemingway's American Wife

My title alludes not to any of the four women to whom Hemingway was married, but to "the American wife" who is twice called by this term in his short story, "Cat in the Rain." We first meet her in the first sentence of the story ("There were only two Americans stopping at the hotel"), and the next time she is mentioned (apart from a reference to the wife and her husband as "they") it is as "the American wife," at the beginning of the second paragraph of the story. The term is used again at the end of the third paragraph.

She is, then, at least in the early part of this story, just an American or an American wife--someone identified only by her nationality and her marital status, but not at all by her personality, her individuality, her inner self. She first becomes something of an individual when she separates herself from her husband by leaving the hotel room and going to look for a cat that she has seen in the garden, in the rain. This act of separation, however, has not the slightest effect on her husband, who "went on reading" (533).

When she returns, without the cat, he puts down his book and speaks to her, but it is obvious that he has no interest in her, beyond as a physical object ("You look pretty darn nice"). This comment is produced when she says she is thinking of letting her hair grow out, because she is "so tired of looking like a boy" (534). Why, a reader wonders, does her husband, who has paid almost no attention to her up to now, assure her that she looks "pretty darn nice"? I think it is reasonable to conclude that he <u>wants</u> her to look like someone who is not truly a woman, in particular someone who is immature. That she does not feel she has much identity is evident when she continues to talk about letting her hair grow, and she says "I want to pull my hair back tight and smooth and make a big knot at the back that I can feel" (535). Long hair is, or at least was, the traditional sign of a woman; she wants long hair, and at the same time she wants to keep it under her control by tying it in a "big knot," a knot that she can feel, a knot whose presence reminds her, because she can feel it, of her feminine nature.

She goes on to say that she wants to brush her hair "in front of a mirror." That is, she wants to <u>see</u> and to feel her femininity, since her husband apparently--so far as we can see in the story, at least--scarcely recognizes it or her. Perhaps her desire for the cat ("I want a cat") is a veiled way of saying that she wants to express her animal nature, and not be simply a neglected woman who is made by her husband to look like a boy. Hemingway tells us, however, that when she looked for the cat in the garden she could not find it, a sign, I think, of her failure to break from the man. At the end of the story the maid brings her the cat, but a woman cannot just be handed a new nature and accept it, just like that. She has to find it herself, and in herself, so I think the story ends with "the American wife" still nothing more than an American wife.

[New page]

Work Cited

<u>Literature for Composition</u>. Ed. Sylvan Barnet et al. 5th ed. New York:

Longman, 2000.

A few comments and questions may be useful.

- Do you find the essay interesting? Explain your response.
- Do you find the essay well written? Explain.
- Do you find the essay convincing? Can you suggest ways of strengthening it, or do you think its argument is mistaken? Carefully reread "Cat in the Rain," taking note of passages that give further support to this student's argument, or that seem to challenge or qualify it.
- We often say that a good critical essay sends us back to the literary work with a fresh point of view. Our rereading differs from our earlier reading. Does this essay change your reading of Hemingway's story?

✎ Topics for Critical Thinking and Writing

1. Can we be certain that the cat at the end of the story is the cat that the woman saw in the rain? (When we first hear about the cat in the rain we are not told anything about its color, and at the end of the story we are not told that the tortoise-shell cat is wet.) Does it matter if there are two cats?
2. One student argued that the cat represents the child that the girl wants to have. Do you think there is something to this idea? How might you support or refute it?

3. Consider the following passage:

> As the American girl passed the office, the padrone bowed from his desk. Something felt very small and tight inside the girl. The padrone made her feel very small and at the same time really important. She had a momentary feeling of being of supreme importance.

Do you think there is anything sexual here? And if so, that the passage tells us something about her relations with her husband? Support your view.

4. What do you suppose Hemingway's attitude was toward each of the three chief characters? How might you support your hunch?

5. Hemingway wrote the story in Italy, when his wife Hadley was pregnant. In a letter to F. Scott Fitzgerald he said,

> Cat in the Rain wasn't about Hadley. . . . When I wrote that we were at Rapallo but Hadley was 4 months pregnant with Bumby. The Inn Keeper was the one at Cortina D'Ampezzo. . . . Hadley never made a speech in her life about wanting a baby because she had been told various things by her doctor and I'd—no use going into all that. (*Letters* 180)

According to some biographers, the story shows that Hemingway knew his marriage was going on the rocks (Hemingway and Hadley divorced). Does knowing that Hemingway's marriage turned out unhappily help you to understand the story? Does it make the story more interesting? And do you think that the story tells a biographer something about Hemingway's life?

6. It is sometimes said that a good short story does two things at once: It provides a believable picture of the surface of life, and it also illuminates some moral or psychological complexity that we feel is part of the essence of human life. This dual claim may not be true, but for the moment accept it. Do you think that Hemingway's story fulfills either or both of these specifications? Support your view.

A SECOND EXAMPLE: AN ESSAY DRAWING ON RELATED MATERIAL IN THE CHAPTER

Another student, Holly Klein, wrote about "Cat in the Rain," but she thought about it partly in terms of Louis Menand's essay, "Love Stories" (p. 530). She also draws on a quotation that is included in one of the questions given after Menand's essay. Here are her first notes, and the essay that she developed from them.

Journal Entries

Menand: "All the world loves a lover? Not necessarily. In real life, few emotions are less sociable than romantic passion." Certainly there's not much romantic passion in this story (or in Menand either, maybe!). But are these people in love?

Menand may be right in saying that "a love story is usually a story not about how happy two people are but about how unhappy they are" (parag. 3). Or is he? Many lovers may suffer and some even die (Leonardo DiCaprio in Titanic), but aren't they happy anyway?

They are happy in their unhappiness. (And Rose--Kate Winslet--survives, happy and unhappy in her love.)

Is "Cat" really a love story anyway? Yes, in the sense it is about people who must at least at some time in the past have been lovers--happy lovers--but who now seem stuck with each other. The wife still seems to be in love, or maybe she is trying to bring a dead love back to life.

Is there something to the idea (as Wilcox says, page 532) that "love is a mood" to men but is "life or death" to women? Does this add up to saying that for men, love is something of the moment, and is trivial, but for women it is enduring and important? And do men and women react differently to love stories? Menand doesn't say anything about this, but people say Titanic is a "woman's picture." But Mark liked it as much as I did. Or at least he said so.

SAMPLE ESSAY BY A STUDENT: "HEMINGWAY'S UNHAPPY LOVERS"

Here is the final version of Holly Klein's essay:

Hemingway's Unhappy Lovers

Louis Menand says that "a love story is usually a story not about how happy two people are but about how unhappy they are" (530). This statement, which at first I thought was ridiculous, now strikes me as true, or for the most part true. The lovers in Romeo and Juliet, West Side Story, and in the television drama All My Children (Haley, Mateo, Lisa, and several other young adults) would not give up being in love, but during most of the time they are unhappy. I have heard a saying, "Love means not ever having to say you are sorry," but some of these lovers, and other lovers in daytime television programs, are always saying they are sorry, and always feeling sorry for themselves. And we feel sorry for them. Our interest in them is not in their happiness, but in their unhappiness.

Certainly in Ernest Hemingway's "Cat in the Rain" the woman is unhappy--and who wouldn't be unhappy, with a husband like hers? She says she is going out into the rain to get the cat, and he says "Don't get wet" (533), and he goes right on reading, obviously uninterested in what his wife is doing, or in her needs. The wife never explicitly says she is unhappy, but it is obvious that she is. Her husband pays very little attention to her, and then, when he does--he goes so far as to say "You look pretty darn nice"--it's only after she tells him she wants to change her appearance: "I get so tired of looking like a boy." When she adds that she wants to change her hair, his response is, "Yeah?" And a moment later he says, "Oh, shut up and get something to read" (535). I felt like hitting him, and I suddenly realized that, at least for this story, Menand is right. If Hemingway's lovers were happy and spent their time cooing at each other, the story probably would have been boring. What's interesting here is, paradoxically, the man's lack of interest in his wife--he is probably affectionate only when he wants sex--and the woman's basic unhappiness. Her unhappiness is revealed partly by her almost desperate attempt to give affection to the cat, and to receive some affection from it: "I want to have a kitty to sit on my lap and purr when I stroke her" (535). Ella Wheeler Wilcox may be overstating the matter, but, allowing for what is called poetic license, there is something sound in her view that "love is a mood--no more--to man, / And love to a woman is life or death" (532).

Menand does not make a distinction between the attitudes of men and women toward love, and he therefore doesn't distinguish between the responses of men and of women to love stories. I think he is right in saying that most love stories are chiefly about unhappiness, but he probably should have gone further and said (or at least suggested) that women in love are more likely than men to express in words their unhappiness. (I think there are psychological or sociological studies that support this view.) In any case, in support of Louis Menand's generalization about love stories, I can say that "Cat in the Rain" interested me not because the lovers keep expressing their romantic passion but because the man does <u>not</u> express his love, and the woman expresses her frustration. In this story about lovers, the man is in bed--but he spends most of his time <u>reading</u> in bed, and (as I said) about the best he can say to the woman is that she looks "pretty darn nice"). The wife holds our interest because she is unhappy, stuck with this guy, and she is so grateful for a kind word from the hotel-keeper. She doesn't explicitly say that she is desperately unhappy, but she does express very vigorously a desire for a life different from the one she is now living, and we do feel that (at least for her) love is not just a "mood," as it probably is for the man, but is a matter of "life or death." She is, so to speak, dying to be loved.

[New page]

Work Cited

<u>Literature for Composition</u>. Ed. Sylvan Barnet et al. 5th ed. New York: Longman, 2000.

We can ask of this essay the same questions that we asked of an earlier essay:

- Do you find the essay interesting? Explain your response.
- Do you find the essay well written? Explain.
- Do you find the essay convincing? Can you suggest ways of strengthening it, or do you think its argument is mistaken? Carefully reread "Cat in the Rain," taking note of passages that give further support to this student's argument, or that seem to challenge or qualify it.
- We often say that a good critical essay sends us back to the literary work with a fresh point of view. Our rereading differs from our earlier reading. Does this essay change your reading of Hemingway's story?

We can also ask one additional question:

- Sometimes writers make their essays far too impersonal, removing every trace of the writer as an individual human being, a distinct person. Do you think that this writer goes too far in the other direction, making the essay too personal? If you think that she does, what advice would you give her, to help her strike the right balance.

 **OSCAR WILDE**

Oscar Wilde (1854–1900) was born in Dublin, Ireland. He studied at Trinity College, Dublin, and then at Oxford University, where he established himself as a distinguished student. After graduation he settled in London, where he achieved some notice as a poet and essayist, and fame as a playwright and a lecturer. His best play, The Importance of Being Earnest *(1895), still holds the stage. By 1895 he was known as the leading advocate of the aesthetic movement, also called the art for art's sake movement. Briefly, the idea is that beauty has nothing to do with truth or morality; beauty is its own excuse for being. In 1895, at the height of his career, Wilde was arrested on charges of homosexuality, convicted, and sentenced to two years at hard labor. (In 1891 Wilde—already married and the father of two children—had established a relationship with a young man, Lord Alfred Douglas; Douglas's father publicly denounced Wilde, and Wilde sued for libel, lost, and then found himself on trial.) After completing his prison sentence he was in disgrace. He left England and spent his three remaining years in France, living under an assumed name.*

The Happy Prince

High above the city, on a tall column, stood the statue of the Happy Prince. He was gilded all over with thin leaves of fine gold, for eyes he had two bright sapphires, and a large red ruby glowed on his sword-hilt.

He was very much admired indeed. "He is as beautiful as a weather-cock," remarked one of the town councillors who wished to gain a reputation for having artistic tastes; "only not quite so useful," he added, fearing lest people should think him unpractical, which he really was not.

"Why can't you be like the Happy Prince?" asked a sensible mother of her little boy who was crying for the moon. "The Happy Prince never dreams of crying for anything."

"I am glad there is some one in the world who is quite happy," muttered a disappointed man as he gazed at the wonderful statue.

5   "He looks just like an angel," said the charity children as they came out of the cathedral in their bright scarlet cloaks and their clean white pinafores.

"How do you know?" said the Mathematical Master, "you have never seen one."

"Ah! but we have, in our dreams," answered the children; and the Mathematical Master frowned and looked very severe, for he did not approve of children dreaming.

One night there flew over the city a little swallow. His friends had gone away to Egypt six weeks before, but he had stayed behind, for he was in love with the most beautiful reed. He had met her early in the spring as he was flying down the river after a big yellow moth, and had been so attracted by her slender waist that he had stopped to talk to her.

"Shall I love you?" said the swallow, who liked to come to the point at once, and the reed made him a low bow. So he flew round and round her, touching the water with his wings and making silver ripples. This was his courtship, and it lasted all through the summer.

10   "It is a ridiculous attachment," twittered the other swallows; "she has no money, and far too many relations"; and, indeed, the river was quite full of reeds. Then, when the autumn came, they all flew away.

After they had gone he felt lonely, and began to tire of his lady-love. "She has no conversation," he said, "and I am afraid that she is a coquette, for she is always flirting with the wind." And certainly, whenever the wind blew, the reed made the most graceful curtsies. "I admit that she is domestic," he continued, "but I love travelling, and my wife, consequently, should love travelling also."

"Will you come away with me?" he said finally to her; but the reed shook her head, she was so attached to her home.

"You have been trifling with me," he cried, "I am off to the pyramids, Goodbye!" and he flew away.

All day long he flew, and at night-time he arrived at the city. "Where shall I put up?" he said; "I hope the town has made preparations."

15   Then he saw the statue on the tall column. "I will put up there," he cried; "it is a fine position with plenty of fresh air." So he alighted just between the feet of the Happy Prince.

"I have a golden bedroom," he said softly to himself as he looked round, and he prepared to go to sleep; but just as he was putting his head under his wing, a large drop of water fell on him. "What a curious thing!" he cried. "There is not a single cloud in the sky, the stars are quite clear and bright, and yet it is raining.

The climate in the north of Europe is really dreadful. The reed used to like the rain, but that was merely her selfishness."

Then another drop fell.

"What is the use of a statue if it cannot keep the rain off?" he said; "I must look for a good chimney-pot." and he determined to fly away.

But before he had opened his wings, a third drop fell, and he looked up and saw—ah! what did he see?

20   The eyes of the Happy Prince were filled with tears, and tears were running down his golden cheeks. His face was so beautiful in the moonlight that the little swallow was filled with pity.

"Who are you?" he said.

"I am the Happy Prince."

"Why are you weeping then?" asked the swallow; "you have quite drenched me."

"When I was alive and had a human heart," answered the statue, "I did not know what tears were, for I lived in the Palace of Sans-Souci,[1] where sorrow is not allowed to enter. In the day-time I played with my companions in the garden, and in the evening I led the dance in the Great Hall. Round the garden ran a very lofty wall, but I never cared to ask what lay beyond it, everything about me was so beautiful. My courtiers called me the Happy Prince, and happy indeed I was, if pleasure be happiness. So I lived, and so I died. And now that I am dead they have set me up here so high that I can see all the ugliness and all the misery of my city, and though my heart is made of lead, yet I cannot choose but weep."

25   "What, is he not solid gold?" said the swallow to himself. He was too polite to make any personal remarks out loud.

"Far away," continued the statue in a low musical voice, "far away in a little street, there is a poor house. One of the windows is open, and through it I can see a woman seated at a table. Her face is thin and worn, and she has coarse red hands, all pricked by the needle, for she is a seamstress. She is embroidering passion-flowers on a satin gown for the loveliest of the Queen's maids-of-honour to wear at the next Court-ball. In a bed in the corner of the room, her little boy is lying ill. He has a fever, and is asking for oranges. His mother has nothing to give him but river water, so he is crying. Swallow, Swallow, little Swallow, will you not bring her the ruby out of my sword-hilt? My feet are fastened to this pedestal and I cannot move."

"I am waited for in Egypt," said the Swallow. "My friends are flying up and down the Nile and talking to the large lotus-flowers. Soon they will go to sleep in the tomb of the great King. The King is there himself in his painted coffin. He is wrapped in yellow linen and embalmed with spices. Round his neck is a chain of pale green jade, and his hands are like withered leaves."

"Swallow, Swallow, little Swallow," said the Prince, "will you not stay with me for one night and be my messenger? The boy is so thirsty, and the mother so sad."

"I don't think I like boys," answered the swallow. "Last summer, when I was staying on the river, there were two rude boys, the miller's sons, who were always throwing stones at me. They never hit me, of course; we swallows fly far too well for that, and besides, I come of a family famous for its agility; but still, it was a mark of disrespect."

[1]without care (French)

30   But the Happy Prince looked so sad that the little swallow was sorry. "It is very cold here," he said; "but I will stay with you for one night and be your messenger."

"Thank you, little Swallow," said the Prince.

So the swallow picked out the great ruby from the Prince's sword and flew away with it in his beak over the roofs of the town.

He passed by the cathedral tower, where the white marble angels were sculptured. He passed by the palace and heard the sound of dancing. A beautiful girl came out on the balcony with her lover. "How wonderful the stars are," he said to her, "and how wonderful is the power of love!" "I hope my dress will be ready in time for the State-ball," she answered: "I have ordered passion-flowers to be embroidered on it; but the seamstresses are so lazy."

He passed over the river and saw the lanterns hanging to the masts of the ships. He passed over the Ghetto and saw the old Jews bargaining with each other and weighing out money in copper scales. At last he came to the poor house and looked in. The boy was tossing feverishly on his bed, and the mother had fallen asleep, she was so tired. In he hopped, and laid the great ruby on the table beside the woman's thimble. Then he flew gently round the bed, fanning the boy's forehead with his wings. "How cool I feel," said the boy, "I must be getting better"; and he sank into a delicious slumber.

35   Then the swallow flew back to the Happy Prince and told him what he had done. "It is curious," he remarked, "but I feel quite warm now, although it is so cold."

"That is because you have done a good action," said the Prince. And the little swallow began to think, and then he fell asleep. Thinking always made him sleepy.

When day broke, he flew down to the river and had a bath. "What a remarkable phenomenon," said the professor of ornithology as he was passing over the bridge. "A swallow in winter!" And he wrote a long letter about it to the local newspaper. Every one quoted it, it was full of so many words that they could not understand.

"To-night I go to Egypt," said the swallow, and he was in high spirits at the prospect. He visited all the public monuments and sat a long time on top of the church steeple. Wherever he went the sparrows chirruped and said to each other, "What a distinguished stranger!" so he enjoyed himself very much.

When the moon rose, he flew back to the Happy Prince. "Have you any commissions for Egypt?" he cried; "I am just starting."

40   "Swallow, Swallow, little Swallow," said the Prince, "will you not stay with me one night longer?"

"I am waited for in Egypt," answered the swallow. "To-morrow my friends will fly up to the Second Cataract. The river-horse couches there among the bulrushes, and on a great granite throne sits the god Memnon. All night long he watches the stars, and when the morning star shines, he utters one cry of joy, and then he is silent. At noon the yellow lions come down to the water's edge to drink. They have eyes like green beryls, and their roar is louder than the roar of the cataract."

"Swallow, Swallow, little Swallow," said the Prince, "far away across the city I see a young man in a garret. He is leaning over a desk covered with papers, and in a tumbler by his side there is a bunch of withered violets. His hair is brown and crisp, and his lips are red as a pomegranate, and he has large and dreamy eyes. He is trying to finish a play for the director of the theatre, but he is too cold to write any more. There is no fire in the grate, and hunger has made him faint."

"I will wait with you one night longer," said the swallow, who really had a good heart. "Shall I take him another ruby?"

"Alas! I have no ruby now," said the Prince; "my eyes are all that I have left. They are made of rare sapphires, which were brought out of India a thousand years ago. Pluck out one of them and take it to him. He will sell it to the jeweller, and buy food and firewood, and finish his play."

45   "Dear Prince," said the swallow, "I cannot do that"; and he began to weep.

"Swallow, Swallow, little Swallow," said the Prince, "do as I command you."

So the swallow plucked out the Prince's eye and flew away to the student's garret. It was easy enough to get in, as there was a hole in the roof. Through this he darted, and came into the room. The young man had his head buried in his hands, so he did not hear the flutter of the bird's wings, and when he looked up, he found the beautiful sapphire lying on the withered violets.

"I am beginning to be appreciated," he cried; "this is from some great admirer. Now I can finish my play," and he looked quite happy.

The next day the swallow flew down to the harbour. He sat on the mast of a large vessel and watched the sailors hauling big chests out of the hold with ropes. "Heave a-hoy!" they shouted as each chest came up. "I am going to Egypt!" cried the swallow, but nobody minded, and when the moon rose, he flew back to the Happy Prince.

50   "I am come to bid you good-bye," he cried.

"Swallow, Swallow, little Swallow," said the Prince, "will you not stay with me one night longer?"

"It is winter," answered the swallow, "and the chill snow will soon be here. In Egypt the sun is warm on the green palm-trees, and the crocodiles lie in the mud and look lazily about them. My companions are building a nest in the Temple of Baalbec, and the pink and white doves are watching them and cooing to each other. Dear Prince. I must leave you, but I will never forget you, and next spring I will bring you back two beautiful jewels in place of those you have given away. The ruby shall be redder than a red rose, and the sapphire shall be as blue as the great sea."

"In the square below," said the Happy Prince, "there stands a little match-girl. She has let her matches fall in the gutter, and they are all spoiled. Her father will beat her if she does not bring home some money, and she is crying. She has no shoes or stockings, and her little head is bare. Pluck out my other eye, and give it to her, and her father will not beat her."

"I will stay with you one night longer," said the swallow, "but I cannot pluck out your eye. You would be quite blind then."

55   "Swallow, Swallow, little Swallow," said the Prince, "do as I command you."

So he plucked out the Prince's other eye and darted down with it. He swooped past the match-girl and slipped the jewel into the palm of her hand. "What a lovely bit of glass," cried the little girl; and she ran home, laughing.

Then the swallow came back to the Prince. "You are blind now," he said, "so I will stay with you always."

"No, little Swallow," said the poor Prince, "you must go away to Egypt."

"I will stay with you always," said the swallow, and he slept at the Prince's feet.

60   All the next day he sat on the Prince's shoulder and told him stories of what he had seen in strange lands. He told him of the red ibises, who stand in long rows on the banks of the Nile and catch gold fish in their beaks; of the Sphinx, who is as old as the world itself, and lives in the desert, and knows everything; of

the merchants, who walk slowly by the side of their camels and carry amber beads in their hands; of the King of the Mountains of the Moon, who is as black as ebony and worships a large crystal; of the great green snake that sleeps in a palm-tree and has twenty priests to feed it with honey-cakes; and of the pygmies, who sail over a big lake on large flat leaves and are always at war with the butterflies.

"Dear little Swallow," said the Prince, "you tell me of marvellous things, but more marvellous than anything is the suffering of men and of women. There is no mystery so great as misery. Fly over my city, little Swallow, and tell me what you see there."

So the swallow flew over the great city and saw the rich making merry in their beautiful houses, while the beggars were sitting at the gates. He flew into dark lanes and saw the white faces of starving children looking out listlessly at the black streets. Under the archway of a bridge, two little boys were lying in one another's arms to try and keep themselves warm. "How hungry we are!" they said. "You must not lie here," shouted the watchman, and they wandered out into the rain.

Then he flew back and told the Prince what he had seen.

"I am covered with fine gold," said the Prince, "you must take it off, leaf by leaf, and give it to my poor; the living always think that gold can make them happy."

65   Leaf after leaf of the fine gold the Swallow picked off, till the Happy Prince looked quite dull and grey. Leaf after leaf of the fine gold he brought to the poor, and the children's faces grew rosier, and they laughed and played games in the street. "We have bread now!" they cried.

Then the snow came, and after the snow came the frost. The streets looked as if they were made of silver, they were so bright and glistening; long icicles like crystal daggers hung down from the eaves of the houses, everybody went about in furs; and the little boys wore scarlet caps and skated on the ice.

The poor little swallow grew colder and colder, but he would not leave the Prince, he loved him too well. He picked up crumbs outside the baker's door when the baker was not looking, and tried to keep himself warm by flapping his wings.

But at last he knew that he was going to die. He had just strength to fly up to the Prince's shoulder once more. "Good-bye, dear Prince!" he murmured, "will you let me kiss your hand?"

"I am glad that you are going to Egypt at last, little Swallow," said the Prince, "you have stayed too long here; but you must kiss me on the lips, for I love you."

70   "It is not to Egypt that I am going," said the swallow. "I am going to the house of death. Death is the brother of sleep, is he not?"

And he kissed the Happy Prince on the lips and fell down dead at his feet.

At that moment a curious crack sounded inside the statue, as if something had broken. The fact is that the leaden heart had snapped right in two. It certainly was a dreadfully hard frost.

Early the next morning the mayor was walking in the square below in company with the town councillors. As they passed the column, he looked up at the statue: "Dear me! how shabby the Happy Prince looks!" he said.

"How shabby indeed!" cried the town councillors, who always agreed with the mayor, and they went up to look at it.

75   "The ruby has fallen out of his sword, his eyes are gone, and he is golden no longer," said the mayor; "in fact, he is little better than a beggar!"

"Little better than a beggar," said the town councillors.

"And here is actually a dead bird at his feet!" continued the mayor. "We must really issue a proclamation that birds are not allowed to die here." And the town clerk made a note of the suggestion.

So they pulled down the statue of the Happy Prince. "As he is no longer beautiful, he is no longer useful," said the art professor at the university.

Then they melted the statue in a furnace, and the mayor held a meeting of the corporation to decide what was to be done with the metal. "We must have another statue, of course," he said, "and it shall be a statue of myself."

"Of myself," said each of the town councillors, and they quarrelled. When I last heard of them, they were quarrelling still.

"What a strange thing!" said the overseer of the workmen at the foundry. "This broken lead heart will not melt in the furnace. We must throw it away." So they threw it on a dust-heap where the dead swallow was also lying.

"Bring me the two most precious things in the city," said God to one of His Angels; and the Angel brought Him the leaden heart and the dead bird.

"You have rightly chosen," said God, "for in my garden of Paradise this little bird shall sing for evermore, and in my city of gold the Happy Prince shall praise me."

[1886]

✐ Topics for Critical Thinking and Writing

1. Do you think this story has a moral? If so, what is the moral?
2. Think of some fairy tale that you know rather well, perhaps *Cinderella* or *Sleeping Beauty* or *Rumpelstiltskin.* Does it have a moral? If so, what is the moral? If it has a moral, is the moral partly what makes it interesting? If it doesn't have a moral, what makes the story interesting?
3. As the brief biographical note indicates. Oscar Wilde was homosexual. Do you think that the story in any way(s) reveals his sexual orientation? Do you think that straights and gays read the story in pretty much the same way? Explain.

📖 VIRGINIA WOOLF

Virginia Woolf (1882–1941) is known chiefly as a novelist, but she was also the author of short stories and essays, and in recent years the range of her power has been increasingly recognized.

Woolf was self-educated in the library of her father, Leslie Stephen, an important English scholar, literary critic, and biographer. In 1907 she married Leonard Woolf, with whom ten years later she established the Hogarth Press, which published some of the most interesting literature of the period, including her own novels. Woolf experienced several mental breakdowns, and in 1941, fearing yet another, she drowned herself.

Lappin and Lapinova*

They were married. The wedding march pealed out. The pigeons fluttered. Small boys in Eton jackets threw rice: a fox terrier sauntered across the path; and

---

lapin is French for rabbit

Ernest Thorburn led his bride to the car through the small inquisitive crowd of complete strangers which always collects in London to enjoy other people's happiness or unhappiness. Certainly he looked handsome and she looked shy. More rice was thrown, and the car moved off.

That was on Tuesday. Now it was Saturday. Rosalind had still to get used to the fact that she was Mrs. Ernest Thorburn. Perhaps she never would get used to the fact that she was Mrs. Ernest Anybody, she thought, as she sat in the bow window of the hotel looking over the lake to the mountains, and waited for her husband to come down to breakfast. Ernest was a difficult name to get used to. It was not the name she would have chosen. She would have preferred Timothy, Antony, or Peter. He did not look like Ernest either. The name suggested the Albert Memorial,[1] mahogany sideboards, steel engravings of the Prince Consort with his family—her mother-in-law's dining-room in Porchester Terrace in short.

But here he was. Thank goodness he did not look like Ernest—no. But what did he look like? She glanced at him sideways. Well, when he was eating toast he looked like a rabbit. Not that anyone else would have seen a likeness to a creature so diminutive and timid in this spruce, muscular young man with the straight nose, the blue eyes, and the very firm mouth. But that made it all the more amusing. His nose twitched very slightly when he ate. So did her pet rabbit's. She kept watching his nose twitch; and then she had to explain, when he caught her looking at him, why she laughed.

"It's because you're like a rabbit, Ernest," she said. "Like a wild rabbit," she added, looking at him. "A hunting rabbit; a King Rabbit; a rabbit that makes laws for all the other rabbits."

5   Ernest had no objection to being that kind of rabbit, and since it amused her to see him twitch his nose—he had never known that his nose twitched—he twitched it on purpose. And she laughed and laughed; and he laughed too, so that the maiden ladies and the fishing man and the Swiss waiter in his greasy jacket all guessed right; they were very happy. But how long does such happiness last? they asked themselves; and each answered according to his own circumstances.

At lunch time, seated on a clump of heather beside the lake. "Lettuce, rabbit?" said Rosalind, holding out the lettuce that had been provided to eat with the hard-boiled eggs. "Come and take it out of my hand," she added, and he stretched out and nibbled the lettuce and twitched his nose.

"Good rabbit, nice rabbit," she said, patting him, as she used to pat her tame rabbit at home. But that was absurd. He was not a tame rabbit, whatever he was. She turned it into French. "Lapin," she called him. But whatever he was, he was not a French rabbit. He was simply and solely English—born at Porchester Terrace, educated at Rugby; now a clerk in His Majesty's Civil Service. So she tried "Bunny" next; but that was worse. "Bunny" was someone plump and soft and comic; he was thin and hard and serious. Still, his nose twitched. "Lappin," she exclaimed suddenly; and gave a little cry as if she had found the very word she looked for.

---

[1] a memorial, in Hyde Park, London, dedicated in 1872 to Prince Albert (1819–61), consort of Queen Victoria. A bronze statue of the prince stands in a tabernacle which rests on a platform. The platform's corners are adorned with sculptural groups representing Industry, Commerce, Agriculture, and Science. The whole is a memorial to Victorian culture, which by Woolf's time was much ridiculed.

"Lappin, Lappin, King Lappin," she repeated. It seemed to suit him exactly; he was not Ernest, he was King Lappin. Why? She did not know.

When there was nothing new to talk about on their long solitary walks—and it rained, as everyone had warned them that it would rain; or when they were sitting over the fire in the evening, for it was cold, and the maiden ladies had gone and the fishing man, and the waiter only came if you rang the bell for him, she let her fancy play with the story of the Lappin tribe. Under her hands—she was sewing; he was reading—they became very real, very vivid, very amusing. Ernest put down the paper and helped her. There were the black rabbits and the red; there were the enemy rabbits and the friendly. There were the wood in which they lived and the outlying prairies and the swamp. Above all there was King Lappin, who, far from having only the one trick—that he twitched his nose—became as the days passed an animal of the greatest character; Rosalind was always finding new qualities in him. But above all he was a great hunter.

10 "And what," said Rosalind, on the last day of the honeymoon, "did the King do to-day?"

In fact they had been climbing all day; and she had worn a blister on her heel; but she did not mean that.

"To-day," said Ernest, twitching his nose as he bit the end off his cigar, "he chased a hare." He paused; struck a match, and twitched again.

"A woman hare," he added.

"A white hare!" Rosalind exclaimed, as if she had been expecting this. "Rather a small hare; silver grey; with big bright eyes?"

15 "Yes," said Ernest, looking at her as she had looked at him, "a smallish animal; with eyes popping out of her head, and two little front paws dangling." It was exactly how she sat, with her sewing dangling in her hands; and her eyes, that were so big and bright, were certainly a little prominent.

"Ah, Lapinova," Rosalind murmured.

"Is that what she's called?" said Ernest—"the real Rosalind?" He looked at her. He felt very much in love with her.

"Yes; that's what she's called," said Rosalind. "Lapinova." And before they went to bed that night it was all settled. He was King Lappin; she was Queen Lapinova. They were the opposite of each other; he was bold and determined; she wary and undependable. He ruled over the busy world of rabbits; her world was a desolate, mysterious place, which she ranged mostly by moonlight. All the same, their territories touched; they were King and Queen.

Thus when they came back from their honeymoon they possessed a private world, inhabited, save for the one white hare, entirely by rabbits. No one guessed that there was such a place, and that of course made it all the more amusing. It made them feel, more even than most young married couples, in league together against the rest of the world. Often they looked slyly at each other when people talked about rabbits and woods and traps and shooting. Or they winked furtively across the table when Aunt Mary said that she could never bear to see a hare in a dish—it looked so like a baby; or when John, Ernest's sporting brother, told them what price rabbits were fetching that autumn in Wiltshire, skins and all. Sometimes when they wanted a gamekeeper, or a poacher or a Lord of the Manor, they amused themselves by distributing the parts among their friends. Ernest's mother, Mrs. Reginald Thorburn, for example, fitted the part of the Squire to perfection. But it was all secret—that was the point of it: nobody save themselves knew that such a world existed.

20   Without that world, how, Rosalind wondered, that winter could she have lived at all? For instance, there was the golden-wedding party, when all the Thorburns assembled at Porchester Terrace to celebrate the fiftieth anniversary of that union which had been so blessed—had it not produced Ernest Thorburn? and so fruitful—had it not produced nine other sons and daughters into the bargain, many themselves married and also fruitful? She dreaded that party. But it was inevitable. As she walked upstairs she felt bitterly that she was an only child and an orphan at that; a mere drop among all those Thorburns assembled in the great drawing-room with the shiny satin wallpaper and the lustrous family portraits. The living Thorburns much resembled the painted; save that instead of painted lips they had real lips; out of which came jokes; jokes about schoolrooms, and how they had pulled the chair from under the governess; jokes about frogs and how they had put them between the virgin sheets of maiden ladies. As for herself, she had never even made an apple-pie bed. Holding her present in her hand she advanced toward her mother-in-law sumptuous in yellow satin; and toward her father-in-law decorated with a rich yellow carnation. All round them on tables and chairs there were golden tributes, some nestling in cotton wool; others branching resplendent—candlesticks; cigar boxes; chains; each stamped with the goldsmith's proof that it was solid gold, hallmarked, authentic. But her present was only a little pinchbeck[2] box pierced with holes; an old sand caster, an eighteenth-century relic, once used to sprinkle sand over wet ink. Rather a senseless present she felt—in an age of blotting paper; and as she proffered it, she saw in front of her the stubby black handwriting in which her mother-in-law when they were engaged had expressed the hope that "My son will make you happy." No, she was not happy. Not at all happy. She looked at Ernest, straight as a ramrod with a nose like all the noses in the family portraits; a nose that never twitched at all.

Then they went down to dinner. She was half hidden by the great chrysanthemums that curled their red and gold petals into large tight balls. Everything was gold. A gold-edged card with gold initials intertwined recited the list of all the dishes that would be set one after another before them. She dipped her spoon in a plate of clear golden fluid. The raw white fog outside had been turned by the lamps into a golden mesh that blurred the edges of the plates and gave the pineapples a rough golden skin. Only she herself in her white wedding dress peering ahead of her with her prominent eyes seemed insoluble as an icicle.

As the dinner wore on, however, the room grew steamy with heat. Beads of perspiration stood out on the men's foreheads. She felt that her icicle was being turned to water. She was being melted; dispersed; dissolved into nothingness; and would soon faint. Then through the surge in her head and the din in her ears she heard a woman's voice exclaim, "But they breed so!"

The Thorburns—yes; they breed so, she echoed; looking at all the round red faces that seemed doubled in the giddiness that overcame her; and magnified in the gold mist that enhaloed them. "They breed so." Then John bawled:

"Little devils! . . . Shoot 'em! Jump on 'em with big boots! That's the only way to deal with 'em . . . rabbits!"

25   At that word, that magic word, she revived. Peeping between the chrysanthemums she saw Ernest's nose twitch. It rippled, it ran with successive

[2]imitation gold

twitches. And at that a mysterious catastrophe befell the Thorburns. The golden table became a moor with the gorse in full bloom; the din of voices turned to one peal of lark's laughter ringing down from the sky. It was a blue sky—clouds passed slowly. And they had all been changed—the Thorburns. She looked at her father-in-law, a furtive little man with dyed moustaches. His foible was collecting things—seals, enamel boxes, trifles from eighteenth-century dressing tables which he hid in the drawers of his study from his wife. Now she saw him as he was—a poacher, stealing off with his coat bulging with pheasants and partridges to drop them stealthily into a three-legged pot in his smoky little cottage. That was her real father-in-law—a poacher. And Celia, the unmarried daughter, who always nosed out other people's secrets, the little things they wished to hide—she was a white ferret[3] with pink eyes, and a nose clotted with earth from her horrid underground nosings and pokings. Slung round men's shoulders, in a net, and thrust down a hole—it was a pitiable life—Celia's; it was none of her fault. So she saw Celia. And then she looked at her mother-in-law—whom they dubbed The Squire. Flushed, coarse, a bully—she was all that, as she stood returning thanks, but now that Rosalind—that is Lapinova—saw her, she saw behind her the decayed family mansion, the plaster peeling off the walls, and heard her, with a sob in her voice, giving thanks to her children (who hated her) for a world that had ceased to exist. There was a sudden silence. They all stood with their glasses raised; they all drank; then it was over.

"Oh, King Lappin!" she cried as they went home together in the fog, "if your nose hadn't twitched just at that moment. I should have been trapped!"

"But you're safe," said King Lappin, pressing her paw.

"Quite safe," she answered.

And they drove back through the Park, King and Queen of the marsh, of the mist, and of the gorse-scented moor.

30   Thus time passed; one year; two years of time. And on a winter's night, which happened by a coincidence to be the anniversary of the golden-wedding party—but Mrs. Reginald Thorburn was dead; the house was to let; and there was only a caretaker in residence—Ernest came home from the office. They had a nice little home; half a house above a saddler's shop in South Kensington, not far from the tube[4] station. It was cold, with fog in the air, and Rosalind was sitting over the fire, sewing.

"What d'you think happened to me to-day?" she began as soon as he had settled himself down with his legs stretched to the blaze. "I was crossing the stream when—"

"What stream?" Ernest interrupted her.

"The stream at the bottom, where our wood meets the black wood," she explained.

Ernest looked completely blank for a moment.

35   "What the deuce are you talking about?" he asked.

"My dear Ernest!" she cried in dismay, "King Lappin," she added, dangling her little front paws in the firelight. But his nose did not twitch. Her hands—they turned to hands—clutched the stuff she was holding; her eyes popped half out of her head. It took him five minutes at least to change from Ernest Thor-

[3]white ferrets—albino polecats—were often used to hunt rats and rabbits   [4]subway

burn to King Lappin; and while she waited she felt a load on the back of her neck, as if somebody were about to wring it. At last he changed to King Lappin; his nose twitched; and they spent the evening roaming the woods much as usual.

But she slept badly. In the middle of the night she woke, feeling as if something strange had happened to her. She was stiff and cold. At last she turned on the light and looked at Ernest lying beside her. He was sound asleep. He snored. But even though he snored, his nose remained perfectly still. It looked as if it had never twitched at all. Was it possible that he was really Ernest; and that she was really married to Ernest? A vision of her mother-in-law's dining-room came before her; and there they sat, she and Ernest, grown old, under the engravings, in front of the sideboard. . . . It was their golden-wedding day. She could not bear it.

"Lappin, King Lappin!" she whispered, and for a moment his nose seemed to twitch of its own accord. But he still slept. "Wake up, Lappin, wake up!" she cried.

Ernest woke; and seeing her sitting bolt upright beside him he asked:

40   "What's the matter?"

"I thought my rabbit was dead!" she whimpered. Ernest was angry.

"Don't talk such rubbish. Rosalind," he said. "Lie down and go to sleep."

He turned over. In another moment he was sound asleep and snoring.

But she could not sleep. She lay curled up on her side of the bed, like a hare in its form.[5] She had turned out the light, but the street lamp lit the ceiling faintly, and the trees outside made a lacy network over it as if there were a shadowy grove on the ceiling in which she wandered, turning, twisting, in and out, round and round, hunting, being hunted, hearing the bay of hounds and horns; flying, escaping . . . until the maid drew the blinds and brought their early tea.

45   Next day she could settle to nothing. She seemed to have lost something. She felt as if her body had shrunk; it had grown small, and black and hard. Her joints seemed stiff too, and when she looked in the glass, which she did several times as she wandered about the flat, her eyes seemed to burst out of her head, like currants in a bun. The rooms also seemed to have shrunk. Large pieces of furniture jutted out at odd angles and she found herself knocking against them. At last she put on her hat and went out. She walked along the Cromwell Road; and every room she passed and peered into seemed to be a dining-room where people sat eating under steel engravings, with thick yellow lace curtains, and mahogany sideboards. At last she reached the Natural History Museum; she used to like it when she was a child. But the first thing she saw when she went in was a stuffed hare standing on sham snow with pink glass eyes. Somehow it made her shiver all over. Perhaps it would be better when dusk fell. She went home and sat over the fire, without a light, and tried to imagine that she was out alone on a moor; and there was a stream rushing; and beyond the stream a dark wood. But she could get no further than the stream. At last she squatted down on the bank on the wet grass, and sat crouched in her chair, with her hands dangling empty, and her eyes glazed, like glass eyes, in the firelight. Then there was the crack of a gun. . . . She started as if she had been shot. It was only Ernest, turning his key in the door. She waited, trembling. He came in and switched on the light. There he stood, tall, handsome, rubbing his hands that were red with cold.

[5]the resting place of a hare

"Sitting in the dark?" he said.

"Oh, Ernest, Ernest!" she cried, starting up in her chair.

"Well, what's up now?" he asked briskly, warming his hands at the fire.

"It's Lapinova . . ." she faltered, glancing wildly at him out of her great started eyes. "She's gone. Ernest. I've lost her!"

50   Ernest frowned. He pressed his lips tight together.

"Oh, that's what's up, is it?" he said, smiling rather grimly at his wife. For ten seconds he stood there, silent; and she waited, feeling hands tightening at the back of her neck.

"Yes." he said at length. "Poor Lapinova . . ." He straightened his tie at the looking-glass over the mantelpiece.

"Caught in a trap," he said, "killed," and sat down and read the newspaper. So that was the end of that marriage.

[1938]

Topics for Critical Thinking and Writing

1. What is the point of view and the tone of the first paragraph? Of the second?
2. We are told that Rosalind and Ernest—King Lappin and Queen Lapinova—"were the opposite of each other; he was bold and determined; she wary and undependable." Are these brief characterizations adequate, or are the characters more complex?
3. Why, at the golden-wedding party, does Rosalind feel that she is being "dissolved into nothingness"?
4. The story ends with this sentence: "So that was the end of that marriage." Why did the marriage end? And what, if anything, does this rather flat sentence add to the story?
5. Write a story, a narrative essay, or a journal entry about the end of a relationship. The relationship need not be between husband and wife, or lovers, or friends. It might be between a teacher and a student, a coach and an athlete, or siblings, for example.

WILLIAM FAULKNER

William Faulkner (1897–1962) was brought up in Oxford, Mississippi. His great-grandfather had been a Civil War hero, and his father was treasurer of the University of Mississippi in Oxford; the family was no longer rich, but it was still respected. In 1918 he enrolled in the Royal Canadian Air Force, though he never saw overseas service. After the war he returned to Mississippi and went to the university for two years. He then moved to New Orleans, where he became friendly with Sherwood Anderson, who was already an established writer. In New Orleans Faulkner worked for the Times-Picayune; *still later, even after he had established himself as a major novelist with* The Sound and the Fury *(1929), he had to do some work in Hollywood in order to make ends meet. In 1950 he was awarded the Nobel Prize in Literature.*

Almost all of Faulkner's writing is concerned with the people of Yoknapatawpha, an imaginary county in Mississippi. "I discovered," he said, "that my own little postage stamp of native soil was worth writing about and that I would never live long enough to exhaust it." Though he lived for brief periods in Canada, New Orleans, New York, Hollywood, and Virginia (where he died), he spent most of his life in his native Mississippi.

A Rose for Emily

I

When Miss Emily Grierson died, our whole town went to her funeral: the men through a sort of respectful affection for a fallen monument, the women mostly out of curiosity to see the inside of her house, which no one save an old manservant—a combined gardener and cook—had seen in at least ten years.

It was a big, squarish frame house that had once been white, decorated with cupolas and spires and scrolled balconies in the heavily lightsome style of the seventies, set on what had once been our most select street. But garages and cotton gins had encroached and obliterated even the august names of that neighborhood; only Miss Emily's house was left, lifting its stubborn and coquettish decay above the cotton wagons and the gasoline pumps—an eyesore among eyesores. And now Miss Emily had gone to join the representatives of those august names where they lay in the cedar-bemused cemetery among the ranked and anonymous graves of Union and Confederate soldiers who fell at the battle of Jefferson.

Alive, Miss Emily had been a tradition, a duty, and a care; a sort of hereditary obligation upon the town, dating from that day in 1894 when Colonel Sartoris, the mayor—he who fathered the edict that no Negro woman should appear on the streets without an apron—remitted her taxes, the dispensation dating from the death of her father on into perpetuity. Not that Miss Emily would have accepted charity. Colonel Sartoris invented an involved tale to the effect that Miss Emily's father had loaned money to the town, which the town, as a matter of business, preferred this way of repaying. Only a man of Colonel Sartoris' generation and thought could have invented it, and only a woman could have believed it.

When the next generation, with its more modern ideas, became mayors and aldermen, this arrangement created some little dissatisfaction. On the first of the year they mailed her a tax notice. February came, and there was no reply. They wrote her a formal letter, asking her to call at the sheriff's office at her convenience. A week later the mayor wrote her himself, offering to call or to send his car for her, and received in reply a note on paper of an archaic shape, in a thin, flowing calligraphy in faded ink, to the effect that she no longer went out at all. The tax notice was also enclosed, without comment.

5   They called a special meeting of the Board of Aldermen. A deputation waited upon her, knocked at the door through which no visitor had passed since she ceased giving china-painting lessons eight or ten years earlier. They were admitted by the old Negro into a dim hall from which a staircase mounted into still more shadow. It smelled of dust and disuse—a close, dank smell. The Negro led them into the parlor. It was furnished in heavy, leather-covered furniture. When the Negro opened the blinds of one window they could see that the leather was cracked; and when they sat down, a faint dust rose sluggishly about their thighs, spinning with slow motes in the single sunray. On a tarnished gilt easel before the fireplace stood a crayon portrait of Miss Emily's father.

They rose when she entered—a small, fat woman in black, with a thin gold chain descending to her waist and vanishing into her belt, leaning on an ebony cane with a tarnished gold head. Her skeleton was small and spare; perhaps that was why what would have been merely plumpness in another was obesity in her. She looked bloated, like a body long submerged in motionless water, and of that pallid hue. Her eyes, lost in the fatty ridges of her face, looked like two small pieces of coal pressed into a lump of dough as they moved from one face to another while the visitors stated their errand.

She did not ask them to sit. She just stood in the door and listened quietly until the spokesman came to a stumbling halt. Then they could hear the invisible watch ticking at the end of the gold chain.

Her voice was dry and cold. "I have no taxes in Jefferson. Colonel Sartoris explained it to me. Perhaps one of you can gain access to the city records and satisfy yourselves."

"But we have. We are the city authorities, Miss Emily. Didn't you get a notice from the sheriff, signed by him?"

10   "I received a paper, yes," Miss Emily said. "Perhaps he considers himself the sheriff. . . . I have no taxes in Jefferson."

"But there is nothing on the books to show that, you see. We must go by the—"

"See Colonel Sartoris. I have no taxes in Jefferson."

"But, Miss Emily—"

"See Colonel Sartoris." (Colonel Sartoris had been dead almost ten years.) "I have no taxes in Jefferson. Tobe!" The Negro appeared. "Show these gentlemen out."

II

15   So she vanquished them, horse and foot, just as she had vanquished their fathers thirty years before about the smell. That was two years after her father's death and a short time after her sweetheart—the one we believed would marry her—had deserted her. After her father's death she went out very little; after her sweetheart went away, people hardly saw her at all. A few of the ladies had the temerity to call, but were not received, and the only sign of life about the place was the Negro man—a young man then—going in and out with a market basket.

"Just as if a man—any man—could keep a kitchen properly," the ladies said; so they were not surprised when the smell developed. It was another link between the gross, teeming world and the high and mighty Griersons.

A neighbor, a woman, complained to the mayor, Judge Stevens, eighty years old.

"But what will you have me do about it, madam?" he said.

"Why, send her word to stop it," the woman said. "Isn't there a law?"

20   "I'm sure that won't be necessary," Judge Stevens said. "It's probably just a snake or a rat that nigger of hers killed in the yard. I'll speak to him about it."

The next day he received two more complaints, one from a man who came in diffident deprecation. "We really must do something about it, Judge, I'd be the last one in the world to bother Miss Emily, but we've got to do something." That night the Board of Aldermen met—three gray-beards and one younger man, a member of the rising generation.

"It's simple enough," he said. "Send her word to have her place cleaned up. Given her a certain time to do it in, and if she don't . . ."

"Dammit, sir," Judge Stevens said, "will you accuse a lady to her face of smelling bad?"

So the next night, after midnight, four men crossed Miss Emily's lawn and slunk about the house like burglars, sniffing along the base of the brickwork and at the cellar openings while one of them performed a regular sowing motion with his hand out of a sack slung from his shoulder. They broke open the cellar door and sprinkled lime there, and in all the out-buildings. As they recrossed the lawn, a window that had been dark was lighted and Miss Emily sat in it, the light behind her, and her upright torso motionless as that of an idol. They crept quietly across the lawn and into the shadow of the locusts that lined the street. After a week or two the smell went away.

25   That was when people had begun to feel really sorry for her. People in our town remembering how old lady Wyatt, her great-aunt, had gone completely crazy at last, believed that the Griersons held themselves a little too high for what they really were. None of the young men were quite good enough for Miss Emily and such. We had long thought of them as a tableau; Miss Emily a slender figure in white in the background, her father a spraddled silhouette in the foreground, his back to her and clutching a horsewhip, the two of them framed by the back-flung front door. So when she got to be thirty and was still single, we were not pleased exactly, but vindicated; even with insanity in the family she wouldn't have turned down all of her chances if they had really materialized.

When her father died, it got about that the house was all that was left to her; and in a way, people were glad. At last they could pity Miss Emily. Being left alone, and a pauper, she had become humanized. Now she too would know the old thrill and the old despair of a penny more or less.

The day after his death all the ladies prepared to call at the house and offer condolence and aid, as is our custom. Miss Emily met them at the door, dressed as usual and with no trace of grief on her face. She told them that her father was not dead. She did that for three days, with the ministers calling on her, and the doctors, trying to persuade her to let them dispose of the body. Just as they were about to resort to law and force, she broke down, and they buried her father quickly.

We did not say she was crazy then. We believed she had to do that. We remembered all the young men her father had driven away, and we knew that with nothing left, she would have to cling to that which had robbed her, as people will.

III

She was sick for a long time. When we saw her again, her hair was cut short, making her look like a girl, with a vague resemblance to those angels in colored church windows—sort of tragic and serene.

30   The town had just let the contracts for paving the sidewalks, and in the summer after her father's death they began to work. The construction company came with niggers and mules and machinery, and a foreman named Homer Barron, a Yankee—a big, dark, ready man, with a big voice and eyes lighter than his face. The little boys would follow in groups to hear him cuss the niggers, and the niggers singing in time to the rise and fall of picks. Pretty soon he knew everybody in town. Whenever you heard a lot of laughing anywhere about the square. Homer Barron would be in the center of the group. Presently we began to see him and Miss Emily on Sunday afternoons driving in the yellow-wheeled buggy and the matched team of bays from the livery stable.

At first we were glad that Miss Emily would have an interest, because the ladies all said. "Of course a Grierson would not think seriously of a Northerner, a day laborer." But there were still others, older people, who said that even grief could not cause a real lady to forget *noblesse oblige*—without calling it *noblesse oblige*. They just said, "Poor Emily. Her kinsfolk should come to her." She had some kin in Alabama; but years ago her father had fallen out with them over the estate of old lady Wyatt, the crazy woman, and there was no communication between the two families. They had not even been represented at the funeral.

And as soon as the old people said, "Poor Emily," the whispering began. "Do you suppose it's really so?" they said to one another. "Of course it is . . . ." This behind their hands; rustling of craned silk and satin behind jalousies closed upon the sun of Sunday afternoon as the thin, swift clop-clop-clop of the matched team passed: "Poor Emily."

She carried her head high enough—even when we believed that she was fallen. It was as if she demanded more than ever the recognition of her dignity as the last Grierson; as if it had wanted that touch of earthiness to reaffirm her imperviousness. Like when she bought the rat poison, the arsenic. That was over a year after they had begun to say "Poor Emily," and while the two female cousins were visiting her.

"I want some poison," she said to the druggist. She was over thirty then, still a slight woman, though thinner than usual, with cold, haughty black eyes in a face the flesh of which was strained across the temples and about the eyesockets as you imagine a lighthouse-keeper's face ought to look. "I want some poison," she said.

35   "Yes, Miss Emily. What kind? For rats and such? I'd recom—"

"I want the best you have. I don't care what kind."

The druggist named several. "They'll kill anything up to an elephant. But what you want is—"

"Arsenic." Miss Emily said. "Is that a good one?"

"Is . . . arsenic? Yes ma'am. But what you want—"

40   "I want arsenic."

The druggist looked down at her. She looked back at him, erect, her face like a strained flag. "Why, of course," the druggist said. "If that's what you want. But the law requires you to tell what you are going to use it for."

Miss Emily just stared at him, her head tilted back in order to look him eye for eye, until he looked away and went and got the arsenic and wrapped it up. The Negro delivery boy brought her the package; the druggist didn't come back. When she opened the package at home there was written on the box, under the skull and bones: "For rats."

IV

So the next day we all said. "She will kill herself"; and we said it would be the best thing. When she had first begun to be seen with Homer Barron, we had said, "She will marry him." Then we said, "She will persuade him yet," because Homer himself had remarked—he liked men, and it was known that he drank with the younger men in the Elks' Club—that he was not a marrying man. Later we said, "Poor Emily," behind the jalousies as they passed on Sunday afternoon in the glittering buggy, Miss Emily with her head high and Homer Barron with his hat cocked and a cigar in his teeth, reins and whip in a yellow glove.

Then some of the ladies began to say that it was a disgrace to the town and a bad example to the young people. The men did not want to interfere, but at last the ladies forced the Baptist minister—Miss Emily's people were Episcopal—to call upon her. He would never divulge what happened during that interview, but he refused to go back again. The next Sunday they again drove about the streets, and the following day the minister's wife wrote to Miss Emily's relations in Alabama.

45   So she had blood-kin under her roof again and we sat back to watch developments. At first nothing happened. Then we were sure that they were to be married. We learned that Miss Emily had been to the jeweler's and ordered a man's toilet set in silver, with the letters H.B. on each piece. Two days later we learned that she had bought a complete outfit of men's clothing, including a nightshirt, and we said, "They are married." We were really glad. We were glad because the two female cousins were even more Grierson than Miss Emily had ever been.

    So we were surprised when Homer Barron—the streets had been finished some time since—was gone. We were a little disappointed that there was not a public blowing-off but we believed that he had gone on to prepare for Miss Emily's coming, or to give a chance to get rid of the cousins. (By that time it was a cabal, and we were all Miss Emily's allies to help circumvent the cousins.) Sure enough, after another week they departed. And, as we had expected all along, within three days Homer Barron was back in town. A neighbor saw the Negro man admit him at the kitchen door at dusk one evening.

    And that was the last we saw of Homer Barron. And of Miss Emily for some time. The Negro man went in and out with the market basket, but the front door remained closed. Now and then we would see her at a window for a moment, as the men did that night when they sprinkled the lime, but for almost six months she did not appear on the streets. Then we knew that this was to be expected too; as if that quality of her father which had thwarted her woman's life so many times had been too virulent and too furious to die.

    When we next saw Miss Emily, she had grown fat and her hair was turning gray. During the next few years it grew grayer and grayer until it attained an even pepper-and-salt iron-gray, when it ceased turning. Up to the day of her death at seventy-four it was still that vigorous iron-gray, like the hair of an active man.

    From that time on her front door remained closed, save for a period of six or seven years, when she was about forty, during which she gave lessons in china-painting. She fitted up a studio in one of the downstairs rooms, where the daughters and granddaughters of Colonel Sartoris' contemporaries were sent to her with the same regularity and in the same spirit that they were sent on Sundays with a twenty-five cent piece for the collection plate. Meanwhile her taxes had been remitted.

50   Then the newer generation became the backbone and the spirit of the town, and the painting pupils grew up and fell away and did not send their children to her with boxes of color and tedious brushes and pictures cut from the ladies' magazines. The front door closed upon the last one and remained closed for good. When the town got free postal delivery Miss Emily alone refused to let them fasten the metal numbers above her door and attach a mailbox to it. She would not listen to them.

    Daily, monthly, yearly we watched the Negro grow grayer and more stooped, going in and out with the market basket. Each December we sent her a tax notice, which would be returned by the post office a week later, unclaimed. Now and then we could see her in one of the downstairs windows—she had evidently shut up the top floor of the house—like the carven torso of an idol in a niche, looking or not looking at us, we could never tell which. Thus she passed from generation to generation—dear, inescapable, impervious, tranquil, and perverse.

And so she died. Fell ill in the house filled with dust and shadows, with only a doddering Negro man to wait on her. We did not even know she was sick; we had long since given up trying to get any information from the Negro. He talked to no one, probably not even to her, for his voice had grown harsh and rusty, as if from disuse.

She died in one of the downstairs rooms, in a heavy walnut bed with a curtain, her gray head propped on a pillow yellow and moldy with age and lack of sunlight.

V

The Negro met the first of the ladies at the front door and let them in, with their hushed, sibilant voices and their quick, curious glances, and then he disappeared. He walked right through the house and out the back and was not seen again.

The two female cousins came at once. They held the funeral on the second day, with the town coming to look at Miss Emily beneath a mass of bought flowers, with the crayon face of her father musing profoundly above the bier and the ladies sibilant and macabre; and the very old men—some in their brushed Confederate uniforms—on the porch and the lawn, talking of Miss Emily as if she had been a contemporary of theirs, believing that they had danced with her and courted her perhaps, confusing time with its mathematical progression, as the old do, to whom all the past is not a diminishing road, but, instead, a huge meadow which no winter ever quite touches, divided from them now by the narrow bottleneck of the most recent decade of years.

Already we knew that there was one room in that region above stairs which no one had seen in forty years, and which would have to be forced. They waited until Miss Emily was decently in the ground before they opened it.

The violence of breaking down the door seemed to fill this room with pervading dust. A thin, acrid pall as of the tomb seemed to lie everywhere upon this room decked and furnished as for a bridal: upon the valance curtains of faded rose color, upon the rose-shaded lights, upon the dressing table, upon the delicate array of crystal and the man's toilet things backed with tarnished silver, silver so tarnished that the monogram was obscured. Among them lay a collar and tie, as if they had just been removed, which, lifted, left upon the surface a pale crescent in the dust. Upon a chair hung the suit, carefully folded; beneath it the two mute shoes and the discarded socks.

The man himself lay in the bed.

For a long while we just stood there, looking down at the profound and fleshless grin. The body had apparently once lain in the attitude of an embrace, but now the long sleep that outlasts love, that conquers even the grimace of love, had cuckolded him. What was left of him, rotted beneath what was left of the nightshirt, had become inextricable from the bed in which he lay; and upon him and upon the pillow beside him lay that even coating of the patient and biding dust.

Then we noticed that in the second pillow was the indentation of a head. One of us lifted something from it, and leaning forward, that faint and invisible dust dry and acrid in the nostrils, we saw a long strand of iron-gray hair.

[1930]

dust and shadows, with only a doddering negro man to wait on
her. We did not even know she was sick; we had long since given up
trying to get any information from the negro. He talked to no
one, probably not even to her, for his voice had grown /h/a/r/d/
harsh and /d/r/y rusty, as though with disuse; the sparse words
which he did speak sounded as though he had learned them that
morning by rote---just enough of them to carry him through .
the day.

        She died in one of the downstairs rooms, in a heavy
walnut bed with a curtain, her gray head propped on a pillow
yellow and moldy with age and lack of sunlight, her voice
cold and strong to the last.

        "But not till I'm gone," she said. "Dont you let a
soul in until I'm gone, do you hear?" Standing beside the bed,
his head in the dim light nimbused by a faint halo of napped,
perfectly white hair, the negro made a brief gesture with his
hand. Miss Emily lay with her eyes open, gazing into the opposite shadows of the room. Upon the coverlet her hands lay on
her breast, gnarled, blue with age, motionless. "Hah," she said.
"Then they can. Let 'em go up there and see what's in that
room. /A/n/d/ /l/e/t/ /t/h/e/m/ /b/e/ /t/h/e/ /l/a/s/t/ /o/n/e/ /t/i/m/e/ Fools. /A/n/d/ Let
'em. /A/n/d/ /l/e/t/ /t/h/e/m/ /b/e/ /t/h/e/ /l/a/s/t/ /o/n/e/ Satisfy their minds that
I am crazy. Do you think I am?" The negro made no reply, no
movement. He stood above the bed, /e/x/p/r/e/s/s/i/o/n/l/e/s/s/ /m/o/t/i/o/n/l/e/s/s/ /l/i/k/e/ /a/n/ /a/n/-/
/a/p/e/ motionless, musing: a secret and unfathomable soul behind
the death-mask of an ape and haloed like an angel. "Let 'em
go up there and open that door. And you wont be the last one,

          13.

The printed version of Faulkner's "A Rose for Emily" omitted several passages of dialogue (shown here in pages 13 to 15 of the typed manuscript) between Miss Emily
and her longtime manservant.

either. Will you?"

"I wont have to," the negro said. "I know what's in that room. I dont have to see."

"Hah," Miss Emily said. "You do, do you. How long have you known?" Again he made that brief sign with his hand. Miss Emily had not turned her head. She stared into the shadows where the high ceiling was lost. "You should be glad. Now you can go to Chicago, like you've been talking about for thirty years. And with what you'll get for the house and furniture.... Colonel Sartoris has the will. He'll see they dont rob you."

"I dont want any house," the negro said.

"You cant help yourself. It's signed and sealed thirty-five years ago. Wasn't that our agreement when I found I couldn't pay you any wages? that you were to have everything that was left if you outlived me, and I was to bury you ~~will~~ in a coffin with your name on a gold plate if I outlived you?" He said nothing. "Wasn't it?" Miss Emily said.

"I was young then. Wanted to be rich. But now I dont want any house."

"Not when you have wanted to go to Chicago for thirty years?" Their breathing was alike: each that harsh, rasping breath of the old, the short inhalations that do not reach the bottom of the lungs: tireless, precarious, on the verge of cessation for all time, as if anything might suffice: a word, a look. "What are you going to do, then?"

"Going to the poorhouse."

"The poorhouse? When I'm trying to fix you so you'll

14.

have neither to worry nor lift your hand as long as you live?

    "I dont want nothing," the negro said. "I'm going to the poorhouse. I already told them."

    "Well," Miss Emily said. She had not moved her head, not moved at all. "Do you mind telling me why you want to go to the poorhouse?"

    Again he mused. The room was still save for their breaing: it was as though they had both quitted all living and all dying; all the travail of mortality and of breath. "So I can set on that hill in the sun all day and watch them trains pass. See them at night too, with the engine puffing and lights in all the windows.

    "Oh," Miss Emily said. Motionless, her knotted hands lying on the yellowed coverlet beneath her chin and her chin resting upon her breast, she appeared to muse intently, as though she were listening to dissolution setting up within her. "Hah," she said.

    Then she died, and the negro met the first of the ladies at the front door and let them in, with their hushed sibilant voices and their quick curious glances, and he went on to the back and disappeared. He walked right through the house and out the back and was not seen again.

    The two female cousins came at once. They held the funeral on the second day, with the town coming to look at Miss Emily beneath a mass of bought flowers, with the crayon face of her father musing profoundly above the bier and the la-

grin cemented into what had once been a pillow by a substance like
hardened sealing-wax. One side of the covers was flung back, as
though he were preparing to rise; we lifted the covers completely
away, liberating still another sluggish cloud of infinitesimal
dust, invisible and tainted. The body had apparently once lain
in the attitude of an embrace, but now the long sleep that outlasts love, that conquers even the grimace of love, had cuckolded
him: what was left of him lay beneath what was left of the
nightshirt, become inextricable with the bed in which he lay,
and upon him and upon the pillow beside him lay that even coating of the patient and biding dust. /p/ Then we noticed that in
the second pillow was the indentation of a head; one of us
lifted something from it, and leaning forward, that faint and
invisible dust lean and acrid in the nostrils, we saw a long
strand of iron-gray hair.

The final paragraph of the typed manuscript was reworded and made into two paragraphs in the published version.

Topics for Critical Thinking and Writing

1. Why does the narrator begin with what is almost the end of the story—the death of Miss Emily—rather than save this information for later? What devices does Faulkner use to hold the reader's interest throughout?
2. In a paragraph, offer a conjecture about Miss Emily's attitudes toward Homer Barron after he was last seen alive.
3. In a paragraph or two, characterize Miss Emily, calling attention not only to her eccentricities or even craziness, but also to what you conjecture to be her moral values.
4. In paragraph 44 we are told that the Baptist minister "would never divulge what happened" during the interview with Miss Emily. Why do you suppose Faulkner does not narrate or describe the interview? Let's assume that in his first draft of the story he *did* give a paragraph of narration or a short dramatic scene. Write such an episode.
5. Suppose that Homer Barron's remains had been discovered before Miss Emily died, and that she was arrested and charged with murder. You are the prosecutor and you are running for a statewide political office. In 500 words, set forth your argument that—despite the fact that she is a public monument—she should be convicted. Or: You are the defense attorney, also running for office. In 500 words, set forth your defense.
6. Assume that Miss Emily kept a journal—perhaps even from her days as a young girl. Write some entries for the journal, giving her thoughts about some of the episodes reported in Faulkner's story.

ZORA NEALE HURSTON

 *Zora Neale Hurston (c. 1901–60) was brought up in Eatonville, Florida, a town said to be the first all-black self-governing town in the United States. Her mother died in 1904, and when Hurston's father remarried, Hurston felt out of place. In 1914, then at about the age of fourteen, she joined a traveling theatrical group as a maid, hoping to save money for school. Later, by working at such jobs as manicurist and waitress, she put herself through college, entering Howard University in 1923. After receiving a scholarship, she transferred in 1926 to Barnard College in New York, where she was the first black student in the college. After graduating from Barnard in 1928 she taught drama, worked as an editor, and studied anthropology. But when grant money ran out in 1932 she returned to Eatonville to edit the folk material that she had collected during four years of field-work, and to do some further writing. She steadily published from 1932 to 1938—stories, folklore, and two novels—but she gained very little money. Further, although she played a large role in the Harlem Renaissance in the 1930s, she was criticized by Richard Wright and other influential black authors for portraying blacks as stereotypes and for being politically conservative. To many in the 1950s her writing seemed reactionary, almost embarrassing in an age of black protest, and she herself—working as a domestic, a librarian, and a substitute teacher—was almost forgotten. She died in a county welfare home in Florida and is buried in an unmarked grave.*

Sweat

It was eleven o'clock of a Spring night in Florida. It was Sunday. Any other night, Delia Jones would have been in bed for two hours by this time. But she was a washwoman, and Monday morning meant a great deal to her. So she collected the soiled clothes on Saturday when she returned the clean things. Sunday night after church, she sorted them and put the white things to soak. It saved her almost a half day's start. A great hamper in the bedroom held the clothes that she brought home. It was so much neater than a number of bundles lying around.

She squatted in the kitchen floor beside the great pile of clothes, sorting them into small heaps according to color, and humming a song in a mournful key, but wondering through it all where Sykes, her husband, had gone with her horse and buckboard.[1]

Just then something long, round, limp and black fell upon her shoulders and slithered to the floor beside her. A great terror took hold of her. It softened her knees and dried her mouth so that it was a full minute before she could cry out or move. Then she saw that it was the big bull whip her husband liked to carry when he drove.

She lifted her eyes to the door and saw him standing there bent over with laughter at her fright. She screamed at him.

5   "Sykes, what you throw dat whip on me like dat? You know it would skeer me—looks just like a snake, an' you knows how skeered Ah is of snakes."

"Course Ah knowed it! That's how come Ah done it." He slapped his leg with his hand and almost rolled on the ground in his mirth. "If you such a big fool dat you got to have a fit over a earth worm or a string, Ah don't keer how bad Ah skeer you."

"You aint got no business doing it. Gawd knows it's a sin. Some day Ah'm gointuh drop dead from some of yo' foolishness. 'Nother thing, where you been wid mah rig? Ah feeds dat pony. He aint fuh you to be drivin' wid no bull whip."

"Yo sho is one aggravatin' nigger woman!" he declared and stepped into the room. She resumed her work and did not answer him at once. "Ah done tole you time and again to keep them white folks' clothes outa dis house."

He picked up the whip and glared down at her. Delia went on with her work. She went out into the yard and returned with a galvanized tub and set in on the washbench. She saw that Sykes had kicked all of the clothes together again, and now stood in her way truculently, his whole manner hoping, *praying,* for an argument. But she walked calmly around him and commenced to re-sort the things.

10   "Next time, Ah'm gointer to kick 'em outdoors," he threatened as he struck a match along the leg of his corduroy breeches.

Delia never looked up from her work, and her thin, stooped shoulders sagged further.

"Ah aint for no fuss t'night Sykes. Ah just come from taking sacrament at the church house."

He snorted scornfully. "Yeah, you just come from de church house on a Sunday night, but heah you is gone to work on them clothes. You aint nothing but a hypocrite. One of them amen-corner Christians—sing, whoop, shout, then come home and wash white folks clothes on the Sabbath."

[1]an open wagon

He stepped roughly upon the whitest pile of things, kicking them helter-skelter as he crossed the room. His wife gave a little scream of dismay, and quickly gathered them together again.

15   "Sykes, you quit grindin' dirt into these clothes! How can Ah git through by Sat'day if Ah don't start on Sunday?"

"Ah don't keer if you never git through. Anyhow, Ah done promised Gawd and a couple of other men, Ah aint gointer have it in mah house. Don't gimme no lip neither, else Ah'll throw 'em out and put mah fist up side yo' head to boot."

Delia's habitual meekness seemed to slip from her shoulders like a blown scarf. She was on her feet; her poor little body, her bare knuckly hands bravely defying the strapping hulk before her.

"Looka heah, Sykes, you done gone too fur. Ah been married to you fur fifteen years, and Ah been takin' in washin' for fifteen years. Sweat, sweat, sweat! Work and sweat, cry and sweat, pray and sweat!"

"What's that got to do with me?" he asked brutally.

20   "What's it got to do with you, Sykes? Mah tub of suds is filled yo' belly with vittles more times than yo' hands is filled it. Mah sweat is done paid for this house and Ah reckon Ah kin keep on sweatin in it."

She seized the iron skillet from the stove and struck a defensive pose, which act surprised him greatly, coming from her. It cowed him and he did not strike her as he usually did.

"Naw you won't," she panted, "that ole snaggle-toothed black woman you runnin' with aint comin' heah to pile up on *mah* sweat and blood. You aint paid for nothin' on this place, and Ah'm gointer stay right heah till Ah'm toted out foot foremost."

"Well, you better quit gittin' me riled up, else they'll be totin' you out sooner than you expect. Ah'm so tired of you Ah don't know whut to do. Gawd! how Ah hates skinny wimmen!"

A little awed by this new Delia, he sidled out of the door and slammed the back gate after him. He did not say where he had gone, but she knew too well. She knew very well that he would not return until nearly daybreak also. Her work over, she went on to bed but not to sleep at once. Things had come to a pretty pass!

25   She lay awake, gazing upon the debris that cluttered their matrimonial trail. Not an image left standing along the way. Anything like flowers had long ago been drowned in the salty stream that had been pressed from her heart. Her tears, her sweat, her blood. She had brought love to the union and he had brought a longing for the flesh. Two months after the wedding, he had given her the first brutal beating. She had the memory of numerous trips to Orlando with all of his wages when he had returned to her penniless, even before the first year had passed. She was young and soft then, but now she thought of her knotty, muscled limbs, her harsh knuckly hands, and drew herself up into an unhappy little ball in the middle of the big feather bed. Too late now to hope for love, even if it were not Bertha it would be someone else. This case differed from the others only in that she was bolder than the others. Too late for everything except her little home. She had built it for her old days, and planted one by one the trees and flowers there. It was lovely to her, lovely.

Somehow before sleep came, she found herself saying aloud: "Oh well, whatever goes over the Devil's back, is got to come under his belly. Sometime or ruther, Sykes, like everybody else, is gointer reap his sowing." After that she was able to build a spiritual earthworks against her husband. His shells could no longer reach her. *Amen.* She went to sleep and slept until he announced his presence in bed by kicking her feet and rudely snatching the cover away.

"Gimme some kivah heah, an' git yo' damn foots over on yo' own side! Ah oughter mash you in yo' mouf fuh drawing dat skillet on me."

Delia went clear to the rail without answering him. A triumphant indifference to all that he was or did.

The week was as full of work for Delia as all other weeks, and Saturday found her behind her little pony, collecting and delivering clothes.

30 It was a hot, hot day near the end of July. The village men on Joe Clarke's porch even chewed cane listlessly. They did not hurl the cane-knots as usual. They let them dribble over the edge of the porch. Even conversation had collapsed under the heat.

"Heah comes Delia Jones," Jim Merchant said, as the shaggy pony came round the bend of the road toward them. The rusty buckboard was heaped with baskets of crisp, clean laundry.

"Yep," Joe Lindsay agreed, "Hot or col', rain or shine, jes ez reg'lar ez de weeks roll roun' Delia carries 'em an' fetches 'em on Sat'day."

"She better if she wanter eat," said Moss. "Syke Jones aint wuth de shot an' powder hit would tek tuh kill 'em. Not to *bub* he aint."

"He sho' aint," Walter Thomas chimed in. "It's too bad, too, cause she wuz a right pritty lil trick when he got huh. Ah'd uh mah'ied huh mahseft' it' he hadnter beat me to it."

35 Delia nodded briefly at the men as she drove past.

"Too much knockin will ruin *any* 'oman. He done beat huh nough tuh kill three women. let 'lone change they looks," said Elijah Mosely. "How Syke kin stommuck dat big black greasy Mogu[2] he's layin' roun' wid, gits me. Ah swear dat eight-rock couldn't kiss a sardine can Ah done thowed out de back do' 'way las' yeah."

"Aw, she's fat, thass how come. He's allus been crazy 'bout fat women," put in Merchant. "He'd a' been tied up wid one long time ago if he could a' found one tuh have him. Did Ah tell yuh 'bout him come sidlin' roun' *mah* 'wife—bringin' her a basket uh pee-cans outa his yard fuh a present? Yes-sir, mah wife! She tol' him tuh take 'em right straight back home, cause Delia works so hard ovah dat washtub she reckon everything en de place taste lak sweat an' soapsuds. Ah jus' wisht Ah'd a' caught 'im 'roun' dere! Ah'd a' made his hips ketch on fiah down dat shell road."

"Ah know he done it, too. Ah sees 'im grinnin' at every 'oman dat passes," Walter Thomas said. "But even so, he useter eat some mighty big hunks uh humble pie tuh git dat lil' 'oman he got. She wuz ez pritty ez a speckled pup! Dat wuz fifteen yeahs ago. He useter be so skeered uh losin' huh, she could make him do some parts of a husband's duty. Dey never wuz de same in de mind."

"There oughter be a law about him," said Lindsay. "He aint fit tuh carry guts tuh a bear."

40 Clarke spoke for the first time. "Taint no law on earth dat kin make a man be decent if it aint in 'im. There's plenty men dat takes a wife lak dey do a joint uh sugar-cane. It's round, juicy an' sweet when dey gits it. But dey squeeze an' grind, squeeze an' grind an' wring tell dey wring every drop uh pleasure dat's in 'em out. When dey's satisfied dat dey is wring dry, dey treats 'em jes lak dey do a cane-chew. Dey thows 'em away. Dey knows whut dey is doin' while dey is at it,

---

[2]big person

an' hates theirselves fuh it but they keeps on hangin' after huh tell she's empty. Den dey hates huh fuh bein' a cane-chew an' in de way."

"We oughter take Syke an' dat stray 'oman uh his'n down in Lake Howell swamp an' lay on de rawhide till they cain't say 'Lawd a' mussy.' He allus wuz uh ovahbearin' niggah, but since dat white 'oman from up north done teached 'im how to run a automobile, he done got too biggety to live—an' we oughter kill 'im." Old Man Anderson advised.

A grunt of approval went around the porch. But the heat was melting their civic virtue and Elijah Moseley began to bait Joe Clarke.

"Come on, Joe, git a melon outa dere an' slice it up for yo' customers. We'se all sufferin' wid de heat. De bear's done got *me!*"

"Thass right. Joe, a watermelon is jes' whut Ah needs tuh cure de eppizu-dicks."[3] Walter Thomas joined forces with Moseley. "Come on dere, Joe. We all is steady customers an' you aint set us up in a long time. Ah chooses dat long, bowlegged Floridy favorite."

45 "A god, an' be dough. You all gimme twenty cents and slice away." Clarke retorted. "Ah needs a col' slice m'self. Heah, everybody chip in. Ah'll lend y'll mah meat knife."

The money was quickly subscribed and the huge melon brought forth. At that moment, Sykes and Bertha arrived. A determined silence fell on the porch and the melon was put away again.

Merchant snapped down the blade of his jackknife and moved toward the store door.

"Come on in, Joe, an' gimme a slab uh sow belly an' uh pound uh coffee— almost fuhgot 'twas Sat'day. Got to git on home." Most of the men left also.

Just then Delia drove past on her way home, as Sykes was ordering magnifi-cently for Bertha. It pleased him for Delia to see.

50 "Git whutsoever yo' heart desires, Honey. Wait a minute, Joe. Give huh two bottles uh strawberry soda-water, uh quart uh parched groundpeas, an' a block uh chewin' gum."

With all this they left the store, with Sykes reminding Bertha that this was his town and she could have it if she wanted it.

The men returned soon after they left, and held their watermelon feast. "Where did Syke Jones git dat 'oman from nohow?" Lindsay asked.

"Ovah Apopka. Guess dey musta been cleanin' out de town when she lef. She don't look lak a thing but a hunk uh liver wid hair on it."

"Well, she sho' kin squall," Dave Carter contributed. "When she gits ready tuh laff, she jes' opens huh mouf an' latches it back tuh de las' notch. No ole grandpa alligator down in Lake Bell aint got nothin' on huh."

55 Bertha had been in town three months now. Sykes was still paying her room rent at Della Lewis'—the only house in town that would have taken her in. Sykes took her frequently to Winter Park to "stomps,"[4] He still assured her that he was the swellest man in the state.

"Sho' you kin have dat lil' ole house soon's Ah kin git dat 'oman outa dere. Everything b'longs tuh me an' you sho' kin have it. Ah sho' 'bominates uh skinny 'oman. Lawdy, you sho' is got one portly shape on you! You kin git *anything* you wants. Dis is *mah* town an' you sho' kin have it.

[3]i.e., epizootic, an epidemic among animals   [4]dances

Delia's work-worn knees crawled over the earth in Gethsemane and on the rocks of Calvary[5] many, many times during these months. She avoided the villagers and meeting places in her effort to be blind and deaf. But Bertha nullified this to a degree, by coming to Delia's house to call Sykes out to her at the gate.

Delia and Sykes fought all the time now with no peaceful interludes. They slept and ate in silence. Two or three times Delia had attempted a timid friendliness, but she was repulsed each time. It was plain that the breaches must remain agape.

The sun had burned July to August. The heat streamed down like a million hot arrows, smiting all things living upon the earth. Grass withered, leaves browned, snakes went blind in shedding and men and dogs went mad. Dog days!

60   Delia came home one day and found Sykes there before her. She wondered, but started to go on into the house without speaking, even though he was standing in the kitchen door and she must either stoop under his arm or ask him to move. He made no room for her. She noticed a soap box beside the steps, but paid no particular attention to it, knowing that he must have brought it there. As she was stooping to pass under his outstretched arm, he suddenly pushed her backward, laughingly.

"Look in de box dere Delia. Ah done brung yuh somethin'!"

She nearly fell upon the box in her stumbling, and when she saw what it held, she all but fainted outright.

"Syke! Syke, mah Gawd! You take dat rattlesnake 'way from heah! You *got-tuh.* Oh, Jesus, have mussy!"

"Ah aint gut tuh do nuthin' uh de kin'—fact is Ah aint got tuh do nothin' but die. Taint no use uh you puttin' on airs makin' out lak you sceered uh dat snake—he's gointer stay right heah tell he die. He wouldn't bite me cause Ah knows how tuh handle 'im. Nohow he wouldn't risk breakin' out his fangs 'gin *yo'* skinny laigs."

65   "Naw, now Syke, don't keep dat thing 'roun' heah tuh skeer me tuh death. You knows Ah'm even feared uh earth worms. Thass de biggest snake Ah evah did see. Kill 'im Syke, please."

"Doan ast me tuh do nothin 'fuh yuh. Goin' 'roun' tryin' to be so damn asterperious. Naw, Ah aint gonna kill it. Ah think uh damn sight mo' uh him dan you! Dat's a nice snake an' anybody doan lak 'im kin jes' hit de grit."

The village soon heard that Sykes had the snake, and came to see and ask questions.

"How de hen-fire did you ketch dat six-foot rattler. Syke?" Thomas asked.

"He's full uh frogs so he caint hardly move, thass how Ah eased up on 'm. But Ah'm a snake charmer an' knows how tuh handle 'em. Shux, dat aint nothin'. Ah could ketch one eve'y day if Ah so wanted tuh."

70   "Whut he needs is a heavy hick'ry club leaned real heavy on his head. Dat's de bes 'way tuh charm a rattlesnake."

"Naw, Walt, y'll jes' don't understand dese diamon' backs lak Ah do," said Sykes in a superior tone of voice.

---

[5]Gethsemane was the garden where Jesus prayed just before he was betrayed (Matthew 26:36–47); Calvary was the hill where he was crucified

The village agreed with Walter, but the snake stayed on. His box remained by the kitchen door with its screen wire covering. Two or three days later it had digested its meal of frogs and literally came to life. It rattled at every movement in the kitchen or the yard. One day as Delia came down the kitchen steps she saw his chalky-white fangs curved like scimitars hung in the wire meshes. This time she did not run away with averted eyes as usual. She stood for a long time in the doorway in a red fury that grew bloodier for every second that she regarded the creature that was her torment.

That night she broached the subject as soon as Sykes sat down to the table.

"Syke, Ah wants you tuh take dat snake 'way fum heah. You done starved me an' Ah put up widcher, you done beat me an Ah took dat, but you done kilt all mah insides bringin' dat varmint heah."

75   Sykes poured out a saucer full of coffee and drank it deliberately before he answered her.

"A whole lot Ah keer 'bout how you feels inside uh out. Dat snake aint goin' no damn wheah till Ah gits ready fuh 'im tuh go. So fur as beatin' is concerned, yuh aint took near all dat you gointer take ef yuh stay 'roun' *me*."

Delia pushed back her plate and got up from the table. "Ah hates you. Sykes," she said calmly. "Ah hates you tuh de same degree dat Ah useter love yuh. Ah done took an' took till mah belly is full up tuh mah neck. Dat's de reason Ah got mah letter fum de church an' moved mah membership tuh Woodbridge—so Ah don't haftuh take no sacrament wid yuh. Ah don't wantuh see yuh, 'roun' me atall. Lay 'roun' wid dat 'oman all yuh wants tuh, but gwan 'way fum me an' mah house. Ah hates yuh lak uh suck-egg dog."

Sykes almost let the huge wad of corn bread and collard greens he was chewing fall out of his mouth in amazement. He had a hard time whipping himself to the proper fury to try to answer Delia.

"Well, Ah'm glad you does hate me. Ah'm sho' tiahed uh you hangin' ontuh me. Ah don't want yuh. Look at yuh stringey ole neck! Yo' raw-bony laigs an' arms is enough tuh cut uh man tuh death. You looks jes' lak de devvul's doll-baby tuh *me*. You cain't hate me no worse dan Ah hates you. Ah been hatin' *you* fuh years."

80   "Yo' ole black hide don't look lak nothin' tuh me, but uh passle uh wrinkled up rubber, wid yo' big ole yeahs flappin' on each side lak up paih uh buzzard wings. Don't think Ah'm gointuh be run 'way fum mah house neither. Ah'm goin' tuh de white folks about *you*, mah young man, de very nex' time you lay yo' han's on me. Mah cup is done run ovah." Delia said this with no signs of fear and Sykes departed from the house, threatening her, but made not the slightest move to carry out any of them.

That night he did not return at all, and the next day being Sunday, Delia was glad that she did not have to quarrel before she hitched up her pony and drove the four miles to Woodbridge.

She stayed to the night service—"love feast"—which was very warm and full of spirit. In the emotional winds her domestic trials were borne far and wide so that she sang as she drove homeward.

"Jurden water,[6] black an' col'
Chills de body, not de soul
An' Ah wantah cross Jurden in uh calm time."

[6]the River Jordan, which the Jews had to cross in order to reach the promised land

She came from the barn to the kitchen door and stopped.

"Whut's de mattah, ol' satan, you aint kickin' up yo' racket?" She addressed the snake's box. Complete silence. She went on into the house with a new hope in its birth struggles. Perhaps her threat to go to the white folks had frightened Sykes! Perhaps he was sorry! Fifteen years of misery and suppression had brought Delia to the place where she would hope *anything* that looked towards a way over or through her wall of inhibitions.

85   She felt in the match safe behind the stove at once for a match. There was only one there.

"Dat niggah wouldn't fetch nothin heah tuh save his rotten neck, but he kin run thew whut Ah brings quick enough. Now he done toted off nigh on tuh haff uh box uh matches. He done had dat 'oman heah in mah house, too."

Nobody but a woman could tell how she knew this even before she struck the match. But she did and it put her into a new fury.

Presently she brought in the tubs to put the white things to soak. This time she decided she need not bring the hamper out of the bedroom; she would go in there and do the sorting. She picked up the pot-bellied lamp and went in. The room was small and the hamper stood hard by the foot of the white iron bed. She could sit and reach through the bedposts—resting as she worked.

"Ah wantah cross Jurden in uh calm time." She was singing again. The mood of the "love feast" had returned. She threw back the lid of the basket almost gaily. Then, moved by both horror and terror, she sprang back toward the door. *There lay the snake in the basket!* He moved sluggishly at first, but even as she turned round and round, jumped up and down in an insanity of fear, he began to stir vigorously. She saw him pouring his awful beauty from the basket upon the bed, then she seized the lamp and ran as fast as she could to the kitchen. The wind from the open door blew out the light and the darkness added to her terror. She sped to the darkness of the yard, slamming the door after her before she thought to set down the lamp. She did not feel safe even on the ground, so she climbed up in the hay barn.

90   There for an hour or more she lay sprawled upon the hay a gibbering wreck.

Finally she grew quiet, and after that, coherent thought. With this, stalked through her a cold, bloody rage. Hours of this. A period of introspection, a space of retrospection, then a mixture of both. Out of this an awful calm.

"Well, Ah done de bes' Ah could. If things aint right, Gawd knows taint mah fault."

She went to sleep—a twitchy sleep—and woke up to a faint gray sky. There was a loud hollow sound below. She peered out. Sykes was at the wood-pile, demolishing a wire-covered box.

He hurried to the kitchen door, but hung outside there some minutes before he entered, and stood some minutes more inside before he closed it after him.

95   The gray in the sky was spreading. Delia descended without fear now, and crouched beneath the low bedroom window. The drawn shade shut out the dawn, shut in the night. But the thin walls held back no sound.

"Dat ol' scratch is woke up now!" She mused at the tremendous whirr inside, which every woodsman knows, is one of the sound illusions. The rattler is a ventriloquist. His whirr sounds to the right, to the left, straight ahead, behind, close under foot—everywhere but where it is. Woe to him who guesses wrong unless he is prepared to hold up his end of the argument! Sometimes he strikes without rattling at all.

Inside, Sykes heard nothing until he knocked a pot lid off the stove while trying to reach the match safe in the dark. He had emptied his pockets at Bertha's.

The snake seemed to wake up under the stove and Sykes made a quick leap into the bedroom. In spite of the gin he had had, his head was clearing now.

"Mah Gawd!" he chattered. "ef Ah could only strack uh light!"

100   The rattling ceased for a moment as he stood paralyzed. He waited. It seemed that the snake waited also.

"Oh, fuh de light! Ah thought he'd be too sick"—Sykes was muttering to himself when the whirr began again, closer, right underfoot this time. Long before this, Sykes' ability to think had been flattened down to primitive instinct and he leaped—onto the bed.

Outside Delia heard a cry that might have come from a maddened chimpanzee, a stricken gorilla. All the terror, all the horror, all the rage that man possibly could express, without a recognizable human sound.

A tremendous stir inside there, another series of animal screams, the intermittent whirr of the reptile. The shade torn violently down from the window, letting in the red dawn, a huge brown hand seizing the window stick, great dull blows upon the wooden floor punctuating the gibberish of sound long after the rattle of the snake had abruptly subsided. All this Delia could see and hear from her place beneath the window, and it made her ill. She crept over to the four-o'-clocks[7] and stretched herself on the cool earth to recover.

She lay there, "Delia, Delia!" She could hear Sykes calling in a most despairing tone as one who expected no answer. The sun crept on up, and he called. Delia could not move—her legs were gone flabby. She never moved, he called, and the sun kept rising.

105   "Mah Gawd!" She heard him moan. "Mah Gawd fum Heben!" She heard him stumbling about and got up from her flower-bed. The sun was growing warm. As she approached the door she heard him call out hopefully. "Delia, is dat you Ah heah?"

She saw him on his hands and knees as soon as she reached the door. He crept an inch or two toward her—all that he was able, and she saw his horribly swollen neck and his one open eye shining with hope. A surge of pity too strong to support bore her away from that eye that must, could not, fail to see the tubs. He would see the lamp. Orlando with its doctors was too far. She could scarcely reach the Chinaberry tree, where she waited in the growing heat while inside she knew the cold river was creeping up and up to extinguish that eye which must know by now that she knew.

[1926]

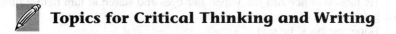

Topics for Critical Thinking and Writing

1. Summarize the relationship of Delia and Sykes before the time of the story.
2. How do the men on Joe Clark's porch further your understanding of Delia and Sykes and of the relationship between the two?

---

[7]flowers that open in the late afternoon

3. To what extent is Delia responsible for Sykes's death? To what extent is Sykes responsible? Do you think that Delia's action (or inaction) at the end of the story is immoral? Why, or why not?

4. To what extent does the relationship between African-Americans and whites play a role in the lives of the characters in "Sweat" and in the outcome of the story?

5. Are the African-Americans in "Sweat" portrayed stereotypically, as some of Hurston's critics charged? (See the biographical note, page 567.) How, on the evidence available in this story, might Hurston's fiction be defended from that charge?

RAYMOND CARVER

Raymond Carver (1938–88) was born in Clatskanie, a logging town in Oregon. In 1963 he graduated from Humboldt State College in northern California and then did further study at the University of Iowa.

His early years were not easy—he married while still in college, divorced a little later, and sometimes suffered from alcoholism. In his last years he found domestic happiness, but he died of cancer at the age of 50.

As a young man he wrote poetry while working at odd jobs (janitor, deliveryman, etc.); later he turned to fiction, though be continued to write poetry. Most of his fiction is of a sort called "minimalist," narrating in a spare, understated style stories about bewildered and sometimes exhausted men and women. His later work, by his own admission, was "larger."

Popular Mechanics

Early that day the weather turned and the snow was melting into dirty water. Streaks of it ran down from the little shoulder-high window that faced the backyard. Cars slushed by on the street outside, where it was getting dark. But it was getting dark on the inside too.

He was in the bedroom pushing clothes into a suitcase when she came to the door.

I'm glad you're leaving! I'm glad you're leaving! she said. Do you hear?

He kept on putting his things into the suitcase.

5   Son of a bitch! I'm so glad you're leaving! She began to cry. You can't even look me in the face, can you?

Then she noticed the baby's picture on the bed and picked it up.

He looked at her and she wiped her eyes and stared at him before turning and going back to the living room.

Bring that back, he said.

Just get your things and get out, she said.

10   He did not answer. He fastened the suitcase, put on his coat, looked around the bedroom before turning off the light. Then he went out to the living room.

She stood in the doorway of the little kitchen, holding the baby.

I want the baby, he said.

Are you crazy?

No, but I want the baby. I'll get someone to come by for his things.

15   You're not touching this baby, she said.

The baby had begun to cry and she uncovered the blanket from around his head.

Oh, oh, she said, looking at the baby.

He moved toward her.

For God's sake! she said. She took a step back into the kitchen.

20 I want the baby.

Get out of here!

She turned and tried to hold the baby over in a corner behind the stove.

But he came up. He reached across the stove and tightened his hands on the baby.

Let go of him, he said.

25 Get away, get away! she cried.

The baby was red-faced and screaming. In the scuffle they knocked down a flowerpot that hung behind the stove.

He crowded her into the wall then, trying to break her grip. He held on to the baby and pushed with all his weight.

Let go of him, he said.

Don't, she said. You're hurting the baby, she said.

30 I'm not hurting the baby, he said.

The kitchen window gave no light. In the near-dark he worked on her fisted fingers with one hand and with the other hand he gripped the screaming baby up under an arm near the shoulder.

She felt her fingers being forced open. She felt the baby going from her.

No! she screamed just as her hands came loose.

She would have it, this baby. She grabbed for the baby's other arm. She caught the baby around the wrist and leaned back.

35 But he would not let go. He felt the baby slipping out of his hands and he pulled back very hard.

In this manner, the issue was decided.

[1981]

 ## Topics for Critical Thinking and Writing

1. Some readers object to "minimalist" writings (briefly defined in the biographical note on p. 576) on the grounds that the stories (1) lack ideas, (2) do not describe the characters in depth, and (3) are written in a drab style. Does Carver's story seem to you to suffer from these alleged weaknesses? Explain.

2. Here is the first paragraph of the story:

> Early that day the weather turned and the snow was melting into dirty water. Streaks of it ran down from the little shoulder-high window that faced the backyard. Cars slushed by on the street outside, where it was getting dark. But it was getting dark on the inside too.

When Carver first published the story, the paragraph was slightly different. Here is the earlier version:

> During the day the sun had come out and the snow melted into dirty water. Streaks of water ran down from the little, shoulder-high

window that faced the back yard. Cars slushed by on the street outside. It was getting dark, outside and inside.

How would you account for the changes?
3. The last line—"In this manner, the issue was decided"—in the original version ran thus:

In this manner they decided the issue.

Do you consider the small change an improvement? Why, or why not?

 RITA DOVE

*Rita Dove (b. 1952) is chiefly known as a poet, but she has also pub-
lished short stories and, most recently, a novel. She was appointed the
nation's poet laureate for 1993–94.*

Second-Hand Man

Virginia couldn't stand it when someone tried to shorten her name—like
Ginny, for example. But James Evans didn't. He set his twelve-string guitar
down real slow.
    "Miss Virginia," he said, "you're a fine piece of woman."
    Seemed he'd been asking around. Knew everything about her. Knew she
was bold and proud and didn't cotton to no silly niggers. Vir-gin-ee-a he said,
nice and slow. Almost Russian, the way he said it. Right then and there she knew
this man was for her.
    He courted her just inside a year, came by nearly every day. First she would-
n't see him for more than half an hour at a time. She'd send him away; he knew
better than to try to force her. Another fellow did that once—kept coming by
when she said she had other things to do. She told him he do it once more, she'd
be waiting at the door with a pot of scalding water to teach him some manners.
Did, too. Fool didn't believe her—she had the pot waiting on the stove and
when he came up those stairs, she was standing in the door. He took one look at
her face and turned and ran. He was lucky those steps were so steep. She only
got a little piece of his pant leg.
5   No, James knew his stuff. He'd come on time and stay till she told him he
needed to go.
    She'd met him out at Summit Beach one day. In the Twenties, that was the
place to go on hot summer days! Clean yellow sand all around the lake, and an
amusement park that ran from morning to midnight. She went there with a couple of girl friends. They were younger than her and a little silly. But they were
sweet. Virginia was nineteen then. "High time," everyone used to say to her, but
she'd just lift her head and go on about her business. She weren't going to marry
just any old Negro. He had to be perfect.
    There was a man who was chasing her around about that time, too. Tall dark
Negro—Sterling Williams was his name. Pretty as a panther. Married, he was.

Least that's what everyone said. Left a wife in Washington, D.C. A little crazy, the wife—poor Sterling was trying to get a divorce.

Well, Sterling was at Summit Beach that day, too. He followed Virginia around, trying to buy her root beer. Everybody loved root beer that summer. Root beer and vanilla ice cream—the Boston Cooler. But she wouldn't pay him no mind. People said she was crazy—Sterling was the best catch in Akron, they said.

"Not for me," Virginia said. "I don't want no second-hand man."

10   But Sterling wouldn't give up. He kept buying root beers and having to drink them himself.

Then she saw James. He'd just come up from Tennessee, working his way up on the riverboats. Folks said his best friend had been lynched down there and he turned his back on the town and said he was never coming back. Well, when she saw this cute little man in a straw hat and a twelve-string guitar under his arm, she got a little flustered. Her girlfriends whispered around to find out who he was, but she acted like she didn't even see him.

He was the hit of Summit Beach. Played that twelve-string guitar like a devil. They'd take off their shoes and sit on the beach toward evening. All the girls loved James. "Oh, Jimmy," they'd squeal, "play us a *loooove* song!" He'd laugh and pick out a tune:

> I'll give you a dollar if you'll come out tonight
> If you'll come out tonight,
> If you'll come out tonight.
> I'll give you a dollar if you'll come out tonight
> And dance by the light of the moon.

Then the girls would giggle. "Jimmy," they screamed, "you outta be 'shamed of yourself!" He'd sing the second verse then:

> I danced with a girl with a hole in her stockin',
> And her heel kep 'a-rockin',
> And her heel kep 'a-rockin';
> I danced with a girl with a hole in her stockin,'
> And we danced by the light of the moon.

Then they'd all priss and preen their feathers and wonder which would be best—to be in fancy clothes and go on being courted by these dull factory fellows, or to have a hole in their stockings and dance with James.

15   Virginia never danced. She sat a bit off to one side and watched them make fools of themselves.

Then one night near season's end, they were all sitting down by the water, and everyone had on sweaters and was in a foul mood because the cold weather was coming and there wouldn't be no more parties. Someone said something about hating having the good times end, and James struck up a nice and easy tune, looking across the fire straight at Virginia:

> As I was lumb'ring down de street,
> Down de street, down de street,
> A han some gal I chanced to meet,
> Oh, she was fair to view!
>
> I'd like to make dat gal my wife,
> Gal my wife, gal my wife.

> I'd be happy all my life
> If I had her by me.

She knew he was the man. She'd known it a long while, but she was just bid-ing her time. He called on her the next day. She said she was busy canning peaches. He came back the day after. They sat on the porch and watched the people go by. He didn't talk much, except to say her name like that: "Vir-gin-ee-a," he said, "you're a mighty fine woman."

She sent him home a little after that. He showed up again a week later. She was angry at him and told him she didn't have time for playing around. But he'd brought his twelve-string guitar, and he said he'd been practicing all week just to play a couple of songs for her. She let him in then and made him sit on the stool while she sat on the porch swing. He sang the first song. It was a floor thumper.

> There is a gal in our town,
> She wears a yellow striped gown,
> And when she walks the streets aroun',
> The hollow of her foot makes a hole in the ground.
>
> Ol' folks, young folks, cl'ar the kitchen,
> Ol' folks, young folks, cl'ar the kitchen,
> Ol' Virginny never tire.

20   She got a little mad then, but she knew he was baiting her. Seeing how much she would take. She knew he wasn't singing about her, and she'd already heard how he said her name. It was time to let the dog in out of the rain, even if he shook his wet all over the floor. So she leaned back and put her hands on her hips, real slow.

"I just *know* you ain't singing about me."

"Virginia," he replied, with a grin would've put Rudolph Valentino to shame, "I'd *never* sing about you that way."

He pulled a yellow scarf out of his trouser pocket. Like melted butter it was, with fringes.

"I saw it yesterday and thought how nice it would look against your skin," he said.

25   That was the first present she ever accepted from a man. Then he sang his other song:

> I'm coming, I'm coming!
> Virginia, I'm coming to stay.
> Don't hold it agin' me
> For running away.
>
> And if I can win ya,
> I'll never more roam,
> I'm coming Virginia,
> My dixie land home.

She was gone for him. Not like those girls on the beach: she had enough sense left to crack a joke or two. "You saying I look like the state of Virginia?" she asked, and he laughed. But she was gone.

She didn't let him know it, though, not for a long while. Even when he asked her to marry him, eight months later, he was trembling and thought she just might refuse out of some woman's whim. No, he courted her proper. Every day for a little while. They'd sit on the porch until it got too cold and then they'd sit in the parlor with two or three bright lamps on. Her mother and father were glad Virginia'd found a beau, but they weren't taking any chances. Everything had to be proper.

He got down, all trembly, on one knee and asked her to be his wife. She said yes. There's a point when all this dignity and stuff get in the way of Destiny. He kept on trembling; he didn't believe her.

"What?" he said.

30   "I said yes," Virginia answered. She was starting to get angry. Then he saw that she meant it, and he went into the other room to ask her father for her hand in marriage.

But people are too curious for their own good, and there's some things they never need to know, but they're going to find them out one way or the other. James had come all the way up from Tennessee and that should have been far enough, but he couldn't hide that snake any more. It just crawled out from under the rock when it was good and ready.

The snake was Jeremiah Morgan. Some fellows from Akron had gone off for work on the riverboats, and some of these fellows had heard about James. That twelve-string guitar and straw hat of his had made him pretty popular. So, story got to town that James had a baby somewhere. And joined up to this baby—but long dead and buried—was a wife.

Virginia had been married six months when she found out from sweettalking, side-stepping Jeremiah Morgan who never liked her no-how after she'd laid his soul to rest one night when he'd taken her home from a dance. (She always carried a brick in her purse—no man could get the best of her!)

Jeremiah must have been the happiest man in Akron the day he found out. He found it out later than most people—things like that have a way of circulating first among those who know how to keep it from spreading to the wrong folks—then when the gossip's gotten to everyone else, it's handed over to the one who knows what to do with it.

35   "Ask that husband of your'n what else he left in Tennessee besides his best friend," was all Jeremiah said at first.

No no-good Negro like Jeremiah Morgan could make Virginia beg for information. She wouldn't bite.

"I ain't got no need for asking my husband nothing," she said, and walked away. She was going to choir practice.

He stood where he was, yelled after her like any old common person. "Mrs. Evans always talking about being Number 1! It looks like she's Number 2 after all."

Her ears burned from the shame of it. She went on to choir practice and sang her prettiest; and straight when she was back home she asked:

40   "What's all this number two business?"

James broke down and told her the whole story—how he'd been married before, when he was seventeen, and his wife dying in childbirth and the child not quite right because of being blue when it was born. And how when his friend was strung up he saw no reason for staying. And how when he met Virginia, he found out pretty quick what she'd done to Sterling Williams and that she'd never have no second-hand man, and he had to have her, so he never said a word about his past.

She took off her coat and hung it in the front closet. She unpinned her hat and set it in its box on the shelf. She reached in the back of the closet and brought out his hunting rifle and the box of bullets. She didn't see no way out but to shoot him.

"Put that down!" he shouted. "I love you!"

"You were right not to tell me," she said, "because I sure as sin wouldn't have married you. I don't want you now."

45   "Virginia!" he said. He was real scared. "How can you shoot me down like this?"

No, she couldn't shoot him when he stood there looking at her with those sweet brown eyes, telling her how much he loved her.

"You have to sleep sometime," she said, and sat down to wait.

He didn't sleep for three nights. He knew she meant business. She sat up in their best chair with the rifle across her lap, but he wouldn't sleep. He sat at the table and told her over and over that he loved her and he hadn't known what else to do at the time.

"When I get through killing you," she told him. "I'm going to write to Tennessee and have them send that baby up here. It won't do, farming a child out to any relative with an extra plate."

50   She held onto that rifle. Not that he would have taken it from her—not that that would've saved him. No, the only thing would've saved him was running away. But he wouldn't run either.

Sitting there, Virginia had lots of time to think. He was afraid of what she might do, but he wouldn't leave her, either. Some of what he was saying began to sink in. He had lied, but that was the only way to get her—she could see the reasoning behind that. And except for that, he was perfect. It was hardly like having a wife before at all. And the baby—anyone could see the marriage wasn't meant to be anyway.

On the third day about midnight, she laid down the rifle.

"You will join the choir and settle down instead of plucking on that guitar anytime anyone drop a hat," she said. "And we will write to your aunt in Tennessee and have that child sent up here." Then she put the rifle back in the closet.

The child never made it up to Ohio—it had died a month before Jeremiah ever opened his mouth. That hit James hard. He thought it was his fault and all, but Virginia made him see the child was sick and was probably better off with its Maker than it would be living out half a life.

55   James made a good tenor in the choir. The next spring, Virginia had her first baby and they decided to name her Belle. That's French for beautiful. And she was, too.

[1985]

✐ Topics for Critical Thinking and Writing

1. From what point of view is the story told? How would you characterize the narrator?

2. If you found some passages that amused you, or that especially amused you, specify two or three and explain *why* you found them amusing.

POETRY

ANONYMOUS
Western Wind

Westron wind, when will thou blow?
The small rain down can rain.
Christ, that my love were in my arms,
And I in my bed again.

[c. 1500]

Topics for Critical Thinking and Writing

1. In "Western Wind," what do you think is the tone of the speaker's voice in the first two lines? Angry? Impatient? Supplicating? Be as precise as possible. What is the tone in the next two lines?
2. In England, the west wind, warmed by the Gulf Stream, rises in the spring. What associations link the wind and rain of lines 1 and 2 with lines 3 and 4?
3. Ought we to have been told why the lovers are separated? Explain.

CHRISTOPHER MARLOWE

Christopher Marlowe (1564–93), English poet and playwright, was born in the same year as Shakespeare. An early death, in a tavern brawl, cut short what might have been a brilliant career.

Marlowe's "Come Live with Me" is a pastoral poem: that is, it depicts shepherds and shepherdesses in an idyllic, timeless setting. This poem engendered many imitations and replies, two of which we reprint after Marlowe's.

Come Live with Me and Be My Love

Come live with me and be my love,
And we will all the pleasures prove,
That hills and valleys, dales and fields,
And all the craggy mountains yields.   4

There we will sit upon the rocks,
And see the shepherds feed their flocks,
By shallow rivers to whose falls
Melodious birds sing madrigals.   8

And I will make thee beds of roses
With a thousand fragrant posies,
A cap of flowers, and a kirtle
Embroidered all with leaves of myrtle;   12

A gown made of the finest wool
Which from our pretty lambs we pull;

Fair lined slippers for the cold,
With buckles of the purest gold; 16

A belt of straw and ivy buds,
With coral clasps and amber studs:
And if these pleasures may thee move,
Come live with me and be my love. 20

The shepherds' swains shall dance and sing
For thy delight each May morning:
If these delights thy mind may move,
Then live with me and be my love. 24

[1599-1600]

Topic for Critical Thinking and Writing

Read the poem two or three times, preferably aloud. Of course Marlowe's poem is not to be taken seriously as a picture of the pastoral (shepherd) life, but if you have enjoyed the poem, exactly what have you enjoyed?

SIR WALTER RALEIGH

Walter Raleigh (1552–1618) is known chiefly as a soldier and a colonizer—he was the founder of the settlement in Virginia, and he introduced tobacco into Europe—but in his own day he was known also as a poet.

The Nymph's Reply to the Shepherd

If all the world and love were young,
And truth in every shepherd's tongue,
These pretty pleasures might me move,
To live with thee, and be thy love. 4

Time drives the flocks from field to fold,
When rivers rage, and rocks grow cold,
And Philomel° becometh dumb,
The rest complains of cares to come. 8

The flowers do fade, and wanton fields,
To wayward winter reckoning yields,
A honey tongue, a heart of gall,
Is fancy's spring, but sorrow's fall. 12

Thy gowns, thy shoes, thy beds of roses,
Thy cap, thy kirtle, and thy posies,

⁷**Philomel** in Greek mythology, Philomela was a beautiful woman who was raped and later transformed into a chattering sparrow, but in most Roman versions she is transformed into the nightingale, noted for its beautiful song

Soon break, soon wither, soon forgotten:
In folly ripe, in reason rotten.   16

Thy belt of straw and ivy buds,
Thy coral clasps and amber studs,
All these in me no means can move,
To come to thee, and be thy love.   20

But could youth last, and love still breed,
Had joys no date, nor age no need,
Then these delights my mind might move,
To live with thee and be thy love.   24

[c. 1600]

Topics for Critical Thinking and Writing

1. What is the season in Marlowe's poem? What season(s) does Raleigh envision?
2. Some readers find puns in line 12, in "fancy's spring, but sorrow's fall." How do you paraphrase and interpret the line?
3. How would you describe the tone of the final stanza?
4. Now that you have read Raleigh's poem, reread Marlowe's. Do you now, in the context of Raleigh's poem, enjoy Marlowe's more than before, or less? Why?

JOHN DONNE

John Donne (1572–1631) wrote religious poetry as well as love poetry. In the following lyric, he alters Marlowe's pastoral setting to a setting involving people engaged in fishing. The poem thus belongs to a type called piscatory lyric (Latin piscis, "fish"). For a fuller biographical note, and a religious poem, see page 1268.

The Bait

Come live with me, and be my love,
And we will some new pleasures prove
Of golden sands, and crystal brooks,
With silken lines, and silver hooks.   4

There will the river whispering run
Warmed by thy eyes, more than the Sun.
And there th'enamored fish will stay,
Begging themselves they may betray.   8

When thou wilt swim in that live bath,
Each fish, which every channel hath,
Will amorously to thee swim,
Gladder to catch thee, than thou him.   12

If thou, to be so seen, beest loath,
By Sun, or Moon, thou darknest both,

And if my self have leave to see,
I need not their light, having thee.   16

Let others freeze with angling reeds,
And cut their legs, with shells and weeds,
Or treacherously poor fish beset,
With strangling snare, or windowy net: 20

Let coarse bold hands, from slimy nest
The bedded fish in banks out-wrest,
Or curious traitors, sleavesilk flies
Bewitch poor fishes' wandring eyes.   24

For thee, thou needst no such deceit,
For thou thy self art thine own bait;
That fish, that is not catched thereby,
Alas, is wiser far than I.   28

[1633]

 ## Topics for Critical Thinking and Writing

1. In Donne's first stanza, which words especially indicate that we are (as in Marlowe's poem) in an idealized world?
2. Which words later in Donne's poem indicate what (for Donne) the real world of fishing is?
3. Paraphrase the last stanza, making it as clear as possible.

WILLIAM SHAKESPEARE

Shakespeare (1564–1616) was born into a middle-class family in Stratford-upon-Avon. Although we have a fair number of records about his life—documents concerning marriage, the birth of children, the purchase of property, and so forth—it is not known exactly why and when he turned to the theater. What we do know, however, is important. He was an actor and a shareholder in a playhouse and he did write the plays that are attributed to him. The dates of some of the plays can be set precisely, but the dates of some others can be only roughly set. Hamlet was probably written between 1600 and 1601. Most of Shakespeare's 154 sonnets were probably written in the late 1590s, but they were not published until 1609.

Sonnet 29

When, in disgrace with Fortune and men's eyes,
I all alone beweep my outcast state,
And trouble deaf heaven with my bootless° cries,
And look upon myself and curse my fate,
Wishing me like to one more rich in hope,   4

---

³**bootless** useless

Featured like him, like him° with friends possessed,
Desiring this man's art and that man's scope,
With what I most enjoy contented least;   8
Yet in these thoughts myself almost despising,
Haply° I think on thee, and then my state,
Like to the lark at break of day arising
From sullen earth, sings hymns at heaven's gate;   12
   For thy sweet love rememb'red such wealth brings,
   That then I scorn to change my state with kings.

[c. 1600]

⁶**like him, like him** like a second man, like a third man   ¹⁰**Haply** perchance

 ## Topics for Critical Thinking and Writing

1. Paraphrase the first eight lines. Then, in a sentence, summarize the speaker's state of mind to this point in the poem.
2. Summarize the speaker's state of mind in lines 9–12. What does "sullen earth" (line 12) suggest to you?
3. Notice that every line in the poem except line 11 ends with a comma or semicolon, indicating a pause. How does the lack of punctuation at the end of line 11 affect your reading of this line and your understanding of the speaker's emotion?
4. In the last two lines of a sonnet Shakespeare often summarizes the preceding lines. In this sonnet, how does the *structure* (the organization) of the summary differ from that of the statement in the first twelve lines? Why? (Try reading the last lines as if they were reversed. Thus:

   For then I scorn to change my state with kings.
   Since thy sweet love rememb'red such wealth brings.

Which version do you like better? Why?
5. The "thee" of this poem is almost certainly a man, not a woman. Is the "love" of the poem erotic love, or can it be taken as something like brotherly love or even as loving-kindness?
6. Write a paragraph (or a sonnet) describing how thinking of someone you love—or hate—changes your mood.

Sonnet 116

Let me not to the marriage of true minds
Admit impediments; love is not love
Which alters when it alteration finds,
Or bends with the remover to remove.   4
O, no, it is an ever-fixèd mark°
That looks on tempests and is never shaken;

⁵**ever-fixèd mark** seamark, guide to mariners

It is the star° to every wand'ring bark,
Whose worth's unknown, although his height be taken. 8
Love's not Time's fool,° though rosy lips and cheeks
Within his bending sickle's compass° come;
Love alters not with his° brief hours and weeks
But bears° it out even to the edge of doom.° 12
    If this be error and upon° me proved,
    I never writ, nor no man ever loved.

[c. 1600]

⁷**the star** the North Star ⁹**fool** plaything ¹⁰**compass** range, circle ¹¹**his** Time's
¹²**bears** survives **doom** Judgment Day ¹³**upon** against

 ## Topics for Critical Thinking and Writing

1. Paraphrase (that is, put into your own words) "Let me not to the marriage of true minds / Admit impediments." Is there more than one appropriate meaning of "Admit"?
2. Notice that the poem celebrates "the marriage of true minds," not bodies. In a sentence or two, using only your own words, summarize Shakespeare's idea of the nature of such love, both what it is and what it is not.
3. Paraphrase lines 13–14. What is the speaker's tone here? Would you say that the tone is different from the tone in the rest of the poem?
4. Write a paragraph or a poem defining either love or hate. Or see if you can find such a definition in a popular song. Bring the lyrics to class.

 # JOHN DONNE

John Donne (1572–1631) was born into a Roman Catholic family in England, but in the 1590s he abandoned that faith. In 1615 he became an Anglican priest and soon was known as a great preacher. A hundred and sixty of his sermons survive, including one with the famous line "No man is an island, entire of itself; every man is a piece of the continent, a part of the main; if a clod be washed away by the sea, Europe is the less . . . ; and therefore never send to know for whom the bell tolls; it tolls for thee." From 1621 until his death he was dean of St. Paul's Cathedral in London. His love poems (often bawdy and cynical) are said to be his early work, and his "Holy Sonnets" (among the greatest religious poems written in English) his later work.

A Valediction: Forbidding Mourning

As virtuous men pass mildly away,
    And whisper to their souls, to go,
Whilst some of their sad friends do say,
    "The breath goes now," and some say, "No": 4

So let us melt, and make no noise.
    No tear-floods, nor sigh-tempests move.

'Twere profanation of our joys
　　To tell the laity our love.   8

Moving of the earth° brings harms and fears,
　　Men reckon what it did and meant;
But trepidation of the spheres,
　　Though greater far, is innocent.°   12

Dull sublunary° lovers' love
　　(Whose soul is sense) cannot admit
Absence, because it doth remove
　　Those things which elemented it.   16

But we, by a love so much refined
　　That our selves know not what it is,
Inter-assurèd of the mind,
　　Care less, eyes, lips, and hands to miss.   20

Our two souls therefore, which are one,
　　Though I must go, endure not yet
A breach, but an expansion,
　　Like gold to airy thinness beat.   24

If they be two, they are two so
　　As stiff twin compasses° are two:
Thy soul, the fixed foot, makes no show
　　To move, but doth, if the other do.   28

And though it in the center sit,
　　Yet when the other far doth roam,
It leans, and hearkens after it,
　　And grows erect, as that comes home.   32

Such wilt thou be to me, who must
　　Like the other foot, obliquely run:
Thy firmness makes my circle just,
　　And makes me end where I begun.   36

[1611]

 ## Topics for Critical Thinking and Writing

1. The first stanza describes the death of "virtuous men." To what is their death compared in the second stanza?
2. Who is the speaker of this poem? To whom does he speak and what is the occasion? Explain the title.
3. What is the meaning of "laity" in line 8? What does it imply about the speaker and his beloved?

---

[9]**Moving of the earth** an earthquake　[11-12]**But trepidation . . . innocent** But the movement of the heavenly spheres (in Ptolemaic astronomy), though far greater, is harmless　[13]**sublunary** under the moon, i.e., earthly　[26]**compasses** i.e., a carpenter's compass

4. In the fourth stanza the speaker contrasts the love of "dull sublunary lovers" (i.e., ordinary mortals) with the love he and his beloved share. What is the difference?
5. In the figure of the carpenter's or draftsperson's compass (lines 25–36) the speaker offers reasons—some stated clearly, some not so clearly—why he will end where he began. In 250 words explain these reasons.
6. In line 35 Donne speaks of his voyage as a "circle." Explain in a paragraph why the circle is traditionally a symbol of perfection.
7. Write a farewell note—or poem—to someone you love (or hate).

 **ANDREW MARVELL**

Born in 1621 near Hull in England, Marvell attended Trinity College, Cambridge, and graduated in 1638. During the Civil War he was tutor to the daughter of Sir Thomas Fairfax in Yorkshire at Nun Appleton House, where most of his best-known poems were written. In 1657 he was appointed assistant to John Milton, the Latin Secretary for the Commonwealth. After the Restoration of the monarchy in 1659 until his death, Marvell represented Hull as a member of parliament. Most of his poems were not published until after his death in 1678.

To His Coy Mistress

Had we but world enough, and time.
This coyness, lady, were no crime.
We would sit down, and think which way
To walk, and pass our long love's day.
Thou by the Indian Ganges' side   5
Should'st rubies find: I by the tide
Of Humber° would complain.° I would
Love you ten years before the Flood,
And you should, if you please, refuse
Till the conversion of the Jews.   10
My vegetable° love should grow
Vaster than empires, and more slow.
An hundred years should go to praise
Thine eyes, and on thy forehead gaze:
Two hundred to adore each breast: 15
But thirty thousand to the rest.
An age at least to every part,
And the last age should show your heart.
For, lady, you deserve this state,
Nor would I love at lower rate,   20
    But at my back I always hear
Time's winged chariot hurrying near;
And yonder all before us lie

---

⁷**Humber** river in England   **complain** write love poems   ¹¹**vegetable** slowly growing

Deserts of vast eternity.
Thy beauty shall no more be found,   25
Nor in thy marble vault shall sound
My echoing song; then worms shall try
That long preserved virginity,
And your quaint honor turn to dust,
And into ashes all my lust.   30
The grave's a fine and private place,
But none, I think, do there embrace.
      Now therefore, while the youthful hue
Sits on thy skin like morning dew,
And while thy willing soul transpires   35
At every pore with instant fires,
Now let us sport us while we may;
And now, like am'rous birds of prey,
Rather at once our time devour,
Than languish in his slow-chapt° power,   40
Let us roll all our strength, and all
Our sweetness, up into one ball;
And tear our pleasures with rough strife
Thorough° the iron gates of life.
Thus, though we cannot make our sun   45
Stand still, yet we will make him run.

[1641]

---

⁴⁰**slow-chapt** slowly devouring   ⁴⁴**thorough** through

Topics for Critical Thinking and Writing

1. What does "coy" mean in the title, and "coyness" in line 2?
2. Do you think that the speaker's claims in lines 1–20 are so inflated that we detect behind them a playfully ironic tone? Explain. Why does the speaker say in line 8 that he would love "ten years before the Flood," rather than merely "since the Flood"?
3. What do you make of lines 21–24? Why is time behind the speaker, and eternity in front of him? Is this "eternity" the same as the period discussed in lines 1–20? Discuss the change in the speaker's tone after line 20.

 WILLIAM BLAKE

William Blake (1757–1827), was born in London and at fourteen was apprenticed for seven years to an engraver. A Christian visionary poet, he made his living by giving drawing lessons and by illustrating books, including his own Songs of Innocence *(1789) and* Songs of Experience *(1794). These two books represent, he said, "two contrary states of the human soul." In 1809 Blake exhibited his art, but the show was*

"The Garden of Love" by William Blake, from *Songs of Experience*. (By permission of the Provost and Fellows of King's College, Cambridge.)

a failure. Not until he was in his sixties, when he stopped writing poetry, did he achieve any public recognition—and then it was as a painter.

The Garden of Love

I went to the Garden of Love,
And saw what I never had seen:
A Chapel was built in the midst,
Where I used to play on the green.

And the gates of this Chapel were shut,
And "Thou shalt not" writ over the door;

4

So I turn'd to the Garden of Love,
That so many sweet flowers bore,   8

And I saw it was filled with graves,
And tomb-stones where flowers should be;
And Priests in black gowns were walking their rounds,
And binding with briars my joys & desires.   12

                                                                   [1794]

Topics for Critical Thinking and Writing

1. What is the speaker's mood as he surveys "the Garden of Love"? What does he report?
2. Does the form of the poem contribute to the speaker's mood? Try taking out the *ands* wherever you can, consistent with the meaning of the sentences. There is a change in effect, but can you say what it is?
3. In a brief essay (500 words) compare Blake's "The Echoing Green" (p. 892) with "The Garden of Love."

A Poison Tree

I was angry with my friend:
I told my wrath, my wrath did end.
I was angry with my foe:
I told it not, my wrath did grow.   4

And I watered it in fears,
Night and morning with my tears:
And I sunnèd it with smiles,
And with soft deceitful wiles.   8

And it grew both day and night,
Till it bore an apple bright.
And my foe beheld it shine,
And he knew that it was mine.   12

And into my garden stole
When the night had veiled the pole:
In the morning glad I see
My foe outstretched beneath the tree.   16

                                                                   [1794]

Topics for Critical Thinking and Writing

1. In the first stanza, the speaker describes two actions. What is the difference between them? Does the poem indicate that we should choose one action over the other?
2. What reaction do you have to the speaker in stanza 2?

3. In stanzas 3 and 4, what does the "foe" do? Paraphrase line 14.
4. The poem ends, "In the morning glad I see / My foe outstretched beneath the tree." Does the reader share this gladness to any degree? Explain.
5. Like many of Blake's other poems, this one has a childlike tone. Does the tone enrich or does it impoverish the poem? Why?

ROBERT BROWNING

Born in a suburb of London into a middle-class family, Browning (1812–89) was educated primarily at home, where he read widely. For a while he wrote for the English stage, but after marrying Elizabeth Barrett in 1846—she too was a poet—he lived with her in Italy until her death in 1861. He then returned to England and settled in London with their son. Regarded as one of the most distinguished poets of the Victorian period, he is buried in Westminster Abbey.

Soliloquy of the Spanish Cloister

I

Gr-r-r—there go, my heart's abhorrence!
　　Water your damned flower-pots, do!
If hate killed men, Brother Lawrence,
　　God's blood, would not mine kill you!　　　　4
What? your myrtle-bush wants trimming?
　　Oh, that rose has prior claims—
Needs its leaden vase filled brimming?
　　Hell dry you up with its flames!　　　　8

II

At the meal we sit together:
　　Salve tibi!° I must hear
Wise talk of the kind of weather.
　　Sort of season, time of year:　　　　12
Not a plenteous cork-crop: scarcely
　　Dare we hope oak-galls,° *I doubt:*
What's the Latin name for "parsley"?
　　What's the Greek name for Swine's Snout?　　　　16

III

Whew! We'll have our platter burnished,
　　Laid with care on our own shelf!
With a fire-new spoon we're furnished,
　　And a goblet for ourself,　　　　20

---

¹⁰**Salve tibi!** Hail to thee!　　¹⁴**oak-galls** growths on oak leaves, used in making ink

Rinsed like something sacrificial
    Ere 'tis fit to touch our chaps—
Marked with L for our initial!
    (He-he! There his lily snaps!)   24

IV

Saint, forsooth! While brown Dolores
    Squats outside the Convent bank
With Sanchicha, telling stories,
    Steeping tresses in the tank,   28
Blue-black, lustrous, thick like horsehairs,
    —Can't I see his dead eye glow,
Bright as 'twere a Barbary corsair's?°
    (That is, if he'd let it show!)   32

V

When he finishes refection.°
    Knife and fork he never lays
Cross-wise, to my recollection,
    As do I, in Jesu's praise.
I the Trinity illustrate,   36
    Drinking watered orange-pulp—
In three sips the Arian° frustrate;
    While he drains his at one gulp.   40

VI

Oh, those melons? If he's able
    We're to have a feast! so nice!
One goes to the Abbot's table,
    All of us get each a slice.
How go on your flowers? None double?   44
    Not one fruit-sort can you spy?
Strange! And I, too, at such trouble,
    Keep them close-nipped on the sly!   48

VII

There's a great text in Galatians,°
    Once you trip on it, entails
Twenty-nine distinct damnations,
    One sure, if another fails: 52

---

[31]**Barbary corsair** Berber pirate [33]**refection** dinner [39]**Arian** Arius, a fourth-century heretic, denied the doctrine of the Trinity [49]**Galatians** a book of the New Testament

If I trip him just a-dying,
    Sure of heaven as sure can be,
Spin him around and send him flying
    Off to hell, a Manichee?°   56

VIII

Or, my scrofulous French novel
    On gray paper with blunt type!
Simply glance at it, you grovel
    Hand and foot in Belial's° gripe: 60
If I double down its pages
    At the woeful sixteenth print,°
When he gathers his greengages,°
    Ope a sieve and slip it in't?   64

IX

Or, there's Satan! One might venture
    Pledge one's soul to him, yet leave
Such a flaw in the indenture
    As he'd miss till, past retrieve,   68
Blasted lay that rose-acacia
    We're so proud of!° *Hy, Zy, Hine*° . . .
'St, there's Vespers! *Plena gratiâ*
    Ave, Virgo!° Gr-r-r—you swine!   72

[1839]

⁵⁶**Manichee** a kind of heretic   ⁶⁰**Belial** a devil   ⁶²**sixteenth print** presumably an obscene picture   ⁶³**greengages** yellowish-green plums   ⁶⁵⁻⁷⁰**Or, . . . proud of** The speaker apparently contemplates pledging his own soul to the devil (who in exchange will snare Lawrence) but leaving a loophole so that he can escape the pledge.   ⁷⁰***Hy, Zy, Hine*** the sound of bells (?) an incantation (?)   ⁷¹⁻⁷²***Plena . . . Virgo!*** "Hail, Virgin, full of grace!"

✏ Topics for Critical Thinking and Writing

1. In which lines does the speaker quote or parody Brother Lawrence?
2. In a paragraph or two, set forth your guesses about why the speaker hates Brother Lawrence.
3. In a paragraph, characterize Brother Lawrence.
4. In an essay of about 500 words, characterize the speaker.

 **WALT WHITMAN**

Walt Whitman (1819–92) was born in a farmhouse in rural Long Island, New York, but was brought up in Brooklyn, then an independent city in New York. He attended

public school for a few years (1825–30), apprenticed as a printer in the 1830s, and then worked as a typesetter, journalist, and newspaper editor. In 1855 he published the first edition of a collection of his poems, Leaves of Grass, *a book that he revised and republished throughout the remainder of his life. During the Civil War, he served as a volunteer nurse for the Union army.*

In the third edition of Leaves of Grass *(1860) Whitman added two groups of poems, one called "Children of Adam" and the other (named for an aromatic grass that grows near ponds and swamps) called "Calamus." "Children of Adam" celebrates heterosexual relations, whereas "Calamus" celebrates what Whitman called "manly love." Although the "Calamus" poems seem clearly homosexual, perhaps the very fact that Whitman published them made them seem relatively innocent; in any case, those nineteenth-century critics who condemned Whitman for the sexuality of his writing concentrated on the poems in "Children of Adam."*

We give two poems from the "Calamus" section. Both were originally published in the third edition of Leaves of Grass *(1860), and both were revised into their final forms in the 1867 edition. We give them in the 1867 versions. We also give the manuscript for one of the poems, showing it in its earliest extant versions.*

When I Heard at the Close of the Day

When I heard at the close of the day how my name had been
    receiv'd with plaudits in the capitol, still it was not a happy
    night for me that follow'd,
And else when I carous'd, or when my plans were accomplish'd,
    still I was not happy,
But the day when I rose at dawn from the bed of perfect health,
    refresh'd, singing, inhaling the ripe breath of autumn,
When I saw the full moon in the west grow pale and disappear in
    the morning light,
When I wander'd alone over the beach, and undressing bathed,
    laughing with the cool waters, and saw the sun rise,   5
And when I thought how my dear friend my lover was on his way
    coming, O then I was happy,
O then each breath tasted sweeter, and all that day my food
    nourish'd me more, and the beautiful day pass'd well.
And the next came with equal joy, and with the next at evening
    came my friend,
And that night while all was still I heard the waters roll slowly
    continually up the shores,
I heard the hissing rustle of the liquid and sands as directed to
    me whispering to congratulate me,   10
For the one I love most lay sleeping by me under the same cover
    in the cool night,
In the stillness in the autumn moonbeams his face was inclined
    toward me,
And his arm lay lightly around my breast—and that night I was
    happy.

[1867]

Topics for Critical Thinking and Writing

1. Let's assume that the word *plot*—the gist of what happens—can be applied not only to prose fiction and to plays but also to lyric poems. How would you summarize the plot of this poem?
2. If someone were to ask you why "When I Heard at the Close of the Day" is regarded as a poem rather than as prose arranged to look like a poem, what would you reply?

I Saw in Louisiana a Live-Oak Growing

I saw in Louisiana a live-oak growing,
All alone stood it and the moss hung down from the branches,
Without any companion it grew there uttering joyous leaves of
    dark green,
And its look, rude, unbending, lusty, made me think of myself,
But I wonder'd how it could utter joyous leaves standing alone
    there without its friend near, for I knew I could not,   5
And I broke off a twig with a certain number of leaves upon it,
    and twined around it a little moss,
And brought it away, and I have placed it in sight in my room,
It is not needed to remind me as of my own dear friends,
(For I believe lately I think of little else than of them,)
Yet it remains to me a curious token, it makes me think of manly
    love;   10
For all that, and though the live-oak glistens there in Louisiana
    solitary in a wide flat space,
Uttering joyous leaves all its life without a friend a lover near,
I know very well I could not.

[1867]

Topic for Critical Thinking and Writing

Compare the final version (1867) of the poem with the manuscript version of 1860. Which version do you prefer? Why?

Calamus 20
p. 36↓

II

I saw in Louisiana a
live-oak growing,
All alone stood it, and the
moss hung down from the
branches,
Without any companion it grew
there, glistening out with
joyous leaves of dark green,
And its look, rude, unbending,
lusty, made me think of
myself;
But I wondered how it could
utter joyous leaves, standing
alone there without its friend,
its lover — For I knew I could
not;
And I plucked a twig with
a certain number of leaves
upon it, and twined around
it a little moss, and brought
it away — And I have placed
it in sight in my room,

2

Walt Whitman, "I Saw in Louisiana a Live-Oak Growing," manuscript of 1860. On the
first leaf, in line 3 Whitman deleted "with." On the second leaf, in the third line (line
8 of the printed text) he added, with a caret, "lately." In the sixth line on this leaf he
deleted, "I write these pieces, and name them after it," replacing the deletion with

(continued)

It is not needed to remind
me as of my friends, (for I
believe lately think of little
else than of them,)
Yet it remains to me a
curious token — it makes
me think of manly love;
~~these pieces and name~~
~~them after it~~;
For all that, and though the
live oak
~~tree~~ glistens there in Louisiana, solitary in a wide
flat space, uttering joyous
leaves all its life, without
a friend, a lover, near — I
know very well I could
not.

"it makes me think of manly love." In the next line he deleted "tree" and inserted "live oak." When he reprinted the poem in the 1867 version of *Leaves of Grass,* he made further changes, as you will see if you compare the printed text with this manuscript version. (Walt Whitman Collection, Clifton Waller Barrett Library, Manuscripts Division, University of Virginia Library)

 **CHRISTINA ROSSETTI**

Christina Rossetti (1830–94) was the daughter of an exiled Italian patriot who lived in London and the sister of the poet and painter Dante Gabriel Rossetti. After her father became an invalid, she led an extremely ascetic life, devoting most of her life to doing charitable work. Her first and best-known volume of poetry, Goblin Market and Other Poems, *was published in 1862.*

A Birthday

My heart is like a singing bird
  Whose nest is in a watered shoot;
My heart is like an apple tree
  Whose boughs are bent with thickset fruit;
My heart is like a rainbow shell   5
  That paddles in a halcyon sea;
My heart is gladder than all these
  Because my love is come to me.

Raise me a dais of silk and down;
  Hang it with vair and purple dyes;   10
Carve it in doves and pomegranates,
  And peacocks with a hundred eyes;
Work it in gold and silver grapes,
  In leaves and silver fleurs-de-lys;
Because the birthday of my life   15
  Is come, my love is come to me.

[1857]

🖋 Topics for Critical Thinking and Writing

1. Some of the words that Rossetti uses may strike you as unusual. Look up the words "halcyon," "vair," "pomegranates," and "fleur-de-lys," and explain how each one contributes to the meaning of the poem.
2. Examine the sequence of similes ("My heart is like . . .") in the first six lines. Describe the implications of each simile, both in its own right and as it is related to the other two.
3. This poem as a whole is joyous and uplifting. But shouldn't a really good poem about love also take into account the dangers and difficulties of being in love?

 T. S. ELIOT

Thomas Stearns Eliot (1888–1965) was born into a New England family that had moved to St. Louis. He attended a preparatory school in Massachusetts, then graduated from Harvard and did further study in literature and philosophy in France, Germany, and England. In 1914 he began working for Lloyd's Bank in London, and three years later he published his first book of poems (it included "Prufrock"). In 1925 he joined a publishing firm, and in 1927 he became a British citizen and a member of the Church of England. Much of his later poetry, unlike "The

Love Song of J. Alfred Prufrock," is highly religious. In 1948 Eliot received the Nobel Prize for Literature.

The Love Song of J. Alfred Prufrock

S'io credesse che mia risposta fosse
A persona che mai tornasse al mondo,
Questa fiamma staria senza piu scosse.
Ma perciocche giammai di questo fondo
Non torno vivo alcun. s'i' odo il vero,
Senza tema d'infama ti rispondo.*

Let us go then, you and I,
When the evening is spread out against the sky
Like a patient etherized upon a table;
Let us go, through certain half-deserted streets,
The muttering retreats   5
Of restless nights in one-night cheap hotels
And sawdust restaurants with oyster-shells:
Streets that follow like a tedious argument
Of insidious intent
To lead you to an overwhelming question . . .   10
Oh. do not ask, "What is it?"
Let us go and make our visit.

In the room the women come and go
Talking of Michelangelo.

The yellow fog that rubs its back upon the window-panes,   15
The yellow smoke that rubs its muzzle on the window-panes
Licked its tongue into the corners of the evening,
Lingered upon the pools that stand in drains,
Let fall upon its back the soot that falls from chimneys,
Slipped by the terrace, made a sudden leap,   20
And seeing that it was a soft October night,
Curled once about the house, and fell asleep.

And indeed there will be time
For the yellow smoke that slides along the street,
Rubbing its back upon the window-panes;   25
There will be time, there will be time
To prepare a face to meet the faces that you meet;
There will be time to murder and create,
And time for all the works and days° of hands
That lift and drop a question on your plate;   30
Time for you and time for me,
And time yet for a hundred indecisions,

---

*In Dante's *Inferno* XXVII:61–66, a damned soul who had sought absolution before committing a crime addresses Dante, thinking that his words will never reach the earth: "If I believed that my answer were to a person who could ever return to the world, this flame would no longer quiver. But because no one ever returned from this depth, if what I hear is true without fear of infamy, I answer you." ²⁹**works and days** "Works and Days" is the title of a poem on farm life by Hesiod (eighth century B.C.).

And for a hundred visions and revisions,
Before the taking of a toast and tea.

In the room the women come and go   35
Talking of Michelangelo.

And indeed there will be time
To wonder, "Do I dare?" and, "Do I dare?"
Time to turn back and descend the stair,
With a bald spot in the middle of my hair—   40
[They will say: "How his hair is growing thin!"]
My morning coat, my collar mounting firmly to the chin,
My necktie rich and modest, but asserted by a simple pin—
[They will say: "But how his arms and legs are thin!"]
Do I dare   45
Disturb the universe?
In a minute there is time
For decisions and revisions which a minute will reverse.

For I have known them all already, known them all:—
Have known the evenings, mornings, afternoons,   50
I have measured out my life with coffee spoons;
I know the voices dying with a dying fall°
Beneath the music from a farther room.
    So how should I presume?

And I have known the eyes already, known them all—   55
The eyes that fix you in a formulated phrase,
And when I am formulated, sprawling on a pin,
When I am pinned and wriggling on the wall,
Then how should I begin
To spit out all the butt-ends of my days and ways?   60
    And how should I presume?

And I have known the arms already, known them all—
Arms that are braceleted and white and bare
[But in the lamplight, downed with light brown hair!]

Is it perfume from a dress   65
That makes me so digress?
Arms that lie along a table, or wrap about a shawl.
    And should I then presume?
    And how should I begin?

                          . . . .

Shall I say, I have gone at dusk through narrow streets   70
And watched the smoke that rises from the pipes
Of lonely men in shirt-sleeves, leaning out of windows? . . .

I should have been a pair of ragged claws
Scuttling across the floors of silent seas.

                          . . . .

And the afternoon, the evening, sleeps so peacefully!   75
Smoothed by long fingers,
Asleep . . . tired . . . or it malingers,

⁵²**dying fall** This line echoes Shakespeare's *Twelfth Night* 1.1.4

Stretched on the floor, here beside you and me.
Should I, after tea and cakes and ices,
Have the strength to force the moment to its crisis?   80
But though I have wept and fasted, wept and prayed,
Though I have seen my head [grown slightly bald]
   brought in upon a platter,°
I am no prophet—and here's no great matter;
I have seen the moment of my greatness flicker,
And I have seen the eternal Footman hold my coat, and snicker,   85
And in short, I was afraid.

And would it have been worth it, after all,
After the cups, the marmalade, the tea,
Among the porcelain, among some talk of you and me,
Would it have been worth while,   90
To have bitten off the matter with a smile,
To have squeezed the universe into a ball°
To roll it toward some overwhelming question,
To say: "I am Lazarus,° come from the dead,
Come back to tell you all, I shall tell you all"—   95
If one, settling a pillow by her head,
   Should say: "That is not what I meant at all.
   That is not it, at all."

And would it have been worth it, after all,
Would it have been worth while,   100
After the sunsets and the dooryards and the sprinkled streets,
After the novels, after the teacups, after the skirts that trial along the floor—
And this, and so much more?—
It is impossible to say just what I mean!
But as if a magic lantern threw the nerves in patterns on a screen: 105
Would it have been worth while
If one, settling a pillow or throwing off a shawl,
And turning toward the window, should say:
   "That is not it at all,
   That is not what I meant at all."   110

No! I am not Prince Hamlet, nor was meant to be;
Am an attendant lord, one that will do
To swell a progress, start a scene or two,
Advise the prince; no doubt, an easy tool,
Deferential, glad to be of use,   115
Politic, cautious, and meticulous;
Full of high sentence,° but a bit obtuse;°
At times, indeed, almost ridiculous—
Almost, at times, the Fool.

[81-83]**But . . . platter** These lines allude to John the Baptist (see Matthew 14.1-11)   [92]**To have . . . ball** this line echoes lines 41-42 of Marvell's "To His Coy Mistress" (see p. 590).   [94]**Lazarus** see Luke 16 and John 11   [117]**full of high sentence** see Chaucer's description of the Clerk of Oxford in the *Canterbury Tales*   [112-117]**Am . . . obtuse** these lines allude to Polonius and perhaps other figures in *Hamlet*

I grow old . . . I grow old . . .   120
I shall wear the bottoms of my trousers rolled.

Shall I part my hair behind? Do I dare to eat a peach?
I shall wear white flannel trousers, and walk upon the beach.
I have heard the mermaids singing, each to each.
I do not think that they will sing to me.   125

I have seen them riding seaward on the waves
Combing the white hair of the waves blown back
When the wind blows the water white and black.

We have lingered in the chambers of the sea
By sea-girls wreathed with seaweed red and brown   130
Till human voices wake us, and we drown.

[1910-11]

Topics for Critical Thinking and Writing

1. How does the speaker's name help to characterize him? What suggestions—of class, race, personality—do you find in it? Does the title of this poem strike you as ironic? If so, how or why?
2. What qualities of big-city life are suggested in the poem? How are these qualities linked to the speaker's mood? What other details of the setting—the weather, the time of day—express or reflect his mood? What images do you find especially striking?
3. The speaker's thoughts are represented in a stream-of-consciousness monologue, that is, in what appears to be an unedited flow of thought. Nevertheless, they reveal a story. What is the story?
4. In a paragraph, characterize Prufrock as he might be characterized by one of the women in the poem, and then, in a paragraph or two, offer your own characterization of him.
5. Consider the possibility that the "you" whom Prufrock is addressing is not a listener but is one aspect of Prufrock, and the "I" is another. Given this possibility, in a paragraph characterize the "you," and in another paragraph characterize the "I."
6. Prufrock has gone to a therapist, a psychiatrist, or a member of the clergy for help. Write a 500-word transcript of their session.

EDNA ST. VINCENT MILLAY

Edna St. Vincent Millay (1892–1950) was born in Rockland, Maine. Even as a child she wrote poetry, and by the time she graduated from Vassar College (1917) she had achieved some note as a poet. Millay settled for a while in Greenwich Village, a center of Bohemian activity in New York City, where she wrote, performed in plays, and engaged in feminist causes. In 1923, the year she married, she became the first woman to win the Pulitzer Prize for Poetry. Numerous other awards followed. Though she is best known as a lyric poet—especially as a writer of sonnets—she also wrote memorable political poetry and nature poetry as well as short stories, plays, and a libretto for an opera.

The Spring and the Fall

In the spring of the year, in the spring of the year,
I walked the road beside my dear.
The trees were black where the bark was wet.
I see them yet, in the spring of the year.
He broke me a bough of the blossoming peach   5
That was out of the way and hard to reach.

In the fall of the year, in the fall of the year,
I walked the road beside my dear.
The rooks went up with a raucous trill.
I hear them still, in the fall of the year.   10
He laughed at all I dared to praise,
And broke my heart, in little ways.

Year be springing or year be falling.
The bark will drip and the birds be calling.
There's much that's fine to see and hear   15
In the spring of a year, in the fall of a year.
'Tis not love's going hurts my days,
But that it went in little ways.

[1923]

✎ Topics for Critical Thinking and Writing

1. The first stanza describes the generally happy beginning of a love story. Where do you find the first hint of an unhappy ending?
2. Describe the rhyme scheme of the first stanza, including internal rhymes. Do the second and third stanzas repeat the pattern, or are there some variations? What repetition of sounds other than rhyme do you note?
3. Paraphrase the last two lines. How do you react to them; that is, do you find the conclusion surprising, satisfying (or unsatisfying), recognizable from your own experience, anticlimactic, or what?
4. In two or three paragraphs explain how the imagery of the poem contributes to its meaning.

Love Is Not All: It Is Not Meat nor Drink

Love is not all: it is not meat nor drink
Nor slumber nor a roof against the rain;
Nor yet a floating spar to men that sink
And rise and sink and rise and sink again;
Love can not fill the thickened lung with breath,   4
Nor clean the blood, nor set the fractured bone;

Yet many a man is making friends with death
Even as I speak, for lack of love alone.   8

It well may be that in a difficult hour,
Pinned down by pain and moaning for release,
Or nagged by want past resolution's power,
I might be driven to sell your love for peace,   12
Or trade the memory of this night for food.
It well may be. I do not think I would.

[1931]

Topics for Critical Thinking and Writing

1. "Love Is Not All" is a sonnet. Using your own words, briefly summarize the argument of the octet (the first 8 lines). Next, paraphrase the sestet, line by line. On the whole, does the sestet repeat the idea of the octet, or does it add a new idea? Whom did you imagine to be speaking the octet? What does the sestet add to your knowledge of the speaker and the occasion? (And how did you paraphrase line 11?)
2. The first and last lines of the poem consist of words of one syllable, and both lines have a distinct pause in the middle. Do you imagine the lines to be spoken in the same tone of voice? If not, can you describe the difference and account for it?
3. Lines 7 and 8 appear to mean that the absence of love can be a cause of death. To what degree do you believe that to be true?
4. Would you call "Love Is Not All" a love poem? Why or why not? Describe the kind of person who might include the poem in a love letter or valentine, or who would be happy to receive it. (One of our friends recited it at her wedding. What do you think of that idea?)

ROBERT FROST

Robert Frost (1874–1963) was born in California. After his father's death in 1885, Frost's mother brought the family to New England, where she taught in high schools in Massachusetts and New Hampshire. Frost studied for part of one term at Dartmouth College in New Hampshire, then did odd jobs (including teaching), and from 1897 to 1899 was enrolled as a special student at Harvard. He later farmed in New Hampshire, published a few poems in local newspapers, left the farm and taught again, and in 1912 left for England, where he hoped to achieve more popular success as a writer. By 1915 be had won a considerable reputation, and he returned to the United States, settling on a farm in New Hampshire and cultivating the image of the country-wise farmer-poet. In fact be was well read in the classics, in the Bible, and in English and American literature.

Among Frost's many comments about literature, here are three: "Writing is unboring to the extent that it is dramatic"; "Every poem is ... a figure of the will braving alien entanglements"; and, finally, a poem "begins in delight and ends in wisdom.... It runs a course of lucky events, and ends in a clarification of life—not necessarily a great clarification, such as sects and cults are founded on, but in a momentary stay against confusion."

Page from Frost's notebooks, showing "The Silken Tent." (Printed with the permission of The Poetry/Rare Books Collection, University Libraries, State University of New York at Buffalo.)

The Silken Tent

She is as in a field a silken tent
At midday when a sunny summer breeze
Has dried the dew and all its ropes relent,
So that in guys it gently sways at ease,   4
And its supporting central cedar pole,
That is its pinnacle to heavenward
And signifies the sureness of the soul,
Seems to owe naught to any single cord,   8
But strictly held by none, is loosely bound
By countless silken ties of love and thought
To everything on earth the compass round,
And only by one's going slightly taut   12
In the capriciousness of summer air
Is of the slightest bondage made aware.

[1943]

Topics for Critical Thinking and Writing

1. The second line places the scene at "midday" in "summer." In addition to giving us the concreteness of a setting, do these words help to characterize the woman whom the speaker describes? If so, how?
2. The tent is supported by "guys" (not men, but the cords or "ties" of line 10) and by its "central cedar pole." What does Frost tell us about these ties? What does he tell us about the pole?
3. What do you make of lines 12–14?
4. In a sentence, a paragraph, or a poem, construct a simile that explains a relationship.

 ADRIENNE RICH

 *Adrienne Rich, born in 1929 in Baltimore, was educated at Radcliffe College. Her first book of poems,* A Change of World, *published in 1951 when she was still an undergraduate, was selected by W. H. Auden for the Yale Series of Younger Poets. In 1953 she married an economist and had three sons, but as she indicates in several books, she felt confined by the full-time domestic role that she was expected to play, and the marriage did not last. Much of her poetry is concerned with issues of gender and power. When her ninth book,* Diving into the Wreck *(1973), won the National Book Award, Rich accepted the award not as an individual but on behalf of women everywhere.*

Diving into the Wreck

First having read the book of myths,
and loaded the camera,
and checked the edge of the knife-blade,
I put on
the body-armor of black rubber   5
the absurd flippers
the grave and awkward mask.
I am having to do this
not like Cousteau° with his
assiduous team   10
aboard the sun-flooded schooner
but here alone.

There is a ladder.
The ladder is always there
hanging innocently   15
close to the side of the schooner.
We know what it is for,
we who have used it.

⁹**Cousteau** Jacques Cousteau (1910–1997) French underwater explorer

Otherwise
it's a piece of maritime floss
some sundry equipment.

I go down.
Rung after rung and still
the oxygen immerses me
the blue light
the clear atoms

of our human air.
I go down.
My flippers cripple me,
I crawl like an insect down the ladder
and there is no one
to tell me when the ocean
will begin.

First the air is blue and then
it is bluer and then green and then
black I am blacking out and yet
my mask is powerful
it pumps my blood with power
the sea is another story
the sea is not a question of power
I have to learn alone
to turn my body without force
in the deep element.

And now: it is easy to forget
what I came for
among so many who have always
lived here
swaying their crenellated fans
between the reefs
and besides
you breathe differently down here.

I came to explore the wreck.
The words are purposes.
The words are maps.
I came to see the damage that was done
and the treasures that prevail.
I stroke the beam of my lamp
slowly along the flank
of something more permanent
than fish or weed

the thing I came for:
the wreck and not the story of the wreck
the thing itself and not the myth
the drowned face always staring
toward the sun
the evidence of damage

worn by salt and sway into this threadbare beauty
the ribs of the disaster
curving their assertion
among the tentative haunters.   70

This is the place.
And I am here, the mermaid whose dark hair
streams black, the merman in his armored body
We circle silently
bout the wreck   75
we dive into the hold.
I am she: I am he

whose drowned face sleeps with open eyes
whose breasts still bear the stress
whose silver. copper, vermeil cargo lies   80
obscurely inside barrels
half-wedged and left to rot
we are the half-destroyed instruments
that once held to a course
the water-eaten log   85
the fouled compass

We are, I am, you are
by cowardice or courage
the one who find our way
back to this scene   90
carrying a knife, a camera
a book of myths
in which
our names do not appear.

                                                        [1973]

Novella

Two people in a room, speaking harshly.
One gets up, goes out to walk.
(That is the man.)
The other goes out into the next room
and washes the dishes, cracking one.   5
(That is the woman.)
It gets dark outside.
The children quarrel in the attic.
She has no blood left in her heart.
The man comes back to a dark house.   10
The only light is in the attic.
He has forgotten his key.
He rings at his own door
and hears sobbing on the stairs.
The lights go on in the house.   15
The door closes behind him.

Outside, separate as minds.
the stars too come alight.

[1967]

XI.*

Every peak is a crater. This is the law of volcanoes,
making them eternally and visibly female.
No height without depth, without a burning core,
though our straw soles shred on the hardened lava.
I want to travel with you to every sacred mountain   5
smoking within like the sibyl stooped over her tripod,
I want to reach for your hand as we scale the path,
to feel your arteries glowing in my clasp,
never failing to note the small, jewel-like flower
unfamiliar to us, nameless till we rename her,   10
that clings to the slowly altering rock—
that detail outside ourselves that brings us to ourselves,
was here before us, knew we would come, and sees beyond us.

[1978]

*From *Twenty-One Love Poems*

 ROBERT PACK

Robert Pack, born in New York City in 1929, was educated at Dart-
mouth College and at Columbia University. The author of several books
of poems, he teaches at Middlebury College in Vermont.

The Frog Prince
(A Speculation on Grimm's Fairy Tale)

Imagine the princess' surprise!
Who would have thought a frog's cold frame
Could hold the sweet and gentle body
Of a prince? How can I name   4
The joy she must have felt to learn
His transformation was the wonder
Of her touch—that she too, in
Her way, had been transformed under   8
Those clean sheets? Such powers were
Like nothing she had ever read.

And in the morning when her mother
Came and saw them there in bed,   12
Heard how a frog became a prince;
What was it that her mother said?

[1980]

Topics for Critical Thinking and Writing

1. Fairy-tale characters seldom have characteristics that go beyond the legend they are in. What characteristics does Pack give to the princess? How do you understand "she too, in / Her way, had been transformed" (lines 7–8)?
2. And "What was it that her mother said?"
3. Transform a fairy tale that you know by giving one character or two some realistic traits. Retell the story, or one scene from it.

JOSEPH BRODSKY

The poet and critic Joseph Brodsky (1940–96) was born in St. Petersburg (then Leningrad), Russia in 1940. Because of his resistance to Soviet authority, he was sentenced in the 1960s to a labor camp and later, in 1972, was expelled from the country. He emigrated to the United States, and taught and lectured at a number of colleges and universities. He received the Nobel Prize for literature in 1987 and was named Poet Laureate by the Library of Congress in 1991. His books include a collection of poems, To Urania *(1988), and* Less Than One: Selected Essays *(1986).*

Love Song

If you were drowning, I'd come to the rescue,
    wrap you in my blanket and pour hot tea.
If I were a sheriff, I'd arrest you
    and keep you in the cell under lock and key.   4

If you were a bird, I'd cut a record
    and listen all night long to your high-pitched trill.
If I were a sergeant, you'd be my recruit,
    and boy I can assure you you'd love the drill.   8

If you were Chinese, I'd learn the language,
    burn a lot of incense, wear funny clothes.
If you were a mirror, I'd storm the Ladies,
    give you my red lipstick and puff your nose.   12

If you loved volcanoes, I'd be lava
    relentlessly erupting from my hidden source.
And if you were my wife, I'd be your lover
    because the church is firmly against divorce.   16

[1996]

Topics for Critical Thinking and Writing

1. This poem is structurally simple: four stanzas long, it is based on a series of if/then sentences (although the "then" is only implied). Start with the first of these in lines 1–2. How does this scene portray the speaker and the person being addressed? Now move to the next, in lines 3–4, and explain as clearly as you can how this if/then differs in tone and emphasis from the one before. And so on through the poem as a whole.

2. Lines 15–16 bring the poem to a close with a line that begins with "And" rather than "If." Put the speaker's witty point here into your own words. Are these final lines comic or serious or both?

 ## ELLEN BRYANT VOIGHT

Ellen Bryant Voight was born in Virginia in 1943 and educated at Converse College and the University of Iowa. She is the author of several books of poems and has taught writing at Massachusetts Institute of Technology and at Warren Wilson College.

Quarrel

Since morning they have been quarreling—
the sun pouring its implacable white bath
over the birches, each one undressing
slyly, from the top down—and they hammer
at each other with their knives, nailfiles,   5
graters of complaint as the day unwinds,
the plush clouds lowering a gray matte°
for the red barn. Lunch, the soup
like batting in their mouths, last week,
last year, they're moving on to always   10
and never, their shrill pitiful children
crowd around but they see the top of this
particular mountain, its glacial headwall,
the pitch is terrific all through dinner,
and they are committed, the sun long gone,   15
the two of them back to back in the blank
constricting bed, like marbles on aluminum—
O this fierce love
that needs to reproduce in one another
wounds inflicted by the world.   20

[1983]

---

⁷**matte** dull paint finish

Topics for Critical Thinking and Writing

1. The quarrel has been going on "Since morning . . . ." What do we know about the people quarreling? When will the quarrel end? What do we know about why they quarrel?
2. The quarrel is set, in part, in a landscape. What does the speaker tell us about the landscape? Is the landscape set off from the quarrel or a part of it?
3. In line 18 did "love" surprise you? On rereading the poem, does the word make sense in the context of the whole? Explain.

 NIKKI GIOVANNI

 *Nikki Giovanni was born in Knoxville, Tennessee, in 1943 and educated at Fisk University, the University of Pennsylvania School of Social Work, and Columbia University. She has taught at Queens College, Rutgers University, and The Ohio State University, and she now teaches creative writing at Mt. St. Joseph on the Ohio. Giovanni has published many books of poems, an autobiography* (Gemini: An Extended Autobiographical Statement on My First Twenty-Five Years of Being a Black Poet), *a book of essays, and a book consisting of a conversation with James Baldwin.*

Love in Place

I really don't remember falling in love all that much
I remember wanting to bake corn bread and boil a ham and I
certainly remember making lemon pie and when I used to smoke I
stopped in the middle of my day to contemplate

I know I must have fallen in love once because I quit biting   5
my cuticles and my hair is gray and that must indicate
something and I all of a sudden had a deeper appreciation
for Billie Holiday° and Billy Strayhorn° so if it wasn't love I don't
know what it was

I see the old photographs and I am smiling and I'm sure quite   10
happy but what I mostly see is me
through your eyes
and I am still young and slim and very much committed to the
love we still have

[1997]

---

⁸**Billie Holiday** jazz singer (1915-59)   **Billy Strayhorn** jazz composer and musician (1915-67)

Topics for Critical Thinking and Writing

1. What reasons does the speaker offer for supposing that she once fell in love? How seriously does she expect us to take those reasons?
2. Read the poem again, but begin with the third stanza and then read the first and second stanzas. Does it make a difference? If so, what is the difference?
3. In line 14 we learn of the "love we still have." Does "still" refer to the present, or to the time of the "old photographs" (10), as the "still" in line 13 does?
4. Why do you suppose Giovanni puts extra space between the words?
5. What do you make of the title?
6. In the first line Giovanni speaks of "falling in love," and she returns to the idea in the fifth line. Judging from your own experience (which includes your knowledge of the people around you), is the term "falling in love" apt, or do people come to love one another in a more gradual fashion than "falling in love" implies? In responding to this question, in an essay of 500 words, you may want to take into consideration a remark by the English essayist William Hazlitt (1778–1830), in his *Table Talk* (1822):

I do not think that what is called *Love at first sight* is so great an absurdity as it is sometimes imagined to be. We generally make up our minds beforehand to the sort of person we should like, grave or gay, black, brown, or fair; with golden tresses or raven locks;—and when we meet with a complete example of the qualities we admire, the bargain is soon struck.

 ## CAROL MUSKE

Carol Muske was born in 1945 in St. Paul, Minnesota, and educated at Creighton University and San Francisco State College (now University). She has taught creative writing at several universities and was the founder and director of Free Space (a creative writing program) at the Women's House of Detention, Riker's Island, New York. She has written several books of poetry (and a novel, Dear Digby *[1989], published under her married name, Carol Muske-Dukes) and has been awarded distinguished fellowships, including a grant from the National Endowment for the Arts.*

Chivalry

In Benares°
the holiest city on earth
I saw an old man
toiling up the stone steps
to the ghat°   5

---

[1]**Benares** one of India's most ancient cities; located on the Ganges River, it is the holy city of the Hindus and the site of pilgrimages   [5]**ghat** a broad flight of steps on an Indian riverbank that provides access to the water

his dead wife in his arms
shrunken to the size
of a child—
lashed to a stretcher.

The sky filled with crows.   10
He held her up for a moment
then placed her
in the flames.

In my time on earth
I have seen few acts of true chivalry,   15
man's reverence
for woman.

But the memory of him
with her
in the cradle of his arms   20
placing her just so in the fire
so she would burn faster
so the kindling of the stretcher
would catch—
is enough for me now,   25
will suffice
for what remains on this earth
a gesture of bereavement
in the familiar carnage of love.

[1997]

 Topics for Critical Thinking and Writing

1. Do you find the poem shocking? Even more to the point: do you find it shocking that the speaker refers to this scene as an example of chivalry?
2. What is the meaning of the final line? Why the word "carnage"? How does this word in particular fit (or, in your view, not fit) in the structure of the poem as a whole?

DRAMA

 WENDY WASSERSTEIN

*Wendy Wasserstein was born in Brooklyn, New York, in 1950, the daughter of immigrants from central Europe. After graduating from Mt. Holyoke College, she took creative writing courses at the City College of New York and then completed a degree program at the Yale School of Drama. Wasserstein has had a highly successful career as a playwright (*The Heidi Chronicles *won a Pulitzer Prize in 1989), and she has also achieved recognition for her television screenplays and a book of essays.*

The Man in a Case *is based on a short story by Anton Chekhov, one of her favorite writers.*

The Man in a Case

LIST OF CHARACTERS
BYELINKOV
VARINKA

SCENE: *A small garden in the village of Mironitski. 1898.*

[BYELINKOV *is pacing. Enter* VARINKA *out of breath.]*

BYELINKOV. You are ten minutes late.

VARINKA. The most amazing thing happened on my way over here. You know the woman who runs the grocery store down the road. She wears a black wig during the week, and a blond wig on Saturday nights. And she has the daughter who married an engineer in Moscow who is doing very well thank you and is living, God bless them, in a three-room apartment. But he really is the most boring man in the world. All he talks about is his future and his station in life. Well, she heard we were to be married and she gave me this basket of apricots to give to you.

BYELINKOV. That is a most amazing thing!

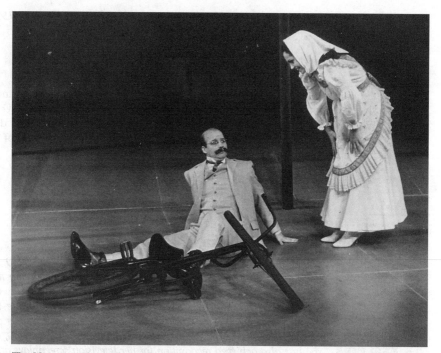

The Man in a Case. The Acting Company, Champaign-Urbana, Illinois, 1985. (Photo by Diane Gorodnitzki. All rights reserved.)

VARINKA. She said to me, Varinka, you are marrying the most honorable man in the entire village. In this village he is the only man fit to speak with my son-in-law.

BYELINKOV. I don't care for apricots. They give me hives.

VARINKA. I can return them. I'm sure if I told her they give you hives she would give me a basket of raisins or a cake.

BYELINKOV. I don't know this woman or her pompous son-in-law. Why would she give me her cakes?

VARINKA. She adores you!

BYELINKOV. She is emotionally loose.

VARINKA. She adores you by reputation. Everyone adores you by reputation. I tell everyone I am to marry Byelinkov, the finest teacher in the country.

BYELINKOV. You tell them this?

VARINKA. If they don't tell me first.

BYELINKOV. Pride can be an imperfect value.

VARINKA. It isn't pride. It is the truth. You are a great man!

BYELINKOV. I am the master of Greek and Latin at a local school at the end of the village of Mironitski.

[VARINKA kisses him.]

VARINKA. And I am to be the master of Greek and Latin's wife!

BYELINKOV. Being married requires a great deal of responsibility. I hope I am able to provide you with all that a married man must properly provide a wife.

VARINKA. We will be very happy.

BYELINKOV. Happiness is for children. We are entering into a social contract, an amicable agreement to provide us with a secure and satisfying future.

VARINKA. You are so sweet! You are the sweetest man in the world!

BYELINKOV. I'm a man set in his ways who saw a chance to provide himself with a small challenge.

VARINKA. Look at you! Look at you! Your sweet round spectacles, your dear collar always starched, always raised, your perfectly pressed pants always creasing at right angles perpendicular to the floor, and my most favorite part, the sweet little galoshes, rain or shine, just in case. My Byelinkov, never taken by surprise. Except by me.

BYELINKOV. You speak about me as if I were your pet.

VARINKA. You are my pet! My little school mouse.

BYELINKOV. A mouse?

VARINKA. My sweetest dancing bear with galoshes, my little stale babka.[1]

BYELINKOV. A stale babka?

VARINKA. I am not Pushkin.[2]

BYELINKOV *[laughs]*. That depends what you think of Pushkin.

VARINKA. You're smiling. I knew I could make you smile today.

BYELINKOV. I am a responsible man. Every day I have for breakfast black bread, fruit, hot tea, and every day I smile three times. I am halfway into my translation of the *Aeneid*[3] from classical Greek hexameter into Russian alexandrines. In twenty years I have never been late to school. I am a responsible man, but no dancing bear.

---

[1]**babka** cake with almonds and raisins   [2]**Pushkin** Alexander Pushkin (1799–1837), Russian poet   [3]*Aeneid* Latin epic poem by the Roman poet Virgil (70–19 B.C.)

VARINKA. Dance with me.

BYELINKOV. Now? It is nearly four weeks before the wedding!

VARINKA. It's a beautiful afternoon. We are in your garden. The roses are in full
bloom.

BYELINKOV. The roses have beetles.

VARINKA. Dance with me!

BYELINKOV. You are a demanding woman.

VARINKA. You chose me. And right. And left. And turn. And right. And left.

BYELINKOV. And turn. Give me your hand. You dance like a school mouse. It's a
beautiful afternoon! We are in my garden. The roses are in full bloom! And
turn. And turn. [*Twirls* VARINKA *around.*]

VARINKA. I am the luckiest woman!

[BYELINKOV *stops dancing.*]

Why are you stopping?

BYELINKOV. To place a lilac in your hair. Every year on this day I will place a lilac
in your hair.

VARINKA. Will you remember?

BYELINKOV. I will write it down. [*Takes a notebook from his pocket.*] Dear
Byelinkov, don't forget the day a young lady, your bride, entered your garden, your peace, and danced on the roses. On that day every year you are
to place a lilac in her hair.

VARINKA. I love you.

BYELINKOV. It is convenient we met.

VARINKA. I love you.

BYELINKOV. You are a girl.

VARINKA. I am thirty.

BYELINKOV. But you think like a girl. That is an attractive attribute.

VARINKA. Do you love me?

BYELINKOV. We've never spoken about housekeeping.

VARINKA. I am an excellent housekeeper. I kept house for my family on the farm
in Gadyatchsky. I can make a beetroot soup with tomatoes and aubergines
which is so nice. Awfully awfully nice.

BYELINKOV. You are fond of expletives.

VARINKA. My beet soup, sir, is excellent!

BYELINKOV. Please don't be cross. I too am an excellent housekeeper. I have a
place for everything in the house. A shelf for each pot, a cubby for every
spoon, a folder for favorite recipes. I have cooked for myself for twenty
years. Though my beet soup is not outstanding, it is sufficient.

VARINKA. I'm sure it's very good.

BYELINKOV. No. It is awfully, awfully not. What I am outstanding in, however,
what gives me greatest pleasure, is preserving those things which are left
over. I wrap each tomato slice I haven't used in a wet cloth and place it in
the coolest corner of the house. I have had my shoes for seven years because I wrap them in the galoshes you are so fond of. And every night before I go to sleep I wrap my bed in quilts and curtains so I never catch a
draft.

VARINKA. You sleep with curtains on your bed?

BYELINKOV. I like to keep warm.

VARINKA. I will make you a new quilt.

BYELINKOV. No. No new quilt. That would be hazardous.

VARINKA. It is hazardous to sleep under curtains.

BYELINKOV. Varinka, I don't like change very much. If one works out the arithmetic the final fraction of improvement is at best less than an eighth of value over the total damage caused by disruption. I never thought of marrying till I saw your eyes dancing among the familiar faces at the headmaster's tea. I assumed I would grow old preserved like those which are left over, wrapped suitably in my case of curtains and quilts.

VARINKA. Byelinkov, I want us to have dinners with friends and summer country visits. I want people to say, "Have you spent time with Varinka and Byelinkov? He is so happy now that they are married. She is just what he needed."

BYELINKOV. You have already brought me some happiness. But I never was a sad man. Don't ever think I thought I was a sad man.

VARINKA. My sweetest darling, you can be whatever you want! If you are sad, they'll say she talks all the time, and he is softspoken and kind.

BYELINKOV. And if I am difficult?

VARINKA. Oh, they'll say he is difficult because he is highly intelligent. All great men are difficult. Look at Lermontov, Tchaikovsky, Peter the Great.

BYELINKOV. Ivan the Terrible.[4]

VARINKA. Yes, him too.

BYELINKOV. Why are you marrying me? I am none of these things.

VARINKA. To me you are.

BYELINKOV. You have imagined this. You have constructed an elaborate romance for yourself. Perhaps you are the great one. You are the one with the great imagination.

VARINKA. Byelinkov, I am a pretty girl of thirty. You're right. I am not a woman. I have not made myself into a woman because I do not deserve that honor. Until I came to this town to visit my brother I lived on my family's farm. As the years passed I became younger and younger in fear that I would never marry. And it wasn't that I wasn't pretty enough or sweet enough, it was just that no man ever looked at me and saw a wife. I was not the woman who would be there when he came home. Until I met you I thought I would lie all my life and say I never married because I never met a man I loved. I will love you, Byelinkov. And I will help you to love me. We deserve the life everyone else has. We deserve not to be different.

BYELINKOV. Yes. We are the same as everyone else.

VARINKA. Tell me you love me.

BYELINKOV. I love you.

VARINKA [*takes his hands*]. We will be very happy. I am very strong. [*Pauses.*] It is time for tea.

BYELINKOV. It is too early for tea. Tea is at half past the hour.

VARINKA. Do you have heavy cream? It will be awfully nice with apricots.

BYELINKOV. Heavy cream is too rich for teatime.

VARINKA. But today is special. Today you placed a lilac in my hair. Write in your note pad. Every year we will celebrate with apricots and heavy cream. I will go to my brother's house and get some.

---

[4]**Lermontov . . . Ivan the Terrible** Mikhail Lermontov (1814–41), poet and novelist; Peter Ilich Tchaikovsky (1840–93), composer; Peter the Great (1672–1725), and Ivan the Terrible (1530–84), czars credited with making Russia a great European power

BYELINKOV. But your brother's house is a mile from here.

VARINKA. Today it is much shorter. Today my brother gave me his bicycle to ride. I will be back very soon.

BYELINKOV. You rode to my house by bicycle! Did anyone see you!

VARINKA. Of course. I had such fun. I told you I saw the grocery store lady with the son-in-law who is doing very well thank you in Moscow, and the head-master's wife.

BYELINKOV. You saw the headmaster's wife!

VARINKA. She smiled at me.

BYELINKOV. Did she laugh or smile?

VARINKA. She laughed a little. She said, "My dear, you are very progressive to ride a bicycle." She said you and your fiancé Byelinkov must ride to-gether sometime. I wonder if he'll take off his galoshes when he rides a bicycle.

BYELINKOV. She said that?

VARINKA. She adores you. We had a good giggle.

BYELINKOV. A woman can be arrested for riding a bicycle. That is not progressive, it is a premeditated revolutionary act. Your brother must be awfully, aw-fully careful on behalf of your behavior. He has been careless—oh so care-less—in giving you the bicycle.

VARINKA. Dearest Byelinkov, you are wrapping yourself under curtains and quilts! I made friends on the bicycle.

BYELINKOV. You saw more than the headmaster's wife and the idiot grocery woman.

VARINKA. She is not an idiot.

BYELINKOV. She is a potato-vending, sausage-armed fool!

VARINKA. Shhhh! My school mouse. Shhh!

BYELINKOV. What other friends did you make on this bicycle?

VARINKA. I saw students from my brother's classes. They waved and shouted, "Anthropos in love! Anthropos in love!!"

BYELINKOV. Where is that bicycle?

VARINKA. I left it outside the gate. Where are you going?

BYELINKOV [*muttering as he exits*]. Anthropos in love, anthropos in love.

VARINKA. They were cheering me on. Careful, you'll trample the roses.

BYELINKOV [*returning with the bicycle*]. Anthropos is the Greek singular for man. Anthropos in love translates as the Greek and Latin master in love. Of course they cheered you. Their instructor, who teaches them the disci-pline and contained beauty of the classics, is in love with a sprite on a bi-cycle. It is a good giggle, isn't it? A very good giggle! I am returning this bi-cycle to your brother.

VARINKA. But it is teatime.

BYELINKOV. Today we will not have tea.

VARINKA. But you will have to walk back a mile.

BYELINKOV. I have my galoshes on. [*Gets on the bicycle.*] Varinka, we deserve not to be different. [*Begins to pedal. The bicycle doesn't move.*]

VARINKA. Put the kickstand up.

BYELINKOV. I beg your pardon.

VARINKA [*giggling*]. Byelinkov, to make the bicycle move, you must put the kick-stand up.

[BYELINKOV *puts it up and awkwardly falls off the bicycle as it moves.*]

[*Laughing.*] Ha ha ha. My little school mouse. You look so funny! You are the sweetest dearest man in the world. Ha ha ha!

[*Pause.*]

BYELINKOV. Please help me up. I'm afraid my galosh is caught.

VARINKA [*trying not to laugh*]. Your galosh is caught! [*Explodes in laughter again.*] Oh, you are so funny! I do love you so. [*Helps* BYELINKOV *up.*] You were right, my pet, as always. We don't need heavy cream for tea. The fraction of improvement isn't worth the damage caused by the disruption.

BYELINKOV. Varinka, it is still too early for tea. I must complete two stanzas of my translation before late afternoon. That is my regular schedule.

VARINKA. Then I will watch while you work.

BYELINKOV. No. You had a good giggle. That is enough.

VARINKA. Then while you work I will work too. I will make lists of guests for our wedding.

BYELINKOV. I can concentrate only when I am alone in my house. Please take your bicycle home to your brother.

VARINKA. But I don't want to leave you. You look so sad.

BYELINKOV. I never was a sad man. Don't ever think I was a sad man.

VARINKA. Byelinkov, it's a beautiful day, we are in your garden. The roses are in bloom.

BYELINKOV. Allow me to help you on to your bicycle. [*Takes* VARINKA'S *hand as she gets on the bike.*]

VARINKA. You are such a gentleman. We will be very happy.

BYELINKOV. You are very strong. Good day, Varinka.

[*VARINKA pedals off.* BYELINKOV, *alone in the garden, takes out his pad and rips up the note about the lilac, strews it over the garden, then carefully picks up each piece of paper and places them all in a small envelope as lights fade to black.*]

[1986]

✏ Topics for Critical Thinking and Writing

1. You will probably agree that the scene where Byelinkov gets on the bicycle and pedals but goes nowhere is funny. But *why* is it funny? Can you formulate some sort of theory of comedy based on this episode?
2. At the end of the play Byelinkov tears up the note but then collects the pieces. What do you interpret these actions to mean?

Gender Roles: Making Men and Women

ESSAYS

KATHA POLLITT

Katha Pollitt (b. 1949) writes chiefly on literary, political, and social topics. In addition to writing essays, she writes poetry; her first collection of poems, Antarctic Traveller *(1982), won the National Book Critics Circle Award. She publishes widely, especially in* The Nation, The New Yorker, *and* The New York Times. *We reprint an article that originally appeared in* The New York Times Magazine.

Why Boys Don't Play with Dolls

It's twenty-eight years since the founding of NOW,* and boys still like trucks and girls still like dolls. Increasingly, we are told that the source of these robust preferences must lie outside society—in prenatal hormonal influences, brain chemistry, genes—and that feminism has reached its natural limits. What else could possibly explain the love of preschool girls for party dresses or the desire of toddler boys to own more guns than Mark from Michigan?

True, recent studies claim to show small cognitive differences between the sexes: He gets around by orienting himself in space; she does it by remembering landmarks. Time will tell if any deserve the hoopla with which each is invariably greeted, over the protests of the researchers themselves. But even if the results hold up (and the history of such research is not encouraging), we don't need studies of sex-differentiated brain activity in reading, say, to understand why boys and girls still seem so unalike.

The feminist movement has done much for some women, and something for every woman, but it has hardly turned America into a playground free of sex roles. It hasn't even got women to stop dieting or men to stop interrupting them.

---

*NOW National Organization for Women (Editors' note)

Instead of looking at kids to "prove" that differences in behavior by sex are innate, we can look at the ways we raise kids as an index to how unfinished the feminist revolution really is, and how tentatively it is embraced even by adults who fully expect their daughters to enter previously male-dominated professions and their sons to change diapers.

5   I'm at a children's birthday party. "I'm sorry," one mom silently mouths to the mother of the birthday girl, who has just torn open her present—Tropical Splash Barbie. Now, you can love Barbie or you can hate Barbie, and there are feminists in both camps. But *apologize* for Barbie? Inflict Barbie, against your own convictions, on the child of a friend you know will be none too pleased?

Every mother in that room had spent years becoming a person who had to be taken seriously, not least by herself. Even the most attractive, I'm willing to bet, had suffered over her body's failure to fit the impossible American ideal. Given all that, it seems crazy to transmit Barbie to the next generation. Yet to reject her is to say that what Barbie represents—being sexy, thin, stylish—is unimportant, which is obviously not true, and children know it's not true.

Women's looks matter terribly in this society, and so Barbie, however ambivalently, must be passed along. After all, there are worse toys. The Cut and Style Barbie styling head, for example, a grotesque object intended to encourage "hair play." The grown-ups who give that probably apologize, too.

How happy would most parents be to have a child who flouted sex conventions? I know a lot of women, feminists, who complain in a comical, eyeball-rolling way about their sons' passion for sports: the ruined weekends, obnoxious coaches, macho values. But they would not think of discouraging their sons from participating in this activity they find so foolish. Or do they? Their husbands are sports fans, too, and they like their husbands a lot.

Could it be that even sports-resistant moms see athletics as part of manliness? That if their sons wanted to spend the weekend writing up their diaries, or reading, or baking, they'd find it disturbing? Too antisocial? Too lonely? Too gay?

10   Theories of innate differences in behavior are appealing. They let parents off the hook—no small recommendation in a culture that holds moms, and sometimes even dads, responsible for their children's every misstep on the road to bliss and success.

They allow grown-ups to take the path of least resistance to the dominant culture, which always requires less psychic effort, even if it means more actual work: Just ask the working mother who comes home exhausted and nonetheless finds it easier to pick up her son's socks than make him do it himself. They let families buy for their children, without *too* much guilt, the unbelievably sexist junk that the kids, who have been watching commercials since birth, understandably crave.

But the thing the theories do most of all is tell adults that the *adult* world—in which moms and dads still play by many of the old rules even as they question and fidget and chafe against them—is the way it's supposed to be. A girl with a doll and a boy with a truck "explain" why men are from Mars and women are from Venus, why wives do housework and husbands just don't understand.

The paradox is that the world of rigid and hierarchical sex roles evoked by determinist theories is already passing away. Three-year-olds may indeed insist that doctors are male and nurses female, even if their own mother is a physician. Six-year-olds know better. These days, something like half of all medical students are female, and male applications to nursing school are inching upward. When tomorrow's three-year-olds play doctor, who's to say how they'll assign the roles?

With sex roles, as in every area of life, people aspire to what is possible, and conform to what is necessary. But these are not fixed, especially today. Biological determinism may reassure some adults about their present, but it is feminism, the ideology of flexible and converging sex roles, that fits out children's future. And the kids, somehow, know this.

15   That's why, if you look carefully, you'll find that for every kid who fits a stereotype, there's another who's breaking one down. Sometimes it's the same kid—the boy who skateboards *and* takes cooking in his afterschool program; the girl who collects stuffed animals *and* A-pluses in science.

Feminists are often accused of imposing their "agenda" on children. Isn't that what adults always do, consciously and unconsciously? Kids aren't born religious, or polite, or kind, or able to remember where they put their sneakers. Inculcating these behaviors, and the values behind them, is a tremendous amount of work, involving many adults. We don't have a choice, really, about *whether* we should give our children messages about what it means to be male and female—they're bombarded with them from morning till night.

[1995]

 Topics for Critical Thinking and Writing

1. In a paragraph set forth Pollitt's answer to the question she poses in her title.
2. In paragraph 7 Pollitt says, "Women's looks matter terribly in this society." Do you agree with this generalization? If they do matter "terribly," do they matter more than men's? What evidence can you give, one way or the other? Set forth your answer in an essay of 250 words.
3. Look at the last sentence in paragraph 12: "A girl with a doll and a boy with a truck 'explain' why men are from Mars and women are from Venus, why wives do housework and husbands just don't understand." Why does Pollitt put "explain" within quotation marks? What is she getting at by speaking of Mars and Venus? "Do housework" and "don't understand" are not the parallel construction that a reader probably expects. Do you think Pollitt's writing is deficient here, or is the variation purposeful? Explain.
4. In paragraph 14 Pollitt says that "the ideology of flexible and converging sex roles" is the one that "fits our children's future." What would be examples of "flexible and converging sex roles"? And do you agree that this ideology is the one that suits the immediate future? Why?
5. Do you believe that you have been influenced by Barbie or by any other toy? Explain.
6. In her final paragraph Pollitt says that adults always impose an "agenda" on their children, consciously or unconsciously. What agenda did your parents (or other adults charged with your upbringing) impose or try to impose? What was your response? As you think back on it, were the agenda and the responses appropriate? Set forth your answers in an essay of 500–750 words.
7. If you have heard that "brain chemistry" or "genes" (paragraph 1) account for "innate differences in behavior" (paragraph 10) in boys and girls, in a

paragraph set forth the view, and in another paragraph evaluate it, drawing perhaps on your reading of Pollitt's essay.

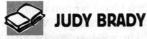

JUDY BRADY

Born in San Francisco in 1937, Judy Brady married in 1960, and two years later earned a bachelor's degree in painting at the University of Iowa. Active in the women's movement and in other political causes, she has worked as an author, an editor, and a secretary. The essay reprinted here, written before she and her husband separated, appeared originally in the first issue of Ms. *in 1971.*

I Want a Wife

I belong to that classification of people known as wives. I am A Wife. And, not altogether incidentally, I am a mother.

Not too long ago a male friend of mine appeared on the scene fresh from a recent divorce. He had one child, who is, of course, with his ex-wife. He is looking for another wife. As I thought about him while I was ironing one evening, it suddenly occurred to me that I, too, would like to have a wife. Why do I want a wife?

I would like to go back to school so that I can become economically independent, support myself, and, if need be, support those dependent upon me. I want a wife who will work and send me to school. And while I am going to school I want a wife to take care of my children. I want a wife to keep track of the children's doctor and dentist appointments. And to keep track of mine, too. I want a wife to make sure my children eat properly and are kept clean. I want a wife who will wash the children's clothes and keep them mended. I want a wife who is a good nurturant attendant to my children, who arranges for their schooling, makes sure that they have an adequate social life with their peers, takes them to the park, the zoo, etc. I want a wife who takes care of the children when they are sick, a wife who arranges to be around when the children need special care, because, of course, I cannot miss classes at school. My wife must arrange to lose time at work and not lose the job. It may mean a small cut in my wife's income from time to time, but I guess I can tolerate that. Needless to say, my wife will arrange and pay for the care of the children while my wife is working.

I want a wife who will take care of *my* physical needs. I want a wife who will keep my house clean. A wife who will pick up after my children, a wife who will pick up after me. I want a wife who will keep my clothes clean, ironed, mended, replaced when need be, and who will see to it that my personal things are kept in their proper place so that I can find what I need the minute I need it. I want a wife who cooks the meals, a wife who is a *good* cook. I want a wife who will plan the menus, do the necessary grocery shopping, prepare the meals, serve them pleasantly, and then do the cleaning up while I do my studying. I want a wife who will care for me when I am sick and sympathize with my pain and loss of time from school. I want a wife to go along when our family takes a vacation so that someone can continue to care for me and my children when I need a rest and change of scene.

5   I want a wife who will not bother me with rambling complaints about a wife's duties. But I want a wife who will listen to me when I feel the need to explain a rather difficult point I have come across in my course of studies. And I want a wife who will type my papers for me when I have written them.

I want a wife who will take care of the details of my social life. When my wife and I are invited out by my friends, I want a wife who will take care of the babysitting arrangements. When I meet people at school that I like and want to entertain, I want a wife who will have the house clean, will prepare a special meal, serve it to me and my friends, and not interrupt when I talk about things that interest me and my friends. I want a wife who will have arranged that the children are fed and ready for bed before my guests arrive so that the children do not bother us. I want a wife who takes care of the needs of my guests so that they feel comfortable, who makes sure that they have an ashtray, that they are passed the hors d'oeuvres, that they are offered a second helping of the food, that their wine glasses are replenished when necessary, that their coffee is served to them as they like it. And I want a wife who knows that sometimes I need a night out by myself.

I want a wife who is sensitive to my sexual needs, a wife who makes love passionately and eagerly when I feel like it, a wife who makes sure that I am satisfied. And, of course, I want a wife who will not demand sexual attention when I am not in the mood for it. I want a wife who assumes the complete responsibility for birth control, because I do not want more children. I want a wife who will remain sexually faithful to me so that I do not have to clutter up my intellectual life with jealousies. And I want a wife who understands that *my* sexual needs may entail more than strict adherence to monogamy. I must, after all, be able to relate to people as fully as possible.

If, by chance, I find another person more suitable as a wife than the wife I already have, I want the liberty to replace my present wife with another one. Naturally, I will expect a fresh, new life; my wife will take the children and be solely responsible for them so that I am left free.

When I am through with school and have a job, I want my wife to quit working and remain at home so that my wife can more fully and completely take care of a wife's duties.

10   My God, who *wouldn't* want a wife?

[1971]

✎ Topics for Critical Thinking and Writing

1. If one were to summarize Brady's first paragraph, one might say it adds up to "I am a wife and a mother." But analyze it closely. Exactly what does the second sentence add to the first? And what does "not altogether incidentally" add to the third sentence?

2. Brady uses the word "wife" in sentences where one ordinarily would use "she" or "her." Why? And why does she begin paragraphs 4, 5, 6, and 7 with the same words, "I want a wife"?

3. In her second paragraph Brady says that the child of her divorced male friend "is, of course, with his ex-wife." In the context of the entire essay, what does this sentence mean?

4. Drawing on your experience as observer of the world around you (and perhaps as husband, wife, or ex-spouse), do you think Brady's picture of a wife's role is grossly exaggerated? Or is it (allowing for some serious playfulness) fairly accurate, even though it was written in 1971? If grossly exaggerated, is the essay therefore meaningless? If fairly accurate, what attitudes and practices does it encourage you to support? Explain.

5. Whether or not you agree with Brady's vision of marriage in our society, write an essay (500 words) titled "I Want a Husband," imitating her style and approach. Write the best possible essay, and then decide which of the two essays—yours or hers—makes a fairer comment on current society. Or, if you believe Brady is utterly misleading, write an essay titled "I Want a Wife," seeing the matter in a different light.

6. If you feel that you have been pressed into an unappreciated, unreasonable role—built-in babysitter, listening post, or girl (or boy or man or woman) Friday—write an essay of 500 words that will help the reader to see both your plight and the injustice of the system. (*Hint:* A little humor will help to keep your essay from seeming to be a prolonged whine.)

 ## SCOTT RUSSELL SANDERS

Scott Russell Sanders first published this essay in Milkweek Chronicle, *Spring/Summer 1984, and then reprinted it in his book* Paradise of Bombs.

The Men We Carry in Our Minds . . . and How They Differ from the Real Lives of Most Men

"This must be a hard time for women," I say to my friend Anneke. "They have so many paths to choose from, and so many voices calling them."

"I think it's a lot harder for men," she replies.

"How do you figure that?"

"The women I know feel excited, innocent, like crusaders in a just cause. The men I know are eaten up with guilt."

5   "Women feel such pressure to be everything, do everything," I say. "Career, kids, art, politics. Have their babies and get back to the office a week later. It's as if they're trying to overcome a million years' worth of evolution in one lifetime."

"But we help one another. And we have this deep-down sense that we're in the *right*—we've been held back, passed over, used—while men feel they're in the wrong. Men are the ones who've been discredited, who have to search their souls."

I search my soul. I discover guilty feelings aplenty—toward the poor, the Vietnamese, Native Americans, the whales, an endless list of debts. But toward women I feel something more confused, a snarl of shame, envy, wary tenderness, and amazement. This muddle troubles me. To hide my unease I say, "You're right, it's tough being a man these days."

"Don't laugh," Anneke frowns at me. "I wouldn't be a man for anything. It's much easier being the victim. All the victim has to do is break free. The persecutor has to live with his past."

How deep is that past? I find myself wondering. How much of an inheritance do I have to throw off?

10   When I was a boy growing up on the back roads of Tennessee and Ohio, the men I knew labored with their bodies. They were marginal farmers, just scraping by, or welders, steelworkers, carpenters; they swept floors, dug ditches, mined coal, or drove trucks, their forearms ropy with muscle; they trained horses, stoked furnaces, made tires, stood on assembly lines wrestling parts onto cars and refrigerators. They got up before light, worked all day long whatever the weather, and when they came home at night they looked as though somebody had been whipping them. In the evenings and on weekends they worked on their own places, tilling gardens that were lumpy with clay, fixing brokendown cars, hammering on houses that were always too drafty, too leaky, too small.

The bodies of the men I knew were twisted and maimed in ways visible and invisible. The nails of their hands were black and split, the hands tattooed with scars. Some had lost fingers. Heavy lifting had given many of them finicky backs and guts weak from hernias. Racing against conveyor belts had given them ulcers. Their ankles and knees ached from years of standing on concrete. Anyone who had worked for long around machines was hard of hearing. They squinted, and the skin of their faces was creased like the leather of old work gloves. There were times, studying them, when I dreaded growing up. Most of them coughed, from dust or cigarettes, and most of them drank cheap wine or whiskey, so their eyes looked bloodshot and bruised. The fathers of my friends always seemed older than the mothers. Men wore out sooner. Only women lived into old age.

As a boy I also knew another sort of men, who did not sweat and break down like mules. They were soldiers, and so far as I could tell they scarcely worked at all. But when the shooting started, many of them would die. This was what soldiers were *for,* just as a hammer was for driving nails.

Warriors and toilers: these seemed, in my boyhood vision, to be the chief destinies for men. They weren't the only destinies, as I learned from having a few male teachers, from reading books, and from watching television. But the men on television—the politicians, the astronauts, the generals, the savvy lawyers, the philosophical doctors, the bosses who gave orders to both soldiers and laborers—seemed as remote and unreal to me as the figures in Renaissance tapestries. I could no more imagine growing up to become one of these cool, potent creatures than I could imagine becoming a prince.

A nearer and more hopeful example was that of my father, who had escaped from a red-dirt farm to a tire factory, and from the assembly line to the front office. Eventually he dressed in a white shirt and tie. He carried himself as if he had been born to work with his mind. But his body, remembering the earlier years of slogging work, began to give out on him in his fifties, and it quit on him entirely before he turned 65.

15   A scholarship enabled me not only to attend college, a rare enough feat in my circle, but even to study in a university meant for the children of the rich.

Here I met for the first time young men who had assumed from birth that they would lead lives of comfort and power. And for the first time I met women who told me that men were guilty of having kept all the joys and privileges of the earth for themselves. I was baffled. What privileges? What joys? I thought about the maimed, dismal lives of most of the men back home. What had they stolen from their wives and daughters? The right to go five days a week, 12 months a year, for 30 or 40 years to a steel mill or a coal mine? The right to drop bombs and die in war? The right to feel every leak in the roof, every gap in the fence, every cough in the engine as a wound they must mend? The right to feel, when the layoff comes or the plant shuts down, not only afraid but ashamed?

I was slow to understand the deep grievances of women. This was because, as a boy, I had envied them. Before college, the only people I had ever known who were interested in art or music or literature, the only ones who read books, the only ones who ever seemed to enjoy a sense of ease and grace were the mothers and daughters. Like the menfolk, they fretted about money, they scrimped and made do. But, when the pay stopped coming in, they were not the ones who had failed. Nor did they have to go to war, and that seemed to me a blessed fact. By comparison with the narrow, ironclad days of fathers, there was an expansiveness, I thought, in the days of mothers. They went to see neighbors, to shop in town, to run errands at school, at the library, at church. No doubt, had I looked harder at their lives, I would have envied them less. It was not my fate to become a woman, so it was easier for me to see the graces. I didn't see, then, what a prison a house could be, since houses seemed to me brighter, handsomer places than any factory. I did not realize—because such things were never spoken of—how often women suffered from men's bullying. Even then I could see how exhausting it was for a mother to cater all day to the needs of young children. But if I had been asked, as a boy, to choose between tending a baby and tending a machine, I think I would have chosen the baby. (Having now tended both, I know I would choose the baby.)

So I was baffled when the women at college accused me and my sex of having cornered the world's pleasures. I think something like my bafflement has been felt by other boys (and by girls as well) who grew up in dirt-poor farm country, in mining country, in black ghettos, in Hispanic barrios, in the shadows of factories, in Third World nations—any place where the fate of men is just as grim and bleak as the fate of women.

When the women I met at college thought about the joys and privileges of men, they did not carry in their minds the sort of men I had known in my childhood. They thought of their fathers, who were bankers, physicians, architects, stockbrokers, the big wheels of the big cities. They were never laid off, never short of cash at month's end, never lined up for welfare. These fathers made decisions that mattered. They ran the world.

The daughters of such men wanted to share in this power, this glory. So did I. They yearned for a say over their future, for jobs worthy of their abilities, for the right to live at peace, unmolested, whole. Yes, I thought, yes yes. The difference between me and these daughters was that they saw me, because of my sex, as destined from birth to become like their fathers, and therefore as an enemy to their desires. But I knew better. I wasn't an enemy, in fact or in feeling. I was an ally. If I had known, then, how to tell them so, would they have believed me? Would they now?

[1984]

Topics for Critical Thinking and Writing

1. Look at Sanders' introductory paragraphs (1–9). What do you think he hoped to accomplish by these paragraphs? To put it another way, suppose the essay began with paragraph 10, "When I was a boy growing up . . . ." What would be changed or lost?

2. Look at the second sentence of paragraph 10. It's a rather long sentence, with three independent clauses and lists of parallel phrases. How would you describe the verbs he uses? What effect does the structure of the sentence produce?

3. What is the topic sentence of paragraph 11? How does Sanders develop the paragraph, and what does the paragraph contribute to his argument?

4. What advantages did women enjoy that Sanders says he envied when he was a boy? What disadvantages does he mention (in paragraph 16)? What disadvantages does he *not* mention?

5. In paragraphs 16, 17, and 18, Sanders shifts from focusing on issues of gender to issues of class. How has he prepared us for this shift?

6. Evaluate Sanders' argument. How would you answer the questions he poses in his final paragraph?

7. When you were growing up, which lives seemed to have the most advantages or disadvantages, those of men or of women? Why did you think so? Did your opinion change as you grew older? Explain.

FICTION

CHARLOTTE PERKINS GILMAN

Charlotte Perkins Gilman (1860–1935), née Charlotte Perkins, was born in Hartford, Connecticut. Her father deserted the family soon after Charlotte's birth; she was brought up by her mother, who found it difficult to make ends meet. For a while Charlotte worked as an artist and teacher of art, and in 1884, when she was twenty-four, she married an artist. In 1885 she had a daughter, but soon after the birth of the girl Charlotte had a nervous breakdown. At her husband's urging she spent a month in the sanitarium of Dr. S. Weir Mitchell, a physician who specialized in treating women with nervous disorders. (Mitchell is specifically named in "The Yellow Wallpaper.") Because the treatment—isolation and total rest—nearly drove her to insanity, she fled Mitchell and her husband. In California she began a career as a lecturer and writer on feminist topics. (She also supported herself by teaching school and by keeping a boardinghouse.) Among her books are Women and Economics *(1899) and* The Man-Made World *(1911), which have been revived by the feminist movement. In 1900 she married a cousin, George Gilman. From all available evidence, the marriage was successful. Certainly it did not restrict her activities as a feminist. In 1935, suffering from inoperable cancer, she took her own life.*

"The Yellow Wallpaper," written in 1892—that is, written after she had been treated by S. Weir Mitchell for her nervous breakdown—was at first interpreted either as a ghost story or as a Poe-like study of insanity. Only in recent years has it

been seen as a feminist story. (One might ask oneself if these interpretations are mutually exclusive.)

The Yellow Wallpaper

It is very seldom that mere ordinary people like John and myself secure ancestral halls for the summer.

A colonial mansion, a hereditary estate. I would say a haunted house, and reach the height of romantic felicity—but that would be asking too much of fate!

Still I will proudly declare that there is something queer about it.

Else, why should it be let so cheaply? And why have stood so long untenanted?

5   John laughs at me, of course, but one expects that in marriage.

John is practical in the extreme. He has no patience with faith, an intense horror of superstition, and he scoffs openly at any talk of things not to be felt and seen and put down in figures.

John is a physician, and *perhaps*—(I would not say it to a living soul, of course, but this is dead paper and a great relief to my mind)—*perhaps* that is one reason I do not get well faster.

You see he does not believe I am sick!

And what can one do?

10   If a physician of high standing, and one's own husband, assures friends and relatives that there is really nothing the matter with one but temporary nervous depression—a slight hysterical tendency—what is one to do?

My brother is also a physician, and also of high standing, and he says the same thing.

So I take phosphates or phosphites—whichever it is, and tonics, and journeys, and air, and exercise, and am absolutely forbidden to "work" until I am well again.

Personally, I disagree with their ideas.

Personally, I believe that congenial work, with excitement and change, would do me good.

15   But what is one to do?

I did write for a while in spite of them: but it *does* exhaust me a good deal—having to be so sly about it, or else meet with heavy opposition.

I sometimes fancy that in my condition if I had less opposition and more society and stimulus—but John says the very worst thing I can do is to think about my condition, and I confess it always makes me feel bad.

So I will let it alone and talk about the house.

The most beautiful place! It is quite alone, standing well back from the road, quite three miles from the village. It makes me think of English places that you read about, for there are hedges and walls and gates that lock, and lots of separate little houses for the gardeners and people.

20   There is a *delicious* garden! I never saw such a garden—large and shady, full of box-bordered paths, and lined with long grapecovered arbors with seats under them.

There were greenhouses, too, but they are all broken now. There was some legal trouble. I believe, something about the heirs and coheirs: anyhow, the place has been empty for years.

That spoils my ghostliness. I am afraid, but I don't care—there is something strange about the house—I can feel it.

I even said so to John one moonlight evening, but he said what I felt was a *draught,* and shut the window.

I get unreasonably angry with John sometimes. I'm sure I never used to be so sensitive. I think it is due to this nervous condition.

25   But John says if I feel so, I shall neglect proper self-control: so I take pains to control myself—before him, at least, and that makes me very tired.

I don't like our room a bit. I wanted one downstairs that opened on the piazza and had roses all over the window, and such pretty old-fashioned chintz hangings! but John would not hear of it.

He said there was only one window and not room for two beds, and no near room for him if he took another.

He is very careful and loving, and hardly lets me stir without special direction.

I have a schedule prescription for each hour in the day: he takes all care from me, and so I feel basely ungrateful not to value it more.

30   He said we came here solely on my account, that I was to have perfect rest and all the air I could get. "Your exercise depends on your strength, my dear," said he, "and your food somewhat on your appetite; but air you can absorb all the time." So we took the nursery at the top of the house.

It is a big, airy room, the whole floor nearly, with windows that look all ways, and air and sunshine galore. It was nursery first and then playroom and gymnasium, I should judge; for the windows are barred for little children, and there are rings and things in the walls.

The paint and paper look as if a boys' school had used it. It is stripped off—the paper—in great patches all around the head of my bed, about as far as I can reach, and in a great place on the other side of the room low down. I never saw a worse paper in my life.

One of those sprawling flamboyant patterns committing every artistic sin.

It is dull enough to confuse the eye in following, pronounced enough to constantly irritate and provoke study, and when you follow the lame uncertain curves for a little distance they suddenly commit suicide—plunge off at outrageous angles, destroy themselves in unheard of contradictions.

35   The color is repellent, almost revolting: a smouldering unclean yellow, strangely faded by the slow-turning sunlight.

It is a dull yet lurid orange in some places, a sickly sulphur tint in others.

No wonder the children hated it! I should hate it myself if I had to live in this room long.

There comes John, and I must put this away,—he hates to have me write a word.

We have been here two weeks, and I haven't felt like writing before, since that first day.

40   I am sitting by the window now, up in this atrocious nursery, and there is nothing to hinder my writing as much as I please, save lack of strength.

John is away all day, and even some nights when his cases are serious.

I am glad my case is not serious!

But these nervous troubles are dreadfully depressing.

John does not know how much I really suffer. He knows there is no *reason* to suffer, and that satisfies him.

45   Of course it is only nervousness. It does weigh on me so not to do my duty in any way!

I meant to be such a help to John, such a real rest and comfort, and here I am a comparative burden already!

Nobody would believe what an effort it is to do what little I am able,—to dress and entertain, and order things.

It is fortunate Mary is so good with the baby. Such a dear baby!

And yet I *cannot* be with him, it makes me so nervous.

50   I suppose John never was nervous in his life. He laughs at me so about this wallpaper!

At first he meant to repaper the room, but afterwards he said that I was letting it get the better of me, and that nothing was worse for a nervous patient than to give way to such fancies.

He said that after the wallpaper was changed it would be the heavy bedstead, and then the barred windows, and then that gate at the head of the stairs, and so on.

"You know the place is doing you good," he said, "and really, dear, I don't care to renovate the house just for a three months' rental."

"Then do let us go downstairs." I said, "there are such pretty rooms there."

55   Then he took me in his arms and called me a blessed little goose, and said he would go down to the cellar, if I wished, and have it whitewashed into the bargain.

But he is right enough about the beds and windows and things.

It is an airy and comfortable room as any one need wish, and, of course, I would not be so silly as to make him uncomfortable just for a whim.

I'm really getting quite fond of the big room, all but that horrid paper.

Out of one window I can see the garden, those mysterious deep-shaded arbors, the riotous old-fashioned flowers, and bushes and gnarly trees.

60   Out of another I get a lovely view of the bay and a little private wharf belonging to the estate. There is a beautiful shaded lane that runs down there from the house. I always fancy I see people walking in these numerous paths and arbors, but John has cautioned me not to give way to fancy in the least. He says that with my imaginative power and habit of story-making, a nervous weakness like mine is sure to lead to all manner of excited fancies, and that I ought to use my will and good sense to check the tendency. So I try.

I think sometimes that if I were only well enough to write a little it would relieve the press of ideas and rest me.

But I find I get pretty tired when I try.

It is so discouraging not to have any advice and companionship about my work. When I get really well, John says we will ask Cousin Henry and Julia down for a long visit; but he says he would as soon put fireworks in my pillow-case as to let me have those stimulating people about now.

I wish I could get well faster.

65   But I must not think about that. This paper looks to me as if it *knew* what a vicious influence it had!

There is a recurrent spot where the pattern lolls like a broken neck and two bulbous eyes stare at you upside down.

I get positively angry with the impertinence of it and the everlastingness. Up and down and sideways they crawl, and those absurd, unblinking eyes are everywhere. There is one place where two breadths didn't match, and the eyes go all up and down the line, one a little higher than the other.

I never saw so much expression in an inanimate thing before, and we all know how much expression they have! I used to lie awake as a child and get more entertainment and terror out of blank walls and plain furniture than most children could find in a toystore.

I remember what a kindly wink the knobs of our big, old bureau used to have, and there was one chair that always seemed like a strong friend.

70   I used to feel that if any of the other things looked too fierce I could always hop into that chair and be safe.

The furniture in this room is no worse than inharmonious, however, for we had to bring it all from downstairs. I suppose when this was used as a playroom they had to take the nursery things out, and no wonder! I never saw such ravages as the children have made here.

The wallpaper, as I said before, is torn off in spots, and it sticketh closer than a brother—they must have had perseverance as well as hatred.

Then the floor is scratched and gouged and splintered, the plaster itself is dug out here and there, and this great heavy bed which is all we found in the room, looks as if it had been through the wars.

But I don't mind it a bit—only the paper.

75   There comes John's sister. Such a dear girl as she is, and so careful of me! I must not let her find me writing.

She is a perfect and enthusiastic housekeeper, and hopes for no better profession. I verily believe she thinks it is the writing which made me sick!

But I can write when she is out, and see her a long way off from these windows.

There is one that commands the road, a lovely shaded winding road, and one that just looks off over the country. A lovely country, too, full of great elms and velvet meadows.

This wallpaper has a kind of sub-pattern in a different shade, a particularly irritating one, for you can only see it in certain lights, and not clearly then.

80   But in the places where it isn't faded and where the sun is just so—I can see a strange, provoking, formless sort of figure, that seems to skulk about behind that silly and conspicuous front design.

There's sister on the stairs!

Well, the Fourth of July is over! The people are all gone and I am tired out. John thought it might do me good to see a little company, so we just had mother and Nellie and the children down for a week.

Of course I didn't do a thing. Jennie sees to everything now. But it tired me all the same.

John says if I don't pick up faster he shall send me to Weir Mitchell in the fall.

85   But I don't want to go there at all. I had a friend who was in his hands once, and she says he is just like John and my brother, only more so!

Besides, it is such an undertaking to go so far.

I don't feel as if it was worth while to turn my hand over for anything, and I'm getting dreadfully fretful and querulous.

I cry at nothing, and cry most of the time.

Of course I don't when John is here, or anybody else, but when I am alone.

90   And I am alone a good deal just now. John is kept in town very often by serious cases, and Jennie is good and lets me alone when I want her to.

So I walk a little in the garden or down that lovely lane, sit on the porch under the roses, and lie down up here a good deal.

I'm getting really fond of the room in spite of the wallpaper. Perhaps *because* of the wallpaper.

It dwells in my mind so!

I lie here on this great immovable bed—it is nailed down, I believe—and follow that pattern about by the hour. It is as good as gymnastics, I assure you. I start, we'll say, at the bottom, down in the corner over there where it has not been touched, and I determine for the thousandth time that I *will* follow that pointless pattern to some sort of a conclusion.

95   I know a little of the principle of design, and I know this thing was not arranged on any laws of radiation, or alternation, or repetition, or symmetry, or anything else that I ever heard of.

It is repeated, of course, by the breadths, but not otherwise.

Looked at in one way each breadth stands alone, the bloated curves and flourishes—a kind of "debased Romanesque" with *delirium tremens*—go waddling up and down in isolated columns of fatuity.

But, on the other hand, they connect diagonally, and the sprawling outlines run off in great slanting waves of optic horror, like a lot of wallowing seaweeds in full chase.

The whole thing goes horizontally, too, at least it seems so, and I exhaust myself in trying to distinguish the order of its going in that direction.

100   They have used a horizontal breadth for a frieze, and that adds wonderfully to the confusion.

There is one end of the room where it is almost intact, and there, when the crosslights fade and the low sun shines directly upon it, I can almost fancy radiation after all,—the interminable grotesques seem to form around a common center and rush off in headlong plunges of equal distraction.

It makes me tired to follow it. I will take a nap I guess.

I don't know why I should write this.

I don't want to.

105   I don't feel able.

And I know John would think it absurd. But I *must* say what I feel and think in some way—it is such a relief.

But the effort is getting to be greater than the relief!

Half the time now I am awfully lazy, and lie down ever so much.

John says I mustn't lose my strength, and has me take cod liver oil and lots of tonics and things, to say nothing of ale and wine and rare meat.

110   Dear John! He loves me very dearly, and hates to have me sick. I tried to have a real earnest reasonable talk with him the other day, and tell him how I wish he would let me go and make a visit to Cousin Henry and Julia.

But he said I wasn't able to go, nor able to stand it after I got there: and I did not make out a very good case for myself, for I was crying before I had finished.

It is getting to be a great effort for me to think straight. Just this nervous weakness I suppose.

And dear John gathered me up in his arms, and just carried me upstairs and laid me on the bed, and sat by me and read to me till it tired my head.

He said I was his darling and his comfort and all he had, and that I must take care of myself for his sake, and keep well.

115   He says no one but myself can help me out of it, that I must use my will and self-control and not let any silly fancies run away with me.

There's one comfort, the baby is well and happy, and does not have to occupy this nursery with the horrid wallpaper.

If we had not used it, that blessed child would have! What a fortunate escape! Why, I wouldn't have a child of mine, an impressionable little thing, live in such a room for worlds.

I never thought of it before, but it is lucky that John kept me here after all. I can stand it so much easier than a baby, you see.

Of course I never mention it to them any more—I am too wise,—but I keep watch of it all the same.

120   There are things in that paper that nobody knows but me, or ever will.

Behind that outside pattern the dim shapes get clearer every day.

It is always the same shape, only very numerous.

And it is like a woman stooping down and creeping about behind that pattern. I don't like it a bit. I wonder—I begin to think—I wish John would take me away from here!

It is so hard to talk with John about my case, because he is so wise, and because he loves me so.

125   But I tried last night.

It was moonlight. The moon shines in all around just as the sun does.

I hate to see it sometimes, it creeps so slowly, and always comes in by one window or another.

John was asleep and I hated to waken him, so I kept still and watched the moonlight on that undulating wallpaper till I felt creepy.

The faint figure behind seemed to shake the pattern, just as if she wanted to get out.

130   I got up softly and went to feel and see if the paper *did* move, and when I came back John was awake.

"What is it, little girl?" he said. "Don't go walking about like that—you'll get cold."

I thought it was a good time to talk, so I told him that I really was not gaining here, and that I wished he would take me away.

"Why darling!" said he, "our lease will be up in three weeks, and I can't see how to leave before."

"The repairs are not done at home, and I cannot possibly leave town just now. Of course if you were in any danger, I could and would, but you really are better, dear, whether you can see it or not. I am a doctor, dear, and I know. You are gaining flesh and color, your appetite is better, I feel really much easier about you."

135   "I don't weigh a bit more," said I, "nor as much: and my appetite may be better in the evening when you are here, but it is worse in the morning when you are away!"

"Bless her little heart!" said he with a big hug, "she shall be as sick as she pleases! But now let's improve the shining hours by going to sleep, and talk about it in the morning!"

"And you won't go away?" I asked gloomily.

"Why, how can I, dear? It is only three weeks more and then we will take a nice little trip of a few days while Jennie is getting the house ready. Really dear you are better!"

"Better in body perhaps—". I began, and stopped short, for he sat up straight and looked at me with such a stern, reproachful look that I could not say another word.

140   "My darling," said he, "I beg of you, for my sake and for our child's sake, as well as for your own, that you will never for one instant let that idea enter your mind! There is nothing so dangerous, so fascinating, to a temperament like yours. It is a false and foolish fancy. Can you not trust me as a physician when I tell you so?"

So of course I said no more on that score, and we went to sleep before long. He thought I was asleep first, but I wasn't and lay there for hours trying to decide whether that front pattern and the back pattern really did move together or separately.

On a pattern like this, by daylight, there is a lack of sequence, a defiance of law, that is a constant irritant to a normal mind.

The color is hideous enough, and unreliable enough, and infuriating enough, but the pattern is torturing.

You think you have mastered it, but just as you get well underway in following, it turns a back-somersault and there you are. It slaps you in the face, knocks you down, and tramples upon you. It is like a bad dream.

145   The outside pattern is a florid arabesque, reminding one of a fungus. If you can imagine a toadstool in joints, an interminable string of toadstools, budding and sprouting in endless convolutions—why, that is something like it.

That is, sometimes!

There is one marked peculiarity about this paper, a thing nobody seems to notice but myself, and that is that it changes as the light changes.

When the sun shoots in through the east window—I always watch for that first long, straight ray—it changes so quickly that I never can quite believe it.

That is why I watch it always.

150   By moonlight—the moon shines in all night when there is a moon—I wouldn't know it was the same paper.

At night in any kind of light, in twilight, candle light, lamplight, and worst of all by moonlight, it becomes bars! The outside pattern I mean, and the woman behind it is as plain as can be.

I didn't realize for a long time what the thing was that showed behind, that dim sub-pattern, but now I am quite sure it is a woman.

By daylight she is subdued, quiet. I fancy it is the pattern that keeps her so still. It is so puzzling. It keeps me quiet by the hour.

I lie down ever so much now. John says it is good for me, and to sleep all I can.

155   Indeed he started the habit by making me lie down for an hour after each meal.

It is a very bad habit I am convinced, for you see I don't sleep.

And that cultivates deceit, for I don't tell them I'm awake—O no!

The fact is I am getting a little afraid of John.

He seems very queer sometimes, and even Jennie has an inexplicable look.

160   It strikes me occasionally, just as a scientific hypothesis—that perhaps it is the paper!

I have watched John when he did not know I was looking, and come into the room suddenly on the most innocent excuses, and I've caught him several times *looking at the paper!* And Jennie too. I caught Jennie with her hand on it once.

She didn't know I was in the room, and when I asked her in a quiet, a very quiet voice, with the most restrained manner possible, what she was doing with the paper—she turned around as if she had been caught stealing, and looked quite angry—asked me why I should frighten her so!

Then she said that the paper stained everything it touched, that she had found yellow smooches on all my clothes and John's, and she wished we would be more careful!

Did not that sound innocent? But I know she was studying that pattern, and I am determined that nobody shall find it out but myself!

165   Life is very much more exciting now than it used to be. You see I have something more to expect, to look forward to, to watch. I really do eat better, and am more quiet than I was.

John is so pleased to see me improve! He laughed a little the other day, and said I seemed to be flourishing in spite of my wallpaper.

I turned it off with a laugh. I had no intention of telling him it was *because* of the wallpaper—he would make fun of me. He might even want to take me away.

I don't want to leave now until I have found it out. There is a week more, and I think that will be enough.

I'm feeling ever so much better! I don't sleep much at night, for it is so interesting to watch developments, but I sleep a good deal in the daytime.

170   In the daytime it is tiresome and perplexing.

There are always new shoots on the fungus, and new shades of yellow all over it. I cannot keep count of them, though I have tried conscientiously.

It is the strangest yellow, that wallpaper! It makes me think of all the yellow things I ever saw—not beautiful ones like buttercups, but old foul, bad yellow things.

But there is something else about that paper—the smell! I noticed it the moment we came into the room, but with so much air and sun it was not bad. Now we have had a week of fog and rain, and whether the windows are open or not, the smell is here.

It creeps all over the house.

175   I find it hovering in the dining-room, skulking in the parlor, hiding in the hall, lying in wait for me on the stairs.

It gets into my hair.

Even when I go to ride, if I turn my head suddenly and surprise it—there is that smell!

Such a peculiar odor, too! I have spent hours in trying to analyze it, to find what it smelled like.

It is not bad—at first, and very gentle, but quite the subtlest, most enduring odor I ever met.

180   In this damp weather it is awful, I wake up in the night and find it hanging over me.

It used to disturb me at first. I thought seriously of burning the house—to reach the smell.

But now I am used to it. The only thing I can think of that it is like is the *color* of the paper! A yellow smell.

There is a very funny mark on this wall, low down, near the mopboard. A streak that runs round the room. It goes behind every piece of furniture, except the bed, a long, straight, even *smooch*, as if it had been rubbed over and over.

I wonder how it was done and who did it, and what they did it for. Round and round and round—round and round and round—it makes me dizzy!

185   I really have discovered something at last.

Through watching so much at night, when it changes so, I have finally found out.

The front pattern *does* move—and no wonder! The woman behind shakes it!

Sometimes I think there are a great many women behind, and sometimes only one, and she crawls around fast, and her crawling shakes it all over.

Then in the very bright spots she keeps still, and in the very shady spots she just takes hold of the bars and shakes them hard.

190   And she is all the time trying to climb through. But nobody could climb through that pattern—it strangles so: I think that is why it has so many heads.

They get through, and then the pattern strangles them off and turns them upside down, and makes their eyes white!

If those heads were covered or taken off it would not be half so bad.

I think that woman gets out in the daytime!

And I'll tell you why—privately—I've seen her!

195 I can see her out of every one of my windows!

It is the same woman, I know, for she is always creeping, and most women do not creep by daylight.

I see her on that long road under the trees, creeping along, and when a carriage comes she hides under the blackberry vines.

I don't blame her a bit. It must be very humiliating to be caught creeping by daylight!

I always lock the door when I creep by daylight. I can't do it at night, for I know John would suspect something at once.

200 And John is so queer now, that I don't want to irritate him. I wish he would take another room! Besides, I don't want anybody to get that woman out at night but myself.

I often wonder if I could see her out of all the windows at once.

But, turn as fast as I can, I can only see out of one at one time. And though I always see her, she *may* be able to creep faster than I can turn!

I have watched her sometimes away off in the open country, creeping as fast as a cloud shadow in a high wind.

If only that top pattern could be gotten off from the under one! I mean to try it, little by little.

205 I have found out another funny thing, but I shan't tell at this time! It does not do to trust people too much.

There are only two more days to get this paper off, and I believe John is beginning to notice. I don't like the look in his eyes.

And I heard him ask Jennie a lot of professional questions about me. She had a very good report to give.

She said I slept a good deal in the daytime.

John knows I don't sleep very well at night, for all I'm so quiet!

210 He asked me all sorts of questions, too, and pretended to be very loving and kind.

As if I couldn't see through him!

Still, I don't wonder he acts so, sleeping under this paper for three months.

It only interests me, but I feel sure John and Jennie are secretly affected by it.

Hurrah! This is the last day, but it is enough. John is to stay in town over night, and won't be out until this evening.

215 Jennie wanted to sleep with me—the sly thing! But I told her I should undoubtedly rest better for a night all alone.

That was clever, for really I wasn't alone a bit! As soon as it was moonlight and that poor thing began to crawl and shake the pattern, I got up and ran to help her.

I pulled and she shook, I shook and she pulled, and before morning we had peeled off yards of that paper.

A strip about as high as my head and half round the room. And then when the sun came and that awful pattern began to laugh at me, I declared I would finish it to-day!

We go away to-morrow, and they are moving all the furniture down again to leave things as they were before.

220 Jennie looked at the wall in amazement, but I told her merrily that I did it out of pure spite at the vicious thing.

She laughed and said she wouldn't mind doing it herself, but I must not get tired.

How she betrayed herself that time!

But I am here, and no person touches this paper but me—not *alive!*

She tried to get me out of the room—it was too patent! But I said it was so quiet and empty and clean now that I believed I would lie down again and sleep all I could; and not to wake me even for dinner—I would call when I woke.

225 So now she is gone, and the servants are gone, and the things are gone, and there is nothing left but that great bedstead nailed down, with the canvas mattress we found on it.

We shall sleep downstairs to-night, and take the boat home to-morrow.

I quite enjoy the room, now it is bare again.

How those children did tear about here!

This bedstead is fairly gnawed!

230 But I must get to work.

I have locked the door and thrown the key down into the front path.

I don't want to go out, and I don't want to have anybody come in, till John comes.

I want to astonish him.

I've got a rope up here that even Jennie did not find. If that woman does get out, and tries to get away, I can tie her!

235 But I forgot I could not reach far without anything to stand on! This bed will *not* move!

I tried to lift and push it until I was lame, and then I got so angry I bit off a little piece at one corner—but it hurt my teeth.

Then I peeled off all the paper I could reach standing on the floor. It sticks horribly and the pattern just enjoys it! All those strangled heads and bulbous eyes and waddling fungus growths just shriek with derision!

I am getting angry enough to do something desperate. To jump out of the window would be admirable exercise, but the bars are too strong even to try.

Besides I wouldn't do it. Of course not, I know well enough that a step like that is improper and might be misconstrued.

240 I don't like to *look* out of the windows even—there are so many of those creeping women, and they creep so fast.

I wonder if they all come out of that wallpaper as I did?

But I am securely fastened now by my well-hidden rope—you don't get *me* out in the road there!

I suppose I shall have to get back behind the pattern when it comes night, and that is hard!

It is so pleasant to be out in this great room and creep around as I please!

245 I don't want to go outside. I won't, even if Jennie asks me to.

For outside you have to creep on the ground, and everything is green instead of yellow.

But here I can creep smoothly on the floor, and my shoulder just fits in that long smooch around the wall, so I cannot lose my way.

Why there's John at the door!

It is no use, young man, you can't open it!

250 How he does call and pound!

Now he's crying for an axe.

It would be a shame to break down that beautiful door!

"John dear!" said I in the gentlest voice, "the key is down by the front steps, under a plantain leaf!"

That silenced him for a few moments.

255 Then he said—very quietly indeed, "Open the door, my darling!"

I can't," said I. "The key is down by the front door under a plantain leaf!"

And then I said it again, several times, very gently and slowly, and said it so often that he had to go and see, and he got it of course, and came in. He stopped short by the door.

"What is the matter?" he cried. "For God's sake, what are you doing!"

I kept on creeping just the same, but I looked at him over my shoulder.

260 "I've got out at last," said I, "in spite of you and Jane. And I've pulled off most of the paper, so you can't put me back!"

Now why should that man have fainted? But he did, and right across my path by the wall, so that I had to creep over him every time!

[1892]

Topics for Critical Thinking and Writing

1. Is the narrator insane at the start of the story, or does she become insane at some point during the narrative? Or can't we be sure? Support your view with evidence from the story.
2. How reliable do you think the narrator's characterization of her husband is? Support your answer with reasons.
3. The narrator says that she cannot get better because her husband is a physician. What do you take this to mean? Do you think the story is about a husband who deliberately drives his wife insane?

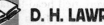

D. H. LAWRENCE

D[avid] H[erbert] Lawrence (1885–1930) was born in a Nottinghamshire (England) coal-mining district. His father was a miner, his mother a schoolteacher with cultural aspirations. When his father died, David had to leave high school, though he later earned a degree and completed a two-year program (1908) at Nottingham University College. Encouraged by his mother, he wrote and painted: in 1911, a year after his mother's death, he published his first novel, The White Peacock, *and in the following year he published another novel,* The Trespasser. *His first major novel,* Sons and Lovers *(1913), draws heavily on his experiences with his parents: it concerns the conflicts between a coarse but vital father and a refined mother who seeks to possess her son with her love.*

In addition to writing stories and such novels as Women in Love *(1920) and* Lady Chatterley's Lover *(1928) Lawrence produced travel books, criticism (*Studies in Classic American Literature*), and poetry.*

"My great religion," he wrote, "is a belief in the blood, the flesh, as being wiser than the intellect."

The Horse Dealer's Daughter

"Well, Mabel, and what are you going to do with yourself?" asked Joe, with foolish flippancy. He felt quite safe himself. Without listening for an answer, he turned aside, worked a grain of tobacco to the tip of his tongue and spat it out. He did not care about anything, since he felt safe himself.

The three brothers and the sister sat round the desolate breakfast table, attempting some sort of desultory consultation. The morning's post had given the final tap to the family fortune, and all was over. The dreary dining room itself, with its heavy mahogany furniture, looked as if it were waiting to be done away with.

But the consultation amounted to nothing. There was a strange air of ineffectuality about the three men, as they sprawled at table, smoking and reflecting vaguely on their own condition. The girl was alone, a rather short, sullen-looking young woman of twenty-seven. She did not share the same life as her brothers. She would have been good-looking, save for the impassive fixity of her face, "bull-dog," as her brothers called it.

There was a confused tramping of horses' feet outside. The three men all sprawled round in their chairs to watch. Beyond the dark holly bushes that separated the strip of lawn from the highroad, they could see a cavalcade of shire horses swinging out of their own yard, being taken for exercise. This was the last time. These were the last horses that would go through their hands. The young men watched with critical, callous looks. They were all frightened at the collapse of their lives, and the sense of disaster in which they were involved left them no inner freedom.

5   Yet they were three fine, well-set fellows enough. Joe, the eldest, was a man of thirty-three, broad and handsome in a hot, flushed way. His face was red, he twisted his black moustache over a thick finger, his eyes were shallow and restless. He had a sensual way of uncovering his teeth when he laughed, and his bearing was stupid. Now he watched the horses with a glazed look of helplessness in his eyes, a certain stupor of downfall.

The great draught-horses swung past. They were tied head to tail, four of them, and they heaved along to where a lane branched off from the highroad, planting their great hoofs floutingly in the fine black mud, swinging their great rounded haunches sumptuously, and trotting a few sudden steps as they were led into the lane, round the corner. Every movement showed a massive, slumbrous strength, and a stupidity which held them in subjection. The groom at the head looked back, jerking the leading rope. And the cavalcade moved out of sight up the lane, the tail of the last horse, bobbed up tight and stiff, held out taut from the swinging great haunches as they rocked behind the hedges in a motion-like sleep.

Joe watched with glazed hopeless eyes. The horses were almost like his own body to him. He felt he was done for now. Luckily he was engaged to a woman as old as himself, and therefore her father, who was steward of a neighboring estate, would provide him with a job. He would marry and go into harness. His life was over, he would be a subject animal now.

He turned uneasily aside, the retreating steps of the horses echoing in his ears. Then, with foolish restlessness, he reached for the scraps of bacon rind from the plates, and making a faint whistling sound, flung them to the terrier that lay against the fender. He watched the dog swallow them, and waited till the creature looked into his eyes. Then a faint grin came on his face, and in a high, foolish voice he said:

"You won't get much more bacon, shall you, you little bitch?"

10   The dog faintly and dismally wagged its tail, then lowered its haunches, circled round, and lay down again.

There was another helpless silence at the table. Joe sprawled uneasily in his seat, not willing to go till the family conclave was dissolved. Fred Henry, the second brother, was erect, cleanlimbed, alert. He had watched the passing of the horses with more sangfroid. If he was an animal, like Joe, he was an animal which controls, not one which is controlled. He was master of any horse, and he carried himself with a well-tempered air of mastery. But he was not master of the situations of life. He pushed his coarse brown moustache upwards, off his lip, and glanced irritably at his sister, who sat impassive and inscrutable.

"You'll go and stop with Lucy for a bit, shan't you?" he asked. The girl did not answer.

"I don't see what else you can do," persisted Fred Henry.

"Go as a skivvy," Joe interpolated laconically.

15   The girl did not move a muscle.

"If I was her, I should go in for training for a nurse," said Malcolm, the youngest of them all. He was the baby of the family, a young man of twenty-two, with a fresh, jaunty *museau*.[1]

But Mabel did not take any notice of him. They had talked at her and round her for so many years, that she hardly heard them at all.

The marble clock on the mantelpiece softly chimed the half-hour, the dog rose uneasily from the hearthrug and looked at the party at the breakfast table. But still they sat on in effectual conclave.

"Oh, all right," said Joe suddenly, apropos of nothing. "I'll get a move on."

20   He pushed back his chair, straddled his knees with a downward jerk, to get them free, in horsey fashion, and went to the fire. Still he did not go out of the room; he was curious to know what the others would do or say. He began to charge his pipe, looking down at the dog and saying, in a high, affected voice:

"Going wi' me? Going wi' me are ter? Tha'rt goin' further tha that counts on just now, dost hear?"

The dog faintly wagged its tail, the man stuck out his jaw and covered his pipe with his hands, and puffed intently, losing himself in the tobacco, looking down all the while at the dog with an absent brown eye. The dog looked at him in mournful distrust. Joe stood with his knees stuck out, in real horsey fashion.

"Have you had a letter from Lucy?" Fred Henry asked of his sister.

"Last week," came the neutral reply.

25   "And what does she say?"

There was no answer.

"Does she *ask* you to go and stop there?" persisted Fred Henry.

"She says I can if I like."

"Well, then, you'd better. Tell her you'll come on Monday." This was received in silence.

30   "That's what you'll do then, is it?" said Fred Henry, in some exasperation.

But she made no answer. There was a silence of futility and irritation in the room. Malcolm grinned fatuously.

"You'll have to make up your mind between now and next Wednesday," said Joe loudly, "or else find yourself lodgings on the curbstone."

The face of the young woman darkened, but she sat on immutable.

---

[1]**museau** jaw (literally muzzle or snout of a beast)

"Here's Jack Fergusson!" exclaimed Malcolm, who was looking aimlessly out of the window.

35 "Where?" exclaimed Joe, loudly.

"Just gone past."

"Coming in?"

Malcolm craned his neck to see the gate.

"Yes." he said.

40 There was a silence. Mabel sat on like one condemned, at the head of the table. Then a whistle was heard from the kitchen. The dog got up and barked sharply. Joe opened the door and shouted:

"Come on."

After a moment a young man entered. He was muffled up in overcoat and a purple woolen scarf, and his tweed cap, which he did not remove, was pulled down on his head. He was of medium height, his face was rather long and pale, his eyes looked tired.

"Hello, Jack! Well, Jack!" exclaimed Malcolm and Joe. Fred Henry merely said, "Jack."

"What's doing?" asked the newcomer, evidently addressing Fred Henry.

45 "Same. We've got to be out by Wednesday. Got a cold?"

"I have—got it bad, too."

"Why don't you stop in?"

"*Me* stop in? When I can't stand on my legs, perhaps I shall have a chance." The young man spoke huskily. He had a slight Scotch accent.

"It's a knock-out, isn't it," said Joe, boisterously, "if a doctor goes round croaking with a cold. Looks bad for the patients, doesn't it?"

50 The young doctor looked at him slowly.

"Anything the matter with *you,* then?" he asked sarcastically.

"Not as I know of. Damn your eyes. I hope not. Why?"

"I thought you were very concerned about the patients, wondered if you might be one yourself."

"Damn it, no, I've never been patient to no flaming doctor, and hope I never shall be," returned Joe.

55 At this point Mabel rose from the table, and they all seemed to become aware of her existence. She began putting the dishes together. The young doctor looked at her, but did not address her. He had not greeted her. She went out of the room with the tray, her face impassive and unchanged.

"When are you off then, all of you?" asked the doctor.

"I'm catching the eleven-forty," replied Malcolm. "Are you goin down wi'th trap, Joe?"

"Yes, I've told you I'm going down wi'th trap, haven't I?"

"We'd better be getting her in then. So long, Jack, if I don't see you before I go," said Malcolm, shaking hands.

60 He went out, followed by Joe, who seemed to have his tail between his legs.

"Well, this is the devil's own," exclaimed the doctor, when he was left alone with Fred Henry. "Going before Wednesday, are you?"

"That's the orders," replied the other.

"Where, to Northampton?"

"That's it."

65 "The devil!" exclaimed Fergusson, with quiet chagrin.

And there was silence between the two.

"All settled up, are you?" asked Fergusson.

"About."

There was another pause.

70　　"Well, I shall miss yer, Freddy, boy," said the young doctor.

"And I shall miss thee, Jack," returned the other.

"Miss you like hell," mused the doctor.

Fred Henry turned aside. There was nothing to say. Mabel came in again, to finish clearing the table.

"What are *you* going to do, then, Miss Pervin?" asked Fergusson. "Going to your sister's, are you?"

75　　Mabel looked at him with her steady, dangerous eyes, that always made him uncomfortable, unsettling his superficial ease.

"No," she said.

"Well, what in the name of fortune *are* you going to do? Say what you mean to do," cried Fred Henry, with futile intensity.

But she only averted her head, and continued her work. She folded the white table-cloth, and put on the chenille cloth.

"The sulkiest bitch that ever trod!" muttered her brother.

80　　But she finished her task with perfectly impassive face, the young doctor watching her interestedly all the while. Then she went out.

Fred Henry stared after her, clenching his lips, his blue eyes fixing in sharp antagonism, as he made a grimace of sour exasperation.

"You could bray her into bits, and that's all you'd get out of her," he said in a small, narrowed tone.

The doctor smiled faintly.

"What's she *going* to do, then?" he asked.

85　　"Strike me if *I* know!" returned the other.

There was a pause. Then the doctor stirred.

"I'll be seeing you to-night, shall I?" he said to his friend.

"Ay—where's it to be? Are we going over to Jessdale?"

"I don't know. I've got such a cold on me. I'll come round to the Moon and Stars, anyway."

90　　"Let Lizzie and May miss their night for once, eh?"

"That's it—if I feel as I do now."

"All's one—"

The two young men went through the passage and down to the back door together. The house was large, but it was servantless now, and desolate. At the back was a small bricked house-yard, and beyond that a big square, graveled fine and red, and having stables on two sides. Sloping, dank, winter-dark fields stretched away on the open sides.

But the stables were empty. Joseph Pervin, the father of the family, had been a man of no education, who had become a fairly large horse dealer. The stables had been full of horses, there was a great turmoil and come-and-go of horses and of dealers and grooms. Then the kitchen was full of servants. But of late things had declined. The old man had married a second time, to retrieve his fortunes. Now he was dead and everything was gone to the dogs, there was nothing but debt and threatening.

95　　For months, Mabel had been servantless in the big house, keeping the home together in penury for her ineffectual brothers. She had kept house for ten years. But previously it was with unstinted means. Then, however brutal and coarse everything was, the sense of money had kept her proud, confident. The men might be foul-mouthed, the women in the kitchen might have bad reputations, her brothers might have illegitimate children. But so long as there was money, the girl felt herself established, and brutally proud, reserved.

No company came to the house, save dealers and coarse men. Mabel had no associates of her own sex, after her sister went away. But she did not mind. She went regularly to church, she attended to her father. And she lived in the memory of her mother, who had died when she was fourteen, and whom she had loved. She had loved her father, too, in a different way, depending upon him, and feeling secure in him, until at the age of fifty-four he married again. And then she had set hard against him. Now he had died and left them all hopelessly in debt.

She had suffered badly during the period of poverty. Nothing, however, could shake the curious sullen, animal pride that dominated each member of the family. Now, for Mabel, the end had come. Still she would not cast about her. She would follow her own way just the same. She would always hold the keys of her own situation. Mindless and persistent, she endured from day to day. Why should she think? Why should she answer anybody? It was enough that this was the end, and there was no way out. She need not pass any more darkly along the main street of the small town, avoiding every eye. She need not demean herself any more, going into the shops and buying the cheapest food. This was at an end. She thought of nobody, not even of herself. Mindless and persistent, she seemed in a sort of ecstasy to be coming nearer to her fulfillment, her own glorification, approaching her dead mother, who was glorified.

In the afternoon she took a little bag, with shears and sponge and a small scrubbing brush, and went out. It was a gray, wintry day, with saddened, dark green fields and an atmosphere blackened by the smoke of foundries not far off. She went quickly, darkly along the causeway, heeding nobody, through the town to the churchyard.

There she always felt secure, as if no one could see her, although as a matter of fact she was exposed to the stare of every one who passed along under the churchyard wall. Nevertheless, once under the shadow of the great looming church, among the graves, she felt immune from the world, reserved within the thick churchyard wall as in another country.

100   Carefully she clipped the grass from the grave, and arranged the pinky white, small chrysanthemums in the tin cross. When this was done, she took an empty jar from a neighboring grave, brought water, and carefully, most scrupulously sponged the marble headstone and the coping-stone. It gave her sincere satisfaction to do this. She felt in immediate contact with the world of her mother. She took minute pains, went through the park in a state bordering on pure happiness, as if in performing this task she came into a subtle, intimate connection with her mother. For the life she followed here in the world was far less real than the world of death she inherited from her mother.

The doctor's house was just by the church. Fergusson, being a mere hired assistant, was slave to the countryside. As he hurried now to attend to the outpatients in the surgery, glancing across the graveyard with his quick eyes, he saw the girl at her task at the grave. She seemed so intent and remote, it was like looking into another world. Some mystical element was touched in him. He slowed down as he walked, watching her as if spellbound.

She lifted her eyes, feeling him looking. Their eyes met. And each looked away again at once, each feeling, in some way, found out by the other. He lifted his cap and passed on down the road. There remained distinct in his consciousness, like a vision, the memory of her face, lifted from the tombstone in the churchyard, and looking at him with slow, large, portentous eyes. It *was* portentous, her face. It seemed to mesmerize him. There was a heavy power in her eyes which laid hold of his whole being, as if he had drunk some powerful drug. He had been feeling weak and done before. Now the life came back into him, he felt delivered from his own fretted, daily self.

He finished his duties at the surgery as quickly as might be, hastily filling up the bottles of the waiting people with cheap drugs. Then, in perpetual haste, he set off again to visit several cases in another part of his round, before teatime. At all times he preferred to walk if he could, but particularly when he was not well. He fancied the motion restored him.

The afternoon was falling. It was gray, deadened, and wintry, with a slow, moist, heavy coldness sinking in and deadening all the faculties. But why should he think or notice? He hastily climbed the hill and turned across the dark green fields, following the black cindertrack. In the distance, across a shallow dip in the country, the small town was clustered like smouldering ash, a tower, a spire, a heap of low, raw, extinct houses. And on the nearest fringe of the town, sloping into the dip, was Oldmeadow, the Pervins's house. He could see the stables and the outbuildings distinctly, as they lay towards him on the slope. Well, he would not go there many more times! Another resource would be lost to him, another place gone: the only company he cared for in the alien, ugly little town he was losing. Nothing but work, drudgery, constant hastening from dwelling to dwelling among the colliers and the iron-workers. It wore him out, but at the same time he had a craving for it. It was a stimulant to him to be in the homes of the working people, moving as it were through the innermost body of their life. His nerves were excited and gratified. He could come so near, into the very lives of the rough, inarticulate, powerfully emotional men and women. He grumbled, he said he hated the hellish hole. But as a matter of fact it excited him, the contact with the rough, strongly-feeling people was a stimulant applied direct to his nerves.

105   Below Oldmeadow, in the green, shallow, soddened hollow of fields, lay a square, deep pond. Roving across the landscape, the doctor's quick eye detected a figure in black passing through the gate of the field, down towards the pond. He looked again. It would be Mabel Pervin. His mind suddenly became alive and attentive.

Why was she going down there? He pulled up on the path on the slope above, and stood staring. He could just make sure of the small black figure moving in the hollow of the failing day. He seemed to see her in the midst of such obscurity, that he was like a clairvoyant, seeing rather with the mind's eye than with ordinary sight. Yet he could see her positively enough, while he kept his eye attentive. He felt, if he looked away from her, in the thick, ugly falling dusk, he would lose her altogether.

He followed her minutely as she moved, direct and intent, like something transmitted rather than stirring in voluntary activity, straight down the field towards the pond. There she stood on the bank for a moment. She never raised her head. Then she waded slowly into the water.

He stood motionless as the small black figure walked slowly and deliberately towards the center of the pond, very slowly, gradually moving deeper into the motionless water, and still moving forward as the water got up to her breast. Then he could see her no more in the dusk of the dead afternoon.

"There!" he exclaimed. "Would you believe it?"

110   And he hastened straight down, running over the wet soddened fields, pushing through the hedges, down into the depression of callous wintry obscurity. It

took him several minutes to come to the pond. He stood on the bank, breathing heavily. He could see nothing. His eyes seemed to penetrate the dead water. Yes, perhaps that was the dark shadow of her black clothing beneath the surface of the water.

He slowly ventured into the pond. The bottom was deep, soft clay, he sank in, and the water clasped dead cold round his legs. As he stirred he could smell the cold, rotten clay that fouled up into the water. It was objectionable in his lungs. Still, repelled and yet not heeding, he moved deeper into the pond. The cold water rose over his thighs, over his loins, upon his abdomen. The lower part of his body was all sunk in the hideous cold element. And the bottom was so deeply soft and uncertain he was afraid of pitching with his mouth underneath. He could not swim, and was afraid.

He crouched a little, spreading his hands under the water and moving them round, trying to feel for her. The dead cold pond swayed upon his chest. He moved again, a little deeper, and again, with his hands underneath, he felt all around under the water. And he touched her clothing. But it evaded his fingers. He made a desperate effort to grasp it.

And so doing he lost his balance and went under, horribly, suffocating in the foul earthy water, struggling madly for a few moments. At last, after what seemed an eternity, he got his footing, rose again into the air and looked around. He gasped, and knew he was in the world. Then he looked at the water. She had risen near him. He grasped her clothing, and drawing her nearer, turned to take his way to land again.

He went very slowly, carefully, absorbed in the slow progress. He rose higher, climbing out of the pond. The water was now only about his legs: he was thankful, full of relief to be out of the clutches of the pond. He lifted her and staggered on to the bank, out of the horror of wet, gray clay.

115   He laid her down on the bank. She was quite unconscious and running with water. He made the water come from her mouth, he worked to restore her. He did not have to work very long before he could feel the breathing begin again in her: she was breathing naturally. He worked a little longer. He could feel her live beneath his hands: she was coming back. He wiped her face, wrapped her in his overcoat, looked round into the dim, dark gray world, then lifted her and staggered down the bank and across the fields.

It seemed an unthinkably long way, and his burden so heavy he felt he would never get to the house. But at last he was in the stableyard, and then in the house-yard. He opened the door and went into the house. In the kitchen he laid her down on the hearthrug, and called. The house was empty. But the fire was burning in the grate.

Then again he kneeled to attend to her. She was breathing regularly, her eyes were wide open and as if conscious, but there seemed something missing in her look. She was conscious in herself, but unconscious of her surroundings.

He ran upstairs, took blankets from a bed, and put them before the fire to warm. Then he removed her saturated, earthy-smelling clothing, rubbed her dry with a towel, and wrapped her naked in the blankets. Then he went into the dining-room, to look for spirits. There was a little whisky. He drank a gulp himself, and put some into her mouth.

The effect was instantaneous. She looked full into his face, as if she had been seeing him for some time, and yet had only just become conscious of him.

120   "Dr. Fergusson?" she said.

"What?" he answered.

He was divesting himself of his coat, intending to find some dry clothing upstairs. He could not bear the smell of the dead, clayey water, and he was mortally afraid of his own health.

"What did I do?" she asked.

"Walked into the pond," he replied. He had begun to shudder like one sick, and could hardly attend to her. Her eyes remained full on him, he seemed to be going dark in his mind, looking back at her helplessly. The shuddering became quieter in him, his life came back in him, dark and unknowing, but strong again.

125   "Was I out of my mind?" she asked, while her eyes were fixed on him all the time.

"Maybe, for the moment," he replied. He felt quiet, because his strength came back. The strange fretful strain had left him.

"Am I out of my mind now?" she asked.

"Are you?" he reflected a moment. "No." he answered truthfully. "I don't see that you are." He turned his face aside. He was afraid now, because he felt dazed, and felt dimly that her power was stronger than his, in this issue. And she continued to look at him fixedly all the time. "Can you tell me where I shall find some dry things to put on?" he asked.

"Did you dive into the pond for me?" she asked.

130   "No," he answered. "I walked in. But I went in overhead as well."

There was silence for a moment. He hesitated. He very much wanted to go upstairs to get into dry clothing. But there was another desire in him. And she seemed to hold him. His will seemed to have gone to sleep, and left him, standing there slack before her. But he felt warm inside himself. He did not shudder at all, though his clothes were sodden on him.

"Why did you?" she asked.

"Because I didn't want you to do such a foolish thing," he said.

"It wasn't foolish," she said, still gazing at him as she lay on the floor, with a sofa cushion under her head. "It was the right thing to do. *I* knew best, then."

135   "I'll go and shift these wet things," he said. But still he had not the power to move out of her presence, until she sent him. It was as if she had the life of his body in her hands, and he could not extricate himself. Or perhaps he did not want to.

Suddenly she sat up. Then she became aware of her own immediate condition. She felt the blankets about her, she knew her own limbs. For a moment it seemed as if her reason were going. She looked round, with wild eye, as if seeking something. He stood still with fear. She saw her clothing lying scattered.

"Who undressed me?" she asked, her eyes resting full and inevitable on his face.

"I did," he replied, "to bring you round."

For some moments she sat and gazed at him awfully, her lips parted.

140   "Do you love me, then?" she asked.

He only stood and stared at her, fascinated. His soul seemed to melt.

She shuffled forward on her knees, and put her arms round him, round his legs, as he stood there, pressing her breasts against his knees and thighs, clutching him with strange, convulsive certainty, pressing his thighs against her, drawing him to her face, her throat, as she looked up at him with flaring, humble eyes of transfiguration, triumphant in first possession.

"You love me." she murmured, in strange transport, yearning and triumphant and confident. "You love me. I know you love me, I know."

And she was passionately kissing his knees, through the wet clothing, passionately and indiscriminately kissing his knees, his legs, as if unaware of everything.

145   He looked down at the tangled wet hair, the wild, bare, animal shoulders. He was amazed, bewildered, and afraid. He had never thought of loving her. He had never wanted to love her. When he rescued her and restored her, he was a doctor, and she was a patient. He had had no single personal thought of her. Nay, this introduction of the personal element was very distasteful to him, a violation of his professional honor. It was horrible to have her there embracing his knees. It was horrible. He revolted from it, violently. And yet—and yet—he had not the power to break away.

She looked at him again, with the same supplication of powerful love, and that same transcendent, frightening light of triumph. In view of the delicate flame which seemed to come from her face like a light, he was powerless. And yet he had never intended to love her. He had never intended. And something stubborn in him could not give way.

"You love me," she repeated, in a murmur of deep, rhapsodic assurance. "You love me."

Her hands were drawing him, drawing him down to her. He was afraid, even a little horrified. For he had, really, no intention of loving her. Yet her hands were drawing him towards her. He put out his hand quickly to steady himself, and grasped her bare shoulder. A flame seemed to burn the hand that grasped her soft shoulder. He had no intention of loving her: his whole will was against his yielding. It was horrible. And yet wonderful was the touch of her shoulders, beautiful the shining of her face. Was she perhaps mad? He had a horror of yielding to her. Yet something in him ached also.

He had been staring away at the door, away from her. But his hand remained on her shoulder. She had gone suddenly very still. He looked down at her. Her eyes were now wide with fear, with doubt, the light was dying from her face, a shadow of terrible grayness was returning. He could not bear the touch of her eyes' question upon him, and the look of death behind the question.

150   With an inward groan he gave way, and let his heart yield towards her. A sudden gentle smile came on his face. And her eyes, which never left his face, slowly, slowly filled with tears. He watched the strange water rise in her eyes, like some slow fountain coming up. And his heart seemed to burn and melt away in his breast.

He could not bear to look at her any more. He dropped on his knees and caught her head with his arms and pressed her face against his throat. She was very still. His heart, which seemed to have broken, was burning with a kind of agony in his breast. And he felt her slow, hot tears wetting his throat. But he could not move.

He felt the hot tears wet his neck and the hollows of his neck, and he remained motionless, suspended through one of man's eternities. Only now it had become indispensable to him to have her face pressed close to him; he could never let her go again. He could never let her head go away from the close clutch of his arm. He wanted to remain like that for ever, with his heart hurting him in a pain that was also life to him. Without knowing, he was looking down on her damp, soft brown hair.

Then, as it were suddenly, he smelt the horrid stagnant smell of that water. And at the same moment she drew away from him and looked at him. Her eyes were wistful and unfathomable. He was afraid of them, and he fell to kissing her, not knowing what he was doing. He wanted her eyes not to have that terrible, wistful, unfathomable look:

When she turned her face to him again, a faint delicate flush was glowing, and there was again dawning that terrible shining of joy in her eyes, which really terrified him, and yet which he now wanted to see, because he feared the look of doubt still more.

155   "You love me?" she said, rather faltering.

"Yes." The word cost him a painful effort. Not because it wasn't true. But because it was too newly true, the *saying* seemed to tear open again his newly torn heart. And he hardly wanted it to be true, even now.

She lifted her face to him, and he bent forward and kissed her on the mouth, gently, with the one kiss that is an eternal pledge. And as he kissed her his heart strained again in his breast. He never intended to love her. But now it was over. He had crossed over the gulf to her, and all that he had left behind had shriveled and become void.

After the kiss, her eyes again slowly filled with tears. She sat still, away from him, with her face drooped aside, and her hands folded in her lap. The tears fell very slowly. There was complete silence. He too sat there motionless and silent on the hearthrug. The strange pain of his heart that was broken seemed to consume him. That he should love her? That this was love! That he should be ripped open in this way! Him, a doctor! How they would all jeer if they knew! It was agony to him to think they might know.

In the curious naked pain of the thought he looked again to her. She was sitting there drooped into a muse. He saw a tear fall, and his heart flared hot. He saw for the first time that one of her shoulders was quite uncovered, one arm bare, he could see one of her small breasts; dimly, because it had become almost dark in the room.

160   "Why are you crying?" he asked, in an altered voice.

She looked up at him, and behind her tears the consciousness of her situation for the first time brought a dark look of shame to her eyes.

"I'm not crying, really," she said, watching him half frightened.

He reached his hand, and softly closed it on her bare arm.

"I love you! I love you!" he said in a soft, low vibrating voice, unlike himself.

165   She shrank and dropped her head. The soft, penetrating grip of his hand on her arm distressed her. She looked up at him.

"I want to go," she said. "I want to go and get you some dry things."

"Why?" he said. "I'm all right."

"But I want to go," she said. "And I want you to change your things."

He released her arm, and she wrapped herself in the blanket, looking at him rather frightened. And still she did not rise.

170   "Kiss me." she said wistfully.

He kissed her, but briefly, half in anger.

Then, after a second, she rose nervously, all mixed up in the blanket. He watched her in her confusion, as she tried to extricate herself and wrap herself up so that she could walk. He watched her relentlessly, as she knew. And as she went, the blanket trailing, and as he saw a glimpse of her feet and her white leg, he tried to remember her as she was when he had wrapped her in the blanket. But then he didn't want to remember, because she had been nothing to him then, and his nature revolted from remembering her as she was when she was nothing to him.

A tumbling, muffled noise from within the dark house startled him. Then he heard her voice:—"There are clothes." He rose and went to the foot of the stairs, and gathered up the garments she had thrown down. Then he came back to the fire, to rub himself down and dress. He grinned at his own appearance when he had finished.

The fire was sinking, so he put on coal. The house was now quite dark, save for the light of a street-lamp that shone in faintly from beyond the holly trees. He lit the gas with matches he found on the mantelpiece. Then he emptied the pockets of his own clothes, and threw all his wet things in a heap into the scullery. After which he gathered up her sodden clothes, gently, and put them in a separate heap on the copper-top in the scullery.

175   It was six o'clock on the clock. His own watch had stopped. He ought to go back to the surgery. He waited, and still she did not come down. So he went to the foot of the stairs and called:

"I shall have to go."

Almost immediately he heard her coming down. She had on her best dress of black voile, and her hair was tidy, but still damp. She looked at him—and in spite of herself, smiled.

"I don't like you in those clothes," she said.

"Do I look a sight?" he answered.

180   They were shy of one another.

"I'll make you some tea," she said.

"No, I must go."

"Must you?" And she looked at him again with the wide, strained, doubtful eyes. And again, from the pain of his breast, he knew how he loved her. He went and bent to kiss her, gently, passionately, with his heart's painful kiss.

"And my hair smells so horrible," she murmured in distraction. "And I'm so awful. I'm so awful! Oh, no, I'm too awful." And she broke into bitter, heart-broken sobbing. "You can't want to love me, I'm horrible."

185   "Don't be silly, don't be silly," he said, trying to comfort her, kissing her, holding her in his arms. "I want you, I want to marry you, we're going to be married, quickly, quickly—tomorrow if I can."

But she only sobbed terribly, and cried:

"I feel awful. I feel awful. I feel I'm horrible to you."

"No, I want you, I want you," was all he answered, blindly, with that terrible intonation which frightened her almost more than her horror lest he should *not* want her.

[1922]

✎ Topics for Critical Thinking and Writing

1. In the opening scene, what is the attitude of the men toward Mabel? What was it like to be a daughter in this family? In the context of the entire story, why is it important that the family is breaking up?

2. Briefly characterize each of Mabel's brothers, and then, more fully, characterize Mabel, pointing out the ways in which she differs from them. You may want to emphasize the ways in which her relations with her mother and father help to differentiate her from them.

3. During what season is the story set? How is this setting relevant?

4. Many psychologists and sociologists say that love is not an instinct but a learned behavior. Basing your views on "The Horse Dealer's Daughter," in-

dicate whether or not, in your opinion, Lawrence would have subscribed to such a view.

 ## RICHARD WRIGHT

Richard Wright (1908–1960), the grandson of a slave and the son of an impoverished sharecropper family, was born on a cotton plantation near Natchez, Mississippi. When Richard was five his father deserted the family; five years later his mother suffered the first of a series of strokes that left her partly paralyzed. Richard was then brought up by relatives in Jackson, Mississippi, and Memphis, Tennessee. He dropped out of school after completing the ninth grade, took a variety of odd jobs, and in 1927 moved to Chicago, where he worked as a porter, dishwasher, burial-insurance salesman, and postal clerk. He also worked for the WPA, first as a writer of guidebooks and then as a director of the Federal Negro Theater. In 1932 he joined the John Reed Club, a left-wing organization. In 1937 he moved to New York, where he became the Harlem editor of The Daily Worker, *a Communist newspaper. In the following year he published his first book,* Uncle Tom's Children: Four Novellas. *In 1947 Wright and his family moved to Paris, where they lived until he suffered a fatal heart attack in 1960.*

With Native Son *(1940), a novel about a black man who murders a white woman, Wright became the first black writer to reach a large white audience with a militant attack on racism. In the following year he wrote the text for* Twelve Million Black Voices, *a pictorial "folk history of the Negro in the United States." His next best-selling work was an autobiography,* Black Boy *(1945). Wright had already left the Communist party in 1944, but material about his disillusionment with Communism was deleted from the manuscript of* Black Boy *and was first published in a posthumous book,* American Hunger *(1977). By the time he moved to France, then, Wright was strongly anti-Communist. He continued to write novels, though he also wrote nonfiction, including an account of a trip to Ghana.*

The Man Who Was Almost a Man

Dave struck out across the fields, looking homeward through paling light. Whut's the use talkin wid em niggers in the field? Anyhow, his mother was putting supper on the table. Them niggers can't understan nothing. One of these days he was going to get a gun and practice shooting, then they couldn't talk to him as though he were a little boy. He slowed, looking at the ground. Shucks, Ah ain scareda them even if they are biggern me! Aw, Ah know what Ahma do. Ahm going by ol Joe's sto n git that Sears Roebuck catlog n look at them guns. Mebbe Ma will lemme buy one when she gits mah pay from ol man Hawkins. Ahma beg her t gimme some money. Ahm ol ernough to hava gun. Ahm seventeen. Almost a man. He strode, feeling his long loose-jointed limbs. Shucks, a man oughta hava little gun aftah he done worked hard all day.

He came in sight of Joe's store. A yellow lantern glowed on the front porch. He mounted steps and went through the screen door, hearing it bang behind him. There was a strong smell of coal oil and mackerel fish. He felt very confident until he saw fat Joe walk in through the rear door, then his courage began to ooze.

"Howdy, Dave! Whutcha want?"

"How yuh, Mistah Joe? Aw, Ah don wanna buy nothing. Ah jus wanted t see ef yuhd lemme look at tha catlog erwhile."

5 "Sure! You wanna see it here?"

"Nawsuh. Ah wants t take it home wid me. Ah'll bring it back termorrow when Ah come in from the fiels."

"You plannin on buying something."

"Yessuh."

"Your ma lettin you have your own money now?"

10 "Shucks. Mistah Joe, Ahm gittin t be a man like anybody else!"

Joe laughed and wiped his greasy white face with a red bandanna.

"Whut you plannin on buyin?"

Dave looked at the floor, scratched his head, scratched his thigh, and smiled. Then he looked up shyly.

"Ah'll tell yuh, Mistah Joe, ef yuh promise yuh won't tell."

15 "I promise."

"Waal, Ahma buy a gun."

"A gun? What you want with a gun?"

"Ah wanna keep it."

"You ain't nothing but a boy. You don't need a gun."

20 "Aw, lemme have the catlog, Mistah Joe. Ah'll bring it back."

Joe walked through the rear door. Dave was elated. He looked around at barrels of sugar and flour. He heard Joe coming back. He craned his neck to see if he were bringing the book. Yeah, he's got it. Gawddog, he's got it!

"Here, but be sure you bring it back. It's the only one I got."

"Sho, Mistah Joe."

"Say, if you wanna buy a gun, why don't you buy one from me? I gotta gun to sell."

25 "Will it shoot?"

"Sure it'll shoot."

"Whut kind is it?"

"Oh, it's kinda old . . . a left-hand Wheeler. A pistol. A big one."

"Is it got bullets in it?"

30 "It's loaded."

"Kin Ah see it?"

"Where's your money?"

"Whut yuh wan fer it?"

"I'll let you have it for two dollars."

35 "Just two dollahs? Shucks, Ah could buy tha when Ah git mah pay."

"I'll have it here when you want it."

"Awright, suh. Ah be in fer it."

He went through the door, hearing it slam again behind him. Ahma git some money from Ma n buy me a gun! Only two dollars! He tucked the thick catalogue under his arm and hurried.

"Where yuh been, boy?" His mother held a steaming dish of blackeyed peas.

40 "Aw, Ma, Ah jus stopped down the road t talk wid the boys."

"Yuh know bettah t keep suppah waitin."

He sat down, resting the catalogue on the edge of the table.

"Yuh git up from there and git to the well n wash yosef! Ah ain feedin no hogs in mah house!"

She grabbed his shoulder and pushed him. He stumbled out of the room, then came back to get the catalogue.

45   "Whut this?"

"Aw, Ma, it's jusa catlog."

"Who yuh git it from?"

"From Joe, down at the sto."

"Waal, thas good. We kin use it in the outhouse."

50   "Naw, Ma." He grabbed for it. "Gimme ma catlog, Ma."

She held onto it and glared at him.

"Quit hollerin at me! Whut's wrong wid yuh? Yuh crazy?"

"But Ma, please. It ain mine! It's Joe's! He tol me t bring it back t im termorrow."

She gave up the book. He stumbled down the back steps, hugging the thick
book under his arm. When he had splashed water on his face and hands, he
groped back to the kitchen and fumbled in a corner for the towel. He bumped
into a chair; it clattered to the floor. The catalogue sprawled at his feet. When he
had dried his eyes he snatched up the book and held it again under his arm. His
mother stood watching him.

55   Now, ef yuh gonna act a fool over that ol book, Ah'll take it n burn it up."

"Naw, Ma, please."

"Waal, set down n be still!"

He sat down and drew the oil lamp close. He thumbed page after page, unaware of the food his mother set on the table. His father came in. Then his small
brother.

"Whutcha got there, Dave?" his father asked.

60   "Jusa catlog," he answered, not looking up.

"Yeah, here they is!" His eyes glowed at blue-and-black revolvers. He
glanced up, feeling sudden guilt. His father was watching him. He eased the
book under the table and rested it on his knees. After the blessing was asked, he
ate. He scooped up peas and swallowed fat meat without chewing. Buttermilk
helped to wash it down. He did not want to mention money before his father. He
would do much better by cornering his mother when she was alone. He looked
at his father uneasily out of the edge of his eye.

"Boy, how come yuh don quit foolin wid tha book n eat yo suppah?"

"Yessuh."

"How you n ol man Hawkins gitten erlong?"

65   "Suh?"

"Can't yuh hear? Why don yuh lissen? Ah ast yu how wuz yuh n ol man
Hawkins gittin erlong?"

"Oh, swell, Pa. Ah plows mo lan than anybody over there."

"Waal, yuh oughta keep you mind on what yuh doin."

"Yessuh."

70   He poured his plate full of molasses and sopped it up slowly with a chunk of
cornbread. When his father and brother had left the kitchen, he still sat and
looked again at the guns in the catalogue, longing to muster courage enough to
present his case to his mother. Lawd, ef Ah only had tha pretty one! He could almost feel the slickness of the weapon with his fingers. If he had a gun like that he
would polish it and keep it shining so it would never rust! N Ah'd keep it loaded,
by Gawd!

"Ma?" His voice was hesitant.

"Hunh?"

"Ol man Hawkins give yuh mah money yit?"

"Yeah, but ain no usa yuh thinking bout throwin nona it erway. Ahm keeping tha money sos yuh kin have cloes t go to school this winter."

75   He rose and went to her side with the open catalogue in his palms. She was washing dishes, her head bent low over a pan. Shyly he raised the book. When he spoke, his voice was husky, faint.

"Ma, Gawd knows Ah wans one of these."

"One of whut?" she asked, not raising her eyes.

"One of these," he said again, not daring even to point. She glanced up at the page, then at him with wide eyes.

"Nigger, is yuh gone plumb crazy?"

80   "Aw, Ma—"

"Git outta here! Don yuh talk t me bout no gun! Yuh a fool!"

"Ma, Ah kin buy one fer two dollahs."

"Not ef Ah knows it, yuh ain!"

"But yuh promised me one—"

85   "Ah don care what Ah promised! Yuh ain nothing but a boy yit!"

"Ma, ef yuh lemme buy one Ah'll *never* ast yuh fer nothing no mo."

"Ah tol yuh t git outta here! Yuh ain gonna toucha penny of tha money fer no gun! Thas how come Ah has Mistah Hawkins t pay yo wages t me, cause Ah knows yuh ain got no sense."

"But, Ma, we needa gun. Pa ain got no gun. We needa gun in the house. Yuh kin never tell whut might happen."

"Now don yuh try to maka fool outta me, boy! Ef we did hava gun, yuh wouldn't have it!"

90   He laid the catalogue down and slipped his arm around her waist.

"Aw, Ma, Ah done worked hard alla summer n ain ast yuh fer nothing, is Ah, now?"

"Thas what yuh spose t do!"

"But Ma, Ah wans a gun. Yuh kin lemme have two dollahs outta mah money. Please, Ma. I kin give it to Pa. . . . Please, Ma! Ah loves yuh, Ma!"

When she spoke her voice came soft and low.

95   "What yu wan wida gun, Dave? Yuh don need no gun. Yuh'll git in trouble. N ef yo pa jus thought Ah let yuh have money t buy a gun he'd hava fit."

"Ah'll hide it, Ma. It ain but two dollahs."

"Lawd, chil, whut's wrong wid yuh?"

"Ain nothin wrong, Ma. Ahm almos a man now. Ah wans a gun."

"Who gonna sell yuh a gun?"

100   "Ol Joe at the sto."

"N it don cos but two dollahs?"

"Thas all, Ma. Jus two dollahs. Please, Ma."

She was stacking the plates away; her hands moved slowly, reflectively. Dave kept an anxious silence. Finally, she turned to him.

"Ah'll let yuh git tha gun if yuh promise me one thing."

105   "What's tha, Ma?"

"Yuh bring it straight back t me, yuh hear? It be fer Pa."

"Yessum! Lemme go now, Ma."

She stooped, turned slightly to one side, raised the hem of her dress, rolled down the top of her stocking, and came up with a slender wad of bills.

"Here," she said. "Lawd knows yuh don need no gun. But yer pa does. Yuh bring it right back t me, yuh hear? Ahma put it up. Now ef yuh don, Ahma have yuh pa lick yuh so hard yuh won fergit it."

110   "Yessum."

He took the money, ran down the steps, and across the yard.

"Dave! Yuuuuuh Daaaaave!"

He heard, but he was not going to stop now. "Naw, Lawd!"

The first movement he made the following morning was to reach under the pillow for the gun. In the gray light of dawn he held it loosely, feeling a sense of power. Could kill a man with a gun like this. Kill anybody, black or white. And if he were holding his gun in his hand, nobody could run over him; they would have to respect him. It was a big gun, with a long barrel and a heavy handle. He raised and lowered it in his hand, marveling at its weight.

115   He had not come straight home with it as his mother had asked; instead he had stayed out in the fields, holding the weapon in his hand, aiming it now and then at some imaginary foe. But he had not fired it; he had been afraid that his father might hear. Also he was not sure he knew how to fire it.

To avoid surrendering the pistol he had not come into the house until he knew that they were all asleep. When his mother had tiptoed to his bedside late that night and demanded the gun, he had first played possum; then he had told her that the gun was hidden outdoors, that he would bring it to her in the morning. Now he lay turning it slowly in his hands. He broke it, took out the cartridges, felt them, and then put them back.

He slid out of bed, got a long strip of old flannel from a trunk, wrapped the gun in it, and tied it to his naked thigh while it was still loaded. He did not go in to breakfast. Even though it was not yet daylight he started for Jim Hawkins' plantation. Just as the sun was rising he reached the barns where the mules and plows were kept.

"Hey! That you, Dave?"

He turned. Jim Hawkins stood eyeing him suspiciously.

120   "What're yuh doing here so early?"

"Ah didn't know Ah wuz gittin up so early, Mistah Hawkins. Ah was fixin t hitch up ol Jenny n take her t the fiels."

"Good. Since you're so early, how about plowing that stretch down by the woods?"

"Suits me, Mistah Hawkins."

"O.K. Go to it!"

125   He hitched Jenny to a plow and started across the fields. Hot dog! This was just what he wanted. If he could get down by the woods, he could shoot his gun and nobody would hear. He walked behind the plow, hearing the traces creaking, feeling the gun tied tight to his thigh.

When he reached the woods, he plowed two whole rows before he decided to take out the gun. Finally, he stopped, looked in all directions, then untied the gun and held it in his hand. He turned to the mule and smiled.

"Know whut this is, Jenny? Naw, yuh wouldn know! Yuhs jusa ol mule! Anyhow, this is a gun, n it kin shoot, by Gawd!"

He held the gun at arm's length. Whut t hell, Ahma shoot this thing! He looked at Jenny again.

"Lissen here, Jenny! When Ah pull this ol trigger, Ah don wan yuh t run n acka fool now!"

130   Jenny stood with head down, her short ears pricked straight. Dave walked off about twenty feet, held the gun far out from him at arm's length, and turned his head. Hell, he told himself, Ah ain afraid. The gun felt loose in his fingers; he waved it wildly for a moment. Then he shut his eyes and tightened his forefinger. Bloom! A report half deafened him and he thought his right

hand was torn from his arm. He heard Jenny whinnying and galloping over the field, and he found himself on his knees, squeezing his fingers hard between his legs. His hand was numb; he jammed it into his mouth, trying to warm it, trying to stop the pain. The gun lay at his feet. He did not quite know what had happened. He stood up and stared at the gun as though it were a living thing. He gritted his teeth and kicked the gun. Yuh almos broke mah arm! He turned to look for Jenny; she was far over the fields, tossing her head and kicking wildly.

"Hol on there, ol mule!"

When he caught up with her she stood trembling, walling her big white eyes at him. The plow was far away; the traces had broken. Then Dave stopped short, looking, not believing. Jenny was bleeding. Her left side was red and wet with blood. He went closer. Lawd, have mercy! Wondah did Ah shoot this mule? He grabbed for Jenny's mane. She flinched, snorted, whirled, tossing her head.

"Hol on now! Hol on."

Then he saw the hole in jenny's side, right between the ribs. It was round, wet, red. A crimson stream streaked down the front leg, flowing fast. Good Gawd! Ah wuzn't shootin at tha mule. He felt panic. He knew he had to stop that blood, or Jenny would bleed to death. He had never seen so much blood in all his life. He chased the mule for half a mile, trying to catch her. Finally she stopped, breathing hard, stumpy tail half arched. He caught her mane and led her back to where the plow and gun lay. Then he stopped and grabbed handfuls of damp black earth and tried to plug the bullet hole. Jenny shuddered, whinnied, and broke from him.

135   "Hol on! Hol on now!"

He tried to plug it again, but blood came anyhow. His fingers were hot and sticky. He rubbed dirt into his palms, trying to dry them. Then again he attempted to plug the bullet hole, but Jenny shied away, kicking her heels high. He stood helpless. He had to do something. He ran at Jenny; she dodged him. He watched a red stream of blood flow down Jenny's leg and form a bright pool at her feet.

"Jenny . . . Jenny," he called weakly.

His lips trembled. She's bleeding t death! He looked in the direction of home, wanting to go back, wanting to get help. But he saw the pistol lying in the damp black clay. He had a queer feeling that if he only did something, this would not be; Jenny would not be there bleeding to death.

When he went to her this time, she did not move. She stood with sleepy, dreamy eyes; and when he touched her she gave a low-pitched whinny and knelt to the ground, her front knees slopping in blood.

140   "Jenny . . . Jenny . . ." he whispered.

For a long time she held her neck erect; then her head sank, slowly. Her ribs swelled with a mighty heave and she went over.

Dave's stomach felt empty, very empty. He picked up the gun and held it gingerly between his thumb and forefinger. He buried it at the foot of a tree. He took a stick and tried to cover the pool of blood with dirt—but what was the use? There was Jenny lying with her mouth open and her eyes walled and glassy. He could not tell Jim Hawkins he had shot his mule. But he had to tell something. Yeah, Ah'll tel'em Jenny started gittin wil n fell on the joint of the plow. . . . But that would hardly happen to a mule. He walked across the field slowly, head down.

It was sunset. Two of Jim Hawkins' men were over near the edge of the woods digging a hole in which to bury Jenny. Dave was surrounded by a knot of people all of whom were looking down at the dead mule.

"I don't see how in the world it happened," said Jim Hawkins for the tenth time.

The crowd parted and Dave's mother, father, and small brother pushed into the center.

145   "Where Dave?" his mother called.

"There he is," said Jim Hawkins.

His mother grabbed him.

"Whut happened, Dave? Whut yuh done?"

"Nothin."

150   "C mon, boy, talk," his father said.

Dave took a deep breath and told the story he knew nobody believed.

"Waal," he drawled. "Ah brung ol Jenny down here sos Ah could do mah plowin. Ah plowed bout two rows, just like yuh see." He stopped and pointed at the long rows of upturned earth. "Then somethin musta been wrong wid ol Jenny. She wouldn ack right a-tall. She started snortin n kickin her heels. Ah tried t hol her, but she pulled erway, tearin n goin in. Then when the point of the plow was stickin up in the air, she swung erroun n twisted herself back on it. . . . She stuck herself n started t bleed. N fo Ah could do anything, she wuz dead."

"Did you ever hear anything like that in all your life?" asked Jim Hawkins.

There were white and black standing in the crowd. They murmured. Dave's mother came close to him and looked hard into his face. "Tell the truth, Dave," she said.

155   "Looks like a bullet hole to me," said one man.

"Dave, whut yuh do wid the gun?" his mother asked.

The crowd surged in, looking at him. He jammed his hands into his pockets, shook his head slowly from left to right, and backed away. His eyes were wide and painful.

"Did he hava gun?" asked Jim Hawkins.

"By Gawd, Ah tol yuh tha wuz a gun wound," said a man, slapping his thigh.

160   His father caught his shoulders and shook him till his teeth rattled.

"Tell whut happened, yuh rascal! Tell whut . . . ."

Dave looked at Jenny's stiff legs and began to cry.

"Whut yuh do wid tha gun?" his mother asked.

"What wuz he doin wida gun?" his father asked.

165   "Come on and tell the truth," said Hawkins. "Ain't nobody going to hurt you . . . ."

His mother crowded close to him.

"Did yuh shoot tha mule, Dave?"

Dave cried, seeing blurred white and black faces.

"Ahh ddinn gggo tt sshooot hher. . . . Ah ssswear ffo Gawd Ahh ddin. . . . Ah wuz a-tryin t sssee ef the old gggun would sshoot—"

170   "Where yuh git the gun from?" his father asked.

"Ah got it from Joe, at the sto."

"Where yuh git the money?"

"Ma give it t me."

"He kept worryin me, Bob. Ah had t. Ah tol im t bring the gun right back t me. . . . It was fer yuh, the gun."

175   "But how yuh happen to shoot that mule?" asked Jim Hawkins.

      "Ah wuzn shootin at the mule, Mistah Hawkins. The gun jumped when Ah pulled the trigger. . . . N fo Ah knowed anythin Jenny was there a-bleedin."

      Somebody in the crowd laughed. Jim Hawkins walked close to Dave and looked into his face.

      "Well, looks like you have bought you a mule, Dave."

      "Ah swear fo Gawd, Ah didn go t kill the mule, Mistah Hawkins!"

      "But you killed her!"

180   All the crowd was laughing now. They stood on tiptoe and poked heads over one another's shoulders.

      "Well, boy, looks like yuh done bought a dead mule! Hahaha!"

      "Ain tha ershame."

      "Hohohohoho."

185   Dave stood, head down, twisting his feet in the dirt.

      "Well, you needn't worry about it, Bob," said Jim Hawkins to Dave's father. "Just let the boy keep on working and pay me two dollars a month."

      "Whut yuh wan fer yo mule, Mistah Hawkins?"

      Jim Hawkins screwed up his eyes.

      "Fifty dollars."

190   "Whut yuh do wid tha gun?" Dave's father demanded.

      Dave said nothing.

      "Yuh wan me t take a tree n beat yuh till yuh talk!"

      "Nawsuh!"

      "Whut yuh do wid it?"

195   "Ah throwed it erway."

      "Where?"

      "Ah . . . Ah throwed it in the creek."

      "Waal, c mon home. N firs thing in the mawnin git to tha creek n fin tha gun."

      "Yessuh."

200   "Whut yuh pay fer it?"

      "Two dollahs."

      "Take tha gun n git yo money back n carry it to Mistah Hawkins, yuh hear? N don fergit Ahma lam you black bottom good fer this! Now march yosef on home, suh!"

      Dave turned and walked slowly. He heard people laughing. Dave glared, his eyes welling with tears. Hot anger bubbled in him. Then he swallowed and stumbled on.

      That night Dave did not sleep. He was glad that he had gotten out of killing the mule so easily, but he was hurt. Something hot seemed to turn over inside him each time he remembered how they had laughed. He tossed on his bed, feeling his hard pillow. N Pa says he's gonna beat me. . . . He remembered other beatings, and his back quivered. Naw, naw, Ah sho don wan im t beat me tha way no mo. Dam em all! Nobody ever gave him anything. All he did was work. They treat me like a mule, n then they beat me. He gritted his teeth. N Ma had t tell on me.

205   Well, if he had to, he would take old man Hawkins that two dollars. But that meant selling the gun. And he wanted to keep that gun. Fifty dollars for a dead mule.

      He turned over, thinking how he had fired the gun. He had an itch to fire it again. Ef other men kin shoota gun, by Gawd, Ah kin! He was still, listening.

Mebbe they all sleepin now. The house was still. He heard the soft breathing of his brother. Yes, now! He would go down and get that gun and see if he could fire it. He eased out of bed and slipped into overalls.

The moon was bright. He ran almost all the way to the edge of the woods: He stumbled over the ground, looking for the spot where he had buried the gun. Yeah, here it is. Like a hungry dog scratching for a bone, he pawed it up. He puffed his black cheeks and blew dirt from the trigger and barrel. He broke it and found four cartridges unshot. He looked around; the fields were filled with silence and moonlight. He clutched the gun stiff and hard in his fingers. But, as soon as he wanted to pull the trigger, he shut his eyes and turned his head. Naw, Ah can't shoot wid mah eyes closed n mah head turned. With effort he held his eyes open: then he squeezed. *Blooooom!* He was stiff, not breathing. The gun was still in his hands. Dammit, he'd done it! He fired again. *Blooooom!* He smiled. *Blooooom! Blooooom! Click, click.* There! It was empty. If anybody could shoot a gun, he could. He put the gun into his hip pocket and started across the fields.

When he reached the top of a ridge he stood straight and proud in the moonlight, looking at Jim Hawkins' big white house, feeling the gun sagging in his pocket. Lawd, ef Ah had just one mo bullet Ah'd taka shot at tha house. Ah'd like t scare ol man Hawkins jusa little. . . . Jusa enough t let im know Dave Saunders is a man.

To his left the road curved, running to the tracks of the Illinois Central. He jerked his head, listening. From far off come a faint *boooof-boooof; boooof-boooof.* . . . He stood rigid. Two dollahs a mont. Les see now. . . . Tha means it'll take bout two years. Shucks! Ah'll be dam!

210 He started down the road, toward the tracks. Yeah, here she comes! He stood beside the track and held himself stiffly. Here she comes, erroun the ben. . . . C mon, yuh slow poke! C mon! He had his hand on his gun; something quivered in his stomach. Then the train thundeted past, the gray and brown box cars tumbling and clinking. He gripped the gun tightly; then he jerked his hand out of his pocket. Ah betcha Bill wouldn't do it? Ah betcha. . . . The cars slid past, steel grinding upon steel. Ahm tidin yuh ternight, so hep me Gawd! He was hot all over. He hesitated just a moment; then he grabbed, pulled atop of a car, and lay flat. He felt his pocket; the gun was still there. Ahead the long rails were glinting in the moonlight, stretching away, away to somewhere, somewhere where he could be a man. . . .

[1940]

 ## Topics for Critical Thinking and Writing

1. Why does Dave place such emphasis on owning a gun?
2. Do you assume that at the end of the story Dave is a man, or that he is only an immature boy who may come to a sad end? Explain.
3. Does the title strike you as odd? Would "The Boy Who Was Almost a Man" be more appropriate?

BOBBIE ANN MASON

Bobbie Ann Mason, born in 1940 in rural western Kentucky and a graduate of the University of Kentucky, now lives in Pennsylvania. She took a master's degree at the State University of New York at Bingham-ton, and a Ph.D. at the University of Connecticut, writing a dissertation on a novel by Vladimir Nabokov. Between graduate degrees she worked for various magazines, including T.V. Star Parade. In 1974 she pub-lished her first book—the dissertation on Nabokov—and in 1975 she published her second, The Girl Sleuth: A Guide to the Bobbsey Twins, Nancy Drew and Their Sisters. *She is, however, most widely known for her fiction, which usually deals with blue-collar people in rural Kentucky. "I write," she says, "about people trapped in circumstances. . . . I identify with people who are ambivalent about their sit-uation. And I guess in my stories, I'm in a way imagining myself as I would have felt if I had not gotten away and gotten a different perspective on things—if, for example, I had gotten pregnant in high school and had to marry a truck driver as the woman did in my story 'Shiloh.'"*

Shiloh

Leroy Moffitt's wife. Norma Jean, is working on her pectorals. She lifts three-pound dumbbells to warm up, then progresses to a twenty-pound barbell. Stand-ing with her legs apart, she reminds Leroy of Wonder Woman.

"I'd give anything if I could just get these muscles to where they're real hard." says Norma Jean. "Feel this arm. It's not as hard as the other one."

"That's cause you're right-handed." says Leroy, dodging as she swings the barbell in an arc.

"Do you think so?"

5   "Sure."

Leroy is a truckdriver. He injured his leg in a highway accident four months ago, and his physical therapy, which involves weights and a pulley, prompted Norma Jean to try building herself up. Now she is attending a body-building class. Leroy has been collecting temporary disability since his tractor-trailer jackknifed in Missouri, badly twisting his left leg in its socket. He has a steel pin in his hip. He will probably not be able to drive his rig again. It sits in the backyard, like a gigan-tic bird that has flown home to roost. Leroy has been home in Kentucky for three months, and his leg is almost healed, but the accident frightened him and he does not want to drive any more long hauls. He is not sure what to do next. In the meantime, he makes things from craft kits. He started by building a miniature log cabin from notched Popsicle sticks. He varnished it and place it on the TV set, where it remains. It reminds him of a rustic Nativity scene. Then he tried string art (sailing ships on black velvet), a macramé owl kit, a snap-together B-17 Flying Fortress, and a lamp made out of a model truck, with a light fixture screwed in the top of the cab. At first the kits were diversions, something to kill time, but now he is thinking about building a full-scale log house from a kit. It would be consider-ably cheaper than building a regular house, and besides, Leroy has grown to ap-preciate how things are put together. He has begun to realize that in all the years he was on the road he never took time to examine anything. He was always flying past scenery.

"They won't let you build a log cabin in any of the new subdivisions," Norma Jean tells him.

"They will if I tell them it's for you," he says, teasing her. Ever since they were married, he has promised Norma Jean he would build her a new home one day. They have always rented, and the house they live in is small and nondescript. It does not even feel like a home, Leroy realizes now.

Norma Jean works at the Rexall drugstore, and she has acquired an amazing amount of information about cosmetics. When she explains to Leroy the three stages of complexion care, involving creams, toners, and moisturizers, he thinks happily of other petroleum products—axle grease, diesel fuel. This is a connection between him and Norma Jean. Since he has been home, he has felt unusually tender about his wife and guilty over his long absences. But he can't tell what she feels about him. Norma Jean has never complained about his traveling; she has never made hurt remarks, like calling his truck a "widow-maker." He is reasonably certain she has been faithful to him, but he wishes she would celebrate his permanent home-coming more happily. Norma Jean is often startled to find Leroy at home, and he thinks she seems a little disappointed about it. Perhaps he reminds her too much of the early days of their marriage, before he went on the road. They had a child who died as an infant, years ago. They never speak about their memories of Randy, which have almost faded, but now that Leroy is home all the time, they sometimes feel awkward around each other, and Leroy wonders if one of them should mention the child. He has the feeling that they are waking up out of a dream together—that they must create a new marriage, start afresh. They are lucky they are still married. Leroy has read that for most people losing a child destroys the marriage—or else he heard this on *Donahue*. He can't always remember where he learns things anymore.

10   At Christmas. Leroy bought an electric organ for Norma Jean. She used to play the piano when she was in high school. "It don't leave you," she told him once. "It's like riding a bicycle."

The new instrument had so many keys and buttons that she was bewildered by it at first. She touched the keys tentatively, pushed some buttons, then pecked out "Chopsticks." It came out in an amplified fox-trot rhythm, with marimba sounds.

"It's an orchestra!" she cried.

The organ had a pecan-look finish and eighteen preset chords, with optional flute, violin, trumpet, clarinet, and banjo accompaniments. Norma Jean mastered the organ almost immediately. At first she played Christmas songs. Then she bought *The Sixties Songbook* and learned every tune in it, adding variations to each with the rows of brightly colored buttons.

"I didn't like these old songs back then." she said. "But I have this crazy feeling I missed something."

15   "You didn't miss a thing," said Leroy.

Leroy likes to lie on the couch and smoke a joint and listen to Norma Jean play "Can't Take My Eyes Off You" and "I'll Be Back." He is back again. After fifteen years on the road, he is finally settling down with the woman he loves. She is still pretty. Her skin is flawless. Her frosted curls resemble pencil trimmings.

Now that Leroy has come home to stay, he notices how much the town has changed. Subdivisions are spreading across western Kentucky like an oil slick. The sign at the edge of town says "Pop: 11,500"—only seven hundred more than it said twenty years before. Leroy can't figure out who is living in all the new

houses. The farmers who used to gather around the courthouse square on Saturday afternoons to play checkers and spit tobacco juice have gone. It has been
years since Leroy has thought about the farmers, and they have disappeared without his noticing.

Leroy meets a kid named Stevie Hamilton in the parking lot at the new
shopping center. While they pretend to be strangers meeting over a stalled car,
Stevie tosses an ounce of marijuana under the front seat of Leroy's car. Stevie is
wearing orange jogging shoes and a T-shirt that says CHATTAHOOCHEE SUPER-RAT.
His father is a prominent doctor who lives in one of the expensive subdivisions
in a new white-columned brick house that looks like a funeral parlor. In the
phone book under his name there is a separate number, with the listing
"Teenagers."

"Where do you get this stuff?" asks Leroy. "From your pappy?"

20   "That's for me to know and you to find out," Stevie says. He is slit-eyed and
skinny.

"What else you got?"

"What you interested in?"

"Nothing special. Just wondered."

Leroy used to take speed on the road. Now he has to go slowly. He needs to
be mellow. He leans back against the car and says. "I'm aiming to build me a log
house, soon as I get time. My wife, though, I don't think she likes the idea."

25   "Well, let me know when you want me again," Stevie says. He has a cigarette
in his cupped palm, as though sheltering it from the wind. He takes a long drag,
then stomps it on the asphalt and slouches away.

Stevie's father was two years ahead of Leroy in high school. Leroy is thirty-
four. He married Norma Jean when they were both eighteen, and their child
Randy was born a few months later, but he died at the age of four months and
three days. He would be about Stevie's age now. Norma Jean and Leroy were at
the drive-in, watching a double feature (*Dr. Strangelove* and *Lover Come Back*),
and the baby was sleeping in the back seat. When the first movie ended, the
baby was dead. It was the sudden infant death syndrome. Leroy remembers
handing Randy to a nurse at the emergency room, as though he were offering
her a large doll as a present. A dead baby feels like a sack of flour. "It just happens sometimes," said the doctor, in what Leroy always recalls as a nonchalant
tone. Leroy can hardly remember the child anymore, but he still sees vividly a
scene from *Dr. Strangelove* in which the President of the United States was talking in a folksy voice on the hot line to the Soviet premier about the bomber accidentally headed toward Russia. He was in the War Room, and the world map
was lit up. Leroy remembers Norma Jean standing catatonically beside him in the
hospital and himself thinking: Who is this strange girl? He had forgotten who she
was. Now scientists are saying that crib death is caused by a virus. Nobody
knows anything, Leroy thinks. The answers are always changing.

When Leroy gets home from the shopping center. Norma Jean's mother,
Mabel Beasley, is there. Until this year. Leroy has not realized how much time
she spends with Norma Jean. When she visits, she inspects the closets and then
the plants, informing Norma Jean when a plant is droopy or yellow. Mabel calls
the plants "flowers," although there are never any blooms. She also notices if
Norma Jean's laundry is piling up. Mabel is a short, overweight woman whose
tight, brown-dyed curls look more like a wig than the actual wig she sometimes
wears. Today she has brought Norma Jean an off-white dust ruffle she made for
the bed; Mabel works in a custom-upholstery shop.

"This is the tenth one I made this year," Mabel says. "I got started and couldn't stop."

"It's real pretty," says Normal Jean.

30   "Now we can hide things under the bed," says Leroy, who gets along with his mother-in-law primarily by joking with her. Mabel has never really forgiven him for disgracing her by getting Norma Jean pregnant. When the baby died, she said that fate was mocking her.

"What's that thing?" Mabel says to Leroy in a loud voice, pointing to a tangle of yarn on a piece of canvas.

Leroy holds it up for Mabel to see. "It's my needlepoint," he explains. "This is a *Star Trek* pillow cover."

"That's what a woman would do," says Mabel. "Great day in the morning!"

"All the big football players on TV do it," he says.

35   "Why, Leroy, you're always trying to fool me. I don't believe you for one minute. You don't know what to do with yourself—that's the whole trouble. Sewing!"

"I'm aiming to build us a log house," says Leroy. "Soon as my plans come."

"Like *heck* you are," says Norma Jean. She takes Leroy's needlepoint and shoves it into a drawer. "You have to find a job first. Nobody can afford to build now anyway."

Mabel straightens her girdle and says. "I still think before you get tied down y'all ought to take a little run to Shiloh."

"One of these days, Mama," Norma Jean says impatiently.

40   Mabel is talking about Shiloh, Tennessee. For the past few years, she has been urging Leroy and Norma Jean to visit the Civil War battleground there. Mabel went there on her honeymoon—the only real trip she ever took. Her husband died of a perforated ulcer when Norma Jean was ten, but Mabel, who was accepted into the United Daughters of the Confederacy in 1975, is still preoccupied with going back to Shiloh.

"I've been to kingdom come and back in that truck out yonder," Leroy says to Mabel, "but we never yet set foot in that battleground. Ain't that something? How did I miss it?"

"It's not even that far," Mabel says.

After Mabel leaves, Norma Jean reads to Leroy from a list she has made. "Things you could do," she announces. "You could get a job as a guard at Union Carbide, where they'd let you set on a stool. You could get on at the lumberyard. You could do a little carpenter work, if you want to build so bad. You could—"

"I can't do something where I'd have to stand up all day."

45   "You ought to try standing up all day behind a cosmetics counter. It's amazing that I have strong feet, coming from two parents that never had strong feet at all." At the moment Norma Jean is holding on to the kitchen counter, raising her knees one at a time as she talks. She is wearing two-pound ankle weights.

"Don't worry," says Leroy. "I'll do something."

"You could truck calves to slaughter for somebody. You wouldn't have to drive any big old truck for that."

"I'm going to build you this house,' says Leroy. "I want to make you a real home."

"I don't want to live in any log cabin."

50   "It's not a cabin. It's a house."

"I don't care. It looks like a cabin."

"You and me together could lift those logs. It's just like lifting weights."

Norma Jean doesn't answer. Under her breath, she is counting. Now she is marching through the kitchen. She is doing goose steps.

Before his accident, when Leroy came home he used to stay in the house with Norma Jean, watching TV in bed and playing cards. She would cook fried chicken, picnic ham, chocolate pie—all his favorites. Now he is home alone much of the time. In the mornings, Norma Jean disappears, leaving a cooling place in the bed. She eats a cereal called Body Buddies, and she leaves the bowl on the table, with the soggy tan balls floating in a milk puddle. He sees things about Norma Jean that he never realized before. When she chops onions, she stares off into a corner, as if she can't bear to look. She puts on her house slippers almost precisely at nine o'clock every evening and nudges her jogging shoes under the couch. She saves bread heels for the birds. Leroy watches the birds at the feeder. He notices the peculiar way goldfinches fly past the window. They close their wings, then fall, then spread their wings to catch and lift themselves. He wonders if they close their eyes when they fall. Norma Jean closes her eyes when they are in bed. She wants the lights turned out. Even then, he is sure she closes her eyes.

55

He goes for long drives around town. He tends to drive a car rather carelessly. Power steering and an automatic shift make a car feel so small and inconsequential that his body is hardly involved in the driving process. His injured leg stretches out comfortably. Once or twice he has almost hit something, but even the prospect of an accident seems minor in a car. He cruises the new subdivisions, feeling like a criminal rehearsing for a robbery. Norma Jean is probably right about a log house being inappropriate here in the new subdivision. All the houses look grand and complicated. They depress him.

One day when Leroy comes home from a drive he finds Norma Jean in tears. She is in the kitchen making a potato and mushroom-soup casserole, with grated cheese topping. She is crying because her mother caught her smoking.

"I didn't hear her coming. I was standing here puffing away pretty as you please," Norma Jean says, wiping her eyes.

"I knew it would happen sooner or later," says Leroy, putting his arm around her.

"She don't know the meaning of the word 'knock,'" says Norma Jean. "It's a wonder she hadn't caught me years ago."

60

"Think of it this way," Leroy says. "What if she caught me with a joint?"

"You better not let her!" Norma Jean shrieks. "I'm warning you, Leroy Moffitt!"

"I'm just kidding. Here, play me a tune. That'll help you relax."

Norma Jean puts the casserole in the oven and sets the timer. Then she plays a ragtime tune, with horns and banjo, as Leroy lights up a joint and lies on the couch, laughing to himself about Mabel's catching him at it. He thinks of Stevie Hamilton—a doctor's son pushing grass. Everything is funny. The whole town seems crazy and small. He is reminded of Virgil Mathis, a boastful policeman Leroy used to shoot pool with. Virgil recently led a drug bust in a back room at a bowling alley, where he seized ten thousand dollars' worth of marijuana. The newspaper had a picture of him holding up the bags of grass and grinning widely. Right now, Leroy can imagine Virgil breaking down the door and arresting him with a lungful of smoke. Virgil would probably have been alerted to the scene because of all the racket Norma Jean is making. Now she sounds like a hard-rock band. Norma Jean is terrific. When she switches to a Latin-rhythm version of "Sunshine Superman," Leroy hums along. Norma Jean's foot goes up and down, up and down.

"Well, what do you think?" Leroy says, when Norma Jean pauses to search through her music.

65   "What do I think about what?"

His mind has gone blank. Then he says. "I'll sell my rig and build us a house." That wasn't what he wanted to say. He wanted to know what she thought—what she *really* thought—about them.

"Don't start in on that again," says Norma Jean. She begins playing "Who'll Be the Next in Line?"

Leroy used to tell hitchhikers his whole life story—about his travels, his hometown, the baby. He would end with a question: "Well, what do you think?" It was just a rhetorical question. In time, he had the feeling that he'd been telling the same story over and over to the same hitchhikers. He quit talking to hitchhikers when he realized how his voice sounded—whining and self-pitying, like some teenage-tragedy song. Now Leroy has the sudden impulse to tell Norma Jean about himself, as if he had just met her. They have known each other so long they have forgotten a lot about each other. They could become reacquainted. But when the oven timer goes off and she runs to the kitchen, he forgets why he wants to do this.

The next day, Mabel drops by. It is Saturday and Norma Jean is cleaning. Leroy is studying the plans of his log house, which have finally come in the mail. He has them spread out on the table—big sheets of stiff blue paper, with diagrams and numbers printed in white. While Norma Jean runs the vacuum, Mabel drinks coffee. She sets her coffee cup on a blueprint.

70   "I'm just waiting for time to pass," she says to Leroy, drumming her fingers on the table.

As soon as Norma Jean switches off the vacuum, Mabel says in a loud voice. "Did you hear about the datsun dog that killed the baby?"

Norma Jean says, "The word is 'dachshund.' "

"They put the dog on trial. It chewed the baby's legs off. The mother was in the next room all the time." She raises her voice. "They thought it was neglect."

Norma Jean is holding her ears. Leroy manages to open the refrigerator and get some Diet Pepsi to offer Mabel. Mabel still has some coffee and she waves away the Pepsi.

75   "Datsuns are like that," Mabel says. "They're jealous dogs. They'll tear a place to pieces if you don't keep an eye on them."

"You better watch out what you're saying, Mabel," says Leroy.

"Well, facts is facts."

Leroy looks out the window at his rig. It is like a huge piece of furniture gathering dust in the backyard. Pretty soon it will be an antique. He hears the vacuum cleaner. Norma Jean seems to be cleaning the living room rug again.

Later, she says to Leroy. "She just said that about the baby because she caught me smoking. She's trying to pay me back."

80   "What are you talking about?" Leroy says, nervously shuffling blueprints.

"You know good and well." Norma Jean says. She is sitting in a kitchen chair with her feet up and her arms wrapped around her knees. She looks small and helpless. She says. "The very idea, her bringing up a subject like that! Saying it was neglect."

"She didn't mean that," Leroy says.

"She might not have *thought* she meant it. She always says things like that. You don't know how she goes on."

"But she didn't really mean it. She was just talking."

85 Leroy opens a king-sized bottle of beer and pours it into two glasses, dividing it carefully. He hands a glass to Norma Jean and she takes it from him mechanically. For a long time, they sit by the kitchen window watching the birds at the feeder.

Something is happening. Norma Jean is going to night school. She has graduated from her six-week body-building course and now she is taking an adult-education course in composition at Paducah Community College. She spends her evenings outlining paragraphs.

"First, you have a topic sentence," she explains to Leroy. "Then you divide it up. Your secondary topic has to be connected to your primary topic."

To Leroy, this sounds intimidating. "I never was any good in English," he says.

"It makes a lot of sense."

90 "What are you doing this for, anyhow?"

She shrugs. "It's something to do." She stands up and lifts her dumbbells a few times.

"Driving a rig, nobody cared about my English."

"I'm not criticizing your English."

Norma Jean used to say, "If I lose ten minutes' sleep, I just drag all day." Now she stays up late, writing compositions. She got a B on her first paper—a how-to theme on soup-based casseroles. Recently Norma Jean has been cooking unusual foods—tacos, lasagna, Bombay chicken. She doesn't play the organ anymore, though her second paper was called "Why Music Is Important to Me." She sits at the kitchen table, concentrating on her outlines, while Leroy plays with his log house plans, practicing with a set of Lincoln Logs. The thought of getting a truckload of notched, numbered logs scares him, and he wants to be prepared. As he and Norma Jean work together at the kitchen table, Leroy has the hopeful thought that they are sharing something, but he knows he is a fool to think this. Norma Jean is miles away. He knows he is going to lose her. Like Mabel, he is just waiting for time to pass.

95 One day, Mabel is there before Norma Jean gets home from work, and Leroy finds himself confiding in her, Mabel, he realizes, must know Norma Jean better than he does.

"I don't know what's got into that girl," Mabel says. "She used to go to bed with the chickens. Now you say she's up all hours. Plus her a-smoking. I like to died."

"I want to make her this beautiful home," Leroy says, indicating the Lincoln Logs. "I don't think she even wants it. Maybe she was happier with me gone."

"She don't know what to make of you, coming home like this."

"Is that it?"

100 Mabel takes the roof off his Lincoln Log cabin. "You couldn't get *me* in a log cabin," she says. "I was raised in one. It's no picnic, let me tell you."

"They're different now," says Leroy.

"I tell you what," Mabel says, smiling oddly at Leroy.

"What?"

"Take her on down to Shiloh. Y'all need to get out together, stir a little. Her brain's all balled up over them books."

105 Leroy can see traces of Norma Jean's features in her mother's face. Mabel's worn face has the texture of crinkled cotton, but suddenly she looks pretty. It

occurs to Leroy that Mabel has been hinting all along that she wants them to take her with them to Shiloh.

"Let's all go to Shiloh," he says. "You and me and her. Come Sunday."

Mabel throws up her hand in protest. "Oh, no, not me. Young folks want to be by theirselves."

When Norma Jean comes in with groceries, Leroy says excitedly. "Your mama here's been dying to go to Shiloh for thirty-five years. It's about time we went, don't you think?"

"I'm not going to butt in on anybody's second honeymoon," Mabel says.

110 "Who's going on a honeymoon, for Christ's sake?" Norma Jean says loudly.

"I never raised no daughter of mine to talk that-a-way," Mabel says.

"You ain't seen nothing yet," says Norma Jean. She starts putting away boxes and cans, slamming cabinet doors.

"There's a log cabin at Shiloh," Mabel says. "It was there during the battle. There's bullet holes in it."

"When are you going to *shut up* about Shiloh, Mama?" asks Norma Jean.

115 "I always thought Shiloh was the prettiest place, so full of history," Mabel goes on. "I just hoped y'all could see it once before I die, so you could tell me about it." Later, she whispers to Leroy. "You do what I said. A little change is what she needs."

"Your name means 'the king.'" Norma Jean says to Leroy that evening. He is trying to get her to go to Shiloh, and she is reading a book about another century.

"Well, I reckon I ought to be right proud."

"I guess so."

"Am I still king around here?"

120 Norma Jean flexes her biceps and feels them for hardness. "I'm not fooling around with anybody, if that's what you mean," she says.

"Would you tell me if you were?"

"I don't know."

"What does *your* name mean?"

"It was Marilyn Monroe's real name."

125 "No kidding!"

"Norma comes from the Normans. They were invaders," she says. She closes her book and looks hard at Leroy. "I'll go to Shiloh with you if you'll stop staring at me."

On Sunday, Norma Jean packs a picnic and they go to Shiloh. To Leroy's relief Mabel says she does not want to come with them. Norma Jean drives, and Leroy, sitting beside her, feels like some boring hitchhiker she has picked up. He tries some conversation, but she answers him in monosyllables. At Shiloh, she drives aimlessly through the park, past bluffs and trails and steep ravines. Shiloh is an immense place, and Leroy cannot see it as a battleground. It is not what he expected. He thought it would look like a golf course. Monuments are everywhere, showing through the thick clusters of trees. Norma Jean passes the log cabin Mabel mentioned. It is surrounded by tourists looking for bullet holes.

"That's not the kind of log house I've got in mind," says Leroy apologetically.

"I know *that*."

130 "This is a pretty place. Your mama was right."

"It's O.K.," says Norma Jean. "Well, we've seen it. I hope she's satisfied."

They burst out laughing together.

At the park museum, a movie on Shiloh is shown every half hour, but they decide that they don't want to see it. They buy a souvenir Confederate flag for Mabel, and then they find a picnic spot near the cemetery. Norma Jean has brought a picnic cooler, with pimento sandwiches, soft drinks, and Yodels. Leroy eats a sandwich and then smokes a joint, hiding it behind the picnic cooler. Norma Jean has quit smoking altogether. She is picking cake crumbs from the cellophane wrapper, like a fussy bird.

Leroy says, "So the boys in gray ended up in Corinth. The Union soldiers zapped 'em finally. April 7, 1862."

135   They both know that he doesn't know any history. He is just talking about some of the historical plaques they have read. He feels awkward, like a boy on a date with an older girl. They are still just making conversation.

"Corinth is where Mama eloped to," says Norma Jean.

They sit in silence and stare at the cemetery for the Union dead and, beyond, at a tall cluster of trees. Campers are parked nearby, bumper to bumper, and small children in bright clothing are cavorting and squealing. Norma Jean wads up the cake wrapper and squeezes it tightly in her hand. Without looking at Leroy, she says, "I want to leave you."

Leroy takes a bottle of Coke out of the cooler and flips off the cap. He holds the bottle poised near his mouth but cannot remember to take a drink. Finally he says. "No, you don't."

"Yes, I do."

140   "I won't let you."

"You can't stop me."

"Don't do me that way."

Leroy knows Norma Jean will have her own way. "Didn't I promise to be home from now on?" he says.

"In some ways, a woman prefers a man who wanders," says Norma Jean. "That sounds crazy, I know."

145   "You're not crazy."

Leroy remembers to drink from his Coke. Then he says, "Yes, you *are* crazy. You and me could start all over again. Right back at the beginning."

"We *have* started all over again." says Norma Jean. "And this is how it turned out."

"What did I do wrong?"

"Nothing."

150   "Is this one of those women's lib things?" Leroy asks.

"Don't be funny."

The cemetery, a green slope dotted with white markers, looks like a subdivision site. Leroy is trying to comprehend that his marriage is breaking up, but for some reason he is wondering about white slabs in a graveyard.

"Everything was fine till Mama caught me smoking." says Norma Jean, standing up. "That set something off."

"What are you talking about?"

155   "She won't leave me alone—*you* won't leave me alone." Norma Jean seems to be crying, but she is looking away from him. "I feel eighteen again. I can't face that all over again." She starts walking away. "No, it *wasn't* fine. I don't know what I'm saying. Forget it."

Leroy takes a lungful of smoke and closes his eyes as Norma Jean's words sink in. He tries to focus on the fact that thirty-five hundred soldiers died on the grounds around him. He can only think of that war as a board game with plastic soldiers. Leroy almost smiles, as he compares the Confederates' daring attack on the Union camps and Virgil Mathis's raid on the bowling alley. General Grant, drunk and furious, shoved the Southerners back to Corinth, where Mabel and Jet Beasley were married years later, when Mabel was still thin and good-looking. The next day, Mabel and Jet visited the battleground, and then Norma Jean was born, and then she married Leroy and they had a baby, which they lost, and now Leroy and Norma Jean are here at the same battleground. Leroy knows he is leaving out a lot. He is leaving out the insides of history. History was always just names and dates to him. It occurs to him that building a house of logs is similarly empty—too simple. And the real inner workings of a marriage, like most of history, have escaped him. Now he sees that building a log house is the dumbest idea he could have had. It was clumsy of him to think Norma Jean would want a log house. It was a crazy idea. He'll have to think of something else, quickly. He will wad the blueprints into tight balls and fling them into the lake. Then he'll get moving again. He opens his eyes. Norma Jean has moved away and is walking through the cemetery, following a serpentine brick path.

Leroy gets up to follow his wife, but his good leg is asleep and his bad leg still hurts him. Norma Jean is far away, walking rapidly toward the bluff by the river, and he tries to hobble toward her. Some children run past him, screaming noisily. Norma Jean has reached the bluff, and she is looking out over the Tennessee River. Now she turns toward Leroy and waves her arms. Is she beckoning to him? She seems to be doing an exercise for her chest muscles. The sky is unusually pale—the color of the dust ruffle Mabel made for their bed.

[1982]

Topics for Critical Thinking and Writing

1. Whose feelings—Leroy's or Norma Jean's—are more fully presented in the story? Do we know exactly what Norma Jean wants? Do you think that she herself knows?
2. The story is written in the present tense, for instance, "Leroy Moffitt's wife, Norma Jean, is working on her pectorals," rather than (as would be more common in fiction) ". . . was working on her pectorals." What is gained by using the present in this story?
3. Why is Leroy preoccupied with kits, and why is Norma Jean so eagerly attempting to improve her body and her mind?
4. When we first meet Mabel, Norma Jean's mother, we learn that she has made "an off-white dust ruffle for the bed." Leroy jokes about it, and Mason refers to it in the last line of the story, a place of great emphasis. Why this business about a dust ruffle for a bed?
5. Do you think "Shiloh" is a good title? Why?

 MAX APPLE

Max Apple was born in 1941 in Grand Rapids. Michigan, in a traditional Jewish home—he knew Yiddish before he knew English. He received a B.A. and a Ph.D. in English from the University of Michigan and has taught literature and creative writing at Rice University.

"I admit to experimenting," he has said of his stories and novels, but he adds, "I hope I've never lost sight of the most powerful question in narrative: What happens next? . . . None of the experiments can

work if you don't create a character whom you care about and whom your reader can care about."

Bridging

At the Astrodome, Nolan Ryan is shaving the corners. He's going through the Giants in order. The radio announcer is not even mentioning that by the sixth the Giants haven't had a hit. The K's mount[1] on the scoreboard. Tonight Nolan passes the Big Train[2] and is now the all-time strikeout king. He's almost as old as I am and he still throws nothing but smoke. His fastball is an aspirin; batters tear their tendons lunging for his curve. Jessica and I have season tickets, but tonight she's home listening and I'm in the basement of St. Anne's Church watching Kay Randall's fingertips. Kay is holding her hands out from her chest, her fingertips on each other. Her fingers move a little as she talks and I can hear her nails click when they meet. That's how close I'm sitting.

Kay is talking about "bridging"; that's what her arched fingers represent.

"Bridging," she says, "is the way Brownies become Girl Scouts. It's a slow steady process. It's not easy, but we allow a whole year for bridging."

Eleven girls in brown shirts with red bandannas at their neck are imitating Kay as she talks. They hold their stumpy chewed fingertips out and bridge them. So do I.

5   I brought the paste tonight and the stick-on gold stars and the thread for sewing buttonholes.

"I feel a little awkward," Kay Randall said on the phone, "asking a man to do these errands . . . but that's my problem, not yours. Just bring the supplies and try to be at the church meeting room a few minutes before seven."

I arrive a half hour early.

"You're off your rocker," Jessica says. She begs me to drop her at the Astrodome on my way to the Girl Scout meeting. "After the game, I'll meet you at the main souvenir stand on the first level. They stay open an hour after the game. I'll be all right. There are cops and ushers every five yards."

She can't believe that I am missing this game to perform my functions as an assistant Girl Scout leader. Our Girl Scout battle has been going on for two months.

10   "Girl Scouts is stupid," Jessica says. "Who wants to sell cookies and sew buttons and walk around wearing stupid old badges?"

When she agreed to go to the first meeting, I was so happy I volunteered to become an assistant leader. After the meeting, Jessica went directly to the car the way she does after school, after a birthday party, after a ball game, after anything. A straight line to the car. No jabbering with girlfriends, no smiles, no dallying, just right to the car. She slides into the back seat, belts in, and braces herself for destruction. It has already happened once.

I swoop past five thousand years of stereotypes and accept my assistant leader's packet and credentials.

"I'm sure there have been other men in the movement," Kay says, "we just haven't had any in our district. It will be good for the girls."

Not for my Jessica. She won't bridge, she won't budge.

---

[1]*K* is the symbol for a strikeout (all notes are by the editors)   [2]Walter Johnson (1887–1946), pitcher for the Washington Senators

15   "I know why you're doing this," she says. "You think that because I don't have a mother, Kay Randall and the Girl Scouts will help me. That's crazy. And I know that Sharon is supposed to be like a mother too. Why don't you just leave me alone."

Sharon is Jessica's therapist. Jessica sees her twice a week. Sharon and I have a meeting once a month.

"We have a lot of shy girls," Kay Randall tells me. "Scouting brings them out. Believe me, it's hard to stay shy when you're nine years old and you're sharing a tent with six other girls. You have to count on each other, you have to communicate."

I imagine Jessica zipping up in her sleeping bag, mumbling good night to anyone who first says it to her, then closing her eyes and hating me for sending her out among the happy.

"She likes all sports, especially baseball," I tell my leader.

20   "There's room for baseball in scouting," Kay says. "Once a year the whole district goes to a game. They mention us on the big scoreboard."

"Jessica and I go to all the home games. We're real fans."

Kay smiles.

"That's why I want her in Girl Scouts. You know, I want her to go to things with her girlfriends instead of always hanging around with me at ball games."

"I understand," Kay says. "It's part of bridging."

25   With Sharon the term is "separation anxiety." That's the fastball, "bridging" is the curve. Amid all their magic words I feel as if Jessica and I are standing at home plate blindfolded.

While I await Kay and the members of Troop 111, District 6, I eye St. Anne in her grotto and St. Gregory and St. Thomas. Their hands are folded as if they started out bridging, ended up praying.

In October the principal sent Jessica home from school because Mrs. Simmons caught her in spelling class listening to the World Series through an earphone.

"It's against the school policy," Mrs. Simmons said. "Jessica understands school policy. We confiscate radios and send the child home."

"I'm glad," Jessica said. "It was a cheap-o radio. Now I can watch the TV with you."

30   They sent her home in the middle of the sixth game. I let her stay home for the seventh too.

The Brewers are her favorite American League team. She likes Rollie Fingers, and especially Robin Yount.

"Does Yount go in the hole[3] better than Harvey Kuenn used to?"

"You bet," I tell her. "Kuenn was never a great fielder but he could hit three hundred with his eyes closed."

Kuenn is the Brewers manager. He has an artificial leg and can barely make it up the dugout steps, but when I was Jessica's age and the Tigers were my team, Kuenn used to stand at the plate, tap the corners with his bat, spit some tobacco juice, and knock liners up the alley.

35   She took the Brewers' loss hard.

"If Fingers wasn't hurt they would have squashed the Cards, wouldn't they?"

I agreed.

---

[3]when a shortstop moves to the right and backhands the ball before throwing to first or second

"But I'm glad for Andujar."

We had Andujar's autograph. Once we met him at a McDonald's. He was a relief pitcher then, an erratic right-hander. In St. Louis he improved. I was happy to get his name on a napkin. Jessica shook his hand.

40　　　One night after I read her a story, she said, "Daddy, if we were rich could we go to the away games too? I mean, if you didn't have to be at work every day."

"Probably we could," I said, "but wouldn't it get boring? We'd have to stay at hotels and eat in restaurants. Even the players get sick of it."

"Are you kidding?" she said. "I'd never get sick of it."

"Jessica has fantasies of being with you forever, following baseball or whatever," Sharon says. "All she's trying to do is please you. Since she lost her mother she feels that you and she are alone in the world. She doesn't want to let anyone or anything else into that unit, the two of you. She's afraid of any more losses. And, of course, her greatest worry is about losing you."

"You know," I tell Sharon, "that's pretty much how I feel too."

45　　　"Of course it is," she says. "I'm glad to hear you say it."

Sharon is glad to hear me say almost anything. When I complain that her $100-a-week fee would buy a lot of peanut butter sandwiches, she says she is "glad to hear me expressing my anger."

"Sharon's not fooling me," Jessica says. "I know that she thinks drawing those pictures is supposed to make me feel better or something. You're just wasting your money. There's nothing wrong with me."

"It's a long, difficult, expensive process," Sharon says. "You and Jessica have lost a lot. Jessica is going to have to learn to trust the world again. It would help if you could do it too."

So I decide to trust Girl Scouts. First Girl Scouts, then the world. I make my stand at the meeting of Kay Randall's fingertips. While Nolan Ryan breaks Walter Johnson's strikeout record and pitches a two-hit shutout, I pass out paste and thread to nine-year-olds who are sticking and sewing their lives together in ways Jessica and I can't.

II

50　　Scouting is not altogether new to me. I was a Cub Scout. I owned a blue beanie and I remember very well my den mother, Mrs. Clark. A den mother made perfect sense to me then and still does. Maybe that's why I don't feel uncomfortable being a Girl Scout assistant leader.

We had no den father. Mr. Clark was only a photograph on the living room wall, the tiny living room where we held our monthly meetings. Mr. Clark was killed in the Korean War. His son John was in the troop. John was stocky but Mrs. Clark was huge. She couldn't sit on a regular chair, only on a couch or a stool without sides. She was the cashier in the convenience store beneath their apartment. The story we heard was that Walt, the old man who owned the store, felt sorry for her and gave her the job. He was her landlord too. She sat on a swivel stool and rang up the purchases.

We met at the store and watched while she locked the door; then we followed her up the steep staircase to her three-room apartment. She carried two wet glass bottles of milk. Her body took up the entire width of the staircase. She passed the banisters the way semi trucks pass each other on a narrow highway.

We were ten years old, a time when everything is funny, especially fat people. But I don't remember anyone ever laughing about Mrs. Clark. She had great dignity and character. So did John. I didn't know what to call it then, but I knew John was someone you could always trust.

She passed out milk and cookies, then John collected the cups and washed them. They didn't even have a television set. The only decoration in the room that barely held all of us was Mr. Clark's picture on the wall. We saw him in his uniform and we knew he died in Korea defending his country. We were little boys in blue beanies drinking milk in the apartment of a hero. Through that aura I came to scouting. I wanted Kay Randall to have all of Mrs. Clark's dignity.

55   When she took a deep breath and then bridged, Kay Randall had noticeable armpits. Her wide shoulders slithered into a tiny, rib cage. Her armpits were like bridges. She said "bridging" like a mantra[4] holding her hands before her for about thirty seconds at the start of each meeting.

"A promise is a promise," I told Jessica. "I signed up to be a leader, and I'm going to do it with you or without you."

"But you didn't even ask me if I liked it. You just signed up without talking it over."

"That's true; that's why I'm not going to force you to go along. It was my choice."

"What can you like about it? I hate Melissa Randall. She always has a cold."

60   "Her mother is a good leader."

"How do you know?"

"She's my boss. I've got to like her, don't I?" I hugged Jessica. "C'mon, honey, give it a chance. What do you have to lose?"

"If you make me go I'll do it, but if I have a choice I won't."

Every other Tuesday, Karen, the fifteen-year-old Greek girl who lives on the corner, babysits Jessica while I go to the Scout meetings. We talk about field trips and how to earn merit badges. The girls giggle when Kay pins a promptness badge on me, my first.

65   Jessica thinks it's hilarious. She tells me to wear it to work.

Sometimes when I watch Jessica brush her hair and tie her ponytail and make up her lunch kit I start to think that maybe I should just relax and stop the therapy and the scouting and all my not-so-subtle attempts to get her to invite friends over. I start to think that, in spite of everything, she's a good student and she's got a sense of humor. She's barely nine years old. She'll grow up like everyone else does. John Clark did it without a father; she'll do it without a mother. I start to wonder if Jessica seems to the girls in her class the way John Clark seemed to me: dignified, serious, almost an adult even while we were playing. I admired him. Maybe the girls in her class admire her. But John had that hero on the wall, his father in a uniform, dead for reasons John and all the rest of us understood.

My Jessica had to explain a neurologic disease she couldn't even pronounce. "I hate it when people ask me about Mom," she says. "I just tell them she fell off the Empire State Building."

III

Before our first field trip I go to Kay's house for a planning session. We're going to collect wildflowers in East Texas. It's a one-day trip. I arranged to rent the school bus.

[4]Buddhist charm or magic formula

I told Jessica that she could go on the trip even though she wasn't a troop member, but she refused.

70　We sit on colonial furniture in Kay's den. She brings in coffee and we go over the supply list. Another troop is joining ours so there will be twenty-two girls, three women, and me, a busload among the bluebonnets.

"We have to be sure the girls understand that the bluebonnets they pick are on private land and that we have permission to pick them. Otherwise they might pick them along the roadside, which is against the law."

I imagine all twenty-two of them behind bars for picking bluebonnets and Jessica laughing while I scramble for bail money.

I keep noticing Kay's hands. I notice them as she pours coffee, as she checks off the items on the list, as she gestures. I keep expecting her to bridge. She has large, solid, confident hands. When she finishes bridging I sometimes feel like clapping the way people do after the national anthem.

"I admire you," she tells me. "I admire you for going ahead with Scouts even though your daughter rejects it. She'll get a lot out of it indirectly from you."

75　Kay Randall is thirty-three, divorced, and has a Bluebird too. Her older daughter is one of the stubby-fingered girls, Melissa. Jessica is right: Melissa always has a cold.

Kay teaches fifth grade and has been divorced for three years. I am the first assistant she's ever had.

"My husband, Bill, never helped with Scouts." Kay says. "He was pretty much turned off to everything except his business and drinking. When we separated I can't honestly say I missed him: he'd never been there. I don't think the girls miss him either. He only sees them about once a month. He has girlfriends, and his business is doing very well. I guess he has what he wants."

"And you?"

She uses one of those wonderful hands to move the hair away from her eyes, a gesture that makes her seem very young.

80　"I guess I do too. I've got the girls and my job. I'm lonesome, though. It's not exactly what I wanted."

We both think about what might have been as we sit beside her glass coffeepot with our lists of sachet supplies. If she was Barbra Streisand and I Robert Redford and the music started playing in the background to give us a clue and there was a long close-up of our lips, we might just fade into middle age together. But Melissa called for Mom because her mosquito bite was bleeding where she scratched it. And I had an angry daughter waiting for me. And all Kay and I had in common was Girl Scouts. We were both smart enough to know it. When Kay looked at me before going to put alcohol on the mosquito bite, our mutual sadness dripped from us like the last drops of coffee through the grinds.

"You really missed something tonight," Jessica tells me. "The Astros did a double steal. I've never seen one before. In the fourth they sent Thon and Moreno together, and Moreno stole home."

She knows batting averages and won-lost percentages too, just like the older boys, only they go out to play. Jessica stays in and waits for me.

During the field trip, while the girls pick flowers to dry and then manufacture into sachets, I think about Jessica at home, probably beside the radio. Juana, our once-a-week cleaning lady, agreed to work on Saturday so she could stay with Jessica while I took the all-day field trip.

85　It was no small event. In the eight months since Vicki died I had not gone away for an entire day.

I made waffles in the waffle iron for her before I left, but she hardly ate.

"If you want anything, just ask Juana."

"Juana doesn't speak English."

"She understands, that's enough."

90   "Maybe for you it's enough."

"Honey, I told you, you can come; there's plenty of room on the bus. It's not too late for you to change your mind."

"It's not too late for you either. There's going to be plenty of other leaders there. You don't have to go. You're just doing this to be mean to me."

I'm ready for this. I spent an hour with Sharon steeling myself. "Before she can leave you," Sharon said, "you'll have to show her that you can leave. Nothing's going to happen to her. And don't let her be sick that day either."

Jessica is too smart to pull the "I don't feel good" routine. Instead she becomes more silent, more unhappy looking than usual. She stays in her pajamas while I wash the dishes and get ready to leave.

95   I didn't notice the sadness as it was coming upon Jessica. It must have happened gradually in the years of Vicki's decline the years in which I paid so little attention to my daughter. There were times when Jessica seemed to recognize the truth more than I did.

As my Scouts picked their wildflowers, I remembered the last outing I had planned for us. It was going to be a Fourth of July picnic with some friends in Austin. I stopped at the bank and got $200 in cash for the long weekend. But when I came home Vicki was too sick to move and the air conditioner had broken. I called our friends to cancel the picnic; then I took Jessica to the mall with me to buy a fan. I bought the biggest one they had, a 58-inch oscillating model that sounded like a hurricane. It could cool 10,000 square feet, but it wasn't enough.

Vicki was home sitting blankly in front of the TV set. The fan could move eight tons of air an hour, but I wanted it to save my wife. I wanted a fan that would blow the whole earth out of its orbit.

I had $50 left. I gave it to Jessica and told her to buy anything she wanted.

"Whenever you're sad, Daddy, you want to buy me things." She put the money back in my pocket. "It won't help." She was seven years old, holding my hand tightly in the appliance department at J. C. Penney's.

100   I watched Melissa sniffle even more among the wildflowers, and I pointed out the names of various flowers to Carol and JoAnne and Sue and Linda and Rebecca, who were by now used to me and treated me pretty much as they treated Kay. I noticed that the Girl Scout flower book had very accurate photographs that made it easy to identify the bluebonnets and buttercups and poppies. There were also several varieties of wild grasses.

We were only 70 miles from home on some land a wealthy rancher long ago donated to the Girl Scouts. The girls bending among the flowers seemed to have been quickly transformed by the colorful meadow. The gigglers and monotonous singers on the bus were now, like the bees, sucking strength from the beauty around them. Kay was in the midst of them and so, I realized, was I, not watching and keeping score and admiring from the distance but a participant, a player.

JoAnne and Carol sneaked up from behind me and dropped some dandelions down my back. I chased them; then I helped the other leaders pour the Kool-Aid and distribute the Baggies and the name tags for each girl's flowers.

My daughter is home listening to a ball game, I thought, and I'm out here having fun with nine-year-olds. It's upside down.

When I came home with dandelion fragments still on my back, Juana had cleaned the house and I could smell the taco sauce in the kitchen. Jessica was in her room. I suspected that she had spent the day listless and tearful, although I had asked her to invite a friend over.

105   "I had a lot of fun, honey, but I missed you."

She hugged me and cried against my shoulder. I felt like holding her the way I used to when she was an infant, the way I rocked her to sleep. But she was a big girl now and needed not sleep but wakefulness.

"I heard on the news that the Rockets signed Ralph Sampson," she sobbed, "and you hardly ever take me to any pro basketball games."

"But if they have a new center things will be different. With Sampson we'll be contenders. Sure I'll take you."

"Promise?"

110   "Promise." I promise to take you everywhere, my lovely child, and then to leave you. I'm learning to be a leader.

[1984]

Topics for Critical Thinking and Writing

1. Jessica refuses to go to the meetings of the Brownies. Why, then, in your opinion, does the narrator continue to work with the Brownies?
2. In the context of the story, what does "bridging" mean? What bridges are being made, or not made?
3. How would you characterize the narrator's tone? How does the tone in which he tells his story shape your sense of the meaning of the story?

JOHN UPDIKE

John Updike (b. 1932) grew up in Shillington, Pennsylvania, where his father was a teacher and his mother a writer. After receiving a B.A. degree in 1954 from Harvard, where he edited the Harvard Lampoon *(for which he both wrote and drew), he studied drawing at Oxford for a year, but an offer from* The New Yorker *brought him back to the United States. He was hired as a reporter for the magazine but soon began contributing poetry, essays, and fiction. In 1957 he left* The New Yorker *in order to write independently full-time, though his stories and book reviews appear regularly in it.*

*In 1959 Updike published his first book of stories (*The Same Door*) and also his first novel (*The Poorhouse Fair*); the next year he published* Rabbit, Run, *a highly successful novel whose protagonist, "Rabbit" Angstrom, has reappeared in three later novels.* Rabbit Redux *(1971),* Rabbit Is Rich *(1981), and* Rabbit at Rest *(1990). The first and the last Rabbit books each won a Pulitzer Prize.*

The Rumor

Frank and Sharon Whittier had come from the Cincinnati area and, with an inheritance of hers and a sum borrowed from his father, had opened a small art gallery on the fourth floor of a narrow building on West Fifty-seventh Street.

They had known each other as children; their families had been in the same country-club set. They had married in 1971, when Frank was freshly graduated from Oberlin and Vietnam-vulnerable and Sharon was only nineteen, a sophomore at Antioch majoring in dance. By the time, six years later, they arrived in New York, they had two small children; the birth of a third led them to give up their apartment and the city struggle and move to a house in Hastings, a low stucco house with a wide-eaved Wright-style roof and a view, through massive beeches at the bottom of the yard, of the leaden, ongliding Hudson. They were happy, surely. They had dry midwestern taste, and by sticking to representational painters and abstract sculptors they managed to survive the uglier Eighties styles—faux graffiti, neo-German expressionism, cathode-ray prole play, ecological-protest trash art—and bring their quiet, chaste string of fourth-floor rooms into the calm lagoon of Nineties eclectic revivalism and subdued recession chic. They prospered; their youngest child turned twelve, their oldest was filling out college applications.

When Sharon first heard the rumor that Frank had left her for a young homosexual with whom he was having an affair, she had to laugh, for, far from having left her, there he was, right in the lamplit study with her, ripping pages out of *ARTnews*.

"I don't think so, Avis," she said to the graphic artist on the other end of the line. "He's right here with me. Would you like to say hello?" The easy refutation was made additionally sweet by the fact that, some years before there had been a brief (Sharon thought) romantic flare-up between her husband and this caller, an overanimated redhead with protuberant cheeks and chin. Avis was a second-wave appropriationist who made color Xeroxes of masterpieces out of art books and then signed them in an ink mixed of her own blood and urine. How could she, who had actually slept with Frank, be imagining this grotesque thing?

The voice on the phone gushed as if relieved and pleased. "I know, it's wildly absurd, but I heard it from two sources, with absolutely solemn assurance."

5   "Who were these sources?"

"I'm not sure they'd like you to know. But it was Ed Jaffrey and then that boy who's been living with Walton Forney, what does he call himself, one of those single names like Madonna—Jojo!"

"Well, then," Sharon began.

"But I've heard it from still others," Avis insisted. "All over town—it's in the air. Couldn't you and Frank *do* something about it, if it's not true?"

"If," Sharon protested, and her thrust of impatience carried, when she put down the receiver, into her conversation with Frank. "Avis says you're supposed to have run off with your homosexual lover."

10   "I don't have a homosexual lover," Frank said, too calmly, ripping an auction ad out of the magazine.

"She says all New York says you do."

"Well, what are you going to believe, all New York or your own experience? Here I sit, faithful to a fault, straight as a die, whatever that means. We made love just two nights ago."

It seemed possibly revealing to her that he so distinctly remembered, as if heterosexual performance were a duty he checked off. He was—had always been, for over twenty years—a slim blond man several inches under six feet tall, with a narrow head he liked to keep trim, even during those years when long hair was in fashion, milky-blue eyes set at a slight tilt, such as you see on certain taut Slavic or Norwegian faces, and a small, precise mouth he kept pursed over teeth a shade too prominent and yellow. He was reluctant to smile, as if giving something away, and was vain of his flat belly and lithe collegiate condition. He weighed himself every morning on the bathroom scale, and if he weighed a pound more than yesterday, he skipped lunch. In this, and in his general attention to his own person, he was as quietly fanatic as—it for the first time occurred to her—a woman.

"You know I've never liked the queer side of this business," he went on. "I've just gotten used to it. I don't even think anymore, who's gay and who isn't."

15   "Avis was *jubilant*." Sharon said. "How could she think it?"

It took him a moment to focus on the question and realize that his answer was important to her. He became nettled. "Ask *her* how," he said. "Our brief and regrettable relationship, if that's what interests you, seemed satisfactory to me at least. What troubles and amazes me, if I may say so, is how *you* can be taking this ridiculous rumor so seriously."

"I'm *not*, Frank," she insisted, then backtracked. "But why would such a rumor come out of thin air? Doesn't there have to be *something*? Since we moved up here, we're not together so much, naturally, some days when I can't come into town you're gone sixteen hours . . . ."

"But *Shar*on," he said, like a teacher restoring discipline, removing his reading glasses from his almond-shaped eyes, with their stubby fair lashes. "Don't you *know* me? Ever since after that dance when you were sixteen, that time by the lake? . . ."

She didn't want to reminisce. Their early sex had been difficult for her; she had submitted to his advances out of a larger, more social, rather idealistic attraction. She knew that together they would have the strength to get out of Cincinnati and, singly or married to others, they would stay. "Well," she said, enjoying this sensation, despite the chill the rumor had awakened in her, of descending to a deeper level of intimacy than usual, "how well do you know even your own spouse? People are fooled all the time. Peggy Jacobson, for instance, when Henry ran off with that physical therapist, couldn't believe, even when the evidence was right there in front of her—"

20   "I'm *deeply* insulted," Frank interrupted, his mouth tense in that way he had when making a joke but not wanting to show his teeth. "My masculinity is insulted." But he couldn't deny himself a downward glance into his magazine; his tidy white hand jerked, as if wanting to tear out yet another item that might be useful to their business. Intimacy had always made him nervous. She kept at it, rather hopelessly. "Avis said two separate people had solemnly assured her."

"Who, exactly?"

When she told him, he said, exactly as she had done. "Well, then." He added. "You know how gays are. Malicious. Mischievous. They have all that time and money on their hands."

"You sound jealous." Something about the way he was arguing with her strengthened Sharon's suspicion that, outrageous as the rumor was—indeed, *because* it was outrageous—it was true.

In the days that followed, now that she was alert to the rumor's vaporous presence, she imagined it everywhere—on the poised young faces of their staff, in the delicate negotiatory accents of their artists' agents, in the heartier tones of their repeat customers, even in the gruff, self-occupied ramblings of the artists themselves. People seemed startled when she and Frank entered a room together: The desk receptionist and the security guard in their gallery halted their daily morning banter, and the waiters in their pet restaurant, over on Fifty-ninth, appeared especially effusive and attentive. Handshakes lasted a second too long, women embraced her with an extra squeeze, she felt herself ensnared in a soft net of unspoken pity.

25   Frank sensed her discomfort and took a certain malicious pleasure in it, enacting all the while his perfect innocence. He composed himself to appear, from her angle, aloof above the rumor. Dealing professionally in so much absurdity— the art world's frantic attention-getting, studied grotesqueries—he merely intensified the fastidious dryness that had sustained their gallery through wave after wave of changing fashion, and that had, like a rocket's heat-resistant skin, insulated their launch, their escape from the comfortable riverine smugness of this metropolis of dreadful freedom. The rumor amused him, and it amused him, too, to notice how she helplessly watched to see if in the metropolitan throngs his eyes now followed young men as once they had noticed and followed young women. She observed his gestures—always a bit excessively graceful and precise—distrustfully, and listened for the buttery, reedy tone of voice that might signal an invisible sex change.

That even in some small fraction of her she was willing to believe the rumor justified a certain maliciousness on his part. He couldn't help teasing her—glancing over at her, say, when an especially magnetic young waiter served them, or at home, in their bedroom, pushing more brusquely than was his style at her increasing sexual unwillingness. More than once, at last away from the countless knowing eyes of their New York milieu, in the privacy of their Hastings upstairs, beneath the wide midwestern eaves, she burst into tears and struck out at him, his infuriating, impervious apparent blamelessness. He was like one of those photo-realist nudes, merciless in every detail and yet subtly, defiantly not there, not human. "You're distant," she accused him. "You've always been."

"I don't mean to be. You didn't used to mind my manner. You thought it was quietly masterful."

"I was a teenage girl. I deferred to you."

"It worked out," he pointed out, lifting his hands in an effete, disclaiming way from his sides, to take in their room, their expensive house, their joint career. "What is it that bothers you, Sharon? The idea of losing me? Or the insult to your female pride? The people who started this ridiculous rumor don't even *see* women. Women to them are just background noise."

30   "It's *not* ridiculous—if it were, why does it keep on and on, even though we're seen together all the time?"

For, ostensibly to quiet her and to quench the rumor, he had all but ceased to go to the city alone, and took her with him even though it meant some neglect of the house and their sons.

Frank asked. "Who *says* it keeps on all the time? I've *never* heard it, never once, except from you. Who's mentioned it lately?"

"Nobody."

"Well, then." He smiled, his lips not quite parting on his curved teeth. tawny like a beaver's.

35   "You bastard!" Sharon burst out. "You have some stinking little secret!"

"I don't," he serenely half-lied.

The rumor had no factual basis. But was there, Frank asked himself, some truth to it after all? Not circumstantial truth, but some higher, inner truth? As a young man, slight of build, with artistic interests, had he not been fearful of

being mistaken for a homosexual? Had he not responded to homosexual over-
tures as they arose, in bars and locker rooms, with a disproportionate terror and
repugnance? Had not his early marriage, and then, ten years later, his flurry of
adulterous womanizing, been an escape of sorts, into safe, socially approved ter-
rain? When he fantasized, or saw a pornographic movie, was not the male organ
the hero of the occasion for him, at the center of every scene? Were not those
slavish, lapping starlets his robotlike delegates, with glazed eyes and undisturbed
coiffures venturing where he did not dare? Did he not, perhaps, envy women
their privilege of worshipping the phallus? But, Frank asked himself, in fairness,
arguing both sides of the case, can homosexual strands be entirely disentangled
from heterosexual in that pink muck of carnal excitement, of dream made flesh,
of return to the presexual womb?

More broadly, had he not felt more comfortable with his father than with his
mother? Was not this in itself a sinister reversal of the usual biology? His father
had been a genteel Fourth Street lawyer, of no particular effectuality save that
most of his clients were from the same social class, with the same accents and
comfortably narrowed aspirations, here on this plateau by the swelling Ohio.
Darker and taller than Frank, with the same long teeth and primly set mouth, his
father had had the lawyer's gift of silence, of judicious withholding, and in his
son's scattered memories of times together—a trip downtown on the trolley to
buy Frank his first suit, each summer's one or two excursions to see the Reds
play at old Crosley Field—the man said little. This prim reserve, letting so much
go unstated and unacknowledged, was a relief after the daily shower of words
and affection and advice Frank received from his mother. As an adult he was attracted, he had noticed, to stoical men, taller than he and nursing an unex-
pressed sadness; his favorite college roommate had been of this saturnine type,
and his pet tennis partner in Hastings, and artists he especially favored and encouraged—dour, weathered landscapists and virtually illiterate sculptors, welded
solid into their crafts and stubborn obsessions. With these men he became a
catering, wifely, subtly agitated presence that Sharon would scarcely recognize.

Frank's mother, once a fluffy belle from Louisville, had been gaudy, strident,
sardonic, volatile, needy, demanding, loving; from her he had inherited his "artistic" side, as well as his pretty blondness, but he was not especially grateful.
Less—as was proposed by a famous formula he didn't know as a boy—would
have been more. His mother had given him an impression of women as complex, brightly-colored traps, attractive but treacherous, their petals apt to harden
in an instant into knives. A certain wistful pallor, indeed, a limp helplessness, had
drawn him to Sharon and, after the initial dazzlement of the Avises of the world
faded and fizzled, always drew him back. Other women asked more than he
could provide; he was aware of other, bigger, warmer men they had had. But
with Sharon he had been a rescuing knight, slaying the dragon of the winding
Ohio. Yet what more devastatingly, and less forgivably, confirmed the rumor's
essential truth than her willingness, she who knew him best and owed him most,
to entertain it? Her instinct had been to believe Avis even though, far from run
off, he was sitting there right in front of her eyes.

40   He was unreal to her, he could not help but conclude: all those years of ux-
orious cohabitation, those nights of lovemaking and days of homemaking un-
gratefully absorbed and now suddenly dismissed because of an apparition, a
shadow of gossip. On the other hand, now that the rumor existed, Frank had become more real in the eyes of José, the younger, daintier of the two security
guards, whose daily greetings had edged beyond the perfunctory; a certain mischievous dance in the boy's sable eyes animated their employer-employee cour-

tesies. And Jennifer, too, the severely beautiful receptionist, with her rather Sixties-reminiscent bangs and shawls and serapes, now treated him more relaxedly, even offhandedly, as if he had somehow dropped out of her calculations. She assumed with him a comradely slanginess—"The boss was in earlier but she went out to exchange something at Bergdorf's"—as if both he and she were in roughly parallel ironic bondage to "the boss." Frank's heart felt a reflex loyalty to Sharon, a single sharp beat, but then he too relaxed, as if his phantom male lover and the weightless, scandal-veiled life that lived with him in some glowing apartment had bestowed at last what the city had withheld from the overworked, child-burdened married couple who had arrived fourteen years ago—a halo of glamour, of debonair uncaring.

In Hastings, when he and his wife attended a suburban party, the effect was less flattering. The other couples, he imagined, were slightly unsettled by the Whittiers' stubbornly appearing together and became disjointed in their presence, the men drifting off in distaste, the women turning supernormal and laying up a chinkless wall of conversation about children's college applications, local zoning, and Wall Street layoffs. The women, it seemed to Frank, edged, with an instinctive animal movement, a few inches closer to Sharon and touched her with a deft, protective flicking on the shoulder or forearm, to express solidarity and sympathy.

Wes Robertson, Frank's favorite tennis partner, came over to him and grunted. "How's it going?"

"Fine," Frank said, staring up at Wes with what he hoped weren't unduly starry eyes. Wes, who had recently turned fifty, had an old motorcycle-accident scar on one side of his chin, a small pale rose of discoloration that seemed to concentrate the man's self-careless manliness. Frank gave him more of an answer than he might have wanted: "In the art game we're feeling the slowdown like everybody else, but the Japanese are keeping the roof from caving in. The trouble with the Japanese, though, is, from the standpoint of a marginal gallery like ours, they aren't adventurous—they want blue chips, they want guaranteed value, they can't grasp that in art, value has to be subjective to an extent. Look at their own stuff—it's all standardized. Who the hell can tell a Hiroshige from a Hokusai?[1] When you think about it, their whole society, their whole success, really, is based on everybody being alike, everybody agreeing. The notion of art as a struggle, a gamble, as the dynamic embodiment of an existential problem, they just don't get it." He was talking too much, he knew, but he couldn't help it; Wes's scowling presence, his melancholy scarred face, and his stringy alcoholic body, which nevertheless could still whip a backhand right across the forecourt, perversely excited Frank, made him want to flirt.

Wes grimaced and contemplated Frank glumly. "Be around for a game Sunday?" Meaning, had he really run off?

45 "Of course, Why wouldn't I be?" This was teasing the issue, and Frank tried to sober up, to rein in. He felt a flush on his face and a stammer coming on. He asked. "The usual time? Ten forty-five, more or less?"

Wes nodded. "Sure."

Frank chattered on: "Let's try to get court 5 this time. Those brats having their lessons on court 2 drove me crazy last time. We spent all our time retrieving their damn balls. And listening to their moronic chatter."

[1]**Hiroshige . . . Hokusai** Ando Hiroshige (1797–1858) and Katsushika Hokusai (1760–1849) are chiefly known as designers of landscape prints.

Wes didn't grant this attempt at evocation of past liaisons even a word, just continued his melancholy, stoical nodding. This was one of the things, it occurred to Frank, that he liked about men: their relational minimalism, their gender-based realization that the cupboard of life, emotionally speaking, was pretty near bare. There wasn't that tireless, irksome, bright-eyed *hope* women kept fluttering at you.

Once, years ago, on a stag golfing trip to Bermuda, he and Wes had shared a room with two single beds, and Wes had fallen asleep within a minute and started snoring, keeping Frank awake for much of the night. Contemplating the unconscious male body on its moonlit bed, Frank had been struck by the tragic dignity of this supine form, like a stone knight eroding on a tomb—the snoring profile in motionless gray silhouette, the massive, sacred warrior weight helpless as Wes's breathing struggled from phase to phase of the sleep cycle, from deep to REM to a near-wakefulness that brought a few merciful minutes of silence. The next morning, Wes said Frank should have reached over and poked him in the side; that's what his wife did. But he wasn't his wife, Frank thought, though in the course of that night's ordeal, he had felt his heart make many curious motions, among them the heaving, all-but-impossible effort women's hearts make in overcoming men's heavy grayness and achieving—a rainbow born of drizzle—love.

50   At the opening of Ned Forschheimer's show—Forschheimer, a shy, rude, stubborn, and now elderly painter of tea-colored, wintry Connecticut landscapes, was one of Frank's pets, unfashionable yet sneakily salable—none other than Walton Forney came up to Frank, his round face lit by white wine and odd, unquenchable self-delight, and said, "Say, Frank, old boy. Methinks I owe you an apology. It was Charlie Whit*field*, who used to run that framing shop down on Eighth Street, who left his wife suddenly, with some little Guatemalan boy he was putting through CCNY on the side. They took off for Mexico and left the missus sitting with the shop mortgaged up to its attic and about a hundred prints of wild ducks left unframed. The thing that must have confused me, Charlie came from Ohio, too—Columbus or Cleveland, one of those. It was—what do they call it—a Freudian slip, an understandable confusion. Avis Wasserman told me Sharon wasn't all that thrilled to get the word a while ago, and you must have wondered yourself what the hell was up."

"We ignored it." Frank said, in a voice firmer and less catering than his usual one. "We rose above it." Walton was a number of inches shorter than Frank, with yet a bigger head; his gleaming, thin-skinned face, bearing smooth jowls that had climbed into his sideburns, was shadowed blue here and there, like the moon. His bruised and powdered look somehow went with his small, spaced teeth and the horizontal red tracks his glasses had left in the fat in front of his ears.

The man gazed at Frank with a gleaming, sagging lower lip, his nearsighted little eyes trying to assess the damage, the depth of the grudge. "Well, mea culpa, mea culpa, I guess, though I *didn't* tell Jojo and that *poisonous* Ed Jaffrey to go blabbing it all over town."

"Well, thanks for telling me, Wally, I guess." Depending on which man he was standing with, Frank felt large and straight and sonorous or, as with Wes, gracile and flighty. Sharon, scenting blood amid the vacuous burble of the party, pushed herself through the crowd and joined the two men. To deny Walton the pleasure, Frank quickly told her, "Wally just confessed to me he started the rumor because Charlie Whitfield downtown, who did run off with somebody, came from Ohio, too. Toledo, as I remember."

"Oh, that rumor," Sharon said, blinking once, as if her party mascara were sticking. "I'd forgotten it. Who could believe it, of Frank?"

55   "Everybody, evidently," Frank said. It was possible, given the strange, willful ways of women, that she had forgotten it, even while Frank had been brooding over its possible justice. If the rumor were truly dispersed—and Walton would undoubtedly tell the story of his Freudian slip around town as a self-promoting joke on himself—Frank would feel diminished. He would lose that small sadistic power to make her watch him watching waiters in restaurants, and to bring her into town as his chaperon. He would feel emasculated if she no longer thought he had a secret. Yet that night, at the party, Walton Forney's Jojo had come up to him. He had seemed, despite an earring the size of a faucet washer and a stripe of bleach in the center of his hair, unexpectedly intelligent and low-key, offering, not in so many words, a kind of apology, and praising the tea-colored landscapes being offered for sale. "I've been thinking, in my own work, of going, you know, more traditional. You get this feeling of, like, a dead end with abstraction." The boy had a bony, rueful face, with a silvery line of a scar under one eye, and seemed uncertain in manner, hesitantly murmurous, as if at a point in life where he needed direction. The fat fool Forney could certainly not provide that, and it pleased Frank to imagine that Jojo was beginning to realize it.

The car as he and Sharon drove home together along the Hudson felt close; the heater fan blew oppressively, parchingly. "*You* were willing to believe it at first," he reminded her.

"Well, Avis seemed so definite. But you convinced me."

"How?"

She placed her hand high on his thigh and dug her fingers in, annoyingly, infuriatingly. "You know," she said, in a lower register, meant to be sexy, but almost inaudible with the noise of the heater fan.

60   "That could be mere performance," he warned her. "Women are fooled that way all the time."

"Who says?"

"Everybody. Books. Proust.[2] People aren't that simple."

"They're simple enough." Sharon said, in a neutral, defensive tone, removing her presumptuous hand.

"If you say so," he said, somewhat stoically, his mind drifting. That silvery line of a scar under Jojo's left eye . . . lean long muscles snugly wrapped in white skin . . . lofts . . . Hellenic fellowship,[3] exercise machines . . . direct negotiations, a simple transaction among equals. The rumor might be dead in the world, but in him it had come alive.

[1990]

✏ Topics for Critical Thinking and Writing

1. What point of view is used in the first paragraph of the story?
2. Consider the following line from the story:

---

[2]**Proust** Marcel Proust (1871–1922), French homosexual novelist   [3]**Hellenic fellowship** Greek friendship, with the implication of erotic love between a mature man and a youth

"I don't have a homosexual lover," Frank said, too calmly, ripping an auction ad out of the catalog.

What is the point of view?

3. How would you characterize the point of view in the following passage, from near the end of the story?

She placed her hand high on his thigh and dug her fingers in, annoyingly, infuriatingly. "You know," she said in a lower register, meant to be sexy, but almost inaudible with the noise of the heater fan.

4. Suppose the story had been told entirely from Sharon's point of view. What might have been gained? What might have been lost?
5. In an essay on fiction. Updike wrote:

I want stories to startle and engage me within the first few sentences, and in their middle to widen or deepen or sharpen my knowledge of human activity, and to end by giving me a sensation of completed statement.

Is this what you want from stories? If not, in what ways do your desires differ from Updike's? A second question: Do you think "The Rumor" meets Updike's criteria? Explain.

 ## DAVID LEAVITT

 David Leavitt was twenty and still an undergraduate at Yale when in 1982 be published "Territory" in The New Yorker. *The New Yorker had been publishing serious fiction for decades, but "Territory" was the first openly gay story to appear in the magazine. Two years later the story was reprinted in a collection of Leavitt's stories,* Family Dancing. *In addition to publishing stories, Leavitt has also published two novels* (The Lost Language of Cranes *[1986] and* Equal Affections *[1989]). both about gay life.*

Territory

Neil's mother, Mrs. Campbell, sits on her lawn chair behind a card table outside the food co-op. Every few minutes, as the sun shifts, she moves the chair and table several inches back so as to remain in the shade. It is a hundred degrees outside, and bright white. Each time someone goes in or out of the co-op a gust of air-conditioning flies out of the automatic doors, raising dust from the cement.

Neil stands just inside, poised over a water fountain, and watches her. She has on a sun hat, and a sweatshirt over her tennis dress; her legs are bare, and shiny with cocoa butter. In front of her, propped against the table, a sign proclaims: MOTHERS, FIGHT FOR YOUR CHILDREN'S RIGHTS—SUPPORT A NON-NUCLEAR FUTURE. Women dressed exactly like her pass by, notice the sign, listen to her brief spiel, finger pamphlets, sign petitions or don't sign petitions, never give money. Her weary eyes are masked by dark glasses. In the age of Reagan, she has declared, keeping up the causes of peace and justice is a futile, tiresome, and unrewarding effort; it is therefore an effort fit only for mothers to keep up. The sun bounces off the window glass through which Neil watches her. His own reflection lines up with her profile.

Later that afternoon. Neil spreads himself out alongside the pool and imagines he is being watched by the shirtless Chicago gardener. But the gardener, concentrating on his pruning, is neither seductive nor seducible. On the lawn, his mother's large Airedales—Abigail. Lucille. Fern—amble, sniff, urinate. Occasionally, they accost the gardener, who yells at them in Spanish.

After two years' absence. Neil reasons, he should feel nostalgia, regret, gladness upon returning home. He closes his eyes and tries to muster the proper background music for the cinematic scene of return. His rhapsody, however, is interrupted by the noises of his mother's trio—the scratchy cello, whining violin, stumbling piano—as she and Lillian Havalard and Charlotte Feder plunge through Mozart. The tune is cheery, in a Germanic sort of way, and utterly inappropriate to what Neil is trying to feel. Yet it *is* the music of his adolescence; they have played it for years, bent over the notes, their heads bobbing in silent time to the metronome.

5   It is getting darker. Every few minutes, he must move his towel so as to remain within the narrowing patch of sunlight. In four hours, Wayne, his lover of ten months and the only person he has ever imagined he could spend his life with, will be in this house, where no lover of his has ever set foot. The thought fills him with a sense of grand terror and curiosity. He stretches, tries to feel seductive, desirable. The gardener's shears whack at the ferns; the music above him rushes to a loud, premature conclusion. The women laugh and applaud themselves as they give up for the day. He hears Charlotte Feder's full nasal twang, the voice of a fat woman in a pink pants suit—odd, since she is a scrawny, arthritic old bird, rarely clad in anything other than tennis shorts and a blouse. Lillian is the fat woman in the pink pants suit; her voice is thin and warped by too much crying. Drink in hand, she calls out from the porch, "Hot enough!" and waves. He lifts himself up and nods to her.

The women sit on the porch and chatter; their voices blend with the clink of ice in glasses. They belong to a small circle of ladies all of whom, with the exception of Neil's mother, are widows and divorcées. Lillian's husband left her twenty-two years ago, and sends her a check every month to live on; Charlotte has been divorced twice as long as she was married, and has a daughter serving a long sentence for terrorist acts committed when she was nineteen. Only Neil's mother has a husband, a distant sort of husband, away often on business. He is away on business now. All of them feel betrayed—by husbands, by children, by history.

Neil closes his eyes, tries to hear the words only as sounds. Soon, a new noise accosts him: his mother arguing with the gardener in Spanish. He leans on his elbows and watches them; the syllables are loud, heated, and compressed, and seem on the verge of explosion. But the argument ends happily; they shake hands. The gardener collects his check and walks out the gate without so much as looking at Neil.

He does not know the gardener's name; as his mother has reminded him, he does not know most of what has gone on since he moved away. Her life has gone on, unaffected by his absence. He flinches at his own egotism, the egoism of sons.

"Neil! Did you call the airport to make sure the plane's coming in on time?"

10   "Yes," he shouts to her. "It is."

"Good. Well, I'll have dinner ready when you get back."

"Mom—"

"What?" The word comes out in a weary wail that is more of an answer than a question.

"What's wrong?" he says, forgetting his original question.

15 "Nothing's wrong," she declares in a tone that indicates that everything is wrong. "The dogs have to be fed, dinner has to be made, and I've got people here. Nothing's wrong."

"I hope things will be as comfortable as possible when Wayne gets here."

"Is that a request or a threat?"

"Mom—"

Behind her sunglasses, her eyes are inscrutable. "I'm tired," she says. "It's been a long day. I . . . I'm anxious to meet Wayne. I'm sure he'll be wonderful, and we'll all have a wonderful, wonderful time. I'm sorry. I'm just tired."

20 She heads up the stairs. He suddenly feels an urge to cover himself; his body embarrasses him, as it has in her presence since the day she saw him shirtless and said with delight. "Neil! You're growing hair under your arms!"

Before he can get up, the dogs gather round him and begin to sniff and lick at him. He wriggles to get away from them, but Abigail, the largest and stupidest, straddles his stomach and nuzzles his mouth. He splutters and, laughing, throws her off. "Get away from me, you goddamn dogs," he shouts, and swats at them. They are new dogs, not the dog of his childhood, not dogs he trusts.

He stands, and the dogs circle him, looking up at his face expectantly. He feels renewed terror at the thought that Wayne will be here so soon: Will they sleep in the same room? Will they make love? He has never had sex in his parents' house. How can he be expected to be a lover here, in this place of his childhood, of his earliest shame, in this household of mothers and dogs?

"Dinnertime! Abbylucyferny. Abbylucyferny, dinnertime!"

"Do you realize," he shouts to her, "that no matter how much those dogs love you they'd probably kill you for the leg of lamb in the freezer?"

25 Neil was twelve the first time he recognized in himself something like sexuality. He was lying outside, on the grass, when Rasputin—the dog, long dead, of his childhood—began licking his face. He felt a tingle he did not recognize, pulled off his shirt to give the dog access to more of him. Rasputin's tongue tickled coolly. A wet nose started to sniff down his body, toward his bathing suit. What he felt frightened him, but he couldn't bring himself to push the dog away. Then his mother called out. "Dinner," and Rasputin was gone, more interested in food than in him.

It was the day after Rasputin was put to sleep, years later, that Neil finally stood in the kitchen, his back turned to his parents, and said, with unexpected ease. "I'm a homosexual." The words seemed insufficient, reductive. For years, he had believed his sexuality to be detachable from the essential him, but now he realized that it was part of him. He had the sudden, despairing sensation that though the words had been easy to say, the fact of their having been aired was incurably damning. Only then, for the first time, did he admit that they were true, and he shook and wept in regret for what he would not be for his mother, for having failed her. His father hung back, silent; he was absent for that moment as he was mostly absent—a strong absence. Neil always thought of him sitting on the edge of the bed in his underwear, captivated by something on television. He said. "It's O.K., Neil." But his mother was resolute; her lower lip didn't quaver. She had enormous reserves of strength to which she only gained access at moments like this one. She hugged him from behind, wrapped him in the childhood smells of perfume and brownies, and whispered. "It's O.K., honey." For once, her words seemed as inadequate as his. Neil felt himself shrunk to an embarrassed adolescent, hating her sympathy, not wanting her to touch him. It was the way he would feel from then on whenever he was in her presence—even now, at twenty-three, bringing home his lover to meet her.

All through his childhood, she had packed only the most nutritious lunches, had served on the PTA, had volunteered at the children's library and at his school, had organized a successful campaign to ban a racist history textbook. The day after he told her, she located and got in touch with an organization called the Coalition of Parents of Lesbians and Gays. Within a year, she was president of it. On weekends, she and the other mothers drove their station wagons to San Francisco, set up their card tables in front of the Bulldog Baths, the Liberty Baths, passed out literature to men in leather and denim who were loath to admit they even had mothers. These men, who would habitually do violence to each other, were strangely cowed by the suburban ladies with their informational booklets, and bent their heads. Neil was a sophomore in college then, and lived in San Francisco. She brought him pamphlets detailing the dangers of bathhouses and back rooms, enemas and poppers, wordless sex in alleyways. His excursion into that world had been brief and lamentable, and was over. He winced at the thought that she knew all his sexual secrets, and vowed to move to the East Coast to escape her. It was not very different from the days when she had campaigned for a better playground, or tutored the Hispanic children in the audiovisual room. Those days, as well, he had run away from her concern. Even today, perched in front of the co-op, collecting signatures for nuclear disarmament, she was quintessentially a mother. And if the lot of mothers was to expect nothing in return, was the lot of sons to return nothing?

Driving across the Dumbarton Bridge on his way to the airport, Neil thinks, I have returned nothing; I have simply returned. He wonders if she would have given birth to him had she known what he would grow up to be.

Then he berates himself: Why should he assume himself to be the cause of her sorrow? She has told him that her life is full of secrets. She has changed since he left home—grown thinner, more rigid, harder to hug. She has given up baking, taken up tennis; her skin has browned and tightened. She is no longer the woman who hugged him and kissed him, who said. "As long as you're happy, that's all that's important to us."

30   The flats spread out around him; the bridge floats on purple and green silt, and spongy bay fill, not water at all. Only ten miles north, a whole city has been built on gunk dredged up from the bay.

He arrives at the airport ten minutes early, to discover that the plane has landed twenty minutes early. His first view of Wayne is from behind, by the baggage belt. Wayne looks as he always looks—slightly windblown—and is wearing the ratty leather jacket he was wearing the night they met. Neil sneaks up on him and puts his hands on his shoulders; when Wayne turns around, he looks relieved to see him.

They hug like brothers; only in the safety of Neil's mother's car do they dare to kiss. They recognize each other's smells, and grow comfortable again. "I never imagined I'd actually see you out here," Neil says, "but you're exactly the same here as there."

"It's only been a week."

They kiss again. Neil wants to go to a motel, but Wayne insists on being pragmatic. "We'll be there soon. Don't worry."

35   "We could go to one of the bathhouses in the city and take a room for a couple of aeons," Neil says. "Christ, I'm hard up. I don't even know if we're going to be in the same bedroom."

"Well, if we're not," Wayne says, "we'll sneak around. It'll be romantic."

They cling to each other for a few more minutes, until they realize that people are looking in the car window. Reluctantly, they pull apart. Neil reminds himself that he loves this man, that there is a reason for him to bring this man home.

He takes the scenic route on the way back. The car careers over foothills, through forests, along white four-lane highways high in the mountains. Wayne tells Neil that he sat next to a woman on the plane who was once Marilyn Monroe's psychiatrist's nurse. He slips his foot out of his shoe and nudges Neil's ankle, pulling Neil's sock down with his toe.

"I have to drive," Neil says. "I'm very glad you're here."

40   There is a comfort in the privacy of the car. They have a common fear of walking hand in hand, of publicly showing physical affection, even in the permissive West Seventies of New York—a fear that they have admitted only to one another. They slip through a pass between two hills, and are suddenly in residential Northern California, the land of expensive ranch-style houses.

As they pull into Neil's mother's driveway, the dogs run barking toward the car. When Wayne opens the door, they jump and lap at him, and he tries to close it again. "Don't worry. Abbylucyferny! Get in the house, damn it!"

His mother descends from the porch. She has changed into a blue flower-print dress, which Neil doesn't recognize. He gets out of the car and halfheartedly chastises the dogs. Crickets chirp in the trees. His mother looks radiant, even beautiful, illuminated by the headlights, surrounded by the now quiet dogs, like a Circe with her slaves. When she walks over to Wayne, offering her hand, and says, "Wayne, I'm Barbara," Neil forgets that she is his mother.

"Good to meet you, Barbara," Wayne says, and reaches out his hand. Craftier than she, he whirls around to kiss her cheek.

Barbara! He is calling his mother Barbara! Then he remembers that Wayne is five years older than he is. They chat by the open car door, and Neil shrinks back—the embarrassed adolescent, uncomfortable, unwanted.

45   So the dreaded moment passes and he might as well not have been there. At dinner, Wayne keeps the conversation smooth, like a captivated courtier seeking Neil's mother's hand. A faggot son's sodomist—such words spit into Neil's head. She has prepared tiny meatballs with fresh coriander, fettucine with pesto. Wayne talks about the street people in New York; El Salvador is a tragedy; if only Sadat had lived; Phyllis Schlafly[1]—what can you do?

"It's a losing battle," she tells him. "Every day I'm out there with my card table, me and the other mothers, but I tell you, Wayne, it's a losing battle. Sometimes I think us old ladies are the only ones with enough patience to fight."

Occasionally, Neil says something, but his comments seem stupid and clumsy. Wayne continues to call her Barbara. No one under forty has ever called her Barbara as long as Neil can remember. They drink wine; he does not.

Now is the time for drastic action. He contemplates taking Wayne's hand, then checks himself. He has never done anything in her presence to indicate that

[1]**Phyllis Schlafly** a vigorous opponent of feminist movements

the sexuality he confessed to five years ago was a reality and not an invention. Even now, he and Wayne might as well be friends, college roommates. Then Wayne, his savior, with a single, sweeping gesture, reaches for his hand, and clasps it, in the midst of a joke he is telling about Saudi Arabians. By the time he is laughing, their hands are joined. Neil's throat contracts; his heart begins to beat violently. He notices his mother's eyes flicker, glance downward; she never breaks the stride of her sentence. The dinner goes on, and every taboo nurtured since childhood falls quietly away.

She removes the dishes. Their hands grow sticky; he cannot tell which fingers are his and which Wayne's. She clears the rest of the table and rounds up the dogs.

50   "Well, boys, I'm very tired, and I've got a long day ahead of me tomorrow, so I think I'll hit the sack. There are extra towels for you in Neil's bathroom, Wayne. Sleep well."

"Good night, Barbara," Wayne calls out. "It's been wonderful meeting you."

They are alone. Now they can disentangle their hands.

"No problem about where we sleep, is there?"

"No," Neil says. "I just can't imagine sleeping with someone in this house."

55   His leg shakes violently. Wayne takes Neil's hand in a firm grasp and hauls him up.

Later that night, they lie outside, under redwood trees, listening to the hysteria of the crickets, the hum of the pool cleaning itself. Redwood leaves prick their skin. They fell in love in bars and apartments, and this is the first time that they have made love outdoors. Neil is not sure he has enjoyed the experience. He kept sensing eyes, imagined that the neighborhood cats were staring at them from behind a fence of brambles. He remembers he once hid in this spot when he and some of the children from the neighborhood were playing sardines, remembers the intoxication of small bodies packed together, the warm breath of suppressed laughter on his neck. "The loser had to go through the spanking machine," he tells Wayne.

"Did you lose often?"

"Most of the time. The spanking machine never really hurt—just a whirl of hands. If you moved fast enough, no one could actually get you. Sometimes, though, late in the afternoon, we'd get naughty. We'd chase each other and pull each other's pants down. That was all. Boys and girls together!"

"Listen to the insects," Wayne says, and closes his eyes.

60   Neil turns to examine Wayne's face, notices a single, small pimple. Their lovemaking usually begins in a wrestle, a struggle for dominance, and ends with a somewhat confusing loss of identity—as now, when Neil sees a foot on the grass, resting against his leg, and tries to determine if it is his own or Wayne's.

From inside the house, the dogs begin to bark. Their yelps grow into alarmed falsettos. Neil lifts himself up. "I wonder if they smell something," he says.

"Probably just us," says Wayne.

"My mother will wake up. She hates getting waked up."

Lights go on in the house; the door to the porch opens.

65   "What's wrong, Abby? What's wrong?" his mother's voice calls softly.

Wayne clamps his hand over Neil's mouth. "Don't say anything," he whispers.

"I can't just—" Neil begins to say, but Wayne's hand closes over his mouth again. He bites it, and Wayne starts laughing.

"What was that?" Her voice projects into the garden. "Hello?" she says.

The dogs yelp louder. "Abbylucyferny, it's O.K., it's O.K." Her voice is soft and panicked. "Is anyone there?" she asks loudly.

70   The brambles shake. She takes a flashlight, shines it around the garden. Wayne and Neil duck down; the light lands on them and hovers for a few seconds. Then it clicks off and they are in the dark—a new dark, a darker dark, which their eyes must readjust to.

"Let's go to bed. Abbylucyferny," she says gently. Neil and Wayne hear her pad into the house. The dogs whimper as they follow her, and the lights go off.

Once before, Neil and his mother had stared at each other in the glare of bright lights. Four years ago, they stood in the arena created by the headlights of her car, waiting for the train. He was on his way back to San Francisco, where he was marching in a Gay Pride Parade the next day. The train station was next door to the food co-op and shared its parking lot. The co-op, familiar and boring by day, took on a certain mystery in the night. Neil recognized the spot where he had skidded on his bicycle and broken his leg. Through the glass doors, the brightly lit interior of the store glowed, its rows and rows of cans and boxes forming their own horizon, each can illuminated so that even from outside Neil could read the labels. All that was missing was the ladies in tennis dresses and sweatshirts, pushing their carts past bins of nuts and dried fruits.

"Your train is late," his mother said. Her hair fell loosely on her shoulders, and her legs were tanned. Neil looked at her and tried to imagine her in labor with him—bucking and struggling with his birth. He felt then the strange, sexless love for women which through his whole adolescence he had mistaken for heterosexual desire.

A single bright light approached them; it preceded the low, haunting sound of the whistle. Neil kissed his mother, and waved goodbye as he ran to meet the train. It was an old train, with windows tinted a sort of horrible lemon-lime. It stopped only long enough for him to hoist himself on board, and then it was moving again. He hurried to a window, hoping to see her drive off, but the tint of the window made it possible for him to make out only vague patches of light—street lamps, cars, the co-op.

75   He sank into the hard, green seat. The train was almost entirely empty; the only other passenger was a dark-skinned man wearing bluejeans and a leather jacket. He sat directly across the aisle from Neil, next to the window. He had rough skin and a thick mustache. Neil discovered that by pretending to look out the window he could study the man's reflection in the lemon-lime glass. It was only slightly hazy—the quality of a bad photograph. Neil felt his mouth open, felt sleep closing in on him. Hazy red and gold flashes through the glass pulsed in the face of the man in the window, giving the curious impression of muscle spasms. It took Neil a few minutes to realize that the man was staring at him, or, rather, staring at the back of his head—staring at his staring. The man smiled as though to say, I know exactly what you're staring at, and Neil felt the sickening sensation of desire rise in his throat.

Right before they reached the city, the man stood up and sat down in the seat next to Neil's. The man's thigh brushed deliberately against his own. Neil's eyes were watering; he felt sick to his stomach. Taking Neil's hand, the man said. "Why so nervous, honey? Relax."

Neil woke up the next morning with the taste of ashes in his mouth. He was lying on the floor, without blankets or sheets or pillows. Instinctively, he reached for his pants, and as he pulled them on came face to face with the man from the train. His name was Luis; he turned out to be a dog groomer. His apartment smelled of dog.

"Why such a hurry?" Luis said.

"The parade. The Gay Pride Parade. I'm meeting some friends to march."

80   "I'll come with you," Luis said. "I think I'm too old for these things, but why not?"

Neil did not want Luis to come with him, but he found it impossible to say so. Luis looked older by day, more likely to carry diseases. He dressed again in a torn T-shirt, leather jacket, bluejeans. "It's my everyday apparel," he said, and laughed. Neil buttoned his pants, aware that they had been washed by his mother the day before. Luis possessed the peculiar combination of hypermasculinity and effeminacy which exemplifies faggotry. Neil wanted to be rid of him, but Luis's mark was on him, he could see that much. They would become lovers whether Neil liked it or not.

They joined the parade midway. Neil hoped he wouldn't meet anyone he knew; he did not want to have to explain Luis, who clung to him. The parade was full of shirtless men with oiled, muscular shoulders. Neil's back ached. There were floats carrying garishly dressed prom queens and cheerleaders, some with beards, some actually looking like women. Luis said. "It makes me proud, makes me glad to be what I am." Neil supposed that by darting into the crowd ahead of him he might be able to lose Luis forever, but he found it difficult to let him go; the prospect of being alone seemed unbearable.

Neil was startled to see his mother watching the parade, holding up a sign. She was with the Coalition of Parents of Lesbians and Gays; they had posted a huge banner on the wall behind them proclaiming: OUR SONS AND DAUGHTERS, WE ARE PROUD OF YOU. She spotted him; she waved, and jumped up and down.

"Who's that woman?" Luis asked.

85   "My mother. I should go say hello to her."

"O.K.," Luis said. He followed Neil to the side of the parade. Neil kissed his mother. Luis took off his shirt, wiped his face with it, smiled.

"I'm glad you came," Neil said.

"I wouldn't have missed it, Neil. I wanted to show you I cared."

He smiled, and kissed her again. He showed no intention of introducing Luis, so Luis introduced himself.

90   "Hello, Luis," Mrs. Campbell said. Neil looked away. Luis shook her hand, and Neil wanted to warn his mother to wash it, warned himself to check with a V.D. clinic first thing Monday.

"Neil, this is Carmen Bologna, another one of the mothers," Mrs. Campbell said. She introduced him to a fat Italian woman with flushed cheeks, and hair arranged in the shape of a clamshell.

"Good to meet you, Neil, good to meet you," said Carmen Bologna. "You know my son, Michael? I'm so proud of Michael! He's doing so well now. I'm proud of him, proud to be his mother I am, and your mother's proud, too!"

The woman smiled at him, and Neil could think of nothing to say but "Thank you." He looked uncomfortably toward his mother, who stood listening to Luis. It occurred to him that the worst period of his life was probably about to begin and he had no way to stop it.

A group of drag queens ambled over to where the mothers were standing. "Michael! Michael!" shouted Carmen Bologna, and embraced a sticklike man wrapped in green satin. Michael's eyes were heavily dosed with green eyeshadow, and his lips were painted pink.

95   Neil turned and saw his mother staring, her mouth open. He marched over to where Luis was standing, and they moved back into the parade. He turned and

waved to her. She waved back; he saw pain in her face, and then, briefly, regret. That day, he felt she would have traded him for any other son. Later, she said to him. "Carmen Bologna really was proud, and, speaking as a mother, let me tell you, you have to be brave to feel such pride."

Neil was never proud. It took him a year to dump Luis, another year to leave California. The sick taste of ashes was still in his mouth. On the plane, he envisioned his mother sitting alone in the dark, smoking. She did not leave his mind until he was circling New York, staring down at the dawn rising over Queens. The song playing in his earphones would remain hovering on the edges of his memory, always associated with her absence. After collecting his baggage, he took a bus into the city. Boys were selling newspapers in the middle of highways, through the windows of stopped cars. It was seven in the morning when he reached Manhattan. He stood for ten minutes on East Thirty-fourth Street, breathed the cold air, and felt bubbles rising in his blood.

Neil got a job as a paralegal—a temporary job, he told himself. When he met Wayne a year later, the sensations of that first morning returned to him. They'd been up all night, and at six they walked across the park to Wayne's apartment with the nervous, deliberate gait of people aching to make love for the first time. Joggers ran by with their dogs. None of them knew what Wayne and he were about to do, and the secrecy excited him. His mother came to mind, and the song, and the whirling vision of Queens coming alive below him. His breath solidified into clouds, and he felt happier than he had ever felt before in his life.

The second day of Wayne's visit, he and Neil go with Mrs. Campbell to pick up the dogs at the dog parlor. The grooming establishment is decorated with pink ribbons and photographs of the owner's champion pit bulls. A fat, middle-aged woman appears from the back, leading the newly trimmed and fluffed Abigail, Lucille, and Fern by three leashes. The dogs struggle frantically when they see Neil's mother, tangling the woman up in their leashes. "Ladies, behave!" Mrs. Campbell commands, and collects the dogs. She gives Fern to Neil and Abigail to Wayne. In the car on the way back. Abigail begins pawing to get on Wayne's lap.

"Just push her off." Mrs. Campbell says. "She knows she's not supposed to do that."

100   "You never groomed Rasputin," Neil complains.

"Rasputin was a mutt."

"Rasputin was a beautiful dog, even if he did smell."

"Do you remember when you were a little kid, Neil, you used to make Rasputin dance with you? Once you tried to dress him up in one of my blouses."

"I don't remember that," Neil says.

105   "Yes. I remember," says Mrs. Campbell. "Then you tried to organize a dog beauty contest in the neighborhood. You wanted to have runners-up—everything."

"A dog beauty contest?" Wayne says.

"Mother, do we have to—"

"I think it's a mother's privilege to embarrass her son," Mrs. Campbell says, and smiles.

When they are about to pull into the driveway, Wayne starts screaming, and pushes Abigail off his lap. "Oh, my God!" he says. "The dog just pissed all over me."

110   Neil turns around and sees a puddle seeping into Wayne's slacks. He suppresses his laughter, and Mrs. Campbell hands him a rag.

"I'm sorry, Wayne," she says. "It goes with the territory."

"This is really disgusting," Wayne says, swatting at himself with the rag.

Neil keeps his eyes on his own reflection in the rearview mirror and smiles.

At home, while Wayne cleans himself in the bathroom, Neil watches his mother cook lunch—Japanese noodles in soup. "When you went off to college," she says. "I went to the grocery store. I was going to buy you ramen noodles, and I suddenly realized you weren't going to be around to eat them. I started crying right then, blubbering like an idiot."

115   Neil clenches his fists inside his pockets. She has a way of telling him little sad stories when he doesn't want to hear them—stories of dolls broken by her brothers, lunches stolen by neighborhood boys on the way to school. Now he has joined the ranks of male children who have made her cry.

"Mama, I'm sorry," he says.

She is bent over the noodles, which steam in her face. "I didn't want to say anything in front of Wayne, but I wish you had answered me last night. I was very frightened—and worried."

"I'm sorry," he says, but it's not convincing. His fingers prickle. He senses a great sorrow about to be born.

"I lead a quiet life," she says. "I don't want to be a disciplinarian. I just don't have the energy for these—shenanigans. Please don't frighten me that way again."

120   "If you were so upset, why didn't you say something?"

"I'd rather not discuss it. I lead a quiet life. I'm not used to getting woken up late at night. I'm not used—"

"To my having a lover?"

"No, I'm not used to having other people around, that's all. Wayne is charming. A wonderful young man."

"He likes you, too."

125   "I'm sure we'll get along fine."

She scoops the steaming noodles into ceramic bowls. Wayne returns, wearing shorts. His white, hairy legs are a shocking contrast to hers, which are brown and sleek.

"I'll wash those pants, Wayne." Mrs. Campbell says. "I have a special detergent that'll take out the stain."

She gives Neil a look to indicate that the subject should be dropped. He looks at Wayne, looks at his mother; his initial embarrassment gives way to a fierce pride—the arrogance of mastery. He is glad his mother knows that he is desired, glad it makes her flinch.

Later, he steps into the back yard: the gardener is back, whacking at the bushes with his shears. Neil walks by him in his bathing suit, imagining he is on parade.

130   That afternoon, he finds his mother's daily list on the kitchen table:

TUESDAY
7:00—breakfast
Take dogs to groomer
Groceries (?)

Campaign against Draft—4–7
Buy underwear
Trios—2:00

Spaghetti
Fruit

Asparagus if sale
Peanuts
Milk

Doctor's Appointment (make)
Write Cranston/Hayakawa
re disarmament

Handi-Wraps
Mozart
Abigail
Top Ramen
Pedro

Her desk and trash can are full of such lists; he remembers them from the earliest days of his childhood. He had learned to read from them. In his own life, too, there have been endless lists—covered with check marks and arrows, at least one item always spilling over onto the next day's agenda. From September to November, "Buy plane ticket for Christmas" floated from list to list to list.

The last item puzzles him: Pedro. Pedro must be the gardener. He observes the accretion of names, the arbitrary specifics that give a sense of his mother's life. He could make a list of his own selves: the child, the adolescent, the promiscuous faggot son, and finally the good son, settled, relatively successful. But the divisions wouldn't work; he is today and will always be the child being licked by the dog, the boy on the floor with Luis; he will still be everything he is ashamed of. The other lists—the lists of things done and undone—tell their own truth: that his life is measured more properly in objects than in stages. He knows himself as "jump rope," "book," "sunglasses," "underwear."

"Tell me about your family, Wayne," Mrs. Campbell says that night, as they drive toward town. They are going to see an Esther Williams movie at the local revival house: an underwater musical, populated by mermaids, underwater Rockettes.

"My father was a lawyer," Wayne says. "He had an office in Queens, with a neon sign. I think he's probably the only lawyer in the world who had a neon sign. Anyway, he died when I was ten. My mother never remarried. She lives in Queens. Her great claim to fame is that when she was twenty-two she went on 'The $64,000 Question.' Her category was mystery novels. She made it to sixteen thousand before she got tripped up."

135 "When I was about ten, I wanted you to go on 'Jeopardy.'" Neil says to his mother. "You really should have, you know. You would have won."

"You certainly loved 'Jeopardy,'" Mrs. Campbell says. "You used to watch it during dinner. Wayne, does your mother work?"

"No," he says. "She lives off investments."

"You're both only children," Mrs. Campbell says. Neil wonders if she is ruminating on the possible connection between that coincidence and their "alternative life style."

The movie theater is nearly empty. Neil sits between Wayne and his mother. There are pillows on the floor at the front of the theater, and a cat is prowling over them. It casts a monstrous shadow every now and then on the screen, disturbing the sedative effect of water ballet. Like a teen-ager, Neil cautiously reaches his arm around Wayne's shoulder. Wayne takes his hand immediately. Next to them. Neil's mother breathes in, out, in, out. Neil timorously moves his other arm and lifts it behind his mother's neck. He does not look at her, but he can tell from her breathing that she senses what he is doing. Slowly, carefully, he lets his hand drop on her shoulder; it twitches spasmodically, and he jumps, as if he had received an electric shock. His mother's quiet breathing is broken by a gasp; even Wayne notices. A sudden brightness on the screen illuminates the panic in her eyes. Neil's arm frozen above her, about to fall again. Slowly, he lowers his arm until his fingertips touch her skin, the fabric of her dress. He has gone too far to go back now; they are all too far.

140   Wayne and Mrs. Campbell sink into their seats, but Neil remains stiff, holding up his arms, which rest on nothing. The movie ends, and they go on sitting just like that.

      "I'm old." Mrs. Campbell says later, as they drive back home. "I remember when those films were new. Your father and I went to one on our first date. I loved them, because I could pretend that those women underwater were flying—they were so graceful. They really took advantage of Technicolor in those days. Color was something to appreciate. You can't know what it was like to see a color movie for the first time, after years of black-and-white. It's like trying to explain the surprise of snow to an East Coaster. Very little is new anymore. I fear."

      Neil would like to tell her about his own nostalgia, but how can he explain that all of it revolves around her? The idea of her life before he was born pleases him. "Tell Wayne how you used to look like Esther Williams," he asks her.

      She blushes. "I was told I looked like Esther Williams, but really more like Gene Tierney," she says. "Not beautiful, but interesting. I like to think I had a certain magnetism."

      "You still do," Wayne says, and instantly recognizes the wrongness of his comment. Silence and a nervous laugh indicate that he has not yet mastered the family vocabulary.

145   When they got home, the night is once again full of the sound of crickets. Mrs. Campbell picks up a flashlight and calls the dogs. "Abbylucyferny, Abbylucyferny," she shouts, and the dogs amble from their various corners. She pushes them out the door to the back yard and follows them. Neil follows her. Wayne follows Neil, but hovers on the porch. Neil walks behind her as she tramps through the garden. She holds out her flashlight, and snails slide from behind bushes, from under rocks, to where she stands. When the snails become visible, she crushes them underfoot. They make a wet, cracking noise, like eggs being broken.

      "Nights like this," she says, "I think of children without pants on, in hot South American countries. I have nightmares about tanks rolling down our street."

      "The weather's never like this in New York." Neil says. "When it's hot, it's humid and sticky. You don't want to go outdoors."

      "I could never live anywhere else but here. I think I'd die. I'm too used to the climate."

      "Don't be silly."

150   "No. I mean it," she says. "I have adjusted too well to the weather."

      The dogs bark and howl by the fence. "A cat, I suspect," she says. She aims her flashlight at a rock, and more snails emerge—uncountable numbers, too stupid to have learned not to trust light.

"I know what you were doing at the movie," she says.

"What?"

"I know what you were doing."

155 "What? I put my arm around you."

"I'm sorry, Neil," she says. "I can only take so much. Just so much."

"What do you mean?" he says. "I was only trying to show affection."

"Oh, affection—I know about affection."

He looks up at the porch, sees Wayne moving toward the door, trying not to listen.

160 "What do you mean?" Neil says to her.

She puts down the flashlight and wraps her arms around herself. "I remember when you were a little boy," she says. "I remember, and I have to stop remembering. I wanted you to grow up happy. And I'm very tolerant, very understanding. But I can only take so much."

His heart seems to have risen into his throat. "Mother," he says. "I think you know my life isn't your fault. But for God's sake, don't say that your life is my fault."

"It's not a question of fault," she says. She extracts a Kleenex from her pocket and blows her nose. "I'm sorry, Neil. I guess I'm just an old woman with too much on her mind and not enough to do." She laughs halfheartedly. "Don't worry. Don't say anything," she says. "Abbylucyferny, Abbylucyferny, time for bed!"

He watches her as she walks toward the porch, silent and regal. There is the pad of feet, the clinking of dog tags as the dogs run for the house.

165 He was twelve the first time she saw him march in a parade. He played the tuba, and as his elementary-school band lumbered down the streets of their then small town she stood on the sidelines and waved. Afterward, she had taken him out for ice cream. He spilled some on his red uniform, and she swiped at it with a napkin. She had been there for him that day, as well as years later, at that more memorable parade; she had been there for him every day.

Somewhere over Iowa, a week later, Neil remembers this scene, remembers other days, when he would find her sitting in the dark, crying. She had to take time out of her own private sorrow to appease his anxiety. "It was part of it," she told him later. "Part of being a mother."

"The scariest thing in the world is the thought that you could unknowingly ruin someone's life," Neil tells Wayne. "Or even change someone's life. I hate the thought of having such control. I'd make a rotten mother."

"You're crazy," Wayne says. "You have this great mother, and all you do is complain. I know people whose mothers have disowned them."

"Guilt goes with the territory," Neil says.

170 "Why?" Wayne asks, perfectly seriously.

Neil doesn't answer. He lies back in his seat, closes his eyes, imagines he grew up in a house in the mountains of Colorado, surrounded by snow—endless white snow on hills. No flat places, and no trees; just white hills. Every time he has flown away, she has come into his mind, usually sitting alone in the dark, smoking. Today she is outside at dusk, skimming leaves from the pool.

"I want to get a dog," Neil says.

Wayne laughs. "In the city? It'd suffocate."

The hum of the airplane is druglike, dazing. "I want to stay with you a long time," Neil says.

175 "I know." Imperceptibly, Wayne takes his hand.

"It's very hot there in the summer, too. You know, I'm not thinking about my mother now."

"It's O.K."

For a moment, Neil wonders what the stewardess or the old woman on the way to the bathroom will think, but then he laughs and relaxes.

Later, the plane makes a slow circle over New York City, and on it two men hold hands, eyes closed, and breathe in unison.

[1982]

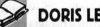

Topics for Critical Thinking and Writing

1. What does Neil mean by saying, on the flight back to New York, that "Guilt goes with the territory"? What judgment on Neil's statement is implied by Wayne's response: "'Why' Wayne asks, perfectly seriously"?
2. What does Neil's attitude toward Luis tell us about Neil?
3. Why do you think Neil put his arm around his mother in the theater?
4. What is Neil's mother's attitude toward her son's homosexuality? How does it compare with Carmen Bologna's?
5. What significance, if any, do you attach to the episode, near the end, when Neil's mother crushes the snails who are attracted by her flashlight?
6. Why, on the flight to New York, does Neil say that he wants to get a dog?

DORIS LESSING

Doris Lessing (b. 1919, née Tayler), was born of British parents in Kermanshah, Persia (now Iran), where her father ran a bank. In 1924 her family moved to a farm in Rhodesia (now Zimbabwe), where she educated herself by reading the classics of European and American literature. During her twenty-five years in Rhodesia she married, was active in the Communist party, held various jobs, divorced, married and divorced a second time (though she retains the last name of her second husband), and wrote. (She says she had always wanted to be a writer, but didn't seriously get down to the business of writing until she was twenty-six or twenty-seven.) In 1949 she moved with her son to London (where she separated from the Communist party) and has continued to live in London. In 1950 she published her first novel, The Grass Is Singing. Her best-known novels are Martha Quest (1952), The Golden Notebook (1962) and The Four-Gated City (1969).

In a collection of her nonfiction, A Small Personal Voice (1975), she says that when she reads a contemporary work of fiction she looks for "the warmth, the compassion, the humanity, the love of people which illuminates the literature of the nineteenth century. . . . Literature should be committed. It is these qualities which I demand."

A Woman on a Roof

It was during the week of hot sun, that June.

Three men were at work on the roof, where the leads got so hot they had the idea of throwing water on to cool them. But the water steamed, then sizzled; and they made jokes about getting an egg from some woman in the flats under

them, to poach it for their dinner. By two it was not possible to touch the guttering they were replacing, and they speculated about what workmen did in regularly hot countries. Perhaps they should borrow kitchen gloves with the egg?
They were all a bit dizzy, not used to the heat; and they shed their coats and
stood side by side squeezing themselves into a foot-wide patch of shade against a
chimney, careful to keep their feet in the thick socks and boots out of the sun.
There was a fine view across several acres of roofs. Not far off a man sat in a deck
chair reading the newspapers. Then they saw her, between chimneys, about fifty
yards away. She lay face down on a brown blanket. They could see the top part
of her; black hair, a flushed solid back, arms spread out.

"She's stark naked," said Stanley, sounding annoyed.

Harry, the oldest, a man of about forty-five, said: "Looks like it."

Young Tom, seventeen, said nothing, but he was excited and grinning.

Stanley said: "Someone'll report her if she doesn't watch out."

"She thinks no one can see," said Tom, craning his head all ways to see more.

At this point the woman, still lying prone, brought her two hands up behind
her shoulders with the ends of a scarf in them, tied it behind her back, and sat
up. She wore a red scarf tied around her breasts and brief red bikini pants. This
being the first day of the sun she was white, flushing red. She sat smoking, and
did not look up when Stanley let out a wolf whistle. Harry said: "Small things
amuse small minds," leading the way back to their part of the roof, but it was
scorching. Harry said: "Wait, I'm going to rig up some shade," and disappeared
down the skylight into the building. Now that he'd gone, Stanley and Tom went
to the farthest point they could to peer at the woman. She had moved, and all
they could see were two pink legs stretched on the blanket. They whistled and
shouted but the legs did not move. Harry came back with a blanket and shouted:
"Come on, then." He sounded irritated with them. They clambered back to him
and he said to Stanley: "What about your missus?" Stanley was newly married,
about three months. Stanley said, jeering: "What about my missus?"—preserving
his independence. Tom said nothing, but his mind was full of the nearly naked
woman. Harry slung the blanket, which he had borrowed from a friendly woman
downstairs, from the stem of a television aerial to a row of chimney-pots. This
shade fell across the piece of gutter they had to replace. But the shade kept moving, they had to adjust the blanket, and not much progress was made. At last
some of the heat left the roof, and they worked fast, making up for lost time.
First Stanley, then Tom, made a trip to the end of the roof to see the woman.
"She's on her back." Stanley said, adding a jest which made Tom snicker, and the
older man smile tolerantly. Tom's report was that she hadn't moved, but it was a
lie. He wanted to keep what he had seen to himself: he had caught her in the act
of rolling down the little red pants over her hips, till they were no more than a
small triangle. She was on her back, fully visible, glistening with oil.

Next morning, as soon as they came up, they went to look. She was already
there, face down, arms spread out, naked except for the little red pants. She had
turned brown in the night. Yesterday she was a scarlet-and-white woman, today
she was a brown woman. Stanley let out a whistle. She lifted her head, startled,
as if she'd been asleep, and looked straight over at him. The sun was in her eyes,
she blinked and stared, then she dropped her head again. At this gesture of indifference, they all three, Stanley, Tom and old Harry, let out whistles and yells.
Harry was doing it in parody of the younger men, making fun of them, but he
was also angry. They were all angry because of her utter indifference to the three
men watching her.

10   "Bitch," said Stanley.

"She should ask us over," said Tom, snickering.

Harry recovered himself and reminded Stanley: "If she's married, her old man wouldn't like that."

"Christ," said Stanley virtuously, "if my wife lay about like that, for everyone to see, I'd soon stop her."

Harry said, smiling: "How do you know, perhaps she's sunning herself at this very moment?"

15   "Not a chance, not on our roof." The safety of his wife put Stanley into a good humor, and they went to work. But today it was hotter than yesterday; and several times one or the other suggested they should tell Matthew, the foreman, and ask to leave the roof until the heat wave was over. But they didn't. There was work to be done in the basement of the big block of flats, but up here they felt free, on a different level from ordinary humanity shut in the streets or the buildings. A lot more people came out on to the roofs that day, for an hour at midday. Some married couples sat side by side in deck chairs, the women's legs stockingless and scarlet, the men in vests with reddening shoulders.

The woman stayed on her blanket, turning herself over and over. She ignored them, no matter what they did. When Harry went off to fetch more screws, Stanley said: "Come on." Her roof belonged to a different system of roofs, separated from theirs at one point by about twenty feet. It meant a scrambling climb from one level to another, edging along parapets, clinging to chimneys, while their big boots slipped and slithered, but at last they stood on a small square projecting roof looking straight down at her, close. She sat smoking, reading a book. Tom thought she looked like a poster, or a magazine cover, with the blue sky behind her and her legs stretched out. Behind her a great crane at work on a new building in Oxford Street swung its black arm across roofs in a great arc. Tom imagined himself at work on the crane, adjusting the arm to swing over and pick her up and swing her back across the sky to drop her near him.

They whistled. She looked up at them, cool and remote, then went on reading. Again, they were furious. Or, rather, Stanley was. His sun-heated face was screwed into a rage as he whistled again and again, trying to make her look up. Young Tom stopped whistling. He stood beside Stanley, excited, grinning; but he felt as if he were saying to the woman: Don't associate me with *him,* for his grin was apologetic. Last night he had thought of the unknown woman before he slept, and she had been tender with him. This tenderness he was remembering as he shifted his feet by the jeering, whistling Stanley, and watched the indifferent, healthy brown woman a few feet off, with the gap that plunged to the street between them. Tom thought it was romantic, it was like being high on two hilltops. But there was a shout from Harry, and they clambered back. Stanley's face was hard, really angry. The boy kept looking at him and wondered why he hated the woman so much, for by now he loved her.

They played their little games with the blanket, trying to trap shade to work under; but again it was not until nearly four that they could work seriously, and they were exhausted, all three of them. They were grumbling about the weather by now. Stanley was in a thoroughly bad humor. When they made their routine trip to see the woman before they packed up for the day, she was apparently asleep, face down, her back all naked save for the scarlet triangle on her buttocks. "I've got a good mind to report her to the police," said Stanley, and Harry said: "What's eating you? What harm's she doing?"

"I tell you, if she was my wife!"

20 "But she isn't, is she?" Tom knew that Harry, like himself, was uneasy at Stanley's reaction. He was normally a sharp young man, quick at his work, making a lot of jokes, good company.

"Perhaps it will be cooler tomorrow," said Harry.

But it wasn't; it was hotter, if anything, and the weather forecast said the good weather would last. As soon as they were on the roof, Harry went over to see if the woman was there, and Tom knew it was to prevent Stanley going, to put off his bad humor. Harry had grownup children, a boy the same age as Tom, and the youth trusted and looked up to him.

Harry came back and said: "She's not there."

"I bet her old man has put his foot down," said Stanley, and Harry and Tom caught each other's eyes and smiled behind the young married man's back.

25 Harry suggested they should get permission to work in the basement, and they did, that day. But before packing up Stanley said: "Let's have a breath of fresh air." Again Harry and Tom smiled at each other as they followed Stanley up to the roof, Tom in the devout conviction that he was there to protect the woman from Stanley. It was about five-thirty, and a calm, full sunlight lay over the roofs. The great crane still swung its black arm from Oxford Street to above their heads. She was not there. Then there was a flutter of white from behind a parapet, and she stood up, in a belted, white dressing-gown. She had been there all day, probably, but on a different patch of roof, to hide from them. Stanley did not whistle; he said nothing, but watched the woman bend to collect papers, books, cigarettes, then fold the blanket over her arm. Tom was thinking: If they weren't here, I'd go over and say . . . what? But he knew from his nightly dreams of her that she was kind and friendly. Perhaps she would ask him down to her flat? Perhaps . . . He stood watching her disappear down the skylight. As she went, Stanley let out a shrill derisive yell: she started, and it seemed as if she nearly fell. She clutched to save herself, they could hear things falling. She looked straight at them, angry. Harry said, facetiously: "Better be careful on those slippery ladders, love." Tom knew he said it to save her from Stanley, but she could not know it. She vanished, frowning. Tom was full of a secret delight, because he knew her anger was for the others, not for him.

"Roll on some rain," said Stanley, bitter, looking at the blue evening sky.

Next day was cloudless, and they decided to finish the work in the basement. They felt excluded, shut in the grey cement basement fitting pipes, from the holiday atmosphere in London in a heat wave. At lunchtime they came up for some air, but while the married couples, and the men in shirt-sleeves or vests, were there, she was not there, either on her usual patch of roof or where she had been yesterday. They all, even Harry, clambered about, between chimney-pots, over parapets, the hot leads stinging their fingers. There was not a sign of her. They took off their shirts and vests and exposed their chests, feeling their feet sweaty and hot. They did not mention the woman. But Tom felt alone again. Last night she had him into her flat: it was big and had fitted white carpets and a bed with a padded white leather headboard. She wore a black filmy negligée and her kindness to Tom thickened his throat as he remembered it. He felt she had betrayed him by not being there.

And again after work they climbed up, but still there was nothing to be seen of her. Stanley kept repeating that if it was as hot as this tomorrow he wasn't going to work and that's all there was to it. But they were all there next day. By ten the temperature was in the middle seventies, and it was eighty long before noon. Harry went to the foreman to say it was impossible to work on the leads in that heat; but the foreman said there was nothing else he could put them on, and they'd have to. At midday they stood, silent, watching the skylight on her roof open, and then she slowly emerged in her white gown, holding a bundle of blanket. She looked at them, gravely, then went to the part of the roof where she was hidden from them. Tom was pleased. He felt she was more his when the other men couldn't see her. They had taken off their shirts and vests, but now they put them back again, for they felt the sun bruising their flesh. "She must have the hide of a rhino," said Stanley, tugging at guttering and swearing. They stopped work, and sat in the shade, moving around behind chimney stacks. A woman came to water a yellow window box opposite them. She was middleaged, wearing a flowered summer dress. Stanley said to her: "We need a drink more than them." She smiled and said: "Better drop down to the pub quick, it'll be closing in a minute." They exchanged pleasantries, and she left them with a smile and a wave.

"Not likely Lady Godiva," said Stanley. "She can give us a bit of a chat and a smile."

30   "You didn't whistle at *her,*" said Tom, reproving.

"Listen to him," said Stanley, "you didn't whistle, then?"

But the boy felt as if he hadn't whistled, as if only Harry and Stanley had. He was making plans, when it was time to knock off work, to get left behind and somehow make his way over to the woman. The weather report said the hot spell was due to break, so he had to move quickly. But there was no chance of being left. The other two decided to knock off work at four, because they were exhausted. As they went down, Tom quickly climbed a parapet and hoisted himself higher by pulling his weight up a chimney. He caught a glimpse of her lying on her back, her knees up, eyes closed, a brown woman lolling in the sun. He slipped and clattered down, as Stanley looked for information: "She's gone down," he said. He felt as if he had protected her from Stanley, and that she must be grateful to him. He could feel the bond between the woman and himself.

Next day, they stood around on the landing below the roof, reluctant to climb up into the heat. The woman who had lent Harry the blanket came out and offered them a cup of tea. They accepted gratefully, and sat around Mrs. Pritchett's kitchen an hour or so, chatting. She was married to an airline pilot. A smart blonde, of about thirty, she had an eye for the handsome sharp-eyed Stanley; and the two teased each other while Harry sat in a corner, watching, indulgent, though his expression reminded Stanley that he was married. And young Tom felt envious of Stanley's ease in badinage;[1] felt, too, that Stanley's getting off with Mrs. Pritchett left his romance with the woman on the roof safe and intact.

"I thought they said the heat wave'd break," said Stanley, sullen, as the time approached when they really would have to climb up into the sunlight.

35   "You don't like it, then?" asked Mrs. Pritchett.

"All right for some," said Stanley. "Nothing to do but lie about as if it was a beach up there. Do you ever go up?"

"Went up once," said Mrs. Pritchett. "But it's a dirty place up there, and it's too hot."

"Quite right too," said Stanley.

Then they went up, leaving the cool neat little flat and the friendly Mrs. Pritchett.

---

[1]**badinage** teasing conversation (French; editors' note)

40   As soon as they were up they saw her. The three men looked at her, resentful at her ease in this punishing sun. Then Harry said, because of the expression on Stanley's face: "Come on, we've got to pretend to work, at least."

They had to wrench another length of guttering that ran beside a parapet out of its bed, so that they could replace it. Stanley took it in his two hands, tugged, swore, stood up. "Fuck it," he said, and sat down under a chimney. He lit a cigarette. "Fuck them," he said. "What do they think we are, lizards? I've got blisters all over my hands." Then he jumped up and climbed over the roofs and stood with his back to them. He put his fingers either side of his mouth and let out a shrill whistle. Tom and Harry squatted, not looking at each other, watching him. They could just see the woman's head, the beginnings of her brown shoulders. Stanley whistled again. Then he began stamping with his feet, and whistled and yelled and screamed at the woman, his face getting scarlet. He seemed quite mad, as he stamped and whistled, while the woman did not move, she did not move a muscle.

"Barmy," said Tom.

"Yes," said Harry, disapproving.

Suddenly the older man came to a decision. It was, Tom knew, to save some sort of scandal or real trouble over the woman. Harry stood up and began packing tools into a length of oily cloth. "Stanley," he said, commanding. At first Stanley took no notice, but Harry said: "Stanley, we're packing it in, I'll tell Matthew."

45   Stanley came back, cheeks mottled, eyes glaring.

"Can't go on like this," said Harry. "It'll break in a day or so. I'm going to tell Matthew we've got sunstroke, and if he doesn't like it, it's too bad." Even Harry sounded aggrieved, Tom noted. The small, competent man, the family man with his grey hair, who was never at a loss, sounded really off balance. "Come on," he said, angry. He fitted himself into the open square in the roof, and went down, watching his feet on the ladder. Then Stanley went, with not a glance at the woman. Then Tom, who, his throat beating with excitement, silently promised her on a backward glance: Wait for me, wait, I'm coming.

On the pavement Stanley said: "I'm going home." He looked white now, so perhaps he really did have sunstroke. Harry went off to find the foreman, who was at work on the plumbing of some flats down the street. Tom slipped back, not into the building they had been working on, but the building on whose roof the woman lay. He went straight up, no one stopping him. The skylight stood open, with an iron ladder leading up. He emerged on to the roof a couple of yards from her. She sat up, pushing back her black hair with both hands. The scarf across her breasts bound them tight, and brown flesh bulged around it. Her legs were brown and smooth. She stared at him in silence. The boy stood grinning, foolish, claiming the tenderness he expected from her.

"What do you want?" she asked.

"I . . . I came to . . . make your acquaintance," he stammered, grinning, pleading with her.

50   They looked at each other, the slight, scarlet-faced excited boy, and the serious, nearly naked woman. Then, without a word, she lay down on her brown blanket, ignoring him.

"You like the sun, do you?" he enquired of her glistening back.

Not a word. He felt panic, thinking of how she had held him in her arms, stroked his hair, brought him where he sat, lordly, in her bed, a glass of some exhilarating liquor he had never tasted in life. He felt that if he knelt down, stroked her shoulders, her hair, she would turn and clasp him in her arms.

He said: "The sun's all right for you, isn't it?"

She raised her head, set her chin on two small fists: "Go away," she said. He did not move. "Listen," she said, in a slow reasonable voice, where anger was kept in check, though with difficulty; looking at him, her face weary with anger, "if you get a kick out of seeing women in bikinis, why don't you take a sixpenny bus ride to the Lido? You'd see dozens of them, without all this mountaineering."

55   She hadn't understood him. He felt her unfairness pale him. He stammered: "But I like you, I've been watching you and . . ."

"Thanks," she said, and dropped her face again, turned away from him.

She lay there. He stood there. She said nothing. She had simply shut him out. He stood, saying nothing at all, for some minutes. He thought: She'll have to say something if I stay. But the minutes went past, with no sign of them in her, except in the tension of her back, her thighs, her arms—the tension of waiting for him to go.

He looked up at the sky, where the sun seemed to spin in heat; and over the roofs where he and his mates had been earlier. He could see the heat quivering where they had worked. And they expect us to work in these conditions! he thought, filled with righteous indignation. The woman hadn't moved. A bit of hot wind blew her black hair softly; it shone, and was iridescent. He remembered how he had stroked it last night.

Resentment of her at last moved him off and away down the ladder, through the building, into the street. He got drunk then, in hatred of her.

60   Next day when he woke the sky was grey. He looked at the wet grey and thought, vicious: Well, that's fixed you, hasn't it now? That's fixed you good and proper.

The three men were at work early on the cool leads, surrounded by damp drizzling roofs where no one came to sun themselves, black roofs, slimy with rain. Because it was cool now, they would finish the job that day, if they hurried.

[1963]

Topics for Critical Thinking and Writing

1. Is the story chiefly about one character? If so, which one?
2. Stanley mentions Lady Godiva. Do you recall the name of the man who peeped at her in the legend? How does his name fit in with Lessing's story?
3. What does Mrs. Pritchett contribute to the story?
4. The last line of the story is, "Because it was cool now, they would finish the job that day, if they hurried." Do you assume that they hurried? Why or why not?

 **GLORIA NAYLOR**

 *Gloria Naylor (b. 1950), a native of New York City, holds a bachelor's degree from Brooklyn College and a master's degree in Afro-American Studies from Yale University. "The Two" comes from* The Women of Brewster Place *(1982), a book that won the American Book Award for First Fiction. Naylor has subsequently published two novels and Centennial (1986), a work of nonfiction.*

The Two

At first they seemed like such nice girls. No one could remember exactly when they had moved into Brewster. It was earlier in the year before Ben[1] was killed—of course, it had to be before Ben's death. But no one remembered if it was in the winter or spring of that year that the two had come. People often came and went on Brewster Place like a restless night's dream, moving in and out in the dark to avoid eviction notices or neighborhood bulletins about the dilapidated condition of their furnishings. So it wasn't until the two were clocked leaving in the mornings and returning in the evenings at regular intervals that it was quietly absorbed that they now claimed Brewster as home. And Brewster waited, cautiously prepared to claim them, because you never knew about young women, and obviously single at that. But when no wild music or drunken friends careened out of the corner building on weekends, and especially, when no slightly eager husbands were encouraged to linger around that first-floor apartment and run errands for them, a suspended sigh of relief floated around the two when they dumped their garbage, did their shopping, and headed for the morning bus.

The women of Brewster had readily accepted the lighter, skinny one. There wasn't much threat in her timid mincing walk and the slightly protruding teeth she seemed so eager to show everyone in her bell-like good mornings and evenings. Breaths were held a little longer in the direction of the short dark one—too pretty, and too much behind. And she insisted on wearing those thin Qiana dresses that the summer breeze molded against the maddening rhythm of the twenty pounds of rounded flesh that she swung steadily down the street. Through slitted eyes, the women watched their men watching her pass, knowing the bastards were praying for a wind. But since she seemed oblivious to whether these supplications went answered, their sighs settled around her shoulders too. Nice girls.

And so no one even cared to remember exactly when they had moved into Brewster Place, until the rumor started. It had first spread through the block like a sour odor that's only faintly perceptible and easily ignored until it starts growing in strength from the dozen mouths it had been lying in, among clammy gums and scum-coated teeth. And then it was everywhere—lining the mouths and whitening the lips of everyone as they wrinkled up their noses at its pervading smell, unable to pinpoint the source or time of its initial arrival. Sophie could—she had been there.

It wasn't that the rumor had actually begun with Sophie. A rumor needs no true parent. It only needs a willing carrier, and it found one in Sophie. She had been there—on one of those August evenings when the sun's absence is a mockery because the heat leaves the air so heavy it presses the naked skin down on your body, to the point that a sheet becomes unbearable and sleep impossible. So most of Brewster was outside that night when the two had come in together, probably from one of those air-conditioned movies downtown, and had greeted the ones who were loitering around their building. And they had started up the steps when the skinny one tripped over a child's ball and the darker one had grabbed her by the arm and around the waist to break her fall. "Careful, don't wanna lose you now." And the two of them had laughed into each other's eyes and went into the building.

[1] the custodian of Brewster Place

5 The smell had begun there. It outlined the image of the stumbling woman and the one who had broken her fall. Sophie and a few other women sniffed at the spot and then, perplexed, silently looked at each other. Where had they seen that before? They had often laughed and touched each other—held each other in joy or its dark twin—but where had they seen *that* before? It came to them as the scent drifted down the steps and entered their nostrils on the way to their inner mouths. They had seen that—done that—with their men. That shared moment of invisible communion reserved for two and hidden from the rest of the world behind laughter or tears or a touch. In the days before babies, miscarriages, and other broken dreams, after stolen caresses in barn stalls and cotton houses, after intimate walks from church and secret kisses with boys who were now long forgotten or permanently fixed in their lives—that was where. They could almost feel the odor moving about in their mouths, and they slowly knitted themselves together and let it out into the air like a yellow mist that began to cling to the bricks on Brewster.

So it got around that the two in 312 were *that* way. And they had seemed like such nice girls. Their regular exits and entrances to the block were viewed with a jaundiced eye. The quiet that rested around their door on the weekends hinted of all sorts of secret rituals, and their friendly indifference to the men on the street was an insult to the women as a brazen flaunting of unnatural ways.

Since Sophie's apartment windows faced theirs from across the air shaft, she became the official watchman for the block, and her opinions were deferred to whenever the two came up in conversation. Sophie took her position seriously and was constantly alert for any telltale signs that might creep out around their drawn shades, across from which she kept a religious vigil. An entire week of drawn shades was evidence enough to send her flying around with reports that as soon as it got dark they pulled their shades down and put on the lights. Heads nodded in knowing unison—a definite sign. If doubt was voiced with a "But I pull my shades down at night too," a whispered "Yeah, but you're not *that* way" was argument enough to win them over.

Sophie watched the lighter one dumping their garbage, and she went outside and opened the lid. Her eyes darted over the crushed tin cans, vegetable peelings, and empty chocolate chip cookie boxes. What do they do with all them chocolate chip cookies? It was surely a sign, but it would take some time to figure that one out. She saw Ben go into their apartment, and she waited and blocked his path as he came out, carrying his toolbox.

"What ya see?" She grabbed his arm and whispered wetly in his face.

10 Ben stared at her squinted eyes and drooping lips and shook his head slowly. "Uh, uh, uh, it was terrible."

"Yeah?" She moved in a little closer.

"Worst busted faucet I seen in my whole life." He shook her hand off his arm and left her standing in the middle of the block.

"You old sop bucket," she muttered, as she went back up on her stoop. A broken faucet, huh? Why did they need to use so much water?

Sophie had plenty to report that day. Ben had said it was terrible in there. No, she didn't know exactly what he had seen, but you can imagine—and they did. Confronted with the difference that had been thrust into their predictable world, they reached into their imaginations and, using an ancient pattern, weaved themselves a reason for its existence. Out of necessity they stitched all of their secret fears and lingering childhood nightmares into this existence, because even though it was deceptive enough to try and look as they looked, talk as they talked, and do as they did, it had to have some hidden stain to invalidate it—it was impossible for them both to be right. So they leaned back, supported by the sheer weight of their numbers and comforted by the woven barrier that kept them protected from the yellow mist that enshrouded the two as they came and went on Brewster Place.

15   Lorraine was the first to notice the change in the people on Brewster Place. She was a shy but naturally friendly woman who got up early, and had read the morning paper and done fifty sit-ups before it was time to leave for work. She came out of her apartment eager to start her day by greeting any of her neighbors who were outside. But she noticed that some of the people who had spoken to her before made a point of having something else to do with their eyes when she passed, although she could almost feel them staring at her back as she moved on. The ones who still spoke only did so after an uncomfortable pause, in which they seemed to be peering through her before they begrudged her a good morning or evening. She wondered if it was all in her mind and she thought about mentioning it to Theresa, but she didn't want to be accused of being too sensitive again. And how would Tee even notice anything like that anyway? She had a lousy attitude and hardly ever spoke to people. She stayed in that bed until the last moment and rushed out of the house fogged-up and grumpy, and she was used to being stared at—by men at least—because of her body.

Lorraine thought about these things as she came up the block from work, carrying a large paper bag. The group of women on her stoop parted silently and let her pass.

"Good evening," she said, as she climbed the steps.

Sophie was standing on the top step and tried to peek into the bag. "You been shopping, huh? What ya buy?" It was almost an accusation.

"Groceries." Lorraine shielded the top of the bag from view and squeezed past her with a confused frown. She saw Sophie throw a knowing glance to the others at the bottom of the stoop. What was wrong with this old woman? Was she crazy or something?

20   Lorraine went into her apartment. Theresa was sitting by the window, reading a copy of *Mademoiselle*. She glanced up from her magazine. "Did you get my chocolate chip cookies?"

"Why good evening to you, too, Tee. And how was my day? Just wonderful." She sat the bag down on the couch. "The little Baxter boy brought in a puppy for show-and-tell, and the damn thing pissed all over the floor and then proceeded to chew the heel off my shoe, but, yes, I managed to hobble to the store and bring you your chocolate chip cookies."

Oh, Jesus, Theresa thought, she's got a bug up her ass tonight.

"Well, you should speak to Mrs. Baxter. She ought to train her kid better than that." She didn't wait for Lorraine to stop laughing before she tried to stretch her good mood. "Here, I'll put those things away. Want me to make dinner so you can rest? I only worked half a day, and the most tragic thing that went down was a broken fingernail and that got caught in my typewriter."

Lorraine followed Theresa into the kitchen. "No, I'm not really tired, and fair's fair, you cooked last night. I didn't mean to tick off like that; it's just that . . . well, Tee, have you noticed that people aren't as nice as they used to be?"

25   Theresa stiffened. Oh, God, here she goes again. "What people, Lorraine? Nice in what way?"

"Well, the people in this building and on the street. No one hardly speaks anymore. I mean, I'll come in and say good evening—and just silence. It wasn't like that when we first moved in. I don't know, it just makes you wonder; that's all. What are they thinking?"

"I personally don't give a shit what they're thinking. And their good evenings don't put any bread on my table."

"Yeah, but you didn't see the way that woman looked at me out there. They must feel something or know something. They probably—"

"They, they, they!" Theresa exploded. "You know, I'm not starting up with this again, Lorraine. Who in the hell are they? And where in the hell are we? Living in some dump of a building in this God-forsaken part of town around a bunch of ignorant niggers with the cotton still under their fingernails because of you and your theys. They knew something in Linden Hills, so I gave up an apartment for you that I'd been in for the last four years. And then they knew in Park Heights, and you made me so miserable there we had to leave. Now these mysterious theys are on Brewster Place. Well, look out that window, kid. There's a big wall down that block, and this is the end of the line for me. I'm not moving anymore, so if that's what you're working yourself up to—save it!"

30   When Theresa became angry she was like a lump of smoldering coal, and her fierce bursts of temper always unsettled Lorraine.

"You see, that's why I didn't want to mention it." Lorraine began to pull at her fingers nervously. "You're always flying up and jumping to conclusions—no one said anything about moving. And I didn't know your life has been so miserable since you met me. I'm sorry about that," she finished tearfully.

Theresa looked at Lorraine, standing in the kitchen door like a wilted leaf, and she wanted to throw something at her. Why didn't she ever fight back? The very softness that had first attracted her to Lorraine was now a frequent cause for irritation. Smoked honey. That's what Lorraine had reminded her of, sitting in her office clutching that application. Dry autumn days in Georgia woods, thick bloated smoke under a beehive, and the first glimpse of amber honey just faintly darkened about the edges by the burning twigs. She had flowed just that heavily into Theresa's mind and had stuck there with a persistent sweetness.

But Theresa hadn't known then that this softness filled Lorraine up to the very middle and that she would bend at the slightest pressure, would be constantly seeking to surround herself with the comfort of everyone's goodwill, and would shrivel up at the least touch of disapproval. It was becoming a drain to be continually called upon for this nurturing and support that she just didn't understand. She had supplied it at first out of love for Lorraine, hoping that she would harden eventually, even as honey does when exposed to the cold. Theresa was growing tired of being clung to—of being the one who was leaned on. She didn't want a child—she wanted someone who could stand toe to toe with her and be willing to slug it out at times. If they practiced that way with each other, then they could turn back to back and beat the hell out of the world for trying to invade their territory. But she had found no such sparring partner in Lorraine, and the strain of fighting alone was beginning to show on her.

"Well, if it was that miserable, I would have been gone a long time ago," she said, watching her words refresh Lorraine like a gentle shower.

35   "I guess you think I'm some sort of a sick paranoid, but I can't afford to have people calling my job or writing letters to my principal. You know I've already lost a position like that in Detroit. And teaching is my whole life, Tee."

"I know," she sighed, not really knowing at all. There was no danger of that ever happening on Brewster Place. Lorraine taught too far from this neighborhood for anyone here to recognize her in that school. No, it wasn't her job she feared losing this time, but their approval. She wanted to stand out there and chat and trade makeup secrets and cake recipes. She wanted to be secretary of their block association and be asked to mind their kids while they ran to the store. And none of that was going to happen if they couldn't even bring themselves to accept her good evenings.

Theresa silently finished unpacking the groceries. "Why did you buy cottage cheese? Who eats that stuff?"

"Well, I thought we should go on a diet."

"If *we* go on a diet, then you'll disappear. You've got nothing to lose but your hair."

40   "Oh, I don't know. I thought that we might want to try and reduce our hips or something." Lorraine shrugged playfully.

"No, thank you. We are very happy with our hips the way they are," Theresa said, as she shoved the cottage cheese to the back of the refrigerator. "And even when I lose weight, it never comes off there. My chest and arms just get smaller, and I start looking like a bottle of salad dressing."

The two women laughed, and Theresa sat down to watch Lorraine fix dinner. "You know, this behind has always been my downfall. When I was coming up in Georgia with my grandmother, the boys used to promise me penny candy if I would let them pat my behind. And I used to love those jawbreakers—you know, the kind that lasted all day and kept changing colors in your mouth. So I was glad to oblige them, because in one afternoon I could collect a whole week's worth of jawbreakers."

"Really. That's funny to you? Having some boy feeling all over you."

Theresa sucked her teeth. "We were only kids, Lorraine. You know, you remind me of my grandmother. That was one straight-laced old lady. She had a fit when my brother told her what I was doing. She called me into the smokehouse and told me in this real scary whisper that I could get pregnant from letting little boys pat my butt and that I'd end up like my cousin Willa. But Willa and I had been thick as fleas, and she had already given me a step-by-step summary of how she'd gotten into her predicament. But I sneaked around to her house that night just to double-check her story, since that old lady had seemed so earnest. 'Willa, are you sure?' I whispered through her bedroom window. 'I'm tellin' ya, Tee,' she said. 'Just keep both feet on the ground and you home free.' Much later I learned that advice wasn't too biologically sound, but it worked in Georgia because those country boys didn't have much imagination."

45   Theresa's laughter bounced off of Lorraine's silent, rigid back and died in her throat. She angrily tore open a pack of the chocolate chip cookies.

"Yeah," she said, staring at Lorraine's back and biting down hard into the cookie, "it wasn't until I came up north to college that I found out there's a whole lot of things that a dude with a little imagination can do to you even with both feet on the ground. You see, Willa forgot to tell me not to bend over or squat or—"

"Must you!" Lorraine turned around from the stove with her teeth clenched tightly together.

"Must I what, Lorraine? Must I talk about things that are as much a part of life as eating or breathing or growing old? Why are you always so uptight about sex or men?"

"I'm not uptight about anything. I just think its disgusting when you go on and on about—"

"There's nothing disgusting about it, Lorraine. You've never been with a man, but I've been with quite a few—some better than others. There were a couple who I still hope to this day will die a slow, painful death, but then there were some who were good to me—in and out of bed."

"If they were so great, then why are you with me?" Lorraine's lips were trembling.

"Because—" Theresa looked steadily into her eyes and then down at the cookie she was twirling on the table. "Because," she continued slowly, "you can take a chocolate chip cookie and put holes in it and attach it to your ears and call it an earring, or hang it around your neck on a silver chain and pretend it's a necklace—but it's still a cookie. See—you can toss it in the air and call it a Frisbee or even a flying saucer, if the mood hits you, and it's still just a cookie. Send it spinning on a table—like this—until it's a wonderful blur of amber and brown light that you can imagine to be a topaz or rusted gold or old crystal, but the law of gravity has got to come into play, sometime, and it's got to come to rest— sometime. Then all the spinning and pretending and hoopla is over with. And you know what you got?"

"A chocolate chip cookie," Lorraine said.

"Uh-huh." Theresa put the cookie in her mouth and winked. "A lesbian." She got up from the table. "Call me when dinner's ready. I'm going back to read." She stopped at the kitchen door. "Now, why are you putting gravy on that chicken, Lorraine? You know it's fattening."

[1982]

✎ Topics for Critical Thinking and Writing

1. The first sentence says. "At first they seemed like such nice girls." What do we know about the person who says it? What does it tell us (and imply) about the "nice girls"?

2. What is Sophie's role in the story?

3. In the second part of the story, who is the narrator? Does she or he know Theresa's thoughts, or Lorraine's, or both?

4. How does the story end? What do you think will happen between Lorraine and Theresa?

5. Try writing a page or less that is the *end* of a story about two people (men, women, children—but *people*) whose relationship is going to end soon, or is going to survive, because of, or despite, its difficulties.

A Casebook on Alice Munro

This casebook consists of three short stories ("Boys and Girls," "How I Met My Husband," and "The Children Stay"), a lecture ("What Is Real?"), and an interview. We accompany the first two stories with Topics for Critical Thinking and Writing.

 ALICE MUNRO

 *Alice Munroe was born in 1931 in Wingham, Ontario, Canada, a relatively rural community and the sort of place in which she sets much of her fiction. She began publishing stories when she was an undergraduate at the University of Western Ontario. She left Western after two years, worked in a library and in a bookstore, then married, moved to Victoria, British Columbia, and founded a bookstore there. She continued to write while raising three children. She divorced and remarried; much of her fiction concerns marriage or divorce, which is to say it concerns shifting relationships in a baffling world.*

Boys and Girls

My father was a fox farmer. That is, he raised silver foxes, in pens; and in the fall and early winter, when their fur was prime, he killed them and skinned them and sold their pelts to the Hudson's Bay Company or the Montreal Fur Traders. These companies supplied us with heroic calendars to hang, one on each side of the kitchen door. Against a background of cold blue sky and black pine forests and treacherous northern rivers, plumed adventurers planted the flags of England or of France: magnificent savages bent their backs to the portage.

For several weeks before Christmas, my father worked after supper in the cellar of our house. The cellar was whitewashed, and lit by a hundred-watt bulb over the worktable. My brother Laird and I sat on the top step and watched. My father removed the pelt inside-out from the body of the fox which looked surprisingly small, mean and rat-like, deprived of its arrogant weight of fur. The naked, slippery bodies were collected in a sack and buried at the dump. One time the hired man, Henry Bailey, had taken a swipe at me with this sack, saying, "Christmas present!" My mother thought that was not funny. In fact she disliked the whole pelting operation—that was what the killing, skinning, and preparation of the furs was called—and wished it did not have to take place in the house. There was the smell. After the pelt had been stretched inside-out on a long board my father scraped away delicately, removing the little clotted webs of blood vessels, the bubbles of fat; the smell of blood and animal fat, with the strong primitive odor of the fox itself, penetrated all parts of the house. I found it reassuringly seasonal, like the smell of oranges and pine needles.

Henry Bailey suffered from bronchial troubles. He would cough and cough until his narrow face turned scarlet, and his light blue, derisive eyes filled up with tears; then he took the lid off the stove, and, standing well back, shot out a great clot of phlegm—hsss—straight into the heart of the flames. We admired him for this performance and for his ability to make his stomach growl at will, and for his laughter, which was full of high whistlings and gurglings and involved the whole faulty machinery of his chest. It was sometimes hard to tell what he was laughing at, and always possible that it might be us.

After we had been sent to bed we could still smell fox and still hear Henry's laugh, but these things, reminders of the warm, safe, brightly lit downstairs world, seemed lost and diminished, floating on the stale cold air upstairs. We were afraid at night in the winter. We were not afraid of *outside* though this was the time of year when snowdrifts curled around our house like sleeping whales and the wind harassed us all night, coming up from the buried fields, the frozen swamp, with its old bugbear chorus of threats and misery. We were afraid of *inside,* the room where we slept. At this time the upstairs of our house was not finished. A brick chimney went up one wall. In the middle of the floor was a square hole, with a wooden railing around it; that was where the stairs came up. On the other side of the stairwell were the things that nobody had any use for any more—a soldiery roll of linoleum, standing on end, a wicker baby carriage, a fern basket, china jugs and basins with cracks in them, a picture of the Battle of Balaclava, very sad to look at. I had told Laird, as soon as he was old enough to understand such things, that bats and skeletons lived over there; whenever a man escaped from the country jail, twenty miles away, I imagined that he had somehow let himself in the window and was hiding behind the linoleum. But we had rules to keep us safe. When the light was on, we were safe as long as we did not step off the square of worn carpet which defined our bedroom-space; when the light was off no place was safe but the beds themselves. I had to turn out the light kneeling on the end of my bed, and stretching as far as I could to reach the cord.

5 In the dark we lay on our beds, our narrow life rafts, and fixed our eyes on the faint light coming up the stairwell, and sang songs. Laird sang "Jingle Bells," which he would sing any time, whether it was Christmas or not, and I sang "Danny Boy." I loved the sound of my own voice, frail and supplicating, rising in the dark. We could make out the tall frosted shapes of the windows now, gloomy and white. When I came to the part, *When I am dead, as dead I well may be*—a fit of shivering caused not by the cold sheets but by pleasurable emotion almost silenced me. *You'll kneel and say, an Ave there above me*—What was an Ave? Every day I forgot to find out.

Laird went straight from singing to sleep. I could hear his long, satisfied, bubbly breaths. Now for the time that remained to me, the most perfectly private and perhaps the best time of the whole day, I arranged myself tightly under the covers and went on with one of the stories I was telling myself from night to night. These stories were about myself, when I had grown a little older; they took place in a world that was recognizably mine, yet one that presented opportunities for courage, boldness and self-sacrifice, as mine never did. I rescued people from a bombed building (it discouraged me that the real war had gone on so far away from Jubilee). I shot two rabid wolves who were menacing the schoolyard (the teachers cowered terrified at my back). I rode a fine horse spiritedly down the main street of Jubilee, acknowledging the townspeople's gratitude for some yet-to-be-worked-out piece of heroism (nobody ever rode a horse there, except King Billy in the Orangemen's Day[1] parade). There was always riding and shooting in these stories, though I had only been on a horse twice—bareback because we did not own a saddle—and the second time I had slid right around and

[1]The Orange Society is named for William of Orange. who. as King William III of England, defeated James II of England at the Battle of the Boyne on 12 July 1609. It sponsors an annual procession on 12 July. (All notes to this reading are by the editors.)

dropped under the horse's feet; it had stepped placidly over me. I really was learning to shoot, but I could not hit anything yet, not even tin cans on fence posts.

Alive, the foxes inhabited a world my father made for them. It was surrounded by a high guard fence, like a medieval town, with a gate that was padlocked at night. Along the streets of this town were ranged large, sturdy pens. Each of them had a real door that a man could go through, a wooden ramp along the wire, for the foxes to run up and down on, and a kennel—something like a clothes chest with airholes—where they slept and stayed in winter and had their young. There were feeding and watering dishes attached to the wire in such a way that they could be emptied and cleaned from the outside. The dishes were made of old tin cans, and the ramps and kennels of odds and ends of old lumber. Everything was tidy and ingenious; my father was tirelessly inventive and his favorite book in the world was Robinson Crusoe. He had fitted a tin drum on a wheelbarrow, for bringing water to the pens. This was my job in summer, when the foxes had to have water twice a day. Between nine and ten o'clock in the morning, and again after supper, I filled the drum at the pump and trundled it down through the barnyard to the pens, where I parked it, and filled my watering can and went along the streets. Laird came too, with his little cream and green gardening can, filled too full and knocking against his legs and slopping water on his canvas shoes. I had the real watering can, my father's, though I could only carry it three-quarters full.

The foxes all had names, which were printed on a tin plate and hung beside their doors. They were not named when they were born, but when they survived the first year's pelting and were added to the breeding stock. Those my father had named were called names like Prince, Bob, Wally and Betty. Those I had named were called Star or Turk, or Maureen or Diana. Laird named one Maud after a hired girl we had when he was little, one Harold after a boy at school, and one Mexico, he did not say why.

Naming them did not make pets out of them, or anything like it. Nobody but my father ever went into the pens, and he had twice had blood-poisoning from bites. When I was bringing them their water they prowled up and down on the paths they had made inside their pens, barking seldom—they saved that for night-time, when they might get up a chorus of community frenzy—but always watching me, their eyes burning, clear gold, in their pointed, malevolent faces. They were beautiful for their delicate legs and heavy, aristocratic tails and the bright fur sprinkled on dark down their backs—which gave them their name—but especially for their faces, drawn exquisitely sharp in pure hostility, and their golden eyes.

10   Besides carrying water I helped my father when he cut the long grass, and the lamb's quarter and flowering money-musk, that grew between the pens. He cut with the scythe and I raked into piles. Then he took a pitchfork and threw fresh-cut grass all over the top of the pens to keep the foxes cooler and shade their coats, which were browned by too much sun. My father did not talk to me unless it was about the job we were doing. In this he was quite different from my mother, who, if she was feeling cheerful, would tell me all sorts of things—the name of a dog she had when she was a little girl, the names of boys she had gone out with later on when she was grown up, and what certain dresses of hers had looked like—she could not imagine now what had become of them. Whatever thoughts and stories my father had were private, and I was shy of him and would never ask him questions. Nevertheless I worked willingly under his eyes, and

with a feeling of pride. One time a feed salesman came down into the pens to talk to him and my father said, "Like to have you meet my new hired man." I turned away and raked furiously, red in the face with pleasure.

"Could of fooled me," said the salesman. "I thought it was only a girl."

After the grass was cut, it seemed suddenly much later in the year. I walked on stubble in the earlier evening, aware of the reddening skies, the entering silences, of fall. When I wheeled the tank out of the gate and put the padlock on, it was almost dark. One night at this time I saw my mother and father standing on the little rise of ground we called the gangway, in front of the barn. My father had just come from the meathouse; he had his stiff bloody apron on, and a pail of cut-up meat in his hand.

It was an odd thing to see my mother down at the barn. She did not often come out of the house unless it was to do something—hang out the wash or dig potatoes in the garden. She looked out of place, with her bare lumpy legs, not touched by the sun, her apron still on and damp across the stomach from the supper dishes. Her hair was tied up in a kerchief, wisps of it falling out. She would tie her hair up like this in the morning, saying she did not have time to do it properly, and it would stay tied up all day. It was true, too; she really did not have time. These days our back porch was piled with baskets of peaches and grapes and pears, bought in town, and onions and tomatoes and cucumbers grown at home, all waiting to be made into jelly and jam and preserves, pickles and chili sauce. In the kitchen there was a fire in the stove all day, jars clinked in boiling water, sometimes a cheesecloth bag was strung on a pole between two chairs straining blue-black grape pulp for jelly. I was given jobs to do and I would sit at the table peeling peaches that had been soaked in the hot water, or cutting up onions, my eyes smarting and streaming. As soon as I was done I ran out of the house, trying to get out of earshot before my mother thought of what she wanted me to do next. I hated the hot dark kitchen in summer, the green blinds and the flypapers, the same old oilcloth table and wavy mirror and bumpy linoleum. My mother was too tired and preoccupied to talk to me, she had no heart to tell about the Normal School Graduation Dance; sweat trickled over her face and she was always counting under her breath, pointing at jars, dumping cups of sugar. It seemed to me that work in the house was endless, dreary and peculiarly depressing; work done out of doors, and in my father's service, was ritualistically important.

I wheeled the tank up to the barn, where it was kept, and I heard my mother saying, "Wait till Laird gets a little bigger, then you'll have a real help."

15   What my father said I did not hear. I was pleased by the way he stood listening, politely as he would to a salesman or a stranger, but with an air of wanting to get on with his real work. I felt my mother had no business down here and I wanted him to feel the same way. What did she mean about Laird? He was no help to anybody. Where was he now? Swinging himself sick on the swing, going around in circles, or trying to catch caterpillars. He never once stayed with me till I was finished.

"And then I can use her more in the house," I heard my mother say. She had a dead-quiet, regretful way of talking about me that always made me uneasy. "I just get my back turned and she runs off. It's not like I had a girl in the family at all."

I went and sat on a feed bag in the corner of the barn, not wanting to appear when this conversation was going on. My mother, I felt, was not to be trusted. She was kinder than my father and more easily fooled, but you could not depend on her, and the real reasons for the things she said and did were not to be known. She loved me, and she sat up late at night making a dress of the difficult style I wanted, for me to wear when school started, but she was also my enemy. She was always plotting. She was plotting now to get me to stay in the house more, although she knew I hated it (*because* she knew I hated it) and keep me from working for my father. It seemed to me she would do this simply out of perversity, and to try her power. It did not occur to me that she could be lonely, or jealous. No grown-up could be; they were too fortunate. I sat and kicked my heels monotonously against a feed bag, raising dust, and did not come out till she was gone.

At any rate, I did not expect my father to pay any attention to what she said. Who could imagine Laird doing my work—Laird remembering the padlock and cleaning out the watering dishes with a leaf on the end of a stick, or even wheeling the tank without it tumbling over? It showed how little my mother knew about the way things really were.

I have forgotten to say what the foxes were fed. My father's bloody apron reminded me. They were fed horsemeat. At this time most farmers still kept horses, and when a horse got too old to work, or broke a leg or got down and would not get up, as they sometimes did, the owner would call my father, and he and Henry went out to the farm in the truck. Usually they shot and butchered the horse there, paying the farmer from five to twelve dollars. If they had already too much meat on hand, they would bring the horse back alive, and keep it for a few days or weeks in our stable, until the meat was needed. After the war the farmers were buying tractors and gradually getting rid of horses altogether, so it sometimes happened that we got a good healthy horse, that there was just no use for any more. If this happened in the winter we might keep the horse in our stable till spring, for we had plenty of hay and if there was a lot of snow—and the plow did not always get out road cleared—it was convenient to be able to go to town with a horse and cutter.[2]

20   The winter I was eleven years old we had two horses in the stable. We did not know what names they had had before, so we called them Mack and Flora. Mack was an old black workhorse, sooty and indifferent. Flora was a sorrel mare, a driver. We took them both out in the cutter. Mack was slow and easy to handle. Flora was given to fits of violent alarm, veering at cars and even at other horses, but we loved her speed and high-stepping, her general air of gallantry and abandon. On Saturdays we went down to the stable and as soon as we opened the door on its cosy, animal-smelling darkness Flora threw up her head, rolled her eyes, whinnied despairingly and pulled herself through a crisis of nerves on the spot. It was not safe to go into her stall; she would kick.

This winter also I began to hear a great deal more on the theme my mother had sounded when she had been talking in front of the barn. I no longer felt safe. It seemed that in the minds of the people around me there was a steady undercurrent of thought, not to be deflected, on this one subject. The word *girl* had formerly seemed to me innocent and unburdened, like the word *child;* now it appeared that it was no such thing. A girl was not, as I had supposed, simply what I was; it was what I had to become. It was a definition, always touched with emphasis, with reproach and disappointment. Also it was a joke on me. Once Laird

[2]A small sleigh

and I were fighting, and for the first time ever I had to use all my strength against him; even so, he caught and pinned my arm for a moment, really hurting me. Henry saw this, and laughed, saying, "Oh, that there Laird's gonna show you, one of these days!" Laird was getting a lot bigger. But I was getting bigger too.

My grandmother came to stay with us for a few weeks and I heard other things. "Girls don't slam doors like that." "Girls keep their knees together when they sit down." And worse still, when I asked some questions, "That's none of girls' business." I continued to slam the doors and sit as awkwardly as possible, thinking by such measures I kept myself free.

When spring came, the horses were let out in the barnyard. Mack stood against the barn wall trying to scratch his neck and haunches, but Flora trotted up and down and reared at the fences, clattering her hooves against the rails. Snow drifts dwindled quickly, revealing the hard gray and brown earth, the familiar rise and fall of the ground, plain and bare after the fantastic landscape of winter. There was a great feeling of opening-out, of release. We just wore rubbers now, over our shoes; our feet felt ridiculously light. One Saturday we went to the stable and found all the doors open, letting in the unaccustomed sunlight and fresh air. Henry was there, just idling around looking at his collection of calendars which were tacked up behind the stalls in a part of the stable my mother had probably never seen.

"Come to say goodbye to your old friend Mack?" Henry said. "Here you give him a taste of oats." He poured some oats in Laird's cupped hands and Laird went to feed Mack. Mack's teeth were in bad shape. He ate very slowly, patiently shifting the oats around in his mouth, trying to find a stump of a molar to grind it on. "Poor old Mac," said Henry mournfully. "When a horse's teeth's gone, he's gone. That's about the way."

25   "Are you going to shoot him today?" I said. Mack and Flora had been in the stable so long I had almost forgotten they were going to be shot.

Henry didn't answer me. Instead he started to sing in a high, trembly, mocking-sorrowful voice. *Oh, there's no more work, for poor Uncle Ned, he's gone where the good darkies go.* Mack's thick, blackish tongue worked diligently at Laird's hand. I went out before the song was ended and sat down on the gangway.

I had never seen them shoot a horse, but I knew where it was done. Last summer Laird and I had come upon a horse's entrails before they were buried. We had thought it was a big black snake, coiled up in the sun. That was around in the field that ran up beside the barn. I thought that if we went inside the barn, and found a wide crack or a knothole to look through, we would be able to see them do it. It was not something I wanted to see; just the same, if a thing really happened, it was better to see, and know.

My father came down from the house, carrying the gun.

"What are you doing here?" he said.

30   "Nothing."

"Go on up and play around the house."

He sent Laird out of the stable. I said to Laird. "Do you want to see them shoot Mack?" and without waiting for an answer led him around to the front door of the barn, opened it carefully, and went in. "Be quiet or they'll hear us," I said. We could hear Henry and my father talking in the stable; then the heavy, shuffling steps of Mack being backed out of his stall.

In the loft it was cold and dark. Thin crisscrossed beams of sunlight fell through the cracks. The hay was low. It was a rolling country, hills and hollows, slipping under our feet. About four feet up was a beam going around the walls. We piled hay up in one corner and I boosted Laird up and hoisted myself. The beam was not very wide; we crept along it with our hands flat on the barn walls. There were plenty of knotholes, and I found one that gave me the view I wanted—a corner of the barnyard, the gate, part of the field. Laird did not have a knothole and began to complain.

I showed him a widened crack between two boards. "Be quiet and wait. If they hear you you'll get us in trouble."

35 My father came in sight carrying the gun. Henry was leading Mack by the halter. He dropped it and took out his cigarette papers and tobacco; he rolled cigarettes for my father and himself. While this was going on Mack nosed around in the old, dead grass along the fence. Then my father opened the gate and they took Mack through. Henry led Mack away from the path to a patch of ground and they talked together, not loud enough for us to hear. Mack again began searching for a mouthful of fresh grass, which was not to be found. My father walked away in a straight line, and stopped short a distance which seemed to suit him. Henry was walking away from Mack too, but sideways, still negligently holding on to the halter. My father raised the gun and Mack looked up as if he had noticed something and my father shot him.

Mack did not collapse at once but swayed, lurched sideways and fell, first on his side; then he rolled over on his back and, amazingly, kicked his legs for a few seconds in the air. At this Henry laughed, as if Mack had done a trick for him. Laird, who had drawn a long, groaning breath of surprise when the shot was fired, said out loud, "He's not dead." And it seemed to me it might be true. But his legs stopped, he rolled on his side again, his muscles quivered and sank. The two men walked over and looked at him in a business-like way; they bent down and examined his forehead where the bullet had gone in, and now I saw his blood on the brown grass.

"Now they just skin him and cut him up," I said. "Let's go." My legs were a little shaky and I jumped gratefully down into the hay. "Now you've seen how they shoot a horse," I said in a congratulatory way, as if I had seen it many times before. "Let's see if any barn cat's had kittens in the hay." Laird jumped. He seemed young and obedient again. Suddenly I remembered how, when he was little, I had brought him into the barn and told him to climb the ladder to the top beam. That was in the spring, too, when the hay was low. I had done it out of a need for excitement, a desire for something to happen so that I could tell about it. He was wearing a little bulky brown and white checked coat, made down from one of mine. He went all the way up just as I told him, and sat down on the top beam with the hay far below him on one side, and the barn floor and some old machinery on the other. Then I ran screaming to my father. "Laird's up on the top beam!" My father came, my mother came, my father went up the ladder talking very quietly and brought Laird down under his arm, at which my mother leaned against the ladder and began to cry. They said to me, "Why weren't you watching him?" but nobody ever knew the truth. Laird did not know enough to tell. But whenever I saw the brown and white checked coat hanging in the closet, or at the bottom of the rag bag, which was where it ended up, I felt a weight in my stomach, the sadness of unexorcised guilt.

I looked at Laird, who did not even remember this, and I did not like the look on this thin, winter-pale face. His expression was not frightened or upset, but remote, concentrating. "Listen," I said, in an unusually bright and friendly voice, "you aren't going to tell, are you?"

"No," he said absently.

40   "Promise."

"Promise," he said. I grabbed the hand behind his back to make sure he was not crossing his fingers. Even so, he might have a nightmare; it might come out that way. I decided I had better work hard to get all thoughts of what he had seen out of his mind—which, it seemed to me, could not hold very many things at a time. I got some money I had saved and that afternoon we went into Jubilee and saw a show, with Judy Canova,[3] at which we both laughed a great deal. After that I thought it would be all right.

Two weeks later I knew they were going to shoot Flora. I knew from the night before, when I heard my mother ask if the hay was holding out all right, and my father said. "Well, after tomorrow there'll just be the cow, and we should be able to put her out to grass in another week." So I knew it was Flora's turn in the morning.

This time I didn't think of watching it. That was something to see just one time. I had not thought about it very often since, but sometimes when I was busy working at school, or standing in front of the mirror combing my hair and wondering if I would be pretty when I grew up, the whole scene would flash into my mind: I would see the easy, practiced way my father raised the gun, and hear Henry laughing when Mack kicked his legs in the air. I did not have any great feeling of horror and opposition, such as a city child might have had; I was too used to seeing the death of animals as a necessity by which we lived. Yet I felt a little ashamed, and there was a new wariness, a sense of holding-off, in my attitude to my father and his work.

It was a fine day, and we were going around the yard picking up tree branches that had been torn off in winter storms. This was something we had been told to do, and also we wanted to use them to make a teepee. We heard Flora whinny, and then my father's voice and Henry's shouting, and we ran down to the barnyard to see what was going on.

45   The stable door was open. Henry had just brought Flora out, and she had broken away from him. She was running free in the barnyard, from one end to the other. We climbed up on the fence. It was exciting to see her running, whinnying, going up on her hind legs, prancing and threatening like a horse in a Western movie, an unbroken ranch horse, though she was just an old driver, an old sorrel mare. My father and Henry ran after her and tried to grab the dangling halter. They tried to work her into a corner, and they had almost succeeded when she made a run between them, wild-eyed, and disappeared around the corner of the barn. We heard the rail clatter down as she got over the fence, and Henry yelled. "She's into the field now!"

That meant she was in the long L-shaped field that ran up by the house. If she got around the center, heading toward the lane, the gate was open; the truck had been driven into the field this morning. My father shouted to me, because I was on the other side of the fence, nearest the lane. "Go shut the gate!"

I could run very fast. I ran across the garden, past the tree where our swing was hung, and jumped across a ditch into the lane. There was the open gate. She had not got out, I could not see her up the road; she must have run to the other end of the field. The gate was heavy, I lifted it out of the gravel and carried it across the roadway. I had it halfway across when she came in sight, galloping straight toward me. There was just time to get the chain on. Laird came scrambling through the ditch to help me.

[3]American comedian, popular in films in the 1940s

Instead of shutting the gate, I opened it as wide as I could. I did not make any decision to do this, it was just what I did. Flora never slowed down; she galloped straight past me, and Laird jumped up and down, yelling "Shut it, shut it!" even after it was too late. My father and Henry appeared in the field a moment too late to see what I had done. They only saw Flora heading for the township road. They would think I had not got there in time.

They did not waste any time asking about it. They went back to the barn and got the gun and the knives they used, and put these in the truck; then they turned the truck around and came bouncing up the field toward us. Laird called to them. "Let me go too, let me go too!" and Henry stopped the truck and they took him in. I shut the gate after they were all gone.

50   I supposed Laird would tell. I wondered what would happen to me. I had never disobeyed my father before, and I could not understand why I had done it. Flora would not really get away. They would catch up with her in the truck. Or if they did not catch her this morning somebody would see her and telephone us this afternoon or tomorrow. There was no wild country here for her to run to, only farms. What was more, my father had paid for her, we needed the meat to feed the foxes, we needed the foxes to make our living. All I had done was make more work for my father who worked hard enough already. And when my father found out about it he was not going to trust me any more; he would know that I was not entirely on his side. I was on Flora's side, and that made me no use to anybody, not even to her. Just the same, I did not regret it; when she came running at me and I held the gate open, that was the only thing I could do.

I went back to the house, and my mother said. "What's all the commotion?" I told her that Flora had kicked down the fence and got away. "Your poor father," she said, "now he'll have to go chasing over the countryside. Well, there isn't any use planning dinner before one." She put up the ironing board. I wanted to tell her, but thought better of it and went upstairs, and sat on my bed.

Lately I had been trying to make my part of the room fancy, spreading the bed with old lace curtains, and fixing myself a dressing table with some leftovers of cretonne for a skirt. I planned to put up some kind of barricade between my bed and Laird's, to keep my section separate from his. In the sunlight, the lace curtains were just dusty rags. We did not sing at night any more. One night when I was singing Laird said. "You sound silly," and I went right on but the next night I did not start. There was not so much need to anyway, we were no longer afraid. We knew it was just old furniture over there, old jumble and confusion. We did not keep to the rules. I still stayed awake after Laird was asleep and told myself stories, but even in these stories something different was happening, mysterious alterations took place. A story might start off in the old way, with a spectacular danger, a fire or wild animals, and for a while I might rescue people; then things would change around, and instead, somebody would be rescuing me. It might be a boy from our class at school, or even Mr. Campbell, our teacher, who tickled girls under the arms. And at this point the story concerned itself at great length with what I looked like—how long my hair was, and what kind of dress I had on; by the time I had these details worked out the real excitement of the story was lost.

It was later than one o'clock when the truck came back. The tarpaulin was over the back, which meant there was meat in it. My mother had to heat dinner up all over again. Henry and my father had changed from their bloody overalls into ordinary working overalls in the barn, and they washed their arms and necks and faces at the sink, and splashed water on their hair and combed it. Laird lifted his arm to show off a streak of blood. "We shot old Flora," he said, "and cut her up in fifty pieces."

"Well I don't want to hear about it," my mother said. "And don't come to my table like that."

55 My father made him go and wash the blood off.

We sat down and my father said grace and Henry pasted his chewing gum on the end of his fork, the way he always did; when he took it off he would have us admire the pattern. We began to pass the bowls of steaming, overcooked vegetables. Laird looked across the table at me and said proudly, distinctly. "Anyway it was her fault Flora got away."

"What?" my father said.

"She could of shut the gate and she didn't. She just open' it up and Flora run out."

"Is that right?" my father said.

60 Everybody at the table was looking at me. I nodded, swallowing food with great difficulty. To my shame, tears flooded my eyes.

My father made a curt sound of disgust. "What did you do that for?"

I did not answer. I put down my fork and waited to be sent from the table, still not looking up.

But this did not happen. For some time nobody said anything, then Laird said matter-of-factly, "She's crying."

"Never mind," my father said. He spoke with resignation, even good humor, the words which absolved and dismissed me for good. "She's only a girl," he said.

65 I didn't protest that, even in my heart. Maybe it was true.

[1968]

 ## Topics for Critical Thinking and Writing

1. Explain, in a paragraph, what the narrator means when she says (paragraph 21), "The word *girl* had formerly seemed to me innocent and unburdened, like the world *child;* now it appeared that it was no such thing. A girl was not, as I had supposed, simply what I was; it was what I had to become."

2. The narrator says that she "could not understand" why she disobeyed her father and allowed the horse to escape. Can you explain her action to her? If so, do so.

3. In a paragraph, characterize the mother.

How I Met My Husband

We heard the plane come over at noon, roaring through the radio news, and we were sure it was going to hit the house, so we all ran out into the yard. We saw it come in over the treetops, all red and silver, the first closeup plane I ever saw. Mrs. Peebles screamed.

"Crash landing," their little boy said. Joey was his name.

"It's okay," said Dr. Peebles. "He knows what he's doing." Dr. Peebles was only an animal doctor, but had a calming way of talking, like any doctor.

This was my first job—working for Dr. and Mrs. Peebles, who had bought an old house out on the Fifth Line, about five miles out of town. It was just when the trend was starting of town people buying up old farms, not to work them but to live on them.

5 We watched the plane land across the road, where the fairgrounds used to be. It did make a good landing field, nice and level for the old race track, and the

barns and display sheds torn down now for scrap lumber so there was nothing in the way. Even the old grandstand bays had burned.

"All right," said Mrs. Peebles, snappy as she always was when she got over her nerves. "Let's go back in the house. Let's not stand here gawking like a set of farmers."

She didn't say that to hurt my feelings. It never occurred to her.

I was just setting the dessert down when Loretta Bird arrived, out of breath, at the screen door.

"I thought it was going to crash into the house and kill youse all!"

10   She lived on the next place and the Peebleses thought she was a country-woman, they didn't know the difference. She and her husband didn't farm, he worked on the roads and had a bad name for drinking. They had seven children and couldn't get credit at the HiWay Grocery. The Peebleses made her welcome, not knowing any better, as I say, and offered her dessert.

Dessert was never anything to write home about, at their place. A dish of Jello-O or sliced bananas or fruit out of a tin. "Have a house without a pie, be ashamed until you die," my mother used to say, but Mrs. Peebles operated differently.

Loretta Bird saw me getting the can of peaches.

"Oh, never mind," she said. "I haven't got the right kind of stomach to trust what comes out of those tins. I can only eat home canning."

I could have slapped her. I bet she never put down fruit in her life.

15   "I know what he's landed here for," she said. "He's got permission to use the fairgrounds and take people up for rides. It costs a dollar. It's the same fellow who was over at Palmerston[1] last week and was up the lakeshore before that. I wouldn't go up, if you paid me."

"I'd jump at the chance," Dr. Peebles said. "I'd like to see this neighborhood from the air."

Mrs. Peebles said she would just as soon see it from the ground. Joey said he wanted to go and Heather did, too. Joey was nine and Heather was seven.

"Would you, Edie?" Heather said.

I said I didn't know. I was scared, but I never admitted that, especially in front of children I was taking care of.

20   "People are going to be coming out here in their cars raising dust and trampling your property, if I was you I would complain," Loretta said. She hooked her legs around the chair rung and I knew we were in for a lengthy visit. After Dr. Peebles went back to his office or out on his next call and Mrs. Peebles went for her nap, she would hang around me while I was trying to do the dishes. She would pass remarks about the Peebleses in their own house.

"She wouldn't find time to lay down in the middle of the day, if she had seven kids like I got."

She asked me did they fight and did they keep things in the dresser drawer not to have babies with. She said it was a sin if they did. I pretended I didn't know what she was talking about.

I was fifteen and away from home for the first time. My parents had made the effort and sent me to high school for a year, but I didn't like it. I was shy of strangers and the work was hard, they didn't make it nice for you or explain the way they do now. At the end of the year the averages were published in the paper, and mine came out on the very bottom, 37 percent. My father said that's

---

[1]a town in Ontario, Canada (All notes are by the editors.)

enough and I didn't blame him. The last thing I wanted, anyway, was to go on and end up teaching school. It happened the very day the paper came out with my disgrace in it, Dr. Peebles was staying at our place for dinner, having just helped one of our cows have twins, and he said I looked smart to him and his wife was looking for a girl to help. He said she felt tied down, with the two children, out in the country. I guess she would, my mother said, being polite, though I could tell from her face she was wondering what on earth it would be like to have only two children and no barn work, and then to be complaining.

When I went home I would describe to them the work I had to do, and it made everybody laugh. Mrs. Peebles had an automatic washer and dryer, the first I ever saw. I have had those in my own home for such a long time now it's hard to remember how much of a miracle it was to me, not having to struggle with the wringer and hang up and haul down. Let alone not having to heat water. Then there was practically no baking. Mrs. Peebles said she couldn't make pie crust, the most amazing thing I ever heard a woman admit. I could, of course, and I could make light biscuits and a white cake and dark cake, but they didn't want it, she said they watched their figures. The only thing I didn't like about working there, in fact, was feeling half hungry a lot of the time. I used to bring back a box of doughnuts made out at home, and hide them under my bed. The children found out, and I didn't mind sharing, but I thought I better bind them to secrecy.

25   The day after the plane landed Mrs. Peebles put both children in the car and drove over to Chesley, to get their hair cut. There was a good woman then at Chesley for doing hair. She got hers done at the same place, Mrs. Peebles did, and that meant they would be gone a good while. She had to pick a day Dr. Peebles wasn't going out into the country, she didn't have her own car. Cars were still in short supply then, after the war.

I loved being left in the house alone, to do my work at leisure. The kitchen was all white and bright yellow, with fluorescent lights. That was before they ever thought of making the appliances all different colors and doing the cupboards like dark old wood and hiding the lighting. I loved light. I loved the double sink. So would anybody new-come from washing dishes in a dishpan with a rag-plugged hole on an oilcloth-covered table by light of a coal-oil lamp. I kept everything shining.

The bathroom too. I had a bath in there once a week. They wouldn't have minded if I took one oftener, but to me it seemed like asking too much, or maybe risking making it less wonderful. The basin and the tub and the toilet were all pink, and there were glass doors with flamingoes painted on them, to shut off the tub. The light had a rosy cast and the mat sank under your feet like snow, except that it was warm. The mirror was three-way. With the mirror all steamed up and the air like a perfume cloud, from things I was allowed to use. I stood up on the side of the tub and admired myself naked, from three directions. Sometimes I thought about the way we lived out at home and the way we lived here and how one way was so hard to imagine when you were living the other way. But I thought it was still a lot easier, living the way we lived at home, to picture something like this, the painted flamingoes and the warmth and the soft mat, than it was anybody knowing only things like this to picture how it was the other way. And why was that?

I was through my jobs in no time, and had the vegetables peeled for supper and sitting in cold water besides. Then I went into Mrs. Peebles' bedroom. I had been in there plenty of times, cleaning, and I always took a good look in her closet, at the clothes she had hanging there. I wouldn't have looked in her drawers, but a closet is open to anybody. That's a lie. I would have looked in drawers, but I would have felt worse doing it and been more scared she could tell.

Some clothes in her closet she wore all the time. I was quite familiar with them. Others she never put on, they were pushed to the back. I was disappointed to see no wedding dress. But there was one long dress I could just see the skirt of, and I was hungering to see the rest. Now I took note of where it hung and lifted it out. It was satin, a lovely weight on my arm, light bluish-green in color, almost silvery. It had a fitted, pointed waist and a full skirt and an off-the-shoulder fold hiding the little sleeves.

30   Next thing was easy. I got out of my own things and slipped it on. I was slimmer at fifteen than anybody would believe who knows me now and the fit was beautiful. I didn't, of course, have a strapless bra on, which was what it needed. I just had to slide my straps down my arms under the material. Then I tried pinning up my hair, to get the effect. One thing led to another, I put on rouge and lipstick and eyebrow pencil from her dresser. The heat of the day and the weight of the satin and all the excitement made me thirsty, and I went out to the kitchen, got-up as I was, to get a glass of ginger ale with ice cubes from the refrigerator. The Peebleses drank ginger ale, or fruit drinks, all day, like water, and I was getting so I did too. Also there was no limit on ice cubes which I was so fond of I would even put them in a glass of milk.

I turned from putting the ice tray back and saw a man watching me through the screen. It was the luckiest thing in the world I didn't spill the ginger ale down the front of me then and there.

"I never meant to scare you. I knocked but you were getting the ice out, you didn't hear me."

I couldn't see what he looked like, he was dark the way somebody is pressed up against a screen door with the bright daylight behind them. I only knew he wasn't from around here.

"I'm from the plane over there. My name is Chris Watters and what I was wondering was if I could use that pump."

35   There was a pump in the yard. That was the way the people used to get their water. Now I noticed he was carrying a pail.

"You're welcome," I said. "I can get it from the tap and save you pumping." I guess I wanted him to know we had piped water, didn't pump ourselves.

"I don't mind the exercise." He didn't move, though, and finally he said "Were you going to a dance?"

Seeing a stranger there had made me entirely forget how I was dressed.

"Or is that the way ladies around here generally get dressed up in the afternoon?"

40   I didn't know how to joke back then. I was too embarrassed.

"You live here? Are you the lady of the house?"

"I'm the hired girl."

Some people change when they find that out, their whole way of looking at you and speaking to you changes, but his didn't.

"Well, I just wanted to tell you you look very nice. I was so surprised when I looked in the door and saw you. Just because you looked so nice and beautiful."

45   I wasn't even old enough then to realize how out of the common it is, for a man to say something like that to a woman, or somebody he is treating like a woman. For a man to say a word like *beautiful*. I wasn't old enough to realize or to say anything back, or in fact to do anything but wish he would go away. Not that I didn't like him, but just that it upset me so, having him look at me, and me trying to think of something to say.

He must have understood. He said good-bye, and thanked me, and went and started filling his pail from the pump. I stood behind the Venetian blinds in the dining room, watching him. When he had gone. I went into the bedroom and took the dress off and put it back in the same place. I dressed in my own clothes and took my hair down and washed my face, wiping it on Kleenex, which I threw in the wastebasket.

The Peebleses asked me what kind of man he was. Young, middle-aged, short, tall? I couldn't say.

"Good-looking?" Dr. Peebles teased me.

I couldn't think a thing but that he would be coming to get his water again, he would be talking to Dr. or Mrs. Peebles, making friends with them, and he would mention seeing me that first afternoon, dressed up. Why not mention it? He would think it was funny. And no idea of the trouble it would get me into.

50   After supper the Peebleses drove into town to go to a movie. She wanted to go somewhere with her hair fresh done. I sat in my bright kitchen wondering what to do, knowing I would never sleep. Mrs. Peebles might not fire me, when she found out, but it would give her a different feeling about me altogether. This was the first place I ever worked but I already had picked up things about the way people feel when you are working for them. They like to think you aren't curious. Not just that you aren't dishonest, that isn't enough. They like to feel you don't notice things, that you don't think or wonder about anything but what they liked to eat and how they liked things ironed, and so on. I don't mean they weren't kind to me, because they were. They had me eat my meals with them (to tell the truth I expected to. I didn't know there were families who don't) and sometimes they took me along in the car. But all the same.

I went up and checked on the children being asleep and then I went out. I had to do it. I crossed the road and went in the old fairgrounds gate. The plane looked unnatural sitting there, and shining with the moon. Off at the far side of the fairgrounds, where the bush was taking over, I saw his tent.

He was sitting outside it smoking a cigarette. He saw me coming.

"Hello, were you looking for a plane ride? I don't start taking people up till tomorrow." Then he looked again and said, "Oh, it's you. I didn't know you without your long dress on."

My heart was knocking away, my tongue was dried up. I had to say something. But I couldn't. My throat was closed and I was like a deaf-and-dumb.

55   "Did you want a ride? Sit down. Have a cigarette."

I couldn't even shake my head to say no, so he gave me one.

"Put it in your mouth or I can't light it. It's a good thing I'm used to shy ladies."

I did. It wasn't the first time I had smoked a cigarette, actually. My girlfriend out home, Muriel Lowe, used to steal them from her brother.

"Look at your hand shaking. Did you just want to have a chat, or what?"

60   In one burst I said. "I wish you wouldn't say anything about that dress."

"What dress? Oh, the long dress."

"It's Mrs. Peebles'."

"Whose? Oh, the lady you work for? Is that it? She wasn't home so you got dressed up in her dress, eh? You got dressed up and played queen. I don't blame you. You're not smoking the cigarette right. Don't just puff. Draw it in. Did anybody ever show you how to inhale? Are you scared I'll tell on you? Is that it?"

I was so ashamed at having to ask him to connive this way I couldn't nod. I just looked at him and he saw *yes*.

65   "Well I won't. I won't in the slightest way mention it or embarrass you. I give you my word of honor."

Then he changed the subject, to help me out, seeing I couldn't even thank him.

"What do you think of this sign?"

It was a board sign lying practically at my feet.

SEE THE WORLD FROM THE SKY, ADULTS $1.00. CHILDREN 50¢. QUALIFIED PILOT.

70   "My old sign was getting pretty beat up, I thought I'd make a new one. That's what I've been doing with my time today."

The lettering wasn't all that handsome, I thought. I could have done a better one in half an hour.

"I'm not an expert at sign making."

"It's very good," I said.

"I don't need it for publicity, word of mouth is usually enough. I turned away two carloads tonight. I felt like taking it easy. I didn't tell them ladies were dropping in to visit me."

75   Now I remembered the children and I was scared again, in case one of them had waked up and called me and I wasn't there.

"Do you have to go so soon?"

I remembered some manners. "Thank you for the cigarette."

"Don't forget. You have my word of honor."

I tore off across the fairgrounds, scared I'd see the car heading home from town. My sense of time was mixed up, I didn't know how long I'd been out of the house. But it was all right, it wasn't late, the children were asleep. I got in bed myself and lay thinking what a lucky end to the day, after all, and among things to be grateful for I could be grateful Loretta Bird hadn't been the one who caught me.

80   The yard and borders didn't get trampled, it wasn't as bad as that. All the same it seemed very public, around the house. The sign was on the fairgrounds gate. People came mostly after supper but a good many in the afternoon, too. The Bird children all came without fifty cents between them and hung on the gate. We got used to the excitement of the plane coming in and taking off, it wasn't excitement anymore. I never went over, after that one time, but would see him when he came to get his water. I would be out on the steps doing sitting-down work, like preparing vegetables, if I could.

"Why don't you come over? I'll take you up in my plane."

"I'm saving my money," I said, because I couldn't think of anything else.

"For what? For getting married?"

I shook my head.

85   "I'll take you up for free if you come sometime when it's slack. I thought you would come, and have another cigarette."

I made a face to hush him, because you never could tell when the children would be sneaking around the porch, or Mrs. Peebles herself listening in the house. Sometimes she came out and had a conversation with him. He told her things he hadn't bothered to tell me. But then I hadn't thought to ask. He told her he had been in the war, that was where he learned to fly a plane, and now he couldn't settle down to ordinary life, this was what he liked. She said she couldn't imagine anybody liking such a thing. Though sometimes, she said, she was almost bored enough to try anything herself, she wasn't brought up to living in the country. It's all my husband's idea, she said. This was news to me.

"Maybe you ought to give flying lessons," she said.

"Would you take them?"

She just laughed.

90   Sunday was a busy flying day in spite of it being preached against from two pulpits. We were all sitting out watching. Joey and Heather were over on the fence with the Bird kids. Their father had said they could go, after their mother saying all week they couldn't.

A car came down the road past the parked cars and pulled up right in the drive. It was Loretta Bird who got out, all importance, and on the driver's side another woman got out, more sedately. She was wearing sunglasses.

"This is a lady looking for the man that flies the plane," Loretta Bird said. "I heard her inquire in the hotel coffee shop where I was having a Coke and I brought her out."

"I'm sorry to bother you." the lady said. "I'm Alice Kelling, Mr. Watters' fiancée."

This Alice Kelling had on a pair of brown and white checked slacks and a yellow top. Her bust looked to me rather low and bumpy. She had a worried face. Her hair had had a permanent, but had grown out, and she wore a yellow band to keep it off her face. Nothing in the least pretty or even young-looking about her. But you could tell from how she talked she was from the city, or educated, or both.

95   Dr. Peebles stood up and introduced himself and his wife and me and asked her to be seated.

"He's up in the air right now, but you're welcome to sit and wait. He gets his water here and he hasn't been yet. He'll probably take his break about five."

"That is him, then?" said Alice Kelling, wrinkling and straining at the sky.

"He's not in the habit of running out on you, taking a different name?" Dr. Peebles laughed. He was the one, not his wife, to offer iced tea. Then she sent me into the kitchen to fix it. She smiled. She was wearing sunglasses too.

"He never mentioned his fiancée," she said.

100   I loved fixing iced tea with lots of ice and slices of lemon in tall glasses. I ought to have mentioned before. Dr. Peebles was an abstainer, at least around the house, or I wouldn't have been allowed to take the place. I had to fix a glass for Loretta Bird too, though it galled me, and when I went out she had settled in my lawn chair, leaving me the steps.

"I knew you was a nurse when I first heard you in that coffee shop."

"How would you know a thing like that?"

"I get my hunches about people. Was that how you met him, nursing?"

"Chris? Well yes. Yes, it was."

105   "Oh, were you overseas?" said Mrs. Peebles.

"No, it was before he went overseas. I nursed him when he was stationed at Centralia and had a ruptured appendix. We got engaged and then he went overseas. My, this is refreshing, after a long drive."

"He'll be glad to see you," Dr. Peebles said. "It's a rackety kind of life, isn't it, not staying one place long enough to really make friends."

"Youse've had a long engagement," Loretta Bird said.

Alice Kelling passed that over. "I was going to get a room at the hotel, but when I was offered directions I came on out. Do you think I could phone them?"

110   "No need," Dr. Peebles said. "You're five miles away from him if you stay at the hotel. Here, you're right across the road. Stay with us. We've got rooms on rooms, look at this big house."

Asking people to stay, just like that, is certainly a country thing, and maybe seemed natural to him now, but not to Mrs. Peebles, from the way she said, oh yes, we have plenty of room. Or to Alice Kelling, who kept protesting, but let herself be worn down. I got the feeling it was a temptation to her to be that close. I was trying for a look at her ring. Her nails were painted red, her fingers were freckled and wrinkled. It was a tiny stone. Muriel Lowe's cousin had one twice as big.

Chris came to get his water, late in the afternoon just as Dr. Peebles had predicted. He must have recognized the car from a way off. He came smiling.

"Here I am chasing after you to see what you're up to," called Alice Kelling. She got up and went to meet him and they kissed, just touched, in front of us.

"You're going to spend a lot on gas that way," Chris said.

115   Dr. Peebles invited Chris to stay for supper since he had already put up the sign that said: NO MORE RIDES TILL 7 P.M. Mrs. Peebles wanted it served in the yard, in spite of the bugs. One thing strange to anybody from the country is this eating outside. I had made a potato salad earlier and she had made a jellied salad, that was one thing she could do, so it was just a matter of getting those out, and some sliced meat and cucumbers and fresh leaf lettuce. Loretta Bird hung around for some time saying, "Oh, well, I guess I better get home to those yappers," and, "It's so nice just sitting here. I sure hate to get up," but nobody invited her, I was relieved to see, and finally she had to go.

That night after rides were finished Alice Kelling and Chris went off somewhere in her car. I lay awake till they got back. When I saw the car lights sweep my ceiling I got up to look down on them through the slats of my blind. I don't know what I thought I was going to see. Muriel Lowe and I used to sleep on her front veranda and watch her sister and her sister's boyfriend saying good night. Afterward we couldn't get to sleep, for longing for somebody to kiss us and rub up against us and we would talk about suppose you were out in a boat with a boy and he wouldn't bring you in to shore unless you did it, or what if somebody got you trapped in a barn, you would have to, wouldn't you, it wouldn't be your fault. Muriel said her two girl cousins used to try with a toilet paper roll that one of them was a boy. We wouldn't do anything like that; just lay and wondered.

All that happened was that Chris got out of the car on one side and she got out on the other and they walked off separately—him toward the fairgrounds and her toward the house. I got back in bed and imagined about me coming home with him, not like that.

Next morning Alice Kelling got up late and I fixed a grapefruit for her the way I had learned and Mrs. Peebles sat down with her to visit and have another cup of coffee. Mrs. Peebles seemed pleased enough now, having company. Alice Kelling said she guessed she better get used to putting in a day just watching Chris take off and come down, and Mrs. Peebles said she didn't know if she should suggest it because Alice Kelling was the one with the car, but the lake was only twenty-five miles away and what a good day for a picnic.

Alice Kelling took her up on the idea and by eleven o'clock they were in the car, with Joey and Heather and a sandwich lunch I had made. The only thing was that Chris hadn't come down, and she wanted to tell him where they were going.

120   "Edie'll go over and tell him," Mrs. Peebles said. "There's no problem."

Alice Kelling wrinkled her face and agreed.

"Be sure and tell him we'll be back by five!"

I didn't see that he would be concerned about knowing this right away, and I thought of him eating whatever he ate over there, alone, cooking on his camp stove, so I got to work and mixed up a crumb cake and baked it, in between the other work I had to do; then, when it was a bit cooled, wrapped it in a tea towel. I didn't do anything to myself but take off my apron and comb my hair. I would like to have put some makeup on, but I was too afraid it would remind him of the way he first saw me, and that would humiliate me all over again.

He had come and put another sign on the gate: NO RIDES THIS P.M. APOLOGIES. I worried that he wasn't feeling well. No sign of him outside and the tent flap was down. I knocked on the pole.

125 "Come in," he said, in a voice that would just as soon have said *Stay out.*

I lifted the flap.

"Oh, it's you. I'm sorry. I didn't know it was you."

He had been just sitting on the side of the bed, smoking. Why not at least sit and smoke in the fresh air?

"I brought a cake and hope you're not sick," I said.

130 "Why would I be sick? Oh—that sign. That's all right. I'm just tired of talking to people. I don't mean you. Have a seat." He pinned back the tent flap. "Get some fresh air in here."

I sat on the edge of the bed, there was no place else. It was one of those fold-up cots, really: I remembered and gave him his fiancée's message.

He ate some of the cake. "Good."

"Put the rest away for when you're hungry later."

"I'll tell you a secret. I won't be around here much longer."

135 "Are you getting married?"

"Ha ha. What time did you say they'd be back?"

"Five o'clock."

"Well, by that time this place will have seen the last of me. A plane can get further than a car." He unwrapped the cake and ate another piece of it, absentmindedly.

"Now you'll be thirsty."

140 "There's some water in the pail."

"It won't be very cold. I could bring some fresh. I could bring some ice from the refrigerator."

"No," he said. "I don't want you to go. I want a nice long time of saying good-bye to you."

He put the cake away carefully and sat beside me and started those little kisses, so soft. I can't ever let myself think about them, such kindness in his face and lovely kisses, all over my eyelids and neck and ears, all over, then me kissing back as well as I could (I had only kissed a boy on a dare before, and kissed my own arms for practice) and we lay back on the cot and pressed together, just gently, and he did some other things, not bad things or not in a bad way. It was lovely in the tent, that smell of grass and hot tent cloth with the sun beating down on it, and he said, "I wouldn't do you any harm for the world." Once, when he had rolled on top of me and we were sort of rocking together on the cot, he said softly, "Oh, no," and freed himself and jumped up and got the water pail. He splashed some of it on his neck and face, and the little bit left, on me lying there.

"That's to cool us off, miss."

145 When we said good-bye I wasn't at all sad, because he held my face and said, "I'm going to write you a letter. I'll tell you where I am and maybe you can come and see me. Would you like that? Okay then. You wait." I was really glad I think

to get away from him, it was like he was piling presents on me I couldn't get the pleasure of till I considered them alone.

No consternation at first about the plane being gone. They thought he had taken somebody up, and I didn't enlighten them. Dr. Peebles had phoned he had to go to the country, so there was just us having supper, and then Loretta Bird thrusting her head in the door and saying. "I see he's took off."

"What?" said Alice Kelling, and pushed back her chair.

"The kids come and told me this afternoon he was taking down his tent. Did he think he'd run through all the business there was around here? He didn't take off without letting you know, did he?"

"He'll send me word," Alice Kelling said. "He'll probably phone tonight. He's terribly restless, since the war."

150 "Edie, he didn't mention to you, did he?" Mrs. Peebles said. "When you took over the message?"

"Yes," I said. So far so true.

"Well why didn't you say?" All of them were looking at me. "Did he say where he was going?"

"He said he might try Bayfield," I said. What made me tell such a lie? I didn't intend it.

"Bayfield, how far is that?" said Alice Kelling.

155 Mrs. Peebles said, "Thirty, thirty-five miles."

"That's not far. Oh, well, that's really not far at all. It's on the lake, isn't it?"

You'd think I'd be ashamed of myself, setting her on the wrong track. I did it to give him more time, whatever time he needed. I lied for him, and also, I have to admit, for me. Women should stick together and not do things like that. I see that now, but didn't then. I never thought of myself as being in any way like her, or coming to the same troubles, ever.

She hadn't taken her eyes off me. I thought she suspected my lie.

"When did he mention this to you?"

160 "Earlier."

"When you were over at the plane?"

"Yes."

"You must've stayed and had a chat." She smiled at me, not a nice smile. "You must've stayed and had a little visit with him."

"I took a cake," I said, thinking that telling some truth would spare me telling the rest.

165 "We didn't have a cake," said Mrs. Peebles rather sharply.

"I baked one."

Alice Kelling said, "That was very friendly of you."

"Did you get permission," said Loretta Bird. "You never know what these girls'll do next," she said. "It's not they mean harm so much, as they're ignorant."

"The cake is neither here nor there," Mrs. Peebles broke in. "Edie, I wasn't aware you knew Chris that well."

170 I didn't know what to say.

"I'm not surprised." Alice Kelling said in a high voice. "I knew by the look of her as soon as I saw her. We get them at the hospital all the time." She looked hard at me with a stretched smile. "Having their babies. We have to put them in a special ward because of their diseases. Little country tramps. Fourteen and fifteen years old. You should see the babies they have, too."

"There was a bad woman here in town had a baby that pus was running out of its eyes," Loretta Bird put in.

"Wait a minute," said Mrs. Peebles. "What is this talk? Edie. What about you and Mr. Watters? Were you intimate with him?"

"Yes," I said. I was thinking of us lying on the cot and kissing, wasn't that intimate? And I would never deny it.

175   They were all one minute quiet, even Loretta Bird.

"Well," said Mrs. Peebles. "I am surprised. I think I need a cigarette. This is the first of any such tendencies I've seen in her," she said, speaking to Alice Kelling, but Alice Kelling was looking at me.

"Loose little bitch." Tears ran down her face. "Loose little bitch, aren't you? I knew as soon as I saw you. Men despise girls like you. He just made use of you and went off, you know that, don't you? Girls like you are just nothing, they're just public conveniences, just filthy little rags!"

"Oh now," said Mrs. Peebles.

"Filthy." Alice Kelling sobbed. "Filthy little rags!"

180   "Don't get yourself upset," Loretta Bird said. She was swollen up with pleasure at being in on this scene. "Men are all the same."

"Edie, I'm very surprised," Mrs. Peebles said. "I thought your parents were so strict. You don't want to have a baby, do you?"

I'm still ashamed of what happened next. I lost control, just like a six-year-old. I started howling. "You don't get a baby from just doing that!"

"You see. Some of them are that ignorant," Loretta Bird said.

But Mrs. Peebles jumped up and caught my arms and shook me.

185   "Calm down. Don't get hysterical. Calm down. Stop crying. Listen to me. Listen. I'm wondering, if you know what being intimate means. Now tell me. What did you think it meant?"

"Kissing," I howled.

She let go. "Oh, Edie. Stop it. Don't be silly. It's all right. It's all a misunderstanding. Being intimate means a lot more than that. Oh I *wondered*."

"She's trying to cover up, now," said Alice Kelling. "Yes. She's not so stupid. She sees she got herself in trouble."

"I believe her," Mrs. Peebles said. "This is an awful scene."

190   "Well there is one way to find out," said Alice Kelling, getting up. "After all, I am a nurse."

Mrs. Peebles drew a breath and said. "No. No. Go to your room, Edie. And stop that noise. This is too disgusting."

I heard the car start in a little while. I tried to stop crying, pulling back each wave as it started over me. Finally I succeeded, and lay heaving on the bed.

Mrs. Peebles came and stood in the doorway.

"She's gone," she said. "That Bird woman too. Of course, you know you should never have gone near that man and that is the cause of all this trouble. I have a headache. As soon as you can, go and wash your face in cold water and get at the dishes and we will not say any more about this."

195   Nor we didn't. I didn't figure out till years later the extent of what I had been saved from. Mrs. Peebles was not very friendly to me afterward, but she was fair. Not very friendly is the wrong way of describing what she was. She had never been very friendly. It was just that now she had to see me all the time and it got on her nerves, a little.

As for me, I put it all out of my mind like a bad dream and concentrated on waiting for my letter. The mail came every day except Sunday, between one-thirty and two in the afternoon, a good time for me because Mrs. Peebles was always having her nap. I would get the kitchen all cleaned and then go up to the mailbox and sit in the grass, waiting. I was perfectly happy, waiting. I forgot all about Alice Kelling and her misery and awful talk and Mrs. Peebles and her chilliness and the embarrassment of whether she told Dr. Peebles and the face of Loretta Bird, getting her fill of other people's troubles. I was always smiling when the mailman got there, and continued smiling even after he gave me the mail and I saw today wasn't the day. The mailman was a Carmichael. I knew by his face because there are a lot of Carmichaels living out by us and so many of them have a sort of sticking-out top lip. So I asked his name (he was a young man, shy, but good-humored, anybody could ask him anything) and then I said, "I knew by your face!" He was pleased by that and always glad to see me and got a little less shy. "You've got the smile I've been waiting on all day!" he used to holler out the car window.

It never crossed my mind for a long time a letter might not come. I believed in it coming just like I believed the sun would rise in the morning. I just put off my hope from day to day, and there was the goldenrod out around the mailbox and the children gone back to school, and the leaves turning, and I was wearing a sweater when I went to wait. One day walking back with the hydro bill stuck in my hand, that was all, looking across at the fairgrounds with the full-blown milkweed and dark teasels, so much like fall, it just struck me: *No letter was ever going to come.* It was an impossible idea to get used to. No, not impossible. If I thought about Chris's face when he said he was going to write to me, it was impossible, but if I forgot that and thought about the actual tin mailbox, empty, it was plain and true. I kept on going to meet the mail, but my heart was heavy now like a lump of lead. I only smiled because I thought of the mailman counting on it, and he didn't have an easy life, with the winter driving ahead.

Till it came to me one day there were women doing this with their lives, all over. There were women just waiting and waiting by mailboxes for one letter or another. I imagined me making this journey day after day and year after year, and my hair starting to go gray, and I thought, I was never made to go on like that. So I stopped meeting the mail. If there were women all through life waiting, and women busy and not waiting, I knew which I had to be. Even though there might be things the second kind of women have to pass up and never know about, it still is better.

I was surprised when the mailman phoned the Peebleses' place in the evening and asked for me. He said he missed me. He asked if I would like to go to Goderich, where some well-known movie was on. I forget now what. So I said yes, and I went out with him for two years and he asked me to marry him, and we were engaged a year more while I got my things together, and then we did marry. He always tells the children the story of how I went after him by sitting by the mailbox every day, and naturally I laugh and let him, because I like for people to think what pleases them and makes them happy.

[1974]

✏ Topics for Critical Thinking and Writing

1. Since Edie tells the story, we know about the other characters only as much as she tells us. Do you think her view of Mrs. Peebles and of Loretta Bird is accurate? On what do you base your answer?
2. Edie offers explicit comments about Mrs. Peebles and Loretta Bird, but not about Alice Kelling, or at least not to the same degree. Why?
3. Characterize Edie.
4. What do you think of the title? Why?

The Children Stay

Thirty years ago, a family was spending a holiday together on the east coast of Vancouver Island. A young father and mother, their two small daughters, and an older couple, the husband's parents.

What perfect weather. Every morning, every morning it's like this, the first pure sunlight falling through the high branches, burning away the mist over the still water of Georgia Strait.

If it weren't for the tide, it would be hard to remember that this is the sea. You look across the water to the mountains on the mainland, the ranges that are the western wall of the continent of North America. These humps and peaks coming clear now through the mist are of interest to the grandfather and to his son, Brian. The two men are continually trying to decide which of these shapes are actual continental mountains and which are improbable heights of the islands that ride in front of the shore.

There is a map, set up under glass, between the cottages and the beach. You can stand there looking at the map, then looking at what's in front of you and back at the map again, until you get things sorted out. The grandfather and Brian usually get into an argument—though you'd think there would not be much room for disagreement with the map right there.

5   Brian's mother won't look at the map. She says it boggles her mind. Her concern is always about whether anybody is hungry yet, or thirsty, whether the children have their sun hats on and have been rubbed with protective lotion. She makes her husband wear a floppy cotton hat and thinks that Brian should wear one, too—she reminds him of how sick he got from the sun that summer they went to the Okanagan, when he was a child. Sometimes Brian says to her, "Oh, dry up, Mother." His tone is mostly affectionate, but his father may ask him if that's the way he thinks he can talk to his mother nowadays.

"She doesn't mind," says Brian.

"How do you know?" says his father.

"Oh, for Pete's sake," says his mother.

Pauline, the young mother, slides out of bed as soon as she's awake every morning, slides out of reach of Brian's long, sleepily searching arms and legs. What wakes her is the first squeaks and mutters of the baby, Mara, in the children's room, then the creak of the crib as Mara—sixteen months old now, getting to the end of babyhood—pulls herself up to stand hanging on to the railing. She continues her soft amiable talk as Pauline lifts her out—Caitlin, nearly five, shifting about but not waking, in her nearby bed—and as she is carried into the kitchen to be changed, on the floor. Then she is settled into her stroller, with a biscuit and a bottle of apple juice, while Pauline gets into her sundress and sandals, goes to the bathroom, combs out her hair—all as quickly and quietly as possible. They leave the cottage and head for the bumpy unpaved road that runs behind the cottages, a mile or so north till it stops at the bank of the little river that runs into the sea. The road is still mostly in deep morning shadow, the floor of a tunnel under fir and cedar trees.

10   The grandfather, also an early riser, sees them from the porch of his cottage, and Pauline sees him. But all that is necessary is a wave. He and Pauline never have much to say to each other (though sometimes there's an affinity they feel, in the midst of some long-drawn-out antics of Brian's or some apologetic but insistent fuss made by the grandmother, there's an awareness of not looking at each other, lest their look reveal a bleakness that would discredit others).

On this holiday Pauline steals time to be by herself—being with Mara is still almost the same thing as being by herself. Early morning walks, the late morning hour when she washes and hangs out the diapers. She could have had another hour or so in the afternoons, while Mara is napping. But Brian has fixed up a shelter on the beach, and he carries the playpen down every day, so that Mara can nap there and Pauline won't have to absent herself. He says his parents might be offended if she's always sneaking off. He agrees, though, that she does need some time to go over her lines for the play she's going to be in, back in Victoria, this September.

Pauline is not an actress. This is an amateur production, and she didn't even try out for the role. She was asked if she would like to be in this play by a man she met at a barbecue, in June. The people there were mostly teachers, and their wives or husbands—it was held at the house of the principal of the high school where Brian taught. The woman who taught French was a widow—she had brought her grown son, who was staying for the summer with her and working as a night clerk in a downtown hotel. She told everybody that he had got a job teaching at a college in western Washington State and would be going there in the fall.

Jeffrey Toom was his name. "Without the 'b,' " he said, as if the staleness of the joke wounded him.

What was he going to teach?

15   "Dram-ah," he said, drawing the word out in a mocking way.

He spoke of his present job disparagingly as well.

"It's a pretty sordid place," he said. "Maybe you heard—a hooker was killed there last February. And then we get the usual losers checking in to O.D. or bump themselves off."

People did not quite know what to make of this way of talking and drifted away from him. Except for Pauline.

"I'm thinking about putting on a play," he said. He asked her if she had ever heard of "Eurydice."

20   Pauline said, "You mean Anouilh's?" and he was unflatteringly surprised. He immediately said he didn't know if it would ever work out. "I just thought it might be interesting to see if you could do something different here in the land of Noël Coward."

Pauline did not remember when there had been a play by Noël Coward put on in Victoria, though she supposed there had been several. She said, "We saw 'The Duchess of Malfi' last winter at the college."

"Yeah. Well," he said, flushing. She had thought he was older than she was, at least as old as Brian—who was thirty, though people were apt to say he didn't act it—but as soon as he started talking to her, in this offhand, dismissive way, never quite meeting her eyes, she suspected that he was younger than he'd like to appear. Now, with that flush, she was sure of it.

As it turned out, he was a year younger than she was. Twenty-five.

She said that she couldn't be Eurydice—she couldn't act. But Brian came over to see what the conversation was about and said at once that she must try it.

25   "She just needs a kick in the behind," Brian said to Jeffrey. "She's like a little mule—it's hard to get her started. No, seriously, she's too self-effacing. I tell her that all the time. She's very smart. She's actually a lot smarter than I am."

At that Jeffrey did look directly into Pauline's eyes—impertinently and searchingly—and she was the one who was flushing.

He had chosen her immediately as his Eurydice because of the way she looked. But it was not because she was beautiful. "I'd never put a beautiful girl in that part," he said. "I don't know if I'd ever put a beautiful girl onstage in anything. It's distracting."

So what did he mean about the way she looked? He said it was her hair, which was long and dark and rather bushy (not in style at that time), and her pale skin ("Stay out of the sun this summer") and, most of all, her eyebrows.

"I never liked them," said Pauline, not quite sincerely. Her eyebrows were level, dark, luxuriant. They dominated her face. Like her hair, they were not in style. But if she had really disliked them, wouldn't she have plucked them?

30   Jeffrey seemed not to have heard her. "They give you a sulky look and that's disturbing," he said. "Also your jaw's a little heavy and that's sort of Greek. It would be better in a movie, where I could get you close up. The routine thing for Eurydice would be a girl who looked ethereal. I don't want ethereal."

As she walked Mara along the road, Pauline did work at the lines. There was a long speech at the end that was giving her trouble. She bumped the stroller along and repeated to herself, "You are terrible, you know, you are terrible like the angels. You think everybody's going forward, as brave and bright as you are—oh, don't look at me, please, darling, don't look at me—Perhaps I'm not what you wish I was, but I'm here, and I'm warm, I'm kind, and I love you. I'll give you all the happiness I can. Don't look at me. Don't look. Let me live."

She had left something out. "Perhaps I'm not what you wish I was, but you feel me here, don't you? I'm warm and I'm kind—"

She had told Jeffrey that she thought the play was beautiful.

He said, "Really?" What she'd said didn't please or surprise him—he seemed to feel it was predictable, superfluous. He would never describe a play in that way. He spoke of it more as a hurdle to be got over. Also a challenge to be flung at various enemies. At the academic snots, as he called them, who had done "The Duchess of Malfi." And at the social twits, as he called them, in the little theatre. He saw himself as an outsider heaving his weight against these people, putting on his play—he called it his—in the teeth of their contempt and opposition. In the beginning Pauline thought that this must be all in his imagination. Then something would happen that could be, but might not be, a coincidence—repairs to be done on the church hall where the play was to be performed, making it unobtainable, an unexpected increase in the cost of printing advertising posters—and she found herself seeing it his way. If you were going to be around him much, you almost had to see it his way—arguing was dangerous and exhausting.

35   "Sons of bitches," said Jeffrey between his teeth, but with some satisfaction. "I'm not surprised. I'm going to get to the bottom of this."

The rehearsals were held upstairs in an old building on Fisgard Street. Sunday afternoon was the only time that everybody could get there, though there were fragmentary rehearsals during the week. Pauline had to depend on sometimes undependable high-school babysitters—for the first six weeks of the summer Brian was busy teaching summer school. And Jeffrey himself had to be at his hotel job by eight o'clock in the evening. But on Sunday afternoons they were all there, laboring in the dusty high-ceilinged room on Fisgard Street. The windows were rounded at the top as in some plain and dignified church, and propped open in the heat with whatever objects could be found—ledger books from the nineteen-twenties, belonging to the hat shop that had once operated downstairs, pieces of wood left over from the picture frames made by the artist whose canvases were now stacked against one wall and apparently abandoned. The glass was grimy, but outside the sunlight bounced off the sidewalks, the empty gravelled parking lots, the low stuccoed buildings, with what seemed a special Sunday brightness. Hardly anybody moved through these downtown streets. Nothing was open except the occasional hole-in-the-wall coffee shop or lackadaisical, flyspecked convenience store.

Pauline was the one who went out at the break to get soft drinks and coffee. She was the one who had the least to say about the play and the way it was going—even though she was the only one who had read it before—because she alone had never done any acting. So it seemed proper for her to volunteer. She enjoyed her short walk in the empty streets—she felt as if she had become an urban person, someone detached and solitary, who lived in the glare of an important dream. Sometimes she thought of Brian at home, working in the garden and keeping an eye on the children. Or perhaps he had taken them to Dallas Road—she recalled a promise—to sail boats on the pond. That life seemed ragged and tedious compared to what went on in the rehearsal room—the hours of effort, the concentration, the sharp exchanges, the sweating and tension. Even the taste of the coffee, its scalding bitterness, and the fact that it was chosen by nearly everybody in preference to a fresher-tasting and maybe more healthful drink out of the cooler, seemed satisfying to her.

When she said that she had to go away for the two-week holiday, Jeffrey looked thunderstruck, as if he had never imagined that things like holidays could come into her life. Then he turned grim and slightly satirical, as if this were just another blow that he might have expected. Pauline explained that she would miss only the one Sunday—the one in the middle of the two weeks—because she and Brian were driving up the Island on a Monday and coming back on a Sunday morning. She promised to get back in time for rehearsal. Privately she wondered how she would do this—it always took so much longer than you expected to pack up and get away. She wondered if she could possibly come back by herself, on the morning bus. That would probably be too much to ask for. She didn't mention it.

She couldn't ask him if it was only the play he was thinking about, only her absence from a rehearsal that caused the thundercloud. At the moment, it very likely was. When he spoke to her at rehearsals there was never any suggestion that he ever spoke to her in any other way. The only difference in his treatment of her was that perhaps he expected less of her, of her acting, than he did of the others. And that would be understandable to anybody. She was the only one chosen out of the blue, for the way she looked—the others had all shown up at the audition he had advertised on signs put up in cafés and bookstores around town.

40   Yet she thought they all knew what was going on, in spite of Jeffrey's offhand and abrupt and none too civil ways. They knew that after every one of them had straggled off home he would walk across the room and bolt the staircase door. (At first Pauline had pretended to leave with the rest and had even got into her car and circled the block, but later such a trick had come to seem insulting, not just to herself and Jeffrey but to the others, whom she was sure would never betray her, bound as they all were under the temporary but potent spell of the play.)

Jeffrey crossed the room and bolted the door. Every time, this was like a new decision that he had to make. Until it was done, she wouldn't look at him. The sound of the bolt being pushed into place, the ominous or fatalistic sound of metal hitting metal, gave her a localized shock of capitulation. But she didn't make a move, she waited for him to come back to her with the whole story of the afternoon's labor draining out of his face, the expression of matter-of-fact and customary disappointment cleared away, replaced by the live energy she always found surprising.

"So. Tell us what this play of yours is about," Brian's father said. "Is it one of those ones where they take their clothes off on the stage?"

"Now, don't tease her," said Brian's mother.

Brian and Pauline had put the children to bed and walked over to his parents' cottage for an evening drink. The sunset was behind them, behind the forests of Vancouver Island, but the mountains in front of them, all clear now and hard cut against the sky, shone in its pink light. Some high inland mountains were capped with pink summer snow.

45   "The story of Orpheus and Eurydice is that Eurydice died," Pauline said. "And Orpheus goes down to the underworld to try to get her back. And his wish is granted, but only if he promises not to look at her. Not to look back at her. She's walking behind him—"

"Twelve paces," said Brian. "As is only right."

"It's a Greek story, but it's set in modern times," said Pauline. "At least this version is. More or less modern. Orpheus is a musician travelling around with his father—they're both musicians—and Eurydice is an actress. This is in France."

"Translated?" Brian's father said.

"No," said Brian. "But don't worry, it's not in French. It was written in Transylvanian."

50   "It's so hard to make sense of anything," Brian's mother said with a worried laugh. "It's so hard, with Brian around."

"It's in English," Pauline said.

"And you're what's-her-name?"

She said, "I'm Eurydice."

"He get you back O.K.?"

55   "No," she said. "He looks back at me and then I have to stay dead."

"Oh, an unhappy ending," Brian's mother said.

"You're so gorgeous?" said Brian's father skeptically. "He can't stop himself from looking back?"

"It's not that," said Pauline. But at this point she felt that something had been achieved by her father-in-law, he had done what he meant to do, which was the same thing that he nearly always meant to do, in any conversation she had with him. And that was to break through the careful structure of some explanation he had asked her for, and she had unwillingly but patiently given, and with a seemingly negligent kick knock it into rubble. He had been dangerous to her for a long time in this way, though he wasn't particularly so tonight.

But Brian did not know that. Brian was still figuring out how to come to her rescue.

60   "Pauline is gorgeous," Brian said.

"Yes indeed," said his mother.

"Maybe if she'd go to the hairdresser," his father said. But Pauline's long hair was such an old objection of his that it had become a family joke. Even Pauline laughed. She said, "I can't afford to till we get the veranda roof fixed." And Brian laughed boisterously, full of relief that she was able to take all this as a joke. It was what he had always told her to do.

"Just kid him back. It's the only way to handle him."

"Yeah, well, if you'd got yourselves a decent house," said his father. But this, like Pauline's hair, was such a familiar sore point that it couldn't rouse anybody.

Brian and Pauline had bought a handsome house in bad repair on a street in Victoria where old mansions were being turned into ill-used apartment buildings. The house, the street, the messy old Garry oaks, the fact that no basement had been blasted out under the house, was all a horror to Brian's father. So what he said now about a decent house might be some kind of peace signal. Or could be taken so.

65   Brian was an only son. He was a math teacher. His father was a civil engineer, and part owner of a contracting company. If he had hoped that he would have a son who was an engineer and might come into the company, there was never any mention of it. Pauline had asked Brian whether he thought the carping about their house, and her hair, and the books she read, might be a cover for this larger disappointment, but Brian had said, "Nope. In our family we complain about just whatever we want to complain about. We ain't subtle, Ma'am."

Pauline still wondered, when she heard his mother talking about how teachers ought to be the most honored people in the world and they did not get half the credit they deserved and that she didn't know how Brian managed it, day after day. Then his father might say, "That's right," or "I sure wouldn't want to do it, I can tell you that. They couldn't pay me to do it."

And Brian would turn that into a joke, as he turned nearly everything into a joke.

"Don't worry, Dad. They don't pay you much."

Brian in his everyday life was a much more dramatic person than Jeffrey. He dominated his classes by keeping up a parade of jokes and antics, extending the role that he had always played, Pauline believed, with his mother and father. He acted dumb, he bounced back from pretended humiliations, he traded insults. He was a bully in a good cause—a chivying, cheerful, indestructible bully.

70   "Your boy has certainly made his mark with us," the principal said to Pauline. "He has not just survived, which is something in itself. He has made his mark."

Your boy.

He called his students boneheads. His tone was affectionate, fatalistic. He said that his father was the King of the Philistines, a pure and natural barbarian. And that his mother was a dishrag, good-natured and worn out. But however he dismissed such people, he could not be long without them. He took his students on camping trips. And he could not imagine a summer without this shared holiday. He was mortally afraid, every year, that Pauline would refuse to go along. Or that, having agreed to go, she was going to be miserable, take offense at something his father said, complain about how much time she had to spend with his mother, sulk because there was no way they could do anything by themselves. She might decide to spend all day in their own cottage, reading, and pretending to have a sunburn.

All those things had happened, on previous holidays. But this year she was easing up. He told her he could see that, and he was grateful to her.

"I know it's an effort," he said. "It's different for me. They're my parents and I'm used to not taking them seriously."

75   Pauline came from a family that took things so seriously that her parents had got a divorce. Her mother was now dead. She had a distant, though cordial, relationship with her father and her two much older sisters. She said that they had nothing in common. She knew Brian could not understand how that could be a reason. She saw what comfort it gave him, this year, to see things going so well. She had thought it was laziness or cowardice that kept him from breaking the arrangement, but now she saw that it was something far more positive. He needed to have his wife and his parents and his children bound together like this, he needed to involve Pauline in his life with his parents and to bring his par-

ents to some recognition of her—though the recognition, from his father, would always be muffled and contrary, and from his mother too profuse, too easily come by, to mean much. Also he wanted Pauline to be connected—and the children, too—to his own childhood. He wanted these holidays to be linked to the holidays of his youth with their lucky or unlucky weather, car troubles, boating scares, bee stings, marathon Monopoly games, to all the things that he told his mother he was bored to death hearing about. He wanted pictures from this summer to be taken, and fitted into his mother's album, a continuation of all the other pictures that he groaned at the mention of.

The only time they could talk to each other was in bed, late at night. But they did talk then, more than was usual with them at home, where Brian was so tired that often he fell immediately asleep. And in ordinary daylight it was hard to talk to him because of his jokes. She could see the joke brightening his eyes. (His coloring was very like hers—dark hair and pale skin and gray eyes—but her eyes were cloudy and his were light, like clear water over stones.) She could see it pulling at the corners of his mouth as he foraged among your words to catch a pun or the start of a rhyme—anything that could take the conversation away, into absurdity. His whole body, tall and loosely joined together and still almost as skinny as a teenager's, twitched with comic propensity. Before she married him, Pauline had a friend named Gracie, a rather grumpy-looking girl, subversive about men. Brian had thought her a girl whose spirits needed a boost, and so he made even more than the usual effort. And Gracie said to Pauline, "How can you stand the non-stop show?"

"That's not the real Brian," Pauline had said. "He's different when we're alone." But, looking back, she wondered how true that had ever been. Had she said it simply to defend her choice, as you did when you had made up your mind to get married?

Even in the cottage, with the window open on the unfamiliar darkness and stillness of the night, he teased a little. He had to speak of Jeffrey as Monsieur le Directeur, which made the play, or the fact that it was a French play, slightly ridiculous. Or perhaps it was Jeffrey himself, Jeffrey's seriousness about the play, that had to be called into question.

Pauline didn't care. It was such a pleasure and a relief to her to mention Jeffrey's name.

80   Though most of the time she didn't mention him, she circled around that pleasure. She described all the others instead. The hairdresser and the harbor pilot and the busboy and the old man who claimed to have once acted on the radio. He played Orphée's father, and gave Jeffrey the most trouble, because he had the stubbornest notions of his own about acting.

The middle-aged impresario, M. Dulac, was played by a twenty-four-year-old travel agent. And Mathias, who was Eurydice's former boyfriend, presumably around her own age, was played by the manager of a shoe store, who was married and a father.

"Why didn't Monsieur le Directeur cast those two the other way round?" said Brian.

"That's the way he does things," Pauline said. "What he sees in us is something different from the obvious."

For instance, she said, the busboy was a difficult Orphée.

85   "He's only nineteen, he's terribly shy, but he's determined to be an actor. Even if it's like making love to his grandmother. Jeffrey has to keep at him. 'Keep your arms around her a little longer, stroke her a little—'"

"He might get to like it," Brian said. "Maybe I should come around and keep an eye on him."

At this Pauline snorted. When she had started to quote Jeffrey she had felt a giving-way in her womb or the bottom of her stomach, a shock that had travelled oddly upward and hit her vocal cords. She had to cover up this quaking by growling in a way that was supposed to be an imitation (though Jeffrey never growled or ranted or carried on in any theatrical way at all).

Stroke her a little.

"But there's a point about him being so innocent," she said hurriedly. "Being not so physical. Being awkward." She began to talk about Orphée in the play, not the busboy—Orphée's problems with love and reality. Orphée will not put up with anything less than perfection. He wants a love that is outside of ordinary life. He wants a perfect Eurydice.

90   "Eurydice is more realistic. She's carried on with Mathias and with M. Dulac. She's been around her mother and her mother's lover. She knows what people are like. But she loves Orphée. She loves him better, in a way, than he loves her. She loves him better because she's not such a fool. She loves him like a human person."

"She's slept with those other guys?"

"Well, with M. Dulac she had to, she couldn't get out of it. She didn't want to, but probably after a while she enjoyed it, because after a certain point she couldn't help enjoying it. Just because she's slept with those men doesn't mean she's corrupt," Pauline said. "She wasn't in love then. She hadn't met Orphée. There's one speech where he tells her that everything she's done is sticking to her, and it's disgusting. Lies she's told him. The other men. It's all sticking to her forever. And then of course M. Henri plays up to that. He tells Orphée that he'll be just as bad and that one day he'll walk down the street with Eurydice and he'll look like a man with a dog he's trying to lose."

Brian laughed. He said, "That could be true."

"But not inevitably," said Pauline. "That's what's silly. It's not inevitable at all."

95   So Orphée is at fault, Pauline said decidedly. He looks back at Eurydice on purpose to kill her and get rid of her because she isn't perfect. Because of him she has to die a second time.

Brian, on his back and with his eyes wide open (she knew that because of the tone of his voice), said, "But doesn't he die, too?"

"Yes. He chooses to."

"So then they're together?"

"Yes. Like Romeo and Juliet. Orphée is with Eurydice at last. That's what M. Henri says. That's the last line of the play. That's the end." Pauline rolled over onto her side and touched her cheek to Brian's shoulder—not to start anything but to emphasize what she said next. "It's a beautiful play in one way but in another it's so silly. And it isn't really like 'Romeo and Juliet,' because it isn't bad luck or circumstances. It's on purpose. So they don't have to go on with life and get married and have kids and buy an old house and fix it up and—"

100   "And have affairs," said Brian. "After all, they're French."

Then he said, "And be like my parents."

Pauline laughed. "Do they have affairs? I can't imagine."

"Oh, sure," said Brian. "I meant their life."

"Oh."

105   "Logically I can see killing yourself so you won't turn into your parents. I just don't believe anybody would do it."

They went on speculating, and comfortably arguing, in a way that was not usual, but not altogether unfamiliar to them. They had done this before, at long intervals in their married life—talked half the night about God or fear of death or how children should be educated or whether money was important. At last they admitted to being too tired to make sense any longer, and arranged themselves in a comradely cuddle and went to sleep.

Finally a rainy day. Brian and his parents were driving into Campbell River to get groceries, and gin, and to take Brian's father's car to a garage. Brian had to go along, with his car, just in case the other car had to be left in the garage overnight. Pauline said that she had to stay home because of Mara's nap.

She persuaded Caitlin to lie down, too—allowing her to take her music box to bed with her if she played it under the covers. Then Pauline spread the script on the kitchen table, and drank coffee and went over the scene in which Orphée says that it's intolerable, at last, to stay in two skins, two envelopes with their own blood and oxygen sealed up in their solitude, and Eurydice tells him to be quiet.

"Don't talk. Don't think. Just let your hand wander, let it be happy on its own."

110   Your hand is my happiness, says Eurydice. Accept that. Accept your happiness.

Of course he says he cannot.

Caitlin called out frequently to ask what time it was, and Pauline could hear the music box. She hurried to the bedroom door and hissed at her to turn it off, not to wake Mara.

"If you play it like that again I'll take it away from you. O.K.?"

But Mara was already rustling around in her crib and in the next few minutes there were sounds of soft, encouraging conversation from Caitlin, designed to get her sister wide awake. Then of Mara rattling the crib railing, pulling herself up, throwing her bottle out onto the floor, and starting the bird cries that would grow more and more desolate until they brought her mother.

115   "I didn't wake her," Caitlin said. "She was awake all by herself. It's not raining anymore. Can we go down to the beach?"

She was right. It wasn't raining. Pauline changed Mara, told Caitlin to get her bathing suit on and find her sand pail. She got into her own bathing suit and put on her shorts on top of it, in case the rest of the family arrived home while she was down there. ("Dad doesn't like the way some women just go right out of their cottages in their bathing suits," Brian's mother had said to her. "I guess he and I just grew up in other times.") She picked up the script to take it along, then laid it down. She was afraid that she would get too absorbed in it and take her eye off the children for a moment too long.

The thoughts that came to her, of Jeffrey, were not really thoughts at all—they were more like alterations in her body. This could happen when she was sitting on the beach (trying to stay in the half shade of a bush and so preserve her pallor, as Jeffrey had ordered). Or when she was wringing out diapers, or when she and Brian were visiting his parents. In the middle of Monopoly games, Scrabble games, card games. She went right on talking, listening, working, keeping track of the children, while some memory of her secret life disturbed her like a radiant explosion. Then a warm weight settled, reassurance filling up all her hollows. But it didn't last, this comfort leaked away, and she was like a miser whose windfall has vanished and who is convinced such luck can never strike again. Longing buckled her up and drove her to the discipline of counting days. Sometimes she even cut the days into fractions to figure out more exactly how much time had gone.

She thought of going in to Campbell River, making some excuse, so that she could get to a phone booth and call him. The cottages had no phones—the only public phone was in the hall of the Lodge, across from the entrance to the dining room. But she did not have the number of the hotel where Jeffrey worked. And, besides that, she could never get away to Campbell River in the evening. She was afraid that if she called him at home in the daytime his mother the French teacher might answer. He said he hardly ever left the house in the summer. Just once, she had taken the ferry to Vancouver for the day. Jeffrey had phoned Pauline to ask her to come over. Brian was teaching and Caitlin was at her play group.

Pauline said, "I can't. I have Mara."

120   "Couldn't you bring her along?" he asked.

She said no.

"Why not? Couldn't you bring some things for her to play with?"

No, said Pauline. "I couldn't," she said. "I just couldn't." It seemed too dangerous to her, to trundle her baby along on such a guilty expedition. To a house where cleaning fluids would not be bestowed on high shelves and all pills and cough syrups and cigarettes and buttons put safely out of reach. And even if she escaped poisoning or choking, Mara might be storing up time bombs—memories of a strange house where she was strangely disregarded, of a closed door, noises on the other side of it.

"I just wanted you," Jeffrey said. "I just wanted you in my bed."

125   She said again, weakly, "No."

Those words of his kept coming back to her. *I wanted you in my bed.* A half-joking urgency in his voice but also a determination, a practicality, as if "in my bed" meant something more, the bed he spoke of taking on larger, less material dimensions.

Had she made a great mistake, with that refusal? With that reminder of how fenced in she was, in what anybody would call her real life?

The beach was nearly empty—people had got used to its being a rainy day. The sand was too heavy for Caitlin to make a castle or dig an irrigation system—projects she would undertake only with her father, anyway, because she sensed that his interest in them was wholehearted, and Pauline's was not. She wandered a bit forlornly at the edge of the water, missing the presence of other children, the nameless instant friends and occasional stone-throwing, water-kicking enemies, the shrieking and splashing and falling about. A boy a little bigger than she was and apparently all by himself stood knee deep in the water farther down the beach. If these two could get together it might be all right, the whole beach experience might be retrieved. Pauline couldn't tell if Caitlin was now making those little splashy runs into the water for his benefit, or whether he was watching her with interest or scorn.

Mara didn't need company, at least for now. She stumbled toward the water, felt it touch her feet and changed her mind, stopped, looked around, and spotted Pauline. "Paw. Paw," she said, in happy recognition. "Paw" was what she said for "Pauline," instead of "Mother" or "Mommy." Looking around overbalanced her; she sat down half on the sand and half in the water, made a squawk of surprise which turned into an announcement, and then, by some determined ungraceful maneuvers that involved putting her weight on her hands, rose to her feet, wavering and triumphant. She had been walking for half a year, but getting around on the sand was still a challenge. Now she came back toward Pauline, making some reasonable casual remarks in her own language.

130   "Sand," said Pauline, holding up a clot of it. "Look. Mara. Sand."

Mara corrected her, calling it something else—it sounded like "whap." Her thick diaper under her plastic pants and her terry-cloth playsuit gave her a fat bottom, and that, along with her plump cheeks and shoulders and her sidelong important expression, made her look like a roguish matron.

Pauline became aware of someone calling her name. It had been called two or three times, but because the voice was unfamiliar she had not recognized it. She stood up and waved. It was the woman who worked in the store at the Lodge. She was leaning over the porch rail and calling, "Mrs. Keating. Mrs. Keating? Telephone, Mrs. Keating."

Pauline hoisted Mara onto her hip and summoned Caitlin. She and the little boy were aware of each other now: they were both picking up stones from the bottom and flinging them out into the water. At first she didn't hear Pauline, or pretended not to hear.

"Store," called Pauline. "Caitlin. Store." When she was sure Caitlin would follow—it was the word "store" that had done it, the reminder of the tiny store in the Lodge where you could buy ice cream and candy—she began the trek across the sand and up the flight of wooden steps. Halfway up she stopped, said, "Mara, you weigh a ton," and shifted the baby to her other hip. Caitlin followed, banging a stick against the railing.

135   "Can I have a Fudgsicle? Mother? Can I?"

"We'll see."

The public phone was beside a bulletin board on the other side of the main hall and across from the door to the dining room. A bingo game had been set up in there, because of the rain.

"Hope he's still hanging on," the woman who worked in the store called out. She was unseen now behind her counter.

Pauline, still holding Mara, picked up the dangling receiver and said breathlessly, "Hello?" She was expecting to hear Brian telling her about some delay in Campbell River or asking her what it was she had wanted him to get at the drugstore. It was just the one thing—calamine lotion—so he had not written it down.

140   "Pauline," said Jeffrey. "It's me."

Mara was bumping and scrambling along Pauline's side, eager to get down. Caitlin came along the hall and went into the store, leaving wet sandy footprints. Pauline said, "Just a minute, just a minute." She let Mara slide down and hurried to close the door that led to the steps. She did not remember telling Jeffrey the name of this place, though she had told him roughly where it was. She heard the woman in the store speaking to Caitlin in a sharper voice than she would use to children whose parents were beside them.

"Did you forget to put your feet under the tap?"

"I'm here," said Jeffrey. "I didn't get along so well without you. I didn't get along at all."

Mara made for the dining room, as if the male voice calling out "Under the N" were a direct invitation to her.

145   "Here. Where?" said Pauline.

She read the signs that were tacked up on the bulletin board beside the phone:

> No Person Under Fourteen Years of Age Not Accompanied by Adult Allowed in Boats or Canoes.
> Fishing Derby.
> Bake and Craft Sale, St. Bartholomew's Church.
> Your life is in your hands. Palms and Cards read. Reasonable and Accurate. Call Claire.

"In a motel. In Campbell River."

Pauline knows where she is before she opens her eyes. Nothing surprises her. She has slept, but not deeply enough to let go of anything.

She had waited for Brian in the parking area of the Lodge, with the children in tow, and then she had asked for the keys. She told him in front of his parents that there was something else she needed, from Campbell River. He asked what was it? And did she have any money?

"Just something," she said, so he would think that it was tampons or birth-control supplies, something that she didn't want to mention.

150   "Sure. O.K., but you'll have to put some gas in," he said.

Later she had to speak to him on the phone. Jeffrey said she had to do it.

"Because he won't take it from me. He'll think I kidnapped you or something. He won't believe it."

But the strangest thing of all the things that day was that Brian did seem, immediately, to believe it. Standing where she had stood not so long before, in the public hallway of the Lodge—the bingo game over now, but people going past, she could hear them, people on their way out of the dining room after dinner—Brian had said, "Oh. Oh. Oh. O.K.," in a voice that would have to be quickly controlled but that seemed to draw on a supply of fatalism or foreknowledge that went far beyond that necessity.

"O.K.," he said. "What about the car?"

155   He said something else, something impossible, and then hung up, and she came out of the phone booth beside a row of gas pumps in Campbell River.

"That was quick," Jeffrey said. "Easier than you expected?"

Pauline said, "I don't know."

"He may have known it subconsciously. People do know."

She shook her head, to tell him not to say any more, and he said, "Sorry." They walked along the street not touching or talking.

160   Now, looking around at leisure—the first real leisure or freedom she's had since she came into that room—Pauline sees that there isn't much of anything in it. Just a junky dresser, the bed without a headboard, an armless upholstered chair. On the window a Venetian blind with a broken slat. Also a noisy air-conditioner—Jeffrey turned it off in the night and left the door open on the chain, since the window was sealed. The door is shut now. He must have got up in the night and shut it.

This is all she has. Her connection with the cottage where Brian lies now asleep or not asleep is broken. Also her connection with the house that has been an expression of her life with Brian, of the way they wanted to live. She has cut herself off from all the large solid acquisitions, like the washer and dryer and the oak table and the refinished wardrobe and the chandelier that is a copy of the one in a painting by Vermeer. And just as much from those things that were particularly hers—the pressed-glass tumblers that she had been collecting and the prayer rug that was probably not authentic, but beautiful. Especially from those things. The skirt and blouse and sandals she put on for the trip to Campbell River might as well be all she has now to her name. She would never go back to lay claim to anything. If Brian got in touch with her to ask what was to be done with things, she would tell him to do what he liked—throw everything into garbage bags and take it to the dump, if that was what he liked. (In fact she knows that he will probably pack up a trunk, which he does, sending on, scrupulously, not only her winter coat and boots but things like the waist cincher she wore at her wedding and never since, with the prayer rug draped on top of everything like a final statement of his generosity, either natural or calculated.)

She believes that she will never again care about what sort of rooms she lives in or what sort of clothes she puts on. She will not be looking for that sort of help to give anybody an idea of who she is, what she is like. Not even to give herself an idea. What she has done will be enough, it will be the whole thing.

What she has done will be what she has heard about and read about. It will be what Anna Karenina did and what Mme. Bovary wanted to do. And what a teacher at Brian's school did, with the school secretary. He ran off with her. That was what it was called. Running off with. Taking off with. It was spoken of disparagingly, humorously, enviously. It was adultery taken one step further. The people who did it had almost certainly been having an affair already, committing adultery for quite some time before they became desperate or courageous enough to take this step. Once in a long while a couple might claim their love was unconsummated and technically pure, but these people would be thought of—if anybody believed them—as being not only very serious and high-minded but almost devastatingly foolish, almost in a class with those who gave up everything to go and work in some poor and dangerous country.

The others, the adulterers, were seen as irresponsible, immature, selfish, or even cruel. Also lucky. They were lucky because the sex they had been having in parked cars or the long grass or in each other's sullied marriage beds or most likely in motels like this one must surely have been splendid. Otherwise they would never have got such a yearning for each other's company at all costs or such a faith that their shared future would be altogether better and different in kind from what they had in the past.

165   Different in kind. That is what Pauline must believe now—that there is this major difference in lives or in marriages or unions between people. That some of them have a necessity, a fatefulness about them, which others do not have. Of course she would have said the same thing a year ago. People did say that, they seemed to believe that, and to believe that their own cases were all of the first, the special kind, even when anybody could see that they were not.

It is too warm in the room. Jeffrey's body is too warm. Conviction and contentiousness seem to radiate from it, even in sleep. His torso is thicker than Brian's, he is pudgier around the waist. More flesh on the bones, yet not so slack to the touch. Not so good-looking in general—she is sure most people would say that. And not so fastidious. Brian in bed smells of nothing. Jeffrey's skin, every time she's been with him, has had a baked-in, slightly oily or nutty smell. He didn't wash last night—but, then, neither did she. There wasn't time. Did he even have a toothbrush with him? She didn't, but she had not known she was staying.

When she met Jeffrey here it was still in the back of her mind that she had to concoct some colossal lie to serve her when she got home. And she—they—had to hurry. When Jeffrey said to her that he had decided that they must stay together, that she would come with him to Washington State, that they would have to drop the play because things would be too difficult for them in Victoria, she had looked at him just in the blank way you'd look at somebody the moment that an earthquake started. She was ready to tell him all the reasons why this was not possible, she still thought she was going to tell him that, but her life was coming adrift in that moment. To go back would be like tying a sack over her head.

All she said was "Are you sure?"

He said, "Sure." He said sincerely, "I'll never leave you."

170   That did not seem the sort of thing that he would say. Then she realized he was quoting—maybe ironically—from the play. It was what Orphée says to Eurydice within a few moments of their first meeting in the station buffet.

So her life was falling forward, she was becoming one of those people who ran away. A woman who shockingly and incomprehensibly gave everything up. For love, observers would say wryly. Meaning, for sex. None of this would happen if it weren't for sex.

And yet what's the great difference there? It's not such a variable procedure, in spite of what you're told. Skins, motions, contact, results. Pauline isn't a woman from whom it's difficult to get results. Brian got them. Probably anybody would, who wasn't wildly inept or morally disgusting.

But nothing's the same, really. With Brian—especially with Brian, to whom she has dedicated a selfish sort of good will, with whom she's lived in married complicity—there can never be this stripping away, the inevitable flight, the feelings she doesn't have to strive for but only to give in to like breathing or dying. That she believes can only come when the skin is on Jeffrey, the motions made by Jeffrey, and the weight that bears down on her has Jeffrey's heart in it, also his habits, thoughts, peculiarities, his ambition and loneliness (that for all she knows may have mostly to do with his youth).

For all she knows. There's a lot she doesn't know. She hardly knows anything about what he likes to eat or what music he likes to listen to or what role his mother plays in his life (no doubt a mysterious but important one, like the role of Brian's parents). One thing she's pretty sure of: whatever preferences or prohibitions he has will be definite. Plates in his armor.

195   She slides out from under Jeffrey's hand and from under the top sheet, which has a harsh smell of bleach, slips down to the floor where the bedspread is lying and wraps herself quickly in that rag of greenish-yellow chenille. She doesn't want him to open his eyes and see her from behind and note the droop of her buttocks. He's seen her naked before, but generally in a more forgiving moment.

She rinses her mouth and washes herself, using the bar of soap that is about the size of two thin squares of chocolate and firm as stone. She's hard used between the legs, swollen and stinking. Urinating takes an effort and it seems she's constipated. Last night when they went out and got hamburgers she found she could not eat. Presumably she'll learn to do all these things again, they'll resume their natural importance in her life. At the moment it's as if she can't quite spare the attention.

She has some money in her purse. She has to go out and buy a toothbrush, toothpaste, deodorant, shampoo. Also vaginal jelly. Last night they used condoms the first two times but nothing the third time.

She didn't bring her watch and Jeffrey doesn't wear one. There's no clock in the room, of course. She thinks it's early—there's still an early look to the light in spite of the heat. The stores probably won't be open, but there'll be someplace where she can get coffee.

Jeffrey has turned onto his other side. She must have wakened him, just for a moment.

180   They'll have a bedroom. A kitchen, an address. He'll go to work. She'll go to the laundromat. Maybe she'll go to work, too. Selling things, waiting on tables, tutoring students. She knows French and Latin—do they teach French and Latin in American high schools? Can you get a job if you're not an American? Jeffrey isn't.

She leaves him the key. She'll have to wake him to get back in. There's nothing to write a note with, or on.

It is early. The motel is on the highway at the north end of town, beside the bridge. There's no traffic yet. She scuffs back and forth under the cottonwood trees at the edge of the lot for quite a while before a vehicle of any kind rumbles over the bridge—though the traffic on it shook their bed regularly late into the night.

Something is coming now. A truck. But not just a truck—there's a large bleak fact coming at her. And it has not arrived out of nowhere—it's been waiting, cruelly nudging at her ever since she woke up or even all night.

Caitlin and Mara.

185 Last night on the phone, after speaking in such a flat and controlled and almost agreeable voice—as if he prided himself on not being shocked, not objecting or pleading—Brian cracked open. He said with contempt and fury and no concern for whoever might hear him, "Well, then—what about the kids?"

The receiver began to shake against Pauline's ear.

She said, "We'll talk—" but he did not seem to hear her.

"The children," he said, in this same shivering and vindictive voice. Changing the word "kids" to "children" was like slamming a board down on her—a heavy, formal, righteous threat.

"The children stay," Brian said. "Pauline. Did you hear me?"

190 "No," said Pauline. "Yes. I heard you, but—"

"All right. You heard me. Remember. The children stay."

It was all he could do. To make her see what she was doing, what she was ending, and to punish her if she did so. Nobody would blame him. There might be finagling, there might be bargaining, there would certainly be humbling of herself, but there it was, like a round cold stone in her gullet, like a cannonball. And it would remain there unless she changed her mind entirely. The children stay.

Their car—hers and Brian's—is still sitting in the motel parking lot. Brian will have to ask his father or his mother to drive him up here today to get it. She has the keys in her purse. There are spare keys—he will surely bring them. She unlocks the car door and throws her keys on the seat, then locks the door from the inside and shuts it.

Now she can't go back. She can't get into the car and drive back and say that she'd been insane. If she did that he would forgive her but he'd never get over it and neither would she. They'd go on, though, as people did.

195 She walks out of the parking lot, she walks along the sidewalk, into town.

The weight of Mara on her hip yesterday. The sight of Caitlin's footprints on the floor.

Paw. Paw.

She doesn't need the keys to get back to them, she doesn't need the car. She could beg a ride on the highway. Give in, give in, get back to them any way at all—how can she not do that?

A sack over her head.

200 This is acute pain. It will become chronic. Chronic means that it will be permanent but perhaps not constant. It may also mean that you won't die of it. You won't get free of it but you won't die of it. You won't feel it every minute but you won't spend many days without it, either. And you'll learn some tricks to dull it or banish it or else you'll end up destroying what you've got. What you incurred this pain to get. It isn't his fault. He's still an innocent or a savage, who doesn't know there's a pain so durable in the world. Say to yourself, You lose them anyway. They grow up. For a mother there's always waiting this private, slightly ridiculous desolation. They'll forget this time, in one way or another

they'll disown you. Or hang around till you don't know what to do about them, the way Brian has.

And, still, what pain. To carry along and get used to until it's only the past you're grieving for and no longer any possible present.

Her children have grown up. They don't hate her. For going away or staying away. They don't forgive her, either. Perhaps they wouldn't have forgiven her anyway, but it would have been about something different.

Caitlin remembers a little about the summer at the Lodge, Mara nothing. Caitlin calls it "that place Grandma and Grandpa stayed at."

"The place we were at when you went away," she says. "Only we didn't know you went away with the man who was Orphée."

205   Pauline has told them about the play.

Pauline says, "It wasn't Orphée."

"It wasn't Orphée? Oh, well. I thought it was."

"No."

"Who was it, then?"

210   "Just a man connected," says Pauline. "It wasn't him."

[1997]

ALICE MUNRO

This essay originated as a lecture that was revised for publication in John Metcalf's Making It New: Contemporary Canadian Stories *(1982).*

What Is Real?

Whenever people get an opportunity to ask me questions about my writing, I can be sure that some of the questions asked will be these:

"Do you write about real people?"

"Did those things really happen?"

"When you write about a small town are you really writing about Wingham?" (Wingham is the small town in Ontario where I was born and grew up, and it has often been assumed, by people who should know better, that I have simply "fictionalized" this place in my work. Indeed, the local newspaper has taken me to task for making it the "butt of a soured and cruel introspection.")

5   The usual thing, for writers, is to regard these either as very naive questions, asked by people who really don't understand the difference between autobiography and fiction, who can't recognize the device of the first-person narrator, or else as catch-you-out questions posed by journalists who hope to stir up exactly the sort of dreary (and to outsiders, slightly comic) indignation voiced by my home-town paper. Writers answer such questions patiently or crossly according to temperament and the mood they're in. They say, no, you must understand, my characters are composites; no, those things didn't happen the way I wrote about them; no, of course not, that isn't Wingham (or whatever other place it may be that has had the queer unsought-after distinction of hatching a writer). Or the writer may, riskily, ask the questioners what is real, anyway? None of this seems to be very satisfactory. People go on asking these same questions because the subject really does interest and bewilder them. It would seem to be quite true that they don't know what fiction is.

And how could they know, when what it is, is changing all the time, and we differ among ourselves, and we don't really try to explain because it is too difficult?

What I would like to do here is what I can't do in two or three sentences at the end of a reading. I won't try to explain what fiction is, and what short stories are (assuming, which we can't, that there is any fixed thing that it is and they are), but what short stories are to me, and how I write them, and how I use things that are "real." I will start by explaining how I read stories written by other people. For one thing, I can start reading them anywhere; from beginning to end, from end to beginning, from any point in between in either direction. So obviously I don't take up a story and follow it as if it were a road, taking me somewhere, with views and neat diversions along the way. I go into it, and move back and forth and settle here and there, and stay in it for a while. It's more like a house. Everybody knows what a house does, how it encloses space and makes connections between one enclosed space and another and presents what is outside in a new way. This is the nearest I can come to explaining what a story does for me, and what I want my stories to do for other people.

So when I write a story I want to make a certain kind of structure, and I know the feeling I want to get from being inside that structure. This is the hard part of the explanation, where I have to use a word like "feeling," which is not very precise, because if I attempt to be more intellectually respectable I will have to be dishonest. "Feeling" will have to do.

There is no blueprint for the structure. It's not a question of, "I'll make this kind of house because if I do it right it will have this effect." I've got to make, I've got to build up, a house, a story, to fit around the indescribable "feeling" that is like the soul of the story, and which I must insist upon in a dogged, embarrassed way, as being no more definable than that. And I don't know where it comes from. It seems to be already there, and some unlikely clue, such as a shop window or a bit of conversation, makes me aware of it. Then I start accumulating the material and putting it together. Some of the material I may have lying around already, in memories and observations, and some I invent, and some I have to go diligently looking for (factual details), while some is dumped in my lap (anecdotes, bits of speech). I see how this material might go together to make the shape I need, and I try it. I keep trying and seeing where I went wrong and trying again.

10   I suppose this is the place where I should talk about technical problems and how I solve them. The main reason I can't is that I'm never sure I do solve anything. Even when I say that I see where I went wrong, I'm being misleading. I never figure out how I'm gong to change things, I never say to myself, "That page is heavy going, that paragraph's clumsy, I need some dialogue and shorter sentences." I feel a part that's wrong, like a soggy weight; then I pay attention to the story, as if it were really happening somewhere, not just in my head, and in its own way, not mine. As a result, the sentences may indeed get shorter, there may be more dialogue, and so on. But though I've tried to pay attention to the story, I may not have got it right; those shorter sentences may be an evasion, a mistake. Every final draft, every published story, is still only an attempt, an approach, to the story.

I did promise to talk about using reality. "Why, if Jubilee isn't Wingham, has it got Shuter Street in it?" people want to know. Why have I described somebody's real ceramic elephant sitting on the mantelpiece? I could say I get momentum from doing things like this. The fictional room, town, world, needs a bit of starter dough from the real world. It's a device to help the writer—at least it helps me—but it arouses a certain baulked fury in the people who really do live on Shuter Street and the lady who owns the ceramic elephant. "Why do you put in something true and then go on and tell lies?" they say, and anybody who has been on the receiving end of this kind of thing knows how they feel.

"I do it for the sake of my art and to make this structure which encloses the soul of my story, that I've been telling you about," says the writer. "That is more important than anything."

Not to everybody, it isn't.

So I can see there might be a case, once you've written the story and got the momentum, for going back and changing the elephant to a camel (though there's always a chance the lady might complain that you made a nasty camel out of a beautiful elephant), and changing Shuter Street to Blank Street. But what about the big chunks of reality, without which your story can't exist? In the story *Royal Beatings,* I use a big chunk of reality: the story of the butcher, and of the young men who may have been egged on to "get" him. This is a story out of an old newspaper; it really did happen in a town I know. There is no legal difficulty about using it because it has been printed in a newspaper, and besides, the people who figure in it are all long dead. But there is a difficulty about offending people in that town who would feel that use of this story is a deliberate exposure, taunt and insult. Other people who have no connection with the real happening would say, "Why write about anything so hideous?" And lest you think that such an objection could only be raised by simple folk who read nothing but Harlequin Romances, let me tell you that one of the questions most frequently asked at universities is, "Why do you write about things that are so depressing?" People can accept almost any amount of ugliness if it is contained in a familiar formula, as it is on television, but when they come closer to their own place, their own lives, they are much offended by a lack of editing.

15   There are ways I can defend myself against such objections. I can say, "I do it in the interests of historical reality. That is what the old days were really like." Or, "I do it to show the dark side of human nature, the beast let loose, the evil we can run up against in communities and families." In certain countries I could say, "I do it to show how bad things were under the old system when there were prosperous butchers and young fellows hanging around livery stables and nobody thought about building a new society." But the fact is, the minute I say *to show* I am telling a lie. I don't do it to show anything. I put this story at the heart of my story because I need it there and it belongs there. It is the black room at the center of the house with all other rooms leading to and away from it. That is all. A strange defense. Who told me to write this story? Who feels any need of it before it is written? I do. I do, so that I might grab off this piece of horrid reality and install it where I see fit, even if Hat Nettleton and his friends were still around to make me sorry.

The answer seems to be as confusing as ever. Lots of true answers are. Yes and no. Yes, I use bits of what is real, in the sense of being really there and really happening, in the world, as most people see it, and I transform it into something that is really there and really happening, in my story. No, I am not concerned with using what is real to make any sort of record or prove any sort of point, and I am not concerned with any methods of selection but my own, which I can't fully explain. This is quite presumptuous, and if writers are not allowed to be so—and quite often, in many places, they are not—I see no point in the writing of fiction.

[1982]

 **ALICE MUNRO**

John Metcalf interviewed Alice Munro and published the interview in the Journal of Canadian Fiction *1:4 (Fall, 1972): 54–62. We reprint a passage that is especially concerned with differences between men and women as writers.*

A Conversation

METCALF: How has being a woman affected the acceptance of your work or the rate of work produced by you?

MUNRO: I don't think it's affected the acceptance at all but I suppose it's affected the rate, you know, my productivity because of my life as a child-rearing person but on the other hand I have not had to be a wage-earning person so I always wonder about this . . . if I have any right to claim that I've had a tougher time. Though I think it's possible if you are a man to get a Canada Council Grant and say this is the year I'm going to write and usually one has a co-operative wife who keeps the kids away. This is my, perhaps, my . . . quite unreal vision of a man's life in that he goes into his room and locks the door and he writes. Well, a woman never does this.

METCALF: Would you describe yourself as a feminist?

MUNRO: I'm not really sure what a feminist is. You've got to define that further.

METCALF: O.K. Have you had any formal relationship with the Women's Liberation movement?

MUNRO: Yes I'm in general, sympathetic.

METCALF: But not particularly active in any political sort of . . . ?

MUNRO: But not active because I'm not a political person. Maybe this is a cop out. Maybe I should be active but I don't have enough energy to stand off in any other direction.

METCALF: Do you think it's really possible for a woman to combine being married in a conventional, traditional sense of what being married has meant and being a writer?

MUNRO: It's very hard . . . um . . . it's not just hard in the question of when do I get time to write or will my writing affect my husband's ego or, you know, all these sort of surface problems you can deal with. But I think it's hard to be a married woman and a writer because I feel that in traditional marriage, as it's been up to now, as it is with most women in my generation . . . a woman abdicates, in a way, . . . she . . . This is turning out to be hard to say . . . she is no longer a completely unbiased observer. She has something to defend. There may be truths that she sees that she would prefer not to see; that she can't see if she wants to maintain her situation and a writer, of course, has to be free of shackles of this sort. I don't know if the same might apply to a married man but I have noticed that men have . . . always seem freer to tell the truth. They tell the truth about their marriages and about themselves, about their bodies. Men write these novels in which they tell about how . . . they feel physically and about how hellish they look when they look in the mirror . . . and all this sort of crap. Women have been bound by quite a different set of conventions. It's much more difficult to explore your life honestly and if you're married it is just that much more difficult because you live within a certain framework that is pretty hard to question because if you start questioning it too far you may be in big trouble. Or your marriage may be in trouble.

METCALF: Does it frighten you that many successful women writers have led very a-typical lives?

MUNRO: Yes. It does frighten me because I'm a fairly security-demanding person. I don't think I'm in any danger of ever leading a bizarre life. I tend to be a person of rather dull habits just because I want to work so much. I don't endanger this by having an exciting life.

METCALF: Do you feel that it's purely and *simply* the traditional social set up and the traditional roles which are played by men and women which have driven women writers in the past into rather strange lifestyles? Is it *merely* the conflict between "a woman's place" and . . .

MUNRO: No. I think it's a conflict for all writers. Really, isn't it, for men *and* women? Don't almost as many men writers lead fairly a-typical lives?

METCALF: Well, in terms of the work-a-day world, yes. Writers are usually extremely egotistical people. When you come across a woman who has said I am this and I am creating this and I am doing this a traditional male reaction to this is to say this woman is insane or . . . voracious or destructive or . . .

MUNRO: Yeah. So if you are a woman who is like this, you either become blatantly so and say to hell with them or you develop disguises which is the way I've managed so far. But there is probably a contradiction in many women writers in the woman *herself* . . . Between the woman who is ambitious and the woman who is there who is also . . . well, what, was called traditionally feminine, who is passive, who wants to be dominated, who wants to have someone between her and the world. And I know *I'm* like this. I have the two women. So . . .

METCALF: Various people, not in the academic world, but people who have read *Lives of Girls and Women* with delight and interest have remarked to me that they were surprised by the way in which the brother and the father seemed to disappear somehow . . . or were shunted off to the fox farm. They don't seem to figure very largely. Now I don't really know if I'm asking an autobiographical question here or a question which is concerned with the artistic purpose of the book. Could you comment on that?

MUNRO: Well, I'm not sure what the answer is either. In the book, I found, I didn't really intend to do this at the beginning, but I found that my emphasis, my interest was shifting so much to the mother that I had to be able to deal with her alone. I couldn't deal with both parents. I have a fairly narrow focus or something so the father tended to, sort of, fade away. But I think there is . . . well, you can see this in "Boys and Girls" too, the father picks the brother and their life is separated.

METCALF: He trains the son into the model that he is to become.

MUNRO: This is certainly what happened in my family and what happens in most traditional, say, farm families.

METCALF: I heard a tape that you made some time ago that was on the C.B.C. where I believe you said that women cannot create men characters as well as men can create women characters.

MUNRO: Hell! Did I say *that!* Well, I must have been crazy because I don't think men can create women characters either. I must have been worn down when I said that . . . because when people come up to me and say, as people have, you know at cocktail parties and things and say . . . well there aren't any real men in that book . . . I say, well, show me the real woman in a man's book. Not very many writers, the great ones *can* create characters of both sexes. But it doesn't often happen, I think.

METCALF: What do you think of D. H. Lawrence's women? I've always found them the most bizzare and peculiar creatures.

MUNRO: Oh. They're impossible. But there again, I suppose they're personifications of ideas. Except for the mother in *Sons and Lovers,* I find a real character. She is the only one I can think of. Can you think of any very good and convincing female characters created by men?

[1972]

POETRY

Three Nursery Rhymes

Nursery rhymes are of course found in books, but they survive because children find them memorable and pass them on to their playmates and, when they become adults, to their children. Nursery rhymes include lullabies ("Rockaby baby, on the tree tops"), counting-out rhymes ("eeny, meeny, miny, mo," "One potato, two potato"), charms ("rain, rain, go away"), short narratives ("Jack and Jill," "Mary had a little lamb"), and they are marked by emphatic rhymes. Scholars believe that perhaps half of the best-loved nursery rhymes of today go back to the eighteenth century, and many to the seventeenth. The earliest printed collections are *Tommy Thumb's Pretty Song Book* (1744) and *Mother Goose's Melody: or Sonnets for the Cradle* (1781).

The illustration for "What are little boys made of" comes from a book of 1825; the illustration for "The Milk Maid" is by John Bewick, in a book of 1792.

✎ Topic for Critical Thinking and Writing

When you read the following nursery rhymes (or call to mind others that you know), ask yourself this question: Do nursery rhymes indoctrinate children— that is, do they engender or reinforce attitudes about age, gender, and class? If so, how? And what should be done about it? Explain, using as examples these rhymes or others that you know.

Illustrations from a book published in 1825.

What Are Little Boys Made Of

What are little boys made of, made of?
What are little boys made of?
    Snips and snails
    And puppy-dogs' tails,
That's what little boys are made of.

What are little girls made of, made of?
What are little girls made of?
    Sugar and spice
    And all things nice,
That's what little girls are made of.

Topics for Critical Thinking and Writing

1. Do you imagine that boys like the description of what boys are made of? Do girls like the description of what girls are made of? Or is it only grown-ups who like these descriptions? Explain.
2. A version in 1846 gives two additional stanzas: "What are young men made of? / Sighs and leers and crocodile tears," and "What are young women made of? / Ribbons and laces, and sweet pretty faces." To the best of our knowledge, these two verses are not nearly so widely known as the first two? Why do you think this is so?

Georgie Porgie

Georgie Porgie, pudding and pie,
Kissed the girls and made them cry;
When the boys came out to play,
Georgie Porgie ran away.

Topics for Critical Thinking and Writing

1. What do you think a child does while reciting "Georgie Porgie"?
2. What do "pudding and pie" have to do with Georgie? How did they get into the line?

3. How old are the girls whom Georgie kisses (offer a guess), and why do they cry?
4. Why does Georgie run away? Is he running to be with the boys, or away from them?

An engraving from a book published in 1792.

The Milk Maid

Where are you going to, my pretty maid?
I'm going a-milking, sir, she said,
Sir, she said, sir, she said,
I'm going a-milking, sir, she said.   4

May I go with you, my pretty maid?
You're kindly welcome, sir, she said,
Sir, she said, sir, she said,
You're kindly welcome, sir, she said.   8

Say, will you marry me, my pretty maid?
Yes, if you please, kind sir, she said,
Sir, she said, sir, she said,
Yes, if you please, kind sir, she said.   12

What is your father, my pretty maid?
My father's a farmer, sir, she said,
Sir, she said, sir, she said,
My father's a farmer, sir, she said.   16

What is your fortune, my pretty maid?
My face is my fortune, sir, she said,
Sir, she said, sir, she said,
My face is my fortune, sir, she said.   20

Then I can't marry you, my pretty maid.
Nobody asked you, sir, she said,
Sir, she said, sir, she said,
Nobody asked you, sir, she said.   24

 ## Topics for Critical Thinking and Writing

1. Do you enjoy the repetition of "Sir, she said, sir, she said"? Why or why not? What gestures might accompany the words?
2. Is it fair to say that this nursery rhyme represents not only gender but also class? Explain.

RITA DOVE

Rita Dove was born in 1952 in Akron, Ohio. After graduating summa cum laude from Miami University (Ohio) she earned an M.F.A. at the Iowa Writers' Workshop. She has been awarded fellowships from the Guggenheim Foundation and the National Endowment for the Arts, and she now teaches at the University of Virginia. In 1993 she was appointed poet laureate for 1993–94. Dove is currently writing a book about the experiences of an African-American volunteer regiment in France during World War I.

Daystar

She wanted a little room for thinking:
but she saw diapers steaming on the line,
a doll slumped behind the door.
So she lugged a chair behind the garage
to sit out the children's naps.   5

Sometimes there were things to watch—
the pinched armor of a vanished cricket,
a floating maple leaf. Other days
she stared until she was assured
when she closed her eyes   10
she'd see only her own vivid blood.

She had an hour, at best, before Liza appeared
pouting from the top of the stairs.
And just *what* was mother doing
out back with the field mice? Why,   15

building a palace. Later
that night when Thomas rolled over and
lurched into her, she would open her eyes
and think of the place that was hers
for an hour—where   20
she was nothing,
pure nothing, in the middle of the day.

[1986]

Topics for Critical Thinking and Writing

1. How would you characterize the woman who is the subject of the poem?
2. What do you make of the title?

ROBERT HAYDEN

Robert Hayden (1913–80) was born in Detroit, Michigan. His parents divorced when he was a child, and he was brought up by a neighboring family, whose name he adopted. In 1942, at the age of 29, he graduated from Detroit City College (now Wayne State University), and he received a master's degree from the University of Michigan. He taught at Fisk University from 1946 to 1969 and after that, for the remainder of his life, at the University of Michigan. In 1979 he was appointed Consultant in Poetry to the Library of Congress, the first African American to hold the post.

Those Winter Sundays

Sundays too my father got up early
and put his clothes on in the blueblack cold,
then with cracked hands that ached
from labor in the weekday weather made
banked fires blaze. No one ever thanked him.   5

I'd wake and hear the cold splintering, breaking.
When the rooms were warm, he'd call,
and slowly I would rise and dress,
fearing the chronic angers of that house.

Speaking indifferently to him,   10
who had driven out the cold
and polished my good shoes as well.
What did I know, what did I know
of love's austere and lonely offices?

[1962]

Topics for Critical Thinking and Writing

1. In line 1, what does the word "too" tell us about the father? What does it suggest about the speaker and the implied hearer of the poem?
2. How old do you believe the speaker was at the time he recalls in the second and third stanzas? What details suggest this age?
3. What is the meaning of "offices" in the last line? What does this word suggest that other words Hayden might have chosen do not?
4. What do you take to be the speaker's present attitude toward his father? What circumstances, do you imagine, prompted his memory of "Those Winter Sundays"?
5. In a page or two, try to get down the exact circumstances when you spoke "indifferently," or not at all, to someone who had deserved your gratitude.

MURIEL RUKEYSER

Muriel Rukeyser (1913–80) was born in New York City and educated at Vassar College (where she knew Elizabeth Bishop) and at Columbia University. In addition to teaching at Sarah Lawrence College, she published fifteen books of poetry, a novel, biographies, books for children, and translations. She was also active in behalf of left-wing causes throughout her adult life.

The myth that Rukeyser refers to in this poem is the story of Oedipus. Oedipus, en route to Thebes, killed a stranger in an angry encounter on the road. He then solved the riddle of the Sphinx, a monster with the face and breasts of a woman, the body and paws of a lion, and the wings of a bird of prey. The riddle was "What walks on four legs in the morning, two at noon, and three in the evening?" The Sphinx posed this question to everyone who approached Thebes; when the traveler could not answer it, the Sphinx devoured him or her. Oedipus was the first to give the correct answer: Man (who crawls on all fours in his infancy, later walks upright, and finally, in the "evening" of his life, totters along with the aid of a staff or cane). When Oedipus arrived in Thebes, he was made the king—the king had recently died—and he married the widowed queen. Ultimately he learned that he had killed his father, the king, on the road, and that he had married his own mother—events that had been prophesied at his birth. When he learned that his actions fulfilled the prophecy, he blinded himself and became a wanderer. (For Sophocles's tragic drama on this legend, see page 280.)

Myth

Long afterward, Oedipus, old and blinded, walked the
roads. He smelled a familiar smell. It was
the Sphinx. Oedipus said, "I want to ask one question.
Why didn't I recognize my mother?" "You gave the
wrong answer," said the Sphinx. "But that was what   5
made everything possible," said Oedipus. "No," she said.
"When I asked, What walks on four legs in the morning.
two at noon, and three in the evening, you answered.
Man. You didn't say anything about woman."
"When you say Man," said Oedipus, "you include women   10
too. Everyone knows that." She said, "That's what
you think."

(1973)

Topics for Critical Thinking and Writing

1. In lines 7–8 Rukeyser sets forth the Sphinx's riddle. Here is a rhyming version:

   What goes on four feet, on two feet,
   and three, But the more feet it goes on the weaker it be?

   What do you think of the idea of including this rhyming version within Rukeyser's version, in place of lines 7–8? Explain.

2. Rukeyser's first sentence is probably of about average length, but it is slightly complicated, since it does not begin with the subject. Her second sentence is shorter and more usual—it *does* begin with the subject ("He"). Her third sentence is still shorter, and again it begins with the subject ("It"). What effects are gained by this arrangement. Try rewriting the passage, perhaps beginning with a very short and simple sentence, and following it with more complex sentences. Then compare (and evaluate) the versions.

3. It is often said that we learn through suffering. For instance, in *Adam Bede* George Eliot writes, "Deep, unspeakable suffering may well be called a baptism, a regeneration, the initiation into a new state." In Rukeyser's poem, what has Oedipus learned? Now that the Sphinx has again spoken to him, do you suppose he learns anything useful?

 THEODORE ROETHKE

Theodore Roethke (1908–63) was born in Saginaw, Michigan, and educated at the University of Michigan and Harvard. From 1947 until his death he taught at the University of Washington in Seattle, where he exerted considerable influence on the next generation of poets. Many of Roethke's best poems are lyrical memories of his childhood.

My Papa's Waltz

The whiskey on your breath
Could make a small boy dizzy;
but I hung on like death:
Such waltzing was not easy.   4

We romped until the pans
Slid from the kitchen shelf;
My mother's countenance
Could not unfrown itself.   8

The hand that held my wrist
Was battered on one knuckle;
At every step you missed
My right ear scraped a buckle.   12

You beat time on my head
With a palm caked hard by dirt,
Then waltzed me off to bed
Still clinging to your shirt.   16

[1948]

Topics for Critical Thinking and Writing

1. Do the syntactical pauses vary much from stanza to stanza? Be specific. Would you say that the rhythm suggests lightness? Why?
2. Does the rhythm parallel or ironically contrast with the episode described? Was the dance a graceful waltz? Explain.
3. What would you say is the function of the stresses in lines 13–14?
4. How different would the poem be if the speaker were a female, and "girl" instead of "boy" appeared in line 2?

 ## LUCILLE CLIFTON

 *Lucille Clifton (née Sayles) was born in New York State in 1936 and educated at Howard University and Fredonia State Teachers College. In addition to publishing 7 books of poetry, she has written 15 children's books. Clifton has received numerous awards, including a grant from the National Endowment for the Arts. She teaches creative writing at the University of California, Santa Cruz.*

wishes for sons

i wish them cramps.
i wish them a strange town
and the last tampon.
i wish them no 7-11.   4

i wish them one week early
and wearing a white skirt.
i wish them one week late.

later i wish them hot flashes   8
and clots like you
wouldn't believe. let the
flashes come when they
meet someone special.   12
let the clots come
when they want to.

let them think they have accepted
arrogance in the universe,   16
then bring them to gynecologists
not unlike themselves.

[1990]

Topics for Critical Thinking and Writing

1. How would you characterize Clifton's "wishes for sons"? Are the wishes sympathetic, hostile, or what?
2. How would you paraphrase or interpret the last two lines?
3. The poem, including the title, has no capital letters. But it does have periods. What other rhythms does it have?
4. Try freewriting a page or two of wishes: for someone you love, or don't love, or both; for someone in the news. Your wishes can be for more than one person; they can be practical, or not.

 SHARON OLDS

Sharon Olds, born in San Francisco in 1942, and educated at Stanford University and Columbia University, has published several volumes of poetry and has received major awards.

Rites of Passage

As the guests arrive at my son's party
They gather in the living room—
short men, men in first grade
with smooth jaws and chins.
Hands in pockets, they stand around   5
jostling, jockeying for place, small fights
breaking out and calming. One says to another
How old are you? Six. I'm seven. So?
They eye each other, seeing themselves
tiny in the other's pupils. They clear their   10
throats a lot, a room of small bankers,
they fold their arms and frown. *I could beat you*
up, a seven says to a six,
the dark cake, round and heavy as a
turret, behind them on the table. My son,   15
freckles like specks of nutmeg on his cheeks,
chest narrow as the balsa keel of a
model boat, long hands
cool and thin as the day they guided him
out of me, speaks up as a host   20
for the sake of the group.
We could easily kill a two-year-old,
he says in his clear voice. The other
men agree, they clear their throats
like Generals, they relax and get down to   25
playing war, celebrating my son's life.

[1983]

Topics for Critical Thinking and Writing

1. Focus on the details that the speaker provides about the boys—how they look, how they speak. What do the details reveal about them?
2. Is the speaker's son the same as or different from the other boys?
3. Some readers find the ironies in this poem (e.g., "short men") to be somewhat comical, while others, noting such phrases as "kill a two-year-old" and "playing war," conclude that the poem as a whole is meant to be upsetting, even frightening. How would you describe the kinds of irony that Olds uses here?
4. An experiment in irony and point of view: Try writing a poem like this one, from the point of view of a father about the birthday party of his son, and then try writing another one, by either a father or mother about a daughter's party.

 **FRANK O'HARA**

Frank O'Hara (1926–1966), was born in Baltimore, and died in a tragic accident—he was run over by a beach vehicle—on Fire Island, New York. O'Hara was not only a prolific writer of verse but also an astute critic of sculpture and painting who worked as an assistant curator at the Museum of Modern Art, in New York, and also as an editor of Art News. *O'Hara's first volume of poetry was* A City Winter, and Other Poems *(1952);* Collected Poems *was issued in 1971, but it was not complete. It has been supplemented by two additional volumes,* Early Poems *(1977) and* Poems Retrieved *(1977).*

Homosexuality

So we are taking off our masks, are we, and keeping
our mouths shut? as if we'd been pierced by a glance!

The song of an old cow is not more full of judgment
than the vapors which escape one's soul when one is sick;

so I pull the shadows around me like a puff   5
and crinkle my eyes as if at the most exquisite moment

of a very long opera, and then we are off!
without reproach and without hope that our delicate feet

will touch the earth again, let alone "very soon."
It is the law of my own voice I shall investigate.   10

I start like ice, my finger to my ear, my ear
to my heart, that proud cur at the garbage can

in the rain. It's wonderful to admire oneself
with complete candor, tallying up the merits of each

of the latrines. 14th Street is drunken and credulous,   15
53rd tries to tremble but is too at rest. The good

love a park and the inept a railway station,
and there are the divine ones who drag themselves up

and down the lengthening shadow of an Abyssinian head
in the dust, trailing their long elegant heels of hot air   20

crying to confuse the brave "It's a summer day,
and I want to be wanted more than anything else in the world."

[1971]

Topics for Critical Thinking and Writing

1. Describe your response to the word that O'Hara chooses for his title. In
   what ways does the poem define and explore the meanings of this word and
   our responses to it?
2. Characterize the point of view and tone of the speaker. Who is or are the
   "we" named in line 1?
3. In line 1 the speaker declares that "we are taking off our masks," but then
   immediately seems to confuse or contradict his point when he says "we" are
   "keeping / our mouths shut." Explain as clearly as you can what the speaker
   is suggesting in this first stanza.
4. Some of the language in this poem is ugly or unpleasant—for example, the
   "cur at the garbage can," "the latrines." What is the purpose of such language? What is its place in the structure of the poem as a whole?

SHEL SILVERSTEIN

*The composer, poet, and cartoonist Shel Silverstein (1932–99) was
born in Chicago. After serving in the 1950s in Japan and Korea as a
cartoonist for the U. S. armed forces' magazine* Stars and Stripes, *he
returned to New York City and became a folksinger and composer. His
book* Where the Sidewalk Ends: The Poems and Drawings of Shel
Silverstein, *published in 1974, has sold 4.5 million copies—the most
ever of any book of poetry for children.*

A Boy Named Sue

My daddy left home when I was three
And he didn't leave much to ma and me
Just this old guitar and an empty bottle of booze.
Now, I don't blame him cause he run and hid
But the meanest thing that he ever did
Was before he left, he went and named me "Sue."
Well, he must o' thought that is was quite a joke
And it got a lot of laughs from a' lots of folk.
It seems I had to fight my whole life through.
Some gal would giggle and I'd get red
And some guy'd laugh and I'd bust his head.

I tell ya, life ain't easy for a boy named "Sue."
Well, I grew up quick and I grew up mean.
My fist got hard and my wits got keen.
I'd roam from town to town to hide my shame.
But I made me a vow to the moon and stars
That I'd search the honky-tonks and bars

And kill that man that give me that awful name.
Well, it was Gatlinburg in mid-July
And I just hit town and my throat was dry,
I thought I'd stop and have myself a brew.
At an old saloon on a street of mud,
There at a table, dealing stud,
Sat the dirty, mangy dog that named me "Sue."
Well, I knew that snake was my own sweet dad
From a worn-out picture that my mother'd had,
And I knew that scar on his cheek and his evil eye.
He was big and bent and gray and old,
And I looked at him and my blood ran cold
And I said: "My name is 'Sue!' How do you do! Now you gonna die!!"
Well, I hit him hard right between the eyes
And he went down but, to my surprise,
He come up with a knife and cut off a piece of my ear.
But I busted a chair right across his teeth
And we crashed through the wall and into the street
Kicking and a' gouging in the mud and the blood and the beer.
I tell ya, I've fought tougher men
But I really can't remember when,
He kicked like a mule and he bit like a crocodile.
I heard him laugh and then I heard him cuss, so He went for his gun and I
pulled mine first.
He stood there lookin' at me and I saw him smile.
And he said: "Son, this world is rough
And if a man's gonna make it, he's gotta be tough
And I know I wouldn't be there to help ya along.
So I give ya that name and I said goodbye
I knew you'd have to get tough or die
And it's that name that helped to make you strong."
He said: "Now you just fought one hell of a fight
And I know you hate me, and you got the right
To kill me now, and I wouldn't blame you if you do.
But ya ought to thank me before I die.
For the gravel in ya guts and the spit in ya eye
Cause I'm the son-of-a-bitch that named you 'Sue.' "
I got all choked up and I threw down my gun
And I called him my pa, and he called me his son.
And I come away with a different point of view.
And I think about him, now and then,
Every time I try and every time I win,
And if I ever have a son, I think I'm gonna name him
Bill or George! Anything but Sue! I still hate that name!

[*1974*]

Topics for Critical Thinking and Writing

1. How does the poem show the power of a name? Can a name be as powerful in shaping a personality as this speaker claims? A Latin proverb runs, *Nomen atque omen.* "The name is an omen." If you can think of someone with an appropriate name (an undertaker named Digger, a baker named Baker, a zookeeper named Fox, an equestrian named Rider or Ryder), in a paragraph describe the person and the degree to which the name fits. Consider especially names that may designate psychological states, such as Moody, Grave, Happy, and Joy.

2. The actions described in this poem are violent and frightening. What makes the poem more than just a horror story?

3. Think about a mother/daughter situation that would be analogous to the battle that concludes Silverstein's poem, and then write a complementary poem based on the naming of a daughter by her mother.

 TESS GALLAGHER

Tess Gallagher, born in 1943 in Port Angeles, Washington, was educated at the University of Washington and the University of Iowa. The author of books of poems and of short stories, she has taught creative writing at several major universities.

I Stop Writing the Poem

to fold the clothes. No matter who lives
or who dies, I'm still a woman.
I'll always have plenty to do.
I bring the arms of his shirt
together. Nothing can stop   5
our tenderness. I'll get back
to the poem. I'll get back to being
a woman. But for now
there's a shirt, a giant shirt
in my hands, and somewhere a small girl   10
standing next to her mother
watching to see how it's done.

[1992]

Topics for Critical Thinking and Writing

1. Why does the speaker say in line 2, "I'm still a woman"? How is this phrase connected to the phrase that precedes it?

2. Gallagher uses only two adjectives. Circle them and explain why they are there. How would the poem be different without them?

3. Is this a protest poem? If you think it is, explain what the nature of the speaker's protest is. If you do not think it is, then explain the point and purpose of the poem as you interpret it.

JULIA ALVAREZ

The Latina author Julia Alvarez has written fiction, poetry, and non-fictional prose. Her books include the novel How the Garcia Girls Lost Their Accents *(1991), which tells the story of four sisters and their parents who emigrate from the Dominican Republic to the United States;* Something to Declare: Essays *(1998); and* Homecoming: New and Collected Poems, *which includes her first book,* Homecoming *(1984), as well as more recent work, and from which the poem below is taken.*

Woman's Work

Who says a woman's work isn't high art?
She'd challenge as she scrubbed the bathroom tiles.
Keep house as if the address were your heart.   3

We'd clean the whole upstairs before we'd start
downstairs. I'd sigh, hearing my friends outside.
Doing her woman's work was a hard art   6

to practice when the summer sun would bar
the floor I swept till she was satisfied.
She kept me prisoner in her housebound heart.   9

She'd shine the tines of forks, the wheels of carts,
cut lacy lattices for all her pies.
Her woman's work was nothing less than art.   12

And, I, her masterpiece since I was smart,
was primed, praised, polished, scolded and advised
to keep a house much better than my heart.   15

I did not want to be her counterpart!
I struck out . . . but became my mother's child:
a woman working at home on her art,   18
housekeeping paper as if it were her heart.

[1996]

Topics for Critical Thinking and Writing

1. The poet explores the relationship between mother and daughter through the work that each performs. Describe this work, and in particular the lessons that the mother teaches through what she does and how she does it.
2. What is the meaning of line 3?
3. How do you interpret the phrase "I struck out"?

MAUDE MEEHAN

The poet and activist Maude Meehan is the author of two books of poetry, Chipping Bone *(1985) and* Before the Snow *(1991). A number of poems from these books, as well as new work, is included in* Washing the Stones: Selected Poems, 1975–1995 *(1996).*

Is There Life After Feminism
(or how to wear boots and still be politically incorrect)

I like to wear boots.
I like the noise they make.
I walk real uppity in boots.
I walk strong.
If pressed   5
I can land a punch, a kick,
demolish a rapist,
and if I want to
I can go to bed in boots.

I cook without Tofu or eggplant   10
and I hate alfalfa sprouts. Call it heresy.
I hug my husband, my sons,
and send my daughter radical feminist literature.
I hug her too. I hug my gay friends,
and don't apologize for being straight.   15
I hug my friends of color
and won't apologize for being white.
How can we stand up together
if we're putting each other down?

I am a senior citizen.   20
There are advantages.
I get ten percent off on pancakes at Golden West
and a dollar off at the Nickelodeon.
Sometimes I wear lipstick, mascara
and don't ask anyone's pardon.   25
I wear a dress when I visit my mother.
She's ninety-six, I'm sixty-five.
Spare me your arguments. Where is it written
that any one of us has all the right answers
for anyone else?   30

I am a good citizen.
There are *dis*advantages.
I write to presidents and politicians
and they do what they want anyway.
I go to marches, to meetings, to jail,   35
and I have a file in Washington in my very own name

which I refuse to send for.
I know who I am.
Even when I do dishes, mind kids or wear high heels
I know who I am.   40
But what I like about wearing boots is,
there's no confusion.
Everyone knows who I am. Watch out!

[1985]

 **Topics for Critical Thinking and Writing**

1. How does the poem answer the question raised in the title?
2. The first thing (and just about the last thing, too) that the speaker tells us is that she "like[s] to wear boots." Why does she emphasize this fact about herself?
3. What does the phrase "politically correct" mean? In what ways does the speaker show that she is politically incorrect?
4. Do you like the person who gives her self-portrait in this poem? Does the speaker care about your response to her? Point to specific details in the text to explain your answers to these questions.

MARGE PIERCY

Marge Piercy, born in Detroit in 1936, was the first member of her family to attend college. After earning a bachelor's degree from the University of Michigan in 1957 and a master's degree from Northwestern University in 1958, she moved to Chicago. There she worked at odd jobs while writing novels (unpublished) and engaging in action on behalf of women and African Americans and against the war in Vietnam. In 1970—the year she moved to Wellfleet, Massachusetts, where she still lives—she published her first book, a novel. Since then she has published other novels, short stories, poems, and essays.

Barbie Doll

This girlchild was born as usual
and presented dolls that did pee-pee
and miniature GE stoves and irons
and wee lipsticks the color of cherry candy.
Then in the magic of puberty, a classmate said: 5
You have a great big nose and fat legs.

She was healthy, tested intelligent,
possessed strong arms and back,
abundant sexual drive and manual dexterity.
She went to and fro apologizing.   10
Everyone saw a fat nose on thick legs.

She was advised to play coy,
exhorted to come on hearty,
exercise, diet, smile and wheedle.
Her good nature wore out   15
like a fan belt.
So she cut off her nose and her legs
and offered them up.

In the casket displayed on satin she lay
with the undertaker's cosmetics painted on,   20
a turned-up putty nose,
dressed in a pink and white nightie.
Doesn't she look pretty? everyone said.
Consummation at last.
To every woman a happy ending.   25

[1969]

Topics for Critical Thinking and Writing

1. The poem begins "This girlchild was born as usual" and ends with everyone admiring a woman in her casket. Overall, in a sentence, what has the poem been about?

2. In "the magic of puberty" (line 5), a classmate makes a remark. What was the remark? And how do you read the word "magic"? Does it describe supernatural effects? A quality that lends enchantment? Or what?

3. In stanza 2 we're given some "social science" facts (lines 7-9). In the same stanza we're also told what the girl does ("She went to and fro apologizing"). Why are we given these two rather different views of her?

4. Why is the poem called "Barbie Doll"?

5. In an essay of 500–750 words, explain what Piercy is saying about women in this poem. Does her view seem to you fair, slightly exaggerated, or greatly exaggerated?

6. Write a poem—or an essay of 500 words—about Ken, Barbie's companion doll. If you wish, closely imitate Marge Piercy's poem.

A Work of Artifice

The bonsai tree
in the attractive pot
could have grown eighty feet tall
on the side of a mountain
till split by lightning.   5
But a gardener
carefully pruned it.
It is nine inches high.
Every day as he
whittles back the branches   10
the gardener croons,

It is your nature
to be small and cozy,
domestic and weak;
how lucky, little tree,   15
to have a pot to grow in.
With living creatures
one must begin very early
to dwarf their growth:
the bound feet,   20
the crippled brain,
the hair in curlers,
the hands you
love to touch.

[1973]

 ## Topics for Critical Thinking and Writing

1. Piercy uses a bonsai tree as a metaphor—but a metaphor for what? (If you have
   never seen a bonsai tree, try to visit a florist or a nursery to take a close look at
   one. You can find a picture of a bonsai in *The American Heritage Dictionary.*)
2. The gardener "croons" (line 11) a song to the bonsai tree. If the tree could
   respond, what might it say?
3. Explain lines 17–24 to someone who doesn't get the point. In your response, explain how these lines are connected with "hair in curlers." Explain, too, what "the hands you / love to touch" has to do with the rest of the
   poem. What tone of voice do you hear in "the hands you / love to touch"?
4. How does the form of the poem suggest its subject?

DRAMA

 **HENRIK IBSEN**

*Henrik Ibsen (1828–1906) was born in Skien, Norway, of wealthy parents who soon
after his birth lost their money. Ibsen worked as a pharmacist's apprentice, but at the
age of 22 he had written his first play, a promising melodrama entitled* Cataline. *He
engaged in theater work first in Norway and then in Denmark and Germany. By 1865
his plays had won him a state pension that enabled him to settle in Rome. After writing
romantic, historic, and poetic plays, he turned to realistic drama with* The League of
Youth *(1869). Among the major realistic "problem plays" are* A Doll's House *(1879),*
Ghosts *(1881), and* An Enemy of the People *(1882). In* The Wild Duck *(1884) he
moved toward a more symbolic tragic comedy, and his last plays, written in the
nineties, are highly symbolic.* Hedda Gabler *(1890) looks backward to the plays of
the eighties rather than forward to the plays of the nineties.*

A Doll's House (Harvard Theatre Collection)

A Doll's House
Translated by James McFarlane

CHARACTERS

Torvald Helmer, a lawyer
Nora, his wife
Dr. Rank
Mrs. Kristine Linde
Nils Krogstad
Anne Marie, the nursemaid
Helene, the maid
The Helmers' three children
A Porter

The action takes place in the Helmers' flat.

Act I

 A pleasant room, tastefully but not expensively furnished. On the back wall, one door on the right leads to the entrance hall, a second door on the left leads to Helmer's study. Between these two doors, a piano. In the middle of the left wall, a door; and downstage from it, a window. Near the window a round table with armchairs and a small sofa. In the right wall, upstage, a door; and on the same wall downstage, a porcelain stove with a couple of armchairs and a rocking chair. Between the stove and the door a small table. Etchings on the walls. A whatnot with china and other small objets d'art; a small bookcase with books in handsome bindings. Carpet on the floor; a fire burns in the stove. A winter's day.

The front door-bell rings in the hall; a moment later, there is the sound of the front door being opened. Nora comes into the room, happily humming to herself. She is dressed in her outdoor things, and is carrying lots of parcels which she then puts down on the table, right. She leaves the door into the hall standing open; a Porter can be seen outside holding a Christmas tree and a basket; he hands them to the Maid who has opened the door for them.

NORA. Hide the Christmas tree away carefully, Helene. The children mustn't see it till this evening when it's decorated. [*To the Porter, taking out her purse.*] How much?

PORTER. Fifty öre.

NORA. There's a crown. Keep the change.

[The Porter thanks her and goes. Nora shuts the door. She continues to laugh quietly and happily to herself as she takes off her things. She takes a bag of macaroons out of her pocket and eats one or two; then she walks stealthily across and listens at her husband's door.]

NORA. Yes, he's in.

[She begins humming again as she walks over to the table, right.]

HELMER [*in his study*]. Is that my little sky-lark chirruping out there?

NORA [*busy opening some of the parcels*]. Yes, it is.

HELMER. Is that my little squirrel frisking about?

NORA. Yes!

HELMER. When did my little squirrel get home?

NORA. Just this minute. [*She stuffs the bag of macaroons in her pocket and wipes her mouth.*] Come on out, Torvald, and see what I've bought.

HELMER. I don't want to be disturbed! [*A moment later, he opens the door and looks out, his pen in his hand.*] 'Bought', did you say? All that? Has my little spendthrift been out squandering money again?

NORA. But, Torvald, surely this year we can spread ourselves just a little. This is the first Christmas we haven't had to go carefully.

HELMER. Ah, but that doesn't mean we can afford to be extravagant, you know.

NORA. Oh yes, Torvald, surely we can afford to be just a little bit extravagant now, can't we? Just a teeny-weeny bit. You are getting quite a good salary now, and you are going to earn lots and lots of money.

HELMER. Yes, after the New Year. But it's going to be three whole months before the first pay cheque comes in.

NORA. Pooh! We can always borrow in the meantime.

HELMER. Nora! [*Crosses to her and takes her playfully by the ear.*] Here we go again, you and your frivolous ideas! Suppose I went and borrowed a thousand crowns today, and you went and spent it all over Christmas, then on New Year's Eve a slate fell and hit me on the head and there I was. . . .

NORA [*putting her hand over his mouth*]. Sh! Don't say such horrid things.

HELMER. Yes, but supposing something like that did happen . . . what then?

NORA. If anything as awful as that did happen, I wouldn't care if I owed anybody anything or not.

HELMER. Yes, but what about the people I'd borrowed from?

NORA. Them? Who cares about them! They are only strangers!

HELMER. Nora, Nora! Just like a woman! Seriously though, Nora, you know what I think about these things. No debts! Never borrow! There's always something inhibited, something unpleasant, about a home built on credit and borrowed money. We two have managed to stick it out so far, and that's the way we'll go on for the little time that remains.

NORA [*walks over to the stove*]. Very well, just as you say, Torvald.

HELMER [*following her*]. There, there! My little singing bird mustn't go drooping her wings, eh? Has it got the sulks, that little squirrel of mine? [*Takes out his wallet.*] Nora, what do you think I've got here?

NORA [*quickly turning round*]. Money!

HELMER. There! [*He hands her some notes*]. Good heavens, I know only too well how Christmas runs away with the housekeeping.

NORA [*counts*]. Ten, twenty, thirty, forty. Oh, thank you, thank you, Torvald! This will see me quite a long way.

HELMER. Yes, it'll have to.

NORA. Yes, yes, I'll see that it does. But come over here, I want to show you all the things I've bought. And so cheap! Look, some new clothes for Ivar . . . and a little sword. There's a horse and a trumpet for Bob. And a doll and a doll's cot for Emmy. They are not very grand but she'll have them all broken before long anyway. And I've got some dress material and some handkerchiefs for the maids. Though, really, dear old Anne Marie should have had something better.

HELMER. And what's in this parcel here?

NORA [*shrieking*]. No, Torvald! You mustn't see that till tonight!

HELMER. All right. But tell me now, what did my little spendthrift fancy for herself?

NORA. For me? Puh, I don't really want anything.

HELMER. Of course you do. Anything reasonable that you think you might like, just tell me.

NORA. Well, I don't really know. As a matter of fact, though, Torvald . . .

HELMER. Well?

NORA [*toying with his coat buttons, and without looking at him*]. If you did want to give me something, you could . . . you could always . . .

HELMER. Well, well, out with it!

NORA [*quickly*]. You could always give me money, Torvald. Only what you think you could spare. And then I could buy myself something with it later on.

HELMER. But Nora. . . .

NORA. Oh, please, Torvald dear! Please! I beg you. Then I'd wrap the money up in some pretty gilt paper and hang it on the Christmas tree. Wouldn't that be fun?

HELMER. What do we call my pretty little pet when it runs away with all the money?

NORA. I know, I know, we call it a spendthrift. But please let's do what I said, Torvald. Then I'll have a bit of time to think about what I need most. Isn't that awfully sensible, now, eh?

HELMER [*smiling*]. Yes, it is indeed—that is, if only you really could hold on to the money I gave you, and really did buy something for yourself with it. But it just gets mixed up with the housekeeping and frittered away on all sorts of useless things, and then I have to dig into my pocket all over again.

NORA. Oh but, Torvald. . . .

HELMER. You can't deny it, Nora dear. [*Puts his arm round her waist.*] My pretty little pet is very sweet, but it runs away with an awful lot of money. It's incredible how expensive it is for a man to keep such a pet.

NORA. For shame! How can you say such a thing? As a matter of fact I save everything I can.

HELMER [*laughs*]. Yes, you are right there. Everything you *can*. But you simply can't.

NORA [*hums and smiles quietly and happily*]. Ah, if you only knew how many expenses the likes of us sky-larks and squirrels have, Torvald!

HELMER. What a funny little one you are! Just like your father. Always on the look-out for money, wherever you can lay your hands on it; but as soon as you've got it, it just seems to slip through your fingers. You never seem to know what you've done with it. Well, one must accept you as you are. It's in the blood. Oh yes, it is, Nora. That sort of thing is hereditary.

NORA. Oh, I only wish I'd inherited a few more of Daddy's qualities.

HELMER. And I wouldn't want my pretty little song-bird to be the least bit differ-ent from what she is now. But come to think of it, you look rather . . . rather . . . how shall I put it? . . . rather guilty today. . . .

NORA. Do I?

HELMER. Yes, you do indeed. Look me straight in the eye.

NORA [*looks at him*]. Well?

HELMER [*wagging his finger at her*]. My little sweet-tooth surely didn't forget herself in town today?

NORA. No, whatever makes you think that?

HELMER. She didn't just pop into the confectioner's for a moment?

NORA. No, I assure you, Torvald . . . !

HELMER. Didn't try sampling the preserves?

NORA. No, really I didn't.

HELMER. Didn't go nibbling a macaroon or two?

NORA. No, Torvald, honestly, you must believe me . . . !

HELMER. All right then! It's really just my little joke. . . .

NORA [*crosses to the table*]. I would never dream of doing anything you didn't want me to.

HELMER. Of course not, I know that. And then you've given me your word. . . . [*Crosses to her.*] Well then, Nora dearest, you shall keep your little Christ-mas secrets. They'll all come out tonight, I dare say, when we light the tree.

NORA. Did you remember to invite Dr. Rank?

HELMER. No. But there's really no need. Of course he'll come and have dinner with us. Anyway, I can ask him when he looks in this morning. I've or-dered some good wine. Nora, you can't imagine how I am looking forward to this evening.

NORA. So am I. And won't the children enjoy it, Torvald!

HELMER. Oh, what a glorious feeling it is, knowing you've got a nice, safe job, and a good fat income. Don't you agree? Isn't it wonderful, just thinking about it?

NORA. Oh, it's marvellous!

HELMER. Do you remember last Christmas? Three whole weeks beforehand you shut yourself up every evening till after midnight making flowers for the Christmas tree and all the other splendid things you wanted to surprise us with. Ugh, I never felt so bored in all my life.

NORA. I wasn't the least bit bored.

HELMER [*smiling*]. But it turned out a bit of an anticlimax, Nora.

NORA. Oh, you are not going to tease me about that again! How was I to know the cat would get in and pull everything to bits?

HELMER. No, of course you weren't. Poor little Nora! All you wanted was for us to have a nice time—and it's the thought behind it that counts, after all. All the same, it's a good thing we've seen the back of those lean times.

NORA. Yes, really it's marvellous.

HELMER. Now there's no need for me to sit here all on my own, bored to tears. And you don't have to strain your dear little eyes, and work those dainty little fingers to the bone. . . .

NORA [*clapping her hands*]. No, Torvald, I don't, do I? Not any more. Oh, how marvellous it is to hear that! [*Takes his arm.*] Now I want to tell you how I've been thinking we might arrange things, Torvald. As soon as Christmas is over. . . . [*The door-bell rings in the hall.*] Oh, there's the bell. [*Tidies one or two things in the room.*] It's probably a visitor. What a nuisance!

HELMER. Remember I'm not at home to callers.

MAID [*in the doorway*]. There's a lady to see you, ma'am.

NORA. Show her in, please.

MAID [*to Helmer*]. And the doctor's just arrived, too, sir.

HELMER. Did he go straight into my room?

MAID. Yes, he did, sir.

[*Helmer goes into his study. The Maid shows in Mrs. Linde, who is in travelling clothes, and closes the door after her.*]

MRS. LINDE [*subdued and rather hesitantly*]. How do you do, Nora?

NORA [*uncertainly*]. How do you do?

MRS. LINDE. I'm afraid you don't recognize me.

NORA. No, I don't think I . . . And yet I seem to. . . . [*Bursts out suddenly.*] Why! Kristine! Is it really you?

MRS. LINDE. Yes, it's me.

NORA. Kristine! Fancy not recognizing you again! But how was I to, when . . . [*Gently.*] How you've changed, Kristine!

MRS. LINDE. I dare say I have. In nine . . . ten years. . . .

NORA. Is it so long since we last saw each other? Yes, it must be. Oh, believe me these last eight years have been such a happy time. And now you've come up to town, too? All that long journey in wintertime. That took courage.

MRS. LINDE. I just arrived this morning on the steamer.

NORA. To enjoy yourself over Christmas, of course. How lovely! Oh, we'll have such fun, you'll see. Do take off your things. You are not cold, are you? [*Helps her.*] There now! Now let's sit down here in comfort beside the stove. No, here, you take the armchair, I'll sit here on the rocking chair. [*Takes her hands.*] Ah, now you look a bit more like your old self again. It was just that when I first saw you. . . . But you are a little paler, Kristine . . . and perhaps even a bit thinner!

MRS. LINDE. And much, much older, Nora.

NORA. Yes, perhaps a little older . . . very, very little, not really very much. [*Stops suddenly and looks serious.*] Oh, what a thoughtless creature I am, sitting here chattering on like this! Dear, sweet Kristine, can you forgive me?

MRS. LINDE. What do you mean, Nora?

NORA [*gently*]. Poor Kristine, of course you're a widow now.

MRS. LINDE. Yes, my husband died three years ago.

NORA. Oh, I remember now. I read about it in the papers. Oh, Kristine, believe me I often thought at the time of writing to you. But I kept putting it off, something always seemed to crop up.

MRS. LINDE. My dear Nora, I understand so well.

NORA. No, it wasn't very nice of me, Kristine. Oh, you poor thing, what you must have gone through. And didn't he leave you anything?

MRS. LINDE. No.

NORA. And no children?

MRS. LINDE. No.

NORA. Absolutely nothing?

MRS. LINDE. Nothing at all . . . not even a broken heart to grieve over.

NORA [*looks at her incredulously*]. But, Kristine, is that possible?

MRS. LINDE [*smiles sadly and strokes Nora's hair*]. Oh, it sometimes happens, Nora.

NORA. So utterly alone. How terribly sad that must be for you. I have three lovely children. You can't see them for the moment, because they're out with their nanny. But now you must tell me all about yourself. . . .

MRS. LINDE. No, no, I want to hear about you.

NORA. No, you start. I won't be selfish today. I must think only about your affairs today. But there's just one thing I really must tell you. Have you heard about the great stroke of luck we've had in the last few days?

MRS. LINDE. No. What is it?

NORA. What do you think? My husband has just been made Bank Manager!

MRS. LINDE. Your husband? How splendid!

NORA. Isn't it tremendous! It's not a very steady way of making a living, you know, being a lawyer, especially if he refuses to take on anything that's the least bit shady—which of course is what Torvald does, and I think he's quite right. You can imagine how pleased we are! He starts at the Bank straight after New Year, and he's getting a big salary and lots of commission. From now on we'll be able to live quite differently . . . we'll do just what we want. Oh, Kristine, I'm so happy and relieved. I must say it's lovely to have plenty of money and not have to worry. Isn't it?

MRS. LINDE. Yes. It must be nice to have enough, at any rate.

NORA. No, not just enough, but pots and pots of money.

MRS. LINDE [*smiles*]. Nora, Nora, haven't you learned any sense yet? At school you used to be an awful spendthrift.

NORA. Yes, Torvald still says I am. [*Wags her finger.*] But little Nora isn't as stupid as everybody thinks. Oh, we haven't really been in a position where I could afford to spend a lot of money. We've both had to work.

MRS. LINDE. You too?

NORA. Yes, odd jobs—sewing, crochet-work, embroidery and things like that. [*Casually.*] And one or two other things, besides. I suppose you know that Torvald left the Ministry when we got married. There weren't any prospects of promotion in his department, and of course he needed to earn more money than he had before. But the first year he wore himself out completely. He had to take on all kinds of extra jobs, you know, and he found himself working all hours of the day and night. But he couldn't go on like that; and he became seriously ill. The doctors said it was essential for him to go South.

MRS. LINDE. Yes, I believe you spent a whole year in Italy, didn't you?

NORA. That's right. It wasn't easy to get away, I can tell you. It was just after I'd had Ivar. But of course we had to go. Oh, it was an absolutely marvellous trip. And it saved Torvald's life. But it cost an awful lot of money, Kristine.

MRS. LINDE. That I can well imagine.

NORA. Twelve hundred dollars. Four thousand eight hundred crowns. That's a lot of money, Kristine.

MRS. LINDE. Yes, but in such circumstances, one is very lucky if one has it.

NORA. Well, we got it from Daddy, you see.

MRS. LINDE. Ah, that was it. It was just about then your father died, I believe, wasn't it?

NORA. Yes, Kristine, just about then. And do you know, I couldn't even go and look after him. Here was I expecting Ivar any day. And I also had poor Torvald, gravely ill, on my hands. Dear, kind Daddy! I never saw him again, Kristine. Oh, that's the saddest thing that has happened to me in all my married life.

MRS. LINDE. I know you were very fond of him. But after that you left for Italy?

NORA. Yes, we had the money then, and the doctors said it was urgent. We left a month later.

MRS. LINDE. And your husband came back completely cured?

NORA. Fit as a fiddle!

MRS. LINDE. But . . . what about the doctor?

NORA. How do you mean?

MRS. LINDE. I thought the maid said something about the gentleman who came at the same time as me being a doctor.

NORA. Yes, that was Dr. Rank. But this isn't a professional visit. He's our best friend and he always looks in at least once a day. No, Torvald has never had a day's illness since. And the children are fit and healthy, and so am I. [*Jumps up and claps her hands.*] Oh God, oh God, isn't it marvellous to be alive, and to be happy, Kristine! . . . Oh, but I ought to be ashamed of myself . . . Here I go on talking about nothing but myself. [*She sits on a low stool near Mrs. Linde and lays her arms on her lap.*] Oh, please, you mustn't be angry with me! Tell me, is it really true that you didn't love your husband? What made you marry him, then?

MRS. LINDE. My mother was still alive; she was bedridden and helpless. And then I had my two young brothers to look after as well. I didn't think I would be justified in refusing him.

NORA. No, I dare say you are right. I suppose he was fairly wealthy then?

MRS. LINDE. He was quite well off, I believe. But the business was shaky. When he died, it went all to pieces, and there just wasn't anything left.

NORA. What then?

MRS. LINDE. Well, I had to fend for myself, opening a little shop, running a little school, anything I could turn my hand to. These last three years have been one long relentless drudge. But now it's finished, Nora. My poor dear mother doesn't need me any more, she's passed away. Nor the boys either; they're at work now, they can look after themselves.

NORA. What a relief you must find it. . . .

MRS. LINDE. No, Nora! Just unutterably empty. Nobody to live for any more. [*Stands up restless.*] That's why I couldn't stand it any longer being cut off up there. Surely it must be a bit easier here to find something to occupy your mind. If only I could manage to find a steady job of some kind, in an office perhaps. . . .

NORA. But, Kristine, that's terribly exhausting; and you look so worn out even before you start. The best thing for you would be a little holiday at some quiet little resort.

MRS. LINDE [*crosses to the window*]. I haven't any father I can fall back on for the money, Nora.

NORA [*rises*]. Oh, please, you mustn't be angry with me!

MRS. LINDE [*goes to her*]. My dear Nora, you mustn't be angry with me either. That's the worst thing about people in my position, they become so bitter. One has nobody to work for, yet one has to be on the look-out all the time. Life has to go on, and one starts thinking only of oneself. Believe it or not,

when you told me the good news about your step up, I was pleased not so
much for your sake as for mine.

NORA. How do you mean? Ah, I see. You think Torvald might be able to do something for you.

MRS. LINDE. Yes, that's exactly what I thought.

NORA. And so he shall, Kristine. Just leave things to me. I'll bring it up so clev-
erly . . . I'll think up something to put him in a good mood. Oh, I do so
much want to help you.

MRS. LINDE. It is awfully kind of you, Nora, offering to do all this for me, particularly in your case, where you haven't known much trouble or hardship in
your own life.

NORA. When I . . . ? I haven't known much . . . ?

MRS. LINDE [*smiling*]. Well, good heavens, a little bit of sewing to do and a few
things like that. What a child you are, Nora!

NORA [*tosses her head and walks across the room*]. I wouldn't be too sure of
that, if I were you.

MRS. LINDE. Oh?

NORA. You're just like the rest of them. You all think I'm useless when it comes
to anything really serious. . . .

MRS. LINDE. Come, come. . . .

NORA. You think I've never had anything much to contend with in this hard world.

MRS. LINDE. Nora dear, you've only just been telling me all the things you've had
to put up with.

NORA. Pooh! They were just trivialities! [*Softly.*] I haven't told you about the really big thing.

MRS. LINDE. What big thing? What do you mean?

NORA. I know you rather tend to look down on me, Kristine. But you shouldn't, you
know. You are proud of having worked so hard and so long for your mother.

MRS. LINDE. I'm sure I don't look down on anybody. But it's true what you say: I
am both proud and happy when I think of how I was able to make
Mother's life a little easier towards the end.

NORA. And you are proud when you think of what you have done for your brothers, too.

MRS. LINDE. I think I have every right to be.

NORA. I think so too. But now I'm going to tell you something, Kristine. I too
have something to be proud and happy about.

MRS. LINDE. I don't doubt that. But what is it you mean?

NORA. Not so loud. Imagine if Torvald were to hear! He must never on any account . . . nobody must know about it, Kristine, nobody but you.

MRS. LINDE. But what is it?

NORA. Come over here. [*She pulls her down on the sofa beside her.*] Yes, Kristine, I too have something to be proud and happy about. I was the one
who saved Torvald's life.

MRS. LINDE. Saved . . . ? How . . . ?

NORA. I told you about our trip to Italy. Torvald would never have recovered but
for that. . . .

MRS. LINDE. Well? Your father gave you what money was necessary. . . .

NORA [*smiles*]. That's what Torvald thinks, and everybody else. But . . .

MRS. LINDE. But . . . ?

NORA. Daddy never gave us a penny. I was the one who raised the money.

MRS. LINDE. You? All that money?

NORA. Twelve hundred dollars. Four thousand eight hundred crowns. What do you say to that!

MRS. LINDE. But, Nora, how was it possible? Had you won a sweepstake or something?

NORA [*contemptuously*]. A sweepstake? Pooh! There would have been nothing to it then.

MRS. LINDE. Where did you get it from, then?

NORA [*hums and smiles secretively*]. H'm, tra-la-la!

MRS. LINDE. Because what you couldn't do was borrow it.

NORA. Oh? Why not?

MRS. LINDE. Well, a wife can't borrow without her husband's consent.

NORA [*tossing her head*]. Ah, but when it happens to be a wife with a bit of a sense for business . . . a wife who knows her way about things, then. . . .

MRS. LINDE. But, Nora, I just don't understand. . . .

NORA. You don't have to. I haven't said I did borrow the money. I might have got it some other way. [*Throws herself back on the sofa.*] I might even have got it from some admirer. Anyone as reasonably attractive as I am. . . .

MRS. LINDE. Don't be so silly!

NORA. Now you must be dying of curiosity, Kristine.

MRS. LINDE. Listen to me now, Nora dear—you haven't done anything rash, have you?

NORA [*sitting up again*]. Is it rash to save your husband's life?

MRS. LINDE. I think it was rash to do anything without telling him. . . .

NORA. But the whole point was that he mustn't know anything. Good heavens, can't you see! He wasn't even supposed to know how desperately ill he was. It was me the doctors came and told his life was in danger, that the only way to save him was to go South for a while. Do you think I didn't try talking him into it first? I began dropping hints about how nice it would be if I could be taken on a little trip abroad, like other young wives. I wept, I pleaded. I told him he ought to show some consideration for my condition, and let me have a bit of my own way. And then I suggested he might take out a loan. But at that he nearly lost his temper, Kristine. He said I was being frivolous, that it was his duty as a husband not to give in to all these whims and fancies of mine—as I do believe he called them. All right, I thought, somehow you've got to be saved. And it was then I found a way. . . .

MRS. LINDE. Did your husband never find out from your father that the money hadn't come from him?

NORA. No, never. It was just about the time Daddy died. I'd intended letting him into the secret and asking him not to give me away. But when he was so ill . . . I'm sorry to say it never became necessary.

MRS. LINDE. And you never confided in your husband?

NORA. Good heavens, how could you ever imagine such a thing! When he's so strict about such matters! Besides, Torvald is a man with a good deal of pride—it would be terribly embarrassing and humiliating for him if he thought he owed anything to me. It would spoil everything between us; this happy home of ours would never be the same again.

MRS. LINDE. Are you never going to tell him?

NORA [*reflectively, half-smiling*]. Oh yes, some day perhaps . . . in many years time, when I'm no longer as pretty as I am now. You mustn't laugh! What

I mean of course is when Torvald isn't quite so much in love with me as he is now, when he's lost interest in watching me dance, or get dressed up, or recite. Then it might be a good thing to have something in reserve. . . . [*Breaks off.*] What nonsense! That day will never come. Well, what have you got to say to my big secret, Kristine? Still think I'm not much good for anything? One thing, though, it's meant a lot of worry for me, I can tell you. It hasn't always been easy to meet my obligations when the time came. You know in business there is something called quarterly interest, and other things called instalments, and these are always terribly difficult things to cope with. So what I've had to do is save a little here and there, you see, wherever I could. I couldn't really save anything out of the house-keeping, because Torvald has to live in decent style. I couldn't let the children go about badly dressed either—I felt any money I got for them had to go on them alone. Such sweet little things!

MRS. LINDE. Poor Nora! So it had to come out of your own allowance?

NORA. Of course. After all, I was the one it concerned most. Whenever Torvald gave me money for new clothes and such-like, I never spent more than half. And always I bought the simplest and cheapest things. It's a blessing most things look well on me, so Torvald never noticed anything. But sometimes I did feel it was a bit hard, Kristine, because it is nice to be well dressed, isn't it?

MRS. LINDE. Yes, I suppose it is.

NORA. I have had some other sources of income, of course. Last winter I was lucky enough to get quite a bit of copying to do. So I shut myself up every night and sat and wrote through to the small hours of the morning. Oh, sometimes I was so tired, so tired. But it was tremendous fun all the same, sitting there working and earning money like that. It was almost like being a man.

MRS. LINDE. And how much have you been able to pay off like this?

NORA. Well, I can't tell exactly. It's not easy to know where you are with transactions of this kind, you understand. All I know is I've paid off just as much as I could scrape together. Many's the time I was at my wit's end. [*Smiles.*] Then I used to sit here and pretend that some rich old gentleman had fallen in love with me. . . .

MRS. LINDE. What! What gentleman?

NORA. Oh, rubbish! . . . and that now he had died, and when they opened his will, there in big letters were the words: 'My entire fortune is to be paid over, immediately and in cash, to charming Mrs. Nora Helmer.'

MRS. LINDE. But my dear Nora—who is this man?

NORA. Good heavens, don't you understand? There never was any old gentleman; it was just something I used to sit here pretending, time and time again, when I didn't know where to turn next for money. But it doesn't make very much difference; as far as I'm concerned, the old boy can do what he likes, I'm tired of him; I can't be bothered any more with him or his will. Because now all my worries are over. [*Jumping up.*] Oh God, what a glorious thought, Kristine! No more worries! Just think of being without a care in the world . . . being able to romp with the children, and making the house nice and attractive, and having things just as Torvald likes to have them! And then spring will soon be here, and blue skies. And maybe we can go away somewhere. I might even see something of the sea again. Oh yes! When you're happy, life is a wonderful thing!

[The door-bell is heard in the hall.]

MRS. LINDE [*gets up*]. There's the bell. Perhaps I'd better go.

NORA. No, do stay, please. I don't suppose it's for me; it's probably somebody for Torvald . . .

MAID [*in the doorway*]. Excuse me, ma'am, but there's a gentleman here wants to see Mr. Helmer, and I didn't quite know . . . because the Doctor is in there. . . .

NORA. Who is the gentleman?

KROGSTAD [*in the doorway*]. It's me, Mrs. Helmer.

[Mrs. Linde starts, then turns away to the window.]

NORA [*tense, takes a step towards him and speaks in a low voice*]. You? What is it? What do you want to talk to my husband about?

KROGSTAD. Bank matters . . . in a manner of speaking. I work at the bank, and I hear your husband is to be the new manager. . . .

NORA. So it's . . .

KROGSTAD. Just routine business matters, Mrs. Helmer. Absolutely nothing else.

NORA. Well then, please go into his study.

[She nods impassively and shuts the hall door behind him; then she walks across and sees to the stove.]

MRS. LINDE. Nora . . . who was that man?

NORA. His name is Krogstad.

MRS. LINDE. So it really was him.

NORA. Do you know the man?

MRS. LINDE. I used to know him . . . a good many years ago. He was a solicitor's clerk in our district for a while.

NORA. Yes, so he was.

MRS. LINDE. How he's changed!

NORA. His marriage wasn't a very happy one, I believe.

MRS. LINDE. He's a widower now, isn't he?

NORA. With a lot of children. There, it'll burn better now.

[She closes the stove door and moves the rocking chair a little to one side.]

MRS. LINDE. He does a certain amount of business on the side, they say?

NORA. Oh? Yes, it's always possible. I just don't know. . . . But let's not think about business . . . it's all so dull.

[Dr. Rank comes in from Helmer's study.]

DR. RANK [*still in the doorway*]. No, no, Torvald, I won't intrude. I'll just look in on your wife for a moment. [*Shuts the door and notices Mrs. Linde.*] Oh, I beg your pardon. I'm afraid I'm intruding here as well.

NORA. No, not at all! [*Introduces them.*] Dr. Rank . . . Mrs. Linde.

RANK. Ah! A name I've often heard mentioned in this house. I believe I came past you on the stairs as I came in.

MRS. LINDE. I have to take things slowly going upstairs. I find it rather a trial.

RANK. Ah, some little disability somewhere, eh?

MRS. LINDE. Just a bit run down, I think, actually.

RANK. Is that all? Then I suppose you've come to town for a good rest—doing the rounds of the parties?

MRS. LINDE. I have come to look for work.

RANK. Is that supposed to be some kind of sovereign remedy for being run down?

MRS. LINDE. One must live, Doctor.

RANK. Yes, it's generally thought to be necessary.

NORA. Come, come, Dr. Rank. You are quite as keen to live as anybody.

RANK. Quite keen, yes. Miserable as I am, I'm quite ready to let things drag on as long as possible. All my patients are the same. Even those with a moral affliction are no different. As a matter of fact, there's a bad case of that kind in talking with Helmer at this very moment . . .

MRS. LINDE [*softly*]. Ah!

NORA. Whom do you mean?

RANK. A person called Krogstad—nobody you would know. He's rotten to the core. But even he began talking about having to *live*, as though it were something terribly important.

NORA. Oh? And what did he want to talk to Torvald about?

RANK. I honestly don't know. All I heard was something about the Bank.

NORA. I didn't know that Krog . . . that this Mr. Krogstad had anything to do with the Bank.

RANK. Oh yes, he's got some kind of job down there. [*To Mrs. Linde.*] I wonder if you've got people in your part of the country too who go rushing round sniffing out cases of moral corruption, and then installing the individuals concerned in nice, well-paid jobs where they can keep them under observation. Sound, decent people have to be content to stay out in the cold.

MRS. LINDE. Yet surely it's the sick who most need to be brought in.

RANK [*shrugs his shoulders*]. Well, there we have it. It's that attitude that's turning society into a clinic.

[*Nora, lost in her own thoughts, breaks into smothered laughter and claps her hands.*]

RANK. Why are you laughing at that? Do you know in fact what society is?

NORA. What do I care about your silly old society? I was laughing about something quite different . . . something frightfully funny. Tell me, Dr. Rank, are all the people who work at the Bank dependent on Torvald now?

RANK. Is that what you find so frightfully funny?

NORA [*smiles and hums*]. Never you mind! Never you mind! [*Walks about the room.*] Yes, it really is terribly amusing to think that we . . . that Torvald now has power over so many people. [*She takes the bag out of her pocket.*] Dr. Rank, what about a little macaroon?

RANK. Look at this, eh? Macaroons. I thought they were forbidden here.

NORA. Yes, but these are some Kristine gave me.

MRS. LINDE. What? I . . . ?

NORA. Now, now, you needn't be alarmed. You weren't to know that Torvald had forbidden them. He's worried in case they ruin my teeth, you know. Still . . . what's it matter once in a while! Don't you think so, Dr. Rank? Here! [*She pops a macaroon into his mouth.*] And you too, Kristine. And I shall have one as well; just a little one . . . or two at the most. [*She walks about the room again.*] Really I am so happy. There's just one little thing I'd love to do now.

RANK. What's that?

NORA. Something I'd love to say in front of Torvald.

RANK. Then why can't you?

NORA. No, I daren't. It's not very nice.

MRS. LINDE. Not very nice?

RANK. Well, in that case it might not be wise. But to us, I don't see why. . . . What is this you would love to say in front of Helmer?

NORA. I would simply love to say: 'Damn.'

RANK. Are you mad!

MRS. LINDE. Good gracious, Nora . . . !

RANK. Say it! Here he is!

NORA [*hiding the bag of macaroons*]. Sh! Sh!

[*Helmer comes out of his room, his overcoat over his arm and his hat in his hand.*]

NORA [*going over to him*]. Well, Torvald dear, did you get rid of him?

HELMER. Yes, he's just gone.

NORA. Let me introduce you. This is Kristine, who has just arrived in town. . . .

HELMER. Kristine . . . ? You must forgive me, but I don't think I know . . .

NORA. Mrs. Linde, Torvald dear. Kristine Linde.

HELMER. Ah, indeed. A school-friend of my wife's, presumably.

MRS. LINDE. Yes, we were girls together.

NORA. Fancy, Torvald, she's come all this long way just to have a word with you.

HELMER. How is that?

MRS. LINDE. Well, it wasn't really . . .

NORA. The thing is, Kristine is terribly clever at office work, and she's frightfully keen on finding a job with some efficient man, so that she can learn even more. . . .

HELMER. Very sensible, Mrs. Linde.

NORA. And then when she heard you'd been made Bank Manager—there was a bit in the paper about it—she set off at once. Torvald please! You *will* try and do something for Kristine, won't you? For my sake?

HELMER. Well, that's not altogether impossible. You are a widow, I presume?

MRS. LINDE. Yes.

HELMER. And you've had some experience in business?

MRS. LINDE. A fair amount.

HELMER. Well, it's quite probable I can find you a job, I think. . . .

NORA [*clapping her hands*]. There, you see!

HELMER. You have come at a fortunate moment, Mrs. Linde. . . .

MRS. LINDE. Oh, how can I ever thank you . . . ?

HELMER. Not a bit. [*He puts on his overcoat.*] But for the present I must ask you to excuse me. . . .

RANK. Wait. I'm coming with you.

[*He fetches his fur coat from the hall and warms it at the stove.*]

NORA. Don't be long, Torvald dear.

HELMER. Not more than an hour, that's all.

NORA. Are you leaving too, Kristine?

MRS. LINDE [*putting on her things*]. Yes, I must go and see if I can't find myself a room.

HELMER. Perhaps we can all walk down the road together.

NORA [*helping her*]. What a nuisance we are so limited for space here. I'm afraid it just isn't possible. . . .

MRS. LINDE. Oh, you mustn't dream of it! Goodbye, Nora dear, and thanks for everything.

NORA. Goodbye for the present. But . . . you'll be coming back this evening, of course. And you too, Dr. Rank? What's that? If you are up to it? Of course you'll be up to it. Just wrap yourself up well.

[They go out, talking, into the hall; children's voices can be heard on the stairs.]

NORA. Here they are! Here they are! [*She runs to the front door and opens it. Anne Marie, the nursemaid, enters with the children.*] Come in! Come in! [*She bends down and kisses them.*] Ah! my sweet little darlings. . . . You see them, Kristine? Aren't they lovely!

RANK. Don't stand here chattering in this draught!

HELMER. Come along, Mrs. Linde. The place now becomes unbearable for anybody except mothers.

[Dr. Rank, Helmer and Mrs. Linde go down the stairs: the Nursemaid comes into the room with the children, then Nora, shutting the door behind her.]

NORA. How fresh and bright you look! My, what red cheeks you've got! Like apples and roses. [*During the following, the children keep chattering away to her.*] Have you had a nice time? That's splendid. And you gave Emmy and Bob a ride on your sledge? Did you now! Both together! Fancy that! There's a clever boy, Ivar. Oh, let me take her a little while, Anne Marie. There's my sweet little baby-doll! [*She takes the youngest of the children from the nursemaid and dances with her.*] All right, Mummy will dance with Bobby too. What? You've been throwing snowballs? Oh, I wish I'd been there. No, don't bother, Anne Marie, I'll help them off with their things. No, please, let me—I like doing it. You go on in, you look frozen. You'll find some hot coffee on the stove. [*The nursemaid goes into the room, left. Nora takes off the children's coats and hats and throws them down anywhere, while the children all talk at once.*] Really! A great big dog came running after you? But he didn't bite. No, the doggies wouldn't bite my pretty little dollies. You mustn't touch the parcels, Ivar! What are they? Wouldn't you like to know! No, no, that's nasty. Now? Shall we play something? What shall we play? Hide and seek? Yes, let's play hide and seek. Bob can hide first. Me first? All right, let me hide first.

[She and the children play, laughing and shrieking, in this room and in the adjacent room on the right. Finally Nora hides under the table; the children come rushing in to look for her but cannot find her; they hear her stifled laughter, rush to the table, lift up the tablecloth and find her. Tremendous shouts of delight. She creeps out and pretends to frighten them. More shouts. Meanwhile there has been a knock at the front door, which nobody has heard. The door half opens, and Krogstad can be seen. He waits a little; the game continues.]

KROGSTAD. I beg your pardon, Mrs. Helmer. . . .

NORA [*turns with a stifled cry and half jumps up*]. Ah! What do you want?

KROGSTAD. Excuse me. The front door was standing open. Somebody must have forgotten to shut it. . . .

NORA [*standing up*]. My husband isn't at home, Mr. Krogstad.

KROGSTAD. I know.

NORA. Well . . . what are you doing here?

KROGSTAD. I want a word with you.

NORA. With . . . ? [*Quietly, to the children.*] Go to Anne Marie. What? No, the strange man won't do anything to Mummy. When he's gone we'll have another game. [*She leads the children into the room, left, and shuts the door after them; tense and uneasy.*] You want to speak to me?

KROGSTAD. Yes, I do.

NORA. Today? But it isn't the first of the month yet. . . .

KROGSTAD. No, it's Christmas Eve. It depends entirely on you what sort of Christmas you have.

NORA. What do you want? Today I can't possibly . . .

KROGSTAD. Let's not talk about that for the moment. It's something else. You've got a moment to spare?

NORA. Yes, I suppose so, though . . .

KROGSTAD. Good. I was sitting in Olsen's café, and I saw your husband go down the road . . .

NORA. Did you?

KROGSTAD. . . . with a lady.

NORA. Well?

KROGSTAD. May I be so bold as to ask whether that lady was a Mrs. Linde?

NORA. Yes.

KROGSTAD. Just arrived in town?

NORA. Yes, today.

KROGSTAD. And she's a good friend of yours?

NORA. Yes, she is. But I can't see . . .

KROGSTAD. I also knew her once.

NORA. I know.

KROGSTAD. Oh? So you know all about it. I thought as much. Well, I want to ask you straight: is Mrs. Linde getting a job in the Bank?

NORA. How dare you cross-examine me like this, Mr. Krogstad? You, one of my husband's subordinates? But since you've asked me, I'll tell you. Yes, Mrs. Linde *has* got a job. And I'm the one who got it for her, Mr. Krogstad. Now you know.

KROGSTAD. So my guess was right.

NORA [*walking up and down*]. Oh, I think I can say that some of us have a little influence now and again. Just because one happens to be a woman, that doesn't mean. . . . People in subordinate positions, ought to take care they don't offend anybody . . . who . . . hm . . .

KROGSTAD. . . . has influence?

NORA. Exactly.

KROGSTAD [*changing his tone*]. Mrs. Helmer, will you have the goodness to use your influence on my behalf?

NORA. What? What do you mean?

KROGSTAD. Will you be so good as to see that I keep my modest little job at the Bank?

NORA. What do you mean? Who wants to take it away from you?

KROGSTAD. Oh, you needn't try and pretend to me you don't know. I can quite see that this friend of yours isn't particularly anxious to bump up against me. And I can also see now whom I can thank for being given the sack.

NORA. But I assure you. . . .

KROGSTAD. All right, all right. But to come to the point: there's still time. And I advise you to use your influence to stop it.

NORA. But, Mr. Krogstad, I *have* no influence.

KROGSTAD. Haven't you? I thought just now you said yourself . . .

NORA. I didn't mean it that way, of course. Me? What makes you think I've got any influence of that kind over my husband?

KROGSTAD. I know your husband from our student days. I don't suppose he is any more steadfast than other married men.

NORA. You speak disrespectfully of my husband like that and I'll show you the door.

KROGSTAD. So the lady's got courage.

NORA. I'm not frightened of you any more. After New Year's I'll soon be finished with the whole business.

KROGSTAD [*controlling himself*]. Listen to me, Mrs. Helmer. If necessary I shall fight for my little job in the Bank as if I were fighting for my life.

NORA. So it seems.

KROGSTAD. It's not just for the money, that's the last thing I care about. There's something else . . . well, I might as well out with it. You see it's like this. You know as well as anybody that some years ago I got myself mixed up in a bit of trouble.

NORA. I believe I've heard something of the sort.

KROGSTAD. It never got as far as the courts; but immediately it was as if all paths were barred to me. So I started going in for the sort of business you know about. I had to do something, and I think I can say I haven't been one of the worst. But now I have to get out of it. My sons are growing up; for their sake I must try and win back what respectability I can. That job in the Bank was like the first step on the ladder for me. And now your husband wants to kick me off the ladder again, back into the mud.

NORA. But in God's name, Mr. Krogstad, it's quite beyond my power to help you.

KROGSTAD. That's because you haven't the will to help me. But I have ways of making you.

NORA. You wouldn't go and tell my husband I owe you money?

KROGSTAD. Suppose I did tell him?

NORA. It would be a rotten shame. [*Half choking with tears.*] That secret is all my pride and joy—why should he have to hear about it in this nasty, horrid way . . . hear about it from *you*. You would make things horribly unpleasant for me. . . .

KROGSTAD. Merely unpleasant?

NORA [*vehemently*]. Go on, do it then! It'll be all the worse for you. Because then my husband will see for himself what a bad man you are, and then you certainly won't be able to keep your job.

KROGSTAD. I asked whether it was only a bit of domestic unpleasantness you were afraid of?

NORA. If my husband gets to know about it, he'll pay off what's owing at once. And then we'd have nothing more to do with you.

KROGSTAD [*taking a pace towards her*]. Listen, Mrs. Helmer, either you haven't a very good memory, or else you don't understand much about business. I'd better make the position a little bit clearer for you.

NORA. How do you mean?

KROGSTAD. When your husband was ill, you came to me for the loan of twelve hundred dollars.

NORA. I didn't know of anybody else.

KROGSTAD. I promised to find you the money. . . .

NORA. And you did find it.

KROGSTAD. I promised to find you the money on certain conditions. At the time you were so concerned about your husband's illness, and so anxious to get the money for going away with, that I don't think you paid very much attention to all the incidentals. So there is perhaps some point in reminding you of them. Well, I promised to find you the money against an IOU which I drew up for you.

NORA. Yes, and which I signed.

KROGSTAD. Very good. But below that I added a few lines, by which your father was to stand security. This your father was to sign.

NORA. Was to . . . ? He did sign it.

KROGSTAD. I had left the date blank. The idea was that your father was to add the date himself when he signed it. Remember?

NORA. Yes, I think. . . .

KROGSTAD. I then gave you the IOU to post to your father. Wasn't that so?

NORA. Yes.

KROGSTAD. Which of course you did at once. Because only about five or six days later you brought it back to me with your father's signature. I then paid out the money.

NORA. Well? Haven't I paid the instalments regularly?

KROGSTAD. Yes, fairly. But . . . coming back to what we were talking about . . . that was a pretty bad period you were going through then, Mrs. Helmer.

NORA. Yes, it was.

KROGSTAD. Your father was seriously ill, I believe.

NORA. He was very near the end.

KROGSTAD. And died shortly afterwards?

NORA. Yes.

KROGSTAD. Tell me, Mrs. Helmer, do you happen to remember which day your father died? The exact date, I mean.

NORA. Daddy died on 29 September.

KROGSTAD. Quite correct. I made some inquiries. Which brings up a rather curious point [*takes out a paper*] which I simply cannot explain.

NORA. Curious . . . ? I don't know . . .

KROGSTAD. The curious thing is, Mrs. Helmer, that your father signed this document three days after his death.

NORA. What? I don't understand. . . .

KROGSTAD. Your father died on 29 September. But look here. Your father has dated his signature 2 October. Isn't that rather curious, Mrs. Helmer? [*Nora remains silent.*] It's also remarkable that the words '2 October' and the year are not in your father's handwriting, but in a handwriting I rather think I recognize. Well, perhaps that could be explained. Your father might have forgotten to date his signature, and then somebody else might have made a guess at the date later, before the fact of your father's death was known. There is nothing wrong in that. What really matters is the signature. And *that* is of course genuine, Mrs. Helmer? It really was your father who wrote his name here?

NORA [*after a moment's silence, throws her head back and looks at him defiantly*]. No, it wasn't. It was me who signed father's name.

KROGSTAD. Listen to me. I suppose you realize that that is a very dangerous confession?

NORA. Why? You'll soon have all your money back.

KROGSTAD. Let me ask you a question: why didn't you send that document to your father?

NORA. It was impossible. Daddy was ill. If I'd asked him for his signature, I'd have to tell him what the money was for. Don't you see, when he was as ill as that I couldn't go and tell him that my husband's life was in danger. It was simply impossible.

KROGSTAD. It would have been better for you if you had abandoned the whole trip.

NORA. No, that was impossible. This was the thing that was to save my husband's life. I couldn't give it up.

KROGSTAD. But did it never strike you that this was fraudulent . . . ?

NORA. That wouldn't have meant anything to me. Why should I worry about you? I couldn't stand you, not when you insisted on going through with all those cold-blooded formalities, knowing all the time what a critical state my husband was in.

KROGSTAD. Mrs. Helmer, it's quite clear you still haven't the faintest idea what it is you've committed. But let me tell you, my own offence was no more and no worse than that, and it ruined my entire reputation.

NORA. You? Are you trying to tell me that you once risked everything to save your wife's life?

KROGSTAD. The law takes no account of motives.

NORA. Then they must be very bad laws.

KROGSTAD. Bad or not, if I produce this document in court, you'll be condemned according to them.

NORA. I don't believe it. Isn't a daughter entitled to try and save her father from worry and anxiety on his deathbed? Isn't a wife entitled to save her husband's life? I might not know very much about the law, but I feel sure of one thing: it must say somewhere that things like this are allowed. You mean to say you don't know that—you, when it's your job? You must be a rotten lawyer, Mr. Krogstad.

KROGSTAD. That may be. But when it comes to business transactions—like the sort between us two—perhaps you'll admit I know something about *them?* Good. Now you must please yourself. But I tell you this: if I'm pitched out a second time, you are going to keep me company.

[He bows and goes out through the hall.]

NORA [*stands thoughtfully for a moment, then tosses her head*]. Rubbish! He's just trying to scare me. I'm not such a fool as all that. [*Begins gathering up the children's clothes; after a moment she stops.*] Yet . . . ? No, it's impossible! I did it for love, didn't I?

THE CHILDREN [*in the doorway, left*]. Mummy, the gentleman's just gone out of the gate.

NORA. Yes, I know. But you mustn't say anything to anybody about that gentleman. You hear? Not even to Daddy!

THE CHILDREN. All right, Mummy. Are you going to play again?

NORA. No, not just now.

THE CHILDREN. But Mummy, you promised!

NORA. Yes, but I can't just now. Off you go now, I have a lot to do. Off you go, my darlings. [*She herds them carefully into the other room and shuts the door behind them. She sits down on the sofa, picks up her embroidery and works a few stitches, but soon stops.*] No! [*She flings her work down, stands up, goes to the hall door and calls out.*] Helene! Fetch the tree in for me, please. [*She walks across to the table, left, and opens the drawer; again pauses.*] No, really, it's quite impossible!

MAID [*with the Christmas tree*]. Where shall I put it, ma'am?

NORA. On the floor there, in the middle.

MAID. Anything else you want me to bring?

NORA. No, thank you. I've got what I want.

[*The maid has put the tree down and goes out.*]

NORA [*busy decorating the tree*]. Candles here . . . and flowers here—Revolting man! It's all nonsense! There's nothing to worry about. We'll have a lovely Christmas tree. And I'll do anything you want me to, Torvald; I'll sing for you, dance for you . . . .

[*Helmer, with a bundle of documents under his arm, comes in by the hall door.*]

NORA. Ah, back again already?

HELMER. Yes. Anybody been?

NORA. Here? No.

HELMER. That's funny. I just saw Krogstad leave the house.

NORA. Oh? O yes, that's right. Krogstad was here a minute.

HELMER. Nora, I can tell by your face he's been asking you to put a good word in for him.

NORA. Yes.

HELMER. And you were to pretend it was your own idea? You were to keep quiet about his having been here. He asked you to do that as well, didn't he?

NORA. Yes, Torvald. But . . .

HELMER. Nora, Nora, what possessed you to do a thing like that? Talking to a person like him, making him promises? And then on top of everything, to tell me a lie!

NORA. A lie . . . ?

HELMER. Didn't you say that nobody had been here? [*Wagging his finger at her.*] Never again must my little song-bird do a thing like that! Little song-birds must keep their pretty little beaks out of mischief; no chirruping out of tune! [*Puts his arm round her waist.*] Isn't that the way we want things to be? Yes, of course it is. [*Lets her go.*] So let's say no more about it. [*Sits down by the stove.*] Ah, nice and cosy here!

[*He glances through his papers.*]

NORA [*busy with the Christmas tree, after a short pause*]. Torvald!

HELMER. Yes.

NORA. I'm so looking forward to the fancy dress ball at the Stenborgs on Boxing Day.

HELMER. And I'm terribly curious to see what sort of surprise you've got for me.

NORA. Oh, it's too silly.

HELMER. Oh?

NORA. I just can't think of anything suitable. Everything seems so absurd, so pointless.

HELMER. Has my little Nora come to *that* conclusion?

NORA [*behind his chair, her arms on the chairback*]. Are you very busy, Torvald?

HELMER. Oh. . . .

NORA. What are all those papers?

HELMER. Bank matters.

NORA. Already?

HELMER. I have persuaded the retiring manager to give me authority to make any changes in organisation or personnel I think necessary. I have to work on it over the Christmas week. I want everything straight by the New Year.

NORA. So that was why that poor Krogstad. . . .

HELMER. Hm!

NORA [*still leaning against the back of the chair, running her fingers through his hair*]. If you hadn't been so busy, Torvald, I'd have asked you to do me an awfully big favour.

HELMER. Let me hear it. What's it to be?

NORA. Nobody's got such good taste as you. And the thing is I do so want to look my best at the fancy dress ball. Torvald, couldn't you give me some advice and tell me what you think I ought to go as, and how I should arrange my costume?

HELMER. Aha! So my impulsive little woman is asking for somebody to come to her rescue, eh?

NORA. Please, Torvald, I never get anywhere without your help.

HELMER. Very well, I'll think about it. We'll find something.

NORA. That's sweet of you. [*She goes across to the tree again; pause.*] How pretty these red flowers look.—Tell me, was it really something terribly wrong this man Krogstad did?

HELMER. Forgery. Have you any idea what that means?

NORA. Perhaps circumstances left him no choice?

HELMER. Maybe. Or perhaps, like so many others, he just didn't think. I am not so heartless that I would necessarily want to condemn a man for a single mistake like that.

NORA. Oh no, Torvald, of course not!

HELMER. Many a man might be able to redeem himself, if he honestly confessed his guilt and took his punishment.

NORA. Punishment?

HELMER. But that wasn't the way Krogstad chose. He dodged what was due to him by a cunning trick. And that's what has been the cause of his corruption.

NORA. Do you think it would . . . ?

HELMER. Just think how a man with a thing like that on his conscience will always be having to lie and cheat and dissemble; he can never drop the mask, not even with his own wife and children. And the children—*that's* the most terrible part of it, Nora.

NORA. Why?

HELMER. A fog of lies like that in a household, and it spreads disease and infection to every part of it. Every breath the children take in that kind of house is reeking with evil germs.

NORA [*closer behind him*]. Are you sure of that?

HELMER. My dear Nora, as a lawyer I know what I'm talking about. Practically all juvenile delinquents come from homes where the mother is dishonest.

NORA. Why mothers particularly?

HELMER. It's generally traceable to the mothers, but of course fathers can have the same influence. Every lawyer knows that only too well. And yet there's Krogstad been poisoning his own children for years with lies and deceit. That's the reason I call him morally depraved. [*Holds out his hands to her.*] That's why my sweet little Nora must promise me not to try putting in any more good words for him. Shake hands on it. Well? What's this? Give me your hand. There now! That's settled. I assure you I would have found it impossible to work with him. I quite literally feel physically sick in the presence of such people.

NORA [*draws her hand away and walks over to the other side of the Christmas tree*]. How hot it is in here! And I still have such a lot to do.

HELMER [*stands up and collects his papers together*]. Yes, I'd better think of getting some of this read before dinner. I must also think about your costume. And I might even be able to lay my hands on something to wrap in gold paper and hang on the Christmas tree. [*He lays his hand on her head.*] My precious little singing bird.

[He goes into his study and shuts the door behind him.]

NORA [*quietly, after a pause*]. Nonsense! It can't be. It's impossible. It *must* be impossible.

MAID [*in the doorway, left*]. The children keep asking so nicely if they can come in and see Mummy.

NORA. No, no, don't let them in! You stay with them, Anne Marie.

MAID. Very well, ma'am.

[She shuts the door.]

NORA [*pale with terror*]. Corrupt my children . . . ! Poison my home? [*Short pause; she throws back her head.*] It's not true! It could never, never be true!

Act II

The same room. In the corner beside the piano stands the Christmas tree, stripped, bedraggled and with its candles burnt out. Nora's outdoor things lie on the sofa. Nora, alone there, walks about restlessly; at last she stops by the sofa and picks up her coat.

NORA [*putting her coat down again*]. Somebody's coming! [*Crosses to the door, listens.*] No, it's nobody. Nobody will come today, of course, Christmas Day—nor tomorrow, either. But perhaps. . . . [*She opens the door and looks out.*] No, nothing in the letter box; quite empty. [*Comes forward.*] Oh, nonsense! He didn't mean it seriously. Things like that *can't* happen. It's impossible. Why, I have three small children.

[The Nursemaid comes from the room, left, carrying a big cardboard box.]

NURSEMAID. I finally found it, the box with the fancy dress costumes.

NORA. Thank you. Put it on the table, please.

NURSEMAID [*does this*]. But I'm afraid they are in an awful mess.

NORA. Oh, if only I could rip them up into a thousand pieces!

NURSEMAID. Good heavens, they can be mended all right, with a bit of patience.

NORA. Yes, I'll go over and get Mrs. Linde to help me.

NURSEMAID. Out again? In this terrible weather? You'll catch your death of cold, Ma'am.

NORA. Oh, worse things might happen.—How are the children?

NURSEMAID. Playing with their Christmas presents, poor little things, but . . .

NORA. Do they keep asking for me?

NURSEMAID. They are so used to being with their Mummy.

NORA. Yes, Anne Marie, from now on I can't be with them as often as I was before.

NURSEMAID. Ah well, children get used to anything in time.

NORA. Do you think so? Do you think they would forget their Mummy if she went away for good?

NURSEMAID. Good gracious—for good?

NORA. Tell me, Anne Marie—I've often wondered—how on earth could you bear to hand your child over to strangers?

NURSEMAID. Well, there was nothing else for it when I had to come and nurse my little Nora.

NORA. Yes but . . . how could you *bring* yourself to do it?

NURSEMAID. When I had the chance of such a good place? When a poor girl's been in trouble she must make the best of things. Because *he* didn't help, the rotter.

NORA. But your daughter will have forgotten you.

NURSEMAID. Oh no, she hasn't. She wrote to me when she got confirmed, and again when she got married.

NORA [*putting her arms round her neck*]. Dear old Anne Marie, you were a good mother to me when I was little.

NURSEMAID. My poor little Nora never had any other mother but me.

NORA. And if my little ones only had you, I know you would. . . . Oh, what am I talking about! [*She opens the box.*] Go in to them. I must . . . Tomorrow I'll let you see how pretty I am going to look.

NURSEMAID. Ah, there'll be nobody at the ball as pretty as my Nora.

[*She goes into the room, left.*]

NORA [*begins unpacking the box, but soon throws it down*]. Oh, if only I dare go out. If only I could be sure nobody would come. And that nothing would happen in the meantime here at home. Rubbish—nobody's going to come. I mustn't think about it. Brush this muff. Pretty gloves, pretty gloves! I'll put it right out of my mind. One, two, three, four, five, six. . . . [*Screams.*] Ah, they are coming. . . . [*She starts towards the door, but stops irresolute. Mrs. Linde comes from the hall, where she has taken off her things.*] Oh, it's you, Kristine. There's nobody else out there, is there? I'm so glad you've come.

MRS. LINDE. I heard you'd been over looking for me.

NORA. Yes, I was just passing. There's something you must help me with. Come and sit beside me on the sofa here. You see, the Stenborgs are having a fancy dress party upstairs tomorrow evening, and now Torvald wants me to go as a Neapolitan fisher lass and dance the tarantella. I learned it in Capri, you know.

MRS. LINDE. Well, well! So you are going to do a party piece?

NORA. Torvald says I should. Look, here's the costume, Torvald had it made for me down there. But it's got all torn and I simply don't know. . . .

MRS. LINDE. We'll soon have that put right. It's only the trimming come away here and there. Got a needle and thread? Ah, here's what we are after.

NORA. It's awfully kind of you.

MRS. LINDE. So you are going to be all dressed up tomorrow, Nora? Tell you what—I'll pop over for a minute to see you in all your finery. But I'm quite forgetting to thank you for the pleasant time we had last night.

NORA [*gets up and walks across the room*]. Somehow I didn't think yesterday was as nice as things generally are.—You should have come to town a little earlier, Kristine.—Yes, Torvald certainly knows how to make things pleasant about the place.

MRS. LINDE. You too, I should say. You are not your father's daughter for nothing. But tell me, is Dr. Rank always as depressed as he was last night?

NORA. No, last night it was rather obvious. He's got something seriously wrong with him, you know. Tuberculosis of the spine, poor fellow. His father was a horrible man, who used to have mistresses and things like that. That's why the son was always ailing, right from being a child.

MRS. LINDE [*lowering her sewing*]. But my dear Nora, how do you come to know about things like that?

NORA [*walking about the room*]. Huh! When you've got three children, you get these visits from . . . women who have had a certain amount of medical training. And you hear all sorts of things from them.

MRS. LINDE [*begins sewing again; short silence*]. Does Dr. Rank call in every day?

NORA. Every single day. He was Torvald's best friend as a boy, and he's a good friend of *mine*, too. Dr. Rank is almost like one of the family.

MRS. LINDE. But tell me—is he really genuine? What I mean is: doesn't he sometimes rather turn on the charm?

NORA. No, on the contrary. What makes you think that?

MRS. LINDE. When you introduced me yesterday, he claimed he'd often heard my name in this house. But afterwards I noticed your husband hadn't the faintest idea who I was. Then how is it that Dr. Rank should. . . .

NORA. Oh yes, it was quite right what he said, Kristine. You see Torvald is so terribly in love with me that he says he wants me all to himself. When we were first married, it even used to make him sort of jealous if I only as much as mentioned any of my old friends from back home. So of course I stopped doing it. But I often talk to Dr. Rank about such things. He likes hearing about them.

MRS. LINDE. Listen, Nora! In lots of ways you are still a child. Now, I'm a good deal older than you, and a bit more experienced. I'll tell you something: I think you ought to give up all this business with Dr. Rank.

NORA. Give up what business?

MRS. LINDE. The whole thing, I should say. Weren't you saying yesterday something about a rich admirer who was to provide you with money. . . .

NORA. One who's never existed, I regret to say. But what of it?

MRS. LINDE. Has Dr. Rank money?

NORA. Yes, he has.

MRS. LINDE. And no dependents?

NORA. No, nobody. But . . . ?

MRS. LINDE. And he comes to the house every day?

NORA. Yes, I told you.

MRS. LINDE. But how can a man of his position want to pester you like this?

NORA. I simply don't understand.

MRS. LINDE. Don't pretend, Nora. Do you think I don't see now who you borrowed the twelve hundred from?

NORA. Are you out of your mind? Do you really think that? A friend of ours who comes here every day? The whole situation would have been absolutely intolerable.

MRS. LINDE. It *really* isn't him?

NORA. No, I give you my word. It would never have occurred to me for one moment. . . . Anyway, he didn't have the money to lend then. He didn't inherit it till later.

MRS. LINDE. Just as well for you, I'd say, my dear Nora.

NORA. No, it would never have occurred to me to ask Dr. Rank. . . . All the same I'm pretty certain if I were to ask him . . .

MRS. LINDE. But of course you won't.

NORA. No, of course not. I can't ever imagine it being necessary. But I'm quite certain if ever I were to mention it to Dr. Rank. . . .

MRS. LINDE. Behind your husband's back?

NORA. I have to get myself out of that other business. That's also behind his back. I *must* get myself out of that.

MRS. LINDE. Yes, that's what I said yesterday. But . . .

NORA [*walking up and down*]. A man's better at coping with these things than a woman. . . .

MRS. LINDE. Your own husband, yes.

NORA. Nonsense! [*Stops.*] When you've paid everything you owe, you do get your IOU back again, don't you?

MRS. LINDE. Of course.

NORA. And you can tear it up into a thousand pieces and burn it—the nasty, filthy thing!

MRS. LINDE [*looking fixedly at her, puts down her sewing and slowly rises*]. Nora, you are hiding something from me.

NORA. Is it so obvious?

MRS. LINDE. Something has happened to you since yesterday morning. Nora, what is it?

NORA [*going towards her*]. Kristine! [*Listens.*] Hush! There's Torvald back. Look, you go and sit in there beside the children for the time being. Torvald can't stand the sight of mending lying about. Get Anne Marie to help you.

MRS. LINDE [*gathering a lot of the things together*]. All right, but I'm not leaving until we have thrashed this thing out.

[*She goes into the room, left; at the same time Helmer comes in from the hall.*]

NORA [*goes to meet him*]. I've been longing for you to be back, Torvald, dear.

HELMER. Was that the dressmaker . . . ?

NORA. No, it was Kristine; she's helping me with my costume. I think it's going to look very nice . . .

HELMER. Wasn't that a good idea of mine, now?

NORA. Wonderful! But wasn't it also nice of me to let you have your way?

HELMER [*taking her under the chin*]. Nice of you—because you let your husband have his way? All right, you little rogue, I know you didn't mean it that way. But I don't want to disturb you. You'll be wanting to try the costume on, I suppose.

NORA. And I dare say you've got work to do?

HELMER. Yes. [*Shows her a bundle of papers.*] Look at this. I've been down at the Bank . . . .

[*He turns to go into his study.*]

NORA. Torvald!

HELMER [*stopping*]. Yes.

NORA. If a little squirrel were to ask ever so nicely . . . ?

HELMER. Well?

NORA. Would you do something for it?

HELMER. Naturally I would first have to know what it is.

NORA. Please, if only you would let it have its way, and do what it wants, it'd scamper about and do all sorts of marvellous tricks.

HELMER. What is it?

NORA. And the pretty little sky-lark would sing all day long. . . .

HELMER. Huh! It does that anyway.

NORA. I'd pretend I was an elfin child and dance a moonlight dance for you, Torvald.

HELMER. Nora—I hope it's not that business you started on this morning?

NORA [coming closer]. Yes, it is, Torvald. I implore you!

HELMER. You have the nerve to bring that up again?

NORA. Yes, yes, you *must* listen to me. You must let Krogstad keep his job at the Bank.

HELMER. My dear Nora, I'm giving his job to Mrs. Linde.

NORA. Yes, it's awfully sweet of you. But couldn't you get rid of somebody else in the office instead of Krogstad?

HELMER. This really is the most incredible obstinacy! Just because you go and make some thoughtless promise to put in a good word for him, you expect me . . .

NORA. It's not that, Torvald. It's for your own sake. That man writes in all the nastiest papers, you told me that yourself. He can do you no end of harm. He terrifies me to death. . . .

HELMER. Aha, now I see. It's your memories of what happened before that are frightening you.

NORA. What do you mean?

HELMER. It's your father you are thinking of.

NORA. Yes . . . yes, that's right. You remember all the nasty insinuations those wicked people put in the papers about Daddy? I honestly think they would have had him dismissed if the Ministry hadn't sent you down to investigate, and you hadn't been so kind and helpful.

HELMER. My dear little Nora, there is a considerable difference between your father and me. Your father's professional conduct was not entirely above suspicion. Mine is. And I hope it's going to stay that way as long as I hold this position.

NORA. But nobody knows what some of these evil people are capable of. Things could be so nice and pleasant for us here, in the peace and quiet of our home—you and me and the children, Torvald! That's why I implore you. . . .

HELMER. The more you plead for him, the more impossible you make it for me to keep him on. It's already known down at the Bank that I am going to give Krogstad his notice. If it ever got around that the new manager had been talked over by his wife. . . .

NORA. What of it?

HELMER. Oh, nothing! As long as the little woman gets her own stubborn way . . . ! Do you want me to make myself a laughing stock in the office? . . . Give people the idea that I am susceptible to any kind of outside pressure? You can imagine how soon I'd feel the consequences of that! Anyway, there's one other consideration that makes it impossible to have Krogstad in the Bank as long as I am manager.

NORA. What's that?

HELMER. At a pinch I might have overlooked his past lapses. . . .

NORA. Of course you could, Torvald!

HELMER. And I'm told he's not bad at his job, either. But we knew each other rather well when we were younger. It was one of those rather rash friendships that prove embarrassing in later life. There's no reason why you shouldn't know we were once on terms of some familiarity. And he, in his tactless way, makes no attempt to hide the fact, particularly when other people are present. On the contrary, he thinks he has every right to treat me as an equal, with his 'Torvald this' and 'Torvald that' every time he opens his mouth. I find it extremely irritating, I can tell you. He would make my position at the Bank absolutely intolerable.

NORA. Torvald, surely you aren't serious?

HELMER. Oh? Why not?

NORA. Well, it's all so petty.

HELMER. What's that you say? Petty? Do you think I'm petty?

NORA. No, not at all, Torvald dear! And that's why . . .

HELMER. Doesn't make any difference! . . . You call my motives petty; so I must be petty too. Petty! Indeed! Well, we'll put a stop to that, once and for all. [*He opens the hall door and calls.*] Helene!

NORA. What are you going to do?

HELMER [*searching among his papers*]. Settle things. [*The Maid comes in.*] See this letter? I want you to take it down at once. Get hold of a messenger and get him to deliver it. Quickly. The address is on the outside. There's the money.

MAID. Very good, sir.

[She goes with the letter.]

HELMER [*putting his papers together*]. There now, my stubborn little miss.

NORA [*breathless*]. Torvald . . . what was that letter?

HELMER. Krogstad's notice.

NORA. Get it back, Torvald! There's still time! Oh, Torvald, get it back! Please for my sake, for your sake, for the sake of the children! Listen, Torvald, please! You don't realize what it can do to us.

HELMER. Too late.

NORA. Yes, too late.

HELMER. My dear Nora, I forgive you this anxiety of yours, although it is actually a bit of an insult. Oh, but it is, I tell you! It's hardly flattering to suppose that anything this miserable pen-pusher wrote could frighten *me!* But I forgive you all the same, because it is rather a sweet way of showing how much you love me. [*He takes her in his arms.*] This is how things must be, my own darling Nora. When it comes to the point, I've enough strength and enough courage, believe me, for whatever happens. You'll find I'm man enough to take everything on myself.

NORA [*terrified*]. What do you mean?

HELMER. Everything, I said. . . .

NORA [*in command of herself*]. That is something you shall never, never do.

HELMER. All right, then we'll share it, Nora—as man and wife. That's what we'll do. [*Caressing her.*] Does that make you happy now? There, there, don't look at me with those eyes, like a little frightened dove. The whole thing is sheer imagination.—Why don't you run through the tarantella and try out the tambourine? I'll go into my study and shut both the doors, then I won't hear anything. You can make all the noise you want. [*Turns in the doorway.*] And when Rank comes, tell him where he can find me.

[He nods to her, goes with his papers into his room, and shuts the door behind him.]

NORA [*wild-eyed with terror, stands as though transfixed*]. He's quite capable of doing it! He would do it! No matter what, he'd do it.—No, never in this world! Anything but that! Help? Some way out . . . ? [*The door-bell rings in the hall.*] Dr. Rank . . . ! Anything but that, *anything*! [*She brushes her hands over her face, pulls herself together and opens the door into the hall. Dr. Rank is standing outside hanging up his fur coat. During what follows it begins to grow dark.*] Hello, Dr. Rank. I recognized your ring. Do you mind not going in to Torvald just yet, I think he's busy.

RANK. And you?

[*Dr. Rank comes into the room and she closes the door behind him.*]

NORA. Oh, you know very well I've always got time for you.

RANK. Thank you. A privilege I shall take advantage of as long as I am able.

NORA. What do you mean—as long as you are able?

RANK. Does that frighten you?

NORA. Well, it's just that it sounds so strange. Is anything likely to happen?

RANK. Only what I have long expected. But I didn't think it would come quite so soon.

NORA [*catching at his arm*]. What have you found out? Dr. Rank, you must tell me!

RANK. I'm slowly sinking. There's nothing to be done about it.

NORA [*with a sigh of relief*]. Oh, it's *you* you're . . . ?

RANK. Who else? No point in deceiving oneself. I am the most wretched of all my patients, Mrs. Helmer. These last few days I've made a careful analysis of my internal economy. Bankrupt! Within a month I shall probably be lying rotting up there in the churchyard.

NORA. Come now, what a ghastly thing to say!

RANK. The whole damned thing is ghastly. But the worst thing is all the ghastliness that has to be gone through first. I only have one more test to make; and when that's done I'll know pretty well when the final disintegration will start. There's something I want to ask you. Helmer is a sensitive soul; he loathes anything that's ugly. I don't want him visiting me. . . .

NORA. But Dr. Rank. . . .

RANK. On no account must he. I won't have it. I'll lock the door on him.—As soon as I'm absolutely certain of the worst, I'll send you my visiting card with a black cross on it. You'll know then the final horrible disintegration has begun.

NORA. Really, you are being quite absurd today. And here was I hoping you would be in a thoroughly good mood.

RANK. With death staring me in the face? Why should I suffer for another man's sins? What justice is there in that? Somewhere, somehow, every single family must be suffering some such cruel retribution. . . .

NORA [*stopping up her ears*]. Rubbish! Do cheer up!

RANK. Yes, really the whole thing's nothing but a huge joke. My poor innocent spine must do penance for my father's gay subaltern life.

NORA [*by the table, left*]. Wasn't he rather partial to asparagus and *pâté de foie gras?*

RANK. Yes, he was. And truffles.

NORA. Truffles, yes. And oysters, too, I believe?

RANK. Yes, oysters, oysters, of course.

NORA. And all the port and champagne that goes with them. It does seem a pity all these delicious things should attack the spine.

RANK. Especially when they attack a poor spine that never had any fun out of them.

NORA. Yes, that is an awful pity.

RANK. [*looks at her sharply*]. Hm. . . .

NORA. [*after a pause*]. Why did you smile?

RANK. No, it was you who laughed.

NORA. No, it was you who smiled, Dr. Rank!

RANK. [*getting up*]. You are a bigger rascal than I thought you were.

NORA. I feel full of mischief today.

RANK. So it seems.

NORA. [*putting her hands on his shoulders*]. Dear, dear Dr. Rank, you mustn't go and die on Torvald and me.

RANK. You wouldn't miss me for long. When you are gone, you are soon forgotten.

NORA. [*looking at him anxiously*]. Do you think so?

RANK. People make new contacts, then . . .

NORA. Who make new contacts?

RANK. Both you and Helmer will, when I'm gone. You yourself are already well on the way, it seems to me. What was this Mrs. Linde doing here last night?

NORA. Surely you aren't jealous of poor Kristine?

RANK. Yes, I am. She'll be my successor in this house. When I'm done for, I can see this woman. . . .

NORA. Hush! Don't talk so loud, she's in there.

RANK. Today as well? There you are, you see!

NORA. Just to do some sewing on my dress. Good Lord, how absurd you are! [*She sits down on the sofa.*] Now Dr. Rank, cheer up. You'll see tomorrow how nicely I can dance. And you can pretend I'm doing it just for you—and for Torvald as well, of course. [*She takes various things out of the box.*] Come here, Dr. Rank. I want to show you something.

RANK. [*sits*]. What is it?

NORA. Look!

RANK. Silk stockings.

NORA. Flesh-coloured! Aren't they lovely! Of course, it's dark here now, but tomorrow. . . . No, no, no, you can only look at the feet. Oh well, you might as well see a bit higher up, too.

RANK. Hm. . . .

NORA. Why are you looking so critical? Don't you think they'll fit?

RANK. I couldn't possibly offer any informed opinion about that.

NORA. [*looks at him for a moment*]. Shame on you. [*Hits him lightly across the ear with the stockings.*] Take that! [*Folds them up again.*]

RANK. And what other delights am I to be allowed to see?

NORA. Not another thing. You are too naughty. [*She hums a little and searches among her things.*]

RANK. [*after a short pause*]. Sitting here so intimately like this with you, I can't imagine . . . I simply cannot conceive what would have become of me if I had never come to this house.

NORA. [*smiles*]. Yes, I rather think you do enjoy coming here.

RANK. [*in a low voice, looking fixedly ahead*]. And the thought of having to leave it all . . .

NORA.   Nonsense. You aren't leaving.

RANK [*in the same tone*].   . . . without being able to leave behind even the slightest token of gratitude, hardly a fleeting regret even . . . nothing but an empty place to be filled by the first person that comes along.

NORA.   Supposing I were to ask you to . . . ? No . . .

RANK.   What?

NORA.   . . . to show me the extent of your friendship . . .

RANK.   Yes?

NORA.   I mean . . . to do me a tremendous favour. . . .

RANK.   Would you really, for once, give me that pleasure?

NORA.   You have no idea what it is.

RANK.   All right, tell me.

NORA.   No, really I can't, Dr. Rank. It's altogether too much to ask . . . because I need your advice and help as well. . . .

RANK.   The more the better. I cannot imagine what you have in mind. But tell me anyway. You do trust me, don't you?

NORA.   Yes, I trust you more than anybody I know. You are my best and my most faithful friend. I know that. So I will tell you. Well then, Dr. Rank, there is something you must help me to prevent. You know how deeply, how passionately Torvald is in love with me. He would never hesitate for a moment to sacrifice his life for my sake.

RANK [*bending towards her*].   Nora . . . do you think he's the only one who . . . ?

NORA [*stiffening slightly*].   Who . . . ?

RANK.   Who wouldn't gladly give his life for your sake.

NORA [*sadly*].   Oh!

RANK.   I swore to myself you would know before I went. I'll never have a better opportunity. Well, Nora! Now you know. And now you know too that you can confide in me as in nobody else.

NORA [*rises and speaks evenly and calmly*].   Let me past.

RANK [*makes way for her, but remains seated*].   Nora. . . .

NORA [*in the hall doorway*].   Helene, bring the lamp in, please. [*Walks over to the stove.*] Oh, my dear Dr. Rank, that really was rather horrid of you.

RANK [*getting up*].   That I have loved you every bit as much as anybody? Is *that* horrid?

NORA.   No, but that you had to go and tell me. When it was all so unnecessary. . . .

RANK.   What do you mean? Did you know . . . ?

[The Maid comes in with the lamp, puts it on the table, and goes out again.]

RANK.   Nora . . . Mrs. Helmer . . . I'm asking you if you knew?

NORA.   How can I tell whether I did or didn't. I simply can't tell you. . . . Oh, how could you be so clumsy, Dr. Rank! When everything was so nice.

RANK.   Anyway, you know now that I'm at your service, body and soul. So you can speak out.

NORA [*looking at him*].   After this?

RANK.   I beg you to tell me what it is.

NORA.   I can tell you nothing now.

RANK.   You must. You can't torment me like this. Give me a chance—I'll do anything that's humanly possible.

NORA.   You can do nothing for me now. Actually, I don't really need any help. It's all just my imagination, really it is. Of course! [*She sits down in the rock-*

ing chair, looks at him and smiles.] I must say, you are a nice one, Dr. Rank! Don't you feel ashamed of yourself, now the lamp's been brought in?

RANK. No, not exactly. But perhaps I ought to go—for good?

NORA. No, you mustn't do that. You must keep coming just as you've always done. You know very well Torvald would miss you terribly.

RANK. And *you?*

NORA. I always think it's tremendous fun having you.

RANK. That's exactly what gave me wrong ideas. I just can't puzzle you out. I often used to feel you'd just as soon be with me as with Helmer.

NORA. Well, you see, there are those people you love and those people you'd almost rather *be* with.

RANK. Yes, there's something in that.

NORA. When I was a girl at home, I loved Daddy best, of course. But I also thought it great fun if I could slip into the maids' room. For one thing they never preached at me. And they always talked about such exciting things.

RANK. Aha! So it's their role I've taken over!

NORA [*jumps up and crosses to him*]. Oh, my dear, kind Dr. Rank, I didn't mean that at all. But you can see how it's a bit with Torvald as it was with Daddy . . . .

[The Maid comes in from the hall.]

MAID. Please, ma'am . . . !

[She whispers and hands her a card.]

NORA [*glances at the card*]. Ah!

[She puts it in her pocket.]

RANK. Anything wrong?

NORA. No, no, not at all. It's just . . . it's my new costume. . . .

RANK. How is that? There's your costume in there.

NORA. That one, yes. But this is another one. I've ordered it. Torvald mustn't hear about it. . . .

RANK. Ah, so that's the big secret, is it!

NORA. Yes, that's right. Just go in and see him, will you? He's in the study. Keep him occupied for the time being. . . .

RANK. Don't worry. He shan't escape me.

[He goes into Helmer's study.]

NORA [*to the maid*]. Is he waiting in the kitchen?

MAID. Yes, he came up the back stairs. . . .

NORA. But didn't you tell him somebody was here?

MAID. Yes, but it was no good.

NORA. Won't he go?

MAID. No, he won't till he's seen you.

NORA. Let him in, then. But quietly. Helene, you mustn't tell anybody about this. It's a surprise for my husband.

MAID. I understand, ma'am . . . .

[She goes out.]

NORA. Here it comes! What I've been dreading! No, no, it can't happen, it *can't* happen.

[*She walks over and bolts Helmer's door. The maid opens the hall door for Krogstad and shuts it again behind him. He is wearing a fur coat, over-shoes, and a fur cap.*]

NORA [*goes towards him*]. Keep your voice down, my husband is at home.

KROGSTAD. What if he is?

NORA. What do you want with me?

KROGSTAD. To find out something.

NORA. Hurry, then. What is it?

KROGSTAD. You know I've been given notice.

NORA. I couldn't prevent it, Mr. Krogstad, I did my utmost for you, but it was no use.

KROGSTAD. Has your husband so little affection for you? He knows what I can do to you, yet he dares. . . .

NORA. You don't imagine he knows about it!

KROGSTAD. No, I didn't imagine he did. It didn't seem a bit like my good friend Torvald Helmer to show that much courage. . . .

NORA. Mr. Krogstad, I must ask you to show some respect for my husband.

KROGSTAD. Oh, sure! All due respect! But since you are so anxious to keep this business quiet, Mrs. Helmer, I take it you now have a rather clearer idea of just what it is you've done, than you had yesterday.

NORA. Clearer than *you* could ever have given me.

KROGSTAD. Yes, being as I am such a rotten lawyer. . . .

NORA. What do you want with me?

KROGSTAD. I just wanted to see how things stood, Mrs. Helmer. I've been thinking about you all day. Even a mere money-lender, a hack journalist, a—well, even somebody like me has a bit of what you might call feeling.

NORA. Show it then. Think of my little children.

KROGSTAD. Did you or your husband think of mine? But what does it matter now? There was just one thing I wanted to say: you needn't take this business too seriously. I shan't start any proceedings, for the present.

NORA. Ah, I knew you wouldn't.

KROGSTAD. The whole thing can be arranged quite amicably. Nobody need know. Just the three of us.

NORA. My husband must never know.

KROGSTAD. How can you prevent it? Can you pay off the balance?

NORA. No, not immediately.

KROGSTAD. Perhaps you've some way of getting hold of the money in the next few days.

NORA. None I want to make use of.

KROGSTAD. Well, it wouldn't have been very much help to you if you had. Even if you stood there with the cash in your hand and to spare, you still wouldn't get your IOU back from me now.

NORA. What are you going to do with it?

KROGSTAD. Just keep it—have it in my possession. Nobody who isn't implicated need know about it. So if you are thinking of trying any desperate remedies . . .

NORA. Which I am. . . .

KROGSTAD. . . . if you happen to be thinking of running away . . .

NORA. Which I am!

KROGSTAD. . . . or anything worse . . .

NORA. How did you know?

KROGSTAD. . . . forget it!

NORA. How did you know I was thinking of *that?*

KROGSTAD. Most of us think of *that,* to begin with. I did, too; but I didn't have the courage. . . .

NORA. [*tonelessly*]. I haven't either.

KROGSTAD. [*relieved*]. So you haven't the courage either, eh?

NORA. No, I haven't! I haven't!

KROGSTAD. It would also be very stupid. There'd only be the first domestic storm to get over. . . . I've got a letter to your husband in my pocket here. . . .

NORA. And it's all in there?

KROGSTAD. In as tactful a way as possible.

NORA. [*quickly*]. He must never read that letter. Tear it up. I'll find the money somehow.

KROGSTAD. Excuse me, Mrs. Helmer, but I've just told you. . . .

NORA. I'm not talking about the money I owe you. I want to know how much you are demanding from my husband, and I'll get the money.

KROGSTAD. I want no money from your husband.

NORA. What do you want?

KROGSTAD. I'll tell you. I want to get on my feet again, Mrs. Helmer; I want to get to the top. And your husband is going to help me. For the last eighteen months I've gone straight; all that time it's been hard going; I was content to work my way up, step by step. Now I'm being kicked out, and I won't stand for being taken back again as an act of charity. I'm going to get to the top, I tell you. I'm going back into that Bank—with a better job. Your husband is going to create a new vacancy, just for me. . . .

NORA. He'll never do that!

KROGSTAD. He will do it. I know him. He'll do it without so much as a whimper. And once I'm in there with him, you'll see what's what. In less than a year I'll be his right-hand man. It'll be Nils Krogstad, not Torvald Helmer, who'll be running that Bank.

NORA. You'll never live to see that day!

KROGSTAD. You mean you . . . ?

NORA. Now I have the courage.

KROGSTAD. You can't frighten me! A precious pampered little thing like you. . . .

NORA. I'll show you! I'll show you!

KROGSTAD. Under the ice, maybe? Down in the cold, black water? Then being washed up in the spring, bloated, hairless, unrecognizable. . . .

NORA. You can't frighten me.

KROGSTAD. You can't frighten me, either. People don't do that sort of thing, Mrs. Helmer. There wouldn't be any point to it, anyway, I'd still have him right in my pocket.

NORA. Afterwards? When I'm no longer . . .

KROGSTAD. Aren't you forgetting that your reputation would then be entirely in my hands? [*Nora stands looking at him, speechless.*] Well, I've warned you. Don't do anything silly. When Helmer gets my letter, I expect to hear from him. And don't forget: it's him who is forcing me off the straight and narrow again, your own husband! That's something I'll never forgive him for. Goodbye, Mrs. Helmer.

[He goes out through the hall. NORA *crosses to the door, opens it slightly, and listens.]*

NORA. He's going. He hasn't left the letter. No, no, that would be impossible! *[Opens the door further and further.]* What's he doing? He's stopped outside. He's not going down the stairs. Has he changed his mind? Is he . . . ? *[A letter falls into the letter-box. Then Krogstad's footsteps are heard receding as he walks downstairs. Nora gives a stifled cry, runs across the room to the sofa table; pause.]* In the letter-box! *[She creeps stealthily across to the hall door.]* There it is! Torvald, Torvald! It's hopeless now!

MRS. LINDE *[comes into the room, left, carrying the costume]*. There, I think that's everything. Shall we try it on?

NORA. *[in a low, hoarse voice]*. Kristine, come here.

MRS. LINDE *[throws the dress down on the sofa]*. What's wrong with you? You look upset.

NORA. Come here. Do you see that letter? *There,* look! Through the glass in the letter-box.

MRS. LINDE. Yes, yes, I can see it.

NORA. It's a letter from Krogstad.

MRS. LINDE. Nora! It was Krogstad who lent you the money!

NORA. Yes. And now Torvald will get to know everything.

MRS. LINDE. Believe me, Nora, it's best for you both.

NORA. But there's more to it than that. I forged a signature. . . .

MRS. LINDE. Heavens above!

NORA. Listen, I want to tell you something, Kristine, so you can be my witness.

MRS. LINDE. What do you mean 'witness'? What do you want me to . . . ?

NORA. If I should go mad . . . which might easily happen . . .

MRS. LINDE. Nora!

NORA. Or if anything happened to me . . . which meant I couldn't be here. . . .

MRS. LINDE. Nora, Nora! Are you out of your mind?

NORA. And if somebody else wanted to take it all upon himself, the whole blame, you understand. . . .

MRS. LINDE. Yes, yes. But what makes you think . . . ?

NORA. Then you must testify that it isn't true, Kristine. I'm not out of my mind; I'm quite sane now. And I tell you this: nobody else knew anything, I alone was responsible for the whole thing. Remember that!

MRS. LINDE. I will. But I don't understand a word of it.

NORA. Why should you? You see something miraculous is going to happen.

MRS. LINDE. Something miraculous?

NORA. Yes, a miracle. But something so terrible as well, Kristine—oh, it must *never* happen, not for anything.

MRS. LINDE. I'm going straight over to talk to Krogstad.

NORA. Don't go. He'll only do you harm.

MRS. LINDE. There was a time when he would have done anything for me.

NORA. Him!

MRS. LINDE. Where does he live?

NORA. How do I know . . . ? Wait a minute. *[She feels in her pocket.]* Here's his card. But the letter, the letter . . . !

HELMER *[from his study, knocking on the door]*. Nora!

NORA *[cries out in terror]*. What's that? What do you want?

HELMER. Don't be frightened. We're not coming in. You've locked the door. Are you trying on?

NORA. Yes, yes, I'm trying on. It looks so nice on me, Torvald.

MRS. LINDE [*who has read the card*]. He lives just round the corner.

NORA. It's no use. It's hopeless. The letter is there in the box.

MRS. LINDE. Your husband keeps the key?

NORA. Always.

MRS. LINDE. Krogstad must ask for his letter back unread, he must find some sort of excuse. . . .

NORA. But this is just the time that Torvald generally . . .

MRS. LINDE. Put him off! Go in and keep him busy. I'll be back as soon as I can.

[*She goes out hastily by the hall door. Nora walks over to Helmer's door, opens it and peeps in.*]

NORA. Torvald!

HELMER [*in the study*]. Well, can a man get into his own living-room again now? Come along, Rank, now we'll see . . . [*In the doorway.*] But what's this?

NORA. What, Torvald dear?

HELMER. Rank led me to expect some kind of marvellous transformation.

RANK [*in the doorway*]. That's what I thought too, but I must have been mistaken.

NORA. I'm not showing myself off to anybody before tomorrow.

HELMER. Nora dear, you look tired. You haven't been practising too hard?

NORA. No, I haven't practised at all yet.

HELMER. You'll have to, though.

NORA. Yes, I certainly must, Torvald. But I just can't get anywhere without your help: I've completely forgotten it.

HELMER. We'll soon polish it up.

NORA. Yes, do help me, Torvald. Promise? I'm so nervous. All those people. . . . You must devote yourself exclusively to me this evening. Pens away! Forget all about the office! Promise me, Torvald dear!

HELMER. I promise. This evening I am wholly and entirely at your service . . . helpless little thing that you are. Oh, but while I remember, I'll just look first . . .

[*He goes towards the hall door.*]

NORA. What do you want out there?

HELMER. Just want to see if there are any letters.

NORA. No, don't, Torvald!

HELMER. Why not?

NORA. Torvald, *please!* There aren't any.

HELMER. Just let me see.

[*He starts to go. Nora, at the piano, plays the opening bars of the tarantella.*]

HELMER [*at the door, stops*]. Aha!

NORA. I shan't be able to dance tomorrow if I don't rehearse it with you.

HELMER. [*walks to her*]. Are you really so nervous, Nora dear?

NORA. Terribly nervous. Let me run through it now. There's still time before supper. Come and sit here and play for me, Torvald dear. Tell me what to do, keep me right—as you always do.

HELMER. Certainly, with pleasure, if that's what you want.

[He sits at the piano. Nora snatches the tambourine out of the box, and also a long gaily-coloured shawl which she drapes round herself, then with a bound she leaps forward.]

NORA. *[shouts].* Now play for me! Now I'll dance!

[Helmer plays and Nora dances; Dr. Rank stands at the piano behind Helmer and looks on.]

HELMER *[playing].* Not so fast! Not so fast!

NORA. I can't help it.

HELMER. Not so wild, Nora!

NORA. This is how it has to be.

HELMER *[stops].* No, no, that won't do at all.

NORA *[laughs and swings the tambourine].* Didn't I tell you?

RANK. Let me play for her.

HELMER *[gets up].* Yes, do. Then I'll be better able to tell her what to do.

[Rank sits down at the piano and plays. Nora dances more and more wildly. Helmer stands by the stove giving her repeated directions as she dances; she does not seem to hear them. Her hair comes undone and falls about her shoulders; she pays no attention and goes on dancing. Mrs. Linde enters.]

MRS. LINDE *[standing as though spellbound in the doorway].* Ah . . . !

NORA *[dancing].* See what fun we are having, Kristine.

HELMER. But my dear darling Nora, you are dancing as though your life depended on it.

NORA. It does.

HELMER. Stop, Rank! This is sheer madness. Stop, I say.

[Rank stops playing and Nora comes to a sudden halt.]

HELMER *[crosses to her].* I would never have believed it. You have forgotten everything I ever taught you.

NORA *[throwing away the tambourine].* There you are, you see.

HELMER. Well, some more instruction is certainly needed there.

NORA. Yes, you see how necessary it is. You must go on coaching me right up to the last minute. Promise me, Torvald?

HELMER. You can rely on me.

NORA. You mustn't think about anything else but me until after tomorrow . . . mustn't open any letters . . . mustn't touch the letter-box.

HELMER. Ah, you are still frightened of what that man might . . .

NORA. Yes, yes, I am.

HELMER. I can see from your face there's already a letter there from him.

NORA. I don't know. I think so. But you mustn't read anything like that now. We don't want anything horrid coming between us until all this is over.

RANK *[softly to Helmer].* I shouldn't cross her.

HELMER *[puts his arm round her].* The child must have her way. But tomorrow night, when your dance is done. . . .

NORA. Then you are free.

MAID *[in the doorway, right].* Dinner is served, madam.

NORA. We'll have champagne, Helene.

MAID. Very good, madam.

[She goes.]

HELMER. Aha! It's to be quite a banquet, eh?

NORA. With champagne flowing until dawn. [*Shouts.*] And some macaroons, Helene . . . lots of them, for once in a while.

HELMER [*seizing her hands*]. Now, now, not so wild and excitable! Let me see you being my own little singing bird again.

NORA. Oh yes, I will. And if you'll just go in . . . you, too, Dr. Rank. Kristine, you must help me to do my hair.

RANK [*softly, as they leave*]. There isn't anything . . . anything as it were, impending, is there?

HELMER. No, not at all, my dear fellow. It's nothing but these childish fears I was telling you about.

[They go out to the right.]

NORA. Well?

MRS. LINDE. He's left town.

NORA. I saw it in your face.

MRS. LINDE. He's coming back tomorrow evening. I left a note for him.

NORA. You shouldn't have done that. You must let things take their course. Because really it's a case for rejoicing, waiting like this for the miracle.

MRS. LINDE. What is it you are waiting for?

NORA. Oh, you wouldn't understand. Go and join the other two. I'll be there in a minute.

[Mrs. Linde goes into the dining-room. Nora stands for a moment as though to collect herself, then looks at her watch.]

NORA. Five. Seven hours to midnight. Then twenty-four hours till the next midnight. Then the tarantella will be over. Twenty-four and seven? Thirty-one hours to live.

HELMER [*in the doorway, right*]. What's happened to our little sky-lark?

NORA [*running towards him with open arms*]. Here she is!

Act III

The same room. The round table has been moved to the centre of the room, and the chairs placed round it. A lamp is burning on the table. The door to the hall stands open. Dance music can be heard coming from the floor above. Mrs. Linde is sitting by the table, idly turning over the pages of a book; she tries to read, but does not seem able to concentrate. Once or twice she listens, tensely, for a sound at the front door.

MRS. LINDE [*looking at her watch*]. Still not here. There isn't much time left. I only hope he hasn't . . . [*She listens again.*] Ah, there he is. [*She goes out into the hall, and cautiously opens the front door. Soft footsteps can be heard on the stairs. She whispers.*] Come in. There's nobody here.

KROGSTAD [*in the doorway*]. I found a note from you at home. What does it all mean?

MRS. LINDE. I *had* to talk to you.

KROGSTAD. Oh? And did it have to be here, in this house?

MRS. LINDE. It wasn't possible over at my place, it hasn't a separate entrance. Come in. We are quite alone. The maid's asleep and the Helmers are at a party upstairs.

KROGSTAD [*comes into the room*]. Well, well! So the Helmers are out dancing tonight! Really?

MRS. LINDE. Yes, why not?

KROGSTAD. Why not indeed!

MRS. LINDE. Well then, Nils. Let's talk.

KROGSTAD. Have we two anything more to talk about?

MRS. LINDE. We have a great deal to talk about.

KROGSTAD. I shouldn't have thought so.

MRS. LINDE. That's because you never really understood me.

KROGSTAD. What else was there to understand, apart from the old, old story? A heartless woman throws a man over the moment something more profitable offers itself.

MRS. LINDE. Do you really think I'm so heartless? Do you think I found it easy to break it off.

KROGSTAD. Didn't you?

MRS. LINDE. You didn't really believe that?

KROGSTAD. If that wasn't the case, why did you write to me as you did?

MRS. LINDE. There was nothing else I could do. If I had to make the break, I felt in duty bound to destroy any feeling that you had for me.

KROGSTAD [*clenching his hands*]. So that's how it was. And all that . . . was for money!

MRS. LINDE. You mustn't forget I had a helpless mother and two young brothers. We couldn't wait for you, Nils. At that time you hadn't much immediate prospect of anything.

KROGSTAD. That may be. But you had no right to throw me over for somebody else.

MRS. LINDE. Well, I don't know. Many's the time I've asked myself whether I was justified.

KROGSTAD [*more quietly*]. When I lost you, it was just as if the ground had slipped away from under my feet. Look at me now: a broken man clinging to the wreck of his life.

MRS. LINDE. Help might be near.

KROGSTAD. It was near. Then you came along and got in the way.

MRS. LINDE. Quite without knowing, Nils. I only heard today it's you I'm supposed to be replacing at the Bank.

KROGSTAD. If you say so, I believe you. But now you do know, aren't you going to withdraw?

MRS. LINDE. No, that wouldn't benefit you in the slightest.

KROGSTAD. Benefit, benefit . . . ! I would do it just the same.

MRS. LINDE. I have learned to go carefully. Life and hard, bitter necessity have taught me that.

KROGSTAD. And life has taught me not to believe in pretty speeches.

MRS. LINDE. Then life has taught you a very sensible thing. But deeds are something you surely must believe in?

KROGSTAD. How do you mean?

MRS. LINDE. You said you were like a broken man clinging to the wreck of his life.

KROGSTAD. And I said it with good reason.

MRS. LINDE. And I am like a broken woman clinging to the wreck of her life. Nobody to care about, and nobody to care for.

KROGSTAD. It was your own choice.

MRS. LINDE. At the time there was no other choice.

KROGSTAD. Well, what of it?

MRS. LINDE. Nils, what about us two castaways joining forces.

KROGSTAD. What's that you say?

MRS. LINDE. Two of us on one wreck surely stand a better chance than each on his own.

KROGSTAD. Kristine!

MRS. LINDE. Why do you suppose I came to town?

KROGSTAD. You mean, you thought of me?

MRS. LINDE. Without work I couldn't live. All my life I have worked, for as long as I can remember; that has always been my one great joy. But now I'm completely alone in the world, and feeling horribly empty and forlorn. There's no pleasure in working only for yourself. Nils, give me somebody and something to work for.

KROGSTAD. I don't believe all this. It's only a woman's hysteria, wanting to be all magnanimous and self-sacrificing.

MRS. LINDE. Have you ever known me hysterical before?

KROGSTAD. Would you really do this? Tell me—do you know all about my past?

MRS. LINDE. Yes.

KROGSTAD. And you know what people think about me?

MRS. LINDE. Just now you hinted you thought you might have been a different person with me.

KROGSTAD. I'm convinced I would.

MRS. LINDE. Couldn't it still happen?

KROGSTAD. Kristine! You know what you are saying, don't you? Yes, you do. I can see you do. Have you really the courage . . . ?

MRS. LINDE. I need someone to mother, and your children need a mother. We two need each other. Nils, I have faith in what, deep down, you are. With you I can face anything.

KROGSTAD [seizing her hands]. Thank you, thank you, Kristine. And I'll soon have everybody looking up to me, or I'll know the reason why. Ah, but I was forgetting. . . .

MRS. LINDE. Hush! The tarantella! You must go!

KROGSTAD. Why? What is it?

MRS. LINDE. You hear that dance upstairs? When it's finished they'll be coming.

KROGSTAD. Yes, I'll go. It's too late to do anything. Of course, you know nothing about what steps I've taken against the Helmers.

MRS. LINDE. Yes, Nils, I do know.

KROGSTAD. Yet you still want to go on. . . .

MRS. LINDE. I know how far a man like you can be driven by despair.

KROGSTAD. Oh, if only I could undo what I've done!

MRS. LINDE. You still can. Your letter is still there in the box.

KROGSTAD. Are you sure?

MRS. LINDE. Quite sure. But . . .

KROGSTAD [regards her searchingly]. Is that how things are? You want to save your friend at any price? Tell me straight. Is that it?

MRS. LINDE. When you've sold yourself once for other people's sake, you don't do it again.

KROGSTAD. I shall demand my letter back.

MRS. LINDE. No, no.

KROGSTAD. Of course I will, I'll wait here till Helmer comes. I'll tell him he has to give me my letter back . . . that it's only about my notice . . . that he mustn't read it. . . .

MRS. LINDE. No, Nils, don't ask for it back.

KROGSTAD. But wasn't that the very reason you got me here?

MRS. LINDE. Yes, that was my first terrified reaction. But that was yesterday, and it's quite incredible the things I've witnessed in this house in the last twenty-four hours. Helmer must know everything. This unhappy secret must come out. Those two must have the whole thing out between them. All this secrecy and deception, it just can't go on.

KROGSTAD. Well, if you want to risk it. . . . But one thing I can do, and I'll do it at once. . . .

MRS. LINDE [*listening*]. Hurry! Go, go! The dance has stopped. We aren't safe a moment longer.

KROGSTAD. I'll wait for you downstairs.

MRS. LINDE. Yes, do. You must see me home.

KROGSTAD. I've never been so incredibly happy before.

[*He goes out by the front door. The door out into the hall remains standing open.*]

MRS. LINDE [*tidies the room a little and gets her hat and coat ready*]. How things change! How things change! Somebody to work for . . . to live for. A home to bring happiness into. Just let me get down to it. . . . I wish they'd come. . . . [*Listens.*] Ah, there they are. . . . Get my things.

[*She takes her coat and hat. The voices of Helmer and Nora are heard outside. A key is turned and Helmer pushes Nora almost forcibly into the hall. She is dressed in the Italian costume, with a big black shawl over it. He is in evening dress, and over it a black cloak, open.*]

NORA [*still in the doorway, reluctantly*]. No, no, not in here! I want to go back up again. I don't want to leave so early.

HELMER. But my dearest Nora . . .

NORA. Oh, please, Torvald, I beg you. . . . *Please,* just for another hour.

HELMER. Not another minute, Nora my sweet. You remember what we agreed. There now, come along in. You'll catch cold standing there.

[*He leads her, in spite of her resistance, gently but firmly into the room.*]

MRS. LINDE. Good evening.

NORA. Kristine!

HELMER. Why, Mrs. Linde. You here so late?

MRS. LINDE. Yes. You must forgive me but I did so want to see Nora all dressed up.

NORA. Have you been sitting here waiting for me?

MRS. LINDE. Yes, I'm afraid I wasn't in time to catch you before you went upstairs. And I felt I couldn't leave again without seeing you.

HELMER [*removing Nora's shawl*]. Well take a good look at her. I think I can say she's worth looking at. Isn't she lovely, Mrs. Linde?

MRS. LINDE. Yes, I must say. . . .

HELMER. Isn't she quite extraordinarily lovely? That's what everybody at the party thought, too. But she's dreadfully stubborn . . . the sweet little thing! And what shall we do about that? Would you believe it, I nearly had to use force to get her away.

NORA. Oh Torvald, you'll be sorry you didn't let me stay, even for half an hour.

HELMER. You hear that, Mrs. Linde? She dances her tarantella, there's wild applause—which was well deserved, although the performance was perhaps rather realistic . . . I mean, rather more so than was strictly necessary from the artistic point of view. But anyway! The main thing is she was a success, a tremendous success. Was I supposed to let her stay after that? Spoil the effect? No thank you! I took my lovely little Capri girl—my capricious little Capri girl, I might say—by the arm, whisked her once round the room, a curtsey all round, and then—as they say in novels—the beautiful vision vanished. An exit should always be effective, Mrs. Linde. But I just can't get Nora to see that. Phew! It's warm in here. [*He throws his cloak over a chair and opens the door to his study.*] What? It's dark. Oh yes, of course. Excuse me . . . .

[*He goes in and lights a few candles.*]

NORA [*quickly, in a breathless whisper*]. Well?

MRS. LINDE [*softly*]. I've spoken to him.

NORA. And . . . ?

MRS. LINDE. Nora . . . you must tell your husband everything.

NORA [*tonelessly*]. I knew it.

MRS. LINDE. You've got nothing to fear from Krogstad. But you must speak.

NORA. I won't.

MRS. LINDE. Then the letter will.

NORA. Thank you, Kristine. Now I know what's to be done. Hush . . . !

HELMER [*comes in again*]. Well, Mrs. Linde, have you finished admiring her?

MRS. LINDE. Yes. And now I must say good night.

HELMER. Oh, already? Is this yours, this knitting?

MRS. LINDE [*takes it*]. Yes, thank you. I nearly forgot it.

HELMER. So you knit, eh?

MRS. LINDE. Yes.

HELMER. You should embroider instead, you know.

MRS. LINDE. Oh? Why?

HELMER. So much prettier. Watch! You hold the embroidery like this in the left hand, and then you take the needle in the right hand, like this, and you describe a long, graceful curve. Isn't that right?

MRS. LINDE. Yes, I suppose so. . . .

HELMER. Whereas knitting on the other hand just can't help being ugly. Look! Arms pressed into the sides, the knitting needles going up and down—there's something Chinese about it. . . . Ah, that was marvellous champagne they served tonight.

MRS. LINDE. Well, good night, Nora! And stop being so stubborn.

HELMER. Well said, Mrs. Linde!

MRS. LINDE. Good night, Mr. Helmer.

HELMER [*accompanying her to the door*]. Good night, good night! You'll get home all right, I hope? I'd be only too pleased to. . . . But you haven't far to walk. Good night, good night! [*She goes; he shuts the door behind her and comes in again.*] There we are, got rid of her at last. She's a frightful bore, that woman.

NORA. Aren't you very tired, Torvald?

HELMER. Not in the least.

NORA. Not sleepy?

HELMER. Not at all. On the contrary, I feel extremely lively. What about you? Yes, you look quite tired and sleepy.

NORA. Yes, I'm very tired. I just want to fall straight off to sleep.

HELMER. There you are, you see! Wasn't I right in thinking we shouldn't stay any longer.

NORA. Oh, everything you do is right.

HELMER [*kissing her forehead*]. There's my little sky-lark talking common sense. Did you notice how gay Rank was this evening?

NORA. Oh, was he? I didn't get a chance to talk to him.

HELMER. I hardly did either. But it's a long time since I saw him in such a good mood. [*Looks at Nora for a moment or two, then comes nearer her.*] Ah, it's wonderful to be back in our own home again, and quite alone with you. How irresistibly lovely you are, Nora!

NORA. Don't look at me like that, Torvald!

HELMER. Can't I look at my most treasured possession? At all this loveliness that's mine and mine alone, completely and utterly mine.

NORA. [*walks round to the other side of the table*]. You mustn't talk to me like that tonight.

HELMER [*following her*]. You still have the tarantella in your blood, I see. And that makes you even more desirable. Listen! The guests are beginning to leave now. [*Softly.*] Nora . . . soon the whole house will be silent.

NORA. I should hope so.

HELMER. Of course you do, don't you, Nora my darling? You know, whenever I'm out at a party with you . . . do you know why I never talk to you very much, why I always stand away from you and only steal a quick glance at you now and then . . . do you know why I do that? It's because I'm pretending we are secretly in love, secretly engaged and nobody suspects there is anything between us.

NORA. Yes, yes. I know your thoughts are always with me, of course.

HELMER. And when it's time to go, and I lay your shawl round those shapely, young shoulders, round the exquisite curve of your neck . . . I pretend that you are my young bride, that we are just leaving our wedding, that I am taking you to our new home for the first time . . . to be alone with you for the first time . . . quite alone with your young and trembling loveliness! All evening I've been longing for you, and nothing else. And as I watched you darting and swaying in the tarantella, my blood was on fire . . . I couldn't bear it any longer . . . and that's why I brought you down here with me so early. . . .

NORA. Go away, Torvald! Please leave me alone. I won't have it.

HELMER. What's this? It's just your little game isn't it, my little Nora. Won't! Won't! Am I not your husband . . . ?

[*There is a knock on the front door.*]

NORA [*startled*]. Listen . . . !

HELMER [*going towards the hall*]. Who's there?

RANK [*outside*]. It's me. Can I come in for a minute?

HELMER [*in a low voice, annoyed*]. Oh, what does he want now? [*Aloud*] Wait a moment. [*He walks across and opens the door.*] How nice of you to look in on your way out.

RANK. I fancied I heard your voice and I thought I would just look in. [*He takes a quick glance round.*] Ah yes, this dear, familiar old place! How cosy and comfortable you've got things here, you two.

HELMER. You seemed to be having a pretty good time upstairs yourself.

RANK. Capital! Why shouldn't I? Why not make the most of things in this world? At least as much as one can, and for as long as one can. The wine was excellent. . . .

HELMER. Especially the champagne.

RANK. You noticed that too, did you? It's incredible the amount I was able to put away.

NORA. Torvald also drank a lot of champagne this evening.

RANK. Oh?

NORA. Yes, and that always makes him quite merry.

RANK. Well, why shouldn't a man allow himself a jolly evening after a day well spent?

HELMER. Well spent? I'm afraid I can't exactly claim that.

RANK [clapping him on the shoulder]. But I can, you see!

NORA. Dr. Rank, am I right in thinking you carried out a certain laboratory test today?

RANK. Exactly.

HELMER. Look at our little Nora talking about laboratory tests!

NORA. And may I congratulate you on the result?

RANK. You may indeed.

NORA. So it was good?

RANK. The best possible, for both doctor and patient—certainty!

NORA [quickly and searchingly]. Certainty?

RANK. Absolute certainty. So why shouldn't I allow myself a jolly evening after that?

NORA. Quite right, Dr. Rank.

HELMER. I quite agree. As long as you don't suffer for it in the morning.

RANK. Well, you never get anything for nothing in this life.

NORA. Dr. Rank . . . you are very fond of masquerades, aren't you?

RANK. Yes, when there are plenty of amusing disguises. . . .

NORA. Tell me, what shall we two go as next time?

HELMER. There's frivolity for you . . . thinking about the next time already!

RANK. We two? I'll tell you. You must go as Lady Luck. . . .

HELMER. Yes, but how do you find a costume to suggest *that?*

RANK. Your wife could simply go in her everyday clothes. . . .

HELMER. That was nicely said. But don't you know what you would be?

RANK. Yes, my dear friend, I know exactly what I shall be.

HELMER. Well?

RANK. At the next masquerade, I shall be invisible.

HELMER. That's a funny idea!

RANK. There's a big black cloak . . . haven't you heard of the cloak of invisibility? That comes right down over you, and then nobody can see you.

HELMER [suppressing a smile]. Of course, that's right.

RANK. But I'm clean forgetting what I came for. Helmer, give me a cigar, one of the dark Havanas.

HELMER. With the greatest of pleasure.

[He offers his case.]

RANK [takes one and cuts the end off]. Thanks.

NORA [strikes a match]. Let me give you a light.

RANK. Thank you. [She holds out the match and he lights his cigar.] And now, goodbye!

HELMER. Goodbye, goodbye, my dear fellow!

NORA. Sleep well, Dr. Rank.

RANK. Thank you for that wish.

NORA. Wish me the same.

RANK. You? All right, if you want me to. . . . Sleep well. And thanks for the light.

[He nods to them both, and goes.]

HELMER *[subdued]*. He's had a lot to drink.
NORA *[absently]*. Very likely.

[Helmer takes a bunch of keys out of his pocket and goes out into the hall.]

NORA. Torvald . . . what do you want there?
HELMER. I must empty the letter-box, it's quite full. There'll be no room for the papers in the morning. . . .
NORA. Are you going to work tonight?
HELMER. You know very well I'm not. Hello, what's this? Somebody's been at the lock.
NORA. At the lock?
HELMER. Yes, I'm sure of it. Why should that be? I'd hardly have thought the maids . . . ? Here's a broken hair-pin. Nora, it's one of yours. . . .
NORA *[quickly]*. It must have been the children. . . .
HELMER. Then you'd better tell them not to. Ah . . . there . . . I've managed to get it open. *[He takes the things out and shouts into the kitchen.]* Helene! . . . Helene, put the light out in the hall. *[He comes into the room again with the letters in his hand and shuts the hall door.]* Look how it all mounts up. *[Runs through them.]* What's this?
NORA. The letter! Oh no, Torvald, no!
HELMER. Two visiting cards . . . from Dr. Rank.
NORA. From Dr. Rank?
HELMER *[looking at them]*. Dr. Rank, Medical Practitioner. They were on top. He must have put them in as he left.
NORA. Is there anything on them?
HELMER. There's a black cross above his name. Look. What an uncanny idea. It's just as if he were announcing his own death.
NORA. He is.
HELMER. What? What do you know about it? Has he said anything to you?
NORA. Yes. He said when these cards came, he would have taken his last leave of us. He was going to shut himself up and die.
HELMER. Poor fellow! Of course I knew we couldn't keep him with us very long. But so soon. . . . And hiding himself away like a wounded animal.
NORA. When it has to happen, it's best that it should happen without words. Don't you think so, Torvald?
HELMER *[walking up and down]*. He had grown so close to us. I don't think I can imagine him gone. His suffering and his loneliness seemed almost to provide a background of dark cloud to the sunshine of our lives. Well, perhaps it's all for the best. For him at any rate. *[Pauses.]* And maybe for us as well, Nora. Now there's just the two of us. *[Puts his arms round her.]* Oh, my darling wife, I can't hold you close enough. You know, Nora . . . many's the time I wish you were threatened by some terrible danger so I could risk everything, body and soul, for your sake.
NORA *[tears herself free and says firmly and decisively]*. Now you must read your letters, Torvald.
HELMER. No, no, not tonight. I want to be with you, my darling wife.

NORA. Knowing all the time your friend is dying . . . ?

HELMER. You are right. It's been a shock to both of us. This ugly thing has come between us . . . thoughts of death and decay. We must try to free ourselves from it. Until then . . . we shall go our separate ways.

NORA [*her arms round his neck*]. Torvald . . . good night! Good night!

HELMER [*kisses her forehead*]. Goodnight, my little singing bird. Sleep well, Nora, I'll just read through my letters.

[He takes the letters into his room and shuts the door behind him.]

NORA [*gropes around her, wild-eyed, seizes Helmer's cloak, wraps it round herself, and whispers quickly, hoarsely, spasmodically*]. Never see him again. Never, never, never. [*Throws her shawl over her head.*] And never see the children again either. Never, never. Oh, that black icy water. Oh, that bottomless . . . ! If only it were all over! He's got it now. Now he's reading it. Oh no, no! Not yet! Torvald, goodbye . . . and my children . . . .

[She rushes out in the direction of the hall; at the same moment Helmer flings open his door and stands there with an open letter in his hand.]

HELMER. Nora!

NORA [*shrieks*]. Ah!

HELMER. What is this? Do you know what is in this letter?

NORA. Yes, I know. Let me go! Let me out!

HELMER [*holds her back*]. Where are you going?

NORA [*trying to tear herself free*]. You mustn't try to save me, Torvald!

HELMER [*reels back*]. True! Is it true what he writes? How dreadful! No, no, it can't possibly be true.

NORA. It *is* true. I loved you more than anything else in the world.

HELMER. Don't come to me with a lot of paltry excuses!

NORA [*taking a step towards him*]. Torvald . . . !

HELMER. Miserable woman . . . what is this you have done?

NORA. Let me go. I won't have you taking the blame for me. You mustn't take it on yourself.

HELMER. Stop play-acting! [*Locks the front door.*] You are staying here to give an account of yourself. Do you understand what you have done? Answer me! Do you understand?

NORA [*looking fixedly at him, her face hardening*]. Yes, now I'm really beginning to understand.

HELMER [*walking up and down*]. Oh, what a terrible awakening this is. All these eight years . . . this woman who was my pride and joy . . . a hypocrite, a liar, worse than that, a criminal! Oh, how utterly squalid it all is! Ugh! Ugh! [*Nora remains silent and looks fixedly at him.*] I should have realized something like this would happen. I should have seen it coming. All your father's irresponsible ways. . . . Quiet! All your father's irresponsible ways are coming out in you. No religion, no morals, no sense of duty. . . . Oh, this is my punishment for turning a blind eye to him. It was for your sake I did it, and this is what I get for it.

NORA. Yes, this.

HELMER. Now you have ruined my entire happiness, jeopardized my whole future. It's terrible to think of. Here I am, at the mercy of a thoroughly unscrupulous person; he can do whatever he likes with me, demand anything he wants, order me about just as he chooses . . . and I daren't even whimper. I'm done for, a miserable failure, and it's all the fault of a feather-brained woman!

NORA. When I've left this world behind, you will be free.

HELMER. Oh, stop pretending! Your father was just the same, always ready with fine phrases. What good would it do me if you left this world behind, as you put it? Not the slightest bit of good. He can still let it all come out, if he likes; and if he does, people might even suspect me of being an accomplice in these criminal acts of yours. They might even think I was the one behind it all, that it was I who pushed you into it! And it's you I have to thank for this . . . and when I've taken such good care of you, all our married life. Now do you understand what you have done to me?

NORA [*coldly and calmly*]. Yes.

HELMER. I just can't understand it, it's so incredible. But we must see about putting things right. Take that shawl off. Take it off, I tell you! I must see if I can't find some way or other of appeasing him. The thing must be hushed up at all costs. And as far as you and I are concerned, things must appear to go on exactly as before. But only in the eyes of the world, of course. In other words you'll go on living here; that's understood. But you will not be allowed to bring up the children, I can't trust you with them. . . . Oh, that I should have to say this to the woman I loved so dearly, the woman I still. . . . Well, that must be all over and done with. From now on, there can be no question of happiness. All we can do is save the bits and pieces from the wreck, preserve appearances. . . . [*The front door-bell rings. Helmer gives a start.*] What's that? So late? How terrible, supposing. . . . If he should . . . ? Hide, Nora! Say you are not well.

[*Nora stands motionless. Helmer walks across and opens the door into the hall.*]

MAID [*half dressed, in the hall*]. It's a note for Mrs. Helmer.

HELMER. Give it to me. [*He snatches the note and shuts the door.*] Yes, it's from him. You can't have it. I want to read it myself.

NORA. You read it then.

HELMER [*by the lamp*]. I hardly dare. Perhaps this is the end, for both of us. Well, I must know. [*He opens the note hurriedly, reads a few lines, looks at another enclosed sheet, and gives a cry of joy.*] Nora! [*Nora looks at him inquiringly.*] Nora! I must read it again. Yes, yes, it's true! I am saved! Nora, I am saved!

NORA. And me?

HELMER. You too, of course, we are both saved, you as well as me. Look, he's sent your IOU back. He sends his regrets and apologies for what he has done. . . . His luck has changed. . . . Oh, what does it matter what he says. We are saved, Nora! Nobody can do anything to you now. Oh, Nora, Nora . . . but let's get rid of this disgusting thing first. Let me see. . . . [*He glances at the IOU.*] No, I don't want to see it. I don't want it to be anything but a dream. [*He tears up the IOU and both letters, throws all the pieces into the stove and watches them burn.*] Well, that's the end of that. He said in his note you'd known since Christmas Eve. . . . You must have had three terrible days of it, Nora.

NORA. These three days haven't been easy.

HELMER. The agonies you must have gone through! When the only way out seemed to be. . . . No, let's forget the whole ghastly thing. We can rejoice and say: It's all over! It's all over! Listen to me, Nora! You don't seem to understand: it's all over! Why this grim look on your face? Oh, poor little Nora, of course I understand. You can't bring yourself to believe I've forgiven you. But I have, Nora, I swear it. I forgive you everything. I know you did what you did because you loved me.

NORA. That's true.

HELMER. You loved me as a wife should love her husband. It was simply that you didn't have the experience to judge what was the best way of going about things. But do you think I love you any the less for that; just because you don't know how to act on your own responsibility? No, no, you just lean on me, I shall give you all the advice and guidance you need. I wouldn't be a proper man if I didn't find a woman doubly attractive for being so obviously helpless. You mustn't dwell on the harsh things I said in that first moment of horror, when I thought everything was going to come crashing down about my ears. I have forgiven you, Nora, I swear it! I have forgiven you!

NORA. Thank you for your forgiveness.

[She goes out through the door, right.]

HELMER. No, don't go! [He looks through the doorway.] What are you doing in the spare room?

NORA. Taking off this fancy dress.

HELMER [standing at the open door]. Yes, do. You try and get some rest, and set your mind at peace again, my frightened little song-bird. Have a good long sleep; you know you are safe and sound under my wing. [Walks up and down near the door.] What a nice, cosy little home we have here, Nora! Here you can find refuge. Here I shall hold you like a hunted dove I have rescued unscathed from the cruel talons of the hawk, and calm your poor beating heart. And that will come, gradually, Nora, believe me. Tomorrow you'll see everything quite differently. Soon everything will be just as it was before. You won't need me to keep on telling you I've forgiven you; you'll feel convinced of it in your own heart. You don't really imagine me ever thinking of turning you out, or even of reproaching you? Oh, a real man isn't made that way, you know, Nora. For a man, there's something indescribably moving and very satisfying in knowing that he has forgiven his wife—forgiven her, completely and genuinely, from the depths of his heart. It's as though it made her his property in a double sense: he has, as it were, given her a new life, and she becomes in a way both his wife and at the same time his child. That is how you will seem to me after today, helpless, perplexed little thing that you are. Don't you worry your pretty little head about anything, Nora. Just you be frank with me, and I'll take all the decisions for you. . . . What's this? Not in bed? You've changed your things?

NORA [in her everyday dress]. Yes, Torvald, I've changed.

HELMER. What for? It's late.

NORA. I shan't sleep tonight.

HELMER. But my dear Nora. . . .

NORA [looks at her watch]. It's not so terribly late. Sit down, Torvald. We two have a lot to talk about.

[She sits down at one side of the table.]

HELMER. Nora, what is all this? Why so grim?

NORA. Sit down. It'll take some time. I have a lot to say to you.

HELMER *[sits down at the table opposite her]*. You frighten me, Nora. I don't understand you.

NORA. Exactly. You don't understand me. And I have never understood you, either—until tonight. No, don't interrupt. I just want you to listen to what I have to say. We are going to have things out, Torvald.

HELMER. What do you mean?

NORA. Isn't there anything that strikes you about the way we two are sitting here?

HELMER. What's that?

NORA. We have now been married eight years. Hasn't it struck you this is the first time you and I, man and wife, have had a serious talk together?

HELMER. Depends what you mean by 'serious.'

NORA. Eight whole years—no, more, ever since we first knew each other—and never have we exchanged one serious word about serious things.

HELMER. What did you want me to do? Get you involved in worries that you couldn't possibly help me to bear?

NORA. I'm not talking about worries. I say we've never once sat down together and seriously tried to get to the bottom of anything.

HELMER. But, my dear Nora, would that have been a thing for you?

NORA. That's just it. You have never understood me . . . I've been greatly wronged, Torvald. First by my father, and then by you.

HELMER. What! Us two! The two people who loved you more than anybody?

NORA *[shakes her head]*. You two never loved me. You only thought how nice it was to be in love with me.

HELMER. But, Nora, what's this you are saying?

NORA. It's right, you know, Torvald. At home, Daddy used to tell me what he thought, then I thought the same. And if I thought differently, I kept quiet about it, because he wouldn't have liked it. He used to call me his baby doll, and he played with me as I used to play with my dolls. Then I came to live in your house. . . .

HELMER. What way is that to talk about our marriage?

NORA *[imperturbably]*. What I mean is: I passed out of Daddy's hands into yours. You arranged everything to your tastes, and I acquired the same tastes. Or I pretended to . . . I don't really know . . . I think it was a bit of both, sometimes one thing and sometimes the other. When I look back, it seems to me I have been living here like a beggar, from hand to mouth. I lived by doing tricks for you, Torvald. But that's the way you wanted it. You and Daddy did me a great wrong. It's your fault that I've never made anything of my life.

HELMER. Nora, how unreasonable . . . how ungrateful you are! Haven't you been happy here?

NORA. No, never. I thought I was, but I wasn't really.

HELMER. Not . . . not happy!

NORA. No, just gay. And you've always been so kind to me. But our house has never been anything but a play-room. I have been your doll wife, just as at home I was Daddy's doll child. And the children in turn have been my dolls. I thought it was fun when you came and played with me, just as they thought it was fun when I went and played with them. That's been our marriage, Torvald.

HELMER. There is some truth in what you say, exaggerated and hysterical though it is. But from now on it will be different. Play-time is over; now comes the time for lessons.

NORA. Whose lessons? Mine or the children's?

HELMER. Both yours and the children's, my dear Nora.

NORA. Ah, Torvald, you are not the man to teach me to be a good wife for you.

HELMER. How can you say that?

NORA. And what sort of qualifications have I to teach the children?

HELMER. Nora!

NORA. Didn't you say yourself, a minute or two ago, that you couldn't trust me with that job.

HELMER. In the heat of the moment! You shouldn't pay any attention to that.

NORA. On the contrary, you were quite right. I'm not up to it. There's another problem needs solving first. I must take steps to educate myself. You are not the man to help me there. That's something I must do on my own. That's why I'm leaving you.

HELMER [*jumps up*]. What did you say?

NORA. If I'm ever to reach any understanding of myself and the things around me, I must learn to stand alone. That's why I can't stay here with you any longer.

HELMER. Nora! Nora!

NORA. I'm leaving here at once. I dare say Kristine will put me up for tonight. . . .

HELMER. You are out of your mind! I won't let you! I forbid you!

NORA. It's no use forbidding me anything now. I'm taking with me my own personal belongings. I don't want anything of yours, either now or later.

HELMER. This is madness!

NORA. Tomorrow I'm going home—to what used to be my home, I mean. It will be easier for me to find something to do there.

HELMER. Oh, you blind, inexperienced . . .

NORA. I must set about *getting* experience, Torvald.

HELMER. And leave your home, your husband and your children? Don't you care what people will say?

NORA. That's no concern of mine. All I know is that this is necessary for me.

HELMER. This is outrageous! You are betraying your most sacred duty.

NORA. And what do you consider to be my most sacred duty?

HELMER. Does it take me to tell you that? Isn't it your duty to your husband and your children?

NORA. I have another duty equally sacred.

HELMER. You have not. What duty might *that* be?

NORA. My duty to myself.

HELMER. First and foremost, you are a wife and mother.

NORA. That I don't believe any more. I believe that first and foremost I am an individual, just as much as you are—or at least I'm going to try to be. I know most people agree with you, Torvald, and that's also what it says in books. But I'm not content any more with what most people say, or with what it says in books. I have to think things out for myself, and get things clear.

HELMER. Surely you are clear about your position in your own home? Haven't you an infallible guide in questions like these? Haven't you your religion?

NORA. Oh, Torvald, I don't really know what religion is.

HELMER. What do you say!

NORA. All I know is what Pastor Hansen said when I was confirmed. He said religion was this, that and the other. When I'm away from all this and on my own, I'll go into that, too. I want to find out whether what Pastor Hansen told me was right—or at least whether it's right for *me*.

HELMER. This is incredible talk from a young woman! But if religion cannot keep you on the right path, let me at least stir your conscience. I suppose you do have some moral sense? Or tell me—perhaps you don't?

NORA. Well, Torvald, that's not easy to say. I simply don't know. I'm really very confused about such things. All I know is my ideas about such things are very different from yours. I've also learnt that the law is different from what I thought; but I simply can't get it into my head that that particular law is right. Apparently a woman has no right to spare her old father on his deathbed, or to save her husband's life, even. I just don't believe it.

HELMER. You are talking like a child. You understand nothing about the society you live in.

NORA. No, I don't. But I shall go into that too. I must try to discover who is right, society or me.

HELMER. You are ill, Nora. You are delirious. I'm half inclined to think you are out of your mind.

NORA. Never have I felt so calm and collected as I do tonight.

HELMER. Calm and collected enough to leave your husband and children?

NORA. Yes.

HELMER. Then only one explanation is possible.

NORA. And that is?

HELMER. You don't love me any more.

NORA. Exactly.

HELMER. Nora! Can you say that!

NORA. I'm desperately sorry, Torvald. Because you have always been so kind to me. But I can't help it. I don't love you any more.

HELMER [*struggling to keep his composure*]. Is that also a 'calm and collected' decision you've made?

NORA. Yes, absolutely calm and collected. That's why I don't want to stay here.

HELMER. And can you also account for how I forfeited your love?

NORA. Yes, very easily. It was tonight, when the miracle didn't happen. It was then I realized you weren't the man I thought you were.

HELMER. Explain yourself more clearly. I don't understand.

NORA. For eight years I have been patiently waiting. Because, heavens, I knew miracles didn't happen every day. Then this devastating business started, and I became absolutely convinced the miracle *would* happen. All the time Krogstad's letter lay there, it never so much as crossed my mind that you would ever submit to that man's conditions. I was absolutely convinced you would say to him: Tell the whole wide world if you like. And when that was done . . .

HELMER. Yes, then what? After I had exposed my own wife to dishonour and shame . . . !

NORA. When that was done, I was absolutely convinced you would come forward and take everything on yourself, and say: I am the guilty one.

HELMER. Nora!

NORA. You mean I'd never let you make such a sacrifice for my sake? Of course not. But what would my story have counted for against yours?—That was the miracle I went in hope and dread of. It was to prevent it that I was ready to end my life.

HELMER. I would gladly toil day and night for you, Nora, enduring all manner of sorrow and distress. But nobody sacrifices his *honour* for the one he loves.

NORA. Hundreds and thousands of women have.

HELMER. Oh, you think and talk like a stupid child.

NORA. All right. But you neither think nor talk like the man I would want to share my life with. When you had got over your fright—and you weren't concerned about me but only about what might happen to you—and when all danger was past, you acted as though nothing had happened. I was your little sky-lark again, your little doll, exactly as before; except you would have to protect it twice as carefully as before, now that it had shown itself to be so weak and fragile. [*Rises.*] Torvald, that was the moment I realised that for eight years I'd been living with a stranger, and had borne him three children. . . . Oh, I can't bear to think about it! I could tear myself to shreds.

HELMER. [*sadly*]. I see. I see. There is a tremendous gulf dividing us. But, Nora, is there no way we might bridge it?

NORA. As I am now, I am no wife for you.

HELMER. I still have it in me to change.

NORA. Perhaps . . . if you have your doll taken away.

HELMER. And be separated from you! No, no, Nora, the very thought of it is inconceivable.

NORA [*goes into the room, right*]. All the more reason why it must be done.

[*She comes back with her outdoor things and a small travelling bag which she puts on the chair beside the table.*]

HELMER. Nora, Nora, not now! Wait till the morning.

NORA [*putting on her coat*]. I can't spend the night in a strange man's room.

HELMER. Couldn't we go on living here like brother and sister . . . ?

NORA. [*tying on her hat*]. You know very well that wouldn't last. [*She draws the shawl round her.*] Goodbye, Torvald. I don't want to see the children. I know they are in better hands than mine. As I am now, I can never be anything to them.

HELMER. But some day, Nora, some day . . . ?

NORA. How should I know? I've no idea what I might turn out to be.

HELMER. But you are my wife, whatever you are.

NORA. Listen, Torvald, from what I've heard, when a wife leaves her husband's house as I am doing now, he is absolved by law of all responsibility for her. I can at any rate free you from all responsibility. You must not feel in any way bound, any more than I shall. There must be full freedom on both sides. Look, here's your ring back. Give me mine.

HELMER. That too?

NORA. That too.

HELMER. There it is.

NORA. Well, that's the end of that. I'll put the keys down here. The maids know where everything is in the house—better than I do, in fact. Kristine will come in the morning after I've left to pack up the few things I brought with me from home. I want them sent on.

HELMER. The end! Nora, will you never think of me?

NORA. I dare say I'll often think about you and the children and this house.

HELMER. May I write to you, Nora?

NORA. No, never. I won't let you.

HELMER. But surely I can send you . . .

NORA. Nothing, nothing.

HELMER. Can't I help you if ever you need it?

NORA. I said 'no.' I don't accept things from strangers.

HELMER. Nora, can I never be anything more to you than a stranger?

NORA [*takes her bag*]. Ah, Torvald, only by a miracle of miracles . . .

HELMER. Name it, this miracle of miracles!

NORA. Both you and I would have to change to the point where. . . . Oh, Torvald, I don't believe in miracles any more.

HELMER. But I *will* believe. Name it! Change to the point where . . . ?

NORA. Where we could make a real marriage of our lives together. Goodbye!

[She goes out through the hall door.]

HELMER [*sinks down on a chair near the door, and covers his face with his hands*]. Nora! Nora! [*He rises and looks round.*] Empty! She's gone! [*With sudden hope.*] The miracle of miracles . . . ?

[The heavy sound of a door being slammed is heard from below.]

[1879]

🖋 Topics for Critical Thinking and Writing

1. Near the beginning of the play, how does Mrs. Linde's presence help to define Nora's character? How does Nora's response to Krogstad's entrance tell us something about Nora?

2. What does Dr. Rank contribute to the play? If he were eliminated, what would be lost?

3. Can it be argued that although at the end Nora goes out to achieve self-realization, her abandonment of her children—especially to Torvald's loathsome conventional morality—is a crime? (By the way, exactly why does Nora leave the children? She seems to imply, in some passages, that because she forged a signature she is unfit to bring them up. But do you agree with her?)

4. Michael Meyer, in his splendid biography *Henrik Ibsen,* says that the play is not so much about women's rights as about "the need of every individual to find out the kind of person he or she really is, and to strive to become that person." What evidence can you offer to support or refute this interpretation?

5. In *The Quintessence of Ibsenism* Bernard Shaw says that Ibsen, reacting against a common theatrical preference for strange situations, "saw that . . . the more familiar the situation, the more interesting the play. Shakespear had put ourselves on the stage but not our situations. Our uncles seldom murder our fathers and . . . marry our mothers. . . . Ibsen . . . gives us not only ourselves, but ourselves in our own situations. The things that happen to his stage figures are things that happen to us. One consequence is that his plays are much more important to us than Shakespear's. Another is that they are capable both of hurting us cruelly and of filling us with excited hopes of escape from idealistic tyrannies, and with visions of intenser life in the future." How much of this do you believe?

DAVID MAMET

David Mamet was born in Chicago in 1947, and was educated at Goddard College. A screenwriter and director as well as a playwright, he has occasionally taught courses in film. In 1976 his play American Buffalo *won the New York Drama Critics Circle Award for the best American play, and in 1984* Glengarry Glen Ross *won the Pulitzer Prize.* Oleanna *was first produced in 1992. "All my plays,"* he has said, "attempt to bring out the poetry in the plain, everyday language people use."

Oleanna

The want of fresh air does not seem much to affect the happiness of children in a London alley: the greater part of them sing and play as though they were on a moor in Scotland. So the absence of a genial mental atmosphere is not commonly recognized by children who have never known it. Young people have a marvelous faculty of either dying or adapting themselves to circumstances. Even if they are unhappy—very unhappy— it is astonishing how easily they can be prevented from finding it out, or at any rate from attributing it to any other cause than their own sinfulness.

—Samuel Butler, The Way of All Flesh

"Oh, to be in Oleanna,
That's where I would rather be.
Than be bound in Norway
And drag the chains of slavery."

—Folk Song

CHARACTERS
CAROL A woman of twenty
JOHN A man in his forties

The play takes place in John's office.

One

John is talking on the phone. Carol is seated across the desk from him.

JOHN [*on phone*]. And what about the land. [*Pause*] The land. And what about the land? [*Pause*] What about it? [*Pause*] No. I don't understand. Well, yes, I'm I'm . . . no, I'm *sure* it's signif . . . I'm sure it's significant. [*Pause*] Because it's significant to mmmmmm . . . did you call Jerry? [*Pause*] Because . . . no, no, no, no, no. What did they say . . . ? Did you speak to the *real* estate . . . where *is* she . . . ? Well, well, all right. Where are her notes? Where are the notes we took with her. [*Pause*] I thought you were? No. No, I'm sorry, I didn't mean that, I just thought that I saw you, when we were there . . . what . . . ? I thought I saw you with a *pencil.* WHY NOW? is what I'm say . . . well, that's why I say "call Jerry." Well, I can't right now, be . . . no, I *didn't* schedule any . . . Grace: I *didn't* . . . I'm well aware . . . Look: Look. Did you call Jerry? Will you call Jerry . . . ? Because I can't now. I'll be there, I'm sure I'll be there in fifteen, in twenty. I intend to. No, we aren't *going* to lose the, we aren't *going* to lose the house. Look: Look, I'm

Rebecca Pidgeon and W. H. Macy in *Oleanna*, 1992. (© Brigitte Lacombe)

not minimizing it. The "easement." Did she say "easement"? [*Pause*] What did she *say; is* it a "term of art," are we *bound* by it . . . I'm sorry . . . [*Pause*] are: we: yes. *Bound* by . . . Look: [*He checks his watch.*] before the other side *goes home,* all right? "a term of art." Because: that's right [*Pause*] The yard for the boy. Well, that's the whole . . . Look: I'm going to meet you there . . . [*He checks his watch.*] Is the realtor there? All right, tell her to show you the basement again. Look at the *this* because . . . Bec . . . I'm leaving in, I'm leaving in ten or fifteen . . . Yes. No, no, I'll meet you at the new . . . That's a good. If he thinks it's necc . . . you tell Jerry to meet . . . All right? We *aren't* going to lose the deposit. All right? I'm sure it's going to be . . . [*Pause*] I hope so. [*Pause*] I love you, too. [*Pause*] I love you, too. As soon as . . . I will.

[*He hangs up.*] [*He bends over the desk and makes a note.*] [*He looks up.*] [*To Carol:*] I'm sorry . . .

CAROL. [*Pause*] What is a "term of art"?

JOHN. [*Pause*] I'm sorry . . . ?

CAROL. [*Pause*] What is a "term of art"?

JOHN. Is that what you want to talk about?

CAROL. . . . to talk about . . . ?

JOHN. Let's take the mysticism out of it, shall we? Carol? [*Pause*] Don't you think? I'll tell you: when you have some "thing." Which must be broached. [*Pause*] Don't you think . . . ? [*Pause*]

CAROL. . . . don't I think . . . ?

JOHN. Mmm?

CAROL. . . . did I . . . ?

JOHN. . . . what?

CAROL. Did . . . did I . . . did I say something wr . . .

JOHN. [*Pause*] No. I'm sorry. No. You're right. I'm very sorry. I'm somewhat rushed. As you see. I'm sorry. You're right. [*Pause*] What is a "term of art"? It seems to mean a *term,* which has come, through its use, to mean something *more specific* than the words would, to someone *not acquainted* with them . . . indicate. That, I believe, is what a "term of art," would mean. [*Pause*]

CAROL. You don't know what it means . . . ?

JOHN. I'm not sure that I know what it means. It's one of those things, perhaps you've had them, that, you look them up, or have someone explain them to you, and you say "aha," and, you immediately *forget* what . . .

CAROL. You don't do that.

JOHN. . . . I . . . ?

CAROL. You don't do . . .

JOHN. . . . I don't, what . . . ?

CAROL. . . . for . . .

JOHN. . . . I don't for . . .

CAROL. . . . no . . .

JOHN. . . . forget things? Everybody does that.

CAROL. No, they don't.

JOHN. They don't . . .

CAROL. No.

JOHN. [*Pause*] No. Everybody does that.

CAROL. Why would they do that . . . ?

JOHN. Because. I don't know. Because it doesn't interest them.

CAROL. No.

JOHN. I think so, though. [*Pause*] I'm sorry that I was distracted.

CAROL. You don't have to say that to me.

JOHN. You paid me the compliment, or the "obeisance"—all right—of coming in here . . . All right. *Carol.* I find that I am at a *standstill.* I find that I . . .

CAROL. . . . what . . .

JOHN. . . . one moment. In regard to your . . . to your . . .

CAROL. Oh, oh. You're buying a new house!

JOHN. No, let's get on with it.

CAROL. "Get on"? [*Pause*]

JOHN. I know how . . . *believe* me. I know how . . . potentially *humiliating* these . . . I have no desire to . . . I have no desire other than to help you. But: [*He picks up some papers on his desk.*] I won't even say "but." I'll say that as I go back over the . . .

CAROL. I'm just, I'm just trying to . . .

JOHN. . . . no, it will not do.

CAROL. . . . what? What will . . . ?

JOHN. No. I see, I see what you, it . . . [*He gestures to the papers.*] but your work . . .

CAROL. I'm just: I sit in class I . . . [*She holds up her notebook.*] I take notes . . .

JOHN. [*simultaneously with "notes"*]. Yes. I understand. What I am trying to *tell* you is that some, some basic . . .

CAROL. . . . I . . .

JOHN. . . . one moment: some basic missed communi . . .

CAROL. I'm doing what I'm told. I bought your book, I read your . . .

JOHN. No, I'm sure you . . .

CAROL. No, no, no. I'm doing what I'm told. It's *difficult* for me. It's *difficult* . . .

JOHN. . . . but . . .

CAROL. I don't . . . lots of the *language* . . .

JOHN. . . . please . . .

CAROL. The *language,* the "things" that you say . . .

JOHN. I'm sorry. No. I don't think that that's true.

CAROL. It *is* true. I . . .

JOHN. I think . . .

CAROL. It *is* true.

JOHN. . . . I . . .

CAROL. Why would I . . . ?

JOHN. I'll tell you why: you're an incredibly bright girl.

CAROL. . . . I . . .

JOHN. You're an incredibly . . . you have no problem with the . . . Who's kidding who?

CAROL. . . . I . . .

JOHN. No. No. I'll tell you why. I'll tell . . . I think you're *angry,* I . . .

CAROL. . . . why would I . . .

JOHN. . . . wait one moment. I . . .

CAROL. It *is* true. I have *problems* . . .

JOHN. . . . every . . .

CAROL. . . . I come from a different *social* . . .

JOHN. . . . ev . . .

CAROL. a different economic . . .

JOHN. . . . Look:

CAROL. No. I: when I *came* to this school:

JOHN. Yes. Quite . . . [*Pause*]

CAROL. . . . does that mean nothing . . . ?

JOHN. . . . but look: look . . .

CAROL. . . . I . . .

JOHN. [*Picks up paper.*] Here: Please: Sit down. [*Pause*] Sit down. [*Reads from her paper.*] "I think that the ideas contained in this work express the author's feelings in a way that he intended, based on his results." What can that mean? Do you see? What . . .

CAROL. I, the best that I . . .

JOHN. I'm saying, that perhaps this course . . .

CAROL. No, no, no, you can't, you can't . . . I have to . . .

JOHN. . . . how . . .

CAROL. . . . I have to pass it . . .

JOHN. Carol, I:

CAROL. I *have* to pass this course, I . . .

JOHN. Well.

CAROL. . . . don't you . . .

JOHN. Either the . . .

CAROL. . . . I . . .

JOHN. . . . either the, I . . . either the *criteria* for judging progress in the class are . . .

CAROL. No, no, no, no, I have to pass it.

JOHN. Now, look: I'm a human being, I . . .

CAROL. I did what you told me. I did, I did everything that, I read your *book,* you told me to buy your book and read it. Everything you *say* I . . . [*She gestures to her notebook.*] [*The phone rings.*] I do. . . . Ev . . .

JOHN. . . . look:

CAROL. . . . everything I'm told . . .

JOHN. Look. Look. I'm not your *father*. [*Pause*]

CAROL. What?

JOHN. I'm.

CAROL. Did I say you were my father?

JOHN. . . . no . . .

CAROL. Why did you say that . . . ?

JOHN. I . . .

CAROL. . . . why . . . ?

JOHN. . . . in class I . . . [*He picks up the phone.*] [*Into phone:*] Hello. I can't talk now. Jerry? Yes? I underst . . . I can't talk now. I know . . . I know . . . Jerry. I can't *talk* now. Yes, I. Call me back in . . . Thank you. [*He hangs up.*] [*To Carol:*] What do you want me to do? We are two people, all right? Both of whom have subscribed to . . .

CAROL. No, no . . .

JOHN. . . . certain arbitrary . . .

CAROL. No. You have to help me.

JOHN. Certain institutional . . . you tell me what you want me to do. . . . You tell me what you want me to . . .

CAROL. How can I go back and tell them the *grades* that I . . .

JOHN. . . . what can I do . . . ?

CAROL. *Teach* me. *Teach* me.

JOHN. . . . I'm trying to teach you.

CAROL. I read your book. I read it. I don't under . . .

JOHN. . . . you don't understand it.

CAROL. No.

JOHN. Well, perhaps it's not well *written* . . .

CAROL [*simultaneously with "written"*]. No. No. No. I want to *understand* it.

JOHN. What don't you understand? [*Pause*]

CAROL. *Any* of it. What you're trying to say. When you talk about . . .

JOHN. . . . yes . . . ? [*She consults her notes.*]

CAROL. "Virtual warehousing of the young" . . .

JOHN. "Virtual warehousing of the young." If we artificially prolong adolescence . . .

CAROL. . . . and about "The Curse of Modern Education."

JOHN. . . . well . . .

CAROL. I don't . . .

JOHN. Look. It's just a *course*, it's just a *book*, it's just a . . .

CAROL. No. No. There are *people* out there. People who came *here*. To know something they didn't *know*. Who *came* here. To be *helped*. To be *helped*. So someone would *help* them. To *do* something. To *know* something. To get, what do they say? "To get on in the world." How can I do that if I don't, if I fail? But I don't *understand*. I don't *understand*. I don't understand what anything means . . . and I walk around. From morning 'til night: with this one thought in my head. I'm *stupid*.

JOHN. No one thinks you're stupid.

CAROL. No? What am I . . . ?

JOHN. I . . .

CAROL. . . . what am I, then?

JOHN. I think you're angry. Many people are. I have a *telephone* call that I have to make. And an *appointment*, which is rather *pressing*; though I sympathize with your concerns, and though I wish I had the time, this was not a previously scheduled meeting and I . . .

CAROL.   . . . you think I'm nothing . . .

JOHN.   . . . have an appointment with a *realtor,* and with my wife and . . .

CAROL.   You think that I'm stupid.

JOHN.   No. I certainly don't.

CAROL.   You said it.

JOHN.   No. I did not.

CAROL.   You did.

JOHN.   When?

CAROL.   . . . you . . .

JOHN.   No. I never did, or never would say that to a student, and . . .

CAROL.   You said, "What can that mean?" [*Pause*] "What can that mean?" . . . [*Pause*]

JOHN.   . . . and what did that mean to you . . . ?

CAROL.   That meant I'm stupid. And I'll never learn. That's what that meant. And you're right.

JOHN.   . . . I . . .

CAROL.   But then. But then, what am I doing here . . . ?

JOHN.   . . . if you thought that I . . .

CAROL.   . . . when nobody wants me, and . . .

JOHN.   . . . if you interpreted . . .

CAROL.   Nobody *tells* me anything. And I *sit* there . . . in the *corner.* In the *back.* And everybody's talking about "this" all the time. And "concepts," and "precepts" and, and, and, and, and, WHAT IN THE WORLD ARE YOU *TALKING* ABOUT? And I read your book. And they said, "Fine, go in that class." Because you talked about responsibility to the young. I DON'T KNOW WHAT IT MEANS AND I'M *FAILING* . . .

JOHN.   May . . .

CAROL.   No, you're right. "Oh, hell." I failed. Flunk me out of it. It's garbage. Everything I do. "The ideas contained in this work express the author's feelings." That's right. That's right. I know I'm stupid. I know what I am. [*Pause*] I know what I am, Professor. You don't have to tell me. [*Pause*] It's pathetic. Isn't it?

JOHN.   . . . Aha . . . [*Pause*] Sit down. Sit down. Please. [*Pause*] Please sit down.

CAROL.   Why?

JOHN.   I want to talk to you.

CAROL.   Why?

JOHN.   Just sit down. [*Pause*] Please. Sit down. Will you, please . . . ? [*Pause. She does so.*] Thank you.

CAROL.   What?

JOHN.   I want to tell you something.

CAROL.   [*Pause*] What?

JOHN.   Well, I know what you're talking about.

CAROL.   No. You don't.

JOHN.   I think I do. [*Pause*]

CAROL.   How can you?

JOHN.   I'll tell you a story about myself. [*Pause*] Do you mind? [*Pause*] I was raised to think myself stupid. That's what I want to tell you. [*Pause*]

CAROL.   What do you mean?

JOHN.   Just what I said. I was brought up, and my earliest, and most persistent memories are of being told that I was stupid. "You have such *intelligence.* Why must you behave so *stupidly?*" Or, "Can't you *understand?* Can't you *understand?*" And I could *not* understand. I could *not* understand.

CAROL. What?

JOHN. The simplest problem. Was beyond me. It was a mystery.

CAROL. What was a mystery?

JOHN. How people learn. How *I* could learn. Which is what I've been speaking of in class. And of *course* you can't hear it. Carol. Of *course* you can't. [*Pause*] I used to speak of "real people," and wonder what the *real* people did. The *real* people. Who were they? *They* were the people other than myself. The *good* people. The *capable* people. The people who could do the things, *I* could not do: learn, study, retain . . . all that *garbage*—which is what I have been talking of in class, and that's *exactly* what I have been talking of—If you are told . . . Listen to this. If the young child is told he cannot understand. Then he takes it as a *description* of himself. What am I? I am *that which can not understand.* And I saw you out there, when we were speaking of the concepts of . . .

CAROL. I can't understand any of them.

JOHN. Well, then, that's *my* fault. That's not your fault. And that is not verbiage. That's what I firmly hold to be the truth. And I am sorry, and I owe you an apology.

CAROL. Why?

JOHN. And I suppose that I have had some *things* on my mind. . . . We're buying a *house,* and . . .

CAROL. People said that you were stupid . . . ?

JOHN. Yes.

CAROL. When?

JOHN. I'll tell you when. Through my life. In my childhood; and, perhaps, they stopped. But I heard them continue.

CAROL. And what did they say?

JOHN. They said I was incompetent. Do you see? And when I'm tested the, the, the *feelings* of my youth about the *very subject of learning* come up. And I . . . I become, I feel "unworthy," and "unprepared." . . .

CAROL. . . . yes.

JOHN. . . . eh?

CAROL. . . . yes.

JOHN. And I feel that I must fail. [*Pause*]

CAROL. . . . but then you *do* fail. [*Pause*] You have to. [*Pause*] Don't you?

JOHN. A *pilot.* Flying a plane. The pilot is flying the plane. He thinks: Oh, my *God,* my mind's been drifting! Oh, my God! What kind of a cursed imbecile am I, that I, with this so precious cargo of *Life* in my charge, would allow my attention to wander. Why was I born? How deluded are those who put their trust in me, . . . et cetera, so on, and he crashes the plane.

CAROL. [*Pause*] He could just . . .

JOHN. That's right.

CAROL. He could say:

JOHN. My attention *wandered* for a moment . . .

CAROL. . . . uh huh . . .

JOHN. I had a *thought* I did not like . . . but now:

CAROL. . . . but now it's . . .

JOHN. That's what I'm telling you. It's time to put my attention . . . see: it is not: this is what I learned. It is Not Magic. Yes. Yes. *You.* You are going to be frightened. When faced with what may or may not be but which you are going to perceive as a test. You will become frightened. And you will say: "I am incapable of . . ." and everything *in* you will think these two things.

"I must. But I can't." And you will think: Why was I born to be the laughingstock of a world in which everyone is better than I? In which I am entitled to nothing. Where I can not learn.

[Pause]

CAROL. Is that . . . *[Pause]* Is that what I have . . . ?

JOHN. Well. I don't know if I'd put it that way. Listen: I'm talking to you as I'd talk to my son. Because that's what I'd like him to have that I never had. I'm talking to you the way I wish that someone had talked to me. I don't know how to do it, other than to be *personal,* . . . but . . .

CAROL. Why would you want to be personal with me?

JOHN. Well, you see? That's what I'm saying. We can only interpret the behavior of others through the screen we . . . *[The phone rings.]* Through . . . *[To phone:]* Hello . . . ? *[To Carol:]* Through the screen we create. *[To phone:]* Hello. *[To Carol:]* Excuse me a moment. *[To phone:]* Hello? No, I can't talk nnn . . . I know I did. In a few . . . I'm . . . is he coming to the . . . yes. I talked to him. We'll meet you at the No, because I'm with a *student.* It's going to be fff . . . This is important, too. I'm with a *student,* Jerry's going to . . . Listen: the sooner I get off, the sooner I'll be down, all right. I love you. Listen, listen, I said "I love you," it's going to work *out* with the, because I feel that it is, I'll be right down. All right? Well, then it's going to take as long as it takes. *[He hangs up.]* *[To Carol:]* I'm sorry.

CAROL. What was that?

JOHN. There are some problems, as there usually are, about the final agreements for the new house.

CAROL. You're buying a new house.

JOHN. That's right.

CAROL. Because of your promotion.

JOHN. Well, I suppose that that's right.

CAROL. Why did you stay here with me?

JOHN. Stay here.

CAROL. Yes. When you should have gone.

JOHN. Because I like you.

CAROL. You like me.

JOHN. Yes.

CAROL. Why?

JOHN. Why? Well? Perhaps we're similar. *[Pause]* Yes. *[Pause]*

CAROL. You said "everyone has problems."

JOHN. Everyone has problems.

CAROL. Do they?

JOHN. Certainly.

CAROL. You do?

JOHN. Yes.

CAROL. What are they?

JOHN. Well. *[Pause]* Well, you're perfectly right. *[Pause]* If we're going to take off the Artificial *Stricture,* of "Teacher," and "Student," why should *my* problems be any more a mystery than your own? Of *course* I have problems. As you saw.

CAROL. . . . with what?

JOHN. With my *wife* . . . with *work* . . .

CAROL. With work?

JOHN. Yes. And, and, perhaps my problems are, do you see? *Similar* to yours.

CAROL. Would you tell me?

JOHN. All right. [*Pause*] I came *late* to teaching. And I found it Artificial. The notion of "I know and you do not"; and I saw an *exploitation* in the education process. I told you. I hated school, I hated teachers. I hated everyone who was in the position of a "boss" because I *knew*—I didn't *think,* mind you, I *knew* I was going to fail. Because I was a fuckup. I was just no goddamned good. When I . . . late in life . . . [*Pause*] When I *got out from under* . . . when I worked my way out of the need to fail. When I . . .

CAROL. How do you do that? [*Pause*]

JOHN. You have to look at what you are, and what you feel, and how you act. And, finally, you have to look at how you act. And say: If that's what I *did,* that must be how I think of myself.

CAROL. I don't understand.

JOHN. If I fail all the time, it must be that I think of myself as a failure. If I do not want to think of myself as a failure, perhaps I should begin by *succeeding* now and again. Look. The tests, you see, which you encounter, in school, in college, in life, were designed, in the most part, for idiots. *By* idiots. There is no need to fail at them. They are not a test of your worth. They are a test of your ability to retain and spout back misinformation. Of *course* you fail them. They're *nonsense.* And I . . .

CAROL. . . . no . . .

JOHN. Yes. They're *garbage.* They're a *joke.* Look at me. Look at me. The Tenure Committee. The Tenure Committee. Come to judge me. The Bad Tenure Committee.

The "Test." Do you see? They put me to the test. Why, they had people voting on me I wouldn't employ to wax my car. And yet, I go before the Great Tenure Committee, and I have an urge, to *vomit,* to, to, to puke my *badness* on the table, to show them: "I'm no good. Why would you pick *me?*"

CAROL. They granted you tenure.

JOHN. Oh no, they announced it, but they haven't *signed.* Do you see? "At any moment . . ."

CAROL. . . . mmm . . .

JOHN. "They might not *sign*" . . . I might not . . . the *house* might not go through . . . Eh? Eh? They'll find out my "dark secret." [*Pause*]

CAROL. . . . what is it . . . ?

JOHN. There *isn't* one. But *they* will find an index of my badness . . .

CAROL. Index?

JOHN. A ". . . pointer." A "Pointer." You see? Do you see? I *understand* you. I. Know. That. Feeling. Am I entitled to my job, and my nice *home,* and my *wife,* and my *family,* and so on. This is what I'm saying: That theory of education which, that *theory:*

CAROL. I . . . I . . . [*Pause*]

JOHN. What?

CAROL. I . . .

JOHN. What?

CAROL. I want to know about my grade. [*Long pause*]

JOHN. Of course you do.

CAROL. Is that bad?

JOHN. No.

CAROL. Is it bad that I asked you that?

JOHN. No.

CAROL. Did I upset you?

JOHN. No. And I apologize. Of *course* you want to know about your grade. And, of course, you can't concentrate on anyth . . . [*The telephone starts to ring.*] Wait a moment.

CAROL. I should go.

JOHN. I'll make you a deal.

CAROL. No, you have to . . .

JOHN. Let it ring. I'll make you a deal. You stay here. We'll start the whole course over. I'm going to say it was not you, it was I who was not paying attention. We'll start the whole course over. Your grade is an "A." Your final grade is an "A." [*The phone stops ringing.*]

CAROL. But the class is only half over . . .

JOHN [*simultaneously with "over"*]. Your grade for the whole term is an "A." If you will come back and meet with me. A few more times. Your grade's an "A." Forget about the paper. You didn't like it, you didn't like writing it. It's not important. What's important is that I awake your interest, if I can, and that I answer your questions. Let's start over. [*Pause*]

CAROL. Over. With what?

JOHN. Say this is the beginning.

CAROL. The beginning.

JOHN. Yes.

CAROL. Of what?

JOHN. Of the class.

CAROL. But we can't start over.

JOHN. I say we can. [*Pause*] I say we can.

CAROL. But I don't believe it.

JOHN. Yes, I know that. But it's true. What is The Class but you and me? [*Pause*]

CAROL. There are rules.

JOHN. Well. We'll break them.

CAROL. How can we?

JOHN. We won't tell anybody.

CAROL. Is that all right?

JOHN. I say that it's fine.

CAROL. Why would you do this for me?

JOHN. I like you. Is that so difficult for you to . . .

CAROL. Um . . .

JOHN. There's no one here but you and me. [*Pause*]

CAROL. All right. I did not understand. When you referred . . .

JOHN. All right, yes?

CAROL. When you referred to hazing.

JOHN. Hazing.

CAROL. You wrote, in your book. About the comparative . . . the comparative . . . [*She checks her notes.*]

JOHN. Are you checking your notes . . . ?

CAROL. Yes.

JOHN. Tell me in your own . . .

CAROL. I want to make sure that I have it right.

JOHN. No. Of course. You want to be exact.

CAROL. I want to know everything that went on.

JOHN. . . . that's good.

CAROL. . . . so I . . .

JOHN. That's very good. But I was suggesting, many times, that that which we wish to retain is retained oftentimes, I think, *better* with less expenditure of effort.

CAROL. [*Of notes*] Here it is: you wrote of *hazing.*

JOHN. . . . that's correct. Now: I said "hazing." It means ritualized annoyance. We shove this book at you, we say read it. Now, you say you've read it? I think that you're *lying.* I'll *grill* you, and when I find you've lied, you'll be disgraced, and your life will be ruined. It's a sick game. Why do we do it? Does it educate? In no sense. Well, then, what is higher education? It is something-other-than-useful.

CAROL. What is "something-other-than-useful"?

JOHN. It has become a ritual, it has become an article of faith. That all must be subjected to, or to put it differently, that all are entitled to Higher Education. And my point . . .

CAROL. You disagree with that?

JOHN. Well, let's address that. What do you think?

CAROL. I don't know.

JOHN. What do you think, though? [*Pause*]

CAROL. I don't know.

JOHN. I spoke of it in class. Do you remember my example?

CAROL. Justice.

JOHN. Yes. Can you repeat it to me? [*She looks down at her notebook.*] your notes? I ask you as a favor to me, so that I can see if my idea was interesting.

CAROL. You said "justice" . . .

JOHN. Yes?

CAROL. . . . that all are entitled . . . [*Pause*] I . . . I . . . I . . .

JOHN. Yes. To a speedy trial. To a fair trial. But they needn't be given a trial *at all* unless they stand accused. Eh? Justice is their right, should they choose to avail themselves of it, they should have a fair trial. It does not follow, of necessity, a person's life is incomplete without a trial in it. Do you see? My point is a confusion between equity and *utility* arose. So we confound the *usefulness* of higher education with our, granted, right to equal access to the same. We, in effect, create a *prejudice* toward it, completely independent of . . .

CAROL. . . . that it is prejudice that we should go to school?

JOHN. Exactly. [*Pause*]

CAROL. How can you say that? How . . .

JOHN. Good. Good. *Good.* That's right! Speak up! What is a prejudice? An unreasoned belief. We are all subject to it. None of us is not. When it is threatened, or opposed, we feel anger, and feel, do we not? As you do now. Do you not? Good.

CAROL. . . . but how can you . . .

JOHN. . . . let us examine. Good.

CAROL. How . . .

JOHN. Good. Good. When . . .

CAROL. I'M SPEAKING . . . [*Pause*]

JOHN. I'm sorry.

CAROL. How can you . . .

JOHN. . . . I beg your pardon.

CAROL. That's all right.

JOHN. I beg your pardon.

CAROL. That's all right.

JOHN. I'm sorry I interrupted you.

CAROL. That's all right.

JOHN. You were saying?

CAROL. I was saying . . . I was saying . . . [*She checks her notes.*] How can you say in a class. Say in a college class, that college education is prejudice?

JOHN. I said that our predilection for it . . .

CAROL. Predilection . . .

JOHN. . . . you know what that means.

CAROL. Does it mean "liking"?

JOHN. Yes.

CAROL. But how can you say that? That College . . .

JOHN. . . . that's my *job,* don't you know.

CAROL. What is?

JOHN. To provoke you.

CAROL. No.

JOHN. Oh. Yes, though.

CAROL. To provoke me?

JOHN. That's right.

CAROL. To make me mad?

JOHN. That's right. To force you . . .

CAROL. . . . to make me mad is your job?

JOHN. To force you to . . . listen: [*Pause*] Ah. [*Pause*] When I was young somebody told me, are you ready, the rich copulate less often than the poor. But when they do, they take more of their clothes off. Years. Years, mind you, I would compare experiences of my own to this dictum, saying, aha, this fits the norm, or ah, this is a variation from it. What did it mean? Nothing. It was some jerk thing, some school kid told me that took up room inside my head. [*Pause*]

   Somebody told *you,* and you hold it as an article of faith, that higher education is an unassailable good. This notion is so dear to you that when I question it you become angry. Good, Good, I say. Are not those the very things which we should question? I say college education, since the war, has become so a matter of course, and such a fashionable necessity, for those either of or aspiring *to* the new vast middle class, that we *espouse* it, as a matter of right, and have ceased to ask, "What is it good for?" [*Pause*]

   What might be some reasons for pursuit of higher education?

   One: A love of learning.

   Two: The wish for mastery of a skill.

   Three: For economic betterment.

[*Stops. Makes a note.*]

CAROL. I'm keeping you.

JOHN. One moment. I have to make a note . . .

CAROL. It's something that I said?

JOHN. No, we're buying a house.

CAROL. You're buying the new house.

JOHN. To go with the tenure. That's right. Nice *house,* close to the *private school* . . . [*He continues making his note.*] . . . We were talking of economic betterment [*Carol writes in her notebook.*] . . . I was thinking of the School Tax. [*He continues writing.*] [*To himself:*] . . . *where is it written* that I have to send my child to public school. . . . Is it a law that I have to improve the City Schools at the expense of my own interest? And, is this

not simply *The White Man's Burden?* Good. And [*Looks up to Carol*] . . .
does this interest you?

CAROL. No. I'm taking notes . . .

JOHN. You don't have to take notes, you know, you can just listen.

CAROL. I want to make sure I remember it. [*Pause*]

JOHN. I'm not lecturing you, I'm just trying to tell you some things I think.

CAROL. What do you think?

JOHN. Should all kids go to college? *Why* . . .

CAROL. [*Pause*] To learn.

JOHN. But if he does not learn.

CAROL. If the child does not learn?

JOHN. Then why is he in college? Because he was told it was his "right"?

CAROL. Some might find college instructive.

JOHN. I would hope so.

CAROL. But how do they feel? Being told they are wasting their time?

JOHN. I don't think I'm telling them that.

CAROL. You said that education was "prolonged and systematic hazing."

JOHN. Yes. It can be so.

CAROL. . . . if education is so *bad*, why do you do it?

JOHN. I do it *because I love it.* [*Pause*] Let's . . . I suggest you look at the demographics, wage-earning capacity, college- and non-college-educated men and women, 1855 to 1980, and let's see if we can wring some worth from the statistics. Eh? And . . .

CAROL. No.

JOHN. What?

CAROL. I can't understand them.

JOHN. . . . you . . . ?

CAROL. . . . the "charts." The *Concepts,* the . . .

JOHN. "Charts" are simply . . .

CAROL. When I leave here . . .

JOHN. Charts, do you see . . .

CAROL. No, I can't . . .

JOHN. You can, though.

CAROL. NO, NO—I DON'T UNDERSTAND. DO YOU SEE??? I DON'T *UNDERSTAND* . . .

JOHN. What?

CAROL. *Any* of it. *Any* of it. I'm *smiling* in class, I'm *smiling,* the whole time. What are you *talking* about? What is everyone *talking* about? I don't *understand.* I don't know what it *means.* I don't know what it means to *be* here . . . you tell me I'm intelligent, and then you tell me I should not be *here,* what do you *want* with me? What does it *mean?* Who should I *listen* to . . . I . . .

[*He goes over to her and puts his arm around her shoulder.*]

NO! [*She walks away from him.*]

JOHN. Sshhhh.

CAROL. No, I don't under . . .

JOHN. Sshhhh.

CAROL. I don't know what you're *saying* . . .

JOHN. Sshhhh. It's all right.

CAROL. . . . I have no . . .

JOHN. Sshhhhh. Sshhhhh. Let it go a moment. [*Pause*] Sshhhhh . . . let it go. [*Pause*] Just let it go. [*Pause*] Just let it go. It's all right. [*Pause*] Sshhhhh. [*Pause*] I understand . . . [*Pause*] What do you feel?

CAROL. I feel bad.

JOHN. I know. It's all right.

CAROL. I . . . [*Pause*]

JOHN. What?

CAROL. I . . .

JOHN. What? Tell me.

CAROL. I don't understand you.

JOHN. I know. It's all right.

CAROL. I . . .

JOHN. What? [*Pause*] What? *Tell* me.

CAROL. I can't tell you.

JOHN. No, you must.

CAROL. I can't.

JOHN. No. Tell me. [*Pause*]

CAROL. I'm bad. [*Pause*] Oh, God. [*Pause*]

JOHN. It's all right.

CAROL. I'm . . .

JOHN. It's all right.

CAROL. I can't talk about this.

JOHN. It's all right. Tell me.

CAROL. Why do you want to know this?

JOHN. I don't want to know. I want to know whatever you . . .

CAROL. I always . . .

JOHN. . . . good . . .

CAROL. I always . . . all my life . . . I have never told anyone this . . .

JOHN. Yes. Go on. [*Pause*] Go on.

CAROL. All of my life . . . [*The phone rings.*] [*Pause. John goes to the phone and picks it up.*]

JOHN. [*into phone.*] I can't talk now. [*Pause*] What? [*Pause*] Hmm. [*Pause*] All right, I . . . I. Can't. Talk. Now. No, no, no, I *Know* I did, but. . . . What? Hello. What? She *what?* She *can't,* she said the agreement is void? How, how is the agreement *void? That's Our House.*

    I have the *paper;* when we come down, next week, with the payment, and the paper, that house is . . . wait, wait, wait, wait, wait, wait, wait: Did Jerry . . . is Jerry there? [*Pause*] Is *she* there . . . ? Does she have a *lawyer* . . . ? How the *hell,* how the *Hell.* That is . . . it's a question, you said, of the *easement.* I don't underst . . . it's not the *whole agreement.* It's just the *easement,* why would she? Put, put, put, *Jerry* on. [*Pause*] Jer, *Jerry:* What the *Hell* . . . that's my *house.* That's . . . Well, I'm no, no, no, I'm *not* coming ddd . . . List, *Listen, screw* her. You *tell* her. You, listen: I want you to take *Grace,* you take Grace, and get out of that house. You *leave* her there. Her and her lawyer, and you *tell* them, we'll see them in court next . . . no. No. Leave her there, leave her to *stew* in it: You tell her, we're *getting* that house, and we are going to . . . No. I'm *not* coming down. I'll be damned if I'll sit in the same rrr . . . the next, you tell her the next time I *see* her is in court . . . I . . . [*Pause*] What? [*Pause*] What? I don't understand. [*Pause*] Well, what about the house? [*Pause*] There isn't any problem with the hhh . . . [*Pause*] No, no, no, that's all right. All ri . . . All right . . . [*Pause*] Of course. Tha . . . Thank you. No, I will. Right away, [*He hangs up.*] [*Pause*]

CAROL. What is it? [*Pause*]

JOHN. It's a surprise party.

CAROL. It is.

JOHN. Yes.

CAROL. A party for you.

JOHN. Yes.

CAROL. Is it your birthday?

JOHN. No.

CAROL. What is it?

JOHN. The tenure announcement.

CAROL. The tenure announcement.

JOHN. They're throwing a party for us in our new house.

CAROL. Your new house.

JOHN. The house that we're buying.

CAROL. You have to go.

JOHN. It seems that I do.

CAROL. [*Pause*] They're proud of you.

JOHN. Well, there are those who would say it's a form of aggression.

CAROL. What is?

JOHN. A surprise.

Two

John and Carol seated across the desk from each other.

JOHN. You see, [*Pause*] I love to teach. And flatter myself I am *skilled* at it. And I love the, the aspect of *performance*. I think I must confess that.

When I found I loved to teach I swore that I would not become that cold, rigid automaton of an instructor which I had encountered as a child.

Now, I was not unconscious that it was given me to err upon the other side. And, so, I asked and *ask* myself if I engaged in heterodoxy, I will not say "gratuitously" for I do not care to posit orthodoxy as a given good—but, "to the detriment of, of my students." [*Pause*]

As I said. When the possibility of tenure opened, and, of course, I'd long pursued it, I was, of course *happy,* and *covetous* of it.

I asked myself if I was wrong to covet it. And thought about it long, and, I hope, truthfully, and saw in myself several things in, I think, no particular order. [*Pause*]

That I *would* pursue it. That I *desired* it, that I was not pure of longing for security, and that that, perhaps, was not reprehensible in me. That I had duties *beyond* the school, and that my duty to my home, for instance, was, or should be, if it were not, of an equal weight. That tenure, and security, and yes, and *comfort,* were not, of themselves, to be scorned; and were even worthy of honorable pursuit. And that it was given me. Here, in this place, which I enjoy, and in which I find comfort, to assure myself of—as far as it rests in The Material—a continuation of that joy and comfort. In exchange for what? Teaching. Which I love.

What was the price of this security? To obtain *tenure.* Which tenure the committee is in the process of granting me. And on the basis of which I contracted to purchase a house. Now, as you don't have your own family, at this point, you may not know what that means. But to me it is important. A home. A Good Home. To raise my family. Now: The Tenure Committee will meet. This is the process, and a *good* process. Under which the school has functioned for quite a long time. They will meet, and hear your complaint—which you have the right to make; and they will dismiss it. They will *dismiss* your complaint; and, in the intervening period, I will lose my house. I will not be able to close on my house. I will lose my *deposit,* and the home I'd picked out for my wife and son will go by the boards. Now: I see I have angered you. I understand your anger at teachers. I was angry with mine. I felt hurt and humiliated by them. Which is one of the reasons that I went into education.

CAROL. What do you want of me?

JOHN. [*Pause*] I was hurt. When I received the report. Of the tenure committee. I was shocked. And I was hurt. No, I don't mean to subject you to my weak sensibilities. All right. Finally, I didn't understand. Then I thought: is it not always at those points at which we reckon ourselves unassailable that we are most vulnerable and ... [*Pause*] Yes. All right. You find me pedantic. Yes. I am. By nature, by *birth,* by profession, I don't know ... I'm always looking for a *paradigm* for ...

CAROL. I don't know what a paradigm is.

JOHN. It's a model.

CAROL. Then why can't you use that word? [*Pause*]

JOHN. If it is important to you. Yes, all right. I was looking for a model. To continue: I feel that one point ...

CAROL. I ...

JOHN. One second ... upon which I am unassailable is my unflinching concern for my students' dignity. I asked you here to ... in the spirit of *investigation,* to ask you ... to ask ... [*Pause*] What have I done to you? [*Pause*] And, and, I suppose, how I can make amends. Can we not settle this now? It's pointless, really, and I want to know.

CAROL. What you can do to force me to retract?

JOHN. That is not what I meant at all.

CAROL. To bribe me, to convince me ...

JOHN. ... No.

CAROL. To retract ...

JOHN. That is not what I meant at all. I think that you know it is not.

CAROL. That is not what I know. I *wish* I ...

JOHN. I do not want to ... you wish what?

CAROL. No, you said what amends can you make. To force me to retract.

JOHN. That is not what I said.

CAROL. I have my notes.

JOHN. Look. Look. The Stoics say ...

CAROL. The Stoics?

JOHN. The Stoical Philosophers say if you remove the phrase "I have been injured," you have removed the injury. Now: Think: I know that you're upset. Just tell me. Literally. Literally: what wrong have I done you?

CAROL. Whatever you have done to me—to the extent that you've done it to *me,* do you know, rather than to me as a *student,* and, so, to the student body, is contained in my report. To the tenure committee.

JOHN. Well, all right. [*Pause*] Let's see. [*He reads.*] I find that I am sexist. That I am *elitist.* I'm not sure I know what that means, other than it's a derogatory word, meaning "bad." That I ... That I insist on wasting time, in nonprescribed, in self-aggrandizing and theatrical *diversions* from the prescribed *text* ... that these have taken both sexist and pornographic forms ... here we find listed ... [*Pause*] Here we find listed ... instances "... closeted with a student" ... "Told a rambling, sexually explicit story, in which the frequency and attitudes of fornication of the poor and rich are, it would seem, the central point ... moved to *embrace* said student and ... all part of a pattern ..." [*Pause*]

    [*He reads.*] That I used the phrase "The White Man's Burden" ... that I told you how I'd asked you to my room because I quote like you. [*Pause*]

    [*He reads.*] "He said he 'liked' me. That he 'liked being with me.'" He'd let me write my examination paper over, if I could come back oftener to see him in his office." [*Pause*] [*To Carol:*] It's *ludicrous,* Don't you know that? It's not *necessary.* It's going to *humiliate* you, and it's going to cost me my *house,* and ...

CAROL. It's "*ludicrous* ..."?

[*John picks up the report and reads again.*]

JOHN. "He told me he had problems with his wife; and that he wanted to take off the artificial stricture of Teacher and Student. He put his arm around me ..."

CAROL. Do you deny it? Can you deny it ... ? Do you see? [*Pause*] Don't you see? You don't see, do you?

JOHN. I don't see ...

CAROL. You think, you think you can deny that these things happened; or, if they *did,* if they *did,* that they meant what you *said* they meant. Don't you see? You drag me in here, you drag us, to listen to you "go on;" and "go on" about this, or that, or we don't "express" ourselves very well. We don't say what we mean. Don't we? Don't we? We *do* say what we mean. And you say that "I don't understand you ...": Then *you* ... [*Points.*]

JOHN. "Consult the Report"?

CAROL. ... that's right.

JOHN. You see. You see. Can't you ... You see what I'm saying? Can't you tell me in your own words?

CAROL. Those are my own words. [*Pause*]

JOHN. [*He reads.*] "He told me that if I would stay alone with him in his office, he would change my grade to an A." [*To Carol:*] What have I done to you? Oh. My God, are you so hurt?

CAROL. What I "feel" is irrelevant. [*Pause*]

JOHN. Do you know that I tried to help you?

CAROL. What I know I have reported.

JOHN. I would like to help you now. I would. Before this escalates.

CAROL [*simultaneously with "escalates"*]. You see. I don't think that I need your help. I don't think I need anything you have.

JOHN. I feel ...

CAROL. I don't *care* what you feel. Do you see? DO YOU SEE? You can't *do* that anymore. You. Do. Not. Have. The. Power. Did you misuse it? *Someone* did. Are you part of that group? *Yes. Yes.* You Are. You've *done* these things. And to say, and to say, "Oh. Let me help you with your problem ..."

JOHN. Yes. I understand. I understand. You're *hurt.* You're *angry.* Yes. I think your *anger* is *betraying* you. Down a path which helps no one.

CAROL. I don't *care* what you think.

JOHN. You don't? [*Pause*] But you talk of *rights.* Don't you see? *I* have rights too. Do you see? I have a *house* ... part of the *real* world; and The Tenure Committee, Good Men and True ...

CAROL. . . . Professor . . .

JOHN. . . . Please: *Also* part of that world: you understand? This is my *life*. I'm not a *bogeyman*. I don't "stand" for something, I . . .

CAROL. . . . Professor . . .

JOHN. . . . I . . .

CAROL. Professor. I came here as a *favor*. At your personal request. Perhaps I should not have done so. But I did. On my behalf, and on behalf of my group. And you speak of the tenure committee, one of whose members is a woman, as you know. And though you might call it Good Fun, or An Historical Phrase, or An Oversight, or, All of the Above, to refer to the committee as Good Men and True, it is a demeaning remark. It is a sexist remark, and to overlook it is to countenance continuation of that method of thought. It's a remark . . .

JOHN. OH COME ON. Come on. . . . Sufficient to deprive a family of . . .

CAROL. Sufficient? Sufficient? Sufficient? Yes. It is a *fact* . . . and that story, which I quote, is *vile* and *classist*, and *manipulative* and *pornographic*. It . . .

JOHN. . . . it's pornographic . . . ?

CAROL. What gives you the *right*. Yes. To speak to a *woman* in your private . . . Yes. Yes. I'm sorry. I'm sorry. You feel yourself empowered . . . you say so yourself. To *strut*. To *posture*. To "perform." To "Call me in here . . ." Eh? You say that higher education is a joke. And treat it as such, you *treat* it as such. And *confess* to a taste to play the *Patriarch* in your class. To grant *this*. To deny *that*. To embrace your students.

JOHN. How can you assert. How can you stand there and . . .

CAROL. How can you *deny* it. You did it to me. *Here*. You *did*. . . . You *confess*. You love the Power. To *deviate*. To *invent*, to transgress . . . to *transgress* whatever norms have been established for us. And you think it's charming to "question" in yourself this taste to mock and destroy. But you should question it. Professor. And you pick those things which you feel *advance* you: publication, *tenure*, and the steps to get them you call "harmless rituals." And you perform those steps. Although you say it is hypocrisy. But to the aspirations of your students. Of *hardworking students,* who come here, who *slave* to come here—you have no idea what it cost me to come to this school—you *mock* us. You call education "hazing," and from your so-protected, so-elitist seat you hold our confusion as a *joke,* and our hopes and efforts with it. Then you sit there and say "what have I done?" And ask me to understand that *you* have aspirations too. But I tell you. I tell you. That you are vile. And that you are exploitative. And if you possess one ounce of that inner honesty you describe in your book, you can look in yourself and see those things that I see. And you can find revulsion equal to my own. Good day. [*She prepares to leave the room.*]

JOHN. Wait a second, will you, just one moment. [*Pause*] Nice day today.

CAROL. What?

JOHN. You said "Good day." I think that it is a nice day today.

CAROL. *Is* it?

JOHN. Yes, I think it is.

CAROL. And why is that important?

JOHN. Because it is the essence of all human communication. I say something conventional, you respond, and the information we exchange is not about the "weather," but that we both agree to converse. In effect, we agree that we are both human. [*Pause*]

I'm not a . . . "exploiter," and you're not a . . . "deranged," what? *Revolutionary* . . . that we may, that we may have . . . positions, and that we may have . . . desires, which are in *conflict,* but that we're just human. [*Pause*] That means that sometimes we're *imperfect.* [*Pause*] Often we're in conflict . . . [*Pause*] *Much* of what we do, you're right, in the name of "principles" is *self-serving* . . . much of what we do is *conventional.* [*Pause*] You're right. [*Pause*] You said you came in the class because you wanted to learn about *education.* I don't know that I can teach you about education. But I know that I can tell you what I *think* about education, and then *you* decide. And you don't have to fight with me. *I'm* not the subject. [*Pause*] And where I'm *wrong* . . . perhaps it's not your job to "fix" me. I don't want to fix *you.* I would like to tell you what I *think,* because that *is* my job, conventional as it is, and flawed as I may be. And then, if you can show me some better *form,* then we can proceed from there. But, just like "nice day, isn't it . . . ?" I don't think we can proceed until we accept that each of us is human. [*Pause*] And we still can have difficulties. We *will* have them . . . that's all right too. [*Pause*] Now:

CAROL. . . . wait . . .

JOHN. Yes. I want to hear it.

CAROL. . . . the . . .

JOHN. Yes. Tell me frankly.

CAROL. . . . my position . . .

JOHN. I want to hear it. In your own words. What you want. And what you feel.

CAROL. . . . I . . .

JOHN. . . . yes . . .

CAROL. My Group.

JOHN. Your "Group" . . . ? [*Pause*]

CAROL. The people I've been talking to . . .

JOHN. There's no shame in that. Everybody needs advisers. Everyone needs to expose themselves. To various points of view. It's not wrong. It's essential. Good. Good. Now: You and I . . . [*The phone rings.*]

You and I . . .

[*He hesitates for a moment, and then picks it up.*] [*Into phone*] Hello. [*Pause*] Um . . . no, I know they do. [*Pause*] I know she does. Tell her that I . . . can I call you back? . . . Then tell her that I think it's going to be fine. [*Pause*] Tell her just, just hold on, I'll . . . can I get back to you? . . . Well . . . no, no, no, we're *taking* the house . . . we're . . . no, no, nn . . . no, she will nnn, it's not a *question* of refunding the dep . . . no . . . it's not a *question* of the deposit . . . will you call Jerry? Babe, baby, will you just call Jerry? Tell him, nnn . . . tell him they, well, they're to keep the deposit, because the deal, be . . . because the deal is going to go *through* . . . because I know . . . be . . . will you please? Just *trust* me. Be . . . well, I'm dealing with the complaint. Yes. Right *Now.* Which is why I . . . yes, no, no, it's really, I can't *talk* about it now. Call Jerry, and I can't talk now. Ff . . . fine. Gg . . . good-bye. [*Hangs up.*] [*Pause*] I'm sorry we were interrupted.

CAROL. No . . .

JOHN. I . . . I was saying:

CAROL. You said that we should agree to talk about my complaint.

JOHN. That's correct.

CAROL. But we *are* talking about it.

JOHN. Well, that's correct too. You see? This is the *gist* of education.

CAROL. No, no. I mean, we're talking about it at the Tenure Committee Hearing. [*Pause*]

JOHN. Yes, but I'm saying: we can talk about it *now*, as easily as . . .

CAROL. No. I think that we should stick to the process . . .

JOHN. . . . wait a . . .

CAROL. . . . the "conventional" process. As you said. [*She gets up.*] And you're right, I'm sorry if I was, um, if I was "discourteous" to you. You're right.

JOHN. Wait, wait a . . .

CAROL. I really should go.

JOHN. Now, look, granted. I have an interest. In the status quo. All right? Everyone does. But what I'm saying is that the *committee* . . .

CAROL. Professor, you're right. Just don't impinge on me. We'll take our differences, and . . .

JOHN. You're going to make a . . . look, look, look, you're going to . . .

CAROL. I shouldn't have come here. They told me . . .

JOHN. One moment. No. No. There are *norms,* here, and there's no reason. Look: I'm trying to *save* you . . .

CAROL. No one *asked* you to . . . you're trying to save *me?* Do me the courtesy to . . .

JOHN. I *am* doing you the courtesy. I'm talking *straight* to you. We can settle this *now*. And I want you to sit *down* and . . .

CAROL. You must excuse me . . . [*She starts to leave the room.*]

JOHN. Sit down, it seems we each have a . . . Wait one moment. Wait one moment . . . just do me the courtesy to . . .

[*He restrains her from leaving.*]

CAROL. LET ME GO.

JOHN. I have no desire to *hold* you, I just want to *talk* to you . . .

CAROL. LET ME GO. LET ME GO. WOULD SOMEBODY *HELP* ME? WOULD SOMEBODY *HELP* ME PLEASE . . . ?

Three

[*At rise, Carol and John are seated.*]

JOHN. I have asked you here. [*Pause*] I have asked you here against, against my . . .

CAROL. I was most surprised you asked me.

JOHN. . . . against my better *judgment*, against . . .

CAROL. I was most surprised . . .

JOHN. . . . against the . . . yes. I'm sure.

CAROL. . . . If you would like me to leave, I'll leave. I'll go right now . . . [*She rises.*]

JOHN. Let us begin *correctly*, may we? I feel . . .

CAROL. That is what I wished to do. That's why I came here, but now . . .

JOHN. . . . I feel . . .

CAROL. But now perhaps you'd like me to leave . . .

JOHN. I don't want you to leave. I asked you to come . . .

CAROL. I didn't have to come here.

JOHN. No. [*Pause*] Thank you.

CAROL. All right. [*Pause*] [*She sits down.*]

JOHN. Although I feel that it *profits*, it would *profit* you something, to . . .

CAROL. . . . what I . . .

JOHN. If you would hear me out, if you would hear me out.

CAROL. I came here to, the court officers told me not to come.

JOHN. . . . the "court" officers . . . ?

CAROL. I was shocked that you asked.

JOHN. . . . wait . . .

CAROL. Yes. But I did *not* come here to hear what it "profits" me.

JOHN. The "court" officers . . .

CAROL. . . . no, no, perhaps I should leave . . . [*She gets up.*]

JOHN. Wait.

CAROL. No. I shouldn't have . . .

JOHN. . . . wait. Wait. Wait a moment.

CAROL. Yes? What is it you want? [*Pause*] What is it you want?

JOHN. I'd like you to stay.

CAROL. You want me to stay.

JOHN. Yes.

CAROL. You do.

JOHN. Yes. [*Pause*] Yes. I would like to have you hear me out. If you would. [*Pause*] Would you please? If you would do that I would be in your debt. [*Pause*] [*She sits.*] Thank You. [*Pause*]

CAROL. What is it you wish to tell me?

JOHN. All right. I cannot . . . [*Pause*] I cannot help but feel you are owed an apology. [*Pause*] [*Of papers in his hands*] I have read. [*Pause*] And reread these accusations.

CAROL. What "accusations"?

JOHN. The, the tenure comm . . . what other accusations . . . ?

CAROL. The tenure committee . . . ?

JOHN. Yes.

CAROL. Excuse me, but those are not accusations. They have been *proved*. They are facts.

JOHN. . . . I . . .

CAROL. No. Those are not "accusations."

JOHN. . . . those?

CAROL. . . . the committee [*The phone starts to ring.*] the committee has . . .

JOHN. . . . All right . . .

CAROL. . . . those are not accusations. The Tenure Committee.

JOHN. ALL RIGHT. ALL RIGHT. ALL RIGHT. [*He picks up the phone.*] Hello. Yes. No. I'm here. Tell Mister . . . No, I can't talk to him now . . . I'm sure he has, but I'm fff . . . I know . . . No, I have no time t . . . tell Mister . . . tell Mist . . . tell Jerry that I'm *fine* and that I'll call him right aw . . . [*Pause*] My wife . . . Yes. I'm sure she has. Yes, thank you. Yes, I'll call her too. I cannot talk to you now. [*He hangs up.*] [*Pause*] All right. It was good of you to come. Thank you. I have studied. I have spent some time studying the indictment.

CAROL. You will have to explain that word to me.

JOHN. An "indictment" . . .

CAROL. Yes.

JOHN. Is a "bill of particulars." A . . .

CAROL. All right. Yes.

JOHN. In which is alleged . . .

CAROL. No. I cannot allow that. I cannot allow that. Nothing is alleged. Everything is proved . . .

JOHN. Please, wait a sec . . .

CAROL. I cannot *come* to allow . . .

JOHN. If I may . . . If I may, from whatever you feel is "established," by . . .

CAROL. The issue here is not what I "feel." It is not my "feelings," but the feelings of women. And men. Your superiors, who've been "polled," do you see? To whom *evidence* has been presented, who have *ruled,* do you see? Who have weighed the testimony and the evidence, and have *ruled,* do you see? That you are *negligent.* That you are *guilty,* that you are found *wanting,* and in *error;* and are *not,* for the reasons so-told, to be given tenure. That you are to be disciplined. For facts. For *facts.* Not "alleged," what is the word? But *proved.* Do you see? *By your own actions.*

   That is what the tenure committee has said. That is what my lawyer said. For what you did in class. For what you did *in this office.*

JOHN. They're going to discharge me.

CAROL. As full well they should. You don't understand? You're angry? What has *led* you to this place? Not your sex. Not your race. Not your class. YOUR OWN ACTIONS. And you're *angry.* You *ask* me here. What *do* you want? You want to "charm" me. You want to "convince" me. You want me to re- cant. I will *not* recant. Why should I . . . ? What I say is right. You tell me, you are going to tell me that you have a wife and child. You are going to say that you have a career and that you've worked for twenty years for this. Do you know what you've *worked* for? *Power.* For *power.* Do you under- stand? And you sit there, and you tell me *stories.* About your *house,* about all the private *schools,* and about *privilege,* and how you are entitled. To *buy,* to *spend,* to *mock,* to *summon.* All your stories. All your silly weak *guilt,* it's all about *privilege;* and you won't know it. Don't you see? You worked twenty years for the right to *insult* me. And you feel entitled to be *paid* for it. Your Home. Your Wife . . . Your sweet "deposit" on your house . . .

JOHN. Don't you have feelings?

CAROL. That's my point. You see? Don't you have feelings? Your final argument. What is it that has no feelings. *Animals.* I don't take your side, you ques- tion if I'm Human.

JOHN. Don't you have feelings?

CAROL. I have a responsibility. I . . .

JOHN. . . . to . . . ?

CAROL. To? This institution. To the *students.* To my *group.*

JOHN. . . . your "group." . . .

CAROL. Because I speak, yes, not for myself. But for the group; for those who suf- fer what I suffer. On behalf of whom, even if I, were, inclined, to what, forgive? Forget? What? Overlook your . . .

JOHN. . . . my behavior?

CAROL. . . . it would be wrong.

JOHN. Even if you were inclined to "forgive" me.

CAROL. It would be wrong.

JOHN. And what would transpire.

CAROL. Transpire?

JOHN. Yes.

CAROL. "Happen?"

JOHN. Yes.

CAROL. Then *say* it. For Christ's sake. Who the *hell* do you think that you are? You want a post. You want unlimited power. To do and to say what you want. As it pleases you—Testing, Questioning, Flirting . . .

JOHN. I never . . .
CAROL. Excuse me, one moment, will you?

[*She reads from her notes.*]

       The twelfth: "Have a good day, dear."
       The fifteenth: "Now, don't *you* look fetching . . ."
       April seventeenth: "If you girls would come over here . . ." I saw you. I saw you, Professor. For two semesters sit there, stand there and exploit your, as you thought, "paternal prerogative," and what is that but rape; I swear to God. You asked me in here to explain something to me, as a child, that I did not understand. But I came to explain something to you. You Are Not God. You ask me why I came? I came here to instruct you.

[*She produces his book.*]

       And your book? You think you're going to show me some "light"? You *"maverick."* Outside of tradition. No, no, [*She reads from the book's liner notes.*] "*of* that fine tradition of *inquiry*. Of Polite *skepticism*" . . . and you say you believe in free intellectual discourse. YOU BELIEVE IN NOTHING. YOU BELIEVE IN NOTHING AT ALL.
JOHN. I believe in freedom of thought.
CAROL. Isn't that fine. *Do* you?
JOHN. Yes. I do.
CAROL. Then why do you question, for one moment, the committee's decision refusing your tenure? Why do you question your suspension? You believe in what *you call* freedom of thought. Then, fine. *You* believe in freedom-of-thought *and* a home, and, *and* prerogatives for your kid, *and* tenure. And I'm going to tell you. You believe *not* in "freedom of thought," but in an elitist, in, in a protected hierarchy which rewards you. And for whom you are the clown. And you mock and exploit the system which pays your rent. You're wrong. I'm not wrong. You're wrong. You think that I'm full of hatred. I know what you think I am.
JOHN. Do you?
CAROL. You think I'm a, of course I do. You think I am a frightened, repressed, confused, I don't know, abandoned young thing of some doubtful sexuality, who wants, power and revenge. [*Pause*] Don't you? [*Pause*]
JOHN. Yes. I do. [*Pause*]
CAROL. Isn't that better? And I feel that that is the first moment which you've treated me with respect. For you told me the truth. [*Pause*] I did not come here, as you are assured, to gloat. Why would I want to gloat? I've profited nothing from your, your, as you say, your "misfortune." I came here, as you did me the honor to *ask* me here, I came here to *tell* you something.
       [*Pause*] That I think . . . that I think you've been wrong. That I think you've been terribly wrong. Do you hate me now? [*Pause*]
JOHN. Yes.
CAROL. Why do you hate me? Because you think me wrong? No. Because I have, you think, *power* over you. Listen to me. Listen to me, Professor. [*Pause*] It is the power that you hate. So deeply that, that any atmosphere of free discussion is impossible. It's not "unlikely." It's *impossible*. Isn't it?
JOHN. Yes.
CAROL. *Isn't* it . . . ?

JOHN. Yes. I suppose.

CAROL. Now. The thing which you find so cruel is the selfsame process of selection I, and my group, go through *every day of our lives.* In admittance to school. In our tests, in our class rankings. . . . Is it unfair? I can't tell you. But, if it is fair. Or even if it is "unfortunate but necessary" for us, then, by God, so must it be for you. [*Pause*] You write of your "responsibility to the young." Treat us with respect, and that will *show* you your responsibility. You write that education is just hazing. [*Pause*] But we worked to get to this school. [*Pause*] And some of us. [*Pause*] Overcame prejudices. Economic, sexual, you cannot begin to imagine. And endured humiliations I *pray* that you and those you love never will encounter. [*Pause*] To gain admittance here. To pursue that same dream of security *you* pursue. We, who, who are, at any moment, in danger of being deprived of it. By . . .

JOHN. . . . by . . . ?

CAROL. By the administration. By the teachers. By *you.* By, say, one low grade, that keeps us out of graduate school; by one, say, one capricious or inventive answer on our parts, which, perhaps, you don't find amusing. Now you *know,* do you see? What it is to be subject to that power. [*Pause*]

JOHN. I don't understand. [*Pause*]

CAROL. My charges are not trivial. You see that in the haste, I think, with which they were accepted. A *joke* you have told, with a sexist tinge. The language you use, a verbal or physical caress, yes, yes, I know, you say that it is meaningless. I understand. I differ from you. To lay a hand on someone's shoulder.

JOHN. It was devoid of sexual content.

CAROL. I say it was not. I SAY IT WAS NOT: Don't you begin to *see* . . . ? Don't you begin to understand? IT'S NOT FOR YOU TO SAY.

JOHN. I take your point, and I see there is much good in what you refer to.

CAROL. . . . do you think so . . . ?

JOHN. . . . but, and this is not to say that I cannot change, in those things in which I am deficient . . . But, the . . .

CAROL. Do you hold yourself harmless from the charge of sexual exploitativeness . . . ? [*Pause*]

JOHN. Well, I . . . I . . . I . . . You know I, as I said. I . . . think I am not too old to *learn,* and I *can* learn, I . . .

CAROL. Do you hold yourself innocent of the charge of . . .

JOHN. . . . wait, wait, wait . . . All right, let's go back to . . .

CAROL. YOU FOOL. Who do you think I am? To come here and be taken in by a *smile.* You little yapping fool. You think I want "revenge." I don't want revenge. I WANT UNDERSTANDING.

JOHN. . . . *do* you?

CAROL. I do. [*Pause*]

JOHN. What's the use. It's over.

CAROL. Is it? What is?

JOHN. My job.

CAROL. Oh. Your job. That's what you want to talk about. [*Pause*] [*She starts to leave the room. She steps and turns back to him.*] All right. [*Pause*] What if it were possible that my Group withdraws its complaint. [*Pause*]

JOHN. What?

CAROL. That's right. [*Pause*]

JOHN. Why.

CAROL. Well, let's say as an act of friendship.

JOHN. An act of friendship.

CAROL. Yes. [*Pause*]

JOHN. In exchange for what.

CAROL. Yes. But I don't think, "exchange." Not "in exchange." For what do we derive from it? [*Pause*]

JOHN. "Derive."

CAROL. Yes.

JOHN. [*Pause*] Nothing. [*Pause*]

CAROL. That's right. We derive nothing. [*Pause*] Do you see that?

JOHN. Yes.

CAROL. That is a little word, Professor. "Yes." "I see that." But you will.

JOHN. And you might speak to the committee . . . ?

CAROL. To the committee?

JOHN. Yes.

CAROL. Well. Of course. That's on your mind. We might.

JOHN. "If" what?

CAROL. "Given" what. Perhaps. I think that that is more friendly.

JOHN. GIVEN WHAT?

CAROL. And, believe me. I understand your rage. It is not that I don't feel it. But I do not see that it is deserved, so I do not resent it. . . . All right. I have a list.

JOHN. . . . a list.

CAROL. Here is a list of books, which we . . .

JOHN. . . . a list of books . . . ?

CAROL. That's right. Which we find questionable.

JOHN. What?

CAROL. Is this so bizarre . . . ?

JOHN. I can't believe . . .

CAROL. It's not necessary you believe it.

JOHN. Academic freedom . . .

CAROL. Someone chooses the books. If you can choose them, others can. What are you, "God"?

JOHN. . . . no, no, the "dangerous." . . .

CAROL. You have an agenda, we have an agenda. I am not interested in your feelings or your motivation, but your actions. If you would like me to speak to the Tenure Committee, here is my list. You are a Free Person, you decide. [*Pause*]

JOHN. Give me the list. [*She does so. He reads.*]

CAROL. I think you'll find . . .

JOHN. I'm capable of reading it. Thank you.

CAROL. We have a number of *texts* we need re . . .

JOHN. I see that.

CAROL. We're amenable to . . .

JOHN. Aha. Well, let me look over the . . . [*He reads.*]

CAROL. I think that . . .

JOHN. LOOK. I'm reading your demands. All right?! [*He reads.*] [*Pause*] You want to ban my book?

CAROL. We do not . . .

JOHN. [*of list*]. It says here . . .

CAROL. . . . We want it removed from inclusion as a representative example of the university.

JOHN. Get out of here.

CAROL. If you put aside the issues of personalities.

JOHN. Get the fuck out of my office.

CAROL. No, I think I would reconsider.

JOHN. . . . you think you can.

CAROL. We can and we *will.* Do you want our support? That is the only quest . . .

JOHN. . . . to ban my *book* . . . ?

CAROL. . . . that is correct . . .

JOHN. . . . this . . . this is a *university* . . . we . . .

CAROL. . . . and we have a statement . . . which we need you to . . . [*She hands him a sheet of paper.*]

JOHN. No, no. It's out of the question. I'm sorry. I don't know what I was thinking of. I want to tell you something. I'm a teacher. I am a teacher. Eh? It's my *name* on the door, and *I* teach the class, and that's what I do. I've got a book with my name on it. And my son will *see* that *book* someday. And I have a respon . . . No, I'm sorry I have a *responsibility* . . . to *myself,* to my *son,* to my *profession.* . . . I haven't been *home* for two days, do you know that? Thinking this out.

CAROL. . . . you haven't?

JOHN. I've been, no. If it's of interest to you. I've been in a *hotel. Thinking.* [*The phone starts ringing.*] *Thinking* . . .

CAROL. . . . you haven't been home?

JOHN. . . . *thinking,* do you see.

CAROL. Oh.

JOHN. And, and, I owe you a debt, I see that now. [*Pause*] You're *dangerous,* you're *wrong* and it's my *job* . . . to say no to you. That's my job. You are absolutely right. You want to ban my book? Go to *hell,* and they can do whatever they want to me.

CAROL. . . . you haven't been home in two days . . .

JOHN. I think I told you that.

CAROL. . . . you'd better get that phone. [*Pause*] I think that you should pick up the phone. [*Pause*]

[John picks up the phone.]

JOHN [*on phone*]. Yes. [*Pause*] Yes. Wh . . . I. I. I had to be away. All ri . . . did they wor . . . did they worry ab . . . No. I'm all right, now, Jerry. I'm f . . . I got a little turned *around,* but I'm *sitting* here and . . . I've got it figured out. I'm fine. I'm fine don't worry about me. I got a little bit mixed up. But I am not sure that it's not a blessing. It cost me my job? Fine. Then the job was not worth having. Tell Grace that I'm coming home and everything is fff . . . [*Pause*] What? [*Pause*] *What?* [*Pause*] What do you *mean?* WHAT? Jerry . . . Jerry. They . . . Who, who, what can they do . . . ? [*Pause*] NO. [*Pause*] NO. They can't do th . . . What do you mean? [*Pause*] But how . . . [*Pause*] She's, she's, she's *here* with me. To . . . Jerry. I don't underst . . . [*Pause*] [*He hangs up.*]. [*To Carol:*] What does this mean?

CAROL. I thought you knew.

JOHN. What. [*Pause*] What does it mean. [*Pause*]

CAROL. You tried to rape me. [*Pause*] According to the law. [*Pause*]

JOHN. . . . what . . . ?

CAROL. You tried to rape me. I was leaving this office, you "pressed" yourself into me. You "pressed" your body into me.

JOHN. . . . I . . .

CAROL. My Group has told your lawyer that we may pursue criminal charges.

JOHN. . . . no . . .

CAROL.   . . . under the statute. I am told. It was battery.

JOHN.   . . . no . . .

CAROL.   Yes. And attempted rape. That's right. [*Pause*]

JOHN.   I think that you should go.

CAROL.   Of course. I thought you knew.

JOHN.   I have to talk to my lawyer.

CAROL.   Yes. Perhaps you should.

   [*The phone rings again.*] [*Pause*]

JOHN.   [*Picks up phone. Into phone:*] Hello? I . . . Hello . . . ? I . . . Yes, he just
   called. No . . . I. I can't talk to you now, Baby. [*To Carol:*] Get out.

CAROL.   . . . your wife . . . ?

JOHN.   . . . who it is is no concern of yours. Get out. [*To phone:*] No, no, it's
   going to be all right. I. I can't talk now, Baby. [*To Carol:*] Get out of here.

CAROL.   I'm going.

JOHN.   Good.

CAROL [*exiting*].   . . . and don't call your wife "baby."

JOHN.   What?

CAROL.   Don't call your wife baby. You heard what I said.

   [*Carol starts to leave the room. John grabs her and begins to beat her.*]

JOHN.   You vicious little bitch. You think you can come in here with your political correctness and destroy my life?

   [*He knocks her to the floor.*]

After how I treated you . . . ? You should be . . . *Rape you* . . . ? Are you kidding me . . . ?

   [*He picks up a chair, raises it above his head, and advances on her.*]

I wouldn't touch you with a ten-foot pole. You little *cunt* . . .

   [*She cowers on the floor below him. Pause. He looks down at her. He lowers
   the chair. He moves to his desk, and arranges the papers on it. Pause. He looks
   over at her.*]

. . . well . . .

   [*Pause. She looks at him.*]

CAROL.   Yes. That's right.
   [*She looks away from him, and lowers her head. To herself:*] . . . yes.
   That's right.

End

[1992]

 Topics for Critical Thinking and Writing

1. Did you find that on the whole you were on the side of one character rather
   than the other, or did your sympathies change, and if they changed did they
   change once and for all? (Incidentally, Mamet in an interview said that both

characters are "altogether right" and both are "altogether wrong." Does this statement help you?)

2. Each of the three scenes begins with a stage direction informing the reader that the two characters are seated. In the first two scenes, they are "seated across the desk." The third scene does not specify the desk. How would you begin the third scene? Explain your decision.

3. Nothing is said of the costumes. How would you dress the two performers? Would you have them wear the same clothing in all three scenes, or different costumes in each scene? Why?

4. Toward the end of the first scene, John tells Carol that it is his job (as a professor) to "provoke" her, that is, to stimulate students to question traditional values. Reread the play, paying close attention to all of the comments on education, especially to Carol's comments in Scene Two—for instance, to her charge that by saying that education may be a form of "hazing" he mocks "*hardworking students,* who come here." Summarize—if it is possible— John's view of education, and Carol's. In your opinion, how much validity is there to what either character says about education? Explain.

5. Near the end of Scene One, we hear one side of a telephone conversation, which at first seems to suggest that John is in danger of losing the house he is about to buy. It turns out that this is a friendly ruse to get him to come to the house, where he will find a party in his honor. Why do you suppose Mamet included this bit?

6. Although in much of Scene Three Carol is dominant, the play ends with her cowering on the floor, and saying—indeed repeating—"That's right." Mamet said, in an interview, "I think that people are generally more happy with a mystery than with an explanation." Is the ending mysterious? If so, do you agree with Mamet's generalization about mystery? Explain.

7. What do you take to be the relevance of the quotation from Samuel Butler (page 825)? (By the way, we strongly recommend Butler's *The Way of All Flesh,* a witty, highly autobiographical and often moving novel published in 1903, a year after Butler's death.)

8. "Oleanna" is never mentioned in the play, but (as you know) the printed version includes as a sort of preface a quotation from a song, mentioning Oleanna, where it is contrasted with an oppressive Norwegian state. A student tells us of another stanza:

So if you'd like a happy life,
To Oleanna you must go,
The poorest man from the old country
Becomes a king in a year or so.

Judging from this stanza, Oleanna is a never-never land, a dream world. We have also heard that Oleanna was the name of a nineteenth-century Norwegian-American utopian community, and that as a youth Mamet once went camping on the site. In any case, what do you think of the title?

Innocence and Experience

CHAPTER

20

ESSAY

 **MAYA ANGELOU**

Maya Angelou, born Marguerita Johnson in 1928 in St. Louis, spent her early years in California and Arkansas. She has worked as a cook, a streetcar conductor, a television screenwriter, and an actress, and she has written poems and five autobiographical books. The following selection comes from her first autobiography, I Know Why the Caged Bird Sings *(1970).*

Graduation

The children in Stamps trembled visibly with anticipation. Some adults were excited too, but to be certain the whole young population had come down with graduation epidemic. Large classes were graduating from both the grammar school and the high school. Even those who were years removed from their own day of glorious release were anxious to help with preparations as a kind of dry run. The junior students who were moving into the vacating classes' chairs were tradition-bound to show their talents for leadership and management. They strutted through the school and around the campus exerting pressure on the lower grades. Their authority was so new that occasionally if they pressed a little too hard it had to be overlooked. After all, next term was coming, and it never hurt a sixth grader to have a play sister in the eighth grade, or a tenth-year student to be able to call a twelfth grader Bubba. So all was endured in a spirit of shared understanding. But the graduating classes themselves were the nobility. Like travelers with exotic destinations on their minds, the graduates were remarkably forgetful. They came to school without their books, or tablets or even pencils. Volunteers fell over themselves to secure replacements for the missing equipment. When accepted, the willing workers might or might not be thanked, and it was of no importance to the pregraduation rites. Even teachers were respectful of the now quiet and aging seniors, and tended to speak to them, if not as equals, as beings only slightly lower than themselves. After tests were returned and grades given, the student body, which acted like an extended family, knew who did well, who excelled, and what piteous ones had failed.

Unlike the white high school, Lafayette County Training School distinguished itself by having neither lawn, nor hedges, nor tennis court, nor climbing ivy. Its two buildings (main classrooms, the grade school and home economics) were set on a dirt hill with no fence to limit either its boundaries or those of bordering farms. There was a large expanse to the left of the school which was used alternately as a baseball diamond or a basketball court. Rusty hoops on the swaying poles represented the permanent recreational equipment, although bats and balls could be borrowed from the P.E. teacher if the borrower was qualified and if the diamond wasn't occupied.

Over this rocky area relieved by a few shady tall persimmon trees the graduating class walked. The girls often held hands and no longer bothered to speak to the lower students. There was a sadness about them, as if this old world was not their home and they were bound for higher ground. The boys, on the other hand, had become more friendly, more outgoing. A decided change from the closed attitude they projected while studying for finals. Now they seemed not ready to give up the old school, the familiar paths and classrooms. Only a small percentage would be continuing on to college—one of the South's A & M (agricultural and mechanical) schools, which trained Negro youths to be carpenters, farmers, handymen, masons, cooks and baby nurses. Their future rode heavily on their shoulders, and blinded them to the collective joy that had pervaded the lives of the boys and girls in the grammar school graduating class.

Parents who could afford it had ordered new shoes and ready-made clothes for themselves from Sears and Roebuck or Montgomery Ward. They also engaged the best seamstresses to make the floating graduating dresses and to cut down secondhand pants which would be pressed to a military slickness for the important event.

5   Oh, it was important, all right. Whitefolks would attend the ceremony, and two or three would speak of God and home, and the Southern way of life, and Mrs. Parsons, the principal's wife, would play the graduation march while the lower-grade graduates paraded down the aisles and took their seats below the platform. The high school seniors would wait in empty classrooms to make their dramatic entrance.

In the Store I was the person of the moment. The birthday girl. The center. Bailey had graduated the year before, although to do so he had had to forfeit all pleasures to make up for his time lost in Baton Rouge.

My class was wearing butter-yellow piqué dresses, and Momma launched out on mine. She smocked the yoke into tiny crisscrossing puckers, then shirred the rest of the bodice. Her dark fingers ducked in and out of the lemony cloth as she embroidered raised daisies around the hem. Before she considered herself finished she had added a crocheted cuff on the puff sleeves, and a pointy crocheted collar.

I was going to be lovely. A walking model of all the various styles of fine hand sewing and it didn't worry me that I was only twelve years old and merely graduating from the eighth grade. Besides, many teachers in Arkansas Negro schools had only that diploma and were licensed to impart wisdom.

The days had become longer and more noticeable. The faded beige of former times had been replaced with strong and sure colors. I began to see my classmates' clothes, their skin tones, and the dust that waved off pussy willows. Clouds that lazed across the sky were objects of great concern to me. Their shiftier shapes might have held a message that in my new happiness and with a little bit of time I'd soon decipher. During that period I looked at the arch of heaven so religiously my neck kept a steady ache. I had taken to smiling more often, and my jaws hurt from the unaccustomed activity. Between the two physical sore spots, I suppose I could have been uncomfortable, but that was not the case. As a member of the winning team (the graduating class of 1940) I had outdistanced unpleasant sensations by miles. I was headed for the freedom of open fields.

10   Youth and social approval allied themselves with me and we trammeled memories of slights and insults. The wind of our swift passage remodeled my features. Lost tears were pounded to mud and then to dust. Years of withdrawal were brushed aside and left behind, as hanging ropes of parasitic moss.

     My work alone had awarded me a top place and I was going to be one of the first called in the graduating ceremonies. On the classroom blackboard, as well as on the bulletin board in the auditorium, there were blue stars and white stars and red stars. No absences, no tardinesses, and my academic work was among the best of the year. I could say the preamble to the Constitution even faster than Bailey. We timed ourselves often: "We the people of the United States in order to form a more perfect union . . ." I had memorized the Presidents of the United States from Washington to Roosevelt in chronological as well as alphabetical order.

     My hair pleased me too. Gradually the black mass had lengthened and thickened, so that it kept at last to its braided pattern, and I didn't have to yank my scalp off when I tried to comb it.

     Louise and I had rehearsed the exercises until we tired out ourselves. Henry Reed was class valedictorian. He was a small, very black boy with hooded eyes, a long, broad nose and an oddly shaped head. I had admired him for years because each term he and I vied for the best grades in our class. Most often he bested me, but instead of being disappointed I was pleased that we shared top places between us. Like many Southern Black children, he lived with his grandmother, who was as strict as Momma and as kind as she knew how to be. He was courteous, respectful and soft-spoken to elders, but on the playground he chose to play the roughest games. I admired him. Anyone, I reckoned, sufficiently afraid or sufficiently dull could be polite. But to be able to operate at a top level with both adults and children was admirable.

     His valedictory speech was entitled "To Be or Not To Be." The rigid tenth-grade teacher had helped him to write it. He'd been working on the dramatic stresses for months.

15   The weeks until graduation were filled with heady activities. A group of small children were to be presented in a play about buttercups and daisies and bunny rabbits. They could be heard throughout the building practicing their hops and their little songs that sounded like silver bells. The older girls (non-graduates, of course) were assigned the task of making refreshments for the night's festivities. A tangy scent of ginger, cinnamon, nutmeg and chocolate wafted around the home economics building as the budding cooks made samples for themselves and their teachers.

     In every corner of the workshop, axes and saws split fresh timber as the woodshop boys made sets and stage scenery. Only the graduates were left out of the general bustle. We were free to sit in the library at the back of the building or look in quite detachedly, naturally, on the measures being taken for our event.

     Even the minister preached on graduation the Sunday before. His subject was, "Let your light so shine that men will see your good works and praise your Father, Who is in Heaven." Although the sermon was purported to be addressed to us, he used the occasion to speak to backsliders, gamblers, and general ne'er-do-wells. But since he had called our names at the beginning of the service we were mollified.

Among Negroes the tradition was to give presents to children going only from one grade to another. How much more important this was when the person was graduating at the top of the class. Uncle Willie and Momma had sent away for a Mickey Mouse watch like Bailey's. Louise gave me four embroidered handkerchiefs. (I gave her three crocheted doilies.) Mrs. Sneed, the minister's wife, made me an underskirt to wear for graduation, and nearly every customer gave me a nickel or maybe even a dime with the instruction "Keep on moving to high ground," or some such encouragement.

Amazingly the great day finally dawned and I was out of bed before I knew it. I threw open the back door to see it more clearly, but Momma said, "Sister, come away from that door and put your robe on."

20   I hoped the memory of that morning would never leave me. Sunlight was itself still young, and the day had none of the insistence maturity would bring it in a few hours. In my robe and barefoot in the backyard, under cover of going to see about my new beans; I gave myself up to the gentle warmth and thanked God that no matter what evil I had done in my life He had allowed me to live to see this day. Somewhere in my fatalism I had expected to die, accidentally, and never have the chance to walk up the stairs in the auditorium and gracefully receive my hard-earned diploma. Out of God's merciful bosom I had won reprieve.

Bailey came out in his robe and gave me a box wrapped in Christmas paper. He said he had saved his money for months to pay for it. It felt like a box of chocolates, but I knew Bailey wouldn't save money to buy candy when we had all we could want under our noses.

He was as proud of the gift as I. It was a soft-leather-bound copy of a collection of poems by Edgar Allan Poe, or, as Bailey and I called him, "Eap." I turned to "Annabel Lee" and we walked up and down the garden rows, the cool dirt between our toes, reciting the beautifully sad lines.

Momma made a Sunday breakfast although it was only Friday. After we finished the blessing, I opened my eyes to find the watch on my plate. It was a dream of a day. Everything went smoothly and to my credit, I didn't have to be reminded or scolded for anything. Near evening I was too jittery to attend to chores, so Bailey volunteered to do all before his bath.

Days before, we had made a sign for the Store and as we turned out the lights Momma hung the cardboard over the doorknob. It read clearly: CLOSED. GRADUATION.

25   My dress fitted perfectly and everyone said that I looked like a sunbeam in it. On the hill, going toward the school, Bailey walked behind with Uncle Willie, who muttered, "Go on, Ju." He wanted him to walk ahead with us because it embarrassed him to have to walk so slowly. Bailey said he'd let the ladies walk together, and the men would bring up the rear. We all laughed, nicely.

Little children dashed by out of the dark like fireflies. Their crepe-paper dresses and butterfly wings were not made for running and we heard more than one rip, dryly, and the regretful "uh uh" that followed.

The school blazed without gaiety. The windows seemed cold and unfriendly from the lower hill. A sense of ill-fated timing crept over me, and if Momma hadn't reached for my hand I would have drifted back to Bailey and Uncle Willie, and possibly beyond. She made a few slow jokes about my feet getting cold, and tugged me along to the now-strange building.

Around the front steps, assurance came back. There were my fellow "greats," the graduating class. Hair brushed back, legs oiled, new dresses and pressed pleats, fresh pocket handkerchiefs and little handbags, all homesewn. Oh, we were up to snuff, all right. I joined my comrades and didn't even see my family go in to find seats in the crowded auditorium.

The school band struck up a march and all classes filed in as had been rehearsed. We stood in front of our seats, as assigned, and on a signal from the choir director, we sat. No sooner had this been accomplished than the band started to play the national anthem. We rose again and sang the song, after which we recited the pledge of allegiance. We remained standing for a brief minute before the choir director and the principal signaled to us, rather desperately I thought, to take our seats. The command was so unusual that our carefully rehearsed and smooth-running machine was thrown off. For a full minute we fumbled for our chairs and bumped into each other awkwardly. Habits change or solidify under pressure, so in our state of nervous tension we had been ready to follow our usual assembly pattern: the American National Anthem, then the pledge of allegiance, then the song every Black person I knew called the Negro National Anthem. All done in the same key, with the same passion and most often standing on the same foot.

30   Finding my seat at last, I was overcome with a presentiment of worse things to come. Something unrehearsed, unplanned, was going to happen, and we were going to be made to look bad. I distinctly remember being explicit in the choice of pronoun. It was "we," the graduating class, the unit, that concerned me then.

The principal welcomed "parents and friends" and asked the Baptist minister to lead us in prayer. His invocation was brief and punchy, and for a second I thought we were getting back on the high road to right action. When the principal came back to the dais, however, his voice had changed. Sounds always affected me profoundly and the principal's voice was one of my favorites. During assembly it melted and lowed weakly into the audience. It had not been in my plan to listen to him, but my curiosity was piqued and I straightened up to give him my attention.

He was talking about Booker T. Washington, our "late great leader," who said we can be as close as the fingers on the hand, etc. . . . Then he said a few vague things about friendship and the friendship of kindly people to those less fortunate than themselves. With that his voice nearly faded, thin, away. Like a river diminishing to a stream and then to a trickle. But he cleared his throat and said, "Our speaker tonight, who is also our friend, came from Texarkana to deliver the commencement address, but due to the irregularity of the train schedule, he's going to, as they say, 'speak and run.'" He said that we understood and wanted the man to know that we were most grateful for the time he was able to give us and then something about how we were willing always to adjust to another's program, and without more ado—"I give you Mr. Edward Donleavy."

Not one but two white men came through the door offstage. The shorter one walked to the speaker's platform, and the tall one moved over to the center seat and sat down. But that was our principal's seat, and already occupied. The dislodged gentleman bounced around for a long breath or two before the Baptist minister gave him his chair, then with more dignity than the situation deserved, the minister walked off the stage.

Donleavy looked at the audience once (on reflection, I'm sure that he wanted only to reassure himself that we were really there), adjusted his glasses and began to read from a sheaf of papers.

35   He was glad "to be here and to see the work going on just as it was in the other schools."

     At the first "Amen" from the audience I willed the offender to immediate death by choking on the word. But Amen's and Yes, sir's began to fall around the room like rain through a ragged umbrella.

     He told us of the wonderful changes we children in Stamps had in store. The Central School (naturally, the white school was Central) had already been granted improvements that would be in use in the fall. A well-known artist was coming from Little Rock to teach art to them. They were going to have the newest microscopes and chemistry equipment for their laboratory. Mr. Donleavy didn't leave us long in the dark over who made these improvements available to Central High. Nor were we to be ignored in the general betterment scheme he had in mind.

     He said that he had pointed out to people at a very high level that one of the first-line football tacklers at Arkansas Agricultural and Mechanical College had graduated from good old Lafayette County Training School. Here fewer Amen's were heard. Those few that did break through lay dully in the air with the heaviness of habit.

     He went on to praise us. He went on to say how he had bragged that "one of the best basketball players at Fisk sank his first ball right here at Lafayette County Training School."

40   The white kids were going to have a chance to become Galileos and Madame Curies and Edisons and Gauguins, and our boys (the girls weren't even in on it) would try to be Jesse Owenses and Joe Louises.

     Owens and the Brown Bomber were great heroes in our world, but what school official in the white-goddom of Little Rock had the right to decide that those two men must be our only heroes? Who decided that for Henry Reed to become a scientist he had to work like George Washington Carver, as a bootblack, to buy a lousy microscope? Bailey was obviously always going to be too small to be an athlete, so which concrete angel glued to what country seat had decided that if my brother wanted to become a lawyer he had to first pay penance for his skin by picking cotton and hoeing corn and studying correspondence books at night for twenty years?

     The man's dead words fell like bricks around the auditorium and too many settled in my belly. Constrained by hard-learned manners I couldn't look behind me, but to my left and right the proud graduating class of 1940 had dropped their heads. Every girl in my row had found something new to do with her handkerchief. Some folded the tiny squares into love knots, some into triangles, but most were wadding them, then pressing them flat on their yellow laps.

     On the dais, the ancient tragedy was being replayed. Professor Parsons sat, a sculptor's reject, rigid. His large, heavy body seemed devoid of will or willingness, and his eyes said he was no longer with us. The other teachers examined the flag (which was draped stage right) or their notes, or the windows which opened on our now-famous playing diamond.

     Graduation, the hush-hush magic time of frills and gifts and congratulations and diplomas, was finished for me before my name was called. The accomplishment was nothing. The meticulous maps, drawn in three colors of ink, learning and spelling decasyllabic words, memorizing the whole of *The Rape of Lucrece*—it was nothing. Donleavy had exposed us.

45   We were maids and farmers, handymen and washerwomen, and anything higher that we aspired to was farcical and presumptuous. Then I wished that

Gabriel Prosser and Nat Turner had killed all whitefolks in their beds and that Abraham Lincoln had been assassinated before the signing of the Emancipation Proclamation, and that Harriet Tubman had been killed by that blow on her head and Christopher Columbus had drowned in the *Santa Maria.*

It was awful to be Negro and have no control over my life. It was brutal to be young and already trained to sit quietly and listen to charges brought against my color and no chance of defense. We should all be dead. I thought I should like to see us all dead, one on top of the other. A pyramid of flesh with the white-folks on the bottom, as the broad base, then the Indians with their silly toma-hawks and teepees and wigwams and treaties, the Negroes with their mops and recipes and cotton sacks and spirituals sticking out of their mouths. The Dutch children should all stumble in their wooden shoes and break their necks. The French should choke to death on the Louisiana Purchase (1803) while silkworms ate all the Chinese with their stupid pigtails. As a species, we were an abomina-tion. All of us.

Donleavy was running for election, and assured our parents that if he won we could count on having the only colored paved playing field in that part of Arkansas. Also—he never looked up to acknowledge the grunts of acceptance—also, we were bound to get some new equipment for the home economics build-ing and the workshop.

He finished, and since there was no need to give any more than the most perfunctory thank-you's, he nodded to the men on the stage, and the tall white man who was never introduced joined him at the door. They left with the atti-tude that now they were off to something really important. (The graduation cer-emonies at Lafayette County Training School had been a mere preliminary.)

The ugliness they left was palpable. An uninvited guest who wouldn't leave. The choir was summoned and sang a modern arrangement of "Onward, Christ-ian Soldiers," with new words pertaining to graduates seeking their place in the world. But it didn't work. Elouise, the daughter of the Baptist minister, recited "Invictus," and I could have cried at the impertinence of "I am the master of my fate, I am the captain of my soul."

50   My name had lost its ring of familiarity and I had to be nudged to go and re-ceive my diploma. All my preparations had fled. I neither marched up to the stage like a conquering Amazon, nor did I look in the audience for Bailey's nod of approval. Marguerite Johnson, I heard the name again, my honors were read, there were noises in the audience of appreciation, and I took my place on the stage as rehearsed.

I thought about colors I hated: ecru, puce, lavender, beige and black.

There was shuffling and rustling around me, then Henry Reed was giving his valedictory address, "To Be or Not to Be." Hadn't he heard the whitefolks? We couldn't *be,* so the question was a waste of time. Henry's voice came out clear and strong. I feared to look at him. Hadn't he got the message? There was no "no-bler in the mind" for Negroes because the world didn't think we had minds, and they let us know it. "Outrageous fortune"? Now, that was a joke. When the cere-mony was over I had to tell Henry Reed some things. That is, if I still cared. Not "rub," Henry, "erase." "Ah, there's the erase." Us.

Henry had been a good student in elocution. His voice rose on tides of promise and fell on waves of warnings. The English teacher had helped him to create a sermon winging through Hamlet's soliloquy. To be a man, a doer, a builder, a leader, or to be a tool, an unfunny joke, a crusher of funky toadstools. I marveled that Henry could go through with the speech as if we had a choice.

I had been listening and silently rebutting each sentence with my eyes closed; then there was a hush, which in an audience warns that something unplanned is happening. I looked up and saw Henry Reed, the conservative, the proper, the A student, turn his back to the audience and turn to us (the proud graduating class of 1940) and sing, nearly speaking,

> Lift ev'ry voice and sing
> Till earth and heaven ring
> Ring with the harmonies of Liberty . . .

It was the poem written by James Weldon Johnson. It was the music composed by J. Rosamond Johnson. It was the Negro National Anthem. Out of habit we were singing it.

55   Our mothers and fathers stood in the dark hall and joined the hymn of encouragement. A kindergarten teacher led the small children onto the stage and the buttercups and daisies and bunny rabbits marked time and tried to follow:

> Stony the road we trod
> Bitter the chastening rod
> Felt in the days when hope, unborn, had died.
> Yet with a steady beat
> Have not our weary feet
> Come to the place for which our fathers sighed?

Every child I knew had learned that song with his ABC's and along with "Jesus Loves Me This I Know." But I personally had never heard it before. Never heard the words, despite the thousands of times I had sung them. Never thought they had anything to do with me.

On the other hand, the words of Patrick Henry had made such an impression on me that I had been able to stretch myself tall and trembling and say, "I know not what course others may take, but as for me, give me liberty or give me death."

And now I heard, really for the first time:

> We have come over a way that with tears has been watered,
> We have come, treading our path through the blood of the slaughtered.

While echoes of the song shivered in the air, Henry Reed bowed his head, said "Thank you," and returned to his place in the line. The tears that slipped down many faces were not wiped away in shame.

60   We were on top again. As always, again. We survived. The depths had been icy and dark, but now a bright sun spoke to our souls. I was no longer simply a member of the proud graduating class of 1940; I was a proud member of the wonderful, beautiful Negro race.

Oh, Black known and unknown poets, how often have your auctioned pains sustained us? Who will compute the lonely nights made less lonely by your songs, or the empty pots made less tragic by your tales?

If we were a people much given to revealing secrets, we might raise monuments and sacrifice to the memories of our poets, but slavery cured us of that weakness. It may be enough, however, to have it said that we survive in exact relationship to the dedication of our poets (include preachers, musicians and blues singers).

[1969]

Topics for Critical Thinking and Writing

1. In the first paragraph notice such overstatements as "glorious release," "the graduating classes themselves were the nobility," and "exotic destinations." Find further examples in the next few pages. What is the function of this diction?
2. How would you define "poets" as Angelou uses the word in the last sentence?
3. Characterize the writer as you perceive her up to the middle of paragraph 29. Support your characterizations with references to specific passages. Next, characterize her in the paragraph beginning "It was awful to be Negro" (paragraph 46). Next, characterize her on the basis of the entire essay. Finally, in a sentence, try to describe the change, telling the main attitudes or moods that she goes through.

JAMES JOYCE

James Joyce (1882–1941) was born into a middle-class family in Dublin, Ireland. His father drank, became increasingly irresponsible and unemployable, and the family sank in the social order. Still, Joyce received a strong classical education at excellent Jesuit schools and at University College, Dublin, where he studied modern languages. In 1902, at the age of twenty, he left Ireland so that he might spend the rest of his life writing about life in Ireland. ("The shortest way to Tara,"
he said, "is via Holyhead," i.e., the shortest way to the heart of Ireland is to take ship away.) In Trieste, Zurich, and Paris he supported his family in a variety of ways, sometimes teaching English in a Berlitz language school. His fifteen stories, collected under the title of Dubliners, *were written between 1904 and 1907, but he could not get them published until 1914. Next came a highly autobiographical novel,* A Portrait of the Artist as a Young Man *(1916).* Ulysses *(1922), a large novel covering eighteen hours in Dublin, was for some years banned by the United States Post Office, though few if any readers today find it offensive. Joyce spent most of the rest of his life working on* Finnegans Wake *(1939).*

Nine years before he succeeded in getting Dubliners *published he described the manuscript in these terms:*

My intention was to write a chapter of the moral history of my country and I chose Dublin for the scene because that city seemed to me the centre of paralysis. . . . I have written it for the most part in a style of scrupulous meanness and with the conviction that he is a very bold man who dares to alter in the presentment, still more to deform, whatever he has seen and heard.

Araby

North Richmond Street, being blind,[1] was a quiet street except at the hour when the Christian Brothers' School set the boys free. An uninhabited house of two stories stood at the blind end, detached from its neighbors in a square ground.

---

[1]**blind** a dead-end street (All notes are by the editors.)

The other houses of the street, conscious of decent lives within them, gazed at one another with brown imperturbable faces.

The former tenant of our house, a priest, had died in the back drawing-room. Air, musty from having long been enclosed, hung in all the rooms, and the waste room behind the kitchen was littered with old useless papers. Among these I found a few papercovered books, the pages of which were curled and damp: *The Abbot,* by Walter Scott, *The Devout Communicant* and *The Memoirs of Vidocq.*[2] I liked the last best because its leaves were yellow. The wild garden behind the house contained a central apple-tree and a few straggling bushes under one of which I found the late tenant's rusty bicycle-pump. He had been a very charitable priest; in his will he had left all his money to institutions and the furniture of his house to his sister.

When the short days of winter came dusk fell before we had well eaten our dinners. When we met in the street the houses had grown sombre. The space of sky above us was the colour of everchanging violet and towards it the lamps of the street lifted their feeble lanterns. The cold air stung us and we played till our bodies glowed. Our shouts echoed in the silent street. The career of our play brought us through the dark muddy lanes behind the houses where we ran the gauntlet of the rough tribes from the cottages, to the back doors of the dark dripping gardens where odours arose from the ashpits, to the dark odorous stables where a coachman smoothed and combed the horse or shook music from the buckled harness. When we returned to the street light from the kitchen windows had filled the areas. If my uncle was seen turning the corner we hid in the shadow until we had seen him safely housed. Or if Mangan's sister came out on the doorstep to call her brother in to his tea we watched her from our shadow peer up and down the street. We waited to see whether she would remain or go in and, if she remained, we left our shadow and walked up to Mangan's steps resignedly. She was waiting for us, her figure defined by the light from the half-opened door. Her brother always teased her before he obeyed and I stood by the railings looking at her. Her dress swung as she moved her body and the soft rope of her hair tossed from side to side.

Every morning I lay on the floor in the front parlour watching her door. The blind was pulled down to within an inch of the sash so that I could not be seen. When she came out on the doorstep my heart leaped. I ran to the hall, seized my books and followed her. I kept her brown figure always in my eye and, when we came near the point at which our ways diverged, I quickened my pace and passed her. This happened morning after morning. I had never spoken to her, except for a few casual words, and yet her name was like a summons to all my foolish blood.

5   Her image accompanied me even in places the most hostile to romance. On Saturday evenings when my aunt went marketing I had to go to carry some of the parcels. We walked through the flaring streets, jostled by drunken men and bargaining women, amid the curses of labourers, the shrill litanies of shop-boys who stood on 'guard by the barrels of pigs' cheeks, the nasal chanting of street-

---

[2]*The Abbot* was one of Scott's popular historical romances. *The Devout Communicant* was a Catholic religious manual; *The Memoirs of Vidocq* were the memoirs of the chief of the French detective force.

singers, who sang a *come-all-you* about O'Donovan Rossa,[3] or a ballad about the troubles in our native land. These noises converged in a single sensation of life for me: I imagined that I bore my chalice safely through a throng of foes. Her name sprang to my lips at moments in strange prayers and praises which I myself did not understand. My eyes were often full of tears (I could not tell why) and at times a flood from my heart seemed to pour itself out into my bosom. I thought little of the future. I did not know whether I would ever speak to her or not or, if I spoke to her, how I could tell her of my confused adoration. But my body was like a harp and her words and gestures were like fingers running upon the wires.

One evening I went into the back drawing-room in which the priest had died. It was a dark rainy evening and there was no sound in the house. Through one of the broken panes I heard the rain impinge upon the earth, the fine incessant needles of water playing in the sodden beds. Some distant lamp or lighted window gleamed below me. I was thankful that I could see so little. All my senses seemed to desire to veil themselves and, feeling that I was about to slip from them, I pressed the palms of my hands together until they trembled, murmuring: *O love! O love!* many times.

At last she spoke to me. When she addressed the first words to me I was so confused that I did not know what to answer. She asked me was I going to Araby.

I forget whether I answered yes or no. It would be a splendid bazaar, she said; she would love to go.

—And why can't you? I asked.

10   While she spoke she turned a silver bracelet round and round her wrist. She could not go, she said, because there would be a retreat that week in her convent. Her brother and two other boys were fighting for their caps and I was alone at the railings. She held one of the spikes, bowing her head towards me. The light from the lamp opposite our door caught the white curve of her neck, lit up her hair that rested there and, falling, lit up the hand upon the railing. It fell over one side of her dress and caught the white border of a petticoat, just visible as she stood at ease.

—It's well for you, she said.

—If I go, I said, I will bring you something.

What innumerable follies laid waste my waking and sleeping thoughts after that evening! I wished to annihilate the tedious intervening days. I chafed against the work of school. At night in my bedroom and by day in the classroom her image came between me and the page I strove to read. The syllables of the word *Araby* were called to me through the silence in which my soul luxuriated and cast an Eastern enchantment over me. I asked for leave to go to the bazaar on Saturday night. My aunt was surprised and hoped it was not some Freemason[2] affair. I answered few questions in class, I watched my master's face pass from amiability to sternness; he hoped I was not beginning to idle. I could not call my wandering thoughts together. I had hardly any patience with the serious work of life which, now that it stood between me and my desire, seemed to me child's play, ugly monotonous child's play.

---

[3]Jeremiah O'Donovan (1831–1915), a popular Irish leader who was jailed by the British for advocating violent rebellion. A "come-all-you" was a topical song that began "Come all you gallant Irishmen." [2]Irish Catholics viewed the Masons as their Protestant enemies.

On Saturday morning I reminded my uncle that I wished to go to the bazaar in the evening. He was fussing at the hallstand, looking for the hat-brush, and answered me curtly:

15   —Yes, boy, I know.

As he was in the hall I could not go into the front parlour and lie at the window. I left the house in bad humour and walked slowly towards the school. The air was pitilessly raw and already my heart misgave me.

When I came home to dinner my uncle had not yet been home. Still it was early. I sat staring at the clock for some time and, when its ticking began to irritate me, I left the room. I mounted the staircase and gained the upper part of the house. The high cold empty gloomy rooms liberated me and I went from room to room singing. From the front window I saw my companions playing below in the street. Their cries reached me weakened and indistinct and, leaning my forehead against the cool glass, I looked over at the dark house where she lived. I may have stood there for an hour, seeing nothing but the brown-clad figure cast by my imagination, touched discreetly by the lamplight at the curved neck, at the hand upon the railings and at the border below the dress.

When I came downstairs again I found Mrs Mercer sitting at the fire. She was an old garrulous woman, a pawnbroker's widow, who collected used stamps for some pious purpose. I had to endure the gossip of the tea-table. The meal was prolonged beyond an hour and still my uncle did not come. Mrs Mercer stood up to go: she was sorry she couldn't wait any longer, but it was after eight o'clock and she did not like to be out late, as the night air was bad for her. When she had gone I began to walk up and down the room, clenching my fists. My aunt said:

—I'm afraid you may put off your bazaar for this night of Our Lord.

20   At nine o'clock I heard my uncle's latchkey in the halldoor. I heard him talking to himself and heard the hallstand rocking when it had received the weight of his overcoat. I could interpret these signs. When he was midway through his dinner I asked him to give me the money to go to the bazaar. He had forgotten.

—The people are in bed and after their first sleep now, he said.

I did not smile. My aunt said to him energetically:

—Can't you give him the money and let him go? You've kept him late enough as it is.

My uncle said he was very sorry he had forgotten. He said he believed in the old saying: *All work and no play makes Jack a dull boy.* He asked me where I was going and, when I had told him a second time he asked me did I know *The Arab's Farewell to His Steed.*[4] When I left the kitchen he was about to recite the opening lines of the piece to my aunt.

25   I held a florin tightly in my hand as I strode down Buckingham Street towards the station. The sight of the streets thronged with buyers and glaring with gas recalled to me the purpose of my journey. I took my seat in a third-class carriage of a deserted train. After an intolerable delay the train moved out of the station slowly. It crept onward among ruinous houses and over the twinkling river. At Westland Row Station a crowd of people pressed to the carriage doors; but the porters moved them back, saying that it was a special train for the bazaar. I remained alone in the bare carriage. In a few minutes the train drew up beside

---

[4]"The Arab to His Favorite Steed" was a popular sentimental poem by Caroline Norton (1808–1877).

an improvised wooden platform. I passed out on to the road and saw by the lighted dial of a clock that it was ten minutes to ten. In front of me was a large building which displayed the magical name.

I could not find any sixpenny entrance and, fearing that the bazaar would be closed, I passed in quickly through a turnstile, handing a shilling to a weary-looking man. I found myself in a big hall girdled at half its height by a gallery. Nearly all the stalls were closed and the greater part of the hall was in darkness. I recognised a silence like that which pervades a church after a service. I walked into the center of the bazaar timidly. A few people were gathered about the stalls which were still open. Before a curtain, over which the words *Café Chantant* were written in coloured lamps, two men were counting money on a salver. I listened to the fall of the coins.

Remembering with difficulty why I had come I went over to one of the stalls and examined porcelain vases and flowered tea-sets. At the door of the stall a young lady was talking and laughing with two young gentlemen. I remarked their English accents and listened vaguely to their conversation.

—O, I never said such a thing!

—O, but you did!

30 —O, but I didn't!

—Didn't she say that?

—Yes! I heard her.

—O, there's a . . . fib!

Observing me the young lady came over and asked me did I wish to buy anything. The tone of her voice was not encouraging; she seemed to have spoken to me out of a sense of duty. I looked humbly at the great jars that stood like eastern guards at either side of the dark entrance to the stall and murmured:

35 —No, thank you.

The young lady changed the position of one of the vases and went back to the two young men. They began to talk of the same subject. Once or twice the young lady glanced at me over her shoulder.

I lingered before her stall, though I knew my stay was useless, to make my interest in her wares seem the more real. Then I turned away slowly and walked down the middle of the bazaar. I allowed the two pennies to fall against the sixpence in my pocket. I heard a voice call from one end of the gallery that the light was out. The upper part of the hall was now completely dark.

Gazing up into the darkness I saw myself as a creature driven and derided by vanity; and my eyes burned with anguish and anger.

[1905]

 ## Topics for Critical Thinking and Writing

1. Joyce wrote a novel called *A Portrait of the Artist as a Young Man.* Write an essay of about 500 words on "Araby" as a portrait of the artist as a boy.

2. In an essay of about 500 words, consider the role of images of darkness and blindness and what they reveal to us about "Araby" as a story of the fall from innocence into painful awareness.

3. How old, approximately, is the narrator of "Araby" at the time of the experience he describes? How old is he at the time he tells his story? On what evidence do you base your estimates?

4. The boy, apparently an only child, lives with an uncle and aunt, rather than with parents. Why do you suppose Joyce put him in this family setting rather than some other?

5. The story is rich in images of religion. This in itself is not surprising, for the story is set in Roman Catholic Ireland, but the religious images are not simply references to religious persons or objects. In an essay of 500 to 750 words, discuss how these images reveal the narrator's state of mind.

 **LANGSTON HUGHES**

Langston Hughes (1902–67), an African-American writer, was born in Joplin, Missouri, lived part of his youth in Mexico, spent a year at Columbia University, served as a merchant seaman, and worked in a Paris nightclub, where he showed some of his poems to Dr. Alain Locke, a strong advocate of African-American literature. Encouraged by Locke, when Hughes returned to the United States he continued to write, publishing fiction, plays, essays, and biographies; he also founded theaters, gave public readings, and was, in short, a highly visible presence.

One Friday Morning

The thrilling news did not come directly to Nancy Lee, but it came in little indirections that finally added themselves up to one tremendous fact: she had won the prize! But being a calm and quiet young lady, she did not say anything, although the whole high school buzzed with rumors, guesses, reportedly authentic announcements on the part of students who had no right to be making announcements at all—since no student really knew yet who had won this year's art scholarship.

But Nancy Lee's drawing was so good, her lines so sure, her colors so bright and harmonious, that certainly no other student in the senior art class at George Washington High was thought to have very much of a chance. Yet you never could tell. Last year nobody had expected Joe Williams to win the Artist Club scholarship with that funny modernistic water color he had done of the high-level bridge. In fact, it was hard to make out there was a bridge until you had looked at the picture a long time. Still, Joe Williams got the prize, was feted by the community's leading painters, club women, and society folks at a big banquet at the Park-Rose Hotel, and was now an award student at the Art School—the city's only art school.

Nancy Lee Johnson was a colored girl, a few years out of the South. But seldom did her high-school classmates think of her as colored. She was smart, pretty, and brown, and fitted in well with the life of the school. She stood high in scholarship, played a swell game of basketball, had taken part in the senior musical in a soft, velvety voice, and had never seemed to intrude or stand out, except in pleasant ways, so it was seldom even mentioned—her color.

Nancy Lee sometimes forgot she was colored herself. She liked her classmates and her school. Particularly she liked her art teacher, Miss Dietrich, the tall red-haired woman who taught her law and order in doing things; and the beauty of working step by step until a job is done; a picture finished; a design created; or a block print carved out of nothing but an idea and a smooth square of linoleum, inked, proofs made, and finally put down on paper—clean, sharp, beautiful, individual, unlike any other in the world, thus making the paper have a meaning nobody else could give it except Nancy Lee. That was the wonderful thing about true creation. You made something nobody else on earth could make—but you.

5   Miss Dietrich was the kind of teacher who brought out the best in her students—but their own best, not anybody else's copied best. For anybody else's best, great though it might be, even Michelangelo's, wasn't enough to please Miss Dietrich, dealing with the creative impulses of young men and women living in an American city in the Middle West, and being American.

Nancy Lee was proud of being American, a Negro American with blood out of Africa a long time ago, too many generations back to count. But her parents had taught her the beauties of Africa, its strength, its song, its mighty rivers, its early smelting of iron, its building of the pyramids, and its ancient and important civilizations. And Miss Dietrich had discovered for her the sharp and humorous lines of African sculpture, Benin, Congo, Makonde. Nancy Lee's father was a mail carrier, her mother a social worker in a city settlement house. Both parents had been to Negro colleges in the South. And her mother had gotten a further degree in social work from a Northern university. Her parents were, like most Americans, simple, ordinary people who had worked hard and steadily for their education. Now they were trying to make it easier for Nancy Lee to achieve learning than it had been for them. They would be very happy when they heard of the award to their daughter—yet Nancy did not tell them. To surprise them would be better. Besides, there had been a promise.

Casually, one day, Miss Dietrich asked Nancy Lee what color frame she thought would be best on her picture. That had been the first inkling.

"Blue," Nancy Lee said. Although the picture had been entered in the Artist Club contest a month ago, Nancy Lee did not hesitate in her choice of a color for the possible frame, since she could still see her picture clearly in her mind's eye—for that picture waiting for the blue frame had come out of her soul, her own life, and had bloomed into miraculous being with Miss Dietrich's help. It was, she knew, the best water color she had painted in her four years as a high-school art student, and she was glad she had made something Miss Dietrich liked well enough to permit her to enter in the contest before she graduated.

It was not a modernistic picture in the sense that you had to look at it a long time to understand what it meant. It was just a simple scene in the city park on a spring day, with the trees still leaflessly lacy against the sky, the new grass fresh and green, a flag on a tall pole in the center, children playing, and an old Negro woman sitting on a bench with her head turned. A lot for one picture, to be sure, but it was not there in heavy and final detail like a calendar. Its charm was that everything was light and airy, happy like spring, with a lot of blue sky; paper-white clouds, and air showing through. You could tell that the old Negro woman was looking at the flag, and that the flag was proud in the spring breeze, and that the breeze helped to make the children's dresses billow as they played.

10   Miss Dietrich had taught Nancy Lee how to paint spring, people, and a breeze on what was only a plain white piece of paper from the supply closet. But Miss Dietrich had not said make it like any other spring-people-breeze ever seen before. She let it remain Nancy Lee's own. That is how the old Negro woman happened to be there looking at the flag—for in her mind the flag, the spring, and the woman formed a kind of triangle holding a dream Nancy Lee wanted to express. White stars on a blue field, spring, children, ever-growing life, and an old woman. Would the judges at the Artist Club like it?

One wet, rainy April afternoon Miss O'Shay, the girls' vice-principal, sent for Nancy Lee to stop by her office as school closed. Pupils without umbrellas or raincoats were clustered in doorways, hoping to make it home between showers. Outside the skies were gray. Nancy Lee's thoughts were suddenly gray, too.

She did not think she had done anything wrong, yet that tight little knot came in her throat just the same as she approached Miss O'Shay's door. Perhaps she had banged her locker too often and too hard. Perhaps the note in French she had written to Sallie halfway across the study hall just for fun had never gotten to Sallie but into Miss O'Shay's hands instead. Or maybe she was failing in some subject and wouldn't be allowed to graduate. Chemistry! A pang went through the pit of her stomach.

She knocked on Miss O'Shay's door. That familiarly solid and competent voice said, "Come in."

Miss O'Shay had a way of making you feel welcome, even if you came to be expelled.

15   "Sit down, Nancy Lee Johnson," said Miss O'Shay. "I have something to tell you." Nancy Lee sat down. "But I must ask you to promise not to tell anyone yet."

"I won't, Miss O'Shay," Nancy Lee said, wondering what on earth the principal had to say to her.

"You are about to graduate," Miss O'Shay said. "And we shall miss you. You have been an excellent student, Nancy, and you will not be without honors on the senior list, as I am sure you know."

At that point there was a light knock on the door. Miss O'Shay called out, "Come in," and Miss Dietrich entered. "May I be a part of this, too?" she asked, tall and smiling.

"Of course," Miss O'Shay said. "I was just telling Nancy Lee what we thought of her. But I hadn't gotten around to giving her the news. Perhaps, Miss Dietrich, you'd like to tell her yourself."

20   Miss Dietrich was always direct. "Nancy Lee," she said, "your picture has won the Artist Club scholarship."

The slender brown girl's eyes widened, her heart jumped, then her throat tightened again. She tried to smile, but instead tears came to her eyes.

"Dear Nancy Lee," Miss O'Shay said, "we are so happy for you." The elderly white woman took her hand and shook it warmly while Miss Dietrich beamed with pride.

Nancy Lee must have danced all the way home. She never remembered quite how she got there through the rain. She hoped she had been dignified. But certainly she hadn't stopped to tell anybody her secret on the way. Raindrops, smiles, and tears mingled on her brown cheeks. She hoped her mother hadn't yet gotten home and that the house was empty. She wanted to have time to calm down and look natural before she had to see anyone. She didn't want to be bursting with excitement—having a secret to contain.

Miss O'Shay's calling her to the office had been in the nature of a preparation and a warning. The kind, elderly vice-principal said she did not believe in catching, young ladies unawares, even with honors, so she wished her to know about the coming award. In making acceptance speeches she wanted her to be calm, prepared, not nervous, overcome, and frightened. So Nancy Lee was asked to think what she would say when the scholarship was conferred upon her a few days hence, both at the Friday morning high-school assembly hour, when the announcement would be made, and at the evening banquet of the Artist

Club. Nancy Lee promised the vice-principal to think calmly about what she would say.

25   Miss Dietrich had then asked for some facts about her parents, her background, and her life, since such material would probably be desired for the papers. Nancy Lee had told her how, six years before, they had come up from the Deep South, her father having been successful in achieving a transfer from the one post office to another, a thing he had long sought in order to give Nancy Lee a chance to go to school in the North. Now they lived in a modest Negro neighborhood, went to see the best plays when they came to town, and had been saving to send Nancy Lee to art school, in case she were permitted to enter. But the scholarship would help a great deal, for they were not rich people.

"Now Mother can have a new coat next winter," Nancy Lee thought, "because my tuition will all be covered for the first year. And once in art school, there are other scholarships I can win."

Dreams began to dance through her head, plans and ambitions, beauties she would create for herself, her parents, and the Negro people—for Nancy Lee possessed a deep and reverent race pride. She could see the old woman in her picture (really her grandmother in the South) lifting her head to the bright stars on the flag in the distance. A Negro in America! Often hurt, discriminated against, sometimes lynched—but always there were the stars on the blue body of the flag. Was there any other flag in the world that had so many stars? Nancy Lee thought deeply, but she could remember none in all the encyclopedias or geographies she had ever looked into.

"Hitch your wagon to a star," Nancy Lee thought, dancing home in the rain. "Who were our flag-makers?"

Friday morning came, the morning when the world would know—her high-school world, the newspaper world, her mother and dad. Dad could not be there at the assembly to hear the announcement, nor see her prize picture displayed on the stage, nor to listen to Nancy Lee's little speech of acceptance, but Mother would be able to come, although Mother was much puzzled as to why Nancy Lee was so insistent she be at school on that particular Friday morning.

30   When something is happening, something new and fine, something that will change your very life, it is hard to go to sleep at night for thinking about it, and hard to keep your heart from pounding, or a strange little knot of joy from gathering in your throat. Nancy Lee had taken her bath, brushed her hair until it glowed, and had gone to bed thinking about the next day, the big day, when before three thousand students, she would be the one student honored, her painting the one painting to be acclaimed as the best of the year from all the art classes of the city. Her short speech of gratitude was ready. She went over it in her mind, not word for word (because she didn't want it to sound as if she had learned it by heart), but she let the thoughts flow simply and sincerely through her consciousness many times.

When the president of the Artist Club presented her with the medal and scroll of the scholarship award, she would say:

"Judges and members of the Artist Club. I want to thank you for this award that means so much to me personally and through me to my people, the colored people of this city, who, sometimes, are discouraged and bewildered, thinking that color and poverty are against them. I accept this award with gratitude and pride, not for myself alone, but for my race that believes in American opportunity and American fairness—and the bright stars in our flag. I thank Miss Dietrich and the teachers who made it possible for me to have the knowledge and training that lie behind this honor you have conferred upon my painting. When I came here from the South a few years ago, I was not sure how you would receive me. You received me well. You have given me a chance and helped me along the road I wanted to follow. I suppose the judges know that every week here at assembly the students of this school pledge allegiance to the flag. I shall try to be worthy of that pledge, and of the help and friendship and understanding of my fellow citizens of whatever race or creed, and of our American dream of 'Liberty and justice for all!'"

That would be her response before the students in the morning. How proud and happy the Negro pupils would be, perhaps almost as proud as they were of the one colored star on the football team. Her mother would probably cry with happiness. Thus Nancy Lee went to sleep dreaming of a wonderful tomorrow.

The bright sunlight of an April morning woke her. There was breakfast with her parents—their half-amused and puzzled faces across the table, wondering what could be this secret that made her eyes so bright. The swift walk to school; the clock in the tower almost nine; hundreds of pupils streaming into the long, rambling old building that was the city's largest high school; the sudden quiet of the homeroom after the bell rang; then the teacher opening her record book to call the roll. But just before she began, she looked across the room until her eyes located Nancy Lee.

35   "Nancy," she said, "Miss O'Shay would like to see you in her office, please."

Nancy Lee rose and went out while the names were being called and the word *present* added its period to each name. Perhaps, Nancy Lee thought, the reporters from the papers had already come. Maybe they wanted to take her picture before assembly, which wasn't until ten o'clock. (Last year they had had the photograph of the winner of the award in the morning papers as soon as the announcement had been made.)

Nancy Lee knocked at Miss O'Shay's door.

"Come in."

The vice-principal stood at her desk. There was no one else in the room. It was very quiet.

40   "Sit down, Nancy Lee," she said. Miss O'Shay did not smile. There was a long pause. The seconds went by slowly. "I do not know how to tell you what I have to say," the elderly woman began, her eyes on the papers on her desk. "I am indignant and ashamed for myself and for this city." Then she lifted her eyes and looked at Nancy Lee in the neat blue dress, sitting there before her. "You are not to receive the scholarship this morning."

Outside in the hall the electric bells announcing the first period rang, loud and interminably long. Miss O'Shay remained silent. To the brown girl there in the chair, the room, grew suddenly smaller, smaller, smaller, and there was no air. She could not speak.

Miss O'Shay said, "When the committee learned that you were colored, they changed their plans."

Still Nancy Lee said nothing, for there was no air to give breath to her lungs.

"Here is the letter from the committee, Nancy Lee." Miss O'Shay picked it up and read the final paragraph to her.

45   "'It seems to us wiser to arbitrarily rotate the award among the various high schools of the city from now on. And especially in this case since the student chosen happens to be colored, a circumstance which unfortunately, had we known, might have prevented this embarrassment. But there have never been any Negro students in the local art school, and the presence of one there might create difficulties for all concerned. We have high regard for the quality of Nancy

Lee Johnson's talent, but we do not feel it would be fair to honor it with the Artist Club award.'" Miss O'Shay paused. She put the letter down.

"Nancy Lee, I am very sorry to have to give you this message."

"But my speech," Nancy Lee said, "was about . . . ." The words stuck in her throat. ". . . about America . . . ."

Miss O'Shay had risen; she turned her back and stood looking out the window at the spring tulips in the school yard.

"I thought, since the award would be made at assembly right after our oath of allegiance," the words tumbled almost hysterically from Nancy Lee's throat now, "I would put part of the flag salute in my speech. You know, Miss O'Shay, that part about 'liberty and justice for all.'"

50   "I know," said Miss O'Shay, slowly facing the room again. "But America is only what we who believe in it make it. I am Irish. You may not know, Nancy Lee, but years ago we were called the dirty Irish, and mobs rioted against us in the big cities, and we were invited to go back where we came from. But we didn't go. And we didn't give up, because we believed in the American dream, and in our power to make that dream come true. Difficulties, yes. Mountains to climb, yes. Discouragements to face, yes. Democracy to make, yes. That is it, Nancy Lee! We still have in this world of ours democracy to *make*. You and I, Nancy Lee. But the premise and the base are here, the lines of the Declaration of Independence and the words of Lincoln are here, and the stars in our flag. Those who deny you this scholarship do not know the meaning of those stars, but it's up to us to make them know. As a teacher in the public schools of this city, I myself will go before the school board and ask them to remove from our system the offer of any prizes or awards denied to any student because of race or color."

Suddenly Miss O'Shay stopped speaking. Her clear, clear blue eyes looked into those of the girl before her. The woman's eyes were full of strength and courage. "Lift up your head, Nancy Lee, and smile at me."

Miss O'Shay stood against the open window with the green lawn and the tulips beyond, the sunlight tangled in her gray hair, her voice an electric flow of strength to the hurt spirit of Nancy Lee. The Abolitionists who believed in freedom when there was slavery must have been like that. The first white teachers who went into the Deep South to teach the freed slaves must have been like that. All those who stand against ignorance, narrowness, hate, and mud on stars must be like that.

Nancy Lee lifted her head and smiled. The bell for assembly rang. She went through the long hall filled with students, toward the auditorium.

"There will be other awards," Nancy Lee thought. "There're schools in other cities. This won't keep me down. But when I'm a woman, I'll fight to see that these things don't happen to other girls as this has happened to me. And men and women like Miss O'Shay will help me."

55   She took her seat among the seniors. The doors of the auditorium closed. As the principal came onto the platform, the students rose and turned their eyes to the flag on the stage.

One hand went to the heart, the other outstretched toward the flag. Three thousand voices spoke. Among them was the voice of a dark girl whose cheeks were suddenly wet with tears, ". . . one nation indivisible, with liberty and justice for all."

"That is the land we must make," she thought.

[1941]

Topics for Critical Thinking and Writing

1. The third paragraph begins: "Nancy Lee Johnson was a colored girl . . . ." How would your response to the opening of the story change if this paragraph were placed at the very beginning?
2. Nancy Lee takes pride in her identity as both a "Negro" and an "American." How does she define and understand each of these terms? Does she perceive them to be at all at odds with one another? Is she admirable in her convictions, or is she simply naive?
3. This is a story about racism, but it is also a study (and an affirmation) of American ideals and principles. What is your response to Miss O'Shay's inspiring words to Nancy Lee at the end of the story? What is Nancy Lee's response to them, and your response to her? Does Hughes succeed in making us believe in, and accept, Nancy Lee's feelings at the conclusion?

 ## HISAYE YAMAMOTO

Hisaye Yamamoto was born in 1921 in Redondo Beach, California. Before the Second World War she contributed to the Japan-California Daily News, but when the United States entered the war she and her family were interned, along with more than a hundred thousand other persons of Japanese ancestry. She was sent to the Colorado River Relocation Center in Poston, Arizona, where she wrote for the camp's newspaper.

Yamamoto writes chiefly of rural Japanese Americans, usually setting her stories in the Depression or in the 1940s. "Yoneko's Earthquake" appeared in Best American Short Stories of 1952. *Five of her stories have been collected in a volume called* Seventeen Syllables *(1985).*

Yoneko's Earthquake

Yoneko Hosoume became a free-thinker on the night of March 10, 1933, only a few months after her first actual recognition of God. Ten years old at the time, of course she had heard rumors about God all along, long before Marpo came. Her cousins who lived in the city were all Christians, living as they did right next door to a Baptist church exclusively for Japanese people. These city cousins, of whom there were several, had been baptized en masse, and were very proud of their condition. Yoneko was impressed when she heard of this and thereafter was given to referring to them as "my cousins, the Christians." She, too, yearned at times after Christianity, but she realized the absurdity of her whim, seeing that there was no Baptist church for Japanese in the rural community she lived in. Such a church would have been impractical, moreover, since Yoneko, her father, her mother, and her little brother Seigo were the only Japanese thereabouts. They were the only ones, too, whose agriculture was so diverse as to include blackberries, cabbages, rhubarb, potatoes, cucumbers, onions, and cantaloupes. The rest of the countryside there was like one vast orange grove.

Yoneko had entered her cousins' church once, but she could not recall the sacred occasion without mortification. It had been one day when the cousins had taken her and Seigo along with them to Sunday school. The church was a narrow, wooden building mysterious-looking because of its unusual bluish-gray paint and its steeple, but the basement schoolroom inside had been disappointingly ordinary, with desks, a blackboard, and erasers. They had all sung "Let Us Gather at the River" in Japanese. This goes:

> *Mamonaku kanata no*
> *Nagare no soba de*
> *Tanoshiku ai-masho*
> *Mata tomodachi to*
>
> *Mamonaku ai-masho*
> *Kirei-na, kirei-na kawa de*
> *Tanoshiku ai-masho*
> *Mata tomodachi to.*

Yoneko had not known the words at all, but always clever in such situations, she had opened her mouth and grimaced nonchalantly to the rhythm. What with everyone else singing at the top of his lungs, no one had noticed that she was not making a peep. Then everyone had sat down again and the man had suggested, "Let us pray." Her cousins and the rest had promptly curled their arms on the desks to make nests for their heads, and Yoneko had done the same. But not Seigo. Because when the room had become so still that one was aware of the breathing, the creaking, and the chittering in the trees outside, Seigo, sitting with her, had suddenly flung his arm around her neck and said with concern, "Sis, what are you crying for? Don't cry." Even the man had laughed and Yoneko had been terribly ashamed that Seigo should thus disclose them to be interlopers. She had pinched him fiercely and he had begun to cry, so she had had to drag him outside, which was a fortunate move, because he had immediately wet his pants. But he had been only three then, so it was not very fair to expect dignity of him.

So it remained for Marpo to bring the word of God to Yoneko, Marpo with the face like brown leather, the thin mustache like Edmund Lowe's,[1] and the rare, breathtaking smile like white gold. Marpo, who was twenty-seven years old, was a Filipino and his last name was lovely, something like Humming Wing, but no one ever ascertained the spelling of it. He ate principally rice, just as though he were Japanese, but he never sat down to the Hosoume table, because he lived in the bunkhouse out by the barn and cooked on his own kerosene stove. Once Yoneko read somewhere that Filipinos trapped wild dogs, starved them for a time, then, feeding them mountains of rice, killed them at the peak of their bloatedness, thus insuring themselves meat ready to roast, stuffing and all, without further ado. This, the book said, was considered a delicacy. Unable to hide her disgust and her fascination, Yoneko went straightway to Marpo and asked, "Marpo, is it true that you eat dogs?" and he, flashing that smile, answered, "Don't be funny, honey!" This caused her no end of amusement, because it was a poem, and she completely forgot about the wild dogs.

Well, there seemed to be nothing Marpo could not do. Mr. Hosoume said Marpo was the best hired man he had ever had, and he said this often, because it was an irrefutable fact among Japanese in general that Filipinos in general were

---

[1] a movie actor popular in the 1930s

an indolent lot. Mr. Hosoume ascribed Marpo's industry to his having grown up in Hawaii, where there is known to be considerable Japanese influence. Marpo had gone to a missionary school there and he owned a Bible given him by one of his teachers. This had black leather covers that gave as easily as cloth, golden edges, and a slim purple ribbon for a marker. He always kept it on the little table by his bunk, which was not a bed with springs but a low, three-plank shelf with a mattress only. On the first page of the book, which was stiff and black, his teacher had written in large swirls of white ink, "As we draw near to God, He will draw near to us."

5   What, for instance, could Marpo do? Why, it would take an entire, leisurely evening to go into his accomplishments adequately, because there was not only Marpo the Christian and Marpo the best hired man, but Marpo the athlete, Marpo the musician (both instrumental and vocal), Marpo the artist, and Marpo the radio technician:

(1) As an athlete, Marpo owned a special pair of black shoes, equipped with sharp nails on the soles, which he kept in shape with the regular application of neatsfoot oil. Putting these on, he would dash down the dirt road to the highway, a distance of perhaps half a mile, and back again. When he first came to work for the Hosoumes, he undertook this sprint every evening before he went to get his supper but, as time went on, he referred to these shoes less and less and, in the end, when he left, he had not touched them for months. He also owned a muscle-builder sent him by Charles Atlas which, despite his unassuming size, he could stretch the length of his outspread arms; his teeth gritted then and his whole body became temporarily victim to a jerky vibration. (2) As an artist, Marpo painted larger-than-life water colors of his favorite movie stars, all of whom were women and all of whom were blonde, like Ann Harding and Jean Harlow, and tacked them up on his walls. He also made for Yoneko a folding contraption of wood holding two pencils, one with lead and one without, with which she, too, could obtain double-sized likenesses of any picture she wished. It was a fragile instrument, however, and Seigo splintered it to pieces one day when Yoneko was away at school. He claimed he was only trying to copy Boob McNutt from the funny paper when it failed. (3) As a musician, Marpo owned a violin for which he had paid over one hundred dollars. He kept this in a case whose lining was red velvet, first wrapping it gently in a brilliant red silk scarf. This scarf, which weighed nothing, he tucked under his chin when he played, gathering it up delicately by the center and flicking it once to unfurl it—a gesture Yoneko prized. In addition to this, Marpo was a singer, with a soft tenor which came out in professional quavers and rolled r's when he applied a slight pressure to his Adam's apple with thumb and forefinger. His violin and vocal repertoire consisted of the same numbers, mostly hymns and Irish folk airs. He was especially addicted to "The Rose of Tralee" and the "Londonderry Air." (4) Finally, as a radio technician who had spent two previous winters at a specialists' school in the city, Marpo had put together a bulky table-size radio which brought in equal proportions of static and entertainment. He never got around to building a cabinet to house it and its innards of metal and glass remained public throughout its lifetime. This was just as well, for not a week passed without Marpo's deciding to solder one bit or another. Yoneko and Seigo became a part of the great listening audience with such fidelity that Mr. Hosoume began remarking the fact that they dwelt more with Marpo than with their own parents. He eventually took a serious view of the matter and bought the naked radio

from Marpo, who thereupon put away his radio manuals and his soldering iron in the bottom of his steamer trunk and divided more time among his other interests.

However, Marpo's versatility was not revealed, as it is here, in a lump. Yoneko uncovered it fragment by fragment every day, by dint of unabashed questions, explorations among his possessions, and even silent observation, although this last was rare. In fact, she and Seigo visited with Marpo at least once a day and both of them regularly came away amazed with their findings. The most surprising thing was that Marpo was, after all this, a rather shy young man meek to the point of speechlessness in the presence of Mr. and Mrs. Hosoume. With Yoneko and Seigo, he was somewhat more self-confident and at ease.

It is not remembered now just how Yoneko and Marpo came to open their protracted discussion on religion. It is sufficient here to note that Yoneko was an ideal apostle, adoring Jesus, desiring Heaven, and fearing Hell. Once Marpo had enlightened her on these basics, Yoneko never questioned their truth. The questions she put up to him, therefore, sought neither proof of her exegeses nor balm for her doubts, but simply additional color to round out her mental images. For example, who did Marpo suppose was God's favorite movie star? Or, what sound did Jesus' laughter have (it must be like music, she added, nodding sagely, answering herself to her own satisfaction), and did Marpo suppose that God's sense of humor would have appreciated the delicious chant she had learned from friends at school today:

There ain't no bugs on us,
There ain't no bugs on us,
There may be bugs on the rest of you mugs,
But there ain't no bugs on us!

Or, did Marpo believe Jesus to have been exempt from stinging eyes when he shampooed that long, naturally wavy hair of his?

To shake such faith, there would have been required a most monstrous upheaval of some sort, and it might be said that this is just what happened. For early on the evening of March 10, 1933, a little after five o'clock this was, as Mrs. Hosoume was getting supper, as Marpo was finishing up in the fields alone because Mr. Hosoume had gone to order some chicken fertilizer, and as Yoneko and Seigo were listening to Skippy, a tremendous roar came out of nowhere and the Hosoume house began shuddering violently as though some giant had seized it in his two hands and was giving it a good shaking. Mrs. Hosoume, who remembered similar, although milder experiences, from her childhood in Japan, screamed, *"Jishin, jishin!"*[2] before she ran and grabbed Yoneko and Seigo each by a hand and dragged them outside with her. She took them as far as the middle of the rhubarb patch near the house, and there they all crouched, pressed together, watching the world about them rock and sway. In a few minutes, Marpo, stumbling in from the fields, joined them, saying, "Earthquake, earthquake!" and he gathered them all in his arms, as much to protect them as to support himself.

---

[2]earthquake (Japanese)

10   Mr. Hosoume came home later that evening in a stranger's car, with another stranger driving the family Reo. Pallid, trembling, his eyes wildly staring, he could have been mistaken for a drunkard, except that he was famous as a teetotaler. It seemed that he had been on the way home when the first jolt came, that the old green Reo had been kissed by a broken live wire dangling from a suddenly leaning pole. Mr. Hosoume, knowing that the end had come by electrocution, had begun to writhe and kick and this had been his salvation. His hands had flown from the wheel, the car had swerved into a ditch, freeing itself from the sputtering wire. Later, it was found that he was left permanently inhibited about driving automobiles and permanently incapable of considering electricity with calmness. He spent the larger part of his later life weakly, wandering about the house or fields and lying down frequently to rest because of splitting headaches and sudden dizzy spells.

So it was Marpo who went back into the house as Yoneko screamed, "No, Marpo, no!" and brought out the Hosoumes' kerosene stove, the food, the blankets, while Mr. Hosoume huddled on the ground near his family.

The earth trembled for days afterwards. The Hosoumes and Marpo Humming Wing lived during that time on a natural patch of Bermuda grass between the house and the rhubarb patch remembering to take three meals a day and retire at night. Marpo ventured inside the house many times despite Yoneko's protests and reported the damage slight: a few dishes had been broken; a gallon jug of mayonnaise had fallen from the top pantry shelf and spattered the kitchen floor with yellow blobs and pieces of glass.

Yoneko was in constant terror during this experience. Immediately on learning what all the commotion was about, she began praying to God to end this violence. She entreated God, flattered Him, wheedled Him, commanded Him, but He did not listen to her at all—inexorably, the earth went on rumbling. After three solid hours of silent, desperate prayer, without any results whatsoever, Yoneko began to suspect that God was either powerless, callous, downright cruel, or nonexistent. In the murky night, under a strange moon wearing a pale ring of light, she decided upon the last as the most plausible theory. "Ha," was one of the things she said tremulously to Marpo, when she was not begging him to stay out of the house, "you and your God!"

The others soon oriented themselves to the catastrophe with philosophy, saying how fortunate they were to live in the country where the peril was less than in the city and going so far as to regard the period as a sort of vacation from work, with their enforced alfresco existence a sort of camping trip. They tried to bring Yoneko to partake of this pleasant outlook, but she, shivering with each new quiver, looked on them as dreamers who refused to see things as they really were. Indeed, Yoneko's reaction was so notable that the Hosoume household thereafter spoke of the event as "Yoneko's earthquake."

15   After the earth subsided and the mayonnaise was mopped off the kitchen floor, life returned to normal, except that Mr. Hosoume stayed at home most of the time. Sometimes, if he had a relatively painless day, he would have supper on the stove when Mrs. Hosoume came in from the fields. Mrs. Hosoume and Marpo did all the field labor now, except on certain overwhelming days when several Mexicans were hired to assist them. Marpo did most of the driving, too, and it was now he and Mrs. Hosoume who went into town on the weekly trip for groceries. In fact, Marpo became indispensable and both Mr. and Mrs. Hosoume often told each other how grateful they were for Marpo.

When summer vacation began and Yoneko stayed at home, too, she found the new arrangement rather inconvenient. Her father's presence cramped her style: for instance, once when her friends came over and it was decided to make fudge, he would not permit them, saying fudge used too much sugar and that sugar was not a plaything; once when they were playing paper dolls, he came along and stuck his finger up his nose and pretended he was going to rub some snot off onto the dolls. Things like that. So, on some days, she was very much annoyed with her father.

Therefore when her mother came home breathless from the fields one day and pushed a ring at her, a gold-colored ring with a tiny glasslike stone in it, saying, "Look, Yoneko, I'm going to give you this ring. If your father asks where you got it, say you found it on the street." Yoneko was perplexed but delighted both by the unexpected gift and the chance to have some secret revenge on her father, and she said, certainly, she was willing to comply with her mother's request. Her mother went back to the fields then and Yoneko put the pretty ring on her middle finger, taking up the loose space with a bit of newspaper. It was similar to the rings found occasionally in boxes of Crackerjack, except that it appeared a bit more substantial.

Mr. Hosoume never asked about the ring; in fact, he never noticed she was wearing one. Yoneko thought he was about to, once, but he only reproved her for the flamingo nail polish she was wearing, which she had applied from a vial brought over by Yvonne Fournier, the French girl two orange groves away. "You look like a Filipino," Mr. Hosoume said sternly, for it was another irrefutable fact among Japanese in general that Filipinos in general were a gaudy lot. Mrs. Hosoume immediately came to her defense, saying that in Japan, if she remembered correctly, young girls did the same thing. In fact, she remembered having gone to elaborate lengths to tint her fingernails: she used to gather, she said, the petals of the red *tsubobana* or the purple *kogane* (which grows on the underside of stones), grind them well, mix them with some alum powder, then cook the mixture and leave it to stand overnight in an envelope of either persimmon or sugar potato leaves (both very strong leaves). The second night, just before going to bed, she used to obtain threads by ripping a palm leaf (because real thread was dear) and tightly bind the paste to her fingernails under shields of persimmon or sugar potato leaves. She would be helpless for the night, the fingertips bound so well that they were alternately numb or aching, but she would grit her teeth and tell herself that the discomfort indicated the success of the operation. In the morning, finally releasing her fingers, she would find the nails shining with a translucent red-orange color.

Yoneko was fascinated, because she usually thought of her parents as having been adults all their lives. She thought that her mother must have been a beautiful child, with or without bright fingernails, because, though surely past thirty, she was even yet a beautiful person. When she herself was younger, she remembered, she had at times been so struck with her mother's appearance that she had dropped to her knees and mutely clasped her mother's legs in her arms. She had left off this habit as she learned to control her emotions, because at such times her mother had usually walked away, saying, "My, what a clinging child you are. You've got to learn to be a little more independent." She also remembered she had once heard someone comparing her mother to "a dewy, half-opened rosebud."

20   Mr. Hosoume, however, was irritated. "That's no excuse for Yoneko to begin using paint on her fingernails," he said. "She's only ten."

"Her Japanese age is eleven,[3] and we weren't much older," Mrs. Hosoume said.

"Look," Mr. Hosoume said, "if you're going to contradict every piece of advice I give the children, they'll end up disobeying us both and doing what they very well please. Just because I'm ill just now is no reason for them to start being disrespectful."

"When have I ever contradicted you before?" Mrs. Hosoume said.

"Countless times," Mr. Hosoume said.

25   "Name one instance," Mrs. Hosoume said.

Certainly there had been times, but Mr. Hosoume could not happen to mention the one requested instance on the spot and he became quite angry. "That's quite enough of your insolence," he said. Since he was speaking in Japanese, his exact accusation was that she was *nama-iki,* which is a shade more revolting than being merely insolent.

"*Nama-iki, nama-iki?*" said Mrs. Hosoume. "How dare you? I'll not have anyone calling me *nama-iki!*"

At that, Mr. Hosoume went up to where his wife was ironing and slapped her smartly on the face. It was the first time he had ever laid hands on her. Mrs. Hosoume was immobile for an instant, but she resumed her ironing as though nothing had happened, although she glanced over at Marpo, who happened to be in the room reading a newspaper. Yoneko and Seigo forgot they were listening to the radio and stared at their parents, thunderstruck.

"Hit me again," said Mrs. Hosoume quietly, as she ironed. "Hit me all you wish."

30   Mr. Hosoume was apparently about to, but Marpo stepped up and put his hand on Mr. Hosoume's shoulder. "The children are here," said Marpo, "the children."

"Mind your own business," said Mr. Hosoume in broken English. "Get out of here!"

Marpo left, and that was about all. Mrs. Hosoume went on ironing, Yoneko and Seigo turned back to the radio, and Mr. Hosoume muttered that Marpo was beginning to forget his place. Now that he thought of it, he said, Marpo had been increasingly impudent towards him since his illness. He said just because he was temporarily an invalid was no reason for Marpo to start being disrespectful. He added that Marpo had better watch his step or that he might find himself jobless one of these fine days.

And something of the sort must have happened. Marpo was here one day and gone the next, without even saying good-bye to Yoneko and Seigo. That was also the day the Hosoume family went to the city on a weekday afternoon, which was most unusual. Mr. Hosoume, who now avoided driving as much as possible, handled the cumbersome Reo as though it were a nervous stallion, sitting on the edge of the seat and hugging the steering wheel. He drove very fast and about halfway to the city struck a beautiful collie which had dashed out barking from someone's yard. The car jerked with the impact, but Mr. Hosoume drove right on and Yoneko, wanting suddenly to vomit, looked back and saw the collie lying very still at the side of the road.

[3]By Japanese reckoning a child becomes one year old on the first New Year's Day following his or her birth.

When they arrived at the Japanese hospital, which was their destination, Mr. Hosoume cautioned Yoneko and Seigo to be exemplary children and wait patiently in the car. It seemed hours before he and Mrs. Hosoume returned, she walking with very small, slow steps and he assisting her. When Mrs. Hosoume got in the car, she leaned back and closed her eyes. Yoneko inquired as to the source of her distress, for she was obviously in pain, but she only answered that she was feeling a little under the weather and that the doctor had administered some necessarily astringent treatment. At that, Mr. Hosoume turned around and advised Yoneko and Seigo that they must tell no one of coming to the city on a weekday afternoon, absolutely no one, and Yoneko and Seigo readily assented. On the way home, they passed the place of the encounter with the collie, and Yoneko looked up and down the stretch of road but the dog was nowhere to be seen.

35   Not long after that, the Hosoumes got a new hired hand, an old Japanese man who wore his gray hair in a military cut and who, unlike Marpo, had no particular interests outside working, eating, sleeping, and playing an occasional game of *goh*[4] with Mr. Hosoume. Before he came Yoneko and Seigo played sometimes in the empty bunkhouse and recalled Marpo's various charms together. Privately, Yoneko was wounded more than she would admit even to herself that Marpo should have subjected her to such an abrupt desertion. Whenever her indignation became too great to endure gracefully, she would console herself by telling Seigo that, after all, Marpo was a mere Filipino, an eater of wild dogs.

Seigo never knew about the disappointing new hired man, because he suddenly died in the night. He and Yoneko had spent the hot morning in the nearest orange grove, she driving him to distraction by repeating certain words he could not bear to hear: she had called him Serge, a name she had read somewhere, instead of Seigo; and she had chanted off the name of the tires they were rolling around like hoops as Goodrich Silver-TO-town, Goodrich Silver-TO-town, instead of Goodrich Silvertown. This had enraged him, and he had chased her around the trees most of the morning. Finally she had taunted him from several trees away by singing "You're a Yellow-streaked Coward," which was one of several small songs she had composed. Seigo had suddenly grinned and shouted, "Sure!" and walked off, leaving her, as he intended, with a sense of emptiness. In the afternoon, they had perspired and followed the potato-digging machine and the Mexican workers, both hired for the day, around the field, delighting in unearthing marble-sized, smooth-skinned potatoes that both the machine and the men had missed. Then, in the middle of the night, Seigo began crying, complaining of a stomach ache. Mrs. Hosoume felt his head and sent her husband for the doctor, who smiled and said Seigo would be fine in the morning. He said it was doubtless the combination of green oranges, raw potatoes, and the July heat. But as soon as the doctor left, Seigo fell into a coma and a drop of red blood stood out on his underlip, where he had evidently bit it. Mr. Hosoume again fetched the doctor, who was this time very grave and wagged his head, saying several times, "It looks very bad." So Seigo died at the age of five.

Mrs. Hosoume was inconsolable and had swollen eyes in the morning for weeks afterwards. She now insisted on visiting the city relatives each Sunday, so that she could attend church services with them. One Sunday, she stood up and

---

[4]a Japanese game for two, played with pebblelike counters on a board

accepted Christ. It was through accompanying her mother to many of these services that Yoneko finally learned the Japanese words to "Let Us Gather at the River." Mrs. Hosoume also did not seem interested in discussing anything but God and Seigo. She was especially fond of reminding visitors how adorable Seigo had been as an infant, how she had been unable to refrain from dressing him as a little girl and fixing his hair in bangs until he was two. Mr. Hosoume was very gentle with her and when Yoneko accidently caused her to giggle once, he nodded and said, "Yes, that's right, Yoneko, we must make your mother laugh and forget about Seigo." Yoneko herself did not think about Seigo at all. Whenever the thought of Seigo crossed her mind, she instantly began composing a new song, and this worked very well.

One evening, when the new hired man had been with them a while, Yoneko was helping her mother with the dishes when she found herself being examined with such peculiarly intent eyes that, with a start of guilt, she began searching in her mind for a possible crime she had lately committed. But Mrs. Hosoume only said, "Never kill a person, Yoneko, because if you do, God will take from you someone you love."

"Oh, that," said Yoneko quickly, "I don't believe in that, I don't believe in God." And her words tumbling pell-mell over one another, she went on eagerly to explain a few of her reasons why. If she neglected to mention the test she had given God during the earthquake, it was probably because she was a little upset. She had believed for a moment that her mother was going to ask about the ring (which, alas, she had lost already, somewhere in the flumes[5] along the cantaloupe patch).

[1951]

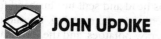

Topics for Critical Thinking and Writing

1. Why does Mrs. Hosoume tell Yoneko not to tell Mr. Hosoume where the ring came from?
2. Why does Mr. Hosoume strike his wife?
3. Why does Marpo disappear on the same day that Mrs. Hosoume goes to the hospital?
4. Why does Mrs. Hosoume say—out of the blue, so far as Yoneko is concerned—"Never kill a person, Yoneko"?

JOHN UPDIKE

John Updike (b. 1932) grew up in Shillington, Pennsylvania, where his father was a teacher and his mother was a writer. After receiving a B.A. degree from Harvard he studied drawing at Oxford for a year, but an offer from The New Yorker *magazine brought him back to the United States. He at first served as a reporter for the magazine, but soon began contributing poetry, essays, and fiction. Today he is one of America's most prolific and well-known writers.*

We print another of his stories on page 680.

[5]irrigation channels

A & P

In walks these three girls in nothing but bathing suits. I'm in the third checkout slot, with my back to the door, so I don't see them until they're over by the bread. The one that caught my eye first was the one in the plaid green two-piece. She was a chunky kid, with a good tan and a sweet broad soft-looking can with those two crescents of white just under it, where the sun never seems to hit, at the top of the backs of her legs. I stood there with my hand on a box of HiHo crackers trying to remember if I rang it up or not. I ring it up again and the customer starts giving me hell. She's one of these cash-register-watchers, a witch about fifty with rouge on her cheekbones and no eyebrows, and I know it made her day to trip me up. She'd been watching cash registers for fifty years and probably never seen a mistake before.

By the time I got her feathers smoothed and her goodies into a bag—she gives me a little snort in passing, if she'd been born at the right time they would have burned her over in Salem—by the time I get her on her way the girls had circled around the bread and were coming back, without a pushcart, back my way along the counters, in the aisle between the checkouts and the Special bins. They didn't even have shoes on. There was this chunky one, with the two-piece—it was bright green and the seams on the bra were still sharp and her belly was still pretty pale so I guessed she just got it (the suit)—there was this one, with one of those chubby berry-faces, the lips all bunched together under her nose, this one, and a tall one, with black hair that hadn't quite frizzed right, and one of these sunburns right across under the eyes, and a chin that was too long—you know, the kind of girl other girls think is very "striking" and "attractive" but never quite makes it, as they very well know, which is why they like her so much—and then the third one, that wasn't quite so tall. She was the queen. She kind of led them, the other two peeking around and making their shoulders round. She didn't look around, not this queen, she just walked straight on slowly, on these long white prima-donna legs. She came down a little hard on her heels, as if she didn't walk in her bare feet that much, putting down her heels and then letting the weight move along to her toes as if she was testing the floor with every step, putting a little deliberate extra action into it. You never know for sure how girls' minds work (do they really think it's a mind in there or just a little buzz like a bee in a glass jar?) but you got the idea she had talked the other two into coming in here with her, and now she was showing them how to do it, walk slow and hold yourself straight.

She had on a kind of dirty pink—beige maybe, I don't know—bathing suit with a little nubble all over it and, what got me, the straps were down. They were off her shoulders looped loose around the cool tops of her arms, and I guess as a result the suit had slipped on her, so all around the top of the cloth there was this shining rim. If it hadn't been there you wouldn't have known there could have been anything whiter than those shoulders. With the straps pushed off, there was nothing between the top of the suit and the top of her head except just *her,* this clean bare plane of the top of her chest down from the shoulder bones like a dented sheet of metal tilted in the light. I mean, it was more than pretty.

She had sort of oaky hair that the sun and salt had bleached, done up in a bun that was unravelling, and a kind of prim face. Walking into the A & P with your straps down, I suppose it's the only kind of face you *can* have. She held her head so high her neck, coming up out of those white shoulders, looked kind of stretched, but I didn't mind. The longer her neck was, the more of her there was.

5   She must have felt in the corner of her eye me and over my shoulder Stokesie in the second slot watching, but she didn't tip. Not this queen. She kept her eyes moving across the racks, and stopped, and turned so slow it made my stomach rub the inside of my apron, and buzzed to the other two, who kind of huddled against her for relief, and then they all three of them went up the cat and dog food-breakfast cereal-macaroni-rice-raisins-seasonings-spreads-spaghetti-soft drinks-crackers-and-cookies aisle. From the third slot I look straight up this aisle to the meat counter, and I watched them all the way. The fat one with the tan sort of fumbled with the cookies, but on second thought she put the package back. The sheep pushing their carts down the aisle—the girls were walking against the usual traffic (not that we have one-way signs or anything)—were pretty hilarious. You could see them, when Queenie's white shoulders dawned on them, kind of jerk, or hop, or hiccup, but their eyes snapped back to their own baskets and on they pushed. I bet you could set off dynamite in the A & P and the people would by and large keep reaching and checking oatmeal off their lists and muttering "Let me see, there was a third thing, began with A, asparagus, no, ah, yes, applesauce!" or whatever it is they do mutter. But there was no doubt, this jiggled them. A few house slaves in pin curlers even look around after pushing their carts past to make sure what they had seen was correct.

You know, it's one thing to have a girl in a bathing suit down on the beach, where what with the glare nobody can look at each other much anyway, and another thing in the cool of the A & P, under the fluorescent lights, against all those stacked packages, with her feet paddling along naked over our checker-board green-and-cream rubber-tile floor.

"Oh, Daddy," Stokesie said beside me. "I feel so faint."

"Darling," I said. "Hold me tight." Stokesie's married, with two babies chalked up on his fuselage already, but as far as I can tell that's the only difference. He's twenty-two, and I was nineteen this April.

"Is it done?" he asks, the responsible married man finding his voice. I forgot to say he thinks he's going to be a manager some sunny day, maybe in 1990 when it's called the Great Alexandrov and Petrooshki Tea Company or something.

10   What he meant was, our town is five miles from a beach, with a big summer colony out on the Point, but we're right in the middle of town, and the women generally put on a shirt or shorts or something before they get out of the car into the street. And anyway these are usually women with six children and varicose veins mapping their legs and nobody, including them, could care less. As I say, we're right in the middle of town, and if you stand at our front doors you can see two banks and the Congregational church and the newspaper store and three real estate offices and about twenty-seven old freeloaders tearing up Central Street because the sewer broke again. It's not as if we're on the Cape; we're north of Boston and there's people in this town haven't seen the ocean for twenty years.

The girls had reached the meat counter and were asking McMahon something. He pointed, they pointed, and they shuffled out of sight behind a pyramid of Diet Delight peaches. All that was left for us to see was old McMahon patting his mouth and looking after them sizing up their joints. Poor kids, I began to feel sorry for them, they couldn't help it.

Now here comes the sad part of the story, at least my family says it's sad, but I don't think it's so sad myself. The store's pretty empty, it being Thursday afternoon, so there was nothing much to do except lean on the register and wait for the girls to show up again. The whole store was like a pinball machine and I didn't know which tunnel they'd come out of. After a while they come around out of the far aisle, around the light bulbs, records at discount of the Caribbean Six or Tony Martin Sings or some such gunk you wonder they waste the wax on, six-packs of candy bars, and plastic toys done up in cellophane that fall apart when a kid looks at them anyway. Around they come, Queenie still leading the way, and holding a little gray jar in her hand. Slots Three through Seven are unmanned and I could see her wondering between Stokes and me, but Stokesie with his usual luck draws an old party in baggy gray pants who stumbles up with four giant cans of pineapple juice (what do these bums *do* with all that pineapple juice? I've often asked myself) so the girls come to me. Queenie puts down the jar and I take it into my fingers icy cold. Kingfish Fancy Herring Snacks in Pure Sour Cream: 49¢. Now her hands are empty, not a ring or a bracelet, bare as God made them, and I wonder where the money's coming from. Still with the prim look she lifts a folded dollar bill out of the hollow at the center of her nubbled pink top. The jar went heavy in my hand. Really, I thought that was so cute.

Then everybody's luck begins to run out. Lengel comes in from haggling with a truck full of cabbages on the lot and is about to scuttle into the door marked MANAGER behind which he hides all day when the girls touch his eye. Lengel's pretty dreary, teaches Sunday school and the rest, but he doesn't miss that much. He comes over and says, "Girls, this isn't the beach."

Queenie blushes, though maybe it's just a brush of sunburn I was noticing for the first time, now that she was so close. "My mother asked me to pick up a jar of herring snacks." Her voice kind of startled me, the way voices do when you see the people first, coming out so flat and dumb yet kind of tony, too, the way it ticked over "pick up" and "snacks." All of a sudden I slid right down her voice into her living room. Her father and the other men were standing around in ice-cream coats and bow ties and the women were in sandals picking up herring snacks on toothpicks off a big glass plate and they were all holding drinks the color of water with olives and sprigs of mint in them. When my parents have somebody over they get lemonade and if it's a real racy affair Schlitz in tall glasses with "They'll Do It Every Time" cartoons stencilled on.

15   "That's all right," Lengel said. "But this isn't the beach." His repeating this struck me as funny, as if it had just occurred to him, and he had been thinking all these years the A & P was a great big dune and he was the head lifeguard. He didn't like my smiling—as I say he doesn't miss much—but he concentrates on giving the girls that sad Sunday-school-superintendent stare.

Queenie's blush was no sunburn now, and the plump one in plaid, that I liked better from the back—a really sweet can—pipes up, "We weren't doing any shopping. We just came in for the one thing."

"That makes no difference," Lengel tells her, and I could see from the way his eyes went that he hadn't noticed she was wearing a two-piece before. "We want you decently dressed when you come in here."

"We *are* decent," Queenie says suddenly, her lower lip pushing, getting sore now that she remembers her place, a place from which the crowd that runs the A & P must look pretty crummy. Fancy Herring Snacks flashed in her very blue eyes.

"Girls, I don't want to argue with you. After this come in here with your shoulders covered. It's our policy." He turns his back. That's policy for you. Policy is what the kingpins want. What the others want is juvenile delinquency.

20   All this while, the customers had been showing up with their carts but, you know, sheep, seeing a scene, they had all bunched up on Stokesie, who shook open a paper bag as gently as peeling a peach, not wanting to miss a word. I could feel in the silence everybody getting nervous, most of all Lengel, who asks me, "Sammy, have you rung up this purchase?"

I thought and said "No" but it wasn't about that I was thinking. I go through the punches, 4, 9, GROC, TOT—it's more complicated than you think and after you do it often enough, it begins to make a little song, that you hear words to, in my case "Hello (*bing*) there, you (*gung*) hap-py *peepul* (*splat*)!"—the *splat* being the drawer flying out. I uncrease the bill, tenderly as you may imagine, it just having come from between the two smoothest scoops of vanilla I had ever known were there, and pass a half and a penny into her narrow pink palm and nestle the herrings in a bag and twist its neck and hand it over, all the time thinking.

The girls, and who'd blame them, are in a hurry to get out, so I say "I quit" to Lengel quick enough for them to hear, hoping they'll stop and watch me, their unsuspected hero. They keep right on going, into the electric eye; the door flies open and they flicker across the lot to their car, Queenie and Plaid and Big Tall Goony-Goony (not that as raw material she was so bad), leaving me with Lengel and a kink in his eyebrow.

"Did you say something, Sammy?"

"I said I quit."

25   "I thought you did."

"You didn't have to embarrass them."

"It was they who were embarrassing us."

I started to say something that came out "Fiddle-de-doo." It's a saying of my grandmother's, and I know she would have been pleased.

"I don't think you know what you're saying," Lengel said.

30   "I know you don't," I said. "But I do." I pull the bow at the back of my apron and start shrugging it off my shoulders. A couple customers that had been heading for my slot begin to knock against each other, like scared pigs in a chute.

Lengel sighs and begins to look very patient and old and gray. He's been a friend of my parents for years. "Sammy, you don't want to do this to your Mom and Dad," he tells me. It's true, I don't. But it seems to me that once you begin a gesture it's fatal not to go through with it. I fold the apron, "Sammy" stitched in red on the pocket, and put it on the counter, and drop the bow tie on top of it. The bow tie is theirs, if you've ever wondered. "You'll feel this for the rest of your life," Lengel says, and I know that's true, too, but remembering how he made that pretty girl blush makes me so scrunchy inside I punch the No Sale tab and the machine whirs "pee-pul" and the drawer splats out. One advantage to this scene taking place in summer, I can follow this up with a clean exit, there's no fumbling around getting your coat and galoshes, I just saunter into the electric eye in my white shirt that my mother ironed the night before, and the door heaves itself open, and outside the sunshine is skating round on the asphalt.

I look around for my girls, but they're gone, of course. There wasn't anybody but some young married screaming with her children about some candy they didn't get by the door of a powder-blue Falcon station wagon. Looking back in the big windows, over the bags of peat moss and aluminum lawn furniture stacked on the pavement, I could see Lengel in my place in the slot, checking the sheep through. His face was dark gray and his back stiff, as if he'd just had an injection of iron, and my stomach kind of fell as I felt how hard the world was going to be to me hereafter.

[1962]

 Topics for Critical Thinking and Writing

1. In what sort of community is this A & P located? To what extent does this community resemble yours?
2. Do you think Sammy is a male chauvinist pig? Why, or why not? And if you think he is, do you find the story offensive? Again, why or why not?
3. In the last line of the story Sammy says, "I felt how hard the world was going to be to me hereafter." Do you think the world is going to be hard to Sammy? Why, or why not? And if it is hard to him, is this because of a virtue or a weakness in Sammy?
4. Write Lengel's version of the story (500–1000 words) as he might narrate it to his wife during dinner. Or write the story from Queenie's point of view.
5. Speaking of contemporary fiction Updike said:

   I want stories to startle and engage me within the first few sentences, and in their middle to widen or deepen or sharpen my knowledge of human activity, and to end by giving me a sensation of completed statement.

   Let's assume that you share Updike's view of what a story should do. To what extent do you think "A & P" fulfills these demands? (You may want to put your response in the form of a letter to Updike.)

 LILIANA HEKER

Liliana Heker, born in Argentina in 1943, achieved fame in 1966 with the publication of her first book. She has continued to write fiction, and she has also been influential in her role as the editor of a literary magazine. "The Stolen Party," first published in Spanish in 1982, was translated and printed in Other Fires: Short Fiction by Latin American Women *(1985), edited and translated by Alberto Manguel.*

The Stolen Party

As soon as she arrived she went straight to the kitchen to see if the monkey was there. It was: what a relief! She wouldn't have liked to admit that her mother had been right. *Monkeys at a birthday?* her mother had sneered. *Get away with you, believing any nonsense you're told!* She was cross, but not because of the monkey, the girl thought; it's just because of the party.

"I don't like you going," she told her. "It's a rich people's party."

"Rich people go to Heaven too," said the girl, who studied religion at school.

"Get away with Heaven," said the mother. "The problem with you, young lady, is that you like to fart higher than your ass."

5   The girl didn't approve of the way her mother spoke. She was barely nine, and one of the best in her class.

"I'm going because I've been invited," she said. "And I've been invited because Luciana is my friend. So there."

"Ah yes, your friend," her mother grumbled. She paused. "Listen, Rosaura," she said at last. "That one's not your friend. You know what you are to them? The maid's daughter, that's what."

Rosaura blinked hard: she wasn't going to cry. Then she yelled: "Shut up! You know nothing about being friends!"

Every afternoon she used to go to Luciana's house and they would both finish their homework while Rosaura's mother did the cleaning. They had their tea in the kitchen and they told each other secrets. Rosaura loved everything in the big house, and she also loved the people who lived there.

10   "I'm going because it will be the most lovely party in the whole world, Luciana told me it would. There will be a magician, and he will bring a monkey and everything."

The mother swung around to take a good look at her child, and pompously put her hands on her hips.

"Monkeys at a birthday?" she said. "Get away with you, believing any nonsense you're told!"

Rosaura was deeply offended. She thought it unfair of her mother to accuse other people of being liars simply because they were rich. Rosaura too wanted to be rich, of course. If one day she managed to live in a beautiful palace, would her mother stop loving her? She felt very sad. She wanted to go to that party more than anything else in the world.

"I'll die if I don't go," she whispered, almost without moving her lips.

15   And she wasn't sure whether she had been heard, but on the morning of the party she discovered that her mother had starched her Christmas dress. And in the afternoon, after washing her hair, her mother rinsed it in apple vinegar so that it would be all nice and shiny. Before going out, Rosaura admired herself in the mirror, with her white dress and glossy hair, and thought she looked terribly pretty.

Señora Ines also seemed to notice. As soon as she saw her, she said:

"How lovely you look today, Rosaura."

Rosaura gave her starched skirt a slight toss with her hands and walked into the party with a firm step. She said hello to Luciana and asked about the monkey. Luciana put on a secretive look and whispered into Rosaura's ear: "He's in the kitchen. But don't tell anyone, because it's a surprise."

Rosaura wanted to make sure. Carefully she entered the kitchen and there she saw it: deep in thought, inside its cage. It looked so funny that the girl stood there for a while, watching it, and later, every so often, she would slip out of the party unseen and go and admire it. Rosaura was the only one allowed into the kitchen. Señora Ines had said: "You yes, but not the others, they're much too boisterous, they might break something." Rosaura had never broken anything. She even managed the jug of orange juice, carrying it from the kitchen into the dining room. She held it carefully and didn't spill a single drop. And Señora Ines had said: "Are you sure you can manage a jug as big as that?" Of course she could manage. She wasn't a butterfingers, like the others. Like that blonde girl with the bow in her hair. As soon as she saw Rosaura, the girl with the bow had said:

20   "And you? Who are you?"

"I'm a friend of Luciana," said Rosaura.

"No," said the girl with the bow, "you are not a friend of Luciana because I'm her cousin and I know all her friends. And I don't know you."

"So what," said Rosaura. "I come here every afternoon with my mother and we do our homework together."

"You and your mother do your homework together?" asked the girl, laughing.

25 "I and Luciana do our homework together," said Rosaura, very seriously.

The girl with the bow shrugged her shoulders.

"That's not being friends," she said. "Do you go to school together?"

"No."

"So where do you know her from?" said the girl, getting impatient.

30 Rosaura remembered her mother's words perfectly. She took a deep breath.

"I'm the daughter of the employee," she said.

Her mother had said very clearly: "If someone asks, you say you're the daughter of the employee; that's all." She also told her to add: "And proud of it." But Rosaura thought that never in her life would she dare say something of the sort.

"What employee?" said the girl with the bow. "Employee in a shop?"

"No," said Rosaura angrily. "My mother doesn't sell anything in any shop, so there."

35 "So how come she's an employee?" said the girl with the bow.

Just then Señora Ines arrived saying *shh shh,* and asked Rosaura if she wouldn't mind helping serve out the hotdogs, as she knew the house so much better than the others.

"See?" said Rosaura to the girl with the bow, and when no one was looking she kicked her in the shin.

Apart from the girl with the bow, all the others were delightful. The one she liked best was Luciana, with her golden birthday crown; and then the boys. Rosaura won the sack race, and nobody managed to catch her when they played tag. When they split into two teams to play charades, all the boys wanted her for their side. Rosaura felt she had never been so happy in all her life.

But the best was still to come. The best came after Luciana blew out the candles. First the cake. Señora Ines had asked her to help pass the cake around, and Rosaura had enjoyed the task immensely, because everyone called out to her, shouting "Me, me!" Rosaura remembered a story in which there was a queen who had the power of life or death over her subjects. She had always loved that, having the power of life or death. To Luciana and the boys she gave the largest pieces, and to the girl with the bow she gave a slice so thin one could see through it.

40 After the cake came the magician, tall and bony, with a fine red cape. A true magician: he could untie handkerchiefs by blowing on them and make a chain with links that had no openings. He could guess what cards were pulled out from a pack, and the monkey was his assistant. He called the monkey "partner." "Let's see here, partner," he would say, "turn over a card." And, "Don't run away, partner: time to work now."

The final trick was wonderful. One of the children had to hold the monkey in his arms and the magician said he would make him disappear.

"What, the boy?" they all shouted.

"No, the monkey!" shouted back the magician.

Rosaura thought that this was truly the most amusing party in the whole world.

45 The magician asked a small fat boy to come and help, but the small fat boy got frightened almost at once and dropped the monkey on the floor. The magician

picked him up carefully, whispered something in his ear, and the monkey nodded almost as if he understood.

"You mustn't be so unmanly, my friend," the magician said to the fat boy.

"What's unmanly?" said the fat boy.

The magician turned around as if to look for spies.

"A sissy," said the magician. "Go sit down."

50   Then he stared at all the faces, one by one. Rosaura felt her heart tremble.

"You, with the Spanish eyes," said the magician. And everyone saw that he was pointing at her.

She wasn't afraid. Neither holding the monkey, nor when the magician made him vanish; not even when, at the end, the magician flung his red cape over Rosaura's head and uttered a few magic words . . . and the monkey reappeared, chattering happily, in her arms. The children clapped furiously. And before Rosaura returned to her seat, the magician said:

"Thank you very much, my little countess."

She was so pleased with the compliment that a while later, when her mother came to fetch her, that was the first thing she told her.

55   "I helped the magician and he said to me, 'Thank you very much, my little countess.'"

It was strange because up to then Rosaura had thought that she was angry with her mother. All along Rosaura had imagined that she would say to her: "See that the monkey wasn't a lie?" But instead she was so thrilled that she told her mother all about the wonderful magician.

Her mother tapped her on the head and said: "So now we're a countess!"

But one could see that she was beaming.

And now they both stood in the entrance, because a moment ago Señora Ines, smiling, had said: "Please wait here a second."

60   Her mother suddenly seemed worried.

"What is it?" she asked Rosaura.

"What is what?" said Rosaura. "It's nothing; she just wants to get the presents for those who are leaving, see?"

She pointed at the fat boy and at a girl with pigtails who were also waiting there, next to their mothers. And she explained about the presents. She knew, because she had been watching those who left before her. When one of the girls was about to leave, Señora Ines would give her a bracelet. When a boy left, Señora Ines gave him a yo-yo. Rosaura preferred the yo-yo because it sparkled, but she didn't mention that to her mother. Her mother might have said: "So why don't you ask for one, you blockhead?" That's what her mother was like. Rosaura didn't feel like explaining that she'd be horribly ashamed to be the odd one out. Instead she said:

"I was the best-behaved at the party."

65   And she said no more because Señora Ines came out into the hall with two bags, one pink and one blue.

First she went up to the fat boy, gave him a yo-yo out of the blue bag, and the fat boy left with his mother. Then she went up to the girl and gave her a bracelet out of the pink bag, and the girl with the pigtails left as well.

Finally she came up to Rosaura and her mother. She had a big smile on her face and Rosaura liked that. Señora Ines looked down at her, then looked up at her mother, and then said something that made Rosaura proud:

"What a marvelous daughter you have, Herminia."

For an instant, Rosaura thought that she'd give her two presents: the bracelet and the yo-yo. Señora Ines bent down as if about to look for something.

Rosaura also leaned forward, stretching out her arm. But she never completed the movement.

70 Señora Ines didn't look in the pink bag. Nor did she look in the blue bag. Instead she rummaged in her purse. In her hand appeared two bills.

"You really and truly earned this," she said handing them over. "Thank you for all your help, my pet."

Rosaura felt her arms stiffen, stick close to her body, and then she noticed her mother's hand on her shoulder. Instinctively she pressed herself against her mother's body. That was all. Except her eyes. Rosaura's eyes had a cold, clear look that fixed itself on Señora Ines's face.

Señora Ines, motionless, stood there with her hand outstretched. As if she didn't dare draw it back. As if the slightest change might shatter an infinitely delicate balance.

[1982]

 Topics for Critical Thinking and Writing

1. The first paragraph tells us, correctly, that Rosaura's mother is wrong about the monkey. By the time the story is over, is the mother right about anything? If so, what?

2. Characterize Señora Ines. Why does she offer Rosaura money instead of a yo-yo or a bracelet? By the way, do you assume she is speaking deceptively when she tells Rosaura that she bars other children from the kitchen on the grounds that "they might break something"? On what do you base your view?

3. What do you make of the last paragraph? Why does Señora Ines stand with her hand outstretched, "as if she didn't dare draw it back"? What "infinitely delicate balance" might be shattered?

POETRY

 **WILLIAM BLAKE**

William Blake (1757–1827) was born in London and at fourteen was apprenticed for seven years to an engraver. A Christian visionary poet, he made his living by giving drawing lessons and by illustrating books, including his own Songs of Innocence *(1789) and* Songs of Experience *(1794). These two books represent, he said, "two contrary states of the human soul." ("Infant Joy" comes from* Innocence, *"Infant Sorrow" and "The Echoing Green" come from* Experience.) *In 1809 Blake exhibited his art, but the show was a failure. Not until he was in his sixties, when he stopped writing poetry, did he achieve any public recognition—and then it was as a painter.*

Infant Joy

"I have no name,
I am but two days old."
What shall I call thee?
"I happy am,

"Infant Joy" by William
Blake, from *Songs of Inno-
cence.* (By permission of the
Provost and Fellows of
King's College, Cambridge)

Joy is my name." 5
Sweet joy befall thee!

Pretty joy!
Sweet joy but two days old,
Sweet joy I call thee;
Thou dost smile, 10
I sing the while—
Sweet joy befall thee.

[1789]

Infant Sorrow

My mother groand! my father wept.
Into the dangerous world I leapt,
Helpless, naked, piping loud;
Like a fiend hid in a cloud. 4

Struggling in my father's hands,
Striving against my swadling bands;

"Infant Sorrow" by William
Blake, from *Songs of Inno-
cence*. By permission of the
Provost and Fellows of
King's College, Cambridge)

Bound and weary I thought best
To sulk upon my mother's breast.   8

[1794]

Topics for Critical Thinking and Writing

1. "Infant Joy" begins "I have no name," but by line 5 the infant says "Joy is my name." What does the mother reply? Does she know the infant's name?
2. In line 9 the mother says, "Sweet joy I call thee." Does the line suggest how the mother has learned the name? What is the child's response?
3. In "Infant Sorrow," why is the infant sorrowful? What does the baby struggle against? Does "Like a fiend" suggest that it is inherently wicked and therefore should be repressed? Or does the adult world wickedly repress energy?
4. Why does the mother groan? Why does the father weep? Is the world "dangerous" to the infant in other than an obviously physical sense? To what degree are its parents its enemies? To what degree does the infant yield to them? In the last line, one might expect a newborn baby to nurse. What does this infant do?

5. Compare "Infant Joy" with "Infant Sorrow." What differences in sound do you hear? In "Infant Sorrow," for instance, look at lines 3, 5, 6, and 7. What repeated sounds do you hear?

The Echoing Green

The Sun does arise,
And make happy the skies;
The merry bells ring
To welcome the Spring;
The skylark and thrush,   5
The birds of the bush,
Sing louder around
To the bells' cheerful sound,
While our sports shall be seen
On the Echoing Green.   10

Old John, with white hair,
Does laugh away 'care,
Sitting under the oak,
Among the old folk.
They laugh at our play,   15
And soon they all say:
"Such, such were the joys
When we all, girls and boys,
In our youth time were seen
On the Echoing Green."   20

Till the little ones, weary,
No more can be merry;
The sun does descend,
And our sports have an end.
Round the laps of their mothers   25
Many sisters and brothers,
Like birds in their nest,
Are ready for rest,
And sport no more seen
On the darkening Green.   30

[1789]

✏ Topics for Critical Thinking and Writing

1. Who speaks the poem? (Go through the poem, picking up the clues that identify the speaker.)
2. When does the poem begin? And when does it end?
3. What is a "green," and why in this poem does it "echo"?
4. Try writing a piece entitled "Such, such were the joys . . ." You may need to affect a few years to write it, but try to get down what really were the joys of your childhood.

 **GERARD MANLEY HOPKINS**

Gerard Manley Hopkins (1844–89) was born near London and was educated at Oxford, where he studied the classics. A convert from Anglicanism to Roman Catholicism, he was ordained a Jesuit priest in 1877. After serving as a parish priest and teacher, he was appointed Professor of Greek at the Catholic University in Dublin.

Hopkins published only a few poems during his lifetime, partly because he believed that the pursuit of literary fame was incompatible with his vocation as a priest, and partly because he was aware that his highly individual style might puzzle readers.

Spring and Fall

To a Young Child

Márgarét áre you griéving
Over Goldengrove unleaving?
Leáves, líke the thíngs of mán, you
With your fresh thoughts care for, can you?
Ah! ás the héart grows older   5
It will come to such sights colder
By and by, nor spare a sigh
Though worlds of wanwood leafmeal lie;
And yet you will weep and know why.
Now no matter, child, the name: 10
Sórrow's springs áre the same.
Nor mouth had, no nor mind, expressed
What héart heárd of, ghost° guéssed:
It iś the blíght mán was bórn for,
It is Margaret you mourn for.   15

[1880]

 Topics for Critical Thinking and Writing

1. What is the speaker's age? His tone? What is the relevance of the title to Margaret? What meanings are in "Fall"? Is there more than one meaning to "spring"? (Notice especially the title and line 11.)
2. What is meant by Margaret's "fresh thoughts" (line 4)? Paraphrase lines 3–4 and lines 12–13.
3. "Wanwood" and "leafmeal" are words coined by Hopkins. What are their suggestions?
4. What does "blight" mean in line 14?
5. Why is it not contradictory for the speaker to say that Margaret weeps for herself (line 15) after saying that she weeps for "Goldengrove unleaving" (line 2)?

¹³**Ghost** spirit

A. E. HOUSMAN

Alfred Edward Housman (1859–1936) was born in rural Shropshire, England, and educated in classics and philosophy at Oxford University. Although he was a brilliant student, his final examination was unexpectedly weak—in fact, he failed—and he did not receive the academic appointment that he had anticipated. He began working as a civil servant at the British Patent Office, but in his spare time he wrote scholarly articles on Latin literature, and these writings in 1892 won him an appointment as Professor of Latin at the University of London. In 1911 he was appointed to Cambridge. During his lifetime he published (in addition to his scholarly writings) only two thin books of poetry, A Shropshire Lad *(1898) and* Last Poems *(1922), and a highly readable lecture called* The Name and Nature of Poetry *(1933). After his death a third book of poems,* More Poems *(1936), was published.*

When I Was One-and-Twenty

When I was one-and-twenty
I heard a wise man say,
"Give crowns and pounds and guineas
But not your heart away;
Give pearls away and rubies   5
But keep your fancy free."
But I was one-and-twenty,
No use to talk to me.

When I was one-and-twenty
I heard him say again,   10
"The heart out of the bosom
Was never given in vain;
'Tis paid with sighs a plenty
And sold for endless rue."
And I am two-and-twenty,   15
And oh, 'tis true, 'tis true.

[1896]

Topics for Critical Thinking and Writing

1. In line 6, what does "fancy" mean?
2. In your own words, what is the advice of the "wise man"?
3. In a paragraph, indicate what you think the speaker's attitude is toward himself. In a second paragraph, indicate what *our* attitude toward him is.

Into My Heart an Air That Kills

Into my heart an air that kills
From yon far country blows:
What are those blue remembered hills,
What spires, what farms are those?

That is the land of lost content
I see it shining plain,
The happy highways where I went
And cannot come again.

[1896]

Topics for Critical Thinking and Writing

1. The "far country" of line 2 is explained by line 5: This far country is "the land of lost content." But what, we might ask, is the land of lost content? Might it be, for instance, sadness induced by the recent death of a mate?
2. Describe the relationship between the question in lines 3–4 and the claim made in line 6.
3. The diction is simple and colloquial, except for "yon" in the second line. Do you think the word is inappropriate here? Support your response with an argument.
4. What is the speaker's tone of voice? What does the word "kills" reveal about the speaker? Do you think he is self-pitying? Point to evidence in the text to explain why, in your view, he is or is not.
5. We print two other poems by Housman, one immediately preceding this poem, and another on page 484. All express a sense of loss. In these three poems is Housman pretty much repeating himself, or is each poem distinctive in a significant way? Support your position.
6. We know from the surviving manuscript that before Housman finally settled, in line 4, on *spires* and *farms,* he jotted down *towns, shires,* and *paths.* And before he settled, in line 7, on *highways,* he jotted down *footpaths* and *wayside.* Do you think he made the right decisions at last? Explain your judgment.

E. E. CUMMINGS

Edwin Estlin Cummings (1894–1962), who used the pen name e. e. cummings, grew up in Cambridge, Massachusetts, and was graduated from Harvard, where he became interested in modern literature and art, especially in the movements called Cubism and Futurism. His father, a conservative clergyman and a professor at Harvard, seems to have been baffled by the youth's interests, but Cummings's mother encouraged his artistic activities, including unconventional punctuation.

Politically liberal in his youth, Cummings became more conservative after a visit to Russia in 1931, but early and late his work emphasizes individuality and freedom of expression.

In Just-

in Just-
spring when the world is mud-
luscious the little
lame balloonman

whistles far and wee   5

and eddieandbill come
running from marbles and
piracies and it's
spring

when the world is puddle-wonderful   10

the queer
old balloonman whistles
far and wee
and bettyandisbel come dancing

from hop-scotch and jump-rope and   15

it's
spring
and
     the
          goat-footed   20

balloonMan whistles
far
and
wee

                                                                                        [1920]

 Topics for Critical Thinking and Writing

1. Why "eddieandbill" and "bettyandisbel" rather than "eddie and bill" and "betty and isabel"? And why not "eddie and betty," and "bill and isabel"?
2. What are some of the effects that Cummings may be getting at by his un-usual arrangement of words on the page? Compare, for instance, the physi-cal appearance of "Whistles far and wee" in line 5 with the appearance of the same words in lines 12–13 and 21–24.
3. Because the balloonman is "lame" (line 4) or "goat-footed" (line 20), many readers find an allusion to the Greek god Pan, the goat-footed god of woods, fields, and flocks, and the inventor of a primitive wind instrument consisting of a series of reeds, "Pan's pipes." (If you are unfamiliar with Pan, consult an encyclopedia or a guide to mythology.) Do you agree that Cummings is al-luding to Pan? If so, what is the point of the allusion?

 LOUISE GLÜCK

Louise Glück (b. 1943) was born in New York City and attended Sarah Lawrence College and Columbia University. She has taught at Goddard College in Vermont and at Warren Wilson College in North Carolina. Her volume of poems, The Triumph of Achilles *(1985), won the Na-tional Book Critics Circle Award for poetry.*

The School Children

The children go forward with their little satchels.
And all morning the mothers have labored
to gather the late apples, red and gold,
like words of another language.

And on the other shore   5
are those who wait behind great desks
to receive these offerings.

How orderly they are—the nails
on which the children hang
their overcoats of blue or yellow wool.   10

And the teachers shall instruct them in silence
and the mothers shall scour the orchards for a way out,
drawing to themselves the gray limbs of the fruit trees
bearing so little ammunition.

[1975]

🖉 Topics for Critical Thinking and Writing

1. Which words in the poem present a cute picture-postcard view of small children going to school?
2. Which words undercut this happy scene?
3. In the last stanza we read that "the teachers shall instruct" and "the mothers shall scour." What, if anything, is changed if we substitute "will" for "shall"?

Gretel in Darkness

This is the world we wanted. All who would have seen us dead
Are dead. I hear the witch's cry
Break in the moonlight through a sheet of sugar: God rewards.
Her tongue shrivels into gas. . . .

                    Now, far from women's arms   5
And memory of women, in our father's hut
We sleep, are never hungry.
Why do I not forget?
My father bars the door, bars harm
From this house, and it is years.   10

No one remembers. Even you, my brother,
Summer afternoons you look at me as though you meant
To leave, as though it never happened. But I killed for you.
I see armed firs, the spires of that gleaming kiln come back, come back—

Nights I turn to you to hold me but you are not there.   15
Am I alone? Spies
Hiss in the stillness, Hansel we are there still, and it is real, real,
That black forest, and the fire in earnest.

[1975]

Topics for Critical Thinking and Writing

1. How, as the poem develops, is the first sentence of the poem modified? Is this the world "we" wanted? What does Gretel believe that Hansel wants?
2. In stanza 3 Gretel says

   But I killed for you.
   I see . . . the spires of that gleaming kiln come back, come back—

   Whether you know the story or not from *Grimm's Fairy Tales,* how do you understand Gretel's plight?
3. Why is the poem called "Gretel in Darkness"? What does the poem seem to tell us about how men and women face danger?

DRAMA

A Casebook on Shakespeare's *Hamlet*

This casebook contains (in addition to illustrations of the original texts of *Hamlet,* the Elizabethan theater, and modern productions) the following material:

1. A note on the Elizabethan theater
2. A note on the text of *Hamlet*
3. The text of *Hamlet*
4. A Freudian interpretation by Ernest Jones
5. Anne Barton's general comments on the play
6. Stanley Wells's analysis of the first soliloquy
7. Elaine Showalter's discussion of Ophelia
8. Claire Bloom's comments on her performance as Gertrude, in the BBC TV production
9. Bernice W. Kliman review of the BBC TV production of *Hamlet* (1980)
10. Stanley Kauffmann's review of Kenneth Branagh's film (1996)
11. A review by a student, Will Saretta, of Branagh's *Hamlet*

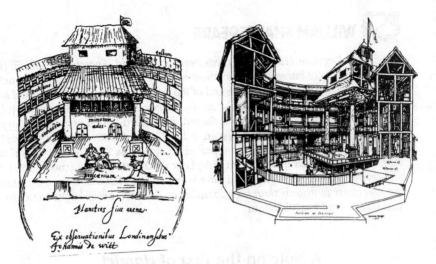

a. Johannes de Witt, a Continental visitor to London, made a drawing of the Swan Theater in about the year 1596. The original drawing is lost; this is Arend van Buchel's copy of it. (Copyright the British Museum.) *b.* C. Walter Hodges's drawing (1965) of an Elizabethan playhouse. (Courtesy C. Walter Hodges)

A Note on the Elizabethan Theater

Shakespeare's theater was wooden, round or polygonal (the Chorus in *Henry V* calls it a "wooden O"). About eight hundred spectators could stand in the yard in front of—and perhaps along the two sides of—the stage that jutted from the rear wall, and another fifteen hundred or so spectators could sit in the three roofed galleries that ringed the stage.

That portion of the galleries that was above the rear of the stage was sometimes used by actors. For instance, in *The Tempest,* 3.3, a stage direction following line 17 mentions "Prospero on the top, invisible," that is, he is imagined to be invisible to the characters in the play.

Entry to the stage was normally gained by doors at the rear, but apparently on rare occasions use was made of a curtained alcove—or perhaps a booth—between the doors, which allowed characters to be "discovered" (revealed) as in the modern proscenium theater, which normally employs a curtain. Such "discovery" scenes are rare.

Although the theater as a whole was unroofed, the stage was protected by a roof, supported by two pillars. These could serve (by an act of imagination) as trees behind which actors might pretend to conceal themselves.

A performance was probably uninterrupted by intermissions or by long pauses for the changing of scenery; a group of characters leaves the stage, another enters, and if the locale has changed the new characters somehow tell us. (Modern editors customarily add indications of locales to help a reader, but it should be remembered that the action on the Elizabethan stage was continuous.)

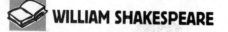 **WILLIAM SHAKESPEARE**

William Shakespeare (1564–1616) was born in Stratford, England, of middle-class parents. Nothing of interest is known about his early years, but by 1590 he was acting and writing plays in London. By the end of the following decade he had worked in all three Elizabethan dramatic genres—tragedy, comedy, and history. Romeo and Juliet, *for example, was written about 1595, the year of* Richard II, *and in the following year he wrote* A Midsummer Night's Dream. Julius Caesar *(1599) probably preceded* As You Like It *by one year, and* Hamlet *probably followed* As You Like It *by less than a year. Among the plays that followed* King Lear *(1605–06) were* Macbeth *(1605–06) and several "romances"—plays that have happy endings but that seem more meditative and closer to tragedy than such comedies as* A Midsummer Night's Dream, As You Like It, *and* Twelfth Night.

A Note on the Text of *Hamlet*

Shakespeare's *Hamlet* comes to us in three versions. The first, known as the First Quarto (Q1), was published in 1603. It is an illegitimate garbled version, perhaps derived from the memory of the actor who played Marcellus (this part is conspicuously more accurate than the rest of the play) in a short version of the play.

The second printed version (Q2), which appeared in 1604, is almost twice as long as Q1; all in all, it is the best text we have, doubtless published (as Q1 was not) with the permission of Shakespeare's theatrical company.

The third printed version, in the First Folio (the collected edition of Shakespeare's plays, published in 1623), is also legitimate, but it seems to be an acting version, for it lacks some two hundred lines of Q2.

On the other hand, the Folio text includes some ninety lines not found in Q2.

Because Q2 is the longest version, giving us more of the play as Shakespeare conceived it than either of the other texts, it serves as the basic version for this text. Unfortunately, the printers of it often worked carelessly: Words and phrases are omitted, there are plain misreadings of what must have been in Shakespeare's manuscript, and speeches are sometimes wrongly assigned. It was therefore necessary to turn to the First Folio for many readings. It has been found useful, also, to divide the play into acts and scenes; these divisions, not found in Q2 (and only a few are found in the Folio), are purely editorial additions, and they are therefore enclosed in square brackets.

We use the text edited by David Bevington.

The Tragedie of Hamlet. 265

With turbulent and dangerous Lunacy.

Rosin. He does confesse he feeles himselfe distracted,
But from what cause he will by no meanes speake.

Guil. Nor do we finde him forward to be sounded,
But with a crafty Madnesse keepes aloofe:
When we would bring him on to some Confession
Of his true state.

Qu. Did he receiue you well?

Rosin. Most like a Gentleman.

Guild. But with much forcing of his disposition.

Rosin. Niggard of question, but of our demands
Most free in his reply.

Qu. Did you assay him to any pastime?

Rosin. Madam, it so fell out, that certaine Players
We ore-wrought on the way : of these we told him,
And there did seeme in him a kinde of ioy
To heare of it : They are about the Court,
And (as I thinke) they haue already order
This night to play before him.

Pol. 'Tis most true:
And he beseech'd me to intreate your Maiesties
To heare, and see the matter.

King. With all my heart, and it doth much content me
To heare him so inclin'd. Good Gentlemen,
Giue him a further edge, and driue his purpose on
To these delights.

Rosin. We shall my Lord.   *Exeunt.*

King. Sweet *Gertrude* leaue vs too,
For we haue closely sent for *Hamlet* hither,
That he, as 'twere by accident, may there
Affront *Ophelia.* Her Father, and my selfe (lawful espials)
Will so bestow our selues, that seeing vnseene
We may of their encounter frankely iudge,
And gather by him, as he is behaued,
If't be th'affliction of his loue, or no.
That thus he suffers for.

Qu. I shall obey you,
And for your part *Ophelia*, I do wish
That your good Beauties be the happy cause
Of *Hamlets* wildenesse : so shall I hope your Vertues
Will bring him to his wonted way againe,
To both your Honors.

Ophe. Madam, I wish it may.

Pol. *Ophelia*, walke you heere. Gracious so please ye
We will bestow our selues : Reade on this booke,
That shew of such an exercise may colour
Your lonelinesse. We are oft too blame in this,
'Tis too much prou'd, that with Deuotions visage,
And pious Action, we do surge o're
The diuell himselfe.

King. Oh 'tis true:
How smart a lash that speech doth giue my Conscience?
The Harlots Cheeke beautied with plaist'ring Art
Is not more vgly to the thing that helpes it,
Then is my deede, to my most painted word.
Oh heauie burthen!

Pol. I heare him comming, let's withdraw my Lord.
                                    Exeunt.

Enter Hamlet.

Ham. To be, or not to be, that is the Question:
Whether tis Nobler in the minde to suffer
The Slings and Arrowes of outragious Fortune,
Or to take Armes against a Sea of troubles,
And by opposing end them : to dye, to sleepe
No more ; and by a sleepe, to say we end
The Heart-ake, and the thousand Naturall shockes

That Flesh is heyre too? 'Tis a consummation
Deuoutly to be wish'd. To dye to sleepe,
To sleepe, perchance to Dreame ; I, there's the rub,
For in that sleepe of death, what dreames may come,
When we haue shuffel'd off this mortall coile,
Must giue vs pawse. There's the respect
That makes Calamity of so long life:
For who would beare the Whips and Scornes of time,
The Oppressors wrong, the poore mans Contumely,
The pangs of dispriz'd Loue, the Lawes delay,
The insolence of Office, and the Spurnes
That patient merit of the vnworthy takes,
When he himselfe might his *Quietus* make
With a bare Bodkin? Who would these Fardles beare
To grunt and sweat vnder a weary life,
But that the dread of something after death,
The vndiscouered Countrey, from whose Borne
No Traueller returnes, Puzels the will,
And makes vs rather beare those illes we haue,
Then flye to others that we know not of.
Thus Conscience does make Cowards of vs all,
And thus the Natiue hew of Resolution
Is sicklied o're, with the pale cast of Thought,
And enterprizes of great pith and moment,
With this regard their Currants turne away,
And loose the name of Action. Soft you now,
The faire *Ophelia*? Nimph, in thy Orizons
Be all my sinnes remembred.

Ophe. Good my Lord,
How does your Honor for this many a day?

Ham. I humbly thanke you : well, well, well.

Ophe. My Lord, I haue Remembrances of yours,
That I haue longed long to re-deliuer.
I pray you now, receiue them.

Ham. No, no, I neuer gaue you ought.

Ophe. My honor'd Lord, I know right well you did,
And with them words of so sweet breath compos'd,
As made the things more rich, then perfume left :
Take these againe, for to the Noble minde
Rich gifts wax poore, when giuers proue vnkinde.
There my Lord.

Ham. Ha, ha : Are you honest?

Ophe. My Lord.

Ham. Are you faire?

Ophe. What meanes your Lordship?

Ham. That if you be honest and faire, your Honesty
should admit no discourse to your Beautie.

Ophe. Could Beautie my Lord, haue better Comerce
then your Honestie?

Ham. I trulie : for the power of Beautie, will sooner
transforme Honestie from what it is, to a Bawd, then the
force of Honestie can translate Beautie into his likenesse.
This was sometime a Paradox, but now the time giues it
proofe. I did loue you once.

Ophe. Indeed my Lord, you made me beleeue so.

Ham. You should not haue beleeued me. For vertue
cannot so innocculate our old stocke, but we shall rellish
of it. I loued you not.

Ophe. I was the more deceiued.

Ham. Get thee to a Nunnerie. Why would'st thou
be a breeder of Sinners? I am my selfe indifferent honest,
but yet I could accuse me of such things, that it were better my Mother had not borne me. I am very prowd, re-
uengefull, Ambitious, with more offences at my becke,
then I haue thoughts to put them in imagination, to giue
them shape, or time to acte them in. What should such
                                                    Fel-

"To be or not to be," as given in the First Folio (F1: 1623).

The Tragedy of Hamlet

And so by continuance, and weakenesse of the braine
Into this frensie, which now possesseth him:
And if this be not true, take this from this.

   King Thinke you t'is so?

   Cor. How? so my Lord, I would very faine know
That thing that I haue saide t'is so, positiuely,
And it hath fallen out otherwise.
Nay, if circumstances leade me on,
Ile finde it out, if it were hid
As deepe as the centre of the earth.

   King. how should wee trie this same?

   Cor. Mary my good lord thus,
The Princes walke is here in the galery,
There let *Ofelia*, walke vntill hee comes:
Your selfe and I will stand close in the study,
There shall you heare the effect of all his hart,
And if it proue any otherwise then loue,
Then let my censure faile an other time.

   King. see where hee comes poring vppon a booke.

           Enter Hamlet.

   Cor. Madame, will it please your grace
To leaue vs here?

   Que. With all my hart.   *exit.*

   Cor. And here *Ofelia*, reade you on this booke,
And walke aloofe, the King shal be vnseene.

   Ham. To be, or not to be, I there's the point,
To Die, to sleepe, is that all? I all:
No, to sleepe, to dreame, I mary there it goes,
For in that dreame of death, when wee awake,
And borne before an euerlasting Iudge,
From whence no passenger euer retur'nd,
The vndiscouered countiy, at whose sight
The happy smile, and the accursed damn'd.
But for this, the ioyfull hope of this,
Whol'd beare the scornes and flattery of the world,
Scorned by the right rich, the rich cursed of the poore?

                         The

"To be or not to be," as given in the First Quarto (Q1, 1603).

The Tragedy of Hamlet

And so by continuance, and weakenesse of the braine
Into this frensie, which now possesseth him:
And if this be not true, take this from this.

    King Thinke you t'is so?

    Cor. How? so my Lord, I would very faine know
That thing that I haue saide t'is so, positiuely,
And it hath fallen out otherwise:
Nay, if circumstances leade me on,
Ile finde it out, if it were hid
As deepe as the centre of the earth.

    King. how should wee trie this same?

    Cor. Mary my good lord this,
The Princes walke is here in the galery,
There let *Ofelia*, walke vntill hee comes:
Your selfe and I will stand close in the study,
There shall you heare the effect of all his hart,
And if it proue any otherwise then loue,
Then let my censure faile an other time.

    King. see where hee comes poring vppon a booke.

Enter Hamlet.

    Cor. Madame, will it please your grace
To leaue vs here?

    Que. With all my hart.   *exit.*

    Cor. And here *Ofelia*, reade you on this booke,
And walke aloose, the King shal be vnseene.

    Ham. To be, or not to be, I there's the point,
To Die, to sleepe, is that all? I all:
No, to sleepe, to dreame, I mary there it goes,
For in that dreame of death, when wee awake,
And borne before an euerlasting Iudge,
From whence no passenger euer return'd,
The vndiscouered country, at whose sight
The happy smile, and the accursed damn'd.
But for this, the ioyfull hope of this,
Whol'd beare the scornes and flattery of the world,
Scorned by the right rich, the rich cursed of the poore?

                        The

That fhow of fuch an exercife may cullour
Your lowlines; we are oft too blame in this,
Tis too much proou'd, that with deuotions vifage
And pious action, we doe fugar ore
The deuill himfelfe.

King. O tis too true,
How fmart a lafh that fpeech doth giue my confcience.
The harlots cheeke beautied with plaftring art,
Is not more ougly to the thing that helps it,
Then is my deede to my moft painted word :
O heauy burthen.

Enter Hamlet.

Pol. I heare him comming, with-draw my Lord.

Ham. To be, or not to be, that is the queftion,
Whether tis nobler in the minde to fuffer
The flings and arrowes of outragious fortune,
Or to take Armes againft a fea of troubles,
And by oppofing, end them; to die to fleepe
No more, and by a fleepe, to fay we end
The hart-ake, and the thoufand naturall fhocks
That flefh is heire to; tis a confumation
Deuoutly to be wifht to die to fleepe,
To fleepe, perchance to dreame, I there's the rub,
For in that fleepe of death what dreames may come
When we haue fhuffled off this mortall coyle
Muft giue vs paufe, there's the refpect
That makes calamitie of fo long life :
For who would beare the whips and fcornes of time,
Th'oppreffors wrong, the proude mans contumely,
The pangs of defpiz'd loue, the lawes delay,
The infolence of office, and the fpurnes
That patient merrit of th'vnworthy takes,
When he himfelfe might his quietas make
With a bare bodkin; who would fardels beare,
To grunt and fweat vnder a wearie life,
But that the dread of fomething after death,
The vndifcouer'd country, from whofe borne.

G 2

"To be or not to be," as given in the Second Quarto (Q2, 1604-05).

The Tragedie of Hamlet

No trauiler returnes, puzzels the will,
And makes vs rather beare those ills we haue,
Then flie to others that we know not of,
Thus conscience dooes make cowards,
And thus the natiue hiew of resolution
Is sickled ore with the pale cast of thought,
And enterprises of great pitch and moment,
With this regard theyr currents turne awry,
And loose the name of action. Soft you now,
The faire *Ophelia*, Nimph in thy orizons
Be all my sinnes remembred.

   Oph. Good my Lord,
How dooes your honour for this many a day?

   Ham. I humbly thanke you well.

   Oph. My Lord, I haue remembrances of yours
That I haue longed long to redeliuer,
I pray you now receiue them.

   Ham. No, not I, I neuer gaue you ought.

   Oph. My honor'd Lord, you know right well you did,
And with them words of so sweet breath compos'd
As made these things more rich, their perfume lost,
Take these againe, for to the noble mind
Rich gifts wax poore when giuers prooue vnkind,
There my Lord.

   Ham. Ha, ha, are you honest.

   Oph. My Lord.

   Ham. Are you faire?

   Oph. What meanes your Lordship?

   Ham. That if you be honest & faire, you should admit
no discourse to your beautie.

   Oph. Could beauty my Lord haue better comerse
Then with honestie?

   Ham. I truly, for the power of beautie will sooner transforme h
nestie from what it is to a bawde, then the force of honestie can tra
late beautie into his likenes, this was sometime a paradox, but now
time giues it proofe, I did loue you once.

   Oph. Indeed my Lord you made me belieue so.

   Ham. You should not haue beleeu'd me, for vertue cannot so
enocutat our old stock, but we shall relish of it, I loued you not.

Figure 1

Hamlet on the Stage

We know that *Hamlet* was popular during Shakespeare's lifetime, but the earliest illustration (1709) showing a scene from the play was engraved more than a century after the play was written, so we know little about what *Hamlet* looked like on Shakespeare's stage. Still, we do have at least a little idea. We know, for instance, that at least in the first scene Hamlet wore black (he speaks of his "inky cloak"), and we know that when the Ghost first appears it is dressed in "the very armor he had on / When he the ambitious Norway combated" (1.1.64–65). We know, too, that when the Ghost appears later, in the Queen's chamber (3.4), he does not wear armor, a sign that his mood is different.

We also have a few tantalizing glimpses of Elizabethan acting. Thus, in the dumb show (pantomime) preceding "The Murder of Gonzago" that the touring players in 3.2 produce for the court, we get this stage direction: "Enter a King and a Queen very lovingly: the Queen embracing him and he her." A little later, when the Queen in this dumb show finds that the King has been poisoned, she "makes passionate action," but then, when the poisoner woos her, "she seems harsh a while but in the end accepts love."

We know something, too, of the sound effects. Possibly the play begins with the bell tolling twelve (in 1.1 Bernardo says, "'Tis now struck twelve"), and certainly in the first scene we hear the crowing of a cock, which causes the Ghost to depart. Later we hear the sound of drums, trumpets, and cannon when Claudius drinks toasts, and the play ends with the sound of cannon, when Fortinbras orders the soldiers to pay tribute to the dead Hamlet.

(continued on p. 908)

Figure 2

Figure 1. "The Murder of Gonzago" in 3.2.   Because this episode is a play-within-the-play, Shakespeare uses a distinctive form of verse (pairs of rhyming line, eight syllables to a line) that sets it off from the language of the rest of the play (chiefly prose, or unrhymed lines of ten syllables). The language, too, is different, for it is conspicuously old-fashioned (the sun is called "Phoebus' cart," the ocean is called "Neptune's salt wash"). In this modern-dress production done at Stratford, England, in 1975, Claudius wore a blue business suit and Fortinbras wore combat gear, but the characters in the play-within-the-play were masked, to emphasize their theatricality.

Figure 2. The "closet" scene," in 3.4.   A line in the preceding scene specifically tells us that Hamlet is "going to his mother's closet." (In Elizabethan language, a "closet" is a private room, as opposed to a public room, for instance a room in which a monarch might pray, or relax, as opposed to an audience chamber in which he or she would engage in official actions.) In the twentieth century, at least as early as John Gielgud's production in New York in 1935, and probably in response to Freudian interpretations of the play, the Queen's "closet" has been fitted with a bed on which Hamlet and Gertrude tussle, and indeed the scene is often wrongly called "the bedroom scene." In this 1989 Royal Shakespeare Company production, with Mark Rylance as Hamlet, a ranting Hamlet (at the left) confronts Gertrude. The Ghost, unknown to Gertrude, sits on the bed, presumably seeking to protect her from Hamlet's assault. The setting was not realistic but expressionistic, that is the curtains stirred and the lighting changed not because a physical wind was blowing or the sources of illumination were changing, but to express the passions of the characters.

Figure 3

What about costumes? In their own day, Elizabethan plays were staged chiefly in contemporary dress—doublet (close-fitting jacket) and hose (tights) for the men, gowns of various sorts for the women (whose roles were played by boy actors)—though for classical plays such as *Julius Caesar* some attempt was made in the direction of ancient costume, at least for the major characters. The seventeenth and eighteenth centuries, too, staged the plays in the costume of the day, which of course was not Elizabethan, but in much of the nineteenth century, and in the first third of the twentieth, a strong sense that the plays were "Elizabethan" caused producers to use Elizabethan costumes, although these costumes—contemporary when the plays were first performed—now had become historical costume, marking the plays as of an age remote from our own. In 1925 Barry Jackson staged a modern-dress production in London, in an effort to emphasize the play's contemporary relevance. Today, productions tend to be in modern dress in the sense that they avoid Elizabethan costume, but usually, in an effort to add some color to the stage and also to add some (but not a great) sense of remoteness, they use costumes of the nineteenth century, which allow for splendid gowns and for military uniforms with sashes.

Figure 4

　　Figures 3 and 4. Hamlet meditates on death in the grave yard, in 5.1.　Both of these productions used costumes that suggested the late nineteenth century. Kenneth Branagh portrayed Hamlet in 1993 for The Royal Shakespeare Theatre. In the photograph showing Kevin Kline as Hamlet (New York Shakespeare Festival), Horatio is played by an African-American. Putting aside plays by black authors, and a very few plays by whites about blacks (such as Eugene O'Neill's *The Emperor Jones*), there are few roles in drama expressly written for blacks. Shakespeare offers only three: Othello, Aaron (a Moor in *Titus Andronicus*), and the Prince of Morocco (in *The Merchant of Venice*). The few black actors who played other Shakespearean roles, such as the great Ira Aldridge who in the nineteenth century was known for his King Lear, performed the roles in whiteface. Since the 1980s, however, directors have engaged in open casting, using blacks (and Asians) in any and all roles, and not requiring white makeup.

Hamlet, Prince of Denmark

[DRAMATIS PERSONAE

GHOST of Hamlet, the former King of Denmark

CLAUDIUS, King of Denmark, the former King's brother

GERTRUDE, Queen of Denmark, widow of the former King and now wife of
    Claudius

HAMLET, Prince of Denmark, son of the late King and of Gertrude

POLONIUS, *councillor to the King*

LAERTES, *his son*

OPHELIA, *his daughter*

REYNALDO, *his servant*

HORATIO, *Hamlet's friend and fellow student*

VOLTIMAND,
CORNELIUS,
ROSENCRANTZ,
GUILDENSTERN,   } *members of the Danish court*
OSRIC,
A GENTLEMAN,
A LORD,

BERNARDO,
FRANCISCO,   } *officers and soldiers on watch*
MARCELLUS,

FORTINBRAS, *Prince of Norway*

CAPTAIN *in his army*

Three or Four PLAYERS, *taking the roles of* PROLOGUE, PLAYER KING, PLAYER QUEEN,
    and LUCIANUS

Two MESSENGERS

FIRST SAILOR

Two CLOWNS, *a gravedigger and his companion*

PRIEST

FIRST AMBASSADOR *from England*

*Lords, Soldiers, Attendants, Guards, other Players, Followers of Laertes, other
    Sailors, another Ambassador or Ambassadors from England*

SCENE: *DENMARK*

    1.1   *Enter* BERNARDO *and* FRANCISCO, *two sentinels [meeting].*

BERNARDO. Who's there?

FRANCISCO. Nay, answer me.° Stand and unfold yourself.°

BERNARDO. Long live the King!

FRANCISCO. Bernardo?

BERNARDO. He.

    5

1.1 Location: Elsinore castle. A guard platform.   **2 me** (Francisco emphasizes that *he*
is the sentry currently on watch.)   **unfold yourself** reveal your identity

FRANCISCO. You come most carefully upon your hour.

BERNARDO. 'Tis now struck twelve. Get thee to bed, Francisco.

FRANCISCO. For this relief much thanks. 'Tis bitter cold,
And I am sick at heart.

BERNARDO. Have you had quiet guard?   10

FRANCISCO. Not a mouse stirring.

BERNARDO. Well, good night.
If you do meet Horatio and Marcellus,
The rivals° of my watch, bid them make haste.

Enter HORATIO *and* MARCELLUS.

FRANCISCO. I think I hear them.—Stand, ho! Who is there?   15

HORATIO. Friends to this ground.°

MARCELLUS. And liegemen to the Dane.°

FRANCISCO. Give° you good night.

MARCELLUS. O, farewell, honest soldier. Who hath relieved you?

FRANCISCO. Bernardo hath my place. Give you good night.   20

Exit FRANCISCO.

MARCELLUS. Holla! Bernardo!

BERNARDO. Say, what, is Horatio there?

HORATIO. A piece of him.

BERNARDO. Welcome, Horatio. Welcome, good Marcellus.

HORATIO. What, has this thing appeared again tonight?   25

BERNARDO. I have seen nothing.

MARCELLUS. Horatio says 'tis but our fantasy,°
And will not let belief take hold of him
Touching this dreaded sight twice seen of us.
Therefore I have entreated him along°   30
With us to watch° the minutes of this night,
That if again this apparition come
He may approve° our eyes and speak to it.

HORATIO. Tush, tush, 'twill not appear.

BERNARDO.   Sit down awhile,
And let us once again assail your ears,   35
That are so fortified against our story,
What° we have two nights seen.

HORATIO.   Well, sit we down,
And let us hear Bernardo speak of this.

BERNARDO. Last night of all,°
When yond same star that's westward from the pole°   40
Had made his° course t' illume° that part of heaven
Where now it burns, Marcellus and myself,
The bell then beating one—

Enter GHOST.

14 rivals partners   **16 ground** country, land   **17 liegemen to the Dane** men sworn to
serve the Danish king   **18 Give** i.e., may God give   **27 fantasy** imagination   **30 along**
to come along   **31 watch** keep watch during   **33 approve** corroborate   **37 What** with
what   **39 Last . . . all** i.e., this *very* last night (Emphatic.)   **40 pole** polestar, north star
41 his its **illume** illuminate

MARCELLUS. Peace, break thee off! Look where it comes again!

BERNARDO. In the same figure like the King that's dead.   45

MARCELLUS. Thou art a scholar.° Speak to it, Horatio.

BERNARDO. Looks 'a° not like the King? Mark it, Horatio.

HORATIO. Most like. It harrows me with fear and wonder.

BERNARDO. It would be spoke to.°

MARCELLUS.   Speak to it, Horatio.

HORATIO. What art thou that usurp'st° this time of night,   50

    Together with that fair and warlike form

    In which the majesty of buried Denmark°

    Did sometime° march? By heaven, I charge thee, speak!

MARCELLUS. It is offended.

BERNARDO.   See, it stalks away.

HORATIO. Stay! Speak, speak! I charge thee, speak!   55

Exit GHOST.

MARCELLUS. 'Tis gone and will not answer.

BERNARDO. How now, Horatio? You tremble and look pale.

    Is not this something more than fantasy?

    What think you on 't?°

HORATIO. Before my God, I might not this believe   60

    Without the sensible° and true avouch°

    Of mine own eyes.

MARCELLUS.   Is it not like the King?

HORATIO. As thou art to thyself.

    Such was the very armor he had on

    When he the ambitious Norway° combated.   65

    So frowned he once when, in an angry parle,°

    He smote the sledded° Polacks° on the ice.

    'Tis strange.

MARCELLUS. Thus twice before, and jump° at this dead hour,

    With martial stalk° hath he gone by our watch.   70

HORATIO. In what particular thought to work° I know not,

    But in the gross and scope° of mine opinion

    This bodes some strange eruption to our state.

MARCELLUS. Good now,° sit down, and tell me, he that knows,

    Why this same strict and most observant watch   75

    So nightly toils° the subject° of the land,

    And why such daily cast° of brazen cannon

    And foreign mart° for implements of war,

---

46 scholar one learned enough to know how to question a ghost properly   **47 'a** he
49 It . . . to (It was commonly believed that a ghost could not speak until spoken to.)
50 usurp'st wrongfully takes over   **52 buried Denmark** the buried King of Denmark
53 sometime formerly   **59 on 't** of it   **61 sensible** confirmed by the senses   **avouch**
warrant, evidence   **65 Norway** King of Norway   **66 parle** parley   **67 sledded** traveling on sleds   **Polacks** Poles   **69 jump** exactly   **70 stalk** stride   **71 to work** i.e., to collect my thoughts and try to understand this   **72 gross and scope** general drift   **74 Good
now** (An expression denoting entreaty or expostulation.)   **76 toils** causes to toil   **subject** subjects   **77 cast** casting   **78 mart** buying and selling

Why such impress° of shipwrights, whose sore task
Does not divide the Sunday from the week.   80
What might be toward,° that this sweaty haste
Doth make the night joint-laborer with the day?
Who is 't that can inform me?

HORATIO.   That can I;
　　　At least, the whisper goes so. Our last king,
　　　Whose image even but now appeared to us,   85
　　　Was, as you know, by Fortinbras of Norway,
　　　Thereto pricked on° by a most emulate° pride,°
　　　Dared to the combat; in which our valiant Hamlet—
　　　For so this side of our known world° esteemed him—
　　　Did slay this Fortinbras; who by a sealed° compact   90
　　　Well ratified by law and heraldry
　　　Did forfeit, with his life, all those his lands
　　　Which he stood seized° of, to the conqueror;
　　　Against the° which a moiety competent°
　　　Was gagèd° by our king, which had returned°   95
　　　To the inheritance° of Fortinbras
　　　Had he been vanquisher, as, by the same cov'nant°
　　　And carriage of the article designed,°
　　　His fell to Hamlet. Now, sir, young Fortinbras,
　　　Of unimprovèd mettle° hot and full,   100
　　　Hath in the skirts° of Norway here and there
　　　Sharked up° a list° of lawless resolutes°
　　　For food and diet° to some enterprise
　　　That hath a stomach° in 't, which is no other—
　　　As it doth well appear unto our state—   105
　　　But to recover of us, by strong hand
　　　And terms compulsatory, those foresaid lands
　　　So by his father lost. And this, I take it,
　　　Is the main motive of our preparations,
　　　The source of this our watch, and the chief head°   110
　　　Of this posthaste and rummage° in the land.

BERNARDO. I think it be no other but e'en so.
　　　Well may it sort° that this portentous figure

---

79 impress impressment, conscription **81 toward** in preparation **87 pricked on** in-
cited **emulate** emulous, ambitious **Thereto . . . pride** (Refers to old Fortinbras, not
the Danish King.) **89 this . . . world** i.e., all Europe, the Western world **90 sealed** cer-
tified, confirmed **93 seized** possessed **94 Against the** in return for **moiety competent** corresponding portion **95 gagèd** engaged, pledged **had returned** would have
passed **96 inheritance** possession **97 cov'nant** i.e., the *sealed compact* of line 90
98 carriage . . . designed carrying out of the article or clause drawn up to cover the
point **100 unimprovèd mettle** untried, undisciplined spirits **101 skirts** outlying regions, outskirts **102 Sharked up** gathered up, as a shark takes fish. **list** i.e., troop
resolutes desperadoes **103 For food and diet** i.e., they are to serve as *food,* or
"means," *to some enterprise;* also they serve in return for the rations they get **104 stomach** (1) a spirit of daring (2) an appetite that is fed by the *lawless resolutes* **110 head**
source **111 rummage** bustle, commotion **113 sort** suit

Comes arméd through our watch so like the King
That was and is the question° of these wars.   115
HORATIO. A mote° it is to trouble the mind's eye.
In the most high and palmy° state of Rome,
A little ere the mightiest Julius fell,
The graves stood tenantless, and the sheeted° dead
Did squeak and gibber in the Roman streets;   120
As° stars with trains° of fire and dews of blood,
Disasters° in the sun; and the moist star°
Upon whose influence Neptune's° empire stands°
Was sick almost to doomsday° with eclipse.
And even the like precurse° of feared events,   125
As harbingers° preceding still° the fates
And prologue to the omen° coming on,
Have heaven and earth together demonstrated
Unto our climatures° and countrymen.

Enter GHOST.

But soft,° behold! Lo, where it comes again!
I'll cross° it, though it blast° me. [*It spreads his° arms.*]   130
   Stay, *illusion!*
If thou hast any sound or use of voice,
Speak to me!
If there be any good thing to be done
That may to thee do ease and grace to me,   135
Speak to me!
If thou art privy to° thy country's fate,
Which, happily,° foreknowing may avoid,
O, speak!
Or if thou hast uphoarded in thy life   140
Extorted treasure in the womb of earth,
For which, they say, you spirits oft walk in death,
   Speak of it! [*The cock crows.*] Stay and speak!—Stop it, Marcellus.
MARCELLUS. Shall I strike at it with my partisan?°
HORATIO. Do, if it will not stand.   *[They strike at it.]* 145
BERNARDO. 'Tis here!
HORATIO. 'Tis here!
MARCELLUS. 'Tis gone.   *[Exit* GHOST.*]*
   We do it wrong, being so majestical,

---

115 question focus of contention **116 mote** speck of dust **117 palmy** flourishing
119 sheeted shrouded **121 As** (This abrupt transition suggests that matter is possibly
omitted between lines 120 and 121.) **trains** trails **122 Disasters** unfavorable signs or
aspects. **moist star** i.e., moon, governing tides **123 Neptune** god of the sea **stands**
depends **124 sick . . . doomsday** (See Matthew 24:29 and Revelation 6:12.) **125 pre-
curse** heralding, foreshadowing **126 harbingers** forerunners **still** continually
127 omen calamitous event **129 climatures** regions **130 soft** i.e., enough, break off
131 cross stand in its path, confront **blast** wither, strike with a curse **s.d. his** its
137 privy to in on the secret of **138 happily** haply, perchance **144 partisan** long-
handled spear

To offer it the show of violence,   150
For it is as the air invulnerable,
And our vain blows malicious mockery.
BERNARDO. It was about to speak when the cock crew.
HORATIO. And then it started like a guilty thing
Upon a fearful summons. I have heard   155
The cock, that is the trumpet° to the morn,
Doth with his lofty and shrill-sounding throat
Awake the god of day, and at his warning,
Whether in sea or fire, in earth or air,
Th' extravagant and erring° spirit hies°   160
To his confine; and of the truth herein
This present object made probation.°
MARCELLUS. It faded on the crowing of the cock.
Some say that ever 'gainst° that season comes
Wherein our Savior's birth is celebrated,   165
This bird of dawning singeth all night long,
And then, they say, no spirit dare stir abroad;
The nights are wholesome, then no planets strike,°
No fairy takes,° nor witch hath power to charm,
So hallowed and so gracious° is that time.   170
HORATIO. So have I heared and do in part believe it.
But, look, the morn in russet mantle clad
Walks o'er the dew of yon high eastward hill.
Break we our watch up, and by my advice
Let us impart what we have seen tonight   175
Unto young Hamlet; for upon my life,
This spirit, dumb to us, will speak to him.
Do you consent we shall acquaint him with it,
As needful in our loves, fitting our duty?
MARCELLUS. Let's do 't, I pray, and I this morning know   180
Where we shall find him most conveniently.

Exeunt.

1.2 Flourish. Enter CLAUDIUS, *King of Denmark,* GERTRUDE *the Queen, [the] Council, as*° POLONIUS *and his son* LAERTES, HAMLET, *cum aliis*° *[including* VOLTIMAND *and* CORNELIUS*].*

KING. Though yet of Hamlet our° dear brother's death
The memory be green, and that it us befitted
To bear our hearts in grief and our whole kingdom
To be contracted in one brow of woe,
Yet so far hath discretion fought with nature   5
That we with wisest sorrow think on him

156 trumpet trumpeter   **160 extravagant and erring** wandering beyond bounds (The words have similar meaning.)   **hies** hastens   **162 probation** proof   **164 'gainst** just before   **168 strike** destroy by evil influence   **169 takes** bewitches   **170 gracious** full of grace   **1.2. Location: The castle.**   **s.d. as** i.e., such as, including   **cum aliis** with others   **1 our** my (The royal "we"; also in the following lines.)

Together with remembrance of ourselves.
Therefore our sometime° sister, now our queen,
Th' imperial jointress° to this warlike state,
Have we, as 'twere with a defeated joy— 10
With an auspicious and a dropping eye,°
With mirth in funeral and with dirge in marriage,
In equal scale weighing delight and dole°—
Taken to wife: Nor have we herein barred
Your better wisdoms, which have freely gone 15
With this affair along. For all, our thanks.
Now follows that you know° young Fortinbras,
Holding a weak supposal° of our worth,
Or thinking by our late dear brother's death
Our state to be disjoint and out of frame, 20
Co-leaguèd with° this dream of his advantage,°
He hath not failed to pester us with message
Importing° the surrender of those lands
Lost by his father, with all bonds° of law,
To our most valiant brother. So much for him. 25
Now for ourself and for this time of meeting.
Thus much the business is: we have here writ
To Norway, uncle of young Fortinbras—
Who, impotent° and bed-rid, scarcely hears
Of this his nephew's purpose—to suppress 30
His° further gait° herein, in that the levies,
The lists, and full proportions are all made
Out of his subject;° and we here dispatch
You, good Cornelius, and you, Voltimand,
For bearers of this greeting to old Norway, 35
Giving to you no further personal power
To business with the King more than the scope
Of these dilated° articles allow.   [*He gives a paper.*]
Farewell, and let your haste commend your duty.°
CORNELIUS, VOLTIMAND. In that, and all things, will we show our duty. 40
KING. We doubt it nothing.° Heartily farewell.

        [*Exeunt* VOLTIMAND *and* CORNELIUS.]
And now, Laertes, what's the news with you?
You told us of some suit; what is 't, Laertes?
You cannot speak of reason to the Dane°

---

8 sometime former   **9 jointress** woman possessing property with her husband   **11 With
. . . eye** with one eye smiling and the other weeping   **13 dole** grief   **17 that you know**
what you know already, that; or, that you be informed as follows   **18 weak supposal** low
estimate   **21 Co-leaguèd with** joined to, allied with   **dream . . . advantage** illusory
hope of having the advantage (His only ally is this hope.)   **23 Importing** pertaining to
24 bonds contracts   **29 impotent** helpless   **31 His** i.e., Fortinbras'   **gait** proceeding
31–33 in that . . . subject since the levying of troops and supplies is drawn entirely from
the King of Norway's own subjects   **38 dilated** set out at length   **39 let . . . duty** let your
swift obeying of orders, rather than mere words, express your dutifulness   **41 nothing** not
at all   **44 the Dane** the Danish king

And lose your voice.° What wouldst thou beg, Laertes,   45
That shall not be my offer, not thy asking?
The head is not more native° to the heart,
The hand more instrumental° to the mouth,
Than is the throne of Denmark to thy father.
What wouldst thou have, Laertes?

LAERTES.   My dread lord,   50
Your leave and favor° to return to France,
From whence though willingly I came to Denmark
To show my duty in your coronation,
Yet now I must confess, that duty done,
My thoughts and wishes bend again toward France   55
And bow them to your gracious leave and pardon.°

KING. Have you your father's leave? What says Polonius?

POLONIUS. H'ath,° my lord, wrung from me my slow leave
By laborsome petition, and at last
Upon his will I sealed° my hard° consent.   60
I do beseech you, give him leave to go.

KING. Take thy fair hour,° Laertes. Time be thine,
And thy best graces spend it at thy will!°
But now, my cousin° Hamlet, and my son—

HAMLET. A little more than kin, and less than kind.°   65

KING. How is it that the clouds still hang on you?

HAMLET. Not so, my lord. I am too much in the sun.°

QUEEN. Good Hamlet, cast thy nighted color° off,
And let thine eye look like a friend on Denmark.°
Do not forever with thy vailèd lids°   70
Seek for thy noble father in the dust.
Thou know'st 'tis common,° all that lives must die,
Passing through nature to eternity.

HAMLET. Ay, madam, it is common.

QUEEN.   If it be,
Why seems it so particular° with thee?   75

HAMLET. Seems, madam? Nay, it is. I know not "seems."
'Tis not alone my inky cloak, good Mother,
Nor customary° suits of solemn black,

45 lose your voice waste your speech   **47 native** closely connected, related   **48 instrumental** serviceable   **51 leave and favor** kind permission   **56 bow . . . pardon** entreatingly make a deep bow, asking your permission to depart   **58 H'ath** he has   **60 sealed** (as if sealing a legal document).   **hard** reluctant   **62 Take thy fair hour** enjoy your time of youth   **63 And . . . will** and may your finest qualities guide the way you choose to spend your time   **64 cousin** any kin not of the immediate family   **65 A little . . . kind** i.e., closer than an ordinary nephew (since I am stepson), and yet more separated in natural feeling (with pun on *kind* meaning "affectionate" and "natural," "lawful." This line is often read as an aside, but it need not be. The King chooses perhaps not to respond to Hamlet's cryptic and bitter remark.)   **67 the sun** i.e., the sunshine of the King's royal favor (with pun on *son*)   **68 nighted color** (1) mourning garments of black (2) dark melancholy   **69 Denmark** the King of Denmark   **70 vailèd lids** lowered eyes   **72 common** of universal occurrence (But Hamlet plays on the sense of "vulgar" in line 74.)   **75 particular** personal   **78 customary** (1) socially conventional (2) habitual with me

Nor windy suspiration° of forced breath,
No, nor the fruitful° river in the eye,   80
Nor the dejected havior° of the visage,
Together with all forms, moods,° shapes of grief,
That can denote me truly. These indeed seem,
For they are actions that a man might play.
But I have that within which passes show;   85
These but the trappings and the suits of woe.

KING. 'Tis sweet and commendable in your nature, Hamlet,
To give these mourning duties to your father.
But you must know your father lost a father,
That father lost, lost his, and the survivor bound   90
In filial obligation for some term
To do obsequious° sorrow. But to persever°
In obstinate condolement° is a course
Of impious stubbornness. 'Tis unmanly grief.
It shows a will most incorrect to heaven,   95
A heart unfortified,° a mind impatient,
An understanding simple° and unschooled.
For what we know must be and is as common
As any the most vulgar thing to sense,°
Why should we in our peevish opposition   100
Take it to heart? Fie, 'tis a fault to heaven,
A fault against the dead, a fault to nature,
To reason most absurd, whose common theme
Is death of fathers, and who still° hath cried,
From the first corpse° till he that died today,   105
"This must be so." We pray you, throw to earth
This unprevailing° woe and think of us
As of a father; for let the world take note,
You are the most immediate° to our throne,
And with no less nobility of love   110
Than that which dearest father bears his son
Do I impart toward° you. For° your intent
In going back to school° in Wittenberg,°
It is most retrograde° to our desire,
And we beseech you bend you° to remain   115
Here in the cheer and comfort of our eye,
Our chiefest courtier, cousin, and our son.

QUEEN. Let not thy mother lose her prayers, Hamlet.
I pray thee, stay with us, go not to Wittenberg.

HAMLET. I shall in all my best° obey you, madam.   120

---

79 suspiration sighing   **80 fruitful** abundant   **81 havior** expression   **82 moods** outward expression of feeling   **92 obsequious** suited to obsequies or funerals   **persever** persevere   **93 condolement** sorrowing   **96 unfortified** i.e., against adversity   **97 simple** ignorant   **99 As ... sense** as the most ordinary experience   **104 still** always   **105 the first corpse** (Abel's)   **107 unprevailing** unavailing, useless   **109 most immediate** next in succession   **112 impart toward** i.e., bestow my affection on   **For** as for   **113 to school** i.e., to your studies   **Wittenberg** famous German university founded in 1502   **114 retrograde** contrary   **115 bend** you incline yourself   **120 in all my best** to the best of my ability

KING. Why, 'tis a loving and a fair reply.
     Be as ourself in Denmark. Madam, come.
     This gentle and unforced accord of Hamlet
     Sits smiling to° my heart, in grace° whereof
     No jocund° health that Denmark drinks today   125
     But the great cannon to the clouds shall tell,
     And the King's rouse° the heaven shall bruit again,°
     Respeaking earthly thunder.° Come away.
                   Flourish. Exeunt all but HAMLET.

HAMLET. O, that this too too sullied° flesh would melt,
     Thaw, and resolve itself into a dew!   130
     Or that the Everlasting had not fixed
     His canon° 'gainst self-slaughter! O God, God,
     How weary, stale, flat, and unprofitable
     Seem to me all the uses° of this world!
     Fie on 't, ah fie! 'Tis an unweeded garden   135
     That grows to seed. Things rank and gross in nature
     Possess it merely.° That it should come to this!
     But two months dead—nay, not so much, not two.
     So excellent a king, that was to° this
     Hyperion° to a satyr,° so loving to my mother   140
     That he might not beteem° the winds of heaven
     Visit her face too roughly. Heaven and earth,
     Must I remember? Why, she would hang on him
     As if increase of appetite had grown
     By what it fed on, and yet within a month—   145
     Let me not think on 't; frailty, thy name is woman!—
     A little month, or ere° those shoes were old
     With which she followed my poor father's body,
     Like Niobe;° all tears, why she, even she—
     O God, a beast, that wants discourse of reason,°   150
     Would have mourned longer—married with my uncle,
     My father's brother, but no more like my father
     Than I to Hercules. Within a month,
     Ere yet the salt of most unrighteous tears
     Had left the flushing in her gallèd° eyes,   155
     She married. O, most wicked speed, to post°
     With such dexterity to incestuous° sheets!

124 to i.e., at   **grace** thanksgiving   **125 jocund** merry   **127 rouse** drinking of a draft of liquor   **bruit again** loudly echo   **128 thunder** i.e., of trumpet and kettledrum, sounded when the King drinks; see 1.4.8-12   **129 sullied** defiled (The early quartos read *sallied;* the Folio, *solid.*)   **132 canon** law   **134 all the uses** the whole routine   **137 merely** completely   **139 to** in comparison to   **140 Hyperion** Titan sun-god, father of Helios **satyr** a lecherous creature of classical mythology, half-human but with a goat's legs, tail, ears, and horns   **141 beteem** allow   **147 or ere** even before   **149 Niobe** Tantalus' daughter, Queen of Thebes, who boasted that she had more sons and daughters than Leto; for this, Apollo and Artemis, children of Leto, slew her fourteen children. She was turned by Zeus into a stone that continually dropped tears.   **150 wants . . . reason** lacks the faculty of reason   **155 gallèd** irritated, inflamed   **156 post** hasten   **157 incestuous** (In Shakespeare's day, the marriage of a man like Claudius to his deceased brother's wife was considered incestuous.)

It is not, nor it cannot come to good.
But break, my heart, for I must hold my tongue.

Enter HORATIO, MARCELLUS *and* BERNARDO.

HORATIO. Hail to your lordship!

HAMLET.   I am glad to see you well.   160
    Horatio!—or I do forget myself.

HORATIO. The same, my lord, and your poor servant ever.

HAMLET. Sir, my good friend; I'll change that name° with you.
    And what make you from° Wittenberg, Horatio?
    Marcellus.   165

MARCELLUS. My good lord.

HAMLET. I am very glad to see you. [*To* BERNARDO.] Good even, sir.—
    But what in faith make you from Wittenberg?

HORATIO. A truant disposition, good my lord.

HAMLET. I would not hear your enemy say so,   170
    Nor shall you do my ear that violence
    To make it truster of your own report
    Against yourself. I know you are no truant.
    But what is your affair in Elsinore?
    We'll teach you to drink deep ere you depart.   175

HORATIO. My lord, I came to see your father's funeral.

HAMLET. I prithee, do not mock me, fellow student;
    I think it was to see my mother's wedding.

HORATIO. Indeed, my lord, it followed hard° upon.

HAMLET. Thrift, thrift, Horatio! The funeral baked meats°   180
    Did coldly° furnish forth the marriage tables.
    Would I had met my dearest° foe in heaven
    Or ever° I had seen that day, Horatio!
    My father!—Methinks I see my father.

HORATIO. Where, my lord?

HAMLET.   In my mind's eye, Horatio.   185

HORATIO. I saw him once. 'A° was a goodly king.

HAMLET. 'A was a man. Take him for all in all,
    I shall not look upon his like again.

HORATIO. My lord, I think I saw him yesternight.

HAMLET. Saw? Who?   190

HORATIO. My lord, the King your father.

HAMLET. The King my father?

HORATIO. Season your admiration° for a while
    With an attent° ear till I may deliver,
    Upon the witness of these gentlemen,   195
    This marvel to you.

HAMLET.   For God's love, let me hear!

---

163 change that name i.e., give and receive reciprocally the name of "friend" (rather than talk of "servant") **164 make you from** are you doing away from **179 hard** close **180 baked meats** meat pies **181 coldly** i.e., as cold leftovers **182 dearest** closest (and therefore deadliest) **183 Or ever** before **186 'A** he **193 Season your admiration** restrain your astonishment **194 attent** attentive

HORATIO. Two nights together had these gentlemen,
　　　　Marcellus and Bernardo, on their watch,
　　　　In the dead waste° and middle of the night,
　　　　Been thus encountered. A figure like your father,   200
　　　　Armèd at point° exactly, cap-à-pie,°
　　　　Appears before them, and with solemn march
　　　　Goes slow and stately by them. Thrice he walked
　　　　By their oppressed and fear-surprisèd eyes
　　　　Within his truncheon's° length, whilst they, distilled°   205
　　　　Almost to jelly with the act° of fear,
　　　　Stand dumb and speak not to him. This to me
　　　　In dreadful° secrecy impart they did,
　　　　And I with them the third night kept the watch,
　　　　Where, as they had delivered, both in time,   210
　　　　Form of the thing, each word made true and good,
　　　　The apparition comes. I knew your father;
　　　　These hands are not more like.
HAMLET.　　　　　　　　　　　　But where was this?
MARCELLUS. My lord, upon the platform where we watch.
HAMLET. Did you not speak to it?
HORATIO.　　　　　　　　　My lord, I did,   215
　　　　But answer made it none. Yet once methought
　　　　It lifted up its head and did address
　　　　Itself to motion, like as it would speak;°
　　　　But even then° the morning cock crew loud,
　　　　And at the sound it shrunk in haste away   220
　　　　And vanished from our sight.
HAMLET.　　　　　　　　　　　　'Tis very strange.
HORATIO. As I do live, my honored lord, 'tis true,
　　　　And we did think it writ down in our duty
　　　　To let you know of it.
HAMLET. Indeed, indeed, sirs. But this troubles me.   225
　　　　Hold you the watch tonight?
ALL.　　　　　　　　　　　　We do, my lord.
HAMLET. Armed, say you?
ALL. Armed, my lord.
HAMLET. From top to toe?
ALL. My lord, from head to foot.   230
HAMLET. Then saw you not his face?
HORATIO. O, yes, my lord, he wore his beaver° up.
HAMLET. What° looked he, frowningly?
HORATIO. A countenance more in sorrow than in anger.
HAMLET. Pale or red?   235
HORATIO. Nay, very pale.
HAMLET. And fixed his eyes upon you?

199 dead waste desolate stillness   **201 at point** correctly in every detail   **cap-à-pie** from head to foot   **205 truncheon** officer's staff   **distilled** dissolved   **206 act** action, operation   **208 dreadful** full of dread   **217–218 did . . . speak** began to move as though it were about to speak   **219 even then** at that very instant   **232 beaver** visor on the helmet   **233 What** how

HORATIO. Most constantly.

HAMLET. I would I had been there.

HORATIO. It would have much amazed you.

HAMLET. Very like, very like. Stayed it long? 240

HORATIO. While one with moderate haste might tell° a hundred.

MARCELLUS, BERNARDO. Longer, longer.

HORATIO. Not when I saw 't.

HAMLET. His beard was grizzled°—no? 245

HORATIO. It was, as I have seen it in his life,
    A sable silvered.°

HAMLET.   I will watch tonight.
    Perchance 'twill walk again.

HORATIO.   I warrant° it will.

HAMLET. If it assume my noble father's person,
    I'll speak to it though hell itself should gape 250
    And bid me hold my peace. I pray you all,
    If you have hitherto concealed this sight,
    Let it be tenable° in your silence still,
    And whatsoever else shall hap tonight,
    Give it an understanding but no tongue. 255
    I will requite your loves. So, fare you well.
    Upon the platform twixt eleven and twelve
    I'll visit you.

ALL.   Our duty to your honor.

HAMLET. Your loves, as mine to you. Farewell.

                     Exeunt [all but HAMLET].

    My father's spirit in arms! All is not well. 260
    I doubt° some foul play. Would the night were come!
    Till then sit still, my soul. Foul deeds will rise,
    Though all the earth o'erwhelm them, to men's eyes.

                          Exit.

      1.3 *Enter* LAERTES *and* OPHELIA, *his sister.*

LAERTES. My necessaries are embarked. Farewell.
    And, sister, as the winds give benefit
    And convoy is assistant,° do not sleep
    But let me hear from you.

OPHELIA.   Do you doubt that?

LAERTES. For Hamlet, and the trifling of his favor, 5
    Hold it a fashion and a toy in blood,°
    A violet in the youth of primy° nature,
    Forward,° not permanent, sweet, not lasting,
    The perfume and suppliance° of a minute—
    No more.

242 tell count   **245 grizzled** gray   **247 sable silvered** black mixed with white **248 warrant** assure you   **253 tenable** held   **261 doubt** suspect   **1.3. Location: Polonius' chambers.**   **3 convoy is assistant** means of conveyance are available   **6 toy in blood** passing amorous fancy   **7 primy** in its prime, springtime   **8 Forward** precocious   **9 suppliance** supply, filler

OPHELIA.   No more but so?

LAERTES.   Think it no more.   10

     For nature crescent° does not grow alone
     In thews° and bulk, but as this temple° waxes
     The inward service of the mind and soul
     Grows wide withal.° Perhaps he loves you now,
     And now no soil° nor cautel° doth besmirch   15
     The virtue of his will,° but you must fear,
     His greatness weighed,° his will is not his own.
     For he himself is subject to his birth.
     He may not, as unvalued persons do,
     Carve° for himself, for on his choice depends   20
     The safety and health of this whole state,
     And therefore must his choice be circumscribed
     Unto the voice and yielding° of that body
     Whereof he is the head. Then if he says he loves you,
     It fits your wisdom so far to believe it   25
     As he in his particular act and place°
     May give his saying deed, which is no further
     Than the main voice° of Denmark goes withal.°
     Then weigh what loss your honor may sustain
     If with too credent° ear you list° his songs,   30
     Or lose your heart, or your chaste treasure open
     To his unmastered importunity.
     Fear it, Ophelia, fear it, my dear sister,
     And keep you in the rear of your affection,°
     Out of the shot and danger of desire.   35
     The chariest° maid is prodigal enough
     If she unmask° her beauty to the moon.°
     Virtue itself scapes not calumnious strokes.
     The canker galls° the infants of the spring
     Too oft before their buttons° be disclosed,°   40
     And in the morn and liquid dew° of youth
     Contagious blastments° are most imminent.
     Be wary then; best safety lies in fear.
     Youth to itself rebels,° though none else near.

OPHELIA.   I shall the effect of this good lesson keep   45
     As watchman to my heart. But, good my brother,
     Do not, as some ungracious° pastors do,

---

11 crescent growing, waxing   **12 thews** bodily strength   **temple** I.e., body   **14 Grows wide withal** grows along with it   **15 soil** blemish   **cautel** deceit   **16 will** desire   **17 His greatness weighed** if you take into account his high position   **20 Carve** i.e., choose   **23 voice and yielding** assent, approval   **26 in . . . place** in his particular restricted circumstances   **28 main voice** general assent   **withal** along with   **30 credent** credulous– **list** listen to   **34 keep . . . affection** don't advance as far as your affection might lead you (A military metaphor.)   **36 chariest** most scrupulously modest   **37 If she unmask** if she does no more than show her beauty   **moon** (Symbol of chastity.)   **39 canker galls** canker-worm destroys   **40 buttons** buds   **disclosed** opened   **41 liquid dew** i.e., time when dew is fresh and bright   **42 blastments** blights   **44 Youth . . . rebels** youth is inherently rebellious   **47 ungracious** ungodly

Show me the steep and thorny way to heaven,
Whiles like a puffed° and reckless libertine
Himself the primrose path of dalliance treads,   50
And recks° not his own rede.°

Enter POLONIUS.

LAERTES.   O, fear me not.°
I stay too long. But here my father comes.
A double° blessing is a double grace;
Occasion smiles upon a second leave.°

POLONIUS. Yet here, Laertes? Aboard, aboard, for shame!   55
The wind sits in the shoulder of your sail,
And you are stayed for. There—my blessing with thee!
And these few precepts in thy memory
Look° thou character.° Give thy thoughts no tongue,
Nor any unproportioned° thought his° act.   60
Be thou familiar,° but by no means vulgar.°
Those friends thou hast, and their adoption tried,°
Grapple them unto thy soul with hoops of steel,
But do not dull thy palm° with entertainment
Of each new-hatched, unfledged courage.° Beware   65
Of entrance to a quarrel, but being in,
Bear 't that° th' opposèd may beware of thee.
Give every man thy ear, but few thy voice;
Take each man's censure,° but reserve thy judgment.
Costly thy habit° as thy purse can buy,   70
But not expressed in fancy;° rich, not gaudy,
For the apparel oft proclaims the man,
And they in France of the best rank and station
Are of a most select and generous chief in that.°
Neither a borrower nor a lender be,   75
For loan oft loses both itself and friend,
And borrowing dulleth edge of husbandry.°
This above all: to thine own self be true,
And it must follow, as the night the day,
Thou canst not then be false to any man.   80
Farewell. My blessing season° this in thee!

LAERTES. Most humbly do I take my leave, my lord.

---

49 puffed bloated, or swollen with pride   **51 recks** heeds   **rede** counsel   **fear me not** don't worry on my account   **53 double** (Laertes has already bid his father good-bye.) **54 Occasion . . . leave** happy is the circumstance that provides a second leave-taking (The goddess Occasion, or Opportunity, smiles.)   **59 Look** be sure that   **character** inscribe   **60 unproportioned** badly calculated, intemperate   **his** its   **61 familiar** sociable   **vulgar** common   **62 and their adoption tried** and also their suitability for adoption as friends having been tested   **64 dull thy palm** i.e., shake hands so often as to make the gesture meaningless   **65 courage** young man of spirit   **67 Bear 't that** manage it so that   **69 censure** opinion, judgment   **70 habit** clothing   **71 fancy** excessive ornament, decadent fashion   **74 Are . . . that** are of a most refined and well-bred preeminence in choosing what to wear   **77 husbandry** thrift   **81 season** mature

POLONIUS. The time invests° you. Go, your servants tend.°
LAERTES. Farewell, Ophelia, and remember well
    What I have said to you.   85
OPHELIA. 'Tis in my memory locked,
    And you yourself shall keep the key of it.
LAERTES. Farewell.

                                            Exit LAERTES.

POLONIUS. What is 't, Ophelia, he hath said to you?
OPHELIA. So please you, something touching the Lord Hamlet.   90
POLONIUS. Marry,° well bethought.
    'Tis told me he hath very oft of late
    Given private time to you, and you yourself
    Have of your audience been most free and bounteous.
    If it be so—as so 'tis put on° me,   95
    And that in way of caution—I must tell you
    You do not understand yourself so clearly
    As it behooves° my daughter and your honor.
    What is between you? Give me up the truth.
OPHELIA. He hath, my lord, of late made many tenders°   100
    Of his affection to me.
POLONIUS. Affection? Pooh! You speak like a green girl,
    Unsifted° in such perilous circumstance.
    Do you believe his tenders, as you call them?
OPHELIA. I do not know, my lord, what I should think.   105
POLONIUS. Marry, I will teach you. Think yourself a baby
    That you have ta'en these tenders for true pay
    Which are not sterling.° Tender° yourself more dearly,
    Or—not to crack the wind° of the poor phrase,
    Running it thus—you'll tender me a fool.°   110
OPHELIA. My lord, he hath importuned me with love
    In honorable fashion.
POLONIUS. Ay, fashion° you may call it. Go to,° go to.
OPHELIA. And hath given countenance° to his speech, my lord,
    With almost all the holy vows of heaven.   115
POLONIUS. Ay, springes° to catch woodcocks.° I do know,
    When the blood burns, how prodigal° the soul
    Lends the tongue vows. These blazes, daughter,
    Giving more light than heat, extinct in both
    Even in their promise as it° is a-making,   120
    You must not take for fire. From this time

83 invests besieges, presses upon   **tend** attend, wait   **91 Marry** i.e., by the Virgin
Mary (A mild oath.)   **95 put on** impressed on, told to   **98 behooves** befits   **100 ten-
ders** offers   **103 Unsifted** i.e., untried   **108 sterling** legal currency   **Tender** hold,
look after, offer   **109 crack the wind** i.e., run it until it is broken-winded   **110 tender
me a fool** (1) show yourself to me as a fool (2) show me up as a fool (3) present me with
a grandchild (*Fool* was a term of endearment for a child.)   **113 fashion** mere form, pretense.   **Go to** (An expression of impatience.)   **114 countenance** credit, confirmation
116 springes snares.   **woodcocks** birds easily caught; here used to connote gullibility
117 prodigal prodigally   **120 it** i.e., the promise

Be something° scanter of your maiden presence.
Set your entreatments° at a higher rate
Than a command to parle.° For Lord Hamlet,
Believe so much in him° that he is young,   125
And with a larger tether may he walk
Than may be given you. In few,° Ophelia,
Do not believe his vows, for they are brokers,°
Not of that dye° which their investments° show,
But mere implorators° of unholy suits,   130
Breathing° like sanctified and pious bawds,
The better to beguile. This is for all:°
I would not, in plain terms, from this time forth
Have you so slander° any moment° leisure
As to give words or talk with the Lord Hamlet.   135
Look to 't, I charge you. Come your ways.°

OPHELIA. I shall obey, my lord.

Exeunt.

1.4   Enter HAMLET, HORATIO, *and* MARCELLUS.

HAMLET. The air bites shrewdly,° it is very cold.
HORATIO. It is a nipping and an eager° air.
HAMLET. What hour now?
HORATIO.   I think it lacks of° twelve.
MARCELLUS. No, it is struck.
HORATIO.   Indeed? I heard it not.
It then draws near the season°   5
Wherein the spirit held his wont° to walk.
A flourish of trumpets, and two pieces° go off [within].
What does this mean, my lord?
HAMLET. The King doth wake° tonight and takes his rouse,°
Keeps wassail,° and the swaggering upspring° reels,°
And as he drains his drafts of Rhenish° down,   10
The kettledrum and trumpet thus bray out
The triumph of his pledge.°
HORATIO.   It is a custom?

---

122 **something** somewhat   123 **entreatments** negotiations for surrender (A military term.)   124 **parle** discuss terms with the enemy (Polonius urges his daughter, in the metaphor of military language, not to meet with Hamlet and consider giving in to him merely because he requests an interview.)   125 **so . . . him** this much concerning him   127 **In few** briefly   128 **brokers** go-betweens, procurers   129 **dye** color or sort   **investments** clothes (The vows are not what they seem.)   130 **mere implorators** out and out solicitors   131 **Breathing** speaking   132 **for all** once for all, in sum   134 **slander** abuse, misuse   **moment** moment's   136 **Come your ways** come along   1.4. **Location: The guard platform.**   1 **shrewdly** keenly, sharply   2 **eager** biting   3 **lacks of** is just short of   5 **season** time   6 **held his wont** was accustomed   **s.d. pieces** i.e., of ordnance, cannon   8 **wake** stay awake and hold revel   **takes his rouse** carouses   9 **wassail** carousal   **upspring** wild German dance   **reels** dances   10 **Rhenish** Rhine wine   12 **The triumph . . . pledge** i.e., his feat in draining the wine in a single draft

HAMLET. Ay, marry, is't,
  But to my mind, though I am native here
  And to the manner° born, it is a custom   15
  More honored in the breach than the observance.°
  This heavy-headed revel east and west°
  Makes us traduced and taxed of° other nations.
  They clepe° us drunkards, and with swinish phrase°
  Soil our addition;° and indeed it takes   20
  From our achievements, though performed at height,°
  The pith and marrow of our attribute.°
  So, oft it chances in particular men,
  That for° some vicious mole of nature° in them,
  As in their birth—wherein they are not guilty,   25
  Since nature cannot choose his° origin—
  By their o'ergrowth of some complexion,°
  Oft breaking down the pales° and forts of reason,
  Or by some habit that too much o'erleavens°
  The form of plausive° manners, that these men,   30
  Carrying, I say, the stamp of one defect,
  Being nature's livery° or fortune's star,°
  His virtues else,° be they as pure as grace,
  As infinite as man may undergo,°
  Shall in the general censure° take corruption   35
  From that particular fault. The dram of evil
  Doth all the noble substance often dout
  To his own scandal.°

  Enter GHOST.

HORATIO.   Look, my lord, it comes!
HAMLET. Angels and ministers° of grace defend us!
  Be thou° a spirit of health° or goblin damned,   40
  Bring° with thee airs from heaven or blasts from hell,

---

15 manner custom (of drinking) **16 More . . . observance** better neglected than followed **17 east and west** i.e., everywhere **18 taxed of** censured by **19 clepe** call **with swinish phrase** i.e., by calling us swine **20 addition** reputation **21 at height** outstandingly **22 The pith . . . attribute** the essence of the reputation that others attribute to us **24 for** on account of **mole of nature** natural blemish in one's constitution **26 his** its **27 their o'ergrowth . . . complexion** the excessive growth in individuals of some natural trait **28 pales** palings, fences (as of a fortification) **29 o'erleavens** induces a change throughout (as yeast works in dough) **30 plausive** pleasing **32 nature's livery** sign of one's servitude to nature **fortune's star** the destiny that chance brings **33 His virtues else** i.e., the other qualities of *these men* (line 30) **34 may undergo** can sustain **35 general censure** general opinion that people have of him **36–38 The dram . . . scandal** i.e., the small drop of evil blots out or works against the noble substance of the whole and brings it into disrepute. To *dout* is to blot out. (A famous crux.) **39 ministers of grace** messengers of God **40 Be thou** whether you are **spirit of health** good angel **41 Bring** whether you bring

Be thy intents° wicked or charitable,
Thou com'st in such a questionable° shape
That I will speak to thee. I'll call thee Hamlet,
King, father, royal Dane. O, answer me!   45
Let me not burst in ignorance, but tell
Why thy canonized° bones, hearsèd° in death,
Have burst their cerements;° why the sepulcher
Wherein we saw thee quietly inurned°
Hath oped his ponderous and marble jaws   50
To cast thee up again. What may this mean,
That thou, dead corpse, again in complete steel,°
Revisits thus the glimpses of the moon,°
Making night hideous, and we fools of nature°
So horridly to shake our disposition°   55
With thoughts beyond the reaches of our souls?
Say, why is this? Wherefore? What should we do?

[The GHOST] *beckons [*HAMLET].*

HORATIO. It beckons you to go away with it,
As if it some impartment° did desire
To you alone.

MARCELLUS.   Look with what courteous action   60
It wafts you to a more removèd ground.
But do not go with it.

HORATIO.   No, by no means.

HAMLET. It will not speak. Then I will follow it.

HORATIO. Do not, my lord!

HAMLET.   Why, what should be the fear?
I do not set my life at a pin's fee,°   65
And for my soul, what can it do to that,
Being a thing immortal as itself?
It waves me forth again. I'll follow it.

HORATIO. What if it tempt you toward the flood,° my lord,
Or to the dreadful summit of the cliff   70
That beetles o'er° his° base into the sea,
And there assume some other horrible form
Which might deprive your sovereignty of reason°
And draw you into madness? Think of it.
The very place puts toys of desperation,°   75
Without more motive, into every brain

42 **Be thy intents** whether your intentions are   43 **questionable** inviting question
47 **canonized** buried according to the canons of the church   **hearsèd** coffined
48 **cerements** grave clothes   49 **inurned** entombed   52 **complete steel** full armor
53 **glimpses of the moon** pale and uncertain moonlight   54 fools of nature   **mere
men, limited to natural knowledge and subject to nature**   55 **So . . . disposition** to
distress our mental composure so violently   59 **impartment** communication   65 **fee**
value   69 **flood** sea   71 **beetles o'er** overhangs threateningly (like bushy eyebrows)
his its   73 **deprive . . . reason** take away the rule of reason over your mind   75 **toys of
desperation** fancies of desperate acts, i.e., suicide

That looks so many fathoms to the sea
And hears it roar beneath.

HAMLET. It wafts me still.—Go on, I'll follow thee.

MARCELLUS. You shall not go, my lord.   *[They try to stop him.]*

HAMLET.   Hold off your hands!   80

HORATIO. Be ruled. You shall not go.

HAMLET.   My fate cries out,°
And makes each petty° artery° in this body
As hardy as the Nemean lion's° nerve.°
Still am I called. Unhand me, gentlemen.
By heaven, I'll make a ghost of him that lets° me!   85
I say, away!—Go on, I'll follow thee.

                                   Exeunt GHOST *and* HAMLET.

HORATIO. He waxes desperate with imagination.

MARCELLUS. Let's follow. 'Tis not fit thus to obey him.

HORATIO. Have after.° To what issue° will this come?

MARCELLUS. Something is rotten in the state of Denmark.   90

HORATIO. Heaven will direct it.°

MARCELLUS.   Nay, let's follow him.

                                             Exeunt.

1.5 *Enter* GHOST *and* HAMLET.

HAMLET. Whither wilt thou lead me? Speak. I'll go no further.

GHOST. Mark me.

HAMLET.   I will.

GHOST.   My hour is almost come,
When I to sulfurous and tormenting flames
Must render up myself.

HAMLET.   Alas, poor ghost!

GHOST. Pity me not, but lend thy serious hearing   5
To what I shall unfold.

HAMLET. Speak. I am bound° to hear.

GHOST. So art thou to revenge, when thou shalt hear.

HAMLET. What?

GHOST. I am thy father's spirit,   10
Doomed for a certain term to walk the night,
And for the day confined to fast° in fires,
Till the foul crimes° done in my days of nature°
Are burnt and purged away. But that° I am forbid
To tell the secrets of my prison house,   15
I could a tale unfold whose lightest word

---

81 My fate cries out my destiny summons me   **82 petty** weak   **artery** (through which the vital spirits were thought to have been conveyed)   **83 Nemean lion** one of the monsters slain by Hercules in his twelve labors   **nerve** sinew   **85 lets** hinders   **89 Have after** let's go after him   **issue** outcome   **91 it** i.e., the outcome   **1.5. Location: The battlements of the castle.**   **7 bound** (1) ready (2) obligated by duty and fate (The Ghost, in line 8, answers in the second sense.)   **12 fast** do penance by fasting   **13 crimes** sins   **of nature** as a mortal   **14 But that** were it not that

Would harrow up° thy soul, freeze thy young blood,
Make thy two eyes like stars start from their spheres,°
Thy knotted and combinèd locks° to part,
And each particular hair to stand on end   20
Like quills upon the fretful porcupine.
But this eternal blazon° must not be
To ears of flesh and blood. List, list, O, list!
If thou didst ever thy dear father love—

HAMLET. O God!   25

GHOST. Revenge his foul and most unnatural murder.

HAMLET. Murder?

GHOST. Murder most foul, as in the best° it is,
But this most foul, strange, and unnatural.

HAMLET. Haste me to know't, that I, with wings as swift   30
As meditation or the thoughts of love,
May sweep to my revenge.

GHOST.   I find thee apt;
And duller shouldst thou be° than the fat° weed
That roots itself in ease on Lethe° wharf,
Wouldst thou not stir in this. Now, Hamlet, hear.   35
'Tis given out that, sleeping in my orchard,°
A serpent stung me. So the whole ear of Denmark
Is by a forgèd process° of my death
Rankly abused.° But know, thou noble youth,
The serpent that did sting thy father's life   40
Now wears his crown.

HAMLET. O, my prophetic soul! My uncle!

GHOST. Ay, that incestuous, that adulterate° beast,
With witchcraft of his wit, with traitorous gifts°—
O wicked wit and gifts, that have the power   45
So to seduce!—won to his shameful lust
The will of my most seeming-virtuous queen.
O Hamlet, what a falling off was there!
From me, whose love was of that dignity
That it went hand in hand even with the vow°   50
I made to her in marriage, and to decline
Upon a wretch whose natural gifts were poor
To° those of mine!
But virtue,° as it° never will be moved,
Though lewdness court it in a shape of heaven,°   55

---

17 **harrow up** lacerate, tear   18 **spheres** i.e., eye-sockets, here compared to the orbits or transparent revolving spheres in which, according to Ptolemaic astronomy, the heavenly bodies were fixed   19 **knotted . . . locks** hair neatly arranged and confined   22 **eternal blazon** revelation of the secrets of eternity   28 **in the best** even at best   33 **shouldst thou be** you would have to be   **fat** torpid, lethargic   34 **Lethe** the river of forgetfulness in Hades   36 **orchard** garden   38 **forgèd process** falsified account   39 **abused** deceived   43 **adulterate** adulterous   44 **gifts** (1) talents (2) presents   50 **even with the vow** with the very vow   53 **To** compared to   54 **virtue, as it** as virtue   55 **shape of heaven** heavenly form

So lust, though to a radiant angel linked,
Will sate itself in a celestial bed°
And prey on garbage.
But soft, methinks I scent the morning air.
Brief let me be. Sleeping within my orchard,   60
My custom always of the afternoon,
Upon my secure° hour thy uncle stole,
With juice of cursèd hebona° in a vial,
And in the porches of my ears° did pour
The leprous distillment,° whose effect   65
Holds such an enmity with blood of man
That swift as quicksilver it courses through
The natural gates and alleys of the body,
And with a sudden vigor it doth posset°
And curd, like eager° droppings into milk,   70
The thin and wholesome blood. So did it mine,
And a most instant tetter° barked° about,
Most lazar-like,° with vile and loathsome crust,
All my smooth body.
Thus was I, sleeping, by a brother's hand   75
Of life, of crown, of queen at once dispatched,°
Cut off even in the blossoms of my sin,
Unhouseled,° disappointed,° unaneled,°
No reckoning° made, but sent to my account
With all my imperfections on my head.   80
O, horrible! O, horrible, most horrible!
If thou hast nature° in thee, bear it not.
Let not the royal bed of Denmark be
A couch for luxury° and damnèd incest.
But, howsoever thou pursues this act,   85
Taint not thy mind nor let thy soul contrive
Against thy mother aught. Leave her to heaven
And to those thorns that in her bosom lodge,
To prick and sting her. Fare thee well at once.
The glowworm shows the matin° to be near,   90
And 'gins to pale his° uneffectual fire.
Adieu, adieu, adieu! Remember me.

                                        [Exit.]

57 sate . . . bed cease to find sexual pleasure in a virtuously lawful marriage **62 secure** confident, unsuspicious **63 hebona** a poison (The word seems to be a form of *ebony,* though it is thought perhaps to be related to *benbane,* a poison, or to *ebenus,* "yew.") **64 porches of my ears** ears as a porch or entrance of the body **65 leprous distillment** distillation causing leprosylike disfigurement **69 posset** coagulate, curdle **70 eager** sour, acid **72 tetter** eruption of scabs **barked** recovered with a rough covering, like bark on a tree **73 lazar-like** leperlike **76 dispatched** suddenly deprived **78 Unhouseled** without having received the Sacrament **disappointment** unready (spiritually) for the last journey **unaneled** without having received extreme unction **79 reckoning** settling of accounts **82 nature** i.e., the promptings of a son **84 luxury** lechery **90 matin** morning **91 his** its

HAMLET. O all you host of heaven! O earth! What else?
        And shall I couple° hell? O, fie! Hold,° hold, my heart,
        And you, my sinews, grow not instant° old,   95
        But bear me stiffly up. Remember thee?
        Ay, thou poor ghost, whiles memory holds a seat
        In this distracted globe.° Remember thee?
        Yea, from the table° of my memory
        I'll wipe away all trivial fond° records,   100
        All saws° of books, all forms,° all pressures° past
        That youth and observation copied there,
        And thy commandment all alone shall live
        Within the book and volume of my brain,
        Unmixed with baser matter. Yes, by heaven!   105
        O most pernicious woman!
        O villain, villain, smiling, damnèd villain!
        My tables°—meet it is° I set it down
        That one may smile, and smile, and be a villain.
        At least I am sure it may be so in Denmark.   110

                                        [Writing.]

        So uncle, there you are.° Now to my word:
        It is "Adieu, adieu! Remember me."
        I have sworn't.

        Enter HORATIO *and* MARCELLUS.

HORATIO. My lord, my lord!
MARCELLUS. Lord Hamlet!   115
HORATIO. Heavens secure him!°
HAMLET. So be it.
MARCELLUS. Hilo, ho, ho, my lord!
HAMLET. Hillo, ho, ho, boy! Come, bird, come.°
MARCELLUS. How is 't, my noble lord?   120
HORATIO. What news, my lord?
HAMLET. O, wonderful!
HORATIO. Good my lord, tell it.
HAMLET. No, you will reveal it.
HORATIO. Not I, my lord, by heaven.   125
MARCELLUS. Nor I, my lord.
HAMLET. How say you, then, would heart of man once° think it?
        But you'll be secret?
HORATIO, MARCELLUS.   Ay, by heaven, my lord.
HAMLET. There's never a villain dwelling in all Denmark
        But he's an arrant° knave.   130

---

94 couple add   **Hold** hold together   **95 instant** instantly   **98 globe** (1) head (2) world
99 table tablet, slate   **100 fond** foolish   **101 saws** wise sayings   **forms** shapes or images copied onto the slate; general ideas   **pressures** impressions stamped   **108 tables**
writing tablets   **meet it is** it is fitting   **111 there you are** i.e., there, I've written that
down against you   **116 secure him** keep him safe   **119 Hilo . . . come** (A falconer's
call to a hawk in air. Hamlet mocks the hallooing as though it were a part of hawking.)
127 once ever   **130 arrant** thoroughgoing

HORATIO. There needs no ghost, my lord, come from the grave
       To tell us this.
HAMLET.   Why, right, you are in the right.
       And so, without more circumstance° at all,
       I hold it fit that we shake hands and part,
       You as your business and desire shall point you—   135
       For every man hath business and desire,
       Such as it is—and for my own poor part,
       Look you, I'll go pray,
HORATIO. These are but wild and whirling words, my lord.
HAMLET. I am sorry they offend you, heartily;   140
       Yes, faith, heartily.
HORATIO.   There's no offense, my lord.
HAMLET. Yes, but Saint Patrick,° but there is, Horatio,
       And much offense° too. Touching this vision here,
       It is an honest ghost,° that let me tell you.
       For your desire to know what is between us,   145
       O'ermaster 't as you may. And now, good friends,
       As you are friends, scholars, and soldiers,
       Give me one poor request.
HORATIO. What is 't, my lord? We will.
HAMLET. Never make known what you have seen tonight.   150
HORATIO, MARCELLUS. My lord, we will not.
HAMLET. Nay, but swear 't.
HORATIO. In faith, my lord, not I.°
MARCELLUS. Nor I, my lord, in faith.
HAMLET. Upon my sword.°   [*He holds out his sword.*]   155
MARCELLUS. We have sworn, my lord, already.°
HAMLET. Indeed, upon my sword, indeed.
GHOST [*cries under the stage*]. Swear.
HAMLET. Ha, ha, boy, sayst thou so? Art thou there, truepenny?°
       Come on, you hear this fellow in the cellarage.   160
       Consent to swear.
HORATIO.   Propose the oath, my lord.
HAMLET. Never to speak of this that you have seen,
       Swear by my sword.
GHOST [*beneath*]. Swear.   [*They swear.*°]
HAMLET. *Hic et ubique?*° Then we'll shift our ground.   165
                         [*He moves to another spot.*]

133 circumstance ceremony, elaboration   **142 Saint Patrick** The keeper of Purgatory
and patron saint of all blunders and confusion.)   **143 offense** (Hamlet deliberately
changes Horatio's "no offense taken" to "an offense against all decency.")   **144 an honest ghost** i.e., a real ghost and not an evil spirit   **153 In faith . . . I** i.e., I swear not to tell
what I have seen (Horatio is not refusing to swear.)   **155 sword** i.e., the hilt in the form
of a cross   **156 We . . . already** i.e., we swore in *faith*   **159 truepenny** honest old fellow   **164 s.d. They swear** (Seemingly they swear here, and at lines 170 and 190, as they
lay their hands on Hamlet's sword. Triple oaths would have particular force; these three
oaths deal with what they have seen, what they have heard, and what they promise about
Hamlet's *antic disposition.*)   **165 Hic et ubique** here and everywhere (Latin.)

Come hither, gentlemen,
And lay your hands again upon my sword.
Swear by my sword
Never to speak of this that you have heard.
GHOST [*beneath*]. Swear by his sword.   [*They swear.*]   170
HAMLET. Well said, old mole. Canst work i' th' earth so fast?
A worthy pioneer!°—Once more removed, good friends.

                                                [*He moves again.*]
HORATIO. O day and night, but this is wondrous strange!
HAMLET. And therefore as a stranger° give it welcome.
There are more things in heaven and earth, Horatio,   175
Than are dreamt of in your philosophy.°
But come;
Here, as before, never, so help you mercy,°
How strange or odd soe'er I bear myself—
As I perchance hereafter shall think meet   180
To put an antic° disposition on—
That you, at such times seeing me, never shall,
With arms encumbered° thus, or this headshake,
Or by pronouncing of some doubtful phrase
As "Well, we know," or "We could, an if° we would,"   185
Or "If we list° to speak," or "There be, an if they might,"°
Or such ambiguous giving out,° to note°
That you know aught° of me—this do swear,
So grace and mercy at your most need help you.
GHOST [*beneath*]. Swear.   [*They swear.*]   190
HAMLET. Rest, rest, perturbèd spirit! So, gentlemen,
With all my love I do commend me to you;°
And what so poor a man as Hamlet is
May do t' express his love and friending° to you,
God willing, shall not lack.° Let us go in together,   195
And still° your fingers on your lips, I pray.
The time° is out of joint. O cursèd spite°
That ever I was born to set it right!
                            [*They wait for him to leave first.*]
Nay, come, let's go together.°
                                                Exeunt.

---

172 pioneer foot soldier assigned to dig tunnels and excavations   **174 as a stranger**
i.e., needing your hospitality   **176 your philosophy** this subject called "natural philosophy" or "science" that people talk about   **178 so help you mercy** as you hope for God's
mercy when you are judged   **181 antic** fantastic   **183 encumbered** folded   **185 an if**
if   **186 list** wished   **There . . . might** i.e., there are people here (we, in fact) who could
tell news if we were at liberty to do so   **187 giving out** intimation   **note** draw attention
to the fact   **188 aught** i.e., something secret   **192 do . . . you** entrust myself to you
194 friending friendliness   **195 lack** be lacking   **196 still** always   **197 The time** the
state of affairs   **spite** i.e., the spite of Fortune   **199 let's go together** (Probably they
wait for him to leave first, but he refuses this ceremoniousness.)

2.1   *Enter old* POLONIUS *with his man* [REYNALDO].

POLONIUS. Give him this money and these notes, Reynaldo.
                                    [He gives money and papers.]
REYNALDO. I will, my lord.
POLONIUS. You shall do marvelous° wisely, good Reynaldo,
    Before you visit him, to make inquire°
    Of his behavior.
REYNALDO.   My lord, I did intend it.   5
POLONIUS. Marry, well said, very well said. Look you, sir,
    Inquire me first what Danskers° are in Paris,
    And how, and who, what means,° and where they keep,°
    What company, at what expense; and finding
    By this encompassment° and drift° of question   10
    That they do know my son, come you more nearer
    Than your particular demands will touch it.°
    Take you,° as 'twere, some distant knowledge of him,
    As thus, "I know his father and his friends,
    And in part him." Do you mark this, Reynaldo?   15
REYNALDO. Ay, very well, my lord.
POLONIUS. "And in part him, but," you may say, "not well.
    But if 't be he I mean, he's very wild,
    Addicted so and so," and there put on° him
    What forgeries° you please—marry, none so rank°   20
    As may dishonor him, take heed of that,
    But, sir, such wanton,° wild, and usual slips
    As are companions noted and most known
    To youth and liberty.
REYNALDO. As gaming, my lord.   25
POLONIUS. Ay, or drinking, fencing, swearing,
    Quarreling, drabbing°—you may go so far.
REYNALDO. My lord, that would dishonor him.
POLONIUS. Faith, no, as you may season° it in the charge.
    You must not put another scandal on him   30
    That he is open to incontinency;°
    That's not my meaning. But breathe his faults so quaintly°
    That they may seem the taints of liberty,°
    The flash and outbreak of a fiery mind,
    A savageness in unreclaimèd blood,   35
    Of general assault.°

2.1 **Location: Polonius' chambers.** 3 **marvelous** marvelously 4 **inquire** inquiry 7 **Danskers** Danes 8 **what means** what wealth (they have) **keep** dwell 10 **encompassment** roundabout talking **drift** gradual approach or course 11–12 **come . . . it** you will find out more this way than by asking pointed questions (*particular demands*) 13 **Take you** assume, pretend 19 **put on** impute to 20 **forgeries** invented tales **rank** gross 22 **wanton** sportive, unrestrained 27 **drabbing** whoring 29 **season** temper, soften 31 **incontinency** habitual sexual excess 32 **quaintly** artfully, subtly 33 **taints of liberty** faults resulting from free living 35–36 **A savageness . . . assault** a wildness in untamed youth that assails all indiscriminately

REYNALDO. But, my good lord—
POLONIUS. Wherefore should you do this?
REYNALDO. Ay, my lord, I would know that.
POLONIUS. Marry, sir, here's my drift,   40
    And I believe it is a fetch of warrant.°
    You laying these slight sullies on my son,
    As 'twere a thing a little soiled wi' the working,°
    Mark you,
    Your party in converse,° him you would sound,°   45
    Having ever° seen in the prenominate crimes°
    The youth you breathe° of guilty, be assured
    He closes with you in this consequence:°
    "Good sir," or so, or "friend," or "gentleman,"
    According to the phrase or the addition°   50
    Of man and country.
REYNALDO.   Very good, my lord.
POLONIUS. And then, sir, does 'a this—'a does—what was I about to
    say? By the Mass, I was about to say something. Where did I
    leave?
REYNALDO. At "closes in the consequence."   55
POLONIUS. At "closes in the consequence," ay, marry.
    He closes thus: "I know the gentleman,
    I saw him yesterday," or "th' other day,"
    Or then, or then, with such or such, "and as you say,
    There was 'a gaming," "there o'ertook in 's rouse,"°   60
    "There falling out° at tennis," or perchance
    "I saw him enter such a house of sale,"
    Videlicet° a brothel, or so forth. See you now,
    Your bait of falsehood takes this carp° of truth;
    And thus do we of wisdom and of reach,°   65
    With windlasses° and with assays of bias,°
    By indirections find directions° out.
    So by my former lecture and advice
    Shall you my son. You have° me, have you not?
REYNALDO. My lord, I have.
POLONIUS.   God b'wi'° ye; fare ye well.   70
REYNALDO. Good my lord.
POLONIUS. Observe his inclination in yourself.°

---

41 fetch of warrant legitimate trick   **43 soiled wi' the working** soiled by handling
while it is being made, i.e., by involvement in the ways of the world   **45 converse** conversation   **sound** i.e., sound out   **46 Having ever** if he has ever   **prenominate
crimes** before-mentioned offenses   **47 breathe** speak   **48 closes . . . consequence**
takes you into his confidence in some fashion, as follows   **50 addition** title   **60 o'er-
took in 's rouse** overcome by drink   **61 falling out** quarreling   **63 Videlicet** namely
64 carp a fish   **65 reach** capacity, ability   **66 windlasses** i.e., circuitous paths. (Literally, circuits made to head off the game in hunting.)   **assays of bias** attempts through in-
direction (like the curving path of the bowling ball, which is biased or weighted to one
side)   **67 directions** i.e., the way things really are   **69 have** understand   **70 b' wi'** be
with   **72 in yourself** in your own person (as well as by asking questions)

REYNALDO. I shall, my lord.
POLONIUS. And let him ply his music.
REYNALDO. Well, my lord.   75
POLONIUS. Farewell.

                                                        Exit REYNALDO.

    Enter OPHELIA.
                    How now, Ophelia, what's the matter?
OPHELIA. O my lord, my lord, I have been so affrighted!
POLONIUS. With what, i' the name of God?
OPHELIA. My lord, as I was sewing in my closet,°
    Lord Hamlet, with his doublet° all unbraced,°   80
    No hat upon his head, his stockings fouled,
    Ungartered, and down-gyvèd° to his ankle,
    Pale as his shirt, his knees knocking each other,
    And with a look so piteous in purport°
    As if he had been loosèd out of hell   85
    To speak of horrors—he comes before me.
POLONIUS. Mad for thy love?
OPHELIA.   My lord, I do not know,
    But truly I do fear it.
POLONIUS.   What said he?
OPHELIA. He took me by the wrist and held me hard.
    Then goes he to the length of all his arm,   90
    And, with his other hand thus o'er his brow
    He falls to such perusal of my face
    As° 'a would draw it. Long stayed he so.
    At last, a little shaking of mine arm
    And thrice his head thus waving up and down,   95
    He raised a sigh so piteous and profound
    As it did seem to shatter all his bulk°
    And end his being. That done, he lets me go,
    And with his head over his shoulder turned
    He seemed to find his way without his eyes,   100
    For out o' doors he went without their helps,
    And to the last bended their light on me.
POLONIUS. Come, go with me. I will go seek the King.
    This is the very ecstasy° of love,
    Whose violent property° fordoes° itself   105
    And leads the will to desperate undertakings
    As oft as any passion under heaven
    That does afflict our natures. I am sorry.
    What, have you given him any hard words of late?
OPHELIA. No, my good lord, but as you did command   110
    I did repel his letters and denied
    His access to me.

---

79 closet private chamber **80 doublet** close-fitting jacket **unbraced** unfastened
82 down-gyvèd fallen to the ankles (like gyves or fetters) **84 in purport** in what it expressed **93 As** as if (also in line 97) **97 bulk** body **104 ecstasy** madness **105 property** nature **fordoes** destroys

POLONIUS.   That hath made him mad.
     I am sorry that with better heed and judgment
     I had not quoted° him. I feared he did but trifle
     And meant to wrack° thee. But beshrew my jealousy!°   115
     By heaven, it is as proper to our age°
     To cast beyond° ourselves in our opinions
     As it is common for the younger sort
     To lack discretion. Come, go we to the King.
     This must be known,° which, being kept close,° might move   120
     More grief to hide than hate to utter love.°
     Come.

                                                           Exeunt.

        2.2 *Flourish. Enter* KING *and* QUEEN, ROSENCRANTZ, *and*
                   GUILDENSTERN *[with others].*

KING. Welcome, dear Rosencrantz and Guildenstern.
     Moreover that° we much did long to see you,
     The need we have to use you did provoke
     Our hasty sending. Something have you heard
     Of Hamlet's transformation—so call it,   5
     Sith nor° th' exterior nor the inward man
     Resembles that° it was. What it should be,
     More than his father's death, that thus hath put him
     So much from th' understanding of himself,
     I cannot dream of. I entreat you both   10
     That, being of so young days° brought up with him,
     And sith so neighbored to° his youth and havior,°
     That you vouchsafe your rest° here in our court
     Some little time, so by your companies
     To draw him on to pleasures, and to gather   15
     So much as from occasion° you may glean,
     Whether aught to us unknown afflicts him thus
     That, opened,° lies within our remedy.
QUEEN. Good gentlemen, he hath much talked of you,
     And sure I am two men there is not living   20
     To whom he more adheres. If it will please you
     To show us so much gentry° and good will

---

114 quoted observed   **115 wrack** ruin, seduce   **beshrew my jealousy** a plague upon
my suspicious nature   **116 proper . . . age** characteristic of us (old) men   **117 cast beyond** overshoot, miscalculate (A metaphor from hunting.)   **120 known** made known (to
the King) **close** secret   **120–121 might . . . love** i.e., might cause more grief (because
of what Hamlet might do) by hiding the knowledge of Hamlet's strange behavior to Ophelia than unpleasantness by telling it   **2.2. Location: The castle.**   **2 Moreover that** besides the fact that   **6 Sith nor** since neither   **7 that** what   **11 of . . . days** from such
early youth   **12 And sith so neighbored to** and since you are (or, and since that time
you are) intimately acquainted with   **havior** demeanor   **13 vouchsafe your rest** please
to stay   **16 occasion** opportunity   **18 opened** being revealed   **22 gentry** courtesy

As to expend your time with us awhile
For the supply and profit of our hope,°
Your visitation shall receive such thanks   25
As fits a king's remembrance.°

ROSENCRANTZ.   Both Your Majesties
Might, by the sovereign power you have of° us,
Put your dread° pleasures more into command
Than to entreaty.

GUILDENSTERN.   But we both obey,
And here give up ourselves in the full bent°   30
To lay our service freely at your feet,
To be commanded.

KING. Thanks, Rosencrantz and gentle Guildenstern.

QUEEN. Thanks, Guildenstern and gentle Rosencrantz.
And I beseech you instantly to visit   35
My too much changèd son. Go, some of you,
And bring these gentlemen where Hamlet is.

GUILDENSTERN. Heavens make our presence and our practices°
Pleasant and helpful to him!

QUEEN.   Ay, amen!
Exeunt ROSENCRANTZ *and* GUILDENSTERN *[with some attendants].*
Enter POLONIUS.

POLONIUS. Th' ambassadors from Norway, my good lord,   40
Are joyfully returned.

KING. Thou still° hast been the father of good news.

POLONIUS. Have I, my lord? I assure my good liege
I hold° my duty, as° I hold my soul,
Both to my God and to my gracious king;   45
And I do think, or else this brain of mine
Hunts not the trail of policy° so sure
As it hath used to do, that I have found
The very cause of Hamlet's lunacy.

KING. O, speak of that! That do I long to hear.   50

POLONIUS. Give first admittance to th' ambassadors.
My news shall be the fruit° to that great feast.

KING. Thyself do grace° to them and bring them in.
                                        [*Exit* POLONIUS.]
He tells me, my dear Gertrude, he hath found
The head and source of all your son's distemper.   55

QUEEN. I doubt° it is no other but the main,°
His father's death and our o'erhasty marriage.

Enter Ambassadors VOLTIMAND *and* CORNELIUS, *with* POLONIUS.

---

24 supply . . . hope aid and furtherance of what we hope for   **26 As fits . . . remembrance** as would be a fitting gift of a king who rewards true service   **27 of** over   **28 dread** inspiring awe   **30 in . . . bent** to the utmost degree of our capacity (An archery metaphor.)   **38 practices** doings   **42 still** always   **44 hold** maintain. **as** firmly as   **47 policy** sagacity   **52 fruit** desert   **53 grace** honor (punning on *grace* said before a *feast*, line 52)   **56 doubt** fear, suspect   **main** chief point, principal concern

KING. Well, we shall sift him.°—Welcome, my good friends!
　　　Say, Voltimand, what from our brother° Norway?
VOLTIMAND. Most fair return of greetings and desires.°   60
　　　Upon our first,° he sent out to suppress
　　　His nephew's levies, which to him appeared
　　　To be a preparation 'gainst the Polack,
　　　But, better looked into, he truly found
　　　It was against Your Highness. Whereat grieved   65
　　　That so his sickness, age, and impotence°
　　　Was falsely borne in hand,° sends out arrests°
　　　On Fortinbras, which he, in brief, obeys,
　　　Receives rebuke from Norway, and in fine°
　　　Makes vow before his uncle never more   70
　　　To give th' assay° of arms against Your Majesty.
　　　Whereon old Norway, overcome with joy,
　　　Gives him three thousand crowns in annual fee
　　　And his commission to employ those soldiers,
　　　So levied as before, against the Polack,   75
　　　With an entreaty, herein further shown,   [*giving a paper*]
　　　That it might please you to give quiet pass
　　　Through your dominions for this enterprise
　　　On such regards of safety and allowance°
　　　As therein are set down.
KING.　　　　　　　　　　It likes° us well,
　　　And at our more considered° time we'll read,   80
　　　Answer, and think upon this business.
　　　Meantime we thank you for your well-took labor.
　　　Go to your rest; at night we'll feast together.
　　　Most welcome home!
　　　　　　　　　　　　　　　　　　　　　Exeunt Ambassadors.
POLONIUS.　　　　　　This business is well ended.
　　　My liege, and madam, to expostulate°   85
　　　What majesty should be, what duty is,
　　　Why day is day, night night, and time is time,
　　　Were nothing but to waste night, day, and time.
　　　Therefore, since brevity is the soul of wit,°
　　　And tediousness the limbs and outward flourishes,   90
　　　I will be brief. Your noble son is mad.
　　　Mad call I it, for, to define true madness,
　　　What is't but to be nothing else but mad?
　　　But let that go.
QUEEN.　　　　　　More matter, with less art.   95

---

58 sift him question Polonius closely　**59 brother** fellow king　**60 desires** good wishes
61 Upon our first at our first words on the business　**66 impotence** helplessness
67 borne in hand deluded, taken advantage of　**arrests** orders to desist　**69 in fine** in
conclusion　**71 give th' assay** make trial of strength, challenge　**78 On . . . allowance**
i.e., with such considerations for the safety of Denmark and permission for Fortinbras
80 likes pleases　**81 considered** suitable for deliberation　**86 expostulate** expound,
inquire into　**90 wit** sense or judgment

POLONIUS. Madam. I swear I use no art at all.
　　　That he's mad, 'tis true; 'tis true 'tis pity.
　　　And pity 'tis 'tis true—a foolish figure,°
　　　But farewell it, for I will use no art.
　　　Mad let us grant him, then, and now remains　　　　　　　　100
　　　That we find out the cause of this effect,
　　　Or rather say, the cause of this defect,
　　　For this effect defective comes by cause.°
　　　Thus it remains, and the remainder thus.
　　　Perpend.°　　　　　　　　　　　　　　　　　　　　　　　　　105
　　　I have a daughter—have while she is mine—
　　　Who, in her duty and obedience, mark,
　　　Hath given me this. Now gather and surmise.°
　　　[He reads the letter.] "To the celestial and my soul's idol, the most
　　　beautified Ophelia"—　　　　　　　　　　　　　　　　　　110
　　　That's an ill phrase, a vile phrase; "beautified" is a vile phrase. But
　　　you shall hear. Thus:　　　　　　　　　　　　　　[He reads.]
　　　"In her excellent white bosom,° these,° etc."
QUEEN. Came this from Hamlet to her?
POLONIUS. Good madam, stay° awhile, I will be faithful.°　　[He reads.]　115

　　　　　"Doubt thou the stars are fire,
　　　　　　　Doubt that the sun doth move,
　　　　　Doubt° truth to be a liar,
　　　　　　　But never doubt I love.

　　　O dear Ophelia, I am ill at these numbers.° I have not art to　　120
　　　reckon° my groans. But that I love thee best, O most best, believe it.
　　　Adieu.
　　　　　Thine evermore, most dear lady, whilst this machine° is to him,
　　　　　　　　　　　　　　　　　　　　　　　　　　Hamlet."

　　　This in obedience hath my daughter shown me,　　　　　　　125
　　　And, more above,° hath his solicitings,
　　　As they fell out° by° time, by means, and place,
　　　All given to mine ear.°
KING.　　　　　　　　　　　　But how hath she
　　　Received his love?
POLONIUS.　　　　　　　　　　What do you think of me?
KING. As of a man faithful and honorable.　　　　　　　　　130
POLONIUS. I would fain° prove so. But what might you think,
　　　When I had seen this hot love on the wing—
　　　As I perceived it, I must tell you that,

98 figure figure of speech　**103 For . . . cause** i.e., for this defective behavior, tis madness, has a cause　**105 Perpend** consider　**108 gather and surmise** draw your own conclusions　**113 In . . . bosom** (The letter is poetically addressed to her heart.)　**these** i.e., the letter　**115 stay** wait　**faithful** i.e., in reading the letter accurately　**118 Doubt** suspect　**120 ill . . . numbers** unskilled at writing verses　**121 reckon** (1) count (2) number metrically, scan　**123 machine** i.e., body　**126 more above** moreover **127 fell out** occurred　**by** according to　**128 given . . . ear** i.e., told me about　**131 fain** gladly

Before my daughter told me—what might you,
Or my dear Majesty your queen here, think,   135
If I had played the desk or table book,°
Or given my heart a winking,° mute and dumb,
Or looked upon this love with idle sight?°
What might you think? No, I went round° to work,
And my young mistress thus I did bespeak:°   140
"Lord Hamlet is a prince out of thy star;°
This must not be." And then I prescripts° gave her,
That she should lock herself from his resort,°
Admit no messengers, receive no tokens.
Which done, she took the fruits of my advice;   145
And he, repelled—a short tale to make—
Fell into a sadness, then into a fast,
Thence to a watch,° thence into a weakness,
Thence to a lightness,° and by this declension°
Into the madness wherein now he raves,   150
And all we° mourn for.

KING [*to the* QUEEN.]   Do you think 'tis this?

QUEEN. It may be, very like.

POLONIUS. Hath there been such a time—I would fain know that—
   That I have positively said "'Tis so,"
   When it proved otherwise?

KING.   Not that I know.   155

POLONIUS. Take this from this,° if this be otherwise.
   If circumstances lead me, I will find
   Where truth is hid, though it were hid indeed
   Within the center.°

KING.   How may we try° it further?

POLONIUS. You know sometimes he walks four hours together   160
   Here in the lobby.

QUEEN.   So he does indeed.

POLONIUS. At such a time I'll loose° my daughter to him.
   Be you and I behind an arras° then.
   Mark the encounter. If he love her not
   And be not from his reason fall'n thereon,°   165
   Let me be no assistant for a state,
   But keep a farm and carters.°

KING.   We will try it.

---

136 played . . . table book i.e., remained shut up, concealing the information   **137 given
. . . winking** closed the eyes of my heart to this   **138 with idle sight** complacently or in-
comprehendingly   **138 round** roundly, plainly   **140 bespeak** address   **141 out of thy
star** above your sphere, position   **142 prescripts** orders   **143 his resort** his visits
148 watch state of sleeplessness   **149 lightness** lightheadedness   **declension** decline,
deterioration (with a pun on the grammatical sense)   **151 all we** all of us, or, into everything that we   **156 Take this from this** (The actor probably gestures, indicating that he
means his head from his shoulders, or his staff of office or chain from his hands or neck,
or something similar.)   **159 center** middle point of the earth (which is also the center of
the Ptolemaic universe)   **try** test, judge   **162 loose** (as one might release an animal that
is being mated)   **163 arras** handing, tapestry   **165 thereon** on that account   **167
carters** wagon drivers

Enter HAMLET *[reading on a book].*

QUEEN. But look where sadly° the poor wretch comes reading.

POLONIUS. Away, I do beseech you both, away.

   I'll board° him presently.° O, give me leave.°   170

         Exeunt KING *and* QUEEN *[with attendants].*

   How does my good Lord Hamlet?

HAMLET. Well, God-a-mercy.°

POLONIUS. Do you know me, my lord?

HAMLET. Excellent well. You are a fishmonger.°

POLONIUS. Not I, my lord.   175

HAMLET. Then I would you were so honest a man.

POLONIUS. Honest, my lord?

HAMLET. Ay, sir. To be honest, as this world goes, is to be one man picked
  out of ten thousand.

POLONIUS. That's very true, my lord.   180

HAMLET. For if the sun breed maggots in a dead dog, being a good kissing
  carrion°—Have you a daughter?

POLONIUS. I have, my lord.

HAMLET. Let her not walk i' the sun.° Conception° is a blessing, but as your
  daughter may conceive, friend, look to 't.   185

POLONIUS *[aside].* How say you by that? Still harping on my daughter. Yet
  he knew me not at first; 'a° said I was a fishmonger. 'A is far gone.
  And truly in my youth I suffered much extremity for love, very near
  this. I'll speak to him again.—What do you read, my lord?

HAMLET. Words, words, words.   190

POLONIUS. What is the matter,° my lord?

HAMLET. Between who?

POLONIUS. I mean, the matter that you read, my lord.

HAMLET. Slanders, sir; for the satirical rogue says here that old men have
  gray beards, that their faces are wrinkled, their eyes purging° thick 195
  amber° and plum-tree gum, and that they have a plentiful lack of
  wit,° together with most weak hams. All which, sir, though I most
  powerfully and potently believe, yet I hold it not honesty° to have
  it thus set down, for yourself, sir, shall grow old° as I am, if like a
  crab you could go backward.   200

POLONIUS *[aside].* Though this be madness, yet there is method in 't.—
  Will you walk out of the air,° my lord?

HAMLET. Into my grave.

POLONIUS. Indeed, that's out of the air. *[Aside.]* How pregnant° sometimes
  his replies are! A happiness° that often madness hits on, which rea- 205

---

168 sadly seriously **170 board** accost **presently** at once **give me leave** i.e., excuse
me, leave me alone (Said to those he hurries offstage, including the King and Queen.)
172 God-a-mercy God have mercy, i.e., thank you **174 fishmonger** fish merchant
181–182 a good kissing carrion i.e., a good piece of flesh for kissing, or for the sun to
kiss **184 i' the sun** in public (with additional implication of the sunshine of princely favors). **Conception** (1) understanding (2) pregnancy **187 'a** he **191 matter** substance (But Hamlet plays on the sense of "basis for a dispute.") **195 purging** discharg-
ing **196 amber** i.e., resin, like the resinous *plum-tree gum* **197 wit** understanding
198 honesty decency, decorum **199 old** as old **202 out of the air** (The open air was
considered dangerous for sick people.) **204 pregnant** quick-witted, full of meaning
205 happiness felicity of expression

son and sanity could not so prosperously° be delivered of. I will leave him and suddenly° contrive the means of meeting between him and my daughter.—My honorable lord, I will most humbly take my leave of you.

HAMLET. You cannot, sir, take from me anything that I will more willingly 210
    part withal°—except my life, except my life, except my life.

    Enter GUILDENSTERN *and* ROSENCRANTZ.

POLONIUS. Fare you well, my lord.
HAMLET. These tedious old fools!°
POLONIUS. You go to seek the Lord Hamlet. There he is.
ROSENCRANTZ [*to* POLONIUS]. God save you, sir! 215

                                    [*Exit* POLONIUS.]

GUILDENSTERN. My honored lord!
ROSENCRANTZ. My most dear lord!
HAMLET. My excellent good friends! How dost thou, Guildenstern? Ah,
    Rosencrantz! Good lads, how do you both?
ROSENCRANTZ. As the indifferent° children of the earth. 220
GUILDENSTERN. Happy in that we are not overhappy.
    On Fortune's cap we are not the very button.
HAMLET. Nor the soles of her shoe?
ROSENCRANTZ. Neither, my lord.
HAMLET. Then you live about her waist, or in the middle of her favors?° 225
GUILDENSTERN. Faith, her privates we.°
HAMLET. In the secret parts of Fortune? O, most true, she is a strumpet.°
    What news?
ROSENCRANTZ. None, my lord, but the world's grown honest.
HAMLET. Then is doomsday near. But your news is not true. Let me ques- 230
    tion more in particular. What have you, my good friends, deserved
    at the hands of Fortune that she sends you to prison hither?
GUILDENSTERN. Prison, my lord?
HAMLET. Denmark's a prison.
ROSENCRANTZ. Then is the world one. 235
HAMLET. A goodly one, in which there are many confines,° wards,° and
    dungeons, Denmark being one o' the worst.
ROSENCRANTZ. We think not so, my lord.
HAMLET. Why then 'tis none to you, for there is nothing either good or bad
    but thinking makes it so. To me it is a prison. 240
ROSENCRANTZ. Why then, your ambition makes it one. 'Tis too narrow for
    your mind.
HAMLET. O God, I could be bounded in a nutshell and count myself a king
    of infinite space, were it not that I have bad dreams.

---

206 prosperously successfully   **207 suddenly** immediately   **211 withal** with   **213 old fools** i.e., old men like Polonius   **220 indifferent** ordinary, at neither extreme of fortune or misfortune   **225 favors** i.e., sexual favors   **226 her privates we** i.e., (1) we are sexually intimate with Fortune, the fickle goddess who bestows her favors indiscriminately (2) we are her private citizens   **227 strumpet** prostitute. (A common epithet for indiscriminate Fortune; see line 452.)   **236 confines** places of confinement   **wards** cells

GUILDENSTERN. Which dreams indeed are ambition, for the very substance   245
    of the ambitious° is merely the shadow of a dream.

HAMLET. A dream itself is but a shadow.

ROSENCRANTZ. Truly, and I hold ambition of so airy and light a quality that
    it is but a shadow's shadow.

HAMLET. Then are our beggars bodies,° and our monarchs and out-   250
    stretched° heroes the beggars' shadows. Shall we to the court? For,
    by my fay,° I cannot reason.

ROSENCRANTZ, GUILDENSTERN. We'll wait upon° you.

HAMLET. No such matter. I will not sort° you with the rest of my servants,
    for, to speak to you like an honest man, I am most dreadfully at-   255
    tended.° But, in the beaten way° of friendship, what make° you at
    Elsinore?

ROSENCRANTZ. To visit you, my lord, no other occasion.

HAMLET. Beggar that I am, I'am even poor in thanks; but I thank you, and
    sure, dear friends, my thanks are too dear a halfpenny.° Were you   260
    not sent for? Is it your own inclining? Is it a free° visitation? Come,
    come, deal justly with me. Come, come. Nay, speak.

GUILDENSTERN. What should we say; my lord?

HAMLET. Anything but to the purpose.° You were sent for, and there is a
    kind of confession in your looks which your modesties° have not   265
    craft enough to color.° I know the good King and Queen have sent
    for you.

ROSENCRANTZ. To what end, my lord?

HAMLET. That you must teach me. But let me conjure° you, by the rights of
    our fellowship, by the consonancy of our youth,° by the obligation   270
    of our ever-preserved love, and by what more dear a better° pro-
    poser could charge° you withal, be even° and direct with me
    whether you were sent for or no.

ROSENCRANTZ [*aside to* GUILDENSTERN.] What say you?

HAMLET [*aside*]. Nay, then, I have an eye of° you.—If you love me, hold   275
    not off.°

GUILDENSTERN. My lord, we were sent for.

HAMLET. I will tell you why; so shall my anticipation prevent your discov-
    ery,° and your secrecy to the King and Queen molt no feather,° I

245–246 the very . . . ambitious that seemingly very substantial thing that the ambitious pursue   **250 bodies** i.e., solid substances rather than shadows (since beggars are not ambitious)   **250–251 outstretched** (1) far-reaching in their ambition (2) elongated as shadows   **252 fay** faith   **253 wait upon** accompany, attend (But Hamlet uses the phrase in the sense of providing menial service.)   **254 sort** class, categorize   **255–256 dreadfully attended** waited upon in slovenly fashion   **256 beaten way** familiar path, tried-and-true course   **make** do   **260 too dear a halfpenny** (1) too expensive at even a halfpenny, i.e., of little worth (2) too expensive *by* a halfpenny in return for worthless kindness   **261 free** voluntary   **264 Anything but to the purpose** anything except a straightforward answer (Said ironically.)   **265 modesties** sense of shame   **266 color** disguise   **269 conjure** adjure, entreat   **270 the consonancy of our youth** our closeness in our younger days   **271 better** more skillful   **272 charge** urge.   **even** straight, honest   **275 of** on   **276 hold not off** don't hold back   **278–279 so . . . discovery** in that way my saying it first will spare you from revealing the truth   **279 molt no feather** i.e., not diminish in the least

have of late—but wherefore I know not—lost all my mirth, for-   280
gone all custom of exercises; and indeed it goes so heavily with my
disposition that this goodly frame, the earth, seems to me a sterile
promontory; this most excellent canopy, the air, look you, this
brave° o'erhanging firmament, this majestical roof fretted° with
golden fire, why, it appeareth nothing to me but a foul and pesti-   285
lent congregation° of vapors. What a piece of work° is a man! How
noble in reason, how infinite in faculties, in form and moving how
express° and admirable, in action how like an angel, in apprehen-
sion° how like a god! The beauty of the world, the paragon of animals! And yet, to me, what is this quintessence° of dust? Man de-   290
lights not me—no, nor woman neither, though by your smiling you
seem to say so.

ROSENCRANTZ. My lord, there was no such stuff in my thoughts.

HAMLET. Why did you laugh, then, when I said man delights not me?

ROSENCRANTZ. To think, my lord, if you delight not in man, what Lenten   295
     entertainment° the players shall receive from you. We coted° them
     on the way, and hither are they coming to offer you service.

HAMLET. He that plays the king shall be welcome; His Majesty shall have
     tribute° of° me. The adventurous knight shall use his foil and tar-
     get,° the lover shall not sigh gratis,° the humorous man° shall end   300
     his part in peace,° the clown shall make those laugh whose lungs
     are tickle o' the sear,° and the lady shall say her mind freely, or the
     blank verse shall halt° for 't. What players are they?

ROSENCRANTZ. Even those you were wont to take such delight in, the trage-
     dians° of the city.   305

HAMLET. How chances it they travel? Their residence,° both in reputation
     and profit, was better both ways.

ROSENCRANTZ. I think their inhibition° comes by the means of the late° in-
     novation.°

HAMLET. Do they hold the same estimation they did when I was in the city?   310
     Are they so followed?

ROSENCRANTZ. No, indeed are they not.

---

284 brave splendid   **fretted** adorned (with fretwork, as in a vaulted ceiling)   **286 congregation** mass   **piece of work** masterpiece   **288 express** well-framed, exact, expressive   **288–289 apprehension** power of comprehending   **290 quintessence** the fifth
essence of ancient philosophy, beyond earth, water, air, and fire, supposed to be the substance of the heavenly bodies and to be latent in all things   **295–296 Lenten
entertainment** meager reception (appropriate to Lent)   **296 coted** over-took and
passed by   **299 tribute** (1) applause (2) homage paid in money   **of** from   **299–300 foil
and target** sword and shield   **300 gratis** for nothing   **humorous man** eccentric character, dominated by one trait or "humor"   **301 in peace** i.e., with full license   **302 tickle
o' the sear** easy on the trigger, ready to laugh easily (A *sear* is part of a gunlock.)   **303 halt**
limp   **305 tragedians** actors   **306 residence** remaining in their usual place, i.e., in the
city   **308 inhibition** formal prohibition (from acting plays in the city)   **late** recent
309 innovation i.e., the new fashion in satirical plays performed by boy actors in the
"private" theaters; or possibly a political uprising; or the strict limitations set on the theaters in London in 1600

HAMLET. How comes it? Do they grow rusty?

ROSENCRANTZ. Nay, their endeavor keeps° in the wonted° pace. But there
is, sir, an aerie° of children, little eyases,° that cry out on the top of   315
question° and are most tyrannically° clapped for 't. These are now
the fashion, and so berattle° the common stages°—so they call
them—that many wearing rapiers° are afraid of goose quills° and
dare scarce come thither.

HAMLET. What, are they children? Who maintains 'em? How are they es-   320
coted?° Will they pursue the quality° no longer than they can sing?°
Will they not say afterwards, if they should grow themselves to
common° players—as it is most like,° if their means are no bet-
ter°—their writers do them wrong to make them exclaim against
their own succession?°   325

ROSENCRANTZ. Faith, there has been much to-do° on both sides, and the nation holds it no sin to tar° them to controversy. There was for a
while no money bid for argument unless the poet and the player
went to cuffs in the question.°

HAMLET. Is 't possible?   330

GUILDENSTERN. O, there has been much throwing about of brains.

HAMLET. Do the boys carry it away?°

ROSENCRANTZ. Ay, that they do, my lord—Hercules and his load° too.°

HAMLET. It is not very strange; for my uncle is King of Denmark, and those
that would make mouths° at him while my father lived give twenty,   335
forty, fifty, a hundred ducats° apiece for his picture in little.°
'Sblood,° there is something in this more than natural, if philoso-
phy° could find it out.

A flourish [of trumpets within].

GUILDENSTERN. There are the players.

HAMLET. Gentlemen, you are welcome to Elsinore. Your hands, come   340
then. Th' appurtenance° of welcome is fashion and ceremony. Let

---

314 keeps continues **wonted** usual   **315 aerie** nest **eyases** young hawks
315–316 cry...question speak shrilly, dominating the controversy (in decrying the
public theaters)   **316 tyrannically** outrageously   **317 berattle** berate, clamor against.
common stages public theaters   **318 many wearing rapiers** i.e., many men of fashion, afraid to patronize the common players for fear of being satirized by the poets writing
for the boy actors.   **goose quills** i.e., pens of satirists   **320–321 escoted** maintained
321 quality (acting) profession   **321–322 no longer ... sing** i.e., only until their voices
change   **323 common** regular, adult   **like** likely   **323–324 if ... better** if they find no
better way to support themselves   **325 succession** i.e., future careers   **326 to-do** ado
327 tar set on (as dogs)   **327–329 There ... question** i.e., for a while, no money was
offered by the acting companies to playwrights for the plot to a play unless the satirical
poets who wrote for the boys and the adult actors came to blows in the play itself
332 carry it away i.e., win the day   **333 Hercules ... load** (Thought to be an allusion
to the sign of the Globe Theatre, which was Hercules bearing the world on his shoulders.)
313–333 How ... load too (The passage, omitted from the early quartos, alludes to the
so-called War of the Theaters, 1599-1602, the rivalry between the children's companies
and the adult actors.)   **335 mouths** faces   **336 ducats** gold coins   **336–337 in little** in
miniature   **337 'Sblood** by God's (Christ's) blood   **338 philosophy** i.e., scientific inquiry   **341 appurtenance** proper accompaniment

me comply° with you in this garb,° lest my extent° to the players, which, I tell you, must show fairly outwards,° should more appear like entertainment° than yours. You are welcome. But my uncle-father and aunt-mother are deceived.   345

GUILDENSTERN. In what, my dear lord?

HAMLET. I am but mad north-north-west.° When the wind is southerly I know a hawk from a handsaw.°

Enter POLONIUS.

POLONIUS. Well be with you, gentlemen!

HAMLET. Hark you, Guildenstern, and you too; at each ear a hearer. That   350
great baby you see there is not yet out of his swaddling clouts.°

ROSENCRANTZ. Haply° he is the second time come to them, for they say an old man is twice a child.

HAMLET. I will prophesy he comes to tell me of the players. Mark it.—You say right, sir, o' Monday morning, 'twas then indeed.   355

POLONIUS. My lord, I have news to tell you.

HAMLET. My lord, I have news to tell you. When Roscius° was an actor in Rome—

POLONIUS. The actors are come hither, my lord.

HAMLET. Buzz,° buzz!   360

POLONIUS. Upon my honor—

HAMLET. Then came each actor on his ass.

POLONIUS. The best actors in the world, either for tragedy, comedy, history, pastoral, pastoral-comical, historical-pastoral, tragical-historical, tragical-comical-historical-pastoral, scene individable,° or poem   365
unlimited.° Seneca° cannot be too heavy, nor Plautus° too light. For the law of writ and the liberty,° these° are the only men.

HAMLET. O Jephthah, judge of Israel,° what a treasure hadst thou!

POLONIUS. What a treasure had he, my lord?

HAMLET. Why,   370

"One fair daughter, and no more,
The which he lovèd passing° well."

POLONIUS [*aside*]. Still on my daughter.

---

342 comply observe the formalities of courtesy **garb** i.e., manner **my extent** that which I extend, i.e., my polite behavior **343 show fairly outwards** show every evidence of cordiality **344 entertainment** a (warm) reception **347 north-north-west** just off true north, only partly **348 hawk, handsaw** i.e., two very different things, though also perhaps meaning a mattock (or *hack*) and a carpenter's cutting tool, respectively; also birds, with a play on *hernshaw*, or heron **351 swaddling clouts** cloths in which to wrap a newborn baby **352 Haply** perhaps **357 Roscius** a famous Roman actor who died in 62 B.C. **360 Buzz** (An interjection used to denote stale news.) **365 scene individable** a play observing the unity of place; or perhaps one that is unclassifiable, or performed without intermission **366 poem unlimited** a play disregarding the unities of time and place; one that is all-inclusive **Seneca** writer of Latin tragedies **Plautus** writer of Latin comedy **367 law . . . liberty** dramatic composition both according to the rules and disregarding the rules **these** i.e., the actors **368 Jephthah . . . Israel** (Jephthah had to sacrifice his daughter; see Judges 11. Hamlet goes on to quote from a ballad on the theme.) **372 passing** surpassingly

HAMLET. Am I not i' the right, old Jephthah?

POLONIUS. If you call me Jephthah, my lord, I have a daughter that I love   375
passing well.

HAMLET. Nay, that follows not.

POLONIUS. What follows then, my lord?

HAMLET. Why,

"As by lot,° God wot,"°   380

and then, you know,

"It came to pass, as most like° it was"—

the first row° of the pious chanson° will show you more, for look
where my abridgement° comes.

Enter the PLAYERS.

You are welcome, masters; welcome, all. I am glad to see thee well.   385
Welcome, good friends. O, old friend! Why, thy face is valanced°
since I saw thee last. Com'st thou to beard° me in Denmark? What,
my young lady° and mistress! By 'r Lady,° your ladyship is nearer to
heaven than when I saw you last, by the altitude of a chopine.°
Pray God your voice, like a piece of uncurrent° gold, be not   390
cracked within the ring.° Masters, you are all welcome. We'll e'en
to 't° like French falconers, fly at anything we see. We'll have a
speech straight.° Come, give us a taste of your quality.° Come, a
passionate speech.

FIRST PLAYER. What speech, my good lord?   395

HAMLET. I heard thee speak me a speech once, but it was never acted, or if
it was, not above once, for the play, I remember, pleased not the
million; 'twas caviar to the general.° But it was—as I received it,
and others, whose judgments in such matters cried in the top of°
mine—an excellent play, well digested° in the scenes, set down   400
with as much modesty° as cunning.° I remember one said there
were no sallets° in the lines to make the matter savory, nor no matter in the phrase that might indict° the author of affectation, but
called it an honest method, as wholesome as sweet, and by very
much more handsome° than fine.° One speech in 't I chiefly loved: 405
'twas Aeneas' tale to Dido, and thereabout of it especially when he

380 lot chance. **wot** knows **382 like** likely, probable **383 row** stanza **chanson**
ballad, song **384 my abridgment** something that cuts short my conversation; also, a di-
version **386 valanced** fringed (with a beard) **387 beard** confront, challenge (with obvious pun) **388 young lady** i.e., boy playing women's parts **By 'r Lady** by Our Lady
389 chopine thick-soled shoe of Italian fashion **390 uncurrent** not passable as lawful
coinage **391 cracked . . . ring** i.e., changed from adolescent to male voice, no longer
suitable for women's roles (Coins featured rings enclosing the sovereign's head; if the coin
was cracked within this ring, it was unfit for currency.) **391–392 e'en to 't** go at it
393 straight at once **quality** professional skill **398 caviar to the general** caviar to
the multitude, i.e., a choice dish too elegant for coarse tastes **399 cried in the top of**
i.e., spoke with greater authority than **400 digested** arranged, ordered **401 modesty**
moderation, restraint **cunning** skill **402 sallets** i.e., something savory, spicy impropri-
eties **403 indict** convict **405 handsome** well-proportioned **fine** elaborately ornamented, showy

speaks of Priam's slaughter.° If it live in your memory, begin at this
line: let me see, let me see—
      "The rugged Pyrrhus,° like th' Hyrcanian° beast"—
'Tis not so. It begins with Pyrrhus: 410
      "The rugged° Pyrrhus, he whose sable° arms,
Black as his purpose, did the night resemble
When he lay couchèd° in the ominous horse,°
Hath now this dread and black complexion smeared
With heraldry more dismal.° Head to foot   415
Now is he total gules,° horridly tricked°
With blood of fathers, mothers, daughters, sons,
Baked and impasted° with the parching streets,°
That lend a tyrannous° and a damnèd light
To their lord's° murder. Roasted in wrath and fire,   420
And thus o'ersizèd° with coagulate gore,
With eyes like carbuncles,° the hellish Pyrrhus
Old grandsire Priam seeks."
      So proceed you.

POLONIUS. 'Fore God, my lord, well spoken, with good accent and good   425
discretion.

FIRST PLAYER.   "Anon he finds him
Striking too short at Greeks. His antique° sword,
Rebellious to his arm, lies where it falls,
Repugnant° to command. Unequal matched,   430
Pyrrhus at Priam drives, in rage strikes wide,
But with the whiff and wind of his fell° sword
Th' unnervèd° father falls. Then senseless Ilium,°
Seeming to feel this blow, with flaming top
Stoops to his° base, and with a hideous crash   435
Takes prisoner Pyrrhus' ear. For, lo! His sword,
Which was declining° on the milky° head
Of reverend Priam, seemed i' th' air to stick.

---

407 Priam's slaughter the slaying of the ruler of Troy, when the Greeks finally took the
city   **409 Pyrrhus** a Greek hero in the Trojan War, also known as Neoptolemus, son of
Achilles—another avenging son   **Hyrcanian beast** i.e., tiger (On the death of Priam, see
Virgil, *Aeneid*, 2.506 ff.; compare the whole speech with Marlowe's *Dido Queen of
Carthage*, 2.1.214. ff. On the *Hyrcanian* tiger, see *Aeneid*, 4.366–367. Hyrcania is on the
Caspian Sea.)   **411 rugged** shaggy, savage   **sable** black (for reasons of camouflage dur-
ing the episode of the Trojan horse)   **413 couchèd** concealed   **ominous horse** fateful
Trojan horse, by which the Greeks gained access to Troy   **415 dismal** ill-omened
416 total gules entirely red (A heraldic term.)   **tricked** spotted and smeared (Heraldic.)
418 impasted crusted, like a thick paste   **with . . . streets** by the parching heat of the
streets (because of the fires everywhere)   **419 tyrannous** cruel   **420 their lord's** i.e.,
Priam's   **421 o'ersizèd** covered as with size or glue   **422 carbuncles** large fiery-red precious stones thought to emit their own light   **428 antique** ancient, long-used   **430 Repugnant** disobedient, resistant   **432 fell** cruel   **433 unnervèd** strengthless   **senseless Ilium** inanimate citadel of Troy   **435 his** its   **437 declining** descending   **milky**
white-haired

So as a painted° tyrant Pyrrhus stood,
And, like a neutral to his will and matter,°   440
Did nothing.
But as we often see against° some storm
A silence in the heavens, the rack° stand still,
The bold winds speechless, and the orb° below
As hush as death, anon the dreadful thunder   445
Doth rend the region,° so, after Pyrrhus' pause,
A rousèd vengeance sets him new a-work
And never did the Cyclops'° hammers fall
On Mars's armor forged for proof eterne°
With less remorse° than Pyrrhus' bleeding sword   450
Now falls on Priam.
Out, out, thou strumpet Fortune! All you gods
In general synod° take away her power!
Break all the spokes and fellies° from her wheel,
And bowl the round nave° down the hill of heaven°   455
As low as to the fiends!"

POLONIUS. This is too long.

HAMLET. It shall to the barber's with your beard.—Prithee, say on. He's
for a jig° or a tale of bawdry, or he sleeps. Say on; come to
Hecuba.°   460

FIRST PLAYER. "But who, ah woe! had° seen the moblèd° queen"—

HAMLET. "The moblèd queen?"

POLONIUS. That's good. "Moblèd queen" is good.

FIRST PLAYER. "Run barefoot up and down, threat'ning the flames°
With bisson rheum,° a clout° upon that head   465
Where late° the diadem stood, and, for a robe,
About her lank and all o'erteemèd° loins
A blanket, in the alarm of fear caught up—
Who this had seen, with tongue in venom steeped,
'Gainst Fortune's state° would treason have pronounced.°   470
But if the gods themselves did see her then
When she saw Pyrrhus make malicious sport
In mincing with his sword her husband's limbs,
The instant burst of clamor that she made,
Unless things mortal move them not at all,   475

---

439 painted i.e., painted in a picture   **440 like . . . matter** i.e., as though suspended between his intention and its fulfillment   **442 against** just before   **443 rack** mass of
clouds   **444 orb** globe, earth   **446 region** sky   **448 Cyclops** giant armor makers in the
smithy of Vulcan   **449 proof eterne** eternal resistance to assault   **450 remorse** pity
453 synod assembly   **454 fellies** pieces of wood forming the rim of a wheel   **455 nave**
hub   **hill of heaven** Mount Olympus   **459 jig** comic song and dance often given at the
end of a play   **460 Hecuba** wife of Priam   **461 who . . . had** anyone who had (also in
line 469)   **moblèd** muffled   **464 threat'ning the flames** i.e., weeping hard enough to
dampen the flames   **465 bisson rheum** blinding tears   **clout** cloth   **466 late** lately
467 all o'erteemèd utterly worn out with bearing children   **470 state** rule, managing.
pronounced proclaimed

Would have made milch° the burning eyes of heaven,°
And passion° in the gods."

POLONIUS.   Look whe'er° he has not turned his color and has tears in 's
eyes. Prithee, no more.

HAMLET.   'Tis well; I'll have thee speak out the rest of this soon.—Good my   480
lord, will you see the players well bestowed?° Do you hear, let
them be well used, for they are the abstract° and brief chronicles of
the time. After your death you were better have a bad epitaph than
their ill report while you live.

POLONIUS. My lord, I will use them according to their desert.   485

HAMLET.   God's bodikin,° man, much better. Use every man after his
desert, and who shall scape whipping? Use them after° your own
honor and dignity. The less they deserve, the more merit is in your
bounty. Take them in.

POLONIUS. Come, sirs.   490

[Exit.]

HAMLET.   Follow him, friends. We'll hear a play tomorrow. [*As they start to
leave,* HAMLET *detains the* FIRST PLAYER.] Dost thou hear me, old
friend? Can you play *The Murder of Gonzago?*

FIRST PLAYER. Ay, my lord.

HAMLET.   We'll ha 't° tomorrow night. You could, for a need, study° a   495
speech of some dozen or sixteen lines which I would set down and
insert in 't, could you not?

FIRST PLAYER. Ay, my lord.

HAMLET.   Very well. Follow that lord, and look you mock him not. (*Exeunt
PLAYERS.*) My good friends, I'll leave you till night. You are welcome   500
to Elsinore.

ROSENCRANTZ. Good my lord!

Exeunt [ROSENCRANTZ *and* GUILDENSTERN].

HAMLET.   Ay, so, goodbye to you.—Now I am alone.
O, what a rogue and peasant slave am I!
Is it not monstrous that this player here,   505
But° in a fiction, in a dream of passion,
Could force his soul so to his own conceit°
That from her working° all his visage wanned,°
Tears in his eyes, distraction in his aspect,°
A broken voice, and his whole function suiting   510
With forms to his conceit?° And all for nothing!
For Hecuba!
What's Hecuba to him, or he to Hecuba,

476 **milch** milky, moist with tears   **burning eyes of heaven** i.e., heavenly bodies
477 **passion** overpowering emotion   478 **whe'er** whether   481 **bestowed** lodged
482 **abstract** summary account   486 **God's bodikin** by God's (Christ's) little body,
bodykin (Not to be confused with *bodkin,* "dagger.")   487 **after** according to   495 **ha 't**
have it   **study** memorize   506 **But** merely   507 **force . . . conceit** bring his innermost
being so entirely into accord with his conception (of the role)   508 **from her working**
as a result of, or in response to, his soul's activity   **wanned** grew pale   509 **aspect** look,
glance   510–511 **his whole . . . conceit** all his bodily powers responding with actions
to suit his thought

That he should weep for her? What would he do
Had he the motive and the cue for passion   515
That I have? He would drown the stage with tears
And cleave the general ear° with horrid° speech,
Make mad the guilty and appall° the free,°
Confound the ignorant,° and amaze° indeed
The very faculties of eyes and ears. Yet I,   520
A dull and muddy-mettled° rascal, peak°
Like John-a-dreams,° unpregnant of° my cause,
And can say nothing—no, not for a king
Upon whose property° and most dear life
A damned defeat° was made. Am I a coward?   525
Who calls me villain? Breaks my pate° across?
Plucks off my beard and blows it in my face?
Tweaks me by the nose? Gives me the lie i' the throat°
As deep as to the lungs? Who does me this?
Ha, 'swounds,° I should take it; for it cannot be   530
But I am pigeon-livered° and lack gall
To make oppression bitter,° or ere this
I should ha' fatted all the region kites°
With this slave's offal.° Bloody, bawdy villain!
Remorseless,° treacherous, lecherous, kindless° villain!   535
O, vengeance!
Why, what an ass am I! This is most brave,°
That I, the son of a dear father murdered,
Prompted to my revenge by heaven and hell,
Must like a whore unpack my heart with words   540
And fall a-cursing, like a very drab,°
A scullion!° Fie upon 't, foh! About,° my brains!
Hum, I have heard
That guilty creatures sitting at a play
Have by the very cunning° of the scene°   545
Been struck so to the soul that presently°
They have proclaimed their malefactions;
For murder, though it have no tongue, will speak
With most miraculous organ. I'll have these players
Play something like the murder of my father   550

---

517 the general ear everyone's ear   **horrid** horrible   **518 appall** (literally, make pale.)
free innocent   **519 Confound the ignorant** i.e., dumbfound those who know nothing of
the crime that has been committed   **amaze** stun   **521 muddy-mettled** dull-spirited
peak mope, pine   **522 John-a-dreams** a sleepy, dreaming idler   **unpregnant of** not
quickened by   **524 property** i.e., the crown; also character, quality   **525 damned defeat**
damnable act of destruction   **526 pate** head   **528 Gives . . . throat** calls me an out-and-out
liar   **530 'swounds** by his (Christ's) wounds   **531 pigeon-livered** (The pigeon or dove
was popularly supposed to be mild because it secreted no gall.)   **532 bitter** i.e., bitter to me
533 region kites kites (birds of prey) of the air   **534 offal** entrails   **535 Remorseless** pitiless   **kindless** unnatural   **537 brave** fine, admirable (Said ironically.)   **541 drab** whore
542 scullion menial kitchen servant (apt to be foul-mouthed)   **About** about it, to work
cunning art, skill   **scene** dramatic presentation   **546 presently** at once

Before mine uncle. I'll observe his looks;
I'll tent° him to the quick.° If 'a do blench,°
I know my course. The spirit that I have seen
May be the devil, and the devil hath power
T' assume a pleasing shape; yea, and perhaps,   555
Out of my weakness and my melancholy,
As he is very potent with such spirits,°
Abuses° me to damn me. I'll have grounds
More relative° than this. The play's the thing
Wherein I'll catch the conscience of the King.   560

Exit.

3.1   *Enter* KING, QUEEN, POLONIUS, OPHELIA, ROSENCRANTZ, GUILDERNSTERN, *lords.*

KING.   And can you by no drift of conference°
Get from him why he puts on this confusion,
Grating so harshly all his days of quiet
With turbulent and dangerous lunacy?
ROSENCRANTZ.   He does confess he feels himself distracted,   5
But from what cause 'a will by no means speak.
GUILDENSTERN.   Nor do we find him forward° to be sounded,°
But with a crafty madness keeps aloof
When we would bring him on to some confession
Of his true state.
QUEEN.   Did he receive you well?   10
ROSENCRANTZ.   Most like a gentleman.
GUILDENSTERN.   But with much forcing of his disposition.°
ROSENCRANTZ.   Niggard° of question,° but of our demands
Most free in his reply.
QUEEN.   Did you assay° him
To any pastime?   15
ROSENCRANTZ.   Madam, it so fell out that certain players
We o'erraught° on the way. Of these we told him,
And there did seem in him a kind of joy
To hear of it. They are here about the court,
And, as I think, they have already order   20
This night to play before him.
POLONIUS.   'Tis most true,
And he beseeched me to entreat Your Majesties
To hear and see the matter.
KING.   With all my heart, and it doth much content me
To hear him so inclined.   25
Good gentlemen, give him a further edge°
And drive his purpose into these delights.

---

552 **tent** probe   **the quick** the tender part of a wound, the core   **blench** quail, flinch
557 **spirits** humors (of melancholy)   **558 Abuses** deludes   **559 relative** cogent, pertinent   **3.1. Location: The castle.**   **1 drift of conference** directing of conversation
7 forward willing   **sounded** questioned   **12 disposition** inclination   **13 Niggard**
stingy   **question** conversation   **14 assay** try to win   BO17 o'er-raught overtook
26 edge incitement

ROSENCRANTZ. We shall, my lord.

Exeunt ROSENCRANTZ *and* GUILDENSTERN.

KING.   Sweet Gertrude, leave us too,
For we have closely° sent for Hamlet hither,
That he, as 'twere by accident, may here   30
Affront° Ophelia.
Her father and myself, lawful espials,°
Will so bestow ourselves that seeing, unseen,
We may of their encounter frankly judge,
And gather by him, as he is behaved,   35
If't be th' affliction of his love or no
That thus he suffers for.

QUEEN.   I shall obey you.
And for your part, Ophelia, I do wish
That your good beauties be the happy cause
Of Hamlet's wildness. So shall I hope your virtues   40
Will bring him to his wonted° way again,
To both your honors.

OPHELIA.   Madam, I wish it may.

[*Exit* QUEEN.]

POLONIUS. Ophelia, walk you here.—Gracious,° so please you,
We will bestow° ourselves. [To OPHELIA.] Read on this book,

[*giving her a book*]

That show of such an exercise° may color°   45
Your loneliness.° We are oft to blame in this—
'Tis too much proved°—that with devotion's visage
And pious action we do sugar o'er
The devil himself.

KING [*aside*]. O 'tis too true!   50
How smart a lash that speech doth give my conscience!
The harlot's cheek, beautied with plastering art,
Is not more ugly to° the thing° that helps it
Than is my deed to my most painted word.
O heavy burden!   55

POLONIUS. I hear him coming. Let's withdraw, my lord.

[*The* KING *and* POLONIUS *withdraw.*°]

Enter HAMLET. *[*OPHELIA *pretends to read a book.]*
HAMLET. To be, or not to be, that is the question:
Whether 'tis nobler in the mind to suffer
The slings° and arrows of outrageous fortune,
Or to take arms against a sea of troubles   60

---

29 closely privately **31 Affront** confront, meet **32 espials** spies **41 wonted** accustomed **43 Gracious** Your Grace (i.e., the King) **44 bestow** conceal **45 exercise** religious exercise (The book she reads is one of devotion.) **color** give a plausible appearance to **46 loneliness** being alone **47 too much proved** too often shown to be true, too often practiced **53 to** compared to **the thing** i.e., the cosmetic **56 s.d. withdraw** (The King and Polonius may retire behind an arras. The stage directions specify that they "enter" again near the end of the scene.) **59 slings** missiles

And by opposing end them. To die, to sleep—
No more—and by a sleep to say we end
The heartache and the thousand natural shocks
That flesh is heir to. 'Tis a consummation
Devoutly to be wished. To die, to sleep;   65
To sleep, perchance to dream. Ay, there's the rub,°
For in that sleep of death what dreams may come,
When we have shuffled° off this mortal coil,°
Must give us pause. There's the respect°
That makes calamity of so long life.°   70
For who would bear the whips and scorns of time,
Th' oppressor's wrong, the proud man's contumely,°
The pangs of disprized° love, the law's delay,
The insolence of office,° and the spurns°
That patient merit of th' unworthy takes,°   75
When he himself might his quietus° make
With a bare bodkin?° Who would fardels° bear,
To grunt and sweat under a weary life,
But that the dread of something after death,
The undiscovered country from whose bourn°   80
No traveler returns, puzzles the will,
And makes us rather bear those ills we have
Than fly to others that we know not of?
Thus conscience does make cowards of us all;
And thus the native hue° of resolution   85
Is sicklied o'er with the pale cast° of thought,
And enterprises of great pitch° and moment°
With this regard° their currents° turn awry
And lose the name of action.—Soft you° now,
The fair Ophelia. Nymph, in thy orisons°   90
Be all my sins remembered.
OPHELIA.   Good my lord,
How does your honor for this many a day?
HAMLET. I humbly thank you; well, well, well.
OPHELIA. My lord, I have remembrances of yours,
That I have longèd long to redeliver.   95
I pray you, now receive them.   [*She offers tokens.*]
HAMLET. No, not I, I never gave you aught.

---

66 **rub** (Literally, an obstacle in the game of bowls.)   68 **shuffled** sloughed, cast.   **coil**
turmoil   69 **respect** consideration   70 **of . . . life** so long-lived, something we willingly
endure for so long (also suggesting that long life is itself a calamity)   72 **contumely** insolent abuse   73 **disprized** unvalued   74 **office** officialdom   **spurns** insults   75 **of . . .
takes** receives from unworthy persons   76 **quietus** acquittance; here, death   77 **a bare
bodkin** a mere dagger, unsheathed   **fardels** burdens   80 **bourn** frontier, boundary
85 **native hue** natural color, complexion   86 **cast** tinge, shade of color   87 **pitch**
height (as of a falcon's flight.)   **moment** importance   88 **regard** respect, consideration
currents courses   89 **Soft you** i.e., wait a minute, gently   90 **orisons** prayers

OPHELIA. My honored lord, you know right well you did,
And with them words of so sweet breath composed
As made the things more rich. Their perfume lost,   100
Take these again, for to the noble mind
Rich gifts wax poor when givers prove unkind.
There, my lord.   [*She gives tokens.*]

HAMLET. Ha, ha! Are you honest?°

OPHELIA. My lord?   105

HAMLET. Are you fair?°

OPHELIA. What means your lordship?

HAMLET. That if you be honest and fair, your honesty° should admit no dis-
course° to your beauty.

OPHELIA. Could beauty, my lord, have better commerce° than with hon-   110
esty?

HAMLET. Ay, truly, for the power of beauty will sooner transform honesty
from what it is to a bawd than the force of honesty can translate
beauty into his° likeness. This was sometime° a paradox,° but now
the time° gives it proof. I did love you once.   115

OPHELIA. Indeed, my lord, you made me believe so.

HAMLET. You should not have believed me, for virtue cannot so inoculate°
our old stock but we shall relish of it.° I loved you not.

OPHELIA. I was the more deceived.

HAMLET. Get thee to a nunnery.° Why wouldst thou be a breeder of sin-   120
ners? I am myself indifferent honest,° but yet I could accuse me of
such things that it were better my mother had not borne me: I am
very proud, revengeful, ambitious, with more offenses at my beck°
than I have thoughts to put them in, imagination to give them
shape, or time to act them in. What should such fellows as I do   125
crawling between earth and heaven? We are arrant knaves all; believe none of us. Go thy ways to a nunnery. Where's your father?

OPHELIA. At home, my lord.

HAMLET. Let the doors be shut upon him, that he may play the fool
nowhere but in's own house. Farewell.   130

OPHELIA. O, help him, you sweet heavens!

HAMLET. If thou dost marry, I'll give thee this plague for thy dowry: be
thou as chaste as ice, as pure as snow, thou shalt not escape
calumny. Get thee to a nunnery, farewell. Or, if thou wilt needs
marry, marry a fool, for wise men know well enough what mon-   135
sters° you make° of them. To a nunnery, go, and quickly too.
Farewell.

---

104 honest (1) truthful (2) chaste   **106 fair** (1) beautiful (2) just, honorable   **108 your honesty** your chastity   **109 discourse** to familiar dealings with   **110 commerce** dealings, intercourse   **114 his** its   **sometime** formerly   **a paradox** a view opposite to commonly held opinion   **115 the time** the present age   **117–118 inoculate** graft, be engrafted to   **118 but . . . it** that we do not still have about us a taste of the old stock. i.e., retain our sinfulness   **120 nunnery** convent (with possibly an awareness that the word was also used derisively to denote a brothel)   **121 indifferent honest** reasonably virtuous   **123 beck** command   **135–136 monsters** (An illusion to the horns of a cuckold.) **you** i.e., you women

OPHELIA. Heavenly powers, restore him!

HAMLET. I have heard of your paintings too, well enough. God hath given
you one face, and you make yourselves another. You jig,° you   140
amble,° and you lisp, you nickname God's creatures,° and make
your wantonness your ignorance.° Go to, I'll no more on 't;° it hath
made me mad. I say we will have no more marriage. Those that are
married already—all but one—shall live. The rest shall keep as they
are. To a nunnery, go.   145

Exit.

OPHELIA. O, what a noble mind is here o'erthrown!
The courtier's, soldier's, scholar's, eye, tongue, sword,
Th' expectancy° and rose° of the fair state,
The glass of fashion and the mold of form,°
Th' observed of all observers,° quite, quite down!   150
And I, of ladies most deject and wretched,
That sucked the honey of his music° vows,
Now see that noble and most sovereign reason
Like sweet bells jangled out of tune and harsh,
That unmatched form and feature of blown° youth   155
Blasted° with ecstasy.° O, woe is me,
T' have seen what I have seen, see what I see!

Enter KING *and* POLONIUS.

KING. Love? His affections° do not that way tend;
Nor what he spake, though it lacked form a little,
Was not like madness. There's something in his soul   160
O'er which his melancholy sits on brood,°
And I do doubt° the hatch and the disclose°
Will be some danger; which for to prevent,
I have in quick determination
Thus set it down:° he shall with speed to England   165
For the demand of° our neglected tribute.
Haply the seas and countries different
With variable objects° shall expel
This something-settled matter in his heart,°
Whereon his brains still° beating puts him thus   170
From fashion of himself.° What think you on 't?

POLONIUS. It shall do well. But yet do I believe
The origin and commencement of his grief

---

140 jig dance   **141 amble** move coyly   **you nickname . . . creatures** i.e., you give
trendy names to things in place of their God-given names   **142 make . . . ignorance** i.e.,
excuse your affectation on the grounds of pretended ignorance   **on 't** of it   **148 expectancy** hope.   **rose** ornament   **149 The glass . . . form** the mirror of true fashioning
and the pattern of courtly behavior   **150 Th' observed . . . observers** i.e., the center of
attention and honor in the court   **152 music** musical, sweetly uttered   **155 blown**
blooming   **156 Blasted** withered   **ecstasy** madness   **158 affections** emotions, feelings   **161 sits on brood** sits like a bird on a nest, about to *hatch* mischief (line 169)
162 doubt fear   **disclose** disclosure, hatching   **165 set it down** resolved   **166 For . . .
of** to demand   **168 variable objects** various sights and surroundings to divert him
169 This something . . . heart the strange matter settled in his heart   **170 still** continually   **171 From . . . himself** out of his natural manner

Sprung from neglected love.—How now, Ophelia?
You need not tell us what Lord Hamlet said;   175
We heard it all.—My lord, do as you please,
But, if you hold it fit, after the play
Let his queen-mother° all alone entreat him
To show his grief. Let her be round° with him;
And I'll be placed, so please you, in the ear   180
Of all their conference. If she find him not,°
To England send him, or confine him where
Your wisdom best shall think.

KING.   It shall be so.
Madness in great ones must not unwatched go.

                                                    Exeunt.

            3.2   Enter HAMLET *and three of the* PLAYERS.

HAMLET. Speak the speech, I pray you, as I pronounced it to you, trippingly
    on the tongue. But if you mouth it, as many of our players° do, I had
    as lief° the town crier spoke my lines. Nor do not saw the air too
    much with your hand, thus, but use all gently; for in the very tor-
    rent, tempest, and, as I may say, whirlwind of your passion, you   5
    must acquire and beget a temperance that may give it smoothness.
    O, it offends me to the soul to hear a robustious° periwig-pated° fel-
    low tear a passion to tatters, to very rags, to split the ears of the
    groundlings,° who for the most part are capable of° nothing but in-
    explicable dumb shows° and noise. I would have such a fellow   10
    whipped for o'erdoing Termagant.° It out-Herods Herod.° Pray you,
    avoid it.

FIRST PLAYER. I warrant your honor.

HAMLET. Be not too tame neither, but let your own discretion be your
    tutor. Suit the action to the word, the word to the action, with this   15
    special observance, that you o'erstep not the modesty° of nature.
    For anything so o'erdone is from° the purpose of playing, whose
    end, both at the first and now, was and is to hold as 't were the mir-
    ror up to nature, to show virtue her feature, scorn° her own image,
    and the very age and body of the time° his° form and pressure.°   20
    Now this overdone or come tardy off,° though it makes the unskill-
    ful° laugh, cannot but make the judicious grieve, the censure of the

178 **queen-mother** queen and mother   179 **round** blunt   181 **find him not** fails to
discover what is troubling him   **3.2. Location: The castle.**   2 **our players** players
nowadays   3 **I had as lief** I would just as soon   7 **robustious** violent, boisterous   **peri-
wig-pated** wearing a wig   9 **groundlings** spectators who paid least and stood in the
yard of the theater   **capable of** able to understand   10 **dumb shows** mimed performances, often used before Shakespeare's time to precede a play or each act   11 **Terma-
gant** a supposed deity of the Mohammedans, not found in any English medieval play but
elsewhere portrayed as violent and blustering   **Herod** Herod of Jewry (A character in *The
Slaughter of the Innocents* and other cycle plays. The part was played with great noise
and fury.)   16 **modesty** restraint, moderation   17 **from** contrary to   19 **scorn** i.e.,
something foolish and deserving of scorn   20 **the very . . . time** i.e., the present state of
affairs   **his** its   **pressure** stamp, impressed character   21 **come tardy off** inadequately
done   21–22 **the unskillful** those lacking in judgment

which one° must in your allowance° o'erweigh a whole theater of others. O, there be players that I have seen play, and heard others praise, and that highly, not to speak it profanely,° that, neither having th' accent of Christians° nor the gait of Christian, pagan, nor man,° have so strutted and bellowed that I have thought some of nature's journeymen° had made men and not made them well, they imitated humanity so abominably.° 25

FIRST PLAYER. I hope we have reformed that indifferently° with us, sir. 30

HAMLET. O, reform it altogether. And let those that play your clowns speak no more than is set down for them; for there be of them° that will themselves laugh, to set on some quantity of barren° spectators to laugh too, though in the meantime some necessary question of the play be then to be considered. That's villainous, and shows a most pitiful ambition in the fool that uses it. Go make you ready. 35

[*Exeunt* PLAYERS.]

Enter POLONIUS, GUILDENSTERN *and* ROSENCRANTZ.

How now, my lord, will the King hear this piece of work?

POLONIUS. And the Queen too, and that presently.°

HAMLET. Bid the players make haste. 40

[*Exit* POLONIUS.]

Will you two help to hasten them?

ROSENCRANTZ. Ay, my lord.

Exeunt they two.

HAMLET.   What ho, Horatio!

Enter HORATIO.

HORATIO. Here, sweet lord, at your service.

HAMLET. Horatio, thou art e'en as just a man
  As e'er my conversation coped withal.° 45

HORATIO. O, my dear lord—

HAMLET.   Nay, do not think I flatter,
  For what advancement may I hope from thee
  That no revenue hast but thy good spirits
  To feed and clothe thee? Why should the poor be flattered?
  No, let the candied° tongue lick absurd pomp, 50
  And crook the pregnant° hinges of the knee
  Where thrift° may follow fawning. Dost thou hear?

22–23 the censure . . . one the judgment of even one of whom   **23 your allowance** your scale of values   **25 not . . . profanely** (Hamlet anticipates his idea in lines 27-29 that some men were not made by God at all.)   **26 Christians** i.e., ordinary decent folk   **26–27 nor man** i.e., nor any human being at all   **28 journeymen** laborers who are not yet masters in their trade   **29 abominably** (Shakespeare's usual spelling, *abhominably,* suggests a literal though etymologically incorrect meaning, "removed from human nature.")   **30 indifferently** tolerably   **32 of them** some among them   **33 barren** i.e., of wit   **39 presently** at once   **45 my . . . withal** my dealings encountered   **50 candied** sugared, flattering   **51 pregnant** compliant   **52 thrift** profit

Since my dear soul was mistress of her choice
And could of men distinguish her election,°
Sh' hath sealed thee° for herself, for thou hast been   55
As one, in suffering all, that suffers nothing,
A man that Fortune's buffets and rewards
Hast ta'en with equal thanks; and blest are those
Whose blood° and judgment are so well commeddled°
That they are not a pipe for Fortune's finger   60
To sound what stop° she please. Give me that man
That is not passion's slave, and I will wear him
In my heart's core, ay, in my heart of heart,
As I do thee.—Something too much of this.—
There is a play tonight before the King.   65
One scene of it comes near the circumstance
Which I have told thee of my father's death.
I prithee, when thou seest that act afoot,
Even with the very comment of thy soul°
Observe my uncle. If his occulted° guilt   70
Do not itself unkennel° in one speech,
It is a damnèd° ghost that we have seen,
And my imaginations are as foul
As Vulcan's stithy.° Give him heedful note,
For I mine eyes will rivet to his face,   75
And after we will both our judgments join
In censure of his seeming.°
HORATIO.   Well, my lord.
If 'a steal aught° the whilst this play is playing
And scape detecting, I will pay the theft.

[Flourish.] Enter trumpets and kettledrums, KING, QUEEN, POLONIUS, OPHELIA,
[ROSENCRANTZ, GUILDENSTERN, *and other lords, with guards carrying torches].*
HAMLET. They are coming to the play. I must be idle.°   80
   Get you a place.   [*The* KING, QUEEN, *and courtiers sit.*]
KING. How fares our cousin° Hamlet?
HAMLET. Excellent, i' faith, of the chameleon's dish:° I eat the air, promise-
   crammed. You cannot feed capons° so.

---

54 could . . . election could make distinguishing choices among persons   **55 sealed thee**
(Literally, as one would seal a legal document to mark possession.)   **59 blood** passion
commeddled commingled   **61 stop** hole in a wind instrument for controlling the sound
69 very . . . soul your most penetrating observation and consideration   **70 occulted** hidden   **71 unkennel** (As one would say of a fox driven from its lair.)   **72 damnèd** in league
with Satan   **74 stithy** smithy, place of stiths (anvils)   **77 censure of his seeming** judgment of his appearance or behavior   **78 If 'a steal aught** if he gets away with anything
80 idle (1) unoccupied (2) mad   **82 cousin** i.e., close relative   **83 chameleon's dish**
(Chameleons were supposed to feed on air. Hamlet deliberately misinterprets the King's
fares as "feeds." By his phrase *eat the air* he also plays on the idea of feeding himself with
the promise of succession, of being the *heir*.)   **84 capons** roosters castrated and *crammed*
with feed to make them succulent

KING. I have nothing with° this answer, Hamlet. These words are not 85
mine.°

HAMLET. No, nor mine now.° [*To* POLONIUS.] My lord, you played once i' th'
university, you say?

POLONIUS. That did I, my lord, and was accounted a good actor.

HAMLET. What did you enact? 90

POLONIUS. I did enact Julius Caesar. I was killed i' the Capitol; Brutus
killed me.

HAMLET. It was a brute° part° of him to kill so capital a calf° there.—Be the
players ready?

ROSENCRANTZ. Ay, my lord. They stay upon° your patience. 95

QUEEN. Come hither, my dear Hamlet, sit by me.

HAMLET. No, good Mother, here's metal° more attractive.

POLONIUS [*to the* KING]. O, ho, do you mark that?

HAMLET. Lady, shall I lie in your lap?

[*Lying down at* OPHELIA's *feet.*]

OPHELIA. No, my lord. 100

HAMLET. I mean, my head upon your lap?

OPHELIA. Ay, my lord.

HAMLET. Do you think I meant country matters?°

OPHELIA. I think nothing, my lord.

HAMLET. That's a fair thought to lie between maids' legs. 105

OPHELIA. What is, my lord?

HAMLET. Nothing.°

OPHELIA. You are merry, my lord.

HAMLET. Who, I?

OPHELIA. Ay, my lord. 110

HAMLET. O God, your only jig maker.° What should a man do but be
merry? For look you how cheerfully my mother looks, and my father died within 's° two hours.

OPHELIA. Nay, 'tis twice two months, my lord.

HAMLET. So long? Nay then, let the devil wear black, for I'll have a suit of 115
sables.° O heavens! Die two months ago, and not forgotten yet?
Then there's hope a great man's memory may outlive his life half a
year. But, by 'r Lady, 'a must build churches, then, or else shall 'a

---

85 have . . . with make nothing of, or gain nothing from **86 are not mine** do not respond to what I asked **87 nor mine now** (Once spoken, words are proverbially no
longer the speaker's own—and hence should be uttered warily.) **93 brute** (The Latin
meaning of *brutus,* "stupid," was often used punningly with the name Brutus.) **part** (1)
deed (2) role **calf** fool **95 stay upon** await **97 metal** substance that is *attractive,*
i.e., magnetic, but with suggestion also of *mettle,* "disposition" **103 country matters**
sexual intercourse (making a bawdy pun on the first syllable of *country*) **107 Nothing**
the figure zero or naught, suggesting the female sexual anatomy. (*Thing* not infrequently
has a bawdy connotation of male or female anatomy, and the reference here could be
male.) **111 only jig maker** very best composer of jigs, i.e., pointless merriment (Hamlet
replies sardonically to Ophelia's observation that he is merry by saying, "If you're looking
for someone who is really merry, you've come to the right person.") **113 within 's**
within this (i.e., these) **115–116 suit of sables** garments trimmed with the fur of the
sable and hence suited for a wealthy person, not a mourner (but with a pun on *sable,*
"black," ironically suggesting mourning once again)

suffer not thinking on,° with the hobbyhorse, whose epitaph is
"For O, for O, the hobbyhorse is forgot."°   120
The trumpets sound. Dumb show follows.
*Enter a King and a Queen [very lovingly]; the Queen embracing him,
and he her. [She kneels, and makes show of protestation unto him.] He
takes her up, and declines his head upon her neck. He lies him down
upon a bank of flowers. She, seeing him asleep, leaves him. Anon comes
in another man, takes off his crown, kisses it, pours poison in the sleeper's
ears, and leaves him. The Queen returns, finds the King dead, makes passionate action. The Poisoner with some three or four come in again, seem
to condole with her. The dead body is carried away. The Poisoner woos
the Queen with gifts; she seems harsh awhile, but in the end accepts love.*
                                                    [*Exeunt* PLAYERS.]
OPHELIA. What means this, my lord?
HAMLET. Marry, this' miching mallico;° it means mischief.
OPHELIA. Belike° this show imports the argument° of the play.

    Enter PROLOGUE.
HAMLET. We shall know by this fellow. The players cannot keep counsel;°
    they'll tell all.   125
OPHELIA. Will 'a tell us what this show meant?
HAMLET. Ay, or any show that you will show him. Be not you° ashamed to
    show, he'll not shame to tell you what it means.
OPHELIA. You are naught,° you are naught. I'll mark the play.
PROLOGUE. For us, and for our tragedy,   130
    Here stooping° to your clemency,
    We beg your hearing patiently.

                                                              [*Exit.*]
HAMLET. Is this a prologue, or the posy of a ring?°
OPHELIA. 'Tis brief, my lord.
HAMLET. As woman's love.   135

    Enter [two PLAYERS *as] King and Queen.*
PLAYER KING. Full thirty times hath Phoebus' cart° gone round
    Neptune's salt wash° and Tellus'° orbèd ground,
    And thirty dozen moons with borrowed° sheen
    About the world have times twelve thirties been,
    Since love our hearts and Hymen° did our hands   140
    Unite commutual° in most sacred bands.°

119 suffer . . . on undergo oblivion   **120 For . . . forgot** (Verse of a song occurring also
in *Love's Labor's Lost*, 3.1.27–28. The hobbyhorse was a character made up to resemble a
horse and rider, appearing in the morris dance and such May-game sports. This song
laments the disappearance of such customs under pressure from the Puritans.)   **122 this'
miching mallico** this is sneaking mischief   **123 Belike** probably   **argument** plot
124–125 counsel secret   **127 Be not you** provided you are not   **129 naught** indecent
(Ophelia is reacting to Hamlet's pointed remarks about not being ashamed to show all.)
131 stooping bowing   **133 posy . . . ring** brief motto in verse inscribed in a ring
136 Phoebus' cart the sun-god's chariot, making its yearly cycle   **137 salt wash** the
sea   **Tellus** goddess of the earth, of the *orbèd ground*   **138 borrowed** i.e., reflected
140 Hymen god of matrimony   **141 commutual** mutually   **bands** bonds

PLAYER QUEEN. So many journeys may the sun and moon
    Make us again count o'er ere love be done!
    But, woe is me, you are so sick of late,
    So far from cheer and from your former state,   145
    That I distrust° you. Yet, though I distrust,
    Discomfort° you, my lord, it nothing° must.
    For women's fear and love hold quantity;°
    In neither aught, or in extremity.°
    Now, what my love is, proof° hath made you know,   150
    And as my love is sized,° my fear is so.
    Where love is great, the littlest doubts are fear;
    Where little fears grow great, great love grows there.
PLAYER KING. Faith, I must leave thee, love, and shortly too;
    My operant powers° their functions leave to do.°   155
    And thou shalt live in this fair world behind,°
    Honored, beloved; and haply one as kind
    For husband shalt thou—
PLAYER QUEEN.   O, confound the rest!
    Such love must needs be treason in my breast.
    In second husband let me be accurst!   160
    None° wed the second but who° killed the first.
HAMLET. Wormwood,° wormwood.
PLAYER QUEEN. The instances° that second marriage move°
    Are base respects of thrift,° but none of love.
    A second time I kill my husband dead   165
    When second husband kisses me in bed.
PLAYER KING. I do believe you think what now you speak,
    But what we do determine oft we break.
    Purpose is but the slave to memory,°
    Of violent birth, but poor validity,°   170
    Which° now, like fruit unripe, sticks on the tree,
    But fall unshaken when they mellow be.
    Most necessary 'tis that we forget
    To pay ourselves what to ourselves is debt.°
    What to ourselves in passion we propose,   175
    The passion ending, doth the purpose lose.
    The violence of either grief or joy
    Their own enactures° with themselves destroy.

---

146 distrust am anxious about   **147 Discomfort** distress   **nothing** not at all   **148 hold quantity** keep proportion with one another   **149 In . . . extremity** i.e., women fear and love either too little or too much, but the two, fear and love, are equal in either case   **150 proof** experience   **151 sized** in size   **155 operant powers** vital functions   **leave to do** cease to perform   **156 behind** after I have gone   **161 None** i.e., let no woman. **but who** except the one who   **162 Wormwood** i.e., how bitter. (Literally, a bitter-tasting plant.)   **163 instances** motives   **move** motivate   **164 base . . . thrift** ignoble considerations of material prosperity   **169 Purpose . . . memory** our good intentions are subject to forgetfulness   **170 validity** strength, durability   **171 Which** i.e., purpose   **173–174 Most . . . debt** it's inevitable that in time we forget the obligations we have imposed on ourselves   **178 enactures** fulfillments

Where joy most revels, grief doth most lament;
Grief joys, joy grieves, on slender accident.° 180
This world is not for aye,° nor 'tis not strange
That even our loves should with our fortunes change;
For 'tis a question left us yet to prove,
Whether love lead fortune, or else fortune love.
The great man down,° you mark his favorite flies; 185
The poor advanced makes friends of enemies.°
And hitherto° doth love on fortune tend;°
For who not needs° shall never lack a friend,
And who in want° a hollow friend doth try°
Directly seasons him° his enemy. 190
But, orderly to end where I begun,
Our wills and fates do so contrary run°
That our devices still° are overthrown;
Our thoughts are ours, their ends° none of our own.
So think thou wilt no second husband wed, 195
But die thy thoughts when thy first lord is dead.
PLAYER QUEEN. Nor° earth to me give food, nor heaven light,
Sport and repose lock from me day and night,°
To desperation turn my trust and hope,
An anchor's cheer° in prison be my scope!° 200
Each opposite that blanks° the face of joy
Meet what I would have well and it destroy!°
Both here and hence° pursue me lasting strife
If, once a widow, ever I be wife!
HAMLET. If she should break it now! 205
PLAYER KING. 'Tis deeply sworn. Sweet, leave me here awhile;
My spirits° grow dull, and fain I would beguile
The tedious day with sleep.
PLAYER QUEEN.   Sleep rock thy brain,
And never come mischance between us twain!
[He sleeps.] Exit [PLAYER QUEEN].
HAMLET. Madam, how like you this play? 210
QUEEN. The lady doth protest too much,° methinks.

179–180 Where . . . accident the capacity for extreme joy and grief go together, and often one extreme is instantly changed into its opposite on the slightest provocation **181 aye** ever **185 down** fallen in fortune **186 The poor . . . enemies** when one of humble station is promoted, you see his enemies suddenly becoming his friends **187 hitherto** up to this point in the argument, or, to this extent **tend** attend **188 who not needs** he who is not in need (of wealth) **189 who in want** he who, being in need **try** test (his generosity) **190 seasons him** ripens him into **192 Our . . . run** what we want and what we get go so contrarily **193 devices still** intentions continually **194 ends** results **197 Nor** let neither **198 Sport . . . night** may day deny me its pastimes and night its repose **200 anchor's cheer** anchorite's or hermit's fare **my scope** the extent of my happiness **201 blanks** causes to blanch or grow pale **201–202 Each . . . destroy** may every adverse thing that causes the face of joy to turn pale meet and destroy everything that I desire to see prosper **203 hence** in the life hereafter **207 spirits** vital spirits **211 doth . . . much** makes too many promises and protestations

HAMLET. O, but she'll keep her word.

KING. Have you heard the argument?° Is there no offense in 't?

HAMLET. No, no, they do but jest,° poison in jest. No offense° i' the
world. 215

KING. What do you call the play?

HAMLET. *The Mousetrap.* Marry, how? Tropically.° This play is the image of
a murder done in Vienna. Gonzago is the Duke's° name, his wife,
Baptista. You shall see anon. 'Tis a knavish piece of work, but what
of that? Your Majesty, and we that have free° souls, it touches us 220
not. Let the galled jade° wince, our withers° are unwrung.°

Enter LUCIANUS.

This is one Lucianus, nephew to the King.

OPHELIA. You are as good as a chorus,° my lord.

HAMLET. I could interpret° between you and your love, if I could see the
puppets dallying.° 225

OPHELIA. You are keen,° my lord, you are keen.

HAMLET. It would cost you a groaning to take off mine edge.

OPHELIA. Still better, and worse.°

HAMLET. So° you mis-take° your husbands. Begin, murder; leave thy
damnable faces and begin. Come, the croaking raven doth bellow 230
for revenge.

LUCIANUS. Thoughts black, hands apt, drugs fit, and time agreeing,
Confederate season,° else° no creature seeing,°
Thou mixture rank, of midnight weeds collected,
With Hecate's ban° thrice blasted, thrice infected, 235
Thy natural magic and dire property°
On wholesome life usurp immediately.

[He pours the poison into the sleeper's ear.]

HAMLET. 'A poisons him i' the garden for his estate.° His° name's Gonzago. The story is extant, and written in very choice Italian. You
shall see anon how the murderer gets the love of Gonzago's 240
wife.

---

213 argument plot **214 jest** make believe **213–214 offense . . . offense** cause for
objection . . . actual injury, crime **217 Tropically** figuratively (The First Quarto reading,
trapically, suggests a pun on *trap* in *Mousetrap.*) **218 Duke's** i.e., King's (A slip that
may be due to Shakespeare's possible source, the alleged murder of the Duke of Urbino by
Luigi Gonzaga in 1538.) **220 free** guiltless **221 galled jade** horse whose hide is
rubbed by saddle or harness **withers** the part between the horse's shoulder blades
unwrung not rubbed sore **223 chorus** (In many Elizabethan plays, the forthcoming action was explained by an actor known as the "chorus"; at a puppet show, the actor who
spoke the dialogue was known as an "interpreter," as indicated by the lines following.)
224 interpret (1) ventriloquize the dialogue, as in puppet show (2) act as pander
225 puppets dallying (With suggestion of sexual play, continued in *keen,* "sexually
aroused," *groaning,* "moaning in pregnancy," and *edge,* "sexual desire" or "impetuosity.")
226 keen sharp, bitter **228 Still . . . worse** more keen, always *bettering* what other
people say with witty wordplay, but at the same time more offensive **229 So** even thus
(in marriage) **mis-take** take falseheartedly and cheat on (The marriage vows say "for better, for worse.") **233 Confederate season** the time and occasion conspiring (to assist
the murderer) **else** otherwise **seeing** seeing me **235 Hecate's ban** the curse of
Hecate, the goddess of witchcraft **236 dire property** baleful quality **238 estate** i.e.,
the kingship **His** i.e., the King's

*[*CLAUDIUS *rises.]*
OPHELIA. The King rises.
HAMLET. What, frighted with false fire?°
QUEEN. How fares my lord?
POLONIUS. Give o'er the play.   245
KING. Give me some light. Away!
POLONIUS. Lights, lights, lights!

Exeunt all but HAMLET *and* HORATIO.

HAMLET. "Why,° let the strucken deer go weep,
      The hart ungallèd° play.
   For some must watch,° while some must sleep;   250
      Thus runs the world away."°
   Would not this,° sir, and a forest of feathers°—if the rest of my for-
   tunes turn Turk with° me—with two Provincial roses° on my
   razed° shoes, get me a fellowship in a cry° of players?°
HORATIO. Half a share.   255
HAMLET. A whole one, I.
   "For thou dost know, O Damon° dear,
      This realm dismantled° was
   Of Jove himself, and now reigns here
      A very, very—pajock."°   260
HORATIO. You might have rhymed.
HAMLET. O good Horatio, I'll take the ghost's word for a thousand pound.
   Didst perceive?
HORATIO. Very well, my lord.
HAMLET. Upon the talk of the poisoning?   265
HORATIO. I did very well note him.

Enter ROSENCRANTZ *and* GUILDENSTERN.

HAMLET. Aha! Come, some music! Come, the recorders.°
   "For if the King like not the comedy,
      Why then, belike, he likes it not, perdy."°
   Come, some music.   270
GUILDENSTERN. Good my lord, vouchsafe me a word with you.
HAMLET. Sir, a whole history.

243 false fire the blank discharge of a gun loaded with powder but no shot   **248–251 Why
. . . away** (Probably from an old ballad, with allusion to the popular belief that a wounded
deer retires to weep and die; compare with *As You Like It*, 2.1.33-66.)   **249 ungallèd**
unafflicted   **250 watch** remain awake   **251 Thus . . . away** thus the world goes   **252 this**
i.e., the play   **feathers** (Allusion to the plumes that Elizabethan actors were fond of wearing.)   **253 turn Turk with** turn renegade against, go back on   **Provincial roses**
rosettes of ribbon, named for roses grown in a part of France   **254 razed** with ornamental slashing   **cry** pack (of hounds)   **fellowship . . . players** partnership in a theatrical
company   **257 Damon** the friend of Pythias, as Horatio is friend of Hamlet; or, a traditional pastoral name   **258 dismantled** stripped, divested   **258–260 This realm . . . pajock** i.e., Jove, representing divine authority and justice, has abandoned this realm to its
own devices, leaving in his stead only a peacock or vain pretender to virtue (though the
rhyme-word expected in place of *pajock* or "peacock" suggests that the realm is now
ruled over by an "ass")   **267 recorders** wind instruments of the flute kind   **269 perdy**
(A corruption of the French *par dieu,* "by God")

GUILDENSTERN. The King, sir—

HAMLET. Ay, sir, what of him?

GUILDENSTERN. Is in his retirement° marvelous distempered.° 275

HAMLET. With drink, sir?

GUILDENSTERN. No, my lord, with choler.°

HAMLET. Your wisdom should show itself more richer to signify this to the
doctor, for for me to put him to his purgation° would perhaps
plunge him into more choler. 280

GUILDENSTERN. Good my lord, put your discourse into some frame° and
start° not so wildly from my affair.

HAMLET. I am tame, sir. Pronounce.

GUILDENSTERN. The Queen, your mother, in most great affliction of spirit,
hath sent me to you. 285

HAMLET. You are welcome.

GUILDENSTERN. Nay, good my lord, this courtesy is not of the right breed.°
If it shall please you to make me a wholesome answer, I will do
your mother's commandment; if not, your pardon° and my return
shall be the end of my business. 290

HAMLET. Sir, I cannot.

ROSENCRANTZ. What, my lord?

HAMLET. Make you a wholesome answer; my wit's diseased. But, sir, such
answer as I can make, you shall command, or rather, as you say,
my mother. Therefore no more, but to the matter. My mother, 295
you say—

ROSENCRANTZ. Then thus she says: your behavior hath struck her into
amazement and admiration.°

HAMLET. O wonderful son, that can so stonish a mother! But is there no
sequel at the heels of this mother's admiration? Impart. 300

ROSENCRANTZ. She desires to speak with you in her closet° ere you go to
bed.

HAMLET. We shall obey, were she ten times our mother. Have you any further trade with us?

ROSENCRANTZ. My lord, you once did love me. 305

HAMLET. And do still, by these pickers and stealers.°

ROSENCRANTZ. Good my lord, what is your cause of distemper? You do
surely bar the door upon your own liberty° if you deny° your griefs
to your friend.

HAMLET. Sir, I lack advancement. 310

---

275 retirement withdrawal to his chambers   **distempered** out of humor (But Hamlet
deliberately plays on the wider application to any illness of mind or body, as in line 308,
especially to drunkenness.)   **277 choler** anger (But Hamlet takes the word in its more
basic humoral sense of "bilious disorder.")   **279 purgation** (Hamlet hints at something
going beyond medical treatment to bloodletting and the extraction of confession.)
281 frame order   **282 start** shy or jump away (like a horse; the opposite of *tame* in
line 283)   **288 breed** (1) kind (2) breeding, manners   **289 pardon** permission to depart   **298 admiration** bewilderment   **301 closet** private chamber   **306 pickers and
stealers** i.e., hands (So called from the catechism, "to keep my hands from picking and
stealing.")   **308 liberty** i.e., being freed from *distemper,* line 307; but perhaps with a
veiled threat as well   **deny** refuse to share

ROSENCRANTZ. How can that be, when you have the voice of the King himself for your succession in Denmark?

HAMLET. Ay, sir, but "While the grass grows"°—the proverb is something° musty.

Enter the PLAYERS° WITH RECORDERS.

    O, the recorders. Let me see one. [*He takes a recorder.*]   315
To withdraw° with you: why do you go about to recover the wind° of me, as if you would drive me into a toil?°

GUILDENSTERN. O, my lord, if my duty be too bold, my love is too unmannerly.°

HAMLET. I do not well understand that.° Will you play upon this pipe?   320

GUILDENSTERN. My lord, I cannot.

HAMLET. I pray you.

GUILDENSTERN. Believe me, I cannot.

HAMLET. I do beseech you.

GUILDENSTERN. I know no touch of it, my lord.   325

HAMLET. It is as easy as lying. Govern these ventages° with your fingers and thumb, give it breath with your mouth, and it will discourse most eloquent music. Look you, these are the stops.

GUILDENSTERN. But these cannot I command to any utterance of harmony. I have not the skill.   330

HAMLET. Why, look you now, how unworthy a thing you make of me! You would play upon me, you would seem to know my stops, you would pluck out the heart of my mystery, you would sound° me from my lowest note to the top of my compass,° and there is much music, excellent voice, in this little organ,° yet cannot you make it   335 speak. 'Sblood, do you think I am easier to be played on than a pipe? Call me what instrument you will, though you can fret° me, you cannot play upon me.

Enter POLONIUS.

    God bless you, sir!

POLONIUS. My lord, the Queen would speak with you, and presently.°   340

HAMLET. Do you see yonder cloud that's almost in shape of a camel?

POLONIUS. By the Mass and 'tis, like a camel indeed.

HAMLET. Methinks it is like a weasel.

POLONIUS. It is backed like a weasel.

HAMLET. Or like a whale.   345

---

313 While . . . grows (The rest of the proverb is "the silly horse starves"; Hamlet may not live long enough to succeed to the kingdom.)   **313–314 something** somewhat   **s.d. Players** actors   **316 withdraw** speak privately   **recover the wind** get to the windward side (thus driving the game into the *toil,* or "net")   **317 toil** snare   **318–319 if . . . unmannerly** if I am using an unmannerly boldness, it is my love that occasion it   **320 I . . . that** i.e., I don't understand how genuine love can be unmannerly   **326 ventages** finger-holes or *stops* (line 328) of the recorder   **333 sound** (1) fathom (2) produce sound in   **334 compass** range (of voice)   **335 organ** musical instrument   **337 fret** irritate (with a quibble on *fret,* meaning the piece of wood, gut, or metal that regulates the fingering on an instrument)   **340 presently** at once

POLONIUS. Very like a whale.

HAMLET. Then I will come to my mother by and by.° [*Aside.*] They fool
    me° to the top of my bent.°—I will come by and by.

POLONIUS. I will say so.

                                              [Exit.]

HAMLET. "By and by" is easily said. Leave me, friends.   350

                            [Exeunt all but HAMLET.*]*

    'Tis now the very witching time° of night,
    When churchyards yawn and hell itself breathes out
    Contagion to this world. Now could I drink hot blood
    And do such bitter business as the day
    Would quake to look on. Soft, now to my mother.   355
    O heart, lose not thy nature!° Let not ever
    The soul of Nero° enter this firm bosom.
    Let me be cruel, not unnatural;
    I will speak daggers to her, but use none.
    My tongue and soul in this be hypocrites: 360
    How in my words soever° she be shent,°
    To give them seals° never my soul consent!

                                        Exit.

    3.3 *Enter* KING, ROSENCRANTZ, *and* GUILDENSTERN.

KING. I like him° not, nor stands it safe with us
    To let his madness range. Therefore prepare you.
    I your commission will forthwith dispatch,°
    And he to England shall along with you.
    The terms of our estate° may not endure   5
    Hazard so near 's as doth hourly grow
    Out of his brows.°

GUILDENSTERN.   We will ourselves provide.
    Most holy and religious fear° it is
    To keep those many many bodies safe
    That live and feed upon Your Majesty.   10

ROSENCRANTZ. The single and peculiar° life is bound
    With all the strength and armor of the mind
    To keep itself from noyance,° but much more
    That spirit upon whose weal depends and rests
    The lives of many. The cess° of majesty   15
    Dies not alone, but like a gulf° doth draw

---

347 by and by quite soon **347–348 fool me** trifle with me, humor my fooling. **348 top of my bent** limit of my ability or endurance (Literally, the extent to which a bow may be bent.) **351 witching time** time when spells are cast and evil is abroad **356 nature** natural feeling **357 Nero** murderer of his mother, Agrippina **361 How . . . soever** however much by my words **shent** rebuked **362 give them seals** i.e., confirm them with deeds **3.3 Location:** The castle. **1 him** i.e., his behavior **3 dispatch** prepare, cause to be drawn up **5 terms of our estate** circumstances of my royal position **7 Out of his brows** i.e., from his brain, in the form of plots and threats **8 religious fear** sacred concern **11 single and peculiar** individual and private **13 noyance** harm **15 cess** decease, cessation **16 gulf** whirlpool

What's near it with it; or it is a massy° wheel
Fixed on the summit of the highest mount,
To whose huge spokes ten thousand lesser things
Are mortised° and adjoined, which, when it falls,°   20
Each small annexment, petty consequence,°
Attends° the boisterous ruin. Never alone
Did the King sigh, but with a general groan.

KING. Arm° you, I pray you, to this speedy voyage,
For we will fetters put about this fear,   25
Which now goes too free-footed.

ROSENCRANTZ.   We will haste us.

Exeunt gentlemen [ROSENCRANTZ *and* GUILDENSTERN].

Enter POLONIUS.

POLONIUS. My lord, he's going to his mother's closet.
Behind the arras° I'll convey myself
To hear the process.° I'll warrant she'll tax him home,°
And, as you said—and wisely was it said—   30
'Tis meet° that some more audience than a mother,
Since nature makes them partial, should o'erhear
The speech, of vantage.° Fare you well, my liege.
I'll call upon you ere you go to bed
And tell you what I know.

KING.   Thanks, dear my lord.   35

Exit [POLONIUS].

O, my offense is rank! It smells to heaven.
It hath the primal eldest curse° upon't,
A brother's murder. Pray can I not,
Though inclination be as sharp as will;°
My stronger guilt defeats my strong intent,   40
And like a man to double business bound°
I stand in pause where I shall first begin,
And both neglect. What if this cursèd hand
Were thicker than itself with brother's blood,
Is there not rain enough in the sweet heavens   45
To wash it white as snow? Whereto serves mercy
But to confront the visage of offense?°

17 **massy** massive   20 **mortised** fastened (as with a fitted joint)   **when it falls** i.e.,
when it descends, like the wheel of Fortune, bringing a king down with it   21 **Each ...
consequence** i.e., every hanger-on and unimportant person or thing connected with the
King   22 **Attends** participates in   24 **Arm** prepare   28 **arras** screen of tapestry placed
around the walls of household apartments (On the Elizabethan stage, the arras was presumably over a door or discovery space in the tiring-house facade.)   29 **process** proceedings   **tax him home** reprove him severely   31 **meet** fitting   33 **of vantage** from
an advantageous place, or, in addition   37 **the primal eldest curse** the curse of Cain,
the first murderer; he killed his brother Abel   39 **Though ... will** though my desire is as
strong as my determination   41 **bound** (1) destined (2) obliged (The King wants to repent and still enjoy what he has gained.)   46–47 **Whereto ... offense** what function
does mercy serve other than to meet sin face to face?

And what's in prayer but this twofold force,
To be forestallèd° ere we come to fall,
Or pardoned being down? Then I'll look up.   50
My fault is past. But O, what form of prayer
Can serve my turn? "Forgive me my foul murder"?
That cannot be, since I am still possessed
Of those effects for which I did the murder:
My crown, mine own ambition, and my Queen.   55
May one be pardoned and retain th' offense?°
In the corrupted currents° of this world
Offense's gilded hand° may shove by° justice,
And oft 'tis seen the wicked prize° itself
Buys out the law. But 'tis not so above.   60
There° is no shuffling,° there the action lies°
In his° true nature, and we ourselves compelled,
Even to the teeth and forehead° of our faults,
To give in° evidence. What then? What rests?°
Try what repentance can. What can it not?   65
Yet what can it, when one cannot repent?
O wretched state, O bosom black as death,
O limèd° soul that, struggling to be free,
Art more engaged!° Help, angels! Make assay.°
Bow, stubborn knees, and heart with strings of steel,   70
Be soft as sinews of the newborn babe!
All may be well.

                                      [He kneels.]

Enter HAMLET.

HAMLET. Now might I do it pat,° now 'a is a-praying;
And now I'll do 't. [*He draws his sword.*] And so 'a goes to heaven,
And so am I revenged. That would be scanned:°   75
A villain kills my father, and for that,
I, his sole son, do this same villain send
To heaven.
Why, this is hire and salary, not revenge.
'A took my father grossly, full of bread,°   80
With all his crimes broad blown,° as flush° as May;
And how his audit° stands who knows save° heaven?

---

49 **forestallèd** prevented (from sinning)   56 **th' offense** the thing for which one offended   57 **currents** courses   58 **gilded hand** hand offering gold as a bribe   **shove by** thrust aside   59 **wicked prize** prize won by wickedness   61 **There** i.e., in heaven.   **shuffling** escape by trickery   **the action lies** the accusation is made manifest (A legal metaphor.)   62 **his** its   63 **to the teeth and forehead** face to face, concealing nothing   64 **give in** provide   **rests** remains   68 **limèd** caught as with birdlime, a sticky substance used to ensnare birds   69 **engaged** entangled   **assay** trial (Said to himself.)   73 **pat** opportunely   75 **would be scanned** needs to be looked into, or, would be interpreted as follows   80 **grossly, full of bread** i.e., enjoying his worldly pleasures rather than fasting (See Ezekiel 16:49.)   81 **crimes broad blown** sins in full bloom.   **flush** vigorous   82 **audit** account   **save** except for

But in our circumstance and course of thought°
'Tis heavy with him. And am I then revenged,
To take him in the purging of his soul,   85
When he is fit and seasoned° for his passage?
No!
Up, sword, and know thou a more horrid hent.°

                            [He puts up his sword.]

When he is drunk asleep, or in his rage,°
Or in th' incestuous pleasure of his bed,   90
At game,° a-swearing, or about some act
That has no relish° of salvation in 't—
Then trip him, that his heels may kick at heaven,
And that his soul may be as damned and black
As hell, whereto it goes. My mother stays.°   95
This physic° but prolongs thy sickly days.

                                                      Exit.

KING. My words fly up, my thoughts remain below.
       Words without thoughts never to heaven go.

                                                      Exit.

               3.4 *Enter [*QUEEN*]* GERTRUDE *and* POLONIUS.

POLONIUS. 'A will come straight. Look you lay home° to him.
       Tell him his pranks have been too broad° to bear with,
       And that Your Grace hath screened and stood between
       Much heat° and him. I'll shroud° me even here.
       Pray you, be round° with him.   5
HAMLET [*within*]. Mother, Mother, Mother!
QUEEN. I'll warrant you, fear me not.
       Withdraw, I hear him coming.

                            *[*POLONIUS *hides behind the arras.]*

       Enter HAMLET.
HAMLET. Now, Mother, what's the matter?
QUEEN. Hamlet, thou hast thy father° much offended.   10
HAMLET. Mother, you have my father much offended.
QUEEN. Come, come, you answer with an idle° tongue.
HAMLET. Go, go, you question with a wicked tongue.
QUEEN. Why, how now, Hamlet?
HAMLET.   What's the matter now?

83 in . . . thought as we see it from our mortal perspective   **86 seasoned** matured, read-
ied   **88 know . . . hent** await to be grasped by me on a more horrid occasion   **hent** act
of seizing   **89 drunk . . . rage** dead drunk, or in a fit of sexual passion   **91 game** gambling   **92 relish** trace, savor   **95 stays** awaits (me)   **96 physic** purging (by prayer), or,
Hamlet's postponement of the killing   **3.4 Location: The Queen's private chamber.**
1 lay home thrust to the heart, reprove him soundly   **2 broad** unrestrained   **4 Much
heat** i.e., the King's anger   **shroud** conceal (with ironic fitness to Polonius' imminent
death. The word is only in the First Quarto: the Second Quarto and the Folio read "silence.")   **5 round** blunt   **10 thy father** i.e., your stepfather, Claudius   **12 idle** foolish

QUEEN. Have you forgot me?°

HAMLET.   No, by the rood,° not so: 15
    You are the Queen your husband's brother's wife,
    And—would it were not so!—you are my mother.

QUEEN. Nay, then, I'll set those to you that can speak.°

HAMLET. Come, come, and sit you down; you shall not budge.
    You go not till I set you up a glass   20
    Where you may see the inmost part of you.

QUEEN. What wilt thou do? Thou wilt not murder me?
    Help, ho!

POLONIUS [*behind the arras*]. What ho! Help!

HAMLET [*drawing*]. How now? A rat? Dead for a ducat,° dead!   25
                [He thrusts his rapier through the arras.]

POLONIUS [*behind the arras*]. O, I am slain!   *[He falls and dies.]*

QUEEN.   O me, what hast thou done?

HAMLET. Nay, I know not. Is it the King?

QUEEN. O, what a rash and bloody deed is this!

HAMLET. A bloody deed—almost as bad, good Mother,
    As kill a King, and marry with his brother.   30

QUEEN. As kill a King!

HAMLET.   Ay, lady, it was my word.
            [He parts the arras and discovers POLONIUS.*]*
    Thou wretched, rash, intruding fool, farewell!
    I took thee for thy better. Take thy fortune.
    Thou find'st to be too busy° is some danger.—
    Leave wringing of your hands. Peace, sit you down,   35
    And let me wring your heart, for so I shall,
    If it be made of penetrable stuff,
    If damnèd custom° have not brazed° it so
    That it be proof° and bulwark against sense.°

QUEEN. What have I done, that thou dar'st wag thy tongue   40
    In noise so rude against me?

HAMLET.   Such an act
    That blurs the grace and blush of modesty,
    Calls virtue hypocrite, takes off the rose
    From the fair forehead of an innocent love
    And sets a blister° there, makes marriage vows   45
    As false as dicers' oaths. O, such a deed
    As from the body of contraction° plucks
    The very soul, and sweet religion makes°
    A rhapsody° of words. Heaven's face does glow
    O'er this solidity and compound mass   50

---

15 forgot me i.e., forgotten that I am your mother   **rood** cross of Christ   **18 speak** i.e., to someone so rude   **25 Dead for a ducat** i.e., I bet a ducat he's dead; or, a ducat is his life's fee   **34 busy** nosey   **38 damnèd custom** habitual wickedness   **brazed** brazened, hardened   **39 proof** armor   **sense** feeling   **45 sets a blister** i.e., brands as a harlot   **47 contraction** the marriage contract   **48 sweet religion makes** i.e., makes marriage vows   **49 rhapsody** senseless string

With tristful visage, as against the doom,
Is thought-sick at the act.°

QUEEN.   Ay me, what act,
That roars so loud and thunders in the index?°

HAMLET [*showing her two likenesses*]. Look here upon this picture, and
on this,
The counterfeit presentment° of two brothers.   55
See what a grace was seated on this brow:
Hyperion's° curls, the front° of Jove himself,
An eye like Mars° to threaten and command,
A station° like the herald Mercury°
New-lighted° on a heaven-kissing hill—   60
A combination and a form indeed
Where every god did seem to set his seal°
To give the world assurance of a man.
This was your husband. Look you now what follows:
Here is your husband, like a mildewed ear,°   65
Blasting° his wholesome brother. Have you eyes?
Could you on this fair mountain leave° to feed
And batten° on this moor?° Ha, have you eyes?
You cannot call it love, for at your age
The heyday° in the blood° is tame, it's humble,   70
And waits upon the judgment, and what judgment
Would step from this to this? Sense,° sure, you have,
Else could you not have motion, but sure that sense
Is apoplexed,° for madness would not err,°
Nor sense to ecstasy was ne'er so thralled,   75
But° it reserved some quantity of choice
To serve in such a difference.° What devil was 't
That thus hath cozened° you at hoodman-blind?°
Eyes without feeling, feeling without sight,
Ears without hands or eyes, smelling sans° all,   80
Or but a sickly part of one true sense

49–52 Heaven's . . . act heaven's face blushes at this solid world compounded of the various elements, with sorrowful face as though the day of doom were near, and is sick with horror at the deed (i.e., Gertrude's marriage) **53 index** table of contents, prelude or preface **55 counterfeit presentment** portrayed representation **57 Hyperion's** the sungod's **front** brow **58 Mars** god of war **59 station** manner of standing **Mercury** winged messenger of the gods **60 New-lighted** newly alighted **62 set his seal** i.e., affix his approval **65 ear** i.e., of grain **66 Blasting** blighting **67 leave** cease **68 batten** gorge **moor** barren or marshy ground (suggesting also "dark-skinned") **70 heyday** state of excitement **blood** passion **72 Sense** perception through the five senses (the functions of the middle or sensible soul) **74 apoplexed** paralyzed (Hamlet goes on to explain that, without such a paralysis of will, mere madness would not so err, nor would the five senses so enthrall themselves to *ecstasy* or lunacy; even such deranged states of mind would be able to make the obvious choice between Hamlet Senior and Claudius.) **err** so err **76 But** but that **77 To . . . difference** to help in making a choice between two such men **78 cozened** cheated **hoodman-blind** blindman's buff (In this game, says Hamlet, the devil must have pushed Claudius toward Gertrude while she was blindfolded.) **80 sans** without

Could not so mope.° O shame, where is thy blush?
Rebellious hell,
If thou canst mutine° in a matron's bones,
To flaming youth let virtue be as wax   85
And melt in her own fire.° Proclaim no shame
When the compulsive ardor gives the charge,
Since frost itself as actively doth burn,
And reason panders will.°

QUEEN.   O Hamlet, speak no more!   90
Thou turn'st mine eyes into my very soul,
And there I see such black and grainèd° spots
As will not leave their tinct.°

HAMLET.   Nay, but to live
In the rank sweat of an enseamèd° bed,
Stewed° in corruption, honeying and making love   95
Over the nasty sty!

QUEEN.   O, speak to me no more!
These words like daggers enter in my ears.
No more, sweet Hamlet!

HAMLET.   A murderer and a villain,
A slave that is not twentieth part the tithe°
Of your precedent lord,° a vice° of kings,   100
A cutpurse of the empire and the rule,
That from a shelf the precious diadem stole
And put it in his pocket!

QUEEN.   No more!   105

Enter GHOST *[in his nightgown].*

HAMLET. A king of shreds and patches°—
Save me, and hover o'er me with your wings,
You heavenly guards! What would your gracious figure?

QUEEN.   Alas, he's mad!

HAMLET. Do you not come your tardy son to chide,   110
That, lapsed° in time and passion, lets go by
Th' important° acting of your dread command?
O, say!

GHOST.   Do not forget. This visitation
Is but to whet thy almost blunted purpose.   115

---

82 mope be dazed, act aimlessly   **84 mutine** incite mutiny   **85–86 be as wax . . .
fire** melt like a candle or stick of sealing wax held over the candle flame   **86–89 Proclaim . . . will** call it no shameful business when the compelling ardor of youth delivers
the attack, i.e., commits lechery, since the *frost* of advanced age burns with as active a fire
of lust and reason perverts itself by fomenting lust rather than restraining it   **92 grainèd**
dyed in grain, indelible   **93 leave their tinct** surrender their color   **94 enseamèd** saturated in the grease and filth of passionate lovemaking   **95 Stewed** soaked, bathed (with a
suggestion of "stew," brothel)   **100 tithe** tenth part   **101 precedent lord** former husband   **vice** buffoon (A reference to the Vice of the morality plays.)   **106 shreds and
patches** i.e., motley, the traditional costume of the clown or fool   **111 lapsed** delaying
112 important importunate, urgent

But look, amazement° on thy mother sits.
O, step between her and her fighting soul!
Conceit° in weakest bodies strongest works.
Speak to her, Hamlet.

HAMLET.   How is it with you, lady?

QUEEN. Alas, how is 't with you,   120
That you do bend your eye on vacancy,
And with th' incorporal° air do hold discourse?
Forth at your eyes your spirits wildly peep,
And, as the sleeping soldiers in th' alarm,°
Your bedded° hair, like life in excrements,°   125
Start up and stand on end. O gentle son,
Upon the heat and flame of thy distemper°
Sprinkle cool patience. Whereon do you look?

HAMLET. On him, on him! Look you how pale he glares!
His form and cause conjoined,° preaching to stones,   130
Would make them capable.°—Do not look upon me,
Lest with this piteous action you convert
My stern effects.° Then what I have to do
Will want true color—tears perchance for blood.°

QUEEN. To whom do you speak this?   135

HAMLET. Do you see nothing there?

QUEEN. Nothing at all, yet all that is I see.

HAMLET. Nor did you nothing hear?

QUEEN. No, nothing but ourselves.

HAMLET. Why, look you there, look how it steals away!   140
My father, in his habit° as° he lived!
Look where he goes even now out at the portal!

                                                        Exit GHOST.

QUEEN. This is the very° coinage of your brain.
This bodiless creation ecstasy
Is very cunning in.°   145

HAMLET. Ecstasy?
My pulse as yours doth temperately keep time,
And makes as healthful music. It is not madness
That I have uttered. Bring me to the test,
And I the matter will reword,° which madness   150
Would gambol° from. Mother, for love of grace,

---

116 amazement distraction   **118 Conceit** imagination   **122 incorporal** immaterial
124 as . . . alarm like soldiers called out of sleep by an alarum   **125 bedded** laid flat
like life in excrements i.e., as though hair, an outgrowth of the body, had a life of its
own (Hair was thought to be lifeless because it lacks sensation, and so its standing on end
would be unnatural and ominous.)   **127 distemper** disorder   **130 His . . . conjoined**
his appearance joined to his cause for speaking   **131 capable** receptive   **132–133 convert . . . effects** divert me from my stern duty   **134 want . . . blood** lack plausibility so
that (with a play on the normal sense of *color*) I shall shed colorless tears instead of blood
141 habit clothes   **as** as when   **143 very** mere   **144–145 This . . . in** madness is skillful in creating this kind of hallucination   **150 reword** repeat word for word   **151 gam-
bol** skip away

Lay not that flattering unction° to your soul
That not your trespass but my madness speaks.
It will but skin° and film the ulcerous place,
Whiles rank corruption, mining° all within,   155
Infects unseen. Confess yourself to heaven,
Repent what's past, avoid what is to come,
And do not spread the compost° on the weeds
To make them ranker. Forgive me this my virtue;°
For in the fatness° of these pursy° times   160
Virtue itself of vice must pardon beg,
Yea, curb° and woo for leave° to do him good.

QUEEN. O Hamlet, thou hast cleft my heart in twain.

HAMLET. O, throw away the worser part of it,
And live the purer with the other half.   165
Good night. But go not to my uncle's bed;
Assume a virtue, if you have it not.
That monster, custom, who all sense doth eat,°
Of habits devil,° is angel yet in this,
That to the use of actions fair and good   170
He likewise gives a frock or livery°
That aptly° is put on. Refrain tonight,
And that shall lend a kind of easiness
To the next abstinence; the next more easy;
For use° almost can change the stamp of nature,°   175
And either° . . . the devil, or throw him out
With wondrous potency. Once more, good night;
And when you are desirous to be blest,
I'll blessing beg of you.° For this same lord,

                              [pointing to POLONIUS.*]*

I do repent; but heaven hath pleased it so   180
To punish me with this, and this with me,
That I must be their scourge and minister.°
I will bestow° him, and will answer° well
The death I gave him. So, again, good night.
I must be cruel only to be kind.   185

---

152 unction ointment   **154 skin** grow a skin for   **155 mining** working under the surface   **158 compost** manure   **159 this my virtue** my virtuous talk in reproving you   **160 fatness** grossness   **pursy** flabby, out of shape   **162 curb** bow, bend the knee   **leave** permission   **168 who . . . eat** which consumes all proper or natural feeling, all sensibility   **169 Of habits devil** devil-like in prompting evil habits   **171 livery** an outer appearance, a customary garb (and hence a predisposition easily assumed in time of stress)   **172 aptly** readily   **175 use** habit   **the stamp of nature** our inborn traits   **176 And either** (A defective line, usually emended by inserting the word *master* after *either,* following the Fourth Quarto and early editors.)   **178–179 when . . . you** i.e., when you are ready to be penitent and seek God's blessing, I will ask your blessing as a dutiful son should   **182 their scourge and minister** i.e., agent of heavenly retribution (By *scourge,* Hamlet also suggests that he himself will eventually suffer punishment in the process of fulfilling heaven's will.)   **183 bestow** stow, dispose of   **answer** account or pay for

This° bad begins, and worse remains behind.°
One word more, good lady.
QUEEN.   What shall I do?
HAMLET. Not this by no means that I bid you do:
Let the bloat° King tempt you again to bed,
Pinch wanton° on your cheek, call you his mouse,   190
And let him, for a pair of reechy° kisses,
Or paddling° in your neck with his damned fingers,
Make you to ravel all this matter out°
That I essentially am not in madness,
But mad in craft.° 'Twere good° you let him know,   195
For who that's but a Queen, fair, sober, wise,
Would from a paddock,° from a bat, a gib,°
Such dear concernings° hide? Who would do so?
No, in despite of sense and secrecy,°
Unpeg the basket° on the house's top,   200
Let the birds fly, and like the famous ape,°
To try conclusions,° in the basket creep
And break your own neck down.°
QUEEN. Be thou assured, if words be made of breath,
And breath of life, I have no life to breathe   205
What thou hast said to me.
HAMLET. I must to England. You know that?
QUEEN.   Alack,
I had forgot. 'Tis so concluded on.
HAMLET. There's letters sealed, and my two schoolfellows,
Whom I will trust as I will adders fanged,   210
They bear the mandate; they must sweep my way
And marshal me to knavery.° Let it work.°
For 'tis the sport to have the enginer°
Hoist with° his own petard,° and 't shall go hard
But I will° delve one yard below their mines°   215

186 **This** i.e., the killing of Polonius **behind** to come 189 **bloat** bloated 190 **Pinch wanton** i.e., leave his love pinches on your cheeks, branding you as wanton 191 **reechy** dirty, filthy 192 **paddling** fingering amorously 193 **ravel . . . out** unravel, disclose 195 **in craft** by cunning **good** (Said sarcastically; also the following eight lines.) 197 **paddock** toad **gib** tomcat 198 **dear concernings** important affairs 199 **sense and secrecy** secrecy that common sense requires 200 **Unpeg the basket** open the cage, i.e., let out the secret 201 **famous ape** (In a story now lost.) 202 **try conclusions** test the outcome (in which the ape apparently enters a cage from which birds have been released and then tries to fly out of the cage as they have done, falling to its death) 203 **down** in the fall; utterly 211–212 **sweep . . . knavery** sweep a path before me and conduct me to some *knavery* or treachery prepared for me 212 **work** proceed 213 **enginer** maker of military contrivances 214 **Hoist with** blown up by **petard** an explosive used to blow in a door or make a breach 214–215 **'t shall . . . will** unless luck is against me, I will 215 **mines** tunnels used in warfare to undermine the enemy's emplacements; Hamlet will countermine by going under their mines

And blow them at the moon. O, 'tis most sweet
When in one line° two crafts° directly meet.
This man shall set me packing.°
I'll lug the guts into the neighbor room.
Mother, good night indeed. This counselor   220
Is now most still, most secret, and most grave,
Who was in life a foolish prating knave.—
Come, sir, to draw toward an end° with you.—
Good night, Mother.

                    Exeunt [separately, HAMLET *dragging in* POLONIUS].

    4.1 *Enter* KING *and* QUEEN,° *with* ROSENCRANTZ *and* GUILDENSTERN.

KING. There's matter° in these sighs, these profound heaves.°
    You must translate; 'tis fit we understand them.
    Where is your son?
QUEEN. Bestow this place on us a little while.

                    [Exeunt ROSENCRANTZ *and* GUILDENSTERN.]
    Ah, mine own lord, what have I seen tonight!   5
KING. What, Gertrude? How does Hamlet?
QUEEN. Mad as the sea and wind when both contend
    Which is the mightier. In his lawless fit,
    Behind the arras hearing something stir,
    Whips out his rapier, cries, "A rat, a rat!"   10
    And in this brainish apprehension° kills
    The unseen good old man.
KING.   O heavy° deed!
    It had been so with us,° had we been there.
    His liberty is full of threats to all—
    To you yourself, to us, to everyone.   15
    Alas, how shall this bloody deed be answered?°
    It will be laid to us, whose providence°
    Should have kept short,° restrained, and out of haunt°
    This mad young man. But so much was our love,
    We would not understand what was most fit,   20
    But, like the owner of a foul disease,
    To keep it from divulging,° let it feed
    Even on the pith of life. Where is he gone?

---

217 in one line i.e., mines and countermines on a collision course, or the countermines directly below the mines   **crafts** acts of guile, plots   **218 set me packing** set me to making schemes, and set me to lugging (him), and, also, send me off in a hurry   **223 draw . . . end** finish up (with a pun on *draw,* "pull")   **4.1 Location: The castle. s.d. Enter . . . Queen** (Some editors argue that Gertrude never exits in 3.4 and that the scene is continuous here, as suggested in the Folio, but the Second Quarto marks an entrance for her and at line 35 Claudius speaks of Gertrude's *closet* as though it were elsewhere. A short time has elapsed, during which the King has become aware of her highly wrought emotional state.) **1 matter** significance   **heaves** heavy sighs   **11 brainish apprehension** headstrong conception   **12 heavy** grievous   **13 us** i.e., me (The royal "we"; also in line 15.) **16 answered** explained   **17 providence** foresight   **18 short** i.e., on a short tether **out of haunt** secluded   **22 divulging** becoming evident

QUEEN. To draw apart the body he hath killed,
O'er whom his very madness, like some ore°   25
Among a mineral° of metals base,
Shows itself pure: 'a weeps for what is done.
KING. O Gertrude, come away!
The sun no sooner shall the mountains touch
But we will ship him hence, and this vile deed   30
We must with all our majesty and skill
Both countenance° and excuse.—Ho, Guildenstern!

Enter ROSENCRANTZ *and* GUILDENSTERN.
Friends both, go join you with some further aid.
Hamlet in madness hath Polonius slain,
And from his mother's closet hath he dragged him.   35
Go seek him out, speak fair, and bring the body
Into the chapel. I pray you, haste in this.
                    [Exeunt ROSENCRANTZ and GUILDENSTERN.]
Come, Gertrude, we'll call up our wisest friends
And let them know both what we mean to do
And what's untimely done°.   40
Whose whisper o'er the world's diameter,°
As level° as the cannon to his blank,°
Transports his poisoned shot, may miss our name
And hit the woundless° air. O, come away!
My soul is full of discord and dismay.   45
                                                    Exeunt.

4.2   *Enter* HAMLET.

HAMLET. Safely stowed.
ROSENCRANTZ, GUILDENSTERN [*within*]. Hamlet! Lord Hamlet!
HAMLET. But soft, what noise? Who calls on Hamlet? O, here they come.

Enter ROSENCRANTZ *and* GUILDENSTERN.
ROSENCRANTZ. What have you done, my lord, with the dead body?
HAMLET. Compounded it with dust, whereto 'tis kin.   5
ROSENCRANTZ. Tell us where 'tis, that we may take it thence
And bear it to the chapel.
HAMLET. Do not believe it.
ROSENCRANTZ. Believe what?
HAMLET. That I can keep your counsel and not mine own.° Besides, to be   10
demanded of° a sponge, what replication° should be made by the
son of a king?

___
25 ore vein of gold   **26 mineral** mine   **32 countenance** put the best face on   **40 And
. . . done** (A defective line; conjectures as to the missing words include *So, haply, slander*
[Capell and others]; *For, haply, slander* [Theobald and others]; and *So envious slander*
[Jenkins].)   **41 diameter** extent from side to side   **42 As level** with as direct aim.   **his
blank** its target at point-blank range   **44 woundless** invulnerable   **4.2. Location:** The
castle.   **10 That . . . own** i.e., that I can follow your advice (by telling where the body is)
and still keep my own secret   **11 demanded of** questioned by   **replication** reply

ROSENCRANTZ. Take you me for a sponge, my lord?

HAMLET. Ay, sir, that soaks up the King's countenance,° his rewards, his
authorities.° But such officers do the King best service in the end.   15
He keeps them, like an ape, an apple, in the corner of his jaw, first
mouthed to be last swallowed. When he needs what you have
gleaned, it is but squeezing you, and, sponge, you shall be dry
again.

ROSENCRANTZ. I understand you not, my lord.   20

HAMLET. I am glad of it. A knavish speech sleeps in° a foolish ear.

ROSENCRANTZ. My lord, you must tell us where the body is and go with us
to the King.

HAMLET. The body is with the King, but the King is not with the body.°
The King is a thing—   25

GUILDENSTERN. A thing, my lord?

HAMLET. Of nothing.° Bring me to him. Hide fox, and all after!°

Exeunt [running].

4.3   *Enter* KING, *and two or three.*

KING. I have sent to seek him, and to find the body.
How dangerous is it that this man goes loose!
Yet must not we put the strong law on him.
He's loved of° the distracted° multitude,
Who like not in their judgment, but their eyes,°   5
And where 'tis so, th' offender's scourge° is weighed,°
But never the offense. To bear all smooth and even,°
This sudden sending him away must seem
Deliberate pause.° Diseases desperate grown
By desperate appliance° are relieved,   10
Or not at all.

Enter ROSENCRANTZ, GUILDENSTERN, *and all the rest.*

How now, what hath befall'n?

ROSENCRANTZ. Where the dead body is bestowed, my lord,
We cannot get from him.

KING.   But where is he?

14 **countenance** favor   15 **authorities** delegated power, influence   21 **sleeps in** has
no meaning to   24 **The . . . body** (Perhaps alludes to the legal commonplace of "the
king's two bodies," which drew a distinction between the sacred office of kingship and
the particular mortal who possessed it at any given time. Hence, although Claudius' body
is necessarily a part of him, true kingship is not contained in it. Similarly, Claudius will
have Polonius' body when it is found, but there is no kingship in this business either.)   27 **Of
nothing** (1) of no account (2) lacking the essence of kingship, as in lines 24–25 and note.
Hide . . . after (An old signal cry in the game of hide-and-seek, suggesting that Hamlet
now runs away from them.)   **4.3 Location: The castle.**   4 **of** by   **distracted** fickle, unstable   5 **Who . . . eyes** who choose not by judgment but by appearance
6 **scourge** punishment (Literally, blow with a whip.)   **weighed** sympathetically considered   7 **To . . . even** to manage the business in an unprovocative way   9 **Deliberate
pause** carefully considered action   10 **appliance** remedies

ROSENCRANTZ. Without, my lord; guarded, to know your pleasure.

KING. Bring him before us.

ROSENCRANTZ.   Ho! Bring in the lord.   15

> *They enter [with* HAMLET*].*

KING. Now, Hamlet, where's Polonius?

HAMLET. At supper.

KING. At supper? Where?

HAMLET. Not where he eats, but where 'a is eaten. A certain convocation
of politic worms° are e'en° at him. Your worm° is your only em-   20
peror for diet.° We fat all creatures else to fat us, and we fat ourselves for maggots. Your fat king and your lean beggar is but variable service°—two dishes, but to one table. That's the end.

KING. Alas, alas!

HAMLET. A man may fish with the worm that hath eat° of a king, and eat of   25
the fish that hath fed of that worm.

KING. What dost thou mean by this?

HAMLET. Nothing but to show you how a king may go a progress° through
the guts of a beggar.

KING. Where is Polonius?   30

HAMLET. In heaven. Send thither to see. If your messenger find him not
there, seek him i' th' other place yourself. But if indeed you find
him not within this month, you shall nose him as you go up the
stairs into the lobby.

KING [*to some attendants*]. Go seek him there.   35

HAMLET. 'A will stay till you come.

> *[Exeunt attendants.]*

KING. Hamlet, this deed, for thine especial safety—
Which we do tender,° as we dearly° grieve
For that which thou hast done—must send thee hence
With fiery quickness. Therefore prepare thyself.   40
The bark° is ready, and the wind at help,
Th' associates tend,° and everything is bent°
For England.

HAMLET. For England!

KING. Ay, Hamlet.   45

HAMLET. Good.

KING. So is it, if thou knew'st our purposes.

HAMLET. I see a cherub° that sees them. But come, for England!
Farewell, dear mother.

KING. Thy loving father, Hamlet.   50

---

20 politic worms crafty worms (suited to a master spy like Polonius) **e'en** even now
Your worm your average worm (Compare *your fat king and your lean beggar* in line
22.) **21 diet** food, eating (with a punning reference to the Diet of Worms, a famous
convocation held in 1521) **22–23 variable service** different courses of a single meal
27 eat eaten (Pronounced *et.*) **28 progress** royal journey of state **38 tender** regard,
hold dear **dearly** intensely **41 bark** sailing vessel **42 tend** wait **bent** in readiness
48 cherub (Cherubim are angels of knowledge. Hamlet hints that both he and heaven
are onto Claudius' tricks.)

HAMLET.   My mother. Father and mother is man and wife, man and wife is
    one flesh, and so, my mother. Come, for England!

                                              Exit.

KING.   Follow him at foot;° tempt him with speed aboard.
    Delay it not. I'll have him hence tonight.
    Away! For everything is sealed and done   55
    That else leans on° th' affair. Pray you, make haste.

                      [Exeunt all but the KING.*]*
    And, England,° if my love thou hold'st at aught°—
    As my great power thereof may give thee sense,°
    Since yet thy cicatrice° looks raw and red
    After the Danish sword, and thy free awe°   60
    Pays homage to us—thou mayst not coldly set°
    Our sovereign process,° which imports at full,°
    By letters congruing° to that effect,
    The present° death of Hamlet. Do it, England,
    For like the hectic° in my blood he rages,   65
    And thou must cure me. Till I know 'tis done,
    Howe'er my haps,° my joys were ne'er begun.

                            Exit.

4.4 *Enter* FORTINBRAS *with his army over the stage.*

FORTINBRAS.   Go, Captain, from me greet the Danish king.
KING.   Tell him that by his license° Fortinbras
    Craves the conveyance of° a promised march
    Over his kingdom. You know the rendezvous.
    If that His Majesty would aught with us,   5
    We shall express our duty° in his eye;°
    And let him know so.
CAPTAIN.   I will do 't, my lord.
FORTINBRAS.   Go softly° on.

                    [Exeunt all but the CAPTAIN.*]*

    Enter HAMLET, ROSENCRANTZ, *[*GUILDENSTERN,*]* etc.
HAMLET.   Good sir, whose powers° are these?   10
CAPTAIN.   They are of Norway, sir.
HAMLET.   How purposed, sir, I pray you?
CAPTAIN.   Against some part of Poland.
HAMLET.   Who commands them, sir?
CAPTAIN.   The nephew to old Norway, Fortinbras.   15

---

53 at foot close behind, at heel **56 leans on** bears upon, is related to **57 England**
i.e., King of England **at aught** at any value **58 As . . . sense** for so my great power
may give you a just appreciation of the importance of valuing my love **59 cicatrice**
scar **60 free awe** voluntary show of respect **61 coldly set** regard with indifference
62 process command. **imports at full** conveys specific directions for **63 congru-
ing** agreeing **64 present** immediate **65 hectic** persistent fever **67 haps** fortunes
4.4 Location: The coast of Denmark. **2 license** permission **3 the conveyance of**
escort during **6 duty** respect **eye** presence **9 softly** slowly, circumspectly
10 powers forces

HAMLET. Goes it against the main° of Poland, sir,
　　　Or for some frontier?
CAPTAIN. Truly to speak, and with no addition,°
　　　We go to gain a little patch of ground
　　　That hath in it no profit but the name.
　　　To pay° five ducats, five, I would not farm it;° 20
　　　Nor will it yield to Norway or the Pole
　　　A ranker° rate, should it be sold in fee.°
HAMLET. Why, then the Polack never will defend it.
CAPTAIN. Yes, it is already garrisoned. 25
HAMLET. Two thousand souls and twenty thousand ducats
　　　Will not debate° the question of this straw.°
　　　This is th' impostume° of much wealth and peace,
　　　That inward breaks, and shows no cause without
　　　Why the man dies. I humbly thank you, sir. 30
CAPTAIN. God b' wi' you, sir.

[Exit.]

ROSENCRANTZ.　　　　　Will 't please you go, my lord?
HAMLET. I'll be with you straight. Go a little before.

[Exeunt all except HAMLET.*]*

　　　How all occasions do inform against° me
　　　And spur my dull revenge! What is a man,
　　　If his chief good and market of° his time 35
　　　Be but to sleep and feed? A beast, no more.
　　　Sure he that made us with such large discourse,°
　　　Looking before and after,° gave us not
　　　That capability and godlike reason
　　　To fust° in us unused. Now, whether it be 40
　　　Bestial oblivion,° or some craven° scruple
　　　Of thinking too precisely° on th' event°—
　　　A thought which, quartered, hath but one part wisdom
　　　And ever three parts coward—I do not know
　　　Why yet I live to say "This thing's to do," 45
　　　Sith° I have cause, and will, and strength, and means
　　　To do 't. Examples gross° as earth exhort me:
　　　Witness this army of such mass and charge,°
　　　Led by a delicate and tender° prince,
　　　Whose spirit with divine ambition puffed 50
　　　Makes mouths° at the invisible event,°

16 main main part **18 addition** exaggeration **21 To pay** i.e., for a yearly rental of.
farm it take a lease of it **23 ranker** higher **in fee** fee simple, outright **27 debate
. . . straw** settle this trifling matter **28 impostume** abscess **33 inform against** denounce, betray; take shape against **35 market of** profit of, compensation for
37 discourse power of reasoning **38 Looking before and after** able to review past
events and anticipate the future **40 fust** grow moldy **41 oblivion** forgetfulness.
craven cowardly **42 precisely** scrupulously. **event** outcome **46 Sith** since
47 gross obvious **48 charge** expense **49 delicate and tender** of fine and youthful
qualities **51 Makes mouths** makes scornful faces **invisible event** unforeseeable
outcome

Exposing what is mortal and unsure
To all that fortune, death, and danger dare,°
Even for an eggshell. Rightly to be great
Is not to stir without great argument,   55
But greatly to find quarrel in a straw
When honor's at the stake.° How stand I, then,
That have a father killed, a mother stained,
Excitements of° my reason and my blood,
And let all sleep, while to my shame I see   60
The imminent death of twenty thousand men
That for a fantasy° and trick° of fame
Go to their graves like beds, fight for a plot°
Whereon the numbers cannot try the cause,°
Which is not tomb enough and continent°   65
To hide the slain? O, from this time forth
My thoughts be bloody or be nothing worth!

Exit.

4.5   *Enter* HORATIO, *[QUEEN]* GERTRUDE, *and a* GENTLEMAN.

QUEEN. I will not speak with her.
GENTLEMAN.   She is importunate,
    Indeed distract.° Her mood will needs be pitied.
QUEEN. What would she have?
GENTLEMAN. She speaks much of her father, says she hears
    There's tricks° i' the world, and hems,° and beats her heart,°   5
    Spurns enviously at straws,° speaks things in doubt°
    That carry but half sense. Her speech is nothing,
    Yet the unshapèd use° of it doth move
    The hearers to collection;° they yawn° at it,
    And botch° the words up fit to their own thoughts,   10
    Which,° as her winks and nods and gestures yield° them,
    Indeed would make one think there might be thought,°
    Though nothing sure, yet much unhappily.°
HORATIO. 'Twere good she were spoken with, for she may strew
    Dangerous conjectures in ill-breeding° minds.   15

---

53 dare could do (to him)   **54–57 Rightly . . . stake** true greatness does not normally
consist of rushing into action over some trivial provocation; however, when one's honor is
involved, even a trifling insult requires that one respond greatly (?)   **at the stake** (A
metaphor from gambling or bear-baiting.)   **59 Excitements of** promptings by   **62 fantasy** fanciful caprice, illusion   **trick** trifle, deceit   **63 plot** plot of ground   **64 Whereon
. . . cause** on which there is insufficient room for the soldiers needed to engage in a military contest   **65 continent** receptacle; container   **4.5. Location: The castle.**   **2 distract** distracted   **5 tricks** deceptions.   **hems** makes "hmm" sounds.   **heart** i.e., breast
6 Spurns . . . straws kicks spitefully, takes offense at trifles   **in doubt** obscurely   **8 un-
shapèd use** incoherent manner   **9 collection** inference, a guess at some sort of meaning.   **yawn** gape, wonder; grasp (The Folio reading, *aim*, is possible.)   **10 botch** patch
11 Which which words   **yield** deliver, represent   **12 thought** intended   **13 unhappily** unpleasantly near the truth, shrewdly   **15 ill-breeding** prone to suspect the worst
and to make mischief

QUEEN. Let her come in.   [*Exit* GENTLEMAN.]

    [*Aside.*] To my sick soul, as sin's true nature is,
    Each toy° seems prologue to some great amiss.°
    So full of artless jealousy is guilt,
    It spills itself in fearing to be spilt.°   20

    Enter OPHELIA° [DISTRACTED].

OPHELIA. Where is the beauteous majesty of Denmark?
QUEEN. How now, Ophelia?
OPHELIA [*she sings*].
    "How should I your true love know
      From another one?
    By his cockle hat° and staff,   25
      And his sandal shoon."°
QUEEN. Alas, sweet lady, what imports this song?
OPHELIA. Say you? Nay, pray you, mark.
    "He is dead and gone, lady,   [*Song.*]
      He is dead and gone;   30
    At his head a grass-green turf,
      At his heels a stone."
    O, ho!
QUEEN. Nay, but Ophelia—
OPHELIA. Pray you, mark.   [*Sings.*]   35
    "White his shroud as the mountain snow"—

    Enter KING.

QUEEN. Alas, look here, my lord.
OPHELIA.
    "Larded° with sweet flowers;   [*Song.*]
    Which bewept to the ground did not go
      With true-love showers."°   40
KING. How do you, pretty lady?
OPHELIA. Well, God 'ild° you! They say the owl° was a baker's daughter.
    Lord, we know what we are, but know not what we may be. God
    be at your table!
KING. Conceit° upon her father.   45
OPHELIA. Pray let's have no words of this; but when they ask you what it
    means, say you this:
    "Tomorrow is Saint Valentine's day,   [*Song.*]
    All in the morning betime,°
    And I a maid at your window,   50

---

18 toy trifle   **amiss** calamity   **19–20 So . . . split** guilt is so full of suspicion that it unskillfully betrays itself in fearing betrayal   **20 s.d. Enter Ophelia** (In the First Quarto, Ophelia enters, "playing on a lute, and her hair down, singing.")   **25 cockle hat** hat with cockle-shell stuck in it as a sign that the wearer had been a pilgrim to the shrine of Saint James of Compostela in Spain   **26 shoon** shoes   **38 Larded** decorated   **40 showers** i.e., tears   **42 God 'ild** God yield or reward   **owl** (Refers to a legend about a baker's daughter who was turned into an owl for being ungenerous when Jesus begged a loaf of bread.)   **45 Conceit** brooding   **49 betime** early

> To be your Valentine.
> Then up he rose, and donned his clothes,
>   And dupped° the chamber door,
> Let in the maid, that out a maid
>   Never departed more." 55

KING. Pretty Ophelia—

OPHELIA. Indeed, la, without an oath, I'll make an end on 't: [*Sings.*]

> "By Gis° and by Saint Charity,
>   Alack, and fie for shame!
> Young men will do 't, if they come to 't; 60
>   By Cock,° they are to blame.
> Quoth she, 'Before you tumbled me,
>   You promised me to wed.'"

He answers:

> "'So would I ha' done, by yonder sun, 65
> An° thou hadst not come to my bed.'"

KING. How long hath she been thus?

OPHELIA. I hope all will be well. We must be patient, but I cannot choose
but weep to think they would lay him i' the cold ground. My
brother shall know of it. And so I thank you for your good counsel. 70
Come, my coach! Good night, ladies, good night, sweet ladies,
good night, good night.

[Exit.]

KING [*to* HORATIO]. Follow her close. Give her good watch, I pray you.

[Exit HORATIO.*]*

> O, this is the poison of deep grief; it springs
> All from her father's death—and now behold!
> O Gertrude, Gertrude, 75
> When sorrows come, they come not single spies,°
> But in battalions. First, her father slain;
> Next, your son gone, and he most violent author
> Of his own just remove;° the people muddied,° 80
> Thick and unwholesome in their thoughts and whispers
> For good Polonius' death—and we have done but greenly,°
> In hugger-mugger° to inter him; poor Ophelia
> Divided from herself and her fair judgment,
> Without the which we are pictures or mere beasts; 85
> Last, and as much containing° as all these,
> Her brother is in secret come from France,
> Feeds on this wonder, keeps himself in clouds,°
> And wants° not buzzers° to infect his ear
> With pestilent speeches of his father's death, 90

---

53 dupped did up, opened   **58 Gis** Jesus   **61 Cock** (A perversion of "God" in oaths; here
also with a quibble on the slang word for penis.)   **66 An** if   **77 spies** scouts sent in advance
of the main force   **80 remove** removal.   **muddied** stirred up, confused   **82 greenly** in an
inexperienced way, foolishly   **83 hugger-mugger** secret haste   **86 as much containing**
as full of serious matter   **88 Feeds . . . clouds** feeds his resentment or shocked grievance,
holds himself inscrutable and aloof amid all this rumor   **89 wants** lacks   **buzzers** gossipers,
informers

Wherein necessity,° of matter beggared,°
Will nothing stick our person to arraign
In ear and ear.° O my dear Gertrude, this,
Like to a murdering piece,° in many places
Gives me superfluous death.°　　　　　*A noise within.*　95

QUEEN. Alack, what noise is this?
KING. Attend!°
　　Where is my Switzers?° Let them guard the door.

Enter a MESSENGER.
　　What is the matter?
MESSENGER.　　　　　Save yourself, my lord!
　　The ocean, overpeering of his list,°　　　　　　　100
　　Eats not the flats° with more impetuous° haste
　　Than young Laertes, in a riotous head,°
　　O'erbears your officers. The rabble call him lord,
　　And, as° the world were now but to begin,
　　Antiquity forgot, custom not known,　　　　　　105
　　The ratifiers and props of every word,°
　　They cry, "Choose we! Laertes shall be king!"
　　Caps,° hands, and tongues applaud it to the clouds,
　　"Laertes shall be king, Laertes king!"
QUEEN. How cheerfully on the false trail they cry!　110
　　　　　　　　　　　　　　A noise within.
　　O, this is counter,° you false Danish dogs!

Enter LAERTES *with others.*
KING. The doors are broke.
LAERTES. Where is this King?—Sirs, stand you all without.
ALL. No, let's come in.
LAERTES. I pray you, give me leave.　　　　　　115
ALL. We will, we will.
LAERTES. I thank you. Keep the door. [*Exeunt followers.*] O thou vile king,
　　Give me my father!
QUEEN [*restraining him*]. Calmly, good Laertes.
LAERTES. That drop of blood that's calm proclaims me bastard,
　　Cries cuckold to my father, brands the harlot　120
　　Even here, between° the chaste unsmirchèd brow
　　Of my true mother.

91 necessity i.e., the need to invent some plausible explanation　**of matter beggared** unprovided with facts　**92–93 Will . . . ear** will not hesitate to accuse my (royal) person in everybody's ears　**94 murdering piece** cannon loaded so as to scatter its shot　**95 Gives . . . death** kills me over and over　**97 Attend** i.e., guard me　**98 Switzers** Swiss guards, mercenaries　**100 overpeering of his list** overflowing its shore, boundary　**101 flats** i.e., flatlands near shore　**impetuous** violent (perhaps also with the meaning of *impiteous* [*impitious*, Q2], "pitiless.")　**102 head** insurrection　**104 as** as if　**106 The ratifiers . . . word** i.e., *antiquity* (or tradition) and *custom* ought to confirm (*ratify*) and underprop our every word or promise　**108 Caps** (The caps are thrown in the air.)　**111 counter** (A hunting term, meaning to follow the trail in a direction opposite to that which the game has taken.)　**121 between** in the middle of

KING.   What is the cause, Laertes,
    That thy rebellion looks so giantlike?
    Let him go, Gertrude. Do not fear our° person.
    There's such divinity doth hedge° a king   125
    That treason can but peep to what it would,°
    Acts little of his will.° Tell me, Laertes,
    Why thou art thus incensed. Let him go, Gertrude.
    Speak, man.

LAERTES.   Where is my father?

KING.   Dead.

QUEEN. But not by him.

KING.   Let him demand his fill.   130

LAERTES. How came he dead? I'll not be juggled with.°
    To hell, allegiance! Vows, to the blackest devil!
    Conscience and grace, to the profoundest pit!
    I dare damnation. To this point I stand,°
    That both the worlds I give to negligence,°   135
    Let come what comes, only I'll be revenged
    Most throughly° for my father.

KING. Who shall stay you?

LAERTES. My will, not all the world's.°
    And for° my means, I'll husband them so well   140
    They shall go far with little.

KING.   Good Laertes,
    If you desire to know the certainty
    Of your dear father, is 't writ in your revenge
    That, swoopstake,° you will draw both friend and foe,
    Winner and loser?   145

LAERTES. None but his enemies.

KING. Will you know them, then?

LAERTES. To his good friends thus wide I'll ope my arms,
    And like the kind life-rendering pelican°
    Repast° them with my blood.

KING.   Why, now you speak   150
    Like a good child and a true gentleman.
    That I am guiltless of your father's death,
    And am most sensibly° in grief for it,
    It shall as level° to your judgment 'pear
    As day does to your eye.   *A noise within.*   155

---

124 fear our fear for my   **125 hedge** protect, as with a surrounding barrier   **126 can . . .
would** can only peep furtively, as through a barrier, at what it would intend   **127 Acts . . .
will** (but) performs little of what it intends   **131 juggled with** cheated, deceived
134 To . . . stand I am resolved in this   **135 both . . . negligence** i.e., both this world
and the next are of no consequence to me   **137 throughly** thoroughly   **139 My will . . .
world's** I'll stop (*stay*) when my will is accomplished, not for anyone else's   **140 for** as
for   **144 swoopstake** i.e., indiscriminately (Literally, taking all stakes on the gambling
table at once. *Draw* is also a gambling term, meaning "take from.")   **149 pelican** (Refers
to the belief that the female pelican fed its young with its own blood.)   **150 Repast** feed
153 sensibly feelingly   **154 level** plain

LAERTES. How now, what noise is that?

   Enter OPHELIA.

KING.   Let her come in.

LAERTES. O heat, dry up my brains! Tears seven times salt
   Burn out the sense and virtue° of mine eye!
   By heaven, thy madness shall be paid with weight°
   Till our scale turn the beam.° O rose of May!   160
   Dear maid, kind sister, sweet Ophelia!
   O heavens, is 't possible a young maid's wits
   Should be as mortal as an old man's life?
   Nature is fine in° love, and where 'tis fine
   It sends some precious instance° of itself   165
   After the thing it loves.°

OPHELIA.   *[Song.]*

     "They bore him barefaced on the bier,
       Hey non nonny, nonny, hey nonny,
       And in his grave rained many a tear—"
   Fare you well, my dove!   170

LAERTES. Hadst thou thy wits and didst persuade° revenge,
   It could not move thus.

OPHELIA. You must sing "A-down a-down," and you "call him a-down-a."°
   O, how the wheel° becomes it! It is the false steward° that stole his 175
   master's daughter.

LAERTES. This nothing's more than matter.°

OPHELIA. There's rosemary,° that's for remembrance; pray you, love, remember. And there is pansies;° that's for thoughts.

LAERTES. A document° in madness, thoughts and remembrance fitted. 180

OPHELIA. There's fennel° for you, and columbines.° There's rue° for you,
   and here's some for me; we may call it herb of grace o' Sundays.
   You must wear your rue with a difference.° There's a daisy.°
   I would give you some violets,° but they withered all when my fa-
   ther died. They say 'a made a good end—   185
   [Sings.] "For bonny sweet Robin is all my joy."

---

158 virtue faculty, power **159 paid with weight** repaid, avenged equally or more
160 beam crossbar of a balance **164 fine in** refined by **165 instance** token **166 After
...loves** i.e., into the grave, along with Polonius **171 persuade** argue cogently for
173–174 You...a-down-a (Ophelia assigns the singing of refrains, like her own "Hey
non nonny," to others present.) **174 wheel** spinning wheel as accompaniment to the
song, or refrain **false steward** (The story is unknown.) **176 This...matter** this
seeming nonsense is more eloquent than sane utterance **177 rosemary** (Used as a symbol of remembrance both at weddings and at funerals.) **178 pansies** (Emblems of love
and courtship; perhaps from French *pensées,* "thoughts.") **179 document** instruction,
lesson **180 fennel** (Emblem of flattery.) **columbines** (Emblems of unchastity or in-
gratitude.) **rue** (Emblem of repentance—a signification that is evident in its popular
name, *herb of grace.*) **182 with a difference** (A device used in heraldry to distinguish
one family from another on the coat of arms, here suggesting that Ophelia and the others
have different causes of sorrow and repentance; perhaps with a play on *rue* in the sense
of "ruth," "pity.") **daisy** (Emblem of dissembling, faithlessness.) **183 violets** (Emblems
of faithfulness.)

LAERTES. Thought° and affliction, passion,° hell itself,
    She turns to favor° and to prettiness.

OPHELIA.   [*Song.*]

    "And will 'a not come again?
    And will 'a not come again?
      No, no, he is dead.   190
      Go to thy deathbed,
    He never will come again.

    "His beard was as white as snow,
    All flaxen was his poll.°
      He is gone, he is gone,   195
      And we cast away moan.
    God ha' mercy on his soul!"

    And of all Christian souls, I pray God. God b' wi' you.

                         [*Exit, followed by* GERTRUDE.]

LAERTES. Do you see this, O God?

KING. Laertes, I must commune with your grief,   200
    Or you deny me right. Go but apart,
    Make choice of whom° your wisest friends you will,
    And they shall hear and judge twixt you and me.
    If by direct or by collateral hand°
    They find us touched,° we will our kingdom give,   205
    Our crown, our life, and all that we call ours
    To you in satisfaction; but if not,
    Be you content to lend your patience to us,
    And we shall jointly labor with your soul
    To give it due content.

LAERTES.   Let this be so.   210
    His means of death, his obscure funeral—
    No trophy,° sword, nor hatchment° o'er his bones,
    No noble rite, nor formal ostentation°—
    Cry to be heard, as 'twere from heaven to earth,
    That° I must call 't in question.°

KING.   So you shall,   215
    And where th' offense is, let the great ax fall.
    I pray you, go with me.

                                     Exeunt.

4.6 *Enter* HORATIO *and others.*

HORATIO. What are they that would speak with me?

GENTLEMAN. Seafaring men, sir. They say they have letters for you.

---

186 Thought melancholy   **passion** suffering   **187 favor** grace, beauty   **194 poll** head
202 whom whichever of   **204 collateral hand** indirect agency   **205 us touched** me
implicated   **213 trophy** memorial   **hatchment** tablet displaying the armorial bearings
of a deceased person   **213 ostentation** ceremony   **215 That** so that   **call 't in ques-**
tion demand an explanation   **4.6. Location: The castle.**

HORATIO. Let them come in.

[*Exit* GENTLEMAN.]

I do not know from what part of the world
I should be greeted, if not from Lord Hamlet.   5

Enter Sailors.

FIRST SAILOR. God bless you, sir.

HORATIO. Let him bless thee too.

FIRST SAILOR. 'A shall, sir, an 't° please him. There's a letter for you, sir—it
came from th' ambassador° that was bound for England—if your
name be Horatio, as I am let to know it is.   [*He gives a letter.*]   10

HORATIO [*reads*]. "Horatio, when thou shalt have overlooked° this, give
these fellows some means° to the King; they have letters for him.
Ere we were two days old at sea, a pirate of very warlike appoint-
ment° gave us chase. Finding ourselves too slow of sail, we put on
a compelled valor, and in the grapple I boarded them. On the in-   15
stant they got clear of our ship, so I alone became their prisoner.
They have dealt with me like thieves of mercy,° but they knew
what they did: I am to do a good turn for them. Let the King have
the letters I have sent, and repair° thou to me with as much speed
as thou wouldest fly death. I have words to speak in thine ear will   20
make thee dumb, yet are they much too light for the bore° of the
matter. These good fellows will bring thee where I am. Rosencrantz and Guildenstern hold their course for England. Of them I
have much to tell thee. Farewell.

He that thou knowest thine, Hamlet."   25

Come, I will give you way° for these your letters,
And do 't the speedier that you may direct me
To him from whom you brought them.

Exeunt.

4.7 *Enter* KING *and* LAERTES.

KING. Now must your conscience my acquittance seal,°
And you must put me in your heart for friend,
Sith° you have heard, and with a knowing ear,
That he which hath your noble father slain
Pursued my life.

LAERTES.   It well appears. But tell me   5
Why you proceeded not against these feats°
So crimeful and so capital° in nature,
As by your safety, greatness, wisdom, all things else,
You mainly° were stirred up.

8 an 't if it   **9 th' ambassador** (Evidently Hamlet. The sailor is being circumspect.)
11 overlooked looked over   **12 means** means of access   **13–14 appointment**
equipage   **17 thieves of mercy** merciful thieves   **19 repair** come   **21 bore** caliber,
i.e., importance   **26 way** means of access   **4.7 Location: The castle.   1 my acquittance seal** confirm or acknowledge my innocence   **3 Sith** since   **6 feats** acts   **7 capital** punishable by death   **9 mainly** greatly

KING. O, for two special reasons,   10
        Which may to you perhaps seem much unsinewed,°
        But yet to me they're strong. The Queen his mother
        Lives almost by his looks, and for myself—
        My virtue or my plague, be it either which—
        She is so conjunctive° to my life and soul   15
        That, as the star moves not but in his° sphere,°
        I could not but by her. The other motive
        Why to a public count° I might not go
        Is the great love the general gender° bear him,
        Who, dipping all his faults in their affection,   20
        Work° like the spring° that turneth wood to stone,
        Convert his gyves° to graces, so that my arrows,
        Too slightly timbered° for so loud° a wind,
        Would have reverted° to my bow again
        But not where I had aimed them.   25
LAERTES. And so have I a noble father lost,
        A sister driven into desperate terms,°
        Whose worth, if praises may go back° again,
        Stood challenger on mount° of all the age
        For her perfections. But my revenge will come.   30
KING. Break not your sleeps for that. You must not think
        That we are made of stuff so flat and dull
        That we can let our beard be shook with danger
        And think it pastime. You shortly shall hear more.
        I loved your father, and we love ourself;   35
        And that, I hope, will teach you to imagine—

        Enter a MESSENGER *with letters.*
How now? What news?
MESSENGER. Letters, my lord, from Hamlet:
        This to Your Majesty, this to the Queen.

                                                [He gives letters.]
KING. From Hamlet? Who brought them?   40
MESSENGER. Sailors, my lord, they say. I saw them not.
        They were given me by Claudio. He received them
        Of him that brought them.
KING.   Laertes, you shall hear them.—
        Leave us.

                                                [Exit MESSENGER.*]*

---

11 unsinewed weak **15 conjunctive** closely united (An astronomical metaphor.)
16 his its **sphere** one of the hollow spheres in which, according to Ptolematic astronomy, the planets were supposed to move **18 count** account, reckoning, indictment
19 general gender common people **21 Work** operate, act **spring** i.e., a spring with
such a concentration of lime that it coats a piece of wood with limestone, in effect gild-
ing and petrifying it **22 gyves** fetters (which, gilded by the people's praise, would look
like badges of honor) **23 slightly timbered** light **loud** (suggesting public outcry on
Hamlet's behalf) **24 reverted** returned **27 terms** state, condition **28 go back** i.e.,
recall what she was **29 on mount** set up on high

[*He reads.*] "High and mighty, you shall know I am set naked° on   45
your kingdom. Tomorrow shall I beg leave to see your kingly eyes,
when I shall, first asking your pardon,° thereunto recount the occasion of my sudden and more strange return.   Hamlet."

What should this mean? Are all the rest come back?
Or is it some abuse,° and no such thing?°   50
LAERTES. Know you the hand?
KING.   'Tis Hamlet's character.° "Naked!"
And in a postscript here he says "alone."
Can you devise° me?
LAERTES. I am lost in it, my lord. But let him come.
It warms the very sickness in my heart   55
That I shall live and tell him to his teeth,
"Thus didst thou."°
KING.   If it be so, Laertes—
As how should it be so? How otherwise?°—
Will you be ruled by me?
LAERTES.   Ay, my lord,
So° you will not o'errule me to a peace.   60
KING. To thine own peace. If he be now returned,
As checking at° his voyage, and that° he means
No more to undertake it, I will work him
To an exploit, now ripe in my device,°
Under the which he shall not choose but fall;   65
And for his death no wind of blame shall breathe,
But even his mother shall uncharge the practice°
And call it accident.
LAERTES.   My lord, I will be ruled,
The rather if you could devise it so
That I might be the organ.°
KING.   It falls right.   70
You have been talked of since your travel much,
And that in Hamlet's hearing, for a quality
Wherein they say you shine. Your sum of parts°
Did not together pluck such envy from him
As did that one, and that, in my regard,   75
Of the unworthiest siege.°
LAERTES. What part is that, my lord?
KING. A very ribbon in the cap of youth,
Yet needful too, for youth no less becomes°

45 naked destitute, unarmed, without following **47 pardon** permission **50 abuse** deceit **no such thing** not what it appears **51 character** handwriting **53 devise** explain to **57 Thus didst thou** i.e., here's for what you did to my father **58 As . . . otherwise** how can this (Hamlet's return) be true? Yet how otherwise than true (since we
have the evidence of his letter)? **60 So** provided that **62 checking at** i.e., turning aside
from (like a falcon leaving the quarry to fly at a chance bird) **that** if **64 device** devising,
invention **67 uncharge the practice** acquit the stratagem of being a plot **70 organ**
agent, instrument **73 Your . . . parts** i.e., all your other virtues **76 unworthiest siege**
least important rank **79 no less becomes** is no less suited by

The light and careless livery that it wears   80
Than settled age his sables° and his weeds°
Importing health and graveness.° Two months since
Here was a gentleman of Normandy.
I have seen myself, and served against, the French,
And they can well° on horseback, but this gallant   85
Had witchcraft in 't; he grew unto his seat,
And to such wondrous doing brought his horse
As had he been incorpsed and demi-natured°
With the brave beast. So far he topped° my thought
That I in forgery° of shapes and tricks   90
Come short of what he did.

LAERTES.   A Norman was 't?

KING. A Norman.

LAERTES. Upon my life, Lamord.

KING.   The very same.

LAERTES. I know him well. He is the brooch° indeed
And gem of all the nation.   95

KING. He made confession° of you,
And gave you such a masterly report
For art and exercise in your defense,°
And for your rapier most especial,
That he cried out 'twould be a sight indeed   100
If one could match you. Th' escrimers° of their nation,
He swore, had neither motion, guard, nor eye
If you opposed them. Sir, this report of his
Did Hamlet so envenom with his envy
That he could nothing do but wish and beg   105
Your sudden° coming o'er, to play° with you.
Now, out of this—

LAERTES.   What out of this, my lord?

KING. Laertes, was your father dear to you?
Or are you like the painting of a sorrow,
A face without a heart?

LAERTES.   Why ask you this?   110

KING. Not that I think you did not love your father,
But that I know love is begun by time,°
And that I see, in passages of proof,°
Time qualifies° the spark and fire of it.
There lives within the very flame of love   115

81 **his sables** its rich robes furred with sable **weeds** garments 82 **Importing . . . graveness** signifying a concern for health and dignified prosperity; also, giving an impression of comfortable prosperity **85 can well** are skilled **88 As . . . deminatured** as if he had been of one body and nearly of one nature (like the centaur) **89 topped** surpassed 90 **forgery** imagining 94 **brooch** ornament 96 **confession** testimonial, admission of superiority 98 **For . . . defense** with respect to your skill and practice with your weapon 101 **escrimers** fencers 106 **sudden** immediate **play** fence 112 **begun by time** i.e., created by the right circumstance and hence subject to change 113 **passages of proof** actual instances that prove it 114 **qualifies** weakens, moderates

A kind of wick or snuff° that will abate it,
And nothing is at a like goodness still,°
For goodness, growing to a pleurisy,°
Dies in his own too much.° That° we would do,
We should do when we would; for this "would" changes   120
And hath abatements° and delays as many
As there are tongues, are hands, are accidents,°
And then this "should" is like a spendthrift sigh,°
That hurts by easing.° But, to the quick o' th' ulcer:°
Hamlet comes back. What would you undertake   125
To show yourself in deed your father's son
More than in words?

LAERTES.   To cut his throat i' the church.

KING. No place, indeed, should murder sanctuarize;°
Revenge should have no bounds. But good Laertes,
Will you do this,° keep close within your chamber.   130
Hamlet returned shall know you are come home.
We'll put on those shall° praise your excellence
And set a double varnish on the fame
The Frenchman gave you, bring you in fine° together,
And wager on your heads. He, being remiss,°   135
Most generous,° and free from all contriving,
Will not peruse the foils, so that with ease,
Or with a little shuffling, you may choose
A sword unbated,° and in a pass of practice°
Requite him for your father.

LAERTES.   I will do 't,   140
And for that purpose I'll anoint my sword.
I bought an unction° of a mountebank°
So mortal that, but dip a knife in it,
Where it draws blood no cataplasm° so rare,
Collected from all simples° that have virtue°   145
Under the moon,° can save the thing from death
That is but scratched withal. I'll touch my point

---

116 **snuff** the charred part of a candlewick   117 **nothing . . . still** nothing remains at a constant level of perfection   118 **pleurisy** excess, plethora (Literally, a chest inflammation.)   119 **in . . . much** of its own excess   **That** that which   121 **abatements** diminutions   122 **As . . . accidents** as there are tongues to dissuade, hands to prevent, and chance events to intervene   123 **spendthrift sigh** (An allusion to the belief that sighs draw blood from the heart.)   124 **hurts by easing** i.e., costs the heart blood and wastes precious opportunity even while it affords emotional relief   **quick o' th' ulcer** i.e., heart of the matter   128 **sanctuarize** protect from punishment (Alludes to the right of sanctuary with which certain religious places were invested.)   130 **Will you do this** if you wish to do this   132 **put on those shall** arrange for some to   134 **in fine** finally   135 **remiss** negligently unsuspicious   136 **generous** noble-minded   139 **unbated** not blunted, having no button.   **pass of practice** treacherous thrust   142 **unction** ointment   **mountebank** quack doctor   144 **cataplasm** plaster or poultice   145 **simples** herbs   **virtue** potency   146 **Under the moon** i.e., anywhere (with reference perhaps to the belief that herbs gathered at night had a special power)

With this contagion, that if I gall° him slightly,
It may be death.

KING.   Let's further think of this,
    Weigh what convenience both of time and means   150
    May fit us to our shape.° If this should fail,
    And that our drift look through our bad performance,°
    'Twere better not assayed. Therefore this project
    Should have a back or second, that might hold
    If this did blast in proof.° Soft, let me see.   155
    We'll make a solemn wager on your cunnings°—
    I ha 't!
    When in your motion you are hot and dry—
    As° make your bouts more violent to that end—
    And that he calls for drink, I'll have prepared him   160
    A chalice for the nonce,° whereon but sipping,
    If he by chance escape your venomed stuck,°
    Our purpose may hold there. [*A cry within.*] But stay, what noise?

    Enter QUEEN.

QUEEN. One woe doth tread upon another's heel,
    So fast they follow. Your sister's drowned, Laertes.   165
LAERTES. Drowned! O, where?
QUEEN. There is a willow grows askant° the brook,
    That shows his hoar leaves° in the glassy stream;
    Therewith fantastic garlands did she make
    Of crowflowers, nettles, daisies, and long purples,°   170
    That liberal° shepherds give a grosser name,°
    But our cold° maids do dead men's fingers call them.
    There on the pendent° boughs her crownet° weeds
    Clamb'ring to hang, an envious sliver° broke,
    When down her weedy° trophies and herself   175
    Fell in the weeping brook. Her clothes spread wide,
    And mermaidlike awhile they bore her up,
    Which time she chanted snatches of old lauds,°
    As one incapable of° her own distress,
    Or like a creature native and endued°   180
    Unto that element. But long it could not be
    Till that her garments, heavy with their drink,

---

148 gall graze, wound   **151 shape** part we propose to act   **152 drift . . . performance**
intention should be made visible by our bungling   **155 blast in proof** burst in the test
(like a cannon)   **156 cunnings** respective skills   **159 As** i.e., and you should   **161 nonce**
occasion   **162 stuck** thrust (From *stoccado,* a fencing term.)   **167 askant** aslant
168 hoar leaves white or gray undersides of the leaves   **170 long purples** early purple
orchids   **171 liberal** free-spoken   **a grosser name** (The testicle-resembling tubers of
the orchid, which also in some cases resemble *dead men's fingers,* have earned various
slang names like "dogstones" and "cullions.")   **172 cold** chaste   **173 pendent** over-
hanging.   **crownet** made into a chaplet or coronet   **174 envious sliver** malicious
branch   **175 weedy** i.e., of plants   **178 lauds** hymns   **179 incapable of** lacking capacity to apprehend   **180 endued** adapted by nature

Pulled the poor wretch from her melodious lay
To muddy death.
LAERTES.   Alas, then she is drowned?
QUEEN. Drowned, drowned.   185
LAERTES. Too much of water hast thou, poor Ophelia,
And therefore I forbid my tears. But yet
It is our trick;° nature her custom holds,
Let shame say what it will. [*He weeps.*] When these are gone,
The woman will be out.° Adieu, my lord.   190
I have a speech of fire that fain would blaze,
But that this folly douts° it.   *Exit.*
KING.   Let's follow, Gertrude.
How much I had to do to calm his rage!
Now fear I this will give it start again;
Therefore let's follow.   195
                                              Exeunt.

5.1 *Enter two* CLOWNS° [WITH SPADES AND MATTOCKS].

FIRST CLOWN. Is she to be buried in Christian burial, when she willfully
    seeks her own salvation?°
SECOND CLOWN. I tell thee she is; therefore make her grave straight.° The
    crowner° hath sat on her,° and finds it° Christian burial.
FIRST CLOWN. How can that be, unless she drowned herself in her own de-   5
    fense?
SECOND CLOWN. Why, 'tis found so.°
FIRST CLOWN. It must be *se offendendo,*° it cannot be else. For here lies the
    point: if I drown myself wittingly, it argues an act, and an act hath
    three branches—it is to act, to do, and to perform. Argal,° she   10
    drowned herself wittingly.
SECOND CLOWN. Nay, but hear you, goodman° delver—
FIRST CLOWN. Give me leave. Here lies the water; good. Here stands the
    man; good. If the man go to this water and drown himself, it is, will
    he, nill he,° he goes, mark you that. But if the water come to him   15
    and drown him, he drowns not himself. Argal, he that is not guilty
    of his own death shortens not his own life.
SECOND CLOWN. But is this law?
FIRST CLOWN. Ay, marry, is 't—crowner's quest° law.

188 It is our trick i.e., weeping is our natural way (when sad)   **189–190 When . . . out**
when my tears are all shed, the woman in me will be expended, satisfied   **192 douts** ex-
tinguishes (The Second Quarto reads "drowns.")   **5.1. Location: A churchyard.   s.d.**
Clowns rustics   **2 salvation** (A blunder for "damnation," or perhaps a suggestion that
Ophelia was taking her own shortcut to heaven.)   **3 straight** straightway, immediately
(But with a pun on *strait,* "narrow.")   **4 crowner** coroner   **sat on her** conducted an inquest on her case   **finds it** gives his official verdict that her means of death was consistent with   **7 found so** determined so in the coroner's verdict   **8 *se offendendo*** (A
comic mistake for *se defendendo,* a term used in verdicts of justifiable homicide.)   **10 Argal**
(Corruption of *ergo,* "therefore.")   **12 goodman** (An honorific title often used with the
name of a profession or craft.)   **15 will he, nill he** whether he will or no, willy-nilly
19 quest inquest

SECOND CLOWN. Will you ha' the truth on 't? If this had not been a gentle-   20
    woman, she should have been buried out o' Christian burial.
FIRST CLOWN. Why, there thou sayst.° And the more pity that great folk
    should have countenance° in this world to drown or hang them-
    selves, more than their even-Christian.° Come, my spade. There is
    no ancient° gentlemen but gardeners, ditchers, and grave makers.   25
    They hold up° Adam's profession.
SECOND CLOWN. Was he a gentleman?
FIRST CLOWN. 'A was the first that ever bore arms.°
SECOND CLOWN. Why, he had none.
FIRST CLOWN. What, art a heathen? How dost thou understand the Scrip-   30
    ture? The Scripture says Adam digged. Could he dig without arms?°
    I'll put another question to thee. If thou answerest me not to the
    purpose, confess thyself°—
SECOND CLOWN. Go to.
FIRST CLOWN. What is he that builds stronger than either the mason, the   35
    shipwright, or the carpenter?
SECOND CLOWN. The gallows maker, for that frame° outlives a thousand
    tenants.
FIRST CLOWN. I like thy wit well, in good faith. The gallows does well.° But
    how does it well? It does well to those that do ill. Now thou dost ill   40
    to say the gallows is built stronger than the church. Argal, the gal-
    lows may do well to thee. To 't again, come.
SECOND CLOWN. "Who builds stronger than a mason, a shipwright, or a car-
    penter?"
FIRST CLOWN. Ay, tell me that, and unyoke.°   45
SECOND CLOWN. Marry, now I can tell.
FIRST CLOWN. To 't.
SECOND CLOWN. Mass,° I cannot tell.

    [Enter HAMLET *and* HORATIO *[at a distance].*
FIRST CLOWN. Cudgel thy brains no more about it, for your dull ass will not
    mend his pace with beating; and when you are asked this question   50
    next, say "a grave maker." The houses he makes lasts till doomsday.
    Go get thee in and fetch me a stoup° of liquor.
            [Exit SECOND CLOWN. FIRST CLOWN *digs.]*
                                            Song.

        "In youth, when I did love, did love,°
            Methought it was very sweet,

---

22 there thou sayst i.e., that's right   **23 countenance** privilege   **24 even-Christ-ian** fellow Christians   **25 ancient** going back to ancient times   **26 hold up** maintain
28 bore arms (To be entitled to bear a coat of arms would make Adam a gentleman, but as one who bore a spade, our common ancestor was an ordinary delver in the earth.)   **31 arms** i.e., the arms of the body   **33 confess thyself** (The saying contin-ues, "and be hanged.")   **37 frame** (1) gallows (2) structure   **39 does well** (1) is an apt answer (2) does a good turn   **45 unyoke** i.e., after this great effort, you may un-harness the team of your wits   **48 Mass** by the Mass   **52 stoup** two-quart measure
53 In . . . love (This and the two following stanzas, with nonsensical variations, are from a poem attributed to Lord Vaux and printed in *Tottel's Miscellany,* 1557. The *O* and *a* [for "ah"] seemingly are the grunts of the digger.)

> To contract—O—the time for—a—my behove,° 55
> O, methought there—a—was nothing—a—meet."°

HAMLET. Has this fellow no feeling of his business, 'a° sings in grave-
making?

HORATIO. Custom hath made it in him a property of easiness.°

HAMLET. 'Tis e'en so. The hand of little employment hath the daintier
sense.° 60

FIRST CLOWN. *Song.*

> "But age with his stealing steps
> Hath clawed me in his clutch,
> And hath shipped me into the land,°
> As if I had never been such."
> 65

[He throws up a skull.]

HAMLET. That skull had a tongue in it and could sing once. How the
knave jowls° it to the ground, as if 'twere Cain's jawbone, that did
the first murder! This might be the pate of a politician,° which
this ass now o'erreaches,° one that would circumvent God, might
it not?

HORATIO. It might, my lord. 70

HAMLET. Or of a courtier, which could say, "Good morrow, sweet lord!
How dost thou, sweet lord?" This might be my Lord Such-a-one,
that praised my Lord Such-a-one's horse when 'a meant to beg it,
might it not?

HORATIO. Ay, my lord. 75

HAMLET. Why, e'en so, and now my Lady Worm's, chapless,° and
knocked about the mazard° with a sexton's spade. Here's fine revolution,° an° we had the trick to see° 't. Did these bones cost no
more the breeding but° to play at loggets° with them? Mine ache
to think on 't. 80

FIRST CLOWN. *Song.*

> "A pickax and a spade, a spade,
> For and° a shrouding sheet;
> O, a pit of clay for to be made
> For such a guest is meet."
> 85

[He throws up another skull.]

55 To contract . . . behove i.e., to shorten the time for my own advantage (Perhaps he
means to *prolong* it.) **56 meet** suitable, i.e., more suitable **57 'a** that he **59 property of easiness** something he can do easily and indifferently **60–61 daintier sense**
more delicate sense of feeling **64 into the land** i.e., toward my grave (?) (But note the
lack of rhyme in *steps, land.*) **67 jowls** dashes (with a pun on *jowl,* "jawbone") **68 politician** schemer, plotter **69 o'erreaches** circumvents, gets the better of (with a quibble
on the literal sense) **77 chapless** having no lower jaw **78 mazard** i.e., head (Literally,
a drinking vessel.) **78–79 revolution** turn of Fortune's wheel, change **79 an** if
trick to see knack of seeing **79–80 cost . . . but** involve so little expense and care in
upbringing that we may **80 loggets** a game in which pieces of hard wood shaped like
Indian clubs or bowling pins are thrown to lie as near as possible to a stake **83 For and**
and moreover

HAMLET. There's another. Why may not that be the skull of a lawyer? Where be his quiddities° now, his quillities,° his cases, his tenures,° and his tricks? Why does he suffer this mad knave now to knock him about the sconce° with a dirty shovel, and will not tell him of his action of battery?° Hum, this fellow might be in 's time a great buyer of land, with his statutes, his recognizances,° his fines, his double° vouchers,° his recoveries.° Is this the fine of his fines and the recovery of his recoveries, to have his fine pate full of fine dirt?° Will his vouchers vouch him no more of his purchases, and double ones too, than the length and breadth of a pair of indentures?° The very conveyances° of his lands will scarcely lie in this box,° and must th' inheritor° himself have no more, ha?   90

    95

HORATIO. Not a jot more, my lord.

HAMLET. Is not parchment made of sheepskins?

HORATIO. Ay, my lord, and of calves' skins too.   100

HAMLET. They are sheep and calves which seek out assurance in that.° I will speak to this fellow.—Whose grave's this, sirrah?°

FIRST CLOWN. Mine, sir.   *[Sings.]*

> "O, pit of clay for to be made
>   For such a guest is meet."   105

HAMLET. I think it be thine, indeed, for thou liest in 't.

FIRST CLOWN. You lie out on 't, sir, and therefore 'tis not yours. For my part, I do not lie in 't, yet it is mine.

HAMLET. Thou dost lie in 't, to be in 't and say it is thine. 'Tis for the dead, not for the quick;° therefore thou liest.   110

FIRST CLOWN. 'Tis a quick lie, sir; 'twill away again from me to you.

HAMLET. What man dost thou dig it for?

FIRST CLOWN. For no man, sir.

HAMLET. What woman, then?

FIRST CLOWN. For none, neither.   115

HAMLET. Who is to be buried in 't?

FIRST CLOWN. One that was a woman, sir, but, rest her soul, she's dead.

---

87 quiddities subtleties, quibbles (From Latin *quid,* "a thing.") **quillities** verbal niceties, subtle distinctions (Variation of *quiddities.*)   **88 tenures** the holding of a piece of property or office, or the conditions or period of such holding   **89 sconce** head   **90 action of battery** lawsuit about physical assault   **91 statutes, recognizances** legal documents guaranteeing a debt by attaching land and property   **91–92 fines, recoveries** ways of converting entailed estates into "fee simple" or freehold   **92 double** signed by two signatories.   **vouchers** guarantees of the legality of a title to real estate   **92–94 fine of his fines . . . fine pate . . . fine dirt** end of his legal maneuvers . . . elegant head . . . minutely sifted dirt   **95–96 pair of indentures** legal document drawn up in duplicate on a single sheet and then cut apart on a zigzag line so that each pair was uniquely matched (Hamlet may refer to two rows of teeth or dentures.)   **96 conveyances** deeds   **97 box** (1) deed box (2) coffin ("Skull" has been suggested.)   **inheritor** possessor, owner   **101 assurance in that** safety in legal parchments   **102 sirrah** (A term of address to inferiors.)   **110 quick** living

HAMLET. How absolute° the knave is! We must speak by the card,° or
   equivocation° will undo us. By the Lord, Horatio, this three years I
   have took° note of it: the age is grown so picked° that the toe of   120
   the peasant comes so near the heel of the courtier, he galls his
   kibe.°—How long hast thou been grave maker?
FIRST CLOWN. Of all the days i' the year, I came to 't that day that our last
   king Hamlet overcame Fortinbras.
HAMLET. How long is that since?   125
FIRST CLOWN. Cannot you tell that? Every fool can tell that. It was that very
   day that young Hamlet was born—he that is mad and sent into
   England.
HAMLET. Ay, marry, why was he sent into England?
FIRST CLOWN. Why, because 'a was mad. 'A shall recover his wits there, or   130
   if 'a do not, 'tis no great matter there.
HAMLET. Why?
FIRST CLOWN. 'Twill not be seen in him there. There the men are as mad
   as he.
HAMLET. How came he mad?   135
FIRST CLOWN. Very strangely, they say.
HAMLET. How strangely?
FIRST CLOWN. Faith, e'en with losing his wits.
HAMLET. Upon what ground?°
FIRST CLOWN. Why, here in Denmark. I have been sexton here, man and   140
   boy, thirty years.
HAMLET. How long will a man lie i' th' earth ere he rot?
FIRST CLOWN. Faith, if 'a be not rotten before 'a die—as we have many
   pocky° corpses nowadays, that will scarce hold the laying in°—'a
   will last you° some eight year or nine year. A tanner will last you   145
   nine year.
HAMLET. Why he more than another?
FIRST CLOWN. Why, sir, his hide is so tanned with his trade that 'a will keep
   out water a great while, and your water is a sore° decayer of your
   whoreson° dead body. [*He picks up a skull.*] Here's a skull now   150
   hath lien you° i' th' earth three-and-twenty years.
HAMLET. Whose was it?
FIRST CLOWN. A whoreson mad fellow's it was. Whose do you think it
   was?
HAMLET. Nay, I know not.   155
FIRST CLOWN. A pestilence on him for a mad rogue! 'A poured a flagon of
   Rhenish° on my head once. This same skull, sir, was, sir, Yorick's
   skull, the King's jester.

118 absolute strict, precise   **by the card** i.e., with precision (Literally, by the mariner's
compass-card, on which the points of the compass were marked.)   **119 equivocation** ambiguity in the use of terms   **120 took** taken   **picked** refined, fastidious   **121–122 galls
his kibe** chafes the courtier's chilblain   **139 ground** cause (But, in the next line, the
gravedigger takes the word in the sense of "land," "country.")   **144 pocky** rotten, diseased (Literally, with the pox, or syphilis.)   **hold the laying in** hold together long enough
to be interred   **145 last you** last (*You* is used colloquially here and in the following lines.)
149 sore i.e., terrible, great   **150 whoreson** i.e., vile, scurvy   **151 lien you** lain (See the
note at line 144.)   **157 Rhenish** Rhine wine

HAMLET. This?

FIRST CLOWN. E'en that.   160

HAMLET. Let me see. [*He takes the skull.*] Alas, poor Yorick! I knew him,
Horatio, a fellow of infinite jest, of most excellent fancy. He hath
bore° me on his back a thousand times, and now how abhorred in
my imagination it is! My gorge rises° at it. Here hung those lips that
I have kissed I know not how oft. Where be your gibes now? Your   165
gambols, your songs, your flashes of merriment that were wont° to
set the table on a roar? Not one now, to mock your own grinning?°
Quite chopfallen?° Now get you to my lady's chamber and tell her,
let her paint an inch thick, to this favor° she must come. Make her
laugh at that. Prithee, Horatio, tell me one thing.   170

HORATIO. What's that, my lord?

HAMLET. Dost thou think Alexander looked o' this fashion i' th' earth?

HORATIO. E'en so.

HAMLET. And smelt so? Pah! [*He throws down the skull.*]

HORATIO. E'en so, my lord.   175

HAMLET. To what base uses we may return, Horatio! Why may not imagination trace the noble dust of Alexander till 'a find it stopping a
bunghole?°

HORATIO. 'Twere to consider too curiously° to consider so.

HAMLET. No, faith, not a jot, but to follow him thither with modesty°   180
enough, and likelihood to lead it. As thus: Alexander died, Alexander was buried, Alexander returneth to dust, the dust is earth, of
earth we make loam,° and why of that loam whereto he was converted might they not stop a beer barrel?
Imperious° Caesar, dead and turned to clay,   185
Might stop a hole to keep the wind away.
O, that that earth which kept the world in awe
Should patch a wall t' expel the winter's flaw!°

Enter KING, QUEEN, LAERTES, *and the corpse [of* OPHELIA, *in procession,
with* PRIEST, *lords, etc.].*

But soft,° but soft awhile! Here comes the King,
The Queen, the courtiers. Who is this they follow?   190
And with such maimèd° rites? This doth betoken
The corpse they follow did with desperate hand
Fordo° its own life. 'Twas of some estate.°
Couch we° awhile and mark.

---

163 **bore** borne   164 **My gorge rises** i.e., I feel nauseated   166 **were wont** used
167 **mock your own grinning** mock at the way your skull seems to be grinning (just as
you used to mock at yourself and those who grinned at you)   168 **chopfallen** (1) lacking the lower jaw (2) dejected   169 **favor** aspect, appearance   178 **bunghole** hole for
filling or emptying a cask   179 **curiously** minutely   180 **modesty** plausible moderation   183 **loam** mortar consisting chiefly of moistened clay and straw   185 **Imperious**
imperial   188 **flaw** gust of wind   189 **soft** i.e., wait, be careful   191 **maimèd** muti-
lated, incomplete   193 **Fordo** destroy   **estate** rank   194 **Couch we** let's hide, lie low

[He and HORATIO *conceal themselves.* OPHELIA*'s body is taken to the grave.]*

LAERTES. What ceremony else? 195

HAMLET [*to* HORATIO]. That is Laertes, a very noble youth. Mark.

LAERTES. What ceremony else?

PRIEST. Her obsequies have been as far enlarged
As we have warranty.° Her death was doubtful,
And but that great command o'ersways the order° 200
She should in ground unsanctified been lodged°
Till the last trumpet. For° charitable prayers,
Shards,° flints, and pebbles should be thrown on her.
Yet here she is allowed her virgin crants,°
Her maiden strewments,° and the bringing home 205
Of bell and burial.°

LAERTES. Must there no more be done?

PRIEST.   No more be done.
We should profane the service of the dead
To sing a requiem and such rest° to her
As to peace-parted souls.°

LAERTES.   Lay her i' th' earth, 210
And from her fair and unpolluted flesh
May violets° spring! I tell thee, churlish priest,
A ministering angel shall my sister be
When thou liest howling.°

HAMLET [*to* HORATIO].   What, the fair Ophelia!

QUEEN [*scattering flowers*]. Sweets to the sweet! Farewell. 215
I hoped thou shouldst have been my Hamlet's wife.
I thought thy bride-bed to have decked, sweet maid,
And not t' have strewed thy grave.

LAERTES.   O, treble woe
Fall ten times treble on that cursèd head
Whose wicked deed thy most ingenious sense° 220
Deprived thee of! Hold off the earth awhile,
Till I have caught her once more in mine arms.

[He leaps into the grave and embraces OPHELIA.*]*
Now pile your dust upon the quick and dead,
Till of this flat a mountain you have made
T' o'ertop old Pelion or the skyish head 225
Of blue Olympus.°

199 warranty i.e., ecclesiastical authority   **200 great...order** orders from on high overrule the prescribed procedures   **201 She should...lodged** she should have been buried in unsanctified ground   **202 For** in place of   **203 Shards** broken bits of pottery   **204 crants** garlands betokening maidenhood   **205 strewments** flowers strewn on a coffin   **205–206 bringing...burial** laying the body to rest, to the sound of the bell   **209 such rest** i.e., to pray for such rest   **210 peace-parted souls** those who have died at peace with God   **212 violets** (See 4.5.183 and note)   **214 howling** i.e., in hell   **220 ingenious sense** a mind that is quick, alert, of fine qualities   **225–226 Pelion, Olympus** sacred mountains in the north of Thessaly; see also *Ossa*, below, at line 257

HAMLET [*coming forward*]. What is he whose grief
    Bears such an emphasis,° whose phrase of sorrow
    Conjures the wandering stars° and makes them stand
    Like wonder-wounded° hearers? This is I,
    Hamlet the Dane.°
LAERTES [*grappling with him*°]. The devil take thy soul!   230
HAMLET. Thou pray'st not well.
    I prithee, take thy fingers from my throat,
    For though I am not splenitive° and rash,
    Yet have I in me something dangerous,
    Which let thy wisdom fear. Hold off thy hand.   235
KING. Pluck them asunder.
QUEEN. Hamlet, Hamlet!
ALL. Gentlemen!
HORATIO. Good my lord, be quiet.

   [HAMLET *and* LAERTES *are parted.*]
HAMLET. Why, I will fight with him upon this theme
    Until my eyelids will no longer wag.°   240
QUEEN. O my son, what theme?
HAMLET. I loved Ophelia. Forty thousand brothers
    Could not with all their quantity of love
    Make up my sum. What wilt thou do for her?   245
KING. O, he is mad, Laertes.
QUEEN. For love of God, forbear him.°
HAMLET. 'Swounds,° show me what thou'lt do.
    Woo't° weep? Woo't fight? Woo't fast? Woo't tear thyself?
    Woo't drink up° eisel?° Eat a crocodile?°   250
    I'll do 't. Dost come here to whine?
    To outface me with leaping in her grave?
    Be buried quick° with her, and so will I.
    And if thou prate of mountains, let them throw
    Millions of acres on us, till our ground,   255
    Singeing his pate° against the burning zone,°

---

227 emphasis i.e., rhetorical and florid emphasis (*Phrase* has a similar rhetorical connotation.) **228 wandering stars** planets **229 wonder-wounded** struck with amazement **230 the Dane** (This title normally signifies the King; see 1.1.17 and note.) **s.d. grappling with him** The testimony of the First Quarto that *"Hamlet leaps in after Laertes"* and the "Elegy on Burbage" ("Oft have I seen him leap into the grave") seem to indicate one way in which this fight was staged; however, the difficulty of fitting two contenders and Ophelia's body into a confined space (probably the trapdoor) suggests to many editors the alternative, that Laertes jumps out of the grave to attack Hamlet.) **233 splenitive** quick-tempered **241 wag** move (A fluttering eyelid is a conventional sign that life has not yet gone.) **247 forbear him** leave him alone **248 'Swounds** by His (Christ's) wounds **249 Woo't** wilt thou **250 drink up** drink deeply. **eisel** vinegar. **crocodile** (Crocodiles were tough and dangerous, and were supposed to shed hypocritical tears.) **253 quick** alive **256 his pate** its head, i.e., top **burning zone** zone in the celestial sphere containing the sun's orbit, between the tropics of Cancer and Capricorn

Make Ossa° like a wart! Nay, an° thou'lt mouth,°
    I'll rant as well as thou.

QUEEN.   This is mere° madness,
    And thus awhile the fit will work on him;
    Anon, as patient as the female dove   260
    When that her golden couplets° are disclosed,°
    His silence will sit drooping.

HAMLET.   Hear you, sir,
    What is the reason that you use me thus?
    I loved you ever. But it is no matter.
    Let Hercules himself do what he may,   265
    The cat will mew, and dog will have his day.°

                             Exit HAMLET.

KING. I pray thee, good Horatio, wait upon him.

                          [*Exit*] HORATIO.

    [*To* LAERTES.] Strengthen your patience in° our last night's speech;
    We'll put the matter to the present push.°—
    Good Gertrude, set some watch over your son.—   270
    This grave shall have a living° monument.
    An hour of quiet° shortly shall we see;
    Till then, in patience our proceeding be.

                               Exeunt.

        5.2 *Enter* HAMLET *and* HORATIO.

HAMLET. So much for this, sir; now shall you see the other.°
    You do remember all the circumstance?

HORATIO. Remember it, my lord!

HAMLET. Sir, in my heart there was a kind of fighting
    That would not let me sleep. Methought I lay   5
    Worse than the mutines° in the bilboes.° Rashly,°
    And praised be rashness for it—let us know°
    Our indiscretion° sometimes serves us well
    When our deep plots do pall,° and that should learn° us
    There's a divinity that shapes our ends,   10
    Rough-hew° them how we will—

---

257 Ossa another mountain in Thessaly (In their war against the Olympian gods, the giants attempted to heap Ossa on Pelion to scale Olympus.) **an** if **mouth** i.e., rant **258 mere** utter **261 golden couplets** two baby pigeons, covered with yellow down. **disclosed** hatched **265–266 Let . . . day** i.e., (1) even Hercules couldn't stop Laertes' theatrical rant (2) I, too, will have my turn; i.e., despite any blustering attempts at interference, every person will sooner or later do what he or she must do **268 in** i.e., by recalling **269 present push** immediate test **271 living** lasting (For Laertes' private understanding, Claudius also hints that Hamlet's death will serve as such a monument.) **272 hour of quiet** time free of conflict **5.2. Location: The castle. 1 see the other** hear the other news **6 mutines** mutineers. **bilboes** shackles. **Rashly** on impulse (This adverb goes with lines 12 ff.) **7 know** acknowledge **8 indiscretion** lack of foresight and judgment (not an indiscreet act) **9 pall** fail, falter, go stale **learn** teach **11 Rough-hew** shape roughly

HORATIO.   That is most certain.

HAMLET. Up from my cabin,
  My sea-gown° scarfed° about me, in the dark
  Groped I to find out them,° had my desire,
  Fingered° their packet, and in fine° withdrew   15
  To mine own room again, making so bold,
  My fears forgetting manners, to unseal
  Their grand commission; where I found, Horatio—
  Ah, royal knavery!—an exact command,
  Larded° with many several° sorts of reasons   20
  Importing° Denmark's health and England's too,
  With, ho! such bugs° and goblins in my life,°
  That on the supervise,° no leisure bated,°
  No, not to stay° the grinding of the ax,
  My head should be struck off.

HORATIO.   Is't possible?   25

HAMLET [*giving a document*].
  Here's the commission. Read it at more leisure.
  But wilt thou hear now how I did proceed?

HORATIO. I beseech you.

HAMLET. Being thus benetted round with villainies—
  Ere I could make a prologue to my brains,   30
  They had begun the play°—I sat me down,
  Devised a new commission, wrote it fair.°
  I once did hold it, as our statists° do,
  A baseness° to write fair, and labored much
  How to forget that learning; but, sir, now   35
  It did me yeoman's° service. Wilt thou know
  Th' effect° of what I wrote?

HORATIO.   Ay, good my lord.

HAMLET. An earnest conjuration° from the King,
  As England was his faithful tributary,
  As love between them like the palm° might flourish,   40
  As peace should still° her wheaten garland° wear
  And stand a comma° 'tween their amities,
  And many suchlike "as"es° of great charge,°
  That on the view and knowing of these contents,

13 sea-gown seaman's coat   **scarfed** loosely wrapped   **14 them** i.e., Rosencrantz and Guildenstern   **15 Fingered** pilfered, pinched   **in fine** finally, in conclusion   **20 Larded** garnished   **several** different   **21 Importing** relating to   **22 bugs** bugbears, hobgoblins **in my life** i.e., to be feared if I were allowed to live   **23 supervise** reading   **leisure bated** delay allowed   **24 stay** await   **30–31 Ere . . . play** before I could consciously turn my brain to the matter, it had started working on a plan   **32 fair** in a clear hand   **33 statists** statesmen   **34 baseness** i.e., lower-class trait   **36 yeoman's** i.e., substantial, faithful, loyal   **37 effect** purport   **38 conjuration** entreaty   **40 palm** (An image of health; see Psalm 92:12)   **41 still** always   **wheaten garland** (Symbolic of fruitful agriculture, of peace and plenty.)   **42 comma** (Indicating continuity, link.)   **43 "as"es** (1) the "whereases" of a formal document (2) asses   **charge** (1) import (2) burden (appropriate to asses)

Without debatement further more or less, 45
He should those bearers put to sudden death,
Not shriving time° allowed.
HORATIO.   How was this sealed?
HAMLET. Why, even in that was heaven ordinant.°
I had my father's signet° in my purse,
Which was the model° of that Danish seal; 50
Folded the writ° up in the form of th' other,
Subscribed° it, gave 't th' impression,° placed it safely,
The changeling° never known. Now, the next day
Was our sea fight, and what to this was sequent°
Thou knowest already. 55
HORATIO. So Guildenstern and Rosencrantz go to 't.
HAMLET. Why, man, they did make love to this employment.
They are not near my conscience. Their defeat°
Does by their own insinuation° grow.
'Tis dangerous when the baser° nature comes 60
Between the pass° and fell° incensèd points
Of mighty opposites.°
HORATIO.   Why, what a king is this!
HAMLET. Does it not, think thee, stand me now upon°—
He that hath killed my king and whored my mother,
Popped in between th' election° and my hopes, 65
Thrown out his angle° for my proper° life,
And with such cozenage°—is 't not perfect conscience
To quit° him with this arm? And is 't not to be damned
To let this canker° of our nature come
In° further evil? 70
HORATIO. It must be shortly known to him from England
What is the issue of the business there.
HAMLET. It will be short. The interim is mine,
And a man's life's no more than to say "one."°
But I am very sorry, good Horatio, 75
That to Laertes I forgot myself,
For by the image of my cause I see
The portraiture of his. I'll court his favors.
But, sure, the bravery° of his grief did put me
Into a tow'ring passion.

47 shriving time time for confession and absolution   **48 ordinant** directing   **49 signet**
small seal   **50 model** replica   **51 writ** writing   **52 Subscribed** signed (with forged signature)   **impression** i.e., with a wax seal   **53 changeling** i.e., substituted letter. (Literally, a fairy child substituted for a human one.)   **54 was sequent** followed   **58 defeat** destruction   **59 insinuation** intrusive intervention, sticking their noses in my business
60 baser of lower social station   **61 pass** thrust   **fell** fierce   **62 opposites** antagonists
63 stand me now upon become incumbent on me now   **65 election** (The Danish
monarch was "elected" by a small number of high-ranking electors.)   **66 angle** fishhook.
proper very   **67 cozenage** trickery   **68 quit** requite, pay back   **69 canker** ulcer
69–70 come In grow into   **74 a man's ... "one"** one's whole life occupies such a short
time, only as long as it takes to count to 1   **79 bravery** bravado

HORATIO.   Peace, who comes here?   80

*Enter a Courtier [*OSRIC*].*

OSRIC. Your lordship is right welcome back to Denmark.

HAMLET. I humbly thank you, sir. [*To* HORATIO.] Dost know this water
    fly?

HORATIO. No, my good lord.

HAMLET. Thy state is the more gracious, for 'tis a vice to know him. He   85
    hath much land, and fertile. Let a beast be lord of beasts, and his
    crib° shall stand at the King's mess.° 'Tis a chuff,° but, as I say, spa-
    cious in the possession of dirt.

OSRIC. Sweet lord, if your lordship were at leisure, I should impart a thing
    to you from His Majesty.   90

HAMLET. I will receive it, sir, with all diligence of spirit.
    Put your bonnet° to his° right use; 'tis for the head.

OSRIC. I thank your lordship, it is very hot.

HAMLET. No, believe me, 'tis very cold. The wind is northerly.

OSRIC. It is indifferent° cold, my lord, indeed.   95

HAMLET. But yet methinks it is very sultry and hot for my complexion.°

OSRIC. Exceedingly, my lord. It is very sultry, as 'twere—I cannot tell how.
    My lord, His Majesty bade me signify to you that 'a has laid a great
    wager on your head. Sir, this is the matter—

HAMLET. I beseech you, remember.   100

*[*HAMLET *moves him to put on his hat.]*

OSRIC. Nay, good my lord; for my ease,° in good faith. Sir, here is newly
    come to court Laertes—believe me, an absolute° gentleman, full of
    most excellent differences,° of very soft society° and great show-
    ing.° Indeed, to speak feelingly° of him, he is the card° or calendar°
    of gentry,° for you shall find in him the continent of what part a   105
    gentleman would see.°

HAMLET. Sir, his definement° suffers no perdition° in you,° though I know
    to divide him inventorially° would dozy° th' arithmetic of memory,
    and yet but yaw° neither° in respect of° his quick sail. But, in the
    verity of extolment,° I take him to be a soul of great article,° and his   110

---

87 crib manger   **86–87 Let . . . mess** i.e., if a man, no matter how beastlike, is as rich in
livestock and possessions as Osric, he may eat at the King's table   **87 chuff** boor, churl
(The Second Quarto spelling, *chough,* is a variant spelling that also suggests the meaning
here of "chattering jackdaw.")   **92 bonnet** any kind of cap or hat   **his** its   **95 indifferent** somewhat   **96 complexion** temperament   **101 for my ease** (A conventional reply
declining the invitation to put his hat back on.)   **102 absolute** perfect   **103 differences**
special qualities   **soft society** agreeable manners   **103–104 great showing** distinguished appearance   **104 feelingly** with just perception   **card** chart, map
104–105 calendar guide   **gentry** good breeding   **105–106 the continent . . . see** one
who contains in him all the qualities a gentleman would like to see (A *continent* is that
which contains.)   **107 definement** definition. (Hamlet proceeds to mock Osric by
throwing his lofty diction back at him.)   **perdition** loss, diminution   **you** your description   **108 divide him inventorially** enumerate his graces   **dozy** dizzy   **109 yaw**
swing unsteadily off course (Said of a ship.)   **neither** for all that   **in respect of** in comparison with   **110 in . . . extolment** in true praise (of him)   **110–111 of great article**
one with many articles in his inventory

infusion° of such dearth and rareness° as, to make true diction° of him, his semblable° is his mirror and who else would trace° him his umbrage,° nothing more.

OSRIC. Your lordship speaks most infallibly of him.

HAMLET. The concernancy,° sir? Why do we wrap the gentleman in our more rawer breath?° 115

OSRIC. Sir?

HORATIO. Is 't not possible to understand in another tongue?° You will do 't,° sir, really.

HAMLET. What imports the nomination° of this gentleman? 120

OSRIC. Of Laertes?

HORATIO [*to* HAMLET]. His purse is empty already; all 's golden words are spent.

HAMLET. Of him, sir.

OSRIC. I know you are not ignorant— 125

HAMLET. I would you did, sir. Yet in faith if you did, it would not much approve° me. Well, sir?

OSRIC. You are not ignorant of what excellence Laertes is—

HAMLET. I dare not confess that, lest I should compare with him in excellence. But to know a man well were to know himself.° 130

OSRIC. I mean, sir, for° his weapon; but in the imputation laid on him by them,° in his meed° he's unfellowed.°

HAMLET. What's his weapon?

OSRIC. Rapier and dagger.

HAMLET. That's two of his weapons—but well.° 135

OSRIC. The King, sir, hath wagered with him six Barbary horses, against the which he° has impawned,° as I take it, six French rapiers and poniards,° with their assigns,° as girdle, hangers,° and so.° Three of the carriages,° in faith, are very dear to fancy,° very responsive° to the hilts, most delicate° carriages, and of very liberal conceit.° 140

---

111 infusion essence, character infused into him by nature **dearth and rareness** rarity **111–112 make true diction** speak truly **112 semblable** only true likeness **112–113 who . . . trace** any other person who would wish to follow **113 umbrage** shadow **115 concernancy** import, relevance **116 rawer breath** unrefined speech that can only come short in praising him **118 to understand . . . tongue** i.e., for you, Osric, to understand when someone else speaks your language. (Horatio twits Osric for not being able to understand the kind of flowery speech he himself uses, when Hamlet speaks in such a vein. Alternatively, all this could be said to Hamlet.) **118–119 You will do 't** i.e., you can if you try, or, you may well have to try (to speak plainly) **120 nomination** naming **127 approve** commend **129–130 I dare . . . himself** I dare not boast of knowing Laertes' excellence lest I seem to imply a comparable excellence in myself. Certainly, to know another person well, one must know oneself. **131 for** i.e., with **131–132 imputation . . . them** reputation given him by others **132 meed** merit **unfellowed** unmatched **135 but well** but never mind **137 he** i.e., Laertes. **impawned** staked, wagered **138 poniards** daggers **assigns** appurtenances **hangers** straps on the sword belt (*girdle*), from which the sword hung **and so** and so on **139 carriages** (An affected way of saying *hangers;* literally, gun carriages.) **dear to fancy** delightful to the fancy **responsive** corresponding closely, matching or well adjusted **140 delicate** (i.e., in workmanship.) **liberal conceit** elaborate design

HAMLET. What call you the carriages?

HORATIO [*to* HAMLET]. I knew you must be edified by the margent° ere you
   had done.

OSRIC. The carriages, sir, are the hangers.

HAMLET. The phrase would be more germane to the matter if we could   145
   carry a cannon by our sides; I would it might be hangers till then.
   But, on: six Barbary horses against six French swords, their assigns,
   and three liberal-conceited carriages; that's the French bet against
   the Danish. Why is this impawned, as you call it?

OSRIC. The King, sir, hath laid,° sir, that in a dozen passes° between your-   150
   self and him, he shall not exceed you three hits. He hath laid on
   twelve for nine, and it would come to immediate trial, if your lordship would vouchsafe the answer.°

HAMLET. How if I answer no?

OSRIC. I mean, my lord, the opposition of your person in trial.   155

HAMLET. Sir, I will walk here in the hall. If it please His Majesty, it is the
   breathing time° of day with me. Let° the foils be brought, the gentleman willing, and the King hold his purpose. I will win for him an
   I can; if not, I will gain nothing but my shame and the odd hits.

OSRIC. Shall I deliver you° so?   160

HAMLET. To this effect, sir—after what flourish your nature will.

OSRIC. I commend° my duty to your lordship.

HAMLET. Yours, yours. [*Exit* OSRIC.] 'A does well to commend it himself;
   there are no tongues else for 's turn.°

HORATIO. This lapwing° runs away with the shell on his head.   165

HAMLET. 'A did comply with his dug° before 'a sucked it. Thus has he—
   and many more of the same breed that I know the drossy° age
   dotes on—only got the tune° of the time and, out of an habit of encounter,° a kind of yeasty° collection,° which carries them through
   and through the most fanned and winnowed opinions;° and do°   170
   but blow them to their trial, the bubbles are out.°

---

142 margent margin of a book, place for explanatory notes   **150 laid** wagered   **passes**
bouts (The odds of the betting are hard to explain. Possibly the King bets that Hamlet will
win at least five out of twelve, at which point Laertes raises the odds against himself by
betting he will win nine.)   **153 vouchsafe the answer** be so good as to accept the challenge (Hamlet deliberately takes the phrase in its literal sense of replying.)   **157 breathing time** exercise period   **Let** i.e., if   **160 deliver you** report what you say   **162 commend** commit to your favor (A conventional salutation, but Hamlet wryly uses a more
literal meaning, "recommend," "praise," in line 163.)   **164 for 's turn** for his purposes,
i.e., to do it for him   **165 lapwing** (A proverbial type of youthful forwardness. Also, a
bird that draws intruders away from its nest and was thought to run about with its head in
the shell when newly hatched; a seeming reference to Osric's hat.)   **166 comply . . .
dug** observe ceremonious formality toward his nurse's or mother's teat
167 drossy laden with scum and impurities, frivolous   **168 tune** temper, mood, manner
of speech   **168–169 an habit of encounter** a demeanor in conversing (with courtiers of
his own kind)   **169 yeasty** frothy   **collection** i.e., of current phrases   **169–170 carries . . . opinions** sustains them right through the scrutiny of persons whose opinions are
select and refined (Literally, like grain separated from its chaff. Osric is both the chaff and
the bubbly froth on the surface of the liquor that is soon blown away.)   **171 and do** yet
do   **blow . . . out** test them by merely blowing on them, and their bubbles burst

Enter a LORD.

LORD. My lord, His Majesty commended him to you by young Osric, who
    brings back to him that you attend him in the hall. He sends to
    know if your pleasure hold to play with Laertes, or that° you will
    take longer time.   175
HAMLET. I am constant to my purposes; they follow the King's pleasure. If
    his fitness speaks, mine is ready;° now or whensoever, provided I
    be so able as now.
LORD. The King and Queen and all are coming down.
HAMLET. In happy time.°   180
LORD. The Queen desires you to use some gentle entertainment° to
    Laertes before you fall to play.
HAMLET. She well instructs me.   [*Exit* LORD.]
HORATIO. You will lose, my lord.
HAMLET. I do not think so. Since he went into France, I have been in con-   185
    tinual practice; I shall win at the odds. But thou wouldst not think
    how ill all's here about my heart; but it is no matter.
HORATIO. Nay, good my lord—
HAMLET. It is but foolery, but it is such a kind of gaingiving° as would per-
    haps trouble a woman.   190
HORATIO. If your mind dislike anything, obey it. I will forestall their repair°
    hither and say you are not fit.
HAMLET. Not a whit, we defy augury. There is special providence in the fall
    of a sparrow. If it be now, 'tis not to come; if it be not to come, it
    will be now; if it be not now, yet it will come. The readiness is all.   195
    Since no man of aught he leaves knows, what is 't to leave betimes?
    Let be.°

    A table prepared. [Enter] trumpets, drums, and officers with cush-
ions; KING, QUEEN, *[*OSRIC,*] and all the state; foils, daggers, [and wine*
borne in;] and LAERTES.

KING. Come, Hamlet, come and take this hand from me.

    [The KING *puts* LAERTES' *hand into* HAMLET*'s.]*

HAMLET [*to* LAERTES]. Give me your pardon, sir. I have done you wrong,
    But pardon 't as you are a gentleman.   200
    This presence° knows,
    And you must needs have heard, how I am punished°
    With a sore distraction. What I have done
    That might your nature, honor, and exception°
    Roughly awake, I here proclaim was madness.   205
    Was 't Hamlet wronged Laertes? Never Hamlet.
    If Hamlet from himself be ta'en away,
    And when he's not himself does wrong Laertes,

---

174 that if **177 If . . . ready** if he declares his readiness, my convenience waits on
his **180 In happy time** (A phrase of courtesy indicating that the time is convenient.)
181 entertainment greeting **189 gaingiving** misgiving **191–192 repair** coming
196–197 Since . . . Let be since no one has knowledge of what he is leaving behind, what
does an early death matter after all? Enough; don't struggle against it **201 presence** royal
assembly **202 punished** afflicted **204 exception** disapproval

Then Hamlet does it not, Hamlet denies it.
Who does it, then? His madness. If 't be so,   210
Hamlet is of the faction° that is wronged;
His madness is poor Hamlet's enemy.
Sir, in this audience
Let my disclaiming from a purposed evil
Free me so far in your most generous thoughts   215
That I have° shot my arrow o'er the house
And hurt my brother.

LAERTES.   I am satisfied in nature,°
Whose motive° in this case should stir me most
To my revenge. But in my terms of honor
I stand aloof, and will no reconcilement   220
Till by some elder masters of known honor
I have a voice° and precedent of peace°
To keep my name ungored.° But till that time
I do receive your offered love like love,
And will not wrong it.

HAMLET.   I embrace it freely,   225
And will this brothers' wager frankly° play.—
Give us the foils. Come on.

LAERTES.   Come, one for me.

HAMLET.   I'll be your foil,° Laertes. In mine ignorance
Your skill shall, like a star i' the darkest night,
Stick fiery off° indeed.

LAERTES.   You mock me, sir.   230

HAMLET.   No, by this hand.

KING.   Give them the foils, young Osric. Cousin Hamlet,
You know the wager?

HAMLET.   Very well, my lord.
Your Grace has laid the odds o'° the weaker side.

KING.   I do not fear it; I have seen you both.   235
But since he is bettered,° we have therefore odds.

LAERTES.   This is too heavy. Let me see another.

                              [*He exchanges his foil for another.*]

HAMLET.   This likes me° well. These foils have all a length?

                              [*They prepare to play.*]

OSRIC.   Ay, my good lord.

KING.   Set me the stoups of wine upon that table.   240
If Hamlet give the first or second hit,

---

211 faction party   **216 That I have** as if I had   **217 in nature** i.e., as to my personal
feelings   **218 motive** prompting   **222 voice** authoritative pronouncement.   **of peace**
for reconciliation   **223 name ungored** reputation unwounded   **226 frankly** without
ill feeling or the burden of rancor   **228 foil** thin metal background which sets a jewel off
(with pun on the blunted rapier for fencing)   **230 Stick fiery off** stand out brilliantly
234 laid the odds o' bet on, backed   **236 is bettered** has improved; is the odds-on favorite. (Laertes' handicap is the "three hits" specified in line 151.)   **238 likes me**
pleases me

Or quit in answer of the third exchange,°
Let all the battlements their ordnance fire.
The King shall drink to Hamlet's better breath,°
And in the cup an union° shall he throw   245
Richer than that which four successive kings
In Denmark's crown have worn. Give me the cups,
And let the kettle° to the trumpet speak,
The trumpet to the cannoneer without,
The cannons to the heavens, the heaven to earth,   250
"Now the King drinks to Hamlet." Come, begin.

Trumpets the while.

And you, the judges, bear a wary eye.

HAMLET. Come on, sir.

LAERTES. Come, my lord.   [*They play.* HAMLET *scores a hit.*]

HAMLET. One.   255

LAERTES. No.

HAMLET. Judgment.

OSRIC.   A hit, a very palpable hit.

Drum, trumpets, and shot. Flourish. A piece goes off.

LAERTES. Well, again.

KING. Stay, give me drink. Hamlet, this pearl is thine.

[He drinks, and throws a pearl in HAMLET'*s cup.]*

Here's to thy health. Give him the cup.   260

HAMLET. I'll play this bout first. Set it by awhile.
Come. [*They play.*] Another hit; what say you?

LAERTES. A touch, a touch, I do confess 't.

KING. Our son shall win.

QUEEN.   He's fat° and scant of breath.
Here, Hamlet, take my napkin,° rub thy brows.   265
The Queen carouses° to thy fortune, Hamlet.

HAMLET. Good, madam!

KING. Gertrude, do not drink.

QUEEN. I will, my lord, I pray you pardon me.   [*She drinks.*]

KING [*aside*]. It is the poisoned cup. It is too late.   270

HAMLET. I dare not drink yet, madam; by and by.

QUEEN. Come, let me wipe thy face.

LAERTES [*to* KING]. My lord, I'll hit him now.

KING.   I do not think 't.

LAERTES [*aside*]. And yet it is almost against my conscience.

HAMLET. Come, for the third, Laertes. You do but dally.   275
I pray you, pass° with your best violence;
I am afeard you make a wanton of me.°

---

242 Or . . . exchange i.e., or requites Laertes in the third bout for having won the first
two **244 better breath** improved vigor **245 union** pearl (So called, according to
Pliny's *Natural History,* 9, because pearls are *unique,* never identical.) **248 kettle**
kettledrum **264 fat** not physically fit, out of training **265 napkin** handkerchief
266 carouses drinks a toast **276 pass** thrust **277 make . . . me** i.e., treat me like a
spoiled child, trifle with me

LAERTES. Say you so? Come on.   [*They play.*]

OSRIC. Nothing neither way.

LAERTES. Have at you now!

   [LAERTES *wounds* HAMLET; *then, in scuffling, they change rapiers,°*
   and HAMLET *wounds* LAERTES.]

KING.   Part them! They are incensed.   280

HAMLET. Nay, come, again.   [*The* QUEEN *falls.*]

OSRIC.   Look to the Queen there, ho!

HORATIO. They bleed on both sides. How is it, my lord?

OSRIC. How is 't, Laertes?

LAERTES. Why, as a woodcock° to mine own springe,° Osric;
   I am justly killed with mine own treachery.   285

HAMLET. How does the Queen?

KING.   She swoons to see them bleed.

QUEEN. No, no, the drink, the drink—O my dear Hamlet—
   The drink, the drink! I am poisoned.   [*She dies.*]

HAMLET. O villainy! Ho, let the door be locked!
   Treachery! Seek it out.   290

                [LAERTES *falls. Exit* OSRIC.]

LAERTES. It is here, Hamlet. Hamlet, thou art slain.
   No med'cine in the world can do thee good;
   In thee there is not half an hour's life.
   The treacherous instrument is in thy hand,
   Unbated° and envenomed. The foul practice°   295
   Hath turned itself on me. Lo, here I lie,
   Never to rise again. Thy mother's poisoned.
   I can no more. The King, the King's to blame.

HAMLET. The point envenomed too? Then, venom, to thy work.

                [*He stabs the* KING.]

ALL. Treason! Treason!   300

KING. O, yet defend me, friends! I am but hurt.

HAMLET [*forcing the* KING *to drink.*]
   Here, thou incestuous, murderous, damnèd Dane,
   Drink off this potion. Is thy union° here?
   Follow my mother.   [*The* KING *dies.*]

LAERTES.   He is justly served.
   It is a poison tempered° by himself.   305
   Exchange forgiveness with me, noble Hamlet.
   Mine and my father's death come not upon thee,
   Nor thine on me!   [*He dies.*]

HAMLET. Heaven make thee free of it! I follow thee.
   I am dead, Horatio. Wretched Queen, adieu!   310

---

280 s.d. in scuffling, they change rapiers (This stage direction occurs in the Folio. According to a widespread stage tradition, Hamlet receives a scratch, realizes that Laertes'
sword is unbated, and accordingly forces an exchange.)   **284 woodcock** a bird, a type of
stupidity or as a decoy   **springe** trap, snare   **295 Unbated** not blunted with a button
practice plot   **303 union** pearl (See line 245; with grim puns on the word's other meanings: marriage, shared death.)   **305 tempered** mixed

You that look pale and tremble at this chance,°
That are but mutes° or audience to this act,
Had I but time—as this fell° sergeant,° Death,
Is strict° in his arrest°—O, I could tell you—
But let it be. Horatio, I am dead;   315
Thou livest. Report me and my cause aright
To the unsatisfied.

HORATIO.   Never believe it.
I am more an antique Roman° than a Dane.
Here's yet some liquor left.

[*He attempts to drink from the poisoned cup.* HAMLET *prevents him.*]

HAMLET.   As thou'rt a man,
Give me the cup! Let go! By heaven, I'll ha 't.   320
O God, Horatio, what a wounded name,
Things standing thus unknown, shall I leave behind me!
If thou didst ever hold me in thy heart,
Absent thee from felicity awhile,
And in this harsh world draw thy breath in pain   325
To tell my story. *A march afar off [and a volley within].*
What warlike noise is this?

Enter OSRIC.

OSRIC. Young Fortinbras, with conquest come from Poland,
To th' ambassadors of England gives
This warlike volley.

HAMLET.   O, I die, Horatio!
The potent poison quite o'ercrows° my spirit.   330
I cannot live to hear the news from England,
But I do prophesy th' election lights
On Fortinbras. He has my dying voice.°
So tell him, with th' occurents° more and less
Which have solicited°—the rest is silence.   [*He dies.*]   335

HORATIO. Now cracks a noble heart. Good night, sweet prince,
And flights of angels sing thee to thy rest!

[*March within.*]

Why does the drum come hither?

Enter FORTINBRAS, *with the [English] Ambassadors
[with drum, colors, and attendants].*

FORTINBRAS. Where is this sight?

HORATIO.   What is it you would see?
If aught of woe or wonder, cease your search.   340

---

311 chance mischance   **312 mutes** silent observers (Literally, actors with nonspeaking
parts.)   **313 fell** cruel   **sergeant** sheriffs officer   **314 strict** (1) severely just (2) un-
avoidable   **arrest** (1) taking into custody (2) stopping my speech   **318 Roman** (Suicide
was an honorable choice for many Romans as an alternative to a dishonorable life.)
330 o'ercrows triumphs over (like the winner in a cockfight)   **333 voice** vote   **334 oc-
currents** events, incidents   **335 solicited** moved, urged (Hamlet doesn't finish saying
what the events have prompted—presumably, his acts of vengeance, or his reporting of
those events to Fortinbras.)

FORTINBRAS.   This quarry° cries on havoc.° O proud Death,
　　　　What feast° is toward° in thine eternal cell,
　　　　That thou so many princes at a shot
　　　　So bloodily hast struck?

FIRST AMBASSADOR.　　　　　　The sight is dismal,
　　　　And our affairs from England come too late.　　　　　　　　345
　　　　The ears are senseless that should give us hearing,
　　　　To tell him his commandment is fulfilled,
　　　　That Rosencrantz and Guildenstern are dead.
　　　　Where should we have our thanks?

HORATIO.　　　　　　　　　　　Not from his° mouth,
　　　　Had it th' ability of life to thank you.　　　　　　　　　350
　　　　He never gave commandment for their death.
　　　　But since, so jump° upon this bloody question,°
　　　　You from the Polack wars, and you from England,
　　　　And here arrived, give order that these bodies
　　　　High on a stage° be placèd to the view,　　　　　　　　355
　　　　And let me speak to th' yet unknowing world
　　　　How these things came about. So shall you hear
　　　　Of carnal, bloody, and unnatural acts,
　　　　Of accidental judgments,° casual° slaughters,
　　　　Of deaths put on° by cunning and forced cause,°　　　　360
　　　　And, in this upshot, purposes mistook
　　　　Fall'n on th' inventors' heads. All this can I
　　　　Truly deliver.

FORTINBRAS.　　　　Let us haste to hear it,
　　　　And call the noblest to the audience.
　　　　For me, with sorrow I embrace my fortune.　　　　　　365
　　　　I have some rights of memory° in this kingdom,
　　　　Which now to claim my vantage° doth invite me.

HORATIO.   Of that I shall have also cause to speak,
　　　　And from his mouth whose voice will draw on more.°
　　　　But let this same be presently° performed,　　　　　　370
　　　　Even while men's minds are wild, lest more mischance
　　　　On° plots and errors happen.

FORTINBRAS.　　　　　　　　　Let four captains
　　　　Bear Hamlet, like a soldier, to the stage,
　　　　For he was likely, had he been put on,°
　　　　To have proved most royal; and for his passage,°　　　375
　　　　The soldiers' music and the rite of war

341 **quarry** heap of dead   **cries on havoc** proclaims a general slaughter   342 **feast** i.e., Death feasting on those who have fallen   **toward** in preparation   349 **his** i.e., Claudius'   352 **jump** precisely, immediately   **question** dispute, affair   355 **stage** platform   359 **judgments** retributions   **casual** occurring by chance   360 **put on** instigated   **forced cause** contrivance   366 **of memory** traditional, remembered, unforgotten   367 **vantage** favorable opportunity   369 **voice . . . more** vote will influence still others   370 **presently** immediately   372 **On** on the basis of; on top of   374 **put on** i.e., invested in royal office and so put to the test   375 **passage** i.e., from life to death

Speak° loudly for him.
Take up the bodies. Such a sight as this
Becomes the field,° but here shows much amiss.
Go bid the soldiers shoot.   380
Exeunt [marching, bearing off the dead bodies; a peal of ordnance is shot off].

✎ Topics for Critical Thinking and Writing

Act 1

1. The first scene (like many other scenes in this play) is full of expressions of uncertainty. What are some are these uncertainties? The Ghost first appears at 1.1.42. Does his appearance surprise us, or have we been prepared for it? Or is there both preparation and surprise? Do the last four speeches of 1.1 help to introduce a note of hope? If so, how?

2. Does the King's opening speech in 1.2 reveal him to be an accomplished public speaker—or are lines 10-14 offensive? In his second speech (lines 41-49), what is the effect of naming Laertes four times? Claudius sometimes uses the royal pronouns ("we," "our"), sometimes the more intimate "I" and "my." Study his use of these in lines 1-4 and in 106-117. What do you think he is getting at?

3. Hamlet's first soliloquy (1.2.129-159) reveals that more than just his father's death distresses him. Be as specific as possible about the causes of Hamlet's anguish here. What traits does Hamlet reveal in his conversation with Horatio (1.2.160-258)?

4. What do you make of Polonius's advice to Laertes (1.3.55-81)? Is it sound? Sound advice, but here uttered by a fool? Ignoble advice? How would one follow the advice of line 78: "to thine own self be true"? In his words to Ophelia in 1.3.102-136, what does he reveal about himself?

5. Can 1.4.17-38 reasonably be taken as a speech on the "tragic flaw"? (On this idea, see page 268.) Or is the passage a much more limited discussion, a comment simply on Danish drinking habits?

6. Hamlet is convinced in 1.5.93-104 that the Ghost has told the truth, indeed, the only important truth. But do we detect in 105-112 a hint of a tone suggesting that Hamlet delights in hating villainy? If so, can it be said that later this delight grows, and that in some scenes (e.g., 3.3) we feel that Hamlet has almost become a diabolic revenger? Explain.

Act 2

1. Characterize Polonius on the basis of 2.1.1-76.

2. In light of what we have seen of Hamlet, is Ophelia's report of his strange behavior when he visits her understandable?

3. Why does 2.2.33-34 seem almost comic? How do these lines help us to form a view about Rosencrantz and Guildenstern?

---

377 Speak (let them) speak   **379 Becomes the field** suits the field of battle

4. Is "the hellish Pyrrhus" (2.2.422) Hamlet's version of Claudius? Or is he Hamlet, who soon will be responsible for the deaths of Polonius, Rosencrantz and Guildenstern, Claudius, Gertrude, Ophelia, and Laertes? Explain.

5. Is the First Player's speech (2.2.427ff) a huffing speech? If so, why? To distinguish it from the poetry of the play itself? To characterize the bloody deeds that Hamlet cannot descend to?

6. In 2.2.504–42 Hamlet rebukes himself for not acting. Why has he not acted? Because he is a coward (line 531)? Because he has a conscience? Because no action can restore his father and his mother's purity? Because he doubts the Ghost? What reason(s) can you offer?

Act 3

1. What do you make out of Hamlet's assertion to Ophelia: "I loved you not" (3.1.118)? Of his characterization of himself as full of "offenses" (3.1.121–27)? Why is Hamlet so harsh to Ophelia?

2. In 3.3.36–72 Claudius's conscience afflicts him. But is he repentant? What makes you say so?

3. Is Hamlet other than abhorrent in 3.3.73–96? Do we want him to kill Claudius at this moment, when Claudius (presumably with his back to Hamlet) is praying? Why?

4. The Ghost speaks of Hamlet's "almost blunted purpose" (3.4.115). Is the accusation fair? Explain.

5. How would you characterize the Hamlet who speaks in 3.4.209–24?

Act 4

1. Is Gertrude protecting Hamlet when she says he is mad (4.1.7), or does she believe that he is mad? If she believes he is mad, does it follow that she no longer feels ashamed and guilty? Explain.

2. Why should Hamlet hide Polonius's body (in 4.2)? Is he feigning madness? Is he on the edge of madness? Explain.

3. How can we explain Hamlet's willingness to go to England (4.3.52)?

4. Judging from 4.5, what has driven Ophelia mad? Is Laertes heroic, or somewhat foolish? Consider also the way Claudius treats him in 4.7.

Act 5

1. Would anything be lost if the gravediggers in 5.1 were omitted?

2. To what extent do we judge Hamlet severely for sending Rosencrantz and Guildenstern to their deaths, as he reports in 5.2? On the whole, do we think of Hamlet as an intriguer? What other intrigues has he engendered? How successful were they?

3. Does 5.2.193–97 show a paralysis of the will, or a wise recognition that more is needed than mere human scheming? Explain.

4. Does 5.2.280 suggest that Laertes takes advantage of a momentary pause and unfairly stabs Hamlet? Is the exchange of weapons accidental, or does Hamlet (as in Olivier's film version), realizing that he has been betrayed, deliberately get possession of Laertes's deadly weapon?

5. Fortinbras is often cut from the play. How much is lost by the cut? Explain.

6. Fortinbras gives Hamlet a soldier's funeral. Is this ridiculous? Can it fairly be said that, in a sense, Hamlet has been at war? Explain.

General Questions

1. Hamlet in 5.2.10–11 speaks of a "divinity that shapes our ends." To what extent does "divinity" (or Fate or mysterious Chance) play a role in the happenings?
2. How do Laertes, Fortinbras, and Horatio help to define Hamlet for us?
3. T. S. Eliot says (in "Shakespeare and the Stoicism of Seneca") that Hamlet, having made a mess, "dies fairly well pleased with himself." Evaluate.

ERNEST JONES
Hamlet and the Oedipus Complex*

In short, the whole picture presented by Hamlet, his deep depression, the hopeless note in his attitude towards the world and towards the value of life, his dread of death, his repeated reference to bad dreams, his self-accusations, his desperate efforts to get away from the thoughts of his duty, and his vain attempts to find an excuse for his procrastination: all this unequivocally points to a *tortured conscience,* to some hidden ground for shirking his task, a ground which he dare not or cannot avow to himself.

Extensive studies of the past half century, inspired by Freud, have taught us that a psychoneurosis means a state of mind where the person is unduly, and often painfully, driven or thwarted by the "unconscious" part of his mind, that buried part that was once the infant's mind and still lives on side by side with the adult mentality that has developed out of it and should have taken its place. It signifies *internal* mental conflict. We have here the reason why it is impossible to discuss intelligently the state of mind of anyone suffering from a psychoneurosis, whether the description is of a living person or an imagined one, without correlating the manifestations with what must have operated in his infancy and is *still operating.* That is what I propose to attempt here.

For some deep-seated reason, which is to him unacceptable, Hamlet is plunged into anguish at the thought of his father being replaced in his mother's affections by someone else. It is as if his devotion to his mother had made him so jealous for her affection that he had found it hard enough to share this even with his father and could not endure to share it with still another man. Against this thought, however, suggestive as it is, may be urged three objections. First, if it were in itself a full statement of the matter, Hamlet would have been aware of the jealousy, whereas we have concluded that the mental process we are seeking is hidden from him. Secondly, we see in it no evidence of the arousing of an old and forgotten memory. And, thirdly, Hamlet is being deprived by Claudius of no greater share in the Queen's affection than he had been by his own father, for the two brothers made exactly similar claims in this respect—namely, those of a loved husband. The last-named objection, however, leads us to the heart of the

---

*The title is the editors'. Footnotes are abridged.

situation. How if, in fact, Hamlet had in years gone by, as a child, bitterly resented having had to share his mother's affection even with his own father, had regarded him as a rival, and had secretly wished him out of the way so that he might enjoy undisputed and undisturbed the monopoly of that affection? If such thoughts had been present in his mind in childhood days they evidently would have been "repressed," and all traces of them obliterated, by filial piety and other educative influences. The actual realization of his early wish in the death of his father at the hands of a jealous rival would then have stimulated into activity these "repressed" memories, which would have produced, in the form of depression and other suffering, an obscure aftermath of his childhood's conflict. This is at all events the mechanism that is actually found in the real Hamlets who are investigated psychologically.

The explanation, therefore, of the delay and self-frustration exhibited in the endeavour to fulfil his father's demand for vengeance is that to Hamlet the thought of incest and parricide combined is too intolerable to be borne. One part of him tries to carry out the task, the other flinches inexorably from the thought of it. How fain would he blot it out in that "bestial oblivion" which unfortunately for him his conscience contemns. He is torn and tortured in an insoluble inner conflict.

Now comes the father's death and the mother's second marriage. The association of the idea of sexuality with his mother, buried since infancy, can no longer be concealed from his consciousness. As Bradley well says: "Her son was forced to see in her action not only an astounding shallowness of feeling, but an eruption of coarse sensuality, 'rank and gross,' speeding post-haste to its horrible delight." Feelings which once, in the infancy of long ago, were pleasurable desires can now, because of his repressions, only fill him with repulsion. The long "repressed" desire to take his father's place in his mother's affection is stimulated to unconscious activity by the sight of someone usurping this place exactly as he himself had once longed to do. More, this someone was a member of the same family, so that the actual usurpation further resembled the imaginary one in being incestuous. Without his being in the least aware of it these ancient desires are ringing in his mind, are once more struggling to find conscious expression, and need such an expenditure of energy again to "repress" them that he is reduced to the deplorable mental state he himself so vividly depicts.

There follows the Ghost's announcement that the father's death was a willed one, was due to murder. Hamlet, having at the moment his mind filled with natural indignation at the news, answers normally enough with the cry (Act I, Sc. 5):

Haste me to know 't, that I with wings as swift
As meditation or the thoughts of love,
May sweep to my revenge.

The momentous words follow revealing who was the guilty person, namely a relative who had committed the deed at the bidding of lust.[1] Hamlet's second guilty wish had thus also been realized by his uncle, namely to procure the fulfilment of the first—the possession of the mother—by a personal deed, in fact by

---

[1] It is not maintained that this was by any means Claudius' whole motive, but it was evidently a powerful one and the one that most impressed Hamlet.

murder of the father. The two recent events, the father's death and the mother's second marriage, seemed to the world to have no inner causal relation to each other, but they represented ideas which in Hamlet's unconscious phantasy had always been closely associated. These ideas now in a moment forced their way to conscious recognition in spite of all "repressing forces," and found immediate expression in his almost reflex cry: "O my prophetic soul! My uncle?" The frightful truth his unconscious had already intuitively divined, his consciousness had now to assimiliate as best it could. For the rest of the interview Hamlet is stunned by the effect of the internal conflict thus re-awakened, which from now on never ceases, and into the essential nature of which he never penetrates.

 ## ANNE BARTON
The Promulgation of Confusion*

The length of the play suggests that it was never, not even in Shakespeare's time, performed uncut. Other plays by Shakespeare are long; no other violates so strikingly the limits of audience attention, or asks for so much from its leading actor. Like *Titus,* like *The Spanish Tragedy* and that lost source play, the so-called *Ur-Hamlet,* which was probably the work of Kyd, Shakespeare's *Hamlet* is a tragedy of revenge. It concentrates, like them, upon a single, essentially sympathetic hero and it confronts precisely the same structural problem: how to linger out his vengeance for the necessary five acts. Kyd's Hieronymo (and probably his Hamlet), Shakespeare's Titus and Hamlet all require proof of the villain's identity before they can act. They are temporarily deflected from their purpose, not only by difficulties of strategy, but by a madness partly assumed and partly real. All make use of some kind of dramatic show to further their intention and all accomplish, in the end, a vengeance which, whatever the original provocation, has by this time become more than a little suspect.

As a tragic predicament, revenge has several inherent advantages. Intrigue and spectacle, madness and violence, are not the only elements native to the genre. The isolation naturally imposed upon the revenger not only encourages introspection, it destroys normal human relationships in a fundamentally tragic way. A detached, satirist's view of the society against which they war almost forces itself upon these characters. Their situation generates a corrosive doubt, reaching out to attack religious, moral and legal institutions. Kyd, Marlowe in *The Jew of Malta,* and the young Shakespeare of *Titus,* had all recognized and explored these inbuilt opportunities, at least to some extent. It was only with *Hamlet,* however, that a dramatist seized upon the form to trigger off an enquiry into the whole basis of human existence. Debate over man's right to encroach upon the prerogative of Heaven by undertaking himself what was properly God's act of retributive justice had been and, in the Jacobean period, would continue to be a feature of revenge tragedy.

. . .

Only *Hamlet* side-steps the ethic of revenge entirely. It is one of several great silences at the heart of this play. Deliberately, Shakespeare has shifted attention away from an expected centre, from the problem of whether the prince

---

*The title is the editors'.

ought to kill Claudius—or even whether in practical terms he *can*—to the far more complicated and subjective issue of whether or not he ultimately *will.* It is not the peculiar status of acts of private vengeance that is under review here, but the validity of all and any human action.

Although other dramatists (Marston, Webster and Tourneur especially) later used *Hamlet* as a spring-board for their own exploration of the revenge form, none of them dared to attempt a focus so wide. The range of the play and, above all, of the role of Hamlet himself, is so great that any performance must necessarily be a matter of selection, of emphases more or less arbitrarily imposed. The impossibility of presenting *Hamlet* whole and uncut is not entirely a feature of its great length. It is also bound up with its inclusiveness, with the fact that Shakespeare seems to have been determined to subject a bewildering number of people, ideas, values, kinds of relationship, emotions and social forms to the distorted but strangely clear scrutiny of a revenger so complicated himself that no attempt to describe, or act, him can be more than partial. Even more than most plays of Shakespeare, *Hamlet* is a warning against the fallacy that any critical interpretation or stage production can be definitive, or even complete.

When Hamlet cautioned Rosencrantz and Guildenstern, after the play scene, against the attempt to "pluck out the heart of my mystery . . . sound me from my lowest note to the top of my compass" (3.2.368-70), he also provided a useful counsel for literary critics. The play as a whole is built upon contradiction, upon the promulgation of confusion. Shakespeare gives every indication of having constructed an imaginary Denmark intended to baffle, to resist explanation as stubbornly as those mysterious facts of human existence which it illuminates without rationalizing. A distrust of what might be described as a "play-shaped" view of the world of the falseness of clearly defined moral, theological or formal patterns imposed upon reality in the interests of art is, I think, characteristic of him throughout his dramatic career. It was to become particularly strong in his Jacobean plays. This antipathy may account, in part, for Shakespeare's apparent suspicion of *tragedy* as a term, and also for the variety and restlessness of his own formal development.

Certainly, the eschatology of *Hamlet* defies explication. The ghost of a murdered king appears from an almost embarrassingly specific Catholic Purgatory, a place of "sulph'rous and tormenting flames" (1.5.3.) to which it has been confined "till the four crimes done in my days of nature / Are burnt and purged away" (1.5.12-13). This spirit urges upon its beloved only son a revenge for which, by immutable Christian law, that son must be damned perpetually—sent not to Purgatory, but to the far greater torments of Hell. Neither Hamlet, the sensible Horatio nor the ghost itself ever remark upon this illogicality. Hamlet's worry is only about the truth of the ghost's accusation. If Claudius is guilty, and the Mouse-trap proves that he is, he must be killed. Not for an instant does Hamlet doubt the justice of such a course, let alone the propriety of a repentant soul spending its time in Purgatory meditating a murder. A similar inconsistency adds complications to what is already, on psychological grounds, a most ambiguous scene in Act 3. Hamlet declines to kill the king at prayers because he fears that Claudius' soul will ascend to Heaven. This, at least, is the reason he gives. He will wait to find his enemy

> drunk asleep, or in his rage,
> Or in th'incestuous pleasure of his bed,
> At game, a-swearing, or about some act

That has no relish of salvation in't,
Then trip him that his heels may kick at heaven,
And that his soul may be as damned and black
As hell whereto it goes.

(3.3.89-95)

Here, the odd fact that Hamlet never considers that his own soul would be damned irrecoverably by the requirements of such a theology, is cunningly mingled with doubts as to whether he really means what he is saying in this speech, or whether it is a feeble excuse for postponing an explicably distasteful task.

In *Hamlet,* Shakespeare affirms a Christian supernatural in one moment to deny it in the next. The hereafter involves Purgatory, hell fire, and flights of angels. It is also silence, an eternal sleep that has nothing to do with punishment or reward. The prince talks about death as "the undiscovered country, from whose bourn / No traveller returns" (3.1.79-80) out of an anguish of mind created by the return of just such a traveller. A special Providence guides the fall of the sparrow, or at least Hamlet asserts that it does just before the fatal game with the foils in Act 5. He seems to die, however, in the agnostic spirit which, a moment later, prompts Horatio's account of the catastrophe as "accidental judgements, casual slaughters" (5.2.380). These conflicting views follow one another so closely in the action, and they are treated by the dramatist with such a non-committal equality, that it becomes impossible to characterize the supernatural in the play. Although we stumble from time to time over the partially submerged rocks of old beliefs, their presence only makes the obscurity of the total picture more poignant. In effect, Shakespeare has created his own, infinitely more complex version of the divided worlds of [Pickering's] *Horestes* and [Kyd's] *The Spanish Tragedy.* Hamlet's questions, instead of being halted artificially as Hieronymo's were by a tidy, Senecan supernatural visible to us in the audience although not to the hero, grope their way into a darkness without form or limit. Like Pickering, Shakespeare placed his spirit of Revenge inside the play itself, as a character who addresses the protagonist directly. Having done so, he proceeded disconcertingly to associate the ghost with a Christian hereafter, and refused to judge its ethic of blood vengeance. *Hamlet* never explains the nature of that silence towards which the hero moves gradually, away from us, and into which he finally vanishes. This is one reason why the tragedy has a terror, and also a relevance to the world as we know it, lacking in Pickering and Kyd.

More perhaps than any other Shakespearean tragedy, *Hamlet* is a play obsessed with words themselves. It displaces the accustomed centre of earlier revenge drama by subordinating plot for its own sake to a new concern with the mysterious gap between thought and action, between the verbal formulation of intent and its concrete realization. The prince himself is the most articulate of Shakespeare's tragic heroes, but he combines verbal fluency with a curious paralysis of the will. When Claudius asks Laertes in Act 4 what he would do "to show yourself your father's son in deed / More than in words" (4.7.124-5), Laertes replies instantly that, to be avenged, he would be happy to cut Hamlet's throat "i' the church." A demonstration that "in deed more than words" he is his father's son is conspicuously what the Hamlet of "O, what a rogue and peasant slave am I" and "How all occasions do inform against me" has not managed. We may respect him for this failing. Certainly, the sharply contrasted readiness of Laertes to act without thinking is unlovely. The fact remains that Hamlet is a man suffering from a peculiar malaise. In his mind, speech and event, language and its realization have become separate and disjunct. He can initiate action only when he has no time to subject it, first, to words: when he stabs impulsively through the arras and kills Polonius, when he sends Rosencrantz and Guildenstern to death *before* "I could make a prologue to my brains" (5.2.30), boards the pirate ship in the heat of the moment or finally, without premeditation, kills the king. The Norwegian captain tells Hamlet in the fourth scene of Act 4 that Fortinbras is hazarding twenty thousand ducats and an army of two thousand men to gain "a little patch of ground / That hath in it no profit but the name" (4.4.18-19). Fortinbras here, as in other respects, is Hamlet's diametric opposite. He has converted a mere word, a name, into a pretext for action. Hamlet, on the other hand, allows a tangible situation, the fact of a father's murder, to dissolve into words alone.

 STANLEY WELLS
On the First Soliloquy

More than most plays, *Hamlet* is a series of opportunities for virtuosity. This is true above all of the role of Hamlet himself. "Hamlet," wrote Max Beerbohm, is "a hoop through which every very eminent actor must, sooner or later, jump." There is no wonder that it has been such a favourite part with actors, and even with actresses. The performer has the opportunity to demonstrate a wide range of ability, to be melancholy and gay, charming and cynical, thoughtful and flippant, tender and cruel, calm and impassioned, noble and vindictive, downcast and witty, all within a few hours. He can wear a variety of costumes, he need not disguise good looks, he can demonstrate athletic ability, he has perhaps the longest role in drama—he could scarcely ask for more, except perhaps the opportunity to sing and dance.

And if the role of Hamlet is the greatest reason for the play's popularity with actors, the character of Hamlet is surely the greatest reason for its popularity with audiences. Hamlet is the most sympathetic of tragic heroes. We are drawn to him by his youth, his intelligence, and his vulnerability. As soon as he appears we are conscious of one of the sources of his appeal: his immense capacity for taking life seriously. It may sound like a slightly repellent quality, but I don't mean to imply that he is excessively gloomy or over-earnest. Often he is deeply dejected: but he has good cause. There is nothing exceptional about his emotional reactions except perhaps their intensity. He has a larger-than-life capacity for experience, a fullness of response, a depth of feeling, a vibrancy of living, which mark him out from the ordinary. He is a raw nerve in the court of Denmark, disconcertingly liable to make the instinctive rather than the conditioned response. This cuts him off from those around him, but it puts him into peculiar contact with the audience. And as Hamlet is to the other figures of the play, so his soliloquies are to the role, for in them Shakespeare shows us the raw nerves of Hamlet himself.

The use of soliloquy is one of the most brilliant features of the play, for in these speeches Shakespeare solves a major technical problem in the presentation of his central character. The young man who takes himself seriously, who persists in explaining himself and his problems, is someone we are apt—perhaps too apt—to regard as a bore. We have all had experience of him, and so probably have most of our friends. On the other hand, the desire to know someone to the depths is fundamental to human nature. Here was both a problem and a challenge: how to let Hamlet reveal himself without becoming an almighty bore? Shakespeare found a double solution. First, he caused Hamlet to conduct his deepest self-communings in solitude, so that there is none of the awkwardness associated with the presence of a confidant. And secondly, the soliloquies are written in a style which presents us not with conclusions but with the very processes of Hamlet's mind.

There had been nothing like this in drama before: nothing which, while retaining a verse form, at the same time so vividly revealed what Shakespeare elsewhere calls "the quick forge and working-house of thought" (*Henry the Fifth* [5.Pro.23]). Vocabulary, syntax, and rhythm all contribute to the effect. Consider the second half of Hamlet's first soliloquy, beginning with his contrast between his uncle and his dead father:

> That it should come to this—
> But two months dead—nay, not so much, not two—
> So excellent a king, that was to this
> Hyperion to a satyr, so loving to my mother
> That he might not beteem the winds of heaven
> Visit her face too roughly! Heaven and earth,
> Must I remember? Why, she would hang on him
> As if increase of appetite had grown
> By what it fed on, and yet within a month—
> Let me not think on't; frailty, thy name is woman—
> A little month, or ere those shoes were old
> With which she followed my poor father's body,
> Like Niobe, all tears, why she, even she—
> O God, a beast that wants discourse of reason
> Would have mourned longer!—married with mine uncle,
> My father's brother, but no more like my father
> Than I to Hercules; within a month,
> Ere yet the salt of most unrighteous tears
> Had left the flushing of her gallèd eyes,
> She married. O most wicked speed, to post
> With such dexterity to incestuous sheets!
> It is not, nor it cannot come to good.
> But break, my heart, for I must hold my tongue.

(1.2.137-59)

The anguish that it causes Hamlet to think of his mother's over-hasty marriage is conveyed as much by the tortured syntax as by direct statement; we share his difficulty as he tries—and fails—to assimilate these unwelcome facts into his consciousness, seeking to bring under emotional control the discordant elements of his disrupted universe: his love of his dead father, his love of his mother combined with disgust at her marriage to the uncle whom he loathes, and the disillusion with womankind that this has provoked in him. The short exclamations interrupting the sentence structure point his horror: the rhythms of ordinary speech within the verse give immediacy to the contrasts in phrases such as "Hyperion to a satyr" and "Than I to Hercules"; and the concreteness of the imagery betrays the effort it costs him to master the unwelcome nature of the facts which it expresses: his mother's haste to marry "or ere those shoes were old / With which she followed my poor father's body"— it is as if only by concentrating on the matter-of-fact, physical aspects of the scene can he bear to contemplate it, or bring it within his belief. He ends on a note of utter helplessness: he alone sees the truth; he knows that his mother's actions, which both he and she see as evil, must bring forth evil; but he, the only emotionally honest person there, cannot express his emotion—except to us.

ELAINE SHOWALTER
Representing Ophelia

"Of all the characters in *Hamlet*," Bridget Lyons has pointed out, "Ophelia is most persistently presented in terms of symbolic meanings." Her behavior, her appearance, her gestures, her costume, her props, are freighted with emblematic significance, and for many generations of Shakespearean critics her part in the play has seemed to be primarily iconographic. Ophelia's symbolic meanings, moreover, are specifically feminine. Whereas for Hamlet madness is metaphysical, linked with culture, for Ophelia it is a product of the female body and female nature, perhaps that nature's purest form. On the Elizabethan stage, the conventions of female insanity were sharply defined. Ophelia dresses in white, decks herself with "fantastical garlands" of wild flowers, and enters, according to the stage directions of the "Bad" Quarto, "distracted" playing on a lute with her "hair down singing." Her speeches are marked by extravagant metaphors, lyrical free associations, and "explosive sexual imagery." She sings wistful and bawdy ballads, and ends her life by drowning.

All of these conventions carry specific messages about femininity and sexuality. Ophelia's virginal and vacant white is contrasted with Hamlet's scholar's garb, his "suits of solemn black." Her flowers suggest the discordant double images of female sexuality as both innocent blossoming and whorish contamination; she is the "green girl" of pastoral, the virginal "Rose of May" and the sexually explicit madwoman who, in giving away her wild flowers and herbs, is symbolically deflowering herself. The "weedy trophies" and phallic "long purples" which she wears to her death intimate an improper and discordant sexuality that Gertrude's lovely elegy cannot quite obscure. In Elizabethan and Jacobean drama, the stage direction that a woman enters with dishevelled hair indicates that she might either be mad or the victim of a rape; the disordered hair, her offense against decorum, suggests sensuality in each case. The mad Ophelia's bawdy songs and verbal license, while they give her access to "an entirely different range of experience" from what she is allowed as the dutiful daughter, seem to be her one sanctioned form of self-assertion as a woman, quickly followed, as if in retribution, by her death.

Drowning too was associated with the feminine, with female fluidity as opposed to masculine aridity. In his discussion of the "Ophelia complex," the phenomenologist Gaston Bachelard traces the symbolic connections between women, water, and death. Drowning, he suggests, becomes the truly feminine death in the dramas of literature and life, one which is a beautiful immersion and submersion in the female element. Water is the profound and organic symbol of the liquid woman whose eyes are so easily drowned in tears, as her body is the repository of blood, amniotic fluid, and milk. A man contemplating this feminine suicide understands it by reaching for what is feminine in himself, like Laertes, by a temporary surrender to his own fluidity—that is, his tears; and he becomes a man again in becoming once more dry—when his tears are stopped.

Clinically speaking, Ophelia's behavior and appearance are characteristic of the malady the Elizabethans would have diagnosed as female love-melancholy, or erotomania. From about 1580, melancholy had become a fashionable disease among young men, especially in London, and Hamlet himself is a prototype of the melancholy hero. Yet the epidemic of melancholy associated with intellectual and imaginative genius "curiously bypassed women." Women's melancholy was seen instead as biological, and emotional in origins.

CLAIRE BLOOM
Playing Gertrude on Television

Editors' note: Claire Bloom played Gertrude in the BBC TV production (1980), directed by Rodney Bennett, with Patrick Stewart as Claudius. In the following passage she discusses the role.

It's very hard to play because strangely enough Gertrude has very few lines; I've always known it was a wonderful part and it *is,* but when you come to play it you realise you have to find many ways around the fact that she in actual fact says little!

You come to rehearse a part like this with certain preconceived notions, which you usually leave! I can only describe them as a battering ram—you knock down the first wall then what is inside is something quite different from what you'd imagined. I was convinced that she was guilty, not of the murder, but certainly that she had found out from Claudius that he had killed her husband. But there's nothing in the text that bears that out and many things that contradict it. I had thought it would make her less of a victim, more of a performer in the world, but [she laughs at herself] it isn't so. Like anyone if you live with a man, she must know there was something more, but I now believe that when Hamlet confronts her with "as kill a king . . . ay, madam, it was my word," it's the first time she's realised. I think from then on she knows and she must accept the fact that Claudius did it, and there is a change in their relationship. But there isn't a break—you don't break with someone suddenly like that. It changes; perhaps if they'd lived another twenty years they would have drifted apart. But there isn't a complete withdrawal. The hold they have on each other is too strong for that to happen. That caused me great difficulty; the scene after the closet scene is with Claudius, when he repeats twice "Gertrude, come away," and she doesn't reply. It's very mysterious. It's a kind of underwritten scene until you realise, or I realised, that there is no real choice for her. For the moment she doesn't go with him, but the next day she does. Hamlet knows it when he says, "Go not to my uncle's bed." She never replies and says "I won't"; she just says, "Thou hast cleft my heart in twain." She's a woman who goes with whatever is happening at the time. She's a weak-willed woman, but most of us are weak-willed if we're in the power of somebody who is very strong—and Claudius and Hamlet are both pretty strong fellows.

The "mysterious" scene with Claudius was one of the hardest to deal with in rehearsal. . . . We tried backwards, forwards, upside down and inside out and didn't really find it until a couple of days before we shot it. The minute we found it we knew it was the right one, but at other times we'd go away saying, "We've got it," then both Patrick and I would come in the next day depressed and say to Rodney, "Could we please do that scene again because it doesn't make sense when you think about it." There are questions that I'm sure have been asked by every cast of every *Hamlet* since Burbage[1] and for Gertrude they are: Was there a decision to go with Claudius or not to go with Claudius? How far was she lying about Hamlet's madness? I do think part of her believes he's mad, but when she says to the king "He's mad," I think that's protection, or overstating a fact she believes is possibly true. And of course she withholds information from Claudius; she says, "Behind the arras hearing something stir . . . [he] kills the unseen good old man," but she *doesn't* say he said "Is it the king?" That is a very important bit of information which she certainly doesn't pass on!

[1]**Burbage** Richard Burbage (c. 1567–1619), the first actor to play Shakepeare's Hamlet

 BERNICE W. KLIMAN
The BBC *Hamlet:* A Television Production

With *Hamlet,* the producers of the BBC Shakespeare Plays have finally met the demands of Shakespeare-on-television by choosing a relatively bare set, conceding only a few richly detailed movable panels and props to shape key locales. By avoiding both location and realistic settings, they point up the natural affinity between Shakespeare's stage and the undisguised sound set. This starkness of setting admits poetry, heightened intensity—and "what not that's sweet and happy."

The producers have thus made a valid choice from among television's three faces: one, broadcast films, whether made for television or not, which exploit location settings, long shots, and all the clichés we associate with movies, including sudden shifts of space and time and full use of distance, from the most extreme long shots to "eyes only" closeups; two, studio-shot television drama with naturalistic settings, such as the hospital corridors and middle-class living rooms of sitcoms and soap operas, mostly in mid- to close-shots, often interspersed, to be sure, with a bit of stock footage of highways and skylines to establish a realistic environment. This second style varies from a close representation of real action to frankly staged action, where canned laughter or even shadowy glimpses of the studio audience can heighten the staged effect. Three, there is bare space with little or no effort made to disguise that this is a televised activity with a television crew out of sight but nearby. News broadcasts, talk shows and some television drama fit into this third category. Because of its patently unrepresentational quality, this last type offers the most freedom in shooting style. To all three kinds of settings we bring particular expectations in response to their conventions.

Shakespeare's plays work best in the last kind of television space, I believe, because it avoids the clash between realism and poetry, between the unity often expected in realistic media and the disunity and ambiguity of many of the plays, especially *Hamlet.* Yet, while closest to the kind of stage Shakespeare wrote for, the bare television set can be stretched through creative camera work. For example, when Hamlet follows the ghost in the BBC play, the two repeatedly walk across the frame and out of it, first from one direction, then from another; framing fosters the illusion of extended space. Freeing this *Hamlet* from location (as in the BBC *As You Like It*) and from realistic sets (as in the BBC *Measure for Measure*—however well those sets worked for that play) allows the play to be as inconsistent as it is, with, as Bernard Beckerman has so brilliantly explained in *Shakespeare at the Globe, 1599-1609,* a rising and falling action in each individual scene rather than through the course of the drama as a whole. It also allows for acting, the bravura kind that Derek Jacobi is so capable of.

Although gradually coalescing like the pointillism of impressionistic paintings into a subtly textured portrait, at first his mannerisms suggesting madness seem excessive. It is to be expected, perhaps, that Hamlet is a bit unhinged after the ghost scene, but Jacobi's rapid, hard blows to his forehead with the flat of his hand as he says "My tables" recall the desperation of Lear's cry: "O, let me not be mad, not mad, sweet heaven." And soon after, following the last couplet of the scene, Hamlet, maniacally playful, widens his eyes and points, pretending to see the ghost again, then guffaws at Marcellus's fears. Even more unsettling is his laughter when he is alone, as while he is saying "The play's the thing / Wherein I'll catch the conscience of the King." More significantly, he breaks up his own "Mousetrap" by getting right into the play, destroying the distance between audience and stage (a very real raked proscenium-arch stage), spoiling it as a test, because Claudius has a right to be incensed at Hamlet's behavior. Of course, Hamlet does so because Claudius never gives himself away, an unusual and provocative but not impossible interpretation. Thus, Claudius can only have the court's sympathy as he calmly calls for light and uses it to examine Hamlet closely. Hamlet, in response, covers his face, then laughs.

Hamlet himself thinks he is mad. To Ophelia he says, as if the realization had suddenly struck him, "It *hath* made me mad [emphasis his]" (III.i.147). To his mother he stresses the word "essentially" in "I *essentially* am not in madness" (III.iv.187). That is, in all essential matters he can be considered sane, though mad around the edges. This indeed turns out to be the explanation.

However doubtful about Hamlet's sanity Jacobi's acting leaves us, in this production this question does not seem to make a difference because it does not have a bearing on the tragedy, and this is true at least partly because in each scene on this nonrealistic set we seem to start anew, ready to let Hamlet's behavior tell us if he is mad or not. Moreover, if Hamlet is mad, it is not so totally as to obscure reason or sensibility. Far from it. It is more as if exacerbated reason and sensibility sometimes tip him into madness. This madness is no excuse for action or delay; it is simply part of the suffering that Hamlet is heir to.

Hamlet, then, is left to struggle against himself—surely where Shakespeare intended the struggle to abide. One of the conflicts in this Hamlet results from his affinity, perhaps, more to the bureaucratic Claudius who handles war-scares with diplomacy and who sits at a desk while brooding over his sins than to the warlike King Hamlet who comes in full armor. Hamlet may admire Fortinbras but is himself more like the bookish Horatio. Through nuance of gesture, through body movement, through a face that is indeed a map of all emotions, Jacobi shapes a Hamlet who loves his father too much to disregard his command, yet who cannot hate his step-father enough to attend to it. Because Jacobi conveys so fully Hamlet's aloneness and vulnerability, one could be struck, for the first time, by the ghost's silence about his son. There is no declaration of love, no concern about Hamlet's ascension to the throne. Hamlet is doomed, it seems, to care about those who consistently care more for others than for him.

All of this production's richness and suggestiveness was realized not only because Jacobi is a marvelous actor—as indeed he is—but also because within the set's spareness that acting could unfold, an acting style that subsumes and transcends the "real." This production's space tells us what is possible for television presentations of Shakespeare. The more bare the set, it seems, the more glowing the words, the more immediate our apprehension of the enacted emotion.

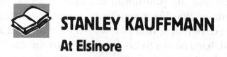

STANLEY KAUFFMANN
At Elsinore

Kenneth Branagh wins two victories in *Hamlet* (Castle Rock [1996]). He has made a vital, exciting film; and he has triumphed over the obstacles he put in his own way.

Let's first rejoice in the virtues. Branagh confirms what was known from the opening shot of *Henry V:* he has fine cinematic skills. His directing keeps *Hamlet* flowing, endows scenes that might become static with germane movement. Many of his touches illuminate. One of them: Hamlet comes into a huge mirrored room in the palace, sees himself full-length and, after a moment, begins "To be or not to be." Two selves speak that speech and give it an added edge.

Then there's the text itself. Branagh has used the complete First Folio text, has included a scene from the Second Quarto that is not in the Folio, to make a film that runs four hours plus intermission. I could find only a few alterations, trifles compared with the chopped, twisted, insulting text that Olivier used in his 155-minute version. Branagh's film looks splendid. He sets it in the mid-nineteenth century—with Blenheim Palace serving as the exterior of Elsinore—and Alex Byrne's costumes fully exploit the period. The cinematographer, Alex Thomson, using 70-mm wide-screen format, has nonetheless created lighting that seems naturally evolved from the hundreds of candles. And as for the music, Patrick Doyle again does wonders. He wrote the scores for Branagh's two previous Shakespeare films, and here again he provides music that rises unobtrusively to benefit scene after scene.

Every supporting role of significance has been superbly cast and is superbly played. I can't imagine a better Claudius than Derek Jacobi, who brings to it force and cunning and manipulative charm. The sequences in which he converts the furious Laertes from enemy to accomplice are masterpieces of guile manifested as honesty. (Jacobi, by the way, was the first Hamlet that Branagh ever saw; and years later Jacobi directed Branagh in a theater production.)

5   Jacobi is no surprise: Julie Christie is. This Golden Girl of the 1960s virtually disappeared for a while, then reappeared in a London production of Pinter's *Old Times*. She was so dull that I thought she was being used just for her name. But here, as Gertrude, she is emotionally rich. She brings to the role the apt quality of overblown sex object, and, presumably with Branagh's help, she completely fulfills the woman. In Gertrude's key moment, the closet scene, Christie bursts with the frightened despair of a guilty woman who thinks that her behavior may have driven her son mad.

Kate Winslet, dear to us already through *Sense and Sensibility* and *Jude,* gives Ophelia the kind of vulnerability that almost invites the man she loves to wound her. Polonius gets the obtuse officiousness that he needs from Richard Briers. It's immediately clear why Horatio, done by Nicholas Farrell, is Hamlet's dearest friend: anybody would want him for a friend. Laertes, a role always in danger of being as much of a blowhard as his father, Polonius, is realized in his confusions by Michael Maloney. Branagh, as he did in *Much Ado About Nothing,* has sprinkled some American actors through his cast. The best of these is Charlton Heston as the Player King, sounding and (even) looking plummy, home at last.

Hamlet is unique in Shakespeare. I can think of no other role in the plays in which an actor is so compelled, commanded, to present *himself.* Macbeth, Othello, Iago, the Richards and the Henrys—run through the roster, and always the actor selects and nurtures what there is in his imagination and experience and technique that will make the man come alive. No such selections for Hamlet. The whole actor is the whole character. So, when we see a Hamlet, we are looking at an actor in a unique way.

Branagh's Hamlet—or, one might say, Hamlet's Branagh—is attractive, keen, nobly intended, tender with regret for Ophelia, torn with disgust for the chicaneries of the world, fiery, quite susceptible to cracking into frenzy. (In appearance, he is fair—not Olivier's platinum blond—with a somewhat darker moustache and goatee.)

This is a man we could meet and understand. What this Hamlet lacks is what possibly we could not understand: his sense of falling upward into the metaphysical. This is what is sometimes called the "poetic" nature of Hamlet, this linkage with a spirit walking the earth in quest of purgation; and this linkage, in mystery and awe and uncertainty, leads to what Granville Barker called "a tragedy of inaction." Branagh's Hamlet doesn't attain this quality: it doesn't quite seem to be in him. Not long ago Ralph Fiennes, burdened with an unworthy director and cast, nevertheless did a Hamlet on Broadway that took us out into the spheres. Not Branagh. Every word he speaks is true. But in Hamlet that is not quite enough.

10   Now the lesser aspects of the film. First, the obverse side of Branagh's directing skill. He is too eager for spectacle, even if it's pointless or harmful. When Gertrude and Claudius exit at the end of the first court scene, confetti rains down on them. For the moment, it's startling, pretty. Then we wonder who planned it and who threw it. Answer: the director. When the Ghost speaks to Hamlet, the earth splits and flames leap. Is this God overseeing unpurged souls? Or the special effects department? Rosencrantz and Guildenstern arrive on a toy locomotive. Who put that model train and tracks on the palace grounds? Old King Hamlet? Claudius? Or the director? When Hamlet and Laertes duel, the civilized sport explodes into Errol Flynn antics, with ropes and chandeliers—another directorial intrusion. Branagh sets the whole film in winter, which allows for some breathtaking vistas but makes us wonder why the old king was sleeping outdoors in his snow-covered orchard on the afternoon of his murder and how the brookside flowers could be present when Ophelia drowns.

Another obverse side, one that may sound odd: the use of the complete text. Admirable though it is in Branagh to aim at "classic" status, not every word is helpful today, especially in a film. To hear Marcellus discourse on "the bird of dawning" at Christmastime, just after the Ghost's second appearance, is a soft indulgence in Elizabethan folklore. To hear Gertrude include a small dirty joke, about "long purples," when she tells Laertes of his sister's death is to coddle the lad from Stratford who couldn't always keep rustic humor out of his plays. And the sad fact is that, when Shakespeare takes time out from drama for moral commentary, the result is sometimes mere homiletics. Hamlet's speech about "the dram of evil" is not only a brusque lapse in the action, it captures perfectly the quality in Shakespeare that Bernard Shaw called "the atmosphere of the rented pew."

Sex. Branagh has searched for chances to get it into the film. While Polonius is warning Ophelia to be careful in her behavior with Hamlet, to avoid the prince completely, Branagh includes flashback shots of her and Hamlet naked in bed together. Presumably Branagh takes his license from the bawdy song that Ophelia later sings when she is mad—"Young men will do't if they come to't," etc.—a song that is usually viewed as the raving of a sexually repressed virgin. Whether or not Hamlet and Ophelia actually had an affair is possibly arguable, but what seems clear is that, if they have made love, it detracts considerably from the fierce, Savonarola-like outburst of the "get thee to a nunnery" passages.

Then, too, Polonius is given a visiting whore in the scene with Reynaldo, who is apparently her pimp. (Ophelia bursts in without knocking—fortuitously, just after Reynaldo and the whore leave.) Branagh's purpose is to lend irony to the old man's instructions to Reynaldo, about checking on Laertes's behavior in Paris, but the episode smacks of opportunism.

Politics. Of course *Hamlet* is, among other elements, a political play. One cause for Hamlet's hatred of Claudius is that his uncle has "popp'd in between th'election and my hopes." Branagh's use of the mid-century period affords the ambiance of the "Age of Metternich," but it misplaces in time the Denmark-England-Norway-Poland relationships of the original. Further, Branagh distorts the political action of the closing scenes. Early in the play we learn that the young Fortinbras of Norway wants to reconquer some lands that his country lost to Denmark, but the Norwegian king dissuades him. Fortinbras swears never to attack Denmark, but he will ask for the right of passage through Denmark to attack Poland. Toward the end of the play Fortinbras leads an army into Denmark and sends a messenger to Claudius to ask for that right of passage.

15   Incomprehensibly, in Branagh's film, Fortinbras then attacks Elsinore. (Real reason: Branagh wants to heat up the film's closing moments.) Shots of this violence are intercut with the Hamlet-Laertes duel. Just as Hamlet dies, the Norwegian soldiers burst into the court, destroying as they come. Fortinbras ought to feel a bit foolish, not only having broken his word but to find out that, just before Hamlet expired, the prince named him as his successor. ("He has my dying voice.") Instead, Fortinbras is shown as a glowering conqueror moderately disturbed by the prince's death. The very last shot is of old King Hamlet's statue being toppled and smashed. Why did Branagh choose that shot as the moment toward which the entire film moved?

Some other points might be called matters of interpretation—Claudius's slapping of Hamlet in anger at the chaffing about Polonius's corpse, the strait-jacketing of Ophelia in a padded cell—but one Branagh touch seems just plain misreading. Claudius (in Act III, Scene 1) says he has "closely sent for Hamlet" so that the prince can meet Ophelia while Claudius and Polonius are hidden and watching. They do hide. Hamlet enters, finds the chamber empty though he has been sent for, muses aloud while waiting ("To be or not to be"). Then Ophelia enters—the girl who, for days, has been forbidden to see him. And it was the king who summoned him here. Surely, in simple reason, Hamlet must be suspicious that this is a set-up from the moment she appears. Instead, Branagh plays it merely petulantly until, after the nunnery speech, he hears a noise behind the door and the deception dawns on him. Branagh's treatment not only makes Hamlet less acute than we are, it takes the bite out of "Are you honest?"

Interpretations and innovations have different weights in a Shakespeare film from such matters in a theater production. When I saw Ingmar Bergman's production of *Hamlet,* with his sluttish Ophelia wandering through scenes in which Shakespeare forgot to include her, I was relieved that Bergman had not filmed it. Branagh's film, warts and all, will be with us for some time to come.

On the whole, this is good news. Though his *Henry V* and *Much Ado About Nothing* were closer to perfection, *Hamlet* is more difficult in every way. Flaws, problems, bumps, yes; but the film surpasses them finally through Branagh's talent and the talents of his colleagues. And, not to be slighted, there is Branagh's infectious joy—the right word even for *Hamlet*—in doing Shakespeare.

WILL SARETTA

What follows is an undergraduate's review, published in a college newspaper, of Kenneth Branagh's film version of Hamlet (1996).

Branagh's Film of *Hamlet*

Kenneth Branagh's *Hamlet* opened last night at the Harmon Auditorium, and will be shown again on Wednesday and Thursday at 7:30 p.m. According to the clock the evening will be long—the film runs for four hours, and in addition there is one ten-minute intermission—but you will enjoy every minute of it.

Well, almost every minute. Curiously, the film begins and ends relatively weakly, but most of what occurs in between is good and much of it is wonderful. The beginning is weak because it is too strong; Bernardo, the sentinel, offstage says "Who's there?" but before he gets a reply he crashes onto the screen and knocks Francisco down. The two soldiers grapple, swords flash in the darkness, and Francisco finally says, "Nay, answer me. Stand and unfold yourself." Presumably Branagh wanted to begin with a bang, but here, as often, more is less. A quieter, less physical opening in which Bernardo, coming on duty, hears a noise and demands that the maker of the noise identify himself, and Francisco, the sentinel on duty, rightly demands that the newcomer identify *himself,* would catch the uneasiness and the mystery that pervades the play much better than does Branagh's showy beginning.

Similarly, at the end of the film, we get too much. For one thing, shots of Fortinbras's army invading Elsinore alternate with shots of the duel between Hamlet and King Claudius's pawn, Laertes, and they merely distract us from what really counts in this scene, the duel itself, which will result in Hamlet's death but also in Hamlet's successful completion of his mission to avenge his father. Second, at the very end we get shots of Fortinbras's men pulling down a massive statue of Hamlet Senior, probably influenced by television and newspaper shots of statues of Lenin being pulled down when the Soviet Union was dissolved a few years earlier. This is ridiculous; *Hamlet* is not a play about the fall of Communism, or about one form of tyranny replacing another. Shakespeare's *Hamlet* is not about the triumph of Fortinbras. It is about Hamlet's brave and ultimately successful efforts to do what is right, against overwhelming odds, and to offer us the consolation that in a world where death always triumphs there nevertheless is something that can be called nobility.

What, then, is good about the film? First of all, the film gives us the whole play, whereas almost all productions, whether on the stage or in the movie house, give us drastically abbreviated versions. Although less is often more, when it comes to the text of *Hamlet,* more is better, and we should be grateful to Branagh for letting us hear all of the lines. Second, it is very well performed, with only a few exceptions. Jack Lemmon as Marcellus is pretty bad, but fortunately the part is small. Other big-name actors in small parts—Charlton Heston as the Player King, Robin Williams as Osric, and Billy Crystal as the First Grave-digger—are admirable. But of course the success or failure of any production of *Hamlet* will depend chiefly on the actor who plays Hamlet, and to a consider-able degree on the actors who play Claudius, Gertrude, Polonius, Ophelia, Laertes, and Horatio. There isn't space here to comment on all of these roles, but let it be said that Branagh's Prince Hamlet is indeed princely, a man who strikes us as having the ability to become a king, not a wimpy whining figure. When at the end Fortinbras says that if Hamlet had lived to become the king, he would "have proved most royal," we believe him. And his adversary, King Claudius, though morally despicable, is a man of great charm and great ability. The two men are indeed "mighty opposites," to use Hamlet's own words.

Branagh's decision to set the play in the late nineteenth century rather than in the Elizabethan period of Shakespeare's day and rather than in our own day contributes to this sense of powerful forces at work. If the play were set in Shakespeare's day, the men would wear tights, and if it were set in our day they would wear suits or trousers and sports jackets and sweaters, but in the film all of the men wear military costumes (black for Hamlet, scarlet for Claudius, white for Laertes) and the women wear ball gowns of the Victorian period. Branagh gives us a world that is closer to our own than would Elizabethan costumes, but yet it is, visually at least, also distant enough to convey a sense of grandeur, which modern dress cannot suggest. Of course *Hamlet* can be done in modern dress, just as *Romeo and Juliet* was done, successfully, in the recent film starring Claire Danes and Leonardo DiCaprio, set in a world that seemed to be Miami Beach, but *Romeo and Juliet* is less concerned with heroism and grandeur than *Hamlet* is, so Branagh probably did well to avoid contemporary costumes.

Although Branagh is faithful to the text, in that he gives us the entire text, he knows that a good film cannot be made merely by recording on film a stage pro-duction, and so he gives us handsome shots of landscape, and of rich interiors—for instance, a great mirrored hall—that would be beyond the resources of any theatrical production. I have already said that at the end, when Fortinbras's army swarms over the countryside and then invades the castle we get material that is distracting, indeed irrelevant, but there are also a few other distractions. It is all very well to let us *see* the content of long narrative speeches (for instance, when the Player King talks of the fall of Troy and the death of King Priam and the lament of Queen Hecuba, Branagh shows us these things, with John Gielgud as Priam and Judi Dench as Hecuba, performing in pantomime), but there surely is no need for us to see a naked Hamlet and a naked Ophelia in bed, when Polonius is warning Ophelia that Hamlet's talk of love cannot be trusted. Polonius's warn-ing is not so long or so undramatic that we need to be entertained visually with an invention that finds not a word of support in the text. On the contrary, all of Ophelia's lines suggest that she would not be other than a dutiful young woman, obedient to the morals of the times and to her father's authority. Yet another of Branagh's unfortunate inventions is the prostitute who appears in Polonius's bedroom, during Polonius's interview with Reynaldo. A final example of unnec-essary spectacle is Hamlet's killing of Claudius: He hurls his rapier the length of the hall, impaling Claudius, and then like some 1930's movie star he swings on the chandelier and drops down on Claudius to finish him off.

But it is wrong to end this review by pointing out faults in Branagh's film of *Hamlet.* There is so much in this film that is exciting, so much that is moving, so much that is . . . , well, so much that is *Hamlet* (which is to say that is a great experience), that the film must be recommended without reservation. Go to see it. The four hours will fly.

A postscript. It is good to see that Branagh uses color-blind casting. Voltemand, Fortinbras's Captain, and the messenger who announces Laertes's return are all blacks—the messenger is a black woman—although of course medieval Denmark and Elizabethan England, and, for that matter, Victorian England, would not have routinely included blacks. These performers are effective, and it is appropriate that actors of color take their place in the world's greatest play.

✏ Topics for Critical Thinking and Writing

1. Does the writer give aequate evidence to support his favorable comments on the play?
2. Does she give evidence to support his unfavorable comments?
3. Given the writer's overall evaluation of the film, do you agree with his strategy of devoting the first and last paragraphs to praising the play?
4. Do you think the writer apportioned his space well, or should he have spent more time on the weaknesses, or more time on the strengths? Why?
5. Do you find the comments about the late-nineteenth-century setting relevant and thoughtful, or irrelevant and not very perceptive? Explain.
6. Do you find the *postscript* intrusive? Explain.
7. If you have seen the film, do you more or less agree with the reviewer? Do you think that the reviewer neglected to make certain points that you would have made in your review?

Identity in Pluralistic America

ESSAYS

 **ZORA NEALE HURSTON**

Zora Neale Hurston (1891–1960) was brought up in Eatonville, Florida, a town said to be the first all-black self-governing town in the United States. Her early years were spent working at odd jobs (domestic servant, manicurist, waitress), but she managed to attend Howard University and then, with the aid of a scholarship, entered Barnard College, where she was the first black student. At Barnard, influenced by the anthropologists Franz Boas and Ruth Benedict, she set out to study the folklore of Eatonville. Later she published several volumes of folklore, as well as stories, novels, and an autobiography (the source of our selection) called Dust Tracks on a Road *(1942).*

In the 1950s her writing seemed reactionary, almost embarrassing in an age of black protest, and she herself—working as a domestic, a librarian, and a substitute teacher—was almost forgotten. She died in a county welfare home in Florida and was buried in an unmarked grave. In the 1980s Hurston was, so to speak, rediscovered, partly because of the attention given to her by Alice Walker.

A Conflict of Interest

An incident happened that made me realize how theories go by the board when a person's livelihood is threatened. A man, a Negro, came into the shop one afternoon and sank down in Banks's chair. Banks was the manager and had the first chair by the door. It was so surprising that for a minute Banks just looked at him and never said a word. Finally, he found his tongue and asked, "What do you want?"

"Hair-cut and shave," the man said belligerently.

"But you can't get no hair-cut and shave here. Mr. Robinson[1] has a fine shop for Negroes on U Street near Fifteenth," Banks told him.

"I know it, but I want one here. The Constitution of the United States—"

5   But by that time, Banks had him by the arm. Not roughly, but he was help-ing him out of his chair, nevertheless.

---

[1]**Robinson:** George Robinson, an African American, owned a chain of barber shops. Most of his shops catered to whites in Washington, D.C.

"I don't know how to cut your hair," Banks objected. "I was trained on straight hair. Nobody in here knows how."

"Oh, don't hand me that stuff!" the crusader snarled. "Don't be such an Uncle Tom."

"Run on, fellow. You can't get waited on in here."

"I'll stay right here until I do. I know my rights. Things like this have got to be broken up. I'll get waited on all right, or sue the place."

10   "Go ahead and sue," Banks retorted. "Go on uptown, and get your hair cut, man. Don't be so hard-headed for nothing."

"I'm getting waited on right here!"

"You're next, Mr. Powell," Banks said to a waiting customer. "Sorry, mister, but you better go on uptown."

"But I have a right to be waited on wherever I please," the Negro said, and started towards Updyke's chair which was being emptied. Updyke whirled his chair around so that he could not sit down and stepped in front of it. "Don't you touch *my* chair!" Updyke glared. "Go on about your business."

But instead of going, he made to get into the chair by force.

15   "Don't argue with him! Throw him out of here!" somebody in the back cried. And in a minute, barbers, customers all lathered and hair half cut, and porters, were all helping to throw the Negro out.

The rush carried him way out into the middle of G street and flung him down. He tried to lie there and be a martyr, but the roar of oncoming cars made him jump up and scurry off. We never heard any more about it. I did not participate in the mêlée, but I wanted him thrown out, too. My business was threatened.

It was only that night in bed that I analyzed the whole thing and realized that I was giving sanction to Jim Crow, which theoretically, I was supposed to resist. But here were ten Negro barbers, three porters and two manicurists all stirred up at the threat of our living through loss of patronage. Nobody thought it out at the moment. It was an instinctive thing. That was the first time it was called to my attention that self-interest rides over all sorts of lines. I have seen the same thing happen hundreds of times since, and now I understand it. One sees it breaking over racial, national, religious and class lines. Anglo-Saxon against Anglo-Saxon, Jew against Jew, Negro against Negro, and all sorts of combinations of the three against other combinations of the three. Offhand, you might say that we fifteen Negroes should have felt the racial thing and served him. He was one of us. Perhaps it would have been a beautiful thing if Banks had turned to the shop crowded with customers and announced that this man was going to be served like everybody else even at the risk of losing their patronage, with all of the other employees lined up in the center of the floor shouting, "So say we all!" It would have been a stirring gesture, and made the headlines for a day. Then we could all have gone home to our unpaid rents and bills and things like that. I could leave school and begin my wanderings again. The "militant" Negro who would have been the cause of it all, would have perched on the smuddled-up wreck of things and crowed. Nobody ever found out who or what he was. Perhaps he did what he did on the spur of the moment, not realizing that serving him would have ruined Mr. Robinson, another Negro who had got what he had the hard way. For not only would the G Street shop have been forced to close, but the F Street shop and all of his other six downtown shops. Wrecking George Robinson like that on a "race" angle would have been ironic tragedy. He always helped out any Negro who was trying to do anything progressive as far as he was able. He had no education himself, but he was for it. He would give any Howard

University student a job in his shops if they could qualify, even if it was only a few hours a week.

So I do not know what was the ultimate right in this case. I do know how I felt at the time. There is always something fiendish and loathsome about a person who threatens to deprive you of your way of making a living. That is just human-like, I reckon.

[1942]

Topics for Critical Thinking and Writing

1. Hurston published this account in 1942, and she was writing about an event that had taken place a couple of decades earlier. Given the period and given Hurston's analysis of her action, do you find her behavior understandable and excusable, or do you think that she is rationalizing cowardice? Explain.

2. Words like *outrageous, ironic, pathetic,* and even *tragic* probably can be appropriately applied to this episode. Would you agree, however, that, as Hurston narrates it, it also has comic elements? If so, explain.

3. Hurston argues that self-interest overrides "racial, national, religious, and class lines." Do you agree? Does she persuade you that at least in this incident it was true, or might there have been other reasons for the employees' actions?

 ## ANNA LISA RAYA

Anna Lisa Raya, daughter of a second-generation Mexican-American father and a Puerto Rican mother, grew up in Los Angeles but went to Columbia University in New York. While an undergraduate at Columbia she wrote and published this essay on identity.

It's Hard Enough Being Me

When I entered college, I *discovered* I was Latina. Until then, I had never questioned who I was or where I was from: My father is a second-generation Mexican-American, born and raised in Los Angeles, and my mother was born in Puerto Rico and raised in Compton, Calif. My home is El Sereno, a predominantly Mexican neighborhood in L.A. Every close friend I have back home is Mexican. So I was always just Mexican. Though sometimes I was just Puerto Rican—like when we would visit Mamo (my grandma) or hang out with my Aunt Titi.

Upon arriving in New York as a first-year student, 3000 miles from home, I not only experienced extreme culture shock, but for the first time I had to define myself according to the broad term "Latina." Although culture shock and identity crisis are common for the newly minted collegian who goes away to school, my experience as a newly minted Latina was, and still is, even more complicating. In El Sereno, I felt like I was part of a majority, whereas at the College I am a minority.

I've discovered that many Latinos like myself have undergone similar experiences. We face discrimination for being a minority in this country while also facing criticism for being "whitewashed" or "sellouts" in the countries of our heritage. But as an ethnic group in college, we are forced to define ourselves according to some vague, generalized Latino experience. This requires us to know our history, our language, our music, and our religion. I can't even be a content "Puerto Mexican" because I have to be a politically-and-socially-aware-Latina-with-a-chip-on-my-shoulder-because-of-how-repressed-I-am-in-this-country.

I am none of the above. I am the quintessential imperfect Latina. I can't dance salsa to save my life, I learned about Montezuma and the Aztecs in sixth grade, and I haven't prayed to the *Virgen de Guadalupe* in years.

5   Apparently I don't even look Latina. I can't count how many times people have just assumed that I'm white or asked me if I'm Asian. True, my friends back home call me *güera* ("whitey") because I have green eyes and pale skin, but that was as bad as it got. I never thought I would wish my skin were a darker shade or my hair a curlier texture, but since I've been in college, I have—many times.

Another thing: my Spanish is terrible. Every time I call home, I berate my mama for not teaching me Spanish when I was a child. In fact, not knowing how to speak the language of my home countries is the biggest problem that I have encountered, as have many Latinos. In Mexico there is a term, *pocha*, which is used by native Mexicans to ridicule Mexican-Americans. It expresses a deep-rooted antagonism and dislike for those of us who were raised on the other side of the border. Our failed attempts to speak pure, Mexican Spanish are largely responsible for the dislike. Other Latin American natives have this same attitude. No matter how well a Latino speaks Spanish, it can never be good enough.

Yet Latinos can't even speak Spanish in the U.S. without running the risk of being called "spic" or "wetback." That is precisely why my mother refused to teach me Spanish when I was a child. The fact that she spoke Spanish was constantly used against her: It prevented her from getting good jobs, and it would have placed me in bilingual education—a construct of the Los Angeles public school system that has proved to be more of a hindrance to intellectual development than a help.

To be fully Latina in college, however, I *must* know Spanish. I must satisfy the equation: Latina [equals] Spanish-speaking.

So I'm stuck in this black hole of an identity crisis, and college isn't making my life any easier, as I thought it would. In high school, I was being prepared for an adulthood in which I would be an individual, in which I wouldn't have to wear a Catholic school uniform anymore. But though I led an anonymous adolescence, I knew who I was. I knew I was different from white, black, or Asian people. I knew there was a language other than English that I could call my own if I only knew how to speak it better. I knew there were historical reasons why I was in this country, distinct reasons that make my existence here easier or more difficult than other people's existence. Ultimately, I was content.

10   Now I feel pushed into a corner, always defining, defending, and proving myself to classmates, professors, or employers. Trying to understand who and why I am, while understanding Plato or Homer, is a lot to ask of myself.

A month ago, I heard three Nuyorican (Puerto Ricans born and raised in New York) writers discuss how New York City has influenced their writing. One problem I have faced as a young writer is finding a voice that is true to my community. I was surprised and reassured to discover that as Latinos, these writers had faced similar pressures and conflicts as myself; some weren't even taught Spanish in childhood. I will never forget the advice that one of them gave me that evening: She said that I need to be true to myself. "Because people will always complain about what you are doing—you're a 'gringa' or a 'spic' no matter what," she explained. "So you might as well do things for yourself and not for them."

I don't know why it has taken 20 years to hear this advice, but I'm going to give it a try. *Soy yo* and no one else. *Punto.*[1]

[1994]

✏ Topics for Critical Thinking and Writing

1. In her first paragraph Raya says that although her parents are American citizens, until she went to New York she "was always just Mexican" or "just Puerto Rican." Why do you suppose she thought this way?

2. In her second paragraph Raya says that in New York she "had to" define herself as "Latina," and in her third paragraph she says that many members of "minority" communities "are forced" to define themselves. In paragraph 10 she says, "Now I feel pushed into a corner, always defining, defending, and proving myself to classmates, professors, or employers. Trying to understand who and why I am, while understanding Plato or Homer, is a lot to ask. . . ." Is Raya saying that both the majority culture and the minority culture force her to define herself? Drawing on your own experience, give your views on whether it is a good thing or a bad thing (or some of each) to be forced to define oneself in terms of ethnicity.

3. Today the words *Latino* and *Latina* are common, but until perhaps ten years ago Spanish-speaking people from Mexico, Central America, and South America were called *Hispanics* or *Latin Americans*. Do you think these terms are useful, or do you think that the differences between, say, a poor black woman from Cuba and a rich white man from Argentina are so great that it makes very little sense to put them into the same category, whether the category is called *Latino, Hispanic,* or *Latin American?* Why, incidentally, do you think that *Latino/Latina* is now preferred to *Hispanic?*

4. In paragraph 7 Raya speaks of the Los Angeles bilingual educational program as "a construct of the Los Angeles public school system that has proved to be more of a hindrance to intellectual development than a help." If you have been in a bilingual educational program, evaluate the program. Did it chiefly help you, or chiefly hinder you? Explain.

5. In her last two paragraphs Raya explains that after an acquaintance told her to be true to herself, she concluded, *Soy yo* ("I'm me," or "I'm myself"). You may recall that in *Hamlet* Polonius says to his son Laertes, "This above all: to thine own self be true" (1.3.79). But what does it mean to be true to oneself? Presumably one doesn't behave immorally, but beyond that, what does one do? For instance, if a friend suggested to Raya that she might enjoy (and intellectually profit from) taking a course in Latin American literature, in making a decision, what *self* would she be true to? In your own life, you make many decisions each day. Are many of them based on being true to yourself? Again, putting aside questions concerning immorality, do you think you have a "self" that you are true to? If so, is this self at least in part based on ethnicity?

[1]*Soy yo . . . Punto* I'm me . . . Period. (Editors' note.)

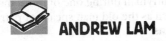

ANDREW LAM

Andrew Lam is an associate editor of the Pacific News Service. This essay originally appeared as an op-ed piece in the New York Times *in 1993.*

Goodbye, Saigon, Finally

Flipping through my United States passport as if it were a comic book, the customs man at the Noi Bai Airport, near Hanoi, appeared curious. "Brother, when did you leave Vietnam?"

"One day before National Defeat Day," I said without thinking. It was an exile's expression, not his.

"God! When did that happen?"

"The 30th of April, 1975."

5   "But, brother, don't you mean National Liberation Day?"

If this conversation had occurred a decade earlier, the difference would have created a dangerous gap between the Vietnamese and the returning Vietnamese-American. But this happened in 1992, when the walls were down, and as I studied the smiling young official, it occurred to me that there was something about this moment, an epiphany. "Yes, brother, I suppose I do mean liberation day."

Not everyone remembers the date with humor. It marked the Vietnamese diaspora, boat people, refugees.

On April 29, 1975, my family and I escaped from Saigon in a crowded C–130. We arrived in Guam the next day, to hear the BBC's tragic account of Saigon's demise: U.S. helicopters flying over the chaotic city, Vietcong tanks rolling in, Vietnamese climbing over the gate into the U.S. Embassy, boats fleeing down the Saigon River toward the South China Sea.

In time, April 30 became the birth date of an exile's culture built on defeatism and a sense of tragic ending. For a while, many Vietnamese in America talked of revenge, of blood debts, of the exile's anguish. Their songs had nostalgic titles: "The Day When I Return" and "Oh, Mother Vietnam, We Are Still Here."

10   April 30, 1976: A child of 12 with nationalistic fervor, I stood in front of San Francisco City Hall with other refugees. I waved the gold flag with three horizontal red stripes. I shouted (to no one in particular): "Give us back South Vietnam!"

April 30, 1979: An uncle told me there was an American plan to retake our homeland by force: "The way Douglas MacArthur did for the South Koreans in the 50's." My 17-year-old brother declared that he would join the anti-Communist guerrilla movement in Vietnam. My father sighed.

April 30, 1983: I stayed awake all night with Vietnamese classmates from Berkeley to listen to monotonous speeches by angry old men. "National defeat must be avenged by sweat and blood!" One vowed.

But through the years, April 30 has come to symbolize something entirely different to me. Although I sometimes mourn the loss of home and land, it's the American landscape and what it offers that solidify my hyphenated identity. This date of tragic ending, from an optimist's point of view, is also an American rebirth, something close to the Fourth of July.

I remember whispering to a young countryman during one of those monotonous April 30 rallies in the mid-1980's: "Even as the old man speaks of patriotic repatriation, we've already become Americans."

15   Assimilation, education, the English language, the American "I"—these have carried me and many others further from that beloved tropical country than the C-130 ever could. Each optimistic step the young Vietnamese takes toward America is tempered with a little betrayal of Little Saigon's parochialism, its sentimentalities and the old man's outdated passion.

When did this happen? Who knows? One night, America quietly seeps in and takes hold of one's mind and body, and the Vietnamese soul of sorrows slowly fades away. In the morning, the Vietnamese American speaks a new language of materialism: his vocabulary includes terms like career choices, down payment, escrow, overtime.

My brother never made it to the Indochinese jungle. The would-be guerrilla fighter became instead a civil engineer. My talk of endless possibilities is punctuated with favorite verbs—transcend, redefine, become. "I want to become a writer," I declared to my parents one morning. My mother gasped.

April 30, 1975: defeat or liberation?

"It was a day of joyous victory," said a retired Communist official in Hanoi. "We fought and realized Uncle Ho's dream of national independence." Then he asked for Marlboro cigarettes and a few precious dollars.

Nhon Nguyen, a real state salesman in San Jose, a former South Vietnamese naval officer, said: "I could never forget the date. So many people died. So much blood. I could never tolerate Communism, you know."

Mai Huong, a young Vietnamese woman in Saigon, said that, of course, it was National Liberation Day. "But it's the South," she said with a wink, "that liberated the North." Indeed, conservative Uncle Ho has slowly admitted defeat to entrepreneurial and cosmopolitan Miss Saigon. She has taken her meaning from a different uncle, you know, Uncle Sam.

"April 30, 1975?" said Bobby To, my 22-year-old cousin in San Francisco. "I don't know that date. I don't remember Vietnam at all." April 29, 1992, is more meaningful to him, Bobby said. "It's when the race riots broke out all over our country. To me it's more realistic to worry about what's going on over here than there."

Sighing, the customs man, who offered me a ride into Hanoi, said: "In truth, there are no liberators. We are all defeated here." There is no job, no future, no direction, only a sense of collective malaise, something akin to the death of the national soul. He added: "You're lucky, brother. You left Vietnam and became an American."

April 30, 1993: My friends and I plan to watch *Gone with the Wind* for the umpteenth time and look for a scene of our unrequited romantic longings: Scarlett, teary-eyed with wind-blown hair, returning to forlorn Tara. We no longer can. Children of defeat, self-liberating adults, we promise to hug instead and recount to each other our own stories of flight.

[1993]

Topics for Critical Thinking and Writing

1. Lam sets up at once the distinction between National Defeat Day and National Liberation Day and calls the moment for him *an epiphany*. How does he do it? And what is an epiphany?

2. In paragraph 8 Lam remembers the escape from Vietnam in 1975, and then April 30 in 1976, 1979, 1983. Assuming that you were not around to notice those dates—or even if you were—what techniques does Lam use to make them vivid?

3. In paragraph 15 Lam says "Each optimistic step the young Vietnamese takes toward America is tempered with a little betrayal of Little Saigon's parochialism, its sentimentalities and the old man's outdated passion." What does he mean?

4. At the essay's conclusion, Lam says that he and his friends will watch *Gone with the Wind* and "recount to each other our own stories of flight." Why do they watch *Gone with the Wind* (instead of a Vietnamese film)? What does Lam's choice of the film tell us?

5. If you have a story similar to Lam's, or one that in many ways is opposed to Lam's, try to tell it in an essay that begins with a narrative and may end with one too.

FICTION

 ## ISAAC BASHEVIS SINGER

 Isaac Bashevis Singer (1904–91) was born in a Jewish village in Poland. His father and both of his grandfathers were Hasidic rabbis, and Singer received a traditional Jewish education in a rabbinical seminary in Warsaw, although he left the seminary after one year and turned to writing fiction and journalism. In 1935 he immigrated to New York, where he wrote articles and essays for the Yiddish Daily Forward *as well as radio scripts for Yiddish soap operas.*

Singer wrote many stories and novels, as well as books for juveniles and four autobiographies (including Lost in America, *1981). In 1978 his work received world attention when he was awarded the Nobel Prize in Literature.*

The Son from America

The village of Lentshin was tiny—a sandy marketplace where the peasants of the area met once a week. It was surrounded by little huts with thatched roofs or shingles green with moss. The chimneys looked like pots. Between the huts there were fields, where the owners planted vegetables or pastured their goats.

In the smallest of these huts lived old Berl, a man in his eighties, and his wife, who was called Berlcha (wife of Berl). Old Berl was one of the Jews who had been driven from their villages in Russia and had settled in Poland. In Lentshin, they mocked the mistakes he made while praying aloud. He spoke with a sharp "r." He was short, broad-shouldered, and had a small white beard, and summer and winter he wore a sheepskin hat, a padded cotton jacket, and stout boots. He walked slowly, shuffling his feet. He had a half acre of field, a cow, a goat, and chickens.

The couple had a son, Samuel, who had gone to America forty years ago. It was said in Lentshin that he became a millionaire there. Every month, the Lentshin letter carrier brought old Berl a money order and a letter that no one could read because many of the words were English. How much money Samuel sent his parents remained a secret. Three times a year, Berl and his wife went on foot to Zakroczym and cashed the money orders there. But they never seemed to use the money. What for? The garden, the cow, and the goat provided most of their needs. Besides, Berlcha sold chickens and eggs, and from these there was enough to buy flour for bread.

No one cared to know where Berl kept the money that his son sent him. There were no thieves in Lentshin. The hut consisted of one room, which contained all their belongings: the table, the shelf for meat, the shelf for milk foods, the two beds, and the clay oven. Sometimes the chickens roosted in the wood-shed and sometimes, when it was cold, in a coop near the oven. The goat, too, found shelter inside when the weather was bad. The more prosperous villages had kerosene lamps, but Berl and his wife did not believe in newfangled gadgets. What was wrong with a wick in a dish of oil? Only for the Sabbath would Berlcha buy three tallow candles at the store. In summer, the couple got up at sunrise and retired with the chickens. In the long winter evenings, Berlcha spun flax at her spinning wheel and Berl sat beside her in the silence of those who enjoy their rest.

5   Once in a while when Berl came home from the synagogue after evening prayers, he brought news to his wife. In Warsaw there were strikers who demanded that the czar abdicate. A heretic by the name of Dr. Herzl[1] had come up with the idea that Jews should settle again in Palestine. Berlcha listened and shook her bonneted head. Her face was yellowish and wrinkled like a cabbage leaf. There were bluish sacks under her eyes. She was half deaf. Berl had to repeat each word he said to her. She would say, "The things that happen in the big cities!"

Here in Lentshin nothing happened except usual events: a cow gave birth to a calf, a young couple had a circumcision party, or a girl was born and there was no party. Occasionally, someone died. Lentshin had no cemetery, and the corpse had to be taken to Zakroczym. Actually, Lentshin had become a village with few young people. The young men left for Zakroczym, for Nowy Dwor, for Warsaw, and sometimes for the United States. Like Samuel's, their letters were illegible, the Yiddish mixed with the languages of the countries where they were now living. They sent photographs in which the men wore top hats and the women fancy dresses like squiresses.

Berl and Berlcha also received such photographs. But their eyes were failing and neither he nor she had glasses. They could barely make out the pictures. Samuel had sons and daughters with gentile names—and grandchildren who had married and had their own offspring. Their names were so strange that Berl and Berlcha could never remember them. But what difference do names make? America was far, far away on the other side of the ocean, at the edge of the world. A Talmud[2] teacher who came to Lentshin had said that Americans walked with their heads down and their feet up. Berl and Berlcha could not grasp this. How was it possible? But since the teacher said so it must be true. Berlcha pondered for some time and then she said, "One can get accustomed to everything."

And so it remained. From too much thinking—God forbid—one may lose one's wits.

---

[1]**Dr. Herzl** Theodore Herzl (1860-1904), the founder of Zionism   [2]**Talmud** the collection of ancient rabbinic writings that constitute the basis of traditional Judaism

One Friday morning, when Berlcha was kneading the dough for the Sabbath loaves, the door opened and a nobleman entered. He was so tall that he had to bend down to get through the door. He wore a beaver hat and a cloak bordered with fur. He was followed by Chazkel, the coachman from Zakroczym, who carried two leather valises with brass locks. In astonishment Berlcha raised her eyes.

10   The nobleman looked around and said to the coachman in Yiddish, "Here it is." He took out a silver ruble and paid him. The coachman tried to hand him change but he said, "You can go now."

When the coachman closed the door, the nobleman said, "Mother, it's me, your son Samuel—Sam."

Berlcha heard the words and her legs grew numb. Her hands, to which pieces of dough were sticking, lost their power. The nobleman hugged her, kissed her forehead, both her cheeks. Berlcha began to cackle like a hen, "My son!" At that moment Berl came in from the woodshed, his arms piled with logs. The goat followed him. When he saw a nobleman kissing his wife, Berl dropped the wood and exclaimed, "What is this?"

The nobleman let go of Berlcha and embraced Berl. "Father!"

For a long time Berl was unable to utter a sound. He wanted to recite holy words that he had read in the Yiddish Bible, but he could remember nothing. Then he asked, "Are you Samuel?"

15   "Yes, Father, I am Samuel."

"Well, peace be with you." Berl grasped his son's hand. He was still not sure that he was not being fooled. Samuel wasn't as tall and heavy as this man, but then Berl reminded himself that Samuel was only fifteen years old when he had left home. He must have grown in that faraway country. Berl asked, "Why didn't you let us know that you were coming?"

"Didn't you receive my cable?" Samuel asked.

Berl did not know what a cable was.

Berlcha had scraped the dough from her hands and enfolded her son. He kissed her again and asked, "Mother, didn't you receive a cable?"

20   "What? If I lived to see this, I am happy to die," Berlcha said, amazed by her own words. Berl, too, was amazed. These were just the words he would have said earlier if he had been able to remember. After a while Berl came to himself and said, "Pescha, you will have to make a double Sabbath pudding in addition to the stew."

It was years since Berl had called Berlcha by her given name. When he wanted to address her, he would say, "Listen," or "Say." It is the young or those from the big cities who call a wife by her name. Only now did Berlcha begin to cry. Yellow tears ran from her eyes, and everything became dim. Then she called out, "It's Friday—I have to prepare for the Sabbath." Yes, she had to knead the dough and braid the loaves. With such a guest, she had to make a larger Sabbath stew. The winter day is short and she must hurry.

Her son understood what was worrying her, because he said, "Mother, I will help you."

Berlcha wanted to laugh, but a choked sob came out. "What are you saying? God forbid."

The nobleman took off his cloak and jacket and remained in his vest, on which hung a solid-gold watch chain. He rolled up his sleeves and came to the trough. "Mother, I was a baker for many years in New York," he said, and he began to knead the dough.

25   "What! You are my darling son who will say Kaddish[3] for me." She wept
raspingly. Her strength left her, and she slumped onto the bed.

Berl said, "Women will always be women." And he went to the shed to get
more wood. The goat sat down near the oven; she gazed with surprise at this
strange man—his height and his bizarre clothes.

The neighbors had heard the good news that Berl's son had arrived from
America and they came to greet him. The women began to help Berlcha prepare
for the Sabbath. Some laughed, some cried. The room was full of people, as at a
wedding. They asked Berl's son, "What is new in America?" And Berl's son answered, "America is all right."

"Do Jews make a living?"

"One eats white bread there on weekdays."[4]

30   "Do they remain Jews?"

"I am not a gentile."

After Berlcha blessed the candles, father and son went to the little synagogue across the street. A new snow had fallen. The son took large steps, but
Berl warned him, "Slow down."

In the synagogue the Jews recited "Let Us Exult" and "Come, My Groom."
All the time, the snow outside kept falling. After prayers, when Berl and Samuel
left the Holy Place, the village was unrecognizable. Everything was covered in
snow. One could see only the contours of the roofs and the candles in the windows. Samuel said, "Nothing has changed here."

Berlcha had prepared gefilte fish, chicken soup with rice, meat, carrot stew.
Berl recited the benediction over a glass of ritual wine. The family ate and drank,
and when it grew quiet for a while one could hear the chirping of the house
cricket. The son talked a lot, but Berl and Berlcha understood little. His Yiddish
was different and contained foreign words.

35   After the final blessing Samuel asked, "Father, what did you do with all the
money I sent you?"

Berl raised his white brows. "It's here."

"Didn't you put it in a bank?"

"There is no bank in Lentshin."

"Where do you keep it?"

40   Berl hesitated. "One is not allowed to touch money on the Sabbath but I will
show you." He crouched beside the bed and began to shove something heavy. A
boot appeared. Its top was stuffed with straw. Berl removed the straw and the
son saw that the boot was full of gold coins. He lifted it.

"Father, this is a treasure!" he called out.

"Well."

"Why didn't you spend it?"

"On what? Thank God, we have everything."

45   "Why didn't you travel somewhere?"

"Where to? This is our home."

The son asked one question after the other, but Berl's answer was always
the same: they wanted for nothing. The garden, the cow, the goat, the chickens

---

[3]**Kaddish** the prayer for the dead   [4]**One eats white bread there on weekdays** in the
poor communities of Europe white bread was a luxury reserved for holidays such as the
Sabbath

provided them with all they needed. The son said, "If thieves knew about this, your lives wouldn't be safe."

"There are no thieves here."

"What will happen to the money?"

50   "You take it."

Slowly, Berl and Berlcha grew accustomed to their son and his American Yiddish. Berlcha could hear him better now. She even recognized his voice. He was saying, "Perhaps we should build a larger synagogue."

"The synagogue is big enough," Berl replied.

"Perhaps a home for old people."

"No one sleeps in the street."

55   The next day after the Sabbath meal was eaten, a gentile from Zakroczym brought a paper—it was the cable. Berl and Berlcha lay down for a nap. They soon began to snore. The goat, too, dozed off. The son put on his cloak and his hat and went for a walk. He strode with his long legs across the marketplace. He stretched out a hand and touched a roof. He wanted to smoke a cigar, but he remembered it was forbidden on the Sabbath. He had a desire to talk to someone, but it seemed that the whole of Lentshin was asleep. He entered the synagogue. An old man was sitting there, reciting psalms. Samuel asked, "Are you praying?"

"What else is there to do when one gets old?"

"Do you make a living?"

The old man did not understand the meaning of those words. He smiled, showing his empty gums, and then he said, "If God gives health, one keeps on living."

Samuel returned home. Dusk had fallen. Berl went to the synagogue for the evening prayers and the son remained with his mother. The room was filled with shadows.

60   Berlcha began to recite in a solemn singsong, "God of Abraham, Isaac, and Jacob, defend the poor people of Israel and Thy name. The Holy Sabbath is departing; the welcome week is coming to us. Let it be one of health, wealth, and good deeds."

"Mother, you don't need to pray for wealth," Samuel said. "You are wealthy already."

Berlcha did not hear—or pretended not to. Her face had turned into a cluster of shadows.

In the twilight Samuel put his hand into his jacket pocket and touched his passport, his checkbook, his letters of credit. He had come here with big plans. He had a valise filled with presents for his parents. He wanted to bestow gifts on the village. He brought not only his own money but funds from the Lentshin Society in New York, which had organized a ball for the benefit of the village. But this village in the hinterland needed nothing. From the synagogue one could hear hoarse chanting. The cricket, silent all day, started again its chirping. Berlcha began to sway and utter holy rhymes inherited from mothers and grandmothers:

Thy holy sheep
In mercy keep,
In Torah[5] good deeds;

---

[5]**Torah** Jewish teachings, especially the first five books of the Hebrew Bible

Provide for all their needs,
Shoes, clothes, and bread
And the Messiah's tread.

[1973]

✏ Topics for Critical Thinking and Writing

1. What is your attitude toward Berl and Berlcha? Admiration? Pity? Or what? (Of course you need not limit your answer to a single word. You may find that your response is complex.) What is your attitude toward Samuel?
2. Compare Samuel's values with those of his parents. What resemblances do you find? What differences?

 DIANA CHANG

Diana Chang, author of several novels and books of poems, teaches creative writing at Barnard College. She identifies herself as an American writer whose background is mostly Chinese.

The Oriental Contingent

Connie couldn't remember whose party it was, whose house. She had an impression of kerosene lamps on brown wicker tables, of shapes talking in doorways. It was summer, almost the only time Connie has run into her since, too, and someone was saying, "You must know Lisa Mallory."

"I don't think so."

"She's here. You must know her."

Later in the evening, it was someone else who introduced her to a figure perched on the balustrade of the steps leading to the lawn where more shapes milled. In stretching out a hand to shake Connie's, the figure almost fell off sideways. Connie pushed her back upright onto her perch and, peering, took in the fact that Lisa Mallory had a Chinese face. For a long instant, she felt nonplussed, and was rendered speechless.

5   But Lisa Mallory was filling in the silence. "Well, now, Connie Sung," she said, not enthusiastically but with a kind of sophisticated interest. "I'm not in music myself, but Paul Wu's my cousin. Guilt by association!" She laughed. "No-tone music, I call his. He studied with John Cage, Varese, and so forth."

Surprised that Lisa knew she was a violinist, Connie murmured something friendly, wondering if she should simply ask outright, "I'm sure I should know, but what do you do?" but she hesitated, taking in her appearance instead, while Lisa went on with, "It's world class composing. Nothing's wrong with the level. But it's hard going for the layman, believe me."

Lisa Mallory wore a one-of-a-kind kimono dress, but it didn't make her look Japanese at all, and her hair was drawn back tightly in a braid which stood out from close to the top of her head horizontally. You could probably lift her off her feet by grasping it, like the handle of a pot.

"You should give a concert here, Connie," she said, using her first name right away, Connie noticed, like any American. "Lots of culturati around." Even when she wasn't actually speaking, she pursued her own line of thought actively and seemed to find herself mildly amusing.

"I'm new to the area," Connie said, deprecatingly. "I've just been a weekend guest, actually, till a month ago."

10   "It's easy to be part of it. Nothing to it. I should know. You'll see."

"I wish it weren't so dark," Connie found herself saying, waving her hand in front of her eyes as if the night were a veil to brush aside. She recognized in herself that intense need to see, to see into fellow Orientals, to fathom them. So far, Lisa Mallory had not given her enough clues, and the darkness itself seemed to be interfering.

Lisa dropped off her perch. "It's important to be true to oneself," she said. "Keep the modern stuff out of your repertory. Be romantic. Don't look like that! You're best at the romantics. Anyhow, take it from me. I know. And *I* like what I like."

Released by her outspokenness, Connie laughed and asked, "I'm sure I should know, but what is it that you do?" She was certain Lisa would say something like, "I'm with a public relations firm." "I'm in city services."

But she replied, "What do all Chinese excel at?" Not as if she'd asked a rhetorical question, she waited, then answered herself. "Well, aren't we all physicists, musicians, architects, or in software?"

15   At that point a voice broke in, followed by a large body which put his arms around both women, "The Oriental contingent! I've got to break this up."

Turning, Lisa kissed him roundly, and said over her shoulder to Connie, "I'll take him away before he tells us we look alike!"

They melted into the steps below, and Connie, feeling put off balance and somehow slow-witted, was left to think over her new acquaintance.

"Hello, Lisa Mallory," Connie Sung always said on the infrequent occasions when they ran into one another. She always said "Hello, Lisa Mallory," with a shyness she did not understand in herself. It was strange, but they had no mutual friends except for Paul Wu, and Connie had not seen him in ages. Connie had no one of whom to ask her questions. But sometime soon, she'd be told Lisa's maiden name. Sometime she'd simply call her Lisa. Sometime what Lisa did with her life would be answered.

Three, four years passed, with their running into one another at receptions and openings, and still Lisa Mallory remained an enigma. Mildly amused herself, Connie wondered if other people, as well, found her inscrutable. But none of her American friends (though, of course, Lisa and she were Americans, too, she had to remind herself), none of their Caucasian friends seemed curious about backgrounds. In their accepting way, they did not wonder about Lisa's background, or about Connie's or Paul Wu's. Perhaps they assumed they were all cut from the same cloth. But to Connie, the Orientals she met were unread books, books she never had the right occasion or time to fully pursue.

20   She didn't even see the humor in her situation—it was such an issue with her. The fact was she felt less, much less, sure of herself when she was with real Chinese.

As she was realizing this, the truth suddenly dawned on her. Lisa Mallory never referred to her own background because it was more Chinese than Connie's, and therefore of a higher order. She was tact incarnate. All along, she had been going out of her way not to embarrass Connie. Yes, yes. Her assurance was definitely uppercrust (perhaps her father had been in the diplomatic service), and her offhand didacticness, her lack of self-doubt, was indeed characteristically Chinese-Chinese. Connie was not only impressed by these traits, but also put on the defensive because of them.

Connie let out a sigh—a sigh that follows the solution to a nagging problem . . . Lisa's mysteriousness. But now Connie knew only too clearly that her own background made her decidedly inferior. Her father was a second-generation gynecologist who spoke hardly any Chinese. Yes, inferior and totally without recourse.

Of course, at one of the gatherings, Connie met Bill Mallory, too. He was simply American, maybe Catholic, possibly lapsed. She was not put off balance by him at all. But most of the time he was away on business, and Lisa cropped up at functions as single as Connie.

Then one day, Lisa had a man in tow—wiry and tall, he looked Chinese from the Shantung area, or perhaps from Beijing, and his styled hair made him appear vaguely artistic.

25   "Connie, I'd like you to meet Eric Li. He got out at the beginning of the *detente,* went to Berkeley, and is assimilating a mile-a-minute," Lisa said, with her usual irony. "Bill found him and is grooming him, though he came with his own charisma."

Eric waved her remark aside. "Lisa has missed her calling. She was born to be in PR," he said, with an accent.

"Is that what she does?" Connie put in at once, looking only at him. "Is that her profession?"

"You don't know?" he asked, with surprise.

Though she was greeting someone else, Lisa turned and answered, "I'm a fabrics tycoon, I think I can say without immodesty." She moved away and continued her conversation with the other friend.

30   Behind his hand, he said, playfully, as though letting Connie in on a secret, "Factories in Hongkong and Taipei, and now he's—Bill, that is—is exploring them on the mainland."

"With her fabulous contacts over there!" Connie exclaimed, now seeing it all. "Of course, what a wonderful business combination they must make."

Eric was about to utter something, but stopped, and said flatly, "I have all the mainland contacts, even though I was only twenty when I left, but my parents . . ."

"How interesting," Connie murmured lamely. "I see," preoccupied as she was with trying to put two and two together.

Lisa was back and said without an introduction, continuing her line of thought, "You two look good together, if I have to say so myself. Why don't you ask him to one of your concerts? And you, Eric, you're in America now, so don't stand on ceremony, or you'll be out in left field." She walked away with someone for another drink.

35   Looking uncomfortable, but recovering himself with a smile, Eric said, "Lisa makes me feel more Chinese than I am becoming—it is her directness, I suspect. In China, we'd say she is too much like a man."

At which Connie found herself saying, "She makes me feel *less* Chinese."

"Less!"

"Less Chinese than she is."

"That is not possible," Eric said, with a shade of contempt—for whom? Lisa or Connie? He barely suppressed a laugh, cold as Chinese laughter could be.

40   Connie blurted out, "I'm a failed Chinese. Yes, and it's to you that I need to say it." She paused and repeated emphatically, "I am a failed Chinese." Her heart was beating quicker, but she was glad to have got that out, a confession and a definition that might begin to free her. "Do you know you make me feel that, too? You've been here only about ten years, right?"

"Right, and I'm thirty-one."

"You know what I think? I think it's harder for a Chinese to do two things."

At that moment, an American moved in closer, looking pleased somehow to be with them.

She continued, "It's harder for us to become American than, say, for a German, and it's also harder not to remain residually Chinese, even if you are third generation."

45   Eric said blandly, "Don't take yourself so seriously. You can't help being an American product."

Trying to be comforting, the American interjected with, "The young lady is not a product, an object. She is a human being, and there is no difference among peoples that I can see."

"I judge myself both as a Chinese and as an American," Connie said.

"You worry too much," Eric said, impatiently. Then he looked around and though she wasn't in sight, he lowered his voice. "She is what she is. I know what she is. But she avoids going to Hongkong. She avoids it."

Connie felt turned around. "Avoids it?"

50   "Bill's in Beijing right now. She's here. How come?"

"I don't know," Connie replied, as though an answer had been required of her.

"She makes up many excuses, reasons. Ask her. Ask her yourself," he said, pointedly.

"Oh, I couldn't do that. By the way, I'm going on a concert tour next year in three cities—Shanghai, Beijing and Nanking," Connie said. "It'll be my first time in China."

"Really! You must be very talented to be touring at your age," he said, genuinely interested for the first time. Because she was going to China, or because she now came across as an over-achiever, even though Chinese American?

55   "I'm just about your age," she said, realizing then that maybe Lisa Mallory had left them alone purposely.

"You could both pass as teenagers!" the American exclaimed.

Two months later, she ran into Lisa again. As usual, Lisa began in the middle of her own thoughts. "Did he call?"

"Who? Oh. No, no."

"Well, it's true he's been in China the last three weeks with Bill. They'll be back this weekend."

60   Connie saw her opportunity. "Are you planning to go to China yourself?"

For the first time, Lisa seemed at a loss for words. She raised her shoulders, than let them drop. Too airily, she said, "You know, there's always Paris. I can't bear not to go to Paris, if I'm to take a trip."

"But you're Chinese. You *have* been to China, you came from China originally, didn't you?"

"I could go to Paris twice a year, I love it so," Lisa said. "And then there's London, Florence, Venice."

"But—but your business contacts?"

65   "*My* contacts? Bill, he's the businessman who makes the contacts. Always has. I take care of the New York office, which is a considerable job. We have a staff of eighty-five."

Connie said, "I told Eric I'll be giving a tour in China. I'm taking Chinese lessons right now."

Lisa Mallory laughed. "Save your time. They'll still be disdainful over there. See, *they* don't care," and she waved her hand at the crowd. "Some of them have been born in Buffalo, too! It's the Chinese you can't fool. They know you're not the genuine article—you and I."

Her face was suddenly heightened in color, and she was breathing as if ready to flee from something. "Yes, you heard right. I was born in Buffalo."

"You were!" Connie exclaimed before she could control her amazement.

70   "Well, what about you?" Lisa retorted. She was actually shaking and trying to hide it by making sudden gestures.

"Westchester."

"But your parents at least were Chinese."

"Well, so were, so are, yours!"

"I was adopted by Americans. My full name is Lisa Warren Mallory."

75   Incredulous, Connie said, "I'm more Chinese than you!"

"Who isn't?" She laughed, unhappily. "Having Chinese parents makes all the difference. We're worlds apart."

"And all the time I thought . . . never mind what I thought."

"You have it over me. It's written all over you. I could tell even in the dark that night."

"Oh, Lisa," Connie said to comfort her, "none of this matters to anybody except us. Really and truly. They're too busy with their own problems."

80   "The only time I feel Chinese is when I'm embarrassed I'm not more Chinese—which is a totally Chinese reflex I'd give anything to be rid of!"

"I know what you mean."

"And as for Eric looking down his nose at me, he's knocking himself out to be so American, *but as a secure Chinese!* What's so genuine about that article?"

Both of them struck their heads laughing, but their eyes were not merry.

"Say it again," Connie asked of her, "say it again that my being more Chinese is written all over me."

85   "Consider it said," Lisa said. "My natural mother happened to be there at the time—I can't help being born in Buffalo."

"I know, I know," Connie said with feeling. "If only you had had some say in the matter."

"It's only Orientals who haunt me!" Lisa stamped her foot. "Only them!"

"I'm so sorry," Connie Sung said, for all of them. "It's all so turned around."

"So I'm made in America, so there!" Lisa Mallory declared, making a sniffing sound, and seemed to be recovering her sangfroid.

90   Connie felt tired—as if she'd traveled—but a lot had been settled on the way.

[1989]

Topics for Critical Thinking and Writing

1. In the first paragraph, a person (whose name we don't know) says, "You must know Lisa Mallory." Why does she make that assumption?
2. During their first meeting Connie thinks "She recognized in herself that intense need to see, to see into fellow Orientals, to fathom them" and she waves "her hand in front of her eyes." Does she know what she is looking for?
3. What does Eric do in the story? What is his function? And "the American" (paragraph 43)?
4. In paragraph 88 we read, "'I'm so sorry,' Connie Sung said, for all of them. 'It's all so turned around.'" What does the writer mean by "for all of them"? And what does Connie mean by "It's all so turned around"?

 ## RAYMOND CARVER

Raymond Carver (1938–88) was born in Clatskanie, a logging town in Oregon. In 1963 he graduated from Humboldt State College in northern California and then did further study at the University of Iowa.

His early years were not easy—he married while still in college, divorced a little later, and sometimes suffered from alcoholism. In his last years he found domestic happiness, but he died of cancer at the age of fifty.

As a young man he wrote poetry while working at odd jobs (janitor, deliveryman, etc.); later he turned to fiction, though he continued to write poetry. Most of his fiction is of a sort called "minimalist," narrating in a spare, understated style stories about bewildered and sometimes exhausted men and women. "Popular Mechanics" (p. 576) is a good example. His later work, beginning with "Cathedral" in 1983, by his own admission was "larger."

Cathedral

This blind man, an old friend of my wife's, he was on his way to spend the night. His wife had died. So he was visiting the dead wife's relatives in Connecticut. He called my wife from his in-laws'. Arrangements were made. He would come by train, a five-hour trip, and my wife would meet him at the station. She hadn't seen him since she worked for him one summer in Seattle ten years ago. But she and the blind man had kept in touch. They made tapes and mailed them back and forth. I wasn't enthusiastic about his visit. He was no one I knew. And his being blind bothered me. My idea of blindness came from the movies. In the movies, the blind moved slowly and never laughed. Sometimes they were led by seeing-eye dogs. A blind man in my house was not something I looked forward to.

That summer in Seattle she had needed a job. She didn't have any money. The man she was going to marry at the end of the summer was in officers' training school. He didn't have any money, either. But she was in love with the guy, and he was in love with her, etc. She'd seen something in the paper: HELP WANTED—*Reading to Blind Man*, and a telephone number. She phoned and went over, was hired on the spot. She'd worked with this blind man all summer.

She read stuff to him, case studies, reports, that sort of thing. She helped him organize his little office in the county social-service department. They'd become good friends, my wife and the blind man. How do I know these things? She told me. And she told me something else. On her last day in the office, the blind man asked if he could touch her face. She agreed to this. She told me he touched his fingers to every part of her face, her nose—even her neck! She never forgot it. She even tried to write a poem about it. She was always trying to write a poem. She wrote a poem or two every year, usually after something really important had happened to her.

When we first started going out together, she showed me the poem. In the poem, she recalled his fingers and the way they had moved around over her face. In the poem, she talked about what she had felt at the time, about what went through her mind when the blind man touched her nose and lips. I can remember I didn't think much of the poem. Of course, I didn't tell her that. Maybe I just don't understand poetry. I admit it's not the first thing I reach for when I pick up something to read.

Anyway, this man who'd first enjoyed her favors, the officer-to-be, he'd been her childhood sweetheart. So okay. I'm saying that at the end of the summer she let the blind man run his hands over her face, said goodbye to him, married her childhood etc., who was now a commissioned officer, and she moved away from Seattle. But they'd kept in touch, she and the blind man. She made the first contact after a year or so. She called him up one night from an Air Force base in Alabama. She wanted to talk. They talked. He asked her to send a tape and tell him about her life. She did this. She sent the tape. On the tape, she told the blind man about her husband and about their life together in the military. She told the blind man she loved her husband but she didn't like it where they lived and she didn't like it that he was part of the military-industrial thing. She told the blind man she'd written a poem and he was in it. She told him that she was writing a poem about what it was like to be an Air Force officer's wife. The poem wasn't finished yet. She was still writing it. The blind man made a tape. He sent her the tape. She made a tape. This went on for years. My wife's officer was posted to one base and then another. She sent tapes from Moody AFB, McGuire, McConnell, and finally Travis, near Sacramento, where one night she got to feeling lonely and cut off from people she kept losing in that moving-around life. She got to feeling she couldn't go it another step. She went in and swallowed all the pills and capsules in the medicine chest and washed them down with a bottle of gin. Then she got into a hot bath and passed out.

5   But instead of dying, she got sick. She threw up. Her officer—why should he have a name? he was the childhood sweetheart, and what more does he want?—came home from somewhere, found her, and called the ambulance. In time, she put it all on a tape and sent the tape to the blind man. Over the years, she put all kinds of stuff on tapes and sent the tapes off lickety-split. Next to writing a poem every year, I think it was her chief means of recreation. On one tape, she told the blind man she'd decided to live away from her officer for a time. On another tape, she told him about her divorce. She and I began going out, and of course she told her blind man about it. She told him everything, or so it seemed to me. Once she asked me if I'd like to hear the latest tape from the blind man. This was a year ago. I was on the tape, she said. So I said okay, I'd listen to it. I got us drinks and we settled down in the living room. We made ready to listen. First she inserted the tape into the player and adjusted a couple of dials. Then she pushed a lever. The tape squeaked and someone began to talk in this loud voice. She

lowered the volume. After a few minutes of harmless chitchat, I heard my own name in the mouth of this stranger, this blind man I didn't even know! And then this: "From all you've said about him, I can only conclude—" But we were interrupted, a knock at the door, something, and we didn't ever get back to the tape. Maybe it was just as well. I'd heard all I wanted to.

Now this same blind man was coming to sleep in my house.

"Maybe I could take him bowling," I said to my wife. She was at the draining board doing scalloped potatoes. She put down the knife she was using and turned around.

"If you love me," she said, "you can do this for me. If you don't love me, okay. But if you had a friend, any friend, and the friend came to visit, I'd make him feel comfortable." She wiped her hands with the dish towel.

"I don't have any blind friends," I said.

10 "You don't have *any* friends," she said. "Period. Besides," she said, "goddamn it, his wife's just died! Don't you understand that? The man's lost his wife!"

I didn't answer. She'd told me a little about the blind man's wife. Her name was Beulah. Beulah! That's a name for a colored woman.

"Was his wife a Negro?" I asked.

"Are you crazy?" my wife said. "Have you just flipped or something?" She picked up a potato. I saw it hit the floor, then roll under the stove. "What's wrong with you?" she said. "Are you drunk?"

"I'm just asking," I said.

15 Right then my wife filled me in with more detail than I cared to know. I made a drink and sat at the kitchen table to listen. Pieces of the story began to fall into place.

Beulah had gone to work for the blind man the summer after my wife had stopped working for him. Pretty soon Beulah and the blind man had themselves a church wedding. It was a little wedding—who'd want to go to such a wedding in the first place?—just the two of them, plus the minister and the minister's wife. But it was a church wedding just the same. It was what Beulah had wanted, he'd said. But even then Beulah must have been carrying the cancer in her glands. After they had been inseparable for eight years—my wife's word, *inseparable*—Beulah's health went into a rapid decline. She died in a Seattle hospital room, the blind man sitting beside the bed and holding on to her hand. They'd married, lived and worked together, slept together—had sex, sure—and then the blind man had to bury her. All this without his having ever seen what the goddamned woman looked like. It was beyond my understanding. Hearing this, I felt sorry for the blind man for a little bit. And then I found myself thinking what a pitiful life this woman must have led. Imagine a woman who could never see herself as she was seen in the eyes of her loved one. A woman who could go on day after day and never receive the smallest compliment from her beloved. A woman whose husband could never read the expression on her face, be it misery or something better. Someone who could wear makeup or not—what difference to him? She could, if she wanted, wear green eye-shadow around one eye, a straight pin in her nostril, yellow slacks, and purple shoes, no matter. And then to slip off into death, the blind man's hand on her hand, his blind eyes streaming tears—I'm imaging now—her last thought maybe this: that he never even knew what she looked like, and she on an express to the grave. Robert was left with a small insurance policy and a half of a twenty-peso Mexican coin. The other half of the coin went into the box with her. Pathetic.

So when the time rolled around, my wife went to the depot to pick him up. With nothing to do but wait—sure, I blamed him for that—I was having a drink and watching the TV when I heard the car pull into the drive. I got up from the sofa with my drink and went to the window to have a look.

I saw my wife laughing as she parked the car. I saw her get out of the car and shut the door. She was still wearing a smile. Just amazing. She went around to the other side of the car to where the blind man was already starting to get out. This blind man, feature this, he was wearing a full beard! A beard on a blind man! Too much, I say. The blind man reached into the back seat and dragged out a suitcase. My wife took his arm, shut the car door, and, talking all the way, moved him down the drive and then up the steps to the front porch. I turned off the TV. I finished my drink, rinsed the glass, dried my hands. Then I went to the door.

My wife said, "I want you to meet Robert. Robert, this is my husband. I've told you all about him." She was beaming. She had this blind man by his coat sleeve.

20   The blind man let go of his suitcase and up came his hand. I took it. He squeezed hard, held my hand, and then he let it go.

"I feel like we've already met," he boomed.

"Likewise," I said. I didn't know what else to say. Then I said, "Welcome. I've heard a lot about you." We began to move then, a little group, from the porch into the living room, my wife guiding him by the arm. The blind man was carrying his suitcase in his other hand. My wife said things like, "To your left here, Robert. That's right. Now watch it, there's a chair. That's it. Sit down right here. This is the sofa. We just bought this sofa two weeks ago."

I started to say something about the old sofa. I'd liked that old sofa. But I didn't say anything. Then I wanted to say something else, small-talk, about the scenic ride along the Hudson. How going *to* New York, you should sit on the right-hand side of the train, and coming *from* New York, the left-hand side.

"Did you have a good train ride?" I said. "Which side of the train did you sit on, by the way?"

25   "What a question, which side!" my wife said. "What's it matter which side?" she said.

"I just asked," I said.

"Right side," the blind man said. "I hadn't been on a train in nearly forty years. Not since I was a kid. With my folks. That's been a long time. I'd nearly forgotten the sensation. I have winter in my beard now," he said. "So I've been told, anyway. Do I look distinguished, my dear?" the blind man said to my wife.

"You look distinguished, Robert," she said. "Robert," she said. "Robert, it's just so good to see you."

My wife finally took her eyes off the blind man and looked at me. I had the feeling she didn't like what she saw. I shrugged.

30   I've never met, or personally known, anyone who was blind. This blind man was late forties, a heavy-set, balding man with stooped shoulders, as if he carried a great weight there. He wore brown slacks, brown shoes, a light-brown shirt, a tie, a sports coat. Spiffy. He also had this full beard. But he didn't use a cane and he didn't wear dark glasses. I'd always thought dark glasses were a must for the blind. Fact was, I wished he had a pair. At first glance, his eyes looked like anyone else's eyes. But if you looked close, there was something different about them. Too much white in the iris, for one thing, and the pupils seemed to move around in the sockets without his knowing it or being able to stop it. Creepy. As I stared at his face, I saw the left pupil turn in toward his nose while the other

made an effort to keep in one place. But it was only an effort, for that eye was on the roam without his knowing it or wanting it to be.

I said, "Let me get you a drink. What's your pleasure? We have a little of everything. It's one of our pastimes."

"Bub, I'm a Scotch man myself," he said fast enough in this big voice.

"Right," I said. Bub! "Sure you are. I knew it."

He let his fingers touch his suitcase, which was sitting alongside the sofa. He was taking his bearings. I didn't blame him for that.

35   "I'll move that up to your room," my wife said.

"No, that's fine," the blind man said loudly. "It can go up when I go up."

"A little water with the Scotch?" I said.

"Very little," he said.

"I knew it," I said.

40   He said, "Just a tad. The Irish actor, Barry Fitzgerald? I'm like that fellow. When I drink water, Fitzgerald said, I drink water. When I drink whiskey, I drink whiskey." My wife laughed. The blind man brought his hand up under his beard. He lifted his beard slowly and let it drop.

I did the drinks, three big glasses of Scotch with a splash of water in each. Then we made ourselves comfortable and talked about Robert's travels. First the long flight from the West Coast to Connecticut, we covered that. Then from Connecticut up here by train. We had another drink concerning that leg of the trip.

I remembered having read somewhere that the blind didn't smoke because, as speculation had it, they couldn't see the smoke they exhaled. I thought I knew that much and that much only about blind people. But this blind man smoked his cigarette down to the nubbin and then lit another one. This blind man filled his ashtray and my wife emptied it.

When we sat down at the table for dinner, we had another drink. My wife heaped Robert's plate with cube steak, scalloped potatoes, green beans. I buttered him up two slices of bread. I said, "Here's bread and butter for you." I swallowed some of my drink. "Now let us pray," I said, and the blind man lowered his head. My wife looked at me, her mouth agape. "Pray the phone won't ring and the food doesn't get cold," I said.

We dug in. We ate everything there was to eat on the table. We ate like there was no tomorrow. We didn't talk. We ate. We scarfed. We grazed that table. We were into serious eating. The blind man had right away located his foods, he knew just where everything was on his plate. I watched with admiration as he used his knife and fork on the meat. He'd cut two pieces of meat, fork the meat into his mouth, and then go all out for the scalloped potatoes, the beans next, and then he'd tear off a hunk of buttered bread and eat that. He'd follow this up with a big drink of milk. It didn't seem to bother him to use his fingers once in a while, either.

45   We finished everything, including half a strawberry pie. For a few moments, we sat as if stunned. Sweat beaded on our faces. Finally, we got up from the table and left the dirty places. We didn't look back. We took ourselves into the living room and sank into our places again. Robert and my wife sat on the sofa. I took the big chair. We had us two or three more drinks while they talked about the major things that had come to pass for them in the past ten years. For the most part, I just listened. Now and then I joined in. I didn't want him to think I'd left the room, and I didn't want her to think I was feeling left out. They talked of things that had happened to them—to them!—these past ten years. I waited in vain to hear my name on my wife's sweet lips: "And then my dear husband came

into my life"—something like that. But I heard nothing of the sort. More talk of Robert. Robert had done a little of everything, it seemed, a regular blind jack-of-all-trades. But most recently he and his wife had had an Amway distributorship, from which, I gathered, they'd earned their living, such as it was. The blind man was also a ham radio operator. He talked in his loud voice about conversations he'd had with fellow operators in Guam, in the Philippines, in Alaska, and even in Tahiti. He said he'd have a lot of friends there if he ever wanted to go visit those places. From time to time, he'd turn his blind face toward me, put his hand under his beard, ask me something. How long had I been in my present position? (Three years.) Did I like my work? (I didn't.) Was I going to stay with it? (What were the options?) Finally, when I thought he was beginning to run down, I got up and turned on the TV.

My wife looked at me with irritation. She was heading toward a boil. Then she looked at the blind man and said, "Robert, do you have a TV?"

The blind man said, "My dear, I have two TVs. I have a color set and a black-and-white thing, an old relic. It's funny, but if I turn the TV on, and I'm always turning it on, I turn on the color set. It's funny, don't you think?"

I didn't know what to say to that. I had absolutely nothing to say to that. No opinion. So I watched the news program and tried to listen to what the announcer was saying.

"This is a color TV," the blind man said. "Don't ask me how, but I can tell."

50   "We traded up a while ago," I said.

The blind man had another taste of his drink. He lifted his beard, sniffed it, and let it fall. He leaned forward on the sofa. He positioned his ashtray on the coffee table, then put the lighter to his cigarette. He leaned back on the sofa and crossed his legs at the ankles.

My wife covered her mouth, and then she yawned. She stretched. She said, "I think I'll go upstairs and put on my robe. I think I'll change into something else. Robert, you make yourself comfortable," she said.

"I'm comfortable," the blind man said.

"I want you to feel comfortable in this house," she said.

55   "I am comfortable," the blind man said.

After she'd left the room, he and I listened to the weather report and then to the sports roundup. By that time, she'd been gone so long I didn't know if she was going to come back. I thought she might have gone to bed. I wished she'd come back downstairs. I didn't want to be left alone with a blind man. I asked him if he wanted another drink, and he said sure. Then I asked if he wanted to smoke some dope with me. I said I'd just rolled a number. I hadn't, but I planned to do so in about two shakes.

"I'll try some with you," he said.

"Damn right," I said. "That's the stuff."

I got our drinks and sat down on the sofa with him. Then I rolled us two fat numbers. I lit one and passed it. I brought it to his fingers. He took it and inhaled.

60   "Hold it as long as you can," I said. I could tell he didn't know the first thing.

My wife came back downstairs wearing her pink robe and her pink slippers.

"What do I smell?" she said.

"We thought we'd have us some cannabis," I said.

My wife gave me a savage look. Then she looked at the blind man and said, "Robert, I didn't know you smoked."

65   He said, "I do now, my dear. There's a first time for everything. But I don't feel anything yet."

"This stuff is pretty mellow," I said. "This stuff is mild. It's dope you can reason with," I said. "It doesn't mess you up."

"Not much it doesn't, bub," he said, and laughed.

My wife sat on the sofa between the blind man and me. I passed her the number. She took it and toked and then passed it back to me. "Which way is this going?" she said. Then she said, "I shouldn't be smoking this. I can hardly keep my eyes open as it is. That dinner did me in. I shouldn't have eaten so much."

"It was the strawberry pie," the blind man said. "That's what did it," he said, and he laughed his big laugh. Then he shook his head.

70   "There's more strawberry pie," I said.

"Do you want some more, Robert?" my wife said.

"Maybe in a little while," he said.

We gave our attention to the TV. My wife yawned again. She said, "Your bed is made up when you feel like going to bed, Robert. I know you must have had a long day. When you're ready to go to bed, say so." She pulled his arm. "Robert?"

He came to and said, "I've had a real nice time. This beats tapes, doesn't it?"

75   I said, "Coming at you," and I put the number between his fingers. He inhaled, held the smoke, and then let it go. It was like he'd been doing it since he was nine years old.

"Thanks, bub," he said. "But I think this is all for me. I think I'm beginning to feel it," he said. He held the burning roach out for my wife.

"Same here," she said. "Ditto. Me, too." She took the roach and passed it to me. "I may just sit here for a while between you two guys with my eyes closed. But don't let me bother you, okay? Either one of you. If it bothers you, say so. Otherwise, I may just sit here with my eyes closed until you're ready to go to bed," she said. "Your bed's made up, Robert, when you're ready. It's right next to our room at the top of the stairs. We'll show you up when you're ready. You wake me up now, you guys, if I fall asleep." She said that and then she closed her eyes and went to sleep.

The news program ended. I got up and changed the channel. I sat back down on the sofa. I wished my wife hadn't pooped out. Her head lay across the back of the sofa, her mouth open. She'd turned so that her robe slipped away from her legs, exposing a juicy thigh. I reached to draw her robe back over her, and it was then that I glanced at the blind man. What the hell! I flipped the robe open again.

"You say when you want some strawberry pie," I said.

80   "I will," he said.

I said, "Are you tired? Do you want me to take you up to your bed? Are you ready to hit the hay?"

"Not yet," he said. "No, I'll stay up with you, bub. If that's all right. I'll stay up until you're ready to turn in. We haven't had a chance to talk. Know what I mean? I feel like me and her monopolized the evening." He lifted his beard and he let it fall. He picked up his cigarettes and his lighter.

"That's all right," I said. Then I said, "I'm glad for the company."

And I guess I was. Every night I smoked dope and stayed up as long as I could before I fell asleep. My wife and I hardly ever went to bed at the same time. When I did go to sleep, I had these dreams. Sometimes I'd wake up from one of them, my heart going crazy.

85   Something about the church and the Middle Ages was on the TV. Not your run-of-the-mill TV fare. I wanted to watch something else. I turned to the other channels. But there was nothing on them, either. So I turned back to the first channel and apologized.

"Bub, it's all right," the blind man said. "It's fine with me. Whatever you want to watch is okay. I'm always learning something. Learning never ends. It won't hurt me to learn something tonight. I got ears," he said.

We didn't say anything for a time. He was leaning forward with his head turned at me, his right ear aimed in the direction of the set. Very disconcerting. Now and then his eyelids drooped and then they snapped open again. Now and then he put his fingers into his beard and tugged, like he was thinking about something he was hearing on the television.

On the screen, a group of men wearing cowls was being set upon and tormented by men dressed in skeleton costumes and men dressed as devils. The men dressed as devils wore devil masks, horns, and long tails. This pageant was part of a procession. The Englishman who was narrating the thing said it took place in Spain once a year. I tried to explain to the blind man what was happening.

"Skeletons," he said. "I know about skeletons," he said, and he nodded.

90   The TV showed this one cathedral. Then there was a long, slow look at another one. Finally, the picture switched to the famous one in Paris, with its flying buttresses and its spires reaching up to the clouds. The camera pulled away to show the whole of the cathedral rising above the skyline.

There were times when the Englishman who was telling the thing would shut up, would simply let the camera move around the cathedrals. Or else the camera would tour the countryside, men in fields walking behind oxen. I waited as long as I could. Then I felt I had to say something. I said, "They're showing the outside of this cathedral now. Gargoyles. Little statues carved to look like monsters. Now I guess they're in Italy. Yeah, they're in Italy. There's paintings on the walls of this one church."

"Are those fresco paintings, bub?" he asked, and he sipped from his drink.

I reached for my glass. But it was empty. I tried to remember what I could remember. "You're asking me are those frescoes?" I said. "That's a good question. I don't know."

The camera moved to a cathedral outside Lisbon. The differences in the Portuguese cathedral compared with the French and Italian were not that great. But they were there. Mostly the interior stuff. Then something occurred to me, and I said, "Something has occurred to me. Do you have any idea what a cathedral is? What they look like, that is? Do you follow me? If somebody says cathedral to you, do you have any notion what they're talking about? Do you know the difference between that and a Baptist church, say?"

95   He let the smoke dribble from his mouth. "I know they took hundreds of workers fifty or a hundred years to build," he said. "I just heard the man say that, of course. I know generations of the same families worked on a cathedral. I heard him say that, too. The men who began their life's work on them, they never lived to see the completion of their work. In that wise, bub, they're no different from the rest of us, right?" He laughed. Then his eyelids drooped again. His head nodded. He seemed to be snoozing. Maybe he was imagining himself in Portugal. The TV was showing another cathedral now. This one was in Germany. The Englishman's voice droned on. "Cathedrals," the blind man said. He sat up and rolled his head back and forth. "If you want the truth, bub, that's about all I know. What I just said. What I heard him say. But maybe you could describe one to me? I wish you'd do it. I'd like that. If you want to know, I really don't have a good idea."

I stared hard at the shot of the cathedral on the TV. How could I even begin to describe it? But say my life depended on it. Say my life was being threatened by an insane guy who said I had to do it or else.

I stared some more at the cathedral before the picture flipped off into the countryside. There was no use. I turned to the blind man and said, "To begin with, they're very tall." I was looking around the room for clues. "They reach way up. Up and up. Toward the sky. They're so big, some of them, they have to have these supports. To help hold them up, so to speak. These supports are called buttresses. They remind me of viaducts, for some reason. But maybe you don't know viaducts, either? Sometimes the cathedrals have devils and such carved into the front. Sometimes lords and ladies. Don't ask me why this is," I said.

He was nodding. The whole upper part of his body seemed to be moving back and forth.

"I'm not doing so good, am I?" I said.

100 He stopped nodding and leaned forward on the edge of the sofa. As he listened to me, he was running his fingers through his beard. I wasn't getting through to him, I could see that. But he waited for me to go on just the same. He nodded, like he was trying to encourage me. I tried to think what else to say. "They're really big," I said. "They're massive. They're built of stone. Marble, too, sometimes. In those olden days, when they built cathedrals, men wanted to be close to God. In those olden days, God was an important part of everyone's life. You could tell this from their cathedral-building. I'm sorry," I said, "but it looks like that's the best I can do for you. I'm just no good at it."

"That's all right, bub," the blind man said. "Hey, listen. I hope you don't mind my asking you. Can I ask you something? Let me ask you a simple question, yes or no. I'm just curious and there's no offense. You're my host. But let me ask if you are in any way religious? You don't mind my asking?"

I shook my head. He couldn't see that, though. A wink is the same as a nod to a blind man. "I guess I don't believe in it. In anything. Sometimes it's hard. You know what I'm saying?"

"Sure, I do," he said.

"Right," I said.

105 The Englishman was still holding forth. My wife sighed in her sleep. She drew a long breath and went on with her sleeping.

"You'll have to forgive me," I said. "But I can't tell you what a cathedral looks like. It just isn't in me to do it. I can't do any more than I've done."

The blind man sat very still, his head down, as he listened to me.

I said, "The truth is, cathedrals don't mean anything special to me. Nothing. Cathedrals. They're something to look at on late-night TV. That's all they are."

It was then that the blind man cleared his throat. He brought something up. He took a handkerchief from his back pocket. Then he said, "I get it, bub. It's okay. It happens. Don't worry about it," he said. "Hey, listen to me. Will you do me a favor? I got an idea. Why don't you find us some heavy paper? And a pen. We'll do something. We'll draw one together. Get us a pen and some heavy paper. Go on, bub, get the stuff," he said.

110 So I went upstairs. My legs felt like they didn't have any strength in them. They felt like they did after I'd done some running. In my wife's room, I looked around. I found some ballpoints in a little basket on her table. And then I tried to think where to look for the kind of paper he was talking about.

Downstairs, in the kitchen, I found a shopping bag with onion skins in the bottom of the bag. I emptied the bag and shook it. I brought it into the living room and sat down with it near his legs. I moved some things, smoothed the wrinkles from the bag, spread it out on the coffee table.

The blind man got down from the sofa and sat next to me on the carpet.

He ran his fingers over the paper. He went up and down the sides of the paper. The edges, even the edges. He fingered the corners.

"All right," he said. "All right, let's do her."

He found my hand, the hand with the pen. He closed his hand over my hand. "Go ahead, bub, draw," he said. "Draw. You'll see. I'll follow along with you. It'll be okay. Just begin now like I'm telling you. You'll see. Draw," the blind man said.

So I began. First I drew a box that looked like a house. It could have been the house I lived in. Then I put a roof on it. At either end of the roof, I drew spires. Crazy.

"Swell," he said. "Terrific. You're doing fine," he said. "Never thought anything like this could happen in your lifetime, did you, bub? Well, it's a strange life, we all know that. Go on now. Keep it up."

I put in windows with arches. I drew flying buttresses. I hung great doors. I couldn't stop. The TV station went off the air. I put down the pen and closed and opened my fingers. The blind man felt around over the paper. He moved the tips of his fingers over the paper, all over what I had drawn, and he nodded.

"Doing fine," the blind man said.

I took up the pen again, and he found my hand. I kept at it. I'm no artist. But I kept drawing just the same.

My wife opened up her eyes and gazed at us. She sat up on the sofa, her robe hanging open. She said, "What are you doing? Tell me, I want to know."

I didn't answer her.

The blind man said, "We're drawing a cathedral. Me and him are working on it. Press hard," he said to me. "That's right. That's good," he said. "Sure. You got it, bub, I can tell. You didn't think you could. But you can, can't you? You're cooking with gas now. You know what I'm saying? We're going to really have us something here in a minute. How's the old arm?" he said. "Put some people in there now. What's a cathedral without people?"

My wife said, "What's going on? Robert, what are you doing? What's going on?"

"It's all right," he said to her. "Close your eyes now," the blind man said to me.

I did it. I closed them just like he said.

"Are they closed?" he said. "Don't fudge."

"They're closed," I said.

"Keep them that way," he said. He said, "Don't stop now. Draw."

So we kept on with it. His fingers rode my fingers as my hand went over the paper. It was like nothing else in my life up to now.

Then he said, "I think that's it. I think you got it," he said. "Take a look. What do you think?"

But I had my eyes closed. I thought I'd keep them that way for a little longer. I thought it was something I ought to do.

"Well?" he said. "Are you looking?"

My eyes were still closed. I was in my house. I knew that. But I didn't feel like I was inside anything.

"It's really something," I said.

[1983]

Topics for Critical Thinking and Writing

1. Describe your response to the narrator in the opening paragraphs of the story. What is his tone of voice? What is his attitude toward himself and toward his wife and the blind man?
2. Does the narrator know who he is, or is he hiding from who he is?
3. The narrator has a lot to say, much of it unpleasant, about his wife. Write a page or two in the wife's voice, expressing her view of him.
4. Why does Carver want a blind man in this story? Wouldn't the story have worked just as effectively if the character had some other disability or affliction?
5. The narrator and the blind man make an important connection at the end, but what kind of connection is it? Is Carver suggesting that the narrator is now on the path to becoming a better person? Do you find this change convincing, or not?

 **AMY TAN**

 *Amy Tan was born in 1952 in Oakland, California, 2½ years after her parents had emigrated from China. She entered Linfield College in Oregon but then followed a boyfriend to California State University at San Jose, where she shifted her major from premedical studies to English. After earning a master's degree in linguistics from San Jose, Tan worked as a language consultant and then, under the name of May Brown, as a freelance business writer.*

In 1985, having decided to try her hand at fiction, she joined the Squaw Valley Community of Writers, a fiction workshop. In 1987 she visited China with her mother; on her return to the United States she learned that her agent had sold her first book, The Joy Luck Club, *a collection of 16 interwoven stories (including "Two Kinds") about four Chinese mothers and their four American daughters. In 1991 she published a second book,* The Kitchen God's Wife.

Two Kinds

My mother believed you could be anything you wanted to be in America. You could open a restaurant. You could work for the government and get good retirement. You could buy a house with almost no money down. You could become rich. You could become instantly famous.

"Of course, you can be prodigy, too," my mother told me when I was nine. "You can be best anything. What does Auntie Lindo know? Her daughter, she is only best tricky."

America was where all my mother's hopes lay. She had come to San Francisco in 1949 after losing everything in China: her mother and father, her family home, her first husband, and two daughters, twin baby girls. But she never looked back with regret. Things could get better in so many ways.

We didn't immediately pick the right kind of prodigy. At first my mother thought I could be a Chinese Shirley Temple. We'd watch Shirley's old movies on TV as though they were training films. My mother would poke my arm and say, "*Ni kan.* You watch." And I would see Shirley tapping her feet, or singing a sailor song, or pursing her lips into a very round O while saying "Oh, my goodness."

5   "*Ni kan,*" my mother said, as Shirley's eyes flooded with tears. "You already know how. Don't need talent for crying!"

    Soon after my mother got this idea about Shirley Temple, she took me to the beauty training school in the Mission District and put me in the hands of a student who could barely hold the scissors without shaking. Instead of getting big fat curls, I emerged with an uneven mass of crinkly black fuzz. My mother dragged me off to the bathroom and tried to wet down my hair.

    "You look like Negro Chinese," she lamented, as if I had done this on purpose.

    The instructor of the beauty training school had to lop off these soggy clumps to make my hair even again. "Peter Pan is very popular these days," the instructor assured my mother. I now had hair the length of a boy's, with curly bangs that hung at a slant two inches above my eyebrows. I liked the haircut, and it made me actually look forward to my future fame.

    In fact, in the beginning I was just as excited as my mother, maybe even more so. I pictured this prodigy part of me as many different images, and I tried each one on for size. I was a dainty ballerina girl standing by the curtain, waiting to hear the music that would send me floating on my tiptoes. I was like the Christ child lifted out of the straw manger, crying with holy indignity. I was Cinderella stepping from her pumpkin carriage with sparkly cartoon music filling the air.

10   In all of my imaginings I was filled with a sense that I would soon become perfect. My mother and father would adore me. I would be beyond reproach. I would never feel the need to sulk, or to clamor for anything.

    But sometimes the prodigy in me became impatient. "If you don't hurry up and get me out of here, I'm disappearing for good," it warned. "And then you'll always be nothing."

    Every night after dinner my mother and I would sit at the Formica-topped kitchen table. She would present new tests, taking her examples from stories of amazing children that she had read in *Ripley's Believe It or Not* or *Good Housekeeping, Reader's Digest,* or any of a dozen other magazines she kept in a pile in our bathroom. My mother got these magazines from people whose houses she cleaned. And since she cleaned many houses each week, we had a great assortment. She would look through them all, searching for stories about remarkable children.

    The first night she brought out a story about a three-year-old boy who knew the capitals of all the states and even of most of the European countries. A teacher was quoted as saying that the little boy could also pronounce the names of the foreign cities correctly. "What's the capital of Finland?" my mother asked me, looking at the story.

    All I knew was the capital of California, because Sacramento was the name of the street we lived on in Chinatown. "Nairobi!" I guessed, saying the most foreign word I could think of. She checked to see if that might be one way to pronounce *Helsinki* before showing me the answer.

15   The tests got harder—multiplying numbers in my head, finding the queen of hearts in a deck of cards, trying to stand on my head without using my hands, predicting the daily temperatures in Los Angeles, New York, and London. One

night I had to look at a page from the Bible for three minutes and then report everything I could remember. "Now Jehoshaphat had riches and honor in abundance and . . . that's all I remember, Ma," I said.

And after seeing, once again, my mother's disappointed face, something inside me began to die. I hated the tests, the raised hopes and failed expectations. Before going to bed that night I looked in the mirror above the bathroom sink, and when I saw only my face staring back—and understood that it would always be this ordinary face—I began to cry. Such a sad, ugly girl! I made high-pitched noises like a crazed animal, trying to scratch out the face in the mirror.

And then I saw what seemed to be the prodigy side of me—a face I had never seen before. I looked at my reflection, blinking so that I could see more clearly. The girl staring back at me was angry, powerful. She and I were the same. I had new thoughts, willful thoughts—or, rather, thoughts filled with lots of won'ts. I won't let her change me, I promised myself. I won't be what I'm not.

So now when my mother presented her tests, I performed listlessly, my head propped on one arm. I pretended to be bored. And I was. I got so bored that I started counting the bellows of the foghorns out on the bay while my mother drilled me in other areas. The sound was comforting and reminded me of the cow jumping over the moon. And the next day I played a game with myself, seeing if my mother would give up on me before eight bellows. After a while I usually counted only one bellow, maybe two at most. At last she was beginning to give up hope.

Two or three months went by without any mention of my being a prodigy. And then one day my mother was watching the *Ed Sullivan Show* on TV. The TV was old and the sound kept shorting out. Every time my mother got halfway up from the sofa to adjust the set, the sound would come back on and Sullivan would be talking. As soon as she sat down, Sullivan would go silent again. She got up—the TV broke into loud piano music. She sat down—silence. Up and down, back and forth, quiet and loud. It was like a stiff, embraceless dance between her and the TV set. Finally, she stood by the set with her hand on the sound dial.

20   She seemed entranced by the music, a frenzied little piano piece with a mesmerizing quality, which alternated between quick, playful passages and teasing, lilting ones.

"*Ni kan,*" my mother said, calling me over with hurried hand gestures. "Look here."

I could see why my mother was fascinated by the music. It was being pounded out by a little Chinese girl, about nine years old, with a Peter Pan haircut. The girl had the sauciness of a Shirley Temple. She was proudly modest, like a proper Chinese child. And she also did a fancy sweep of a curtsy, so that the fluffy skirt of her white dress cascaded to the floor like the petals of a large carnation.

In spite of these warning signs, I wasn't worried. Our family had no piano and we couldn't afford to buy one, let alone reams of sheet music and piano lessons. So I could be generous in my comments when my mother badmouthed the little girl on TV.

"Play note right, but doesn't sound good!" my mother complained. "No singing sound."

25   "What are you picking on her for?" I said carelessly. "She's pretty good. Maybe she's not the best, but she's trying hard." I knew almost immediately that I would be sorry I had said that.

"Just like you," she said. "Not the best. Because you not trying." She gave a little huff as she let go of the sound dial and sat down on the sofa.

The little Chinese girl sat down also, to play an encore of "Anitra's Tanz," by Grieg.[1] I remember the song, because later on I had to learn how to play it.

Three days after watching the *Ed Sullivan Show* my mother told me what my schedule would be for piano lessons and piano practice. She had talked to Mr. Chong, who lived on the first floor of our apartment building. Mr. Chong was a retired piano teacher, and my mother had traded housecleaning services for weekly lessons and a piano for me to practice on every day, two hours a day, from four until six.

When my mother told me this, I felt as though I had been sent to hell. I whined, and then kicked my foot a little when I couldn't stand it anymore.

30   "Why don't you like me the way I am?" I cried. "I'm *not* a genius! I can't play the piano. And even if I could, I wouldn't go on TV if you paid me a million dollars!"

My mother slapped me. "Who ask you to be genius?" she shouted. "Only ask you be your best. For you sake. You think I want you to be genius? Hnnh! What for! Who ask you!"

"So ungrateful," I heard her mutter in Chinese. "If she had as much talent as she has temper, she'd be famous now."

Mr. Chong, whom I secretly nicknamed Old Chong, was very strange, always tapping his fingers to the silent music of an invisible orchestra. He looked ancient in my eyes. He had lost most of the hair on the top of his head, and he wore thick glasses and had eyes that always looked tired. But he must have been younger than I thought, since he lived with his mother and was not yet married.

I met Old Lady Chong once, and that was enough. She had a peculiar smell, like a baby that had done something in its pants, and her fingers felt like a dead person's, like an old peach I once found in the back of the refrigerator; its skin just slid off the flesh when I picked it up.

35   I soon found out why Old Chong had retired from teaching piano. He was deaf. "Like Beethoven!" he shouted to me. "We're both listening only in our head!" And he would start to conduct his frantic silent sonatas.

Our lessons went like this. He would open the book and point to different things, explaining their purpose: "Key! Treble! Bass! No sharps or flats! So this is C major! Listen now and play after me!"

And then he would play the C scale a few times, a simple chord, and then, as if inspired by an old unreachable itch, he would gradually add more notes and running trills and a pounding bass until the music was really something quite grand.

I would play after him, the simple scale, the simple chord, and then just play some nonsense that sounded like a cat running up and down on top of garbage cans. Old Chong would smile and applaud and say, "Very good! But now you must learn to keep time!"

So that's how I discovered Old Chong's eyes were too slow to keep up with the wrong notes I was playing. He went through the motions in half time. To

[1] a section from the incidental music that Edward Grieg (1843-1907) wrote for *Peer Gynt,* a play by Henrik Ibsen

help me keep rhythm, he stood behind me and pushed down on my right shoulder for every beat. He balanced pennies on top of my wrists so that I would keep them still as I slowly played scales and arpeggios. He had me curve my hand around an apple and keep that shape when playing chords. He marched stiffly to show me how to make each finger dance up and down, staccato, like an obedient little soldier.

40   He taught me all these things, and that was how I also learned I could be lazy and get away with mistakes, lots of mistakes. If I hit the wrong notes because I hadn't practiced enough, I never corrected myself. I just kept playing in rhythm. And Old Chong kept conducting his own private reverie.

    So maybe I never really gave myself a fair chance. I did pick up the basics pretty quickly, and I might have become a good pianist at that young age. But I was so determined not to try, not to be anybody different, that I learned to play only the most ear-splitting preludes, the most discordant hymns.

    Over the next year I practiced like this, dutifully in my own way. And then one day I heard my mother and her friend Lindo Jong both talking in a loud, bragging tone of voice so that others could hear. It was after church, and I was leaning against a brick wall, wearing a dress with stiff white petticoats. Auntie Lindo's daughter, Waverly, who was my age, was standing farther down the wall, about five feet away. We had grown up together and shared all the closeness of two sisters, squabbling over crayons and dolls. In other words, for the most part, we hated each other. I thought she was snotty. Waverly Jong had gained a certain amount of fame as "Chinatown's Littlest Chinese Chess Champion."

    "She bring home too many trophy," Auntie Lindo lamented that Sunday. "All day she play chess. All day I have no time do nothing but dust off her winnings." She threw a scolding look at Waverly, who pretended not to see her.

    "You lucky you don't have this problem," Auntie Lindo said with a sigh to my mother.

45   And my mother squared her shoulders and bragged: "Our problem worser than yours. If we ask Jing-mei wash dish, she hear nothing but music. It's like you can't stop this natural talent."

    And right then I was determined to put a stop to her foolish pride.

    A few weeks later Old Chong and my mother conspired to have me play in a talent show that was to be held in the church hall. By then my parents had saved up enough to buy me a secondhand piano, a black Wurlitzer spinet with a scarred bench. It was the showpiece of our living room.

    For the talent show I was to play a piece called "Pleading Child," from Schumann's *Scenes From Childhood*.[2] It was a simple, moody piece that sounded more difficult than it was. I was supposed to memorize the whole thing. But I dawdled over it, playing a few bars and then cheating, looking up to see what notes followed. I never really listened to what I was playing. I daydreamed about being somewhere else, about being someone else.

    The part I liked to practice best was the fancy curtsy: right foot out, touch the rose on the carpet with a pointed foot, sweep to the side, bend left leg, look up, and smile.

50   My parents invited all the couples from their social club to witness my debut. Auntie Lindo and Uncle Tin were there. Waverly and her two older broth-

---

[2]a piano work by Robert Schumann (1810–56) with twelve titled sections and an epilogue

ers had also come. The first two rows were filled with children either younger or older than I was. The littlest ones got to go first. They recited simple nursery rhymes, squawked out tunes on miniature violins, and twirled hula hoops in pink ballet tutus, and when they bowed or curtsied, the audience would sigh in unison, *"Awww,"* and then clap enthusiastically.

When my turn came, I was very confident. I remember my childish excitement. It was as if I knew, without a doubt, that the prodigy side of me really did exist. I had no fear whatsoever, no nervousness. I remember thinking, This is it! This is it! I looked out over the audience, at my mother's blank face, my father's yawn, Auntie Lindo's stiff-lipped smile, Waverly's sulky expression. I had on a white dress, layered with sheets of lace, and a pink bow in my Peter Pan haircut. As I sat down, I envisioned people jumping to their feet and Ed Sullivan rushing up to introduce me to everyone on TV.

And I started to play. Everything was so beautiful. I was so caught up in how lovely I looked that I wasn't worried about how I would sound. So I was surprised when I hit the first wrong note. And then I hit another, and another. A chill started at the top of my head and began to trickle down. Yet I couldn't stop playing, as though my hands were bewitched. I kept thinking my fingers would adjust themselves back, like a train switching to the right track. I played this strange jumble through to the end, the sour notes staying with me all the way.

When I stood up, I discovered my legs were shaking. Maybe I had just been nervous, and the audience, like Old Chong, had seen me go through the right motions and had not heard anything wrong at all. I swept my right foot out, went down on my knee, looked up, and smiled. The room was quiet, except for Old Chong, who was beaming and shouting, "Bravo! Bravo! Well done!" But then I saw my mother's face, her stricken face. The audience clapped weakly, and as I walked back to my chair, with my whole face quivering as I tried not to cry, I heard a little boy whisper loudly to his mother, "That was awful," and the mother whispered, "Well, she certainly tried."

And now I realized how many people were in the audience—the whole world, it seemed. I was aware of eyes burning into my back. I felt the shame of my mother and father as they sat stiffly through the rest of the show.

55   We could have escaped during intermission. Pride and some strange sense of honor must have anchored my parents to their chairs. And so we watched it all: The eighteen-year-old boy with a fake moustache who did a magic show and juggled flaming hoops while riding a unicycle. The breasted girl with white makeup who sang an aria from *Madame Butterfly* and got an honorable mention. And the eleven-year-old boy who won first prize playing a tricky violin song that sounded like a busy bee.

After the show the Hsus, the Jongs, and the St. Clairs, from the Joy Luck Club, came up to my mother and father.

"Lots of talented kids," Auntie Lindo said vaguely, smiling broadly.

"That was somethin' else," my father said, and I wondered if he was referring to me in a humorous way, or whether he even remembered what I had done.

Waverly looked at me and shrugged her shoulders. "You aren't a genius like me," she said matter-of-factly. And if I hadn't felt so bad, I would have pulled her braids and punched her stomach.

60   But my mother's expression was what devastated me: a quiet, blank look that said she had lost everything. I felt the same way, and everybody seemed now to be coming up, like gawkers at the scene of an accident, to see what parts were actually missing.

When we got on the bus to go home, my father was humming the busy-bee tune and my mother was silent. I kept thinking she wanted to wait until we got home before shouting at me. But when my father unlocked the door to our apartment, my mother walked in and went straight to the back, into the bedroom. No accusations. No blame. And in a way, I felt disappointed. I had been waiting for her to start shouting, so that I could shout back and cry and blame her for all my misery.

I had assumed that my talent-show fiasco meant that I would never have to play the piano again. But two days later, after school, my mother came out of the kitchen and saw me watching TV.

"Four clock," she reminded me, as if it were any other day. I was stunned, as though she were asking me to go through the talent-show torture again. I planted myself more squarely in front of the TV.

"Turn off TV," she called from the kitchen five minutes later.

65   I didn't budge. And then I decided. I didn't have to do what my mother said anymore. I wasn't her slave. This wasn't China. I had listened to her before, and look what happened. She was the stupid one.

She came out of the kitchen and stood in the arched entryway of the living room. "Four clock," she said once again, louder.

"I'm not going to play anymore," I said nonchalantly. "Why should I? I'm not a genius."

She stood in front of the TV. I saw that her chest was heaving up and down in an angry way.

"No!" I said, and I now felt stronger, as if my true self had finally emerged. So this was what had been inside me all along.

70   "No! I won't!" I screamed.

She snapped off the TV, yanked me by the arm and pulled me off the floor. She was frighteningly strong, half pulling, half carrying me toward the piano as I kicked the throw rugs under my feet. She lifted me up and onto the hard bench. I was sobbing by now, looking at her bitterly. Her chest was heaving even more and her mouth was open, smiling crazily as if she were pleased that I was crying.

"You want me to be someone that I'm not!" I sobbed. "I'll never be the kind of daughter you want me to be!"

"Only two kinds of daughters," she shouted in Chinese. "Those who are obedient and those who follow their own mind! Only one kind of daughter can live in this house. Obedient daughter!"

"Then I wish I weren't your daughter. I wish you weren't my mother," I shouted. As I said these things I got scared. It felt like worms and toads and slimy things crawling out of my chest, but it also felt good, that this awful side of me had surfaced, at last.

75   "Too late change this," my mother said shrilly.

And I could sense her anger rising to its breaking point. I wanted to see it spill over. And that's when I remembered the babies she had lost in China, the ones we never talked about. "Then I wish I'd never been born!" I shouted. "I wish I were dead! Like them."

It was as if I had said magic words. Alakazam!—her face went blank, her mouth closed, her arms went slack, and she backed out of the room, stunned, as if she were blowing away like a small brown leaf, thin, brittle, lifeless.

It was not the only disappointment my mother felt in me. In the years that followed, I failed her many times, each time asserting my will, my right to fall short of expectations. I didn't get straight As. I didn't become class president. I didn't get into Stanford. I dropped out of college.

Unlike my mother, I did not believe I could be anything I wanted to be. I could only be me.

80 And for all those years we never talked about the disaster at the recital or my terrible declarations afterward at the piano bench. Neither of us talked about it again, as if it were a betrayal that was now unspeakable. So I never found a way to ask her why she had hoped for something so large that failure was inevitable.

And even worse, I never asked her about what frightened me the most: Why had she given up hope? For after our struggle at the piano, she never mentioned my playing again. The lessons stopped. The lid to the piano was closed, shutting out the dust, my misery, and her dreams.

So she surprised me. A few years ago she offered to give me the piano, for my thirtieth birthday. I had not played in all those years. I saw the offer as a sign of forgiveness, a tremendous burden removed.

"Are you sure?" I asked shyly. "I mean, won't you and Dad miss it?"

"No, this your piano," she said firmly. "Always your piano. You only one can play."

85 "Well, I probably can't play anymore," I said. "It's been years."

"You pick up fast," my mother said, as if she knew this was certain. "You have natural talent. You could be genius if you want to."

"No, I couldn't."

"You just not trying," my mother said. And she was neither angry nor sad. She said it as if announcing a fact that could never be disproved. "Take it," she said.

But I didn't at first. It was enough that she had offered it to me. And after that, every time I saw it in my parents' living room, standing in front of the bay window, it made me feel proud, as if it were a shiny trophy that I had won back.

90 Last week I sent a tuner over to my parents' apartment and had the piano reconditioned, for purely sentimental reasons. My mother had died a few months before, and I had been getting things in order for my father, a little bit at a time. I put the jewelry in special silk pouches. The sweaters she had knitted in yellow, pink, bright orange—all the colors I hated—I put in mothproof boxes. I found some old Chinese silk dresses, the kind with little slits up the sides. I rubbed the old silk against my skin, and then wrapped them in tissue and decided to take them home with me.

After I had the piano tuned, I opened the lid and touched the keys. It sounded even richer than I remembered. Really, it was a very good piano. Inside the bench were the same exercise notes with handwritten scales, the same secondhand music books with their covers held together with yellow tape.

I opened up the Schumann book to the dark little piece I had played at the recital. It was on the left-hand page, "Pleading Child." It looked more difficult than I remembered. I played a few bars, surprised at how easily the notes came back to me.

And for the first time, or so it seemed, I noticed the piece on the right-hand side. It was called "Perfectly Contented." I tried to play this one as well. It had a lighter melody but with the same flowing rhythm and turned out to be quite easy. "Pleading Child" was shorter but slower; "Perfectly Contented" was longer but faster. And after I had played them both a few times, I realized they were two halves of the same song.

[1989]

Topics for Critical Thinking and Writing

1. Try to recall your responses when you had finished reading the first three paragraphs. At that point, how did the mother strike you? Now that you have read the entire story, is your view of her different? If so, in what way(s)?
2. When the narrator looks in the mirror, she discovers "the prodigy side," a face she "had never seen before." What do you think she is discovering?
3. If you enjoyed the story, point out two or three passages that you found particularly engaging, and briefly explain why they appeal to you.
4. Do you think this story is interesting only because it may give a glimpse of life in a Chinese-American family? Or do you find it interesting for additional reasons? Explain.
5. Conceivably the story could have ended with the fourth paragraph from the end. What do the last three paragraphs contribute?

LOUISE ERDRICH

Louise Erdrich, born in 1954 in Little Falls, Minnesota, grew up in North Dakota, a member of the Turtle Mountain Band of Chippewa. Her father had been born in Germany; her mother was French Ojibwe; both parents taught at the Bureau of Indian Affairs School. After graduating from Dartmouth College (major in anthropology) in 1976, Erdrich returned briefly to North Dakota to teach in the Poetry in the Schools Program, and went to Johns Hopkins University, where she earned a master's degree in creative writing. She now lives in Minneapolis, Minnesota.

Erdrich has published two books of poems and several novels, one of which, Love Medicine *(1986), won the National Book Critics Circle Award. "The Red Convertible" is a self-contained story, but it is also part of* Love Medicine, *which consists of narratives about life on a North Dakota reservation.*

The Red Convertible

Lyman Lamartine

I was the first one to drive a convertible on my reservation. And of course it was red, a red Olds. I owned that car along with my brother Henry Junior. We owned it together until his boots filled with water on a windy night and he bought out my share. Now Henry owns the whole car, and his youngest brother Lyman (that's myself), Lyman walks everywhere he goes.

How did I earn enough money to buy my share in the first place? My own talent was I could always make money. I had a touch for it, unusual in a Chippewa. From the first I was different that way, and everyone recognized it. I was the only kid they let in the American Legion Hall to shine shoes, for example, and one Christmas I sold spiritual bouquets for the mission door to door. The nuns let me keep a percentage. Once I started, it seemed the more money I made the easier the money came. Everyone encouraged it. When I was fifteen I got a job washing dishes at the Joliet Café, and that was where my first big break happened.

It wasn't long before I was promoted to bussing tables, and then the short-order cook quit and I was hired to take her place. No sooner than you know it I was managing the Joliet. The rest is history. I went on managing. I soon became part owner, and of course there was no stopping me then. It wasn't long before the whole thing was mine.

After I'd owned the Joliet for one year, it blew over in the worst tornado ever seen around here. The whole operation was smashed to bits. A total loss. The fryalator was up in a tree, the grill torn in half like it was paper. I was only sixteen. I had it all in my mother's name, and I lost it quick, but before I lost it I had every one of my relatives, and their relatives, to dinner, and I also bought that red Olds I mentioned, along with Henry.

5   The first time we saw it! I'll tell you when we first saw it. We had gotten a ride up to Winnipeg, and both of us had money. Don't ask me why, because we never mentioned a car or anything, we just had all our money. Mine was cash, a big bankroll from the Joliet's insurance. Henry had two checks—a week's extra pay for being laid off, and his regular check from the Jewel Bearing Plant.

We were walking down Portage anyway, seeing the sights, when we saw it. There it was, parked, large as life. Really as *if* it was alive. I thought of the word *repose,* because the car wasn't simply stopped, parked, or whatever. That car re-posed, calm and gleaming, a FOR SALE sign in its left front window. Then, before we had thought it over at all, the car belonged to us and our pockets were empty. We had just enough money for gas back home.

We went places in that car, me and Henry. We took off driving all one whole summer. We started off toward the Little Knife River and Mandaree in Fort Berthold and then we found ourselves down in Wakpala somehow, and then suddenly we were over in Montana on the Rocky Boys, and yet the summer was not even half over. Some people hang on to details when they travel, but we didn't let them bother us and just lived our everyday lives here to there.

I do remember this one place with willows. I remember I laid under those trees and it was comfortable. So comfortable. The branches bent down all around me like a tent or a stable. And quiet, it was quiet, even though there was a powwow close enough so I could see it going on. The air was not too still, not too windy either. When the dust rises up and hangs in the air around the dancers like that, I feel good. Henry was asleep with his arms thrown wide. Later on, he woke up and we started driving again. We were somewhere in Montana, or maybe on the Blood Reserve—it could have been anywhere. Anyway it was where we met the girl.

All her hair was in buns around her ears, that's the first thing I noticed about her. She was posed alongside the road with her arm out, so we stopped. That girl was short, so short her lumber shirt looked comical on her, like a nightgown. She had jeans on and fancy moccasins and she carried a little suitcase.

10   "Hop on in," says Henry. So she climbs in between us.

"We'll take you home," I says. "Where do you live?"

"Chicken," she says.

"Where the hell's that?" I ask her.

"Alaska."

15   "Okay," says Henry, and we drive.

We got up there and never wanted to leave. The sun doesn't truly set there in summer, and the night is more a soft dusk. You might doze off, sometimes, but before you know it you're up again, like an animal in nature. You never feel like you have to sleep hard or put away the world. And things would grow up there. One day just dirt or moss, the next day flowers and long grass. The girl's name was Susy. Her family really took to us. They fed us and put us up. We had our own tent to live in by their house, and the kids would be in and out of there all day and night. They couldn't get over me and Henry being brothers, we looked so different. We told them we knew we had the same mother, anyway.

One night Susy came in to visit us. We sat around in the tent talking of this thing and that. The season was changing. It was getting darker by that time, and the cold was even getting just a little mean. I told her it was time for us to go. She stood up on a chair.

"You never seen my hair," Susy said.

That was true. She was standing on a chair, but still, when she unclipped her buns the hair reached all the way to the ground. Our eyes opened. You couldn't tell how much hair she had when it was rolled up so neatly. Then my brother Henry did something funny. He went up to the chair and said, "Jump on my shoulders." So she did that, and her hair reached down past his waist, and he started twirling, this way and that, so her hair was flung out from side to side.

20 "I always wondered what it was like to have long pretty hair," Henry says. Well we laughed. It was a funny sight, the way he did it. The next morning we got up and took leave of those people.

On to greener pastures, as they say. It was down through Spokane and across Idaho then Montana and very soon we were racing the weather right along under the Canadian border through Columbus, Des Lacs, and then we were in Bottineau County and soon home. We'd made most of the trip, that summer, without putting up the car hood at all. We got home just in time, it turned out, for the army to remember Henry had signed up to join it.

I don't wonder that the army was so glad to get my brother that they turned him into a Marine. He was built like a brick outhouse anyway. We liked to tease him that they really wanted him for his Indian nose. He had a nose big and sharp as a hatchet, like the nose on Red Tomahawk, the Indian who killed Sitting Bull, whose profile is on signs all along the North Dakota highways. Henry went off to training camp, came home once during Christmas, then the next thing you know we got an overseas letter from him. It was 1970, and he said he was stationed up in the northern hill country. Whereabouts I did not know. He wasn't such a hot letter writer, and only got off two before the enemy caught him. I could never keep it straight, which direction those good Vietnam soldiers were from.

I wrote him back several times, even though I didn't know if those letters would get through. I kept him informed all about the car. Most of the time I had it up on blocks in the yard or half taken apart, because that long trip did a hard job on it under the hood.

I always had good luck with numbers, and never worried about the draft myself. I never even had to think about what my number was. But Henry was never lucky in the same way as me. It was at least three years before Henry came home. By then I guess the whole war was solved in the government's mind, but for him it would keep on going. In those years I'd put his car into almost perfect shape. I always thought of it as his car while he was gone, even though when he left he said, "Now it's yours," and threw me his key.

25 "Thanks for the extra key," I'd say. "I'll put it up in your drawer just in case I need it." He laughed.

When he came home, though, Henry was very different, and I'll say this: the change was no good. You could hardly expect him to change for the better, I know. But he was quiet, so quiet, and never comfortable sitting still anywhere but always up and moving around. I thought back to times we'd sat still for whole afternoons, never moving a muscle, just shifting our weight along the ground, talking to whoever sat with us, watching things. He'd always had a joke, then, too, and now you couldn't get him to laugh, or when he did it was more the sound of a man choking, a sound that stopped up the throats of other people around him. They got to leaving him alone most of the time, and I didn't blame them. It was a fact: Henry was jumpy and mean.

I'd bought a color TV set for my mom and the rest of us while Henry was away. Money still came very easy. I was sorry I'd ever bought it though, because of Henry. I was also sorry I'd bought color, because with black-and-white the pictures seem older and farther away. But what are you going to do? He sat in front of it, watching it, and that was the only time he was completely still. But it was the kind of stillness that you see in a rabbit when it freezes and before it will bolt. He was not easy. He sat in his chair gripping the armrests with all his might, as if the chair itself was moving at a high speed and if he let go at all he would rocket forward and maybe crash right through the set.

Once I was in the room watching TV with Henry and I heard his teeth click at something. I looked over, and he'd bitten through his lip. Blood was going down his chin. I tell you right then I wanted to smash that tube to pieces. I went over to it but Henry must have known what I was up to. He rushed from his chair and shoved me out of the way, against the wall. I told myself he didn't know what he was doing.

My mom came in, turned the set off real quiet, and told us she had made something for supper. So we went and sat down. There was still blood going down Henry's chin, but he didn't notice it and no one said anything, even though every time he took a bit of his bread his blood fell onto it until he was eating his own blood mixed in with the food.

30   While Henry was not around we talked about what was going to happen to him. There were no Indian doctors on the reservation, and my mom was afraid of trusting Old Man Pillager because he courted her long ago and was jealous of her husbands. He might take revenge through her son. We were afraid that if we brought Henry to a regular hospital they would keep him.

"They don't fix them in those places," Mom said; "they just give them drugs."

"We wouldn't get him there in the first place," I agreed, "so let's just forget about it."

Then I thought about the car.

Henry had not even looked at the car since he'd gotten home, though like I said, it was in tip-top condition and ready to drive. I thought the car might bring the old Henry back somehow. So I bided my time and waited for my chance to interest him in the vehicle.

35   One night Henry was off somewhere. I took myself a hammer. I went out to that car and I did a number on its underside. Whacked it up. Bent the tail pipe double. Ripped the muffler loose. By the time I was done with the car it looked worse than any typical Indian car that has been driven all its life on reservation roads, which they always say are like government promises—full of holes. It just about hurt me, I'll tell you that! I threw dirt in the carburetor and I ripped all the electric tape off the seats. I made it look just as beat up as I could. Then I sat back and waited for Henry to find it.

Still, it took him over a month. That was all right, because it was just getting warm enough, not melting, but warm enough to work outside.

"Lyman," he says, walking in one day, "that red car looks like shit."

"Well it's old," I says. "You got to expect that."

"No way!" says Henry. "That car's a classic! But you went and ran the piss right out of it, Lyman, and you know it don't deserve that. I kept that car in A-one shape. You don't remember. You're too young. But when I left, that car was running like a watch. Now I don't even know if I can get it to start again, let alone get it anywhere near its old condition."

40   "Well you try," I said, like I was getting mad, "but I say it's a piece of junk."

Then I walked out before he could realize I knew he'd strung together more than six words at once.

After that I thought he'd freeze himself to death working on that car. He was out there all day, and at night he rigged up a little lamp, ran a cord out the window, and had himself some light to see by while he worked. He was better than he had been before, but that's still not saying much. It was easier for him to do the things the rest of us did. He ate more slowly and didn't jump up and down during the meal to get this or that or look out the window. I put my hand in the back of the TV set, I admit, and fiddled around with it good, so that it was almost impossible now to get a clear picture. He didn't look at it very often anyway. He was always out with that car or going off to get parts for it. By the time it was really melting outside, he had it fixed.

I had been feeling down in the dumps about Henry around this time. We had always been together before. Henry and Lyman. But he was such a loner now that I didn't know how to take it. So I jumped at the chance one day when Henry seemed friendly. It's not that he smiled or anything. He just said, "Let's take that old shitbox for a spin." Just the way he said it made me think he could be coming around.

We went out to the car. It was spring. The sun was shining very bright. My only sister, Bonita, who was just eleven years old, came out and made us stand together for a picture. Henry leaned his elbow on the red car's windshield, and he took his other arm and put it over my shoulder, very carefully, as though it was heavy for him to lift and he didn't want to bring the weight down all at once.

45   "Smile," Bonita said, and he did.

That picture, I never look at it anymore. A few months ago, I don't know why, I got his picture out and tacked it on the wall. I felt good about Henry at the time, close to him. I felt good having his picture on the wall, until one night when I was looking at television. I was a little drunk and stoned. I looked up at the wall and Henry was staring at me. I don't know what it was, but his smile had changed, or maybe it was gone. All I know is I couldn't stay in the same room with that picture. I was shaking. I got up, closed the door, and went into the kitchen. A little later my friend Ray came over and we both went back into that room. We put the picture in a brown bag, folded the bag over and over tightly, then put it way back in a closet.

I still see that picture now, as if it tugs at me, whenever I pass that closet door. The picture is very clear in my mind. It was so sunny that day Henry had to squint against the glare. Or maybe the camera Bonita held flashed like a mirror, blinding him, before she snapped the picture. My face is right out in the sun, big and round. But he might have drawn back, because the shadows on his face are deep as holes. There are two shadows curved like little hooks around the ends of his smile, as if to frame it and try to keep it there—that one, first smile that looked like it might have hurt his face. He has his field jacket on and the worn-in clothes he'd come back in and kept wearing ever since. After Bonita took the picture, she went into the house and we got into the car. There was a full cooler in the trunk. We started off, east, toward Pembina and the Red River because Henry said he wanted to see the high water.

The trip over there was beautiful. When everything starts changing, drying up, clearing off, you feel like your whole life is starting. Henry felt it, too. The top was down and the car hummed like a top. He'd really put it back in shape, even the tape on the seats was very carefully put down and glued back in layers. It's not that he smiled again or even joked, but his face looked to me as if it was clear, more peaceful. It looked as though he wasn't thinking of anything in particular except the bare fields and windbreaks and houses we were passing.

The river was high and full of winter trash when we got there. The sun was still out, but it was colder by the river. There were still little clumps of dirty snow here and there on the banks. The water hadn't gone over the banks yet, but it would, you could tell. It was just at its limit, hard swollen glossy like an old gray scar. We made ourselves a fire, and we sat down and watched the current go. As I watched it I felt something squeezing inside me and tightening and trying to let go all at the same time. I knew I was not just feeling it myself; I knew I was feeling what Henry was going through at that moment. Except that I couldn't stand it, the closing and opening. I jumped to my feet. I took Henry by the shoulders and I started shaking him. "Wake up," I says, "wake up, wake up, wake up!" I didn't know what had come over me. I sat down beside him again.

50   His face was totally white and hard. Then it broke, like stones break all of a sudden when water boils up inside them.

"I know it," he says. "I know it. I can't help it. It's no use."

We start talking. He said he knew what I'd done with the car. It was obvious it had been whacked out of shape and not just neglected. He said he wanted to give the car to me for good now, it was no use. He said he'd fixed it just to give it back and I should take it.

"No way," I says, "I don't want it."

"That's okay," he says, "you take it."

55   "I don't want it, though," I says back to him, and then to emphasize, just to emphasize, you understand, I touch his shoulder. He slaps my hand off.

"Take that car," he says.

"No," I say, "make me," I say, and then he grabs my jacket and rips the arm loose. That jacket is a class act, suede with tags and zippers. I push Henry backwards, off the log. He jumps up and bowls me over. We go down in a clinch and come up swinging hard, for all we're worth, with our fists. He socks my jaw so hard I feel like it swings loose. Then I'm at his ribcage and land a good one under his chin so his head snaps back. He's dazzled. He looks at me and I look at him and then his eyes are full of tears and blood and at first I think he's crying. But no, he's laughing. "Ha! Ha!" he says. "Ha! Ha! Take good care of it."

"Okay," I says, "okay, no problem. Ha! Ha!"

I can't help it, and I start laughing, too. My face feels fat and strange, and after a while I get a beer from the cooler in the trunk, and when I hand it to Henry he takes his shirt and wipes my germs off. "Hoof-and-mouth disease," he says. For some reason this cracks me up, and so we're really laughing for a while, and then we drink all the rest of the beers one by one and throw them in the river and see how far, how fast, the current takes them before they fill up and sink.

60   "You want to go on back?" I ask after a while. "Maybe we could snag a couple nice Kashpaw girls."

He says nothing. But I can tell his mood is turning again.

"They're all crazy, the girls up here, every damn one of them."

"You're crazy too," I say, to jolly him up. "Crazy Lamartine boys!"

He looks as though he will take this wrong at first. His face twists, then clears, and he jumps up on his feet. "That's right!" he says. "Crazier 'n hell. Crazy Indians!"

65   I think it's the old Henry again. He throws off his jacket and starts swinging his legs out from the knees like a fancy dancer. He's down doing something between a grouse dance and a bunny hop, no kind of dance I ever saw before, but neither has anyone else on all this green growing earth. He's wild. He wants to pitch whoopee! He's up and at me and all over. All this time I'm laughing so hard, so hard my belly is getting tied up in a knot.

"Got to cool me off!" he shouts all of a sudden. Then he runs over to the river and jumps in.

There's boards and other things in the current. It's so high. No sound comes from the river after the splash he makes, so I run right over. I look around. It's getting dark. I see he's halfway across the water already, and I know he didn't swim there but the current took him. It's far. I hear his voice, though, very clearly across it.

"My boots are filling," he says.

He says this in a normal voice, like he just noticed and he doesn't know what to think of it. Then he's gone. A branch comes by. Another branch. And I go in.

70   By the time I get out of the river, off the snag I pulled myself onto, the sun is down. I walk back to the car, turn on the high beams, and drive it up the bank. I put it in first gear and then I take my foot off the clutch. I get out, close the door, and watch it plow softly into the water. The headlights reach in as they go down, searching, still lighted even after the water swirls over the back end. I wait. The wires short out. It is all finally dark. And then there is only the water, the sound of it going and running and going and running and running.

[1984]

Topics for Critical Thinking and Writing

1. Did the ending of the story surprise or perhaps even shock you? When you reread the story, what details do you notice that foreshadow the ending?
2. Why does Lyman let the red convertible roll into the river? Why with the lights on?
3. Is the fact that Lyman and Henry are Indians important to the story? Explain.
4. In the first paragraph Lyman speaks of himself in the third person. What is the effect of this device? Taking the story as a whole, how would you characterize the tone of this first-person narrator? Focus on specific phrases and sentences that enable us to know and to understand the narrator and, in particular, the nature of his relationship with his brother.

POETRY

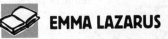 EMMA LAZARUS

Emma Lazarus (1849–1887) was of German-Jewish descent on her mother's side, and of Sephardic descent on her father's side. (Sephardic Jews trace their ancestry back to Spain under Moslem rule, before the Jews were expelled by the Christians in 1492.)

In 1883 a committee was formed to raise funds for a pedestal for the largest statue in the world, Liberty Enlightening the People, to be installed on a small island in New York Harbor. Authors were asked to donate manuscripts which then were auctioned to raise money. Emma Lazarus, keenly aware of ancient persecutions and of contemporary Jewish refugees fleeing Russian persecutions, contributed the following poem. It was read when the statue was unveiled in 1886, and the words of Liberty, spoken in the last five lines, were embossed on a plaque inside the pedestal.

For the ancients, a colossus was a statue larger than life. "The brazen giant of Greek fame," mentioned in Lazarus's first line, was a statue of the sun god, erected in the harbor of the Greek island of Rhodes, celebrating the island's success in resisting the Macedonians in 305–04 B.C. More than 100 feet tall, it stood in the harbor until it toppled during an earthquake in 225 B.C. In later years its size became mythical; it was said to have straddled the harbor (Lazarus speaks of "limbs astride from land to land"), so that ships supposedly entered the harbor by sailing between its legs.

In Lazarus's poem, the "imprisoned lightning" (line 5) in the torch is electricity. The harbor is said to be "air-bridged" because in 1883, the year of the poem, the Brooklyn Bridge was completed, connecting Brooklyn with New York. (These are the "twin cities" of the poem.)

The New Colossus

Not like the brazen giant of Greek fame,
With conquering limbs astride from land to land;
Here at our sea-washed, sunset gates shall stand
A mighty woman with a torch, whose flame
Is the imprisoned lightning, and her name   5
Mother of Exiles. From her beacon-hand

Tseng Kwong Chi, "Statue of Liberty, New York City." (© 1995 Estate of Tseng Kwong Chi. MTDP/Artists Rights Society [ARS]. New York)

Glows world-wide welcome; her mild eyes command
The air-bridged harbor that twin cities frame.
"Keep, ancient lands, your storied pomp!" cries she
With silent lips. "Give me your tired, your poor,   10
Your huddled masses yearning to breathe free,
The wretched refuse of your teeming shore.
Send these, the homeless, tempest-tost to me,
I lift my lamp beside the golden door!"

[1883]

THOMAS BAILEY ALDRICH

Thomas Bailey Aldrich (1836–1907) was born in Portsmouth, New Hampshire. He wrote poetry from his youth to his old age, and he also wrote short stories and essays, but his literary career was chiefly that of a journalist and an editor. (One magazine that he edited from 1881 to 1890, Atlantic Monthly, *continues to be important.) As the following poem indicates, Aldrich was deeply conservative. The view that he here expresses is known as Nativism, or the Nativist view.*

The Unguarded Gates

Wide open and unguarded stand our gates,
And through them press a wild, a motley throng—
Men from the Volga and the Tartar steppes,
Featureless figures of the Hoang-Ho,
Malayan, Scythian, Teuton, Kelt, and Slav,   5
Flying the Old World's poverty and scorn;
These bringing with them unknown gods and rites,
Those tiger passions, here to stretch their claws.
In street and alley what strange tongues are these,
Accents of menace alien to our air,   10
Voices that once the tower of Babel knew!

O, Liberty, white goddess, is it well
To leave the gate unguarded? On thy breast
Fold sorrow's children, soothe the hurts of fate,
Lift the downtrodden, but with the hand of steel   15
Stay those who to thy sacred portals come
To waste the fight of freedom. Have a care
Lest from thy brow the clustered stars be torn
And trampled in the dust. For so of old
The thronging Goth and Vandal trampled Rome,   20
And where the temples of the Caesars stood
The lean wolf unmolested made her lair.

[1885]

JOSEPH BRUCHAC III

Joseph Bruchac III (the name is pronounced "Brewshack") was born in Saratoga Springs, New York, in 1942, and educated at Cornell University, Syracuse University, and Union Graduate School. Like many other Americans, he has a multicultural ethnic heritage, and he includes Native Americans as well as Slovaks among his ancestors. Bruchac, who has taught in Ghana and also in the United States, has chiefly worked as an editor.

"Much of my writing and my life," Bruchac says, "relates to the problem of being an American. . . . While in college I was active in Civil Rights work and in the antiwar movement. . . . I went to Africa to teach—but more than that to be taught. It showed me many things. How much we have as Americans and take for granted. How much our eyes refuse to see because they are blinded to everything in a man's face except his color."

Ellis Island

Beyond the red brick of Ellis Island
where the two Slovak children
who became my grandparents
waited the long days of quarantine,

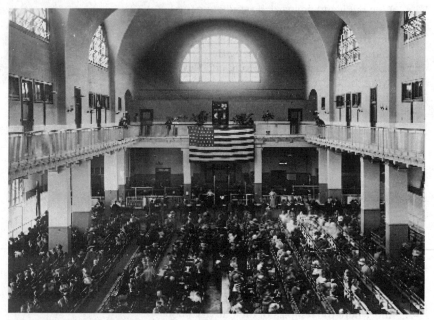

The Registry Room, Ellis Island, ca. 1912. (William Williams Collection of Photographs. Miriam and Ira D. Wallach Division of Art, Prints and Photographs. New York Public Library)

after leaving the sickness,   5
the old Empires of Europe,
a Circle Line ship slips easily
on its way to the island
of the tall woman, green
as dreams of forests and meadows   10
waiting for those who'd worked
a thousand years
yet never owned their own.
Like millions of others,   15
I too come to this island,
nine decades the answerer
of dreams.

Yet only one part of my blood loves that memory.
Another voice speaks
of native lands   20
within this nation.
Lands invaded
when the earth became owned.
Lands of those who followed
the changing Moon,   25
knowledge of the seasons
in their veins.

[1978]

Slavic women arrive at Ellis Island in the winter of 1910. (Brown Brothers)

 **EDWIN ARLINGTON ROBINSON**

Edwin Arlington Robinson (1869–1935) grew up in Gardiner, Maine, spent two years at Harvard, and then returned to Maine, where he published his first book of poetry in 1896. Though he received encouragement from neighbors, his finances were precarious, even after President Theodore Roosevelt, having been made aware of the book, secured for him an appointment as customs inspector in New York from 1905 to 1909. Additional books won fame for Robinson, and in 1922 he was awarded the first of the three Pulitzer Prizes for poetry that he would win.

Richard Cory

Whenever Richard Cory went down town,
We people on the pavement looked at him:
He was a gentleman from sole to crown,
Clean favored, and imperially slim.   4

And he was always quietly arrayed,
And he was always human when he talked;
But still he fluttered pulses when he said,
"Good-morning," and he glittered when he walked.   8

And he was rich—yes, richer than a king—
And admirably schooled in every grace:
In fine,° we thought that he was everything
To make us wish that we were in his place.   12

So on we worked, and waited for the light,
And went without the meat, and cursed the bread;
And Richard Cory, one calm summer night,
Went home and put a bullet through his head.   16

[1896]

 Topics for Critical Thinking and Writing

1. Consult the entry on irony in the glossary. Then read the pages referred to in the entry. Finally, write an essay of 500 words on irony in "Richard Cory."
2. What do you think were Richard Cory's thoughts shortly before he "put a bullet through his head"? In 500 words, set forth his thoughts and actions (what he sees and does). If you wish, you can write in the first person, from Cory's point of view. Further, if you wish, your essay can be in the form of a suicide note.
3. Write a sketch (250–350 words) setting forth your early impression or understanding of someone whose later actions revealed that you had not understood the person.

¹¹**In fine** in short

ALFRED HAYES

Alfred Hayes (1911–85) was born in England but he grew up in New York City, where he worked as a journalist and wrote novels, plays, and film scripts. His most famous work is the song that we reprint below, "Joe Hill."

Joe Hill (1879–1915) was born Joel Emmanuel Hägglund in Sweden, of Lutheran parents. He worked as a laborer, then emigrated in 1902 to the United States, where he again worked at odd jobs, on the docks and in the fields. He seems to have done a good deal of wandering, from New York through Cleveland, Chicago, the Dakotas, and on to Spokane and Portland. Around 1910 he joined the Industrial Workers of the World (IWW, nicknamed the Wobblies), a revolutionary union formed in Chicago in 1905.

Joe Hill became the chief songwriter of the movement ("The Preacher and the Slave," "Casey Jones, the Union Scab"), and his songs were widely distributed in union publications. He was arrested in Utah in 1914, charged with murdering a Salt Lake City grocer, convicted on extremely flimsy evidence—virtually all students of the case agree that he was innocent—and executed by a firing squad in 1915. The day before he was executed he wired the head of the IWW, "Don't waste any time in mourning. Organize!" His ashes, divided into packets and sent to workers in every state except Utah, were scattered on May Day 1916.

Joe Hill

I dreamed I saw Joe Hill last night
Alive as you and me.
Says I, "But Joe, you're ten years dead."
"I never died," says he.
"I never died," says he.   5

"In Salt Lake, Joe, by God," says I,
Him standing by my bed,
"They framed you on a murder charge."
Says Joe, "But I ain't dead."
Says Joe, "But I ain't dead."   10

"The copper bosses killed you, Joe,
They shot you, Joe," says I.
"Takes more than guns to kill a man,"
Says Joe, "I didn't die."
Says Joe, "I didn't die."   15

And standing there as big as life
And smiling with his eyes,
Joe says, "What they forgot to kill
Went on to organize.
Went on to organize."   20

"Joe Hill ain't dead," he says to me,
"Joe Hill ain't never died.
Where working men are out on strike
Joe Hill is at their side.
Joe Hill is at their side."   25

"From San Diego up to Maine
In every mine and mill,
Where workers strike and organize,"
Says he, "You'll find Joe Hill."
Says he, "You'll find Joe Hill."   30

I dreamed I saw Joe Hill last night
Alive as you and me.
Says I, "But Joe, you're ten years dead."

"I never died," says he.
"I never died," says he.   35

[1938]

 ## Topics for Critical Thinking and Writing

1. This song is often called a ballad. In what ways does it resemble songs that
   are called folk ballads, and in what ways does it not resemble them? For
   some observations on folk ballads, see the discussions of Huddie Ledbetter's *"De Titanic"* (page 50) and the anonymous ballad, "Sir Patrick Spence"
   (p. 423).
2. Joe Hill's Industrial Workers of the World stood for a classless society, in
   which everyone was equal and in which everyone worked. It is often said
   that the United States is classless. Do you think this view is correct? Explain.
   (You will probably want to define "class.")

 ## AURORA LEVINS MORALES

*Aurora Levins Morales, born in Puerto Rico in 1954, came to the United
States with her family in 1967. She has lived in Chicago and New
Hampshire and now lives in the San Francisco Bay Area. Levins
Morales has published stories, essays, prose poems, and poems.*

Child of the Americas

I am a child of the Americas,
a light-skinned mestiza of the Caribbean,
a child of many diaspora,° born into this continent at a crossroads.

I am a U.S. Puerto Rican Jew,
a product of the ghettos of New York I have never known.   5
An immigrant and the daughter and granddaughter of immigrants.
I speak English with passion: it's the tongue of my consciousness,
a flashing knife blade of crystal, my tool, my craft.

I am Caribeña,° island grown. Spanish is in my flesh,
ripples from my tongue, lodges in my hips: 10

---

³**diaspora** literally, "scattering"; the term is used especially to refer to the dispersion of
the Jews outside of Israel from the sixth century, when they were exiled to Babylonia, to
the present time   ⁹**Caribeña** Caribbean woman

the language of garlic and mangoes,
the singing in my poetry, the flying gestures of my hands.

I am of Latinoamerica, rooted in the history of my continent:
I speak from that body.

I am not african. African is in me, but I cannot return.   15
I am not taína.° Taíno is in me, but there is no way back.
I am not european. Europe lives in me, but I have no home there.

I am new. History made me. My first language was spanglish.°
I was born at the crossroads
and I am whole.   20

[1986]

 Topics for Critical Thinking and Writing

1. In the first stanza, Levins Morales speaks of herself as "a child of many diaspora." *Diaspora* often means "a scattering," or "a dispersion of a homoge-
   neous people." What does it refer to here?
2. In the second stanza, Levins Morales says that she is "a product of the ghettos of New York I have never known." What does she apparently refer to?
3. What attitude does "Child of the Americas" have toward the writer's ethnicity? What words or lines particularly communicate it?

 GLORIA ANZALDÚA

*Gloria Anzaldúa, a seventh-generation American, was born in 1942 on
a ranch settlement in Texas. When she was 11 her family moved to
Hargill, Texas, and in the next few years the family traveled as migrant
workers between Texas and Arkansas. In 1969 she earned a B.A. from
Pan American University, and later she earned an M.A. from the University of Texas at Austin and did further graduate work at the University of California, Santa Cruz. Anzaldúa has taught at the University of
Texas at Austin; San Francisco State University; Oakes College at the University of California, Santa Cruz; and Vermont College.*

We give a poem from Anzaldúa's Borderlands: La Frontera—The New Mestiza
*(1987), a work that combines seven prose essays with poems. For Anzaldúa—a
woman, a Latina, and a lesbian—the "borderlands" of course are spiritual as well as
geographic.*

To Live in the Borderlands Means You

To live in the Borderlands means you
   are neither *hispana india negra española*

---

¹⁶**taína** the Taínos were the Indian tribe native to Puerto Rico   ¹⁸**spanglish** a mixture of
Spanish and English

ni gabacha, eres mestiza, mulata,° half-breed
caught in the crossfire between camps
while carrying all five races on your back   5
not knowing which side to turn to, run from;

To live in the Borderlands means knowing
that the *india* in you, betrayed for 500 years,
is no longer speaking to you,
that *mexicanas* call you *rajetas,*°   10
that denying the Anglo inside you
is as bad as having denied the Indian or Black;

Cuando vives en la frontera°
people walk through you, the wind steals your voice,
you're a *burra, buey,*° scapegoat,   15
forerunner of a new race,
half and half—both woman and man, neither—
a new gender;

To live in the Borderlands means to
put *chile* in the borscht,   20
eat whole wheat *tortillas,*
speak Tex-Mex with a Brooklyn accent;
be stopped by *la migra*° at the border checkpoints;

Living in the Borderlands means you fight hard to
resist the gold elixer beckoning from the bottle,   25
the pull of the gun barrel,
the rope crushing the hollow of your throat;

In the Borderlands
you are the battleground
where enemies are kin to each other;   30
you are at home, a stranger,
the border disputes have been settled
the volley of shots have shattered the truce
you are wounded, lost in action
dead, fighting back;   35

To live in the Borderlands means
the mill with the razor white teeth wants to shred off
your olive-red skin, crush out the kernel, your heart
pound you pinch you roll you out
smelling like white bread but dead;   40

To survive the Borderlands
you must live *sin fronteras*°
be a crossroads.

[1987]

2-3**neither . . . mulata** neither Spanish indian black Spanish woman, nor white, you are
mixed, a mixed breed   10**rajetas** split, having betrayed your word [author's note]
13**Cuando . . . frontera** when you live in the borderlands   15**burra, buey** donkey, ox
[author's note]   23**la migra** immigration officials   42**sin fronteras** without borders

JIMMY SANTIAGO BACA

Jimmy Santiago Baca, of Chicano and Apache descent, was born in 1952. When be was 2 his parents divorced, and a grandparent brought him up until he was 5, when he was placed in an orphanage in New Mexico. He ran away when he was 11, lived on the streets, took drugs, and at the age of 20 was convicted of drug possession. In prison he taught himself to read and write, and he began to compose poetry. A fellow inmate urged him to send some poems to Mother Jones *magazine, and the work was accepted. In 1979 Louisiana State University Press published a book of his poems,* Immigrants in Our Own Land. *He has since published several other books.*

So Mexicans Are Taking Jobs from Americans

O Yes? Do they come on horses
with rifles, and say,
       Ese gringo,° gimmee your job?
And do you, gringo, take off your ring,
drop your wallet into a blanket   5
spread over the ground, and walk away?

I hear Mexicans are taking your jobs away.
Do they sneak into town at night,
and as you're walking home with a whore,
do they mug you, a knife at your throat,   10
saying, I want your job?
Even on TV, an asthmatic leader
crawls turtle heavy, leaning on an assistant,
and from a nest of wrinkles on his face,
a tongue paddles through flashing waves   15
of lightbulbs, of cameramen, rasping
"They're taking our jobs away."

Well, I've gone about trying to find them,
asking just where the hell are these fighters.

The rifles I hear sound in the night   20
are white farmers shooting blacks and browns
whose ribs I see jutting out
and starving children,
I see the poor marching for a little work,
I see small white farmers selling out   25
to clean-suited farmers living in New York,
who've never been on a farm,
don't know the look of a hoof or the smell
of a woman's body bending all day long in fields.

---

³*Ese gringo* Hey, whitey

I see this, and I hear only a few people   30
got all the money in this world, the rest
count their pennies to buy bread and butter.

Below that cool green sea of money,
millions and millions of people fight to live,
search for pearls in the darkest depths   35
of their dreams, hold their breath for years
trying to cross poverty to just having something.

The children are dead already. We are killing them,
that is what America should be saying;
on TV, in the streets, in offices, should be saying,   40
   "We aren't giving the children a chance to live."

   Mexicans are taking our jobs, they say instead.
   What they really say is, let them die,
   and the children too.

                                                          [1979]

LANGSTON HUGHES

Langston Hughes (1902–1967) was born in Joplin, Missouri. He lived part of his youth in Mexico, spent a year at Columbia University, served as a merchant seaman, and worked in a Paris nightclub, where he showed some of his poems to Dr. Alain Locke, a strong advocate of African-American literature. After returning to the United States, Hughes went on to publish poetry, fiction, plays, essays, and biographies.

Theme for English B

The instructor said,

> *Go home and write*
> *a page tonight.*
> *And let that page come out of you—*
> *Then, it will be true.*   5

I wonder if it's that simple?

I am twenty-two, colored, born in Winston-Salem.
I went to school there, then Durham, then here
to this college on the hill above Harlem.
I am the only colored student in my class.   10
The steps from the hill lead down into Harlem,
through a park, then I cross St. Nicholas,
Eighth Avenue, Seventh, and I come to the Y,
the Harlem Branch Y, where I take the elevator
up to my room, sit down, and write this page: 15

It's not easy to know what is true for you or me
at twenty-two, my age. But I guess I'm what

I feel and see and hear, Harlem, I hear you:
hear you, hear me—we two—you, me, talk on this page.
(I hear New York, too.) Me—who?   20

Well, I like to eat, sleep, drink, and be in love.
I like to work, read, learn, and understand life.
I like a pipe for a Christmas present,
or records—Bessie,° bop, or Bach.
I guess being colored doesn't make me *not* like   25
the same things other folks like who are other races.

So will my page be colored that I write?
Being me, it will not be white.
But it will be
a part of you, instructor.   30

You are white—
yet a part of me, as I am a part of you.
That's American.
Sometimes perhaps you don't want to be a part of me.
Nor do I often want to be a part of you.   35
But we are, that's true!
As I learn from you,
I guess you learn from me—
although you're older—and white—
and somewhat more free.   40

This is my page for English B.

                                                                       [1949]

 Topics for Critical Thinking and Writing

1. The teacher instructs the students (line 4) to "let that page come out of you," and adds, "Then, it will be true" (6). Does it follow that what we let "come" out of us is "true"? If you were a student, what would be your response to the teacher's instruction?

2. In lines 21–24 Hughes specifies some of the things he likes—things that many people who are not black doubtless also like. Why, then, does he say (line 28) that his page "will not be white"?

3. Pretend that you are the English B instructor who received Hughes's theme. What comment (about 250 words) do you put at the end of the theme?

4. Aside from the statement that he is a "colored" student (10, 27) from Harlem (9, 11, 14, 18), is there anything particularly African American about this poem? Putting aside these references, might the poem have been written by an Asian American, or (say) an American of Middle Eastern descent?

5. In line 10 the speaker says he is "the only colored student in [his] class." If you have ever been the only student of your race or religion or ethnic back-

---

²⁴**Bessie** Bessie Smith (1898?–1937), African-American blues singer

ground or sex in a group, in an essay of 250–500 words set forth the feelings you had, and the feelings you now have about the experience.

PAT PARKER

Pat Parker (1944–89), author of several books of poems and essays, was a founder of the Black Women's Revolutionary Council in 1980, and a medical coordinator at the Oakland Feminist Women's Health Center.

For the white person who wants to know how to be my friend

The first thing you do is to forget that i'm Black.
Second, you must never forget that i'm Black.

You should be able to dig Aretha,°
but don't play her every time i come over.
And if you decide to play Beethoven—don't tell me   5
his life story. They made us take music appreciation too.

Eat soul food if you like it, but don't expect me
to locate your restaurants
or cook it for you.

And if some Black person insults you,   10
mugs you, rapes your sister, rapes you,
rips your house or is just being an ass—
please, do not apologize to me
for wanting to do them bodily harm.
It makes me wonder if you're foolish.   15

And even if you really believe Blacks are better lovers than
whites—don't tell me. I start thinking of charging stud fees.

In other words—if you really want to be my friend—*don't*
make a labor of it. I'm lazy. Remember.

[1978]

Topics for Critical Thinking and Writing

1. The first two lines are contradictory. What sense do you make out of them?
2. Explain lines 4–5.

---

[3]**Aretha** Aretha Franklin, African-American singer of blues and rock

3. What stereotypes of African Americans does Parker evoke in the last two stanzas? What is her point?
4. If you have ever been involved in an episode of the sort that Parker mentions in her second stanza, in an essay of 500 words narrate the experience and offer a reflection on it.

 # MITSUYE YAMADA

Mitsuye Yamada, the daughter of Japanese immigrants to the United States, was born in Japan in 1923, during her mother's return visit to her native land. Yamada was raised in Seattle, but in 1942 she and her family were incarcerated and then relocated in a camp in Idaho, when Executive Order 9066 gave military authorities the right to remove any and all persons from "military areas." In 1954 she became an American citizen. A member of the Asian American Studies Program at the University at California at Irvine, she is the author of poems and stories.

For another poem by Yamada, see page 1332.

To the Lady

The one in San Francisco who asked:
Why did the Japanese Americans let
the government put them in
those camps without protest?

Come to think of it I   5
    should've run off to Canada
    should've hijacked a plane to Algeria
    should've pulled myself up from my
    bra straps
    and kicked'm in the groin   10
    should've bombed a bank
    should've tried self-immolation
    should've holed myself up in a
    woodframe house
    and let you watch me
    burn up on the six o'clock news   15
    should've run howling down the street
    naked and assaulted you at breakfast
    by AP wirephoto
    should've screamed bloody murder
    like Kitty Genovese°   20

    Then
    YOU would've

---

[21]**Kitty Genovese** In 1964 Kitty Genovese of Kew Gardens, New York, was stabbed to death when she left her car and walked toward her home. Thirty-eight persons heard her screams, but no one came to her assistance.

Dorothea Lange. "Grandfather and Grandchildren Awaiting Evacuation Bus." (War Relocation Authority/The National Archives)

come to my aid in shining armor
laid yourself across the railroad track   25
marched on Washington
tatooed a Star of David on your arm
written six million enraged
letters to Congress

But we didn't draw the line   30
anywhere
law and order Executive Order 9066°
social order moral order internal order

You let'm   35
I let'm
All are punished.

[1976]

32**Executive Order 9066** an authorization, signed in 1941 by President Franklin D. Roosevelt, allowing military authorities to relocate Japanese and Japanese Americans who
resided on the Pacific Coast of the United States

Topics for Critical Thinking and Writing

1. Has the lady's question (lines 2–4) ever crossed your mind? If so, what answers did you think of?
2. What, in effect, is the speaker really saying in lines 5–21? And in lines 24–29?
3. Explain the last line.

DRAMA

AUGUST WILSON

August Wilson was born in Pittsburgh in 1945, the son of a black woman and a white man. After dropping out of school at the age of 15, Wilson took various odd jobs, such as stock clerk and short-order cook, in his spare time educating himself in the public library, chiefly by reading works by such black writers as Richard Wright, Ralph Ellison, Langston Hughes, and Amiri Baraka (LeRoi Jones). In 1978 the director of a black theater in St. Paul, Minnesota, who had known Wilson in Pittsburgh, invited him to write a play for the theater. Six months later Wilson moved permanently to St. Paul.

The winner of the Pulitzer Prize for drama in 1987, Wilson's Fences *was first presented as a staged reading in 1983 and was later performed in Chicago, Seattle, Rochester (New York), and New Haven (Connecticut) before reaching New York City in 1987. An earlier play,* Ma Rainey's Black Bottom, *was voted Best Play of the Year 1984–85 by the New York Drama Critics' Circle. In 1981 when* Ma Rainey *was first read at the O'Neill Center in Waterford, Connecticut, Wilson met Lloyd Richards, a black director with whom he has continued to work closely. The* Piano Lesson, *directed by Richards, won Wilson a second Pulitzer Prize in 1990.*

Fences

for Lloyd Richards,
who adds to whatever he touches

When the sins of our fathers visit us
We do not have to play host.
We can banish them with forgiveness
As God, in His Largeness and Laws.

—August Wilson

LIST OF CHARACTERS
TROY MAXSON
JIM BONO, *Troy's friend*
ROSE, *Troy's wife*
LYONS, *Troy's oldest son by previous marriage*
GABRIEL, *Troy's brother*
CORY, *Troy and Rose's son*
RAYNELL, *Troy's daughter*

Fences in the Seattle Repertory Theater production with (left to right) Frances Foster as Rose, Keith Amos as Cory, William Jay as Gabriel, and Gilbert Lewis as Troy. (Photo © Chris Bennion)

SETTING: *The setting is the yard which fronts the only entrance to the Maxson household, an ancient two-story brick house set back off a small alley in a big-city neighborhood. The entrance to the house is gained by two or three steps leading to a wooden porch badly in need of paint.*

A relatively recent addition to the house and running its full width, the porch lacks congruence. It is a sturdy porch with a flat roof. One or two chairs of dubious value sit at one end where the kitchen window opens onto the porch. An old-fashioned icebox stands silent guard at the opposite end.

The yard is a small dirt yard, partially fenced, except for the last scene, with a wooden saw horse, a pile of lumber, and other fence-building equipment set off to the side. Opposite is a tree from which hangs a ball made of rags. A baseball bat leans against the tree. Two oil drums serve as garbage receptacles and sit near the house at right to complete the setting.

THE PLAY: *Near the turn of the century, the destitute of Europe sprang on the city with tenacious claws and an honest and solid dream. The city devoured them. They swelled its belly until it burst into a thousand furnaces and sewing machines, a thousand butcher shops and bakers' ovens, a thousand churches and hospitals and funeral parlors and money-lenders. The city grew. It nourished itself and offered each man a partnership limited only by his talent, his guile, and his willingness and capacity for hard work. For the immigrants of Europe, a dream dared and won true.*

The descendants of African slaves were offered no such welcome or participation. They came from places called the Carolinas and the Virginias, Georgia, Alabama, Mississippi, and Tennessee. They came strong, eager, searching. The city rejected them and they fled and settled along the river-

banks and under bridges in shallow, ramshackle houses made of sticks and tarpaper. They collected rags and wood. They sold the use of their muscles and their bodies. They cleaned houses and washed clothes, they shined shoes, and in quiet desperation and vengeful pride, they stole, and lived in pursuit of their own dream. That they could breathe free, finally, and stand to meet life with the force of dignity and whatever eloquence the heart could call upon.

By 1957, the hard-won victories of the European immigrants had solidified the industrial might of America. War had been confronted and won with new energies that used loyalty and patriotism as its fuel. Life was rich, full, and flourishing. The Milwaukee Braves won the World Series, and the hot winds of change that would make the sixties a turbulent, racing, dangerous, and provocative decade had not yet begun to blow full.

Act 1

Scene 1

It is 1957. TROY *and* BONO *enter the yard, engaged in conversation.* TROY *is fifty-three years old, a large man with thick, heavy hands; it is this largeness that he strives to fill out and make an accommodation with. Together with his blackness, his largeness informs his sensibilities and the choices he has made in his life.*

Of the two men, BONO *is obviously the follower. His commitment to their friendship of thirty-odd years is rooted in his admiration of* TROY*'s honesty, capacity for hard work, and his strength, which* BONO *seeks to emulate.*

It is Friday night, payday, and the one night of the week the two men engage in a ritual of talk and drink. TROY *is usually the most talkative and at times he can be crude and almost vulgar, though he is capable of rising to profound heights of expression. The men carry lunch buckets and wear or carry burlap aprons and are dressed in clothes suitable to their jobs as garbage collectors.*

BONO. Troy, you ought to stop that lying!

TROY. I ain't lying! The nigger had a watermelon this big. [*He indicates with his hands.*] Talking about . . . "What watermelon, Mr. Rand?" I liked to fell out! "What watermelon, Mr. Rand?" . . . And it sitting there big as life.

BONO. What did Mr. Rand say?

TROY. Ain't said nothing. Figure if the nigger too dumb to know he carrying a watermelon, he wasn't gonna get much sense out of him. Trying to hide that great big old watermelon under his coat. Afraid to let the white man see him carry it home.

BONO. I'm like you . . . I ain't got no time for them kind of people.

TROY. Now what he look like getting mad cause he see the man from the union talking to Mr. Rand?

BONO. He come to me talking about . . . "Maxson gonna get us fired." I told him to get away from me with that. He walked away from me calling you a troublemaker. What Mr. Rand say?

TROY. Ain't said nothing. He told me to go down the Commissioner's office next Friday. They called me down there to see them.

BONO. Well, as long as you got your complaint filed, they can't fire you. That's what one of them white fellows tell me.

TROY. I ain't worried about them firing me. They gonna fire me cause I asked a question? That's all I did. I went to Mr. Rand and asked him, "Why? Why you got the white mens driving and the colored lifting?" Told him, "What's the matter, don't I count? You think only white fellows got sense enough to drive a truck. That ain't no paper job! Hell, anybody can drive a truck. How come you got all whites driving and the colored lifting?" He told me "take it to the union." Well, hell, that's what I done! Now they wanna come up with this pack of lies.

BONO. I told Brownie if the man come and ask him any questions . . . just tell the truth! It ain't nothing but something they done trumped up on you cause you filed a complaint on them.

TROY. Brownie don't understand nothing. All I want them to do is change the job description. Give everybody a chance to drive the truck. Brownie can't see that. He ain't got that much sense.

BONO. How you figure he be making out with that gal be up at Taylor's all the time . . . that Alberta gal?

TROY. Same as you and me. Getting just as much as we is. Which is to say nothing.

BONO. It is, huh? I figure you doing a little better than me . . . and I ain't saying what I'm doing.

TROY. Aw, nigger, look here . . . I know you. If you had got anywhere near that gal, twenty minutes later you be looking to tell somebody. And the first one you gonna tell . . . that you gonna want to brag to . . . is me.

BONO. I ain't saying that. I see where you be eyeing her.

TROY. I eye all the women. I don't miss nothing. Don't never let nobody tell you Troy Maxson don't eye the women.

BONO. You been doing more than eyeing her. You done bought her a drink or two.

TROY. Hell yeah, I bought her a drink! What that mean? I bought you one, too. What that mean cause I buy her a drink? I'm just being polite.

BONO. It's all right to buy her one drink. That's what you call being polite. But when you wanna be buying two or three . . . that's what you call eyeing her.

TROY. Look here, as long as you known me . . . you ever known me to chase after women?

BONO. Hell yeah! Long as I done known you. You forgetting I knew you when.

TROY. Naw, I'm talking about since I been married to Rose?

BONO. Oh, not since you been married to Rose. Now, that's the truth, there. I can say that.

TROY. All right then! Case closed.

BONO. I see you be walking up around Alberta's house. You supposed to be at Taylors' and you be walking up around there.

TROY. What you watching where I'm walking for? I ain't watching after you.

BONO. I seen you walking around there more than once.

TROY. Hell, you liable to see me walking anywhere! That don't mean nothing cause you see me walking around there.

BONO. Where she come from anyway? She just kinda showed up one day.

TROY. Tallahassee. You can look at her and tell she one of them Florida gals. They got some big healthy women down there. Grow them right up out the ground. Got a little bit of Indian in her. Most of them niggers down in Florida got some Indian in them.

BONO. I don't know about that Indian part. But she damn sure big and healthy. Woman wear some big stockings. Got them great big old legs and hips as wide as the Mississippi River.

TROY. Legs don't mean nothing. You don't do nothing but push them out of the way. But them hips cushion the ride!

BONO. Troy, you ain't got no sense.

TROY. It's the truth! Like you riding on Goodyears!

ROSE *enters from the house. She is ten years younger than* TROY, *her devotion to him stems from her recognition of the possibilities of her life without him: a succession of abusive men and their babies, a life of partying and running the streets, the Church, or aloneness with its attendant pain and frustration. She recognizes* TROY's *spirit as a fine and illuminating one and she either ignores or forgives his faults, only some of which she recognizes. Though she doesn't drink, her presence is an integral part of the Friday night rituals. She alternates between the porch and the kitchen, where supper preparations are under way.*

ROSE. What you all out here getting into?

TROY. What you worried about what we getting into for? This is men talk, woman.

ROSE. What I care what you all talking about? Bono, you gonna stay for supper?

BONO. No, I thank you, Rose. But Lucille say she cooking up a pot of pigfeet.

TROY. Pigfeet! Hell, I'm going home with you! Might even stay the night if you got some pigfeet. You got something in there to top them pigfeet, Rose?

ROSE. I'm cooking up some chicken. I got some chicken and collard greens.

TROY. Well, go on back in the house and let me and Bono finish what we was talking about. This is men talk. I got some talk for you later. You know what kind of talk I mean. You go on and powder it up.

ROSE. Troy Maxson, don't you start that now!

TROY [*puts his arm around her*]. Aw, woman . . . come here. Look here, Bono . . . when I met this woman . . . I got out that place, say, "Hitch up my pony, saddle up my mare . . . there's a woman out there for me somewhere. I looked here. Looked there. Saw Rose and latched on to her." I latched on to her and told her—I'm gonna tell you the truth—I told her, "Baby, I don't wanna marry, I just wanna be your man." Rose told me . . . tell him what you told me, Rose.

ROSE. I told him if he wasn't the marrying kind, then move out the way so the marrying kind could find me.

TROY. That's what she told me. "Nigger, you in my way. You blocking the view! Move out the way so I can find me a husband." I thought it over two or three days. Come back—

ROSE. Ain't no two or three days nothing. You was back the same night.

TROY. Come back, told her . . . "Okay, baby . . . but I'm gonna buy me a banty rooster and put him out there in the backyard . . . and when he see a stranger come, he'll flap his wings and crow . . . ." Look here, Bono, I could watch the front door by myself . . . it was that back door I was worried about.

ROSE. Troy, you ought not talk like that. Troy ain't doing nothing but telling a lie.

TROY. Only thing is . . . when we first got married . . . forget the rooster . . . we ain't had no yard!

BONO. I hear you tell it. Me and Lucille was staying down there on Logan Street. Had two rooms with the outhouse in the back. I ain't mind the outhouse none. But when that goddamn wind blow through there in the winter . . . that's what I'm talking about! To this day I wonder why in the hell I ever stayed down there for six long years. But see, I didn't know I could do no better. I thought only white folks had inside toilets and things.

ROSE. There's a lot of people don't know they can do no better than they doing now. That's just something you got to learn. A lot of folks still shop at Bella's.

TROY. Ain't nothing wrong with shopping at Bella's. She got fresh food.

ROSE. I ain't said nothing about if she got fresh food. I'm talking about what she charge. She charge ten cents more than the A&P.

TROY. The A&P ain't never done nothing for me. I spends my money where I'm treated right. I go down to Bella, say, "I need a loaf of bread, I'll pay you Friday." She give it to me. What sense that make when I got money to go and spend it somewhere else and ignore the person who done right by me? That ain't in the Bible.

ROSE. We ain't talking about what's in the Bible. What sense it make to shop there when she overcharge?

TROY. You shop where you want to. I'll do my shopping where the people been good to me.

ROSE. Well, I don't think it's right for her to overcharge. That's all I was saying.

BONO. Look here . . . I got to get on. Lucille going be raising all kind of hell.

TROY. Where you going, nigger? We ain't finished this pint. Come here, finish this pint.

BONO. Well, hell, I am . . . if you ever turn the bottle loose.

TROY [*hands him the bottle*]. The only thing I say about the A&P is I'm glad Cory got that job down there. Help him take care of his school clothes and things. Gabe done moved out and things getting tight around here. He got that job. . . . He can start to look out for himself.

ROSE. Cory done went and got recruited by a college football team.

TROY. I told that boy about that football stuff. The white man ain't gonna let him get nowhere with that football. I told him when he first come to me with it. Now you come telling me he done went and got more tied up in it. He ought to go and get recruited in how to fix cars or something where he can make a living.

ROSE. He ain't talking about making no living playing football. It's just something the boys in school do. They gonna send a recruiter by to talk to you. He'll tell you he ain't talking about making no living playing football. It's a honor to be recruited.

TROY. It ain't gonna get him nowhere. Bono'll tell you that.

BONO. If he be like you in the sports . . . he's gonna be all right. Ain't but two men ever played baseball as good as you. That's Babe Ruth and Josh Gibson.[1] Them's the only two men ever hit more home runs than you.

TROY. What it ever get me? Ain't got a pot to piss in or a window to throw it out of.

ROSE. Times have changed since you was playing baseball, Troy. That was before the war. Times have changed a lot since then.

TROY. How in hell they done changed?

ROSE. They got lots of colored boys playing ball now. Baseball and football.

BONO. You right about that, Rose. Times have changed, Troy. You just come along too early.

TROY. There ought not never have been no time called too early! Now you take that fellow . . . what's that fellow they had playing right field for the Yankees back then? You know who I'm talking about, Bono. Used to play right field for the Yankees.

---

[1]African-American ballplayer (1911–47), known as the Babe Ruth of the Negro leagues

ROSE. Selkirk?

TROY. Selkirk! That's it! Man batting .269, understand? .269. What kind of sense that make? I was hitting .432 with thirty-seven home runs! Man batting .269 and playing right field for the Yankees! I saw Josh Gibson's daughter yesterday. She walking around with raggedy shoes on her feet. Now I bet you Selkirk's daughter ain't walking around with raggedy shoes on the feet! I bet you that!

ROSE. They got a lot of colored baseball players now. Jackie Robinson[2] was the first. Folks had to wait for Jackie Robinson.

TROY. I done seen a hundred niggers play baseball better than Jackie Robinson. Hell, I know some teams Jackie Robinson couldn't even make! What you talking about Jackie Robinson. Jackie Robinson wasn't nobody. I'm talking about if you could play ball then they ought to have let you play. Don't care what color you were. Come telling me I come along too early. If you could play . . . then they ought to have let you play.

    TROY *takes a long drink from the bottle.*

ROSE. You gonna drink yourself to death. You don't need to be drinking like that.

TROY. Death ain't nothing. I done seen him. Done wrassled with him. You can't tell me nothing about death. Death ain't nothing but a fastball on the outside corner. And you know what I'll do to that! Lookee here, Bono . . . am I lying? You get one of them fastballs, about waist high, over the outside corner of the plate where you can get the meat of the bat on it . . . and good god! You can kiss it goodbye. Now, am I lying?

BONO. Naw, you telling the truth there. I seen you do it.

TROY. If I'm lying . . . that 450 feet worth of lying! [*Pause.*] That's all death is to me. A fastball on the outside corner.

ROSE. I don't know why you want to get on talking about death.

TROY. Ain't nothing wrong with talking about death. That's part of life. Everybody gonna die. You gonna die, I'm gonna die. Bono's gonna die. Hell, we all gonna die.

ROSE. But you ain't got to talk about it. I don't like to talk about it.

TROY. You the one brought it up. Me and Bono was talking about baseball . . . you tell me I'm gonna drink myself to death. Ain't that right, Bono? You know I don't drink this but one night out of the week. That's Friday night. I'm gonna drink just enough to where I can handle it. Then I cuts it loose. I leave it alone. So don't you worry about me drinking myself to death. 'Cause I ain't worried about Death. I done seen him. I done wrestled with him.

    Look here, Bono . . . I looked up one day and Death was marching straight at me. Like Soldiers on Parade! The Army of Death was marching straight at me. The middle of July, 1941. It got real cold just like it be winter. It seem like Death himself reached out and touched me on the shoulder. He touched me just like I touch you. I got cold as ice and Death standing there grinning at me.

ROSE. Troy, why don't you hush that talk.

TROY. I say . . . what you want, Mr. Death? You be wanting me? You done brought your army to be getting me? I looked him dead in the eye. I wasn't fearing

---

[2]In 1947 Robinson (1919–72) became the first African-American to play baseball in the major leagues.

ROSE. nothing. I was ready to tangle. Just like I'm ready to tangle now. The Bible say be ever vigilant. That's why I don't get but so drunk. I got to keep watch.

ROSE. Troy was right down there in Mercy Hospital. You remember he had pneumonia? Laying there with a fever talking plumb out of his head.

TROY. Death standing there staring at me . . . carrying that sickle in his hand. Finally he say, "You want bound over for another year?" See, just like that . . . "You want bound over for another year?" I told him, "Bound over hell! Let's settle this now!"

It seem like he kinda fell back when I said that, and all the cold went out of me. I reached down and grabbed that sickle and threw it just as far as I could throw it . . . and me and him commenced to wrestling.

We wrestled for three days and three nights. I can't say where I found the strength from. Everytime it seemed like he was gonna get the best of me, I'd reach way down deep inside myself and find the strength to do him one better.

ROSE. Everytime Troy tell that story he find different ways to tell it. Different things to make up about it.

TROY. I ain't making up nothing. I'm telling you the facts of what happened. I wrestled with Death for three days and three nights and I'm standing here to tell you about it. [*Pause.*] All right. At the end of the third night we done weakened each other to where we can't hardly move. Death stood up, throwed on his robe . . . had him a white robe with a hood on it. He throwed on that robe and went off to look for his sickle. Say, "I'll be back." Just like that. "I'll be back." I told him, say, "Yeah, but . . . you gonna have to find me!" I wasn't no fool. I wasn't going looking for him. Death ain't nothing to play with. And I know he's gonna get me. I know I got to join his army . . . his camp followers. But as long as I keep my strength and see him coming . . . as long as I keep up my vigilance . . . he's gonna have to fight to get me. I ain't going easy.

BONO. Well, look here, since you got to keep up your vigilance . . . let me have the bottle.

TROY. Aw hell, I shouldn't have told you that part. I should have left out that part.

ROSE. Troy be talking that stuff and half the time don't even know what he be talking about.

TROY. Bono know me better than that.

BONO. That's right. I know you. I know you got some Uncle Remus[3] in your blood. You got more stories than the devil got sinners.

TROY. Aw hell, I done seen him too! Done talked with the devil.

ROSE. Troy, don't nobody wanna be hearing all that stuff.

LYONS *enters the yard from the street. Thirty-four years old,* TROY's *son by a previous marriage, he sports a neatly trimmed goatee, sport coat, white shirt, tieless and buttoned at the collar. Though he fancies himself a musician, he is more caught up in the rituals and "idea" of being a musician than in the actual practice of the music. He has come to borrow money from* TROY, *and while he knows he will be successful, he is uncertain as to what extent his lifestyle will be held up to scrutiny and ridicule.*

LYONS. Hey, Pop.

TROY. What you come "Hey, Popping" me for?

---

[3]Narrator of traditional black tales in a book by Joel Chandler Harris

LYONS. How you doing, Rose? [*He kisses her.*] Mr. Bono. How you doing?

BONO. Hey, Lyons . . . how you been?

TROY. He must have been doing all right. I ain't seen him around here last week.

ROSE. Troy, leave your boy alone. He come by to see you and you wanna start all that nonsense.

TROY. I ain't bothering Lyons. [*Offers him the bottle.*] Here . . . get you a drink. We got an understanding. I know why he come by to see me and he know I know.

LYONS. Come on, Pop . . . I just stopped by to say hi . . . see how you was doing.

TROY. You ain't stopped by yesterday.

ROSE. You gonna stay for supper, Lyons? I got some chicken cooking in the oven.

LYONS. No, Rose . . . thanks. I was just in the neighborhood and thought I'd stop by for a minute.

TROY. You was in the neighborhood all right, nigger. You telling the truth there. You was in the neighborhood cause it's my payday.

LYONS. Well, hell, since you mentioned it . . . let me have ten dollars.

TROY. I'll be damned! I'll die and go to hell and play blackjack with the devil before I give you ten dollars.

BONO. That's what I wanna know about . . . that devil you done seen.

LYONS. What . . . Pop done seen the devil? You too much, Pops.

TROY. Yeah, I done seen him. Talked to him too!

ROSE. You ain't seen no devil. I done told you that man ain't had nothing to do with the devil. Anything you can't understand, you want to call it the devil.

TROY. Look here, Bono . . . I went down to see Hertzberger about some furniture. Got three rooms for two-ninety-eight. That what it say on the radio. "Three rooms . . . two-ninety-eight." Even made up a little song about it. Go down there . . . man tell me I can't get no credit. I'm working every day and can't get no credit. What to do? I got an empty house with some raggedy furniture in it. Cory ain't got no bed. He's sleeping on a pile of rags on the floor. Working every day and can't get no credit. Come back here— Rose'll tell you—madder than hell. Sit down . . . try to figure what I'm gonna do. Come a knock on the door. Ain't been living here but three days. Who know I'm here? Open the door . . . devil standing there bigger than life. White fellow . . . white fellow . . . got on good clothes and everything. Standing there with a clipboard in his hand. I ain't had to say nothing. First words come out of his mouth was . . . "I understand you need some furniture and can't get no credit." I liked to fell over. He say, "I'll give you all the credit you want, but you got to pay the interest on it." I told him, "Give me three rooms worth and charge whatever you want." Next day a truck pulled up here and two men unloaded them three rooms. Man what drove the truck give me a book. Say send ten dollars, first of every month to the address in the book and every thing will be all right. Say if I miss a payment the devil was coming back and it'll be hell to pay. That was fifteen years ago. To this day . . . the first of the month I send my ten dollars, Rose'll tell you.

ROSE. Troy lying.

TROY. I ain't never seen that man since. Now you tell me who else that could have been but the devil? I ain't sold my soul or nothing like that, you understand. Naw, I wouldn't have truck with the devil about nothing like that. I got my furniture and pays my ten dollars the first of the month just like clockwork.

BONO. How long you say you been paying this ten dollars a month?

TROY. Fifteen years!

BONO. Hell, ain't you finished paying for it yet? How much the man done charged you?

TROY. Ah hell, I done paid for it. I done paid for it ten times over! The fact is I'm scared to stop paying it.

ROSE. Troy lying. We got that furniture from Mr. Glickman. He ain't paying no ten dollars a month to nobody.

TROY. Aw hell, woman. Bono know I ain't that big a fool.

LYONS. I was just getting ready to say . . . I know where there's a bridge for sale.

TROY. Look here, I'll tell you this . . . it don't matter to me if he was the devil. It don't matter if the devil give credit. Somebody has got to give it.

ROSE. It ought to matter. You going around talking about having truck with the devil . . . God's the one you gonna have to answer to. He's the one gonna be at the Judgment.

LYONS. Yeah, well, look here, Pop . . . Let me have that ten dollars. I'll give it back to you. Bonnie got a job working at the hospital.

TROY. What I tell you, Bono? The only time I see this nigger is when he wants something. That's the only time I see him.

LYONS. Come on, Pop, Mr. Bono don't want to hear all that. Let me have the ten dollars. I told you Bonnie working.

TROY. What that mean to me? "Bonnie working." I don't care if she working. Go ask her for the ten dollars if she working. Talking about "Bonnie working." Why ain't you working?

LYONS. Aw, Pop, you know I can't find no decent job. Where am I gonna get a job at? You know I can't get no job.

TROY. I told you I know some people down there. I can get you on the rubbish if you want to work. I told you that the last time you came by here asking me for something.

LYONS. Naw, Pop . . . thanks. That ain't for me. I don't wanna be carrying nobody's rubbish. I don't wanna be punching nobody's time clock.

TROY. What's the matter, you too good to carry people's rubbish? Where you think that ten dollars you talking about come from? I'm just supposed to haul people's rubbish and give my money to you cause you too lazy to work. You too lazy to work and wanna know why you ain't got what I got.

ROSE. What hospital Bonnie working at? Mercy?

LYONS. She's down at Passavant working in the laundry.

TROY. I ain't got nothing as it is. I give you that ten dollars and I got to eat beans the rest of the week. Naw . . . you ain't getting no ten dollars here.

LYONS. You ain't got to be eating no beans. I don't know why you wanna say that.

TROY. I ain't got no extra money. Gabe done moved over to Miss Pearl's paying her the rent and things done got tight around here. I can't afford to be giving you every payday.

LYONS. I ain't asked you to give me nothing. I asked you to loan me ten dollars. I know you got ten dollars.

TROY. Yeah, I got it. You know why I got it? Cause I don't throw my money away out there in the streets. You living the fast life . . . wanna be a musician . . . running around in them clubs and things . . . then, you learn to take care of yourself. You ain't gonna find me going and asking nobody for nothing. I done spent too many years without.

LYONS. You and me is two different people, Pop.

TROY. I done learned my mistake and learned to do what's right by it. You still trying to get something for nothing. Life don't owe you nothing. You owe it to yourself. Ask Bono. He'll tell you I'm right.

LYONS. You got your way of dealing with the world . . . I got mine. The only thing that matters to me is the music.

TROY. Yeah, I can see that! It don't matter how you gonna eat . . . where your next dollar is coming from. You telling the truth there.

LYONS. I know I got to eat. But I got to live too. I need something that gonna help me to get out of the bed in the morning. Make me feel like I belong in the world. I don't bother nobody. I just stay with the music cause that's the only way I can find to live in the world. Otherwise there ain't no telling what I might do. Now I don't come criticizing you and how you live. I just come by to ask you for ten dollars. I don't wanna hear all that about how I live.

TROY. Boy, your mamma did a hell of a job raising you.

LYONS. You can't change me, Pop. I'm thirty-four years old. If you wanted to change me, you should have been there when I was growing up. I come by to see you . . . ask for ten dollars and you want to talk about how I was raised. You don't know nothing about how I was raised.

ROSE. Let the boy have ten dollars, Troy.

TROY [*to* LYONS]. What the hell you looking at me for? I ain't got no ten dollars. You know what I do with my money. [*To* ROSE] Give him ten dollars if you want him to have it.

ROSE. I will. Just as soon as you turn it loose.

TROY [*handing* ROSE *the money*]. There it is. Seventy-six dollars and forty-two cents. You see this, Bono? Now, I ain't gonna get but six of that back.

ROSE. You ought to stop telling that lie. Here, Lyons. [*She hands him the money.*]

LYONS. Thanks, Rose. Look . . . I got to run . . . I'll see you later.

TROY. Wait a minute. You gonna say, "thanks, Rose" and ain't gonna look to see where she got that ten dollars from? See how they do me, Bono?

LYONS. I know she got it from you, Pop. Thanks. I'll give it back to you.

TROY. There he go telling another lie. Time I see that ten dollars . . . he'll be owing me thirty more.

LYONS. See you, Mr. Bono.

BONO. Take care, Lyons!

LYONS. Thanks, Pop. I'll see you again.

LYONS *exits the yard.*

TROY. I don't know why he don't go and get him a decent job and take care of that woman he got.

BONO. He'll be all right, Troy. The boy is still young.

TROY. The *boy* is thirty-four years old.

ROSE. Let's not get off into all that.

BONO. Look here . . . I got to be going. I got to be getting on. Lucille gonna be waiting.

TROY [*puts his arm around* ROSE]. See this woman, Bono? I love this woman. I love this woman so much it hurts. I love her so much . . . I done run out of ways of loving her. So I got to go back to basics. Don't you come by my house Monday morning talking about time to go to work . . . 'cause I'm still gonna be stroking!

ROSE. Troy! Stop it now!

BONO. I ain't paying him no mind, Rose. That ain't nothing but gin-talk. Go on, Troy. I'll see you Monday.

TROY. Don't you come by my house, nigger! I done told you what I'm gonna be doing.

The lights go down to black.

Scene 2

The lights come up on ROSE *hanging up clothes. She hums and sings softly to herself. It is the following morning.*

ROSE [*sings*]. Jesus, be a fence all around me every day
    Jesus, I want you to protect me as I travel on my way.
    Jesus, be a fence all around me every day.

TROY *enters from the house.*

    Jesus, I want you to protect me
    As I travel on my way.

    [*To* TROY.] Morning. You ready for breakfast? I can fix it soon as I finish hanging up these clothes?

TROY. I got the coffee on. That'll be all right. I'll just drink some of that this morning.

ROSE. That 651 hit yesterday. That's the second time this month. Miss Pearl hit for a dollar . . . seem like those that need the least always get lucky. Poor folks can't get nothing.

TROY. Them numbers don't know nobody. I don't know why you fool with them. You and Lyons both.

ROSE. It's something to do.

TROY. You ain't doing nothing but throwing your money away.

ROSE. Troy, you know I don't play foolishly. I just play a nickel here and a nickel there.

TROY. That's two nickels you done thrown away.

ROSE. Now I hit sometimes . . . that makes up for it. It always comes in handy when I do hit. I don't hear you complaining then.

TROY. I ain't complaining now. I just say it's foolish. Trying to guess out of six hundred ways which way the number gonna come. If I had all the money niggers, these Negroes, throw away on numbers for one week—just one week—I'd be a rich man.

ROSE. Well, you wishing and calling it foolish ain't gonna stop folks from playing numbers. That's one thing for sure. Besides . . . some good things come from playing numbers. Look where Pope done bought him that restaurant off of numbers.

TROY. I can't stand niggers like that. Man ain't had two dimes to rub together. He walking around with his shoes all run over bumming money for cigarettes. All right. Got lucky there and hit the numbers . . .

ROSE. Troy, I know all about it.

TROY. Had good sense, I'll say that for him. He ain't throwed his money away. I seen niggers hit the numbers and go through two thousand dollars in four days. Man bought him that restaurant down there . . . fixed it up real nice . . . and then didn't want nobody to come in it! A Negro go in there and can't get no kind of service. I seen a white fellow come in there and order a bowl of stew. Pope picked all the meat out of the pot for him. Man ain't had nothing but a bowl of meat! Negro come behind him and ain't got nothing but the potatoes and carrots. Talking about what numbers do for people, you picked a wrong example. Ain't done nothing but make a worser fool out of him than he was before.

ROSE. Troy, you ought to stop worrying about what happened at work yesterday.

TROY. I ain't worried. Just told me to be down there at the Commissioner's office on Friday. Everybody think they gonna fire me. I ain't worried about them firing me. You ain't got to worry about that. [*Pause.*] Where's Cory? Cory in the house? [*Calls.*] Cory?

ROSE. He gone out.

TROY. Out, huh? He gone out 'cause he know I want him to help me with this fence. I know how he is. That boy scared of work.

GABRIEL *enters. He comes halfway down the alley and, hearing* TROY's *voice, stops.*

TROY [*continues*]. He ain't done a lick of work in his life.

ROSE. He had to go to football practice. Coach wanted them to get in a little extra practice before the season start.

TROY. I got his practice . . . running out of here before he get his chores done.

ROSE. Troy, what is wrong with you this morning? Don't nothing set right with you. Go on back in there and go to bed . . . get up on the other side.

TROY. Why something got to be wrong with me? I ain't said nothing wrong with me.

ROSE. You got something to say about everything. First it's the numbers . . . then it's the way the man runs his restaurant . . . then you done got on Cory. What's it gonna be next? Take a look up there and see if the weather suits you . . . or is it gonna be how you gonna put up the fence with the clothes hanging in the yard.

TROY. You hit the nail on the head then.

ROSE. I know you like I know the back of my hand. Go on in there and get you some coffee . . . see if that straighten you up. 'Cause you ain't right this morning.

TROY *starts into the house and sees* GABRIEL. GABRIEL *starts singing.* TROY's *brother, he is seven years younger than* TROY. *Injured in World War II, he has a metal plate in his head. He carries an old trumpet tied around his waist and believes with every fiber of his being that he is the Archangel Gabriel. He carries a chipped basket with an assortment of discarded fruits and vegetables he has picked up in the strip district and which he attempts to sell.*

GABRIEL [*singing*] Yes, ma'am I got plums
    You ask me how I sell them
    Oh ten cents apiece
    Three for a quarter
    Come and buy now
    'Cause I'm here today
    And tomorrow I'll be gone

GABRIEL *enters. Hey, Rose!*

ROSE. How you doing Gabe?

GABRIEL. There's Troy . . . Hey, Troy!

TROY. Hey, Gabe.

Exit into kitchen.

ROSE [*to* GABRIEL]. What you got there?

GABRIEL. You know what I got, Rose. I got fruits and vegetables.

ROSE [*looking in basket*]. Where's all these plums you talking about?

GABRIEL. I ain't got no plums today, Rose. I was just singing that. Have some tomorrow. Put me in a big order for plums. Have enough plums tomorrow
for St. Peter and everybody.

TROY *reenters from kitchen, crosses to steps.*

[*To* ROSE.] Troy's mad at me.

TROY. I ain't mad at you. What I got to be mad at you about? You ain't done nothing to me.

GABRIEL. I just moved over to Miss Pearl's to keep out from in your way. I ain't
mean no harm by it.

TROY. Who said anything about that? I ain't said anything about that.

GABRIEL. You ain't mad at me, is you?

TROY. Naw . . . I ain't mad at you, Gabe. If I was mad at you I'd tell you about it.

GABRIEL. Got me two rooms. In the basement. Got my own door too. Wanna see
my key? [*He holds up a key.*] That's my own key! My two rooms!

TROY. Well, that's good, Gabe. You got your own key . . . that's good.

ROSE. You hungry, Gabe? I was just fixing to cook Troy his breakfast.

GABRIEL. I'll take some biscuits. You got some biscuits? Did you know when I
was in heaven . . . every morning me and St. Peter would sit down by the
gate and eat some big fat biscuits? Oh, yeah! We had us a good time.
We'd sit there and eat us them biscuits and then St. Peter would go off to
sleep and tell me to wake him up when it's time to open the gates for the
judgment.

ROSE. Well, come on . . . I'll make up a batch of biscuits.

ROSE *exits into the house.*

GABRIEL. Troy . . . St. Peter got your name in the book. I seen it. It say . . . Troy
Maxson. I say . . . I know him! He got the same name like what I got. That's
my brother!

TROY. How many times you gonna tell me that, Gabe?

GABRIEL. Ain't got my name in the book. Don't have to have my name. I done
died and went to heaven. He got your name though. One morning St. Peter
was looking at his book . . . marking it up for the judgment . . . and he let
me see your name. Got it in there under M. Got Rose's name . . . I ain't
seen it like I seen yours . . . but I know it's in there. He got a great big
book. Got everybody's name what was ever been born. That's what he
told me. But I seen your name. Seen it with my own eyes.

TROY. Go on in the house there. Rose going to fix you something to eat.

GABRIEL. Oh, I ain't hungry. I done had breakfast with Aunt Jemimah. She come
by and cooked me up a whole mess of flapjacks. Remember how we used
to eat them flapjacks?

TROY. Go on in the house and get you something to eat now.

GABRIEL. I got to sell my plums. I done sold some tomatoes. Got me two quarters.
Wanna see? [*He shows* TROY *his quarters.*] I'm gonna save them and buy

me a new horn so St. Peter can hear me when it's time to open the gates. [GABRIEL *stops suddenly. Listens.*] Hear that? That's the hellhounds. I got to chase them out of here. Go on get out of here! Get out!

GABRIEL *exits singing.*
Better get ready for the judgment
Better get ready for the judgment
My Lord is coming down

ROSE *enters from the house.*

TROY. He's gone off somewhere.

GABRIEL *[offstage].*Better get ready for the judgment
Better get ready for the judgment morning
Better get ready for the judgment
My God is coming down

ROSE. He ain't eating right. Miss Pearl say she can't get him to eat nothing.
TROY. What you want me to do about it, Rose? I done did everything I can for the man. I can't make him get well. Man got half his head blown away . . . what you expect?
ROSE. Seem like something ought to be done to help him.
TROY. Man don't bother nobody. He just mixed up from that metal plate he got in his head. Ain't no sense for him to go back into the hospital.
ROSE. Least he be eating right. They can help him take care of himself.
TROY. Don't nobody wanna be locked up, Rose. What you wanna lock him up for? Man go over there and fight the war . . . messin' around with them Japs, get half his head blow off . . . and they give him a lousy three thousand dollars. And I had to swoop down on that.
ROSE. Is you fixing to go into that again?
TROY. That's the only way I got a roof over my head . . . cause of that metal plate.
ROSE. Ain't no sense you blaming yourself for nothing. Gabe wasn't in no condition to manage that money. You done what was right by him. Can't nobody say you ain't done what was right by him. Look how long you took care of him . . . till he wanted to have his own place and moved over there with Miss Pearl.
TROY. That ain't what I'm saying, woman! I'm just stating the facts. If my brother didn't have that metal plate in his head . . . I wouldn't have a pot to piss in or a window to throw it out of. And I'm fifty-three years old. Now see if you can understand that!

TROY *gets up from the porch and starts to exit the yard.*

ROSE. Where you going off to? You been running out of here every Saturday for weeks. I thought you was gonna work on this fence?
TROY. I'm gonna walk down to Taylor's. Listen to the ball game. I'll be back in a bit. I'll work on it when I get back.

He exits the yard. The lights go to black.

Scene 3

The lights come up on the yard. It is four hours later. ROSE *is taking down the clothes from the line.* CORY *enters carrying his football equipment.*

ROSE. Your daddy like to had a fit with you running out of here this morning without doing your chores.

CORY. I told you I had to go to practice.

ROSE. He say you were supposed to help him with this fence.

CORY. He been saying that the last four or five Saturdays, and then he don't never do nothing, but go down to Taylors'. Did you tell him about the recruiter?

ROSE. Yeah, I told him.

CORY. What he say?

ROSE. He ain't said nothing too much. You get in there and get started on your chores before he gets back. Go on and scrub down them steps before he gets back here hollering and carrying on.

CORY. I'm hungry. What you got to eat, Mama?

ROSE. Go on and get started on your chores. I got some meat loaf in there. Go on and make you a sandwich . . . and don't leave no mess in there.

    CORY *exits into the house.* ROSE *continues to take down the clothes.* TROY *enters the yard and sneaks up and grabs her from behind.*

Troy! Go on, now. You liked to had scared me to death. What was the score of the game? Lucille had me on the phone and I couldn't keep up with it.

TROY. What I care about the game? Come here, woman.

   [He tries to kiss her.]

ROSE. I thought you went down Taylors' to listen to the game. Go on, Troy! You supposed to be putting up this fence.

TROY [*attempting to kiss her again*]. I'll put it up when I finish with what is at hand.

ROSE. Go on, Troy. I ain't studying you.

TROY [*chasing after her*]. I'm studying you . . . fixing to do my homework!

ROSE. Troy, you better leave me alone.

TROY. Where's Cory? That boy brought his butt home yet?

ROSE. He's in the house doing his chores.

TROY [*calling*]. Cory! Get your butt out here, boy!

    ROSE *exits into the house with the laundry.* TROY *goes over to the pile of wood, picks up a board, and starts sawing.* CORY *enters from the house.*

TROY. You just now coming in here from leaving this morning?

CORY. Yeah, I had to go to football practice.

TROY. Yeah, what?

CORY. Yessir.

TROY. I ain't but two seconds off you noway. The garbage sitting in there overflowing . . . you ain't done none of your chores . . . and you come in here talking about "Yeah."

CORY. I was just getting ready to do my chores now, Pop . . .

TROY. Your first chore is to help me with this fence on Saturday. Everything else come after that. Now get that saw and cut them boards.

    CORY *takes the saw and begins cutting the boards.* TROY *continues working. There is a long pause.*

CORY. Hey, Pop . . . why don't you buy a TV?

TROY. What I want with a TV? What I want one of them for?

CORY. Everybody got one. Earl, Ba Bra . . . Jesse!

TROY. I ain't asked you who had one. I say what I want with one?

CORY. So you can watch it. They got lots of things on TV. Baseball games and everything. We could watch the World Series.

TROY. Yeah . . . and how much this TV cost?

CORY. I don't know. They got them on sale for around two hundred dollars.

TROY. Two hundred dollars, huh?

CORY. That ain't that much, Pop.

TROY. Naw, it's just two hundred dollars. See that roof you got over your head at night? Let me tell you something about that roof. It's been over ten years since that roof was last tarred. See now . . . the snow come this winter and sit up there on that roof like it is . . . and it's gonna seep inside. It's just gonna be a little bit . . . ain't gonna hardly notice it. Then the next thing you know, it's gonna be leaking all over the house. Then the wood rot from all that water and you gonna need a whole new roof. Now, how much you think it cost to get that roof tarred?

CORY. I don't know.

TROY. Two hundred and sixty-four dollars . . . cash money. While you thinking about a TV, I got to be thinking about the roof . . . and whatever else go wrong here. Now if you had two hundred dollars, what would you do . . . fix the roof or buy a TV?

CORY. I'd buy a TV. Then when the roof started to leak . . . when it needed fixing . . . I'd fix it.

TROY. Where you gonna get the money from? You done spent it for a TV. You gonna sit up and watch the water run all over your brand new TV.

CORY. Aw, Pop. You got money. I know you do.

TROY. Where I got it at, huh?

CORY. You got it in the bank.

TROY. You wanna see my bankbook? You wanna see that seventy-three dollars and twenty-two cents I got sitting up in there?

CORY. You ain't got to pay for it all at one time. You can put a down payment on it and carry it on home with you.

TROY. Not me. I ain't gonna owe nobody nothing if I can help it. Miss a payment and they come and snatch it right out of your house. Then what you got? Now, soon as I get two hundred dollars clear, then I'll buy a TV. Right now, as soon as I get two hundred and sixty-four dollars, I'm gonna have this roof tarred.

CORY. Aw . . . Pop!

TROY. You go on and get you two hundred dollars and buy one if ya want it. I got better things to do with my money.

CORY. I can't get no two hundred dollars. I ain't never seen two hundred dollars.

TROY. I'll tell you what . . . you get you a hundred dollars and I'll put the other hundred with it.

CORY. All right, I'm gonna show you.

TROY. You gonna show me how you can cut them boards right now.

CORY *begins to cut the boards. There is a long pause.*

CORY. The Pirates won today. That makes five in a row.

TROY. I ain't thinking about the Pirates. Got an all-white team. Got that boy . . . that Puerto Rican boy . . . Clemente. Don't even half-play him. That boy could be something if they give him a chance. Play him one day and sit him on the bench the next.

CORY. He gets a lot of chances to play.

TROY. I'm talking about playing regular. Playing every day so you can get your timing. That's what I'm talking about.

CORY. They got some white guys on the team that don't play every day. You can't play everybody at the same time.

TROY. If they got a white fellow sitting on the bench . . . you can bet your last dollar he can't play! The colored guy got to be twice as good before he get on the team. That's why I don't want you to get all tied up in them sports. Man on the team and what it get him? They got colored on the team and don't use them. Same as not having them. All them teams the same.

CORY. The Braves got Hank Aaron and Wes Covington. Hank Aaron hit two home runs today. That makes forty-three.

TROY. Hank Aaron ain't nobody. That what you supposed to do. That's how you supposed to play the game. Ain't nothing to it. It's just a matter of timing . . . getting the right follow-through. Hell, I can hit forty-three home runs right now!

CORY. Not off no major-league pitching, you couldn't.

TROY. We had better pitching in the Negro leagues. I hit seven home runs off of Satchel Paige.[4] You can't get no better than that!

CORY. Sandy Koufax. He's leading the league in strikeouts.

TROY. I ain't thinking of no Sandy Koufax.

CORY. You got Warren Spahn and Lew Burdette. I bet you couldn't hit no home runs off of Warren Spahn.

TROY. I'm through with it now. You go on and cut them boards. [*Pause.*] Your mama tell me you done got recruited by a college football team? Is that right?

CORY. Yeah. Coach Zellman say the recruiter gonna be coming by to talk to you. Get you to sign the permission papers.

TROY. I thought you supposed to be working down there at the A&P. Ain't you suppose to be working down there after school?

CORY. Mr. Stawicki say he gonna hold my job for me until after the football season. Say starting next week I can work weekends.

TROY. I thought we had an understanding about this football stuff? You suppose to keep up with your chores and hold that job down at the A&P. Ain't been around here all day on a Saturday. Ain't none of your chores done . . . and now you telling me you done quit your job.

CORY. I'm going to be working weekends.

TROY. You damn right you are! And ain't no need for nobody coming around here to talk to me about signing nothing.

CORY. Hey, Pop . . . you can't do that. He's coming all the way from North Carolina.

TROY. I don't care where he coming from. The white man ain't gonna let you get nowhere with that football noway. You go on and get your book-learning so you can work yourself up in that A&P or learn how to fix cars or build houses or something, get you a trade. That way you have something can't nobody take away from you. You go on and learn how to put your hands to some good use. Besides hauling people's garbage.

CORY. I get good grades, Pop. That's why the recruiter wants to talk with you. You got to keep up your grades to get recruited. This way I'll be going to college. I'll get a chance . . .

---

[4]Paige (1906–82) was a pitcher in the Negro leagues

TROY. First you gonna get your butt down there to the A&P and get your job back.

CORY. Mr. Stawicki done already hired somebody else 'cause I told him I was playing football.

TROY. You a bigger fool than I thought . . . to let somebody take away your job so you can play some football. Where you gonna get your money to take out your girlfriend and whatnot? What kind of foolishness is that to let somebody take away your job?

CORY. I'm still gonna be working weekends.

TROY. Naw . . . naw. You getting your butt out of here and finding you another job.

CORY. Come on, Pop! I got to practice. I can't work after school and play football too. The team needs me. That's what Coach Zellman say . . .

TROY. I don't care what nobody else say. I'm the boss . . . you understand? I'm the boss around here. I do the only saying what counts.

CORY. Come on, Pop!

TROY. I asked you . . . did you understand?

CORY. Yeah . . .

TROY. What?!

CORY. Yessir.

TROY. You go on down there to that A&P and see if you can get your job back. If you can't do both . . . then you quit the football team. You've got to take the crookeds with the straights.

CORY. Yessir. [*Pause.*] Can I ask you a question?

TROY. What the hell you wanna ask me? Mr. Stawicki the one you got the questions for.

CORY. How come you ain't never liked me?

TROY. Liked you? Who the hell say I got to like you? What law is there say I got to like you? Wanna stand up in my face and ask a damn foolass question like that. Talking about liking somebody. Come here, boy, when I talk to you.

CORY *comes over to where* TROY *is working. He stands slouched over and* TROY *shoves him on his shoulder.*

Straighten up, goddammit! I asked you a question . . . what law is there say I got to like you?

CORY. None.

TROY. Well, all right then! Don't you eat every day? [*Pause.*] Answer me when I talk to you! Don't you eat every day?

CORY. Yeah.

TROY. Nigger, as long as you in my house, you put that sir on the end of it when you talk to me.

CORY. Yes . . . sir.

TROY. You eat every day.

CORY. Yessir!

TROY. Got a roof over your head.

CORY. Yessir!

TROY. Got clothes on your back.

CORY. Yessir.

TROY. Why you think that is?

CORY. Cause of you.

TROY. Ah, hell I know it's cause of me . . . but why do you think that is?

CORY [*hesitant*]. Cause you like me.

TROY. Like you? I go out of here every morning . . . bust my butt . . . putting up with them crackers every day . . . cause I like you? You are the biggest fool I ever saw. [*Pause.*] It's my job. It's my responsibility! You understand that? A man got to take care of his family. You live in my house . . . sleep you behind on my bedclothes . . . fill you belly up with my food . . . cause you my son. You my flesh and blood. Not cause I like you! Cause it's my duty to take care of you. I owe a responsibility to you! Let's get this straight right here . . . before it go along any further . . . I ain't got to like you. Mr. Rand don't give me my money come payday cause he likes me. He gives me cause he owe me. I done give you everything I had to give you. I gave you your life! Me and your mama worked that out between us. And liking your black ass wasn't part of the bargain. Don't you try and go through life worrying about if somebody like you or not. You best be making sure they doing right by you. You understand what I'm saying boy?

CORY. Yessir.

TROY. Then get the hell out of my face, and get on down to that A&P.

ROSE *has been standing behind the screen door for much of the scene. She enters as* CORY *exits.*

ROSE. Why don't you let the boy go ahead and play football, Troy? Ain't no harm in that. He's just trying to be like you with the sports.

TROY. I don't want him to be like me! I want him to move as far away from my life as he can get. You the only decent thing that ever happened to me. I wish him that. But I don't wish him a thing else from my life. I decided seventeen years ago that boy wasn't getting involved in no sports. Not after what they did to me in the sports.

ROSE. Troy, why don't you admit you was too old to play in the major leagues? For once . . . why don't you admit that?

TROY. What do you mean too old? Don't come telling me I was too old. I just wasn't the right color. Hell, I'm fifty-three years old and can do better than Selkirk's .269 right now!

ROSE. How's was you gonna play ball when you were over forty? Sometimes I can't get no sense out of you.

TROY. I got good sense, woman. I got sense enough not to let my boy get hurt over playing no sports. You been mothering that boy too much. Worried about if people like him.

ROSE. Everything that boy do . . . he do for you. He wants you to say "Good job, son." That's all.

TROY. Rose, I ain't got time for that. He's alive. He's healthy. He's got to make his own way. I made mine. Ain't nobody gonna hold his hand when he get out there in that world.

ROSE. Times have changed from when you was young, Troy. People change. The world's changing around you and you can't even see it.

TROY [*slow, methodical*]. Woman . . . I do the best I can do. I come in here every Friday. I carry a sack of potatoes and a bucket of lard. You all line up at the door with your hands out. I give you the lint from my pockets. I give you my sweat and my blood. I ain't got no tears. I done spent them. We go upstairs in that room at night . . . and I fall down on you and try to blast a hole into forever. I get up Monday morning . . . find my lunch on the table. I go out. Make my way. Find my strength to carry me through to the next Friday. [*Pause.*] That's all I got, Rose. That's all I got to give. I can't give nothing else.

TROY *exits into the house. The lights go down to black.*

Scene 4

It is Friday. Two weeks later. CORY *starts out of the house with his football equipment. The phone rings.*

CORY [*calling*]. I got it! [*He answers the phone and stands in the screen door talking.*] Hello? Hey, Jesse. Naw . . . I was just getting ready to leave now.

ROSE [*calling*]. Cory!

CORY. I told you, man, them spikes is all tore up. You can use them if you want, but they ain't no good. Earl got some spikes.

ROSE [*calling*]. Cory!

CORY [*calling to* ROSE]. Mam? I'm talking to Jesse. [*Into phone.*] When she say that? [*Pause.*] Aw, you lying, man. I'm gonna tell her you said that.

ROSE [*calling*]. Cory, don't you go nowhere!

CORY. I got to go to the game, Ma! [*Into the phone.*] Yeah, hey, look, I'll talk to you later. Yeah, I'll meet you over Earl's house. Later. Bye, Ma.

CORY *exits the house and starts out the yard.*

ROSE. Cory, where you going off to? You got that stuff all pulled out and thrown all over your room.

CORY [*in the yard*]. I was looking for my spikes. Jesse wanted to borrow my spikes.

ROSE. Get up there and get that cleaned up before your daddy get back in here.

CORY. I got to go to the game! I'll clean it up *when I get back.*

CORY *exits.*

ROSE. That's all he need to do is see that room all messed up.

ROSE *exits into the house.* TROY *and* BONO *enter the yard.* TROY *is dressed in clothes other than his work clothes.*

BONO. He told him the same thing he told you. Take it to the union.

TROY. Brownie ain't got that much sense. Man wasn't thinking about nothing. He wait until I confront them on it . . . then he wanna come crying seniority. [*Calls.*] Hey, Rose!

BONO. I wish I could have seen Mr. Rand's face when he told you.

TROY. He couldn't get it out of his mouth! Liked to bit his tongue! When they called me down there to the Commissioner's office . . . he thought they was gonna fire me. Like everybody else.

BONO. I didn't think they was gonna fire you. I thought they was gonna put you on the warning paper.

TROY. Hey, Rose! [*To* BONO.] Yeah, Mr. Rand like to bit his tongue.

TROY *breaks the seal on the bottle, takes a drink, and hands it to* BONO.

BONO. I see you run right down to Taylors' and told that Alberta gal.

TROY [*calling*]. Hey Rose! [*To* BONO.] I told everybody. Hey, Rose! I went down there to cash my check.

ROSE [*entering from the house*]. Hush all that hollering, man! I know you out here. What they say down there at the Commissioner's office?

TROY. You supposed to come when I call you, woman. Bono'll tell you that. [*To* BONO.] Don't Lucille come when you call her?

ROSE. Man, hush your mouth. I ain't no dog . . . talk about "come when you call me."

TROY [*puts his arm around* ROSE]. You hear this, Bono? I had me an old dog used to get uppity like that. You say, "C'mere, Blue!" . . . and he just lay there and look at you. End up getting a stick and chasing him away trying to make him come.

ROSE. I ain't studying you and your dog. I remember you used to sing that old song.

TROY [*he sings*]. Hear it ring! Hear it ring! I had a dog his name was Blue.

ROSE. Don't nobody wanna hear you sing that old song.

TROY [*sings*]. You know Blue was mighty true.

ROSE. Used to have Cory running around here singing that song.

BONO. Hell, I remember that song myself.

TROY [*sings*]. You know Blue was a good old dog.

> Blue treed a possum in a hollow log.
> That was my daddy's song. My daddy made up that song.

ROSE. I don't care who made it up. Don't nobody wanna hear you sing it.

TROY [*makes a song like calling a dog*]. Come here, woman.

ROSE. You come in here carrying on, I reckon they ain't fired you. What they say down there at the Commissioner's office?

TROY. Look here, Rose . . . Mr. Rand called me into his office today when I got back from talking to them people down there . . . it come from up top . . . he called me in and told me they was making me a driver.

ROSE. Troy, you kidding!

TROY. No I ain't. Ask Bono.

ROSE. Well, that's great, Troy. Now you don't have to hassle them people no more.

LYONS *enters from the street.*

TROY. Aw hell, I wasn't looking to see you today. I thought you was in jail. Got it all over the front page of the *Courier* about them raiding Sefus's place . . . where you be hanging out with all them thugs.

LYONS. Hey, Pop . . . that ain't got nothing to do with me. I don't go down there gambling. I go down there to sit in with the band. I ain't got nothing to do with the gambling part. They got some good music down there.

TROY. They got some rogues . . . is what they got.

LYONS. How you been, Mr. Bono? Hi, Rose.

BONO. I see where you playing down at the Crawford Grill tonight.

ROSE. How come you ain't brought Bonnie like I told you? You should have brought Bonnie with you, she ain't been over in a month of Sundays.

LYONS. I was just in the neighborhood . . . thought I'd stop by.

TROY. Here he come . . .

BONO. Your daddy got a promotion on the rubbish. He's gonna be the first colored driver. Ain't got to do nothing but sit up there and read the paper like them white fellows.

LYONS. Hey, Pop . . . if you knew how to read you'd be all right.

BONO. Naw . . . naw . . . you mean if the nigger knew how to drive he'd be all right. Been fighting with them people about driving and ain't even got a license. Mr. Rand know you ain't got no driver's license?

TROY. Driving ain't nothing. All you do is point the truck where you want it to go. Driving ain't nothing.

BONO. Do Mr. Rand know you ain't got no driver's license? That's what I'm talking about. I ain't asked if driving was easy. I asked if Mr. Rand know you ain't got no driver's license.

TROY. He ain't got to know. The man ain't got to know my business. Time he find out, I have two or three driver's licenses.

LYONS [*going into his pocket*]. Say, look here, Pop . . .

TROY. I knew it was coming. Didn't I tell you, Bono? I know what kind of "Look here, Pop" that was. The nigger fixing to ask me for some money. It's Friday night. It's my payday. All them rogues down there on the avenue . . . the ones that ain't in jail . . . and Lyons is hopping in his shoes to get down there with them.

LYONS. See, Pop . . . if you give somebody else a chance to talk sometimes, you'd see that I was fixing to pay you back your ten dollars like I told you. Here . . . I told you I'd pay you when Bonnie got paid.

TROY. Naw . . . you go ahead and keep that ten dollars. Put it in the bank. The next time you feel like you wanna come by here and ask me for something . . . you go on down there and get that.

LYONS. Here's your ten dollars, Pop. I told you I don't want you to give me nothing. I just wanted to borrow ten dollars.

TROY. Naw . . . you go on and keep that for the next time you want to ask me.

LYONS. Come on, Pop . . . here go your ten dollars.

ROSE. Why don't you go on and let the boy pay you back, Troy?

LYONS. Here you go, Rose. If you don't take it I'm gonna have to hear about it for the next six months. [*He hands her the money.*]

ROSE. You can hand yours over here too, Troy.

TROY. You see this, Bono. You see how they do me.

BONO. Yeah, Lucille do me the same way.

GABRIEL *is heard singing off stage. He enters.*

GABRIEL. Better get ready for the Judgment! Better get ready for . . . Hey! . . . Hey! . . . There's Troy's boy!

LYONS. How are you doing, Uncle Gabe?

GABRIEL. Lyons . . . The King of the Jungle! Rose . . . hey, Rose. Got a flower for you. [*He takes a rose from his pocket.*] Picked it myself. That's the same rose like you is!

ROSE. That's right nice of you, Gabe.

LYONS. What you been doing, Uncle Gabe?

GABRIEL. Oh, I been chasing hellhounds and waiting on the time to tell St. Peter to open the gates.

LYONS. You been chasing hellhounds, huh? Well . . . you doing the right thing, Uncle Gabe. Somebody got to chase them.

GABRIEL. Oh, yeah . . . I know it. The devil's strong. The devil ain't no pushover. Hellhounds snipping at everybody's heels. But I got my trumpet waiting on the judgment time.

LYONS. Waiting on the Battle of Armageddon, huh?

GABRIEL. Ain't gonna be too much of a battle when God get to waving that Judgment sword. But the people's gonna have a hell of a time trying to get into heaven if them gates ain't open.

LYONS [*putting his arm around* GABRIEL]. You hear this, Pop. Uncle Gabe, you all right!

GABRIEL. [*laughing with* LYONS]. Lyons! King of the Jungle.

ROSE. You gonna stay for supper, Gabe? Want me to fix you a plate?

GABRIEL. I'll take a sandwich, Rose. Don't want no plate. Just wanna eat with my hands. I'll take a sandwich.

ROSE. How about you, Lyons? You staying? Got some short ribs cooking.

LYONS. Naw, I won't eat nothing till after we finished playing. [*Pause.*] You ought to come down and listen to me play, Pop.

TROY. I don't like that Chinese music. All that noise.

ROSE. Go on in the house and wash up, Gabe . . . I'll fix you a sandwich.

GABRIEL [*to* LYONS, *as he exits*]. Troy's mad at me.

LYONS. What you mad at Uncle Gabe for, Pop?

ROSE. He thinks Troy's mad at him cause he moved over to Miss Pearl's.

TROY. I ain't mad at the man. He can live where he want to live at.

LYONS. What he move over there for? Miss Pearl don't like nobody.

ROSE. She don't mind him none. She treats him real nice. She just don't allow all that singing.

TROY. She don't mind that rent he be paying . . . that's what she don't mind.

ROSE. Troy, I ain't going through that with you no more. He's over there cause he want to have his own place. He can come and go as he please.

TROY. Hell, he could come and go as he please here. I wasn't stopping him. I ain't put no rules on him.

ROSE. It ain't the same thing, Troy. And you know it.

GABRIEL *comes to the door.*

Now, that's the last I wanna hear about that. I don't wanna hear nothing else about Gabe and Miss Pearl. And next week . . .

GABRIEL. I'm ready for my sandwich, Rose.

ROSE. And next week . . . when that recruiter come from that school . . . I want you to sign that paper and go on and let Cory play football. Then that'll be the last I have to hear about that.

TROY [*to* ROSE *as she exits into the house*]. I ain't thinking about Cory nothing.

LYONS. What . . . Cory got recruited? What school he going to?

TROY. That boy walking around here smelling his piss . . . thinking he's grown. Thinking he's gonna do what he want, irrespective of what I say. Look here, Bono . . . I left the Commissioner's office and went down to the A&P . . . that boy ain't working down there. He lying to me. Telling me he got his job back . . . telling me he working weekends . . . telling me he working after school . . . Mr. Stawicki tell me he ain't working down there at all!

LYONS. Cory just growing up. He's just busting at the seams trying to fill out your shoes.

TROY. I don't care what he's doing. When he get to the point where he wanna disobey me . . . then it's time for him to move on. Bono'll tell you that. I bet he ain't never disobeyed his daddy without paying the consequences.

BONO. I ain't never had a chance. My daddy came on through . . . but I ain't never knew him to see him . . . or what he had on his mind or where he went.

Just moving on through. Searching out the New Land. That's what the old folks used to call it. See a fellow moving around from place to place . . . woman to woman . . . called it searching out the New Land. I can't say if he ever found it. I come along, didn't want no kids. Didn't know if I was gonna be in one place long enough to fix on them right as their daddy. I figured I was going searching too. As it turned out I been hooked up with Lucille near about as long as your daddy been with Rose. Going on sixteen years.

TROY. Sometimes I wish I hadn't known my daddy. He ain't cared nothing about no kids. A kid to him wasn't nothing. All he wanted was for you to learn how to walk so he could start you to working. When it come time for eating . . . he ate first. If there was anything left over, that's what you got. Man would sit down and eat two chickens and give you the wing.

LYONS. You ought to stop that, Pop. Everybody feed their kids. No matter how hard times is . . . everybody care about their kids. Make sure they have something to eat.

TROY. The only thing my daddy cared about was getting them bales of cotton in to Mr. Lubin. That's the only thing that mattered to him. Sometimes I used to wonder why he was living. Wonder why the devil hadn't come and got him. "Get them bales of cotton in to Mr. Lubin" and find out he owe him money . . .

LYONS. He should have just went on and left when he saw he couldn't get nowhere. That's what I would have done.

TROY. How he gonna leave with eleven kids? And where he gonna go? He ain't knew how to do nothing but farm. No, he was trapped and I think he knew it. But I'll say this for him . . . he felt a responsibility toward us. Maybe he ain't treated us the way I felt he should have . . . but without that responsibility he could have walked off and left us . . . made his own way.

BONO. A lot of them did. Back in those days what you talking about . . . they walk out their front door and just take on down one road or another and keep on walking.

LYONS. There you go! That's what I'm talking about.

BONO. Just keep on walking till you come to something else. Ain't you never heard of nobody having the walking blues? Well, that's what you call it when you just take off like that.

TROY. My daddy ain't had them walking blues! What you talking about? He stayed right there with his family. But he was just as evil as he could be. My mama couldn't stand him. Couldn't stand that evilness. She run off when I was about eight. She sneaked off one night after he had gone to sleep. Told me she was coming back for me. I ain't never seen her no more. All his women run off and left him. He wasn't good for nobody.

When my turn come to head out, I was fourteen and got to sniffing around Joe Canewell's daughter. Had us an old mule we called Greyboy. My daddy sent me out to do some plowing and I tied up Greyboy and went to fooling around with Joe Canewell's daughter. We done found us a nice little spot, got real cozy with each other. She about thirteen and we done figured we was grown anyway . . . so we down there enjoying ourselves . . . ain't thinking about nothing. We didn't know Greyboy had got loose and wandered back to the house and my daddy was looking for me. We down there by the creek enjoying ourselves when my daddy come up on us. Surprised us. He had them leather straps off the mule and commenced to whupping me like there was no tomorrow. I jumped up, mad and embarrassed. I was scared of my daddy. When he commenced to whupping on me . . . quite naturally I run to get out of the way. [*Pause.*] Now I thought he was mad cause I ain't done my work. But I see where he was chasing me off so he could have the gal for himself. When I see what the matter of it was, I lost all fear of my daddy. Right there is where I become a man . . . at fourteen years of age. [*Pause.*] Now it was my turn to run him off. I picked up them same reins that he had used on me. I picked up them reins and commenced to whupping on him. The gal jumped up and run off . . . and when my daddy turned to face me, I could see why the devil had never come to get him . . . cause he was the devil himself. I don't know what happened. When I woke up, I was laying right there by the creek, and Blue . . . this old dog we had . . . was licking my face. I thought I was blind. I couldn't see nothing. Both my eyes were swollen shut. I laid there and cried. I didn't know what I was gonna do. The only thing I knew was the time had come for me to leave my daddy's house. And right there the world suddenly got big. And it was a long time before I could cut it down to where I could handle it.

Part of that cutting down was when I got to the place where I could feel him kicking in my blood and knew that the only thing that separated us was the matter of a few years.

GABRIEL *enters from the house with a sandwich.*

LYONS. What you got there, Uncle Gabe?

GABRIEL. Got me a ham sandwich. Rose gave me a ham sandwich.

TROY. I don't know what happened to him. I done lost touch with everybody except Gabriel. But I hope he's dead. I hope he found some peace.

LYONS. That's a heavy story, Pop. I didn't know you left home when you was fourteen.

TROY. And didn't know nothing. The only part of the world I knew was the forty-two acres of Mr. Lubin's land. That's all I knew about life.

LYONS. Fourteen's kinda young to be out on your own. [*Phone rings.*] I don't even think I was ready to be out on my own at fourteen. I don't know what I would have done.

TROY. I got up from the creek and walked on down to Mobile. I was through with farming. Figured I could do better in the city. So I walked the two hundred miles to Mobile.

LYONS. Wait a minute . . . you ain't walked no two hundred miles, Pop. Ain't nobody gonna walk no two hundred miles. You talking about some walking there.

BONO. That's the only way you got anywhere back in them days.

LYONS. Shhh. Damn if I wouldn't have hitched a ride with somebody!

TROY. Who you gonna hitch it with? They ain't had no cars and things like they got now. We talking about 1918.

ROSE [*entering*]. What you all out here getting into?

TROY [*to* ROSE]. I'm telling Lyons how good he got it. He don't know nothing about this I'm talking.

ROSE. Lyons, that was Bonnie on the phone. She say you supposed to pick her up.

LYONS. Yeah, okay, Rose.

TROY. I walked on down to Mobile and hitched up with some of them fellows that was heading this way. Got up here and found out . . . not only couldn't you get a job . . . you couldn't find no place to live. I thought I was in freedom. Shhh. Colored folks living down there on the river banks in whatever kind of shelter they could find for themselves. Right down there under the Brady Street Bridge. Living in shacks made of sticks and tarpaper. Messed around there and went from bad to worse. Started stealing. First it was food. Then I figured, hell, if I steal money I can buy me some food. Buy me some shoes too! One thing led to another. Met your mama. I was young and anxious to be a man. Met your mama and had you. What I do that for? Now I got to worry about feeding you and her. Got to steal three times as much. Went out one day looking for somebody to rob . . . that's what I was, a robber. I'll tell you the truth. I'm ashamed of it today. But it's the truth. Went to rob this fellow . . . pulled out my knife . . . and he pulled out a gun. Shot me in the chest. I felt just like somebody had taken a hot branding iron and laid it on me. When he shot me I jumped at him with my knife. They told me I killed him and they put me in the penitentiary and locked me up for fifteen years. That's where I met Bono. That's where I learned how to play baseball. Got out that place and your mama had taken you and went on to make life without me. Fifteen years was a long time for her to wait. But that fifteen years cured me of that robbing stuff. Rose'll tell you. She asked me when I met her if I had gotten all that foolishness out of my system. And I told her, "Baby, it's you and baseball all what count with me." You hear me, Bono? I meant it too. She say, "Which one comes first?" I told her, "Baby, ain't no doubt it's baseball . . . but you stick and get old with me and we'll both outlive this baseball." Am I right, Rose? And it's true.

ROSE. Man, hush your mouth. You ain't said no such thing. Talking about, "Baby you know you'll always be number one with me." That's what you was talking.

TROY. You hear that, Bono. That's why I love her.

BONO. Rose'll keep you straight. You get off the track, she'll straighten you up.

ROSE. Lyons, you better get on up and get Bonnie. She waiting on you.

LYONS [*gets up to go*]. Hey, Pop, why don't you come on down to the Grill and hear me play?

TROY. I ain't going down there. I'm too old to be sitting around in them clubs.

BONO. You got to be good to play down at the Grill.

LYONS. Come on, Pop . . .

TROY. I got to get up in the morning.

LYONS. You ain't got to stay long.

TROY. Naw, I'm gonna get my supper and go on to bed.

LYONS. Well, I got to go. I'll see you again.

TROY. Don't you come around my house on my payday.

ROSE. Pick up the phone and let somebody know you coming. And bring Bonnie with you. You know I'm always glad to see her.

LYONS. Yeah, I'll do that, Rose. You take care now. See you, Pop. See you, Mr. Bono. See you, Uncle Gabe.

GABRIEL. Lyons! King of the Jungle!

LYONS *exits.*

TROY. Is supper ready, woman? Me and you got some business to take care of. I'm gonna tear it up too.

ROSE. Troy, I done told you now!

TROY [*puts his arm around* BONO]. Aw hell, woman . . . this is Bono. Bono like family. I done known this nigger since . . . how long I done know you?

BONO. It's been a long time.

TROY. I done know this nigger since Skippy was a pup. Me and him done been through some times.

BONO. You sure right about that.

TROY. Hell, I done know him longer than I known you. And we still standing shoulder to shoulder. Hey, look here, Bono . . . a man can't ask for no more than that. [*Drinks to him.*] I love you, nigger.

BONO. Hell, I love you too . . . I got to get home see my woman. You got yours in hand. I got to get mine.

BONO *starts to exit as* CORY *enters the yard, dressed in his football uniform. He gives* TROY *a hard, uncompromising look.*

CORY. What you do that for, Pop?

He throws his helmet down in the direction of TROY.

ROSE. What's the matter? Cory . . . what's the matter?

CORY. Papa done went up to the school and told Coach Zellman I can't play football no more. Wouldn't even let me play the game. Told him to tell the recruiter not to come.

ROSE. Troy . . .

TROY. What you Troying me for. Yeah, I did it. And the boy know why I did it.

CORY. Why you wanna do that to me? That was the one chance I had.

ROSE. Ain't nothing wrong with Cory playing football, Troy.

TROY. The boy lied to me. I told the nigger if he wanna play football . . . to keep up his chores and hold down that job at the A&P. That was the conditions. Stopped down there to see Mr. Stawicki . . .

CORY. I can't work after school during the football season, Pop! I tried to tell you that Mr. Stawicki's holding my job for me. You don't never want to listen to nobody. And then you wanna go and do this to me!

TROY. I ain't done nothing to you. You done it to yourself.

CORY. Just cause you didn't have a chance! You just scared I'm gonna be better than you, that's all.

TROY. Come here.

ROSE. Troy . . .

CORY *reluctantly crosses over to* TROY.

TROY. All right! See. You done made a mistake.

CORY. I didn't even do nothing!

TROY. I'm gonna tell you what your mistake was. See . . . you swung at the ball and didn't hit it. That's strike one. See, you in the batter's box now. You swung and you missed. That's strike one. Don't you strike out!

Lights fade to black.

Act 2

Scene 1

The following morning. CORY *is at the tree hitting the ball with the bat. He tries to mimic* TROY, *but his swing is awkward, less sure.* ROSE *enters from the house.*

ROSE. Cory, I want you to help me with this cupboard.

CORY. I ain't quitting the team. I don't care what Poppa say.

ROSE. I'll talk to him when he gets back. He had to go see about your Uncle Gabe. The police done arrested him. Say he was disturbing the peace. He'll be back directly. Come on in here and help me clean out the top of this cupboard.

CORY *exits into the house.* ROSE *sees* TROY *and* BONO *coming down the alley.*

Troy . . . what they say down there?

TROY. Ain't said nothing. I give them fifty dollars and they let him go. I'll talk to you about it. Where's Cory?

ROSE. He's in there helping me clean out these cupboards.

TROY. Tell him to get his butt out here.

TROY *and* BONO *go over to the pile of wood.* BONO *picks up the saw and begins sawing.*

TROY [*to* BONO]. All they want is the money. That makes six or seven times I done went down there and got him. See me coming they stick out their hands.

BONO. Yeah. I know what you mean. That's all they care about . . . that money. They don't care about what's right. [*Pause.*] Nigger, why you got to go and get some hard wood? You ain't doing nothing but building a little old fence. Get you some soft pine wood. That's all you need.

TROY. I know what I'm doing. This is outside wood. You put pine wood inside the house. Pine wood is inside wood. This here is outside wood. Now you tell me where the fence is gonna be?

BONO. You don't need this wood. You can put it up with pine wood and it'll stand as long as you gonna be here looking at it.

TROY. How you know how long I'm gonna be here, nigger? Hell, I might just live forever. Live longer than old man Horsely.

BONO. That's what Magee used to say.

TROY. Magee's damn fool. Now you tell me who you ever heard of gonna pull their own teeth with a pair of rusty pliers.

BONO. The old folks . . . my granddaddy used to pull his teeth with pliers. They ain't had no dentists for the colored folks back then.

TROY. Get clean pliers! You understand? Clean pliers! Sterilize them! Besides we ain't living back then. All Magee had to do was walk over to Doc Goldblum's.

BONO. I see where you and that Tallahassee gal . . . that Alberta . . . I see where you all done got tight.

TROY. What you mean "got tight"?

BONO. I see where you be laughing and joking with her all the time.

TROY. I laughs and jokes with all of them, Bono. You know me.

BONO. That ain't the kind of laughing and joking I'm talking about.

CORY *enters from the house.*

CORY. How you doing. Mr. Bono?

TROY. Cory? Get that saw from Bono and cut some wood. He talking about the wood's too hard to cut. Stand back there, Jim, and let that young boy show you how it's done.

BONO. He's sure welcome to it.

CORY *takes the saw and begins to cut the wood.*

Whew-e-e! Look at that. Big old strong boy. Look like Joe Louis. Hell, must be getting old the way I'm watching that boy whip through that wood.

CORY. I don't see why Mama want a fence around the yard noways.

TROY. Damn if I know either. What the hell she keeping out with it? She ain't got nothing nobody want.

BONO. Some people build fences to keep people out . . . and other people build fences to keep people in. Rose wants to hold on to you all. She loves you.

TROY. Hell, nigger, I don't need nobody to tell me my wife loves me. Cory . . . go on in the house and see if you can find that other saw.

CORY. Where's it at?

TROY. I said find it! Look for it till you find it!

CORY *exits into the house.*

What's that supposed to mean? Wanna keep us in?

BONO. Troy . . . I done known you seem like damn near my whole life. You and Rose both. I done know both of you all for a long time. I remember when you met Rose. When you was hitting them baseball out the park. A lot of them old gals was after you then. You had the pick of the litter. When you picked Rose, I was happy for you. That was the first time I knew you had any sense. I said . . . My man Troy knows what he's doing . . . I'm gonna follow this nigger . . . he might take me somewhere. I been following you too. I done learned a whole heap of things about life watching you. I done learned how to tell where the shit lies. How to tell it from the alfalfa. You done learned me a lot of things. You showed me how to not make the same mistakes . . . to take life as it comes along and keep putting one foot in front of the other. [*Pause.*] Rose a good woman, Troy.

TROY. Hell, nigger, I know she a good woman. I been married to her for eighteen years. What you got on your mind, Bono?

BONO. I just say she a good woman. Just like I say anything. I ain't got to have nothing on my mind.

TROY. You just gonna say she a good woman and leave it hanging out there like that? Why you telling me she a good woman?

BONO. She loves you, Troy. Rose loves you.

TROY. You saying I don't measure up. That's what you trying to say. I don't measure up cause I'm seeing this other gal. I know what you trying to say.

BONO. I know what Rose means to you, Troy. I'm just trying to say I don't want to see you mess up.

TROY. Yeah, I appreciate that, Bono. If you was messing around on Lucille I'd be telling you the same thing.

BONO. Well, that's all I got to say. I just say that because I love you both.

TROY. Hell, you know me . . . I wasn't out there looking for nothing. You can't find a better woman than Rose. I know that. But seems like this woman just stuck onto me where I can't shake her loose. I done wrestled with it, tried to throw her off me . . . but she just stuck on tighter. Now she's stuck on for good.

BONO. You's in control . . . that's what you tell me all the time. You responsible for what you do.

TROY. I ain't ducking the responsibility of it. As long as it sets right in my heart . . . then I'm okay. Cause that's all I listen to. It'll tell me right from wrong every time. And I ain't talking about doing Rose no bad turn. I love Rose. She done carried me a long ways and I love and respect her for that.

BONO. I know you do. That's why I don't want to see you hurt her. But what you gonna do when she find out? What you got then? If you try and juggle both of them . . . sooner or later you gonna drop one of them. That's common sense.

TROY. Yeah, I hear what you saying, Bono. I been trying to figure a way to work it out.

BONO. Work it out right, Troy. I don't want to be getting all up between you and Rose's business . . . but work it so it come out right.

TROY. Ah hell, I get all up between you and Lucille's business. When you gonna get that woman that refrigerator she been wanting? Don't tell me you ain't got no money now. I know who your banker is. Mellon don't need that money bad as Lucille want that refrigerator. I'll tell you that.

BONO. Tell you what I'll do . . . when you finish building this fence for Rose . . . I'll buy Lucille that refrigerator.

TROY. You done stuck your foot in your mouth now!

TROY *grabs up a board and begins to saw.* BONO *starts to walk out the yard.*

Hey, nigger . . . where you going?

BONO. I'm going home. I know you don't expect me to help you now. I'm protecting my money. I wanna see you put that fence up by yourself. That's what I want to see. You'll be here another six months without me.

TROY. Nigger, you ain't right.

BONO. When it comes to my money . . . I'm right as fireworks on the Fourth of July.

TROY. All right, we gonna see now. You better get out your bankbook.

BONO *exits, and* TROY *continues to work.* ROSE *enters from the house.*

ROSE. What they say down there? What's happening with Gabe?

TROY. I went down there and got him out. Cost me fifty dollars. Say he was disturbing the peace. Judge set up a hearing for him in three weeks. Say to show cause why he shouldn't be recommitted.

ROSE. What was he doing that cause them to arrest him?

TROY. Some kids was teasing him and he run them off home. Say he was howling and carrying on. Some folks seen him and called the police. That's all it was.

ROSE. Well, what's you say? What'd you tell the judge?

TROY. Told him I'd look after him. It didn't make no sense to recommit the man. He stuck out his big greasy palm and told me to give him fifty dollars and take him on home.

ROSE. Where's he at now? Where'd he go off to?

TROY. He's gone about his business. He don't need nobody to hold his hand.

ROSE. Well, I don't know. Seem like that would be the best place for him if they did put him into the hospital. I know what you're gonna say. But that's what I think would be best.

TROY. The man done had his life ruined fighting for what? And they wanna take and lock him up. Let him be free. He don't bother nobody.

ROSE. Well, everybody got their own way of looking at it I guess. Come on and get your lunch. I got a bowl of lima beans and some cornbread in the oven. Come and get something to eat. Ain't no sense you fretting over Gabe.

ROSE *turns to go into the house.*

TROY. Rose . . . got something to tell you.

ROSE. Well, come on . . . wait till I get this food on the table.

TROY. Rose!

She stops and turns around.

I don't know how to say this. [*Pause.*] I can't explain it none. It just sort of grows on you till it gets out of hand. It starts out like a little bush . . . and the next thing you know it's a whole forest.

ROSE. Troy . . . what is you talking about?

TROY. I'm talking, woman, let me talk. I'm trying to find a way to tell you . . . I'm gonna be a daddy. I'm gonna be somebody's daddy.

ROSE. Troy . . . you're not telling me this? You're gonna be . . . what?

TROY. Rose . . . now . . . see . . .

ROSE. You telling me you gonna be somebody's daddy? You telling your *wife* this?

GABRIEL *enters from the street. He carries a rose in his hand.*

GABRIEL. Hey, Troy! Hey, Rose!

ROSE. I have to wait eighteen years to hear something like this.

GABRIEL. Hey, Rose . . . I got a flower for you. [*He hands it to her.*] That's a rose. Same rose like you is.

ROSE. Thanks, Gabe.

GABRIEL. Troy, you ain't mad at me is you? Them bad mens come and put me away. You ain't mad at me is you?

TROY. Naw, Gabe, I ain't mad at you.

ROSE. Eighteen years and you wanna come with this.

GABRIEL [*takes a quarter out of his pocket*]. See what I got? Got a brand new quarter.

TROY. Rose . . . it's just . . .

ROSE. Ain't nothing you can say, Troy. Ain't no way of explaining that.

GABRIEL. Fellow that give me this quarter had a whole mess of them. I'm gonna keep this quarter till it stop shining.

ROSE. Gabe, go on in the house there. I got some watermelon in the Frigidaire. Go on and get you a piece.

GABRIEL. Say, Rose . . . you know I was chasing hellhounds and them bad mens come and get me and take me away. Troy helped me. He come down there and told them they better let me go before he beat them up. Yeah, he did!

ROSE. You go on and get you a piece of watermelon, Gabe. Them bad mens is gone now.

GABRIEL. Okay, Rose . . . gonna get me some watermelon. The kind with the stripes on it.

GABRIEL *exits into the house.*

ROSE. Why, Troy? Why? After all these years to come dragging this in to me now. It don't make no sense at your age. I could have expected this ten or fifteen years ago, but not now.

TROY. Age ain't got nothing to do with it, Rose.

ROSE. I done tried to be everything a wife should be. Everything a wife could be. Been married eighteen years and I got to live to see the day you tell me you been seeing another woman and done fathered a child by her. And you know I ain't never wanted no half nothing in my family. My whole family is half. Everybody got different fathers and mothers . . . my two sisters and my brother. Can't hardly tell who's who. Can't never sit down and talk about Papa and Mama. It's your papa and your mama and my papa and my mama . . .

TROY. Rose . . . stop it now.

ROSE. I ain't never wanted that for none of my children. And now you wanna drag your behind in here and tell me something like this.

TROY. You ought to know. It's time for you to know.

ROSE. Well, I don't want to know, goddamn it!

TROY. I can't just make it go away. It's done now. I can't wish the circumstance of the thing away.

ROSE. And you don't want to either. Maybe you want to wish me and my boy away. Maybe that's what you want? Well, you can't wish us away. I've got eighteen years of my life invested in you. You ought to have stayed upstairs in my bed where you belong.

TROY. Rose . . . now listen to me . . . we can get a handle on this thing. We can talk this out . . . come to an understanding.

ROSE. All of a sudden it's "we." Where was "we" at when you was down there rolling around with some godforsaken woman? "We" should have come to an understanding before you started making a damn fool of yourself. You're a day late and a dollar short when it comes to an understanding with me.

TROY. It's just . . . She gives me a different idea . . . a different understanding about myself. I can step out of this house and get away from the pressures and problems . . . be a different man. I ain't got to wonder how I'm gonna pay the bills or get the roof fixed. I can just be a part of myself that I ain't never been.

ROSE. What I want to know . . . is do you plan to continue seeing her. That's all you can say to me.

TROY. I can sit up in her house and laugh. Do you understand what I'm saying. I can laugh out loud . . . and it feels good. It reaches all the way down to the bottom of my shoes. [*Pause.*] Rose, I can't give that up.

ROSE. Maybe you ought to go on and stay down there with her . . . if she's a better woman than me.

TROY. It ain't about nobody being a better woman or nothing. Rose, you ain't the blame. A man couldn't ask for no woman to be a better wife than you've been. I'm responsible for it. I done locked myself into a pattern trying to take care of you all that I forgot about myself.

ROSE. What the hell was I there for? That was my job, not somebody else's.

TROY. Rose, I done tried all my life to live decent . . . to live a clean . . . hard . . . useful life. I tried to be a good husband to you. In every way I knew how. Maybe I come into the world backwards, I don't know. But . . . you born with two strikes on you before you come to the plate. You got to guard it closely . . . always looking for the curve ball on the inside corner. You can't afford to let none get past you. You can't afford a call strike. If you going down . . . you going down swinging. Everything lined up against you. What you gonna do. I fooled them, Rose. I bunted. When I found you and Cory and a halfway decent job . . . I was safe. Couldn't nothing touch me. I wasn't gonna strike out no more. I wasn't going back to the penitentiary. I wasn't gonna lay in the streets with a bottle of wine. I was safe. I had me a family. A job. I wasn't gonna get that last strike. I was on first looking for one of them boys to knock me in. To get me home.

ROSE. You should have stayed in my bed, Troy.

TROY. Then when I saw that gal . . . she firmed up my backbone. And I got to thinking that if I tried . . . I just might be able to steal second. Do you understand after eighteen years I wanted to steal second.

ROSE. You should have held me tight. You should have grabbed me and held on.

TROY. I stood on first base for eighteen years and I thought . . . well, goddamn it . . . go on for it!

ROSE. We're not talking about baseball! We're talking about you going off to lay in bed with another woman . . . and then bring it home to me. That's what we're talking about. We ain't talking about no baseball.

TROY. Rose, you're not listening to me. I'm trying the best I can to explain it to you. It's not easy for me to admit that I been standing in the same place for eighteen years.

ROSE. I been standing with you! I been right here with you, Troy. I got a life too. I gave eighteen years of my life to stand in the same spot with you. Don't you think I ever wanted other things? Don't you think I had dreams and hopes? What about my life? What about me. Don't you think it ever crossed my mind to want to know other men? That I wanted to lay up somewhere and forget about my responsibilities? That I wanted someone to make me laugh so I could feel good? You not the only one who's got wants and needs. But I held on to you, Troy. I took all my feelings, my wants and needs, my dreams . . . and I buried them inside you. I planted a seed and watched and prayed over it. I planted myself inside you and waited to bloom. And it didn't take me no eighteen years to find out the soil was hard and rocky and it wasn't never gonna bloom.

But I held on to you, Troy. I held you tighter. You was my husband. I owed you everything I had. Every part of me I could find to give you. And upstairs in that room . . . with the darkness falling in on me . . . I gave everything I had to try and erase the doubt that you wasn't the finest man in the world. And wherever you was going . . . I wanted to be there with you. Cause you was my husband. Cause that's the only way I was gonna survive as your wife. You always talking about what you give . . . and what you don't have to give. But you take too. You take . . . and don't even know nobody's giving!

ROSE *turns to exit into the house;* TROY *grabs her arm.*

TROY. You say I take and don't give!
ROSE. Troy! You're hurting me!
TROY. You say I take and don't give!
ROSE. Troy . . . you're hurting my arm! Let go!
TROY. I done give you everything I got. Don't you tell that lie on me.
ROSE. Troy!
TROY. Don't you tell that lie on me!

CORY *enters from the house.*

CORY. Mama!
ROSE. Troy. You're hurting me.
TROY. Don't you tell me about no taking and giving.

CORY *comes up behind* TROY *and grabs him.* TROY, *surprised, is thrown off balance just as* CORY *throws a glancing blow that catches him on the chest and knocks him down.* TROY *is stunned, as is* CORY.

ROSE. Troy. Troy. No!

TROY *gets to his feet and starts at* CORY.

Troy . . . no. Please! Troy!

ROSE *pulls on* TROY *to hold him back.* TROY *stops himself.*

TROY [*to* CORY]. All right. That's strike two. You stay away from around me, boy. Don't you strike out. You living with a full count. Don't you strike out.

TROY *exits out the yard as the lights go down.*

Scene 2

It is six months later, early afternoon. TROY *enters from the house and starts to exit the yard.* ROSE *enters from the house.*

ROSE. Troy, I want to talk to you.
TROY. All of a sudden, after all this time, you want to talk to me, huh? You ain't wanted to talk to me for months. You ain't wanted to talk to me last night. You ain't wanted no part of me then. What you wanna talk to me about now?
ROSE. Tomorrow's Friday.
TROY. I know what day tomorrow is. You think I don't know tomorrow's Friday? My whole life I ain't done nothing but look to see Friday coming and you got to tell me it's Friday.
ROSE. I want to know if you're coming home.
TROY. I always come home, Rose. You know that. There ain't never been a night I ain't come home.
ROSE. That ain't what I mean . . . and you know it. I want to know if you're coming straight home after work.
TROY. I figure I'd cash my check . . . hang out at Taylors' with the boys . . . maybe play a game of checkers . . .
ROSE. Troy, I can't live like this. I won't live like this. You livin' on borrowed time with me. It's been going on six months now you ain't been coming home.
TROY. I be here every night. Every night of the year. That's 365 days.
ROSE. I want you to come home tomorrow after work.
TROY. Rose . . . I don't mess up my pay. You know that now. I take my pay and I give it to you. I don't have no money but what you give me back. I just want to have a little time to myself . . . a little time to enjoy life.
ROSE. What about me? When's my time to enjoy life?
TROY. I don't know what to tell you, Rose. I'm doing the best I can.
ROSE. You ain't been home from work but time enough to change your clothes and run out . . . and you wanna call that the best you can do?
TROY. I'm going over to the hospital to see Alberta. She went into the hospital this afternoon. Look like she might have the baby early. I won't be gone long.
ROSE. Well, you ought to know. They went over to Miss Pearl's and got Gabe today. She said you told them to go ahead and lock him up.
TROY. I ain't said no such thing. Whoever told you that is telling a lie. Pearl ain't doing nothing but telling a big fat lie.
ROSE. She ain't had to tell me. I read it on the papers.
TROY. I ain't told them nothing of the kind.
ROSE. I saw it right there on the papers.
TROY. What it say, huh?

ROSE. It said you told them to take him.

TROY. Then they screwed that up, just the way they screw up everything. I ain't worried about what they got on the paper.

ROSE. Say the government send part of his check to the hospital and the other part to you.

TROY. I ain't got nothing to do with that if that's the way it works. I ain't made up the rules about how it work.

ROSE. You did Gabe just like you did Cory. You wouldn't sign the paper for Cory . . . but you signed for Gabe. You signed that paper.

The telephone is heard ringing inside the house.

TROY. I told you I ain't signed nothing, woman! The only thing I signed was the release form. Hell, I can't read, I don't know what they had on that paper! I ain't signed nothing about sending Gabe away.

ROSE. I said send him to the hospital . . . you said let him be free . . . now you done went down there and signed him to the hospital for half his money. You went back on yourself, Troy. You gonna have to answer for that.

TROY. See now . . . you been over there talking to Miss Pearl. She done got mad cause she ain't getting Gabe's rent money. That's all it is. She's liable to say anything.

ROSE. Troy, I seen where you signed the paper.

TROY. You ain't seen nothing I signed. What she doing got papers on my brother anyway? Miss Pearl telling a big fat lie. And I'm gonna tell her about it too! You ain't seen nothing I signed. Say . . . you ain't seen nothing I signed.

ROSE *exists into the house to answer the telephone. Presently she returns.*

ROSE. Troy . . . that was the hospital. Alberta had the baby.

TROY. What she have? What is it?

ROSE. It's a girl.

TROY. I better get on down to the hospital to see her.

ROSE. Troy . . .

TROY. Rose . . . I got to go see her now. That's only right . . . what's the matter . . . the baby's all right, ain't it?

ROSE. Alberta died having the baby.

TROY. Died . . . you say she's dead? Alberta's dead?

ROSE. They said they done all they could. They couldn't do nothing for her.

TROY. The baby? How's the baby?

ROSE. They say it's healthy. I wonder who's gonna bury her.

TROY. She had family, Rose. She wasn't living in the world by herself.

ROSE. I know she wasn't living in the world by herself.

TROY. Next thing you gonna want to know if she had any insurance.

ROSE. Troy, you ain't got to talk like that.

TROY. That's the first thing that jumped out your mouth. "Who's gonna bury her?" Like I'm fixing to take on that task for myself.

ROSE. I am your wife. Don't push me away.

TROY. I ain't pushing nobody away. Just give me some space. That's all. Just give me some room to breathe.

ROSE *exists into the house.* TROY *walks about the yard.*

TROY [*with a quiet rage that threatens to consume him*]. All right . . . Mr. Death. See now . . . I'm gonna tell you what I'm gonna do. I'm gonna take and build me a fence around this yard. See? I'm gonna build me a fence around what belongs to me. And then I want you to stay on the other side. See? You stay over there until you're ready for me. Then you come on. Bring your army. Bring your sickle. Bring your wrestling clothes. I ain't gonna fall down on my vigilance this time. You ain't gonna sneak up on me no more. When you ready for me . . . when the top of your list say Troy Maxson . . . that's when you come around here. You come up and knock on the front door. Ain't nobody else got nothing to do with this. This is between you and me. Man to man. You stay on the other side of that fence until you ready for me. Then you come up and knock on the front door. Anytime you want. I'll be ready for you.

The lights go down to black.

Scene 3

The lights come up on the porch. It is late evening three days later. ROSE *sits listening to the ball game waiting for* TROY. *The final out of the game is made and* ROSE *switches off the radio.* TROY *enters the yard carrying an infant wrapped in blankets. He stands back from the house and calls.*

ROSE *enters and stands on the porch. There is a long, awkward silence, the weight of which grows heavier with each passing second.*

TROY. Rose . . . I'm standing here with my daughter in my arms. She ain't but a wee bittie little old thing. She don't know nothing about grownups' business. She innocent . . . and she ain't got no mama.
ROSE. What you telling me for, Troy?

She turns and exits into the house.

TROY. Well . . . I guess we'll just sit out here on the porch.

He sits down on the porch. There is an awkward indelicateness about the way he handles the baby. His largeness engulfs and seems to swallow it. He speaks loud enough for ROSE *to hear.*

A man's got to do what's right for him. I ain't sorry for nothing I done. It felt right in my heart. [*To the baby.*] What you smiling at? Your daddy's a big man. Got these great big old hands. But sometimes he's scared. And right now your daddy's scared cause we sitting out here and ain't got no home. Oh, I been homeless before. I ain't had no little baby with me. But I been homeless. You just be out on the road by your lonesome and you see one of them trains coming and you just kinda go like this . . .

He sings as a lullaby.

Please, Mr. Engineer let a man ride the line
Please, Mr. Engineer let a man ride the line
I ain't got no ticket please let me ride the blinds.

ROSE *enters from the house.* TROY, *hearing her steps behind him, stands and faces her.*

She's my daughter, Rose. My own flesh and blood. I can't deny her no more than I can deny them boys. [*Pause.*] You and them boys is my family.

You and them and this child is all I got in the world. So I guess what I'm saying is . . . I'd appreciate it if you'd help me take care of her.

ROSE. Okay, Troy . . . you're right. I'll take care of your baby for you . . . cause . . . like you say . . . she's innocent . . . and you can't visit the sins of the father upon the child. A motherless child has got a hard time. [*She takes the baby from him.*] From right now . . . this child got a mother. But you a woman-less man.

ROSE *turns and exits into the house with the baby. Lights go down to black.*

Scene 4

It is two months later. LYONS *enters the street. He knocks on the door and calls.*

LYONS. Hey, Rose! [*Pause.*] Rose!

ROSE [*from inside the house*]. Stop that yelling. You gonna wake up Raynell. I just got her to sleep.

LYONS. I just stopped by to pay Papa this twenty dollars I owe him. Where's Papa at?

ROSE. He should be here in a minute. I'm getting ready to go down to the church. Sit down and wait on him.

LYONS. I got to go pick up Bonnie over her mother's house.

ROSE. Well, sit it down there on the table. He'll get it.

LYONS [*enters the house and sets the money on the table*]. Tell Papa I said thanks. I'll see you again.

ROSE. All right, Lyons. We'll see you.

LYONS *starts to exit as* CORY *enters.*

CORY. Hey, Lyons.

LYONS. What's happening, Cory? Say man, I'm sorry I missed your graduation. You know I had a gig and couldn't get away. Otherwise, I would have been there, man. So what you doing?

CORY. I'm trying to find a job.

LYONS. Yeah I know how that go, man. It's rough out here. Jobs are scarce.

CORY. Yeah, I know.

LYONS. Look here, I got to run. Talk to Papa . . . he know some people. He'll be able to help get you a job. Talk to him . . . see what he say.

CORY. Yeah . . . all right, Lyons.

LYONS. You take care. I'll talk to you soon. We'll find some time to talk.

LYONS *exits the yard.* CORY *wanders over to the tree, picks up the bat, and assumes a batting stance. He studies an imaginary pitcher and swings. Dissatisfied with the result, he tries again.* TROY *enters. They eye each other for a beat.* CORY *puts the bat down and exits the yard.* TROY *starts into the house as* ROSE *exits with* RAYNELL. *She is carrying a cake.*

TROY. I'm coming in and everybody's going out.

ROSE. I'm taking this cake down to the church for the bake sale. Lyons was by to see you. He stopped by to pay you your twenty dollars. It's laying in there on the table.

TROY [*going into his pocket*]. Well . . . here go this money.

ROSE. Put it in there on the table, Troy. I'll get it.

TROY. What time you coming back?

ROSE. Ain't no use in you studying me. It don't matter what time I come back.

TROY. I just asked you a question, woman. What's the matter . . . can't I ask you a question?

ROSE. Troy, I don't want to go into it. Your dinner's in there on the stove. All you got to do is heat it up. And don't you be eating the rest of them cakes in there. I'm coming back for them. We having a bake sale at the church tomorrow.

ROSE *exits the yard.* TROY *sits down on the steps, takes a pint bottle from his pocket, opens it, and drinks. He begins to sing.*

TROY. Hear it ring! Hear it ring!

Had an old dog his name was Blue
You know Blue was mighty true
You know Blue as a good old dog
Blue trees a possum in a hollow log
You know from that he was a good old dog.

BONO *enters the yard.*

BONO. Hey, Troy.

TROY. Hey, what's happening, Bono?

BONO. I just thought I'd stop by to see you.

TROY. What you stop by and see me for? You ain't stopped by in a month of Sundays. Hell, I must owe you money or something.

BONO. Since you got your promotion I can't keep up with you. Used to see you every day. Now I don't even know what route you working.

TROY. They keep switching me around. Got me out in Greentree now . . . hauling white folks' garbage.

BONO. Greentree, huh? You lucky, at least you ain't got to be lifting them barrels. Damn if they ain't getting heavier. I'm gonna put in my two years and call it quits.

TROY. I'm thinking about retiring myself.

BONO. You got it easy. You can drive for another five years.

TROY. It ain't the same, Bono. It ain't like working the back of the truck. Ain't got nobody to talk to . . . feel like you working by yourself. Naw, I'm thinking about retiring. How's Lucille?

BONO. She all right. Her arthritis get to acting up on her sometime. Saw Rose on my way in. She going down to the church, huh?

TROY. Yeah, she took up going down there. All them preachers looking for somebody to fatten their pockets. [*Pause.*] Got some gin here.

BONO. Naw, thanks. I just stopped by to say hello.

TROY. Hell, nigger . . . you can take a drink. I ain't never known you to say no to a drink. You ain't got to work tomorrow.

BONO. I just stopped by. I'm fixing to go over to Skinner's. We got us a domino game going over his house every Friday.

TROY. Nigger, you can't play no dominoes. I used to whup you four games out of five.

BONO. Well, that learned me. I'm getting better.

TROY. Yeah? Well, that's all right.

BONO. Look here . . . I got to be getting on. Stop by sometime, huh?

TROY. Yeah, I'll do that, Bono. Lucille told Rose you bought her a new refrigerator.

BONO. Yeah, Rose told Lucille you had finally built your fence . . . so I figured we'd call it even.

TROY. I knew you would.

BONO. Yeah . . . okay. I'll be talking to you.

TROY. Yeah, take care, Bono. Good to see you. I'm gonna stop over.

BONO. Yeah. Okay, Troy.

BONO *exits.* TROY *drinks from the bottle.*

TROY.

> Old Blue died and I dig his grave
> Let him down with a golden chain
> Every night when I hear old Blue bark
> I know Blue treed a possum in Noah's Ark
> Hear it ring! Hear it ring!

CORY *enters the yard. They eye each other for a beat.* TROY *is sitting in the middle of the steps.* CORY *walks over.*

CORY. I got to get by.

TROY. Say what? What's you say?

CORY. You in my way. I got to get by.

TROY. You got to get by where? This is my house. Bought and paid for. In full. Took me fifteen years. And if you wanna go in my house and I'm sitting on the steps . . . you say excuse me. Like your mama taught you.

CORY. Come on, Pop . . . I got to get by.

CORY *starts to maneuver his way past* TROY. TROY *grabs his leg and shoves him back.*

TROY. You just gonna walk over top of me?

CORY. I live here too!

TROY [*advancing toward him*]. You just gonna walk over top of me in my own house?

CORY. I ain't scared of you.

TROY. I ain't asked if you was scared of me. I asked you if you was fixing to walk over top of me in my own house? That's the question. You ain't gonna say excuse me? You just gonna walk over top of me?

CORY. If you wanna put it like that.

TROY. How else am I gonna put it?

CORY. I was walking by you to go into the house cause you sitting on the steps drunk, singing to yourself. You can put it like that.

TROY. Without saying excuse me???

CORY *doesn't respond.*

I asked you a question. Without saying excuse me???

CORY. I ain't got to say excuse me to you. You don't count around here no more.

TROY. Oh, I see . . . I don't count around here no more. You ain't got to say excuse me to your daddy. All of a sudden you done got so grown that your daddy don't count around here no more . . . Around here in his own house and yard that he done paid for with the sweat of his brow. You done got so grown to where you gonna take over. You gonna take over my house. Is that right? You gonna wear my pants. You gonna go in there and stretch out on my bed. You ain't got to say excuse me cause I don't count around here no more. Is that right?

CORY. That's right. You always talking this dumb stuff. Now, why don't you just get out my way?

TROY. I guess you got someplace to sleep and something to put in your belly. You got that, huh? You got that? That's what you need. You got that, huh?

CORY. You don't know what I got. You ain't got to worry about what I got.

TROY. You right! You one hundred percent right! I done spent the last seventeen years worrying about what you got. Now it's your turn, see? I'll tell you what to do. You grown . . . we done established that. You a man. Now, let's see you act like one. Turn your behind around and walk out this yard. And when you get out there in the alley . . . you can forget about this house. See? Cause this is my house. You go on and be a man and get your own house. You can forget about this. Cause this is mine. You go on and get yours cause I'm through with doing for you.

CORY. You talking about what you did for me . . . what'd you ever give me?

TROY. Them feet and bones! That pumping heart, nigger! I give you more than anybody else is ever gonna give you.

CORY. You ain't never gave me nothing! You ain't never done nothing but hold me back. Afraid I was gonna be better than you. All you ever did was try and make me scared of you. I used to tremble every time you called my name. Every time I heard your footsteps in the house. Wondering all the time . . . what's Papa gonna say if I do this? . . . What's he gonna say if I do that? . . . What's Papa gonna say if I turn on the radio? And Mama, too . . . she tries . . . but she's scared of you.

TROY. You leave your mama out of this. She ain't got nothing to do with this.

CORY. I don't know how she stand you . . . after what you did to her.

TROY. I told you to leave your mama out of this!

He advances toward CORY.

CORY. What you gonna do . . . give me a whupping? You can't whup me no more. You're too old. You just an old man.

TROY [*shoves him on his shoulder*]. Nigger! That's what you are. You just another nigger on the street to me!

CORY. You crazy! You know that?

TROY. Go on now! You got the devil in you. Get on away from me!

CORY. You just a crazy old man . . . talking about I got the devil in me.

TROY. Yeah, I'm crazy! If you don't get on the other side of that yard . . . I'm gonna show you how crazy I am! Go on . . . get the hell out of my yard.

CORY. It ain't your yard. You took Uncle Gabe's money he got from the army to buy this house and then you put him out.

TROY [*advances on* CORY]. Get your black ass out of my yard!

TROY's *advance backs* CORY *up against the tree.* CORY *grabs up the bat.*

CORY. I ain't going nowhere! Come on . . . put me out! I ain't scared of you.

TROY. That's my bat!

CORY. Come on!

TROY. Put my bat down!

CORY. Come on, put me out.

CORY *swings at* TROY, *who backs across the yard.*

What's the matter? You so bad . . . put me out!

TROY *advances toward* CORY.

CORY [*backing up*]. Come on! Come on!
TROY. You're gonna have to use it! You wanna draw that bat back on me . . .
   you're gonna have to use it.
CORY. Come on! . . . Come on!

CORY *swings the bat at* TROY *a second time. He misses.* TROY *continues to advance toward him.*

TROY. You're gonna have to kill me! You wanna draw that bat back on me.
   You're gonna have to kill me.

CORY, *backed up against the tree, can go no farther.* TROY *taunts him. He sticks out his head and offers him a target.*

Come on! Come on!

CORY *is unable to swing the bat.* TROY *grabs it.*

TROY. Then I'll show you.

CORY *and* TROY *struggle over the bat. The struggle is fierce and fully engaged.* TROY *ultimately is the stronger and takes the bat from* CORY *and stands over him ready to swing. He stops himself.*

Go on and get away from around my house.

CORY, *stung by his defeat, picks himself up, walks slowly out of the yard and up the alley.*

CORY. Tell Mama I'll be back for my things.
TROY. They'll be on the other side of that fence.

CORY *exits.*

TROY. I can't taste nothing. Helluljah! I can't taste nothing no more. TROY *assumes a batting posture and begins to taunt Death, the fastball on the outside corner.*] Come on! It's between you and me now! Come on! Anytime you want! Come on! I be ready for you . . . but I ain't gonna be easy.

The lights go down on the scene.

Scene 5

The time is 1965. The lights come up in the yard. It is the morning of TROY's *funeral. A funeral plaque with a light hangs beside the door. There is a small garden plot off to the side. There is noise and activity in the house as* ROSE, LYONS, *and* BONO *have gathered. The door opens and* RAYNELL, *seven years old, enters dressed in a flannel nightgown. She crosses to the garden and pokes around with a stick.* ROSE *calls from the house.*

ROSE. Raynell!

RAYNELL. Mam?

ROSE. What you doing out there?

RAYNELL. Nothing.

ROSE *comes to the door.*

ROSE. Girl, get in here and get dressed. What you doing?

RAYNELL. Seeing if my garden growed.

ROSE. I told you it ain't gonna grow overnight. You got to wait.

RAYNELL. It don't look like it never gonna grow. Dag!

ROSE. I told you a watched pot never boils. Get in here and get dressed.

RAYNELL. This ain't even no pot, Mama.

ROSE. You just have to give it a chance. It'll grow. Now you come on and do
  what I told you. We got to be getting ready. This ain't no morning to be
  playing around. You hear me?

RAYNELL. Yes, mam.

ROSE *exits into the house.* RAYNELL *continues to poke at her garden with a
stick.* CORY *enters. He is dressed in a Marine corporal's uniform, and carries a
duffelbag. His posture is that of a military man, and his speech has a clipped
sternness.*

CORY [*to* RAYNELL]. Hi. [*Pause.*] I bet your name is Raynell.

RAYNELL. Uh huh.

CORY. Is your mama home?

RAYNELL *runs up on the porch and calls through the screen door.*

RAYNELL. Mama . . . there's some man out here. Mama?

ROSE *comes to the door.*

ROSE. Cory? Lord have mercy! Look here, you all!

ROSE *and* CORY *embrace in a tearful reunion as* BONO *and* LYONS *enter from
the house dressed in funeral clothes.*

BONO. Aw, looka here . . .

ROSE. Done got all grown up!

CORY. Don't cry, Mama. What you crying about?

ROSE. I'm just so glad you made it.

CORY. Hey Lyons. How you doing, Mr. Bono.

LYONS *goes to embrace* CORY.

LYONS. Look at you, man. Look at you. Don't he look good, Rose. Got them Corporal stripes.

ROSE. What took you so long?

CORY. You know how the Marines are, Mama. They got to get all their paper-
  work straight before they let you do anything.

ROSE. Well, I'm sure glad you made it. They let Lyons come. Your Uncle Gabe's
  still in the hospital. They don't know if they gonna let him out or not. I just
  talked to them a little while ago.

LYONS. A Corporal in the United States Marines.

BONO. Your daddy knew you had it in you. He used to tell me all the time.

LYONS. Don't he look good, Mr. Bono?

BONO. Yeah, he remind me of Troy when I first met him. [*Pause.*] Say, Rose, Lucille's down at the church with the choir. I'm gonna go down and get the pallbearers lined up. I'll be back to get you all.

ROSE. Thanks, Jim.

CORY. See you, Mr. Bono.

LYONS [*with his arm around* RAYNELL]. Cory . . . look at Raynell. Ain't she precious? She gonna break a whole lot of hearts.

ROSE. Raynell, come and say hello to your brother. This is your brother, Cory. You remember Cory.

RAYNELL. No, Mam.

CORY. She don't remember me, Mama.

ROSE. Well, we talk about you. She heard us talk about you. [*To* RAYNELL.] This is your brother, Cory. Come on and say hello.

RAYNELL. Hi.

CORY. Hi. So you're Raynell. Mama told me a lot about you.

ROSE. You all come on into the house and let me fix you some breakfast. Keep up your strength.

CORY. I ain't hungry, Mama.

LYONS. You can fix me something, Rose. I'll be in there in a minute.

ROSE. Cory, you sure you don't want nothing? I know they ain't feeding you right.

CORY. No, Mama . . . thanks. I don't feel like eating. I'll get something later.

ROSE. Raynell . . . get on upstairs and get that dress on like I told you.

> ROSE *and* RAYNELL *exit into the house.*

LYONS. So . . . I hear you thinking about getting married.

CORY. Yeah, I done found the right one, Lyons. It's about time.

LYONS. Me and Bonnie been split up about four years now. About the time Papa retired. I guess she just got tired of all them changes I was putting her through. [*Pause.*] I always knew you was gonna make something out yourself. Your head was always in the right direction. So . . . you gonna stay in . . . make it a career . . . put in your twenty years?

CORY. I don't know. I got six already, I think that's enough.

LYONS. Stick with Uncle Sam and retire early. Ain't nothing out here. I guess Rose told you what happened with me. They got me down the workhouse. I thought I was being slick cashing other people's checks.

CORY. How much time you doing?

LYONS. They give me three years. I got that beat now. I ain't got but nine more months. It ain't so bad. You learn to deal with it like anything else. You got to take the crookeds with the straights. That's what Papa used to say. He used to say that when he struck out. I seen him strike out three times in a row . . . and the next time up he hit the ball over the grandstand. Right out there in Homestead Field. He wasn't satisfied hitting in the seats . . . he want to hit it over everything! After the game he had two hundred people standing around waiting to shake his hand. You got to take the crookeds with the straights. Yeah, Papa was something else.

CORY. You still playing?

LYONS. Cory . . . you know I'm gonna do that. There's some fellows down there we got us a band . . . we gonna try and stay together when we get out . . . but yeah, I'm still playing. It still helps me to get out of bed in the morning. As long as it do that I'm gonna be right there playing and trying to make some sense out of it.

ROSE. [*calling*]. Lyons, I got these eggs in the pan.

LYONS. Let me go on and get these eggs, man. Get ready to go bury Papa. [*Pause.*] How you doing? You doing all right?

CORY *nods.* LYONS *touches him on the shoulder and they share a moment of silent grief.* LYONS *exits into the house.* CORY *wanders about the yard.* RAYNELL *enters.*

RAYNEL. Hi.

CORY. Hi.

RAYNELL. Did you used to sleep in my room?

CORY. Yeah . . . that used to be my room.

RAYNELL. That's what Papa call it. "Cory's room." It got your football in the closet.

ROSE *comes to the door.*

ROSE. Raynell, get in there and get them good shoes on.

RAYNELL. Mama, can't I wear these? Them other one hurt my feet.

ROSE. Well, they just gonna have to hurt your feet for a while. You ain't said they hurt your feet when you went down to the store and got them.

RAYNELL. They didn't hurt then. My feet done got bigger.

ROSE. Don't you give me no backtalk now. You get in there and get them shoes on.

RAYNELL *exits into the house.*

Ain't too much changed. He still got that piece of rag tied to that tree. He was out here swinging that bat. I was just ready to go back in the house. He swung that bat and then he just fell over. Seem like he swung it and stood there with this grin on his face . . . and then he just fell over. They carried him on down to the hospital, but I knew there wasn't no need . . . why don't you come on in the house?

CORY. Mama . . . I got something to tell you. I don't know how to tell you this . . . but I've got to tell you . . . I'm not going to Papa's funeral.

ROSE. Boy, hush your mouth. That's your daddy you talking about. I don't want hear that kind of talk this morning. I done raised you to come to this? You standing there all healthy and grown talking about you ain't going to your daddy's funeral?

CORY. Mama . . . listen . . .

ROSE. I don't want to hear it, Cory. You just get that thought out of your head.

CORY. I can't drag Papa with me everywhere I go. I've got to say no to him. One time in my life I've got to say no.

ROSE. Don't nobody have to listen to nothing like that. I know you and your daddy ain't seen eye to eye, but I ain't got to listen to that kind of talk this morning. Whatever was between you and your daddy . . . the time has come to put it aside. Just take it and set it over there on the shelf and forget about it. Disrespecting your daddy ain't gonna make you a man, Cory. You got to find a way to come to that on your own. Not going to your daddy's funeral ain't gonna make you a man.

CORY. The whole time I was growing up . . . living in his house . . . Papa was like a shadow that followed you everywhere. It weighed on you and sunk into your flesh. It would wrap around you and lay there until you couldn't tell which one was you anymore. That shadow digging in your flesh. Trying to crawl in. Trying to live through you. Everywhere I looked, Troy Maxson was staring back at me . . . hiding under the bed . . . in the closet. I'm just saying I've got to find a way to get rid of that shadow, Mama.

ROSE. You just like him. You got him in you good.

CORY. Don't tell me that, Mama.

ROSE. You Troy Maxson all over again.

CORY. I don't want to be Troy Maxson. I want to be me.

ROSE. You can't be nobody but who you are, Cory. That shadow wasn't nothing but you growing into yourself. You either got to grow into it or cut it down to fit you. But that's all you got to make life with. That's all you got to measure yourself against that world out there. Your daddy wanted you to be everything he wasn't . . . and at the same time he tried to make you into everything he was. I don't know if he was right or wrong . . . but I do know he meant to do more good than he meant to do harm. He wasn't always right. Sometimes when he touched he bruised. And sometimes when he took me in his arms he cut.

When I first met your daddy I thought . . . Here is a man I can lay down with and make a baby. That's the first thing I thought when I seen him. I was thirty years old and had done seen my share of men. But when he walked up to me and said, "I can dance a waltz that'll make you dizzy," I thought, Rose Lee, here is a man that you can open yourself up to and be filled to bursting. Here is a man that can fill all them empty spaces you been tipping around the edges of. One of them empty spaces was being somebody's mother.

I married your daddy and settled down to cooking his supper and keeping clean sheets on the bed. When your daddy walked through the house he was so big he filled it up. That was my first mistake. Not to make him leave some room for me. For my part in the matter. But at that time I wanted that. I wanted a house that I could sing in. And that's what your daddy gave me. I didn't know to keep up his strength I had to give up little pieces of mine. I did that. I took on his life as mine and mixed up the pieces so that you couldn't hardly tell which was which anymore. It was my choice. It was my life and I didn't have to live it like that. But that's what life offered me in the way of being a woman and I took it. I grabbed hold of it with both hands.

By the time Raynell came into the house, me and your daddy had done lost touch with one another. I didn't want to make my blessing off of nobody's misfortune . . . but I took on to Raynell like she was all them babies I had wanted and never had.

The phone rings.

Like I'd been blessed to relive a part of my life. And if the Lord see fit to keep up my strength . . . I'm gonna do her just like your daddy did you . . . I'm gonna give her the best of what's in me.

RAYNELL [*entering, still with her old shoes*]. Mama . . . Reverend Tollivier on the phone.

ROSE *exits into the house.*

RAYNELL. Hi.

CORY. Hi.

RAYNELL. You in the Army or the Marines?

CORY. Marines.

RAYNELL. Papa said it was the Army. Did you know Blue?

CORY. Blue? Who's Blue?

RAYNELL. Papa's dog what he sing about all the time.

CORY [*singing*].

> Hear it ring! Hear it ring!
> I had a dog his name was Blue
> You know Blue was mighty true
> You know Blue was a good old dog
> Blue treed a possum in a hollow log
> You know from that he was a good old dog.
> Hear it ring! Hear it ring!

RAYNELL *joins in singing.*

CORY AND RAYNELL. Blue treed a possum out on a limb
> Blue looked at me and I looked at him
> Grabbed that possum and put him in a sack
> Blue stayed there till I came back
> Old Blue's feets was big and round
> Never allowed a possum to touch the ground.

> Old Blue died and I dug his grave
> I dug his grave with a silver spade
> Let him down with a golden chain
> And every night I call his name
> Go on Blue, you good dog you
> Go on Blue, you good dog you.

RAYNELL. Blue laid down and died like a man
> Blue laid down and died . . .

BOTH. Blue laid down and died like a man
> Now he's treeing possums in the Promised Land
> I'm gonna tell you this to let you know
> Blue's gone where the good dogs go
> When I hear old Blue bark
> When I hear old Blue bark
> Blue treed a possum in Noah's Ark
> Blue treed a possum in Noah's Ark.

ROSE *comes to the screen door.*

ROSE. Cory, we gonna be ready to go in a minute.

CORY [*to* RAYNELL]. You go on in the house and change them shoes like Mama told you so we can go to Papa's funeral.

RAYNELL. Okay, I'll be back.

RAYNELL *exits into the house.* CORY *gets up and crosses over to the tree.* ROSE *stands in the screen door watching him.* GABRIEL *enters from the alley.*

GABRIEL [*calling*]. Hey, Rose!

ROSE. Gabe?

GABRIEL. I'm here, Rose. Hey Rose, I'm here!

ROSE *enters from the house.*

ROSE. Lord . . . Look here, Lyons!

LYONS. See, I told you, Rose . . . I told you they'd let him come.

CORY. How you doing, Uncle Gabe?

LYONS. How you doing, Uncle Gabe?

GABRIEL. Hey, Rose. It's time. It's time to tell St. Peter to open the gates. Troy,
you ready? You ready, Troy. I'm gonna tell St. Peter to open the gates. You
get ready now.

GABRIEL, *with great fanfare, braces himself to blow. The trumpet is without a mouthpiece. He puts the end of it into his mouth and blows with great
force, like a man who has been waiting some twenty-odd years for this single
moment. No sound comes out of the trumpet. He braces himself and blows
again with the same result. A third time he blows. There is a weight of impossible description that falls away and leaves him bare and exposed to a
frightful realization. It is a trauma that a sane and normal mind would be
unable to withstand. He begins to dance. A slow, strange dance, eerie and
life-giving. A dance of atavistic signature and ritual.* LYONS *attempts to embrace him.* GABRIEL *pushes* LYONS *away. He begins to howl in what is an attempt at song, or perhaps a song turning back into itself in an attempt at
speech. He finishes his dance and the gates of heaven stand open as wide as
God's closet.*

That's the way that go!

(BLACKOUT)

[1987]

Topics for Critical Thinking and Writing

1. What do you think Bono means when he says, early in Act 2 (page 1125),
   "Some people build fences to keep people out . . . and other people build
   fences to keep people in"? Why is the play called *Fences?* What is Troy fencing in? (You'll want to take account of Troy's last speech in 2.2, but don't
   limit your response to this speech.)

2. Would you agree that Troy's refusal to encourage his younger son's aspirations is one of the "fences" of the play? What do you think Troy's reasons
   are—conscious and unconscious—for not wanting Cory to play football at
   college?

3. Compare and contrast Cory and Lyons. Consider, too, in what ways they resemble Troy, and in what ways they differ from him.

4. In what ways is Troy like his father, and in what ways unlike?

5. What do you make of the prominence given to the song about Blue?

6. There is a good deal of anger in the play, but there is also humor. Which passages do you find humorous, and why?

7. Characterize Rose Maxson.

8. Some scenes begin by specifying that "the lights come up." Others do
   not, presumably beginning with an illuminated stage. All scenes except
   the last one—which ends with a sudden blackout—end with the lights
   slowly going down to blackness. How would you explain Wilson's use of
   lighting?

A Casebook on American Indian Identity

First, a word about nomenclature. When Columbus encountered the Caribs in 1492, he thought he had reached India and therefore he called them *Indios* (Indians). Later, efforts to distinguish the peoples of the Western Hemisphere produced the terms *American Indian, Amerindian,* and *Amerind.* More recently, *Native American* has been used, but of course the people who met the European newcomers were themselves descended from persons who had immigrated from eastern Asia in ancient times, and in any case *American* is a word derived from the name of an Italian. On the other hand, anyone born in America, regardless of ethnicity, is a Native American. Further, it appears that most Native Americans (in the new, restricted sense) continue to speak of themselves as Indians (e.g., members of the Navaho Indian Nation), thereby making the use of *Indian* not only acceptable but preferable. Nevertheless, when possible it is advisable to use the name of the specific group, such as Arapaho, Iroquois, or Navaho.

This casebook includes three kinds of material:

- writings by Indians,
- writings by whites, and
- pictures.

Most of the writings are poems, but we also include important prose selections: John Smith's account of his rescue and a review of the Disney film *Pocahontas.* Within the casebook is a mini-casebook on Pocahontas. Although in this abbreviated table of contents we do not list the pictures, they are not only handsome but they also provide opportunities for writing.

The verbal material is as follows:

1. Two anonymous Arapaho Ghost Dance songs
2. Lydia Howard Huntley Sigourney's poem "The Indians' Welcome to the Pilgrim Fathers"
3. Robert Frost's poem "The Vanishing Red"
4. Sherman Alexie's poem "On the Amtrak from Boston to New York City"
5. Mini-casebook—Representations of Pocahontas:
   a. John Smith's account of how Pocahontas saved him
   b. Three early nineteenth-century poems about Pocahontas
   c. Paula Gunn Allen's poem "Pocahontas to Her English Husband, John Rolfe"
   d. A review of the Disney film *Pocahontas*

✎ ANONYMOUS ARAPAHO

The Arapaho are North American Plains Indians of Algonquian (or Algonkian) linguistic stock. Their origins are uncertain, but according to tribal traditions they migrated from northern Minnesota. During their westward migration they divided into northern and southern groups, and they now live chiefly in Wyoming and Oklahoma.

The two songs that we reprint are both from the Ghost Dance ritual, part of a widespread messianic religion that originated in the late nineteenth century, and is especially associated with a Paiute, Wovoka (c. 1858–1932, known also as Jack Wilson), the son of a medicine man. Wovoka, influenced by his father as well as by a Christian family he worked for and by the revivalistic Shaker movement, in 1889 said he had a vision that the earth would soon die and be reborn: All whites would disappear, and all Indians (living and dead) would be reunited. (The "ghosts" of the dance are dead Indians.) The songs were sung throughout the night, by singers in trances. Although Wovoka was a pacifist, the movement became, or seemed to become, warlike, and its adherents wore magic shirts they deemed to be bullet-proof. On December 29, 1890, at Wounded Knee, South Dakota, a group of Sioux were ordered to disarm; a medicine man threw dust into the air; an Indian with a gun wounded an officer; U.S. troops opened fire, and almost two hundred Sioux men, women, and children were killed. The apocalyptic hopes of the Ghost Dance were over.

The songs constitute a dialogue between the Sun ("Father") and the Native Americans ("children"). It is essential to understand that these compositions, like all Native American poetry of the nineteenth century, are oral, not written, and like most oral literature they use repetition and parallelism, as well as contrast. We give two songs in the version of James Mooney, who published his translations in the last decade of the nineteenth century. Inevitably, translators (from any language into any other) consciously or unconsciously impose some of their own aesthetic criteria on the material that they are translating, and in particular translators of Native American material have often somewhat reduced the amount of repetition. Further, many contemporary translators believe that oral material must be presented in such a way as to indicate how it was performed (i.e., with indications of pauses, changes of stress, and so forth). Nevertheless, although Mooney produced his translations about a hundred years ago, and although modern scholars have tools he never dreamed of, Mooney's translations are still highly regarded.

My Children, When at First I Liked the Whites

My children, when at first I liked the whites,
My children, when at first I liked the whites,
I gave them fruits,
I gave them fruits.   4

Father, Have Pity on Me

Father, have pity on me,
Father, have pity on me;
I am crying for thirst,
I am crying for thirst;
All is gone—I have nothing to eat,   4
All is gone—I have nothing to eat.

[c. 1889]

"Ghost Dancers"

![book icon] **LYDIA HOWARD HUNTLEY SIGOURNEY**

Lydia Sigourney (1791–1865), born in Norwich, Connecticut, of humble family, was taken up by her father's employer as a child prodigy and was tutored in Latin and He-brew. She wrote poetry chiefly on public issues, such as historical events and slavery, rather than personal lyric poetry. A fair number of her poems concern the displacement of Native Americans; she did not condemn the settling of the continent, but she did criticize the failure of whites to treat the Native Americans according to Christian ethics.

The Indian's Welcome to the Pilgrim Fathers

> *"On Friday, March 16th, 1622, while the colonists were busied in their usual labors, they were much surprised to see a savage walk boldly to-wards them, and salute them with, 'much welcome, English, much wel-come, Englishmen.'"*

Above them spread a stranger sky
  Around, the sterile plain,
The rock-bound coast rose frowning nigh,
  Beyond,—the wrathful main:
Chill remnants of the wintry snow   5
  Still chok'd the encumber'd soil,
Yet forth these Pilgrim Fathers go,
  To mark their future toil.

'Mid yonder vale their corn must rise
  In Summer's ripening pride,   10

And there the church-spire woo the skies
    Its sister-school beside.
Perchance 'mid England's velvet green
    Some tender thought repos'd,—
Though nought upon their stoic mien   15
    Such soft regret disclos'd.

When sudden from the forest wide
    A red-brow'd chieftain came,
With towering form, and haughty stride,
    And eye like kindling flame: 20
No wrath he breath'd, no conflict sought,
    To no dark ambush drew,
But simply *to the Old World brought,*
    The welcome of the New.

That *welcome* was a blast and ban   25
    Upon thy race unborn.
Was there no seer, thou fated Man!
    Thy lavish zeal to warn?
Thou in thy fearless faith didst hail
    A weak, invading band,   30
But who shall heed thy children's wail,
    Swept from their native land?

Thou gav'st the riches of thy streams,
    The lordship o'er thy waves,
The region of thine infant dreams,   35
    And of thy fathers' graves,
But who to yon proud mansions pil'd
    With wealth of earth and sea,
Poor outcast from thy forest wild,
    Say, who shall welcome thee?   40

                        [1835]

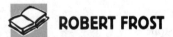 **ROBERT FROST**

For a biographical note on Robert Frost (1875–1963), see pages 461–62.

The Vanishing Red

He is said to have been the last Red Man
In Acton.° And the Miller is said to have laughed—
If you like to call such a sound a laugh.
But he gave no one else a laugher's license.
For he turned suddenly grave as if to say,   5

---

²**Acton** a town in Massachusetts, not far from where Frost spent part of his childhood

Edward S. Curtis. *The Vanishing Race,* c. 1904. (Platinum print. San Francisco Museum of Modern Art; extended loan of Van Deren Coke.)

'Whose business—if I take it on myself,
Whose business—but why talk round the barn?—
When it's just that I hold with getting a thing done with.'
You can't get back and see it as he saw it.
It's too long a story to go into now.   10
You'd have to have been there and lived it.
Then you wouldn't have looked on it as just a matter
Of who began it between the two races.

Some guttural exclamation of surprise
The Red Man gave in poking about the mill   15
Over the great big thumping shuffling mill-stone
Disgusted the Miller physically as coming
From one who had no right to be heard from.
'Come, John,' he said, 'you want to see the wheel pit?'°

He took him down below a cramping rafter,   20
And showed him, through a manhole in the floor,
The water in desperate straits like frantic fish,
Salmon and sturgeon, lashing with their tails.
Then he shut down the trap door with a ring in it

That jangled even above the general noise,   25
And came up stairs alone—and gave that laugh,

---

[19]**wheel pit** the pit containing the wheel that, agitated by the water, drives the mill

And said something to a man with a meal-sack
That the man with the meal-sack didn't catch—then.
Oh, yes, he showed John the wheel pit all right.

[1916]

WENDY ROSE

Wendy Rose, of Hopi and Miwok ancestry, was born in Oakland, California, in 1948. Educated as an anthropologist at the University of California, Berkeley, she has taught at Berkeley and at California State University, and she has edited the American Indian Quarterly. *Rose is the author of several books of poetry. In the course of an interview about the status of American Indian poets, she said, "The usual practice in bookstores upon receiving books of poems by American Indians is to classify them as 'Native Americana' rather than as poetry; the poets are seen as literate fossils more than as living, working artists." In the following poem, the dead are imagined as coming alive.*

Three Thousand Dollar Death Song

> *Nineteen American Indian Skeletons from Nevada . . . valued at $3000 . . .*
>
> —*Museum invoice, 1975*

Is it in cold hard cash? the kind
that dusts the insides of men's pockets
lying silver-polished surface along the cloth.
Or in bills? papering the wallets of they
who thread the night with dark words. Or   5
checks? paper promises weighing the same
as words spoken once on the other side
of the grown grass and damned rivers
of history. However it goes, it goes
Through my body it goes assessing each nerve, running its edges   10
along my arteries, planning ahead
for whose hands will rip me
into pieces of dusty red paper,
whose hands will smooth or smatter me
into traces of rubble. Invoiced now,   15
it's official how our bones are valued
that stretch out pointing to sunrise
or are flexed into one last foetal bend,
that are removed and tossed about,
catalogued, numbered with black ink   20
on newly-white foreheads.
As we were formed to the white soldier's voice,
so we explode under white students' hands.

Death is a long trail of days
in our fleshless prison.   25

From this distant point we watch our bones
auctioned with our careful beadwork,
our quilled medicine bundles, even the bridles
of our shot-down horses. You: who have   30
priced us, you who have removed us: at what cost?
What price the pits where our bones share
a single bit of memory, how one century
turns our dead into specimens, our history
into dust, our survivors into clowns.   35
Our memory might be catching, you know;
picture the mortars, the arrowheads, the labrets°
shaking off their labels like bears
suddenly awake to find the seasons have ended
while they slept. Watch them touch each other,   40
measure reality, march out the museum door!
Watch as they lift their faces
and smell about for us; watch our bones rise
to meet them and mount the horses once again!
The cost, then, will be paid   45
for our sweetgrass-smelling having-been
in clam shell beads and steatite,°
dentalia° and woodpecker scalp, turquoise
and copper, blood and oil, coal
and uranium, children, a universe   50
of stolen things.

[1980]

Topics for Critical Thinking and Writing

1. Why would a museum buy Indian skeletons? Would a museum buy the
   skeletons of whites?
2. What is the real cost of the skeletons?

NILA NORTHSUN

*Nila northSun was born in 1951 in Schurz, Nevada, of Shoshone-Chippewa stock. She
studied at the California State University campuses at Hayward and Humboldt and the
University of Montana at Missoula, beginning as a psychology major but switching to
art history, specializing in Native American art. She is the author of three books of poetry and is director of an emergency youth shelter in Fallon, Nevada.*

---

[37]**labrets** ornaments worn in pierced lips   [47]**steatite** grayish green or brown soapstone
[48]**dentalia** tooth shells (shells of marine mollusks)

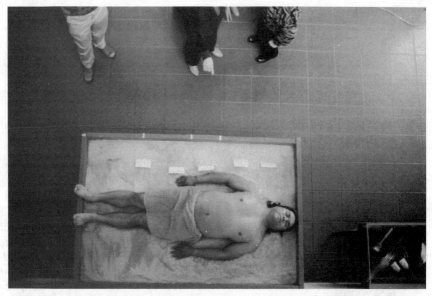

James Luna. *The Artifact Piece.* Luna (b. 1950), a Luiseño 1950 performance artist who lives on the La Jolla Reservation Valley Center, California, exhibited himself in a museum, lying on a bed of sand in an exhibition case (1987–1990).

Moving Camp Too Far

i can't speak of
   many moons
   moving camp on travois°
i can't tell of
   the last great battle   5
   counting coup° or
   taking scalp
i don't know what it
   was to hunt buffalo
   or do the ghost dance   10
but
i can see an eagle
   almost extinct
   on slurpee plastic cups
i can travel to powwows   15
   in campers & winnebagos
i can eat buffalo meat
   at the tourist burger stand
i can dance to indian music
   rock-n-roll hey-a-hey-o   20

¹**travois** a frame slung between trailing poles that are pulled by a horse. Plains Indians used the device to transport their goods.   ⁶**counting coup** recounting one's exploits in battle

i can
  & unfortunately
  i do

[1977]

 Topic for Critical Thinking and Writing

What is the speaker's attitude toward the world she has lost? What is her attitude
toward herself?

 **SHERMAN ALEXIE**

Sherman Alexie, born in 1966 in Spokane, Washington, holds a
B.A. from Washington State University. Author of novels, stories,
and poems, and author and director of the highly praised film
Smoke Signals (1998), Alexie has been awarded a grant from the
National Endowment for the Arts. Of his life and his work he says,
"I am a Spokane Coeur d'Alene Indian. . . . I live on the Spokane In-
dian Reservation. Everything I do now, writing and otherwise, has
its origin in that."

Robin Lloyd. Three American
Indian students at Princeton
(1973).

On the Amtrak from Boston to New York City

The white woman across the aisle from me says, "Look,
look at all the history, that house
on the hill there is over two hundred years old,"
as she points out the window past me   4

into what she has been taught. I have learned
little more about American history during my few days
back East than what I expected and far less
of what we should all know of the tribal stories   8

whose architecture is 15,000 years older
than the corners of the house that sits
museumed on the hill. "Walden Pond,"°
the woman on the train asks, "Did you see Walden Pond?"   12

and I don't have a cruel enough heart to break
her own by telling her there are five Walden Ponds
on my little reservation out West
and at least a hundred more surrounding Spokane,   16

the city I pretend to call my home. "Listen,"
I could have told her. "I don't give a shit
about Walden. I know the Indians were living stories
around that pond before Walden's grandparents were born   20

and before his grandparents' grandparents were born.
I'm tired of hearing about Don-fucking-Henley° saving it, too,
because that's redundant. If Don Henley's brothers and sisters
and mothers and fathers hadn't come here in the first place   24

then nothing would need to be saved."
But I didn't say a word to the woman about Walden
Pond because she smiled so much and seemed delighted
that I thought to bring her an orange juice   28

back from the food car. I respect elders
of every color. All I really did was eat
my tasteless sandwich, drink my Diet Pepsi
and nod my head whenever the woman pointed out   32

another little piece of her country's history
while I, as all Indians have done
since this war began, made plans
for what I would do and say the next time   36

somebody from the enemy thought I was one of their own.

                                                                 [1993]

---

¹¹**Walden Pond** site in Massachusetts where Henry David Thoreau (1817–1862) lived
from 4 July 1845 to 6 September 1847, and about which he wrote in his most famous
book, *Walden* (1854).   ²²**Don Henley** rock singer who was active in preserving Walden
from building developers

REPRESENTATIONS—VISUAL AND VERBAL— OF POCAHONTAS

Captain John Smith (1580–1631), an Englishman, began his career as a soldier of fortune at the age of fifteen in the Netherlands, and he went on to fight in Hungary, France, Germany, Spain, Austria, Rumania, Transylvania, Turkey, and North Africa. Then, back in England, he decided to join the expedition that founded Jamestown colony in 1607. From Jamestown he set out on exploratory expeditions, during one of which, in 1608, he was captured by Chesapeake Indians, who brought him to their chief or king, Powhatan. Years later, in the account he gave in *The Generall Historie of Virginia, New-England, and the Summer Isles* (1624), he says he was condemned to death but saved by Powhatan's daughter, Pocahontas.

The fact that Smith did not report this episode in his earlier account of the Virginia colony, *A True Relation . . . of Virginia* (1608), has caused many historians to doubt it. On the other hand, it has been argued that because the earlier publication was intended to attract colonists to Virginia, Smith may appropriately have omitted a life-threatening event. Another interpretation holds that the episode occurred but was in fact a ritual that Smith did not understand. Historians remain divided on the issue.

Pocahontas (c. 1595–1617), daughter of Powhatan, is said to have originally been named Matoaka, but came to be called Pocahontas ("playful one"). Whatever the truth of Smith's report that she rescued him, it is a fact that in 1613 Pocahontas was captured, taken to Jamestown, and held as hostage for English prisoners held by Powhatan. In Jamestown she was converted to Christianity, baptized, and in 1614, with the permission of her father and of the governor of the colony she was married to John Rolfe, a colonist. In 1616 Pocahontas and several other Indians went to England, where she was presented as a princess to the king and queen, and where, dressed in the English fashion, her portrait was engraved. (See page 1157.) In 1617 she started to return from England, but died before she could embark. She is buried in the parish churchyard at Gravesend, on the Thames River.

 ## JOHN SMITH
John Smith Saved by Pocahontas

At last they brought him[1] to Werowocomoco,[2] where was Powhatan, their Emperor. Here more than two hundred of those grim courtiers stood wondering at him, as [if] he had been a monster, till Powhatan and his train had put themselves in their greatest braveries.[3] Before a fire, upon a seat like a bedstead, he sat covered with a great robe made of Rarowcun[4] skins and all the tails hanging by. On either hand did sit a young wench of sixteen or eighteen years and along each side [of] the house, two rows of men and behind them as many women, with all their heads and shoulders painted red, many of their heads bedecked

---

[1] **him** Smith (throughout the narrative Smith speaks of himself in the third person)
[2] **Werowocomoco** Chief's Town   [3] **braveries** fine costumes   [4] **Rarowcun** raccoon

"King Powhatan commands Capt. Smith to be slain," in John Smith, *The Generall Historie of Virginia* . . . (1624). (Photo courtesy of the Edward E. Ayer Collection, The Newberry Library.)

with the white down of birds; but every one with something, and a great chain of white beads about their necks.

At his entrance before the King, all the people gave a great shout. The Queen of Appomattoc[5] was appointed to bring him water to wash his hands, and another brought him a bunch of feathers, instead of a towel, to dry them; having feasted him after their best barbarous manner they could, a long consultation was held, but the conclusion was, two great stones were brought before Powhatan; then as many as could laid hands on him, dragged him to them, and thereon laid his head, and being ready with their clubs, to beat out his brains. Pocohontas, the King's dearest daughter, when no entreaty could prevail, got his head in her arms and laid her own upon his to save him from death, whereat the Emperor was contented he should live to make him hatchets, and her bells, beads, and copper, for they thought him as well[6] of all occupations as themselves. For the King himself will make his own robes, shoes, bows, arrows, pots; plant, hunt, or do anything so well as the rest.

> They say he bore a pleasant show,
> But sure his heart was sad.
> For who can pleasant be, and rest,
> That lives in fear and dread:
> And having life suspected, doth
> It still suspected lead.

---

[5]**Appomattoc** Powhatan tribe   [6]**as well** as capable

Two days after, Powhatan, having disguised himself in the most fearfulest manner he could, caused Captain Smith to be brought forth to a great house in the woods and there upon a mat by the fire to be left alone. Not long after, from behind a mat that divided the house, was made the most dolefulest noise he ever heard; then Powhatan, more like a devil than a man, with some two hundred more as black as himself, came unto him and told him now they were friends, and presently he should go to Jamestown to send him two great guns and a grindstone for which he would give him the country of Capahowasick and forever esteem him as his son Nantaquond.

So to Jamestown with twelve guides Powhatan sent him. That night they quartered in the woods, he still expecting (as he had done all this long time of his imprisonment) every hour to be put to one death or other, for all their feasting. But almighty God (by His divine providence) had mollified the hearts of those stern barbarians with compassion. The next morning betimes they came to the fort, where Smith having used the savages with what kindness he could, he showed Rawhunt, Powhatan's trusty servant, two demiculverins[7] and a millstone to carry [to] Powhatan; they found them somewhat too heavy, but when they did see him discharge them, being loaded with stones, among the boughs of a great tree loaded with icicles, the ice and branches came so tumbling down that the poor savages ran away half dead with fear. But at last we regained some conference with them and gave them such toys and sent to Powhatan, his women, and children such presents as gave them in general full content.

Now ever once in four or five days, Pocahontas with her attendants brought him so much provision that saved many of their lives, that else for all this had starved with hunger

> Thus from numb death our good God sent relief,
> The sweet assuager of all other grief.

His relation of the plenty he had seen, especially at Werowocomoco, and of the state and bounty of Powhatan, which till that time was unknown, so revived their dead spirits (especially the love of Pocahontas) as all men's fear was abandoned.

[1624]

The next three poems are from the first third of the nineteenth century.

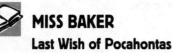

MISS BAKER
Last Wish of Pocahontas

THE setting sun threw a parting ray
O'er the lowly couch where the dying lay;
The fragrant breeze from a rosy bough,

---

[7]**demiculverins** small cannons

Engraving of Pocahontas by Simon
van de Passe, produced in London
in 1616. (Reprinted by permission
of The British Library (G.7037).)

Moved the long, dark locks on the hueless brow;
A tear-drop stood in the swimming eye,   5
And the bosom laboured with a sigh:
Then the dying turn'd to the sunset glow,
And said, with a faltering voice and low—
   "Yon sun goes down—but never to me
Shall the glory of his rising be: 10
For my form is faint, my heart throbs slow,
The fountain of life is chill and low:
The spirit's home looks brightly afar,
And I go to dwell with my kindred there.
I wish for my lowly grave to be made   15
In my native vale, 'neath the wild-wood shade.
When the dying strife in my bosom is o'er,
And closes mine eye to wake no more,
Then bear ye my pallid corse away
To my own green vale, where the sunbeams play—   20
Where the streams with a gentle murmur flow,
The wild birds sing, and the fresh winds blow.
There first I sported when wild and free,
And there may the place of my resting be;
My fathers sleep there 'neath the green oak shade   25
With theirs let my lowly couch be made."

GEORGE P. MORRIS
Pocahontas

UPON the barren sand
  A single captive stood;
Around him came, with bow and brand,
  The red men of the wood.
Like him of old, his doom he hears,   5
  Rock-bound on ocean's brim—
The chieftain's daughter knelt in tears,
  And breathed a prayer for him.

Above his head in air
  The savage war-club swung: 10
The frantic girl, in wild despair,
  Her arms about him flung.
Then shook the warriors of the shade,
  Like leaves on aspen limb,
Subdued by that heroic maid   15
  Who breathed a prayer for him!

"Unbind him!" gasp'd the chief:
  "It is your king's decree!"
He kiss'd away the tears of grief,
  And set the captive free!   20
"Tis ever thus, when in life's storm
  Hope's star to man grows dim,
An angel kneels, in woman's form,
  And breathes a prayer for him.

MOSES Y. SCOTT
Pocahontas

RUDE was the storm, and her fallen hair
Stream'd in the gale from her bosom bare,
As, alone, through the forest's blacken'd shade,
On errand of fear came the Indian maid.   4

Wild was her look; but her eye was bright
With the melting beam of Mercy's light—
Her speech was hurried; but kindness hung
On the accents bland of her warning tongue.   8

"White men, beware of Havoc's sweep!
He is waked in the forest from sullen sleep
He would drink your blood in a guardless hour,
And your wives and slumbering babes devour.   12

"Beware! for the tempest, chain'd so long,
Shall burst to-night, in its fury strong:

John Gadsby Chapman, *The Baptism of Pocahontas at Jamestown, Virginia, 1613*, 1837–40. (Oil on canvas, 12 × 18 ft. United States Capitol Collection, Washington, D.C.; photograph courtesy of the Architect of the Capitol.)

The trees must root them against its sway,
And the branches cling, or be scatter'd away!   16

"The fire shall rage, for the breeze is blowing;
The smoke rolls hither—the flames are glowing;
They climb the hills; to the vales they spread—
The night is black; but the forest is red.   20

White men, beware!—And when, at last,
Your fears are dead, and your dangers past,
Shall the voice of the warner be e'er betray'd?
Shall white men forget the Indian maid?"   24

 PAULA GUNN ALLEN

 *Part Sioux-Laguna and part Lebanese-Jewish, Paula Gunn Allen was born in 1939 in Cubero, New Mexico, into a family that used five languages. Allen, who holds a Ph.D. from the University of New Mexico, teaches Native American Studies at San Francisco State University. She has written several books of poems, a novel, a collection of traditional tales, and a collection of essays,* The Sacred Hoop: Recovering the Feminine in American Indian Traditions *(1986).*

Pocahontas to Her English Husband, John Rolfe

Had I not cradled you in my arms,
oh beloved   perfidious one,
you would have died.
And how many times did I pluck you
from certain death in the wilderness—   5
my world through which you stumbled
as though blind?
Had I not set you tasks
your masters far across the sea
would have abandoned you—   10
did abandon you, as many times they
left you to reap the harvest of their lies;
still you survived   oh my fair husband
and brought them gold
wrung from a harvest I taught you   15
to plant: Tobacco.   It
is not without irony that by this crop
your descendants die, for other powers
than those you know take part in this.
And indeed I did rescue you   20
not once but a thousand thousand times
and in my arms you slept, a foolish child,
and beside me you played,

chattering nonsense about a God
you had not wit to name;   25
and wondered you at my silence—
simple foolish wanton maid you saw,
dusky daughter of heathen sires
who knew not the ways of grace—
no doubt, no doubt.   30
I spoke little, you said.
And you listened less.
But played with your gaudy dreams
and sent ponderous missives to the throne
striving thereby to curry favor   35
with your king.   I saw you well.   I
understood the ploy and still protected you,
going so far as to die in your keeping—
a wasting, putrifying death, and you,
deceiver, my husband, father of my son,   40
survived, your spirit bearing crop
slowly from my teaching, taking
certain life from the wasting of my bones,

[1988]

JOHN D'ENTREMONT

John d'Entremont, a professor at Randolph-Macon Woman's College, here reviews the Disney film. The review was originally published in The Journal of American History *82 (December 1995).*

Review of Disney's *Pocahontas*

Pocahontas, Prod. by James Pentecost. Dir. by Mike Gabriel and Eric Goldberg. Buena Vista. 1995. 80 mins.

Pocahontas is the Walt Disney Company's thirty-third animated feature and its first based on a historical character—a film it describes in its latest, Pocahontas-stuffed gift catalog as "history, folklore and magic rolled up in one—inspiring love and respect for all things of the Earth." The ingredients, though, come not in equal doses. Of history there is almost nothing, and of faithfully transmitted folklore not much more. Apparently the key ingredient in producing love and respect for all things of the Earth is magic—here translated as the art of making almost everything up.

Of all the film's characters, five carry the names of people who once walked on planet Earth. Two are English. One bears the name of John Ratcliffe, chosen obviously for its rodentish, obnoxious sound. In reality, Ratcliffe was a military man about whom we know nothing except that he captained the tiny pinnace *Discovery*—the smallest of the 1607 expedition's three ships—on its transatlantic voyage, followed Edward Wingfield as president of the Virginia Company's resident council, and died under hideous torture by Powhatan women in November 1609. The film's "Governor" Ratcliffe is its one villain, an obese, slightly swishy, gold-obsessed, Indian-hating fop in a lavender suit (the third consecutive Disney animated villain to suggest homosexuality), who struts about proclaiming that Virginia is "mine, mine, mine!"

Ratcliffe's foil is named John Smith. The filmmakers correctly portray Smith as seeking adventure more than money, though they omit his strident, alienating preoccupation with his own fame and reputation, as well as his chronic belligerence. In mid-voyage, the Disney Smith leaps into the sea to save a comrade washed overboard, an outlandish flourish that Smith himself would have loved. As depicted, it seems preposterous until one notices that the short, stubby, ruddy, scraggly-bearded Smith has been transformed into a tall, blond (the film's only blond), clean-shaven, blue-eyed hunk who may well have spent years negotiating the big waves of Malibu.

Finally Smith and Ratcliffe arrive aboard their one nameless vessel at a lush, verdant land of towering firs, majestic waterfalls, rugged mountains, and craggy promontories: the Virginia coastal plain apparently looked just like Norway in the seventeenth century. Here the crew builds a fort and starts maniacally digging for gold on and near the beach.

5   This is all quite alarming to the Indians, led by their wise and noble chief, Powhatan. (The film follows the common error of mistaking Wahunsonacock's title for the man's own name.) The chief's only solace amid this threat is his daughter Pocahontas and his plan to marry her to the earnest, Schwarzeneggeresque warrior Kokoum. Headstrong Pocahontas has other ideas. She is a fun-lover; she finds Kokoum "too serious" and has an intimation—thanks to a dream and the advice of a talking tree—of something better. This is soon fulfilled when she meets John Smith at a crashing waterfall. He is about to shoot her when he becomes mesmerized by her beauty, or perhaps simply by her hair. In the film it cascades, billows, and blows whenever something dramatic is supposed to be happening, always in the same direction and sometimes when nothing else is blowing. In this case it buys her enough time to introduce herself. Within seconds, after remembering the talking tree's advice to "listen with your heart," she is speaking perfect English, and Smith is in love. This bit of magic works vicariously, as well, since we later see that the other Indians can speak perfect English too. Soon she and Smith (whose official duties consist largely of wandering about by himself, allowing him to be the fun guy Pocahontas is after) are exploring the mountains with her cute animal companions. A lovers' spat ensues when the well-meaning Smith calls her people "savages," but she sings him a song as they cavort with some deer and roll giddily in the grass. This transforms him into a heterosexual Walt Whitman (though he is still called John Smith), and soon all is well.

Until, that is, too-serious Kokoum comes on the scene, intending to save his fiancée from the trouble her best girl friend (who, like the great majority of Powhatan women, is sexy, svelte, and twenty) has warned him she is courting. Kokoum sees the two in a passionate kiss and rushes in; Smith's buddy—the very same whose life Smith saved from the briny deep—shoots Kokoum and kills him. Smith, wrongly accused, is brought before Powhatan, who decides to brain the newly ecologically concerned surfer-adventurer himself. Thus, as the movie nears its close, the stage is set for enactment of The Legend.

What history, what folklore, have American family audiences received thus far? Essentially, nothing. The three Indians who bear the names of historical figures are no more faithfully rendered than are Ratcliffe and Smith. All we know of Kokoum is that he was, in colonist William Strachey's words, a "pryvate captaine" to whom Pocahontas was married when she was kidnapped by the English in 1613. Her politically advantageous 1614 marriage to John Rolfe was apparently facilitated by Wahunsonacock's annulment of her marriage to Kokoum. Unlike the soft-hearted, easily swayed, grieving widower and father of one portrayed in the film, Powhatan/Wahunsonacock was a ruthless ruler of not-always-willing Indian groups from the fall line to the Chesapeake Bay, from the Northern Neck nearly to what became North Carolina. He was also a relentless opponent of European intrusion and the initiator of the first major Indian war in Anglo-American history. Implacable to the end, he never consented to visit an English home or settlement. And he had dozens of wives and scores of offspring.

One of them was Matoaka, nicknamed Pocahontas. Far from the lithe supermodel of the film, she was a prepubescent girl of about twelve in 1607, who, like all Powhatan girls, went about naked in summer, her head shaved nearly bald. She did visit Jamestown on occasion, informing her father about what she saw there. But her central significance lies in her capture at age eighteen and in her subsequent Christian conversion and marriage to the remarkable John Rolfe. The latter event brought a truce to an exhausting war under circumstances that saved the face of both sides. Pocahontas and Rolfe, with their infant son, visited England in 1616–1617, acting as a sort of poster family for the cause of Virginia and the possibilities of America before the newly celebrated young woman succumbed to an English respiratory ailment at approximately twenty-one. None of what made Pocahontas significant in American history is included or even hinted at in the film, which closes with her bidding a tearful farewell to an injured John Smith and choosing to remain with her own people rather than follow her European lover to England.

Depictions of Indian culture are little more faithful to reality than are the treatments of individuals, although some brief glimpses of the Powhatan material world are well done. Disney Indians do not hunt. This primary occupation of Powhatan men—central to their masculine identity and reputation as well as to their people's economy—is entirely absent from a film in which Pocahontas prevents Smith from shooting a bear and in which animals are playmates, not prey. The highly developed, polytheistic Powhatan religion is ignored. An old man does some conjuring but is not defined as a priest; there are no temples and no hint of gods as presences in Indians' lives. Attitudes toward gender and family are not perceptibly different from those of Europeans—or, more to the point, from the sensibilities of Americans in the 1990s. Indeed, it is difficult to see just what the difference is that makes the English and Indians initially so mutually hostile. Ratcliffe is greedy and disrespectful of nature, but his men eventually see the evil of his character and refuse to follow him in wickedness. The film does emphasize the distinction of race: "Here's what you get when races are diverse," Ratcliffe complains, and Pocahontas sings of the unity of all, be they "white or copperskinned." No matter that race, as today understood, does not seem in reality to have been central to the problem. The English frequently spoke admiringly of the attractiveness of both male and female Indians. Native Americans were not described as "red" people until the eighteenth century. Most English people found Indians inferior because of a host of differences the film sidesteps, especially religion. But to depict a people's paganism as equal to Christianity would alienate a significant portion of the Disney audience, while to condemn it would irritate the multiculturalists whom the filmmakers wish to placate. Better to leave it alone, favoring instead a safer (if anachronistic) stress on racism in its most crude, uncomplicated form.

10   The effect of this, however, is actually to diminish, not celebrate, the struggle of the various Indians and English, including Pocahontas and Rolfe, who did attempt to build bridges to another, profoundly different culture. In Disney's Virginia the differences are so few, the similarities so many, the hostility so irrational, that Pocahontas barely has to break out in a sweat to bring about a conciliation that is quick, absolutely thorough, and apparently lasting. The lesson Disney supposedly wishes to teach—that we should respect people who are different—is blunted by the patently false evasion that people really *aren't* different. It turns out to be a waste of energy to study other cultures, because there are no other cultures. It's a small world after all.

But are such criticisms too somber and ponderous when directed at an entertainment, and a child's entertainment at that? Are those who make them, like Kokoum, "too serious"? Consider the official characterizations of the film. Powhatan voice Russell Means has been quoted repeatedly as describing *Pocahontas* as "the finest feature film ever done about American Indians in the history of Hollywood" (for example, in *Disney Adventures,* July 31, 1995). Disney animators have widely propagandized about the serious "research" behind the film (for example, in *New York Times,* June 11, 1995); Ratcliffe voice David Ogden Stiers declaimed that the movie "may help us heal from the Oklahoma City bombing" (*USA Today,* June 9, 1995). No criticism could take the film as seriously as the filmmakers wish it to be taken. This does not, of course, prevent them from trying to have it both ways. Listeners to politically influential radio demagogues—broadcasting dubious assertions in deadly earnest and labeling themselves entertainers when challenged—will be familiar with the trick.

Pocahontas, moreover, is less a mere entertainment than it is an event in the history of merchandising—a capitalist spree that makes Disney's Ratcliffe look ascetic. Because of one of the most extensive marketing campaigns in the history of the planet, one may now obtain Pocahontas dolls and hand puppets (from Mattel), keepsake ornaments (Hallmark), trading cards (Skybox), cereal prizes (Cheerios), action figures (Burger King), athletic shoes (Payless), and chocolate bars (Nestlé). This is in addition to Disney's own Pocahontas T-shirts, pins, throw rugs, medallions, watches, dresses, nightgowns, stuffed animals, towels, bedding, and beanbag chairs. The detritus from this movie may endure nearly as long as nuclear waste from the Savannah River Plant; and, as the videocassette makes its way into the homes and minds of generations of children, its image of Pocahontas may prove comparably enduring.

Pocahontas's folklore image began with John Smith's *Generall Historie of Virginia* . . . (1624), in which he first spun the yarn of his last-second rescue by Pocahontas. A yarn it probably was, because, as the anthropologist Helen Rountree emphasizes, the story is entirely incongruent with Powhatan customs and practices; because it was recounted only after many years (and after the death of Pocahontas and all other principals), even though Smith had described his captivity in print as early as 1608; and because of what we know of Smith's propensity to exaggerate, embellish, and prevaricate when it suited his interest. Yet the tale stuck and became enshrined in American mythology—for good reason.

It stuck because it fit with what English colonizers and later generations of Americans wished to believe about themselves. The Pocahontas rescue story placed a gentle, conciliatory veneer on a long interior history of invasion, brutality, and war. The story was cherished by generations of Americans who needed to see themselves and their history as virtuous and well-meaning; it was ultimately embraced even by culturally embattled Native Americans as a means of securing some national acknowledgment, at whatever cost, of their own centrality to the American story. That this myth should be immortalized in a bas-relief in the Capitol rotunda—the *sanctum sanctorum* of American iconography—is entirely appropriate. The rescue tale took hold at the grass roots and was retold independently over the centuries by hundreds of artists and writers and countless thousands of parents and teachers because it resonated with deep and serious cultural need. That, indeed, is the essence of folklore.

Perhaps the most dispiriting thing about Disney's *Pocahontas* is that it is no less contemptuous of folklore than of history. It is not simply the innovative details: the inevitable rocky promontory, or the decision to put the execution club in the hands of Wahunsonacock/Powhatan himself. All narrators of myth fiddle with details. What shocks is the mystifying transformation of Smith from rescued to rescuer, upstaging Pocahontas and mangling both history and myth. For in this version Ratcliffe and his English soldiers march on Powhatan's village, ready to do battle, and witness Pocahontas's act of mercy. Once she melts her father's heart and saves Smith, Ratcliffe sees his chance to start a war slipping away. In desperation he raises his musket and fires at Powhatan. Smith, in his second rescue of the film, bravely leaps in front of the Indian leader and falls, gravely wounded. (This is the movie's substitute for the accidental gunpowder explosion that in reality forced his return to England in October 1609.) The rescue story as hitherto known is thus utterly garbled. Smith, not Pocahontas, becomes the central actor and hero. The Indians become not a proud people choosing to show mercy to a possible enemy, but a lucky people beholden to their English benefactor. In the film's penultimate scene, a grateful Powhatan brings food to the English settlement. "You are always welcome among my people," he tells the departing Smith. "Thank you, my brother."

This did not percolate up from the grass roots in modern America, though it now will seep down. This was hatched in a corporate office by a handful of people with no demonstrable regard for either history or myth. The only pertinent "research," evidently, was market research. This Pocahontas story emerged to serve, not the cultural needs of a society, but the financial imperatives of a corporation.

Perhaps we do inhabit a postmodern age, outgrowing not only objective facts and ultimate truths but also coherent (though argued-about) stories. Perhaps this liberates us; we did pay a price for those stories. But Disney's *Pocahontas* compels us to ponder the price—in cultural illiteracy, intellectual Darwinism, and obliterated collective memory—that we are now to pay for their dismantling.

[1995]

Literary Visions: Poems and Paintings

A WORD ABOUT CONNECTIONS BETWEEN LITERATURE AND THE OTHER ARTS

Although the word *art* perhaps first calls to mind painting and sculpture, it can also be used of music, literature, dance, and architecture. We can even extend the word and (for instance) speak of the art of medicine. Presumably the *science* of medicine is a matter of diligent study of conventional scientific procedures, but the *art* of medicine is a matter of intuition (or of skills developed out of intuitions).

Something of this implication that the arts draw on individual insights is evident, too, in the distinction between **the arts** and **the crafts.** But first we should mention that some people deny that a meaningful distinction can be made. In their view, an elite society snobbishly calls some things that it happens to value "art," and other things that it values less "craft." Thus, in our society, at least until very recently, an oil painting (probably executed by a man) was a work of art, and a quilt (executed by a woman) was a work of craft; a sculpture of a nude male or female (probably executed by a man) was a work of art, and a clothed doll (executed by a woman) was a work of craft. This view has been called the institutional view of art, or the establishment view of art: Something is a work of art if an important institution says it is. Museums tell us what is and is not art; so long as quilts are not exhibited in museums, they are not works of art, but if major museums exhibit quilts, quilts become art. Similarly, it is argued, educational institutions decree what is literature and what is not. If Alice James's *Diary* is not taught in literature courses in colleges and universities, it is not literature; if it *is* taught, it *is* literature. (Of course other institutions also are part of the game; if a major publishing house publishes a book, the act of publication helps to establish the work as a work of literature.) Is this a cynical view? Or is it in fact a realistic view? After all, we do know that works that were ignored in their own day—let's say the paintings of Vincent van Gogh—have come to be highly regarded as works of art. The works did not change—only the attitudes toward them.

Still, can we say that the distinction between a work of art and a work of craft is in the object itself, and not in the viewer? Let's try. Consider the worker in wood who produces something (let's call it a sculpture) that can be said to be in some degree the product of imagination. Now, on the other hand, let's consider the worker in wood who, following a predictable plan, produces something (for instance a handsome, sturdy coffee table) that is very like countless objects that already exist. The wooden object that is a work of art presumably is valued chiefly as a unique object that

- *is expressive* (let's say, of power, or lightness, or energy, or tranquility) and that
- in itself *gives pleasure* by means of its color, its shape, and so on—even though of course we might also stack magazines on it.

The wooden object that is a work of craft is, we might say, not essentially expressive and not essentially an object that gives pleasure. Further, it is *made* by technical skill rather than *created* by the imagination. Technical skill, admirable in itself, is possessed by many people, and can be learned by almost all.

Of course works of art also require technical skill—it's not easy to carve (or to write a sonnet)—and there may be widespread disagreement about whether a particular wooden object is a work of art or a work of craft, but the general idea is clear enough. If we ask a carpenter to copy this coffee table, he or she produces a work of craft; if we ask a carpenter to design a table that will somehow go with the rest of the living room and will "make a statement," the table conceivably may be a work of art. Certainly furniture *can* be expressive. For instance, an overstuffed armchair expresses or says something very different from a typist's chair. In short, the line between the arts and the crafts is not always clear. In fact, sculpting has often been thought of as a craft because there is so much physical labor involved in producing a work of sculpture. (Some sculptors, eager to avoid the stigma attached to physical labor, have produced small clay models and then left to stonemasons the job of making a larger copy in stone.) And—to get back to literature—the very word *playwright* implies craft, since a *wright* is a maker; a playwright (*not* "playwrite") is a *maker* of plays, just as a shipwright is a maker of ships.

No one denies that authors must learn their craft, but most people would agree that the enduring writings—the writings that outlive their own generation—are the products of more than technical competence. Still, a case can be made that there is no sharp distinction between the arts and the crafts—just as a case can be made that there is no sharp distinction between literature and the writing that we all produce, for instance letters, diaries, journal entries, lectures. In this view, "literature," "art," and "craft" are social constructs—things constructed (like, say, educational systems or penal systems) by society. Different societies construct different systems; hence, the canon (the body of accepted work called literature, or called art) may change from decade to decade.

Enough of the philosophizing—or almost enough. Artists (in the broad sense, including not only people who produce paintings and sculptures but also those who produce poems, novels, operas, dances, and so forth) are often tempted to think that artists in other fields have some sort of advantage. Thus, writers—casting envious eyes at painters—may fret that their own audiences are limited to persons who can read the language, whereas painters supposedly work in a "universal language" of line and color.

Are there, one may ask, significant correspondences between the arts? If we talk about *rhythm* in a painting, are we talking about a quality similar to *rhythm* in a poem? Are the painter's colors comparable to the poet's images? Does it make sense to say, as Goethe (1749-1832) said, that architecture is frozen music? Or to call architecture music in space? Many artists of one sort have felt that their abilities *ought* to enable them to move into a "sister art," and they have tried their hand at something outside of their specialty, usually with no great success. (William Blake, represented in this book by several poems and pictures, is often said to be the only figure in English history who is significant both as a poet and as a painter.) For instance, the painter Edgar Degas (1834-1917) tried to write sonnets, but he could not satisfy even himself. When he complained to his friend, the poet Stéphane Mallarmé, that he couldn't write poems even though he had plenty of ideas, Mallarmé replied, "You don't write poems with ideas; you write them with words."

Artists (of all kinds) may be pardoned for feeling that there is a kinship between the arts. The idea can be traced back to Simonides (556-468 B.C.), an ancient Greek poet who is reputed to have said that "painting is mute poetry, poetry a speaking picture." The Roman poet Horace (65-8 B.C.) picked up the idea, saying in *The Art of Poetry* that "a poem is like a picture" (*ut pictura poesis*), an assertion that has been disputed ever since.

Painters have been moved, for many centuries, to illustrate texts—for instance, more than two thousand years ago the painters of Greek vases illustrated the Greek myths, and from the Middle Ages onward artists have illustrated the Bible. In this book we include a mid-twentieth-century painting by Charles Demuth, based on a poem by William Carlos Williams. Conversely, poets have been moved to write about paintings or sculptures. Later in this chapter we reprint several poems about paintings by Botticelli, Brueghel, van Gogh, and others.

THINKING AND WRITING ABOUT POEMS AND PAINTINGS

When you read the poems that we print along with pictures, you might think about some of the following questions:

- What is your own first response to the painting? In interpreting the painting, consider the subject matter, the composition (for instance, balanced masses, as opposed to an apparent lack of equilibrium), the technique (for instance, vigorous brush strokes of thick paint, as opposed to thinly applied strokes that leave no trace of the artist's hand), the color, and the title.
- After having read the poem, do you see the painting in a somewhat different way?
- To what extent does the poem illustrate the painting, and to what extent does it depart from the painting and make a very different statement?
- If the painting is based on a poem (see Demuth's painting on page 1172), to what extent does the painting capture the poem?
- Beyond the subject matter, what (if anything) do the two works have in common?

For an example of an essay by a student discussing a poem and a picture, see page 1193.

Poems and Paintings

Vincent van Gogh. *Vincent's Bed in Arles.* (Oil on canvas, 72 × 90 cm. Vincent van Gogh Foundation/Van Gogh Museum, Amsterdam.)

 **JANE FLANDERS**

Jane Flanders, born in Waynesboro, Pennsylvania, in 1940, and educated at Bryn Mawr College and Columbia University, is the author of three books of poems. Among her awards are poetry fellowships from the National Endowment for the Arts and the New York Foundation for the Arts.

Van Gogh's Bed

is orange,
like Cinderella's coach, like
the sun when he looked it
straight in the eye.   4

is narrow,
he slept alone, tossing
between two pillows, while it carried him
bumpily to the ball.   8

is clumsy,
but friendly. A peasant
built the frame; an old wife beat
the mattress till it rose like meringue.   12

is empty,
morning light pours in
like wine, melody, fragrance,
the memory of happiness.   16

[1985]

✎ Topics for Critical Thinking and Writing

Jane Flanders tells us that the poem is indebted not only to the painting but also to two comments in letters that van Gogh wrote to his brother, Theo:

> I can tell you that for my part I will try to keep a straight course, and will paint the most simple, the most common things.

[December 1884]

> My eyes are still tired, but then I had a new idea in my head and here is the sketch of it. . . . It's just simply my bedroom, only here color is to do everything, and giving by its simplification a grander style to things, is to be suggestive here of *rest* or of sleep in general. In a word, to look at the picture ought to rest the brain or rather the imagination.

[September 1888]

1. Does the painting convey "rest" to you? If not, has van Gogh failed to paint a picture of interest? What *does* the picture convey to you?
2. In an earlier version, the last stanza of the poem went thus:

   empty,
   morning light pours in
   like wine; the sheets are what they are,
   casting no shadows.

   Which version do you prefer? Why?

Charles Demuth. *I Saw the Figure 5 in Gold.* 1928. (Oil on composition board, 36 × 29¾ in. The Metropolitan Museum of Art, New York. The Alfred Stieglitz Collection, 1949. [49.59.1] Photograph © 1979 The Metropolitan Museum of Art)

 ## WILLIAM CARLOS WILLIAMS

William Carlos Williams (1883–1963) was the son of an English traveling salesman and a Basque-Jewish woman. The couple met in Puerto Rico and settled in Rutherford, New Jersey, where Williams was born. He spent his life there, practicing as a pediatrician and writing poems in the moments between seeing patients who were visiting his office.

In his Autobiography *Williams gives an account of the origin of this poem. He was walking in New York City, on his way to visit a friend:*

As I approached his number I heard a great clatter of bells and the roar of a fire engine passing the end of the street down Ninth Avenue. I turned just in time to see a golden 5 on a red background flash by. The impression was so sudden and forceful that I took a piece of paper out of my pocket and wrote a short poem about it.

Several years later his friend Charles Demuth (1883–1939), an American painter who has been called a cubist-realist, painted this picture, inspired by the poem. The picture is one of a series of paintings about Demuth's friends.

The Great Figure

Among the rain
and lights
I saw the figure 5
in gold
on a red   5
fire truck
moving
tense
unheeded
to gong clangs   10
siren howls
and wheels rumbling
through the dark city

[1920]

🖉 Topic for Critical Thinking and Writing

Williams's draft for the poem runs thus:

> Among the rain
> and lights
> I saw the figure 5
> gold on red
> moving
> to gong clangs
> siren howls
> and wheels rumbling
> tense
> unheeded
> through the dark city

Do you think the final version is better in all respects, some respects, or no respect? Explain.

Edwin Romanzo Elmer. *Mourning Picture.* 1890. (Oil on canvas, 28 × 36 in. [71.1 × 91.5 cm.] Smith College Museum of Art, Northampton, Massachusetts. Purchased 1953.)

 **ADRIENNE RICH**

Adrienne Rich, born in 1929 in Baltimore, was educated at Radcliffe College. Her first book of poems, A Change of World, *published in 1951 when she was still an undergraduate, was selected by W. H. Auden for the Yale Series of Younger Poets.*

Mourning Picture

(The picture was painted by Edwin Romanzo Elmer (1850–1923) as a memorial to his daughter Effie. In the poem, it is the dead girl who speaks.)

They have carried the mahogany chair and the cane rocker
out under the lilac bush,
and my father and mother darkly sit there, in black clothes.
Our clapboard house stands fast on its hill,
my doll lies in her wicker pram   5
gazing at western Massachusetts.
This was our world.

I could remake each shaft of grass
feeling its rasp on my fingers,
draw out the map of every lilac leaf   10
or the net of veins on my father's
grief-tranced hand.

Out of my head, half-bursting,
still filling, the dream condenses—
shadows, crystals, ceilings, meadows, globes of dew.   15
Under the dull green of the lilacs, out in the light
carving each spoke of the pram, the turned porch-pillars,
under high early-summer clouds,
I am Effie, visible and invisible,
remembering and remembered.   20

They will move from the house,
give the toys and pets away.
Mute and rigid with loss my mother
will ride the train to Baptist Corner,
the silk-spool will run bare.   25
I tell you, the thread that bound us lies
faint as a web in the dew.
Should I make you, world, again,
could I give back the leaf its skeleton, the air
its early-summer cloud, the house   30
its noonday presence, shadowless,
and leave *this* out? I am Effie, you were my dream.

                                                          [1965]

Kitagawa Utamaro.*
*Two Women Dress-
ing Their Hair.* (Print
collection, Miriam
and Ira D. Wallach
Division of Art, Prints
and Photographs/
New York Public
Library, Astor,
Lenox and Tilden
Foundations)

 **CATHY SONG**

*Cathy Song was born in Honolulu in 1952 of a Chinese mother and a Korean father.
She holds a bachelor's degree from Wellesley College and a master's degree in creative
writing from Boston University. A manuscript that she submitted to the Yale Series of
Younger Poets was chosen as the winner and in 1983 was published under the title of*
Picture Bride.

---

*Kitagawa Utamaro (1754–1806) lived in Edo (now called Tokyo). He specialized in de-
signing pictures of courtesans and actors that were then used to make woodblock prints.
Brothels and the theater were important parts of what was called the Floating World, that
is, the world of transient pleasure.

1176

Beauty and Sadness

for Kitagawa Utamaro

He drew hundreds of women
in studies unfolding
like flowers from a fan.
Teahouse waitresses, actresses,
geishas, courtesans and maids.   5
They arranged themselves
before this quick, nimble man
whose invisible presence
one feels in these prints
is as delicate   10
as the skinlike paper
he used to transfer
and retain their fleeting loveliness.

Crouching like cats,
they purred amid the layers of
          kimono   15
swirling around them
as though they were bathing
in a mountain pool with irises
growing in the silken sunlit water.
Or poised like porcelain vases,   20
slender, erect and tall; their heavy
brocaded hair was piled high
with sandalwood combs and blossom
          sprigs
poking out like antennae.
They resembled beautiful iridescent
          insects,   25
creatures from a floating world.

Utamaro absorbed these women of
          Edo
in their moments of melancholy

He captured the wisp of shadows,   30
the half-draped body
emerging from a bath; whatever
skin was exposed
was powdered white as snow.
A private space disclosed.   35
Portraying another girl
catching a glimpse of her own vulner-
          able
face in the mirror, he transposed
the trembling plum lips
like a drop of blood   40
soaking up the white expanse of paper.

At times, indifferent to his inconsolable
eye, the women drifted
through the soft gray feathered light,
maintaining stillness, the moments in
          between.   45
Like the dusty ash-winged moths
that cling to the screens in summer
and that the Japanese venerate
as ancestors reincarnated;
Utamaro graced these women with
          immortality   50
in the thousand sheaves of prints
fluttering into the reverent hands of
          keepers:
the dwarfed and bespectacled painter
holding up to a square of sunlight
what he had carried home beneath his
          coat   55
one afternoon in winter.

[1983]

✎ Topics for Critical Thinking and Writing

1. In the first stanza the women in Utamaro's prints possess a "fleeting loveliness." What does "fleeting" suggest here? What are Utamaro's characteristics in this stanza?
2. In the second stanza would you say that the women are beautiful, or not?
   And in the third stanza? What do they look like in each stanza?
3. In the last stanza, in the last few lines, we learn that Utamaro was a "dwarfed
   and bespectacled painter." We might have learned this earlier in the poem,
   or not at all. Why does Song wait until this late in the poem to tell us?

Sandro Botticelli. *The Birth of Venus.* About 1480. (5′ 8⅞″ × 9′ ⅞″. Uffizi Gallery, Florence [Scala/Art Resource, New York])

 **MARY JO SALTER**

Mary Jo Salter, born in 1954 in Grand Rapids, Michigan, was raised in Detroit and Baltimore and was educated at Harvard and at Cambridge University. The author of several books of poetry, Salter has received numerous awards, including a fellowship from the National Endowment for the Arts.

The Rebirth of Venus

He's knelt to fish her face up from the sidewalk
all morning, and at last some shoppers gather
to see it drawn—wide-eyed, and dry as chalk—
whole from the sea of dreams. It's she. None other   4

than the other one who's copied in the book
he copies from, that woman men divined
ages before a painter let them look
into the eyes their eyes had had in mind.   8

Love's called him too, today, though she has taught
him in her beauty to love best
the one who first had formed her from a thought.
One square of pavement, like a headstone (lest   12

anyone mistake where credit lies),
reads BOTTICELLI, but the long-closed dates
suggest, instead, a view of centuries
coming unbracketed, as if the gates   16

might swing wide to admit, here, in the sun,
one humble man into the pantheon
older and more exalted than her own.
   Slow gods of Art, late into afternoon   20

let there be light: a few of us drop the wish
into his glinting coinbox like a well,
remembering the forecast. Yet he won't rush
her finish, though it means she'll have no shell   24

to harbor in; it's clear enough the rain
will swamp her like a tide, and lion-hearted
he'll set off, black umbrella sprung again,
envisioning faces where the streets have parted.   28

[1989]

✏ Topics for Critical Thinking and Writing

1. In the first stanza, what words suggest that Venus, whose portrait is being drawn on the sidewalk, is born in the sea? What medium is the artist using?
2. What do you think Salter means when she says (lines 6–8) that the sidewalk artist's picture is of "that woman men divined / ages before a painter let them look / into the eyes their eyes had had in mind"?
3. According to the Hebrew Bible, "let there be light" (line 21) is what God said in Genesis 1.3. In the context of Salter's poem what do the words mean? Does the poet expect her wish (in line 21) to be granted?
4. If you agree that the poem is lighthearted, what makes it so?
5. Botticelli's painting is a great favorite. Why do you suppose it is so popular?

Vincent van Gogh. *The Starry Night.* 1889. (Oil on canvas, 29 × 36¼ in. [73.7 × 92.1 cm.]. Collection, The Museum of Modern Art, New York. Acquired through the Lillie P. Bliss Bequest. Photograph © 1999 The Museum of Modern Art, New York)

 **ANNE SEXTON**

Anne Sexton (1928–75) was born in Newton, Massachusetts. She attended Garland Junior College, married at 20, and began a life as a housewife. After a mental breakdown at the age of 28 she took up writing poetry on the suggestion of a therapist. She published eight books of poetry, the third of which won a Pulitzer Prize. Despite her literary success, her life was deeply troubled, and she attempted suicide on several occasions. At last she succeeded, by carbon monoxide poisoning.

The Starry Night

That does not keep me from having a terrible need of—shall I say the word—religion. Then I go out at night to paint the stars.

—Vincent van Gogh in a letter to his brother

The town does not exist
except where one black-haired tree slips
up like a drowned woman into the hot sky.
The town is silent. The night boils with eleven stars
Oh starry starry night! This is how   5
I want to die.

It moves. They are all alive.
Even the moon bulges in its orange irons
to push children, like a god, from its eye.
The old unseen serpent swallows up the stars.   10
Oh starry starry night! This is how
I want to die:

into that rushing beast of the night,
sucked up by that great dragon, to split
from my life with no flag,   15
no belly,
no cry.

[1961]

✎ Topic for Critical Thinking and Writing

Sexton calls her poem "The Starry Night" and uses an epigraph from van Gogh. In what ways does her poem *not* describe or evoke van Gogh's painting? In what ways *does* it describe the painting?

Pieter Brueghel the Elder. *Landscape with the Fall of Icarus.* (Royal Museum of Fine Arts, Brussels, Belgium)

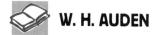 **W. H. AUDEN**

Wystan Hugh Auden (1907–73) was born in York, England, and educated at Oxford. In the 1930s his left-wing poetry earned him wide acclaim as the leading poet of his generation. He went to Spain during the Spanish Civil War, intending to serve as an ambulance driver for the Republicans in their struggle against fascism, but he was so distressed by the violence of the Republicans that he almost immediately returned to England. In 1939 he came to America, and in 1946 he became a citizen of the United States, though he spent his last years in England. Much of his poetry is characterized by a combination of colloquial diction and technical dexterity.

In the following poem, Auden offers a meditation triggered by a painting in the Museum of Fine Arts in Brussels. The painting, by Pieter Brueghel (c. 1525–69), is based on the legend of Icarus, told by the Roman poet Ovid (43 B.C.–A.D. 17) in his Metamorphoses. *The story goes thus: Daedalus, father of Icarus, was confined with his son on the island of Crete. In order to escape, Daedalus made wings for himself and for Icarus by fastening feathers together with wax, but Icarus flew too near the sun, the wax melted, and Icarus fell into the sea. According to Ovid, the event—a boy falling through the sky—was witnessed with amazement by a plowman, a shepherd, and an angler. In the painting, however, these figures seem to pay no attention to Icarus, who is represented not falling through the sky but already in the water (in the lower right corner, near the ship), with only his lower legs still visible.*

Musée des Beaux Arts

About suffering they were never wrong,
The Old Masters: how well they understood
Its human position; how it takes place
While someone else is eating or opening a window or just walking dully along;
How, when the aged are reverently, passionately waiting   5
For the miraculous birth, there always must be
Children who did not specially want it to happen, skating
On a pond at the edge of the wood:
They never forgot
That even the dreadful martyrdom must run its course   10
Anyhow in a corner, some untidy spot
Where the dogs go on with their doggy life and the torturer's horse
Scratches its innocent behind on a tree.

In Brueghel's *Icarus,* for instance: how everything turns away
Quite leisurely from the disaster; the ploughman may   15
Have heard the splash, the forsaken cry,
But for him it was not an important failure; the sun shone
As it had to on the white legs disappearing into the green
Water; and the expensive delicate ship that must have seen
Something amazing, a boy falling out of the sky,   20
Had somewhere to get to and sailed calmly on.

[1938]

✏ Topics for Critical Thinking and Writing

1. In your own words sum up what, according to the speaker (in lines 1-13), the Old Masters understood about human suffering. (The Old Masters were the great European painters who worked from about 1500 to about 1750.)
2. Suppose the first lines read:

   The Old Masters were never wrong about suffering.
   They understood its human position well.

   What (beside the particular rhymes) would change or be lost?
3. Reread the poem (preferably over the course of several days) a number of times, jotting down your chief responses after each reading. Then, in connection with a final reading, study your notes, and write an essay of 500 words setting forth the history of your final response to the poem. For example, you may want to report that certain difficulties soon were clarified and that your enjoyment increased. Or, conversely, you may want to report that the poem became less interesting (for reasons you will set forth) the more you studied it. Probably your history will be somewhat more complicated than these simple examples. Try to find a chief pattern in your experience, and shape it into a thesis.
4. Consider a picture, either in a local museum or reproduced in a book, and write a 500-word reflection on it. If the picture is not well known, include a reproduction (a postcard from the museum or a photocopy of a page of a book).

Marcel Duchamp. *Nude Descending a Staircase, No. 2.* 1912. (Oil on canvas, 58″ × 35″. Philadelphia Museum of Art: The Louise and Walter Arensberg Collection)

 **X. J. KENNEDY**

X. J. Kennedy was born in New Jersey in 1929. He has taught at Tufts University and is the author of several books of poems, books for children, and college textbooks.

Marcel Duchamp's Nude Descending a Staircase No. 2 *(1912) was exhibited in 1913 in the Armory Show, an international exhibition held at an armory in New York, and later in Chicago and Boston. The Armory Show gave America its first good look at contemporary European art, for instance, cubism, which had influenced Duchamp's painting.*

Nude Descending a Staircase

Toe upon toe, a snowing flesh,
A gold of lemon, root and rind,
She sifts in sunlight down the stairs
With nothing on. Nor on her mind.   4

We spy beneath the banister
A constant thresh of thigh on thigh—
Her lips imprint the swinging air
That parts to let her parts go by   8
One-woman waterfall, she wears
Her slow descent like a long cape
And pausing, on the final stair
Collects her motions into shape.   12

[1961]

✏ Topics for Critical Thinking and Writing

1. To what extent does the poem describe the painting? To what extent does it do something else?
2. Some viewers have found Duchamp's painting strange and confusing. Does Kennedy's poem help you to understand Duchamp's style of art? Explain.

John James Audubon.
American Flamingo (hand-colored print). (Courtesy
William S. Reese)

GREG PAPE

Greg Pape was born in 1947 in Eureka, California, and educated at Fresno State College (now California State University, Fresno) and the University of Arizona. The author of several books of poems, he has served as writer-in-residence at several colleges and universities, and now teaches at Northern Arizona University, in Flagstaff.

American Flamingo

I know he shot them to know them.
I did not know the eyes of the flamingo
are blue, a deep live blue.   3

And the tongue is lined with many small
tongues, thirteen, in the sketch
by Audubon,° to function as a sieve.   6

I knew the long rose-pink neck,
the heavy tricolored down-sweeping bill,
the black primaries.   9

But I did not know the blue eye
drawn so passionately by Audubon
it seems to look out, wary, intense,   12

---

[6]**Audubon** John James Audubon American ornithologist and artist (1785–1851), author of
the multivolume *Birds of America* (1827–38)

from the paper it is printed on.
                    —what
Is man but his passion?   15

asked Robert Penn Warren.° In the background
of this sketch, tenderly subtitled *Old Male,*
beneath the over-draping feathered   18

monument of the body, between the long
flexible neck and the long bony legs
covered with pink plates of flesh,   21

Audubon has given us eight postures,
eight stunning movements in the ongoing
dance of the flamingos.   24

Once at Hialeah° in late afternoon
I watched the satin figures of the jockeys
perched like bright beetles on the backs   27

of horses pounding down the home
stretch, a few crops whipping
the lathering flanks, the loud flat   30

metallic voice of the announcer fading
as the flamingos, grazing the pond water
at the far end of the infield, rose   33

in a feathery blush, only a few feet
off the ground, and flew one long
clipped-winged ritual lap   36

in the heavy Miami light, a great
slow swirl of grace from the old world
that made tickets fall from hands,   39

stilled horses, and drew toasts from the stands
as they settled down again
like a rose-colored fog on the pond.   42

                                                            [1998]

 Topics for Critical Thinking and Writing

1. Why is the speaker preoccupied with the flamingo's eyes?
2. A transition occurs in lines 14–15, with the italicized quotation from Robert Penn Warren. What is the relationship of this to the description of the flamingo (and the speaker's reflections) that precede it?
3. From line 25 to the end, the speaker carefully describes a scene at Hialeah. Take note of the specific details and terms that the speaker presents, and explain how these make the poem both a vivid description and something more than that.

---

[16]**Robert Penn Warren** American poet, novelist, and literary critic (1905–89) [25]**Hialeah** city in southeast Florida, site of Hialeah Park racetrack

Edouard Manet. *Déjeuner sur l'herbe.* 1863. (Oil on canvas, 6'9" × 8'10". Louvre, Paris. Scala/Art Resource, New York)

CARL PHILLIPS

Carl Phillips was born in 1959 in Everett, Washington, and was educated at Harvard and at Boston University. African American, gay, a scholar of classical Greek and Latin, and the author of two books of poetry, he has taught creative writing at Harvard, and he now teaches English and African-American Studies at Washington University in St. Louis.

Luncheon on the Grass

They're a curious lot. Manet's scandalous
lunch partners. The two men, lost
in cant and full dress, their legs sprawled
subway-style, as men's legs invariably are, seem
remarkably unruffled, all but oblivious to their nude   5
female companion. Her nudity is puzzling and
correct; clothes for her are surely only needed
to shrug a shoulder out of. She herself appears
baldly there-for-the-ride; her eyes, moving out
toward the viewer, are wide with the most banal,   10
detached surprise, as if to say, "where's
the *real* party?"

Now, in a comparable state of outdoor
undress, I'm beginning to have a fair idea
of what's going on in that scene. Watching   15
you, in clothes, remove one boot to work your
finger toward an itch in your athletic sock,
I look for any similarities between art
and our afternoon here on abandoned
property. The bather in the painting's   20
background, presumably there for a certain
balance of composition, is for us an ungainly,
rusted green dumpster, rising from overgrown
weeds that provide a contrast only remotely
pastoral. We are two to Manet's main group   25
of three, but the hum of the odd car or truck
on the highway below us offers a transient third.
Like the nude, I don't seem especially hungry,
partly because it's difficult eating naked when
everyone else is clothed, partly because   30
you didn't remember I hate chicken salad.
The beer you opened for me sits untouched,
going flat in the sun. I stroke the wet bottle
fitfully, to remind myself just how far
we've come or more probably have always been   35

from the shape of romance. My dear,
this is not art; we're not anywhere close
to Arcadia.°

                                                            [1993]

Topics for Critical Thinking and Writing

1. The author is openly gay. Does knowledge of his sexual orientation affect the way in which you read the poem? Explain.
2. Do you agree that the speaker and the partner are "not anywhere close / to Arcadia"? Support your response with evidence.

38**Arcadia** an ancient region in Greece, traditionally associated in art and literature with the simple, pastoral life, a Golden Age of unfailing romantic love.

 **JOHN UPDIKE**

John Updike, born in 1932, grew up in Shillington, Pennsylvania, where his father was a teacher and his mother was a writer. After receiving a B.A. degree from Harvard he studied drawing at Oxford for a year, but an offer from The New Yorker *magazine brought him back to the United States. He at first served as a reporter for the magazine, but soon began contributing poetry, essays, and fiction. Today he is one of America's most prolific and well-known writers.*

Before the Mirror

How many of us still remember
when Picasso's "Girl Before a Mirror" hung
at the turning of the stairs in the pre-
expansion Museum of Modern Art?
Millions of us, probably, but we form   5
a dwindling population. Garish
and brush-slashed and yet as balanced
as a cardboard Queen in a deck of giant cards,

the painting proclaimed, "Enter here
and abandon preconception." She bounced   10
the erotic balls of herself back and forth
between reflection and reality.

Now I discover, in the recent re-
trospective at the same establishment,
that the vivid painting dates   15
from March of 1932,
the very month in which I first saw light,
squinting in nostalgia for the womb.
I bend closer, inspecting. The blacks,
the stripy cyanide greens are still uncracked,   20
I note with satisfaction; the cherry reds
and lemon yellows full of childish juice.
No sag, no wrinkle. Fresh as paint. Back then
they knew just how, I reflect, to lay it on.

[1996]

✎ Topics for Critical Thinking and Writing

1. The painting shows a young woman looking into a mirror. In viewing a picture with this subject, what associations might reasonably come to mind?
   Vanity? Mortality? Or what?
2. The woman (at the left) has two faces, one in profile. Do you think Picasso
   is showing us two views of the same face, or perhaps two stages in the
   woman's life? And what of the face in the mirror? Do you think it shows either or both of the faces at the left, or a third face or stage?
3. Why do you suppose the woman is reaching out toward the mirror? (There
   cannot be any way of proving whatever you or anyone else might offer as an
   answer, but *why* do you offer the explanation that you do offer?)
4. What do you think the poem is chiefly about? The distinctiveness of modern
   art (meaning the age of Picasso)? The excellent condition of the picture?
   The speaker's response to the picture? Explain.
5. The first twelve lines of this poem describe the speaker's thoughts "then,"
   when he first saw "Girl Before a Mirror"; the last twelve lines describe his
   ideas and feelings "now." In two paragraphs, or in one extended paragraph,
   write a "Then and Now," describing a picture or a song or a scene—a lake, a
   house, a kitchen—or a person, then and now.

Pieter Brueghel the Elder. *Two Monkeys.* 1562. (Oil on wood. Gemäldegalerie, Berlin/Staaliche Museum, Preussicher Kulturbesitz.)

 **WISLAWA SZYMBORSKA**

Wislawa Szymborska (pronounced "Vislawa Zimborska"), born 1923, is one of Poland's leading poets. Her first book published in 1952, she has published seven later volumes. Some of her work is available in English, in Sounds, Feelings, Thoughts *(1981).*

Brueghel's Two Monkeys*

This is what I see in my dream about final exams:
two monkeys, chained to the floor, sit on the windowsill,
the sky behind them flutters,
the sea is taking its bath.

The exam is History of Mankind.   5
I stammer and hedge.

One monkey stares and listens with mocking disdain,
the other seems to be dreaming away—
but when it's clear I don't know what to say
he prompts me with a gentle   10
clinking of his chain.

[1933]

Topics for Critical Thinking and Writing

1. What do we know, or guess, about the speaker from the poem's first line? Are we willing to listen to him (or her)?
2. We are not likely to be examined on "History of Mankind." Why do you suppose the speaker is being quizzed on it? What does the speaker do? (Paraphrase line 6.)
3. In the third stanza the speaker again does not know what to say. Do we know what the question is? Does the prompting (line 10) help?
4. Write a comment, in prose or verse, on Brueghel's painting.

*Translated, from the Polish, by Stanislaw Baranczak and Clare Cavanagh

A SAMPLE ESSAY

On pages 1180–81, read (preferably aloud) Anne Sexton's "The Starry Night," which was inspired by van Gogh's painting of the same name. Then read the following essay.

Tina Washington

English 10G

November 12, 1998

Two Ways of Looking at a Starry Night

About a hundred years ago Vincent van Gogh looked up into the sky at night and painted what he saw, or what he felt. We know that he was a very religious man, but even if we had not heard this in an art course or read it in a book we would know it from his painting The Starry Night, which shows a glorious heaven, with stars so bright that they all have halos. Furthermore, almost in the lower center of the picture is a church, with its steeple rising above the hills and pointing to the heavens.

Anne Sexton's poem is about this painting, and also (we know from the line she quotes above the poem) about van Gogh's religious vision of the stars. But her poem is not about the heavenly comfort that the starry night offered van Gogh. It is a poem about her wish to die. As I understand the poem, she wants to die in a blaze of light, and to become extinct. She says, in the last line of the poem, that she wants to disappear with "no cry," but this seems to me to be very different from anything van Gogh is saying. His picture is about the glorious heavens, not about himself. Or if it is about himself, it is about how wonderful he feels when he sees God's marvelous creation. Van Gogh is concerned with praising God as God expresses himself in nature; Anne Sexton is concerned with expressing her anguish and with her hope that she can find extinction. Sexton's world is not ruled by a benevolent God but is ruled by an "old unseen serpent." The night is a "rushing beast," presided over by a "great dragon."

Sexton has responded to the painting in a highly unique way. She is not trying to put van Gogh's picture into words that he might approve of. Rather, she has boldly used the picture as a point of departure for her own word-picture.

🖉 Topics for Critical Thinking and Writing

1. Do you agree with Tina Washington's analysis, especially her point about Sexton's poem?
2. Has Washington cited and examined passages from the poem in a convincing way?
3. A general question: Do you think poets are obliged to be faithful to the paintings that they write about, or do poets enjoy the freedom—a kind of poetic license—to interpret a painting just as they choose, doing with it whatever the purpose of the poem requires?

Religion and Society

Essays

JILL TWEEDIE

Jill Tweedie (1936–93) was born of an English family in the Middle East. She grew up in England and then lived ten years in Canada before returning to England. The author of a novel and of books of essays (some of the essays have been collected under the title It's Only Me*), she also wrote articles for the* Guardian.

God the Mother Rules—OK?

Recently I read a snippet about women in the United States who were altering prayers and hymns by substituting Her for Him, Mother for Father and Goddess for God. Oh ho ho, did you ever, sniggered the writer. Put them in straitjackets and take them off to the funny farm.

One of the continuing small surprises for the enquiring atheist is the widespread ignorance of believers about their belief. A viewpoint peculiarly limited—parochial is, I suppose, the *mot juste*.[1] Is it wildly unfair to say that if you picked the first avowed Christian off any pew and set him the religious equivalent of the 11-plus,[2] he would fail?

The one I picked was quite hot on the Church version of Jesus's life: who he was born to, where he was born, how he died and where he died, though in between was a bit of a blank, apart from a vague image of white robes, long hair, sheep and children. He knew about Judas and he listed three miracles, including the resurrection, but he didn't know the number of apostles and only remembered five of their names. As to any historical realities of the time, nothing. The Sadducees, the Philistines, the Pharisees and the Samaritans were simply emotive words, the Old Testament an almost complete blank other than the bit about Moses in the cradle and parting the Red Sea. Nor had he any idea at all about the beliefs of the Jews (except that they killed Jesus, of course), the Buddhists, Islam, Taoism, Shintoism, Hinduism or any other ism. Religions that preceded

[1]exact word (French)   [2]school examination

Christianity? The Greeks had a lot of different gods and the Indians (Red) had the totem pole.

Indeed, without wishing to be unduly critical, my experience even of those who have taken up religion fulltime, priests and vicars, monks and nuns, is that though they may have a detailed knowledge of the mystical side of things, the mysteries, the ritual, the dogma, they are almost as ignorant as my random sample of historical realities. Which is, of course, not entirely accidental. Historical realities and, worse, historical perspectives, have a frightening way of shedding light and reason on corners that, to the believer, are best left dark.

5   That reporter from the States automatically assumed that his readers would join him in his titters at the absurdity of women who, not content with equal rights, are now pretending God could be female. He has, like most of us, the comforting idea that history started yesterday and will stay that way for ever. Because God and God's son are male today, so they always were and always will be, amen.

Brother, you couldn't be wronger. Slowly but surely a vast and ancient international jig-saw is being pieced together: antique temples here, swollen statues there, papyri drawings, carvings and writings from all over. And already the puzzle, half-finished though it is, is as exciting and significant as would be the revelation of a mother to a child who supposed itself an orphan from birth. Because it appears increasingly certain that a male God is an *arriviste,* a mere *nouveau riche*[3] upon the contemporary scene. Before Him, for literally thousands of years, disappearing back into the trackless wastes of pre-history, the people of the world shared one central figure of worship. A She, a Her, a Mother. The Goddess.

Merlin Stone, sculptor and art historian, has spent over 10 years on the trail of the Goddess and the results of her detective work in museums and ancient sites in the Near and Middle East have been published in *The Paradise Papers.* It makes a beautiful whole of many scattered clues until now undiscovered, ignored, misinterpreted, or—shamefully often—unacknowledged; an anthology of archaeological material that fairly bellows Ms Stone's central thesis. The impulse to worship came from the mystery of birth and the performer of that mystery, apparently entirely on her own, was woman.

So the explanation of a Goddess, the original Mother of humanity, came about as naturally and, when you think about it, as obviously as all the other apparent miracles of life and the Goddess was made manifest in the millions of statues, large and small, of big-bellied women. Statues we all know about and we have all been encouraged to dismiss as unimportant, mere fertility symbols, evidence only of cults, of strange rites practised in corners by heretics instead of what they surely are—endless variations of the same central belief held by many peoples over anything up to 25,000 years.

The face behind the clouds is a woman's face, women are her chosen priestesses and handmaidens and unto women shall go all kinship lines and rights of inheritance. Call her Ishtar in Babylon, Ashtoreth in Israel, Astarte in Phoenicia, Athar in Syria or Ate in Cicilia, call her what you will in the Mediterranean, the Near or the Middle East, even in old Ireland—by any other name she is the Goddess, the Queen of Heaven.

10   Ms Stone opines that the core of all theological thought is the quest for the ultimate source of life and ancestry worship occurs (and occurred) among tribal

[3]upstart . . . one who has lately become rich (French)

people the world over. Add that fact to the observations of anthropologists like Margaret Mead and James Frazer—that in the most ancient human societies coitus was not linked with reproduction—and you have woman the life-giver, the sex that gives birth.

What, then, more logical than to posit a First Ancestress in the sky? Robertson Smith, writing of the precedence of the female deity among the Arab and Hebrew peoples, says: "It was the mother's, not the father's, blood which formed the original bond of kinship among the Semites as among other early people and in this stage of society, if the tribal deity was thought of as the parent of the stock, a goddess, not a god, would necessarily have been the object of worship."

How did women fare when the Goddess reigned in their lands? Merlin Stone brings together the researches of many archaeologists and anthropologists to find out and the answer is as predictable as it is revealing of the purpose of religion. If you have a God in heaven, men rule on earth. If you have a Goddess, women take charge. Diodorus of Sicily, observant traveller BC, reported that the ladies of Ethiopia carried arms, practised communal marriage and raised their children communally. Of the warrior women in Libya he says: "All authority was vested in the woman, who discharged every kind of public duty. The men looked after domestic affairs and did as they were told by their wives.

"They were not allowed to undertake war service or to exercise any functions of government or to fill any public office, such as might have given them more spirit to set themselves up against the women. The children were handed over immediately after birth to the men." Are you listening, Colonel Gaddafi?

Professor Cyrus Gordon, writing of life in ancient Egypt, says: "In family life women had a peculiarly important position for inheritance passed through the mother . . . this system may well hark back to prehistoric times when only the obvious relationship between mother and child was recognized." The message is as clear and as apposite today as ever. Though you gain power through error (the misunderstanding about the father's part in reproduction), once the system is working for you (matrilineal descent) you can hang on for a very long time in the face of the most damning facts. Patriarchal gods know all about this, too.

15   Mind you, in spite of probable male suppression under a goddess, there is a plethora of evidence that the goddess made it well worth their while and that under her sexually permissive reign there were more tempting compensations for being a mere man than ever there were for a mere woman in a god's world. Subjugation, says the God, is your punishment. Subjugation, said the Goddess, can be fun. Because one thing is certain. It took eons of bloody struggle to put the Goddess down. They came out of the northern countries, those eventual victors, migrating in waves over perhaps a thousand, even three thousand years, to the lands of the Goddess, armed with their God and the realization that power for men could only come when a man knew his own son. And how could a man know his own son? By caging women, by making her male property, by scaring her into believing that all hell would break loose if *she* did, that only by cleaving to one man from virginity to death could she hope to save her soul by a male God's intervention.

So battle commenced, fought as much against the desires of many men as against the sexual freedom of women. All over the territories of the Goddess are the myths that mark the traces of that battle. For years I have wondered at the stories of men fighting dragons—what did a dragon represent, what was its factual origin? Merlin Stone drops in another piece of the puzzle. The snake (serpent, dragon) was the widespread Goddess symbol and the living companion of her priestesses. So what was St. George doing, fighting his dragon? He was the new religion fighting the old, the male squaring off with the female, an historical reality told in snake/man struggles in hundreds of nations and tribes from India to Turkey, from Babylon to Assyria, from Ireland to Israel and Jehovah's battle with the serpent Leviathan.

"But it was upon the last assaults by the Hebrews and eventually by the Christians of the first centuries after Christ that the religion was finally suppressed and nearly forgotten," says Merlin Stone. The struggle rages still in the pages of the Bible, pages that as a girl amazed and fascinated me, with their constant emphasis on whores: whores of Babylon, whores of Sodom and Gomorrah, whores like Lilith and Jezebel, painted whores to be spurned by the sons and daughters of Israel. I had thought it then a sort of kink, a kind of mental aberration common to Jews and Christians. Not at all. The truth is far more tangible. The whore was the Garden, the old religion. The sin—adherence to the old religion. The real sin—ignorance of paternity, female promiscuity.

And that whole battle, so bitterly fought over so many years, produced as its apogee the fable of the Garden of Eden. There is the serpent, creature of the Goddess, of the old religion. There is Eve, the woman, handmaiden to the Goddess and traitress at the heart of the new religion, potentially promiscuous and, therefore, potentially the underminer of male power, of patrilineal descent. She must be warned, threatened, terrified in order to save Adam from the temptations of the Goddess. If she will not accept a male God and reject the Goddess, if she will not accept one man and one man only, all her life, she will be thrown out of Paradise and bear her children in agony.

It is all there in *The Paradise Papers* and, for me at least, Merlin Stone crystallizes what has all along been obvious, however submerged. Even today, in the dour Protestant religions, the last lingering trace of the Goddess (Mary, carefully a virgin) is hardly allowed to surface. The Catholics, always more opportunist, gave Mary her place in the sun but exacted from the ordinary women a terrible price for this concession.

20   Yesterday, I thought the leaders of all contemporary religions a blind and prejudiced lot for their refusal to allow women any more power within their churches than the arrangement of flowers upon the altars. Now I know they are simply afraid, afraid that the Goddess may return from her long exile and take over again, and that is curiously comforting, an explanation from weakness rather than strength.

This, then, was the original battle of the sexes. A Goddess reigned for thousands of years, a God for two thousand. Shall we soon, perhaps, learn to do without either?

[1976]

Topics for Critical Thinking and Writing

1. In paragraph 3 Tweedie ridicules a Christian who didn't know the number of the apostles and could name only five. If you are a Christian, could you pass Tweedie's test? If you are a Christian and couldn't pass, would you agree that you are deficient in essential knowledge of the faith—or, on the other hand, would you argue that her test is invalid? (If you are a member of some faith other than Christianity, apply a comparable test to yourself.)

2. Drawing on the writing of Merlin Stone, in paragraph 7 Tweedie asserts that "the impulse to worship came from the mystery of birth and the performer

of that mystery, apparently entirely on her own, was woman." Given the rest of Tweedie's essay, in an essay of 500 words explain why you are willing or not willing to accept this assertion.

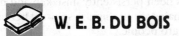 ## W. E. B. DU BOIS

W. E. B. Du Bois (1868–1963) was born in Massachusetts, where he seems to have had a relatively happy early childhood—though in grade school he was shocked to learn that his classmates considered him different because of his color. In 1885 he went to Fisk University in Nashville, Tennessee, and then, for doctoral work, to Harvard University, where be studied history, and to the University of Berlin, where he studied sociology. His doctoral dissertation, The Suppression of the Slave Trade in the United States of America, *was published in* Harvard Historical Studies *in 1896.*

Although Du Bois had embarked on a scholarly career, he became increasingly concerned with the injustices of contemporary society, and his writings were now directed at a general public. In 1903 he published The Souls of Black Folk, *a book challenging Booker T. Washington's more resigned position. From 1910 to the mid-1930s he edited* The Crisis, *the journal of the National Association for the Advancement of Colored People; although he energetically solicited the writings of other people, he wrote so many essays for the journal that he can almost be said to be its author as well as its editor. Eventually Du Bois joined the Communist Party, and in 1963 he left the United States for Ghana, where he died.*

We reprint part of chapter 14 from The Souls of Black Folk.

Of the Sorrow Songs

I walk through the churchyard
To lay this body down;
I know moon-rise, I know star-rise;
I walk in the moonlight, I walk in the starlight;
I'll lie in the grave and stretch out my arms,
I'll go to judgment in the evening of the day,
And my soul and thy soul shall meet that day,
When I lay this body down.

—*Negro Song*

They that walked in darkness sang songs in the olden days—Sorrow Songs—for they were weary at heart. And so before each thought that I have written in this book I have set a phrase, a haunting echo of these weird old songs in which the soul of the black slave spoke to men. Ever since I was a child these songs have stirred me strangely. They came out of the South unknown to me, one by one, and yet at once I knew them as of me and of mine. Then in after years when I came to Nashville I saw the great temple builded of these songs towering over the pale city. To me Jubilee Hall seemed ever made of the songs themselves, and its bricks were red with the blood and dust of toil. Out of them rose for me morning, noon, and night, bursts of wonderful melody, full of the voices of my brothers and sisters, full of the voices of the past.

Little of beauty has America given the world save the rude grandeur God himself stamped on her bosom; the human spirit in this new world has expressed itself in vigor and ingenuity rather than in beauty. And so by fateful chance the Negro folk-song—the rhythmic cry of the slave—stands today not simply as the sole American music, but as the most beautiful expression of human experience born this side of the seas. It has been neglected, it has been, and is, half despised, and above all it has been persistently mistaken and misunderstood; but notwithstanding, it still remains as the singular spiritual heritage of the nation and the greatest gift of the Negro people.

Away back in the thirties the melody of these slave songs stirred the nation, but the songs were soon half forgotten. Some, like "Near the lake where dropped the willow," passed into current airs and their source was forgotten; others were caricatured on the "minstrel" stage and their memory died away. Then in war-time came the singular Port Royal experiment after the capture of Hilton Head, and perhaps for the first time the North met the Southern slave face to face and heart to heart with no third witness. The Sea Islands of the Carolinas, where they met, were filled with a black folk of primitive type, touched and moulded less by the world about them than any others outside the Black Belt. Their appearance was uncouth, their language funny, but their hearts were human and their singing stirred men with a mighty power. Thomas Wentworth Higginson hastened to tell of these songs, and Miss McKim and others urged upon the world their rare beauty. But the world listened only half credulously until the Fisk Jubilee Singers sang the slave songs so deeply into the world's heart that it can never wholly forget them again.

There was once a blacksmith's son born at Cadiz, New York, who in the changes of time taught school in Ohio and helped defend Cincinnati from Kirby Smith. Then he fought at Chancellorsville and Gettysburg and finally served in the Freedman's Bureau at Nashville. Here he formed a Sunday-school class of black children in 1866, and sang with them and taught them to sing. And then they taught him to sing, and when once the glory of the Jubilee songs passed into the soul of George L. White, he knew his life-work was to let those Negroes sing to the world as they had sung to him. So in 1871 the pilgrimage of the Fisk Jubilee Singers began. North to Cincinnati they rode,— four half-clothed black boys and five girl-women,—led by a man with a cause and a purpose. They stopped at Wilberforce, the oldest of Negro schools, where a black bishop blessed them. Then they went, fighting cold and starvation, shut out of hotels, and cheerfully sneered at, ever northward; and ever the magic of their song kept thrilling hearts, until a burst of applause in the Congregational Council at Oberlin revealed them to the world. They came to New York and Henry Ward Beecher dared to welcome them, even though the metropolitan dailies sneered at his "Nigger Minstrels." So their songs conquered till they sang across the land and across the sea, before Queen and Kaiser, in Scotland and Ireland, Holland and Switzerland. Seven years they sang, and brought back a hundred and fifty thousand dollars to found Fisk University. . . .

5   The words that are left to us are not without interest, and, cleared of evident dross, they conceal much of real poetry and meaning beneath conventional theology and unmeaning rhapsody. Like all primitive folk, the slave stood near to Nature's heart. Life was a "rough and rolling sea" like the brown Atlantic of the Sea Islands; the "Wilderness" was the home of God, and the "lonesome valley" led to the way of life. "Winter'll soon be over" was the picture of life and death to a tropical imagination. The sudden wild thunder-storms of the South awed and impressed the Negroes,—at times the rumbling seemed to them "mournful," at times imperious:

"My Lord calls me,
He calls me by the thunder,
The trumpet sounds it in my soul."

The monotonous toil and exposure is painted in many words. One sees the ploughmen in the hot, moist furrow, singing:

"Dere's no rain to wet you,
Dere's no sun to burn you,
Oh, push along, believer,
I want to go home."

The bowed and bent old man cries, with thrice-repeated wail:

"O Lord, keep me from sinking down,"

and he rebukes the devil of doubt who can whisper:

"Jesus is dead and God's gone away."

Yet the soul-hunger is there, the restlessness of the savage, the wail of the wanderer, and the plaint is put in one little phrase:

"My soul wants something that's new, that's new."

Of death the Negro showed little fear, but talked of it familiarly and even fondly as simply a crossing of the waters, perhaps—who knows?—back to his ancient forests again. Later days transfigured his fatalism, and amid the dust and dirt the toiler sang:

"Dust, dust and ashes, fly over my grave,
But the Lord shall bear my spirit home."

The things evidently borrowed from the surrounding world undergo characteristic change when they enter the mouth of the slave. Especially is this true of Bible phrases. "Weep, O captive daughter of Zion," is quaintly turned into "Zion, weep-a-low," and the wheels of Ezekiel are turned every way in the mystic dreaming of the slave, till he says:

"There's a little wheel a-turnin' in-a-my heart."

10   As in olden time, the words of these hymns were improvised by some leading minstrel of the religious band. The circumstances of the gathering, however, the rhythm of the songs, and the limitations of allowable thought, confined the poetry for the most part to single or double lines, and they seldom were expanded to quatrains or longer tales, although there are some few examples of sustained efforts, chiefly paraphrases of the Bible. Three short series of verses have always attracted me,—the one that heads this chapter, of one line of which Thomas Wentworth Higginson has fittingly said, "Never, it seems to me, since man first lived and suffered was his infinite longing for peace uttered more plaintively." The second and third are descriptions of the Last Judgment,—the one a late improvisation, with some traces of outside influence:

"Oh, the stars in the elements are falling,
And the moon drips away into blood,
And the ransomed of the Lord are returning unto God,
Blessed be the name of the Lord."

And the other earlier and homelier picture from the low coast lands:

"Michael, haul the boat ashore,
Then you'll hear the horn they blow,
Then you'll hear the trumpet sound,
Trumpet sound the world around,
Trumpet sound for rich and poor,
Trumpet sound for Jubilee,
Trumpet sound for you and me."

Through all the sorrow of the Sorrow Songs there breathes a hope—a faith in the ultimate justice of things. The minor cadences of despair change often to triumph and calm confidence. Sometimes it is faith in life, sometimes a faith in death, sometimes assurance of boundless justice in some fair world beyond. But whichever it is, the meaning is always clear: that sometime, somewhere, men will judge men by their souls and not by their skins. Is such a hope justified? Do the Sorrow Songs sing true?

The silently growing assumption of this age is that the probation of races is past, and that the backward races of today are of proven inefficiency and not worth the saving. Such an assumption is the arrogance of peoples irreverent toward Time and ignorant of the deeds of men. A thousand years ago such an assumption, easily possible, would have made it difficult for the Teuton to prove his right to life. Two thousand years ago such dogmatism, readily welcome, would have scouted the idea of blond races ever leading civilization. So woefully unorganized is sociological knowledge that the meaning of progress, the meaning of "swift" and "slow" in human doing, and the limits of human perfectability, are veiled, unanswered sphinxes on the shores of science. Why should Aeschylus have sung two thousand years before Shakespeare was born? Why has civilization flourished in Europe, and flickered, flamed, and died in Africa? So long as the world stands meekly dumb before such questions, shall this nation proclaim its ignorance and unhallowed prejudices by denying freedom of opportunity to those who brought the Sorrow Songs to the Seats of the Mighty?

Your country? How came it yours? Before the Pilgrims landed we were here. Here we have brought our three gifts and mingled them with yours: a gift of story and song—soft, stirring melody in an ill-harmonized and unmelodious land; the gift of sweat and brawn to beat back the wilderness, conquer the soil, and lay the foundations of this vast economic empire two hundred years earlier than your weak hands could have done it; the third, a gift of the Spirit. Around us the history of the land has centred for thrice a hundred years; out of the nation's heart we have called all that was best to throttle and subdue all that was worst; fire and blood, prayer and sacrifice, have billowed over this people, and they have found peace only in the altars of the God of Right. Nor has our gift of the Spirit been merely passive. Actively we have woven ourselves with the very warp and woof of this nation,—we fought their battles, shared their sorrow, mingled our blood with theirs, and generation after generation have pleaded with a headstrong, careless people to despise not Justice, Mercy, and Truth, lest the nation be smitten with a curse. Our song, our toil, our cheer, and warning have been given to this nation in blood-brotherhood. Are not these gifts worth the giving? Is not this work and striving? Would America have been America without her Negro people?

Even so is the hope that sang in the songs of my fathers well sung. If some-where in this whirl and chaos of things there dwells Eternal Good, pitiful yet masterful, then anon in His good time America shall rend the Veil and the pris-oned shall be free. Free, free as the sunshine trickling down the morning into these high windows of mine, free as yonder fresh young voices welling up to me from the caverns of brick and mortar below—welling with song, instinct with life, tremulous treble and darkening bass. My children, my little children, are singing to the sunshine, and thus they sing:

> "Let us cheer the weary traveller,
> Cheer the weary traveller,
> Let us cheer the weary traveller
> Along the heavenly way.'

15   And the traveller girds himself, and sets his face toward the Morning, and goes his way.

[1903]

Topics for Critical Thinking and Writing

1. Du Bois uses some terms that may disconcert a reader, such as "primitive folk" and "backward races." Look especially closely at the passages in which these terms occur, and then summarize Du Bois's view of the African Amer-icans of his time. Look closely, too, at passages in which he discusses whites' attitudes toward African Americans, and summarize his views of these whites also.
2. Read the spirituals on pages 1263–66, or, better, hear a performance of spir-ituals. To what extent, if any, has Du Bois helped you to understand and enjoy these works?
3. Alain Locke (1886–1954), African-American educator and literary critic and historian, in *The Negro and His Music,* says this of the spirituals:

   > Over-emphasize the melodic elements of a spiritual, and you get a senti-mental ballad à la Stephen Foster. Stress the harmony and you get a cloying glee or "barber-shop" chorus. Over-emphasize, on the other hand, the rhythmic idiom and instantly you secularize the product and it becomes a syncopated shout, with the religious tone and mood completely evapo-rated.

   If you are familiar with performances of spirituals, test the performances against Locke's words—or test Locke's words against the performances.

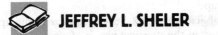

JEFFREY L. SHELER

In the following article, Sheler writes that recent scientific discoveries suggest to some scientists that there is a "grand design" to the universe; further, "modern science has provided a new language and a new set of symbols for believers to more easily imagine

God and eternity." The essay was published in 1997, just before Easter, in U.S. News and World Report.

Heaven in the Age of Reason

Easter at its essence is about a belief in the triumph of life over death. It is one faith's response to the mystery that has haunted humankind since our first contemplative ancestors gazed into the abyss of death and trembled. What, if anything, awaits beyond the grave?

As Christians celebrate the Resurrection this holy season, they will affirm their faith that Jesus Christ arose from the dead and, in doing so, made "life everlasting" a possibility for all. "We are born," says Andrew Greeley, a Roman Catholic priest and University of Chicago sociologist, "with two incurable diseases: life, from which we die, and hope, which says maybe death isn't the end." To hope for life in the hereafter is a part of human nature.

All of this will strike some—as it did Sigmund Freud, Karl Marx, and other noted critics of religion—as wishful, largely superstitious thinking that does little more than sap human creativity and divert attention from earthly misery. It is easy to dismiss belief in the afterlife as a relic of ancient cultures that believed in a celestial city above the clouds and a fiery subterranean hell.

counter for allow for difference of opinion

But to many modern believers, those old ideas are still vital, even if less vivid. While the notion of life after death has roots in ancient Greek philosophy and corollaries in other religions, the primary window on the afterlife for many Christians and Jews remains the Bible. The scriptures present an evolving picture with few concrete details, giving believers broad imaginative license.

5   **Not for human souls.** The Old Testament portrays heaven as a celestial sphere "above the vault of the earth" from which God, surrounded by his angels, rules his creation. But there is no suggestion in the most ancient Hebrew texts that heaven is the final repository of human souls. Throughout most of the Old Testament, deceased humans, good and evil, were said to end up in Sheol, a gloomy netherworld separated from God, much like the Hades of Greek mythology. Only in later Judaism did belief in a final resurrection of the dead and a heavenly "world to come" appear.

In the New Testament, Jesus spoke of the "kingdom of heaven" as a place of eternal reward with "many dwelling places." He tells his followers in the Gospel According to John:

> I go to prepare a place for you, and if I go to prepare a place for you I will come again, and receive you to myself; that where I am there you may be also.

The apostle Paul assured believers that a "house not made with hands, eternal in the heavens" awaited them. Writing to Christians in Corinth, Paul even refers to his own mystical journey into "the third heaven" where he "heard inexpressible words, which a man is not permitted to speak." But he gives no visual description of the heavenly landscape.

The most vivid and familiar biblical images of heaven appear in the apocalyptic book of Revelation. It is there, in the mystical vision of a prophet named John, that we find the often popularized descriptions of pearly gates and streets of gold, of a vast white throne, and of throngs of saints and angels gathered around God at the culmination of history. But the meaning and significance of those images are widely debated and often misunderstood. The picture of the end times in the book of Revelation, says N. T. Wright, dean of the Anglican cathedral in Lichfield, Staffordshire, England, "isn't about humans being snatched up from earth to heaven." Rather, he writes in a recent issue of the *Christian Century,* "the holy city, new Jerusalem, comes down from heaven to earth. God's space and ours are finally married, integrated at last." That, says Wright, is what Christians pray for when they say "thy kingdom come" in the Lord's Prayer.

Christian theologians traditionally have viewed Revelation as a glimpse not just into heaven but into future events, Judgment Day, and the end of the present world. Some scholars, on the other hand, contend it is more properly understood as "resistance literature" intended to exhort first-century Christians living in Asia Minor to "stand firm in the faith" against the threat of Roman persecution. Even so, the evocative imagery of Revelation continues to have a powerful influence on Christian views of the afterlife.

Should believers expect to see alabaster houses and gold-paved streets in heaven? Biblical scholars treat those images as vibrantly metaphorical. They illustrate what theologians regard as perhaps most important to understand about the Judeo-Christian concept of heaven: It means dwelling forever in the presence of God. Without the specific imagery of houses and gates and city streets, says Martin Marty, a University of Chicago religion historian, "we have no way of imagining what it's like being with God" in the hereafter.

10   **Scientific faith.** Strikingly, nearly 80 percent of Americans—of various religious faiths and of none—say they believe in life after death, and two thirds are certain there is a heaven. This may be explained by the religious nature of society today. By almost every measure, the United States is a nation steeped in religion, more so than all other Western nations except Poland and Ireland.

Yet this religious pitch occurs in an epoch of science. We can understand the anguished hope of those among us who, in the midst of pain, grief, or oppression, find solace in anticipating a better shake in the next life. But in an age of cloning and quantum physics, of supercomputers and the Hubble Space Telescope, some might reasonably wonder how "normal," educated people can cling to such archaic beliefs.

Despite the apparent contradiction, during the past half century science has moved from a dogmatic denial of realities beyond its reach toward an appreciation of their possibility. Dialogue between scientists and theologians has become increasingly common. Dozens of organizations worldwide now provide forums for exchanges of religious and scientific views on issues ranging from cosmology to the environment. From Albert Einstein to Stephen Hawking, scientists have grown more comfortable in using the word "God" in pondering questions of meaning and order.

New scientific revelations about supernovas, black holes, quarks, and the big bang even suggest to some scientists that there is a "grand design" in the universe—an argument that theologians like Augustine and Thomas Aquinas advanced centuries ago. The presence of intelligent, self-aware beings in the universe, writes Australian physicist Paul Davies in his 1992 book, *The Mind of God,* "can be no trivial detail, no minor byproduct of mindless, purposeless forces. We are truly meant to be here." Were scientists to discover a long-sought "theory of everything" to explain the workings of the varying mechanisms of the universe, wrote Hawking in his 1988 book, *A Brief History of Time,* "we would truly know the mind of God."

Perhaps as important, modern science has provided a new language and a new set of symbols for believers to more easily imagine God and eternity. Einstein's theory of relativity, which challenged the Newtonian view of absolute time operating everywhere in the universe, suddenly added a new level of meaning to the biblical injunction that "with the Lord, one day is as a thousand years."

15   Speculation in science about such things as parallel universes, new dimensions, and anomalies in the time-space continuum, even if not fully understood by laymen, has provided a conceptual framework for thinking about heaven and post-mortem existence in ways that were not available 100 or even 50 years ago. "We are no longer forced to choose between believing either that heaven is a city in the sky somewhere or that it doesn't exist at all," explains Richard McBrien, a theology professor at the University of Notre Dame. "Now we can think of heaven as an alternate state, perhaps as another dimension." While such imagery is unlikely to foster belief where none exists, says McBrien, "it expands the options for those who are at least open to the possibility" of life after death.

In a society where science and religion flourish side by side, then, remaining open to the idea of the afterlife seems a reasonable posture. Science can't prove the existence of heaven, but its findings have made it easier for some people to believe. While the Christian creed asks adherents to affirm "life everlasting," it requires no assent to the speculative details. It's possible to adhere to the "hope of heaven" and be agnostic about the particulars.

In his book *Teaching Your Children About God,* Rabbi David Wolpe, a professor at the Jewish Theological Seminary of America, recalls an ancient Jewish parable about twin fetuses lying together in the womb. One believes that there is a world beyond the womb, "where people walk upright, where there are mountains and oceans, a sky filled with stars. The other can barely contain his contempt for such foolish ideas."

Suddenly the "believer" is forced through the birth canal leaving behind the only way of life he has known. The remaining fetus is saddened, convinced that a great catastrophe has befallen his companion. "Outside the womb, however, the parents are rejoicing. For what the remaining brother, left behind, has just witnessed is not death but birth." This, Wolpe reminds us, is a classic view of the afterlife—a birth into a world that we on Earth can only try to imagine.

[1997]

 Topics for Critical Thinking and Writing

1. If you are familiar with the view of an afterlife in some religion other than Christianity, set it forth in an essay of 250–500 words. Your imagined readers are your classmates. In your essay indicate whether any of Sheler's comments are relevant also to your topic.

2. In an essay of 500 words set forth your own view of the afterlife. You may, as a writing strategy, think of your essay as a companion piece to Sheler's. That is, you may want to summarize his essay very briefly, show how your view conforms to or departs from his, and explain why.

FICTION

 NATHANIEL HAWTHORNE

Nathaniel Hawthorne (1804–64) was born in Salem, Massachusetts, the son of a sea captain. Two of his ancestors were judges; one had persecuted Quakers, and another had served at the Salem witch trials. After graduating from Bowdoin College in Maine he went back to Salem in order to write in relative seclusion. In 1832 he published "Roger Malvin's Burial" (p. 103), and in 1835 he published "Young Goodman Brown."

From 1839 to 1841 Hawthorne worked in the Boston Customs House and then spent a few months as a member of a communal society, Brook Farm. In 1842 he married. From 1846 to 1849 he was a surveyor at the Salem Customs House; from 1849 to 1850 he wrote The Scarlet Letter, *the book that made him famous. From 1853 to 1857 he served as American consul in Liverpool, England, a plum awarded him in exchange for writing a campaign biography of a former college classmate, President Franklin Pierce. In 1860, after living in England and Italy, he returned to the United States, settling in Concord, Massachusetts.*

In his stories and novels Hawthorne keeps returning to the Puritan past, studying guilt, sin, and isolation.

Young Goodman Brown

Young Goodman Brown came forth at sunset into the street at Salem village; but put his head back, after crossing the threshold, to exchange a parting kiss with his young wife. And Faith, as the wife was aptly named, thrust her own pretty head into the street, letting the wind play with the pink ribbons of her cap while she called to Goodman Brown.

"Dearest heart," whispered she, softly and rather sadly, when her lips were close to his ear, "prithee put off your journey until sunrise and sleep in your own bed to-night. A lone woman is troubled with such dreams and such thoughts that she's afeared of herself sometimes. Pray tarry with me this night, dear husband, of all nights in the year."

"My love and my Faith," replied young Goodman Brown, "of all nights in the year, this one night must I tarry away from thee. My journey, as thou callest it, forth and back again, must needs be done 'twixt now and sunrise. What, my sweet, pretty wife, dost thou doubt me already, and we but three months married?"

"Then God bless you!" said Faith, with the pink ribbons; "and may you find all well when you come back."

5   "Amen!" cried Goodman Brown. "Say thy prayers, dear Faith, and go to bed at dusk, and no harm will come to thee."

So they parted; and the young man pursued his way until, being about to turn the corner by the meeting-house, he looked back and saw the head of Faith still peeping after him with a melancholy air, in spite of her pink ribbons.

"Poor little Faith!" thought he, for his heart smote him. "What a wretch am I to leave her on such an errand! She talks of dreams, too. Methought as she spoke there was trouble in her face, as if a dream had warned her what work is to be done to-night. But no, no; 'twould kill her to think it. Well, she's a blessed angel on earth; and after this one night I'll cling to her skirts and follow her to heaven."

With this excellent resolve for the future, Goodman Brown felt himself justified in making more haste on his present evil purpose. He had taken a dreary road, darkened by all the gloomiest trees of the forest, which barely stood aside to let the narrow path creep through, and closed immediately behind. It was all as lonely as could be; and there is this peculiarity in such a solitude, that the traveler knows not who may be concealed by the innumerable trunks and the thick boughs overhead; so that with lonely footsteps he may yet be passing through an unseen multitude.

"There may be a devilish Indian behind every tree," said Goodman Brown to himself; and he glanced fearfully behind him as he added, "What if the devil himself should be at my very elbow!"

10   His head being turned back, he passed a crook of the road, and, looking forward again, beheld the figure of a man, in grave and decent attire, seated at the foot of an old tree. He arose at Goodman Brown's approach and walked onward side by side with him.

"You are late, Goodman Brown," said he. "The clock of the Old South was striking as I came through Boston, and that is full fifteen minutes agone."

"Faith kept me back a while," replied the young man, with a tremor in his voice, caused by the sudden appearance of his companion, though not wholly unexpected.

It was now deep dusk in the forest, and deepest in that part of it where these two were journeying. As nearly as could be discerned, the second traveller was about fifty years old, apparently in the same rank of life as Goodman Brown, and bearing a considerable resemblance to him, though perhaps more in expression than features. Still they might have been taken for father and son. And yet, though the elder person was as simply clad as the younger, and as simple in manner too, he had an indescribable air of one who knew the world, and who would not have felt abashed at the governor's dinner table or in King William's court, were it possible that his affairs should call him thither. But the only thing about him that could be fixed upon as remarkable was his staff, which bore the likeness of a great black snake, so curiously wrought that it might almost be seen to twist and wriggle itself like a living serpent. This, of course, must have been an ocular deception, assisted by the uncertain light.

"Come, Goodman Brown," cried his fellow-traveller, "this is a dull pace for the beginning of a journey. Take my staff, if you are so soon weary."

15   "Friend," said the other, exchanging his slow pace for a full stop, "Having kept covenant by meeting thee here, it is my purpose now to return whence I came. I have scruples touching the matter thou wot'st of."

"Sayest thou so?" replied he of the serpent, smiling apart. "Let us walk on, nevertheless, reasoning as we go; and if I convince thee not thou shalt turn back. We are but a little way in the forest yet."

"Too far! too far!" exclaimed the goodman, unconsciously resuming his walk. "My father never went into the woods on such an errand, not his father before him. We have been a race of honest men and good Christians since the days of the martyrs; and shall I be the first of the name of Brown that ever took this path and kept—"

"Such company, thou wouldst say," observed the elder person, interpreting his pause. "Well said, Goodman Brown! I have been as well acquainted with your family as with ever a one among the Puritans; and that's no trifle to say. I helped your grandfather, the constable, when he lashed the Quaker woman so smartly through the streets of Salem; and it was I that brought your father a pitch-pine knot, kindled at my own hearth, to set fire to an Indian village, in King Philip's war. They were my good friends, both; and many a pleasant walk have we had along this path, and returned merrily after midnight. I would fain be friends with you for their sake."

"If it be as thou sayest," replied Goodman Brown, "I marvel they never spoke of these matters; or, verily, I marvel not, seeing that the least rumor of the sort would have driven them from New England. We are a people of prayer, and good works to boot, and abide no such wickedness."

20   "Wickedness or not," said the traveller with the twisted staff, "I have a very general acquaintance here in New England. The deacons of many a church have drunk the communion wine with me; the selectmen of divers towns make me their chairman; and a majority of the Great and General Court are firm support-ers of my interest. The governor and I, too—But these are state secrets."

"Can this be so?" cried Goodman Brown, with a stare of amazement at his undisturbed companion. "Howbeit, I have nothing to do with the governor and council; they have their own ways, and are no rule for a simple husbandman like me. But, were I to go on with thee, how should I meet the eye of that good old man, our minister, at Salem village? Oh, his voice would make me tremble both Sabbath day and lecture day."

Thus far the elder traveller had listened with due gravity; but now burst into a fit of irrepressible mirth, shaking himself so violently that his snake-like staff ac-tually seemed to wriggle in sympathy.

"Ha! ha! ha!" shouted he again and again; then composing himself, "Well, go on, Goodman Brown, go on; but, prithee, don't kill me with laughing."

"Well, then, to end the matter at once," said Goodman Brown, considerably nettled, "there is my wife, Faith. It would break her dear little heart; and I'd rather break my own."

25   "Nay, if that be the case," answered the other, "e'en go thy ways, Goodman Brown. I would not for twenty old women like the one hobbling before us that Faith should come to any harm."

As he spoke he pointed his staff at a female figure on the path, in whom Goodman Brown recognized a very pious and exemplary dame, who had taught him his catechism in youth, and was still his moral and spiritual adviser, jointly with the minister and Deacon Gookin.

"A marvel, truly, that Goody Cloyse should be so far in the wilderness at nightfall," said he. "But with your leave, friend, I shall take a cut through the woods until we have left this Christian woman behind. Being a stranger to you, she might ask whom I was consorting with and whither I was going."

"Be it so," said his fellow-traveller. "Betake you the woods, and let me keep the path."

Accordingly the young man turned aside, but took care to watch his com-panion, who advanced softly along the road until he had come within a staff's length of the old dame. She, meanwhile, was making the best of her way, with singular speed for so aged a woman, and mumbling some indistinct words—a prayer, doubtless—as she went. The traveller put forth his staff and touched her withered neck with what seemed the serpent's tail.

30   "The devil!" screamed the pious old lady.

"Then Goody Cloyse knows her old friend?" observed the traveller, con-fronting her and leaning on his writhing stick.

"Ah, forsooth, and is it your worship indeed?" cried the good dame. "Yea, truly is it, and in the very image of my old gossip, Goodman Brown, the grandfather of the silly fellow that now is. But—would your worship believe it?—my broomstick hath strangely disappeared, stolen, as I suspect, by that unhanged witch, Goody Cory, and that, too, when I was all anointed with the juice of smallage, and cinquefoil, and wolf's bane—"

"Mingled with fine wheat and the fat of a new-born babe," said the shape of old Goodman Brown.

"Ah, your worship knows the recipe," cried the old lady, cackling aloud. "So, as I was saying, being all ready for the meeting, and no horse to ride on, I made up my mind to foot it; for they tell me there is a nice young man to be taken into communion to-night. But now your good worship will lend me your arm, and we shall be there in a twinkling."

35   "That can hardly be," answered her friend. "I may not spare you my arm, Goody Cloyse; but here is my staff, if you will."

So saying, he threw it down at her feet, where, perhaps, it assumed life, being one of the rods which its owner had formerly lent to the Egyptian magi. Of this fact, however, Goodman Brown could not take cognizance. He had cast up his eyes in astonishment, and, looking down again, beheld neither Goody Cloyse nor the serpentine staff, but his fellow-traveller alone, who waited for him as calmly as if nothing had happened.

"That old woman taught me my catechism," said the young man; and there was a world of meaning in this simple comment.

They continued to walk onward, while the elder traveller exhorted his companion to make good speed and persevere in the path, discoursing so aptly that his arguments seemed rather to spring up in the bosom of his auditor than to be suggested by himself. As they went, he plucked a branch of maple to serve for a walking stick, and began to strip it of the twigs and the little boughs, which were wet with evening dew. The moment his fingers touched them they became strangely withered and dried up as with a week's sunshine. Thus the pair proceeded, at a good free pace, until suddenly, in a gloomy hollow of the road, Goodman Brown sat himself down on the stump of a tree and refused to go any farther.

"Friend," said he, stubbornly, "my mind is made up. Not another step will I budge on this errand. What if a wretched old woman do choose to go to the devil when I thought she was going to heaven: is that any reason why I should quit my dear Faith and go after her?"

40   "You will think better of this by and by," said his acquaintance, composedly. "Sit here and rest yourself a while; and when you feel like moving again, there is my staff to help you along."

Without more words, he threw his companion the maple stick, and was as speedily out of sight as if he had vanished into the deepening gloom. The young man sat a few moments by the roadside, applauding himself greatly, and thinking with how clear a conscience he should meet the minister in his morning walk, nor shrink from the eye of good old Deacon Gookin. And what calm sleep would be his that very night, which was to have been spent so wickedly, but so purely and sweetly now, in the arms of Faith! Amidst these pleasant and praiseworthy meditations, Goodman Brown heard the tramp of horses along the road, and deemed it advisable to conceal himself within the verge of the forest, conscious of the guilty purpose that had brought him thither, though now so happily turned from it.

On came the hoof tramps and the voices of the riders, two grave old voices, conversing soberly as they drew near. These mingled sounds appeared to pass along the road, within a few yards of the young man's hiding-place; but, owing doubtless to the depth of the gloom at that particular spot, neither the travellers nor their steeds were visible. Though their figures brushed the small boughs by the wayside, it could not be seen that they intercepted, even for a moment, the faint gleam from the strip of bright sky athwart which they must have passed. Goodman Brown alternately crouched and stood on tiptoe, pulling aside the branches and thrusting forth his head as far as he durst without discerning so much as a shadow. It vexed him the more, because he could have sworn, were such a thing possible, that he recognized the voices of the minister and Deacon Gookin, jogging along quietly, as they were wont to do, when bound to some or-dination or ecclesiastical council. While yet within hearing, one of the riders stopped to pluck a switch.

"Of the two, reverend sir," said the voice like the deacon's, "I had rather miss an ordination dinner than to-night's meeting. They tell me that some of our community are to be here from Falmouth and beyond, and others from Con-necticut and Rhode Island, besides several of the Indian powwows, who, after their fashion, know almost as much deviltry as the best of us. Moreover, there is a goodly young woman to be taken into communion."

"Mighty well, Deacon Gookin!" replied the solemn old tones of the minister. "Spur up, or we shall be late. Nothing can be done, you know, until I get on the ground."

45   The hoofs clattered again; and the voices, talking so strangely in the empty air, passed on through the forest, where no church had ever been gathered or solitary Christian prayed. Whither, then, could these holy men be journeying so deep into the heathen wilderness? Young Goodman Brown caught hold of a tree for support, being ready to sink down on the ground, faint and overburdened with the heavy sickness of his heart. He looked up to the sky, doubting whether there really was a heaven above him. Yet there was the blue arch, and the stars brightening in it.

"With heaven above and Faith below, I will yet stand firm against the devil!" cried Goodman Brown.

While he still gazed upward into the deep arch of the firmament and had lifted his hands to pray, a cloud, though no wind was stirring, hurried across the zenith and hid the brightening stars. The blue sky was still visible, except directly overhead, where this black mass of cloud was sweeping swiftly northward. Aloft in the air, as if from the depths of the cloud, came a confused and doubtful sound of voices. Once the listener fancied that he could distinguish the accents of townspeople of his own, men and women, both pious and ungodly, many of whom he had met at the communion table, and had seen others rioting at the tav-ern. The next moment, so indistinct were the sounds, he doubted whether he had heard aught but the murmur of the old forest, whispering without a wind. Then came a stronger swell of those familiar tones, heard daily in the sunshine at Salem village, but never until now from a cloud of night. There was one voice, of a young woman, uttering lamentations, yet with an uncertain sorrow, and en-treating for some favor, which, perhaps, it would grieve her to obtain; and all the unseen multitude, both saints and sinners, seemed to encourage her onward.

"Faith!" shouted Goodman Brown, in a voice of agony and desperation; and the echoes of the forest mocked him, crying, "Faith! Faith!" as if bewildered wretches were seeking her all through the wilderness.

The cry of grief, rage, and terror was yet piercing the night, when the unhappy husband held his breath for a response. There was a scream, drowned immediately in a louder murmur of voices, fading into far-off laughter, as the dark cloud swept away, leaving the clear and silent sky above Goodman Brown. But something fluttered lightly down through the air and caught on the branch of a tree. The young man seized it, and beheld a pink ribbon.

50   "My Faith is gone!" cried he, after one stupefied moment. "There is no good on earth; and sin is but a name. Come, devil; for to thee is this world given."

And, maddened with despair, so that he laughed loud and long, did Goodman Brown grasp his staff and set forth again, at such a rate that he seemed to fly along the forest path rather than to walk or run. The road grew wilder and drearier and more faintly traced, and vanished at length, leaving him in the heart of the dark wilderness, still rushing onward with the instinct that guides mortal man to evil. The whole forest was peopled with frightful sounds—the creaking of the trees, the howling of wild beasts, and the yell of Indians; while sometimes the wind tolled like a distant church bell, and sometimes gave a broad roar around the traveller, as if all Nature were laughing him to scorn. But he was himself the chief horror of the scene, and shrank not from its other horrors.

"Ha! ha! ha!" roared Goodman Brown when the wind laughed at him. "Let us hear which will laugh loudest. Think not to frighten me with your deviltry. Come witch, come wizard, come Indian powwow, come devil himself, and here comes Goodman Brown. You may as well fear him as he fear you."

In truth, all through the haunted forest there could be nothing more frightful than the figure of Goodman Brown. On he flew among the black pines, brandishing his staff with frenzied gestures, now giving vent to an inspiration of horrid blasphemy, and now shouting forth such laughter as set all the echoes of the forest laughing like demons around him. The fiend in his own shape is less hideous than when he rages in the breast of man. Thus sped the demoniac on his course, until, quivering among the trees, he saw a red light before him, as when the felled trunks and branches of a clearing have been set on fire, and throw up their lurid blaze against the sky, at the hour of midnight. He paused, in a lull of the tempest that had driven him onward, and heard the swell of what seemed a hymn, rolling solemnly from a distance with the weight of many voices. He knew the tune; it was a familiar one in the choir of the village meeting-house. The verse died heavily away, and was lengthened by a chorus, not of human voices, but of all the sounds of the benighted wilderness pealing in awful harmony together. Goodman Brown cried out, and his cry was lost to his own ear by its unison with the cry of the desert.

In the interval of silence he stole forward until the light glared full upon his eyes. At one extremity of an open space, hemmed in by the dark wall of the forest, arose a rock, bearing some rude, natural resemblance either to an altar or a pulpit, and surrounded by four blazing pines, their tops aflame, their stems untouched, like candles at an evening meeting. The mass of foliage that had overgrown the summit of the rock was all on fire, blazing high into the night and fitfully illuminating the whole field. Each pendent twig and leafy festoon was in a blaze. As the red light arose and fell, a numerous congregation alternately shone forth, then disappeared in shadow, and again grew, as it were, out of the darkness, peopling the heart of the solitary woods at once.

55   "A grave and dark-clad company," quoth Goodman Brown.

In truth they were such. Among them, quivering to and fro between gloom and splendor, appeared faces that would be seen next day at the council board of the province, and others which, Sabbath after Sabbath, looked devoutly heavenward, and benignantly over the crowded pews, from the holiest pulpits in the land. Some affirm that the lady of the governor was there. At least three were high dames well known to her, and wives of honored husbands, and widows, a great multitude, and ancient maidens, all of excellent repute, and fair young girls, who trembled lest their mothers should espy them. Either the sudden gleams of light flashing over the obscure field bedazzled Goodman Brown, or he recognized a score of the church members of Salem village famous for their especial sanctity. Good old Deacon Gookin had arrived, and waited at the skirts of that venerable saint, his revered pastor. But, irreverently consorting with these grave, reputable, and pious people, these elders of the church, these chaste dames and dewy virgins, there were men of dissolute lives and women of spotted fame, wretches given over to all mean and filthy vice, and suspected even of horrid crimes. It was strange to see that the good shrank not from the wicked, nor were the sinners abashed by the saints. Scattered also among their pale-faced enemies were the Indian priests, or powwows, who had often scared their native forest with more hideous incantations than any known to English witchcraft.

"But where is Faith?" thought Goodman Brown; and, as hope came into his heart, he trembled.

Another verse of the hymn arose, a slow and mournful strain, such as the pious love, but joined to words which expressed all that our nature can conceive of sin, and darkly hinted at far more. Unfathomable to mere mortals is the lore of fiends. Verse after verse was sung; and still the chorus of the desert swelled between like the deepest tone of a mighty organ; and with the final peal of that dreadful anthem there came a sound, as if the roaring wind, the rushing streams, the howling beasts, and every other voice of the unconcerted wilderness were mingling and according with the voice of guilty man in homage to the prince of all. The four blazing pines threw up a loftier flame, and obscurely discovered shapes and visages of horror on the smoke wreaths above the impious assembly. At the same moment the fire on the rock shot redly forth and formed a glowing arch above its base, where now appeared a figure. With reverence be it spoken, the figure bore no slight similitude, both in garb and manner, to some grave divine of the New England churches.

"Bring forth the converts!" cried a voice that echoed through the field and rolled into the forest.

60   At the word, Goodman Brown stepped forth from the shadow of the trees and approached the congregation, with whom he felt a loathful brotherhood by the sympathy of all that was wicked in his heart. He could have well-nigh sworn that the shape of his own dead father beckoned him to advance, looking downward from a smoke wreath, while a woman, with dim features of despair, threw out her hand to warn him back. Was it his mother? But he had no power to retreat one step, nor to resist, even in thought, when the minister and good old Deacon Gookin seized his arms and led him to the blazing rock. Thither came also the slender form of a veiled female, led between Goody Cloyse, that pious teacher of the catechism, and Martha Carrier, who had received the devil's promise to be queen of hell. A rampant hag was she. And there stood the proselytes beneath the canopy of fire.

"Welcome, my children," said the dark figure, "to the communion of your race. Ye have found thus young your nature and your destiny. My children, look behind you!"

They turned; and flashing forth, as it were, in a sheet of flame, the fiend worshippers were seen; the smile of welcome gleamed darkly on every visage.

"There," resumed the sable form, "are all whom ye have reverenced from youth. Ye deemed them holier than yourselves, and shrank from your own sin, contrasting it with their lives of righteousness and prayerful aspirations heavenward. Yet here are they all in my worshipping assembly. This night it shall be granted you to know their secret deeds: how hoary-bearded elders of the church have whispered wanton words to the young maids of their households; how many a woman, eager for widows' weeds, has given her husband a drink at bedtime and let him sleep his last sleep in her bosom; how beardless youths have made haste to inherit their fathers' wealth; and how fair damsels—blush not, sweet ones—have dug little graves in the garden, and bidden me, the sole guest, to an infant's funeral. By the sympathy of your human hearts for sin ye shall scent out all the places—whether in church, bedchamber, street, field, or forest—where crime has been committed, and shall exult to behold the whole earth one stain of guilt, one mighty blood spot. Far more than this. It shall be yours to penetrate, in every bosom, the deep mystery of sin, the fountain of all wicked arts, and which inexhaustibly supplies more evil impulses than human power—than my power at its utmost—can make manifest in deeds. And now, my children, look upon each other."

They did so; and, by the blaze of the hell-kindled torches, the wretched man beheld his Faith, and the wife her husband, trembling before that unhallowed altar.

65   "Lo, there ye stand, my children," said the figure, in a deep and solemn tone, almost sad with its despairing awfulness, as if his once angelic nature could yet mourn for our miserable race. "Depending upon one another's hearts, ye had still hoped that virtue were not all a dream. Now are ye undeceived. Evil is the nature of mankind. Evil must be your only happiness. Welcome again, my children, to the communion of your race."

"Welcome," repeated the fiend worshippers, in one cry of despair and triumph.

And there they stood, the only pair, as it seemed, who were yet hesitating on the verge of wickedness in this dark world. A basin was hollowed, naturally, in the rock. Did it contain water, reddened by the lurid light? or was it blood? or, perchance, a liquid flame? Herein did the shape of evil dip his hand and prepare to lay the mark of baptism upon their foreheads, that they might be partakers of the mystery of sin, more conscious of the secret guilt of others, both in deed and thought, than they could now be of their own. The husband cast one look at his pale wife, and Faith at him. What polluted wretches would the next glance show them to each other, shuddering alike at what they disclosed and what they saw!

"Faith! Faith!" cried the husband, "look up to heaven, and resist the wicked one."

Whether Faith obeyed he knew not. Hardly had he spoken when he found himself amid calm night and solitude, listening to a roar of the wind which died heavily away through the forest. He staggered against the rock, and felt it chill and damp; while a hanging twig, that had been all on fire, besprinkled his cheek with the coldest dew.

70   The next morning young Goodman Brown came slowly into the street of Salem village, staring around him like a bewildered man. The good old minister was taking a walk along the graveyard to get an appetite for breakfast and meditate his sermon, and bestowed a blessing, as he passed, on Goodman Brown. He

shrank from the venerable saint as if to avoid an anathema. Old Deacon Gookin was at domestic worship, and the holy words of his prayer were heard through the open window. "What God doth the wizard pray to?" quoth Goodman Brown. Goody Cloyse, that excellent old Christian, stood in the early sunshine at her own lattice, catechizing a little girl who had brought her a pint of morning's milk. Goodman Brown snatched away the child as from the grasp of the fiend himself. Turning the corner by the meeting-house, he spied the head of Faith, with the pink ribbons, gazing anxiously forth, and bursting into such joy at sight of him that she skipped along the street and almost kissed her husband before the whole village. But Goodman Brown looked sternly and sadly into her face, and passed on without a greeting.

Had Goodman Brown fallen asleep in the forest and only dreamed a wild dream of a witch-meeting?

Be it so if you will; but alas! it was a dream of evil omen for young Goodman Brown. A stern, a sad, a darkly meditative, a distrustful, if not a desperate man did he become from the night of that fearful dream. On the Sabbath day, when the congregation were singing a holy psalm, he could not listen because an anthem of sin rushed loudly upon his ear and drowned all the blessed strain. When the minister spoke from the pulpit with power and fervid eloquence, and, with his hand on the open Bible, of the sacred truths of our religion, and of saint-like lives and triumphant deaths, and of future bliss or misery unutterable, then did Goodman Brown turn pale, dreading lest the roof should thunder down upon the gray blasphemer and his hearers. Often, awaking suddenly at midnight, he shrank from the bosom of Faith; and at morning or eventide, when the family knelt down at prayer, he scowled and muttered to himself, and gazed sternly at his wife, and turned away. And when he had lived long, and was borne to his grave a hoary corpse, followed by Faith, an aged woman, and children and grandchildren, a goodly procession, besides neighbors not a few, they carved no hopeful verse upon his tombstone, for his dying hour was gloom.

[1835]

Topics for Critical Thinking and Writing

1. What do you think Hawthorne gains (or loses) by the last sentence?
2. Evaluate the view that when Young Goodman Brown enters the dark forest he is really entering his own evil mind. Why, by the way, does he go into the forest at night? (Hawthorne gives no explicit reason, but you may want to offer a conjecture.)
3. In a sentence or two summarize the plot, and then in another sentence or two state the theme of the story. (On theme, see pages 199–200.)
4. If you have undergone a religious experience, write an essay discussing your condition before, during, and after the experience.

I. L. PERETZ

Isaac Loeb Peretz (1852–1915), born in Poland and educated as a lawyer, was active as a political radical—he was imprisoned as a socialist agitator—but he devoted most of his professional life to writing fiction, poetry, and plays. He wrote his early work in

Hebrew, but he then turned to writing in Yiddish, and it is as a Yiddish writer that he is remembered.

If Not Higher*

Early every Friday morning, at the time of the Penitential Prayers,[1] the Rabbi of Nemirov would vanish.

He was nowhere to be seen—neither in the synagogue nor in the two Houses of Study nor at a *minyan*.[2] And he was certainly not at home. His door stood open; whoever wished could go in and out; no one would steal from the rabbi. But not a living creature was within.

Where could the rabbi be? Where should he be? In heaven, no doubt. A rabbi has plenty of business to take care of just before the Days of Awe. Jews, God bless them, need livelihood, peace, health, and good matches. They want to be pious and good, but our sins are so great, and Satan of the thousand eyes watches the whole earth from one end to the other. What he sees he reports; he denounces, informs. Who can help us if not the rabbi!

That's what the people thought.

5   But once a Litvak[3] came, and he laughed. You know the Litvaks. They think little of the Holy Books but stuff themselves with Talmud and law. So this Litvak points to a passage in the *Gemarah*[4]—it sticks in your eyes—where it is written that even Moses, our Teacher, did not ascend to heaven during his lifetime but remained suspended two and a half feet below. Go argue with a Litvak!

So where can the rabbi be?

"That's not my business," said the Litvak, shrugging. Yet all the while—what a Litvak can do!—he is scheming to find out.

That same night, right after the evening prayers, the Litvak steals into the rabbi's room, slides under the rabbi's bed, and waits. He'll watch all night and discover where the rabbi vanishes and what he does during the Penitential Prayers.

Someone else might have got drowsy and fallen asleep, but a Litvak is never at a loss; he recites a whole tractate of the Talmud by heart.

10   At dawn he hears the call to prayers.

The rabbi has already been awake for a long time. The Litvak has heard him groaning for a whole hour.

Whoever has heard the Rabbi of Nemirov groan knows how much sorrow for all Israel, how much suffering, lies in each groan. A man's heart might break, hearing it. But a Litvak is made of iron; he listens and remains where he is. The rabbi, long life to him, lies on the bed, and the Litvak under the bed.

Then the Litvak hears the beds in the house begin to creak; he hears people jumping out of their beds, mumbling a few Jewish words, pouring water on their fingernails, banging doors. Everyone has left. It is again quiet and dark; a bit of light from the moon shines through the shutters.

(Afterward the Litvak admitted that when he found himself alone with the rabbi a great fear took hold of him. Goose pimples spread across his skin, and the

---

*Translated by Marie Syrkin   [1]prayers recited in the days preceding the Days of Awe. The Days of Awe extend from the New Year's days (Rosh Hashanah) to the Day of Atonement (Yom Kippur), a period of ten days   [2]the quorum of ten men needed to conduct Jewish public worship   [3]a Lithuanian Jew   [4]part of the Talmud, a commentary on Jewish law

roots of his earlocks pricked him like needles. A trifle: to be alone with the rabbi at the time of the Penitential Prayers! But a Litvak is stubborn. So he quivered like a fish in water and remained where he was.)

15   Finally the rabbi, long life to him, arises. First he does what befits a Jew. Then he goes to the clothes closet and takes out a bundle of peasant clothes: linen trousers, high boots, a coat, a big felt hat, and a long wide leather belt studded with brass nails. The rabbi gets dressed. From his coat pocket dangles the end of a heavy peasant rope.

The rabbi goes out, and the Litvak follows him.

On the way the rabbi stops in the kitchen, bends down, takes an ax from under the bed, puts it in his belt, and leaves the house. The Litvak trembles but continues to follow.

The hushed dread of the Days of Awe hangs over the dark streets. Every once in a while a cry rises from some *minyan* reciting the Penitential Prayers, or from a sickbed. The rabbi hugs the sides of the streets, keeping to the shade of the houses. He glides from house to house, and the Litvak after him. The Litvak hears the sound of his heartbeats mingling with the sound of the rabbi's heavy steps. But he keeps on going and follows the rabbi to the outskirts of the town.

A small wood stands behind the town.

20   The rabbi, long life to him, enters the wood. He takes thirty or forty steps and stops by a small tree. The Litvak, overcome with amazement, watches the rabbi take the ax out of his belt and strike the tree. He hears the tree creak and fall. The rabbi chops the tree into logs and the logs into sticks. Then he makes a bundle of the wood and ties it with the rope in his pocket. He puts the bundle of wood on his back, shoves the ax back into his belt, and returns to the town.

He stops at a back street beside a small broken-down shack and knocks at the window.

"Who is there?" asks a frightened voice. The Litvak recognizes it as the voice of a sick Jewish woman.

"I," answers the rabbi in the accent of a peasant.

"Who is I?"

25   Again the rabbi answers in Russian. "Vassil."

"Who is Vassil, and what do you want?"

"I have wood to sell, very cheap." And, not waiting for the woman's reply, he goes into the house.

The Litvak steals in after him. In the gray light of the early morning he sees a poor room with broken, miserable furnishings. A sick woman, wrapped in rags, lies on the bed. She complains bitterly, "Buy? How can I buy? Where will a poor widow get money?"

"I'll lend it to you," answers the supposed Vassil. "It's only six cents."

30   "And how will I ever pay you back?" said the poor woman, groaning.

"Foolish one," says the rabbi reproachfully. "See, you are a poor sick Jew, and I am ready to trust you with a little wood. I am sure you'll pay. While you, you have such a great and mighty God and you don't trust him for six cents."

"And who will kindle the fire?" said the widow. "Have I the strength to get up? My son is at work."

"I'll kindle the fire," answers the rabbi.

As the rabbi put the wood into the oven he recited, in a groan, the first portion of the Penitential Prayers.

35   As he kindled the fire and the wood burned brightly, he recited, a bit more joyously, the second portion of the Penitential Prayers. When the fire was set he recited the third portion, and then he shut the stove.

The Litvak who saw all this became a disciple of the rabbi.

And ever after, when another disciple tells how the Rabbi of Nemirov ascends to heaven at the time of the Penitential Prayers, the Litvak does not laugh. He only adds quietly, "If not higher."

[1900]

Topics for Critical Thinking and Writing

1. According to the third paragraph, why would a rabbi go to heaven "just before the Days of Awe"? Why does the rabbi of this story *not* go to heaven during this period?
2. In a paragraph characterize the Litvak, taking into account his final speech.

KATHERINE ANNE PORTER

Katherine Anne Porter (1890–1980) had the curious habit of inventing details in her life, but it is true that she was born in a log cabin in Indian Creek, Texas, that she was originally named Callie Russell Porter, that her mother died when the child was 2 years old, and that Callie was brought up by her maternal grandmother in Kyle, Texas. She was sent to convent schools, where, in her words, she received a "strangely useless and ornamental education." When she was 16 she left school, married (and soon divorced), and worked as a reporter, first in Texas and later in Denver and Chicago. She moved around a good deal, both within the United States and abroad; she lived for a while in Mexico, Belgium, Switzerland, France, and Germany.

Even as a child she was interested in writing, but she did not publish her first story until she was 33. She wrote essays and one novel (Ship of Fools), but she is best known for her stories. Porter's Collected Stories *won the Pulitzer Prize and the National Book Award in 1965.*

The Jilting of Granny Weatherall

She flicked her wrist neatly out of Doctor Harry's pudgy careful fingers and pulled the sheet up to her chin. The brat ought to be in knee breeches. Doctoring around the country with spectacles on his nose! "Get along now, take your schoolbooks and go. There's nothing wrong with me."

Doctor Harry spread a warm paw like a cushion on her forehead where the forked green vein danced and made her eyelids twitch. "Now, now, be a good girl, and we'll have you up in no time."

"That's no way to speak to a woman nearly eighty years old just because she's down. I'd have you respect your elders, young man."

"Well, Missy, excuse me." Doctor Harry patted her cheek. "But I've got to warn you, haven't I? You're a marvel, but you must be careful or you're going to be good and sorry."

5   "Don't tell me what I'm going to be. I'm on my feet now, morally speaking. It's Cornelia. I had to go to bed to get rid of her."

Her bones felt loose, and floated around in her skin, and Doctor Harry floated like a balloon around the foot of the bed. He floated and pulled down his waistcoat and swung his glasses on a cord. "Well, stay where you are, it certainly can't hurt you."

"Get along and doctor your sick," said Granny Weatherall. "Leave a well woman alone. I'll call for you when I want you. . . . Where were you forty years ago when I pulled through milk-leg and double pneumonia? You weren't even born. Don't let Cornelia lead you on," she shouted, because Doctor Harry appeared to float up to the ceiling and out. "I pay my own bills, and I don't throw my money away on nonsense!"

She meant to wave good-by, but it was too much trouble. Her eyes closed of themselves, it was like a dark curtain drawn around the bed. The pillow rose and floated under her, pleasant as a hammock in a light wind. She listened to the leaves rustling outside the window. No, somebody was swishing newspapers: no, Cornelia and Doctor Harry were whispering together. She leaped broad awake, thinking they whispered in her ear.

"She was never like this, *never* like this!" "Well, what can we expect?" "Yes, eighty years old. . . ."

10   Well, and what if she was? She still had ears. It was like Cornelia to whisper around doors. She always kept things secret in such a public way. She was always being tactful and kind. Cornelia was dutiful; that was the trouble with her. Dutiful and good: "So good and dutiful," said Granny, "that I'd like to spank her." She saw herself spanking Cornelia and making a fine job of it.

"What'd you say, Mother?"

Granny felt her face tying up in hard knots.

"Can't a body think, I'd like to know?"

"I thought you might want something."

15   "I do. I want a lot of things. First off, go away and don't whisper."

She lay and drowsed, hoping in her sleep that the children would keep out and let her rest a minute. It had been a long day. Not that she was tired. It was always pleasant to snatch a minute now and then. There was always so much to be done, let me see: tomorrow.

Tomorrow was far away and there was nothing to trouble about. Things were finished somehow when the time came; thank God there was always a little margin over for peace: then a person could spread out the plan of life and tuck in the edges orderly. It was good to have everything clean and folded away, with the hair brushes and tonic bottles sitting straight on the white embroidered linen: the day started without fuss and the pantry shelves laid out with rows of jelly glasses and brown jugs and white stone-china jars with blue whirligigs and words painted on them: coffee, tea, sugar, ginger, cinnamon, allspice: and the bronze clock with the lion on top nicely dusted off. The dust that lion could collect in twenty-four hours! The box in the attic with all those letters tied up, well, she'd have to go through that tomorrow. All those letters—George's letters and John's letters and her letters to them both—lying around for the children to find afterwards made her uneasy. Yes, that would be tomorrow's business. No use to let them know how silly she had been once.

While she was rummaging around she found death in her mind and it felt clammy and unfamiliar. She had spent so much time preparing for death there was no need for bringing it up again. Let it take care of itself now. When she was sixty she had felt very old, finished, and went around making farewell trips to see her children and grandchildren, with a secret in her mind: This is the very last of your mother, children! Then she made her will and came down with a long fever. That was all just a notion like a lot of other things, but it was lucky too, for she had once for all got over the idea of dying for a long time. Now she couldn't be worried. She hoped she had better sense now. Her father had lived to be one hundred and two years old and had drunk a noggin of strong hot toddy on his last birthday. He told the reporters it was his daily habit, and he owed his long life to that. He had made quite a scandal and was very pleased about it. She believed she'd just plague Cornelia a little.

"Cornelia! Cornelia!" No footsteps, but a sudden hand on her cheek. "Bless you, where have you been?"

20   "Here, Mother."

"Well, Cornelia, I want a noggin of hot toddy."

"Are you cold, darling?"

"I'm chilly, Cornelia. Lying in bed stops the circulation. I must have told you that a thousand times."

Well, she could just hear Cornelia telling her husband that Mother was getting a little childish and they'd have to humor her. The thing that most annoyed her was that Cornelia thought she was deaf, dumb, and blind. Little hasty glances and tiny gestures tossed around her and over her head saying, "Don't cross her, let her have her way, she's eighty years old," and she sitting there as if she lived in a thin glass cage. Sometimes Granny almost made up her mind to pack up and move back to her own house where nobody could remind her every minute that she was old. Wait, wait, Cornelia, till your own children whisper behind your back!

25   In her day she had kept a better house and had got more work done. She wasn't too old yet for Lydia to be driving eighty miles for advice when one of the children jumped the track, and Jimmy still dropped in and talked things over: "Now, Mammy, you've a good business head, I want to know what you think of this? . . ." Old. Cornelia couldn't change the furniture around without asking. Little things, little things! They had been so sweet when they were little. Granny wished the old days were back again with the children young and everything to be done over. It had been a hard pull, but not too much for her. When she thought of all the food she had cooked, and all the clothes she had cut and sewed, and all the gardens she had made—well, the children showed it. There they were, made out of her, and they couldn't get away from that. Sometimes she wanted to see John again and point to them and say, Well, I didn't do so badly, did I? But that would have to wait. That was for tomorrow. She used to think of him as a man, but now all the children were older than their father, and he would be a child beside her if she saw him now. It seemed strange and there was something wrong in the idea. Why, he couldn't possibly recognize her. She had fenced in a hundred acres once, digging the post holes herself and clamping the wires with just a negro boy to help. That changed a woman. John would be looking for a young woman with the peaked Spanish comb in her hair and the painted fan. Digging post holes changed a woman. Riding country roads in the winter when women had their babies was another thing: sitting up nights with sick horses and sick negroes and sick children and hardly ever losing one. John, I hardly ever lost one of them! John would see that in a minute, that would be something he could understand, she wouldn't have to explain anything!

It made her feel like rolling up her sleeves and putting the whole place to rights again. No matter if Cornelia was determined to be everywhere at once, there were a great many things left undone on this place. She would start tomorrow and do them. It was good to be strong enough for everything, even if all you made melted and changed and slipped under your hands, so that by the time you finished you almost forgot what you were working for. What was it I set out to do? she asked herself intently, but she could not remember. A fog rose over the valley, she saw it marching across the creek swallowing the trees and moving up the hill like an army of ghosts. Soon it would be at the near edge of the orchard, and then it was time to go in and light the lamps. Come in, children, don't stay out in the night air.

Lighting the lamps had been beautiful. The children huddled up to her and breathed like little calves waiting at the bars in the twilight. Their eyes followed the match and watched the flame rise and settle in a blue curve, then they moved away from her. The lamp was lit, they didn't have to be scared and hang on to mother any more. Never, never, never more. God, for all my life I thank Thee. Without Thee, my God, I could never have done it. Hail, Mary, full of grace.

I want you to pick all the fruit this year and see that nothing is wasted. There's always someone who can use it. Don't let good things rot for want of using. You waste life when you waste good food. Don't let things get lost. It's bitter to lose things. Now, don't let me get to thinking, not when I am tired and taking a little nap before supper. . . .

The pillow rose about her shoulders and pressed against her heart and the memory was being squeezed out of it: oh, push down that pillow, somebody: it would smother her if she tried to hold it. Such a fresh breeze blowing and such a green day with no threats in it. But he had not come, just the same. What does a woman do when she has put on the white veil and set out the white cake for a man and he doesn't come? She tried to remember. No, I swear he never harmed me but in that. He never harmed me but in that . . . and what if he did? There was the day, the day, but a whirl of dark smoke rose and covered it, crept up and over into the bright field where everything was planted so carefully in orderly rows. That was hell, she knew hell when she saw it. For sixty years she had prayed against remembering him and against losing her soul in the deep pit of hell, and now the two things were mingled in one and the thought of him was a smoky cloud from hell that moved and crept in her head when she had just got rid of Doctor Harry and was trying to rest a minute. Wounded vanity, Ellen, said a sharp voice in the top of her mind. Don't let your wounded vanity get the upper hand of you. Plenty of girls get jilted. You were jilted, weren't you? Then stand up to it. Her eyelids wavered and let in streamers of blue-gray light like tissue paper over her eyes. She must get up and pull the shades down or she'd never sleep. She was in bed again and the shades were not down. How could that happen? Better turn over, hide from the light, sleeping in the light gave you nightmares. "Mother, how do you feel now?" and a stinging wetness on her forehead. But I don't like having my face washed in cold water!

30   Hapsy? George? Lydia? Jimmy? No, Cornelia, and her features were swollen and full of little puddles. "They're coming, darling, they'll all be here soon." Go wash your face, child, you look funny.

Instead of obeying, Cornelia knelt down and put her head on the pillow. She seemed to be talking but there was no sound. "Well, are you tongue-tied? Whose birthday is it? Are you going to give a party?"

Cornelia's mouth moved urgently in strange shapes. "Don't do that, you bother me, daughter."

"Oh, no, Mother. Oh, no. . . ."

Nonsense. It was strange about children. They disputed your every word. "No what, Cornelia?"

35   "Here's Doctor Harry."

"I won't see that boy again. He just left five minutes ago."

"That was this morning, Mother. It's night now. Here's the nurse."

"This is Doctor Harry, Mrs. Weatherall. I never saw you look so young and happy!"

"Ah, I'll never be young again—but I'd be happy if they'd let me lie in peace and get rested."

40   She thought she spoke up loudly, but no one answered. A warm weight on her forehead, a warm bracelet on her wrist, and a breeze went on whispering, trying to tell her something. A shuffle of leaves in the everlasting hand of God. He blew on them and they danced and rattled. "Mother, don't mind, we're going to give you a little hypodermic." "Look here, daughter, how do ants get in this bed? I saw sugar ants yesterday." Did you send for Hapsy too?

It was Hapsy she really wanted. She had to go a long way back through a great many rooms to find Hapsy standing with a baby on her arm. She seemed to herself to be Hapsy also, and the baby on Hapsy's arm was Hapsy and himself and herself, all at once, and there was no surprise in the meeting. Then Hapsy melted from within and turned flimsy as gray gauze and the baby was a gauzy shadow, and Hapsy came up close and said, "I thought you'd never come," and looked at her very searchingly and said, "You haven't changed a bit!" They leaned forward to kiss, when Cornelia began whispering from a long way off, "Oh, is there anything you want to tell me? Is there anything I can do for you?"

Yes, she had changed her mind after sixty years and she would like to see George. I want you to find George. Find him and be sure to tell him I forgot him. I want him to know I had my husband just the same and my children and my house like any other woman. A good house too and a good husband that I loved and fine children out of him. Better than I hoped for even. Tell him I was given back everything he took away and more. Oh, no, oh, God, no, there was something else besides the house and the man and the children. Oh, surely they were not all? What was it? Something not given back. . . . Her breath crowded down under her ribs and grew into a monstrous frightening shape with cutting edges; it bored up into her head, and the agony was unbelievable: Yes, John, get the doctor now, no more talk, my time has come.

When this one was born it should be the last. The last. It should have been born first, for it was the one she had truly wanted. Everything came in good time. Nothing left out, left over. She was strong, in three days she would be as well as ever. Better. A woman needed milk in her to have her full health.

"Mother, do you hear me?"

45   "I've been telling you—"

"Mother, Father Connolly's here."

"I went to Holy Communion only last week. Tell him I'm not so sinful as all that."

"Father just wants to speak to you."

He could speak as much as he pleased. It was like him to drop in and inquire about her soul as if it were a teething baby, and then stay on for a cup of tea and a round of cards and gossip. He always had a funny story of some sort, usually about an Irishman who made his little mistakes and confessed them, and the point lay in some absurd thing he would blurt out in the confessional showing his struggles between native piety and original sin. Granny felt easy about her soul. Cornelia, where are your manners? Give Father Connolly a chair. She had her secret comfortable understanding with a few favorite saints who cleared a straight road to God for her. All as surely signed and sealed as the papers for the new Forty Acres. Forever . . . heirs and assigns forever. Since the day the wedding cake was not cut, but thrown out and wasted. The whole bottom dropped out of the world, and there she was blind and sweating with nothing under her feet and the walls falling away. His hand had caught her under the breast, she had not fallen, there was the freshly polished floor with the green rug on it, just as before. he had cursed like a sailor's parrot and said, "I'll kill him for you." Don't lay a hand on him, for my sake leave something to God. "Now, Ellen, you must believe what I tell you. . . ."

50   So there was nothing, nothing to worry about any more, except sometimes in the night one of the children screamed in a nightmare, and they both hustled out shaking and hunting for the matches and calling, "There, wait a minute, here we are!" John, get the doctor now, Hapsy's time has come. But there was Hapsy standing by the bed in a white cap. "Cornelia, tell Hapsy to take off her cap. I can't see her plain."

Her eyes opened very wide and the room stood out like a picture she had seen somewhere. Dark colors with the shadows rising toward the ceiling in long angles. The tall black dresser gleamed with nothing on it but John's picture, enlarged from a little one, with John's eyes very black when they should have been blue. You never saw him, so how do you know how he looked? But the man insisted the copy was perfect, it was very rich and handsome. For a picture, yes, but it's not my husband. The table by the bed had a linen cover and a candle and a crucifix. The light was blue from Cornelia's silk lampshades. No sort of light at all, just frippery. You had to live forty years with kerosene lamps to appreciate honest electricity. She felt very strong and she saw Doctor Harry with a rosy nimbus around him.

"You look like a saint, Doctor Harry, and I vow that's as near as you'll ever come to it."

"She's saying something."

"I heard you, Cornelia. What's all this carrying on?"

55   "Father Connolly's saying—"

Cornelia's voice staggered and bumped like a cart in a bad road. It rounded corners and turned back again and arrived nowhere. Granny stepped up in the cart very lightly and reached for the reins, but a man sat beside her and she knew him by his hands, driving the cart. She did not look in his face, for she knew without seeing, but looked instead down the road where the trees leaned over and bowed to each other and a thousand birds were singing a Mass. She felt like singing too, but she put her hand in the bosom of her dress and pulled out a rosary, and Father Connolly murmured Latin in a very solemn voice and tickled her feet. My God, will you stop that nonsense? I'm a married woman. What if he did run away and leave me to face the priest by myself? I found another a whole world better. I wouldn't have exchanged my husband for anybody except St. Michael himself, and you may tell him that for me with a thank you in the bargain.

Light flashed on her closed eyelids, and a deep roaring shook her. Cornelia, is that lightning? I hear thunder. There's going to be a storm. Close all the windows. Call the children in. . . . "Mother, here we are, all of us." "Is that you, Hapsy?" "Oh, no, I'm Lydia. We drove as fast as we could." Their faces drifted above her, drifted away. The rosary fell out of her hands and Lydia put it back. Jimmy tried to help, their hands fumbled together, and Granny closed two fingers around Jimmy's thumb. Beads wouldn't do, it must be something alive. She was so amazed her thoughts ran round and round. So, my dear Lord, this is my death and I wasn't even thinking about it. My children have come to see me die. But I can't, it's not time. Oh, I always hated surprises. I wanted to give Cornelia the amethyst set—Cornelia, you're to have the amethyst set, but Hapsy's to wear it when she wants, and, Doctor Harry, do shut up. Nobody sent for you. Oh, my dear Lord, do wait a minute. I meant to do something about the Forty Acres, Jimmy doesn't need it and Lydia will later on, with that worthless husband of hers. I meant to finish the altar cloth and send six bottles of wine to Sister Borgia for her dyspepsia. I want to send six bottles of wine to Sister Borgia, Father Connolly, now don't let me forget.

Cornelia's voice made short turns and tilted over and crashed. "Oh, Mother, oh, Mother, oh, Mother. . . ."

"I'm not going, Cornelia. I'm taken by surprise. I can't go."

60   You'll see Hapsy again. What about her? "I thought you'd never come." Granny made a long journey outward, looking for Hapsy. What if I don't find her? What then? Her heart sank down and down, there was no bottom to death, she couldn't come to the end of it. The blue light from Cornelia's lampshade drew into a tiny point in the center of her brain, it flickered and winked like an eye, quietly it fluttered and dwindled. Granny lay curled down within herself, amazed and watchful, starting at the point of light that was herself; her body was now only a deeper mass of shadow in an endless darkness and this darkness would curl around the light and swallow it up. God, give a sign!

For the second time there was no sign. Again no bridegroom and the priest in the house. She could not remember any other sorrow because this grief wiped them all away. Oh, no, there's nothing more cruel than this—I'll never forgive it. She stretched herself with a deep breath and blew out the light.

[1929]

 Topics for Critical Thinking and Writing

1. In a paragraph characterize Granny Weatherall. In another paragraph evaluate her claim that the anguish of the jilting has been compensated for by her subsequent life.
2. The final paragraph alludes to Christ's parable of the bridegroom (Matthew 25.1-13). With this allusion in mind, write a paragraph explaining the title of the story.

 **LESLIE MARMON SILKO**

Leslie Marmon Silko was born in 1948 in Albuquerque, New Mexico, and grew up on the Laguna Pueblo Reservation some fifty miles to the west. Of her family she says,

We are mixed blood—Laguna, Mexican, white. . . . All those languages, all those ways of living are combined, and we live somewhere on the fringes of all three. But I don't apologize for this any more—not to whites, not to full bloods—our origin is unlike any other. My poetry, my storytelling rise out of this source.

After graduating from the University of New Mexico in 1969, Silko entered law school but soon left to become a writer. She taught for two years at Navajo Community Col-

lege at Many Farms, Arizona, and then went to Alaska for two years where she studied Eskimo-Aleut culture and worked on a novel, Ceremony. *After returning to the Southwest, she taught at the University of Arizona and then at the University of New Mexico.*

In addition to writing stories, a novel, and poems, Silko has written the screenplay for Marlon Brando's film Black Elk. *In 1981 she was awarded one of the so-called "genius grants" from the MacArthur Foundation, which supports "exceptionally talented individuals."*

The Man to Send Rain Clouds

One

They found him under a big cottonwood tree. His Levi jacket and pants were faded light-blue so that he had been easy to find. The big cottonwood tree stood apart from a small grove of winterbare cottonwoods which grew in the wide, sandy arroyo. He had been dead for a day or more, and the sheep had wandered and scattered up and down the arroyo. Leon and his brother-in-law, Ken, gathered the sheep and left them in the pen at the sheep camp before they returned to the cottonwood tree. Leon waited under the tree while Ken drove the truck through the deep sand to the edge of the arroyo. He squinted up at the sun and unzipped his jacket—it sure was hot for this time of year. But high and northwest the blue mountains were still deep in snow. Ken came sliding down the low, crumbling bank about fifty yards down, and he was bringing the red blanket.

Before they wrapped the old man, Leon took a piece of string out of his pocket and tied a small gray feather in the old man's long white hair. Ken gave him the paint. Across the brown wrinkled forehead he drew a streak of white and along the high cheekbones he drew a strip of blue paint. He paused and watched Ken throw pinches of corn meal and pollen into the wind that fluttered the small gray feather. Then Leon painted with yellow under the old man's broad nose, and finally, when he had painted green across the chin, he smiled.

"Send us rain clouds, Grandfather." They laid the bundle in the back of the pickup and covered it with a heavy tarp before they started back to the pueblo.

They turned off the highway onto the sandy pueblo road. Not long after they passed the store and post office they saw Father Paul's car coming toward them. When he recognized their faces he slowed his car and waved for them to stop. The young priest rolled down the car window.

5   "Did you find old Teofilo?" he asked loudly.

Leon stopped the truck. "Good morning, Father. We were just out to the sheep camp. Everything is O.K. now."

"Thank God for that. Teofilo is a very old man. You really shouldn't allow him to stay at the sheep camp alone."

"No, he won't do that any more now."

"Well, I'm glad you understand. I hope I'll be seeing you at Mass this week—we missed you last Sunday. See if you can get old Teofilo to come with you." The priest smiled and waved at them as they drove away.

Two

10   Louise and Teresa were waiting. The table was set for lunch, and the coffee was boiling on the black iron stove. Leon looked at Louise and then at Teresa.

"We found him under a cottonwood tree in the big arroyo near sheep camp. I guess he sat down to rest in the shade and never got up again." Leon walked toward the old man's head. The red plaid shawl had been shaken and spread carefully over the bed, and a new brown flannel shirt and pair of stiff new Levis were arranged neatly beside the pillow. Louise held the screen door open while Leon and Ken carried in the red blanket. He looked small and shriveled, and after they dressed him in the new shirt and pants he seemed more shrunken.

It was noontime now because the church bells rang the Angelus.[1] They ate the beans with hot bread, and nobody said anything until after Teresa poured the coffee.

Ken stood up and put on his jacket. "I'll see about the gravediggers. Only the top layer of soil is frozen. I think it can be ready before dark."

Leon nodded his head and finished his coffee. After Ken had been gone for a while, the neighbors and clanspeople came quietly to embrace Teofilo's family and to leave food on the table because the grave-diggers would come to eat when they were finished.

Three

15   The sky in the west was full of pale-yellow light. Louise stood outside with her hands in the pockets of Leon's green army jacket that was too big for her. The funeral was over, and the old men had taken their candles and medicine bags and were gone. She waited until the body was laid into the pickup before she said anything to Leon. She touched his arm, and he noticed that her hands were still dusty from the corn meal that she had sprinkled around the old man. When she spoke, Leon could not hear her.

"What did you say? I didn't hear you."

"I said that I had been thinking about something."

"About what?"

"About the priest sprinkling holy water for Grandpa. So he won't be thirsty."

20   Leon stared at the new moccasins that Teofilo had made for the ceremonial dances in the summer. They were nearly hidden by the red blanket. It was getting colder, and the wind pushed gray dust down the narrow pueblo road. The sun was approaching the long mesa where it disappeared during the winter. Louise stood there shivering and watching his face. Then he zipped up his jacket and opened the truck door. "I'll see if he's there."

Ken stopped the pickup at the church, and Leon got out; and then Ken drove down the hill to the graveyard where people were waiting. Leon knocked at the old carved door with its symbols of the Lamb. While he waited he looked up at the twin bells from the king of Spain with the last sunlight pouring around them in their tower.

The priest opened the door and smiled when he saw who it was. "Come in! What brings you here this evening?"

The priest walked toward the kitchen, and Leon stood with his cap in his hand, playing with the earflaps and examining the living room—the brown sofa, the green armchair, and the brass lamp that hung down from the ceiling by links of chain. The priest dragged a chair out of the kitchen and offered it to Leon.

[1]**Angelus** a devotional prayer commemorating the Annunciation (the angel Gabriel's announcement of the Incarnation of God in the human form of Jesus)

"No thank you, Father. I only came to ask you if you would bring your holy water to the graveyard."

The priest turned away from Leon and looked out the window at the patio full of shadows and the dining-room windows of the nuns' cloister across the patio. The curtains were heavy, and the light from within faintly penetrated; it was impossible to see the nuns inside eating supper. "Why didn't you tell me he was dead? I could have brought the Last Rites anyway."

Leon smiled. "It wasn't necessary, Father."

The priest stared down at his scuffed brown loafers and the worn hem of his cassock. "For a Christian burial it was necessary."

His voice was distant, and Leon thought that his blue eyes looked tired.

"It's O.K., Father, we just want him to have plenty of water."

The priest sank down in the green chair and picked up a glossy missionary magazine. He turned the colored pages full of lepers and pagans without looking at them.

"You know I can't do that, Leon. There should have been the Last Rites and a funeral Mass at the very least."

Leon put on his green cap and pulled the flaps down over his ears. "It's getting late, Father. I've got to go."

When Leon opened the door Father Paul stood up and said, "Wait." He left the room and came back wearing a long brown overcoat. He followed Leon out the door and across the dim churchyard to the adobe steps in front of the church. They both stooped to fit through the low adobe entrance. And when they started down the hill to the graveyard only half of the sun was visible above the mesa.

The priest approached the grave slowly, wondering how they had managed to dig into the frozen ground, and then he remembered that this was New Mexico, and saw the pile of cold loose sand beside the hole. The people stood close to each other with little clouds of steam puffing from their faces. The priest looked at them and saw a pile of jackets, gloves, and scarves in the yellow, dry tumbleweeds that grew in the graveyard. He looked at the red blanket, not sure that Teofilo was so small, wondering if it wasn't some perverse Indian trick—something they did in March to ensure a good harvest—wondering if maybe old Teofilo was actually at sheep camp corraling the sheep for the night. But there he was, facing into a cold dry wind and squinting at the last sunlight, ready to bury a red wool blanket while the faces of the parishioners were in shadow with the last warmth of the sun on their backs.

His fingers were stiff, and it took them a long time to twist the lid off the holy water. Drops of water fell on the red blanket and soaked into dark icy spots. He sprinkled the grave and the water disappeared almost before it touched the dim, cold sand; it reminded him of something—he tried to remember what it was, because he thought if he could remember he might understand this. He sprinkled more water; he shook the container until it was empty, and the water fell through the light from sundown like August rain that fell while the sun was still shining, almost evaporating before it touched the wilted squash flowers.

The wind pulled at the priest's brown Franciscan robe and swirled away the corn meal and pollen that had been sprinkled on the blanket. They lowered the bundle into the ground, and they didn't bother to untie the stiff pieces of new rope that were tied around the ends of the blanket. The sun was gone, and over on the highway the eastbound lane was full of headlights. The priest walked away slowly. Leon watched him climb the hill, and when he had disappeared within the tall, thick walls, Leon turned to look up at the high blue mountains in the deep snow that reflected a faint red light from the west. He felt good because it was finished, and he was happy about the sprinkling of the holy water, now the old man could send them big thunderclouds for sure.

[1969]

✏ Topics for Critical Thinking and Writing

1. How would you describe the response of Leon, Ken, Louise, and Teresa to Teofilo's death? To what degree does it resemble or differ from responses to death that you are familiar with?
2. How do the funeral rites resemble or differ from those of your community?
3. How well does Leon understand the priest? How well does the priest understand Leon?
4. At the end of the story we are told that Leon "felt good." Do you assume that the priest also felt good? Why, or why not?
5. From what point of view is the story told? Mark the passages where the narrator enters a character's mind, and then explain what, in your opinion, Silko gains (or loses) by doing so.

A Casebook on Flannery O'Connor

In this casebook we give two short stories and several comments of O'Connor's on literature:

1. "A Good Man Is Hard to Find"
2. "Revelation"
3. Passages from five essays about fiction and a letter on "A Good Man Is Hard to Find"

We also include a page from the manuscript of "A Good Man Is Hard to Find," showing O'Connor's revisions.

Flannery O'Connor (1925–64)—her first name was Mary but she did not use it—was born in Savannah, Georgia, but spent most of her life in Milledgeville, Georgia, where her family moved when she was 12. She was educated in parochial schools and at the local college and then went to the School for Writers at the University of Iowa where she earned an M.F.A. in 1946. For a few months she lived at a writers' colony in Saratoga Springs, New York, and then for a few weeks she lived in New York City, but most of her life was spent back in Milledgeville, where she tended her peacocks and wrote stories, novels, essays (posthumously published as Mystery and Manners *[1970]), and letters (posthumously published under the title* The Habit of Being *[1979]).*

In 1951, when she was 25, Flannery O'Connor discovered that she was a victim of lupus erythematosus, an incurable autoimmune disease that had crippled and then killed her father ten years before. She died at the age of 39. O'Connor faced her illness with stoic courage, Christian fortitude—and tough humor. Here is a glimpse, from one of her letters, of how she dealt with those who pitied her:

An old lady got on the elevator behind me and as soon as I turned around she fixed me with a moist gleaming eye and said in a loud voice, "Bless you, darling!" I felt exactly like the Misfit [in "A Good Man Is Hard to Find"] and I gave her a weakly lethal look, whereupon greatly encouraged she grabbed my arm and whispered (very loud) in my ear, "Remember what they said to John at the gate, darling!" It was not my floor but I got off and I suppose the old lady was astounded at how quick I could get away on crutches. I have a one-legged friend and I asked her what they said to John at the gate. She said she reckoned they said, "The lame shall enter first." This may be because the lame will be able to knock everybody else aside with their crutches.

A devout Catholic, O'Connor forthrightly summarized the relation between her belief and her writing:

I see from the standpoint of Christian orthodoxy. This means that for me the meaning of life is centered in our Redemption by Christ and what I see in the world I see in its relation to that.

A Good Man Is Hard to Find

The grandmother didn't want to go to Florida. She wanted to visit some of her connections in east Tennessee and she was seizing every chance to change Bailey's mind. Bailey was the son she lived with, her only boy. He was sitting on the edge of his chair at the table, bent over the orange sports section of the *Journal.* "Now look here, Bailey," she said, "see here, read this," and she stood with one hand on her thin hip and the other rattling the newspaper at his bald head. "Here this fellow that calls himself The Misfit is aloose from the Federal Pen and headed toward Florida and you read here what it says he did to these people. Just you read it. I wouldn't take my children in any direction with a criminal like that aloose in it. I couldn't answer to my conscience if I did."

Bailey didn't look up from his reading so she wheeled around then and faced the children's mother, a young woman in slacks. whose face was as broad and innocent as a cabbage and was tied around with a green headkerchief that had two points on the top like rabbit's ears. She was sitting on the sofa, feeding the baby his apricots out of a jar. "The children have been to Florida before," the old lady said. "You all ought to take them somewhere else for a change so they would see different parts of the world and be broad. They never have been to east Tennessee."

The children's mother didn't seem to hear her, but the eight-year-old boy, John Wesley, a stocky child with glasses, said. "If you don't want to go to Florida, why dontcha stay at home?" He and the little girl, June Star, were reading the funny papers on the floor.

"She wouldn't stay at home to be queen for a day," June Star said without raising her yellow head.

5 "Yes, and what would you do if this fellow, The Misfit, caught you?" the grandmother said.

"I'd smack his face," John Wesley said.

"She wouldn't stay at home for a million bucks," June Star said. "Afraid she'd miss something. She has to go everywhere we go."

"All right, Miss," the grandmother said. "Just remember that the next time you want me to curl your hair."

2

the grandmother

~~Of course she~~ was the first one ready to load up the next morning at six o'clock. She had Baby Brother's bucking bronco ~~that and maxxxxxx~~ what she called her "F Lee" and Pitty Sing, the cat, ~~xxxxxx~~ packed in the car before Boatwrite had a chance to ~~gxtxxxxthingxxixxxixx~~ ~~come out of the door with the~~ rest of the luggage out of the hall. They got off at seven-thirty, Boatwrite and ~~Baby~~ the children's mother in the front and Granny, John Wesley, Baby Brother Little Sister Mayy Ann, Pitty Sing, and the bucking bronco in the back.

"Why the hell did you bring that goddam rocking horse?" Boatwrite asked because as soon as ~~the car began to move~~, Baby Brother began to squall to get on the bucking bronco. "He can't get on that thing in this car and that's final," his father, who was a stern man said.

"Can we open the lunch now?" Little Sister ~~Mayyxxx~~ asked. "It'll shut Baby Brother up. Mamma, can we open up the lunch?"

"No," their grandmother said. *It's only eight-thirty*

Their mother was ~~xxxll~~ reading SCREEN MOTHERS AND THEIR CHILDREN. "Yeah, sure," she said without looking up. She was all dressed up today. She had on a purple silk dress and a hat and ~~glxxxxxxx~~ a choker of pink beads and a new pocket book, and high heel pumps.

"Let's go through Georgia quick so we won't have to look at it much," John Wesley said. ~~It xxxx xxxxxxxx~~

"You should see Tennessee," his grandmother said. "Now there is a *beautiful* state."

"Like hell," John Wesley said. "That's just a hillbilly dumping ground."

"Yeah," his mother said, and nudged Boatwrite. "Didjer hear that?" *she was from Tennessee*

They ate their lunch and got along fine ~~after that~~ for a while until Pitty Sing who had been asleep jumped into the front of the car and caused Boatwrite to swerve to the right into a ditch. Pitty Sing was a large grey-striped cat with a yellow hind leg and a ~~large~~ soiled white face. Granny thought that she ~~returned was~~ was the only person in the world that he really loved but he had never ~~really~~ looked ~~xxxxxxxxxxxxxxxx~~ any farther than her middle and he didn't even like other cats. He jumped snarling into ~~the front seat and Boatwrite's~~ shoulder

Typescript page from "A Good Man Is Hard to Find" with O'Connor's handwritten changes.

June Star said her hair was naturally curly.

10 The next morning the grandmother was the first one in the car, ready to go. She had her big black valise that looked like the head of a hippopotamus in one corner, and underneath it she was hiding a basket with Pitty Sing, the cat, in it. She didn't intend for the cat to be left alone in the house for three days because he would miss her too much and she was afraid he might brush against one of the gas burners and accidentally asphyxiate himself. Her son, Bailey, didn't like to arrive at a motel with a cat.

She sat in the middle of the back seat with John Wesley and June Star on either side of her. Bailey and the children's mother and the baby sat in front and they left Atlanta at eight forty-five with the mileage on the car at 55890. The grandmother wrote this down because she thought it would be interesting to say how many miles they had been when they got back. It took them twenty minutes to reach the outskirts of the city.

The old lady settled herself comfortably, removing her white cotton gloves and putting them up with her purse on the shelf in front of the back window. The children's mother still had on slacks and still had her head tied up in a green kerchief, but the grandmother had on a navy blue straw sailor hat with a bunch of white violets on the brim and a navy blue dress with a small white dot in the print. Her collars and cuffs were white organdy trimmed with lace and at her neckline she had pinned a purple spray of cloth violets containing a sachet. In case of an accident, anyone seeing her dead on the highway would know at once that she was a lady.

She said she thought it was going to be a good day for driving, neither too hot nor too cold, and she cautioned Bailey that the speed limit was fifty-five miles an hour and that the patrolmen hid themselves behind bill-boards and small clumps of trees and sped out after you before you had a chance to slow down. She pointed out interesting details of the scenery: Stone Mountain; the blue granite that in some places came up to both sides of the highway; the brilliant red clay banks slightly streaked with purple; and the various crops that made rows of green lace-work on the ground. The trees were full of silver-white sunlight and the meanest of them sparkled. The children were reading comic magazines and their mother had gone back to sleep.

"Let's go through Georgia fast so we won't have to look at it much," John Wesley said.

15   "If I were a little boy," said the grandmother, "I wouldn't talk about my native state that way. Tennessee has the mountains and Georgia has the hills."

"Tennessee is just a hillbilly dumping ground," John Wesley said, "and Georgia is a lousy state too."

"You said it," June Star said.

"In my time," said the grandmother, folding her thin veined fingers, "children were more respectful of their native states and their parents and everything else. People did right then. Oh look at the cute little pickaninny!" she said and pointed to a Negro child standing in the door of a shack. "Wouldn't that make a picture, now?" she asked and they all turned and looked at the little Negro out of the back window. He waved.

"He didn't have any britches on," June Star said.

20   "He probably didn't have any," the grandmother explained. "Little niggers in the country don't have things like we do. If I could paint, I'd paint that picture," she said.

The children exchanged comic books.

The grandmother offered to hold the baby and the children's mother passed him over the front seat to her. She set him on her knee and bounced him and told him about the things they were passing. She rolled her eyes and screwed up her mouth and stuck her leathery thin face into his smooth bland one. Occasionally he gave her a faraway smile. They passed a large cotton field with five or six graves fenced in the middle of it, like a small island. "Look at the graveyard!" the grandmother said, pointing it out. "That was the old family burying ground. That belonged to the plantation."

"Where's the plantation?" John Wesley asked.

"Gone With the Wind," said the grandmother. "Ha. Ha."

25   When the children finished all the comic books they had brought, they opened the lunch and ate it. The grandmother ate a peanut butter sandwich and

an olive and would not let the children throw the box and the paper napkins out the window. When there was nothing else to do they played a game by choosing a cloud and making the other two guess what shape it suggested. John Wesley took one the shape of a cow and June Star guessed a cow and John Wesley said, no, an automobile, and June Star said he didn't play fair, and they began to slap each other over the grandmother.

The grandmother said she would tell them a story if they would keep quiet. When she told a story, she rolled her eyes and waved her head and was very dramatic. She said once when she was a maiden lady she had been courted by a Mr. Edgar Atkins Teagarden from Jasper, Georgia. She said he was a very good-looking man and a gentleman and that he brought her a watermelon every Saturday afternoon with his initials cut in it, E.A.T. Well, one Saturday, she said, Mr. Teagarden brought the watermelon and there was nobody at home and he left it on the front porch and returned in his buggy to Jasper, but she never got the watermelon, she said, because a nigger boy ate it when he saw the initials, E.A.T.! This story tickled John Wesley's funny bone and he giggled and giggled but June Star didn't think it was any good. She said she wouldn't marry a man that just brought her a watermelon on Saturday. The grandmother said she would have done well to marry Mr. Teagarden because he was a gentleman and had bought Coca-Cola stock when it first came out and that he had died only a few years ago, a very wealthy man.

They stopped at The Tower for barbecued sandwiches. The Tower was a part-stucco and part-wood filling station and dance hall set in a clearing outside of Timothy. A fat man named Red Sammy Butts ran it and there were signs stuck here and there on the building and for miles up and down the highway saying, TRY RED SAMMY'S FAMOUS BARBECUE. NONE LIKE FAMOUS RED SAMMY'S! RED SAM! THE FAT BOY WITH THE HAPPY LAUGH. A VETERAN! RED SAMMY'S YOUR MAN!

Red Sammy was lying on the bare ground outside The Tower with his head under a truck while a gray monkey about a foot high, chained to a small chinaberry tree, chattered nearby. The monkey sprang back into the tree and got on the highest limb as soon as he saw the children jump out of the car and run toward him.

Inside, The Tower was a long dark room with a counter at one end and tables at the other and dancing space in the middle. They all sat down at a broad table next to the nickelodeon and Red Sam's wife, a tall burnt-brown woman with hair and eyes lighter than her skin, came and took their order. The children's mother put a dime in the machine and played "The Tennessee Waltz," and the grandmother said that tune always made her want to dance. She asked Bailey if he would like to dance but he only glared at her. He didn't have a naturally sunny disposition like she did and trips made him nervous. The grandmother's brown eyes were very bright. She swayed her head from side to side and pretended she was dancing in her chair. June Star said play something she could tap to so the children's mother put in another dime and played a fast number and June Star stepped out onto the dance floor and did her tap routine.

30   "Ain't she cute?" Red Sam's wife said, leaning over the counter. "Would you like to come be my little girl?"

"No, I certainly wouldn't," June Star said. "I wouldn't live in a broken-down place like this for a million bucks!" and she ran back to the table.

"Ain't she cute?" the woman repeated, stretching her mouth politely.

"Aren't you ashamed?" hissed the grandmother.

Red Sam came in and told his wife to quit lounging on the counter and hurry with these people's order. His khaki trousers reached just to his hip bones and his stomach hung over them like a sack of meal swaying under his shirt. He came over and sat down at a table nearby and let out a combination sigh and yodel. "You can't win," he said, "You can't win," and he wiped his sweating red face off with a gray handkerchief. "These days you don't know who to trust," he said. "Ain't that the truth?"

35   "People are certainly not nice like they used to be," said the grandmother.

"Two fellers come in here last week," Red Sammy said, "driving a Chrysler. It was an old beat-up car but it was a good one and these boys looked all right to me. Said they worked at the mill and you know I let them fellers charge the gas they bought? Now why did I do that?"

"Because you're a good man!" the grandmother said at once.

"Yes'm, I suppose so," Red Sam said as if he were struck with this answer.

His wife brought the orders, carrying the five plates all at once without a tray, two in each hand and one balanced on her arm. "It isn't a soul in this green world of God's that you can trust," she said. "And I don't count nobody out of that, not nobody," she repeated, looking at Red Sammy.

40   "Did you read about that criminal, The Misfit, that's escaped?" asked the grandmother.

"I wouldn't be a bit surprised if he didn't attack this place right here," said the woman. "If he hears about it being here, I wouldn't be none surprised to see him. If he hears it's two cent in the cash register, I wouldn't be a tall surprised if he . . ."

"That'll do," Red Sam said. "Go bring these people their Co'Colas," and the woman went off to get the rest of the order.

"A good man is hard to find," Red Sammy said. "Everything is getting terrible. I remember the day you could go off and leave your screen door unlatched. Not no more."

He and the grandmother discussed better times. The old lady said that in her opinion Europe was entirely to blame for the way things were now. She said the way Europe acted you would think we were made of money and Red Sam said it was no use talking about it, she was exactly right. The children ran outside into the white sunlight and looked at the monkey in the lacy chinaberry tree. He was busy catching fleas on himself and biting each one carefully between his teeth as if it were a delicacy.

45   They drove off again into the hot afternoon. The grandmother took cat naps and woke up every five minutes with her own snoring. Outside of Toombsboro she woke up and recalled an old plantation that she had visited in this neighborhood once when she was a young lady. She said the house had six white columns across the front and that there was an avenue of oaks leading up to it and two little wooden trellis arbors on either side in front where you sat down with your suitor after a stroll in the garden. She recalled exactly which road to turn off to get to it. She knew that Bailey would not be willing to lose any time looking at an old house, but the more she talked about it, the more she wanted to see it once again and find out if the little twin arbors were still standing. "There was a secret panel in this house," she said craftily, not telling the truth but wishing that she were, "and the story went that all the family silver was hidden in it when Sherman came through but it was never found . . ."

"Hey!" John Wesley said. "Let's go see it! We'll find it! We'll poke all the woodwork and find it! Who lives there? Where do you turn off at? Hey, Pop, can't we turn off there?"

"We never have seen a house with a secret panel!" June Star shrieked. "Let's go to the house with the secret panel! Hey, Pop, can't we go see the house with the secret panel!"

"It's not far from here, I know," the grandmother said. "It wouldn't take over twenty minutes."

Bailey was looking straight ahead. His jaw was as rigid as a horseshoe. "No," he said.

50   The children began to yell and scream that they wanted to see the house with the secret panel. John Wesley kicked the back of the front seat and June Star hung over her mother's shoulder and whined desperately into her ear that they never had any fun even on their vacation, that they could never do what THEY wanted to do. The baby began to scream and John Wesley kicked the back of the seat so hard that his father could feel the blows in his kidney.

"All right!" he shouted and drew the car to a stop at the side of the road. "Will you all shut up? Will you all just shut up for one second? If you don't shut up, we won't go anywhere."

"It would be very educational for them," the grandmother murmured.

"All right," Bailey said, "but get this. This is the only time we're going to stop for anything like this. This is the one and only time."

"The dirt road that you have to turn down is about a mile back," the grandmother directed. "I marked it when we passed."

55   "A dirt road," Bailey groaned.

After they had turned around and were headed toward the dirt road, the grandmother recalled other points about the house, the beautiful glass over the front doorway and the candle lamp in the hall. John Wesley said that the secret panel was probably in the fireplace.

"You can't go inside this house," Bailey said. "You don't know who lives there."

"While you all talk to the people in front, I'll run around behind and get in a window," John Wesley suggested.

"We'll all stay in the car," his mother said.

60   They turned onto the dirt road and the car raced roughly along in a swirl of pink dust. The grandmother recalled the times when there were no paved roads and thirty miles was a day's journey. The dirt road was hilly and there were sudden washes in it and sharp curves on dangerous embankments. All at once they would be on a hill, looking down over the blue tops of trees for miles around, then the next minute, they would be in a red depression with the dust-coated trees looking down on them.

"This place had better turn up in a minute," Bailey said, "or I'm going to turn around."

The road looked as if no one had traveled on it in months.

"It's not much farther," the grandmother said and just as she said it, a horrible thought came to her. The thought was so embarrassing that she turned red in the face and her eyes dilated and her feet jumped up, upsetting her valise in the corner. The instant the valise moved, the newspaper top she had over the basket under it rose with a snarl and Pitty Sing, the cat, sprang onto Bailey's shoulder.

The children were thrown to the floor and their mother, clutching the baby, was thrown out the door onto the ground; the old lady was thrown into the front seat. The car turned over once and landed right-side-up in a gulch on the side of the road. Bailey remained in the driver's seat with the cat—gray-striped with a broad white face and an orange nose—clinging to his neck like a caterpillar.

65   As soon as the children saw they could move their arms and legs, they scrambled out of the car, shouting, "We've had an ACCIDENT!" The grandmother was curled up under the dashboard, hoping she was injured so that Bailey's wrath would not come down on her all at once. The horrible thought she had had before the accident was that the house she had remembered so vividly was not in Georgia but in Tennessee.

Bailey removed the cat from his neck with both hands and flung it out the window against the side of a pine tree. Then he got out of the car and started looking for the children's mother. She was sitting against the side of the red gutted ditch, holding the screaming baby, but she only had a cut down her face and a broken shoulder. "We've had an ACCIDENT!" the children screamed in a frenzy of delight.

"But nobody's killed," June Star said with disappointment as the grandmother limped out of the car, her hat still pinned to her head but the broken front brim standing up at a jaunty angle and the violet spray hanging off the side. They all sat down in the ditch, except the children, to recover from the shock. They were all shaking.

"Maybe a car will come along," said the children's mother hoarsely.

"I believe I have injured an organ," said the grandmother, pressing her side, but no one answered her. Bailey's teeth were clattering. He had on a yellow sport shirt with bright blue parrots designed in it and his face was as yellow as the shirt. The grandmother decided that she would not mention that the house was in Tennessee.

70   The road was about ten feet above and they could see only the tops of the trees on the other side of it. Behind the ditch they were sitting in there were more woods, tall and dark and deep. In a few minutes they saw a car some distance away on top of a hill, coming slowly as if the occupants were watching them. The grandmother stood up and waved both arms dramatically to attract their attention. The car continued to come on slowly, disappeared around a bend and appeared again, moving even slower on top of the hill they had gone over. It was a big black battered hearselike automobile. There were three men in it.

It came to a stop just over them and for some minutes, the driver looked down with a steady expressionless gaze to where they were sitting, and didn't speak. Then he turned his head and muttered something to the other two and they got out. One was a fat boy in black trousers and a red sweat shirt with a silver stallion embossed on the front of it. He moved around on the right side of them and stood staring, his mouth partly open in a kind of loose grin. The other had on khaki pants and a blue striped coat and a gray hat pulled down very low, hiding most of his face. He came around slowly on the left side. Neither spoke.

The driver got out of the car and stood by the side of it, looking down at them. He was an older man than the other two. His hair was just beginning to gray and he wore silver-rimmed spectacles that gave him a scholarly look. He had a long creased face and didn't have on any shirt or undershirt. He had on blue jeans that were too tight for him and was holding a black hat and a gun. The two boys also had guns.

"We've had an ACCIDENT!" the children screamed.

The grandmother had the peculiar feeling that the bespectacled man was someone she knew. His face was as familiar to her as if she had known him all her life but she could not recall who he was. He moved away from the car and began to come down the embankment, placing his feet carefully so that he wouldn't slip. He had on tan and white shoes and no socks, and his ankles were red and thin. "Good afternoon," he said. "I see you all had you a little spill."

75   "We turned over twice!" said the grandmother.

"Oncet," he corrected. "We seen it happen. Try their car and see will it run, Hiram," he said quietly to the boy with the gray hat.

"What you got that gun for?" John Wesley asked. "Whatcha gonna do with that gun?"

"Lady," the man said to the children's mother, "would you mind calling them children to sit down by you? Children make me nervous. I want all you to sit down right together there where you're at."

"What are you telling us what to do for?" June Star asked.

80   Behind them the line of woods gaped like a dark open mouth. "Come here," said their mother.

"Look here now," Bailey began suddenly, "we're in a predicament! We're in . . ."

The grandmother shrieked. She scrambled to her feet and stood staring. "You're The Misfit!" she said. "I recognized you at once!"

"Yes'm," the man said, smiling slightly as if he were pleased in spite of himself to be known, "but it would have been better for all of you, lady, if you hadn't of reckernized me."

Bailey turned his head sharply and said something to his mother that shocked even the children. The old lady began to cry and The Misfit reddened.

85   "Lady," he said, "don't you get upset. Sometimes a man says things he don't mean. I don't reckon he meant to talk to you thataway."

"You wouldn't shoot a lady, would you?" the grandmother said and removed a clean handkerchief from her cuff and began to slap at her eyes with it.

The Misfit pointed the toe of his shoe into the ground and made a little hole and then covered it up again. "I would hate to have to," he said.

"Listen," the grandmother almost screamed, "I know you're a good man. You don't look a bit like you have common blood. I know you must come from nice people!"

"Yes ma'm," he said, "finest people in the world." When he smiled he showed a row of strong white teeth. "God never made a finer woman than my mother and my daddy's heart was pure gold," he said. The boy with the red sweat shirt had come around behind them and was standing with his gun at his hip. The Misfit squatted down on the ground. "Watch them children, Bobby Lee," he said. "You know they make me nervous." He looked at the six of them huddled together in front of him and he seemed to be embarrassed as if he couldn't think of anything to say. "Ain't a cloud in the sky," he remarked, looking up at it. "Don't see no sun but don't see no cloud neither."

90   "Yes, it's a beautiful day," said the grandmother. "Listen," she said, "you shouldn't call yourself The Misfit because I know you're a good man at heart. I can just look at you and tell."

"Hush!" Bailey yelled, "Hush! Everybody shut up and let me handle this!" He was squatting in the position of a runner about to sprint forward but he didn't move.

"I pre-chate that, lady," The Misfit said and drew a little circle in the ground with the butt of his gun.

"It'll take a half a hour to fix this here car," Hiram called, looking over the raised hood of it.

"Well, first you and Bobby Lee get him and that little boy to step over yonder with you," The Misfit said, pointing to Bailey and John Wesley. "The boys want to ask you something," he said to Bailey. "Would you mind stepping back in them woods there with them?"

95   "Listen," Bailey began, "we're in a terrible predicament! Nobody realizes what this is," and his voice cracked. His eyes were as blue and intense as the parrots in his shirt and he remained perfectly still.

The grandmother reached up to adjust her hat brim as if she were going to the woods with him but it came off in her hand. She stood staring at it and after a second she let it fall on the ground. Hiram pulled Bailey up by the arm as if he were assisting an old man. John Wesley caught hold of his father's hand and Bobby Lee followed. They went off toward the woods and just as they reached the dark edge, Bailey turned and supporting himself against a gray naked pine trunk, he shouted, "I'll be back in a minute, Mamma, wait on me!"

"Come back this instant!" his mother shrilled but they all disappeared into the woods.

"Bailey Boy!" the grandmother called in a tragic voice but she found she was looking at The Misfit squatting on the ground in front of her. "I just know you're a good man," she said desperately. "You're not a bit common!"

"Nome, I ain't a good man," The Misfit said after a second as if he had considered her statement carefully, "but I ain't the worst in the world neither. My daddy said I was a different breed of dog from my brothers and sisters. 'You know,' Daddy said, 'It's some that can live their whole life without asking about it and it's others has to know why it is, and this boy is one of the latters. He's going to be into everything!'" He put on his black hat and looked up suddenly and then away deep into the woods as if he were embarrassed again. "I'm sorry I don't have on a shirt before you ladies," he said, hunching his shoulders slightly. "We buried our clothes that we had on when we escaped and we're just making do until we can get better. We borrowed these from some folks we met," he explained.

100   "That's perfectly all right," the grandmother said. "Maybe Bailey has an extra shirt in his suitcase."

"I'll look and see terrectly," The Misfit said.

"Where are they taking him?" the children's mother screamed.

"Daddy was a card himself," The Misfit said. "You couldn't put anything over on him. He never got in trouble with the Authorities though. Just had the knack of handling them."

"You could be honest too if you'd only try," said the grandmother. "Think how wonderful it would be to settle down and live a comfortable life and not have to think about somebody chasing you all the time."

105   The Misfit kept scratching in the ground with the butt of his gun as if he were thinking about it. "Yes'm, somebody is always after you," he murmured.

The grandmother noticed how thin his shoulder blades were just behind his hat because she was standing up looking down on him. "Do you ever pray?" she asked.

He shook his head. All she saw was the black hat wiggle between his shoulder blades. "Nome," he said.

There was a pistol shot from the woods, followed closely by another. Then silence. The old lady's head jerked around. She could hear the wind move through the tree tops like a long satisfied insuck of breath. "Bailey Boy!" she called.

"I was a gospel singer for a while," The Misfit said. "I been most everything. Been in the arm service, both land and sea, at home and abroad, been twict married, been an undertaker, been with the railroads, plowed Mother Earth, been in a tornado, seen a man burnt alive oncet," and he looked up at the children's mother and the little girl who were sitting close together, their faces white and their eyes glassy; "I even seen a woman flogged," he said.

110 "Pray, pray," the grandmother began, "pray, pray. . . ."

"I never was a bad boy that I remember of," The Misfit said in an almost dreamy voice, "but somewheres along the line I done something wrong and got sent to the penitentiary. I was buried alive," and he looked up and held her attention to him by a steady stare.

"That's when you should have started to pray," she said. "What did you do to get sent up to the penitentiary that first time?"

"Turn to the right, it was a wall," The Misfit said, looking up again at the cloudless sky. "Turn to the left, it was a wall. Look up it was a ceiling, look down it was a floor. I forget what I done, lady. I set there and set there, trying to remember what it was I done and I ain't recalled it to this day. Oncet in a while, I would think it was coming to me, but it never come."

"Maybe they put you in by mistake," the old lady said vaguely.

115 "Nome," he said. "It wasn't no mistake. They had the papers on me."

"You must have stolen something," she said.

The Misfit sneered slightly. "Nobody had nothing I wanted," he said. "It was a head-doctor at the penitentiary said what I had done was kill my daddy but I known that for a lie. My daddy died in nineteen ought nineteen of the epidemic flu and I never had a thing to do with it. He was buried in the Mount Hopewell Baptist churchyard and you can go there and see for yourself."

"If you would pray," the old lady said, "Jesus would help you."

"That's right," The Misfit said.

120 "Well then, why don't you pray?" she asked trembling with delight suddenly.

"I don't want no hep," he said. "I'm doing all right by myself."

Bobby Lee and Hiram came ambling back from the woods. Bobby Lee was dragging a yellow shirt with bright blue parrots in it.

"Throw me that shirt, Bobby Lee," The Misfit said. The shirt came flying at him and landed on his shoulder and he put it on. The grandmother couldn't name what the shirt reminded her of. "No, lady," The Misfit said while he was buttoning it up, "I found out the crime don't matter. You can do one thing or you can do another, kill a man or take a tire off his car, because sooner or later you're going to forget what it was you done and just be punished for it."

The children's mother had begun to make heaving noises as if she couldn't get her breath. "Lady," he asked, "would you and that little girl like to step off yonder with Bobby Lee and Hiram and join your husband?"

125 "Yes, thank you," the mother said faintly. Her left arm dangled helplessly and she was holding the baby, who had gone to sleep, in the other. "Hep that lady up, Hiram," The Misfit said as she struggled to climb out of the ditch, "and Bobby Lee, you hold onto that little girl's hand."

"I don't want to hold hands with him," June Star said. "He reminds me of a pig."

The fat boy blushed and laughed and caught her by the arm and pulled her off into the woods after Hiram and her mother.

Alone with The Misfit, the grandmother found that she had lost her voice. There was not a cloud in the sky nor any sun. There was nothing around her but woods. She wanted to tell him that he must pray. She opened and closed her mouth several times before anything came out. Finally she found herself saying, "Jesus, Jesus," meaning, Jesus will help you, but the way she was saying it, it sounded as if she might be cursing.

"Yes'm," The Misfit said as if he agreed. "Jesus thown everything off balance. It was the same case with Him as with me except He hadn't committed any crime and they could prove I had committed one because they had the papers on me. Of course," he said, "they never shown me my papers. That's why I sign myself now. I said long ago, you get you a signature and sign everything you do and keep a copy of it. Then you'll know what you done and you can hold up the crime to the punishment and see do they match and in the end you'll have something to prove you ain't been treated right. I call myself The Misfit," he said, "because I can't make what all I done wrong fit what all I gone through in punishment."

130   There was a piercing scream from the woods, followed closely by a pistol report. "Does it seem right to you, lady, that one is punished a heap and another ain't punished at all?"

"Jesus!" the old lady cried. "You've got good blood! I know you wouldn't shoot a lady! I know you come from nice people! Pray! Jesus, you ought not to shoot a lady. I'll give you all the money I've got!"

"Lady," The Misfit said, looking beyond her far into the woods, "there never was a body that give the undertaker a tip."

There were two more pistol reports and the grandmother raised her head like a parched old turkey hen crying for water and called, "Bailey Boy, Bailey Boy!" as if her heart would break.

"Jesus was the only One that ever raised the dead," The Misfit continued, "and He shouldn't have done it. He thrown everything off balance. If He did what He said, then it's nothing for you to do but thow away everything and follow Him, and if He didn't, then it's nothing for you to do but enjoy the few minutes you got left the best way you can—by killing somebody or burning down his house or doing some other meanness to him. No pleasure but meanness," he said and his voice had become almost a snarl.

135   "Maybe He didn't raise the dead," the old lady mumbled, not knowing what she was saying and feeling so dizzy that she sank down in the ditch with her legs twisted under her.

"I wasn't there so I can't say He didn't," The Misfit said. "I wisht I had of been there," he said, hitting the ground with his fist. "It ain't right I wasn't there because if I had of been there I would of known. Listen lady," he said in a high voice, "if I had of been there I would of known and I wouldn't be like I am now." His voice seemed about to crack and the grandmother's head cleared for an instant. She saw the man's face twisted close to her own as if he were going to cry and she murmured, "Why you're one of my babies. You're one of my own children!" She reached out and touched him on the shoulder. The Misfit sprang back as if a snake had bitten him and shot her three times through the chest. Then he put his gun down on the ground and took off his glasses and began to clean them.

Hiram and Bobby Lee returned from the woods and stood over the ditch, looking down at the grandmother who half sat and half lay in a puddle of blood with her legs crossed under her like a child's and her face smiling up at the cloudless sky.

Without his glasses, The Misfit's eyes were red-rimmed and pale and defenseless-looking. "Take her off and thow her where you thown the others," he said, picking up the cat that was rubbing itself against his leg.

"She was a talker, wasn't she?" Bobby Lee said, sliding down the ditch with a yodel.

140   "She would of been a good woman," The Misfit said, "if it had been somebody there to shoot her every minute of her life."

"Some fun!" Bobby Lee said.

"Shut up, Bobby Lee," The Misfit said. "It's no real pleasure in life."

[1953]

Revelation

The doctor's waiting room, which was very small, was almost full when the Turpins entered and Mrs. Turpin, who was very large, made it look even smaller by her presence. She stood looming at the head of the magazine table set in the center of it, a living demonstration that the room was inadequate and ridiculous. Her little bright black eyes took in all the patients as she sized up the seating situation. There was one vacant chair and a place on a sofa occupied by a blond child in a dirty blue romper who should have been told to move over and make room for the lady. He was five or six, but Mrs. Turpin saw at once that no one was going to tell him to move over. He was slumped down in the seat, his arms idle at his sides and his eyes idle in his head; his nose ran unchecked.

Mrs. Turpin put a firm hand on Claud's shoulder and said in a voice that included anyone who wanted to listen, "Claud, you sit in that chair there," and gave him a push down into the vacant one. Claud was florid and bald and sturdy, somewhat shorter than Mrs. Turpin, but he sat down as if he were accustomed to doing what she told him to.

Mrs. Turpin remained standing. The only man in the room besides Claud was a lean stringy old fellow with a rusty hand spread out on each knee, whose eyes were closed as if he were asleep or dead or pretending to be so as not to get up and offer her his seat. Her gaze settled agreeably on a well-dressed grey-haired lady whose eyes met hers and whose expression said: If that child belonged to me, he would have some manners and move over—there's plenty of room there for you and him too.

Claud looked up with a sigh and made as if to rise.

5   "Sit down," Mrs. Turpin said. "You know you're not supposed to stand on that leg. He has an ulcer on his leg," she explained.

Claud lifted his foot onto the magazine table and rolled his trouser leg up to reveal a purple swelling on a plump marble-white calf.

"My!" the pleasant lady said. "How did you do that?"

"A cow kicked him," Mrs. Turpin said.

"Goodness!" said the lady.

10   Claud rolled his trouser leg down.

"Maybe the little boy would move over," the lady suggested, but the child did not stir.

"Somebody will be leaving in a minute," Mrs. Turpin said. She could not understand why a doctor—with as much money as they made charging five dollars a day to just stick their head in the hospital door and look at you—couldn't afford a decent-sized waiting room. This one was hardly bigger than a garage. The table was cluttered with limp-looking magazines and at one end of it there was a big green glass ash tray full of cigaret butts and cotton wads with little blood spots on them. If she had had anything to do with the running of the place, that would have been emptied every so often. There were no chairs against the wall at the head of the room. It had a rectangular-shaped panel in it that permitted a view of the office where the nurse came and went and the secretary listened to the radio. A plastic fern in a gold pot sat in the opening and trailed its fronds down almost to the floor. The radio was softly playing gospel music.

Just then the inner door opened and a nurse with the highest stack of yellow hair Mrs. Turpin had ever seen put her face in the crack and called for the next patient. The woman sitting beside Claud grasped the two arms of her chair and hoisted herself up; she pulled her dress free from her legs and lumbered through the door where the nurse had disappeared.

Mrs. Turpin eased into the vacant chair, which held her tight as a corset. "I wish I could reduce," she said, and rolled her eyes and gave a comic sigh.

15   "Oh, *you* aren't fat," the stylish lady said.

"Ooooo I am too," Mrs. Turpin said. "Claud he eats all he wants to and never weighs over one hundred and seventy-five pounds, but me I just look at something good to eat and I gain some weight," and her stomach and shoulders shook with laughter. "You can eat all you want to, can't you, Claud?" she asked, turning to him.

Claud only grinned.

"Well, as long as you have such a good disposition," the stylish lady said, "I don't think it makes a bit of difference what size you are. You just can't beat a good disposition."

Next to her was a fat girl of eighteen or nineteen, scowling into a thick blue book which Mrs. Turpin saw was entitled *Human Development.* The girl raised her head and directed her scowl at Mrs. Turpin as if she did not like her looks. She appeared annoyed that anyone should speak while she tried to read. The poor girl's face was blue with acne and Mrs. Turpin thought how pitiful it was to have a face like that at that age. She gave the girl a friendly smile but the girl only scowled the harder. Mrs. Turpin herself was fat but she had always had good skin, and, though she was forty-seven years old, there was not a wrinkle in her face except around her eyes from laughing too much.

20   Next to the ugly girl was the child, still in exactly the same position, and next to him was a thin leathery old woman in a cotton print dress. She and Claud had three sacks of chicken feed in their pump house that was in the same print. She had seen from the first that the child belonged with the old woman. She could tell by the way they sat—kind of vacant and white-trashy, as if they would sit there until Doomsday if nobody called and told them to get up. And at right angles but next to the well-dressed pleasant lady was a lank-faced woman who was certainly the child's mother. She had on a yellow sweat shirt and wine-colored slacks, both gritty-looking, and the rims of her lips were stained with snuff. Her dirty yellow hair was tied behind with a little piece of red paper ribbon. Worse than niggers any day, Mrs. Turpin thought.

The gospel hymn playing was, "When I looked up and He looked down," and Mrs. Turpin, who knew it, supplied the last line mentally, "And wona these days I know I'll we-era crown."

Without appearing to, Mrs. Turpin always noticed people's feet. The well-dressed lady had on red and grey suede shoes to match her dress. Mrs. Turpin had on her good black patent leather pumps. The ugly girl had on Girl Scout shoes and heavy socks. The old woman had on tennis shoes and the white-trashy mother had on what appeared to be bedroom slippers, black straw with gold braid threaded through them—exactly what you would have expected her to have on.

Sometimes at night when she couldn't go to sleep, Mrs. Turpin would occupy herself with the question of who she would have chosen to be if she couldn't have been herself. If Jesus had said to her before he made her, "There's only two places available for you. You can either be a nigger or white-trash," what would she have said? "Please, Jesus, please," she would have said, "just let me wait until there's another place available," and he would have said, "No, you have to go right now and I have only those two places so make up your mind." She would have wiggled and squirmed and begged and pleaded but it would have been no use and finally she would have said, "All right, make me a nigger then—but that don't mean a trashy one." And he would have made her a neat clean respectable Negro-woman, herself but black.

Next to the child's mother was a red-headed youngish woman, reading one of the magazines and working a piece of chewing gum, hell for leather, as Claud would say. Mrs. Turpin could not see the woman's feet. She was not white-trash, just common. Sometimes Mrs. Turpin occupied herself at night naming the classes of people. On the bottom of the heap were most colored people, not the kind she would have been if she had been one, but most of them; then next to them—not above, just away from—were the white-trash; then above them were the homeowners, and above them the home-and-land owners, to which she and Claud belonged. Above she and Claud were people with a lot of money and much bigger houses and much more land. But here the complexity of it would begin to bear in on her, for some of the people with a lot of money were common and ought to be below she and Claud and some of the people who had good blood had lost their money and had to rent and then there were colored people who owned their homes and land as well. There was a colored dentist in town who had two red Lincolns and a swimming pool and a farm with registered white-face cattle on it. Usually by the time she had fallen asleep all the classes of people were moiling and roiling around in her head, and she would dream they were all crammed in together in a box car, being ridden off to be put in a gas oven.

25   "That's a beautiful clock," she said and nodded to her right. It was a big wall clock, the face encased in a brass sunburst.

"Yes, it's very pretty," the stylish lady said agreeably. "And right on the dot too," she added, glancing at her watch.

The ugly girl beside her cast an eye upward at the clock, smirked, then looked directly at Mrs. Turpin and smirked again. Then she returned her eyes to her book. She was obviously the lady's daughter because, although they didn't look anything alike as to disposition, they both had the same shape of face and the same blue eyes. On the lady they sparkled pleasantly but in the girl's seared face they appeared alternately to smolder and to blaze.

What if Jesus had said, "All right, you can be white-trash or a nigger or ugly"!

Mrs. Turpin felt an awful pity for the girl, though she thought it was one thing to be ugly and another to act ugly.

30   The woman with the snuff-stained lips turned around in her chair and looked up at the clock. Then she turned back and appeared to look a little to the side of Mrs. Turpin. There was a cast in one of her eyes. "You want to know wher you can get one of themther clocks?" she asked in a loud voice.

"No, I already have a nice clock," Mrs. Turpin said. Once somebody like her got a leg in the conversation, she would be all over it.

"You can get you one with green stamps," the woman said. "That's most likely wher he got hisn. Save you up enough, you can get you most anything. I got me some joo'ry."

Ought to have got you a wash rag and some soap, Mrs. Turpin thought.

"I get contour sheets with mine," the pleasant lady said.

35   The daughter slammed her book shut. She looked straight in front of her, directly through Mrs. Turpin and on through the yellow curtain and the plate glass window which made the wall behind her. The girl's eyes seemed lit all of a sudden with a peculiar light, an unnatural light like night road signs give. Mrs. Turpin turned her head to see if there was anything going on outside that she should see, but she could not see anything. Figures passing cast only a pale shadow through the curtain. There was no reason the girl should single her out for her ugly looks.

"Miss Finley," the nurse said, cracking the door. The gum chewing woman got up and passed in front of her and Claud and went into the office. She had on red high-heeled shoes.

Directly across the table, the ugly girl's eyes were fixed on Mrs. Turpin as if she had some very special reason for disliking her.

"This is wonderful weather, isn't it?" the girl's mother said.

"It's good weather for cotton if you can get the niggers to pick it," Mrs. Turpin said, "but niggers don't want to pick cotton any more. You can't get the white folks to pick it and now you can't get the niggers—because they got to be right up there with the white folks."

40   "They gonna *try* anyways," the white-trash woman said, leaning forward.

"Do you have one of those cotton-picking machines?" the pleasant lady asked.

"No," Mrs. Turpin said, "they leave half the cotton in the field. We don't have much cotton anyway. If you want to make it farming now, you have to have a little of everything. We got a couple of acres of cotton and a few hogs and chickens and just enough white-face that Claud can look after them himself."

"One thang I don't want," the white-trash woman said, wiping her mouth with the back of her hand. "Hogs. Nasty stinking things, a-gruntin and a-rootin all over the place."

Mrs. Turpin gave her the merest edge of her attention. "Our hogs are not dirty and they don't stink," she said. "They're cleaner than some children I've seen. Their feet never touch the ground. We have a pig-parlor—that's where you raise them on concrete," she explained to the pleasant lady, "and Claud scoots them down with the hose every afternoon and washes off the floor." Cleaner by far than that child right there, she thought. Poor nasty little thing. He had not moved except to put the thumb of his dirty hand into his mouth.

45   The woman turned her face away from Mrs. Turpin. "I know I wouldn't scoot down no hog with no hose," she said to the wall.

You wouldn't have no hog to scoot down, Mrs. Turpin said to herself.

"A-gruntin and a-rootin and a-groanin," the woman muttered.

"We got a little of everything," Mrs. Turpin said to the pleasant lady. "It's no use in having more than you can handle yourself with help like it is. We found enough niggers to pick our cotton this year but Claud he has to go after them and take them home again in the evening. They can't walk that half a mile. No they can't. I tell you," she said and laughed merrily, "I sure am tired of buttering up niggers, but you got to love em if you want em to work for you. When they come in the morning, I run out and I say, 'Hi yawl this morning?' and when Claud drives them off to the field I just wave to beat the band and they just wave back." And she waved her hand rapidly to illustrate.

"Like you read out of the same book," the lady said, showing she understood perfectly.

50   "Child, yes," Mrs. Turpin said. "And when they come in from the field, I run out with a bucket of icewater. That's the way it's going to be from now on," she said. "You may as well face it."

"One thang I know," the white-trash woman said. "Two thangs I ain't going to do: love no niggers or scoot down no hog with no hose." And she let out a bark of contempt.

The look that Mrs. Turpin and the pleasant lady exchanged indicated they both understood that you had to *have* certain things before you could *know* certain things. But every time Mrs. Turpin exchanged a look with the lady, she was aware that the ugly girl's peculiar eyes were still on her, and she had trouble bringing her attention back to the conversation.

"When you got something," she said, "you got to look after it." And when you ain't got a thing but breath and britches, she added to herself, you can afford to come to town every morning and just sit on the Court House coping and spit.

A grotesque revolving shadow passed across the curtain behind her and was thrown palely on the opposite wall. Then a bicycle clattered down against the outside of the building. The door opened and a colored boy glided in with a tray from the drug store. It had two large red and white paper cups on it with tops on them. He was a tall, very black boy in discolored white pants and a green nylon shirt. He was chewing gum slowly, as if to music. He set the tray down in the office opening next to the fern and stuck his head through to look for the secretary. She was not in there. He rested his arms on the ledge and waited, his narrow bottom stuck out, swaying slowly to the left and right. He raised a hand over his head and scratched the base of his skull.

55   "You see that button there, boy?" Mrs. Turpin said. "You can punch that and she'll come. She's probably in the back somewhere."

"Is that right?" the boy said agreeably, as if he had never seen the button before. He leaned to the right and put his finger on it. "She sometime out," he said and twisted around to face his audience, his elbows behind him on the counter. The nurse appeared and he twisted back again. She handed him a dollar and he rooted in his pocket and made the change and counted it out to her. She gave him fifteen cents for a tip and he went out with the empty tray. The heavy door swung to slowly and closed at length with the sound of suction. For a moment no one spoke.

"They ought to send all them niggers back to Africa," the white-trash woman said. "That's wher they come from in the first place."

"Oh, I couldn't do without my good colored friends," the pleasant lady said.

"There's a heap of things worse than a nigger," Mrs. Turpin agreed. "It's all kinds of them just like it's all kinds of us."

60   "Yes, and it takes all kinds to make the world go round," the lady said in her musical voice.

As she said it, the raw-complexioned girl snapped her teeth together. Her lower lip turned downwards and inside out, revealing the pale pink inside of her mouth. After a second it rolled back up. It was the ugliest face Mrs. Turpin had ever seen anyone make and for a moment she was certain that the girl had made it at her. She was looking at her as if she had known and disliked her all her life—all of Mrs. Turpin's life, it seemed too, not just all the girl's life. Why, girl, I don't even know you, Mrs. Turpin said silently.

She forced her attention back to the discussion. "It wouldn't be practical to send them back to Africa," she said. "They wouldn't want to go. They got it too good here."

"Wouldn't be what they wanted—if I had anythang to do with it," the woman said.

"It wouldn't be a way in the world you could get all the niggers back over there," Mrs. Turpin said. "They'd be hiding out and lying down and turning sick on you and wailing and hollering and raring and pitching. It wouldn't be a way in the world to get them over there."

65   "They got over here," the trashy woman said. "Get back like they got over."

"It wasn't so many of them then," Mrs. Turpin explained.

The woman looked at Mrs. Turpin as if here was an idiot indeed but Mrs. Turpin was not bothered by the look, considering where it came from.

"Nooo," she said, "they're going to stay here where they can go to New York and marry white folks and improve their color. That's what they all want to do, every one of them, improve their color."

"You know what comes of that, don't you?" Claud asked.

70   "No, Claud, what?" Mrs. Turpin said.

Claud's eyes twinkled. "White-faced niggers," he said with never a smile.

Everybody in the office laughed except the white-trash and the ugly girl. The girl gripped the book in her lap with white fingers. The trashy woman looked around her from face to face as if she thought they were all idiots. The old woman in the feed sack dress continued to gaze expressionless across the floor at the high-top shoes of the man opposite her. the one who had been pretending to be asleep when the Turpins came in. He was laughing heartily, his hands still spread out on his knees. The child had fallen to the side and was lying now almost face down in the old woman's lap.

While they recovered from their laughter, the nasal chorus on the radio kept the room from silence.

> You go to blank blank
> And I'll go to mine
> But we'll all blank along
> To-geth-ther,
> And all along the blank
> We'll hep each other out
> Smile-ling in any kind of
> Weath-ther!

Mrs. Turpin didn't catch every word but she caught enough to agree with the spirit of the song and it turned her thoughts sober. To help anybody out that needed it was her philosophy of life. She never spared herself when she found somebody in need, whether they were white or black, trash or decent. And of all she had to be thankful for, she was most thankful that this was so. If Jesus had said, "You can be high society and have all the money you want and be thin and svelte-like, but you can't be a good woman with it," she would have had to say, "Well don't make me that then. Make me a good woman and it don't matter what else, how fat or how ugly or how poor!" Her heart rose. He had not made her a nigger or white-trash or ugly! He had made her herself and given her a little of everything. Jesus, thank you! she said. Thank you thank you thank you! Whenever she counted her blessings she felt as buoyant as if she weighed one hundred and twenty-five pounds instead of one hundred and eighty.

75   "What's wrong with your little boy?" the pleasant lady asked the white-trashy woman.

"He has a ulcer," the woman said proudly. "He ain't give me a minute's peace since he was born. Him and her are just alike," she said, nodding at the old woman, who was running her leathery fingers through the child's pale hair. "Look like I can't get nothing down them two but Co'Cola and candy."

That's all you try to get down em, Mrs. Turpin said to herself. Too lazy to light the fire. There was nothing you could tell her about people like them that she didn't know already. And it was not just that they didn't have anything. Because if you gave them everything, in two weeks it would all be broken or filthy or they would have chopped it up for lightwood. She knew all this from her own experience. Help them you must, but help them you couldn't.

All at once the ugly girl turned her lips inside out again. Her eyes were fixed like two drills on Mrs. Turpin. This time there was no mistaking that there was something urgent behind them.

Girl, Mrs. Turpin exclaimed silently, I haven't done a thing to you! The girl might be confusing her with somebody else. There was no need to sit by and let herself be intimidated. "You must be in college," she said boldly, looking directly at the girl. "I see you reading a book there."

80   The girl continued to stare and pointedly did not answer.

Her mother blushed at this rudeness. "The lady asked you a question, Mary Grace," she said under her breath.

"I have ears," Mary Grace said.

The poor mother blushed again. "Mary Grace goes to Wellesley College," she explained. She twisted one of the buttons on her dress. "In Massachusetts," she added with a grimace. "And in the summer she just keeps right on studying. Just reads all the time, a real book worm. She's done real well at Wellesley; she's taking English and Math and History and Psychology and Social Studies," she rattled on, "and I think it's too much. I think she ought to get out and have fun."

The girl looked as if she would like to hurl them all through the plate glass window.

85   "Way up north," Mrs. Turpin murmured and thought, well, it hasn't done much for her manners.

"I'd almost rather to have him sick," the white-trash woman said, wrenching the attention back to herself. "He's so mean when he ain't. Look like some children just take natural to meanness. It's some gets bad when they get sick but he was the opposite. Took sick and turned good. He don't give me no trouble now. It's me waitin to see the doctor," she said.

If I was going to send anybody back to Africa, Mrs. Turpin thought, it would be your kind, woman. "Yes, indeed," she said aloud, but looking up at the ceiling, "it's a heap of things worse than a nigger." And dirtier than a hog, she added to herself.

"I think people with bad dispositions are more to be pitied than anyone on earth," the pleasant lady said in a voice that was decidedly thin.

"I thank the Lord he has blessed me with a good one," Mrs. Turpin said. "The day has never dawned that I couldn't find something to laugh at."

90 "Not since she married me anyways," Claud said with a comical straight face.

Everybody laughed except the girl and the white-trash.

Mrs. Turpin's stomach shook. "He's such a caution," she said, "that I can't help but laugh at him."

The girl made a loud ugly noise through her teeth.

Her mother's mouth grew thin and tight. "I think the worst thing in the world," she said, "is an ungrateful person. To have everything and not appreciate it. I know a girl," she said, "who has parents who would give her anything, a little brother who loves her dearly, who is getting a good education, who wears the best clothes, but who can never say a kind word to anyone, who never smiles, who just criticizes and complains all day long."

95 "Is she too old to paddle?" Claud asked.

The girl's face was almost purple.

"Yes," the lady said. "I'm afraid there's nothing to do but leave her to her folly. Some day she'll wake up and it'll be too late."

"It never hurt anyone to smile," Mrs. Turpin said. "It just makes you feel better all over."

Of course," the lady said sadly, "but there are just some people you can't tell anything to. They can't take criticism."

100 ""If it's one thing I am," Mrs. Turpin said with feeling, "it's grateful. When I think who all I could have been besides myself and what all I got, a little of everything, and a good disposition besides, I just feel like shouting, 'Thank you, Jesus, for making everything the way it is!' It could have been different!" For one thing, somebody else could have got Claud. At the thought of this, she was flooded with gratitude and a terrible pang of joy ran through her. "Oh thank you, Jesus, Jesus, thank you!" she cried aloud.

The book struck her directly over her left eye. It struck almost at the same instant that she realized the girl was about to hurl it. Before she could utter a sound, the raw face came crashing across the table toward her, howling. The girl's fingers sank like clamps into the soft flesh of her neck. She heard the mother cry out and Claud shout, "Whoa!" There was an instant when she was certain that she was about to be in an earthquake.

All at once her vision narrowed and she saw everything as if it were happening in a small room far away, or as if she were looking at it through the wrong end of a telescope. Claud's face crumpled and fell out of sight. The nurse ran in, then out, then in again. Then the gangling figure of the doctor rushed out of the inner door. Magazines flew this way and that as the table turned over. The girl fell with a thud and Mrs. Turpin's vision suddenly reversed itself and she saw everything large instead of small. The eyes of the white-trashy woman were staring hugely at the floor. There the girl, held down on one side by the nurse and on the other by her mother, was wrenching and turning in their grasp. The doctor was kneeling astride her, trying to hold her arm down. He managed after a second to sink a long needle into it.

Mrs. Turpin felt entirely hollow except for her heart which swung from side to side as if it were agitated in a great empty drum of flesh.

"Somebody that's not busy call for the ambulance," the doctor said in the off-hand voice young doctors adopt for terrible occasions.

105 Mrs. Turpin could not have moved a finger. The old man who had been sitting next to her skipped nimbly into the office and made the call, for the secretary still seemed to be gone.

"Claud!" Mrs. Turpin called.

He was not in his chair. She knew she must jump up and find him but she felt like someone trying to catch a train in a dream, when everything moves in slow motion and the faster you try to run the slower you go.

"Here I am," a suffocated voice, very unlike Claud's, said.

He was doubled up in the corner on the floor, pale as paper, holding his leg. She wanted to get up and go to him but she could not move. Instead, her gaze was drawn slowly downward to the churning face on the floor, which she could see over the doctor's shoulder.

110 The girl's eyes stopped rolling and focused on her. They seemed a much lighter blue than before, as if a door that had been tightly closed behind them was now open to admit light and air.

Mrs. Turpin's head cleared and her power of motion returned. She leaned forward until she was looking directly into the fierce brilliant eyes. There was no doubt in her mind that the girl did know her. knew her in some intense and personal way, beyond time and place and condition. "What you got to say to me?" she asked hoarsely and held her breath, waiting, as for a revelation.

The girl raised her head. Her gaze locked with Mrs. Turpin's. "Go back to hell where you came from, you old wart hog," she whispered. Her voice was low but clear. Her eyes burned for a moment as if she saw with pleasure that her message had struck its target.

Mrs. Turpin sank back in her chair.

After a moment the girl's eyes closed and she turned her head wearily to the side.

115 The doctor rose and handed the nurse the empty syringe. He leaned over and put both hands for a moment on the mother's shoulders, which were shaking. She was sitting on the floor, her lips pressed together, holding Mary Grace's hand in her lap. The girl's fingers were gripped like a baby's around her thumb. "Go on to the hospital," he said. "I'll call and make the arrangements."

"Now let's see that neck," he said in a jovial voice to Mrs. Turpin. He began to inspect her neck with his first two fingers. Two little moonshaped lines like pink fish bones were indented over her windpipe. There was the beginning of an angry red swelling above her eye. His fingers passed over this also.

"Lea' me be," she said thickly and shook him off. "See about Claud. She kicked him."

"I'll see about him in a minute," he said and felt her pulse. He was a thin gray-haired man, given to pleasantries. "Go home and have yourself a vacation the rest of the day," he said and patted her on the shoulder.

Quit your pattin me, Mrs. Turpin growled to herself.

120 "And put an ice pack over that eye," he said. Then he went and squatted down beside Claud and looked at his leg. After a moment he pulled him up and Claud limped after him into the office.

Until the ambulance came, the only sounds in the room were the tremulous moans of the girl's mother, who continued to sit on the floor. The white-trash woman did not take her eyes off the girl. Mrs. Turpin looked straight ahead at nothing. Presently the ambulance drew up, a long dark shadow, behind the curtain. The attendants came in and set the stretcher down beside the girl and lifted her expertly onto it and carried her out. The nurse helped the mother gather up her things. The shadow of the ambulance moved silently away and the nurse came back in the office.

"That ther girl is going to be a lunatic, ain't she?" the white-trash woman asked the nurse, but the nurse kept on to the back and never answered her.

"Yes, she's going to be a lunatic," the white-trash woman said to the rest of them.

"Po' critter," the old woman murmured. The child's face was still in her lap. His eyes looked idly out over her knees. He had not moved during the disturbance except to draw one leg up under him.

125   "I thank Gawd," the white-trash woman said fervently, "I ain't a lunatic."

Claud came limping out and the Turpins went home.

As their pick-up truck turned into their own dirt road and made the crest of the hill, Mrs. Turpin gripped the window ledge and looked out suspiciously. The land sloped gracefully down through a field dotted with lavender weeds and at the start of the rise their small yellow frame house, with its little flower beds spread out around it like a fancy apron, sat primly in its accustomed place between two giant hickory trees. She would not have been startled to see a burnt wound between two blackened chimneys.

Neither of them felt like eating so they put on their house clothes and lowered the shade in the bedroom and lay down, Claud with his leg on a pillow and herself with a damp washcloth over her eye. The instant she was flat on her back, the image of a razor-backed hog with warts on its face and horns coming out behind its ears snorted into her head. She moaned, a low quiet moan.

"I am not," she said tearfully, "a wart hog. From hell." But the denial had no force. The girl's eyes and her words, even the tone of her voice, low but clear, directed only to her, brooked no repudiation. She had been singled out for the message, though there was trash in the room to whom it might justly have been applied. The full force of this fact struck her only now. There was a woman there who was neglecting her own child but she had been overlooked. The message had been given to Ruby Turpin, a respectable, hard-working, church-going woman. The tears dried. Her eyes began to burn instead with wrath.

130   She rose on her elbow and the washcloth fell into her hand. Claud was lying on his back, snoring. She wanted to tell him what the girl had said. At the same time she did not wish to put the image of herself as a wart hog from hell into his mind.

"Hey, Claud," she muttered and pushed his shoulder.

Claud opened one pale baby blue eye.

She looked into it warily. He did not think about anything. He just went his way.

"Wha, whasit?" he said and closed the eye again.

135   "Nothing," she said. "Does your leg pain you?"

"Hurts like hell," Claud said.

"It'll quit terreckly," she said and lay back down. In a moment Claud was snoring again. For the rest of the afternoon they lay there. Claud slept. She scowled at the ceiling. Occasionally she raised her fist and made a small stabbing motion over her chest as if she was defending her innocence to invisible guests who were like the comforters of Job, reasonable-seeming but wrong.

About five-thirty Claud stirred. "Got to go after those niggers," he sighed, not moving.

She was looking straight up as if there were unintelligible handwriting on the ceiling. The protuberance over her eye had turned a greenish-blue. "Listen here," she said.

140   "What?"

"Kiss me."

Claud leaned over and kissed her loudly on the mouth. He pinched her side and their hands interlocked. Her expression of ferocious concentration did not change. Claud got up, groaning and growling, and limped off. She continued to study the ceiling.

She did not get up until she heard the pick-up truck coming back with the Negroes. Then she rose and thrust her feet in her brown oxfords, which she did not bother to lace, and stumped out onto the back porch and got her red plastic bucket. She emptied a tray of ice cubes into it and filled it half full of water and went out into the back yard. Every afternoon after Claud brought the hands in, one of the boys helped him put out hay and the rest waited in the back of the truck until he was ready to take them home. The truck was parked in the shade under one of the hickory trees.

"Hi yawl this evening?" Mrs. Turpin asked grimly, appearing with the bucket and the dipper. There were three women and a boy in the truck.

145   "Us doin nicely," the oldest woman said. "Hi you doin?" and her gaze stuck immediately on the dark lump on Mrs. Turpin's forehead. "You done fell down, ain't you?" she asked in a solicitous voice. The old woman was dark and almost toothless. She had on an old felt hat of Claud's set back on her head. The other two women were younger and lighter and they both had new bright green sun hats. One of them had hers on her head; the other had taken hers off and the boy was grinning beneath it.

Mrs. Turpin set the bucket down on the floor of the truck. "Yawl hep yourselves," she said. She looked around to make sure Claud had gone. "No. I didn't fall down," she said, folding her arms. "It was something worse than that."

"Ain't nothing bad happen to you!" the old woman said. She said it as if they all knew Mrs. Turpin was protected in some special way by Divine Providence. "You just had you a little fall."

"We were in town at the doctor's office for where the cow kicked Mr. Turpin," Mrs. Turpin said in a flat tone that indicated they could leave off their foolishness. "And there was this girl there. A big fat girl with her face all broke out. I could look at that girl and tell she was peculiar but I couldn't tell how. And me and her mama were just talking and going along and all of a sudden WHAM! She throws this big book she was reading at me and . . ."

"Naw!" the old woman cried out.

150   "And then she jumps over the table and commences to choke me."

"Naw!" they all exclaimed, "naw!"

"Hi come she do that?" the old woman asked. "What ail her?"

Mrs. Turpin only glared in front of her.

"Somethin ail her," the old woman said.

155   "They carried her off in an ambulance," Mrs. Turpin continued, "but before she went she was rolling on the floor and they were trying to hold her down to give her a shot and she said something to me." She paused. "You know what she said to me?"

"What she say?" they asked.

"She said," Mrs. Turpin began, and stopped, her face very dark and heavy. The sun was getting whiter and whiter, blanching the sky overhead so that the leaves of the hickory tree were black in the face of it. She could not bring forth the words. "Something real ugly," she muttered.

"She sho shouldn't said nothin ugly to you," the old woman said. "You so sweet. You the sweetest lady I know."

"She pretty too," the one with the hat on said.

160   "And stout," the other one said. "I never knowed no sweeter white lady."

"That's the truth befo' Jesus," the old woman said. "Amen! You des as sweet and pretty as you can be."

Mrs. Turpin knew just exactly how much Negro flattery was worth and it added to her rage. "She said," she began again and finished this time with a fierce rush of breath, "that I was an old wart hog from hell."

There was an astounded silence.

"Where she at?" the youngest woman cried in a piercing voice.

165   "Lemme see her. I'll kill her!"

"I'll kill her with you!" the other one cried.

"She b'long in the sylum," the old woman said emphatically. "You the sweetest white lady I know."

"She pretty too," the other two said. "Stout as she can be and sweet. Jesus satisfied with her!"

"Deed he is," the old woman declared.

170   Idiots! Mrs. Turpin growled to herself. You could never say anything intelligent to a nigger. You could talk at them but not with them. "Yawl ain't drunk your water," she said shortly. "Leave the bucket in the truck when you're finished with it. I got more to do than just stand around and pass the time of day," and she moved off and into the house.

She stood for a moment in the middle of the kitchen. The dark protuberance over her eye looked like a miniature tornado cloud which might any moment sweep across the horizon of her brow. Her lower lip protruded dangerously. She squared her massive shoulders. Then she marched into the front of the house and out the side door and started down the road to the pig parlor. She had the look of a woman going single-handed, weaponless, into battle.

The sun was a deep yellow now like a harvest moon and was riding westward very fast over the far tree line as if it meant to reach the hogs before she did. The road was rutted and she kicked several good-sized stones out of her path as she strode along. The pig parlor was on a little knoll at the end of a lane that ran off from the side of the barn. It was a square of concrete as large as a small room, with a board fence about four feet high around it. The concrete floor sloped slightly so that the hog wash could drain off into a trench where it was carried to the field for fertilizer. Claud was standing on the outside, on the edge of the concrete, hanging onto the top board, hosing down the floor inside. The hose was connected to the faucet of a water trough nearby.

Mrs. Turpin climbed up beside him and glowered down at the hogs inside. There were seven long-snouted bristly shoats in it—tan with liver-colored spots—and an old sow a few weeks off from farrowing. She was lying on her side grunting. The shoats were running about shaking themselves like idiot children, their little slit pig eyes searching the floor for anything left. She had read that pigs were the most intelligent animal. She doubted it. They were supposed to be smarter than dogs. There had even been a pig astronaut. He had performed his assignment perfectly but died of a heart attack afterwards because they left him in his electric suit, sitting upright throughout his examination when naturally a hog should be on all fours.

A-gruntin and a-rootin and a-groanin.

175   "Gimme that hose," she said, yanking it away from Claud. "Go on and carry them niggers home and then get off that leg."

"You look like you might have swallowed a mad dog," Claud observed, but he got down and limped off. He paid no attention to her humors.

Until he was out of earshot, Mrs. Turpin stood on the side of the pen, holding the hose and pointing the stream of water at the hind quarter of any shoat that looked as if it might try to lie down. When he had had time to get over the hill, she turned her head slightly and her wrathful eyes scanned the path. He was nowhere in sight. She turned back again and seemed to gather herself up. Her shoulders rose and she drew in her breath.

"What do you send me a message like that for?" she said in a low fierce voice, barely above a whisper but with the force of a shout in its concentrated fury. "How am I a hog and me both? How am I saved and from hell too?" Her free fist was knotted and with the other she gripped the hose, blindly pointing the stream of water in and out of the eye of the old sow whose outraged squeal she did not hear.

The pig parlor commanded a view of the back pasture where their twenty beef cows were gathered around the hay-bales Claud and the boy had put out. The freshly cut pasture sloped down to the highway. Across it was their cotton field and beyond that a dark green dusty wood which they owned as well. The sun was behind the wood, very red, looking over the paling of trees like a farmer inspecting his own hogs.

180   "Why me?" she rumbled. "It's no trash around here, black or white, that I haven't given to. And break my back to the bone every day working. And do for the church."

She appeared to be the right size woman to command the arena before her. "How am I a hog?" she demanded. "Exactly how am I like them?" and she jabbed the stream of water at the shoats. "There was plenty of trash there. It didn't have to be me."

"If you like trash better, go get yourself some trash then," she railed. "You could have made me trash. Or a nigger. If trash is what you wanted why didn't you make me trash?" She shook her fist with the hose in it and a watery snake appeared momentarily in the air. "I could quit working and take it easy and be filthy," she growled. "Lounge about the sidewalks all day drinking root beer. Dip snuff and spit in every puddle and have it all over my face. I could be nasty."

"Or you could have made me a nigger. It's too late for me to be a nigger," she said with deep sarcasm, "but I could act like one. Lay down in the middle of the road and stop traffic. Roll on the ground."

In the deepening light everything was taking on a mysterious hue. The pasture was growing a peculiar glassy green and the streak of highway had turned lavender. She braced herself for a final assault and this time her voice rolled out over the pasture. "Go on," she yelled, "call me a hog! Call me a hog again. From hell. Call me a wart hog from hell. Put that bottom rail on top. There'll still be a top and bottom!"

185   A garbled echo returned to her.

A final surge of fury shook her and she roared, "Who do you think you are?"

The color of everything, field and crimson sky, burned for a moment with a transparent intensity. The question carried over the pasture and across the highway and the cotton field and returned to her clearly like an answer from beyond the wood.

She opened her mouth but no sound came out of it.

A tiny truck, Claud's, appeared on the highway, heading rapidly out of sight. Its gears scraped thinly. It looked like a child's toy. At any moment a bigger truck might smash into it and scatter Claud's and the niggers' brains all over the road.

190   Mrs. Turpin stood there, her gaze fixed on the highway, all her muscles rigid, until in five or six minutes the truck reappeared, returning. She waited until it had had time to turn into their own road. Then like a monumental statue coming to life, she bent her head slowly and gazed, as if through the very heart of the mystery, down into the pig parlor at the hogs. They had settled all in one corner around the old sow who was grunting softly. A red glow suffused them. They appeared to pant with a secret life.

Until the sun slipped finally behind the tree line, Mrs. Turpin remained there with her gaze bent to them as if she were absorbing some abysmal life-giving knowledge. At last she lifted her head. There was only a purple streak in the sky, cutting through a field of crimson and leading, like an extension of the highway, into the descending dusk. She raised her hands from the side of the pen in a gesture hieratic and profound. A visionary light settled in her eyes. She saw the streak as a vast swinging bridge extending upward from the earth through a field of living fire. Upon it a vast horde of souls were rumbling toward heaven. There were whole companies of white-trash, clean for the first time in their lives, and bands of black niggers in white robes, and battalions of freaks and lunatics shouting and clapping and leaping like frogs. And bringing up the end of the procession was a tribe of people whom she recognized at once as those who, like herself and Claud, had always had a little of everything and the God-given wit to use it right. She leaned forward to observe them closer. They were marching behind the others with great dignity, accountable as they had always been for good order and common sense and respectable behavior. They alone were on key. Yet she could see by their shocked and altered faces that even their virtues were being burned away. She lowered her hands and gripped the rail of the hog pen, her eyes small but fixed unblinkingly on what lay ahead. In a moment the vision faded but she remained where she was, immobile.

At length she got down and turned off the faucet and made her slow way on the darkening path to the house. In the woods around her the invisible cricket choruses had struck up, but what she heard were the voices of the souls climbing upward into the starry field and shouting hallelujah.

[1964]

REMARKS FROM ESSAYS AND LETTERS
From "The Fiction Writer and His Country"

In the greatest fiction, the writer's moral sense coincides with his dramatic sense, and I see no way for it to do this unless his moral judgment is part of the very act of seeing, and he is free to use it. I have heard it said that belief in Christian dogma is a hindrance to the writer, but I myself have found nothing further from the truth. Actually, it frees the storyteller to observe. It is not a set of rules which fixes what he sees in the world. It affects his writing primarily by guaranteeing his respect for mystery. . . .

When I look at stories I have written I find that they are, for the most part, about people who are poor, who are afflicted in both mind and body, who have little—or at best a distorted—sense of spiritual purpose, and whose actions do not apparently give the reader a great assurance of the joy of life.

Yet how is this? For I am no disbeliever in spiritual purpose and no vague believer. I see from the standpoint of Christian orthodoxy. This means that for me the meaning of life is centered in our Redemption by Christ and what I see in the world I see in its relation to that. . . .

The novelist with Christian concerns will find in modern life distortions which are repugnant to him, and his problem will be to make these appear as distortions to an audience which is used to seeing them as natural; and he may well be forced to take ever more violent means to get his vision across to this hostile audience. When you can assume that your audience holds the same beliefs you do, you can relax a little and use more normal means of talking to it; when you have to assume that it does not, then you have to make your vision apparent by shock—to the hard of hearing you shout, and for the almost-blind you draw large and startling figures.

From "Some Aspects of the Grotesque in Southern Fiction"

If the writer believes that our life is and will remain essentially mysterious, if he looks upon us as beings existing in a created order to whose laws we freely respond, then what he sees on the surface will be of interest to him only as he can go through it into an experience of mystery itself. His kind of fiction will always be pushing its own limits outward toward the limits of mystery, because for this kind of writer, the meaning of a story does not begin except at a depth where adequate motivation and adequate psychology and the various determinations have been exhausted. Such a writer will be interested in what we don't understand rather than in what we do. He will be interested in possibility rather than in probability. He will be interested in characters who are forced out to meet evil and grace and who act on a trust beyond themselves—whether they know very clearly what it is they act upon or not. To the modern mind, this kind of character, and his creator, are typical Don Quixotes, tilting at what is not there.

From "The Nature and Aim of Fiction"

The novel works by a slower accumulation of detail than the short story does. The short story requires more drastic procedures than the novel because more has to be accomplished in less space. The details have to carry more immediate weight. In good fiction, certain of the details will tend to accumulate meaning from the story itself, and when this happens, they become symbolic in their action.

Now the word *symbol* scares a good many people off, just as the word *art* does. They seem to feel that a symbol is some mysterious thing put in arbitrarily by the writer to frighten the common reader—sort of a literary Masonic grip that is only for the initiated. They seem to think that it is a way of saying something that you aren't actually saying, and so if they can be got to read a reputedly symbolic work at all, they approach it as if it were a problem in algebra. Find x. And when they do find or think they find this abstraction, x, then they go off with an elaborate sense of satisfaction and the notion that they have "understood" the story. Many students confuse the *process* of understanding a thing with understanding it.

I think that for the fiction writer himself, symbols are something he uses simply as a matter of course. You might say that these are details that, while having their essential place in the literal level of the story, operate in depth as well as on the surface, increasing the story in every direction. . . .

People have a habit of saying, "What is the theme of your story?" and they expect you to give them a statement: "The theme of my story is the economic pressure of the machine on the middle class"—or some such absurdity. And when they've got a statement like that, they go off happy and feel it is no longer necessary to read the story.

Some people have the notion that you read the story and then climb out of it into the meaning, but for the fiction writer himself the whole story is the meaning, because it is an experience, not an abstraction.

From "Writing Short Stories"

Being short does not mean being slight. A short story should be long in depth and should give us an experience of meaning. . . .

Meaning is what keeps the short story from being short. I prefer to talk about the meaning in a story rather than the theme of a story. People talk about the theme of a story as if the theme were like the string that a sack of chicken feed is tied with. They think that if you can pick out the theme, the way you pick the right thread in the chicken-feed sack, you can rip the story open and feed the chickens. But this is not the way meaning works in fiction.

When you can state the theme of a story, when you can separate it from the story itself, then you can be sure the story is not a very good one. The meaning of a story has to be embodied in it, has to be made concrete in it. A story is a way to say something that can't be said any other way, and it takes every word in the story to say what the meaning is. You tell a story because a statement would be inadequate. When anybody asks what a story is about, the only proper thing is to tell him to read the story. The meaning of fiction is not abstract meaning but experienced meaning, and the purpose of making statements about the meaning of a story is only to help you to experience that meaning more fully.

ON INTERPRETING "A GOOD MAN IS HARD TO FIND"

A professor of English had sent Flannery the following letter: "I am writing as spokesman for three members of our department and some ninety university students in three classes who for a week now have been discussing your story 'A Good Man Is Hard to Find.' We have debated at length several possible interpretations, none of which fully satisfies us. In general we believe that the appearance of the Misfit is not 'real' in the same sense that the incidents of the first half of the story are real. Bailey, we believe, imagines the appearance of the Misfit, whose activities have been called to his attention on the night before the trip and again during the stopover at the roadside restaurant. Bailey, we further believe, identifies himself with the Misfit and so plays two roles in the imaginary last half of the story. But we cannot, after great effort, determine the point at which reality fades into illusion or reverie. Does the accident literally occur, or is it a part of Bailey's dream? Please believe me when I say we are not seeking an easy way out of our difficulty. We admire your story and have examined it with great care, but we are convinced that we are missing something important which you intended for us to grasp. We will all be very grateful if you comment on the interpretation which I have outlined above and if you will give us further comments about your intention in writing 'A Good Man Is Hard to Find.'"

She replied:

To a Professor of English

28 March 61

The interpretation of your ninety students and three teachers is fantastic and about as far from my intentions as it could get to be. If it were a legitimate interpretation, the story would be little more than a trick and its interest would be simply for abnormal psychology. I am not interested in abnormal psychology.

There is a change of tension from the first part of the story to the second where the Misfit enters, but this is no lessening of reality. This story is, of course, not meant to be realistic in the sense that it portrays the everyday doings of people in Georgia. It is stylized and its conventions are comic even though its meaning is serious.

Bailey's only importance is as the Grandmother's boy and the driver of the car. It is the Grandmother who first recognizes the Misfit and who is most concerned with him throughout. The story is a duel of sorts between the Grandmother and her superficial beliefs and the Misfit's more profoundly felt involvement with Christ's action which set the world off balance for him.

The meaning of a story should go on expanding for the reader the more he thinks about it, but meaning cannot be captured in an interpretation. If teachers are in the habit of approaching a story as if it were a research problem for which any answer is believable so long as it is not obvious, then I think students will never learn to enjoy fiction. Too much interpretation is certainly worse than too little and where feeling for a story is absent, theory will not supply it.

My tone is not meant to be obnoxious. I am in a state of shock.

"A Reasonable Use of the Unreasonable"

Last fall I received a letter from a student who said she would be "graciously appreciative" if I would tell her "just what enlightenment" I expected her to get from each of my stories. I suspect she had a paper to write. I wrote her back to forget about the enlightenment and just try to enjoy them. I knew that was the most unsatisfactory answer I could have given because, of course, she didn't want to enjoy them, she just wanted to figure them out.

In most English classes the short story has become a kind of literary specimen to be dissected. Every time a story of mine appears in a Freshman anthology, I have a vision of it, with its little organs laid open, like a frog in a bottle.

I realize that a certain amount of this what-is-the-significance has to go on, but I think something has gone wrong in the process when, for so many students, the story becomes simply a problem to be solved, something which you evaporate to get Instant Enlightenment.

A story really isn't any good unless it successfully resists paraphrase, unless it hangs on and expands in the mind. Properly, you analyze to enjoy, but it's equally true that to analyze with any discrimination, you have to have enjoyed already, and I think that the best reason to hear a story read is that it should stimulate that primary enjoyment.

I don't have any pretensions to being an Aeschylus or Sophocles and providing you in this story with a cathartic experience out of your mythic background, though this story I'm going to read certainly calls up a good deal of the South's mythic background, and it should elicit from you a degree of pity and terror, even though its way of being serious is a comic one. I do think, though, that like the Greeks you should know what is going to happen in this story so that any element of suspense in it will be transferred from its surface to its interior.

I would be most happy if you have already read it, happier still if you knew it well, but since experience has taught me to keep my expectations along these lines modest, I'll tell you that this is the story of a family of six which, on its way driving to Florida, gets wiped out by an escaped convict who calls himself the Misfit. The family is made up of the Grandmother and her son, Bailey, and his children, John Wesley and June Star and the baby, and there is also the cat and the children's mother. The cat is named Pitty Sing, and the Grandmother is taking him with them, hidden in a basket.

Now I think it behooves me to try to establish with you the basis on which reason operates in this story. Much of my fiction takes its character from a reasonable use of the unreasonable, though the reasonableness of my use of it may not always be apparent. The assumptions that underlie this use of it, however, are those of the central Christian mysteries. These are assumptions to which a large part of the modern audience takes exception. About this I can only say that there are perhaps other ways than my own in which this story could be read, but none other by which it could have been written. Belief, in my own case anyway, is the engine that makes perception operate.

The heroine of this story, the Grandmother, is in the most significant position life offers the Christian. She is facing death. And to all appearances she, like the rest of us, is not too well prepared for it. She would like to see the event postponed. Indefinitely.

I've talked to a number of teachers who use this story in class and who tell their students that the Grandmother is evil, that in fact, she's a witch, even down to the cat. One of these teachers told me that his students, and particularly his Southern students, resisted this interpretation with a certain bemused vigor, and he didn't understand why. I had to tell him that they resisted it because they all had grandmothers or great-aunts just like her at home, and they knew, from personal experience, that the old lady lacked comprehension, but that she had a good heart. The Southerner is usually tolerant of those weaknesses that proceed from innocence, and he knows that a taste for self-preservation can be readily combined with the missionary spirit.

This same teacher was telling his students that morally the Misfit was several cuts above the Grandmother. He had a really sentimental attachment to the Misfit. But then a prophet gone wrong is almost always more interesting than your grandmother, and you have to let people take their pleasures where they find them.

It is true that the old lady is a hypocritical old soul; her wits are no match for the Misfit's, nor is her capacity for grace equal to his; yet I think the unprejudiced reader will feel that the Grandmother has a special kind of triumph in this story which instinctively we do not allow to someone altogether bad.

I often ask myself what makes a story work, and what makes it hold up as a story, and I have decided that it is probably some action, some gesture of a character that is unlike any other in the story, one which indicates where the real heart of the story lies. This would have to be an action or a gesture which was both totally right and totally unexpected; it would have to be one that was both in character and beyond character; it would have to suggest both the world and eternity. The action or gesture I'm talking about would have to be on the anagogical level, that is, the level which has to do with the Divine life and our participation in it. It would be a gesture that transcended any neat allegory that might have been intended or any pat moral categories a reader could make. It would be a gesture which somehow made contact with mystery.

There is a point in this story where such a gesture occurs. The Grandmother is at last alone, facing the Misfit. Her head clears for an instant and she realizes, even in her limited way, that she is responsible for the man before her and joined to him by ties of kinship which have their roots deep in the mystery she has been merely prattling about so far. And at this point, she does the right thing, she makes the right gesture.

I find that students are often puzzled by what she says and does here, but I think myself that if I took out this gesture and what she says with it, I would have no story. What was left would not be worth your attention. Our age not only does not have a very sharp eye for the almost imperceptible intrusions of grace, it no longer has much feeling for the nature of the violences which precede and follow them. The devil's greatest wile, Baudelaire has said, is to convince us that he does not exist.

I suppose the reasons for the use of so much violence in modern fiction will differ with each writer who uses it, but in my own stories I have found that violence is strangely capable of returning my characters to reality and preparing them to accept their moment of grace. Their heads are so hard that almost nothing else will do the work. This idea, that reality is something to which we must be returned at considerable cost, is one which is seldom understood by the casual reader, but it is one which is implicit in the Christian view of the world.

I don't want to equate the Misfit with the devil. I prefer to think that, however unlikely this may seem, the old lady's gesture, like the mustard-seed, will grow to be a great crow-filled tree in the Misfit's heart, and will be enough of a pain to him there to turn him into the prophet he was meant to become. But that's another story.

This story has been called grotesque, but I prefer to call it literal. A good story is literal in the same sense that a child's drawing is literal. When a child draws, he doesn't intend to distort but to set down exactly what he sees, and as his gaze is direct, he sees the lines that create motion. Now the lines of motion that interest the writer are usually invisible. They are lines of spiritual motion. And in this story you should be on the lookout for such things as the action of grace in the Grandmother's soul, and not for the dead bodies.

We hear many complaints about the prevalence of violence in modern fiction, and it is always assumed that this violence is a bad thing and meant to be an end in itself. With the serious writer, violence is never an end in itself. It is the extreme situation that best reveals what we are essentially, and I believe these are times when writers are more interested in what we are essentially than in the tenor of our daily lives. Violence is a force which can be used for good or evil, and among other things taken by it is the kingdom of heaven. But regardless of what can be taken by it, the man in the violent situation reveals those qualities least dispensable in his personality, those qualities which are all he will have to take into eternity with him; and since the characters in this story are all on the verge of eternity, it is appropriate to think of what they take with them. In any case, I hope that if you consider these points in connection with the story, you will come to see it as something more than an account of a family murdered on the way to Florida.

[1957]

POETRY

A NOTE ON THE PSALMS

The Book of Psalms (*psalm* is from the Greek *psalmoi*, "songs of praise"), or the Psalter (Greek *psalterion*, a stringed instrument), contains about 150 songs, prayers, and meditations. The number is a bit imprecise for several reasons: for instance, in the Hebrew Bible the numbering from Psalm 10 to Psalm 148 is one digit ahead of the numbering in Bibles used in the Christian church, which joins 9 and 10 and 114 and 115 but divides both 116 and 147 into two. It is also a bit imprecise to call the psalms "songs"; although some of them are titled songs and some were certainly sung—the texts include references to instruments and to singing—it is by no means certain that all were sung.

The Hebrew text attributes 73 of the psalms to David, who reigned circa 1010-970 B.C.E., and the Greek text attributes 82 to him. David is said to have been a musician (1 Samuel 16.23, Amos 6.5), but these attributions are not taken very seriously by scholars; some of the psalms may indeed go back to the tenth century B.C.E., though some others may be as late as 200 B.C.E. The book in fact is a compilation of earlier collections from hundreds of years of Hebrew history.

We give the psalms in the King James Version (1611).

Psalm 19

To the chief Musician. A Psalm of David.

1   The heavens declare the glory of God; and the firmament° sheweth his handywork.
2   Day unto day uttereth speech, and night unto night sheweth knowledge.
3   *There is* no speech nor language, *where* their voice is not heard.
4   Their line is gone out through all the earth, and their words to the end of the world. In them hath he set a tabernacle for the sun,
5   Which *is* as a bridegroom coming out of his chamber, *and* rejoiceth as a strong man to run a race.
6   His going forth *is* from the end of the heaven, and his circuit unto the ends of it: and there is nothing hid from the heat thereof.
7   The law of the LORD *is* perfect, converting the soul: the testimony of the LORD *is* sure, making wise the simple.
8   The statutes of the LORD *are* right, rejoicing the heart: the commandment of the LORD *is* pure, enlightening the eyes.
9   The fear° of the LORD *is* clean, enduring for ever: the judgments of the LORD *are* true *and* righteous altogether.
10   More to be desired *are they* than gold, yea, than much fine gold: sweeter also than honey and the honeycomb.

---

¹ **firmament** dome of the sky   ⁹ **fear** often emended in later translations to *word*

11   Moreover by them is thy servant warned: *and* in keeping of them *there is* great reward.

12   Who can understand *his* errors? cleanse thou me from secret *faults.*°

13   Keep back thy servant also from presumptuous *sins;* let them not have dominion over me: then shall I be up-right, and I shall be innocent from the great transgression.

14   Let the words of my mouth, and the meditation of my heart, be acceptable in thy sight, O LORD, my strength, and my redeemer.

¹²**secret faults** unconscious violations of God's will

Psalm 23

1   The LORD *is* my shepherd; I shall not want.

2   He maketh me to lie down in green pastures: he leadeth me beside the still waters.

3   He restoreth my soul: he leadeth me in the paths of righteousness for his name's sake.°

4   Yea, though I walk through the valley of the shadow of death,° I will fear no evil: for thou *art* with me; thy rod° and thy staff° they comfort me.

5   Thou preparest a table° before me in the presence of mine enemies: thou anointest my head with oil; my cup runneth over.

6   Surely goodness and mercy shall follow me° all the days of my life: and I will dwell in the house of the LORD for ever.

³**for his name's sake** because he is that kind of God (the *name* reveals the nature of a person or a god); or in order to exalt his name   ⁴**valley of the shadow of death** a mistranslation—but most readers will not willingly give it up. Modern translations give something like *dark valley* or *valley of deep shadow* (metaphoric for "deep distress").   **rod** a cudgel, to ward off wild animals.   **staff** a pole, probably with a hook at the end, to guide timid sheep.   ⁵**table** probably a table in the temple, prepared for a sacrificial meal.   ⁶**shall follow me** the goodness and mercy experienced in the temple will continue in daily life

Psalm 121

1   I will lift up mine eyes unto the hills, from whence cometh my help.

2   My help *cometh* from the LORD, which made heaven and earth.

3   He will not suffer thy foot to be moved: he that keepeth thee will not slumber.

4   Behold, he that keepeth Israel shall neither slumber nor sleep.

5   The LORD *is* thy keeper: the LORD *is* thy shade upon thy right hand.

6   The sun shall not smite thee by day, nor the moon° by night.

7   The LORD shall preserve thee from all evil: he shall preserve thy soul.

8   The LORD shall preserve thy going out and thy coming in from this time forth, and even for evermore.

⁶**the sun . . . the moon** the sun can cause sunstroke; the moon was thought to cause lunacy

✎ Topics for Critical Thinking and Writing

1. Probably most readers will agree about the structure of Psalm 19: verses 1-6 are on nature, 7-11 are on the Law, and 12-14 are a prayer. Do you think these units cohere into a whole? For instance, does it make sense to say that the second unit is connected to the first by the idea that just as nothing is hidden from the heat of the sun (6), in like manner "the law of the Lord" is everywhere? Is such a reading appropriate, or is it strained? Explain.

2. In Psalm 23, line 1, the speaker says, "I shall not want," that is, "I shall not lack anything." Judging from the rest of the psalm, what does the speaker hope to be granted?

3. Some scholars consider Psalm 121 to contain a question by a pilgrim (in their view, the pilgrim's question is "From whence cometh my help?") and an answer by a priest (in this view, the answer is that help comes not from the hills, with their pagan sanctuaries, but from the Lord). Since the scholars are divided, we may offer our own opinions. Do you think the poem gains or loses by being read as a dialogue? Explain.

FROM THE QU'RAN

The Qu'ran (often spelled *Koran;* from an Arabic verb that means "read" or "recite") is the sacred book of Islam, and for believers it is the highest authority in legal and civil as well as in religious matters. The Qu'ran is held to be the word of God (Allah) itself, as revealed by the angel Gabriel to the prophet Muhammad (c. 570–c. 632), the founder of Islam, during a period from about 610 to 632. There are many translations of the Qu'ran, and through them the poetry and principles of Islam have become known around the world. The translation below is by A. J. Arberry, from *The Koran Interpreted.* But we must remember that because believers consider the Arabic text the word of God, in their view the Qu'ran cannot truly be translated at all, nor can its style ever be imitated.

Muhammad Speaks of Allah: "There Is No God but He . . ."*

God
there is no god but He, the Living, the Everlasting.
Slumber seizes Him not, neither sleep;
to Him belongs
all that is in the heavens and the earth   5
Who is there that shall intercede with Him save by His leave?
He knows what lies before them
and what is after them,
and they comprehend not anything of His knowledge
save such as He wills.   10

---

* Excerpts from Arthur J. Arberry, *The Koran Interpreted,* 2 vols. (New York: Macmillan, 1955). Translation by A. J. Arberry.

His Throne comprises the heavens and earth;
the preserving of them oppresses Him not;
He is the All-high, the All-glorious.

No compulsion is there in religion.
Rectitude has become clear from error.   15
So whosoever disbelieves in idols
and believes in God, has laid hold of
the most firm handle, unbreaking; God is
All-hearing, All-knowing.
God is the protector of the believers;   20
He brings them forth from the shadows
into the light.
And the unbelievers—their protectors are
idols, that bring them forth from the light
into the shadows;   25
those are the inhabitants of the Fire,
therein dwelling forever.

(Qur'an, II, 256–9)

That then is God your Lord;
there is no god but He,
the Creator of everything.   30
So serve Him,
for He is Guardian over everything.
The eyes attain Him not, but He attains the eyes;
He is the All-subtle, the All-aware.

(Qur'an, VI, 102–3)

✐ Topics for Critical Thinking and Writing

1. In the first of these three passages, what is the meaning of line 6 ("Who is there . . .")? What does this line suggest about human beings' relationship to God?

2. Explain the meaning of the final two lines in the third passage. Do you find the idea of a God who is "All-aware" reassuring or disquieting? Is it possible to have both of these responses at one and the same time?

A NOTE ON SPIRITUALS

Spirituals, or sorrow songs, by slaves in the United States, seem to have been created chiefly in the first half of the nineteenth century. Their origins are still a matter of some dispute, but probably most students of the subject agree that the songs represent a distinctive fusion of African rhythms with white hymns, and of course many of the texts derive ultimately from biblical sources. One of the chief themes is the desire for release, sometimes presented with imagery drawn from ancient Israel. Examples include references to crossing the River Jordan (a river that runs from north of the Sea of Galilee to the Dead Sea), the release of the Israelites from slavery in Egypt (Exodus), Jonah's release from the whale (Book of

Jonah), and Daniel's deliverance from the fiery furnace and from the lions' den (Book of Daniel, chapters 3 and 6).

The texts were collected and published, especially in the 1860s and 1870s, for instance in *Slave Songs of the United States* (1867) and in *Jubilee Songs* (1872). These books usually sought to reproduce the singers' pronunciation, and we have followed the early texts here.

ANONYMOUS
Deep River

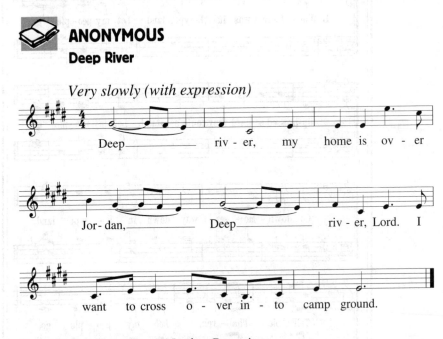

Very slowly (with expression)

Deep_____ riv - er, my home is ov - er

Jor- dan,_____ Deep_____ riv - er, Lord. I

want to cross o - ver in - to camp ground.

Deep river, my home is over Jordan. Deep river,
Lord, I want to cross over into campground,
Lord, I want to cross over into campground,
Lord, I want to cross over into campground.
Oh, chillun, Oh, don't you want to go to that gospel feast,   5
That promised land, that land, where all is peace?
Walk into heaven, and take my seat.
And cast my crown at Jesus' feet,
Lord, I want to cross over into campground,
Lord, I want to cross over into campground,   10
Lord, I want to cross over into campground.
Deep river, my home is over Jordan. Deep river,
Lord, I want to cross over into campground,
Lord, I want to cross over into campground,
Lord, I want to cross over into campground, Lord!   15

Pages from *Jubilee Songs* (1872), one of the earliest printed collections of spirituals.

JUBILEE SONGS.   23

5.
0, 'twas a dark and dismal night,
　Let my people go;
When Moses led the Israelites,
　Let my people go.

6.
'Twas good old Moses and Aaron, too,
　Let my people go;
'Twas they that led the armies through,
　Let my people go.

7.
The Lord told Moses what to do,
　Let my people go;
To lead the children of Israel through,
　Let my people go.

8.
0 come along Moses, you'll not get lost,
　Let my people go;
Stretch out your rod and come across,
　Let my people go.

9.
As Israel stood by the water side,
　Let my people go;
At the command of God it did divide,
　Let my people go.

10.
When they had reached the other shore,
　Let my people go;
They sang a song of triumph o'er,
　Let my people go.

11.
Pharaoh said he would go across,
　Let my people go;
But Pharaoh and his host were lost,
　Let my people go.

12.
0 Moses the cloud shall cleave the way,
　Let my people go;
A fire by night, a shade by day,
　Let my people go.

13.
You'll not get lost in the wilderness,
　Let my people go;
With a lighted candle in your breast,
　Let my people go.

14.
Jordan shall stand up like a wall,
　Let my people go;
And the walls of Jericho shall fall
　Let my people go.

15.
Your foes shall not before you stand,
　Let my people go;
And you'll possess fair Canaan's land,
　Let my people go.

16.
'Twas just about in harvest time,
　Let my people go;
When Joshua led his host divine,
　Let my people go.

17.
0 let us all from bondage flee,
　Let my people go;
And let us all in Christ be free,
　Let my people go

18.
We need not always weep and moan,
　Let my people go;
And wear these slavery chains forlorn,
　Let my people go.

19.
This world's a wilderness of woe,
　Let my people go ;
0, let us on to Canaan go,
　Let my people go.

20.
What a beautiful morning that will be,
　Let my people go ;
When time breaks up in eternity,
　Let my people go.

21.
The Devil he thought he had me fast,
　Let my people go;
But I thought I'd break his chains at
　Let my people go.　　　　[last,

22.
0 take yer shoes from off yer feet,
　Let my people go;
And walk into the golden street,
　Let my people go.

23.
I'll tell you what I likes de best,
　Let my people go ;
It is the shouting Methodist,
　Let my people go.

24.
I do believe without a doubt,
　Let my people go;
That a Christian has the right to shout,
　Let my people go.

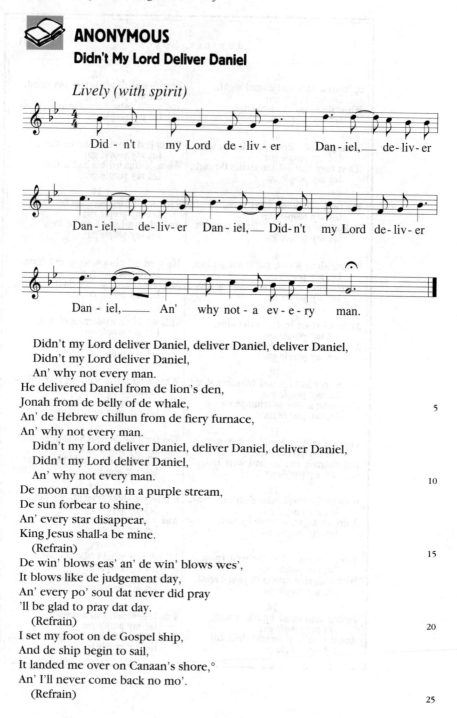

ANONYMOUS
Didn't My Lord Deliver Daniel

Lively (with spirit)

Did-n't my Lord de-liv-er Dan-iel,— de-liv-er
Dan-iel,— de-liv-er Dan-iel,— Did-n't my Lord de-liv-er
Dan-iel,— An' why not-a ev-e-ry man.

Didn't my Lord deliver Daniel, deliver Daniel, deliver Daniel,
Didn't my Lord deliver Daniel,
   An' why not every man.
He delivered Daniel from de lion's den,
Jonah from de belly of de whale,   5
An' de Hebrew chillun from de fiery furnace,
   An' why not every man.
   Didn't my Lord deliver Daniel, deliver Daniel, deliver Daniel,
   Didn't my Lord deliver Daniel,
   An' why not every man.   10
De moon run down in a purple stream,
De sun forbear to shine,
An' every star disappear,
King Jesus shall-a be mine.
   (Refrain)   15
De win' blows eas' an' de win' blows wes',
It blows like de judgement day,
An' every po' soul dat never did pray
'll be glad to pray dat day.
   (Refrain)   20
I set my foot on de Gospel ship,
And de ship begin to sail,
It landed me over on Canaan's shore,°
An' I'll never come back no mo'.
   (Refrain)   25

---

[23]**Canaan's shore** Canaan is the ancient name of a territory that included part of what is
now Israel

🖊 Topic for Critical Thinking and Writing

As we mentioned a moment ago, we give the texts of the songs as they were printed in the second half of the nineteenth century, when an effort to indicate pronunciation was made (e.g., *chillun* for *children*). If you were printing the songs. would you retain these attempts to indicate pronunciation? What, if anything, is gained by keeping them? What, if any, unintentional side effects do you think may be produced?

📖 WILLIAM SHAKESPEARE

William Shakespeare (1564–1616), born in Stratford-upon-Avon in England, is chiefly known as a dramatic poet, but he also wrote nondramatic poetry. In 1609 a volume of 154 of his sonnets was published, apparently without his permission. Probably he chose to keep his sonnets unpublished not because he thought that they were of little value, but because it was more prestigious to be an amateur poet (unpublished) than a professional (published). Although the sonnets were published in 1609, they were probably written in the mid-1590s, when there was a vogue for sonneteering. A contemporary writer in 1598 said that Shakespeare's "sugred Sonnets [circulate] among his private friends."

We print other sonnets on pages 68, 586, and 587.

Sonnet 146

Poor soul, the center of my sinful earth,
[My sinful earth] these rebel pow'rs that thee array,
Why dost thou pine within and suffer dearth,
Painting thy outward walls so costly gay? 4
Why so large cost,° having so short a lease,
Dost thou upon thy fading mansion spend?
Shall worms, inheritors of this excess,
Eat up thy charge? Is this thy body's end? 8
Then, soul, live thou upon thy servant's loss,
And let that pine to aggravate thy store;
Buy terms divine° in selling hours of dross;
Within be fed, without be rich no more. 12
 So shalt thou feed on Death, that feeds on men,
 And death once dead, there's no more dying then.

°cost expense ¹¹**buy terms divine** buy ages of immortality

🖊 Topics for Critical Thinking and Writing

1. "My sinful earth," in line 2, is doubtless an error made by the printer of the first edition (1609), who mistakenly repeated the end of the first line. Among suggested replacements are "Thrall to," "Fooled by," "Rebuke,"

"Leagued with," and "Feeding." If you wish, suggest your own corrections. Which do you prefer?

2. In what tone of voice would you speak the first line? The last line? Trace the speaker's shifts in emotion throughout the poem.

 **JOHN DONNE**

John Donne (1572–1631) was born into a Roman Catholic family in England, but in the 1590s he abandoned that faith. In 1615 he became an Anglican priest and soon was known as a great preacher. One hundred sixty of his sermons survive, including one with the famous line "No man is an island, entire of itself; every man is a piece of the continent, a part of the main; if a clod be washed away by the sea, Europe is the less . . . ; and therefore never send to know for whom the bell tolls; it tolls for thee." From 1621 until his death he was dean of St. Paul's Cathedral in London. His love poems (often bawdy and cynical) are said to be his early work, and his "Holy Sonnets" (among the greatest religious poems written in English) his later work.

Holy Sonnet XIV

Batter my heart, three-personed God; for you
As yet but knock, breathe, shine, and seek to mend;
That I may rise and stand, o'erthrow me, and bend
Your force, to break, blow, burn, and make me new. 4
I, like an usurped town, to another due,
Labor to admit you, but oh, to no end.
Reason, your viceroy in me, me should defend,
But is captived, and proves weak or untrue. 8
Yet dearly I love you, and would be loved fain,
But am betrothed unto your enemy:
Divorce me, untie, or break that knot again,
Take me to you, imprison me, for I 12
Except you enthrall me, never shall be free,
Nor ever chaste, except you ravish me.

[1633]

Topics for Critical Thinking and Writing

1. Explain the paradoxes (apparent contradictions) in lines 2, 3, 13, and 14. Explain the double meanings of "enthrall" (line 13) and "ravish" (line 14).
2. In lines 1–4, what is God implicitly compared to (considering especially lines 2 and 4)? How does this comparison lead into the comparison that dominates lines 5–8? What words in lines 9–12 are especially related to the earlier lines?
3. What is gained by piling up verbs in lines 2–4?
4. Are sexual references necessarily irreverent in a religious poem?

JOHN MILTON

John Milton (1608–74) was born into a well-to-do family in London, where from child-hood he was a student of languages, mastering at an early age Latin, Greek, Hebrew, and a number of modern languages. Instead of becoming a minister in the Anglican Church, he resolved to become a poet and spent five years at his family's country home, reading. His attacks against the monarchy secured him a position in Oliver Cromwell's Puritan government as Latin secretary for foreign affairs. He became totally blind, but he continued his work through secretaries, one of whom was Andrew Marvell, author of "To His Coy Mistress" (page 590). With the restoration of the monarchy in 1660, Milton was for a time confined but was later pardoned in the general amnesty. Until his death he continued to work on many subjects, including his greatest poem, the epic Paradise Lost.

When I Consider How My Light is Spent

When I consider how my light is spent
  Ere half my days, in this dark world and wide,
  And that one talent which is death to hide°
Lodged with me useless,° though my soul more bent   4
To serve therewith my Maker, and present
  My true account, lest he returning chide;
  "Doth God exact day-labor, light denied?"
I fondly° ask; but Patience to prevent°   8
That murmur, soon replies, "God doth not need
  Either man's work or his own gifts; who best
  Bear his mild yoke, they serve him best. His state
Is kingly. Thousands at his bidding speed   12
  And post o'er land and ocean without rest:
  They also serve who only stand and wait."

[1655]

³There is a pun in *talent,* relating Milton's literary talent to Christ's Parable of the Talents (Matthew 25.14 ff.), in which a servant is rebuked for not putting his talent (a unit of money) to use ⁴**useless** a pun on *use,* i.e., usury, interest ⁸**fondly** foolishly. **prevent** forestall

Topics for Critical Thinking and Writing

1. This sonnet is sometimes called "On His Blindness," though Milton never gave it a title. Do you think this title gets toward the heart of the poem? Explain. If you were to give it a title, what would the title be?
2. Read the parable in Matthew 25.14-30, and then consider how close the parable is to Milton's life as Milton describes it in this poem.

 **CHRISTINA ROSSETTI**

Christina Rossetti (1830–94) was the daughter of an exiled Italian patriot who lived in London and the sister of the poet and painter Dante Gabriel Rossetti. After her father became an invalid, she led an extremely ascetic life, devoting most of her life to doing charitable work. Her first and best-known volume of poetry, Goblin Market and Other Poems, *was published in 1862.*

We print other poems by Rossetti on pages 410 and 601.

Uphill

Does the road wind uphill all the way?
   Yes, to the very end.
Will the day's journey take the whole long day?
   From morn to night, my friend.   4

But is there for the night a resting-place?
   A roof for when the slow dark hours begin.
May not the darkness hide it from my face?
   You cannot miss that inn.   8

Shall I meet other wayfarers at night?
   Those who have gone before.
Then must I knock, or call when just in sight?
   They will not keep you standing at that door.   12

Shall I find comfort, travel-sore and weak?
   Of labor you shall find the sum.
Will there be beds for me and all who seek?
   Yea, beds for all who come.   16

[1858]

Topics for Critical Thinking and Writing

1. Suppose that someone told you this poem is about a person preparing to go on a hike. The person is supposedly making inquiries about the road and the possible hotel arrangements. What would you reply?
2. Who is the questioner? A woman? A man? All human beings collectively? "Uphill" does not use quotation marks to distinguish between two speakers. Can one say that in "Uphill" the questioner and the answerer are the same person?
3. Are the answers unambiguously comforting? Or can it, for instance, be argued that the "roof" is (perhaps among other things) the lid of a coffin—hence the questioner will certainly not be kept "standing at that door"? If the poem can be read along these lines, is it chilling rather than comforting?

GERARD MANLEY HOPKINS

Gerard Manley Hopkins (1844–89) was born near London and was educated at Oxford, where he studied Classics. A convert from Anglicanism to Roman Catholicism, he was ordained a Jesuit priest in 1877. After serving as a parish priest and teacher, he was appointed Professor of Greek at the Catholic University in Dublin.

Hopkins published only a few poems during his lifetime, partly because he believed that the pursuit of literary fame was incompatible with his vocation as a priest, and partly because he was aware that his highly individual style might puzzle readers.

We print another poem by Hopkins on page 893.

God's Grandeur

The world is charged with the grandeur of God.
    It will flame out, like shining from shook foil;
    It gathers to a greatness, like the ooze of oil
Crushed. Why do men then now not reck his rod?   4
Generations have trod, have trod, have trod;
    And all is seared with trade; bleared, smeared with toil;
    And wears man's smudge and shares man's smell: the soil
Is bare now nor can foot feel, being shod.   8

And for all this, nature is never spent;
    There lives the dearest freshness deep down things;
And though the last lights off the black West went
    Oh, morning, at the brown brink eastward, springs—   12
Because the Holy Ghost over the bent
    World broods with warm breast and with ah! bright wings.

[1877]

Topics for Critical Thinking and Writing

1. Hopkins, a Roman Catholic priest, lived in England during the last decades of the nineteenth century—that is, in an industrialized society. Where in the poem do you find him commenting on his setting? Circle the words in the poem that can refer both to England's physical appearance and to the sinful condition of human beings.

2. What is the speaker's tone in the first three and one-half lines (through "Crushed.")? In the rest of line 4? In lines 5–8? Is the second part of the sonnet (the next six lines) more unified in *tone* or less? In an essay of 500 words describe the shifting tones of the speaker's voice. Probably after writing a first draft you will be able to form a thesis that describes an overall pattern. As you revise your drafts, make sure that (1) the thesis is clear to the reader, and (2) it is adequately supported by brief quotations.

ROBERT FROST

Robert Frost (1874–1963) was born in California. After his father's death in 1885 Frost's mother brought the family to New England, where she taught in high schools in Massachusetts and New Hampshire. Frost studied for part of one term at Dartmouth College in New Hampshire, then did odd jobs (including teaching), and from 1897 to 1899 was enrolled as a special student at Harvard. He then farmed in New Hampshire, published a few poems in local newspapers, left the farm and taught again, and in 1912 left for England, where he hoped to achieve more popular success as a writer. By 1915 he had won a considerable reputation, and he returned to the United States, settling on a farm in New Hampshire and cultivating the image of the country-wise farmer-poet. In fact he was well read in the classics, the Bible, and English and American literature.

Design

I found a dimpled spider, fat and white,
On a white heal-all, holding up a moth
Like a white piece of rigid satin cloth—
Assorted characters of death and blight   4
Mixed ready to begin the morning right,
Like the ingredients of a witches' broth—
A snow-drop spider, a flower like a froth,
And dead wings carried like a paper kite.   8

What had that flower to do with being white,
The wayside blue and innocent heal-all?
What brought the kindred spider to that height,
Then steered the white moth thither in the night?   12
What but design of darkness to appall?—
If design govern in a thing so small.

[1936]

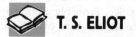

Topics for Critical Thinking and Writing

1. Do you find the spider, as described in line 1, cute or disgusting? Why?
2. What is the effect of "If" in the last line?
3. The word "design" can mean "pattern" (as in "a pretty design"), or it can mean "intention," especially an evil intention (as in "He had designs on her"). Does Frost use the word in one sense or in both? Explain.

T. S. ELIOT

Thomas Stearns Eliot (1888–1965) was born into a New England family that had moved to St. Louis. He attended a preparatory school in Massachusetts; then graduated from Harvard and did further study in literature and philosophy in France, Germany, and England. In 1914 he began working for Lloyd's Bank in London, and three years later he published his first book of poems. In 1925 he joined a publishing firm, and in 1927 he became a British citizen and a member of the Church of England. In 1948 Eliot received the Nobel Prize in Literature.

"Journey of the Magi," published shortly before Eliot announced his conversion, is spoken by one of the Magi, that is, by one of the Wise Men who, according to Matthew 2.1–2, 9–10, followed a star to Bethlehem, where they paid homage to the infant Jesus. The first five lines are enclosed within quotation marks because they are derived, with slight changes, from a sermon on the Nativity by Bishop Lancelot Andrewes

(1555–1626), preached at Christmas in 1622. In line 24 the three trees prefigure the three crosses of Matthew 27.38. The white horse in line 25 is indebted to Revelation 6.2 and 19.11, and perhaps it is also indebted to G. K. Chesterton's The Ballad of the White Horse, in which the disappearance of the horse represents the disappearance of paganism at the advent of Christianity. The vine (line 26) is often associated with Christ; see, for example, John 15.1–6. Line 27 ("dicing for pieces of silver") may allude to Matthew 27.3–6 (Judas is paid in silver) and 35 (the soldiers cast lots for Jesus's clothes).

Journey of the Magi

"A cold coming we had of it,
Just the worst time of the year
For a journey, and such a long journey:
The ways deep and the weather sharp,
The very dead of winter." 5
And the camels galled, sore-footed, refractory,
Lying down in the melting snow.
There were times we regretted
The summer palaces on slopes, the terraces,
And the silken girls bringing sherbet. 10
Then the camel men cursing and grumbling
And running away, and wanting their liquor and women,
And the night-fires going out, and the lack of shelters,
And the cities hostile and the towns unfriendly
And the villages dirty and charging high prices: 15

Sassetta [Stefano di Giovanni], *The Journey of the Magi*, c. 1440.

A hard time we had of it.
At the end we preferred to travel all night,
Sleeping in snatches,
With the voices singing in our ears, saying
That this was all folly.   20

Then at dawn we came down to a temperate valley,
Wet, below the snow line, smelling of vegetation;
With a running stream and a water-mill beating the darkness,
And three trees on the low sky,
And an old white horse galloped away in the meadow.   25
Then we came to a tavern with vine-leaves over the lintel,
Six hands at an open door dicing for pieces of silver,
And feet kicking the empty wine-skins.
But there was no information, and so we continued
And arrived at evening, not a moment too soon   30
Finding the place; it was (you may say) satisfactory.

All this was a long time ago, I remember,
And I would do it again, but set down
This set down
This: were we led all that way for   35
Birth or Death? There was a Birth, certainly,
We had evidence and no doubt. I had seen birth and death,
But had thought they were different; this Birth was
Hard and bitter agony for us, like Death, our death.
We returned to our places, these Kingdoms,   40
But no longer at ease here, in the old dispensation,
With an alien people clutching their gods.
I should be glad of another death.

[1927]

Topic for Critical Thinking and Writing

In the first stanza, what is the speaker's attitude toward the palaces he has left behind? What is his attitude in the last stanza? How do you explain the difference?

 GABRIELA MISTRAL

*The Chilean poet Gabriela Mistral's name at birth in 1889 was Lucila Godoy Alcayaga,
but when she became a writer she adopted a pen-name that acknowledged her respect
for, and literary indebtedness to, the Italian writer Gabriele D'Annunzio and the
Provencal poet Frédéric Mistral. She was a prolific writer of poetry, prose, and books for
children, and in 1957 she was awarded the Nobel Prize in Literature—the first writer
from Latin America to receive this honor. A professor, cultural minister, and diplomat
as well as an author, Mistral was admired throughout Central and South America. Her
books of verse include* Ternura *("Tenderness," 1924; enlarged edition, 1945),* Tala
("Destruction," 1938), and Lagar *("The Wine Press," 1954). She died in 1957. The
following poem was published posthumously. The translation is by Helene Masslo Anderson.*

Nocturne

Our Father who art in heaven.
Why hast Thou forsaken me!°
Thou did'st remember the February fruit,
When torn was its pulp of ruby.
My side is pierced also   5
Yet Thou will'st not look at me!

Thou did'st remember the dark grape cluster
And did'st give it to the crimsoned press,
And Thou did'st fan the poplar leaves
With thy breath of gentleness.   10
Yet in the deep wine press of death
Thou still would'st not my heart express!

As I walked I saw violets open:
And I drank the wine of the wind,
And I have lowered my yellowed eyelids   15
Never more to see Winter or Spring.
And I have tightened my mouth to stifle
The verses I am never to sing.
Thou hast wounded the cloud of Autumn
And Thou will'st not turn toward me!   20

I was sold by the one who kissed my cheek;°
He betrayed me for the tunic vile.
I gave him in my verses, my blood-stained face,
As Thine imprinted on her veil,
And in my night of the Orchard° I have found   25
John reluctant and the Angel hostile.

And now an infinite fatigue
Has come to pierce my eyes:
The fatigue of the day that it dying
And of the dawn that will arise;   30
The fatigue of the sky of metal
The fatigue of indigo skies!

And now I loosen my martyred sandal
And my locks, for I am longing to sleep.
And lost in the night, I lift my voice   35
In the cry I have learned from Thee:
Our Father who art in heaven,
Why hast Thou forsaken me!

²**Why hast thou forsaken me!** Jesus's words of agony and near-despair as he suffered on
the cross (Matthew 27.46)   ²¹**I was sold . . .** For thirty pieces of silver, the disciple Judas
betrayed Jesus (Matthew 26.47-50); later he repented, returned the money, and hanged
himself.   ²⁵**the Orchard** The garden where Jesus prayed before his betrayal and arrest;
see the note to Levertov, "Salvator Mundi: Via Crucis," p. 1276.

Topics for Critical Thinking and Writing

1. What does "nocturne" mean? How does this word prepare the reader for the poem that follows? Do you think a different title would have been more effective?

2. How would you reply to someone who said, "No poet should presume to speak in the voice of Jesus"? Does Mistral succeed in this daring poetic (and religious) act?

3. Focus on the images that Mistral uses in the first three stanzas—for example, "the February fruit" in lines 3–4, and the "grape cluster" and the "poplar leaves" in the second stanza. Describe carefully how Mistral uses these images to articulate and explore Jesus's thoughts and feelings.

4. The final line of the poem repeats line 2, but would you agree that the tone and meaning of these words are different at the end from what they were at the beginning? What is the movement of the poem as a whole: How does it begin? Where does it end?

 ## DENISE LEVERTOV

Denise Levertov was born in England in 1923, the daughter of a Welsh mother and a Russian-Jewish father who became an Anglican clergyman. She served as a nurse during World War II and then, in 1948, emigrated with her husband to New York City, becoming a U.S. citizen a few years later. Levertov taught at a number of colleges and universities, and she spoke and wrote often on social and political issues; in particular, she was a staunch critic of the Vietnam War. She wrote many volumes of verse, including Evening Train *(1992), from which the poem below is reprinted. She died in Seattle, Washington, in 1997.*

Salvator Mundi: Via Crucis°

Maybe He looked indeed
much as Rembrandt° envisioned Him
in those small heads that seem in fact
portraits of more than a model.
A dark, still young, very intelligent face,   5
a soul-mirror gaze of deep understanding, unjudging.
That face, in extremis, would have clenched its teeth
in a grimace not shown in even the great crucifixions.

°**Salvator Mundi: Via Crucis** Savior of the World: The Way of the Cross (Latin)
[2]**Rembrandt** The work of the great Dutch painter Rembrandt Harmensz van Rijn (1606–69) includes many etchings and paintings of scenes from the Bible, including the life of Christ.

The burden of humanness (I begin to see) exacted from Him
that He taste also the humiliation of dread,   10
cold sweat of wanting to let the whole thing go,
like any mortal hero out of his depth,
like anyone who has taken a step too far
and wants herself back.
The painters, even the greatest, don't show how,   15
in the midnight Garden,°
or staggering uphill under the weight of the Cross,
He went through with even the human longing
to simply cease, to not be.
Not torture of body,   20
not the hideous betrayals humans commit
not the faithless weakness of friends, and surely
not the anticipation of death (not then, in agony's grip)
was Incarnation's heaviest weight,
but this sickened desire to renege,   25
to step back from what He, Who was God,
had promised Himself, and had entered
time and flesh to enact.
Sublime acceptance, to be absolute, had to have welled
up from those depths where purpose   30
drifted for mortal moments.

[1992]

¹⁶**midnight Garden** The gospel of John (18.1–11) states that Jesus, fearful and in anguish,
prayed alone in a garden, just before he was betrayed and arrested. In their gospels, Mark
(14.32) and Matthew (26.36) identify the site as Gethsemane (Hebrew for "oil press");
Luke (22.39) places the scene on the Mount of Olives.

 ## Topics for Critical Thinking and Writing

1. This is a poem about Jesus' agony in the Garden and death by crucifixion,
   but it is also a poem about painting. More precisely: It explores the
   strengths and limitations of painters' renderings of what is for Christians the
   most sacred of subjects. What is the speaker's commentary on Rembrandt in
   the opening lines? Is he viewed as similar to, or different from, the painters
   referred to later?
2. This is a poem about poetry too—about its capacity to evoke the thoughts
   and feelings and physical expressions of Jesus. Is Levertov suggesting
   through this poem that as a poet she can do something that even the greatest painters cannot? Can you identify what this "something" is, or might
   be?
3. Why does Levertov write "herself" rather than "himself" in line 14?
4. Explain the meaning of the phrase "this sickened desire to renege" (line 25).
   Why, later on, does the speaker say *"had* to have welled / up"?

 **CARL DENNIS**

Carl Dennis has written seven books of poems, the most recent of which is Ranking the Wishes *(1997).*

On the Bus to Utica

Up to a year ago I'd have driven myself to Utica
As I've always done when visiting Aunt Jeannine.
But since last summer, and the bad experience in my car
With aliens, I prefer bus travel. Do you believe
In intelligent peoples elsewhere in our universe   5
More advanced than we are who might be visiting?
Neither did I till experience forced me
To widen the narrow notion of the possible
Common to people like me who have faith in science.
It happened one night last fall after the Rotary° meeting.   10
I'd lingered, as chapter chairman, to sort my notes,
So I wasn't surprised when I finally got to the lot
To find my car the only one there, though the shadows
Hovering over it should have been a tip-off
And the strong odor I had trouble placing—   15
Salty, ashy, metallic. My thoughts were elsewhere,
Reliving the vote at the meeting to help a restaurant
Take its first steps in a risky neighborhood.
So the element of surprise was theirs, the four of them,
Three who pulled me in when I opened the door   20
And one who drove us out past the town edge
To a cleared field where a three-legged landing craft
Big as a moving van sat idling. In its blue-green light
I caught my first good look of their faces. Like ours,
But with eyes bigger and glossier, and foreheads bumpier   25
With bristles from the eyebrows up, the hair of hedgehogs.
No rudeness from them, no shouting or shoving.
Just quiet gestures signaling me to sit down
And keep calm as we rose in silence to the mother ship.
I remember the red lights of the docking platform,   30
A dark hall, a room with a gurney where it dawned on me
Just before I went under there would be no discussions,
No sharing of thoughts on the fate of the universe,
No messages to bring back to my fellow earthlings.
When I woke from the drug they'd dosed me with   35
I was back in the car, in the Rotary parking lot,
With a splitting headache and a feeling I'd been massaged
Hard for a week or two by giants. Now I feel fine
Though my outlook on life has altered. It rankles
To think that beings have reached us who are smugly certain   40

---

¹⁰**Rotary** the name of a major national and international service club

All they can learn from us is what we can learn
From dissecting sea worms or banding geese.
Let's hope their science is pure at least,
Not a probe for a colony in the Milky Way.
Do you think they've planted a bug inside me?   45
Is that why you're silent? Fear will do us more harm
Than they will. Be brave. Speak out.
Tell me something you won't confide to your friends
Out of fear they may think you strange, eccentric.
If you're waiting for an audience that's more congenial,   50
More sensitive than the one that happens
To be sitting beside you now on this ramshackle bus,
I can sympathize. Once I waited too.
Now, as you see, I take what's offered.

[1998]

✎ Topics for Critical Thinking and Writing

1. How does Dennis characterize the speaker of "On the Bus to Utica"? What kind of person does the speaker believe himself to be?
2. How do you respond to the speaker?
3. The person sitting beside the speaker gives him an audience for his story. What other function does this character serve?
4. The poem could have ended, perhaps quite effectively, at either line 44 or 45. But Dennis wanted to end with the section, beginning in line 46, in which the speaker urges plain speaking and bravery and says he is a sympathetic listener. What does this section contribute to the meaning of the poem as a whole? How would the poem be different without it?

DRAMA

📖 SOPHOCLES

One of the three great writers of tragedies in ancient Greece, Sophocles (496?–406 B.C.) was born in Colonus, near Athens, into a well-to-do family. Well educated, he first won public acclaim as a tragic poet at the age of 27, in 468 B.C., when he defeated Aeschylus in a competition for writing a tragic play. He is said to have written some 120 plays, but only 7 tragedies are extant; among them are Oedipus Rex *(page 280,)* Antigonê, *and* Oedipus at Colonus. *He died, much honored, in his nineteenth year, in Athens, where he had lived his entire life.*

For a Note on Greek Tragedy, and a picture of a Greek theater, see pages 277-79.

Antigonê

An English Version by Dudley Fitts and Robert Fitzgerald

LIST OF CHARACTERS

ANTIGONÊ
ISMENÊ
EURYDICÊ

Jane Lapotaire in *Antigone*. National Theater, London, 1984. (Donald Cooper/Photo-stage)

CREON
HAIMON
TEIRESIAS
A SENTRY
A MESSENGER
CHORUS

> **SCENE:** *Before the palace of* CREON, *king of Thebes. A central double door, and two lateral doors. A platform extends the length of the façade, and from this platform three steps lead down into the "orchestra," or chorus-ground.*
> **TIME:** *Dawn of the day after the repulse of the Argive army from the assault on Thebes.*

Prologue

ANTIGONÊ *and* ISMENÊ *enter from the central door of the palace.*
ANTIGONÊ. Ismenê, dear sister,
　　　You would think that we had already suffered enough
　　　For the curse on Oedipus.°

---

3 Oedipus, once King of Thebes, was the father of Antigonê and Ismenê, and of their brothers Polyneicês and Eteoclês. Oedipus unwittingly killed his father, Laïos, and married his own mother, Iocastê. When he learned what he had done, he blinded himself and left Thebes. Eteoclês and Polyneicês quarreled; Polyneicês was driven out but returned to assault Thebes. In the battle each brother killed the other; Creon became king and ordered that Polyneicês be left to rot unburied on the battlefield as a traitor.

I cannot imagine any grief
That you and I have not gone through. And now—   5
Have they told you of the new decree of our King Creon?
ISMENÊ. I have heard nothing: I know
That two sisters lost two brothers, a double death
In a single hour; and I know that the Argive army
Fled in the night; but beyond this, nothing.   10
ANTIGONÊ. I thought so. And this is why I wanted you
To come out here with me. There is something we must do.
ISMENÊ. Why do you speak so strangely?
ANTIGONÊ. Listen, Ismenê:
Creon buried our brother Eteoclês   15
With military honors, gave him a soldier's funeral,
And it was right that he should; but Polyneicês,
Who fought as bravely and died as miserably,—
They say that Creon has sworn
No one shall bury him, no one mourn for him,   20
But his body must lie in the fields, a sweet treasure
For carrion birds to find as they search for food.
That is what they say, and our good Creon is coming here
To announce it publicly; and the penalty—
Stoning to death in the public square!
                                   There it is,   25
And now you can prove what you are:
A true sister, or a traitor to your family.
ISMENÊ. Antigonê, you are mad! What could I possibly do?
ANTIGONÊ. You must decide whether you will help me or not.
ISMENÊ. I do not understand you. Help you in what?   30
ANTIGONÊ. Ismenê. I am going to bury him. Will you come?
ISMENÊ. Bury him! You have just said the new law forbids it.
ANTIGONÊ. He is my brother. And he is your brother, too.
ISMENÊ. But think of the danger! Think what Creon will do!
ANTIGONÊ. Creon is not strong enough to stand in my way.   35
ISMENÊ. Ah sister!
Oedipus died, everyone hating him
For what his own search brought to light, his eyes
Ripped out by his own hand; and Iocastê died,
His mother and wife at once: she twisted the cords   40
That strangled her life; and our two brothers died,
Each killed by the other's sword. And we are left:
But oh, Antigonê,
Think how much more terrible than these
Our own death would be if we should go against Creon   45
And do what he has forbidden! We are only women,
We cannot fight with men, Antigonê!
The law is strong, we must give in to the law
In this thing, and in worse. I beg the Dead
To forgive me, but I am helpless: I must yield   50
To those in authority. And I think it is dangerous business
To be always meddling.
ANTIGONÊ.   If that is what you think,
I should not want you, even if you asked to come.

You have made your choice, you can be what you want to be.
But I will bury him; and if I must die,   55
I say that this crime is holy: I shall lie down
With him in death, and I shall be as dear
To him as he to me.
                    It is the dead,
Not the living, who make the longest demands:
We die for ever. . . .
                        You may do as you like.   60
Since apparently the laws of the gods mean nothing to you.

ISMENÊ. They mean a great deal to me; but I have no strength
    To break laws that were made for the public good.

ANTIGONÊ. That must be your excuse, I suppose. But as for me,
    I will bury the brother I love.

ISMENÊ.   Antigonê,   65
    I am so afraid for you!

ANTIGONÊ.   You need not be:
    You have yourself to consider, after all.

ISMENÊ. But no one must hear of this, you must tell no one!
    I will keep it a secret, I promise!

ANTIGONÊ.   O tell it! Tell everyone!
    Think how they'll hate you when it all comes out   70
    If they learn that you knew about it all the time!

ISMENÊ. So fiery! You should be cold with fear.

ANTIGONÊ. Perhaps. But I am doing only what I must.

ISMENÊ. But can you do it? I say that you cannot.

ANTIGONÊ. Very well: when my strength gives out,
    I shall do no more.   75

ISMENÊ. Impossible things should not be tried at all.

ANTIGONÊ. Go away, Ismenê:
    I shall be hating you soon, and the dead will too,
    For your words are hateful. Leave me my foolish plan:
    I am not afraid of the danger; if it means death,   80
    It will not be the worst of deaths—death without honor.

ISMENÊ. Go then, if you feel that you must.
    You are unwise,
    But a loyal friend indeed to those who love you.

Exit into the palace. ANTIGONÊ *goes off, left. Enter the* CHORUS.

Párodos

CHORUS. Now the long blade of the sun, lying   *Strophe 1*
    Level east to west, touches with glory
    Thebes of the Seven Gates. Open, unlidded
    Eye of golden day! O marching light
    Across the eddy and rush of Dircê's stream,°   5
    Striking the white shields of the enemy
    Thrown headlong backward from the blaze of morning!

Párodos 5 Dircê's stream a stream west of Thebes

CHORAGOS.° Polyneicês their commander
    Roused them with windy phrases,
    He the wild eagle screaming   10
    Insults above our land,
    His wings their shields of snow,
    His crest their marshalled helms.

CHORUS. Against our seven gates in a yawning ring   *Antistrophe 1*
    The famished spears came onward in the night: 15
    But before his jaws were sated with our blood,
    Or pinefire took the garland of our towers,
    He was thrown back; and as he turned, great Thebes—
    No tender victim for his noisy power—
    Rose like a dragon behind him, shouting war.   20

CHORAGOS. For God hates utterly
    The bray of bragging tongues;
    And when he beheld their smiling,
    Their swagger of golden helms,
    The frown of his thunder blasted   25
    Their first man from our walls.

CHORUS. We heard his shout of triumph high in the air   *Strophe 2*
    Turn to a scream; far out in a flaming arc
    He fell with his windy torch, and the earth struck him.
    And others storming in fury no less than his   30
    Found shock of death in the dusty joy of battle.

CHORAGOS. Seven captains at seven gates
    Yielded their clanging arms to the god
    That bends the battle-line and breaks it.
    These two only, brothers in blood,   35
    Face to face in matchless rage.
    Mirroring each the other's death,
    Clashed in long combat.

CHORUS. But now in the beautiful morning of victory   *Antistrophe 2*
    Let Thebes of the many chariots sing for joy!   40
    With hearts for dancing we'll take leave of war:
    Our temples shall be sweet with hymns of praise,
    And the long nights shall echo with our chorus.

Scene I

CHORAGOS. But now at last our new King is coming:
    Creon of Thebes, Menoikeus' son.
    In this auspicious dawn of his reign
    What are the new complexities
    That shifting Fate has woven for him?   5
    What is his counsel? Why has he summoned
    The old men to hear him?

    Enter CREON *from the palace, center. He addresses the* CHORUS *from the top step.*

8 Choragos leader of the Chorus

CREON. Gentlemen: I have the honor to inform you that our Ship of State, which recent storms have threatened to destroy, has come safely to harbor at last, guided by the merciful wisdom of Heaven. I have   10
summoned you here this morning because I know that I can depend upon you: your devotion to King Laïos was absolute; you never hesitated in your duty to our late ruler Oedipus; and when Oedipus died, your loyalty was transferred to his children. Unfortunately, as you know, his two sons, the princes Eteoclês and Poly-   15
neicês, have killed each other in battle; and I, as the next in blood, have succeeded to the full power of the throne.

I am aware, of course, that no Ruler can expect complete loyalty from his subjects until he has been tested in office. Nevertheless, I say to you at the very outset that I have nothing but contempt for the kind of Governor who is afraid, for whatever reason,   20
to follow the course that he knows is best for the State; and as for the man who sets private friendship above the public welfare,—I have no use for him, either. I call God to witness that if I saw my country headed for ruin, I should not be afraid to speak out plainly;   25
and I need hardly remind you that I would never have any dealings with an enemy of the people. No one values friendship more highly than I: but we must remember that friends made at the risk of wrecking our Ship are not real friends at all.

These are my principles, at any rate, and that is why I have   30
made the following decision concerning the sons of Oedipus: Eteoclês, who died as a man should die, fighting for his country, is to be buried with full military honors, with all the ceremony that is usual when the greatest heroes die; but his brother Polyneicês, who broke his exile to come back with fire and sword against his native   35
city and the shrines of his fathers' gods, whose one idea was to spill the blood of his blood and sell his own people into slavery—Polyneicês, I say, is to have no burial: no man is to touch him or say the least prayer for him; he shall lie on the plain, unburied; and the birds and the scavenging dogs can do with him whatever they like.   40

This is my command, and you can see the wisdom behind it. As long as I am King, no traitor is going to be honored with the loyal man. But whoever shows by word and deed that he is on the side of the State—he shall have my respect while he is living and my reverence when he is dead.   45

CHORAGOS. If that is your will, Creon son of Menoikeus,
You have the right to enforce it: we are yours.

CREON. That is my will. Take care that you do your part.

CHORAGOS. We are old men: let the younger ones carry it out.

CREON. I do not mean that: the sentries have been appointed.   50

CHORAGOS. Then what is it that you would have us do?

CREON. You will give no support to whoever breaks this law.

CHORAGOS. Only a crazy man is in love with death!

CREON. And death it is; yet money talks, and the wisest
Have sometimes been known to count a few coins too many.   55

Enter SENTRY *from left.*

SENTRY. I'll not say that I'm out of breath from running, King, because
every time I stopped to think about what I have to tell you, I felt

like going back. And all the time a voice kept saying, "You fool, don't you know you're walking straight into trouble?"; and then another voice: "Yes, but if you let somebody else get the news to   60
Creon first, it will be even worse than that for you!" But good sense won out, at least I hope it was good sense, and here I am with a story that makes no sense at all; but I'll tell it anyhow, because, as they say, what's going to happen's going to happen and—
CREON. Come to the point. What have you to say?   65
SENTRY. I did not do it. I did not see who did it. You must not punish me for what someone else has done.
CREON. A comprehensive defense! More effective, perhaps, if I knew its purpose. Come: what is it?
SENTRY. A dreadful thing . . . I don't know how to put it—   70
CREON. Out with it!
SENTRY.   Well, then;
    The dead man—
             Polyneicês—

Pause. The SENTRY *is overcome, fumbles for words.* CREON *waits impassively.*

                         out there—
                         someone,—
    New dust on the slimy flesh!

Pause. No sign from CREON
    Someone has given it burial that way, and
    Gone. . . .   75

Long pause. CREON *finally speaks with deadly control.*
CREON. And the man who dared do this?
SENTRY.   I swear I
    Do not know! You must believe me!
                             Listen:
    The ground was dry, not a sign of digging, no,
    Not a wheeltrack in the dust, no trace of anyone.
    It was when they relieved us this morning: and one of them,   80
    The corporal, pointed to it.
                         There it was,
    The strangest—
             Look:
    The body, just mounded over with light dust: you see?
    Not buried really, but as if they'd covered it
    Just enough for the ghost's peace. And no sign   85
    Of dogs or any wild animal that had been there.

    And then what a scene there was! Every man of us
    Accusing the other: we all proved the other man did it,
    We all had proof that we could not have done it.
    We were ready to take hot iron in our hands,   90
    Walk through fire, swear by all the gods,
    It was not I!
    I do not know who it was, but it was not I!

CREON*'s rage has been mounting steadily, but the* SENTRY *is too intent
upon his story to notice it.*

And then, when this came to nothing, someone said
A thing that silenced us and made us stare   95
Down at the ground: you had to be told the news,
And one of us had to do it! We threw the dice,
And the bad luck fell to me. So here I am,
No happier to be here than you are to have me:
Nobody likes the man who brings bad news.   100

CHORAGOS. I have been wondering, King: can it be that the gods have
done this?

CREON [*furiously*]. Stop!
Must you doddering wrecks
Go out of your heads entirely? "The gods"!   105
Intolerable!
The gods favor this corpse? Why? How had he served them?
Tried to loot their temples, burn their images,
Yes, and the whole State, and its laws with it!
Is it your senile opinion that the gods love to honor bad men?   110
A pious thought!—
No, from the very beginning
There have been those who have whispered together,
Stiff-necked anarchists, putting their heads together,
Scheming against me in alleys. These are the men,
And they have bribed my own guard to do this thing.   115
[*Sententiously.*] Money!
There's nothing in the world so demoralizing as money.
Down go your cities,
Homes gone, men gone, honest hearts corrupted.
Crookedness of all kinds, and all for money!
[*To* SENTRY.]   But you—!   120
I swear by God and by the throne of God,
The man who has done this thing shall pay for it!
Find that man, bring him here to me, or your death
Will be the least of your problems: I'll string you up
Alive, and there will be certain ways to make you   125
Discover your employer before you die;
And the process may teach you a lesson you seem to have missed:
The dearest profit is sometimes all too dear:
That depends on the source. Do you understand me?
A fortune won is often misfortune.   130

SENTRY. King, may I speak?

CREON.   Your very voice distresses me.

SENTRY. Are you sure that it is my voice, and not your conscience?

CREON. By God, he wants to analyze me now!

SENTRY. It is not what I say, but what has been done, that hurts you.

CREON. You talk too much.

SENTRY.   Maybe; but I've done nothing.   135

CREON. Sold your soul for some silver: that's all you've done.

SENTRY. How dreadful it is when the right judge judges wrong!

CREON. Your figures of speech

May entertain you now; but unless you bring me the man,
You will get little profit from them in the end.   140

Exit CREON *into the palace.*
SENTRY. "Bring me the man"—!
     I'd like nothing better than bringing him the man!
     But bring him or not, you have seen the last of me here.
     At any rate, I am safe!   *[Exit* SENTRY.*]*

Ode I

CHORUS. Numberless are the world's wonders, but not   *Strophe 1*
     More wonderful than man; the stormgray sea
     Yields to his prows, the huge crests bear him high;
     Earth, holy and inexhaustible, is graven
     With shining furrows where his plows have gone   5
     Year after year, the timeless labor of stallions.

     The lightboned birds and beasts that cling to cover, *Antistrophe 1*
     The lithe fish lighting their reaches of dim water,
     All are taken, tamed in the net of his mind;
     The lion on the hill, the wild horse windy-maned,   10
     Resign to him; and his blunt yoke has broken
     The sultry shoulders of the mountain bull.

     Words also, and thought as rapid as air,   *Strophe 2*
     He fashions to his good use; statecraft is his,
     And his the skill that deflects the arrows of snow,   15
     The spears of winter rain: from every wind
     He has made himself secure—from all but one:
     In the late wind of death he cannot stand.

     O clear intelligence, force beyond all measure!   *Antistrophe 2*
     O fate of man, working both good and evil!   20
     When the laws are kept, how proudly his city stands!
     When the laws are broken, what of his city then?
     Never may the anarchic man find rest at my hearth,
     Never be it said that my thoughts are his thoughts.

Scene II

Reenter SENTRY *leading* ANTIGONÊ.
CHORAGOS. What does this mean? Surely this captive woman
     Is the Princess, Antigonê. Why should she be taken?
SENTRY. Here is the one who did it! We caught her
     In the very act of burying him.—Where is Creon?
CHORAGOS. Just coming from the house.

Enter CREON, *center.*
CREON.   What has happened?   5
     Why have you come back so soon?
SENTRY *[expansively].*   O King,
     A man should never be too sure of anything:
     I would have sworn

That you'd not see me here again: your anger
Frightened me so, and the things you threatened me with;   10
But how could I tell then
That I'd be able to solve the case so soon?
No dice-throwing this time: I was only too glad to come!
Here is this woman. She is the guilty one:
We found her trying to bury him.   15
Take her, then; question her; judge her as you will.
I am through with the whole thing now, and glad of it.

CREON. But this is Antigonê! Why have you brought her here?

SENTRY. She was burying him, I tell you!

CREON [*severely*].   Is this the truth?

SENTRY. I saw her with my own eyes. Can I say more?   20

CREON. The details: come, tell me quickly!

SENTRY.   It was like this:
After those terrible threats of yours, King,
We went back and brushed the dust away from the body.
The flesh was soft by now, and stinking,
So we sat on a hill to windward and kept guard.   25
No napping this time! We kept each other awake.
But nothing happened until the white round sun
Whirled in the center of the round sky over us:
Then, suddenly,
A storm of dust roared up from the earth, and the sky   30
Went out, the plain vanished with all its trees
In the stinging dark. We closed our eyes and endured it.
The whirlwind lasted a long time, but it passed;
And then we looked, and there was Antigonê!
I have seen   35
A mother bird come back to a stripped nest, heard
Her crying bitterly a broken note or two
For the young ones stolen. Just so, when this girl
Found the bare corpse, and all her love's work wasted,
She wept, and cried on heaven to damn the hands   40
That had done this thing.
                        And then she brought more dust
And sprinkled wine three times for her brother's ghost.

We ran and took her at once. She was not afraid,
Not even when we charged her with what she had done.
She denied nothing.
                    And this was a comfort to me,   45
And some uneasiness: for it is a good thing
To escape from death, but it is no great pleasure
To bring death to a friend.
                    Yet I always say
There is nothing so comfortable as your own safe skin!

CREON [*slowly, dangerously*]. And you, Antigonê,   50
You with your head hanging,—do you confess this thing?

ANTIGONÊ. I do. I deny nothing.

CREON [*to* SENTRY].   You may go.

                                      [*Exit* SENTRY.]

[*To* ANTIGONÊ.] Tell me, tell me briefly:
Had you heard my proclamation touching this matter?
ANTIGONÊ. It was public. Could I help hearing it?   55
CREON. And yet you dared defy the law.
ANTIGONÊ.   I dared.
It was not God's proclamation. That final Justice
That rules the world below makes no such laws.

Your edict, King, was strong.
But all your strength is weakness itself against   60
The immortal unrecorded laws of God.
They are not merely now: they were, and shall be,
Operative for ever, beyond man utterly.
I knew I must die, even without your decree:
I am only mortal. And if I must die   65
Now, before it is my time to die,
Surely this is no hardship: can anyone
Living, as I live, with evil all about me,
Think Death less than a friend? This death of mine
Is of no importance; but if I had left my brother   70
Lying in death unburied, I should have suffered.
Now I do not.
                    You smile at me. Ah Creon,
Think me a fool, if you like; but it may well be
That a fool convicts me of folly.
CHORAGOS. Like father, like daughter: both headstrong, deaf to reason!   75
She has never learned to yield.
CREON.   She has much to learn.
The inflexible heart breaks first, the toughest iron
Cracks first, and the wildest horses bend their necks
At the pull of the smallest curb.
                                        Pride? In a slave?
This girl is guilty of a double insolence,   80
Breaking the given laws and boasting of it.
Who is the man here,
She or I, if this crime goes unpunished?
Sister's child, or more than sister's child,
Or closer yet in blood—she and her sister   85
Win bitter death for this!
[*To* SERVANTS.]   Go, some of you,
Arrest Ismenê. I accuse her equally.
Bring her: you will find her sniffling in the house there.

Here mind's a traitor: crimes kept in the dark
Cry for light, and the guardian brain shudders;   90
But how much worse than this
Is brazen boasting of barefaced anarchy!
ANTIGONÊ. Creon, what more do you want than my death?
CREON.   Nothing.
That gives me everything.
ANTIGONÊ.   Then I beg you: kill me.
This talking is a great weariness: your words   95

Are distasteful to me, and I am sure that mine
Seem so to you. And yet they should not seem so:
I should have praise and honor for what I have done.
All these men here would praise me
Were their lips not frozen shut with fear of you.   100
[*Bitterly.*] Ah the good fortune of kings,
Licensed to say and do whatever they please!

CREON. You are alone here in that opinion.

ANTIGONÊ. No, they are with me. But they keep their tongues in leash.

CREON. Maybe. But you are guilty, and they are not.   105

ANTIGONÊ. There is no guilt in reverence for the dead.

CREON. But Eteoclês—was he not your brother too?

ANTIGONÊ. My brother too.

CREON.   And you insult his memory?

ANTIGONÊ [*softly*]. The dead man would not say that I insult it.

CREON. He would: for you honor a traitor as much as him.   110

ANTIGONÊ. His own brother, traitor or not, and equal in blood.

CREON. He made war on his country. Eteoclês defended it.

ANTIGONÊ. Nevertheless, there are honors due all the dead.

CREON. But not the same for the wicked as for the just.

ANTIGONÊ. Ah Creon, Creon,   115
Which of us can say what the gods hold wicked?

CREON. An enemy is an enemy, even dead.

ANTIGONÊ. It is my nature to join in love, not hate.

CREON [*finally losing patience*]. Go join them then; if you must have
your love,
Find it in hell!   120

CHORAGOS. But see, Ismenê comes:

Enter ISMENÊ, *guarded.*
Those tears are sisterly, the cloud
That shadows her eyes rains down gentle sorrow.

CREON. You too, Ismenê,
Snake in my ordered house, sucking my blood   125
Stealthily—and all the time I never knew
That these two sisters were aiming at my throne!
                                                                Ismenê,
Do you confess your share in this crime, or deny it?
Answer me.

ISMENÊ. Yes, if she will let me say so. I am guilty.   130

ANTIGONÊ [*coldly*]. No, Ismenê. You have no right to say so.
You would not help me, and I will not have you help me.

ISMENÊ. But now I know what you meant: and I am here
To join you, to take my share of punishment.

ANTIGONÊ. The dead man and the gods who rule the dead   135
Know whose act this was. Words are not friends.

ISMENÊ. Do you refuse me, Antigonê? I want to die with you:
I too have a duty that I must discharge to the dead.

ANTIGONÊ. You shall not lessen my death by sharing it.

ISMENÊ. What do I care for life when you are dead?   140

ANTIGONÊ. Ask Creon. You're always hanging on his opinions.

ISMENÊ. You are laughing at me. Why, Antigonê?

ANTIGONÊ. It's a joyless laughter, Ismenê.

ISMENÊ.   But can I do nothing?

ANTIGONÊ. Yes. Save yourself. I shall not envy you.

      There are those who will praise you; I shall have honor, too.   145

ISMENÊ. But we are equally guilty!

ANTIGONÊ.   No more, Ismenê.

      You are alive, but I belong to Death.

CREON [*to the* CHORUS]. Gentlemen, I beg you to observe these girls:

      One has just now lost her mind; the other,

      It seems, has never had a mind at all.   150

ISMENÊ. Grief teaches the steadiest minds to waver, King.

CREON. Yours certainly did, when you assumed guilt with the guilty!

ISMENÊ. But how could I go on living without her?

CREON.   You are.

      She is already dead.

ISMENÊ.   But your own son's bride!

CREON. There are places enough for him to push his plow.   155

      I want no wicked women for my sons!

ISMENÊ. O dearest Haimon, how your father wrongs you!

CREON. I've had enough of your childish talk of marriage!

CHORAGOS. Do you really intend to steal this girl from your son?

CREON. No; Death will do that for me.

CHORAGOS.   Then she must die?   160

CREON [*ironically*]. You dazzle me.

                  —But enough of this talk!

      [*To* GUARDS.] You, there, take them away and guard them well:

      For they are but women, and even brave men run

      When they see Death coming.

                     Exeunt ISMENÊ, ANTIGONÊ, *and* GUARDS.

Ode II

CHORUS. Fortunate is the man who has never tasted   *Strophe 1*

      God's vengeance!

      Where once the anger of heaven has struck, that house is shaken

      For ever: damnation rises behind each child

      Like a wave cresting out of the black northeast,

      When the long darkness under sea roars up   5

      And bursts drumming death upon the windwhipped sand.

      I have seen this gathering sorrow from time long past   *Antistrophe 1*

      Loom upon Oedipus' children: generation from generation

      Takes the compulsive rage of the enemy god.

      So lately this last flower of Oedipus' line   10

      Drank the sunlight! but now a passionate word

      And a handful of dust have closed up all its beauty.

      What mortal arrogance   *Strophe 2*

      Transcends the wrath of Zeus?

      Sleep cannot lull him nor the effortless long months   15

      Of the timeless gods: but he is young for ever,

      And his house is the shining day of high Olympos.

      All that is and shall be,

And all the past, is his.
No pride on earth is free of the curse of heaven.   20

The straying dreams of men   *Antistrophe 2*
May bring them ghosts of joy:
But as they drowse, the waking embers burn them;
Or they walk with fixed eyes, as blind men walk.
But the ancient wisdom speaks for our own time: 25

> *Fate works most for woe*
> *With Folly's fairest show.*

Man's little pleasure is the spring of sorrow.

Scene III

CHORAGOS. But here is Haimon, King, the last of all your sons.
Is it grief for Antigonê that brings him here,
And bitterness at being robbed of his bride?

Enter HAIMON.
CREON. We shall soon see, and no need of diviners.
                                        —Son,
You have heard my final judgment on that girl: 5
Have you come here hating me, or have you come
With deference and with love, whatever I do?
HAIMON. I am your son, father. You are my guide.
You make things clear for me, and I obey you.
No marriage means more to me than your continuing wisdom.   10
CREON. Good. That is the way to behave: subordinate
Everything else, my son, to your father's will.
This is what a man prays for, that he may get
Sons attentive and dutiful in his house,
Each one hating his father's enemies,   15
Honoring his father's friends. But if his sons
Fail him, if they turn out unprofitably,
What has he fathered but trouble for himself
And amusement for the malicious?
                              So you are right
Not to lose your head over this woman.   20
Your pleasure with her would soon grow cold, Haimon,
And then you'd have a hellcat in bed and elsewhere.
Let her find her husband in Hell!
Of all the people in this city, only she
Has had contempt for my law and broken it.   25

Do you want me to show myself weak before the people?
Or to break my sworn word? No, and I will not.
The woman dies.
I suppose she'll plead "family ties." Well, let her.
If I permit my own family to rebel,   30
How shall I earn the world's obedience?
Show me the man who keeps his house in hand,

He's fit for public authority.

                I'll have no dealings
With lawbreakers, critics of the government:
Whoever is chosen to govern should be obeyed—   35
Must be obeyed, in all things, great and small,
Just and unjust! O Haimon,
The man who knows how to obey, and that man only,
Knows how to give commands when the time comes.
You can depend on him, no matter how fast   40
The spears come: he's a good soldier, he'll stick it out.

Anarchy, anarchy! Show me a greater evil!
This is why cities tumble and the great houses rain down,
This is what scatters armies!
No, no: good lives are made so by discipline.   45
We keep the laws then, and the lawmakers,
And no woman shall seduce us. If we must lose,
Let's lose to a man, at least! Is a woman stronger than we?

CHORAGOS. Unless time has rusted my wits,
    What you say, King, is said with point and dignity.   50

HAIMON [*boyishly earnest*]. Father:
    Reason is God's crowning gift to man, and you are right
To warn me against losing mine. I cannot say—
I hope that I shall never want to say!—that you
Have reasoned badly. Yet there are other men   55
Who can reason, too; and their opinions might be helpful.
You are not in a position to know everything
That people say or do, or what they feel:
Your temper terrifies—everyone
Will tell you only what you like to hear.   60
But I, at any rate, can listen; and I have heard them
Muttering and whispering in the dark about this girl.
They say no woman has ever, so unreasonably,
Died so shameful a death for a generous act:
"She covered her brother's body. Is this indecent?   65
She kept him from dogs and vultures. Is this a crime?
Death?—She should have all the honor that we can give her!"

This is the way they talk out there in the city.

You must believe me:
Nothing is closer to me than your happiness.   70
What could be closer? Must not any son
Value his father's fortune as his father does his?
I beg you, do not be unchangeable:
Do not believe that you alone can be right.
The man who thinks that,   75
The man who maintains that only he has the power
To reason correctly, the gift to speak, the soul—
A man like that, when you know him, turns out empty.

It is not reason never to yield to reason!

In flood time you can see how some trees bend,   80
And because they bend, even their twigs are safe,
While stubborn trees are torn up, roots and all.
And the same thing happens in sailing:
Make your sheet fast, never slacken,—and over you go,
Head over heels and under: and there's your voyage.   85
Forget you are angry! Let yourself be moved!
I know I am young; but please let me say this:
The ideal condition
Would be, I admit, that men should be right by instinct;
But since we are all too likely to go astray,   90
The reasonable thing is to learn from those who can teach.

CHORAGOS. You will do well to listen to him, King,
If what he says is sensible. And you, Haimon,
Must listen to your father.—Both speak well.

CREON. You consider it right for a man of my years and experience   95
To go to school to a boy?

HAIMON.   It is not right
If I am wrong. But if I am young, and right,
What does my age matter?

CREON. You think it right to stand up for an anarchist?

HAIMON. Not at all. I pay no respect to criminals.   100

CREON. Then she is not a criminal?

HAIMON. The City would deny it, to a man.

CREON. And the City proposes to teach me how to rule?

HAIMON. Ah. Who is it that's talking like a boy now?

CREON. My voice is the one voice giving orders in this City!   105

HAIMON. It is no City if it takes orders from one voice.

CREON. The State is the King!

HAIMON.   Yes, if the State is a desert.

Pause.

CREON. This boy, it seems, has sold out to a woman.

HAIMON. If you are a woman: my concern is only for you.

CREON. So? Your "concern"! In a public brawl with your father!   110

HAIMON. How about you, in a public brawl with justice?

CREON. With justice, when all that I do is within my rights?

HAIMON. You have no right to trample on God's right.

CREON [*completely out of control*]. Fool, adolescent fool! Taken in by a
woman!

HAIMON. You'll never see me taken in by anything vile.   115

CREON. Every word you say is for her!

HAIMON [*quietly, darkly*].   And for you.
And for me. And for the gods under the earth.

CREON. You'll never marry her while she lives.

HAIMON. Then she must die.—But her death will cause another.

CREON. Another?   120
Have you lost your senses? Is this an open threat?

HAIMON. There is no threat in speaking to emptiness.

CREON. I swear you'll regret this superior tone of yours!
You are the empty one!

HAIMON.   If you were not my father,
    I'd say you were perverse.   125
CREON. You girlstruck fool, don't play at words with me!
HAIMON. I am sorry. You prefer silence.
CREON.   Now, by God—
    I swear, by all the gods in heaven above us,
    You'll watch it, I swear you shall!
    [To the SERVANTS.*]* Bring her out!
    Bring the woman out! Let her die before his eyes!   130
    Here, this instant, with her bridegroom beside her!
HAIMON. Not here, no; she will not die here, King.
    And you will never see my face again.
    Go on raving as long as you've a friend to endure you.

                                              Exit HAIMON.

CHORAGOS. Gone, gone.   135
    Creon, a young man in a rage is dangerous!
CREON. Let him do, or dream to do, more than a man can.
    He shall not save these girls from death.
CHORAGOS.   These girls?
    You have sentenced them both?
CREON.   No, you are right.
    I will not kill the one whose hands are clean.   140
CHORAGOS. But Antigonê?
CREON. *[somberly]*.   I will carry her far away
    Out there in the wilderness, and lock her
    Living in a vault of stone. She shall have food,
    As the custom is, to absolve the State of her death.
    And there let her pray to the gods of hell: 145
    They are her only gods:
    Perhaps they will show her an escape from death,
    Or she may learn,
                  though late,
    That piety shown the dead is piety in vain.

                                        [Exit CREON.*]*

Ode III

CHORUS. Love, unconquerable   *Strophe*
    Waster of rich men, keeper
    Of warm lights and all-night vigil
    In the soft face of a girl:
    Sea-wanderer, forest-visitor!   5
    Even the pure Immortals cannot escape you,
    And the mortal man, in his one day's dusk,
    Trembles before your glory.

    Surely you swerve upon ruin   *Antistrophe*
    The just man's consenting heart,   10
    As here you have made bright anger
    Strike between father and son—

And none has conquered by Love!
A girl's glance working the will of heaven:
Pleasure to her alone who mocks us,   15
Merciless Aphroditê.°

                                  Scene IV

CHORAGOS [*as* ANTIGONÊ *enters guarded*]. But I can no longer stand in
          awe of this,
     Nor, seeing what I see, keep back my tears.
     Here is Antigonê, passing to that chamber
     Where all find sleep at last.
ANTIGONÊ. Look upon me, friends, and pity me   *Strophe 1*   5
     Turning back at the night's edge to say
     Good-by to the sun that shines for me no longer;
     Now sleepy Death
     Summons me down to Acheron,° that cold shore:
     There is no bridesong there, nor any music.   10
CHORUS. Yet not unpraised, not without a kind of honor,
     You walk at last into the underworld;
     Untouched by sickness, broken by no sword.
     What woman has ever found your way to death?
ANTIGONÊ. How often I have heard the story of Niobê,°   *Antistrophe 1*   15
     Tantalos' wretched daughter, how the stone
     Clung fast about her, ivy-close: and they say
     The rain falls endlessly
     And sifting soft snow; her tears are never done.
     I feel the loneliness of her death in mine.   20
CHORUS. But she was born of heaven, and you
     Are woman, woman-born. If her death is yours,
     A mortal woman's, is this not for you
     Glory in our world and in the world beyond?
ANTIGONÊ. You laugh at me. Ah, friends, friends   *Strophe 2*   25
     Can you not wait until I am dead? O Thebes,
     O men many-charioted, in love with Fortune,
     Dear springs of Dircê, sacred Theban grove,
     Be witnesses for me, denied all pity,
     Unjustly judged! and think a word of love   30
     For her whose path turns
     Under dark earth, where there are no more tears.
CHORUS. You have passed beyond human daring and come at last
     Into a place of stone where Justice sits.
     I cannot tell   35
     What shape of your father's guilt appears in this.
ANTIGONÊ. You have touched it at last: *Antistrophe 2*

Ode III 16 Aphroditê goddess of love   **9 Acheron** a river of the underworld, which was
ruled by Hades   **15 Niobê** Niobê boasted of her numerous children, provoking Leto, the
mother of Apollo, to destroy them. Niobê wept profusely, and finally was turned to stone
on Mount Sipylus, whose streams are her tears.

That bridal bed
Unspeakable, horror of son and mother mingling:
Their crime, infection of all our family!
O Oedipus, father and brother!   40
Your marriage strikes from the grave to murder mine.
I have been a stranger here in my own land:
All my life
The blasphemy of my birth has followed me.
CHORUS. Reverence is a virtue, but strength
     Lives in established law: that must prevail.
     You have made your choice,
     Your death is the doing of your conscious hand.
ANTIGONÊ. Then let me go, since all your words are bitter,   *Epode*
     And the very light of the sun is cold to me.   50
     Lead me to my vigil, where I must have
     Neither love nor lamentation; no song, but silence.

          CREON *interrupts impatiently.*
CREON. If dirges and planned lamentations could put off death,
     Men would be singing for ever.
     [*To the* SERVANTS.]   Take her, go!
     You know your orders: take her to the vault   55
     And leave her alone there. And if she lives or dies,
     That's her affair, not ours: our hands are clean.

ANTIGONÊ. O tomb, vaulted bride-bed in eternal rock,
     Soon I shall be with my own again
     Where Persephonê° welcomes the thin ghosts underground: 60
     And I shall see my father again, and you, mother,
     And dearest Polyneicês—
                         dearest indeed
     To me, since it was my hand
     That washed him clean and poured the ritual wine:
     And my reward is death before my time!   65

     And yet, as men's hearts know, I have done no wrong,
     I have not sinned before God. Or if I have,
     I shall know the truth in death. But if the guilt
     Lies upon Creon who judged me, then, I pray,
     May his punishment equal my own.
CHORAGOS.   O passionate heart,   70
     Unyielding, tormented still by the same winds!
CREON. Her guards shall have good cause to regret their delaying.
ANTIGONÊ. Ah! That voice is like the voice of death!
CREON. I can give you no reason to think you are mistaken.
ANTIGONÊ. Thebes, and you my fathers' gods,   75
     And rulers of Thebes, you see me now, the last
     Unhappy daughter of a line of kings,
     Your kings, led away to death. You will remember

60 Persephonê queen of the underworld

What things I suffer, and at what men's hands,
Because I would not transgress the laws of heaven.   80
[*To the* GUARDS, *simply.*] Come: let us wait no longer.

[*Exit* ANTIGONÊ, *left, guarded.*]

Ode IV

CHORUS.   All Danaê's beauty was locked away   *Strophe 1*
    In a brazen cell where the sunlight could not come:
    A small room, still as any grave, enclosed her.
    Yet she was a princess too,
    And Zeus in a rain of gold poured love upon her.   5
    O child, child,
    No power in wealth or war
    Or tough sea-blackened ships
    Can prevail against untiring Destiny!

    And Dryas' son° also, that furious king,   *Antistrophe 1*   10
    Bore the god's prisoning anger for his pride:
    Sealed up by Dionysos in deaf stone,
    His madness died among echoes.
    So at the last he learned what dreadful power
    His tongue had mocked: 15
    For he had profaned the revels,
    And fired the wrath of the nine
    Implacable Sisters° that love the sound of the flute.

    And old men tell a half-remembered tale   *Strophe 2*
    Of horror where a dark ledge splits the sea   20
    And a double surf beats on the gray shores:
    How a king's new woman,° sick
    With hatred for the queen he had imprisoned,
    Ripped out his two sons' eyes with her bloody hands
    While grinning Arês° watched the shuttle plunge   25
    Four times: four blind wounds crying for revenge,

    Crying, tears and blood mingled.—Piteously born,   *Antistrophe 2*
    Those sons whose mother was of heavenly birth!
    Her father was the god of the North Wind
    And she was cradled by gales,   30
    She raced with young colts on the glittering hills
    And walked untrammeled in the open light:
    But in her marriage deathless Fate found means
    To build a tomb like yours for all her joy.

---

10 Dryas' son Lycurgus, King of Thrace   **18 Sisters** the Muses   **22 king's new woman** Eidothea, second wife of King Phineus, blinded her stepsons. Their mother, Cleopatra, had been imprisoned in a cave. Phineus was the son of a king, and Cleopatra, his first wife, was the daughter of Boreas, the North Wind, but this illustrious ancestry could not protect his sons from violence and darkness.   **25 Arês** god of war

Scene V

Enter blind TEIRESIAS, *led by a boy. The opening speeches of* TEIRESIAS
should be in singsong contrast to the realistic lines of CREON.
TEIRESIAS. This is the way the blind man comes, Princes, Princes,
    Lock-step, two heads lit by the eyes of one.
CREON. What new thing have you to tell us, old Teiresias?
TEIRESIAS. I have much to tell you: listen to the prophet, Creon.
CREON. I am not aware that I have ever failed to listen.   5
TEIRESIAS. Then you have done wisely, King, and ruled well.
CREON. I admit my debt to you. But what have you to say?
TEIRESIAS. This, Creon: you stand once more on the edge of fate.
CREON. What do you mean? Your words are a kind of dread.
TEIRESIAS. Listen, Creon: 10
    I was sitting in my chair of augury, at the place
    Where the birds gather about me. They were all a-chatter,
    As is their habit, when suddenly I heard
    A strange note in their jangling, a scream, a
    Whirring fury; I knew that they were fighting,   15
    Tearing each other, dying
    In a whirlwind of wings clashing. And I was afraid.
    I began the rites of burnt-offering at the altar,
    But Hephaistos° failed me: instead of bright flame,
    There was only the sputtering slime of the fat thigh-flesh   20
    Melting: the entrails dissolved in gray smoke,
    The bare bone burst from the welter. And no blaze!

    This was a sign from heaven. My boy described it,
    Seeing for me as I see for others.

    I tell you, Creon, you yourself have brought   25
    This new calamity upon us. Our hearths and altars
    Are stained with the corruption of dogs and carrion birds
    That glut themselves on the corpse of Oedipus' son.
    The gods are deaf when we pray to them, their fire
    Recoils from our offering, their birds of omen   30
    Have no cry of comfort, for they are gorged
    With the thick blood of the dead.
                O my son,
    These are no trifles! Think: all men make mistakes,
    But a good man yields when he knows his course is wrong,
    And repairs the evil. The only crime is pride.   35

    Give in to the dead man, then: do not fight with a corpse—
    What glory is it to kill a man who is dead?
    Think, I beg you:
    It is for your own good that I speak as I do.
    You should be able to yield for your own good.   40

19 Hephaistos god of fire

CREON. It seems that prophets have made me their especial province.
    All my life long
    I have been a kind of butt for the dull arrows
    Of doddering fortune-tellers!
                  No, Teiresias:
    If your birds—if the great eagles of God himself   45
    Should carry him stinking bit by bit to heaven,
    I would not yield. I am not afraid of pollution:
    No man can defile the gods.
                 Do what you will,
    Go into business, make money, speculate
    In India gold or that synthetic gold from Sardis,   50
    Get rich otherwise than by my consent to bury him.
    Teiresias, it is a sorry thing when a wise man
    Sells his wisdom, lets out his words for hire!

TEIRESIAS. Ah Creon! Is there no man left in the world—

CREON. To do what?—Come, let's have the aphorism!   55

TEIRESIAS. No man who knows that wisdom outweighs any wealth?

CREON. As surely as bribes are baser than any baseness.

TEIRESIAS. You are sick, Creon! You are deathly sick!

CREON. As you say: it is not my place to challenge a prophet.

TEIRESIAS. Yet you have said my prophecy is for sale.   60

CREON. The generation of prophets has always loved gold.

TEIRESIAS. The generation of kings has always loved brass.

CREON. You forget yourself! You are speaking to your King.

TEIRESIAS. I know it. You are a king because of me.

CREON. You have a certain skill; but you have sold out.   65

TEIRESIAS. King, you will drive me to words that—

CREON.   Say them, say them!
    Only remember: I will not pay you for them.

TEIRESIAS. No, you will find them too costly.

CREON.   No doubt. Speak:
    Whatever you say, you will not change my will.

TEIRESIAS. Then take this, and take it to heart!   70
    The time is not far off when you shall pay back
    Corpse for corpse, flesh of your own flesh.
    You have thrust the child of this world into living night,
    You have kept from the gods below the child that is theirs:
    The one in a grave before her death, the other,   75
    Dead, denied the grave. This is your crime:
    And the Furies and the dark gods of Hell
    Are swift with terrible punishment for you.

    Do you want to buy me now, Creon?

                       Not many days,
    And your house will be full of men and women weeping,   80
    And curses will be hurled at you from far
    Cities grieving for sons unburied, left to rot
    Before the walls of Thebes.

    These are my arrows, Creon: they are all for you.

[*To* BOY.] But come, child: lead me home.   85
Let him waste his fine anger upon younger men.
Maybe he will learn at last
To control a wiser tongue in a better head.   [*Exit* TEIRESIAS.]
CHORAGOS. The old man has gone, King, but his words
Remain to plague us. I am old, too,   90
But I cannot remember that he was ever false.
CREON. That is true. . . . It troubles me.
Oh it is hard to give in! but it is worse
To risk everything for stubborn pride.
CHORAGOS. Creon: take my advice.
CREON.   What shall I do?   95
CHORAGOS. Go quickly: free Antigonê from her vault
And build a tomb for the body of Polyneicês.
CREON. You would have me do this!
CHORAGOS.   Creon, yes!
And it must be done at once: God moves
Switftly to cancel the folly of stubborn men.   100
CREON. It is hard to deny the heart! But I
Will do it: I will not fight with destiny.
CHORAGOS. You must go yourself, you cannot leave it to others.
CREON. I will go.
          —Bring axes, servants:
Come with me to the tomb. I buried her, I   105
Will set her free.
              Oh quickly!
My mind misgives—
The laws of the gods are mighty, and a man must serve them
To the last day of his life!
                                                          [*Exit* CREON.]

Paean°

CHORAGOS. God of many names   *Strophe 1*
CHORUS.   O Iacchos
                    son
of Kadmeian Sémelê
                O born of the Thunder!
Guardian of the West
                Regent
of Eleusis' plain
                O Prince of maenad Thebes
and the Dragon Field by rippling Ismenós:°   5
CHORAGOS. God of many names   *Antistrophe 1*

Paean a hymn (here dedicated to Iacchos, also called Dionysos. His father was Zeus, his
mother was Sémelê, daughter of Kadmos. Iacchos's worshipers were the Maenads, whose
cry was "*Evohé evohé*") **5 Ismenós** a river east of Thebes (from a dragon's teeth, sown
near the river, there sprang men who became the ancestors of the Theban nobility)

CHORUS.   the flame of torches
        flares on our hills
                    the nymphs of Iacchos
        dance at the spring of Castalia:°
        from the vine-close mountain
                            come ah come in ivy:
        Evohé evohé! sings through the streets of Thebes   10
CHORAGOS. God of many names   *Strophe 2*
CHORUS.   Iacchos of Thebes
        heavenly Child
                of Sémelê bride of the Thunderer!
        The shadow of plague is upon us:
                            come
        with clement feet
                    oh come from Parnassos
        down the long slopes
                        across the lamenting water   15
CHORAGOS. Iô Fire! Chorister of the throbbing stars!   *Antistrophe 2*
        O purest among the voices of the night!
        Thou son of God, blaze for us!
CHORUS. Come with choric rapture of circling Maenads
        Who cry *Iô Iacche!*
                        God of many names!   20

Exodos

Enter MESSENGER *from left.*
MESSENGER. Men of the line of Kadmos,° you who live
        Near Amphion's citadel,°
                                I cannot say
        Of any condition of human life "This is fixed,
        This is clearly good, or bad." Fate raises up,
        And Fate casts down the happy and unhappy alike: 5
        No man can foretell his Fate.
                        Take the case of Creon:
        Creon was happy once, as I count happiness:
        Victorious in battle, sole governor of the land,
        Fortunate father of children nobly born.
        And now it has all gone from him! Who can say   10
        That a man is still alive when his life's joy fails?
        He is a walking dead man. Grant him rich,
        Let him live like a king in his great house:
        If his pleasure is gone, I would not give
        So much as the shadow of smoke for all he owns.   15
CHORAGOS. Your words hint at sorrow: what is your news for us?
MESSENGER. They are dead. The living are guilty of their death.

---

8 Paean Castalia a spring on Mount Parnassos   **1 Kadmos,** who sowed the dragon's
teeth, was founder of Thebes   **2 Amphion's citadel** Amphion played so sweetly on his
lyre that he charmed stones to form a wall around Thebes

CHORAGOS. Who is guilty? Who is dead? Speak!

MESSENGER.   Haimon.

    Haimon is dead; and the hand that killed him

    Is his own hand.

CHORAGOS. His father's? or his own?   20

MESSENGER. His own, driven mad by the murder his father had done.

CHORAGOS. Teiresias, Teiresias, how clearly you saw it all!

MESSENGER. This is my news: you must draw what conclusions you can

    from it.

CHORAGOS. But look: Eurydicê, our Queen:

    Has she overheard us?   25

    Enter EURYDICÊ *from the palace, center.*

EURYDICE. I have heard something, friends:

    As I was unlocking the gate of Pallas'° shrine,

    For I needed her help today, I heard a voice

    Telling of some new sorrow. And I fainted

    There at the temple with all my maidens about me.   30

    But speak again: whatever it is, I can bear it:

    Grief and I are no strangers.

MESSENGER.   Dearest Lady,

    I will tell you plainly all that I have seen.

    I shall not try to comfort you: what is the use,

    Since comfort could lie only in what is not true?   35

    The truth is always best.

                    I went with Creon

    To the outer plain where Polyneicês was lying,

    No friend to pity him, his body shredded by dogs.

    We made our prayers in the place to Hecatê

    And Pluto,° that they would be merciful. And we bathed   40

    The corpse with holy water, and we brought

    Fresh-broken branches to burn what was left of it,

    And upon the urn we heaped up a towering barrow

    Of the earth of his own land.

                  When we were done, we ran

    To the vault where Antigonê lay on her couch of stone.   45

    One of the servants had gone ahead,

    And while he was yet far off he heard a voice

    Grieving within the chamber, and he came back

    And told Creon. And as the King went closer,

    The air was full of wailing, the words lost,   50

    And he begged us to make all haste. "Am I a prophet?"

    He said, weeping, "And must I walk this road,

    The saddest of all that I have gone before?

    My son's voice calls me on. Oh quickly, quickly!

    Look through the crevice there, and tell me   55

    If it is Haimon, or some deception of the gods!"

27 Pallas Pallas Athene, goddess of wisdom   **40 Hecatê / And Pluto** Hecatê and Pluto
(also known as Hades) were deities of the underworld

We obeyed; and in the cavern's farthest corner
We saw her lying:
She had made a noose of her fine linen veil
And hanged herself. Haimon lay beside her,   60
His arms about her waist, lamenting her,
His love lost under ground, crying out
That his father had stolen her away from him.

When Creon saw him the tears rushed to his eyes
And he called to him: "What have you done, child?
Speak to me.   65
What are you thinking that makes your eyes so strange?
O my son, my son, I come to you on my knees!"
But Haimon spat in his face. He said not a word,
Staring—
        And suddenly drew his sword
And lunged. Creon shrank back, the blade missed; and the boy,   70
Desperate against himself, drove it half its length
Into his own side, and fell. And as he died
He gathered Antigonê close in his arms again,
Choking, his blood bright red on her white cheek.
And now he lies dead with the dead, and she is his   75
At last, his bride in the house of the dead.

                                            Exit EURYDICÊ *into the palace.*
CHORAGOS. She has left us without a word. What can this mean?
MESSENGER. It troubles me, too; yet she knows what is best,
    Her grief is too great for public lamentation,
    And doubtless she has gone to her chamber to weep   80
    For her dead son, leading her maidens in his dirge.

    Pause.
CHORAGOS. It may be so: but I fear this deep silence.
MESSENGER. I will see what she is doing. I will go in.

                                        Exit MESSENGER *into the palace.*

Enter CREON *with attendants, bearing* HAIMON's *body.*
CHORAGOS. But here is the king himself: on look at him,
    Bearing his own damnation in his arms.   85
CREON. Nothing you say can touch me any more.
    My own blind heart has brought me
    From darkness to final darkness. Here you see
    The father murdering, the murdered son—
    And all my civic wisdom!   90

    Haimon my son, so young, so young to die,
    I was the fool, not you; and you died for me.
CHORAGOS. That is the truth; but you were late in learning it.
CREON. This truth is hard to bear. Surely a god
    Has crushed me beneath the hugest weight of heaven,   95
    And driven me headlong a barbaric way
    To trample out the thing I held most dear.

    The pains that men will take to come to pain!

Enter MESSENGER *from the palace.*

MESSENGER. The burden you carry in your hands is heavy,
But it is not all: you will find more in your house. 100

CREON. What burden worse than this shall I find there?

MESSENGER. The Queen is dead.

CREON. O port of death, deaf world,
Is there no pity for me? And you, Angel of evil,
I was dead, and your words are death again. 105
Is it true, boy? Can it be true?
Is my wife dead? Has death bred death?

MESSENGER. You can see for yourself.

The doors are opened and the body of EURYDICÊ *is disclosed within.*

CREON. Oh pity!
All true, all true, and more than I can bear! 110
O my wife, my son!

MESSENGER. She stood before the altar, and her heart
Welcomed the knife her own hand guided,
And a great cry burst from her lips for Megareus° dead,
And for Haimon dead, her sons; and her last breath 115
Was a curse for their father, the murderer of her sons.
And she fell, and the dark flowed in through her closing eyes.

CREON. O God, I am sick with fear.
Are there no swords here? Has no one a blow for me?

MESSENGER. Her curse is upon you for the deaths of both. 120

CREON. It is right that it should be. I alone am guilty.
I know it, and I say it. Lead me in,
Quickly, friends.
I have neither life nor substance. Lead me in.

CHORAGOS. You are right, if there can be right in so much wrong. 125
The briefest way is best in a world of sorrow.

CREON. Let it come,
Let death come quickly, and be kind to me.
I would not ever see the sun again.

CHORAGOS. All that will come when it will; but we, meanwhile, 130
Have much to do. Leave the future to itself.

CREON. All my heart was in that prayer!

CHORAGOS. Then do not pray any more: the sky is deaf.

CREON. Lead me away. I have been rash and foolish.
I have killed my son and my wife. 135
I look for comfort; my comfort lies here dead.
Whatever my hands have touched has come to nothing.
Fate has brought all my pride to a thought of dust.

As CREON *is being led into the house, the* CHORAGOS *advances and speaks directly to the audience.*

CHORAGOS. There is no happiness where there is no wisdom;
No wisdom but in submission to the gods. 140

114 Megareus Megareus, brother of Haimon, had died in the assault on Thebes

Big words are always punished,
And proud men in old age learn to be wise.

[c. 441 B.C.]

Topics for Critical Thinking and Writing

1. Would you use masks for some (or all) of the characters? If so, would they be masks that fully cover the face, Greek style, or some sort of half-masks? (A full mask enlarges the face, and conceivably the mouthpiece can amplify the voice, but only an exceptionally large theater might require such help. Perhaps half-masks are enough if the aim is chiefly to distance the actors from the audience and from daily reality, and to force the actors to develop resources other than facial gestures. One director, arguing in favor of half-masks, has said that an actor who wears even a half-mask learns to act not with his eyes but with his neck.)

2. How would you costume the players? Would you dress them as the Greeks might have? Why? One argument sometimes used by those who hold the modern productions of Greek drama should use classical costumes is that Greek drama *ought* to be remote and ritualistic. Evaluate this view. What sort of modern dress might be effective?

3. If you were directing a college production of *Antigonê,* how large a chorus would you use? (Sophocles is said to have used a chorus of 15.) Would you have the chorus recite (or chant) the odes in unison, or would you assign lines to single speakers?

4. If you have read *Oedipus Rex,* compare and contrast the Creon of *Antigonê* with the Creon of *Oedipus.*

5. Although Sophocles called his play *Antigonê,* many critics say that Creon is the real tragic hero, pointing out that Antigone is absent from the last third of the play. Evaluate this view.

6. In some Greek tragedies, fate plays a great role in bringing about the downfall of the tragic hero. Though there are references to the curse on the House of Oedipus in *Antigonê,* do we feel that Antigone goes to her death as a result of the workings of fate? Do we feel that fate is responsible for Creon's fall? Are both Antigone and Creon the creators of their own tragedy?

7. Are the words *hamartia* (page 268) and *hubris* (page 267) relevant to Antigone? To Creon?

8. Why does Creon, contrary to the Chorus's advice, bury the body of Polyneices before he releases Antigone? Does his action show a zeal for piety as short-sighted as his earlier zeal for law? Is his action plausible, in view of the facts that Teiresias has dwelt on the wrong done to Polyneices and that Antigone has ritual food to sustain her? Or are we not to worry about Creon's motive?

9. A *foil* is a character who, by contrast, sets off or helps define another character. To what extent is Ismene a foil to Antigone? Is she entirely without courage?

10. What function does Eurydice serve? How deeply do we feel about her fate?

Remarks about Manuscript Form

BASIC MANUSCRIPT FORM

Much of what follows is nothing more than common sense.

- Use good quality $8\frac{1}{2}'' \times 11''$ paper. Make a photocopy, or, if you have written on a word processor print out a second copy, in case the instructor's copy goes astray.
- If you write on a word processor, **double-space,** and print on one side of the page only; set the printer for professional or best quality. If you submit handwritten copy, use lined paper and write on one side of the page only in black or dark blue ink, on every other line.
- Use **one-inch margins** on all sides.
- Within the top margin, put your last name and then (after hitting the space bar twice) the **page number** (in arabic numerals), so that the number is flush with the right-hand margin.
- On the first page, below the top margin and flush with the left-hand margin, put your **full name,** your **instructor's name,** the **course number** (including the section), and the **date,** one item per line, double-spaced.
- **Center the title** of your essay. Remember that the title is important—it gives the readers their first glimpse of your essay. **Create your own title**—one that reflects your topic or thesis. For example, a paper on Charlotte Perkins Gilman's "The Yellow Wallpaper" should not be called "The Yellow Wallpaper" but might be called

  Disguised Tyranny in Gilman's "The Yellow Wallpaper"

  or

  How to Drive a Woman Mad

  These titles do at least a little in the way of rousing a reader's interest.
- **Capitalize the title thus:** Begin the first word of the title with a capital letter, and capitalize each subsequent word except articles (*a, an, the*), conjunctions (*and, but, if, when,* etc.), and prepositions (*in, on, with,* etc.):

A Word on Behalf of Love

Notice that you do *not* enclose your title within quotation marks, and you do *not* underline it—though if it includes the title of a poem or a story, *that* is enclosed within quotation marks, or if it includes the title of a novel or play, *that* is underlined (to indicate italics), thus:

Gilman's "The Yellow Wallpaper" and Medical Practice

and

Gender Stereotypes in <u>Hamlet</u>

- **After writing your title, double-space,** indent five spaces, and begin your first sentence.
- Unless your instructor tells you otherwise, **use a staple** to hold the pages together. (Do not use a stiff binder; it will only add to the bulk of the instructor's stack of papers.)
- Extensive revisions should have been made in your drafts, but minor **last-minute revisions** may be made—neatly—on the finished copy. Proofreading may catch some typographical errors, and you may notice some small weaknesses. You can make corrections using the following proofreader's symbols.

CORRECTIONS IN THE FINAL COPY

Changes in wording may be made by crossing through words and rewriting them:

The influence of Poe and Hawthorne ~~have~~ *has* greatly diminished.

Additions should be made above the line, with a caret below the line at the appropriate place:

The influence of Poe and Hawthorne has *greatly* ^ diminished.

Transpositions of letters may be made thus:

The influence of Poe and Hawthorne has greatly diminished.

Deletions are indicated by a horizontal line through the word or words to be deleted. Delete a single letter by drawing a vertical or diagonal line through it; then indicate whether the letters on either side are to be closed up by drawing a connecting arc:

The influence of Poe and Hawthorne has greatly diminished.

Separation of words accidentally run together is indicated by a vertical line, closure by a curved line connecting the letters to be closed up:

The influence/of Poe and Hawthorne has g reatly diminished.

Paragraphing may be indicated by the symbol ¶ before the word that is to begin the new paragraph:

> The influence of Poe and Hawthorne has greatly diminished. ¶ The
>
> influence of Borges has very largely replaced that of earlier writers
>
> of fantasy.

QUOTATIONS AND QUOTATION MARKS

First, a word about the *point* of using quotations. Don't use quotations to pad the length of a paper. Rather, give quotations from the work you are discussing so that your readers will see the material you are discussing and (especially in a research paper) so that your readers will know what some of the chief interpretations are and what your responses to them are.

Note: The next few paragraphs do *not* discuss how to include citations of pages, a topic taken up in the next chapter under the heading "How to Document: Footnotes and Internal Parenthetical Citations."

The Golden Rule: If you quote, *comment on* the quotation. Let the reader know what you make of it and why you quote it.

Additional principles:

1. **Identify the speaker or writer of the quotation** so that the reader is not left with a sense of uncertainty. Usually, in accordance with the principle of letting readers know where they are going, this identification precedes the quoted material, but occasionally it may follow the quotation, especially if it will provide something of a pleasant surprise. For instance, in a discussion of Flannery O'Connor's stories, you might quote a disparaging comment on one of the stories and then reveal that O'Connor herself was the speaker.

2. If the quotation is part of your own sentence, **be sure to fit the quotation grammatically and logically into your sentence.**

> *Incorrect:* Holden Caulfield tells us very little about "what my lousy childhood was like."
>
> *Correct:* Holden Caulfield tells us very little about what his "lousy childhood was like."

3. **Indicate any omissions or additions.** The quotation must be exact. Any material that you add—even one or two words—must be enclosed within square brackets, thus:

> Hawthorne tells us that "owing doubtless to the depth of the gloom at
>
> that particular spot [in the forest], neither the travellers nor their
>
> steeds were visible."

If you wish to omit material from within a quotation, indicate the ellipsis by three spaced periods. If your sentence ends in an omission, add a closed-up period and then three spaced periods to indicate the omission. The following example is based on a quotation from the sentences immediately above this one:

> The instructions say, "If you . . . omit material from within a quotation,
>
> [you must] indicate the ellipsis. . . . If your sentence ends in an
>
> omission, add a closed-up period and then three spaced periods. . . ."

Notice that although material preceded "If you," periods are not needed to indicate the omission because "If you" began a sentence in the original. Customarily, initial and terminal omissions are indicated only when they are part of the sentence you are quoting. Even such omissions need not be indicated when the quoted material is obviously incomplete—when, for instance, it is a word or phrase.

4. **Distinguish between short and long quotations,** and treat each appropriately. **Short quotations** (usually defined as fewer than five lines of typed prose or three lines of poetry) are enclosed within quotation marks and run into the text (rather than being set off, without quotation marks), as in the following example:

> Hawthorne begins the story by telling us that "Young Goodman
>
> Brown came forth at sunset into the street at Salem village," thus at
>
> the outset connecting the village with daylight. A few paragraphs
>
> later, when Hawthorne tells us that the road Brown takes was
>
> "darkened by all of the gloomiest trees of the forest," he begins to
>
> associate the forest with darkness--and a very little later with evil.

If your short quotation is from a poem, be sure to follow the capitalization of the original, and use a slash mark (with a space before and after it) to indicate separate lines. Give the line numbers, if your source gives them, in parentheses, immediately after the closing quotation marks and before the closing punctuation, thus:

> In "Diving into the Wreck," Adrienne Rich's speaker says that she puts
>
> on "body-armor" (5). Obviously the journey is dangerous.

To set off a **long quotation** (more than four typed lines of prose or more than two lines of poetry), indent the entire quotation ten spaces from the left margin. Usually, a long quotation is introduced by a clause ending with a colon—for instance, "The following passage will make this point clear:" or "The closest we come to hearing an editorial voice is a long passage in the middle of the story:" or some such lead-in. After typing your lead-in, double-space, and then type the quotation, indented and double-spaced.

5. **Commas and periods go inside the quotation marks.**

> Chopin tells us in the first sentence that "Mrs. Mallard was afflicted
>
> with heart trouble," and in the last sentence the doctors say that Mrs.
>
> Mallard "died of heart disease."

Exception: If the quotation is immediately followed by material in parentheses or in square brackets, close the quotation, then give the parenthetic or bracketed material, and then—after closing the parenthesis or bracket—put the comma or period.

> Chopin tells us in the first sentence that "Mrs. Mallard was afflicted
>
> with heart trouble" (17), and in the last sentence the doctors say that
>
> Mrs. Mallard "died of heart disease" (18).

Semicolons, colons, and dashes go outside the closing quotation marks.
Question marks and exclamation points go inside if they are part of the quotation, outside if they are your own.

In the following passage from a student's essay, notice the difference in the position of the question marks. The first question mark is part of the quotation, so it is enclosed within the quotation marks. The second question mark, however, is the student's, so it comes after the closing quotation mark.

> The older man says to Goodman Brown, "Sayest thou so?" Doesn't a
>
> reader become uneasy when the man immediately adds, "We are but a
>
> little way in the forest yet"?

Quotation Marks or Underlining?

Use quotation marks around titles of short stories and other short works—that is, titles of chapters in books, essays, and poems that might not be published by themselves. Underline (to indicate italics) titles of books, periodicals, collections of essays, plays, and long poems such as *The Rime of the Ancient Mariner.* Word processing software will let you use italic type (instead of underlining) if you wish.

A Note on the Possessive

It is awkward to use the possessive case for titles of literary works and secondary sources. Rather than "*The Great Gatsby*'s final chapter," write instead "the final chapter of *The Great Gatsby.*" Not "*The Oxford Companion to American Literature*'s entry on Emerson," but, instead, "the entry on Emerson in *The Oxford Companion to American Literature.*"

Writing a Research Paper

WHAT RESEARCH IS NOT, AND WHAT RESEARCH IS

Because a research paper requires its writer to collect and interpret evidence—usually including the opinions of earlier investigators—one sometimes hears that a research paper, unlike a critical essay, is not the expression of personal opinion. But such a view is unjust both to criticism and to research. A critical essay is not a mere expression of personal opinions; if it is any good, it offers evidence that supports the opinions and thus persuades the reader of their objective rightness. And a research paper is in the final analysis largely personal, because the author continuously uses his or her own judgment to evaluate the evidence, deciding what is relevant and convincing. A research paper is not the mere presentation of what a dozen scholars have already said about a topic; it is a thoughtful evaluation of the available evidence, and so it is, finally, an expression of what the author thinks the evidence adds up to.

PRIMARY AND SECONDARY MATERIALS

The materials of literary research can be conveniently divided into two sorts, primary and secondary. The *primary materials,* or sources, are the real subject of study; the *secondary materials* are critical and historical accounts already written about these primary materials. For example, Langston Hughes wrote poems, stories, plays, and essays. For a student of Hughes, these works are the primary materials. (We include several of his works in this book.) If you want to study his ways of representing African-American speech or his representations of whites, or his collaboration with Zora Neale Hurston, you will read the primary material—his own writings (and Hurston's, in the case of the collaborative work). But in an effort to reach a thoughtful understanding of some aspect of his work, you will also want to look at later biographical and critical studies of his works and perhaps also at scholarly writing on such topics as Black English. You may even find yourself looking at essays on Black English that do not specifically mention Hughes but that nevertheless may prove helpful.

Similarly, if you are writing about Charlotte Perkins Gilman (we include one of her stories), the primary material includes not only other stories but also her social and political writing. If you are writing about her views of medical treatment of women, you will want to look not only at the story we reprint ("The Yellow Wallpaper") but also at her autobiography. Further, you will also want to look at some secondary material, such as recent scholarly books and articles on medical treatment of women in the late nineteenth and early twentieth centuries.

Locating Material: First Steps*

The easiest way to locate articles and books on literature written in a modern language—that is, on a topic other than literature of the ancient world—is to consult the

> *MLA International Bibliography of Books and Articles in the Modern Languages and Literatures* (1922-),

which until 1969 was published as part of *PMLA* (*Publications of the Modern Language Association*) and since 1969 has been published separately. It is also available on CD-ROM through WILSONDISC, and in fact the disc is preferable since it is updated quarterly, whereas the print version is more than a year behind the times. Many college and university libraries also now offer the *MLA International Bibliography* as part of their package of online resources for research.

MLA International Bibliography lists scholarly studies—books as well as articles in academic journals—published in a given year. Because of the great number of items listed, the print version of the bibliography runs to more than one volume, but material on writing in English (including, for instance, South African authors who write in English) is in one volume. To see what has been published on Langston Hughes in a given year, then, in this volume you turn to the section on American literature (as opposed to English, Canadian, Irish, and so forth), and then to the subsection labeled 1900-99, to see if anything that sounds relevant is listed.

Because your time is limited, you probably cannot read everything published on your topic. At least for the moment, therefore, you will use only the last five or ten years of this bibliography. Presumably, any important earlier material will have been incorporated into some of the recent studies listed, and if, when you come to read these recent studies, you find references to an article of, say, 1975 that sounds essential, of course you will read that article too.

Although *MLA International Bibliography* includes works on American literature, if you are doing research on an aspect of American literature you may want to begin with

> *American Literary Scholarship* (1965-),

an annual publication noted for its broad coverage of articles and books on major and minor American writers, and especially valuable for its frank comments on the material that it lists.

On some recent topics—for instance, the arguments for and against dropping *Huckleberry Finn* from high school curricula—there may be few or no books, and there may not even be material in the scholarly journals indexed in

---

*This appendix is devoted to traditional resources. Consult the next two appendices for a detailed introduction to electronic resources.

MLA International Bibliography. Popular magazines, however, such as *Atlantic, Ebony,* and *Newsweek*—unlisted in *MLA*—may include some useful material. These magazines, and about 200 others, are indexed in

Readers' Guide to Periodical Literature (1900–).

If you want to write a research paper on the controversy over *Huckleberry Finn,* or on the popular reception given to Kenneth Branagh's films of Shakespeare's *Henry V, Much Ado about Nothing,* and *Hamlet,* you can locate material (for instance, reviews of Branagh's films) through *Readers' Guide.* For that matter, you can also locate reviews of older films, let's say Olivier's films of Shakespeare's plays, by consulting the volumes for the years in which the films were released.

On many campuses *Readers' Guide* has been supplanted by

InfoTrac (1985–),

on CD-ROM. The disc is preinstalled in a microcomputer that can be accessed from a computer terminal. This index to authors and subjects in popular and scholarly magazines and in newspapers provides access to several database indexes, including:

- The *General Periodicals Index,* available in the Academic Library Edition (about 1,100 general and scholarly periodicals) and in the Public Library Edition (about 1,100 popular magazines).
- The *Academic Index* (400 general-interest publications, all of which are also available in the Academic Library Edition of the *General Periodicals Index*).
- The *Magazine Index Plus* (the four most recent years of the *New York Times,* the two most recent months of the *Wall Street Journal,* and 400 popular magazines, all of which are included in the Public Library Edition of the *General Periodicals Index*).
- The *National Newspaper Index* (the four most recent years of the *New York Times,* the *Christian Science Monitor,* the *Washington Post,* and the *Los Angeles Times*).

Once again, many college and university libraries are now making available online versions of these and similar resources for research. Some students (and faculty) prefer to use the books on the shelf, but the electronic editions do have advantages. Often, it is easier to perform "searches" using them; and in many cases they are updated well before the next print editions are published.

Other Bibliographic Aids

There are hundreds of guides to publications and to reference works. *The Oxford Companion to African American Literature* (1997), edited by William L. Andrews, Frances Smith Foster, and Trudier Harris, provides detailed entries on authors, literary works, and many literary, historical, and cultural topics and terms, as well as suggestions for further reading. *Reader's Guide to Literature in English* (1996), edited by Mark Hawkins-Dady, is a massive work (nearly 1,000 pages) that gives thorough summaries of recent critical and scholarly writing on English and American authors.

How do you find such books? Two invaluable guides to reference works (that is, to bibliographies and to such helpful compilations as handbooks of mythology, place names, and critical terms) are

> James L. Harner, *Literary Research Guide: A Guide to Reference Sources for the Study of Literatures in English and Related Topics,* 3rd ed. (1998)

and

> Michael J. Marcuse, *A Reference Guide for English Studies* (1990).

And there are guides to these guides: reference librarians. If you don't know where to turn to find something, turn to the librarian.

TAKING NOTES

Let's assume now that you have checked some bibliographies and that you have a fair number of references you must read to have a substantial knowledge of the evidence and the common interpretations of the evidence. Most researchers find it convenient, when examining bibliographies and the library catalog, to write down each reference on a $3'' \times 5''$ index card—one title per card. On the card put the author's full name (last name first), the exact title of the book or of the article, and the name of the journal (with dates and pages). Titles of books and periodicals (publications issued periodically—for example, monthly or four times a year) are underlined; titles of articles and of essays in books are put within quotation marks. It's also a good idea to put the library catalog number on the card to save time if you need to get the item for a second look.

Next, start reading or scanning the materials whose titles you have collected. Some of these items will prove irrelevant or silly; others will prove valuable in themselves and also in the leads they give you to further references, which you should duly record on $3'' \times 5''$ cards. Notes—aside from these bibliographic notes—are best taken on $4'' \times 6''$ cards. Smaller cards do not provide enough space for summaries of useful materials, but $4'' \times 6''$ cards—rather than larger cards—will serve to remind you that you should not take notes on everything. Be selective in taking notes.

Two Mechanical Aids: The Photocopier and the Word Processor

Use the photocopier to make copies of material from the library (including material that does not circulate) that you know that you need, or that you later might want to refer to. But remember that sometimes it is even more efficient

- to read the material in the library,
- to select carefully what pertains to the purpose of your research, and
- to take your notes on it.

The word processor or computer is useful not only in the final stage, to produce a neat copy, but also in the early stages of research, when you are getting ideas and taking notes. For a Checklist of tips and suggestions, see pages 26–27.

A Guide to Note-Taking

Some students use note cards for taking notes during the process of research. Others write on separate sheets of a notebook, or on $8\frac{1}{2}'' \times 11''$ yellow sheets. Still others take their notes using a computer or word processor, and then organize and rearrange this body of material by copying and pasting, moving the notes into a co-herent order. (We advise you not to delete material that, when you reread your notes, strikes you as irrelevant. It *probably* is irrelevant, but, on the other hand, it may turn out to be valuable after all. Just put unwanted material into a file called "rejects," or some such thing, until you have completed the paper.)

Whichever method you prefer, keep in mind the following:

1. **For everything you consult or read in detail, always specify the source,** so that you know exactly from where you have taken a key point or a quotation.

2. **Write summaries (abridgments), not paraphrases (restatements).**

3. **Quote sparingly.** Remember that this is *your* paper, it will present your thesis, not the thesis and arguments and analyses of someone else. Quote directly only those passages that are particularly effective, or crucial, or memorable. In your finished paper these quotations will provide authority and emphasis.

4. **Quote accurately.** After copying a quotation, check your card against the original, correct any misquotation, and then put a checkmark after your quotation to indicate that it is accurate. Verify the page number also, and then put a check-mark on your card after the page number. If a quotation runs from the bottom of, say, page 306 to the top of 307, on your card put a distinguishing mark (for in-stance two parallel vertical lines after the last word of the first page), so that if you later use only part of the quotation, you will know the page on which it appeared.

Use ellipses (three spaced periods) to indicate the omission of any words within a sentence. If the omitted words are at the end of the quoted sentence, put a period where you end the sentence, and then add three spaced periods to indicate the omission:

If the . . . words were at the end of the quoted sentence, put a period

where you end. . . .

Use square brackets to indicate your additions to the quotation. Here is an example:

Here is an [uninteresting] example.

5. **Never copy a passage by changing an occasional word,** under the impression that you are thereby putting it into your own words. Notes of this sort may find their way into your paper, your reader will sense a style other than yours, and suspicions of plagiarism may follow. (For a detailed discussion of pla-giarism, see pages 1319-20.)

6. **Comment on your notes** as you do your work, and as you reflect alter on what you have jotted down from the sources. Use a special mark—we rec-ommend that you use double parentheses ((. . .)) or a different color pen to write, for example, "Jones seriously misreads the passage," or "Smith makes a good point but fails to see its implications." As you work, consider it your oblig-ation to *think* about the material, evaluating it and using it as a stimulus to fur-ther thought.

7. **In the upper corner of each note card write a brief key**—for example, "Swordplay in *Hamlet*"—so that later you can tell at a glance what is on the card.

DRAFTING THE PAPER

The difficult job of writing up your findings remains, but if you have taken good notes and have put useful headings on each card, you are well on your way. Read through the cards and sort them into packets of related material. Discard all notes, however interesting, that you now see are irrelevant to your paper. Go through the cards again and again. sorting and re-sorting, putting together what belongs together. Probably you will find that you have to do a little additional research—somehow you aren't quite clear about this or that—but after you have done this additional research, you should be able to arrange the packets into a reasonable and consistent sequence. You now have a kind of first draft, or at least a tentative organization for your paper. Two further pieces of advice:

1. Beware of the compulsion to include every note card in your essay: that is, beware of telling the reader, "*A* says . . . ; *B* says . . . ; *C* says. . . ."
2. You must have a point, a thesis.

The final version of the paper should be a finished piece of work, without the inconsistencies, detours, and occasional dead ends of an early draft. Your readers should feel that they are moving toward a conclusion (by means of your thoughtful evaluation of the evidence) rather than merely reading an anthology of commentary on the topic. And so we should get some such structure as: "There are three common views on . . . The first two are represented by *A* and *B;* the third, and by far the most reasonable, is *C*'s view that . . . *A* argues . . . but . . . The second view, *B*'s, is based on . . . but . . . Although the third view, *C*'s, is not conclusive, still . . . Moreover, *C*'s point can be strengthened when we consider a piece of evidence that she does not make use of. . . ."

Be sure, when you quote, to *write a lead-in,* such as "*X* concisely states the common view" or "*Z*, without offering any proof, asserts that . . ." Let the reader know where you are going, or, to put it a little differently, let the reader know how the quotation fits into your argument.

Quotations and summaries, in short, are accompanied by judicious analyses of your own so that by the end of the paper your readers not only have read a neatly typed paper (see pages 1307–08) and have gained an idea of what previous writers have said, but also are persuaded that under your guidance they have seen the evidence, heard the arguments justly summarized, and reached a sound conclusion.

A bibliography or list of works consulted (see pages 1320–29) is usually appended to a research paper so that readers may easily look further into the primary and secondary material if they wish; but if you have done your job well, readers will be content to leave the subject where you left it, grateful that you have set matters straight.

A SENSE OF PROPORTION

Remember that your paper should highlight *primary* sources. It should be, above all, *your* paper, a paper in which you present a thesis that you have developed about the literary work or works that you have chosen to examine. By using secondary sources, you can enrich your analysis, as you place yourself in the midst of the scholarly community interested in this author or authors. But keep a proper proportion between primary sources—which should receive the greater emphasis—and secondary sources—which should be used selectively.

To help make this come about, when you review your draft, mark with a red pen the quotations from and references to primary sources, and then with a blue pen do the same marking for secondary sources. If, when you scan the pages of your paper-in-progress, you see a lot more blue than red, you should change the emphasis, the proportion, to what it should be. Guard against the tendency to rely more than is proper on the secondary sources you have compiled. The point of view that really counts is your own.

DOCUMENTATION

What to Document: Avoiding Plagiarism

Honesty requires that you acknowledge your indebtedness for material. not only when you quote directly from a work. but also when you appropriate an idea that is not common knowledge. Not to acknowledge such borrowing is plagiarism. If in doubt whether to give credit, give credit.

You ought, however, to develop a sense of what is considered **common knowledge.** Definitions in a dictionary can be considered common knowledge, so there is no need to say, "According to Webster, a novel is. . . ." (This is weak in three ways: It's unnecessary, it's uninteresting, and it's unclear, since "Webster" appears in the titles of several dictionaries, some good and some bad.) Similarly, the date of first publication of *The Scarlet Letter* (1850) can be considered common knowledge. Few can give it when asked, but it can be found out from innumerable sources, and no one need get the credit for providing you with the date. The idea that Hamlet delays is also a matter of common knowledge. But if you are impressed by So-and-so's argument that Claudius has been much maligned, you should give credit to So-and-so.

Suppose that in the course of your research for a paper on Langston Hughes you happen to come across Arnold Rampersad's statement, in an essay in *Voices and Visions* (ed. Helen Vendler), that

> Books alone could not save Hughes from loneliness, let alone give him the strength to be a writer. At least one other factor was essential in priming him for creative obsession. In the place in his heart, or psychology, vacated by his parents entered the black masses. (355)

This is an interesting idea, and in the last sentence the shift from heart to psychology is perhaps especially interesting. You certainly can*not* say—with the implication that the idea and the words are your own—something like

> Hughes let enter into his heart, or his psychology--a place vacated by
>
> his parents--the black masses.

The writer is simply lifting Rampersad's ideas and making only tiny changes in the wording. But even a larger change in the wording is unacceptable unless Rampersad is given credit. Here is a restatement that is an example of plagiarism even though the words differ from Rampersad's:

> Hughes took into himself ordinary black people, thus filling the gap
>
> created by his mother and father.

In this version. the writer presents Rampersad's idea as if it were the writer's own—and presents it less effectively than Rampersad.

What to do? Give Rampersad credit, perhaps along these lines:

> As Arnold Rampersad has said, "in the place in his heart, or his
>
> psychology" where his parents had once been, Hughes now substituted
>
> ordinary black people (355).

You can use another writer's ideas, and even some of the very words, but you must give credit, and you must use quotation marks when you quote.

You can

- give credit and quote directly, or
- give credit and summarize the writer's point, or
- give credit and summarize the point but include—within quotation marks—some phrase you think is especially interesting.

How to Document: Footnotes, Internal Parenthetical Citatations, and a List of Works Cited (MLA Format)

Documentation tells your reader exactly what your sources are. Until recently, the standard form was the footnote, which, for example, told the reader that the source of such and such a quotation was a book by So-and-so. But in 1984 the Modern Language Association. which had established the footnote form used in hundreds of journals. university presses, and classrooms, substituted a new form. It is this new form—parenthetical citation *within* the text (rather than at the foot of the page or the end of the essay)—that we will discuss at length. Keep in mind, though, that footnotes still have their uses.

Footnotes. If you are using only one source, your instructor may advise you to give the source in a footnote. (Check with your instructors to find out their preferred forms of documentation.)

Let's say that your only source is this textbook. Let's say, too, that all of your quotations will be from a single story—Kate Chopin's "The Story of an Hour"—printed in this book on pages 12–13. If you use a word processor, the software program can probably format the note for you. If, however, you are using a typewriter, type the digit 1 (elevated, and *without* a period after it) after your first reference to (or quotation from) the story, and then put a footnote at the bottom of the page, explaining where the story can be found. After your last line of text on the page, triple-space, indent five spaces from the left-hand margin, and write the arabic number 1. Do *not* put a period after it. Then type a statement (double-spaced) to the effect that all references are to this book.

Notice that although the footnote begins by being indented five spaces, if the note runs to more than one line the subsequent lines are given flush left.

[1]Chopin's story appears in Sylvan Barnet et al., eds. Literature

for Composition, 5th ed. (New York: Longman, 2000), 12–13.

(If a book has more than three authors or editors, give the name of only the first author or editor, and follow it with a comma and *et al.,* the Latin abbreviation for "and others.")

Even if you are writing a comparison of, say, two stories in this book, you can use a note of this sort. It might run thus:

[1]All page references given parenthetically within the essay refer

to stories in Sylvan Barnet et al., eds. <u>Literature for Composition</u>, 5th

ed. (New York: Longman, 2000).

If you use such a note, you do not need to use a footnote after each quotation that follows. You can give the citations right in the body of the paper, by putting the page references in parentheses after the quotations.

Internal Parenthetical Citations. On pages 1309–11 we distinguish between embedded quotations (which are short, are run right into your own sentence, and are enclosed within quotation marks) and quotations that are set off on the page and are not enclosed within quotation marks (for example, three or more lines of poetry, five or more lines of typed prose).

For an embedded quotation, put the page reference in parentheses immediately after the closing quotation mark. *without* any intervening punctuation. Then, after the parenthesis that follows the number, put the necessary punctuation (for instance, a comma or a period):

Woolf says that in the struggling moth there was "something

marvelous as well as pathetic" (180). She goes on to explain . . .

The period comes *after* the parenthetical citation. In the next example *no* punctuation comes after the first citation—because none is needed—and a comma comes *after* (not before or within) the second citation, because a comma is needed in the sentence:

This is ironic because almost at the start of the story, in the second

paragraph, Richards with the best of motives "hastened" (12) to bring

his sad message; if he had at the start been "too late" (13), Mallard

would have arrived at home first.

For a quotation that is not embedded within the text but is set off (by being indented ten spaces), put the parenthetical citation on the last line of the quotation. one space *after* the period that ends the quoted sentence.
Four additional points:

1. The abbreviations *p.*, *pg.*, and *pp.* are *not* used in citing pages.
2. If a story is very short—perhaps running for only a page or two—your instructor may tell you there is no need to keep citing the page reference for each quotation. Simply mention in the footnote that the story appears on, say, pages 35–36.
3. If you are referring to a poem, your instructor may tell you to use parenthetical citations of line numbers rather than of page numbers. But, again, your footnote will tell the reader that the poem can be found in this book, and on what page.
4. If you are referring to a play with numbered lines, your instructor may prefer that in your parenthetical citations you give act, scene, and line,

rather than page numbers. Use arabic (not roman) numerals, separating the act from the scene, and the scene from the line, by periods. Here, then, is how a reference to Act 3, Scene 2, line 118 would be given:

(3.2.118)

Parenthetical Citations and List of Works Cited.
Footnotes have fallen into disfavor. Parenthetical citations are now usually clarified not by means of a footnote but by means of a list, headed Works Cited, given at the end of the essay. In this list you give alphabetically (last name first) the authors and titles that you have quoted or referred to in the essay.

Briefly, the idea is that the reader of your paper encounters an author's name and a parenthetical citation of pages. By checking the author's name in Works Cited, the reader can find the passage in the book. Suppose you are writing about Kate Chopin's "The Story of an Hour." Let's assume that you have already mentioned the author and the title of the story—that is, you have let the reader know the subject of the essay—and now you introduce a quotation from the story in a sentence such as this. (Notice the parenthetical citation of page numbers immediately after the quotation.)

True, Mrs. Mallard at first expresses grief when she hears the news,

but soon (unknown to her friends) she finds joy in it. So, Richards's

"sad message" (12), though sad in Richard's eyes, is in fact a happy

message.

Turning to Works Cited, the reader, knowing the quoted words are by Chopin, looks for Chopin and finds the following:

Chopin, Kate. "The Story of an Hour." Literature for Composition, 5th

ed. Ed. Sylvan Barnet et al. New York: Longman, 2000.

Thus the essayist is informing the reader that the quoted words ("sad message") are to be found on page 12 of this anthology.

If you have not mentioned Chopin's name in some sort of lead-in, you will have to give her name within the parentheses so that the reader will know the author of the quoted words:

What are we to make out of a story that ends by telling us that the

leading character has died "of joy that kills" (Chopin 13)?

The closing quotation marks come immediately after the last word of the quotation; the citation and the final punctuation—in this case, the essayist's question mark—come *after* the closing quotation marks.

If you are comparing Chopin's story with Gilman's "The Yellow Wallpaper," in Works Cited you will give a similar entry for Gilman—her name, the title of the story, the book in which it is reprinted, and the page numbers that the story occupies.

If you are referring to several works reprinted within one volume, instead of listing each item fully, it is acceptable in Works Cited to list each item simply by giving the author's name, the title of the work, then a period, a space, and the name of the anthologist, followed by the page numbers that the selection spans. Thus a reference to Chopin's "The Story of an Hour" would be followed only by: Barnet 12-13. This form requires that the anthology. itself be cited under the name of the first-listed editor, thus:

Barnet, Sylvan, et al., eds. Literature for Composition, 5th ed.

New York: Longman, 2000.

If you are writing a research paper, you will use many sources. Within the essay itself you will mention an author's name, quote or summarize from this author, and follow the quotation or summary with a parenthetical citation of the pages. In Works Cited you will give the full title, place of publication, and other bibliographic material.

Here are a few examples, all referring to an article by Joan Templeton. "The *Doll House* Backlash: Criticism, Feminism, and Ibsen." The article appeared in *PMLA* 104 (1989): 28-40, but this information is given only in Works Cited, not within the text of the student's essay.

If in the text of your essay you mention the author's name, the citation following a quotation (or a summary of a passage) is merely a page number in parentheses, followed by a period, thus:

In 1989 Joan Templeton argued that many critics, unhappy with

recognizing Ibsen as a feminist, sought "to render Nora

inconsequential" (29).

Or:

In 1989 Joan Templeton noted that many critics, unhappy with

recognizing Ibsen as a feminist, have sought to make Nora trivial (29).

If you don't mention the name of the author in a lead-in, you will have to give the name within the parenthetical citation:

Many critics, attempting to argue that Ibsen was not a feminist, have

tried to make Nora trivial (Templeton 29).

Notice in all of these examples that the final period comes after the parenthetical citation. *Exception:* If the quotation is longer than four lines and, therefore, is set off by being indented ten spaces from the left margin, end the quotation with the appropriate punctuation (period, question mark, or exclamation mark), hit the space bar twice, and type (in parentheses) the page number. In this case, do not put a period after the citation.

Another point: If your list of Works Cited includes more than one work by an author, in your essay when you quote or refer to one or the other you'll have to identify *which* work you are drawing on. You can provide the title in a lead-in, thus:

In "The <u>Doll House</u> Backlash: Criticism, Feminism, and Ibsen,"

Templeton says, "Nora's detractors have often been, from the first, her

husband's defenders" (30).

Or you can provide the information in the parenthetic citation, giving a shortened version of the title—usually the first word, unless it is *A, An,* or *The,* in which case the second word usually will do, though certain titles may require still another word or two, as in this example:

According to Templeton, "Nora's detractors have often been, from the

first, her husband's defenders" ("<u>Doll House</u> Backlash" 30).

Forms of Citation in Works Cited.   In looking over the following samples of entries in Works Cited, remember:

1. The list of Works Cited appears at the end of the paper. It begins on a new page, and the page continues the numbering of the text.
2. The list of Works Cited is arranged alphabetically by author (last name first).
3. If a work is anonymous, list it under the first word of the title unless the first word is *A, An,* or *The,* in which case list it under the second word.
4. If a work is by two authors, although the book is listed alphabetically under the first author's last name, the second author's name is given in the normal order, first name first.
5. If you list two or more works by the same author, the author's name is not repeated but is represented by three hyphens followed by a period and a space.
6. Each item begins flush left, but if an entry is longer than one line, subsequent lines in the entry are indented five spaces.

For details about almost every imaginable kind of citation, consult Joseph Gibaldi, *MLA Handbook for Writers of Research Papers,* 5th ed. (New York: Modern Language Association, 1999). We give here, however, information concerning the most common kinds of citations.

For citations to electronic sources, see pages 1352–53.

Here are samples of the kinds of citations you are most likely to include in your list of Works Cited.

A book by one author:

Douglas, Ann. <u>The Feminization of American Culture.</u>

New York: Knopf, 1977.

Notice that the author's last name is given first, but otherwise the name is given as on the title page. Do not substitute initials for names written out on the title page, but you may shorten the publisher's name—for example, from Little, Brown and Company to Little.

Take the title from the title page, not from the cover or the spine, but disregard unusual typography—for instance, the use of only capital letters or the use of & for *and.* Underline the title and subtitle with one continuous underline, but do not underline the period. The place of publication is indicated by the name of the city. If the city is not well known or if several cities have the same name (for instance, Cambridge, Massachusetts, and Cambridge, England) the name of the state is added. If the title page lists several cities, give only the first.

A book by more than one author:

Gilbert, Sandra, and Susan Gubar. <u>The Madwoman in the Attic: The</u>

<u>Woman Writer and the Nineteenth-Century Literary</u>

<u>Imagination</u>. New Haven: Yale UP, 1979.

Notice that the book is listed under the last name of the first author (Gilbert) and that the second author's name is then given with first name (Susan) first. *If the book has more than three authors,* give the name of the first author only (last name first) and follow it with *et al.* (Latin for "and others.")

A book in several volumes:

McQuade, Donald, et al., eds. <u>The Harper American Literature</u>. 2nd ed.

2 vols. New York: HarperCollins, 1994.

Pope, Alexander. <u>The Correspondence of Alexander Pope</u>. 5 vols. Ed.

George Sherburn. Oxford: Clarendon, 1955.

The total number of volumes is given after the title, regardless of the number that you have used.

If you have used more than one volume, within your essay you will parenthetically indicate a reference to, for instance, page 30 of volume 3 thus: (3: 30). If you have used only one volume of a multivolume work—let's say you used only volume 2 of McQuade's anthology—in your entry in Works Cited write, after the period following the date, Vol. 2. In your parenthetical citation within the essay you will therefore cite only the page reference (without the volume number), since the reader will (on consulting Works Cited) understand that in this example the reference is in volume 2.

If, instead of using the volumes as a whole, you used only an independent work within one volume—say, an essay in volume 2—in Works Cited omit the abbreviation *Vol.* Instead, give an arabic 2 (indicating volume 2) followed by a colon, a space, and the page numbers that encompass the selection you used:

McPherson, James Alan. "Why I Like Country Music." <u>The Harper</u>

<u>American Literature</u>. 2nd ed. 2 vols. New York: HarperCollins,

1994. 2: 2304-15.

Notice that this entry for McPherson specifies not only that the book consists of two volumes, but also that only one selection ("Why I Like Country Music," occupying pages 2304-15 in volume 2) was used. If you use this sort of citation in

Works Cited, in the body of your essay a documentary reference to this work will be only to the page; the volume number will *not* be added.

A book with a separate title in a set of volumes:

Churchill, Winston. The Age of Revolution. Vol. 3 of A History of the

English-Speaking Peoples. New York: Dodd, 1957.

Jonson, Ben. The Complete Masques. Ed. Stephen Orgel. Vol. 4 of The

Yale Ben Jonson. New Haven: Yale UP, 1969.

A revised edition of a book:

Chaucer, Geoffrey. The Riverside Chaucer. Ed. Larry Benson. 3rd ed.

Boston: Houghton, 1987.

Ellmann, Richard. James Joyce. Rev. ed. New York: Oxford UP, 1982.

A reprint, such as a paperback version of an older hardcover book:

Rourke, Constance. American Humor. 1931. Garden City, New York:

Doubleday, 1953.

Notice that the entry cites the original date (1931) but indicates that the writer is using the Doubleday reprint of 1953.

An edited book other than an anthology:

Keats, John. The Letters of John Keats. Ed. Hyder Edward Rollins. 2

vols. Cambridge, Mass.: Harvard UP, 1958.

An anthology. You can list an anthology either under the editor's name or under the title.

A work in a volume of works by one author:

Sontag, Susan. "The Aesthetics of Silence." In Styles of Radical Will.

New York: Farrar, 1969, 3-34.

This entry indicates that Sontag's essay, called "The Aesthetics of Silence," appears in a book of hers entitled *Styles of Radical Will.* Notice that the page numbers of the short work are cited (not page numbers that you may happen to refer to, but the page numbers of the entire piece).

A work in an anthology, that is, in a collection of works by several authors.
Begin with the author and the title of the work you are citing, not with the name of the anthologist or the title of the anthology. The entry ends with the pages occupied by the selection you are citing:

Ng, Fae Myenne. "A Red Sweater." Charlie Chan Is Dead: An

Anthology of Contemporary Asian American Fiction. Ed. Jessica

Hagedorn. New York: Penguin, 1993. 358-68.

Normally, you will give the title of the work you are citing (probably an essay, short story, or poem) in quotation marks. If you are referring to a book-length work (for instance, a novel or a full-length play), underline it to indicate italics. If the work is translated, after the period that follows the title, write *Trans.* and give the name of the translator, followed by a period and the name of the anthology.

If the collection is a multivolume work and you are using only one volume, in Works Cited you will specify the volume, as in the example (p. 1325) of McPherson's essay. Because the list of Works Cited specifies the volume, your parenthetical documentary reference within your essay will specify (as mentioned earlier) only the page numbers, not the volume. Thus, although McPherson's essay appears on pages 2304-15 in the second volume of a two-volume work, a parenthetical citation will refer only to the page numbers because the citation in Works Cited specifies the volume.

Remember that the pages specified in the entry in your list of Works Cited are to the *entire selection*, not simply to pages you may happen to refer to within your paper.

If you are referring to a *reprint of a scholarly article*, give details of the original publication, as in the following example:

Mack, Maynard. "The World of Hamlet." Yale Review 41 (1952):

502–23. Rpt. in Hamlet. By William Shakespeare. Ed. Sylvan

Barnet. New York: Penguin Putnam, 1998. 265-87.

Two or more works in an anthology. If you are referring to more than one work in an anthology in order to avoid repeating all the information about the anthology in each entry in Works Cited, under each author's name (in the appropriate alphabetical place) give the author and title of the work, then a period, a space, and the name of the anthologist, followed by the page numbers that the selection spans. Thus, a reference to Shakespeare's *Hamlet* would be followed only by

Barnet 910-1019

rather than by a full citation of Barnet's anthology. This form requires that the anthology itself also be listed, under Barnet.

Two or more works by the same author. Notice that the works are given in alphabetical order (*Fables* precedes *Fools*) and that the author's name is not repeated but is represented by three hyphens followed by a period and a space. If the author is the translator or editor of a volume, the three hyphens are followed not by a period but by a comma, then a space, then the appropriate abbreviation (*Trans.* or *Ed.*), then the title:

Frye, Northrop. Fables of Identity: Studies in Poetic Mythology. New

York: Harcourt, 1963.

---. Fools of Time: Studies in Shakespearean Tragedy. Toronto: U of

Toronto P, 1967.

A translated book:

> Gogol, Nikolai. Dead Souls. Trans. Andrew McAndrew. New York:
>
> New American Library, 1961.

If you are discussing the translation itself, as opposed to the book, list the work under the translator's name. Then put a comma, a space, and "trans." After the period following "trans." skip a space, then give the title of the book, a period, a space, and then "By" and the author's name, first name first. Continue with information about the place of publication, publisher, and date, as in any entry to a book.

An introduction, foreword, or afterword, or other editorial apparatus:

> Fromm, Erich. Afterword. 1984. By George Orwell. New American
>
> Library, 1961.

Usually a book with an introduction or some such comparable material is listed under the name of the author of the book rather than the name of the author of the editorial material (see the citation to Pope on p. 1325). But if you are referring to the editor's apparatus rather than to the work itself, use the form just given.

Words such as *preface, introduction, afterword,* and *conclusion* are capitalized in the entry but are neither enclosed within quotation marks nor underlined.

A book review. First, an example of a review that does not have a title:

> Vendler, Helen. Rev. of Essays on Style. Ed. Roger Fowler. Essays in
>
> Criticism 16 (1966): 457-63.

If the review has a title, give the title after the period following the reviewer's name, before "Rev." If the review is unsigned, list it under the first word of the title, or the second word if the first word is *A, An,* or *The.* If an unsigned review has no title, begin the entry with "Rev. of" and alphabetize it under the title of the work being reviewed.

An encyclopedia. The first example is for a signed article, the second for an unsigned article:

> Lang, Andrew. "Ballads." Encyclopaedia Britannica. 1910 ed.

> "Metaphor." The New Encyclopaedia Britannica: Micropaedia. 1974 ed.

An article in a scholarly journal. Some journals are paginated consecutively; that is, the pagination of the second issue picks up where the first issue left off. Other journals begin each issue with a new page 1. The forms of the citations in Works Cited differ slightly.

First, the citation of *a journal that uses continuous pagination:*

> Burbick, Joan. "Emily Dickinson and the Economics of Desire."
>
> American Literature 58 (1986): 361-78.

This article appeared in volume 58, which was published in 1986. (Notice that the volume number is followed by a space, then by the year in parentheses, and then by a colon, a space, and the page numbers of the entire article.) Although each volume consists of four issues, you do *not* specify the issue number when the journal is paginated continuously.

For *a journal that paginates each issue separately* (a quarterly journal will have four page 1's each year), give the issue number directly after the volume number and a period, with no spaces before or after the period:

Spillers, Hortense J. "Martin Luther King and the Style of the Black

Sermon." The Black Scholar 3.1 (1971): 14-27.

An article in a weekly, biweekly, or monthly publication:

McCabe, Bernard. "Taking Dickens Seriously." Commonweal 14 May

1965: 24.

Notice that the volume number and the issue number are omitted for popular weeklies or monthlies such as *Time* and *Atlantic.*

An article in a newspaper. Because newspapers usually consist of several sections, a section number may precede the page number. The example indicates that an article begins on page 3 of section 2 and is continued on a later page:

Wu, Jim. "Authors Praise New Forms." New York Times 8 March 1996,

sec. 2: 3+.

You may also have occasion to cite something other than a printed source, for instance, a lecture. Here are the forms for the chief nonprint sources.

An interview:

Saretta, Howard. Personal interview. 3 Nov. 1998.

A lecture:

Heaney, Seamus. Lecture. Tufts University. 15 Oct. 1998.

A television or radio program:

60 Minutes. CBS. 30 Jan. 1994.

A film or videotape:

Modern Times. Dir. Charles Chaplin. United Artists, 1936.

A recording:

Frost, Robert. "The Road Not Taken." Robert Frost Reads His Poetry.

Caedmon, TC 1060, 1956.

A performance:

<u>The Cherry Orchard</u>. By Anton Chekhov. Dir. Ron Daniels. American

Repertory Theatre, Cambridge, Mass. 3 Feb. 1994.

Reminder: For the form of citations to electronic material, see pages 1352–53.

New Approaches to the Research Paper: Literature, History, and the World Wide Web

The previous section describes the traditional model and methods for writing a literary research paper. But literary research has recently become more wide-ranging and complicated, and a book like this one needs to devote another section to it, in order to take into account important changes in the field of literary study and developments in technology.

Students in both literature and composition courses are now often asked to work with historical and literary materials and to demonstrate skills in interdisciplinary learning—and this educational change has taken place on the introductory as well as the intermediate and advanced levels. Like other fields, literary study is supplementing printed texts with electronic search tools, databases, and resources; literary analysis, writing, and research increasingly take place as much on the World Wide Web as in the library, and, in some cases, through e-mail and e-mail lists devoted to specific subject areas. Historical research can be very rewarding; it opens up new lines of inquiry as it teaches us about the contexts for literary works and enables us to respond to them in more complex ways. But we need the right strategies to perform this research effectively. Students in literature and composition must now possess the insight and understanding to explore, and to make good choices when consulting, ever-multiplying amounts of information.

CASE STUDY ON LITERATURE AND HISTORY: THE INTERNMENT OF JAPANESE AMERICANS

The best means of illustrating the new approach to literature and history, and the process for identifying new kinds of resources, is through a case study, and for this purpose we have chosen the literature and history of the internment of Japanese Americans during World War II. This is a subject for research that a student might select, or be assigned, in a variety of courses—an introduction to literature in which a group of contemporary poems are studied, with some of them related in subject; a first-year writing course in which the subject is the literature of American immigration; a course in American or Asian-American literature; a course in Multicultural literature or in American literature since World War II; a senior seminar that examines twentieth-century literature and history, types of ethnic and minority literatures, or poetry and politics. Many books, articles, and conferences have been devoted to the internment—we can hardly do it justice here. This discussion will outline the nature of the inquiry into the subject that you can undertake, beginning with the analysis of literary texts and moving outward from it into history, and into print and electronic sources.

LITERARY TEXTS

Reprinted below are two poems. The first is Mitsuye Yamada's "The Question of Loyalty," from *Camp Notes and Other Poems* (1992); the second is David Mura's "An Argument: On 1942," from *After We Lost Our Way* (1989).

 ## MITSUYE YAMADA

Mitsuye Yamada, the daughter of Japanese immigrants to the United States, was born in Japan in 1923, during her mother's return visit to her native land. She was raised in Seattle, but in 1942 she and her family were incarcerated and then relocated to an internment camp in Idaho. This was the result of Executive Order 9066, signed by President Franklin Roosevelt in February 1942. This order, in the aftermath of the Japanese attack on Pearl Harbor in December 1941, gave military authorities the right to remove any and all persons from "military areas." In 1954 Yamada became an American citizen. A member of the Asian American Studies Program at the University of California at Irvine, she is the author of many stories and poems. In addition to Camp Notes and Other Poems, *she has written* Desert Run: Poems and Stories *(1988) and edited* Sowing TI Leaves: Writings by Multicultural Women *(1991).*

The Question of Loyalty

I met the deadline
for alien registration
once before
was numbered fingerprinted
and ordered not to travel   5
without permit.

But alien still they said I must
forswear allegiance to the emperor.
for me that was easy
I didn't even know him   10
but my mother who did cried out
   If I sign this
   What will I be?
   I am doubly loyal
   to my American children   15
   also to my own people.
   How can double mean nothing?
   I wish no one to lose this war.
   Everyone does.

I was poor
at math.
I signed
my only ticket out.

20

[1976]

DAVID MURA

David Mura is a sansei, a third-generation Japanese American. He was born in 1952, seven years after the end of the war. In both poetry and prose, he has examined race, ethnicity, and sexuality, and has described his quest for self-knowledge and personal and familial identity. A Male Grief: Notes on Pornography and Addiction *(1987) was his first book. Two years later he published* After We Lost Our Way *in the National Poetry Series, and followed it with a second book of verse,* The Colors of Desire: Poems *(1995). He has also written* Turning Japanese: Memoirs of a Sansei *(1992) and* Where the Body Meets Memory: An Odyssey of Race, Sexuality, and Identity *(1996), which tells of his childhood in Chicago, his parents' recollections of the internment camps, and the impact of internment on several generations of Japanese Americans.*

An Argument: On 1942
For my mother

Near Rose's Chop Suey and Jinosuke's grocery the temple where incense hovered and inspired dense evening chants (prayers for Buddha's mercy, colorless and deep), that day he was fired . . .

—No, no, no, she tells me. Why bring it back?
The camps are over. (Also overly dramatic.)
Forget *shoyu*-stained *furoshiki,*° *mochi*° on a stick:
You're like a terrier, David, gnawing a bone, an old, old trick . . .

Mostly we were bored. Women cooked and sewed,   5
men played blackjack, dug gardens, a *benjo.*°
Who noticed barbed wire, guards in the towers?
We were children, hunting stones, birds, wild flowers.

Yes, Mother hid tins of *tsukemono*° and eel
beneath the bed. And when the last was peeled,   10
clamped tight her lips, growing thinner and thinner.
But cancer not the camps made her throat blacker

. . . And she didn't die then . . . after the war, in St. Paul,
you weren't even born. Oh, I know, I know, it's all
part of your job, your way, but why can't you glean   15
how far we've come, how much I can't recall—

David, it was so long ago—how useless it seems . . .

[1989]

---

³ *shoyu-stained furoshiki* a soy-stained scarf that is used to carry things *mochi* rice cakes ⁶ *benjo* toilet ⁹ *tsukemono* Japanese pickles [All are author's notes.]

Your goal is eventually to move to historical research, but first you must know the poems well. Reflect upon the movement of each one—how it begins, what occupies its middle sections, and how it ends. Consider the relationship of the structure—the length of the lines, the organization of the stanzas, the diction and imagery—to the dramatic situation and themes.

- For this, reread the discussions of speaker, structure, figurative language, and other key terms presented in Chapter 13 of this book, and refer to the Checklist on page 420.

Yamada focuses on the conflict experienced by her mother. The mother expresses her loyalty to her children, to her *American* children, even as she cherishes her loyalty to her own people, the Japanese (though this word, revealingly, is not used). She wants there to be no loser in the war; she hopes for an impossible stalemate, in which neither side loses. The war manifests itself in her own identity, in the tension between the person she has been and the person, it seems, she must become. If the mother signs the form forswearing allegiance to the Japanese emperor, she will be denying her ancestry, forced to disclaim one-half of herself. She cannot be who she is.

Mura describes the conflict between his mother and himself and delves into the struggle that his mother wages with her memories. Unlike Yamada, Mura was not in the camps himself; he is seeking knowledge about an experience that took place before he was born. The mother objects to her son's efforts to make her remember: "You're like a terrier, David, gnawing a bone, an old, old trick." But as her own listing of details shows, the mother, if only to herself, has continued to linger over the internment—the men playing blackjack, the barbed wire. She says there is much she cannot recall, but one feels that there is much that remains keenly present for her, much that she could recall and has recalled. The mother cannot practice the lesson she gives to her son. Nor will he allow her to. He is curious to know what happened; he wants his mother to tell about her experiences and, one suspects, to explain why she and the others did not resist then and have not spoken out since.

These are powerful poems even for a reader who knows only a little about the historical facts to which Yamada and Mura bear witness—a reader who knows only in a general way that many Japanese Americans were forced during World War II to leave their West Coast homes and live in internment camps in the California desert, in other western states, and as far east as Arkansas. But the poems become still more effective for a reader who knows in depth and detail about this episode in American history, and who can bring this knowledge to a reading of the texts and present it in an analytical research paper.

One form of *historical* research is to follow a traditional route for *literary* research. The literary resources and methods described in the previous chapter can lead to secondary sources on the authors and their writings and to information about their careers, the work they have done, and its major themes. There will be historical information in many of these sources, particularly those of a recent date.

By checking in the *MLA International Bibliography* (see the previous appendix, page 1314), you can locate items such as the following:

On Yamada:

Jaskoski, Helen. "Interview with Mitsuye Yamada." *MELUS: The Journal of the Society for the Study of the Multi-Ethnic Literature of the United States.* 15: 1 (Spring 1988): 97–108.

Schweik, Susan. "A Needle with Mama's Voice: Mitsuye Yamada's *Camp Notes* and the American Canon of War Poetry." In *Arms and the Woman: War, Gender, and Literary Representation.* Ed. Helen M. Cooper and Adrienne Auslander Munich. Chapel Hill: U of North Carolina P, 1989.

Usui, Masami. "A Language of Her Own in Mitsuye Yamada's Poetry and Stories." *Studies in Culture and the Humanities: Bulletin of the Faculty of Integrated Arts and Sciences,* Hiroshima University: 5: 3 (1996): 1–17.

On Mura:

Taylor, Gordon O. "'The Country I Had Thought Was My Home': David Mura's *Turning Japanese* and Japanese-American Narrative since World War II." *Connotations: A Journal for Critical Debate* (Münster, Germany): 6:3 (1996–1997): 283–309.

General studies:

Nakanishi, Don T., ed. *Japanese American Internment: Commemorative Issue.* Special issue of *Amerasia Journal* 19: 1 (1993).

Thiesmeyer, Lynn. "The Discourse of Official Violence: Anti-Japanese North American Discourse and the American Internment Camps." *Discourse & Society* 6: 3 (July 1995): 319–52.

Yogi, Stan. "Yearning for the Past: The Dynamics of Memory in Sansei Internment Poetry." *Memory and Cultural Politics: New Approaches to American Ethnic Literatures.* Ed. Amritjit Singh, Joseph T. Skerrett, Jr., and Robert E. Hogan. Boston: Northeastern UP, 1996.

- Through electronic access and interlibrary loan, a student can obtain almost any source, even if it is not carried by a library on campus. But sometimes interlibrary loan can take a few days, a week, or more. Remember the importance of starting early on research projects. Request copies of everything while there is still time before the deadline to examine them.

HISTORICAL SOURCES

The sources in the *MLA International Bibliography,* while promising, may take for granted more than at this stage you know; the discussion and analysis presented in them assumes that readers *already* have the background that you are seeking to acquire. How can you begin to acquire a base of historical knowledge?

Start small. Don't overwhelm yourself with more information than you can handle. Keep in mind as well that you are not aiming to become an historian, but, instead, intend to enrich your literary explorations with knowledge drawn from another field and set of sources.

Basic Reference Books (Short Paper)

It is best to begin with basic reference books, and you can get to them by consulting the following:

Balay, Robert. *Guide to Reference Books,* 11th ed. Chicago: American Library Association, 1996.

Blazek, Ron, and Elizabeth Aversa. *The Humanities: A Selective Guide to Information Sources.* 4th ed. Englewood, Colo.: Libraries Unlimited, 1994.

> This is an annotated guide to research sources in literature, art, and other fields in the humanities.

Or, consult *ARBA Guide to Subject Encyclopedias and Dictionaries* (1986); and *First Stop: The Master Index to Subject Encyclopedias* (1989).

Or, in the online library catalog, check under the subject heading, "history—*dictionaries.*" (You can do the same thing for literature, for titles of reference works in that field.)

You can also refer to Jules R. Benjamin, *A Student's Guide to History,* 6th ed. (1994); and James R. Bracken, *Reference Works in British and American Literature,* 2 vols. (1990). See also M. J. Marcuse, *Reference Guide for English Studies* (1990); and James L. Harner, *Literary Research Guide,* 3rd. ed. (1993).

Browse in the reference section or, better still, talk to a reference librarian— he or she can be a valuable resource and often can direct you quickly to helpful books.

In reply to the question, "Where can I find out about the internment of Japanese Americans during World War II?" the reference librarian recommended to us *The Reader's Companion to American History,* ed. Eric Foner and John A. Garraty (Boston: Houghton Mifflin, 1991), which includes an entry on this subject titled "Japanese American Relocation."

Here is the entry in full:

JAPANESE-AMERICAN RELOCATION

The relocation of thousands of Japanese-Americans into internment camps during World War II marked an ignoble chapter in American history. In 1941 when the Japanese bombed Pearl Harbor, there were 127,000 persons of Japanese ancestry in America, the majority residing on the West Coast. For years they had been denied the right to vote or own land. After Pearl Harbor, rumors spread that a Japanese plot to sabotage the American war effort was afoot. In early 1942, the Roosevelt administration was pressured to remove Japanese-Americans from the West Coast by agricultural interests seeking to eliminate Japanese competition, a public fearing sabotage, and politicians hoping to gain by aligning against this unpopular group.

In February 1942, the federal government forced all Japanese-Americans regardless of loyalty or citizenship to evacuate the West Coast, which was perceived as a vulnerable military area. To justify this move against Americans only of Japanese—not German or Italian—descent, the government claimed that racial ties inclined the Japanese to disloyalty. When neighboring states resisted the incoming refugees, the government established ten internment camps in California, Idaho, Utah, Arizona, Wyoming, Colorado, and Arkansas to receive them. By September, 100,000 people had been moved. The camps resembled prisons, with cramped quarters, communal facilities, and poor food. Generational conflict beset the internees: older Issei (immigrants) were deprived of their traditional respect when their children, the Nisei (American-born), were alone permitted authority positions within the camps. Ultimately, 5,766 Nisei renounced their American citzenship. When internees were given the opportunity to leave the camps by joining the U.S. army, only 1,200 did so.

The U.S. Supreme Court upheld the government's position in two cases challenging the relocation, *Hirabayashi v. United States* and *Korematsu v. United States.* Only after his reelection in 1944 did Franklin D. Roosevelt finally rescind the evacuation order, and by the end of 1945 the camps were closed. In 1968, the Japanese-Americans were reimbursed for property they had lost, and in 1988, Congress enacted legislation awarding resititution payments of twenty thousand dollars each to the 60,000 surviving internees.
See also World War II.
(588–89)

At this point you should remind yourself of the boundaries of the assignment.

- What is the *length* of the essay? Its *due date?*
- *How many* sources did the instructor state that you should use? Did he or she refer to specific kinds of sources that the paper should include—scholarly books and/or articles, other primary sources (literary texts, letters, autobiographies, journals), photographs, and so on?
- The *proportions* of the essay? How much of it should consist of literary analysis, and how much of historical research and context?

For a short paper of three pages that treats one or both of the poems and provides some historical context, the entry from *The Reader's Companion* may be all that you need. It reports what happened, where, and why, emphasizes the outrage done to civil liberties, and highlights an aspect of camp experience that bears on Yamada's and Mura's poems: "Generational conflict beset the internees . . ." (589). You can relate this comment to the differences and struggles between the generations that Yamada and Mura evoke. Here, you have an historical detail that you can develop in your examination of the poems *and,* if the assignment were a longer one calling for extensive research, that you could make the organizing principle for gathering and then sifting through sources.

- It is important, then, to gain basic knowledge of the subject, so that you have a clear, accurate answer to your core question—in this case, What was the internment? But, at the same time, seek to locate in the overview of the subject an idea or issue that is connected to the themes of the specific literary works. *Connect* the literature and the history.

Getting Deeper (Medium Paper)

The entry in *The Reader's Companion to American History* has limitations. It is brief and lacks a bibliography; and the cross-reference leads to an entry on World War II that supplies no further information about the internment. For a medium-length paper, you will need to search elsewhere for more information and, if you require it, for a bibliography. Sources include:

Encyclopedia of the United States in the Twentieth Century. Stanley I. Kutler, general editor. 5 vols. New York: Scribner's, 1996.

> *Harvard Encyclopedia of American Ethnic Groups.* Ed. Stephan
> Thernstrom. Cambridge: Harvard UP, 1980.

> *Oxford Companion to World War II,* general editor, I. C. B. Dear, con-
> sultant editor, M. R. D. Foot. New York: Oxford UP, 1995.

Like *The Reader's Companion to American History,* the *Oxford Companion to World War II* is recent, prepared by eminent scholars, and published by a
reputable press. It is a trustworthy source, and its signed entry on "Japanese-
Americans" (632-34) is longer and more detailed than the entry in *The Reader's
Companion;* it is cross-referenced to a general entry on "internment" and identifies three books for further reading:

> Daniels, Roger. *Asian America: Chinese and Japanese in the United
> States since 1850* (Seattle, Wash., 1988).
>
> ————. *Concentration Camps USA* (New York, 1971).

> Takaki, Ronald. *Strangers from a Different Shore: A History of Asian
> Americans* (Boston, 1989).

Now you can start to compile a bibliography of your own, with these three
books as its foundation. But—here is a key point—note their dates of publication. No doubt these are good sources, but you should be seeking more recent
sources as well to make certain that your knowledge is as up-to-date as possible.

The relevant section in the *Encyclopedia of the United States,* included in
the chapter "Ethnicity and Immigration," is fairly brief (see 1:176-77), about the
same length as (and less detailed than) the entry in *The Reader's Companion*
from which you started. But the chapter closes with a bibliographic essay that includes this important information:

> On Japanese American internment, the essential work is Roger Daniels,
> *Prisoners without Trial: Japanese Americans in World War II* (1993).

This tells you that Daniels has written a book on the subject that is more recent than his 1971 book that the *Oxford Companion* lists. A scholar in the field
of ethnic studies has flagged it as "essential" and thus it is a source you should
highlight in your notes for special attention.

> • Daniels gives a background chapter on the period 1850-1941, four
>   chapters on the internment and its aftermath, an epilogue "Could It Hap-
>   pen Again?" "An Essay in Photographs," "Suggestions for Further Read-
>   ing," and an appendix of "Documents." This is a first-rate book for your
>   purposes; it is recent, concise (150 pages), written by an accomplished
>   scholar who is in full command of primary and secondary sources and
>   whose bibliography will direct you authoritatively to other materials.

The section on the wartime internment of Japanese Americans in *Harvard
Encyclopedia* is part of a long essay devoted to the history of the Japanese in
America (561-71). The author, Harry H. L. Kitano, notes at one point:

> In the camps all Japanese, whether highly educated, wealthy, illiterate,
> or poor, were housed in barracks, ate mess-hall food, and received the
> same rates of pay for work—$16 a month for manual labor and $19 for
> professional work. They used communal toilets, took communal show-
> ers, waited patiently in line for everything; they wore identical clothes,

and the sun, wind, and dust soon endowed them with the same con-
centration-camp complexion. (566)

Kitano helps you grasp the historical setting for Mura's poem, and the next part
of his discussion pertains to it, and to Yamada's poem, even more directly:

> The most difficult problem proved to be the boredom and monotony of
> camp life; it exacerbated tensions and magnified irritations, resulting in
> fights, riots, strikes, and even homicides. Inmates complained con-
> stantly about the food, their neighbors, living conditions, and camp ad-
> ministrators. Conflicts between the Issei [Japanese-born Americans—
> the first or immigrant generation] and Nisei [American-born
> Japanese—the second generation] added to the strain. Ideological argu-
> ments between those loyal to Japan and those who stood with the
> United States grew heated. The derogatory term *inu* [dog] was applied
> to those suspect of being spies or government collaborators, and some
> of the inu were the victims of severe beatings. (566).

"Mostly we were bored," recalls Mura's mother, touching on an aspect of
life in the camps that Kitano stresses in his historical survey. Kitano makes clear
how real and pervasive were the differences between generations, between parents and children. He concludes:

> Family life was disrupted: the authority of the provider-father and the
> housekeeper-mother was undercut by government supervision; chil-
> dren ate in mess halls rather than in the family circle. They were stifled
> in an atmosphere of boredom and stagnation. Gambling became a prob-
> lem, and petty family quarrels often escalated into violence. (567)

Now you can really begin to see the analytical value of historical sources.
Details like these make one wonder if part of the effect of Mura's poem lies in
what we sense the mother is trying *not* to remember—the fact, for example, that
the men playing blackjack were doing something that not only distracted them
but that caused a serious problem in the camps. She acknowledges that life was
boring, but possibly the boredom was even more grave than she reveals to her
son—a boredom that led to arguments among family members and to violence.

Our historical research teaches us about the *contexts* for the Yamada and
Mura poems and alerts us to the power and precision of details that the poets include. Sometimes, too, it helps us sense the pressure of feelings and thoughts
that a writer or speaker is excluding, is holding back or reacting against. The
more we learn about the camps, the more we can perceive what Mura's mother
is referring to and what, on some level, she might be struggling to keep from
speaking about.

Kitano's chapter ends with a bibliographic essay that includes the following
note:

> The internment of the Japanese in relocation camps has received much
> attention. The most perceptive studies of this painful episode are
> Leonard Broom and John I. Kitsuse, *The Managed Casualty: The Japan-
> ese American Family in World War II* (Berkeley, 1956); Audrie Gird-
> ner and Anne Loftis, *The Great Betrayal* (New York, 1969); Jacobus
> Tenbroek, Edward N. Barnhart, and Floyd W. Matson, *Prejudice, War,
> and the Constitution* (Berkeley, 1970); and Michi Weglyn, *Years of In-
> famy: The Untold Story of America's Concentration Camps* (New
> York, 1976).

Now you have additional items for your bibliography.

Checklist: A Review of Researching a Literary-Historical Paper

✔ Consult a range of reference books as you are getting launched on a literary-historical paper—it will take less time than you think, and it will be time invested wisely.

✔ Pay attention to *when* the books were published and how up-to-date they are in their suggestions for additional reading.

✔ Even as you acquire familiarity with the subject in general, take special note of where the historical record *makes connections* to the literature that you are studying. The real reward comes when you can perceive the relationship between history and the structure and themes of the literary works.

Question for Consideration

In *Prisoners Without Trial,* Roger Daniels states:

There were no individual cooking facilities. Everyone ate in the mess hall. Three times a day, prisoners lined up with trays to receive wholesome, starchy, cheap food, not usually prepared in the most appetizing manner. . . . Almost everyone complained about the food, but what the mess halls did to family relationships was worse. Youngsters tended to eat in groups and move around from mess hall to mess hall. The dislocation of the family meal was but another way in which the detention process eroded the dignity and authority of parents. (67)

Write one or two paragraphs in which you connect Daniels's description to details that Mura includes in "An Argument: On 1942." Through your commentary show how the historical context enhances the reader's response to and understanding of the poem.

Other Reference Sources (Long Paper)

If your literary/historical research needs to be extended further, say, for a term paper of 20–25 pages, then you will have to make use of other tools for locating historical sources. The items in the *MLA International Bibliography* and the suggestions for further reading given in reference books are excellent, but there are other routes to follow, especially for historical materials.

Humanities Abstracts, an index of articles in the humanities, with their contents summarized, is a good resource. It gives the following item (among others) on the subject of the internment:

Davidov, Judith Fryer. "'The Color of My Skin, the Shape of My Eyes': Photographs of the Japanese-American Internment by Dorothea

Lange, Ansel Adams, and Toyo Miyatake." *Yale Journal of Criticism* 9 (Fall 1996): 223–44, illustrations.

> A description of the shrouded history of the internment of Japanese-Americans during World War 2 and a discussion of the photographs of these internees taken by Dorothea Lange, Ansel Adams, and Toyo Miyatake. Lange's images are rich in content, demanding an emotional response that seemed to some to be inimical to national security. Adams, whose photographs of the camp at Manzanar, California, were taken with the sanction of the authorities, contributed to the official presentation of the internment as humane, orderly, and even beneficial to the internees. Miyatake, who was an internee, took his photographs with smuggled materials, and his images, which are dense in detail, insistently show the fallaciousness of demarcating otherness.

The "abstract" or summary of the author's main points is a valuable feature of this reference work. Here you are told about an essay that deals with visual materials—a type of source you have not yet encountered. In the essay the author reproduces some of the photographs (note the reference to "illustrations") and no doubt refers her readers to the collections where the photographs can be found.

Here are several more items from *Humanities Abstracts* (for these, we have cut the abstracts slightly to save space). When you read an abstract, keep in mind that you are seeking sources that bear on the issues in the literary works that you have chosen to examine. The abstract may tell you about a source that, while interesting, is not pertinent to your research needs for this particular paper. For many topics, there is a great deal of material that you could draw upon if your time were limitless; but because you must use your limited time well, you should be focused and selective. Fasten on the best sources for the nature of the research task at hand.

Yoshino, Ronald W. "Barbed Wire and Beyond: A Sojourn through Internment—in Personal Recollection." *Journal of the West* 35 (January 1996): 34–43, illustrations.

> . . . The clash with the federal government and the ensuing incarceration pointed to the importance of the Nisei, the Americanized, second generation Japanese who acted for most internees. With more power as a result of increased responsibility, the Nisei led the Japanese Americans into the postwar era, speeding up the process of acculturation. . . .

Now you have another personal story to place alongside the one that Mura's and Yamada's speakers present, and this story, like that in the poems, calls attention to the differences between generations. The reference in the title to "barbed wire" may even remind you of the "barbed wire" in Mura's poem.

Kuramitsu, Kristine C. "Internment and Identity in Japanese American Art." *American Quarterly* 47 (Dec. 1995): 619–58, illustrations.

> . . . Examines an exhibition of hitherto unseen art from the camps, "The View from Within: Japanese American Art from the Internment Camps 1942–1945," and looks at these artworks as aesthetic expressions of personal and cultural identity. She concludes by discussing Japanese American artists who are one or two generations removed from this event and how they deal with the issues surrounding it, with reference to the 1992 exhibition "Relocations and Revisions: The Japanese American Internment Reconsidered." . . .

Works of art, a special exhibition—through this article you can learn about still other perspectives on the subject. Like the article by Davidov cited above, this source might be an especially good one if you were asked to give an oral report in class about your research. By making copies for your classmates of some of the illustrations, you can give a visual dimension to the report, making your analysis all the more attention-getting and interesting to the audience.

> Greenberg, Cheryl. "Black and Jewish Responses to Japanese Internment." *Journal of American Ethnic History* 14 (Winter 1995): 3-37.
>> . . . Argues that many of the most prominent and outspoken black and Jewish civil rights organizations did not perceive the injustice of this racially based policy, although they did support fair treatment for individual Japanese Americans not living in militarily sensitive areas . . . .

Now you have a source that places the internment in the context of American ethnic and minority history.

> Sundquist, Eric J. "The Japanese-American Internment: A Reappraisal." *The American Scholar* 57 (Autumn 1988): 529-47.

There is no summary given in *Humanities Abstracts* for this item, but you do not need one. The key word "reappraisal" indicates that the author will be discussing the events themselves and the current state of scholarly work.

- Look for key words in titles of books and articles listed in bibliographies that offer clues about the author's point of view, approach, or treatment of the subject.

If the paper requires sustained research, your best next step might be to perform a "subject" search in the online card catalogs of your own and other research libraries. It is always tempting to do a search by subject first, before anything else and without bothering to check reference books. While convenient, this method has disadvantages. Your subject search for Japanese American internment might not turn up Daniels's 1993 book at all—maybe your library does not own it. Or, if it does, this book might be in the middle of a long subject list: You would not know that it has been praised as an "essential" source and that— given that you must make choices—you would be better off zeroing in on this source than others on the list.

- When you check the online catalog for one of the books already on your bibliography, you will see on the entry the *subject* category for it. You can then use this category for your more complete *subject* search. The librarian can also assist you in identifying the phrases for the subject you are researching; the *Library of Congress Subject Headings* (*LCSH*) is another resource.

Too Much Information?

At this point, you may be wondering, "How do I know when to stop?" A good question, but not one with a simple answer. We have known students who have become gripped by a subject and have read everything they can about it. But however excited about a subject you become, in the midst of a busy semester you will need to make choices and budget your time.

- "How do I know when to stop?" Stop when you have acquired the historical knowledge that strengthens your analysis of the literary texts— the knowledge that deepens your understanding of the issues that the authors have treated, and the knowledge that is sufficient for you to meet the terms (that is, the boundaries) of the assignment.

Question for Consideration

As you perform your research, you will often be confronted with lists of sources. It is important to become aware of how you might evaluate these sources and determine which of the items on a list might be most relevant. Review the following items chosen from a lengthy list produced by a subject search for "Japanese Americans—Evacuation and Relocation, 1942–1945." Consider the type of each source and its area of emphasis, the publication date, and the nature of the connection (if any) to the themes in the poem you plan to examine.

Conrat, Maisie. *Executive Order 9066: The Internment of 110,000 Japanese Americans.* With an introd. by Edison Uno and an epilogue by Tom C. Clark. Photographs by Dorothea Lange and others. Cambridge, Mass.: MIT P for the California Historical Society, 1972.

Daniels, Roger, ed. *American Concentration Camps: A Documentary History of the Relocation and Incarceration of Japanese Americans.* 9 vols. New York: Garland, 1989.

Gesensway, Deborah. *Beyond Words: Images from America's Concentration Camps.* Ithaca, N.Y.: Cornell UP, 1987.

Hansen, Arthur A., ed. *Japanese American World War II Evacuation Oral History Project.* 5 vols. Westport, Conn.: Meckler, 1991–93.

Ichihashi, Yamato. *Morning Glory, Evening Shadow: Yamato Ichihashi and His Internment Writings, 1942–1945,* edited, annotated, and with a biographical essay by Gordon H. Chang. Stanford, Calif.: Stanford UP, 1997.

Mills, Denice Lee. *The Evacuation and Relocation of Japanese Americans During World War II: A Bibliography.* Public Administration Series—Bibliography, P 2788, 1989.

Nagata, Donna K. *Legacy of Injustice: Exploring the Cross-Generational Impact of the Japanese American Internment.* New York: Plenum, 1993.

Smith, Page. *Democracy on Trial: The Japanese American Evacuation and Relocation in World War II.* New York: Simon & Schuster, 1995.

Uchida, Yoshiko. *Desert Exile: The Uprooting of a Japanese American Family.* Seattle: U of Washington P, 1984.

ELECTRONIC SOURCES

Encyclopedias: Print and Electronic Versions

Encyclopedias can give you the basics about a subject, but like all resources, they have limitations. An encyclopedia may not cover the subject that you are researching or not cover it in adequate depth. Knowledge expands rapidly, and because it does, even a good encyclopedia lags somewhat behind current scholarship. A number of encyclopedias are now in CD-ROM form, preloaded on a personal computer, and the CD makes searches for information easier. Many such encyclopedias can also be connected to the World Wide Web, where updated information and links to reference and research resources are listed. It is helpful to have the updated information and links, but only when they are reliable. More on this point in a moment.

Perhaps the most popular CD-ROM encyclopedia is the *Grolier Multimedia Encyclopedia* (current edition 1998, 2 CDs). But for the internment of Japanese Americans, there is no specific entry; brief discussions are located within other entries, the most comprehensive of which is for Asian Americans. Here is the relevant paragraph:

> The most traumatic blow against Japanese Americans was struck soon after Japan bombed Pearl Harbor. More than 2,000 community leaders along the Pacific Coast and in Hawaii were rounded up by the Federal Bureau of Investigation and imprisoned. On Feb. 19, 1942, President Franklin D. Roosevelt signed Executive Order 9066 authorizing the secretary of war or any military commander designated by him to establish "military areas" and to "exclude any and all persons" from them. In the next few months, 112,000 persons of Japanese ancestry—two-thirds of them American citizens—were forcibly removed from the western half of Washington, Oregon, and California and the southern third of Arizona and incarcerated first in temporary assembly centers and eventually in ten relocation camps. The vast majority of Japanese Americans in Hawaii were not interned, as they made up 40 percent of the islands' labor force and their removal would have crippled Hawaii. Despite the maltreatment they received, some 23,000 Nisei served in the U.S. Army, fighting in both Europe and Asia. The unit in Europe received more decorations than any unit of comparable size during World War II.
> (© 1998 Grolier Interactive Inc.)

This is less informative than print sources we have discussed, and the thinness of the entry helps to make clear that electronic sources have not yet done away with the need to go to the library.

The value of *Grolier* lies less in this entry's information than in the fact that through the CD-ROM, you can access (or so it appears) other sources and links on the World Wide Web. For "Asian Americans," *Grolier* provides WWW links to two directories:

1. *Asian American Resources.*
Diverse collection of links to clubs, organizations, media, personal home pages, FAQs [frequently asked questions], event listings, news about Asian Americans.
—Reading level: General.

2. *WWW Virtual Library: Migration and Ethnic Relations.*
Directory includes research institutes, academic departments, journals, conferences, data archives, mailing lists, related sites for study of ethnic groups, diversity, and migration.
—Reading level: General.

Asian American Resources—this sounds promising. But when we tried several times to link to this site (January 1998), it had expired. It was a dead-end, and this kind of experience is fairly common when conducting research through the World Wide Web. When we attempted to access *WWW Virtual Library: Migration and Ethnic Relations* (again, January 1998), we received the message, "Document contains no data."
There are two things to do when a link does not work:

1. Type in the link but end with *.edu* or *.com* or *.org* to specify it further. The internal architecture of the site may have changed, but the information you are seeking might still be there, accessible through a different link.
2. Go to a search engine, such as Yahoo! ⟨http://www.yahoo.com/⟩ or Infoseek ⟨http://www.infoseek.com/⟩; type in the exact name of the site and see what you get. Sometimes the link that you tried at first will have expired, but you will manage, via a search engine, to reach the site under its name.

Note on terms:

- *URL* (Uniform Resource Locator): the Web address, the location, that your browser points to in order to access a file on an Internet computer.
- *Internet* and *World Wide Web* (WWW): The Internet is the global network that connects networks of many thousands of computers that communicate with one another; the World Wide Web is a complex system for delivering files of hypertext and multimedia on the Internet. These terms are not identical but are often used as if they were.
- *Web page:* a single screen, whatever its length.
- *Web site:* a collection of Web pages, usually includes a main or "home" page for the site.

The best encyclopedia is the *Encyclopaedia Britannica,* and it is available both on the library shelves and on CD-ROM (1997). But, like *Grolier,* it does not supply an entry on the internment; the user must first "search" the database and find information among a number of items. For example:

Manzanar Relocation Center—an internment facility for Japanese Americans during World War II. In March 1942 the U.S. War Relocation Authority was set up; it established 10 relocation centres for persons of Japanese ancestry, located in California, Arizona, Idaho, Utah, Wyoming, and Arkansas. The best known of these, and the first to be established, was the Manzanar Relocation Center near Lone Pine, Calif.; it operated from March 1942 to November 1945. During this time more than 11,000 persons were confined there.

Not much here, but through the CD-ROM you can link to the *Encyclopaedia Britannica*'s WWW site and discover a link for the Manzanar Relocation Center:

MANZANAR NATIONAL HISTORIC SITE

Manzanar War Relocation Center was one of ten camps at which Japanese American citizens and Japanese aliens were interned during World War II. Located at the foot of the imposing Sierra Nevada in eastern California's Owens Valley, Manzanar has been identified as the best preserved of these camps. http://www.nps.gov/manz/

This is an interesting site to visit briefly on the WWW, but it contains little information about the internment itself; in its current form (February 1998), it is not a good source.

The Internet/World Wide Web

Because of the ease of using the Internet, with its access to electronic mail (e-mail), newsgroups, mailing lists, and, especially, sites and links on the World Wide Web, many students now make it their first—and, unfortunately, too often their *only*—stop for research.

All of us, however, must be *critical* users of the materials we find on the WWW. The WWW is up-to-date *and* out-of-date, helpful *and* disappointing. It can be a researcher's dream come true, and a source of errors and a time-waster.

Let's work a bit on the literature and history of the internment by means of the WWW and see what we discover.

Start a search using a popular "search engine," such as Yahoo!, with the search phrase *Japanese and internment.*

- Search engines make use of logical operators, such as *and, or, not, near. And* searches the field for any uses of both keywords you have specified. *Or* searches for either of the keywords. *Not* enables you to restrict the search—e.g., *minority not European. Near* looks for the keywords within a certain range (e.g., ten words) of one another. These operators can help you to tailor a search, and most search engines accept them and offer other refinements. Placing a phrase in quotations, for instance, means that the search will produce items using that specific phrase: e.g., "internment of Japanese Americans."

Here are the results of our search on 1/28/98:

> Yahoo! Category Matches (1 - 1 of 1)

Arts: Humanities: History: 20th Century: World War II: Internment Camps: Japanese-American

> Yahoo! Site Matches (1 - 7 of 7)

Arts: Humanities: History: 20th Century: World War II: Internment Camps: Japanese-American

- *Japanese-American Internment* - from the Random House Kid's Encyclopedia.
- *Japanese American Internment* - collecting information on America's concentration camps.
- *Camp Harmony* - documents, letters and photographs from the Puyallup Assembly Center, a Japanese-American internment camp.
- *Topaz: 1942-1946* - remembering the Japanese-Americans imprisoned in Utah by their own government during World War II.

Arts: Humanities: History: Regional: U.S. States: Washington: Complete Listing:

- *Camp Harmony* - documents, letters and photographs from the Puyallup Assembly Center, a Japanese-American internment camp.

Entertainment: Cool Links: Arts and Humanities: History

- *Camp Harmony* - documents, letters and photographs from the Puyallup Assembly Center, a Japanese-American internment camp.

Regional: U.S. States: Washington: Cities: Puyallup: History

- *Camp Harmony* - documents, letters and photographs from the Puyallup Assembly Center, a Japanese-American internment camp.

Perhaps the most promising-looking site on this list is *Japanese American Internment* - collecting information. . . . Its URL is ⟨http://www.geocities.com/Athens/8420/main.html⟩. Once there, here is what we find:

CONTENTS
CONTRIBUTIONS & REQUESTS UPDATED: 10/6/97

Pre-War Intelligence Updated: 4/15/96
The Politics Updated: 2/3/97
An Exclusion Poster Updated: 4/22/96
The Camps Updated: 10/6/97
Memories Updated: 1/13/97
Disillusionment Updated: 2/2/97

Timeline Updated: 10/6/97
Glossary Updated: 11/23/96
Gallery Updated: 6/3/96

Next, there follows a list (too long to reproduce here) of twenty-four Web sites and twenty-one Web documents, some of which turn out to be useful. For example, the Dorothea Lange site at the Library of Congress ⟨http://lcweb.loc.gov/exhibits/wcf/wcf0013.html⟩ presents a biography of this famous photographer and a few of her photographs, including several of the internment experience. Other sites, however, are poorly constructed, not maintained, sketchy, or not relevant at all. By the time you consult the list for yourself, some of the sites and documents almost surely will have disappeared.

Notice that nowhere on this list is the Camp Harmony link. When you see it on the Yahoo! list, it may strike you as overspecific, not as promising as the more general categories, and you might overlook it if you proceed too quickly. Be patient; take some time to do some browsing and exploring, and use more than one search engine, since each one may turn up sites that the others do not. Try also to evaluate the merits of the sites based on the brief descriptions given of them. Yahoo! supplies a summary for its lists of sites, and Infoseek includes text from the sites themselves. Take note also of whether the URL includes .edu since such sites are likely to be more scholarly than others. You should also evaluate the site when you link to it, and later we will offer some guidelines (see page 1352). But first let's consider what the Camp Harmony site contributes to our specific research project.

Camp Harmony
http://weber.u.washington.edu/~mudrock/ALLEN/Exhibit/index.html

Camp Harmony

In the spring of 1942, just months after the bombing of Pearl Harbor, more than 100,000 residents of Japanese ancestry were forcefully evicted by the army from their homes in Washington, Oregon, California, Arizona and Alaska, and sent to nearby temporary assembly centers. From there they were sent by trains to American-style concentration camps at remote inland sites where many people spent the remainder of the war. This exhibit tells the story of Seattle's Japanese American community in the spring and summer of 1942 and their four-month sojourn at the Puyallup Assembly Center known as "Camp Harmony."

Photograph of Japanese-Americans surrendering cameras and radios in 1942, available via World Wide Web (http://WWW.lib.washington.edu/exhibits/harmony/Photo/ m28030.gif). (Photograph from *Seattle Post-Intelligencer* collection, University of Washington Libraries and the Museum of History and Industry.)

Photograph of a family in an apartment in internment camp, available via World Wide Web (http://www.lib.washington.edu/exhibits/harmony/Image/uw526.jpg). (Photograph by Howard Clifford, *Tacoma News Tribune*. Available in Special Collections and Preservation Division of the University of Washington Libraries.)

Overview
Bainbridge Island
Round-Up to the Camp
The Camp: Administration & Physical Layout
Civil Liberties
Children: Miss Evanson's Class
Students: Mrs. Willis's Class
The Essentials: Housing & Food
The Rhythm of Life: Work, School and Play
The Cycle of Life: Birth, Marriage & Death
The Move to Minidoka

The exhibit is based on materials located in the University of Washington Libraries, including newspapers, photographs, correspondence, books, and documents.

Camp Harmony Newsletter
Photographs & Drawings
Documents

The Overview is a well-written page with an informative map of the relocation centers. The page includes lengthy quotations from primary sources, and the sources are identified with complete bibliographic information. The other links take you to cogently written and organized Web pages, filled with primary sources (books, letters, government reports and documents, etc., and, again, these are fully documented), as well as photographs, drawings, and maps.

The Camp Harmony site—presented and sponsored by a major university and prepared on a high scholarly level—displays the interdisciplinary enrichment that the WWW can provide. The letters from the University of Washington archives, for example, are moving and suggestive—and they bear upon the themes of parents and children, the nature of camp life, and the relationship of the Japanese and Japanese Americans to the United States that Yamada and Mura explore in their poems. Here is a section of one letter (the site does not include the author's name) to Elizabeth Bayley Willis, a teacher of art, Latin, and English at Garfield High School in Seattle, whose students described their Cape Harmony experiences in letters written between 1942 and 1943.

> . . . Some of the Isseis volunteered in the last war. They were promised their citizenship to this country. They were promised better treatment.
>
> Now these old folks say, what of us now. Have we got our American citizenship? Are we getting better treatment? What of our businesses? Our children are Americans yet they are being kicked around like dogs—by Americans. The American government made a lot of promises in the last war. It is again making the same promises. The promises of today will be as good as the promises of the last war.
>
> Do you wonder why so many of the first generation feel so bitter, Mrs. Willis?
>
> But that is not all. When we moved into this relocation camp, the camp was still being constructed and many, many families had to share rooms with totally strange families while others lived in recreation buildings with a number of others. The days were hot. The wind blew constantly and dust was always fogging up the rooms. It was impossible to keep rooms free of dust. I remember my mother mopping our room about a half dozen times in one day trying to settle some of the dust. We had no hot water. Our cold water contained chlorine and the smell and taste were repulsive. Our latrines were outdoor affairs. The men had not partitions (we still haven't). It was cold going to the toilets in sub-zero weather. There was a coal shortage. Rain settled the dust but made the ground so muddy people had to wear boots. In general, people suffered so much unnecessary uncomfortable situations that no one can really blame them for being bitter. . . .
>
> (Letter dated April 11, 1943. Elizabeth Bayley Willis Papers.
> Box 1. Manuscripts and University Archives, UW Libraries)

Here, as elsewhere in the process of research, our quest is for particular kinds of historical knowledge that can illuminate the interpretation of the literary works. The details in this letter about the loyalty that the Issei showed toward the U.S. government, and the betrayal of that loyalty, connect it to one of the central themes in Yamada's "The Question of Loyalty." The letter's emphasis on conflict and disagreement between the generations furnishes a point of comparison not only with Yamada's poem but also with Mura's "An Argument: On 1942." And the vivid details about the conditions of life in this camp are described with a bitterness and anger that the mother in Mura's poem, as she recalls the camp, continues on some level to feel but wants to locate at a distance, in the past, long ago.

In this instance, the WWW turns out to be an excellent resource. Wherever he or she might be, a student can in effect undertake research in the University of Washington's holdings on the internment experience, reading primary and secondary materials, viewing photographs and artworks and making copies of (or downloading) them for papers and presentations. Many universities have well-designed sites like this one, affiliated with a department or the library, and they offer a wide array of visual materials and texts on all sorts of subjects. Because academic institutions maintain these sites, they are very likely to be scholarly, up-to-date, and reliable in the information they assemble.

After completing a search using Yahoo!, you could conduct the same search through another search engine, such as Infoseek, which gathers sites from its own pool and allows you to narrow from the initial search results. You can find good material this way, but for the AltaVista search ⟨http://www.altavista.digital.com/⟩ *Japanese and internment,* you get the following (from 5/4/98 search):

> About 1100931 documents match your query.

True, the sites are rated or graded, with the best presented first. But your own idea about what's best may not match the rating of the list. You will have to do lots of browsing or else—the better path—you will need to narrow down and/or experiment with other search words and phrases. By refining and altering the words and phrases for the search, you can make the search more specific and exclude sites not relevant to your direct interest.

- Each search engine has its own forms and criteria; and each has its own categories and indexes. Consult the Help pages for each search engine so that you will perform your search as effectively as possible.
- It is worth noting once again that Web sites are a supplement to print sources, not a substitute for them, and the search tools and bibliographical pathways to print sources are now easier to negotiate than are those for the WWW.
- Keeping this point in mind, we recommend to students that for each WWW site they consult (e.g., the Camp Harmony site), they should consult three print sources.

EVALUATING SOURCES ON THE WORLD WIDE WEB

The case study we have presented in this chapter proves the value of integrating literary analysis and historical research. It also shows that for sources on the World Wide Web, as with print sources, you must evaluate what you have located and gauge how much or how little it will contribute to your literary analysis and argument. In the words of one reference librarian, Joan Stockard (Wellesley College), "The most serious mistake students make when they use the Internet for research is to assume everything is of equal (and acceptable) quality. They need to establish who wrote the material, the qualifications of the author to write on the topic, whether any bias is likely, how current the information is, and how other resources compare."

 ## Checklist: A Review of Using the WWW

✔ *Focus* the topic of your research as precisely as you can before you embark on a WWW search. Lots of surfing and browsing can sometimes turn up good material, but using the WWW without a focus can prove distracting and unproductive. It takes you away from library research (where the results might be better) and from the actual planning and writing of the paper.
✔ Ask the following questions:

- Does this site or page look like it can help me in my assignment?
- Whose site or page is this?
- The intended audience?
- Point of view? Signs of a specific slant or bias?
- Detail, depth, and quality of the material presented?
- Well-constructed and well-organized?
- Is the text well-written?
- Can this WWW information be corroborated or supported by print sources?
- When was the site or page made available? Has it been recently revised or updated? *Note:* Your browser will enable you to get this information; if you are using Netscape 4.01, for example, go to View, and choose Page Info.
- Can the person or institution, company, or agency responsible for this site or page receive e-mail comments, questions, criticisms?

DOCUMENTATION: CITING A WWW SOURCE

Scholars and reference librarians have not reached a consensus about the correct form—what should be included, and in what order—for the citation of WWW sources. But all agree on two principles: (1) Give as much information as you can; (2) Make certain that your readers can retrieve the source themselves—which means that you should check the URL carefully. For accuracy's sake, it is a good idea to copy the URL from the Location line of your browser and paste it into your list of works cited.

✔ Checklist: Citing WWW Sources

Provide the following information:
- ✔ Author
- ✔ Title
- ✔ Publication information
- ✔ Title of archive or database
- ✔ Date (if given) when the site was posted; sometimes termed the "revision" or "modification" date
- ✔ Name of institution/organization that supports or is associated with this site
- ✔ Date that you accessed this source
- ✔ URL

Here, for example, is how you would cite the letter written by an internee that we quoted on page 1350:

> Letter (name withheld) to Elizabeth Bayley Willis. April 11, 1943. Elizabeth Bayley Willis Papers. Box 1. Manuscripts and University Archives, University of Washington Libraries. Online. WWW 27 February 1998 ⟨http://www.lib.washington.edu/exhibits/harmony/Documents/willis4.html⟩.

Many Web sites and pages are not prepared according to the style and form in which you want to cite them. Sometimes the name of the author is unknown, and other information may be missing or hard to find as well. It is worth repeating that while you may cite the source, including the URL, accurately, you cannot be certain that the site will exist at this URL (or at all) when your readers attempt to access it for themselves. These difficulties aside, perhaps the main point to remember is that a source on the WWW is as much a source as is a book or article that you can track down and read in the library. If you have made use of it, you must acknowledge that you have done so and include the bibliographical information, as fully as you can, in your list of works cited for the paper.

We will conclude this chapter by noting additional print and electronic resources that can aid you in a literary and historical project like the one we have undertaken on the Japanese-American internment.

ADDITIONAL PRINT AND ELECTRONIC SOURCES

Some Search Engines and Directories

All-In-One Search Page

http://www.albany.net/allinone/
> Gathers together search forms for all search engines.

The Argus Clearinghouse

http://www.clearinghouse.net
> A directory of subject guides to resources; especially useful for scholars.

Britannica Internet Guide

http://www.ebig.com/
> A directory of sites reviewed by the *Encyclopaedia Britannica*.

Galaxy

http://www.einet.net/
> Directory for resources in many subjects and fields, including Humanities–Literature.

Libweb:Library WWW Servers

http://sunsite.Berkeley.EDU/Libweb/
> List of 2,000+ home pages of libraries in over seventy countries

Yahoo!

http:/www.yahoo.com/
> A guide by subject to the WWW, with links to other sites and an array of search engines.

Print Directories

The following books include listings of Web sites on a wide range of topics; as the titles suggest, a number also supply tips and suggestions for effective research. Such books can be great time-savers in identifying for you the names and URLs of sites you can consult for your research. Rather than the hundreds, even thousands, of sites that a search engine might turn up, these books will be much more focused and selective in their listings. Their limitation is that however carefully they have been compiled, they always fall behind the ever-changing nature of the WWW.

Calishain, Tara, *Official Netscape Guide to Internet Research.* Research Triangle Park, N.C.: Ventana, 1997.

Clark, Michael. *Cultural Treasures of the Internet.* 2nd ed. Upper Saddle River, N.J.: Prentice Hall, 1997.

Hahn, Harley. *Harley Hahn's Internet & Web Yellow Pages: 1998.* 5th ed. Berkeley, Calif.: Osborne McGraw-Hill, 1997.

Krol, Ed, and Bruce C. Klopfenstein. *The Whole Internet User's Guide & Catalog.* Wadsworth, 1996.

Levine, John R., Carol Baroudi, and Margaret Levine Young. *The Internet for Dummies.* 4th ed. IDGB Books Worldwide, 1997.

Morris, Evan. *The Book Lover's Guide to the Internet.* New York: Fawcett, 1996.

Rositano, Dean J., Robert A. Rositano, and Jay Lee. *Que's Mega Web Directory.* Cupetino, Calif.: Que, 1996.

Stout, Rick. *The World Wide Web Complete Reference.* Berkeley, Calif.: Osborne McGraw-Hill, 1996.

The magazines *Yahoo!: Internet Life* and *The Web Magazine* review and compile lists of sites on a wide range of subjects. These are mass-circulation magazines, and thus many of their listings and reviews will not be pertinent to academic work. But the editors realize that the WWW is now used often for research, and increasingly they are providing advice and commentary on WWW resources in the humanities and other fields.

Print articles on Literature, History, and the WWW

These expert articles give overviews of WWW (and CD-ROM) resources for research, in particular for literature and history. The authors describe the kinds of material now available and supply bibliographies:

Gates, Joanne E. "Literature in Electronic Format: The Traditional English and American Canon." *Choice* April 1997: 1279–96.

Juhl, Beth. "Red, White, and Boolean: Electronic Resources for American History." *Choice* April 1998: 1313–26

New Technologies and the Practice of History. Special issue of *Perspectives: American Historical Association Newsletter* 36:2 (February 1998).

O'Malley, Michael, and Roy Rosenzweig. "Brave New World or Blind Alley?: American History on the World Wide Web." *The Journal of American History* 84: 1 (June 1997).

The Web Issue. Special supplement of *Choice* 34 (1997).

These following sites, prepared by research librarians, provide excellent advice for evaluating WWW sites and materials they contain:

Evaluating Internet Resources **(University at Albany Libraries)**

http://www.albany.edu/library/internet/evaluate.html

Thinking Critically about World Wide Web Resources **(UCLA College Library)**

http://www.library.ucla.edu/libraries/college/instruct/critical.htm

Thinking Critically about Discipline-Based World Wide Web Resources **(UCLA College Library)**

http://www.library.ucla.edu/libraries/college/instruct/discp.htm

Recommended WWW Sites for Scholarly Citation and the Internet/WWW

Longman Web site

http://longman.awl.com/englishpages/
> Includes a range of resources in five areas: Online Citation Guide; Composition; Literature; Basic Skills; Technical Writing.

MLA on the Web

http://www.mla.org/
> Includes a link to a site of guidelines for MLA (Modern Language Association) documentation style, for example, Citing Sources from the World Wide Web.

Literary Research: Print and Electronic Resources

The more you gain experience as a student and writer in literature courses, the more you will want to know about reference and bibliographical works for your field. We described a number of print and electronic sources in Appendices B and C. Here is a supplementary list and guide that will direct you to yet more resources in both print and electronic forms.

LITERATURE—PRINT REFERENCE SOURCES

Oxford University Press has published many volumes in its *Companion* reference series, quite a few of them keyed to literary subjects. Each title begins with the words *The Oxford Companion to. . . .*

The series includes: *African American Literature* (1997), *American Literature* (6th ed., 1995), *American Theater* (2nd ed., 1992), *English Language* (1992), *English Literature* (5th ed., rev., 1995), *Theater* (4th ed., 1983), *Twentieth-Century Literature in English* (1996), *Twentieth-Century Poetry in English* (1994), and *Women's Writing in the United States* (1995).

There are also *Oxford Companion* volumes for: *Australian Literature* (2nd ed., 1994), the Bible (1993), *Canadian Literature* (1983), *Children's Literature* (1984), *Classical Literature* (1989), *Film* (1976), *German Literature* (3rd ed., 1997), *Irish Literature* (1996), *Literature in French* (1995), and *Spanish Literature* (1978).

Cambridge University Press also publishes many reference books, including its *Cambridge Guide* series; each title begins with the words *The Cambridge Guide to. . .*: *African and Caribbean Theatre* (1994), *American Theatre* (1993), *Asian Theatre* (1993), *Literature in English* (1988), and the *Theatre* (1992).

See also:

The Bloomsbury Guide to Women's Literature. Ed. Claire Buck. New York: Prentice Hall, 1992.

Encyclopedia of Post-Colonial Literatures in English. 2 vols. Ed. Eugene Benson and L. W. Conolly. New York: Routledge, 1994.

The Feminist Companion to Literature in English: Women Writers from the Middle Ages to the Present. Ed. Virginia Blain, Isobel Grundy, and Patricia Clements. New Haven: Yale UP, 1990.

For more on the literatures of other nations:

Encyclopedia of World Literature in the Twentieth Century. Ed.
Leonard S. Klein. 4 vols. New York: Continuum, 1983.

European Writers. 7 vols. Ed. George Stade and William T. Jackson.
New York: Macmillan, 1983–85.

The New Guide to Modern World Literature. 4 vols. Ed. Martin Sey-
mour-Smith. New York: Peter Bedrick, 1970; rpt. 1985.

The Penguin Companion to World Literature. 4 vols. 1969–71.
This work covers American, English, European, African, Asian, and classical
literature.

Other Reference Resources

*American Women Writers: A Critical Reference Guide from Colonial
Times to the Present.* 4 vols. Ed. Lina Mainero. New York: Ungar,
1979–82; supplement, 1994.

Contemporary Literary Criticism. Detroit: Gale, 1973–.
This series, still in progress, runs to many volumes. Brief biographies, plus extensive selections from reviews and critical essays.

Dictionary of American Biography. 22 vols. New York, 1928–58, with
supplements published since.

Dictionary of National Biography. 22 vols. London, 1908–09, with
multivolume supplements published since.

Dictionary of Literary Biography. Detroit: Gale, 1978–.
Many volumes, series in progress. Detailed biographies of American, British,
and foreign-language literary authors, as well as critics, journalists, historians.
Includes critical analysis of their writings and primary and secondary bibliographies.

The Oxford English Dictionary 2nd. ed. Oxford: Clarendon, 1989;
available online and CD-ROM.
The *OED* defines words historically from time of first appearance, and supported by quotations.

Bibliographies

For extensive bibliographical coverage (to supplement the *MLA International
Bibliography*) in a variety of literary subjects and fields:

American Literary Scholarship. Durham, N.C.: Duke UP, 1963–.
Published annually, bibliographical essays.

American Literature and Language: A Guide to Information Sources.
Detroit: Gale, 1982.

Annual Bibliography of English Language and Literature. Cambridge: Modern Humanities Research Association, 1921–.
Well-indexed; covers books, articles, dissertations, and pamphlets on English
and American literatures.

Bibliographic Index: A Cumulative Bibliography of Bibliographies. New York: Wilson, 1937–; online 1984–.
Lists bibliographies published as books, parts of books, or in periodicals (coverage, 2,000+ periodicals, including foreign languages).

Bibliographical Guide to the Study of the Literature of the USA. Ed. Clarence Godhes and Sanford E. Marovitz. 5th ed. Durham, N.C.: Duke UP, 1984.

Bibliography of Bibliographies in American Literature. Ed. Charles H. Nilon. New York: Bowker, 1970.

Bibliography of British Literary Bibliographies. 2nd ed. Ed. Trevor H. Howard-Hill. Oxford: Clarendon, 1986.
Lists bibliographies for English literature that were published after 1890; covers authors from 1475 to the present.

A Guide to Basic Information Sources in English Literature. By Paul Doyle. New York, Wiley, 1976.
Focuses on English and American literature, but some coverage of Australian, Canadian, and Irish literature.

A Guide to English and American Literature. 3rd ed. By F. W. Bateson and Harrison T. Meserole. 3rd ed. New York: Longman, 1976.
Literary history and bibliography.

A Guide to Serial Bibliographies for Modern Literatures. 2nd ed. By William A. Wortman. New York: MLA, 1995.

Literary Criticism Index. 2nd ed. By Alan R. Weiner and Spencer Means. Metuchen, N.J.: Scarecrow, 1994.
Indexes 85 bibliographies of literary criticism.

A Literary History of England. 2nd ed. Ed. Albert C. Baugh. New York: Appleton-Century-Crofts, 1967.
Literary history by period, with extensive (if dated) bibliographies.

Literary History of the United States Ed. Robert E. Spiller et al. 4th ed. 2 vols. New York: Macmillan, 1974. Supplement with: *Columbia Literary History of the United States,* ed. Emory Elliot et al. New York: Columbia UP, 1988.
Both present historical coverage of authors, periods, and movements. The *Literary History* includes bibliographies; the *Columbia* history does not.

The New Cambridge Bibliography of English Literature. 5 vols. Cambridge, Eng.: Cambridge UP, 1969–77.

The Oxford History of English Literature. 13 vols. 1945–.
Histories of literary periods, supplemented by full bibliographies.

Problems in Literary Research: A Guide to Selected Reference Works. 4th ed. By Dorothea Kehler. Lanham: Scarecrow, 1996.

A Research Guide for Undergraduate Students. By Nancy L. Baker and Nancy Huling. 4th ed. New York: MLA, 1995.

Selective Bibliography for the Study of English and American Literature. 6th ed. Ed. Richard D. Altick and Andrew Wright. New York: Macmillan, 1979.
Lists bibliographies and reference works; includes a glossary of bibliographic and literary terms.

The Year's Work in English Studies. London: Blackwell, 1921-.

>   Bibliographical essays on studies in books and periodicals on English and American literatures.

Note: You can locate additional dictionaries, encyclopedias, bibliographies, and reference tools by checking in the Subject category of the library catalog:

literature—dictionaries
literature—bio bibliography

LITERATURE—ELECTRONIC SOURCES

For research in the Humanities, with an emphasis on literary studies:

The Electronic Text Center at the University of Virginia

http://etext.lib.virginia.edu/

>   Some databases are restricted, but access to others is free to all users; for example, British Poetry 1780-1910.

The English Server (Carnegie Mellon University)

http://english-www.hss.cmu.edu/

>   Wide-ranging index to electronic texts, sites, and links in fiction, drama, feminism, cultural theory, and many other subject areas.

Literature Webliography

http://www.lib.lsu.edu/hum/lit.html

>   Includes general guides, bibliographies, dictionaries, and other subject headings.

On-Line Literary Resources

http://www.english.upenn.edu/[~asciitilde]jlynch/Lit/

Project Bartleby Archive (Columbia University)

http://www.cc.columbia.edu/acis/bartleby/

>   Electronic archive of literary texts (e.g., the complete works of Shelley and Wordsworth); the editions used are in the public domain, hence are not always as reliable as a recent scholarly edition.

The Voice of the Shuttle: Web Page for Humanities Research

http://humanitas.ucsb.edu/

>   Well-organized guide to sites in literary studies.

Some of the best WWW sites are devoted to authors; often these are maintained and updated by scholars or by persons affiliated with a professional organization or academic institution, research library, museum, or archive.

There are several good Shakespeare sites, for example. One of the resources they offer is keyword searching through the complete works, individual plays, or any subset of them (e.g., the tragedies).

The Collected Works of Shakespeare
http://www.gh.cs.su.oz.au/~matty/Shakespeare/Shakespeare.html

Mr. William Shakespeare and the Internet
http://daphne.palomar.edu/shakespeare/

Shakespeare
http://the-tech.mit.edu/Shakespeare/works.html

Note: A Yahoo! search (31 January 1998), for the words *Hamlet and quarto and folio* turned up one item:

Enfolded Hamlet: Enfolded Texts of the Second Quarto and First Folio
http://narp.oed.com/enfolded.html

This site, by Bernice Kliman, enables you to view the Second Quarto (1604) or First Folio (1623) text, or both at the same time. It is the kind of outstanding source that with careful searching, and some luck, you might be able to locate.
Also recommended:

The Julius Caesar Site
http://www.perseus.tufts.edu/JC/

This wonderful site includes (as of 12 February 1998) the Variorum edition of the play, a modern edition, classical sources—and much more is to come. We learned about it through an electronic mailing list to which we belong. The site does not appear in any search engine for the phrase *"Julius Caesar" and Shakespeare*. Nor does any search engine turn it up even if you conduct the search using the exact name of the site.

Other Useful Sites on Authors

Herman Melville: *The Life and Works of Herman Melville*
http://www.melville.org/

John Milton: *The Milton-L Home Page*
http://www.urich.edu/[~asciitilde]creamer/milton.html

Mark Twain
http://marktwain.miningco.com/

Sites for three authors discussed in this book are:

Langston Hughes
http://history.hanover.edu/20th/hughes.htm

James Joyce: *The Brazen Head: A James Joyce Public House*
http://rpg.net/quail/libyrinth/joyce/

Eudora Welty: *Eudora's Wide Net*
http://www.geocities.com/BourbonStreet/3156/welty.html

You can locate many more author sites by checking the directories at Yahoo! and *The Voice of the Shuttle.*
Sites for other fields and disciplines include:

Bible Gateway

http://bible.gospelcom.net/bible?
   Search the Bible in nine languages and multiple Bible versions.

The Internet Movie Database

http://www.us.imdb.com/
   A comprehensive, detailed database of more than 125,000 movies.

Perseus Project **(Classics Department, Tufts University)**

http://www.perseus.tufts.edu/
   Includes Greek and Latin texts in the original and in translation, and many
   other resources for classical art, literature, archaeology.

HISTORY—REFERENCE AND BIBLIOGRAPHY SOURCES

America: History and Life. Santa Barbara, Calif.: ABC-Clio, 1964–.
   Published annually in three volumes: article abstracts and citations, index to
   book reviews, and bibliography.

American Historical Association Guide to Historical Literature. 2
   vols. Ed. Mary Beth Norton. 3rd ed. New York: Oxford UP, 1995.

The Columbia Companion to British History. Ed. Juliet Gardiner and
   Neil Wenborn. New York: Columbia UP, 1997.

A Companion to American Thought. Ed. Richard Wightman Fox and
   James T. Kloppenberg. Cambridge, Mass.: Blackwell, 1995.

Encyclopedia of American History. 7th ed. Ed. Jeffrey B. Morris and
   Richard B. Morris. New York: HarperCollins, 1996.

Encyclopedia of American Social History. 3 vols. Ed. Mary Kupiec Cay-
   ton. New York: Scribner's, 1993.

Harvard Guide to American History. 2 vols. Ed. Frank B. Freidel. Cambridge: Harvard UP, 1980.

The Oxford Companion to British History. Ed. John Cannon. New York: Oxford UP, 1997.

The Reader's Companion to American History. Ed. Eric Foner and John A. Garraty. Boston: Houghton Mifflin, 1991.

WWW Sites for History

Index of Resources for History
http://kuhttp.cc.ukans.edu/history/index.html.

Library of Congress Home Page
http://www.loc.gov/
Includes the site *American Memory,* a treasury of documents, photographs, works of art, films, and sound recordings.

Organization of American Historians
http://www.indiana.edu/[~asciitilde]oah/
Includes excellent, up-to-date list of Web sites for historians.

The Smithsonian Institution Home Page
http://www.si.edu/newstart.htm

For news and current events take a look at:

Time Warner's Pathfinder Network
http://www.pathfinder.com/welcome/
News and links to CNN, *Time, Fortune,* and other magazines and news sources.

TotalNEWS
http://www.totalnews.com/
News and links to many national and international news services; allows for keyword searches.

Periodicals: Print and Electronic Sources

MLA Directory of Periodicals: A Guide to Journals and Series in Languages and Literatures 1993-95: Complete International Listings
Standard source for information about journals and series concerned with literature, language, linguistics, and folklore.

Ulrich's Periodicals Directory
Multivolume series, regularly updated; classified guide to a selected list of current periodicals, foreign and domestic.

Directory of Electronic Journals, Newsletters, and Academic Discussion Lists. 6th ed., 1996.

Directory of Online Journals and Periodicals
http://eserver.org/journals/

FOR GENERAL BIBLIOGRAPHY IN THE HUMANITIES

Arts and Humanities Citation Index. Philadelphia: Institute for Scientific Information, 1977–.
>   Index listing names of authors cited by other writers in their own work.

Biography Index. New York: Wilson, 1946–; online, 1984–.
>   Information on persons written about in books and 1000+ scholarly journals and popular magazines.

Book Review Digest. 1905–; CD-ROM and online, 1983–.
>   Includes brief excerpts from the reviews.

Book Review Index. 1965–; online, 1969–.
>   Lists book reviews, in 500+ periodicals, of fiction and nonfiction books.

Current Book Review Citations. 1976–

Essay and General Literature Index. New York: Wilson, 1900–.
>   Locates often hard-to-find articles and chapters in or parts of books; helpful in identifying items not covered by the usual key word and title searches.

Expanded Humanities Index. 1984–.
>   Citations to articles and reviews; covers 1500+ scholarly and popular periodicals.

Historical Abstracts. 1955–; CD-ROM, 1982–.

Humanities Index. 1974–; online, 1984–.
>   Covers more than 300 journals in literature, history, philosophy, and other subjects.

An Index to Book Reviews in the Humanities. 1969–90.
>   Lists book reviews in 700+ scholarly periodicals.

The Readers' Guide to Periodical Literature. 1900–; CD-ROM and online, 1983–.
>   Covers 200+ popular periodicals. Best for current topics and issues.

For periodicals not covered by *The Readers' Guide* look at:

Access: The Supplementary Index to Periodicals (1979–)

For radical and alternative publications, go to:

The Alternative Press Index (1970–).

Specialized periodical indexes include:

Index to Black Periodicals. 1984–.
>   Scholarly and popular articles about African Americans.

Left Index. 1982–.
>   Index by author and subject to 80+ radical, Marxist, and left-wing periodicals.

Chicano Index. 1967–; before 1989, titled *Chicano Periodical Index.*

For facts, statistics, and other information, see:

Statistical Abstract of the United States. U.S. Bureau of the Census. Washington, D.C.: Government Printing Office.

World Almanac and Book of Facts.

Information Please Almanac, Atlas, and Yearbook.

Statistical Abstract—U.S. Census Bureau.
http://www.census.gov/

Nexis. 1977-.
> Online service, indexes 50+ national newspapers.

FOR EVALUATING THE POINT OF VIEW, THE CONTENT, AND THE INTENDED AUDIENCE OF SOURCES

Gale Directory of Publications and Broadcast Media (1990).
> Focuses on newspapers and magazines.

Magazines for Libraries (1992).
> Lists 6,500 periodicals, arranged by academic discipline.

Note: There are thousands of electronic-mail discussion lists through which professional scholars, students, and nonacademic readers share information and ideas about a subject. As your interests develop—perhaps you find you have a special interest in Shakespeare, or American literature, or literary theory—you might decide to join one of them. There are a number of WWW sites for the names, subject areas, and criteria for these lists:

The Directory of Scholarly and Professional E-Conferences
http://www.n2h2.com/KOVACS/

Tile.net/lists
http://www.tile.net/listserv/
> Reference source for Internet discussion lists.

OTHER RESOURCES

Encyclopedia of Associations. 32nd ed. Ed. Sandra Jaszczak. Detroit: Gale, 1997, published in three parts.
> Find out if there is an organization devoted to a subject that interests you; it might provide good leads or resources for your work.

Research Centers Directory, 22nd ed. 2 vols. Ed. Anthony Gerring. Detroit: Gale, 1997.
> Lists centers for scholarly and other kinds of research.

WHAT DOES YOUR OWN INSTITUTION OFFER?

Colleges and universities now offer as part of their resources for research a wide range of electronic materials and databases. Ask the reference librarian about them, take a library tutorial, browse in and examine both the Library's home page and the online catalog's options and directories.

At Wellesley College, the Library's home page first offers a general list of Internet Research Resources, and a second list follows that is arranged according to department or interdisciplinary program. The majority of these are open or free sites, available to anyone with a connection to the WWW. But others are by "subscription only"—which means that only members of this academic community can access them.

One of the best sites, to which your institution may subscribe, is the *First-Search* commercial database service, and it is available through both a telnet connection (which connects two computers on the Internet) and on the WWW.

FirstSearch enables you to find books, articles, theses, films, computer software, and other types of material for just about any field, subject, or topic.

Its categories include:

Arts & Humanities
Business & Economics
Conferences & Proceedings
Consumer Affairs & People
Education
Engineering & Technology
General & Reference
General Science
Life Sciences
Medicine & Health
News & Current Events
Public Affairs & Law
Social Sciences

Within Arts & Humanities, you will find:

WorldCat: Books and other materials in libraries worldwide.
Article 1st: Index of articles from nearly 12,500 journals.
Contents 1st: Table of contents of nearly 12,500 journals.
A&H Search: Arts & Humanities Search. A citation index.
ArtAbstracts: Leading publications in the world of the arts.
HumanitiesAbs: An index of articles in the humanities.
MLA: Literature, languages, linguistics, folklore.
PerContentsIndx: Periodicals Contents Index—1961–1991.
RILM: RILM Abstracts of Music Literature.

The General & Reference category includes (this is only a partial list):

BookRevDigst: Reviews of fiction and nonfiction books.
BooksInPrint: R. R. Bowker's Books In Print.
Diss: Dissertation Abstracts Online.

Note: Both *Books in Print* (New York: Bowker, 1948–) and the *Subject Guide to Books in Print* (New York: Bowker, 1957–) can be helpful in locating new books on the subject of your research.

Your school may also subscribe to more specialized electronic services and WWW sites for literature and the humanities. For example:

Literature On-Line (Chadwyck-Healey Ltd.)

http://lion.chadwyck.com/

This site offers an extraordinary array of literary databases, reference works, and lists of Web sites for literature. Also included are "featured" databases; in February 1998, one of these was *LionHeart,* a "fully searchable subset of 1,000 love poems extracted from English, American, and African American poetry, featuring Shakespeare, Keats, Donne, Browning, and others."

APPENDIX

Glossary of Literary Terms

The terms briefly defined here are for the most part more fully defined earlier in the text. Hence many of the entries below are followed by page references to the earlier discussions.

accent stress given to a syllable (415)

act a major division of a play

action (1) the happenings in a narrative or drama, usually physical events (*B* marries *C, D* kills *E*), but also mental changes (*F* moves from innocence to experience); in short, the answer to the question, "What happens?" (2) less commonly, the theme or underlying idea of a work (270)

allegory a work in which concrete elements (for instance, a pilgrim, a road, a splendid city) stand for abstractions (humanity, life, salvation), usually in an unambiguous, one-to-one relationship. The literal items (the pilgrim, and so on) thus convey a meaning, which is usually moral, religious, or political. To take a nonliterary example: The Statue of Liberty holds a torch (enlightenment, showing the rest of the world the way to freedom), and at her feet are broken chains (tyranny overcome). A caution: Not all of the details in an allegorical work are meant to be interpreted. For example, the hollowness of the Statue of Liberty does not stand for the insubstantiality or emptiness of liberty.

alliteration repetition of consonant sounds, especially at the beginnings of words (*f*ree, *f*orm, *ph*antom) (419)

allusion an indirect reference; thus when Lincoln spoke of "a nation dedicated to the proposition that all men are created equal," he was making an allusion to the Declaration of Independence.

ambiguity multiplicity of meaning, often deliberate, that leaves the reader uncertain about the intended significance

anagnorisis a recognition or discovery, especially in tragedy—for example when the hero understands the reason for his or her fall (268)

analysis an examination, which usually proceeds by separating the object of study into parts (25, 61, 73-98, 150)

anapest a metrical foot consisting of two unaccented syllables followed by an accented one. Example, showing three anapests: "As I came / to the edge / of the wood" (416)

anecdote a short narrative, usually reporting an amusing event in the life of an important person

antagonist a character or force that opposes (literally, "wrestles") the protagonist (the main character). Thus, in *Hamlet* the antagonist is King Claudius, the protagonist is Hamlet; in *Antigonê,* the antagonist is Creon, the protagonist Antigonê.

antecedent action happenings (especially in a play) that occurred before the present action (270)

apostrophe address to an absent figure or to a thing as if it were present and could listen. Example: "O rose, thou art sick!" (405)

approximate rhyme see *half-rhyme*

archetype a theme, image, motive, or pattern that occurs so often in literary works it seems to be universal. Examples: a dark forest (for mental confusion), the sun (for illumination) (503-04)

aside in the theater, words spoken by a character in the presence of other characters, but directed to the spectators—i.e., understood by the audience to be inaudible to the other characters

assonance repetition of similar vowel sounds in stressed syllables. Example: *light/bride* (419)

atmosphere the emotional tone (for instance, joy, or horror) in a work, most often established by the setting (195)

ballad a short narrative poem, especially one that is sung or recited, often in a stanza of four lines, with 8, 6, 8, 6 syllables, with the second and fourth lines rhyming. A **folk** or **popular ballad** is a narrative song that has been transmitted orally by what used to be called "the folk"; a **literary ballad** is a conscious imitation (without music) of such a work, often with complex symbolism. (46-47, 422-23)

blank verse unrhymed iambic pentameter—that is, unrhymed lines of ten syllables, with every second syllable stressed (420)

cacophony an unpleasant combination of sounds

caesura a strong pause within a line of verse (417)

canon a term originally used to refer to those books accepted as Holy Scripture by the Christian church. The term has come to be applied to literary works thought to have a special merit by a given culture—for instance, the body of literature traditionally taught in colleges and universities. Such works are sometimes called "classics" and their authors are "major authors." As conceived in the United States until recently, the canon consisted chiefly of works by dead white European and American males—partly, of course, because middle-class and upper-class white males were in fact the people who did most of the writing in the Western Hemisphere, but also because white males (for instance, college professors) were the people who chiefly established the canon. Not surprisingly the canon-makers valued (or valorized or "privileged") writings that revealed, asserted, or reinforced the canon-makers own values. From about the 1960s feminists and Marxists and others argued that these works had been regarded as central not because they were inherently better than other works but because they reflected the interests of the dominant culture, and that other work, such as slave narratives and the diaries of women, had been "marginalized."

In fact, the literary canon has never been static (in contrast to the biblical canon, which has not changed for more than a thousand years), but it is true that certain authors, such as Homer, Chaucer, and Shakespeare have been permanent fixtures. Why? Partly because they do indeed support the values of those who in large measure control the high cultural purse strings, and perhaps partly because these books are rich enough to invite constant reinterpretation from age to age—that is, to allow each generation to find its needs and its values in them. (37-38, 472-73)

catastrophe the concluding action, especially in a tragedy

catharsis Aristotle's term for the purgation or purification of the pity and terror supposedly experienced while witnessing a tragedy

character (1) a person in a literary work (Romeo); (2) the personality of such a figure (sentimental lover, or whatever). Characters (in the first sense) are sometimes classified as either "flat" (one-dimensional) or "round" (fully realized, complex). (192-95, 201, 273, 276-77)

characterization the presentation of a character, whether by direct description, by showing the character in action, or by the presentation of other characters who help to define each other (193-94)

cliché an expression that through overuse has ceased to be effective. Examples: *acid test, sigh of relief, the proud possessor*

climax the culmination of a conflict; a turning point, often the point of greatest tension in a plot (270)

comedy a literary work, especially a play, characterized by humor and by a happy ending (267-69)

comparison and contrast to compare is strictly to note similarities; to contrast is to note differences. But *compare* is now often used for both activities. (79-84)

complication an entanglement in a narrative or dramatic work that causes a conflict

conflict a struggle between a character and some obstacle (for example, another character or fate) or between internal forces, such as divided loyalties (270, 276)

connotation the associations (suggestions, overtones) of a word or expression. Thus *seventy* and *three score and ten* both mean "one more than sixty-nine," but because *three score and ten* is a biblical expression, it has an association of holiness; see also *denotation*. (405)

consistency building the process engaged in during the act of reading, of reevaluating the details that one has just read in order to make them consistent with the new information that the text is providing (6)

consonance repetition of consonant sounds, especially in stressed syllables. Also called *half-rhyme* or slant rhyme. Example: *arouse/doze* (419)

convention a pattern (for instance, the 14-line poem, or sonnet) or motif (for instance, the bumbling police officer in detective fiction) or other device occurring so often that it is taken for granted. Thus it is a convention that actors in a performance of *Julius Caesar* are understood to be speaking Latin, though in fact they are speaking English. Similarly, the soliloquy (a character alone on the stage speaks his or her thoughts aloud) is a convention, for in real life sane people rarely talk aloud to themselves.

couplet a pair of lines of verse, usually rhyming (419)

crisis a high point in the conflict that leads to the turning point (270)

criticism the analysis or evaluation of a literary work (495-518)

cultural criticism criticism that sets literature in a social context, often of economics or politics or gender. Borrowing some of the methods of anthropology, cultural criticism usually extends the canon to include popular material—for instance, comic books and soap operas

dactyl a metrical foot consisting of a stressed syllable followed by two unstressed syllables. Example: *underwear* (416)

deconstruction a critical approach that assumes language is unstable and ambiguous and is therefore inherently contradictory. Because authors cannot control their language, texts reveal more than their authors are aware of. For instance, texts (like such institutions as the law, the churches, and the schools) are likely, when closely scrutinized, to reveal connections to a society's economic system, even though the authors may have believed they were outside of the system. (499-500)

denotation the dictionary meaning of a word. Thus *soap opera* and *daytime serial* have the same denotation, but the connotations (associations, emotional overtones) of *soap opera* are less favorable. (405)

dénouement the resolution or the outcome (literally, the "unknotting") of a plot (270)

deus ex machina literally, "a god out of a machine"; any unexpected and artificial way of resolving the plot—for example, by introducing a rich uncle, thought to be dead, who arrives on the scene and pays the debts that otherwise would overwhelm the young hero

dialogue exchange of words between characters; speech

diction the choice of vocabulary and of sentence structure. There is a difference in diction between "One never knows" and "You never can tell." (399-400)

didactic pertaining to teaching; having a moral purpose

dimeter a line of poetry containing two feet

discovery see *anagnorisis*

drama (1) a play; (2) conflict or tension, as in "The story lacks drama."

dramatic irony see *irony*

dramatic monologue a poem spoken entirely by one character but addressed to one or more other characters whose presence is strongly felt

effaced narrator a narrator who reports but who does not editorialize or enter into the minds of any of the characters in the story

elegy a lyric poem, usually a meditation on a death

elision omission (usually of a vowel or unstressed syllable), as in *o'er* (for *over*) and in "Th' inevitable hour"

end rhyme identical sounds at the ends of lines of poetry (418)

end-stopped line a line of poetry that ends with a pause (usually marked by a comma, semicolon, or period) because the grammatical structure and the sense reach (at least to some degree) completion. It is contrasted with a *run-on line*. (417)

English (or Shakespearean) sonnet a poem of 14 lines (three quatrains and a couplet), rhyming *ababcdcdefefgg* (420)

enjambment a line of poetry in which the grammatical and logical sense run on, without pause, into the next line or lines (417)

epic a long narrative, especially in verse, that usually records heroic material in an elevated style

epigram a brief, witty poem or saying

epigraph a quotation at the beginning of the work, just after the title, often giving a clue to the theme

epiphany a "showing forth," as when an action reveals a character with particular clarity

episode an incident or scene that has unity in itself but is also a part of a larger action

epistle a letter, in prose or verse

essay a work, usually in prose and usually fairly short, that purports to be true and that treats its subject tentatively. In most literary essays the reader's interest is as much in the speaker's personality as in any argument that is offered. (161–64)

euphony literally, "good sound," a pleasant combination of sounds

explication a line-by-line unfolding of the meaning of a text (60–67, 84, 411–14)

exposition a setting forth of information. In fiction and drama, introductory material introducing characters and the situation; in an essay, the presentation of information, as opposed to the telling of a story or the setting forth of an argument. (162, 270)

eye rhyme words that look as though they rhyme, but do not rhyme when pronounced. Example: *come/home* (418)

fable a short story (often involving speaking animals) with an easily grasped moral

farce comedy based not on clever language or on subtleties of characters but on broadly humorous situations (for instance, a man mistakenly enters the women's locker room)

feminine rhyme a rhyme of two or more syllables, with the stress falling on a syllable other than the last. Examples: *fatter/batter, tenderly/slenderly* (418)

feminist criticism an approach especially concerned with analyzing the depiction of women in literature—what images do male authors present of female characters?—and also with the reappraisal of work by female authors (508–11)

fiction an imaginative work, usually a prose narrative (novel, short story), that reports incidents that did not in fact occur. The term may include all works that invent a world, such as a lyric poem or a play.

figurative language words intended to be understood in a way that is other than literal. Thus *lemon* used literally refers to a citrus fruit, but *lemon* used figuratively refers to a defective machine, especially a defective automobile. Other examples: "He's a beast." "She's a witch." "A sea of troubles." Literally, such expressions are nonsense, but writers use them to express meanings inexpressible in literal speech. Among the commonest kinds of figures of speech are *apostrophe, metaphor,* and *simile* (see the discussions of these words in this glossary). (403–06)

flashback an interruption in a narrative that presents an earlier episode

flat character a one-dimensional character (for instance, the figure who is only and always the jealous husband or the flirtatious wife) as opposed to a round or many-sided character (193)

fly-on-the-wall narrator a narrator who never editorializes and never enters a character's mind but reports only what is said and done (199)

foil a character who makes a contrast with another, especially a minor character who helps to set off a major character (194)

foot a metrical unit, consisting of two or three syllables, with a specified arrangement of the stressed syllable or syllables. Thus the iambic foot consists of an unstressed syllable followed by a stressed syllable. (416)

foreshadowing suggestions of what is to come (194–95)

formalist criticism analysis that assumes a work of art is a constructed object with a stable meaning that can be ascertained by studying the relationships between the elements of the work. Thus a poem is like a chair: a chair *can* of course be stood on, or used for firewood, but it was created with a specific purpose that was evident and remains evident to all viewers. (497–99)

free verse poetry in lines of irregular length, usually unrhymed (420)

gap a term from reader-response criticism, referring to a reader's perception that something is unstated in the text, requiring the reader to fill in the material—for instance, to draw a conclusion as to why a character behaves as she does. Filling in the gaps is a matter of "consistency building." Different readers of course may fill the gaps differently, and readers may even differ as to whether a gap exists at a particular point in the text. (6, 502)

gay criticism see *gender criticism*

gender criticism criticism concerned especially with alleged differences in the ways that males and females read and write, and also with the representations of gender (straight, bisexual, gay, lesbian) in literature (508-14)

genre kind or type, roughly analogous to the biological term *species*. The four chief literary genres are nonfiction, fiction, poetry, and drama, but these can be subdivided into further genres. Thus fiction obviously can be divided into the short story and the novel, and drama obviously can be divided into tragedy and comedy. But these can be still further divided—for instance, tragedy into heroic tragedy and bourgeois tragedy, comedy into romantic comedy and satirical comedy.

gesture physical movement, especially in a play (271-72)

haiku a Japanese form having three unrhymed lines of five, seven, and five syllables (434-35)

half-rhyme repetition in accented syllables of the final consonant sound but without identity in the preceding vowel sound; words of similar but not identical sound. Also called near rhyme, slant rhyme, approximate rhyme, and off-rhyme. See also *consonance*. Examples: *light/bet; affirm/perform* (418)

hamartia a flaw in the tragic hero, or an error made by the tragic hero (268)

heptameter a metrical line of seven feet (417)

hero, heroine the main character (not necessarily heroic or even admirable) in a work: cf. *protagonist*

heroic couplet an end-stopped pair of rhyming lines of iambic pentameter (419)

hexameter a metrical line of six feet (417)

historical criticism the attempt to illuminate a literary work by placing it in its historical context (504-05)

hubris, hybris a Greek word, usually translated as "overweening pride," "arrogance," "excessive ambition," and often said to be characteristic of tragic figures (267)

hyperbole figurative language using overstatement, as in "He died a thousand deaths" (407)

iamb, iambic a poetic foot consisting of an unaccented syllable followed by an accented one. Example: *alone* (416)

image, imagery imagery is established by language that appeals to the senses, especially sight ("deep blue sea") but also other senses ("tinkling bells," "perfumes of Arabia") (405-06)

indeterminacy a passage that careful readers agree is open to more than one interpretation. According to some poststructural critics, because language is unstable and because contexts can never be objectively viewed, all texts are indeterminate. (6, 502)

innocent eye a naive narrator in whose narration the reader sees more than the narrator sees

internal rhyme rhyme within a line (418)

interpretation the assignment of meaning to a text (455-68)

intertextuality all works show the influence of other works. If an author writes (say) a short story, no matter how original she thinks she is, she inevitably brings to her own story a knowledge of other stories—for example, a conception of what a short story is, and, speaking more generally, an idea of what a story (long or short, written or oral) is. In opposition to formalist critics, who see a literary work as an independent whole containing a fixed meaning, some contemporary critics emphasize the work's *intertextuality*—that is, its connections with a vast context of writings and indeed of all aspects of culture, and in part depending also on what the reader brings to the work. Because different readers bring different things, meaning is thus ever-changing. In this view, then, no text is self-sufficient, and no writer fully controls the meaning of the text. Because we are talking about connections of which the writer is unaware, and because "meaning" is in part the creation of the reader, the author is by no means an authority. Thus the critic should see a novel (for instance) in connection not only with other novels, past and present, but also in connection with other kinds of narratives, such as TV dramas and films, even though the author of the book lived before the age of film and TV. See Jay Clayton and Eric Rothstein, eds., *Influences and Intertextuality in Literary History* (1991).

irony a contrast of some sort. For instance, in **verbal irony** or **Socratic irony** (268n, 407), the contrast is between what is said and what is meant ("You're a great guy," meant bitterly). In **dramatic irony** or **Sophoclean irony** (also called **tragic irony**) (268), the contrast is between what is intended and what is accomplished (Macbeth usurps the throne, thinking he will then be happy, but the action leads him to misery), or between what the audience knows (a murderer waits in the bedroom) and what a character says (the victim enters the bedroom, innocently saying, "I think I'll have a long sleep").

Italian (or Petrarchan) sonnet a poem of 14 lines, consisting of an octave (rhyming *abbaabba*) and a sestet (usually *cdecde* or *cdccdc*) (420)

lesbian criticism see *gender criticism*

litotes a form of understatement in which an affirmation is made by means of a negation; thus "He was not underweight," meaning "He was grossly overweight."

lyric poem a short poem, often songlike, with the emphasis not on narrative but on the speaker's emotion or reverie

Marxist criticism the study of literature in the light of Karl Marx's view that economic forces, controlled by the dominant class, shape the literature (as well as the law, philosophy, religion, etc.) of a society (505–06)

masculine rhyme rhyme of one-syllable words (*lies/cries*) or, if more than one syllable, words ending with accented syllables (*behold/foretold*) (418)

mask a term used to designate the speaker of a poem, equivalent to *persona* or *voice* (397–400)

meaning critics seek to interpret "meaning," variously defined as what the writer intended the work to say about the world and human experience, or as what the work says to the reader irrespective of the writer's intention. Both versions imply that a literary work is a nut to be cracked, with a kernel that is to be extracted. Because few critics today hold that meaning is clear and unchanging, the tendency now is to say that a critic offers "an interpretation" or "a reading" rather than a "statement of the meaning of a work." Many critics today would say that an alleged interpretation is really a creation of meaning. (4–6, 34–37, 455–68)

melodrama a narrative, usually in dramatic form, involving threatening situations but ending happily. The characters are usually stock figures (virtuous heroine, villainous landlord).

metaphor a kind of figurative language equating one thing with another: "This novel is garbage" (a book is equated with discarded and probably inedible food), "a piercing cry" (a cry is equated with a spear or other sharp instrument) (404)

meter a pattern of stressed and unstressed syllables (416–18)

metonymy a kind of figurative language in which a word or phrase stands not for itself but for something closely related to it: *saber rattling* means "militaristic talk or action" (404)

monologue a relatively long, uninterrupted speech by a character

monometer a metrical line consisting of only one foot (417)

montage in film, quick cutting: in fiction, quick shifts

mood the atmosphere, usually created by descriptions of the settings and characters

motif a recurrent theme within a work, or a theme common to many works

motivation grounds for a character's action (194–95, 273)

myth (1) a traditional story reflecting primitive beliefs, especially explaining the mysteries of the natural world (why it rains, or the origin of mountains); (2) a body of belief, not necessarily false, especially as set forth by a writer. Thus one may speak of Yeats and Alice Walker as myth-makers, referring to the visions of reality that they set forth in their works.

myth criticism see *archetype*

narrative, narrator a narrative is a story (an anecdote, a novel); a narrator is one who tells a story (not the author, but the invented speaker of the story). On kinds of narrators, see *point of view.* (195–97, 201–02)

New Criticism a mid-twentieth-century movement (also called formalist criticism) that regarded a literary work as an independent, carefully constructed object; hence it made little or no use of the author's biography or of historical context and it relied chiefly on explication. (497–99)

New Historicism a school of criticism holding that the past cannot be known objectively. According to this view, because historians project their own "narrative"—their own invention or "construction"—on the happenings of the past, historical writings are not objective but are, at bottom, political statements. (506–07)

novel a long work of prose fiction, especially one that is relatively realistic

novella a work of prose fiction longer than a short story but shorter than a novel—say, about 40 to 80 pages

objective point of view a narrator reports but does not editorialize or enter into the minds of any of the characters in the story (199)

octave, octet an eight-line stanza, or the first eight lines of a sonnet, especially of an Italian sonnet (420)

octosyllabic couplet a pair of rhyming lines, each line with four iambic feet (419)

ode a lyric exalting someone (for instance, a hero) or something (for instance, a season)

off-rhyme see *half-rhyme*

omniscient narrator a speaker who knows the thoughts of all of the characters in the narrative (198)

onomatopoeia words (or the use of words) that sound like what they mean. Examples: *buzz, whirr* (419)

open form poetry whose form seems spontaneous rather than highly patterned

oxymoron a compact paradox, as in *a mute cry, a pleasing pain, proud humility*

parable a short narrative that is at least in part allegorical and that illustrates a moral or spiritual lesson (77–78)

paradox an apparent contradiction, as in Jesus's words "Whosoever will save his life shall lose it; but whosoever will lose his life for my sake, the same shall save it." (407)

paraphrase a restatement that sets forth an idea in diction other than that of the original (33, 134-35, 411)

parody a humorous imitation of a literary work, especially of its style (141-42)

pathos pity, sadness

pentameter a line of verse containing five feet (417)

peripeteia a reversal in the action (268)

persona literally, a mask; the "I" or speaker of a work, sometimes identified with the author but usually better regarded as the voice or mouthpiece created by the author (162-63, 397-400)

personification a kind of figurative language in which an inanimate object, animal, or other nonhuman is given human traits. Examples: *the creeping tide* (the tide is imagined as having feet), *the cruel sea* (the sea is imagined as having moral qualities) (404)

Petrarchan sonnet see *Italian sonnet*

plot the episodes in a narrative or dramatic work—that is, what happens. (But even a lyric poem can be said to have a plot; for instance, the speaker's mood changes from anger to resignation.) Sometimes *plot* is defined as the author's particular arrangement (sequence) of these episodes, and *story* is the episodes in their chronological sequence. Until recently it was widely believed that a good plot had a logical structure: *A* caused *B* (*B* did not simply happen to follow *A*), but in the last few decades some critics have argued that such a concept merely represents the white male's view of experience. (191-92, 200-01, 276)

poem an imaginative work in meter or in free verse, usually employing figurative language (397-422)

point of view the perspective from which a story is told—for example, by a major character or a minor character or a fly on the wall; see also *narrative, narrator, omniscient narrator* (197-99, 201-02)

postmodernism the term came into prominence in the 1960s, to distinguish the contemporary experimental writing of such authors as Samuel Beckett and Jorge Luis Borges from such early twentieth-century classics of modernism as James Joyce's *Ulysses* (1922) and T. S. Eliot's *The Waste Land* (1922). Although the classic modernists had been thought to be revolutionary in their day, after World War II they seemed to be conservative, and their works seemed remote from today's society with its new interests in such things as feminism, gay and lesbian rights, and pop culture. Postmodernist literature, though widely varied and not always clearly distinct from modernist literature, usually is more politically concerned, more playful—it is given to parody and pastiche—and more closely related to the art forms of popular culture than is modernist literature.

prosody the principles of versification (414-20)

protagonist the chief actor in any literary work. The term is usually preferable to *hero* and *heroine* because it can include characters—for example, villainous or weak ones—who are not aptly called heroes or heroines.

psychological criticism a form of analysis especially concerned both with the ways in which authors unconsciously leave traces of their inner lives in their works and with the ways in which readers respond, consciously and unconsciously, to works (507–08)

pyrrhic foot   in poetry, a foot consisting of two unstressed syllables (417)

quatrain   a stanza of four lines (420)

reader-response criticism   criticism emphasizing the idea that various readers respond in various ways and therefore that readers as well as authors "create" meaning (500–03)

realism   presentation of plausible characters (usually middle class) in plausible (usually everyday) circumstances, as opposed, for example, to heroic characters engaged in improbable adventures. Realism in literature seeks to give the illusion of reality.

recognition   see *anagnorisis*

refrain   a repeated phrase, line, or group of lines in a poem, especially in a ballad

resolution   the dénouement or untying of the complication of the plot

reversal   a change in fortune, often an ironic twist (268)

rhetorical question   a question to which no answer is expected or to which only one answer is plausible. Example: "Do you think I am unaware of your goings-on?"

rhyme   similarity or identity of accented sounds in corresponding positions, as, for example, at the ends of lines: *love/dove; tender/slender* (418)

rhythm   in poetry, a pattern of stressed and unstressed sounds; in prose, some sort of recurrence (for example, of a motif) at approximately identical intervals (414–15)

rising action   in a story or play, the events that lead up to the *climax* (270)

rising meter   a foot (for example, iambic or anapestic) ending with a stressed syllable

romance   narrative fiction, usually characterized by improbable adventures and love

round character   a many-sided character, one who does not always act predictably, as opposed to a "flat" or one-dimensional, unchanging character (193)

run-on line   a line of verse whose syntax and meaning require the reader to go on, without a pause, to the next line; an *enjambed* line (417)

sarcasm   crudely mocking or contemptuous language; heavy verbal irony

satire   literature that entertainingly attacks folly or vice; amusingly abusive writing

scansion   description of rhythm in poetry: metrical analysis (415–18)

scene   (1) a unit of a play, in which the setting is unchanged and the time continuous; (2) the setting (locale, and time of the action); (3) in fiction, a dramatic passage, as opposed to a passage of description or of summary

selective omniscience   a point of view in which the author enters the mind of one character and for the most part sees the other characters only from the outside (198)

sentimentality   excessive emotion, especially excessive pity, treated as appropriate rather than as disproportionate (477–81)

sestet   a six-line stanza, or the last six lines of an Italian sonnet (420)

sestina   a poem with six stanzas of six lines each and a concluding stanza of three lines. The last word of each line in the first stanza appears as the last word of a line in each of the next five stanzas but in a different order. In the final (three-line) stanza, each line ends with one of these six words, and each line includes in the middle of the line one of the other three words.

setting the time and place of a story, play, or poem (for instance, a Texas town in winter, about 1900) (192, 195, 202, 272-73)

Shakespearean sonnet see *English sonnet*

short story a fictional narrative, usually in prose, rarely longer than 30 pages and often much briefer (190)

simile a kind of figurative language explicitly making a comparison—for example, by using *as, like,* or a verb such as *seems* (403-04)

soliloquy a speech in a play, in which a character alone on the stage speaks his or her thoughts aloud

sonnet a lyric poem of 14 lines; see *English sonnet, Italian sonnet*

speaker see *persona*

spondee a metrical foot consisting of two stressed syllables (417)

stage direction a playwright's indication to the actors or readers—for example, offering information about how an actor is to speak a line (272-73)

stanza a group of lines forming a unit that is repeated in a poem (419-20)

stereotype a simplified conception, especially an oversimplification—for example, a stock character such as the heartless landlord, the kindly old teacher, the prostitute with a heart of gold. Such a character usually has only one personality trait, and this is boldly exaggerated.

stream of consciousness the presentation of a character's unrestricted flow of thought, often with free associations, and often without punctuation (198-99)

stress relative emphasis on one syllable as compared with another (416)

structuralism a critical theory holding that a literary work consists of conventional elements that, taken together by a reader familiar with the conventions, give the work its meaning. Thus just as a spectator must know the rules of a game (e.g., three strikes and you're out) in order to enjoy the game, so a reader must know the rules of, say, a novel (coherent, realistic, adequately motivated characters, a plausible plot, for instance *The Color Purple*) or of a satire (caricatures of contemptible figures in amusing situations that need not be at all plausible, for instance *Gulliver's Travels*). Structuralists normally have no interest in the origins of a work (i.e., in the historical background, or in the author's biography), and no interest in the degree to which a work of art seems to correspond to reality. The interest normally is in the work as a self-sufficient construction. Consult Robert Scholes. *Structuralism in Literature: An Introduction,* and two books by Jonathan Culler, *Structuralist Poetics* (1976) and (for the critical shift from structuralism to poststructuralism) *On Deconstruction* (1982).

structure the organization of a work, the relationship between the chief parts, the large-scale pattern—for instance, a rising action or complication followed by a crisis and then a resolution (407-10, 421)

style the manner of expression, evident not only in the choice of certain words (for instance, colloquial language) but also in the choice of certain kinds of sentence structure, characters, settings, and themes

subplot a sequence of events often paralleling or in some way resembling the main story

summary a synopsis or condensation (133-34, 166-70)

symbol a person, object, action, or situation that, charged with meaning, suggests another thing (for example, a dark forest may suggest confusion, or perhaps evil), though usually with less specificity and more ambiguity than an allegory. A symbol usually differs from a metaphor in that a symbol is expanded or repeated and works by accumulating associations. (195-97, 202)

synecdoche a kind of figurative language in which the whole stands for a part (*the law,* for a police officer), or a part (*all hands on deck,* for all persons) stands for the whole (404)

tale a short narrative, usually less realistic and more romantic than a short story; a yarn

tercet see *triplet*

tetrameter a verse line of four feet (417)

theme what the work is about; an underlying idea of a work; a conception of human experience suggested by the concrete details. Thus the theme of *Macbeth* is often said to be that "vaulting ambition o'erleaps itself." (199-200, 202, 269-70)

thesis the point or argument that a writer announces and develops. A thesis differs from a *topic* by making an assertion. "The fall of Oedipus" is a topic, but "Oedipus falls because he is impetuous" is a thesis, as is "Oedipus is impetuous, but his impetuosity has nothing to do with his fall." (18-19, 85-87, 464)

thesis sentence a sentence summarizing, as specifically as possible, the writer's chief point (argument and perhaps purpose) (18-19, 168-169)

third-person narrator the teller of a story who does not participate in the happenings (197-98)

tone the prevailing attitude (for instance, ironic, genial, objective) as perceived by the reader. Notice that a reader may feel that the tone of the persona of the work is genial while the tone of the author of the same work is ironic. (163-64, 399-400)

topic a subject, such as "Hamlet's relation to Horatio." A topic becomes a *thesis* when a predicate is added to this subject, thus: "Hamlet's relation to Horatio helps to define Hamlet."

tragedy a serious play showing the protagonist moving from good fortune to bad and ending in death or a deathlike state (267-68, 277-78)

tragic flaw a supposed weakness (for example, arrogance) in the tragic protagonist. If the tragedy results from an intellectual error rather than from a moral weakness, it is better to speak of "a tragic error." (268)

tragicomedy a mixture of tragedy and comedy, usually a play with serious happenings that expose the characters to the threat of death but that ends happily

transition a connection between one passage and the next

trimeter a verse line with three feet (417)

triplet a group of three lines of verse, usually rhyming (419)

trochee a metrical foot consisting of a stressed syllable followed by an unstressed syllable. Example: *garden* (416)

understatement a figure of speech in which the speaker says less than what he or she means; an ironic minimizing, as in "You've done fairly well for yourself" said to the winner of a multimillion-dollar lottery (407)

unity harmony and coherence of parts, absence of irrelevance (21)

unreliable narrator a narrator whose report a reader cannot accept at face value, perhaps because the narrator is naive or is too deeply implicated in the action to report it objectively

verbal irony see *irony*

verse (1) a line of poetry; (2) a stanza of a poem (414, 419)

vers libre free verse, unrhymed poetry (420)

villanelle a poem with five stanzas of three lines rhyming *aba,* and a concluding stanza of four lines, rhyming *abaa.* The entire first line is repeated as
the third line of the second and fourth stanzas; the entire third line is repeated as the third line of the third and fifth stanzas. These two lines form
the final two lines of the last (four-line) stanza.

voice see *persona, style,* and *tone* (397–400)

Literary Credits

Sherman Alexie, "On the Amtrak from Boston to New York" from FIRST INDIAN ON THE MOON. © 1993 by Sherman Alexie, by permission of Hanging Loose Press.

Paula Gunn Allen, "Pocahontas to Her English Husband, John Rolfe" from SKINS AND BONES (West End Press). Reprinted by permission of the author.

Julia Alvarez, "Woman's Work" from HOMECOMING by Julia Alvarez. Copyright © 1984, 1996 by Julia Alvarez. Published by Plume, an imprint of Dutton Signet, a division of Penguin USA; originally published by Grove Press. Reprinted by permission of Susan Bergholz Literary Services, New York. All rights reserved.

Maya Angelou, excerpt from I KNOW WHY THE CAGED BIRD SINGS by Maya Angelou. Copyright © 1969 and renewed 1997 by Maya Angelou. Reprinted by permission of Random House, Inc.

Anonymous, "The Titanic" sung by Huddie Ledbetter (Lead Belly) in NEGRO FOLK SONGS AS SUNG BY LEAD BELLY, TRANSCRIBED, SELECTED AND EDITED BY JOHN LOMAX. (Macmillan, 1936). Reprinted by permission of Alan Lomax.

Anonymous, excerpt from THE AMERICAN SONGBAG, copyright 1927 by Harcourt Brace & Company and renewed 1955 by Carl Sandburg, reproduced by permission of Harcourt Brace & Company.

Gloria Anzaldúa, "To live in the Borderlands means you" from BORDERLANDS/LA FRONTERA: THE NEW MESTIZA © 1987 by Gloria Anzaldúa. Reprinted by permission of Aunt Lute Books.

Max Apple, "Bridging" from FREE AGENTS by Max Apple. Copyright © 1984 by Max Apple. Reprinted by permission of HarperCollins Publishers, Inc.

A. J. Arberry, excerpts from THE KORAN INTERPRETED, translated by A. J. Arberry. Copyright © 1955 by George Allen and Unwin, Ltd. Reprinted with the permission of Simon & Schuster and HarperCollins Publishers Ltd.

José Armas, "El Tonto del Barrio" originally published in *Pajarito* publications, 1979, from CUENTOS CHICANOS, Revised Edition, 1984, edited by Rudolfo A. Anaya and Antonio Marques, University of New Mexico Press. Reprinted by permission of José Armas.

W. H. Auden, "Musée des Beaux Arts" from W. H. Auden: COLLECTED POEMS by W. H. Auden, edited by Edward Mendelson. Copyright © 1940 and renewed 1968 by W. H. Auden. Reprinted by permission of Random House, Inc.

Jimmy Santiago Baca, "So Mexicans Are Taking Jobs from Americans" from IMMIGRANTS IN OUR OWN LAND. Copyright © 1982 by Jimmy Santiago Baca. Reprinted by permission of New Directions Publishing Corp.

Toni Cade Bambara, "The Lesson" copyright © 1972 by Toni Cade Bambara from GORILLA, MY LOVE by Toni Cade Bambara. Reprinted by permission of Random House, Inc.

Anne Barton, "The Promulgation of Confusion" from ENGLISH DRAMA TO 1710, edited by Christopher Ricks. Penguin Books UK Ltd.

Photo Credits

41: Private Collection. Photograph courtesy R.M.S. Titanic Inc.; 42: ©1912 by *The New York Times.* Reprinted by permission; 43: Collection of Richard Faber; 50: American Folklife Center, Smithsonian Institution, Washington, D.C.; 54: Louisiana State University Press. Photograph by Bernard Gotfryd; 57: Photofest; 70: Photograph by Dorothy Alexander; 115: AP/Wide World Photos; 122: Photograph courtesy José Armas; 127: Thomas Victor; 151: Buffalo Bill Historical Center, Cody, WY; 154: By permission of the Houghton Library, Harvard University. bMS Am 1823.7 (21), 80; 155: *Harvard Library Bulletin*, for permission to reprint a transcription of the manuscript draft of E. E. Cummings's "Buffalo Bill 's," originally published in Rushworth M. Kidder, " 'Buffalo Bill 's'— An Early E. E. Cummings Manuscript," *Harvard Library Bulletin* 24:4 (1976): 373-380; 156: Buffalo Bill Historical Center, Cody, WY; 157: Buffalo Bill Historical Center, Cody, WY; 158: McCord Museum of Canadian History, Montreal; 179: AP/Wide World Photos; 181: Corbis-Bettmann; 183: AP/Wide World Photos; 187: Photograph by Jay Ann Cox; 212: AP/Wide World Photos; 218: Photograph by Annie Valva; 223: AP/Wide World Photos; 226: Photograph © Jerry Bauer; 240: Photograph © Gordon Parks; 254: Courtesy of Tuskegee University. Photograph by Eric J. Sundquist; 278: Frederick Ayers/Photo Researchers; 279: Photography by John Vickers; 315: AP/Wide World Photos; 316: New York Public Library for the Performing Arts; 325: Corbis; 326: Peter Cunningham; 349: Corbis; 350: New York Public Library for the Performing Arts; 428: AP/Wide World Photos; 429: AP/Wide World Photos; 431: Courtesy HarperCollins; 433: Photograph © Nancy Crampton; 435: Photograph © Nancy Crampton; 437: AP/Wide World Photos; 441: AP/Wide World Photos; 444: Amherst College; 445: Harvard University Press; 461 (bottom): Courtesy of The Jones Library, Amherst, Massachusetts; 461 (top): Brown Brothers; 482: Photograph by Dorothy Alexander; 487: AP/Wide World Photos; 522: Photograph by Rick O'Quinn; 526: Photograph by M. L. Marinelli; 533: Corbis-Bettmann; 556: Bern Keating/Black Star; 563-566: University of Virginia Library, Faulkner Collection; 592: By kind permission of the Provost and Fellows of King's College Cambridge; 599-600: University of Virginia Library, Walt Whitman Collection; 601: AP/Wide World Photos; 605: AP/Wide World Photos; 608: Printed with the permission of The Poetry/Rare Books Collection, University Libraries, State University of New York at Buffalo; 609: Stanford University News Service; 612: David Bain/Courtesy University of Chicago Press; 613: Photograph © Nancy Crampton; 614: Photograph © Nancy Crampton; 615: Photograph © Nancy Crampton; 616: Photograph by Dorothy Alexander; 618: Photograph by Diane Gorodnitzki/Acting Company, Champaign-Urbana; 624: AP/Wide World Photos; 627: Courtesy Judy Brady; 629: Photograph by Eve Sanders; 632: Corbis; 643: Corbis; 655: Corbis/Bettmann; 664: Photograph © Jerry Bauer; 673: K. Krueger Jones/Courtesy Warner Books; 680: Corbis; 688: Photograph © Nancy Crampton; 701: Corbis; 707: AP/Wide World Photos; 714: Outline; 761: AP/Wide World Photos; 762: Courtesy Doubleday; 763: Photograph by Dorothy Alexander; 764: Photograph © Nancy Crampton; 767: Photograph by Larry Moyer; 768: Photograph by Dorothy Alexander;

769: Photograph by Dorothy Alexander; 770: Courtesy Maude Meehan; 771: AP/Wide World Photos; 774: The Harvard Theater Collection, The Houghton Library; 826: © Brigitte Lacombe; 872: Courtesy Rutgers University Press; 885: Photograph © 1999 Layle Silbert; 890: By kind permission of the Provost and Fellows of King's College Cambridge; 891: By kind permission of the Provost and Fellows of King's College Cambridge; 896: Photograph by Dorothy Alexander; 899 (left): © The British Museum; 899 (right): Drawing of an Elizabethan playhouse by C. Walter Hodges, 1965. Courtesy C. Walter Hodges; 906: © Joe Cocks Studio Collection/Shakespeare Centre Library; 907: © Joe Cocks Studio Collection/Shakespeare Centre Library; 908: Mark Douet/Performing Arts Library; 1045: Photograph © Jerry Bauer; 1050: Gordon Robotham; 1065: Courtesy Putnam & Grosset Group; 1080: © 1995 Estate of Tsend Kwong Chi. MTD/Artists Rights Society (ARS), New York; 1082 (top): Photograph by Carol Bruchac; 1082 (bottom): William Williams Collection of Photographs. Miriam and Ira D. Wallach Division of Art, Prints and Photographs. New York Public Library. Astor, Lenox and Tilden Foundations; 1083: Brown Brothers; 1087: Photograph by Linda Haas; 1088: Photograph by Jean Weisinger/Courtesy Aunt Lute Books; 1090: AP/Wide World Photos; 1094: Courtesy Rutgers University Press; 1095: Dorothea Lange/War Relocation Authority/National Archives; 1096: AP/Wide World Photos; 1097: Chris Bennion/Seattle Repertory Theater; 1146: James Mooney/National Anthropological Archive, Smithsonian Institution, Washington D.C.; 1148: Courtesy Christopher Cardozo; 1151: James Luna. *The Artifact Piece*, 1987-90. San Diego Museum of Man; 1152: Princeton University Library, Department of Rare Books and Special Collections; 1155: Photo courtesy of the Edward E. Ayer Collection, The Newberry Library; 1157: Rare Books and Manuscripts Division, New York Public Library, Astor, Lenox and Tilden Foundations; 1159: Architect of the Capitol; 1160: © Courtesy Museum of Art, Brigham Young University. All rights reserved; 1170: Vincent van Gogh. *Vincent's Bed in Arles*. Oil on canvas 72 x 90 cm. Vincent Van Gogh Foundation/Van Gogh Museum, Amsterdam; 1172: Charles Demuth. *I Saw the Figure 5 in Gold*. Oil on composition board, 36 x 29¾ in. The Metropolitan Museum of Art, Alfred Stieglitz Collection, 1949. (49.59.1) Photograph © 1979 The Metropolitan Museum of Art; 1174: Edwin Romanzo Elmer. *Mourning Picture*, 1890. Oil on canvas 28 x 36 in. Smith College Museum of Art, Northampton, Massachusetts; 1176: Kitagawa Utamaro. *Two Women Dressing Their Hair*. Print Collection, Miriam and Ira D. Wallach Division of Art, Prints and Photographs. The New York Public Library. Astor, Lenox and Tilden Foundations; 1178: Sandro Botticelli. *The Birth of Venus*, c. 1480. Uffizi Gallery, Florence/Scala/Art Resource, New York; 1180: Vincent van Gogh. *The Starry Night*. (1889) Oil on canvas, 29 x 36¼ (73.7 x 92.1 cm). The Museum of Modern Art, New York. Acquired through the Lillie P. Bliss Bequest. Photograph © 1999 The Museum of Modern Art, New York; 1182: Pieter Brueghel. *Landscape with the Fall of Icarus*. Royal Museum of Fine Arts, Brussels, Belgium; 1184: Marcel Duchamp. *Nude Descending Staircase, No. 2*, 1912. Oil on canvas, 58 x 35 in. Philadelphia Museum of Art. The Louise and Walter Arensberg Collection; 1186: Courtesy of the William S. Reese Collection; 1188: Edouard Manet. *Déjeuner sur l'herbe*, 1863. Louvre, Paris/Scala/Art Resource, New York; 1190: Museum of Modern Art, New York/ © 1999 The Estate of Pablo Picasso/ Artist Rights Society (ARS), New York; 1192: Pieter Brueghel, the Elder. *Two Monkeys*. Gemäldegalerie, Berlin/Staatliche Museum, Preussicher Kulturbesitz; 1195: Photograph © Jerry Bauer; 1218: Jill Krementz, Inc.; 1224: Photograph © Nancy Crampton; 1228: AP/Wide World Photos; 1273: Sasetta (Stefano di Giovanni). "The Journey of the Magi." c. 1440. Tempera on wood, 8½ x 11¾ in. The Metropolitan Museum of Art, Maitland F. Griggs Collection, Bequest of Maitland F. Griggs. (43.98.1); 1276: Photograph © Nancy Crampton; 1280: Donald Cooper/Photostage; 1348: Photo from the Seattle Post Intelligencer Collection, The University of Washington Library and the Museum of History and Industry; 1349: Photo by Howard Clifford, *Tacoma News Tribune*. Available in Special Collections and Preservation Division of the University of Washington Libraries.

Index of Authors, Titles, and First Lines of Poems

Index of Terms